1879 - Gottlob Frege founds the modern discipline of mathematical logic
1937 - Alan Turing presents the concept of the Turing machine
1941 - Alfred Tarski applies model theory to the Calculus of Binary Relations
1962 - Charles Bachman develops the Integrated Data Management System (IDMS) network database
1966 - Indexed Sequential Access Method (ISAM) is developed at IBM
1970-1971 - Edgar F. Codd introduces the Relational Model along with Relational Algebra and Relational calculus
1971 - Rudolf Bayer and Edward McCreight publish paper on B-trees, the basic indexing mechanism in modern database systems
1972 - Boyce-Codd normal form for database design is introduced
1973 - Charles Bachman wins Turing Award for his work on network databases
1974 - The theory of functional dependencies and relational normalization theory taking shape
1976 - Eswaran, Gray, Lorie, and Traiger define isolation levels, serializability, and two-phase locking

Database Principles

Supplements

For Instructors

- Online PowerPoint slides for all chapters
- Online PowerPoint slides for all figures in the textbook
- Online Solutions Manual containing solutions for all problems in the textbook
- Online Test Bank containing projects (some with downloadable implementation details) and extra problems with solutions

Instructor supplements for this text are available online. Visit www.aw-bc.com or contact your Addison-Wesley sales representative.

(continued)

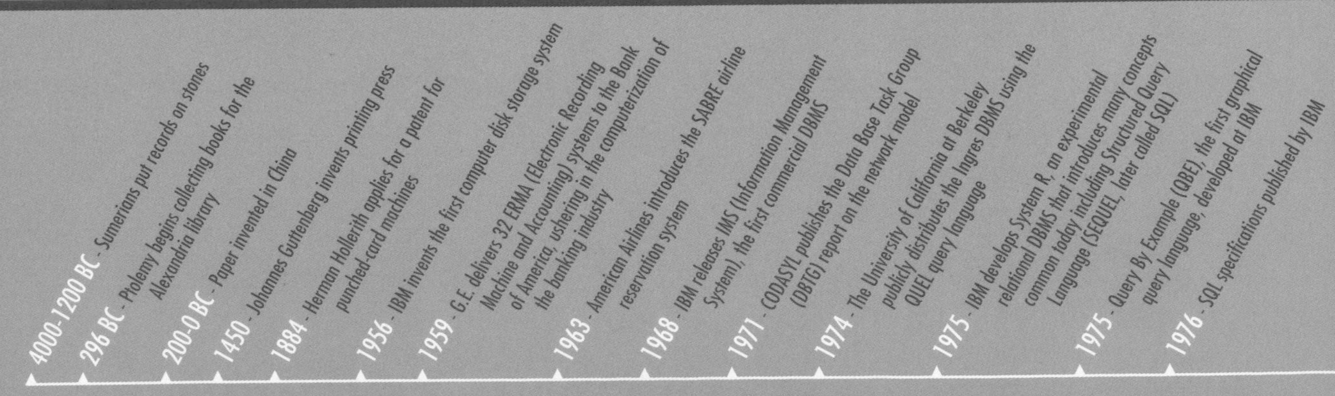

Mid 1970s - Two-phase commit introduced and implemented in a number of systems

1976 - Peter Chen introduces the Entity-Relationship model

1977 - Akifumi Makinouchi describes a nested relational model, a precursor of the object-relational model

1979 - Home H. Gallaire and Jack Minker introduce logic-based databases, also known as deductive databases

1979 - Fagin, Nievergelt, Pippenger and Strong define Extensible Hashing

1981 - Edgar F. Codd wins the Turing Award for his contributions to database theory

1985 - Active databases introduced

1988 - Deductive and object-oriented databases unified in one model

1985-1993 - Object-oriented and object-relational database technologies are developed

1995 - Datacube OLAP operators introduced

1995 - The semi-structured data model is developed

1998 - Jim Gray wins the Turing Award for his contributions to the fields of databases and transaction processing

For Students

- Three Web appendices entitled *An Overview of Transaction Processing*; *Requirements and Specifications*; and *Design, Coding, and Testing*
- Additional practice problems and solutions
- Online PowerPoint slides for all figures in the textbook
- A Practice Case Study
- Glossary

These student supplements are available at www.aw-bc.com/kifer.

Database Place, a series of online database tutorials, offers additional help mastering SQL, normalization, and modeling. A complimentary subscription is offered when an access code is bundled with a new copy of this text. Subscriptions may also be purchased online. For more information, visit www.aw-bc.com/databaseplace.

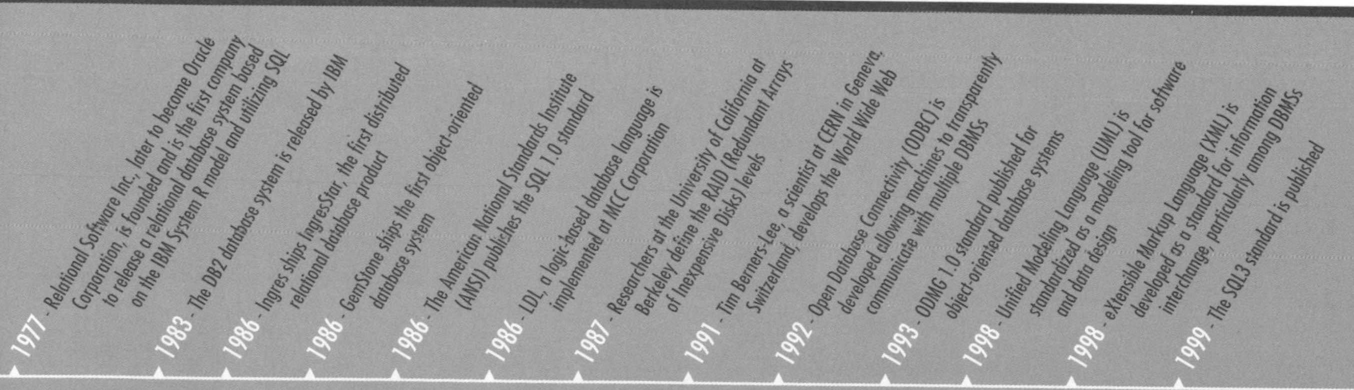
1977 - Relational Software Inc., later to become Oracle Corporation, is founded and is the first company to release a relational database system based on the IBM System R model and utilizing SQL
1983 - The DB2 database system is released by IBM
1986 - Ingres ships IngresStar, the first distributed relational database product
1986 - GemStone ships the first object-oriented database system
1986 - The American National Standards Institute (ANSI) publishes the SQL 1.0 standard
1986 - LDL, a logic-based database language is implemented at MCC Corporation
1987 - Researchers at the University of California at Berkeley define the RAID (Redundant Arrays of Inexpensive Disks) levels
1991 - Tim Berners-Lee, a scientist at CERN in Geneva, Switzerland, develops the World Wide Web
1992 - Open Database Connectivity (ODBC) is developed allowing machines to transparently communicate with multiple DBMSs
1993 - ODMG 1.0 standard published for object-oriented database systems
1998 - Unified Modeling Language (UML) is standardized as a modeling tool for software and data design
1998 - eXtensible Markup Language (XML) is developed as a standard for information interchange, particularly among DBMSs
1999 - The SQL3 standard is published

Online Access for *Database Systems*

Thank you for purchasing a new copy of *Database Systems: An Application Oriented Approach, Complete Version*, Second Edition. Your textbook includes six months of prepaid access to the book's Companion Website. This prepaid subscription provides you with full access to all student support areas, including:

- Three Web appendices entitled *An Overview of Transaction Processing*; *Requirements and Specifications*; and *Design, Coding, and Testing*
- Additional practice problems and solutions
- Online PowerPoint slides for all figures in the textbook
- A Practice Case Study
- Glossary

To access the *Database Systems: An Application-Oriented Approach, Complete Version*, Second Edition Companion Website for the first time:

You will need to register online using a computer with an Internet connection and a Web browser. The process takes just a couple of minutes and only needs to be completed once.

1. Go to **http://www.aw-bc.com/kifer**.
2. Click the **Register** button.
3. Use a coin to scratch off the gray coating below and reveal your student access code.* Do not use a knife or other sharp object, which can damage the code.

WSKDSS-CHOLI-BOTHA-TYPED-ABBOT-LINES

4. On the registration page, enter your student access code. Do not type the dashes. You can use lowercase or uppercase letters.
5. Follow the on-screen instructions. If you need help at any time during the online registration process, simply click the **Need Help?** icon.
6. Once your personal Login Name and Password are confirmed, you can begin using the *Database Systems: An Application-Oriented Approach, Complete Version*, Second Edition Companion Website!

To log in to this Website after you've registered:

You only need to register for this Companion Website once. After that, you can access the site by going to http://www.aw-bc.com/kifer and providing your Login Name and Password when prompted.

*IMPORTANT: The access code on this page can only be used once to establish a subscription to the *Database Systems: An Application-Oriented Approach, Complete Version*, Second Edition Companion Website. This subscription is valid for six months upon activation and is not transferable. If this access code has already been scratched off, it may no longer be valid. If this is the case, you can purchase a subscription by going to http://www.aw-bc.com/kifer and clicking "Buy Now."

COMPLETE VERSION

Database Systems

An Application-Oriented Approach

SECOND EDITION

COMPLETE VERSION

Database Systems

An Application-Oriented Approach

SECOND EDITION

Michael Kifer Arthur Bernstein Philip M. Lewis

STATE UNIVERSITY OF NEW YORK, STONY BROOK

Boston San Francisco New York
London Toronto Sydney Tokyo Singapore Madrid
Mexico City Munich Paris Cape Town Hong Kong Montreal

Acquisitions Editor	Matt Goldstein
Project Editor	Katherine Harutunian
Production Supervisor	Marilyn Lloyd
Marketing Manager	Michelle Brown
Marketing Coordinator	Jake Zavracky
Project Management	Windfall Software
Text Designer	Paul C. Anagnostopoulos
Copyeditor	Elisabeth Beller
Composition	Windfall Software, using ZzTEX
Proofreader	Jennifer McClain
Cover Designer	Joyce Cosentino Wells
Cover Image	© 2005 Greg Paprocki/Photodisc
Prepress and Manufacturing	Caroline Fell
Printer	Hamilton Printing

Access the latest information about Addison-Wesley titles from our World Wide Web site: http://www.aw-bc.com/computing

ISBN 0-321-31256-2
1 2 3 4 5 6 7 8 9 10—HAM—08 07 06 05

In memory of my late parents, Luba and Isaac;
and to my wife, Lora, and my children. M.K.

To my wife, Edie, my children, and my grandchildren. A.J.B.

To my wife, Rhoda, my children, and my grandchildren. P.M.L.

Contents

Preface xxiii

PART ONE Introduction 1

1 Overview of Databases and Transactions 3

1.1 What Are Databases and Transactions? 3
1.2 Features of Modern Database and Transaction Processing Systems 6
1.3 Major Players in the Implementation and Support of Database and Transaction Processing Systems 7
1.4 Decision Support Systems—OLAP and OLTP 9

2 The Big Picture 13

CS 2.1 Case Study: A Student Registration System 13
2.2 Introduction to Relational Databases 14
2.3 What Makes a Program a Transaction—The ACID Properties 20
Bibliographic Notes 25
Exercises 25

PART TWO Database Management 29

3 The Relational Data Model 31

3.1 What Is a Data Model? 31
3.2 The Relational Model 35
3.2.1 Basic Concepts 35
3.2.2 Integrity Constraints 38
3.3 SQL—Data Definition Sublanguage 46
3.3.1 Specifying the Relation Type 46

3.3.2 The System Catalog 46
3.3.3 Key Constraints 47
3.3.4 Dealing with Missing Information 48
3.3.5 Semantic Constraints 49
3.3.6 User-Defined Domains 53
3.3.7 Foreign-Key Constraints 53
3.3.8 Reactive Constraints 56
3.3.9 Database Views 59
3.3.10 Modifying Existing Definitions 60
3.3.11 SQL-Schemas 62
3.3.12 Access Control 63
Bibliographic Notes 65
Exercises 66

4 Conceptual Modeling of Databases with Entity-Relationship Diagrams and the Unified Modeling Language 69

4.1 Conceptual Modeling with the E-R Approach 70
4.2 Entities and Entity Types 70
4.3 Relationships and Relationship Types 73
4.4 Advanced Features in Conceptual Data Modeling 78
4.4.1 Entity Type Hierarchies 78
4.4.2 Participation Constraints 81
4.4.3 The Part-of Relationship 83
4.5 From E-R Diagrams to Relational Database Schemas 86
4.5.1 Representation of Entities 86
4.5.2 Representation of Relationships 88
4.5.3 Representing IsA Hierarchies in the Relational Model 90
4.5.4 Representation of Participation Constraints 92
4.5.5 Representation of the Part-of Relationship 94
★ **4.6** UML: A New Kid on the Block 95
4.6.1 Representing Entities in UML 96
4.6.2 Representing Relationships in UML 97
4.6.3 Advanced Modeling Concepts in UML 101
4.6.4 Translation to SQL 105
4.7 A Brokerage Firm Example 106
4.7.1 An Entity-Relationship Design 106
★ 4.7.2 A UML Design 110
CS **4.8** Case Study: A Database Design for the Student Registration System 111
4.8.1 The Database Part of the Requirements Document 112
4.8.2 The Database Design 113

4.9 Limitations of Data Modeling Methodologies 119
Bibliographic Notes 123
Exercises 123

5 Relational Algebra and SQL 127

5.1 Relational Algebra: Under the Hood of SQL 128
5.1.1 Basic Operators 128
5.1.2 Derived Operators 137
5.2 The Query Sublanguage of SQL 147
5.2.1 Simple SQL Queries 148
5.2.2 Set Operations 154
5.2.3 Nested Queries 157
5.2.4 Quantified Predicates 163
5.2.5 Aggregation over Data 164
5.2.6 A Query Evaluation Algorithm for SQL with Aggregates 170
5.2.7 Join Expressions in the FROM Clause 173
5.2.8 More on Views in SQL 174
5.2.9 Materialized Views 177
5.2.10 The Null Value Quandary 181
5.3 Modifying Relation Instances in SQL 182
5.3.1 Inserting Data 182
5.3.2 Deleting Data 184
5.3.3 Updating Existing Data 185
5.3.4 Updates on Views 185
Bibliographic Notes 187
Exercises 188

6 Database Design with the Relational Normalization Theory 193

6.1 The Problem of Redundancy 193
6.2 Decompositions 195
6.3 Functional Dependencies 198
6.4 Properties of Functional Dependencies 200
6.5 Normal Forms 207
6.5.1 The Boyce-Codd Normal Form 208
6.5.2 The Third Normal Form 210
6.6 Properties of Decompositions 211
6.6.1 Lossless and Lossy Decompositions 212
6.6.2 Dependency-Preserving Decompositions 215
6.7 An Algorithm for BCNF Decomposition 219

6.8 Synthesis of 3NF Schemas 222
6.8.1 Minimal Cover 222
6.8.2 3NF Decomposition through Schema Synthesis 224
6.8.3 BCNF Decomposition through 3NF Synthesis 227
★ 6.9 The Fourth Normal Form 229
★ 6.10 Advanced 4NF Design 235
6.10.1 MVDs and Their Properties 235
6.10.2 The Difficulty of Designing for 4NF 236
6.10.3 A 4NF Decomposition How-To 240
6.11 Summary of Normal Form Decomposition 242
CS 6.12 Case Study: Schema Refinement for the Student Registration System 242
6.13 Tuning Issues: To Decompose or Not to Decompose? 245
Bibliographic Notes 246
Exercises 247

7 Triggers and Active Databases 251

7.1 What Is a Trigger? 251
7.2 Semantic Issues in Trigger Handling 252
7.3 Triggers in SQL 256
7.4 Avoiding a Chain Reaction 264
Bibliographic Notes 265
Exercises 265

8 Using SQL in an Application 267

8.1 What Are the Issues Involved? 267
8.2 Embedded SQL 268
8.2.1 Status Processing 271
8.2.2 Sessions, Connections, and Transactions 273
8.2.3 Executing Transactions 274
8.2.4 Cursors 276
8.2.5 Stored Procedures on the Server 282
8.3 More on Integrity Constraints 285
8.4 Dynamic SQL 286
8.4.1 Statement Preparation in Dynamic SQL 287
★ 8.4.2 Prepared Statements and the Descriptor Area 290
8.4.3 Cursors 293
8.4.4 Stored Procedures on the Server 293
8.5 JDBC and SQLJ 294
8.5.1 JDBC Basics 294

8.5.2 Prepared Statements 297
8.5.3 Result Sets and Cursors 297
8.5.4 Obtaining Information about a Result Set 300
8.5.5 Status Processing 300
8.5.6 Executing Transactions 301
8.5.7 Stored Procedures on the Server 302
8.5.8 An Example 303
8.5.9 SQLJ: Statement-Level Interface to Java 303

★ 8.6 ODBC 307
8.6.1 Prepared Statements 309
8.6.2 Cursors 309
8.6.3 Status Processing 312
8.6.4 Executing Transactions 312
8.6.5 Stored Procedures on the Server 313
8.6.6 An Example 313

8.7 Comparison 315

Bibliographic Notes 316

Exercises 316

PART THREE Optimizing DBMS Performance 319

9 Physical Data Organization and Indexing 321

9.1 Disk Organization 322
9.1.1 RAID Systems 326

9.2 Heap Files 329

9.3 Sorted Files 333

9.4 Indices 337
9.4.1 Clustered versus Unclustered Indices 340
9.4.2 Sparse versus Dense Indices 342
9.4.3 Search Keys Containing Multiple Attributes 344

9.5 Multilevel Indexing 347
9.5.1 Index-Sequential Access 350
9.5.2 B^+ Trees 353

9.6 Hash Indexing 363
9.6.1 Static Hashing 364
★ 9.6.2 Dynamic Hashing Algorithms 366

★ 9.7 Special-Purpose Indices 375
9.7.1 Bitmap Indices 375
9.7.2 Join Indices 376

9.8 Tuning Issues: Choosing Indices for an Application 377
Bibliographic Notes 378
Exercises 378

10 The Basics of Query Processing **383**

10.1 Overview of Query Processing 383
10.2 External Sorting 384
10.3 Computing Projection, Union, and Set Difference 388
10.4 Computing Selection 390
10.4.1 Selections with Simple Conditions 391
10.4.2 Access Paths 393
10.4.3 Selections with Complex Conditions 395
10.5 Computing Joins 396
10.5.1 Computing Joins Using Simple Nested Loops 397
10.5.2 Sort-Merge Join 400
10.5.3 Hash Join 402
★ 10.6 Multirelational Joins 403
10.7 Computing Aggregate Functions 405
Bibliographic Notes 405
Exercises 405

11 An Overview of Query Optimization **409**

11.1 Query Processing Architecture 409
11.2 Heuristic Optimization Based on Algebraic Equivalences 411
11.3 Estimating the Cost of a Query Execution Plan 414
11.4 Estimating the Size of the Output 422
11.5 Choosing a Plan 424
Bibliographic Notes 429
Exercises 429

12 Database Tuning **433**

12.1 Disk Caches 434
12.1.1 Tuning the Cache 435
12.2 Tuning the Schema 437
12.2.1 Indices 437
12.2.2 Denormalization 444
12.2.3 Repeating Groups 446
12.2.4 Partitioning 446
12.3 Tuning the Data Manipulation Language 447
12.4 Tools 451

12.5 Managing Physical Resources 451
12.6 Influencing the Optimizer 453
Bibliographic Notes 455
Exercises 455

PART FOUR Advanced Topics in Databases 459

13 Relational Calculus, Visual Query Languages, and Deductive Databases 461

13.1 Tuple Relational Calculus 461
13.2 Understanding SQL through Tuple Relational Calculus 471
13.3 Domain Relational Calculus and Visual Query Languages 474
13.4 Visual Query Languages: QBE and PC Databases 479
13.5 The Relationship between Relational Algebra and the Calculi 486
★ 13.6 Deductive Databases 488
13.6.1 Limitations of Relational Query Languages 488
13.6.2 Recursive Queries in SQL 490
13.6.3 Datalog 496
Bibliographic Notes 510
Exercises 510

14 Object Databases 515

14.1 Limitations of the Relational Data Model 515
14.2 Object Databases versus Relational Databases 521
14.3 The Conceptual Object Data Model 523
14.3.1 Objects and Values 523
14.3.2 Classes 525
14.3.3 Types 526
14.3.4 Object-Relational Databases 529
14.4 Objects in SQL:1999 and SQL:2003 530
14.4.1 Row Types 531
14.4.2 User-Defined Types 531
14.4.3 Objects 533
14.4.4 Querying User-Defined Types 534
14.4.5 Updating User-Defined Types 535
14.4.6 Reference Types 538
14.4.7 Inheritance 540
14.4.8 Collection Types 540

14.5 The ODMG Standard 543
14.5.1 ODL—The ODMG Object Definition Language 546
14.5.2 OQL—The ODMG Object Query Language 552
14.5.3 Transactions in ODMG 557
14.5.4 Object Manipulation in ODMG 557
14.5.5 Language Bindings 558
★ 14.6 Common Object Request Broker Architecture 562
14.6.1 CORBA Basics 563
14.6.2 CORBA and Databases 569
Bibliographic Notes 573
Exercises 575

15 XML and Web Data **579**

15.1 Semistructured Data 579
15.2 Overview of XML 582
15.2.1 XML Elements and Database Objects 585
15.2.2 XML Attributes 587
15.2.3 Namespaces 589
15.2.4 Document Type Definitions 594
15.2.5 Inadequacy of DTDs as a Data Definition Language 596
15.3 XML Schema 599
15.3.1 XML Schema and Namespaces 599
15.3.2 Simple Types 603
15.3.3 Complex Types 608
15.3.4 Putting It Together 616
15.3.5 Shortcuts: Anonymous Types and Element References 616
15.3.6 Integrity Constraints 620
15.4 XML Query Languages 627
15.4.1 XPath: A Lightweight XML Query Language 628
★ 15.4.2 XSLT: A Transformation Language for XML 637
15.4.3 XQuery: A Full-Featured Query Language for XML 649
15.4.4 SQL/XML 668
Bibliographic Notes 679
Exercises 680

16 Distributed Databases **687**

16.1 The Application Designer's View of the Database 688
16.2 Distributing Data among Different Databases 691
16.2.1 Partitioning 692
16.2.2 Updates and Partitioning 695

16.2.3 Replication 696
16.3 Query Planning Strategies 698
16.3.1 Global Query Optimization 698
16.3.2 Strategies for a Multidatabase System 705
16.3.3 Tuning Issues: Database Design and Query Planning in a Distributed Environment 706
Bibliographic Notes 707
Exercises 707

17 OLAP and Data Mining **711**

17.1 OLAP and Data Warehouses—Old and New 711
17.2 A Multidimensional Model for OLAP Applications 713
17.3 Aggregation 717
17.3.1 Drilling, Slicing, Rolling, and Dicing 718
17.3.2 The CUBE Operator 721
17.4 ROLAP and MOLAP 725
17.5 Implementation Issues 727
17.6 Populating a Data Warehouse 728
17.7 Data Mining Tasks 730
17.8 Mining Associations 731
17.9 Classification and Prediction Using Decision Trees 734
★ 17.10 Classification and Prediction Using Neural Nets 744
17.11 Clustering 752
Bibliographic Notes 757
Exercises 757

PART FIVE Transaction Processing **761**

18 ACID Properties of Transactions **763**

18.1 Consistency 764
18.1.1 Checking Integrity Constraints 765
18.1.2 A Transaction as a Unit of Work 766
18.2 Atomicity 767
18.3 Durability 768
18.4 Isolation 769
18.5 The ACID Properties 773
Bibliographic Notes 774
Exercises 774

19 Models of Transactions 777

19.1 Flat Transactions 777
19.2 Providing Structure within a Transaction 779
19.2.1 Savepoints 779
19.2.2 Distributed Transactions 781
19.2.3 Nested Transactions 785
19.3 Structuring an Application as Multiple Transactions 787
19.3.1 Chained Transactions 788
19.3.2 Sagas and Compensation 791
19.3.3 Declarative Transaction Demarcation 793
★ 19.3.4 Multilevel Transactions 796
19.3.5 Transaction Scheduling with Recoverable Queues 799
19.3.6 Workflows and Workflow Management Systems 804
Bibliographic Notes 809
Exercises 810

20 Implementing Isolation 813

20.1 Schedules and Schedule Equivalence 815
20.1.1 Serializability 819
20.1.2 Conflict Equivalence and View Equivalence 821
20.1.3 Serialization Graphs 822
20.2 Recoverability, Cascaded Aborts, and Strictness 824
20.3 Models for Concurrency Control 827
20.4 A Strategy for Immediate-Update Pessimistic Concurrency Controls 829
20.4.1 Conflict Avoidance 830
20.4.2 Deadlocks 832
20.5 Design of an Immediate-Update Pessimistic Concurrency Control 834
20.5.1 An Implementation Using Lock Sets and Wait Sets 834
20.5.2 Two-Phase Locking 836
20.5.3 Lock Granularity 838
20.6 Objects and Semantic Commutativity 839
★ 20.6.1 Partial Operations and Backward-Commutativity 840
20.7 Atomicity, Recoverability, and Compensating Operations 842
20.8 Isolation in Structured Transaction Models 848
20.8.1 Savepoints 848
20.8.2 Chained Transactions 849
20.8.3 Recoverable Queues 849

20.8.4 Nested Transactions 850
★ 20.8.5 Multilevel Transactions 851
20.9 Other Concurrency Controls 856
20.9.1 Timestamp-Ordered Concurrency Controls 856
20.9.2 Optimistic Concurrency Controls 859
Bibliographic Notes 863
Exercises 863

21 Isolation in Relational Databases **869**

21.1 Conflicts in a Relational Database 869
21.1.1 Phantoms 870
21.1.2 Predicate Locking 872
21.2 Locking and the SQL Isolation Levels 875
21.2.1 Lost Updates, Cursor Stability, and Update Locks 880
CS 21.2.2 Case Study: Correctness and NonSERIALIZABLE Schedules—The Student Registration System 883
21.2.3 Serializable, SERIALIZABLE, and Correct 887
21.3 Granular Locking: Intention Locks and Index Locks 887
21.3.1 Index Locks: Granular Locking without Phantoms 890
★ 21.3.2 Granular Locking in an Object Database 900
21.4 Tuning Transactions 901
21.5 Multiversion Concurrency Controls 903
21.5.1 Read-Only Multiversion Concurrency Control 904
21.5.2 Read-Consistency Multiversion Concurrency Controls 906
CS 21.5.3 Case Study: SNAPSHOT Isolation 906
Bibliographic Notes 912
Exercises 912

22 Atomicity and Durability **919**

22.1 Crash, Abort, and Media Failure 919
22.2 Immediate-Update Systems and Write-Ahead Logs 921
22.2.1 Performance and Write-Ahead Logging 925
22.2.2 Checkpoints and Recovery 928
★ 22.2.3 Logical and Physiological Logging 934
22.3 Recovery in Deferred-Update Systems 936
22.4 Recovery from Media Failure 937
Bibliographic Notes 941
Exercises 941

PART SIX Distributed Applications and the Web 945

23 Architecture of Transaction Processing Systems 947

23.1 Transaction Processing in a Centralized System 947
23.1.1 Organization of a Single-User System 947
23.1.2 Organization of a Centralized Multiuser System 949
23.2 Transaction Processing in a Distributed System 950
23.2.1 Organization of a Distributed System 951
23.2.2 Sessions and Context 957
23.2.3 Queued Transaction Processing 960
23.3 The TP Monitor: An Overview 961
23.3.1 The Services Provided by a TP Monitor 963
23.4 The TP Monitor: Global Atomicity and the Transaction Manager 965
23.5 The TP Monitor: Remote Procedure Call 967
23.5.1 Implementation of Remote Procedure Call 968
23.5.2 Directory Services 970
23.5.3 The Transaction Manager and Transactional RPC 971
23.6 The TP Monitor: Peer-to-Peer Communication 974
23.6.1 Establishing a Connection 975
23.6.2 Distributed Commitment 976
23.7 The TP Monitor: Event Communication 977
23.7.1 Event Broker 979
23.8 Storage Architectures 981
23.9 Transaction Processing on the Internet 982
23.9.1 Architectures for C2B Transaction Processing Systems on the Internet 983
23.10 Web Application Servers—J2EE 985
23.10.1 Enterprise Java Beans 986
23.10.2 The EJB Container 992
23.10.3 Using Java Beans 1001
Bibliographic Notes 1002
Exercises 1003

24 Implementing Distributed Transactions 1005

24.1 Implementing the ACID Properties 1005
24.2 Atomic Termination 1007
24.2.1 The Two-Phase Commit Protocol 1008
24.2.2 Dealing with Failures in the Two-Phase Commit Protocol 1013
24.2.3 The Peer-to-Peer Atomic Commit Protocol 1020
24.3 Transfer of Coordination 1021

24.3.1 The Linear Commit Protocol 1022
24.3.2 Two-Phase Commit without a Prepared State 1023
24.4 Distributed Deadlock 1023
24.5 Global Serialization 1024
24.6 When Global Atomicity Cannot Be Guaranteed 1026
24.6.1 Weaker Commit Protocols 1027
24.7 Replicated Databases 1028
24.7.1 Synchronous-Update Replication Systems 1031
24.7.2 Asynchronous-Update Replication Systems 1033
24.8 Distributed Transactions in the Real World 1038
Bibliographic Notes 1038
Exercises 1038

25 Web Services 1043

25.1 The Basic Idea 1043
25.2 Web Basics 1047
25.3 Hypertext Transfer Protocol 1048
25.4 SOAP: Message Passing 1051
25.4.1 SOAP and Remote Procedure Call 1053
25.4.2 SOAP Extensibility 1055
25.4.3 SOAP Faults 1061
25.4.4 SOAP Binding 1061
25.5 WSDL: Specifying Web Services 1063
25.5.1 The Abstract Level 1063
25.5.2 The Concrete Level 1067
25.5.3 Putting It All Together 1077
25.5.4 WSDL Version 2.0 1078
25.6 BPEL: Specifying Business Processes 1080
25.6.1 Communication 1082
25.6.2 Processes 1088
25.6.3 Structured Activities 1092
25.6.4 Links 1095
25.6.5 BPEL and WS-Addressing 1097
25.6.6 Handling Errors 1099
25.6.7 Handling Multiple Requests 1105
25.6.8 Front-End and Back-End Systems 1108
25.6.9 Interacting with a Web Service: Projection of a BPEL Process 1109
25.7 UDDI: Publishing and Discovering Information about Services 1110
25.7.1 Data Structures in the UDDI Registry 1111
25.7.2 The Inquiry Interface (Query Language) 1117
25.7.3 The Publisher Interface (Update Language) 1120

25.7.4 Some Final Observations about UDDI 1123
25.8 WS-Coordination: Transactional Web Services 1123
Bibliographic Notes 1131
Exercises 1131

26 Security and Electronic Commerce 1135

26.1 Authentication, Authorization, and Encryption 1135
26.2 Encryption 1136
26.3 Digital Signatures 1141
26.4 Key Distribution and Authentication 1143
26.4.1 The Kerberos Protocol: Tickets 1144
26.4.2 Nonces 1148
26.5 Authorization 1149
26.6 Authenticated Remote Procedure Call 1151
26.7 Electronic Commerce 1152
26.8 The Secure Sockets Layer Protocol: Certificates 1153
26.9 Passport: Single Sign-On 1155
26.10 Keeping Credit Card Numbers Private 1157
★ 26.11 The Secure Electronic Transaction Protocol: Dual Signatures 1158
★ 26.12 Goods Atomicity, Certified Delivery, and Escrow 1162
★ 26.13 Electronic Cash: Blind Signatures 1165
26.14 Security in XML-Based Web Services 1171
26.14.1 Encryption and Signatures—XML Encryption and XML Signature 1171
26.14.2 Encrypting and Signing SOAP Messages—WS-Security 1176
26.14.3 SAML: Authentication, Authorization, and Single Sign-On 1180
Bibliographic Notes 1184
Exercises 1185

Bibliography 1187

Index 1203

Appendices, available on the Web[1]

A An Overview of Transaction Processing A-1

A.1 Isolation A-1
A.1.1 Serializability A-2

[1] Available on the Web at *http://www.aw-bc.com/kifer*

A.1.2 Two-Phase Locking A-4
A.1.3 Deadlock A-8
A.1.4 Locking in Relational Databases A-9
A.1.5 Isolation Levels A-11
A.1.6 Lock Granularity and Intention Locks A-14
A.1.7 Summary A-17
A.2 Atomicity and Durability A-18
A.2.1 The Write-Ahead Log A-18
A.2.2 Recovery from Mass Storage Failure A-22
A.3 Implementing Distributed Transactions A-23
A.3.1 Atomicity and Durability—The Two-Phase Commit Protocol A-24
A.3.2 Global Serializability and Deadlock A-26
A.3.3 Replication A-28
A.3.4 Summary A-30
Bibliographic Notes A-30
Exercises A-31

B Requirements and Specifications B-1

B.1 Software Engineering Methodology B-1
B.1.1 UML Use Cases B-2
CS B.2 The Requirements Document for the Student Registration System B-5
CS B.3 Requirements Analysis—New Issues B-12
CS B.4 Specifying the Student Registration System B-14
B.4.1 UML Sequence Diagrams B-15
CS B.5 The Specification Document for the Student Registration System: Section III B-16
B.6 The Next Step in the Software Engineering Process B-18
Bibliographic Notes B-18
Exercises B-19

C Design, Coding, and Testing C-1

C.1 The Design Process C-1
C.1.1 Database Design C-2
C.1.2 Describing the Behavior of Objects with UML State Diagrams C-2
C.1.3 Structure of the Design Document C-4
C.1.4 Design Review C-6
C.2 Test Plan C-7
C.3 Project Planning C-10

C.4 Coding C-13
C.5 Incremental Development C-15
C.6 The Project Management Plan C-16
CS C.7 Design and Code for the Student Registration System C-17
C.7.1 Completing the Database Design: Integrity Constraints C-18
C.7.2 Design of the Registration Transaction C-20
C.7.3 Partial Code for the Registration Transaction C-22
Bibliographic Notes C-25
Exercises C-25

Preface

Database systems occupy a central position in our information-based society. Virtually every large system with which we interact in our daily lives has a database at its core. The systems range from those that control the most trivial aspects of our lives (e.g., supermarket checkout systems) to those on which our lives depend (e.g., air traffic control systems). Over the next decades, we will become increasingly dependent on the correctness and efficiency of these systems.

We believe that every computer scientist and information systems professional should be familiar with the theoretical and engineering concepts that underlie these highly complex systems since these are the people who will be designing, building, maintaining, and administering them.

First and foremost, our goal in writing this book is to present these concepts clearly in a textbook for an introductory undergraduate or graduate course in a computer science or information systems curriculum.

Rather than focusing on how to build a database management system (DBMS), our approach focuses on how to build applications that use such a system. We believe that many more students will be implementing database applications than building DBMSs. We emphasize application issues early in the book. In addition to the standard material, this emphasis is reflected in the extensive coverage of both the UML and E-R approaches to database modeling, both SQL and the techniques for embedding SQL in host languages, and database tuning.

To enhance students' understanding of the technical material, we have included a case study of a transaction processing application, the Student Registration System, which is carried throughout the book. While a student registration system can hardly be considered glamorous, it has a unique advantage - all students have interacted with such a system as users. More important, it turns out to be a surprisingly rich application, so we can use it to illustrate many of the issues in database design, query processing, and transaction processing.

We supplement this material with three chapters specifically intended to support a first course in databases. The chapters are contained in appendices. In them we cover software engineering as it relates to database applications and we provide a brief introduction to transaction processing.

The transaction processing chapter summarizes a more extensive treatment of this subject that appears in the second half of the book. It provides a brief and accessible discussion suitable for use in a course primarily devoted to databases. We have placed it in an appendix because it repeats material that appears elsewhere in the book.

Two chapters deal with software engineering concepts using the Student Registration System as an example. Since the implementations of many information systems fail because of poor project management and inadequate attention to the principles of software engineering, we feel that these topics should be an important part of a student's education. Our treatment of this subject is brief, as many students will have studied it in a separate course. However, we believe that they will be better able to understand and apply the material when they see it presented in the context of an information system implementation. The chapters can be covered in class, or students can simply be asked to read them. Either way, we feel that instructors should require students to use good software engineering practice in their class projects. We have placed these chapters in appendices since software engineering is not within the main thrust of the book.

The second half of the book is devoted to advanced material and can serve as the basis for several advanced undergraduate or graduate courses. Topics such as the theory of relational databases, object and object relational databases, XML and document processing over the Internet, transactions and transaction processing systems, Web services, and e-commerce are given extensive coverage.

Although we discuss many practical aspects of database applications, we are primarily concerned with the concepts that underlie these topics rather than with the details of particular commercial systems or applications. Thus, in the database portion of the book we concentrate on the concepts underlying the relational and object data models rather than on any particular commercial DBMS. These concepts will remain the foundation of database processing long after SQL is obsolete. (Recall the generation of programmers who were trained in COBOL and found it extremely difficult to learn any other language.) In a similar way, in the transaction processing portion of the book, we concentrate on the concepts underlying the ACID properties and the technical issues involved in their implementation rather than on any particular commercial DBMS or transaction processing monitor.

In addition to an introductory database course, the book contains enough advanced material so that it can be used for the following courses:

- An undergraduate or graduate course in transaction processing for students who have had an introductory course in databases
- An advanced undergraduate or a first graduate course in databases for students who have had an introductory course in databases
- A course in electronic commerce and Web services

CHANGES IN THE SECOND EDITION

We have decided to publish the second edition in two versions:

- This version, which is the complete book, is appropriate for all of the courses listed above.

- Roughly the first half of the complete book, which consists of introductory material, is appropriate for a first undergraduate or graduate course in databases. Our goal here is to produce a more affordable book for students who would be taking only an introductory course.

The technology underlying the development of database applications is moving so rapidly that we have made a large number of changes and additions to the material of the first edition. One rapidly advancing technology is the Unified Modeling Language (UML). Hence, both versions have been updated with a substantial amount of material on UML. This appears in Chapter 4 on database design, where it is presented in parallel with the material on E-R diagrams that was already there. We also added UML to the material on software engineering in Appendices B and C. We added a new chapter, Chapter 12, on database tuning, because so much effort in the real world is spent increasing the throughput of database and transaction processing applications.

Perhaps the most extensive additions to the complete version are in the area of XML-based Web services. In the first edition, we had a chapter on XML. In this edition, we added a large amount of material on Web services based on XML technology. We updated the chapter on XML, Chapter 15, bringing the coverage of XQuery to the latest recommendation and adding a section on SQL/XML. We added a new chapter on Web Services, Chapter 25, which includes material on SOAP, WSDL, BPEL, UDDI, and XML-based transaction processing. In Chapter 26, on security and internet commerce, we added a section on XML-based security, using XML-Encryption, XML-Signature, WS-Security, and SAML. And in the architecture chapter, Chapter 23, we added material on Web Application Servers and J2EE, which are used to implement the back-end of many Web services.

Finally, material has been added and updated in almost all the chapters. In particular, we updated the material on object databases in Chapter 14 to bring the coverage of the object-relational aspects of SQL to the latest SQL:2003 standard. In Chapter 17, on OLAP and data mining, we included additional material on decision trees and clustering.

Note that these enhancements to the first edition are all designed to make the book more suitable for use in an applications-oriented course.

ORGANIZATION OF A FIRST COURSE IN DATABASES

This course can be taught in three different ways depending on the goals of the instructor, as summarized in the Figure P.1.

Chapters 1 through 7 and 9 through 12 should be taught in the order in which they appear in the book. Chapter 8 contains much of the information that students need in order to put the knowledge they acquired in the preceding chapters into practice. However, subsequent chapters do not significantly depend on Chapter 8. The software engineering appendices utilize some of the material of the chapters in Parts 2 and 3, but can be read in parallel with them.

TEACHING ADVANCED COURSES OUT OF THE BOOK

The book contains material for at least three advanced courses: an advanced course in databases, a transaction processing course, and a course on electronic commerce. A possible chapter layout for each of these courses is shown in Figure P.1.

The advanced database course is primarily based on Part 4, which can be augmented with material from Chapters 11, 12, and parts of earlier chapters. An in-depth course on transaction processing can be based on Parts 5 and 6. Chapters 8 and 9 are useful for projects in both of these courses and can be assigned as independent reading or can be partially covered in class. The course on electronic commerce is primarily based on Chapter 15 and the chapters in Part 6. Appendix A can also be covered in class or assigned as independent reading to students who did not have prior exposure to transaction processing.

SUPPLEMENTS

In addition to the text, the following supplementary materials are available to assist instructors:

- Three appendices, available on the Web at *http://www.aw-bc.com/kifer*, summarizing elementary transaction processing and software engineering
- Online PowerPoint presentations for all chapters
- Online PowerPoint slides of all figures
- An online solution manual containing solutions for all end-of-chapter exercises
- Solutions to sample problems, which can be given to the students in order to help them prepare for the exams. Note that these problems are *disjoint* from the end-of-chapter problems whose solutions appear in the online solution manual. Therefore, the end-of-chapter problems can be safely given in the exams.
- A test bank containing *additional* problems drawn from material in each chapter. Like the end-of-chapter problems, the test bank problems can be used for exams.
- Material describing possible course projects, including solutions (code and design documents) for some of the projects.

For more information on obtaining these supplements, please visit this book's companion Web site at *http://www.aw-bc.com/kifer*. The solutions manual, test bank, project descriptions, and PowerPoint presentations are available only to instructors through your Addison-Wesley sales representative. To contact your representative, please visit *www.aw-bc.com*.

CHAPTER DEPENDENCIES

The text can be used in a number of different ways depending on the goals of the course. To provide some guidance to the instructor, Figure P.1 shows the chapters that

Chapter	Courses					
	DB/Intro	DB/ Applications	DB/Theory	DB/Advanced	Transactions	E-commerce
1	yes	yes	yes		yes	
2	yes	yes	yes			
3	yes	yes	yes			
4	yes	yes	yes			
5	yes	yes	yes			
6		parts	yes	parts		
7	parts	parts	yes	parts		
8		yes	yes	parts	yes	
9	parts	yes		parts	yes	
10	yes	yes	yes			
11	yes	yes	yes	yes		
12	parts	yes	yes	yes		
13				yes		
14				yes		
15				yes		yes
16				yes		
17				yes		
18					yes	
19					yes	parts
20					yes	
21					yes	
22					yes	
23					yes	yes
24					yes	yes
25				yes		yes
26				yes	parts	yes
App. A		parts	yes			read
App. B	read	read	read		read	
App. C	read	read	read		read	

FIGURE P.1 Chapters for various courses.

might be included in six different courses that address different student populations and attempt to emphasize different aspects of the subject. In this table, "yes" means that all parts of the chapter should be covered by the lectures. "Parts" means that the instructor can select only parts of the material presented in the chapter. "Read" means that the chapter can be given as a reading assignment to the students.

Column 1 marks chapters that would be covered in a slow-paced introductory database course. In such a course, for instance, only parts of Chapter 6 on normalization theory might be included—perhaps only the introductory sections. Similarly, only some parts of Chapter 8, on various ways in which SQL can be combined with a host language, might be covered—perhaps only one approach, the one required for the course project.

Columns 2 and 3 outline two more-intensive introductory database courses. Column 2 expands the material covered in the introductory course in the direction of database applications, while Column 3 describes a more theory-oriented version of the course. It provides a more in-depth coverage of the normalization theory, foundations of query languages, and query optimization at the expense of the application-oriented material in Chapter 8. Although we have characterized this material as theory-oriented, we might also have characterized it as system-oriented because it covers issues involved in the design of a DBMS.

Column 4 describes an advanced database course. The course might start by reviewing or filling in material that the instructor judges the students might not have covered in a prerequisite, introductory database course. Such material would probably be found in Chapters 6, 7, 8, 11, and 13. The body of the course then continues with advanced database topics and some material on transactions in electronic commerce. At Stony Brook, this course is taught to graduate students who have had a database course in their undergraduate years.

Column 5 describes a course on transaction processing that also assumes that students have had an introductory database course as a prerequisite. At Stony Brook, we teach both an undergraduate and a graduate version of this course. The material on transaction processing can be supplemented with related material that might not have been covered in the student's prerequisite database course, for example, some material from Chapters 7 and 8.

Column 6 describes a course on electronic commerce and Web services. The course assumes a rudimentary knowledge of transactions (such as that provided in Appendix A or in an undergraduate course in databases). This should be supplemented by material with which the student might not be familiar that is covered in Chapter 19 (distributed transactions, compensation, declarative transaction semantics, recoverable queues, and workflows). Web services are heavily dependent on XML, and so Chapter 15 forms the basis of the material in Part 7.

For further fine-tuning of courses, the chapter dependency diagram in Figure P.2 can be of help. The figure identifies two kinds of dependencies. Solid arrows indicate that one chapter depends on much of the material presented in another chapter, except for the sections marked as optional. Dotted arrows indicate weak dependency, which means that only a few concepts developed in the prerequisite chapter are used in the dependent chapter, and those concepts can be covered quickly. The dependencies involving Chapter 26 are a special case. It can be taught either at the end of a transaction processing course, in which case it depends on Chapters 19, 22, and 23, or at the end of a database course, in which case it depends on Appendix A.

Finally we note that the sections in this book that are marked with the ⊛ icon in the table of contents are optional and can be omitted if the instructor prefers to

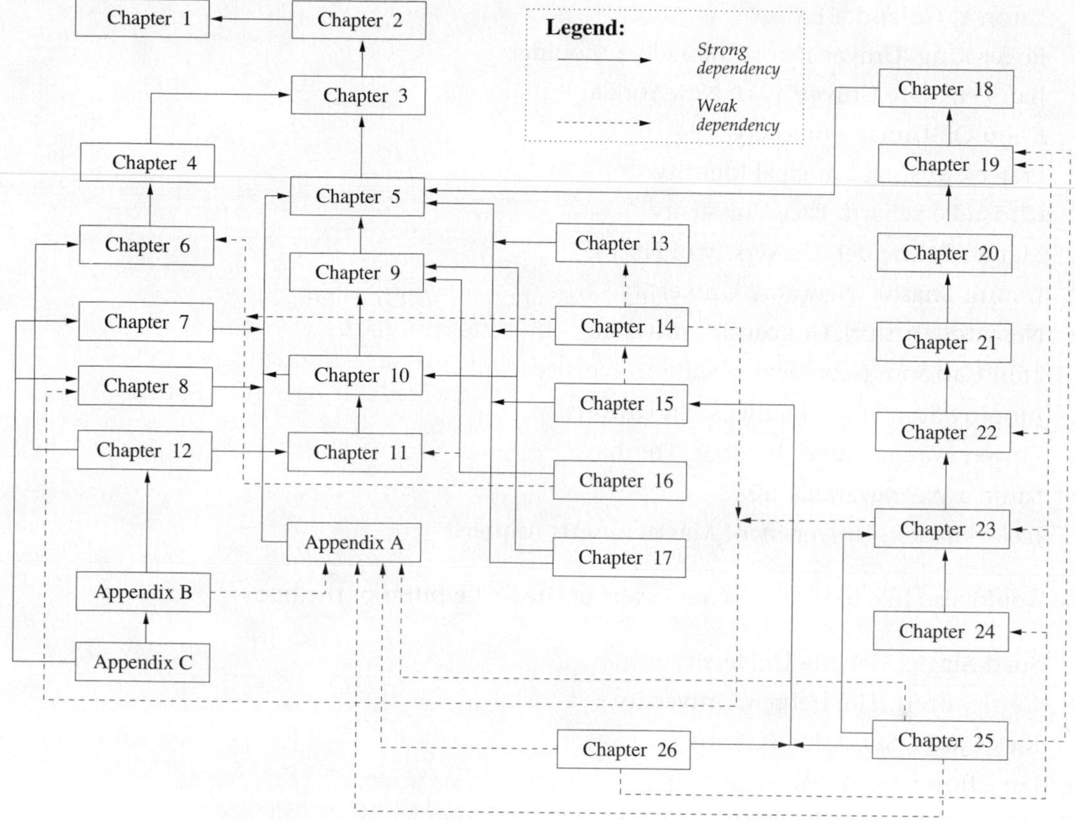

FIGURE P.2 The chapter dependency diagram.

do so. Sections marked with the Ⓒⓢ icon in the table of contents deal with the case study. Also, exercises that are marked with an asterisk are slightly harder than the rest, and exercises that are marked with two asterisks are even harder.

ACKNOWLEDGMENTS

We would like to thank the following reviewers, whose comments and suggestions significantly improved the second edition of the book:

Sibel Adali, Rensselaer Polytechnic Institute

Philip Cannata, Sun Microsystems

Mike Champion, Microsoft Corporation

Francisco Curbera, IBM

Frantisek Franek, McMaster University

Yaron Y. Goland, BEA
Roger King, University of Colorado at Boulder
Jian Pei, State University of New York at Buffalo
Dehu Qi, Lamar University
Prateek Mishra, Principal Identity
Christelle Scharff, Pace University
Markus Schneider, University of Florida
Dennis Shasha, New York University
Nematollah Shiri, Concordia University
Tran Cao Son, New Mexico State University
Junping Sun, Nova Southeastern University
Zhiwei Wang, University of St. Thomas
Sanjiva Weerawarana, IBM
Jack Wileden, University of Massachusetts Amherst

We would also like to thank the reviewers of the first edition of the book:

Suad Alagic, Wichita University
Catriel Beeri, The Hebrew University
Rick Cattel, Sun Microsystems
Jan Chomicki, SUNY Buffalo
Henry A. Etlinger, Rochester Institute of Technology
Leonidas Fegaras, University of Texas at Arlington
Alan Fekete, University of Sidney
Johannes Gehrke, Cornell University
Hershel Gottesman, consultant
Jiawei Han, Simon Fraser University
Peter Honeyman, University of Michigan
Vijay Kumar, University of Missouri–Kansas City
Jonathan Lazar, Towson University
Dennis McLeod, University of Southern California
Rokia Missaoui, University of Quebec in Montreal
Clifford Neuman, University of Southern California
Fabian Pascal, consultant
Sudha Ram, University of Arizona
Krithi Ramamritham, University of Massachusetts–Amherst, and IIT Bombay
Andreas Reuter, International University in Germany, Bruchsal

Arijit Sengupta, Georgia State University

Munindar P. Singh, North Carolina State University

Greg Speegle, Baylor University

Junping Sun, Nova Southeastern University

Joe Trubicz, consultant

Vassilis J. Tsotras, University of California, Riverside

Emilia E. Villarreal, California Polytechnic State University

We thank the following people who were kind enough to provide us with additional information, answer our questions, and suggest improvements: Don Chamberlin, Daniela Florescu, Eric Gossett, Jim Gray, Pankaj Gupta, Rob Kelly, and C. Mohan.

Two people taught out of beta versions of the book and made useful comments and suggestions: David S. Warren and Radu Grosu. Joe Trubicz served not only as a reviewer when the manuscript was complete, but provided critical comments on early versions of many of the chapters.

A number of students were very helpful in reading and checking the correctness of various parts of the book: Ziyang Duan, Shiyong Lu, Swapnil Patil, Guizhen Yang, and Yan Zhang.

Many thanks to the staff of the Computer Science Department at Stony Brook, and in particular Kathy Germana, who helped make things happen at work.

We would particularly like to thank Matt Goldstein and Maite Suarez-Rivas, our editors at Addison-Wesley, who played an important role in shaping the contents and approach of the book in its early stages and throughout the time we were writing it. We would also like to thank the various staff members of Addison-Wesley and Windfall Software, who did an excellent job of editing and producing the book: Paul Anagnostopoulos, Elisabeth Beller, Katherine Harutunian, Marilyn Lloyd, MaryEllen Oliver, John Sanderson, Jacqui Scarlott, and Joe Snowden.

Last, but not least, we would like to thank our wives, Lora, Edie, and Rhoda, who provided much-needed support and encouragement while we were writing the book.

COMPLETE VERSION

Database Systems

An Application-Oriented Approach

SECOND EDITION

PART ONE
Introduction

THE INTRODUCTORY PART of the book consists of two chapters.

In Chapter 1, we will try to get you excited about the fields of databases and transaction processing by giving you some idea of what the book is all about.

In Chapter 2, we will introduce many of the technical concepts underlying the fields of databases and transaction processing, including the SQL language and the ACID properties of transactions. We will expand on these concepts in the rest of the book.

1 Overview of Databases and Transactions

1.1 What Are Databases and Transactions?

During your vacation, you stand at the checkout counter of a department store in Tokyo, hand the clerk your credit card, and wait anxiously for your purchases to be approved. In the few seconds you have to wait, messages are sent around the world to one or more banks and clearinghouses, accessing and updating a number of databases until finally the system approves your purchase. Over 100 million such credit card transactions are processed each day from over 10 million merchants through more than 20 thousand banks. Billions of dollars are involved, and the only record of what happens is stored in the databases on the network. The accuracy, security, and availability of these databases and the correctness and performance characteristics of the transactions that access them are critical to the entire credit card business.

What is a database? A **database** is a collection of data items related to some enterprise—for example, the depositor account information in a bank. A database might be stored on cards in a Rolodex or on paper in a file cabinet, but we are particularly interested in databases stored as bits and bytes in a computer. Such a database can be **centralized** on one computer or **distributed** over several, perhaps widely separated geographically.

An increasing number of enterprises depend on such databases for their very existence. No paper records exist within the enterprise; the only up-to-date record of its current status—for example, the balance of each bank customer's checking account—is stored in its databases. Many enterprises view their databases as their most important asset.

For example, the database of the company that manufactured the airplane on which you flew to Tokyo contains the only record of information about the engineering design, manufacturing processes, and subassembly suppliers involved in producing that plane 10 years ago, together with every test made on it over its lifetime. If, at some time in the future, a test shows that a turbine blade on one of the plane's jet engines has failed, the company can determine from its database which subcontractor supplied that particular engine, and the subcontractor can determine from its database the date on which that turbine blade was manufactured, the machines and people involved, the source of the materials from which the blade was fabricated, and the results of quality assurance tests made while the blade was being manufactured. In this way it can determine the cause of the failure and increase the quality of future planes. The existence of these detailed historical databases, as well as the ability to search them for information about the fabrication of a specific turbine blade in a specific jet engine on a specific airplane manufactured 10 years ago, gives the airplane manufacturer a significant strategic advantage over any other manufacturer that does not maintain such databases.

In some cases, a database is the major asset of an enterprise—for example, the database of the credit history company that your credit card company consulted when you applied for your card. In other cases, the accuracy of the information in the database is critical for human life—for example, the database in the air traffic control system at the Tokyo airport.

What is a database management system? To make access to them convenient, databases are generally encapsulated within a **database management system (DBMS)**. The DBMS supports a high-level language in which the application programmer describes the database access it wishes to perform. Typically, all database access is classified into two broad categories: **queries** and **updates**. A query is a request to retrieve data, and an update is a request to insert, delete, or modify existing data items. The most commonly used data access language, and the one we study the most in this text, is the Structured Query Language (**SQL**). Although it is called a *query* language, updates are also done through SQL. The beauty of SQL lies in its declarative nature: the application programmer need only state what is to be done; the DBMS figures out how to do it efficiently. The DBMS interprets each SQL statement and performs the action it describes. The application programmer need not know the details of how the database is stored, need not formulate the algorithm for performing the access, and need not be concerned about many other aspects of managing the database. Compare this to the regular file systems where the programmer not only has to know the details of the file structure but also provide the algorithms to search the files to retrieve the desired information.

What is a transaction? Databases frequently store information that describes the current state of an enterprise. For example, a bank's database stores the current balance in each depositor's account. When an event happens in the real world that changes the state of the enterprise, a corresponding change must be made to the information stored in the database. With online DBMSs, these changes are made in real time by programs called **transactions**, which execute when the real-world event occurs. For example, when a customer deposits money in a bank (an event in the real world), a deposit transaction is executed. Each transaction must be designed so that it maintains the correctness of the relationship between the database state and the real-world enterprise it is modeling. In addition to changing the state of the database, the transaction itself might initiate some events in the real world. For example, a withdraw transaction at an automated teller machine (ATM) initiates the event of dispensing cash, and a transaction that establishes a connection for a telephone call requires the allocation of resources (bandwidth on a long-distance link) in the telephone company's infrastructure.

Credit card approval is only one example of a transaction that you executed on your vacation in Tokyo. Your flight arrangements involved a transaction with the airline's reservation database, your passage through passport control at the airport involved a transaction with the immigration services database, and your check-in at the hotel involved a transaction with the hotel reservation database. Even the phone call you made from your hotel room to tell your family you had arrived safely involved transactions with the hotel billing database and with a long-distance carrier to arrange billing and to establish the call.

Other examples of transactions you probably execute regularly involve ATM systems, supermarket scanning systems, and university registration and billing systems. Increasingly, these transactions entail access to **distributed databases**: multiple databases managed by different DBMSs stored at different geographical locations. Your phone call transaction at the Tokyo hotel is an example.

What is a transaction processing system? A **transaction processing system** (**TPS**) includes one or more databases that store the state of an enterprise, the software for managing the transactions that manipulate that state, and the transactions themselves that constitute the application code. In its simplest form the TPS involves a single DBMS that contains the software for managing transactions. More complex systems involve several DBMSs. In this case, transaction management is handled both within the DBMSs and without, by additional code called a **TP monitor** that coordinates transactions across multiple sites (see Figure 1.1).

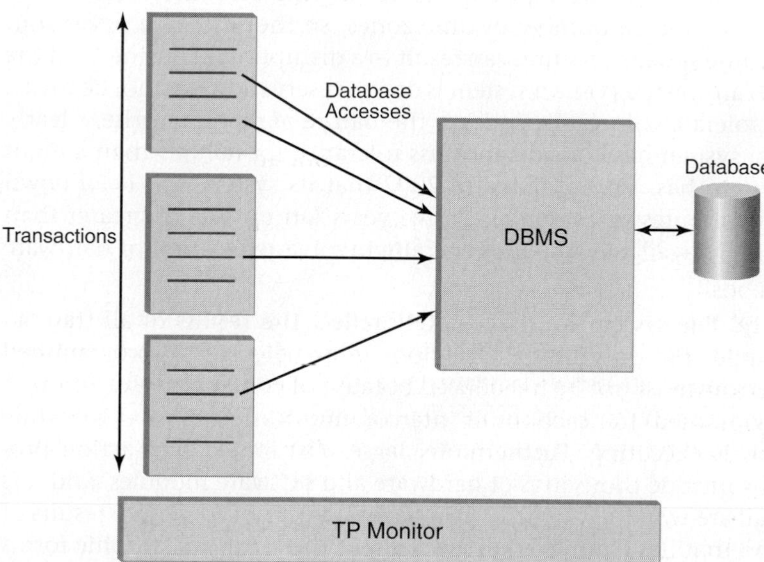

FIGURE 1.1 The structure of a transaction processing system.

The database is at the heart of a transaction processing system because it persists beyond the lifetime of any particular transaction. An increasing number of enterprises depend on such systems for their business. For example, one might say that the credit card transaction processing system *is* the credit card business.

Our concern in this book is with the technical aspects of databases and the transaction processing systems that use them. Specifically, we are interested in the design and implementation of applications, including the organization of the application database, but we are not concerned with the algorithms and data structures used to implement the underlying DBMS and transaction processing system modules. Nevertheless, we must learn enough about these underlying systems so that we can use them intelligently in an application.

1.2 Features of Modern Database and Transaction Processing Systems

Modern computer and communication technology has led to significant advances in the architecture, design, and use of database and transaction processing systems. Their enhanced functionality has lead to important new business opportunities for the enterprises that deploy them and, in turn, implies a number of additional requirements on their operation:

- ***High availability.*** Because the system is online, it must be operational at all times when the enterprise is open for business. In some enterprises, this means that the system must always be available. For example, an airline reservation system might be required to accept requests for flight reservations from ticket offices spread over a large number of time zones, so the system is never shut down. With online systems, failures can result in a disruption of business—if the computer in an airline reservation system is down, reservations cannot be made. The ability to tolerate failures depends on the nature of the enterprise. Clearly a flight control system has considerably less tolerance for failures than a flight reservation system has. VISA claimed in 2002 that its system had been down a total of eight minutes in the previous five years (an uptime of greater than 99.9999%). Highly available systems generally involve replication of hardware and software.
- ***High reliability.*** The system must accurately reflect the results of all transactions. This implies not only that transactions must be correctly programmed but also that errors must not be introduced because of concurrent execution of (correctly programmed) transactions or intercommunication of modules while the transaction is executing. Furthermore, large, distributed transaction processing systems include thousands of hardware and software modules, and it is unlikely that all are working correctly. The system must not forget the results of any transaction that has completed despite all but the most catastrophic forms of failure. For example, the database in a banking system must accurately reflect

the effect of all the deposits and withdrawals that have completed and cannot lose the results of any such transactions should it subsequently crash.

- ***High throughput.*** Because the enterprise has many customers who must use the transaction processing system, the system must be capable of performing many transactions per second. For example, a credit card approval system might perform thousands of transactions per second during its busiest periods. As we shall see, this requirement implies that individual transactions cannot be executed sequentially but must be executed concurrently—thus significantly complicating the design of the system.
- ***Low response time.*** Because customers might be waiting for a response from it, the system must respond quickly. Response requirements may differ depending on the application. Whereas you might be willing to wait fifteen seconds for an ATM to output cash, you expect a telephone connection to be made in no more than one or two seconds. Furthermore, in some applications, if the response does not occur within a fixed period of time, the transaction will not perform properly. For example, in a factory automation system the transaction might be required to actuate a device before some unit passes a particular position on the conveyor belt. Applications of this type are said to have **hard real-time** constraints.
- ***Long lifetime.*** Transaction processing systems are complex and not easily replaced. They must be designed in such a way that individual hardware or software modules can be replaced with newer versions (that perform better or have additional functionality) without necessitating major changes to the surrounding system.
- ***Security.*** Many transaction processing systems contain information about the private concerns of individuals (e.g., the items they purchase, their credit card number, the videos they view, and their health and financial records). Because these systems can be accessed by a large number of people from a large number of places (perhaps over the Internet), security is important. Individual users must be authenticated (are they who they claim to be?), users must be allowed to execute only those transactions they are authorized to execute (only a bank teller can execute a transaction to generate a certified check), the information in the database must not be corrupted or read by an attacker, and the information transmitted between the user and the system must not be altered or overheard by an eavesdropper.

1.3 Major Players in the Implementation and Support of Database and Transaction Processing Systems

A transaction processing system, together with its associated databases, can be an immensely complex assemblage of hardware and software, with which many different types of people interact in various roles. Examining these roles is a useful way of understanding what a transaction processing system is. First consider the people involved in the design and implementation of a transaction processing system:

- ***System analyst.*** The system analyst works with the customer of a proposed application system to develop formal requirements and specifications for it. He or she must understand both the business rules of the enterprise for which the application is being implemented and the database and transaction processing technology underlying the implementation so that the application will meet the customer's needs and execute efficiently. The specifications developed by the system analyst are then refined into the design of the database formats and the individual transactions that will access the database.
- ***Database designer.*** The database designer specifies the structure of the database appropriate for an application. The database contains the information that describes the current state of the real-world application. The structure must support the accesses required by the transactions and allow those accesses to be performed in a timely manner.
- ***Application programmer.*** The application programmer implements the graphical user interface and the individual transactions in the system. He or she must ensure that the transactions maintain the correspondence between the state of the real-world application and the state of the database. Together with the database designer, the application programmer must ensure that the rules governing the workings of the enterprise are enforced. For example, in the Student Registration System, to be discussed in Section 2.1, the number of students enrolled in a course should not exceed the number of seats in the room assigned to the course.
- ***Project manager.*** The project manager is responsible for the successful completion of the implementation project. He or she prepares schedules and budgets, assigns people to tasks, and monitors day-to-day project operation. Project management is surprisingly difficult. According to a widely quoted report of the Standish Group, an Information Technology (IT) consulting group, of the more than eight thousand IT projects the group surveyed, only 16% completed successfully—on time and on budget [Standish 2000]. The primary reason for the failures was almost always poor project management.[1]

The people interacting with (as opposed to building) an operational transaction processing system include the following:

- ***User.*** The user causes the execution of individual transactions, usually by interacting through some graphical user interface. The user interface must be

[1] For large companies, the success rate dropped to 9%. For projects that completed late or over budget, the average completion time was 222% of the scheduled time and the average cost was 189% of the budgeted cost. An astonishing 31% of the projects were canceled before they were completed. At the time this book was written, information about this study, called Chaos, could be found in [Standish 2000].

appropriate to the capabilities of the intended class of users. As an example, the user interface presented by an ATM is simple enough that an average person can use the system to perform bank deposit and withdraw transactions without any training or instructions except those presented on the screen. By contrast, the interface to an airline reservation system, which is used by reservation clerks or travel agents, requires advanced training. In both cases, however, most of the complexities of the system are hidden from the user.

- ***Database administrator.*** The database administrator is responsible for supporting the database while the system is running. Among his or her concerns are allocating storage space for the database, monitoring and optimizing database performance, and monitoring and controlling database security. In addition, the database administrator might modify the structure of the database to accommodate changes in the enterprise or to handle performance bottlenecks.
- ***System administrator.*** The system administrator is responsible for supporting the system as a whole while it is running. Among the things he or she must keep track of are
  - ***System architecture.*** What hardware and software modules are connected to the system at any instant, and how are they interconnected?
  - ***Configuration management.*** What version of each software module exists on each machine?
  - ***System status.*** What is the health of the system? Which systems and communication links are operational or congested, and what is being done to repair the situation? How is the system currently performing?

Our main interest in this book lies at the application level. Thus, we are particularly concerned with the roles of the system analyst, the application programmer, and the database designer. However, in order for someone working at the application level to take full advantage of the capabilities of the underlying system, he or she must be knowledgeable about the other roles as well.

1.4 Decision Support Systems—OLAP and OLTP

Transaction processing is not the only application domain in which databases play a key role. Another such domain is **decision support**. While transaction processing is concerned with using a database to maintain an accurate model of some real-world situation, decision support is concerned with using the information in a database to guide management decisions. To illustrate the differences between these two domains, we discuss the roles they might play in the operation of a national supermarket chain.

Transaction processing. Each local supermarket in a chain maintains a database of the prices and current inventory of all the items it sells. It uses that database (together with a bar code scanner) as part of a transaction processing system at the checkout counters. One transaction in this system might be, "Three cans of Campbell soup and one box of Ritz crackers were purchased; compute the price, print out a receipt, update the balance in the cash drawer, and subtract these items from the store's inventory." The customer expects this transaction to complete in a few seconds.

The main goal of such a transaction processing system is to maintain the correspondence between the database and the real-world situation it is modeling as events occur in the real world. In this case, the event is the customer's purchase, and the real-world situation is the store's inventory and the amount of cash in the cash drawer.

Decision support. The managers of the supermarket chain might want to analyze the data stored in the databases in each store to help them make decisions for the chain as a whole. Such decision support applications are becoming increasingly important as enterprises attempt to turn the *data* in their databases into *information* they can use to advance their long-term strategic goals.

Decision support applications involve queries to one or more databases, possibly followed by some mathematical analysis of the information returned by the queries. Decision support applications are sometimes called **online analytic processing** (**OLAP**), in contrast with the **online transaction processing** (**OLTP**) applications we have been discussing.

In some decision support applications, the queries are so simple they can be implemented as transactions in the same local database used for OLTP applications—for example, "Print out a report of the weekly produce sales in Store 27 for the past six months."

In many applications, however, the queries are quite complex and cannot be efficiently executed against the local databases. They take too long to execute (because the database has been optimized for OLTP transactions) and cause the local transactions—for example, the checkout transactions—to execute too slowly. The supermarket chain therefore maintains a separate database specifically for such complex OLAP queries. The database contains historical information about sales and inventory from all its branches for the past 10 years. This information is extracted from the individual store databases at various times and updated once a day. Such a database is called a **data warehouse**.

A manager can enter a complex query about the data in the data warehouse—for example, "During the winter months of the last five years, what is the percentage of customers in northeast urban supermarkets who bought crackers at the same time they bought soup?" (Perhaps these items should be placed near each other on the shelves.)

Data warehouses can contain terabytes (10^{12} bytes) of data and require special hardware to maintain that data. An OLAP query might be quite difficult to formulate and might require query language concepts more powerful than those needed for OLTP queries. OLAP queries usually do not have severe constraints on execution time and might take several hours to execute. The warehouse database might have been structured to speed up the execution of such queries. The database need be updated only periodically because minute-by-minute correctness is not needed for the types of queries it supports—satisfactory responses might be obtained even if the database is less than 100% accurate.

Data mining. A manager might also be interested in making a much less structured query about the data in the warehouse database—for example, "Are there *any* interesting combinations of items bought by customers?" Such queries are called **data mining**. In contrast with OLAP, in which requests are made to obtain specific information, data mining can be viewed as knowledge discovery—an attempt to extract new knowledge from the data stored in the database.

Data mining queries can be extremely difficult to formulate and might require sophisticated mathematics or techniques from the field of artificial intelligence. A query might require many hours to execute and might involve several interactions with the manager for obtaining additional information or reformulating parts of the query.

One widely repeated but perhaps apocryphal success story of data mining is that a convenience store chain used the above query ("Are there *any* interesting combinations . . . ") and found an unexpected correlation. In the early evenings, a high percentage of male customers who bought diapers also bought beer—presumably these customers were fathers who were going to stay home that night with their babies.

2

The Big Picture

2.1 Case Study: A Student Registration System

Your university is interested in implementing a student registration system so that students can register for courses from their home PCs. You have been asked to build a prototype of that system as a project in this course. The registrar has prepared the following preliminary **Statement of Objectives** for the system.

> The objectives of the Student Registration System are to allow students and faculty (as appropriate) to
>
> 1. Authenticate themselves as users of the system
> 2. Register and deregister for courses (offered for the next semester)
> 3. Obtain reports on a particular student's status
> 4. Maintain information about students and courses
> 5. Enter final grades for courses that a student has completed

This brief description is typical of what might be supplied as a starting point for a system implementation project, but it is not specific or detailed enough to serve as the basis for the project's design and coding phases. We will be developing the student registration scenario throughout this book and will be using it to illustrate the various concepts in databases and transaction processing.

Our next step is to meet with the registrar, faculty, and students to expand this brief description into a formal Requirements Document for the system. We will discuss the Requirements Document in Appendix B,[1] which we expect you to read at appropriate times as you proceed through the rest of the book. In this chapter, we will take a closer look at some of the underlying concepts of databases and transaction processing that are needed for that system.

The following sections provide a brief overview of these concepts. Although we will revisit these concepts in a more detailed fashion in subsequent chapters, an overview will help you see the big picture and will set the stage for better understanding of the following chapters.

[1] The appendices are available on the Web at *http://www.aw-bc.com/kifer*

2.2 Introduction to Relational Databases

A database is at the heart of most transaction processing systems. At every instant of time, the database must contain an accurate description—often the only one—of the real-world enterprise the transaction processing system is modeling. For example, in the Student Registration System the database is the only source of information about which students have registered for each course.

Relations and tuples. We are particularly interested in databases that use the **relational model** [Codd 1970, 1990], in which data is stored in **tables**. The Student Registration System, for example, might include the STUDENT table, shown in Figure 2.1. A table contains a set of **rows**. In the figure, each row contains information about one student. Each **column** of the table describes the student in a particular way. In the example, the columns are `Id`, `Name`, `Address`, and `Status`. Each column has an associated type, called its **domain**, from which the value in a particular row for that column is drawn. For example, the domain for `Id` is integer and the domain for `Name` is string.

This database model is called "relational" because it is based on the mathematical concept of a relation. A **mathematical relation** captures the notion that elements of different sets are related to one another. For example, `John Doe`, an element of the set of all humans, is related to `123 Main St.`, an element of the set of all addresses, and to `111111111`, an element of the set of all Ids. A relation is a set of **tuples**. Following the example of the table STUDENT, we might define a relation called STUDENT containing the tuple ⟨`111111111, John Doe, 123 Main St., Freshman`⟩. The STUDENT relation presumably contains a tuple describing every student.

We can view a relation as a predicate. A **predicate** is a declarative statement that is either true or false depending on the values of its arguments—for example, the predicate "It rained in Detroit on date X" is either true or false depending on the value chosen for the argument X. When we view a relation as a predicate, the arguments of the predicate correspond to the elements of a tuple, and the predicate is defined to be true for arguments $a_1, \ldots, a_n$ exactly when the tuple $\langle a_1, \ldots, a_n \rangle$ is in the relation. For instance, we might define the predicate STUDENT

Id	Name	Address	Status
111111111	John Doe	123 Main St.	Freshman
666666666	Joseph Public	666 Hollow Rd.	Sophomore
111223344	Mary Smith	1 Lake St.	Freshman
987654321	Bart Simpson	Fox 5 TV	Senior
023456789	Homer Simpson	Fox 5 TV	Senior
123454321	Joe Blow	6 Yard Ct.	Junior

FIGURE 2.1 The table STUDENT. Each row describes a single student.

with arguments `Id`, `Name`, `Address`, and `Status`. Then we can say that the predicate STUDENT ⟨`111111111, John Doe, 123 Main St., Freshman`⟩ is true, because the tuple ⟨`111111111, John Doe, 123 Main St., Freshman`⟩ is in the table STUDENT shown in Figure 2.1.

The correspondence between tables and relations should now be clear: the tuples of a relation correspond to the rows of a table, and the column names of a table are the names of the **attributes** of the relation. Thus, the rows of the STUDENT table can be viewed as enumerating the set of all 4-tuples (tuples with four attributes of the appropriate types) that satisfy the STUDENT relation (i.e., the Id, Name, Address, and Status of a student).

Operations on tables are mathematically defined. In real applications, tables can become quite large—a STUDENT table for our university would contain over 15 thousand rows, and each row would likely contain much more information about each student than is shown here. In addition to the STUDENT table, the complete database for the Student Registration System at our university would contain a number of other tables, each with a large number of rows, containing information about other aspects of student registration. For example, a TRANSCRIPT table might contain a row for each course that every student has ever taken. Hence, the databases for most applications contain a large amount of information and are generally held in mass storage.

In most applications, the database is under the control of a database management system (DBMS), which is supplied by a commercial vendor. When an application wants to perform an operation on the database, it does so by making a request to the DBMS. A typical operation might extract some information from the rows of one or more tables, modify some rows, or add or delete rows. For example, when a new student is admitted to the university, a row is added to the STUDENT table.

In addition to the fact that tables in the database can be modeled by mathematical relations, operations on the tables can also be modeled as mathematical operations on the corresponding relations. Thus, a particular unary operation might take a table, T, as an argument and produce a result table containing a subset of the rows of T. For example, an instructor might want to display the roster of students registered for a course. Such a request might involve scanning the TRANSCRIPT table, locating the rows corresponding to the course, and returning them to the application. A particular binary operation might take two tables as arguments and construct a new table containing the union of the rows of the argument tables. A complex query against a database might be equivalent to an expression involving many such relational operations involving many tables.

Because of this mathematical description, relational operations can be precisely defined and their mathematical properties, such as commutativity and associativity, can be proven. As we shall see, this mathematical description has important practical implications. Commercial DBMSs contain a **query optimizer** module that converts queries into expressions involving relational operations and then uses these mathematical properties to simplify those expressions and thus optimize query execution.

SQL: Basic SELECT statement. An application describes the access that it wants the DBMS to perform on its behalf in a language supported by the DBMS. We are particularly interested in SQL, the most commonly used database language, which provides facilities for accessing a relational database and is supported by almost all commercial DBMSs.

The basic structure of the SQL statements for manipulating data is straightforward and easy to understand. Each statement takes one or more tables as arguments and produces a table as a result. For example, to find the name of the student whose Id is 987654321, we might use the statement

```
SELECT   Name
FROM     STUDENT                                    2.1
WHERE    Id = 987654321
```

More precisely, this statement asks the DBMS to extract from the table named in the FROM clause—that is, the table STUDENT—all rows satisfying the condition in the WHERE clause—that is, all rows whose Id column has value 987654321—and then from each such row to delete all columns except those named in the SELECT clause—that is, Name. The resulting rows are placed in a result table produced by the statement. In this case, because Ids are unique, at most one row of STUDENT can satisfy the condition, and so the result of the statement is a table with one column and at most one row.

Thus, the FROM clause identifies the table to be used as input, the WHERE clause identifies the rows of that table from which the answer is to be generated, and the SELECT clause identifies the columns of those rows that are to be output in the result table.

The result table generated by this example contains only one column and at most one row. As a somewhat more complex example, the statement

```
SELECT   Id, Name
FROM     STUDENT                                    2.2
WHERE    Status = 'senior'
```

returns a result table (shown in Figure 2.2) containing two columns and multiple rows: the Ids and names of all seniors. If we want to produce a table containing all the columns of STUDENT but describing only seniors, we use the statement

```
SELECT   *
FROM     STUDENT
WHERE    Status = 'senior'
```

Id	Name
987654321	Bart Simpson
023456789	Homer Simpson

FIGURE 2.2 The database table returned by the SQL SELECT statement (2.2).

The asterisk is simply shorthand that allows us to avoid listing the names of all the columns of STUDENT.

In some situations the user is interested not in outputting a result table but in information *about* the result table. An example is the statement

```
SELECT  COUNT(*)
FROM    STUDENT
WHERE   Status = 'senior'
```

which returns the number of rows in the result table (i.e., the number of seniors). COUNT is referred to as an **aggregate** function because it produces a value that is a function of all the rows in the result table. Note that in this case, the SELECT statement produces a table that has only one row and one column.

The WHERE clause is the most interesting component of the SELECT statement; it contains a general condition that is evaluated over each row of the table named in the FROM clause. Column values from the row are substituted into the condition, yielding an expression that has either a true or a false value. If the condition evaluates to true, the row is retained for processing by the SELECT clause and then stored in the result table. Hence, the WHERE clause acts as a filter.

Conditions can be much more complex than we have seen so far: A condition can be a Boolean combination of terms. If we want the result table to contain information describing seniors whose Ids are in a particular range, for example, we might use

```
WHERE  Status = 'senior' AND Id > '888888888'
```

OR and NOT can also be used. Furthermore, a number of predicates are provided in the language for expressing particular relationships. For example, the IN predicate tests set membership.

```
WHERE  Status IN ('freshman', 'sophomore')
```

Additional aggregates and predicates and the full complexity of the WHERE clause are discussed in Chapter 5.

Multi-table SELECT statements. The result table can contain information extracted from several base tables. Thus, if we have a table TRANSCRIPT with columns StudId, CrsCode, Semester, and Grade, the statement

```
SELECT   Name, CrsCode, Grade
FROM     STUDENT, TRANSCRIPT
WHERE    StudId = Id AND Status = 'senior'
```

can be used to form a result table in which each row contains the name of a senior, a particular course she took, and the grade she received.

The first thing to note is that the attribute values in the result table come from different base tables: Name comes from STUDENT; CrsCode and Grade come from TRANSCRIPT. As in the previous examples, the FROM clause produces a table whose rows are input to the WHERE clause. In this case the table is the Cartesian product of the tables listed in the FROM clause: a row of this table is the concatenation of a row of STUDENT and a row of TRANSCRIPT. Many of these rows make no sense. For example, Bart Simpson's row in STUDENT is not related to a row in TRANSCRIPT describing a course that Bart did not take. The first conjunct of the WHERE clause ensures that the rows of TRANSCRIPT for a particular student are associated with the appropriate row of STUDENT by matching the Id values of the rows of the two tables. For example, if TRANSCRIPT has a row ⟨987654321, CS305, F1995, C⟩, it will match only Bart Simpson's row in STUDENT, producing the row ⟨Bart Simpson, CS305, C⟩ in the result table.

Query optimization. One very important feature of SQL is that the programmer does not have to specify the algorithm the DBMS should use to satisfy a particular query. For example, tables are frequently defined to include auxiliary data structures, called **indices**, which make it possible to locate particular rows without using lengthy searches through the entire table. Thus, an index on the Id column of the STUDENT table might contain a list of pairs ⟨*Id, pointer*⟩ where the pointer points to the row of the table containing the corresponding Id. If such an index were present, the DBMS would automatically use it to find the row that satisfies the query (2.1). If the table also had an index on the column Status, the DBMS would use that index to find the rows that satisfy the query (2.2). If this second index did not exist, the DBMS would automatically use some other method to satisfy (2.2)—for example, it might look at every row in the table in order to locate all rows having the value senior in the Status column. The programmer does not specify what method to use—just the condition the desired result table must satisfy.

In addition to selecting appropriate indices to use, the query optimizer uses the properties of the relational operations to further improve the efficiency with which a query can be processed—again, without any intervention by the programmer. Nevertheless, programmers should have some understanding of the strategies the DBMS uses to satisfy queries so they can design the database tables, indices, and

SQL statements in such a way that they will be executed in an efficient manner consistent with the requirements of the application.

Changing the contents of tables. The following examples illustrate the SQL statements for modifying the contents of a table. The statement

```
UPDATE   STUDENT
SET      Status = 'sophomore'
WHERE    Id = '111111111'
```

updates the STUDENT table to make John Doe a sophomore. The statement

```
INSERT
INTO     STUDENT (Id, Name, Address, Status)
VALUES   ('999999999', 'Winston Churchill', '10 Downing St',
         'senior')
```

inserts a new row for Winston Churchill in the STUDENT table. The statement

```
DELETE
FROM     STUDENT
WHERE    Id = '111111111'
```

deletes the row for John Doe from the STUDENT table. Again, the details of how these operations are to be performed need not be specified by the programmer.

Creating tables and specifying constraints. Before you can store data in a table, the table structure must be created. For instance, the STUDENT table could have been created with the SQL statement

```
CREATE TABLE  STUDENT (
Id            INTEGER,
Name          CHAR(20),
Address       CHAR(50),
Status        CHAR(10),
PRIMARY KEY (Id) )
```

where we have declared the name of each column and the domain (type) of the data that can be stored in that column. We have also declared the Id column to be a **primary key** to the table, which means that each row of the table must have a unique value in that column and the DBMS will (most probably) automatically construct an index on that column. The DBMS will enforce this uniqueness constraint by not allowing any INSERT or UPDATE statement to produce a row with a value in the Id column that duplicates a value of Id in another row. This requirement is an example of an **integrity constraint** (sometimes called a **consistency constraint**)—an application-based restriction on the values that can appear as entries in the database. We discuss integrity constraints in more detail in the next section.

We have given simple examples of each statement type to highlight the conceptual simplicity of the basic ideas underlying SQL, but be aware that the complete language has many subtleties. Each statement type has a large number of options that allow very complex queries and updates. For this reason, mastery of SQL requires significant effort. We continue our discussion of relational databases and SQL in Chapter 3.

2.3 What Makes a Program a Transaction—The ACID Properties

In many applications, a database is used to model the state of some real-world enterprise. In such applications, a transaction is a program that interacts with that database so as to maintain the correspondence between the state of the enterprise and the state of the database. In particular, a transaction might update the database to reflect the occurrence of a real-world event that affects the enterprise state. An example is a deposit transaction at a bank. The event is that the customer gives the teller the cash and a deposit slip. The transaction updates the customer's account information in the database to reflect the deposit.

Transactions, however, are not just ordinary programs. Requirements are placed on them, particularly on the way they are executed, that go beyond what is normally expected of regular programs. These requirements are enforced by the DBMS and the TP monitor.

Consistency. A transaction must access and update the database in such a way that it preserves all database integrity constraints. Every real-world enterprise is organized in accordance with certain rules that restrict the possible states of the enterprise. For example, the number of students registered for a course cannot exceed the number of seats in the room assigned to the course. When such a rule exists, the possible states of the database are similarly restricted.

The restrictions are stated as integrity constraints. The integrity constraint corresponding to the above rule asserts that the value of the database item that records the number of course registrants must not exceed the value of the item that records the room size. Thus, when the registration transaction completes, the database must satisfy this integrity constraint (assuming that the constraint was satisfied when the transaction started).

Although we have not yet designed the database for the Student Registration System, we can make some assumptions about the data that will be stored and postulate some additional integrity constraints:

- *IC0.* The database contains the Id of each student. These Ids must be unique.
- *IC1.* The database contains a list of prerequisites for each course and, for each student, a list of completed courses. A student cannot register for a course without having taken all prerequisite courses.

- *IC2.* The database contains the maximum number of students allowed to take each course and the number of students who are currently registered for each course. The number of students registered for each course cannot be greater than the maximum number allowed for that course.
- *IC3.* It might be possible to determine the number of students registered for (or enrolled in) a particular course from the database in two ways: the number is stored as a count in the information describing the course, and it can be calculated from the information describing each student by counting the number of student records that indicate that the student is registered for (or enrolled in) the course. These two determinations must yield the same result.

In addition to maintaining the integrity constraints, each transaction must update the database in such a way that the new database state reflects the state of the real-world enterprise that it models. If John Doe registers for CS305, but the registration transaction records Mary Smith as the new student in the class, the integrity constraints will be satisfied but the new state will be incorrect. Hence, consistency has two dimensions.

> ***Consistency.*** The transaction designer can assume that when execution of the transaction is initiated, the database is in a state in which all integrity constraints are satisfied and, in addition, the database correctly models the current state of the enterprise. The designer has the responsibility of ensuring that when execution has completed, the database is once again in a state in which all integrity constraints are satisfied and, in addition, that the new state reflects the transformation described in the transaction's specification (in other words, that the database still correctly models the state of the enterprise).

SQL provides some support for the transaction designer in maintaining consistency. When the database is being designed, the database designer can specify certain types of integrity constraints and include them within the statements that declare the format of the various tables in the database. The primary key constraint of the SQL statement (2.3) is an example of this. Later, as each transaction is executed, the DBMS automatically checks that each specified constraint is not violated and prevents completion of any transaction that would cause a constraint violation.

Atomicity. In addition to the transaction designer's responsibility for consistency, the TP monitor must provide certain guarantees concerning the manner in which transactions are executed. One such condition is atomicity.

> ***Atomicity.*** The system must ensure that the transaction either runs to completion or, if it does not complete, has no effect at all (as if it had never been started).

In the Student Registration System, either a student has registered for a course or he has not registered for a course. Partial registration makes no sense and might leave the database in an inconsistent state. For example, as indicated by constraint IC3, two items of information in the database must be updated when a student registers.

If a registration transaction were to have a partial execution in which one update completed but the system crashed before the second update could be executed, the resulting database would be inconsistent.

When a transaction has successfully completed, we say that it has **committed**. If the transaction does not successfully complete, we say that it has **aborted** and the TP monitor has the responsibility of ensuring that whatever partial changes the transaction has made to the database are undone, or **rolled back. Atomic execution** means that every transaction either commits or aborts.

Notice that ordinary programs do not necessarily have the property of atomicity. For example, if the system were to crash while a program that was updating a file was executing, the file could be left in a partially updated state when the system recovered.

Durability. A second requirement of the transaction processing system is that it does not lose information.

> ***Durability.*** The system must ensure that once the transaction commits, its effects remain in the database even if the computer, or the medium on which the database is stored, subsequently crashes.

For example, if you successfully register for a course, you expect the system to remember that you are registered even if it later crashes. Notice that ordinary programs do not necessarily have the property of durability either. For example, if a media failure occurs after a program that has updated a file has completed, the file might be restored to a state that does not include the update.

Isolation. In discussing consistency, we concentrated on the effect of a single transaction. We next examine the effect of executing a set of transactions. We say that a set of transactions is executed sequentially, or **serially**, if one transaction in the set is executed to completion before another is started. The good news about serial execution is that if all transactions are consistent and the database is initially in a consistent state, serial execution maintains consistency. When the first transaction in the set starts, the database is in a consistent state and, since the transaction is consistent, the database will be consistent when the transaction completes. Because the database is consistent when the second transaction starts, it too will perform correctly and the argument will repeat.

Serial execution is adequate for applications that have modest performance requirements. However, many applications have strict requirements on response time and throughput, and often the only way to meet the requirements is to process transactions concurrently. Modern computing systems are capable of servicing more than one transaction simultaneously, and we refer to this mode of execution as **concurrent**. Concurrent execution is appropriate in a transaction processing system serving many users. In this case, there will be many active, partially completed transactions at any given time.

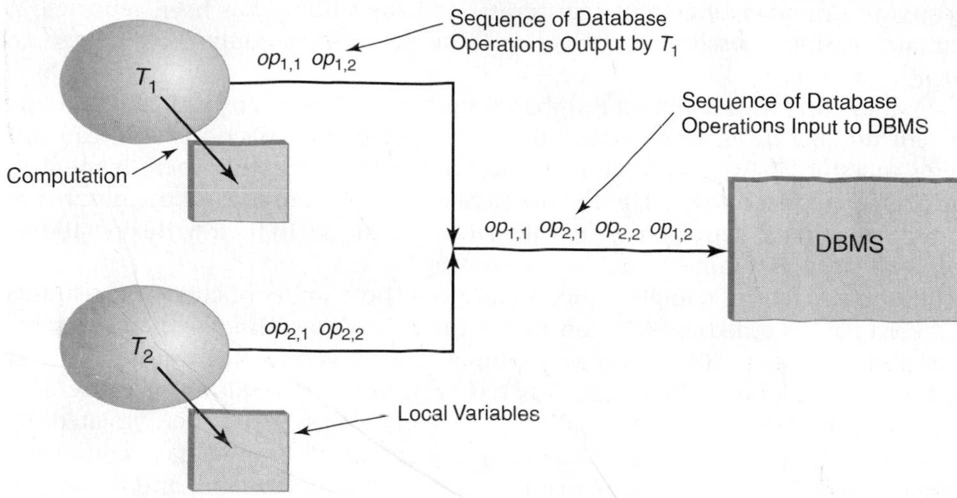

FIGURE 2.3 The database operations output by two transactions in a concurrent schedule might be interleaved in time. (Note that the figure should be interpreted as meaning that $op_{1,1}$ arrives first at the DBMS, followed by $op_{2,1}$, etc.)

In concurrent execution, the database operations of different transactions are effectively interleaved in time, a situation shown in Figure 2.3. Transaction T_1 alternately computes using its local variables and sends requests to the database system to transfer data between the database and its local variables. The requests are made in the sequence $op_{1,1}$, $op_{1,2}$. We refer to that sequence as a **transaction schedule**. T_2 performs its computation in a similar way. Because the execution of the two transactions is not synchronized, the sequence of operations arriving at the database, called a **schedule**, is an arbitrary merge of the two transaction schedules. The schedule in the figure is $op_{1,1}$, $op_{2,1}$, $op_{2,2}$, $op_{1,2}$.

When transactions are executed concurrently, the consistency of each transaction is not sufficient to guarantee that the database that exists after both have completed correctly reflects the state of the enterprise. For example, suppose that T_1 and T_2 are two instances of the registration transaction invoked by two students who want to register for the same course. A possible schedule of these transactions is shown in Figure 2.4, where time progresses from left to right and the notation $r(cur\_reg : n)$ means that a transaction has read the database object *cur_reg*, which

FIGURE 2.4 A schedule in which two registration transactions are not isolated from each other.

$T_1 : r(cur\_reg: 29)$ $\qquad$ $w(cur\_reg: 30)$

$T_2 :$ $\qquad$ $r(cur\_reg: 29)$ $\qquad$ $w(cur\_reg: 30)$

records the number of current registrants, and the value n has been returned. A similar notation is used for $w(cur\_reg : n)$. The figure shows only the accesses[2] to cur_reg.

Assume that the maximum number of students allowed to register is 30 and the current number is 29. In its first step, each of the two transactions will read this value and store it in its local variable, and both will decide that there is room in the course. In its second step, each will increment its private copy of the number of current registrants; hence, both will calculate the value 30. In their write operations, both will write that same value, 30, into cur_reg.

Both transactions complete successfully, but the number of current registrants is incorrectly recorded as 30 when it is actually 31 (even though the maximum allowable number is 30). This is an example of what is often referred to as a **lost update** because one of the increments has been lost. The resulting database does not reflect the real-world state, and integrity constraint IC2 has been violated. By contrast, if the transactions had executed sequentially, T_1 would have completed before T_2 was allowed to start. Hence, T_2 would find the course full and would not register the student.

As this example demonstrates, we must specify some restriction on concurrent execution that is guaranteed to maintain the consistency of the database and the correspondence between the enterprise state and the database state. One such restriction that is obviously sufficient follows.

> ***Isolation.*** Even though transactions are executed concurrently, the overall effect of the schedule must be the same as if the transactions had executed serially in some order.

It should be evident that if the transactions are consistent and if the overall effect of a concurrent schedule is the same as that of some serial schedule, the concurrent schedule will maintain consistency. Concurrent schedules that satisfy this condition are called **serializable**.

As was the case with atomicity and durability, ordinary programs do not necessarily have the property of isolation. For example, if programs that update a common set of files are executed concurrently, updates might be interleaved and produce an outcome that is quite different from that obtained if they had been executed in any serial order. That result might be totally unacceptable.

ACID properties. The features that distinguish transactions from ordinary programs are frequently referred to by the acronym **ACID** [Haerder and Reuter 1983]:

- ***Atomic.*** Each transaction is executed completely or not at all.
- ***Consistent.*** Each transaction maintains database consistency.
- ***Isolated.*** The concurrent execution of a set of transactions has the same effect as some serial execution of that set.

[2] In a relational database, r and w represent SELECT and UPDATE statements.

- ***Durable.*** The effects of committed transactions are permanently recorded in the database.

When a transaction processing system supports the ACID properties, the database maintains a consistent and up-to-date model of the real world and the transactions supply responses to users that are always correct and up to date.

BIBLIOGRAPHIC NOTES

The relational model for databases was introduced in [Codd 1970, 1990]. The SQL language is described by the various SQL standards, such as [SQL 1992]. The term "ACID" was coined by [Haerder and Reuter 1983], but the individual components of ACID were introduced in earlier papers—for example, [Gray et al. 1976] and [Eswaran et al. 1976].

EXERCISES

2.1 Design the following two tables (in addition to that in Figure 2.1) that might be used in the Student Registration System. Note that the same student Id might appear in many rows of each of these tables.

a. A table implementing the relation COURSESREGISTEREDFOR, relating a student's Id and the identifying numbers of the courses for which she is registered

b. A table implementing the relation COURSESTAKEN, relating a student's Id, the identifying numbers of the courses he has taken, and the grade received in each course

Specify the predicate corresponding to each of these tables.

2.2 Write an SQL statement that

a. Returns the Ids of all seniors in the table STUDENT

b. Deletes all seniors from STUDENT

c. Promotes all juniors in the table STUDENT to seniors

2.3 Write an SQL statement that creates the TRANSCRIPT table.

2.4 Using the TRANSCRIPT table, write an SQL statement that

a. Deregisters the student with `Id = 123456789` from the course `CS305` for the fall of 2001

b. Changes to an A the grade assigned to the student with `Id = 123456789` for the course `CS305` taken in the fall of 2000

c. Returns the Id of all students who took `CS305` in the fall of 2000

*2.5 Given the relation MARRIED that consists of tuples of the form $\langle a, b \rangle$, where a is the husband and b is the wife, the relation BROTHER that has tuples of the form $\langle c, d \rangle$, where c is the brother of d, and the relation SIBLING, which has tuples of the form $\langle e, f \rangle$, where e and f are siblings, use SQL to define the relation BROTHER-IN-LAW, where tuples have the form $\langle x, y \rangle$ with x being the brother-in-law of y.

2.6 Write an SQL statement that returns the names (not the Ids) of all students who received an A in `CS305` in the fall of 2000.

2.7 State whether or not each of the following statements could be an integrity constraint of a checking account database for a banking application. Give reasons for your answers.

a. The value stored in the `balance` column of an account is greater than or equal to `$0`.
b. The value stored in the `balance` column of an account is greater than it was last week at this time.
c. The value stored in the `balance` column of an account is `$128.32`.
d. The value stored in the `balance` column of an account is a decimal number with two digits following the decimal point.
e. The `social_security_number` column of an account is defined and contains a nine-digit number.
f. The value stored in the `check_credit_in_use` column of an account is less than or equal to the value stored in the `total_approved_check_credit` column. (These columns have their obvious meanings.)

2.8 State five integrity constraints, other than those given in the text, for the database in the Student Registration System.

2.9 Give an example in the Student Registration System where the database satisfies the integrity constraints IC0–IC3 but its state does not reflect the state of the real world.

2.10 State five (possible) integrity constraints for the database in an airline reservation system.

2.11 A reservation transaction in an airline reservation system makes a reservation on a flight, reserves a seat on the plane, issues a ticket, and debits the appropriate credit card account. Assume that one of the integrity constraints of the reservation database is that the number of reservations on each flight does not exceed the number of seats on the plane. (Of course, many airlines purposely over-book and so do not use this integrity constraint.) Explain how transactions running on this system might violate

a. Atomicity
b. Consistency
c. Isolation
d. Durability

2.12 Describe informally in what ways the following events differ from or are similar to transactions with respect to atomicity and durability.

a. A telephone call from a pay phone (Consider line busy, no answer, and wrong number situations. When does this transaction "commit?")
b. A wedding ceremony (Suppose that the groom refuses to say "I do." When does this transaction "commit?")
c. The purchase of a house (Suppose that, after a purchase agreement is signed, the buyer is unable to obtain a mortgage. Suppose that the buyer backs out during the closing. Suppose that two years later the buyer does not make the mortgage payments and the bank forecloses.)
d. A baseball game (Suppose that it rains.)

2.13 Assume that, in addition to storing the grade a student has received in every course he has completed, the system stores the student's cumulative GPA. Describe an integrity constraint that relates this information. Describe how the constraint would be violated if the transaction that records a new grade were not atomic.

2.14 Explain how a lost update could occur if, under the circumstances of the previous problem, two transactions that were recording grades for a particular student (in different courses) were run concurrently.

PART TWO

Database Management

Now we are ready to begin a more in-depth study of databases.

In Chapter 3, we will discuss how data items are specified in modern database management systems and how they appear to the transactions that use them. In other words, we will learn a few things about data models and data definition languages.

In Chapter 4, we will study conceptual database design, which includes methodologies for organizing data around a set of high-level concepts.

In Chapter 5, we will discuss how transactions access and modify data in a DBMS using data manipulation and query languages—in particular, SQL.

In Chapter 6, we will resume the design theme and will talk about the Relational Normalization Theory. This theory provides algorithms and objective measures for improving the quality of database design.

Chapter 7 introduces the mechanism of triggers—a powerful device for maintaining the consistency of databases and for enabling databases to react to external events.

Chapter 8 concludes this part of the book with a discussion of how SQL statements can be executed from within a host language, such as C or Java.

3

The Relational Data Model

This chapter is an introduction to the relational data model. First we define its main abstract concepts, and then we show how these concepts are embodied in the concrete syntax of SQL. Specifically, this chapter covers the data definition subset of SQL, which is used to specify data structures, constraints, and authorization policies in databases.

3.1 What Is a Data Model?

Data independence. Ultimately, all data is recorded as bytes on a disk. However, as a programmer you know that working with data at this low level of abstraction is quite tedious. Few people are interested in how sectors, tracks, and cylinders are allocated for storing information. Most programmers much prefer to work with data stored in *files*, which is a more reasonable abstraction for many applications.

From a course on file structures, you might be familiar with a variety of methods for storing data in files. **Sequential** files are best for applications that access records in the order in which they are stored. **Direct access** (or **random access**) files are best when records are accessed in a more or less unpredictable order. Files might have **indices**, which are auxiliary data structures that enable applications to retrieve records based on the value of a **search key**. We will discuss various index types in Chapter 9. Files might also consist of fixed-length records or records that have variable lengths.

The details of how data is stored in files belong to the **physical level** of data modeling. This level is specified using a **physical schema**, which in the field of databases refers to the syntax that describes the structure of files and indices.

Early data-intensive applications worked directly with the physical schema instead of the higher levels of abstraction provided by a modern DBMS. This choice was made for a number of reasons. First, commercial database systems were rare and costly. Second, computers were slow, and working directly with the file system offered a performance advantage. Third, most early applications were primitive by today's standards, and building a level of abstraction between those programs and the file system did not seem justified.

A serious drawback of this approach is that changes to the file format at the physical level could have costly repercussions for software maintenance. The "year 2000 problem" was a good example of such repercussions. In the 1960s and 1970s, it was common to write programs in which the data item representing the calendar year was hard-coded as a two-digit number. The rationale was that these programs would be replaced within fifteen to twenty years, so using four digits (or using a data abstraction for the DATE data type) was a waste of precious disk space. The result was that every routine that worked with dates expected to find the year in the two-digit format. Hence, any change to that format implied finding and changing code throughout the application. The consequence of these past decisions was the multibillion-dollar bill presented to the industry in the late 1990s for fixing outdated software.

If a data abstraction, DATE, had been used in those programs, the whole problem could have been avoided. Applications would have viewed years as four-digit numbers, even though they had been physically stored in the database as two-digit numbers. To adjust to the change of millennium, designers could have changed the underlying physical representation of years in the database to four-digit numbers by (1) building a simple program that converted the database by adding "1900" to every existing year field and (2) correspondingly changing the implementations of the appropriate functions within the DATE data type to access the new physical representation. None of the existing applications would have had to be modified because they could still use the same DATE data abstraction.

When the underlying data structures are subject to change (even infrequently), basing the design of data-intensive applications on a bare file system becomes problematic. Even trivial changes, such as adding or deleting a field in a file, imply that every application that uses this file must be manually updated, recompiled, and retested. Less trivial changes, such as merging two fields or splitting a field into two, might impact the existing applications quite significantly. Accommodating such changes can be labor intensive and error prone. In addition, the data in the original file needs to be converted to the new representation, and without the appropriate tools such conversion can be costly.

Also, the file system offers too low a level of abstraction to support the development of an application that requires frequent and rapid implementation of new queries. For such applications, the **conceptual level** of data modeling becomes appropriate.

The conceptual model hides the details of the physical data representation and instead describes data in terms of higher-level concepts that are closer to the way humans view it. For instance, the **conceptual schema**—the syntax used to describe the data at the conceptual level—could represent some of the information about students as

```
STUDENT (Id: INT, Name: STRING, Address: STRING, Status: STRING)
```

While this schema might look similar to the way file records are represented, the important point is that the different pieces of information it describes might be *physically* stored in a different way than that described in the schema. Indeed, these pieces of information might not even reside in the same file (perhaps not even on the same computer!).

The possibility of having separate schemas at the physical and conceptual levels leads to the simple, yet powerful, idea of **physical data independence**. Instead of working directly with the file system, applications see only the conceptual schema. The DBMS maps data between the conceptual and physical levels *automatically*. If the physical representation changes, all that needs to be done is to change the mapping between the levels, and *all* applications that deal exclusively with the conceptual schema will continue to work with the new physical data structures.

The conceptual schema is not the last word in the game of data abstraction. The third level of abstraction is called the **external schema** (also known as the **user** or **view** abstraction level). The external schema is used to customize the conceptual schema to the needs of various classes of users, and it also plays a role in database security (as we will see later).

The external schema looks and feels like a conceptual schema, and both are defined in essentially the same way in modern DBMSs. However, while there is a single conceptual schema per database, there might be several external schemas (i.e., views on the conceptual schema), usually one per user category. For example, to generate proper student billing information, the bursar's office might need to know each student's GPA and status and the total number of credits the student has taken, but not the names of the courses and the grades received. Even though the GPA and total number of credits might not be stored in the database explicitly, the bursar's office can be presented with a view in which these items appear as regular fields (whose values are calculated at run time when the field is accessed), and all fields and relations that are irrelevant to billing are omitted. Similarly, an academic advisor does not need to know anything about billing, so much of this information can be omitted from the advisor's view of the registration system.

These ideas lead to the principle of **conceptual data independence**: Applications tailored to the needs of specific user groups can be designed to use the external schemas appropriate for these groups. The mapping between the external and conceptual schemas is the responsibility of the DBMS, so applications are insulated from changes in the conceptual schema *as well as* from changes in the physical schema. The overall picture is shown in Figure 3.1.

Data model. A **data model** consists of a set of concepts and languages for describing

1. **Conceptual and external schemas**. A schema specifies the structure of the data stored in the database. Schemas are described using a **data definition language** (DDL).

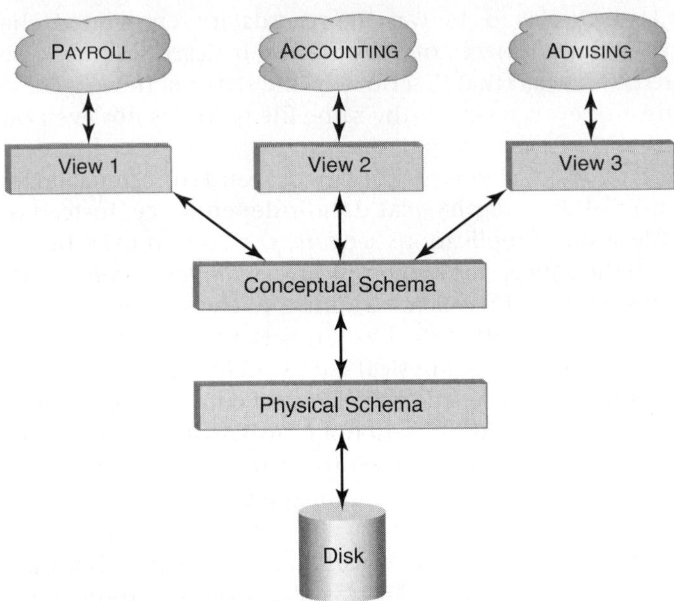

FIGURE 3.1 Levels of data independence.

2. **Constraints**. A constraint specifies a condition that the data items in the database must satisfy. A constraint specification sublanguage is usually part of the DDL.
3. **Operations on data**. Operations on database items are described using a **data manipulation language** (**DML**). The DML is usually the most important and interesting part of any data model because it is the set of operations that ultimately gives us the high-level data abstraction.

In addition, all commercial systems provide some kind of **storage definition language** (**SDL**), which allows the database designer to *influence* the physical schema (although most systems reserve the final say). The SDL is usually tightly integrated with the DDL. Changes in the physical schema that might occur if the database administrator introduces new SDL statements into a database do not affect the semantics of the applications because physical data independence shields the application from changes at the storage level. Hence, although the performance of an application might change, the results it produces do not.

In Sections 3.2 and 3.3, we describe the mother of all data models used by commercial DBMSs, the *relational model*, and the *lingua franca* these DBMS speak, **Structured Query Language** (**SQL**). Be aware, however, that despite its name SQL is not *just* a query language; it is an amalgamation of a DML, a DDL, and an SDL—three for the price of one!

3.2 The Relational Model

The *relational data model* was proposed in 1970 by E. F. Codd and was considered a major breakthrough at the time. In fact, database research and development in the 1970s and 1980s was largely shaped by the ideas presented in Codd's original work [Codd 1970, 1990]. Even today, most commercial DBMSs are based on the relational model, although they are beginning to acquire object-oriented features, especially due to the increased use of XML-based data.

The main attraction of the relational model is that it is built around a simple and natural mathematical structure—the *relation* (or table). Relations have a set of powerful, high-level operators, and data manipulation languages are deeply rooted in mathematical logic. This solid mathematical background means that relational expressions (i.e., queries) can be analyzed. Hence, any expression can potentially be transformed (by the DBMS itself) into another, *equivalent*, expression that can be executed more efficiently, in a process called *query optimization*. Thus, application programmers need not study the nitty-gritty details of the internals of each database and need not be aware of how query evaluators work. The application programmer can formulate a query in a simple and natural way and leave it to the query optimizer to find an equivalent query that is more efficient to execute.

Nevertheless, query optimizers have limitations that can result in performance penalties for certain classes of complex queries. It is therefore important for both programmers and database designers to understand the heuristics they use. With this knowledge, programmers can formulate queries that the DBMS can optimize more easily, and database designers can speed up the evaluation of important queries by adding appropriate indices and using other design techniques.

3.2.1 Basic Concepts

The central construct in the relational model is the **relation**. A relation is two things in one: a **schema** and an **instance** of that schema.

Relation instance. A **relation instance** is nothing more than a table with rows and named columns. When no confusion arises, we refer to relation instances as just "relations." The rows in a relation are called *tuples*; they are similar to *records* in a file, but unlike file records all tuples have the same number of columns (this number is called the **arity** of the relation), and no two tuples in a relation instance can be the same. In other words, a relational instance is a *set* of unique tuples. The **cardinality** of a relation instance is the number of tuples in it.

Figure 3.2 shows one possible instance for the STUDENT relation. The columns in this relation are named, which is the usual convention in the relational model. These named columns are also known as **attributes**. Because relations are sets of tuples, the order of these tuples is considered immaterial. Similarly, because columns are named, their order in a table is of no importance either. The relations in Figures 3.2 and 3.3 are thus considered to be the same relation.

STUDENT	Id	Name	Address	Status
	111111111	John Doe	123 Main St.	Freshman
	666666666	Joseph Public	666 Hollow Rd.	Sophomore
	111223344	Mary Smith	1 Lake St.	Freshman
	987654321	Bart Simpson	Fox 5 TV	Senior
	023456789	Homer Simpson	Fox 5 TV	Senior
	123454321	Joe Blow	6 Yard Ct.	Junior

FIGURE 3.2 Instance of the STUDENT relation.

STUDENT	Id	Name	Status	Address
	111223344	Mary Smith	Freshman	1 Lake St.
	987654321	Bart Simpson	Senior	Fox 5 TV
	111111111	John Doe	Freshman	123 Main St.
	023456789	Homer Simpson	Senior	Fox 5 TV
	666666666	Joseph Public	Sophomore	666 Hollow Rd.
	123454321	Joe Blow	Junior	6 Yard Ct.

FIGURE 3.3 STUDENT relation with different order of columns and tuples.

We should note that the terms "tuple," "attribute," and "relation" are preferred in relational database theory, while "row," "column," and "table" are the terms used in SQL. However, it is common to use these terms interchangeably.

The value of a particular attribute in any row of a relation is drawn from a set called the **attribute domain**—for example, the `Address` attribute of the STUDENT relation has as its domain the set of all strings. One important requirement placed on the values in a domain is **data atomicity**.[1] Data atomicity does not mean that these values are not decomposable. After all, we have seen that the values can be strings of characters, which means that they *are* decomposable. Rather, data atomicity means that the relational model does not specify any means for looking into the internal structure of the values, so that the values appear indivisible to the relational operators.

This atomicity restriction is sometimes seen as a shortcoming of the relational model, and most commercial systems relax it in various ways. Some remove it altogether, which leads to a breed of data models known as *object-relational*. We will return to the object-relational model in Chapter 14.

[1] The notion of *data atomicity* should not be confused with the unrelated notion of *transaction atomicity*, which we discussed in Section 2.3.

Brain Teaser: Can a relation have zero attributes?

Relation schema. A **relation schema** consists of

1. The **name** of the relation. Relation names must be unique across the database.
2. The names of the *attributes* in the relation along with their associated *domain names*. An **attribute** is simply the name given to a column in a relation instance. All columns in a relation must be named, and no two columns in the same relation can have the same name. A **domain name** is just a name given to some well-defined set of values. In programming languages, domain names are usually called *types*. Examples are INTEGER, REAL, and STRING.
3. The *integrity constraints* (*IC*). **Integrity constraints** are restrictions on the relational instances of this schema (i.e., restrictions on which tuples can appear in an instance of the relation). An instance of a schema is said to be **legal** if it satisfies all ICs associated with the schema.

To illustrate, let us revisit the schema that was mentioned before:

```
STUDENT(Id:INTEGER, Name:STRING, Address:STRING, Status:STRING)
```

This schema states that STUDENT relations must have exactly four attributes: `Id`, `Name`, `Address`, and `Status` with associated domains INTEGER and STRING. As seen from this example, different attributes in the same schema must have distinct names but can share domains.

The domains specify that in STUDENT relations all values in the column `Id` must belong to the domain INTEGER, while the values in all other columns must belong to the domain STRING. Naturally, we assume that the domain INTEGER consists of all integers and that the domain STRING consists of all character strings. However, schemas can also have *user-defined* domains, such as SSN or STATUS, that can be constrained to contain precisely the values appropriate for the attributes at hand. For instance, the domain STATUS can be defined to consist just of the symbols "freshman," "sophomore," and so forth, and the domain SSN can be defined to contain all (and only) nine-digit positive numbers. The point of this discussion is that relation schemas impose so-called type constraints.

A **type constraint** is a requirement that if **S** is a relation schema and **s** is a relation instance, then **s** must satisfy the following two conditions:

1. *Column naming.* Each column in **s** must correspond to an attribute in **S** (and vice versa), and the column names must be the same as the names of the corresponding attributes.
2. *Domain constraints.* For each attribute-domain pair, `attr`: DOM, in **S**, the values that appear in the column `attr` in **s** must belong to the domain DOM.

FIGURE 3.4 Fragment of the Student Registration database schema.

STUDENT (Id:INTEGER, Name:STRING, Address:STRING, Status:STRING)
PROFESSOR (Id:INTEGER, Name:STRING, DeptId:STRING)
COURSE (DeptId:STRING, CrsCode:STRING, CrsName:STRING, Descr:STRING)
TRANSCRIPT (StudId:INTEGER, CrsCode:STRING, Semester:STRING, Grade:STRING)
TEACHING (ProfId:INTEGER, CrsCode:STRING, Semester:STRING)

As we shall see, typing is just one of the several classes of constraints associated with relation schemas. To be legal, a schema instance must therefore satisfy typing as well as those additional constraints.

Relational database. A **relational database** is a finite set of relations. Because a relation is two things in one, a database is also two things: a set of relation schemas (and other entities that we will describe shortly)—called a **database schema**—and a set of corresponding relation instances—called a **database instance**. When confusion does not arise, it is common to use the term "database" to refer to database instances only. Figure 3.4 depicts one possible fragment of a database schema for our Student Registration System. Figure 3.5 gives examples of instances corresponding to these relation schemas. Observe that each relation satisfies the type constraint specified by the corresponding schema.

Brain Teaser: If you solved the previous teaser, what are the tuples of a 0-ary relation? How many tuples can such a relation have?

3.2.2 Integrity Constraints

We discussed the role that integrity constraints play in an application in Section 2.2. Now we have to fit these constraints into the database schema that supports that application. An **integrity constraint** (IC) is a statement about all *legal instances* of a database. That is, to be qualified as a legal instance a set of relations must satisfy all ICs associated with the database schema. We have already seen the type and domain constraints, and we will discuss several other kinds of constraints later.

Some integrity constraints are based on the business rules of the enterprise. The statement "No employee can earn more than his boss" is one example. Such constraints are often listed in the Requirements Document of the application. Other constraints, such as type and domain constraints, are based on the schema design and are specified by the database designer.

Since ICs are part of the database schema, they are usually specified in the original schema design. It is also possible to add or remove ICs later, after the database has been created and populated with data. Once constraints have been specified in the schema, it is the responsibility of the DBMS to make sure that they are not violated by the execution of any transactions.

PROFESSOR	Id	Name	DeptId
	101202303	John Smyth	CS
	783432188	Adrian Jones	MGT
	121232343	David Jones	EE
	864297531	Qi Chen	MAT
	555666777	Mary Doe	CS
	009406321	Jacob Taylor	MGT
	900120450	Ann White	MAT

COURSE	CrsCode	DeptId	CrsName	Descr
	CS305	CS	Database Systems	On the road to high-paying job
	CS315	CS	Transaction Processing	Recover from your worst crashes
	MGT123	MGT	Market Analysis	Get rich quick
	EE101	EE	Electronic Circuits	Build your own computer
	MAT123	MAT	Algebra	The world where $2 * 2 \neq 4$

TRANSCRIPT	StudId	CrsCode	Semester	Grade
	666666666	MGT123	F1994	A
	666666666	EE101	S1991	B
	666666666	MAT123	F1997	B
	987654321	CS305	F1995	C
	987654321	MGT123	F1994	B
	123454321	CS315	S1997	A
	123454321	CS305	S1996	A
	123454321	MAT123	S1996	C
	023456789	EE101	F1995	B
	023456789	CS305	S1996	A
	111111111	EE101	F1997	A
	111111111	MAT123	F1997	B
	111111111	MGT123	F1997	B

FIGURE 3.5 Examples of database instances.

TEACHING	ProfId	CrsCode	Semester
	009406321	MGT123	F1994
	121232343	EE101	S1991
	555666777	CS305	F1995
	101202303	CS315	S1997
	900120450	MAT123	S1996
	121232343	EE101	F1995
	101202303	CS305	S1996
	900120450	MAT123	F1997
	783432188	MGT123	F1997

FIGURE 3.5 (continued)

An IC can be **intrarelational**, meaning that it involves only one relation, or it can be **interrelational**, meaning that it involves more than one relation. The type constraint is an example of an intrarelational constraint; another example is a constraint that states that the value of the Id attribute in all rows of an instance of the STUDENT table must be unique. The latter is called a *key constraint* (discussed later). The constraint that asserts that the value of the attribute Id of each professor shown as teaching a course must appear as the value of the Id attribute of some row of the table PROFESSOR is an example of an interrelational constraint called a *foreign-key constraint* (discussed later). It expresses the requirement that each faculty member teaching a course must be described by some row of the table that describes all faculty members. The constraint that no employee can earn more than the boss[2] can be intrarelational or interrelational, depending on whether the salary information and the management structure information are stored in the same or different relations. This constraint belongs to the class of **semantic constraints**, which we will discuss later in this section.

The constraints up to this point were **static ICs**. **Dynamic ICs** are different: instead of restricting the legal instances of a database, they restrict the evolution of legal instances. This type of constraint is particularly useful for representing the business rules of an enterprise. An example is a rule that salaries must not increase or decrease by more than 5% per transaction. Another example is a rule that the marital status of a person cannot change from single to divorced. A bank might have a rule that if an overdraft has been made, it must be covered by the end of the next business day through a transfer of funds from the line-of-credit account.

[2] Let us not worry about such subtleties as how this constraint applies to the company president, who has no boss.

Unfortunately, the mainstream data manipulation languages (such as SQL) and commercial DBMSs provide little support for automatic enforcement of dynamic constraints. Therefore, application designers must provide code that enforces such constraints within the transactions that update the database. Because there is no easy way to verify that the transactions actually obey those rules, the integrity of such databases depends on the competence of the design, coding, and quality assurance groups that implement the transactions.

The situation with static ICs is much more satisfactory. Such constraints are both easier to specify and—in most cases—easier to enforce than dynamic ICs. In this section, we discuss the most common static integrity constraints. Section 3.3 shows how they are specified in SQL.

Key constraints. We have already seen one example of a key constraint: values of the `Id` attribute in an instance of the STUDENT table must be unique. For a more complex example, consider the TRANSCRIPT relation. Because it seems reasonable to assume that a student can get only one (final) grade for any course in any given semester, we can specify that {`StudId`, `CrsCode`, `Semester`} is a key. This specification ensures that for any given value for `StudId`, `CrsCode`, and `Semester`, there is *at most* one transcript record with these values. If such a tuple actually exists, it specifies the one and only grade that a given student got for a given course in a given semester.

With this intuition in mind, we can give a more precise definition of a key constraint. A **key constraint**, key($\overline{K}$), associated with a relation schema, **S**, consists of a subset, $\overline{K}$ (called a **key**), of attributes in **S** with the following **minimality property**: if $\overline{L}$ is a proper subset of $\overline{K}$ then key($\overline{L}$) cannot be specified as a key constraint in the same schema **S**. A relation instance, s, of the schema **S satisfies** the constraint key($\overline{K}$) if it has the following **uniqueness property**: s does not contain a pair of distinct tuples whose values agree on *all* of the attributes in $\overline{K}$.

Therefore, it is an error to specify, for example, both `key(A)` and `key(A,B)` as key constraints in the same relation schema. Also, if `{A,B}` is a key, then at most one tuple can have a given pair of values, *a* and *b*, in attributes `A` and `B`, respectively. However, it is possible for two different tuples to have the same value in the attribute `A` but not in `B`, and vice versa.

Example 3.2.1 (Key Constraint). The TRANSCRIPT relation of Figure 3.5 satisfies the uniqueness property for the constraint `key(StudId,CrsCode,Semester)` since there are no distinct tuples whose values agree on each of these three attributes. On the other hand, this relation does not satisfy the constraint `key(StudId,CrsCode)` because, for example, tuples 1 and 3 are distinct and yet their values over `StudId` and `CrsCode` are the same. Similarly, the constraint `key(StudId,Semester)` is not satisfied because of, say, the last two tuples.

Note that some particular instance of TRANSCRIPT *could* satisfy the uniqueness property for, say, `key(StudId,CrsCode)`. However, since this is not a reasonable constraint (since it implies that students are not allowed to re-take courses), it is unlikely to appear as one of the constraints for the Student Registration System. Note also that if this *were* specified as a constraint after all, then `key(StudId,CrsCode,`

Semester) could not have been a constraint at the same time, due to the minimality property.

Thus, if we decided to adopt the constraint key(StudId,CrsCode,Semester) for our system, then it would be allowed to have different tuples that record the same course taken by the same student, provided that this course was taken in different semesters (this would correspond to re-taking the course). It would also be allowed for any student to take several different courses during the same semester. However, it would not be possible for a student to get two different grades for the same course in the same semester. ■

The following points are important for understanding the notion of a key:

1. *Superset of a key has key-like properties.* If key($\overline{K}$) is a key constraint in schema **S**, and $\overline{L}$ is a set of attributes in **S** that *contains* $\overline{K}$, then legal instances of **S** cannot have *distinct* tuples that agree on every attribute in $\overline{L}$. Indeed, if t and s are tuples that have the same values for each attribute in $\overline{L}$, then they must have the same values for each attribute in $\overline{K}$. But because key($\overline{K}$) is a key constraint, it must have the uniqueness property, and thus t and s must be the same tuple.

   These ideas lead to the following notion: a set of attributes in **S** that contains a key is called a **superkey** of **S**. Thus, every key is also a superkey. The converse is not always true. For instance, in our TRANSCRIPT example, {StudId, CrsCode, Semester, Grade} is a superkey but not a key (because {StudId, CrsCode, Semester} is said to be a key, and they both cannot be keys at the same time, due to the minimality property). In other words, a superkey is like a key but without the minimality condition.

2. *Every relation has a key (and hence a superkey).* Indeed, the set of all attributes in a schema, **S**, is always a superkey because if a legal instance of **S** has a pair of tuples that agree on all attributes in **S**, then these must be identical tuples: since relations are sets, they cannot have identical elements. Now, if the set of all attributes in **S** is not a minimal superkey, there must be a superkey that is a strict subset of **S**. If that superkey is not a minimal superkey, there must be an even smaller superkey. As the number of attributes in a relation is finite, we will eventually hit the minimal superkey, which must then be a key, by definition.

3. *A schema can have several different keys.* For instance, in the COURSE relation, CrsCode can be one key. But because it is unlikely that the same department will offer two different courses with the same name, we can specify that {DeptId, CrsName} is also a key in the same relation.

   If a relation has several keys, they are referred to as **candidate keys**. However, one key is often designated as the **primary key**. A primary key might or might not have any particular semantic significance in the application (often a primary key is just the first among equals). However, commercial DBMSs treat primary keys as hints for optimizing the storage structures to enable efficient access to data whenever the value of a primary key is given. Thus, the choice of a primary key affects the physical schema and may affect performance.

FIGURE 3.6 Fragment of the Student Registration database with key constraints.

```
STUDENT(Id:INTEGER, Name:STRING, Address:STRING, Status:STRING)
    Key: {Id}
PROFESSOR(Id:INTEGER, Name:STRING, DeptId:STRING)
    Key: {Id}
COURSE(CrsCode:STRING, DeptId:STRING, CrsName:STRING, Descr:STRING)
    Keys: {CrsCode}, {DeptId,CrsName}
TRANSCRIPT(StudId:INTEGER, CrsCode:STRING, Semester:STRING, Grade:STRING)
    Key: {StudId,CrsCode,Semester}
TEACHING(ProfId:INTEGER, CrsCode:STRING, Semester:STRING)
    Key: {CrsCode,Semester}
```

Our fragment of the student registration database schema, with all of the key constraints included, is summarized in Figure 3.6. Note that the relation COURSE has two keys.

Referential integrity. In relational databases, it is common for tuples in one relation to reference tuples in the same or other relations. For instance, the value 009406321 of ProfId in the first tuple in TEACHING (Figure 3.5) refers to Professor Jacob Taylor, whose tuple in the table PROFESSOR has the same value in the Id field. Likewise, the value MGT123 in the first tuple of TEACHING references the Market Analysis course described by a tuple in the COURSE table.

In many situations, it is a violation of data integrity if the referenced tuple does not exist in the appropriate relation. For instance, it makes little sense to have a TEACHING tuple ⟨009406321, MGT123, F1994⟩ and not have the tuple describing MGT123 in the COURSE relation: otherwise, which course is Jacob Taylor teaching? Likewise, if the PROFESSOR relation has no tuple with Id 009406321, who is said to be teaching Market Analysis?

The requirement that the referenced tuples must exist (when the semantics of the data so requires) is called **referential integrity**. One important type of referential integrity is the *foreign-key constraint*.

Suppose that **S** and **T** are relation schemas, $\overline{F}$ is a list of attributes in **S**, and key($\overline{K}$) is a key constraint in **T**. Suppose further that there is a known 1-1 correspondence between the attributes of $\overline{F}$ and $\overline{K}$ (but the names of the attributes in $\overline{F}$ and $\overline{K}$ need not be the same). We say that relation instances **s** and **t** (over schemas **S** and **T**, respectively) satisfy the **foreign-key constraint** "**S**($\overline{F}$) references **T**($\overline{K}$)" and that $\overline{F}$ is a **foreign key** if and only if, for every tuple $s \in$ **s**, there is a tuple $t \in$ **t** that has the same values over the attributes in $\overline{K}$ as does s over the corresponding attributes in $\overline{F}$.

The concept of a foreign-key constraint is illustrated in Figure 3.7, where attribute D in table T_1 has been declared a foreign key that refers to attribute E in table T_2. E must be a candidate (or primary) key of T_2, but note that the names of the referring and referenced attributes (D and E) in the two tables need not be the same. Note also that, although each row of T_1 must reference exactly one row of T_2, not all

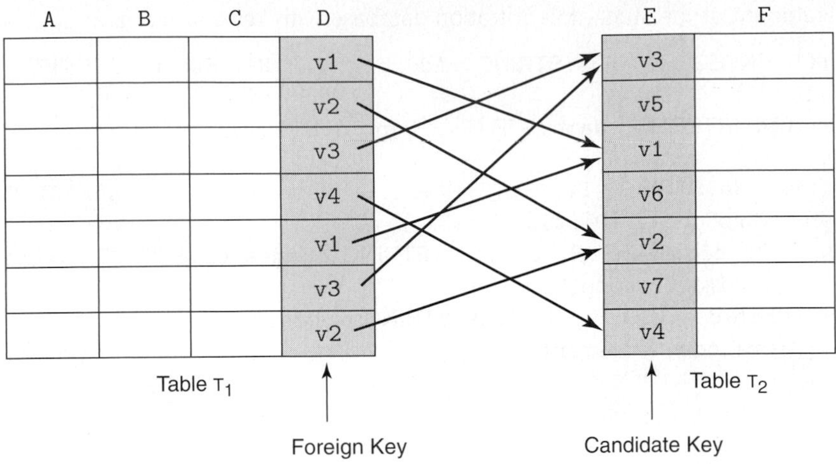

FIGURE 3.7 Attribute D in Table T_1 is a foreign key that refers to the candidate key, attribute E, in Table T_2.

rows of T_2 need be referenced, and two or more rows in T_1 can reference the same row in T_2.

In Section 3.3, we will show how foreign-key constraints are specified in SQL and will discuss the precise semantics of such constraints (which are slightly more permissive than the definition we have just given).

In a foreign-key constraint, the referring and the referenced relations need not be distinct. For instance, in the schema

```
EMPLOYEE(Id:INTEGER, Name:STRING, MngrId:INTEGER)
```

with the key {Id} the supervisor is also an employee. Thus, we have the constraint "EMPLOYEE (MngrId) references EMPLOYEE(Id)." This constraint implies that in every tuple of the EMPLOYEE relation—for example, ⟨....., ..., 998877665⟩—the MngrId value 998877665 must occur in the Id field in this or some other tuple of the same relation.

Example 3.2.2 (Foreign Keys for the Student Registration System). The following is a set of foreign-key constraints that is appropriate for the schema of the fragment of our Student Registration System shown in Figure 3.6.

```
TRANSCRIPT(StudId) references STUDENT(Id)
TRANSCRIPT(CrsCode) references COURSE(CrsCode)
TEACHING(ProfId) references PROFESSOR(Id)
TEACHING(CrsCode) references COURSE(CrsCode)
TRANSCRIPT(CrsCode,Semester) references TEACHING(CrsCode,Semester)
```

These constraints illustrate several important points. First, the attributes used to cross-reference relations need not have the same name. For instance, the attribute StudId of TRANSCRIPT references a STUDENT attribute named Id, not StudId. The foreign-key constraint in the EMPLOYEE relation above is another example of the same phenomenon.

Second, a foreign key can consist of more than one attribute, as in the last constraint. In plain English, this constraint says that if a student took a course in a particular semester, there must be a professor who taught that course in that semester. ■

Not all referential constraints are foreign-key constraints. Indeed, contrary to a popular belief, professors do not teach empty classes—at least at some universities. In other words,

```
TEACHING(CrsCode,Semester)
        references TRANSCRIPT(CrsCode,Semester)          3.1
```

appears to be an appropriate constraint for our database: at least one student must have taken (or be taking) the course named in each tuple of TEACHING. Hence, (3.1) is a referential integrity constraint, but is it a foreign-key constraint? The definition of foreign keys requires that the set of the *referenced* attributes must be a candidate key in the referenced relation.

The set ⟨CrsCode, Semester⟩ is not a candidate key of TRANSCRIPT because, naturally, we must allow several students to take the same course in any given semester. Thus, (3.1) is a referential integrity constraint, but not a foreign-key constraint.

The above constraint is known as an **inclusion dependency** in the database theory. A foreign-key constraint is just a special kind of inclusion dependency, one where the referenced attribute set is a key. Unfortunately, because of the complexity of automatic enforcement of general inclusion dependencies, such dependencies are not part of SQL's DDL. However, they can be expressed using SQL's assertion mechanism. This is illustrated later in this chapter: the CREATE ASSERTION statement (3.4) is one possible representation of constraint (3.1).

Semantic constraints. Type, domain, key, and foreign-key constraints deal with the structure of the data. Other types of constraints might have little to do with structure but rather implement a business rule or convention in a particular enterprise. Such constraints are *semantic* because they are derived from the particular application domain being modeled by the database.

Some semantic constraints were mentioned earlier: the number of students registered for a course must not exceed the capacity of the classroom where the course is scheduled to meet; a student registered for a course must meet all the prerequisites for the course; no employee can earn more than the boss; and so forth.

As we will see later, SQL provides support for specifying a wide range of semantic constraints.

3.3 SQL—Data Definition Sublanguage

Having familiarized ourselves with the basic concepts of the relational model—tables and constraints—we are now ready to look at how these concepts are specified in the "real world"—the data definition sublanguage of SQL. We base our discussion on the SQL-92 standard, but be aware that most database vendors do not fully support this standard. Because most SQL manuals are hundreds of pages long (and the actual standard has several thousand pages), we discuss only the most salient points of the language. You will need a vendor-specific reference manual if you plan to undertake serious SQL projects.

Still, SQL-92 belongs to the past, while we are planning for the future. So, to prepare for the things to come, we will also be peeking into the new standards, SQL:1999 and SQL:2003. We will discuss other parts of SQL:1999 and SQL:2003 later in the book. The most significant of those are triggers in Section 7.3 and object-relational databases in Section 14.4. Some vendors are beginning to support parts of this standard in their latest releases.

Schemas are specified using the CREATE TABLE statement of SQL. This statement has a rich syntax, which we will introduce gradually. As a bare minimum, CREATE TABLE specifies the typing constraint: the name of a relation and the names of the attributes with their associated domains. However, the same statement can also specify primary and candidate keys, foreign-key constraints, and even certain semantic constraints.

3.3.1 Specifying the Relation Type

The type for the STUDENT relation is defined as follows.

```
CREATE TABLE  STUDENT (
      Id            INTEGER,
      Name          CHAR(20),
      Address       CHAR(50),
      Status        CHAR(10) )
```

You should have no difficulty relating this SQL schema to earlier examples. Note that SQL allows the same symbolic name to be used for the name of a relation, an attribute, or even an attribute domain. Therefore, to distinguish the different parts of an SQL clause, we will be using different fonts for different syntactic categories.

3.3.2 The System Catalog

A DBMS must use information describing the structure of the database when it translates a statement of the DML into an executable program. It finds this information

COLUMNS	AttrName	RelName	Position	Format
	AttrName	Columns	1	CHAR(255)
	RelName	Columns	2	CHAR(255)
	Position	Columns	3	CHAR(255)
	Format	Columns	4	CHAR(255)
	CrsCode	Course	1	CHAR(6)
	DeptId	Course	2	CHAR(4)
	CrsName	Course	3	CHAR(20)
	Descr	Course	4	CHAR(100)
	Id	Student	1	INTEGER
	Name	Student	2	CHAR(20)
	Address	Student	3	CHAR(50)
	Status	Student	4	CHAR(10)
	...	...	...	...

FIGURE 3.8 Catalog relation.

in the **system catalog**. Therefore, while conceptually the purpose of the CREATE TABLE clause is to define a schema, technically this means inserting rows that describe the schema of a created table into the catalog. The catalog is a collection of special relations with their own schema. Figure 3.8 shows a table, called COLUMNS, which could be part of a catalog. Each row of COLUMNS contains information about a column in some database table, and all columns in all database tables are described in this way. The four columns of the table COURSE, for example, are described by four rows in the middle of the COLUMNS table.

Because COLUMNS is a table itself, its description must also be recorded. Rather than creating special machinery for this purpose, it is convenient to describe COLUMNS (and the other tables of the catalog) as a set of tuples in the catalog itself! Thus, the first few rows of COLUMNS describe the schema of that very relation. For example, the first row says that the first column of COLUMNS has the attribute name AttrName and the domain CHAR (255).

How then does all this referential complexity get bootstrapped? The catalog schema of a DBMS is designed by the vendor, and an instance of the catalog is created automatically whenever a new database is created by the database administrator.

3.3.3 Key Constraints

Primary keys and candidate keys are specified in SQL using two separate statements: PRIMARY KEY and UNIQUE. For instance, the schema of the table COURSE might look like this:

```
CREATE TABLE COURSE (
    CrsCode       CHAR(6),
    DeptId        CHAR(4),
    CrsName       CHAR(20),
    Descr         CHAR(100),
    PRIMARY KEY   (CrsCode),
    UNIQUE        (DeptId,CrsName) )
```

3.3.4 Dealing with Missing Information

Relations, as we have defined them, consist of tuples, which in turn are sequences of *known* values. For instance, in tuple ⟨111111111, Doe John, 123 Main St., freshman⟩, we have known values for Id, Name, Address, and so forth. In practice, the values of certain attributes might not be known. For example, when John Doe initially registers as a student we might not know his address. We might ask him to supply it as soon as possible, but we do not want to keep him out of our database until he complies. Instead, we use a placeholder, called NULL, and store it in place of the address until more information becomes available. Similarly, a tuple is entered in the TRANSCRIPT relation when a student registers for a course, but the Grade attribute for that tuple has no value until the semester completes.

The NULL placeholder is commonly referred to as a **null value**, but this is somewhat misleading because NULL is not a value—it indicates the *absence* of a "normal" value. In database theory and practice, NULL is treated as a special value that is a member of every attribute domain but is different from any other value in any domain. In fact, as we will see in Chapter 5, NULL is not even considered to be equal to itself!

In our example, null values arise because of a lack of information. In other situations, they arise by design. For instance, the attribute MaidenName is applicable to females but not to males. A database designer might decide that the schema

```
EMPLOYEE(Id:INT, Name:STRING, MaidenName:STRING)
```

is an appropriate description of a company's employees. If such a relation includes tuples for male employees, those tuples will not and cannot have any value for the MaidenName attribute. Again, we can use NULL here.

As we will show later, null values often introduce additional problems, especially in query processing. For these reasons and others, it is sometimes desirable not to allow null values in certain sensitive places, such as the primary key. Indeed, how can we interpret a row of STUDENT of the form ⟨NULL, Doe John, 123 Main St., freshman⟩? What if John Doe is sharing a room with a friend, also John Doe, who attends the same university and is a freshman? In this case, we might end up having two identical tuples in the same relation (each representing a different John Doe) and yet not being able to tell which John is represented by which tuple.

To preclude the above semantic difficulty, it is necessary to ensure that there is at least one key in each relation where null values are prohibited, and the primary key is the logical choice for this. Thus, the SQL standard does not permit any attribute of a primary key to have a null value. In addition to the primary key, there may be other places where NULL is inappropriate. For instance, while it might be acceptable to temporarily allow NULL in the address field, a missing student name would certainly be a problem.

Although null values are not allowed in primary keys, they are allowed in other candidate keys (unless the database designer explicitly prohibits this). Note that a null in a candidate key does not violate the definition of a key. Indeed, as mentioned earlier, NULL is not equal to itself. Therefore, if a null value occurs in a candidate key of a tuple, *t*, no other tuple can agree with *t* on that candidate key.

In summary, database designers can deal with the null value problem by not allowing nulls in attributes that are deemed crucial to the semantic integrity of the database. We can, for instance, banish the nulls from the Name field as follows.

```
CREATE TABLE STUDENT (
    Id          INTEGER,
    Name        CHAR(20)  NOT NULL,
    Address     CHAR(50),
    Status      CHAR(10) DEFAULT 'freshman',
    PRIMARY KEY (Id) )
```

In this example, null values are not allowed in the primary key, Id (which we do *not* need to specify explicitly), or in Name (which we *do* need to specify). One additional feature to note: The user can specify a *default* value for an attribute. This value will be automatically assigned to the attribute of a tuple should the tuple be inserted without this attribute being given a specific value.

3.3.5 Semantic Constraints

Semantic constraints are specified using the CHECK clause, whose basic syntax is

```
CHECK ( conditional expression )
```

The conditional expression can be any predicate or Boolean combination of predicates that can appear in the WHERE clause of an SQL statement. The integrity constraint is said to be violated if the conditional expression evaluates to false.

The CHECK clause is not used as a stand-alone statement: it is either attached to a CREATE TABLE statement, in which case it serves as an *intra*relational constraint on that particular relation, or it can be attached to a CREATE ASSERTION statement, in which case it is an *inter*relational constraint.

CHECK constraints in table definitions. CHECK constraints attached to CREATE TABLE statements are generally used to impose conditions on the content of individual relations. The following example illustrates how the CHECK clause can limit the range of an attribute.

```
CREATE TABLE TRANSCRIPT (
    StudId   INTEGER,
    CrsCode  CHAR(6),
    Semester CHAR(6),                                          3.2
    Grade    CHAR(1),
    CHECK ( Grade IN ('A', 'B', 'C', 'D', 'F') ),
    CHECK ( StudId > 0 AND StudId < 1000000000 ) )
```

Restricting the applicable range of attributes is not the only use of the CHECK constraint in the above context. Using the somewhat contrived relation schema below, we can express the constraint that managers must always earn more than their subordinates.

```
CREATE TABLE EMPLOYEE (
    Id           INTEGER,
    Name         CHAR(20),
    Salary       INTEGER,
    MngrSalary   INTEGER,
    CHECK ( MngrSalary > Salary ) )
```

The semantics of the CHECK clause inside the CREATE TABLE statement requires that *every tuple* in the corresponding relation satisfy all of the conditional expressions associated with all CHECK clauses in the corresponding CREATE TABLE statement.

One important consequence of this semantics is that the *empty relation*—a relation that contains no tuples—*always satisfies all* CHECK *constraints* as there are no tuples to check. This can lead to certain unexpected results. Consider the following syntactically correct schema definition.

```
CREATE TABLE EMPLOYEE (
    Id           INTEGER,
    Name         CHAR(20),
    Salary       INTEGER,
    DepartmentId CHAR(4),                                      3.3
    MngrId       INTEGER,
    CHECK ( 0 < (SELECT COUNT(*) FROM EMPLOYEE) ),
    CHECK ( (SELECT COUNT(*) FROM MANAGER)
                 < (SELECT COUNT(*)FROM EMPLOYEE) ) )
```

Both CHECK clauses involve SELECT statements that count the number of rows in the named relation. Hence, the first CHECK clause presumably says that the EMPLOYEE relation cannot be empty. However natural this constraint may seem to be, it *does not* achieve its intended goal. Indeed, as we have remarked, this condition is supposed to be satisfied by *every tuple* in the EMPLOYEE relation, *not* by the relation itself. Therefore, if the relation is empty, it satisfies every CHECK constraint, even the one that supposedly says that the relation must not be empty!

The second CHECK clause in (3.3) shows that in principle nothing stops us from trying to (mis)use this facility for interrelational constraints. We have assumed that there is a relation, MANAGER, that has a tuple for each manager in the company. The constraint presumably says that there must be more employees than managers, which it in fact does, but only if the EMPLOYEE relation is not empty.

General constraints: ASSERTIONS. Apart from the subtle bug, the second constraint in (3.3) looks particularly unintuitive because it is symmetric by nature and yet it is asymmetrically hardwired into the table definition of just one of the two relations involved. To overcome this problem, SQL provides one more way to use the CHECK clause—inside the CREATE ASSERTION statement. An assertion is a component of the database schema, like a table, so incorporating the CHECK clause within it puts the constraint in a symmetric relationship with the two tables. Thus, the two constraints can be restated as follows (and this time correctly!):

```
CREATE ASSERTION  THOUSHALTNOTFIREEVERYONE
    CHECK ( 0 < (SELECT COUNT(*) FROM EMPLOYEE) )
CREATE ASSERTION  WATCHADMINCOSTS
    CHECK ( (SELECT COUNT(*) FROM MANAGER)
          < (SELECT COUNT(*) FROM EMPLOYEE) ) )
```

Unlike the CHECK conditions that appear inside a table definition, those in the CREATE ASSERTION statement must be satisfied by the contents of the entire database rather than by individual tuples of a host table. Thus, a database satisfies the first assertion (above) if and only if the number of tuples in the EMPLOYEE relation is greater than zero. Likewise, the second assertion is satisfied whenever the MANAGER relation has fewer tuples than the EMPLOYEE relation has.

For another example of the use of assertions, suppose that the salary information about managers and employees is kept in different relations. We can then state our rule about who should earn more using the following assertion, which literally says that there must not exist an employee who has a boss who earns less. For the sake of this example, we assume that the MANAGER relation has the attributes Id and Salary.

```
CREATE ASSERTION  THOUSHALTNOTOUTEARNYOURBOSS
    CHECK ( NOT EXISTS
            (SELECT * FROM EMPLOYEE, MANAGER
             WHERE EMPLOYEE.Salary > MANAGER.Salary
                 AND EMPLOYEE.MngrId = MANAGER.Id ))
```

An interesting question now is, what if, at the time of specifying the constraint THOUSHALTNOTFIREEVERYONE, the EMPLOYEE relation is empty? And what if, at the time of specifying THOUSHALTNOTOUTEARNYOURBOSS, there already is an employee who earns more than the boss? The SQL standard states that if a new constraint is defined and the existing database does not satisfy it, the constraint is *rejected*. The database designer then has to find out the cause of constraint violation and either amend the constraint or rectify the database.

Our last example is a little more complex.[3] It shows how assertions can be used to specify inclusion dependencies that are not foreign-key constraints. More specifically, we express the inclusion dependency (3.1) on page 45 using the assertion statement of SQL.

```
CREATE ASSERTION  COURSESSHALLNOTBEEMPTY
    CHECK (NOT EXISTS (
        SELECT * FROM TEACHING
        WHERE NOT EXISTS (                                      3.4
            SELECT * FROM TRANSCRIPT
            WHERE Teaching.CrsCode = Transcript.CrsCode
                AND Teaching.Semester = Transcript.Semester)))
```

The CHECK constraint here verifies that there is no tuple in the TEACHING relation (the outer NOT EXISTS statement) for which no matching class exists in the TRANSCRIPT relation (the inner NOT EXISTS statement). A tuple in the TEACHING relation refers to the same class as does a tuple in the TRANSCRIPT relation if in both tuples the CrsCode and Semester components are equal. This test is performed in the innermost WHERE clause.

Different assertions have different maintenance costs (the time required for the DBMS to check that the assertion is satisfied). Generally, intrarelational constraints come cheaper than do interrelational constraints. Among the interrelational constraints, those that are based on keys are easier to enforce than those that are not. Thus, for instance, foreign-key constraints come cheaper than do general inclusion dependencies, such as (3.4).

The automatic checking of integrity constraints by a DBMS is one of the more powerful features of SQL. It not only protects the database from errors that might be introduced by untrustworthy users (or sloppy application programmers) but can simplify access to the database as well. For example, a primary key constraint ensures that at most one tuple containing a particular primary key value exists in a table. If a DBMS did not automatically check this constraint, an application program attempting to insert a new tuple or to update the key attributes of an existing tuple would have to scan the table first to ensure that the primary key constraint is maintained.

[3] It involves the use of a nested, correlated subquery. If you do not understand (3.4), plan to come back here after reading Chapter 5.

3.3.6 User-Defined Domains

We have already seen how the CHECK clause lets us limit the range of the attributes in a table. SQL provides an alternative way to enforce such constraints by allowing the user to define appropriate ranges of values, give them domain names, and then use these names in various table definitions. This approach makes the design more modular. We could, for example, create the domain GRADES and use it in the TRANSCRIPT relation instead of using the CHECK constraint directly in the definition of that relation.

```
CREATE DOMAIN   GRADES CHAR(1)
      CHECK ( VALUE IN ('A', 'B', 'C', 'D', 'F', 'I') )
```

The only difference between this and the previous constraint (3.2) on page 50, which was directly imposed on the table STUDENT, is that here we use a special keyword, VALUE, instead of the attribute name—we cannot use attribute names here, because the domain is not attached to any particular table. Now we can add

```
Grade GRADES
```

to the definition of STUDENT. The overall effect is the same, but we can use this predefined domain name in several tables without having to repeat the definition. At a later time, if we need to change this domain definition, the change will automatically propagate to all the tables that use that domain. A domain is a component of the database schema, like a table or an assertion.

Note that, as with assertions, we can use complex queries to define fairly nontrivial domains.

```
CREATE DOMAIN   UPPERDIVISIONSTUDENT INTEGER
      CHECK ( VALUE  IN (SELECT Id FROM STUDENT
                              WHERE Status IN ('senior', 'junior')
                                    AND  VALUE IS NOT NULL ) )
```

The domain UPPERDIVISIONSTUDENT consists of student Ids that belong to students whose status is either senior or junior. In addition, the last clause excludes NULL from that domain. Observe that, in order to verify that the constraint imposed by this domain is satisfied, a query against the database is run. Since such queries might be quite expensive, not every vendor supports the creation of such "virtual" domains.

3.3.7 Foreign-Key Constraints

SQL provides a simple and natural way of specifying foreign keys. The following statement makes CrsCode a foreign key referencing COURSE and makes ProfId a foreign key referencing the PROFESSOR relation.

```
CREATE TABLE TEACHING (
    ProfId   INTEGER,
    CrsCode  CHAR(6),
    Semester CHAR(6),
    PRIMARY KEY (CrsCode, Semester),
    FOREIGN KEY (CrsCode) REFERENCES COURSE,
    FOREIGN KEY (ProfId) REFERENCES PROFESSOR (Id)  )
```

If the names of the referring and the referenced attributes are the same, the referenced attribute can be omitted. The attribute CrsCode above is an example of this situation. If the referenced attribute has a different name than that of the referring attribute, both attributes must be specified. The term PROFESSOR (Id) in the second FOREIGN KEY clause shows how this is done.

It should be noted that, although the SQL standard does not require that the referenced attributes form a *primary* key (they can form *any candidate* key), some database vendors impose the primary key restriction.

In the above example, whenever a TEACHING tuple has a course code in it, the actual course record with this course code must exist in the COURSE relation. Similarly, the professor's Id in a TEACHING tuple must reference an existing tuple in the PROFESSOR relation. The DBMS is expected to enforce these constraints automatically once they are specified. Thus, as part of the procedure for deleting a tuple in the PROFESSOR relation, a check is made to ensure that there is no corresponding tuple in the TEACHING relation.

Foreign keys and nulls. What if, in a particular tuple, the value of an attribute in a foreign key is NULL? Should we insist that there be a corresponding tuple in the referenced relation with a null value in a key attribute? Not a good idea, especially if the referenced key is a primary key. Therefore, SQL *relaxes the foreign-key constraint* by letting foreign keys have null values. In this case there need not be a corresponding tuple in the referenced relation.

Chicken-and-egg problems. Foreign-key constraints raise other subtle issues too. Consider the table EMPLOYEE defined in (3.3). Suppose that we also have a table that describes departments.

```
CREATE TABLE  DEPARTMENT  (
    DeptId   CHAR(4),
    Name     CHAR(40)
    Budget   INTEGER,
    MngrId   INTEGER,
    FOREIGN KEY (MngrId) REFERENCES EMPLOYEE (Id) )
```

Now, if we look back at the DepartmentId attribute of the EMPLOYEE table, it is clear that this attribute is intended to represent valid department Ids (i.e., Ids of the departments stored in the DEPARTMENT relation). In other words, the constraint

```
FOREIGN KEY (DepartmentId) REFERENCES DEPARTMENT (DeptId)
```

is in order as part of the CREATE TABLE EMPLOYEE statement.

The problem is that either EMPLOYEE or DEPARTMENT has to be defined first. If EMPLOYEE comes first, we cannot have the above foreign-key constraint in the CREATE TABLE EMPLOYEE statement because it refers to the yet-to-be-defined table DEPARTMENT. If DEPARTMENT is defined before EMPLOYEE, the DBMS will issue an error trying to process the foreign-key constraint in the CREATE TABLE DEPARTMENT statement because this constraint references the yet-to-be-defined table EMPLOYEE. We are facing a chicken-and-egg problem.

The solution is to *postpone* the introduction of the foreign-key constraint in the first table. That is, if CREATE TABLE EMPLOYEE is executed first, we should not have the FOREIGN KEY clause in it. However, after CREATE TABLE DEPARTMENT has been processed, we can *add* the desired constraint to EMPLOYEE using the ALTER TABLE directive. This directive will be described in detail later in this section. Here we give only the final result.

```
ALTER TABLE  EMPLOYEE
  ADD CONSTRAINT  EMPDEPTCONSTR
    FOREIGN KEY (DepartmentId) REFERENCES DEPARTMENT (DeptId)
```

If, after settling this circular reference problem, we now want to start populating the database, we are in for another surprise. Suppose that we want to put the first tuple, ⟨000000007, James Bond, 7000000, B007, 000000000⟩, into the EMPLOYEE relation. Since at this moment the DEPARTMENT table is empty, the foreign-key constraint that prescribes that B007 must refer to a valid tuple in the DEPARTMENT relation is violated.

One solution is to initially replace the DepartmentId component in all tuples in the EMPLOYEE relation with NULL. Then, when DEPARTMENT is populated with appropriate tuples, we can scan the EMPLOYEE relation and replace the null values with valid department Ids. However, this solution is awkward and error-prone. A better solution is to use a transaction and deferred checking of integrity constraints.

In Chapter 2, we pointed out that the intermediate states of the database produced by a transaction might be inconsistent—they might temporarily violate integrity constraints. The only important thing is that constraints must be preserved when the transaction commits. To accommodate the possibility of temporary constraint violations, SQL allows the programmer to specify the mode of a particular integrity constraint to be either IMMEDIATE, in which case a check is made after each SQL statement that changes the database, or DEFERRED, in which case a check is made only when a transaction commits. Then, to deal with the circular reference problem just described, we can

1. Declare the foreign-key constraints in the two tables, EMPLOYEE and DEPARTMENT, as INITIALLY DEFERRED to set the initial mode of constraint checking.
2. Make the updates that populate these tables part of the same transaction. This will allow the intermediate states to be temporarily inconsistent.
3. Make sure that when all updates are done, the foreign-key constraints are satisfied. Otherwise, the transaction will be aborted when it terminates.

The full details of how transactions are defined in SQL and how they interact with constraints will be discussed in Chapter 8.

3.3.8 Reactive Constraints

When a constraint is violated, the corresponding transaction is typically aborted. However, in some cases, other remedial actions are more appropriate. Foreign-key constraints are one example of this situation.

Suppose that a tuple ⟨`007007007`, `MGT123`, `F1994`⟩ is inserted into the TEACHING relation. Because the table PROFESSOR does not have a professor with the Id `007007007`, this insertion violates the foreign-key constraint that requires all non-NULL values in the `ProfId` field of TEACHING to reference existing professors. In such a case, the semantics of SQL is very simple: the insertion is rejected.

When constraint violation occurs because of deletion of a referenced tuple, SQL offers more choices. Consider the tuple $t =$ ⟨`009406321`, `MGT123`, `F1994`⟩ in the table TEACHING. According to Figure 3.5, t references Professor Taylor in the PROFESSOR relation, and the course Market Analysis in the COURSE relation. Suppose that Professor Taylor leaves the university. What should happen to t? One solution is to temporarily set the value of `ProfId` in t to NULL until a replacement lecturer is found. Another solution is to have the attempt to delete Professor Taylor's tuple from the PROFESSOR relation fail, which might reflect the policy that professors are not allowed to leave in the middle of a semester. Finally, if Professor Taylor is the only faculty member capable of teaching the course, we might remove `MGT123` from the curriculum altogether. By deleting the referencing tuple, t, the violation of referential integrity is resolved.

These possibilities can be rephrased as **reactive constraints**. A reactive constraint is a static constraint coupled with a specification of *what to do* if a certain event happens. For instance, the first alternative above is a constraint that requires that whenever a PROFESSOR tuple is deleted, the field `ProfId` of all the referencing tuples in TEACHING must be set to NULL. The second alternative is a constraint that asserts that if a referencing tuple exists it cannot be deleted. The third alternative asserts that all referencing tuples are deleted when the referenced tuple is deleted.

We can specify the appropriate response to an event using **triggers**, which are statements of the form

```
WHENEVER event DO action
```

Triggers attached to foreign-key constraints. SQL supports a special kind of triggers, which are attached to foreign-key constraints. These triggers are specified as part of the FOREIGN KEY clause using the options ON DELETE and ON UPDATE, which indicate what to do if a referenced tuple is deleted or updated. To illustrate, let us revisit the definition of TEACHING.

```
CREATE TABLE  TEACHING  (
    ProfId    INTEGER,
    CrsCode   CHAR(6),
    Semester  CHAR(6),
    PRIMARY KEY (CrsCode, Semester),
    FOREIGN KEY (ProfId) REFERENCES PROFESSOR(Id)
        ON DELETE NO ACTION
        ON UPDATE CASCADE,
    FOREIGN KEY (CrsCode) REFERENCES COURSE (CrsCode)
        ON DELETE SET NULL
        ON UPDATE CASCADE )
```

Here we have specified four triggers. One is **fired** (i.e., executed) whenever a PROFESSOR tuple is deleted, one whenever a PROFESSOR tuple is modified, one when a COURSE tuple is deleted, and one when a COURSE tuple is modified. The clause ON DELETE NO ACTION means that any attempt to remove a PROFESSOR tuple must be rejected outright if the professor is referenced by a TEACHING tuple. NO ACTION is the default situation when an ON DELETE or ON UPDATE clause is not specified. The clause ON UPDATE CASCADE means that if the Id number of a PROFESSOR tuple is changed, the change must be propagated to all referencing TEACHING tuples (i.e., the new Id must be stored in the referencing tuples). Hence, the same professor is recorded as teaching the course. (Similarly, a specification ON DELETE CASCADE causes the referencing tuple to be deleted.) ON DELETE SET NULL tells the DBMS that if a COURSE tuple is removed and there is a referencing TEACHING tuple, the referencing attribute, CrsCode, in that tuple must be set to NULL. Alternatively, the designer can specify SET DEFAULT (instead of SET NULL): if CrsCode was defined with a DEFAULT option (e.g., the Status attribute in the STUDENT relation), then it will be reset to its default value if the referenced tuple is deleted; otherwise, it will be set to NULL (which is the default value for the DEFAULT option).

Any combination of DELETE or UPDATE triggers with NO ACTION, CASCADE, or SET NULL/DEFAULT options is allowed in foreign-key triggers. The action taken to repair a foreign-key violation in one table, T_2, in response to a change in another table, T_1, (e.g., delete a row in T_2 if a row is deleted in T_1) might cause a violation of a foreign-key constraint in T_3 that refers to T_2. The action specified in T_3 controls how that violation is handled. If the entire chain of violations cannot be resolved (e.g., the action specified in T_3 is NO ACTION), the initial deletion from T_1 is rejected.

General triggers. The ON DELETE/UPDATE triggers are simple and powerful, but they are not powerful enough to capture a wide variety of constraint violations that arise in database applications and are not due to foreign keys. For instance, the referential integrity constraint (3.1) on page 45 is *not* a foreign-key constraint and yet the same problems arise here when tuples of the TRANSCRIPT relation are modified or deleted. More importantly, foreign-key triggers cannot even begin to address common needs such as preventing salaries from changing by more than 5% in the same transaction.

To handle these needs, all major database vendors took destiny into their own hands and retrofitted their products with trigger mechanisms. Interestingly, the original design of SQL—before there was an SQL-92 standard—did have relatively powerful triggers. Triggers reappeared in SQL with the SQL:1999 standard, but some vendors are yet to align their offerings with the new standard. We will briefly describe the general trigger mechanism here and leave the details to Chapter 7.

The basic idea behind triggers is simple: whenever a specified *event* occurs, execute some specified *action*. Consider the following simple trigger defined using the syntax of SQL:1999. The trigger fires whenever CrsCode or Semester is changed in a tuple in the TRANSCRIPT relation. When the trigger fires and the grade recorded for the course is not NULL, an exception is raised and the changes made by the transaction are rolled back. Otherwise (if the grade *is* NULL), we interpret the change as a student dropping one course in favor of another, so the trigger does nothing and the change is allowed to take hold. This trigger is created with the statement

```
CREATE TRIGGER  CRSCHANGETRIGGER
    AFTER UPDATE OF  CrsCode, Semester  ON TRANSCRIPT
    WHEN  ( Grade IS NOT NULL )
        ROLLBACK
```

This definition is self-explanatory except, perhaps, for the WHEN clause, which acts as a guard, that is, as a precondition that must be satisfied in order for the trigger to fire. If the precondition is true, the statements following WHEN are executed. In our case, the statement aborts the transaction.

In general, many more details might need to be specified in order to define a trigger. For instance, should the action be executed just before the triggering update is applied to the database or after it? Should this action be executed immediately after the event or at some later time? Can a triggered action trigger another action? Moreover, to specify the guard in the WHEN clause, we might need to refer to both the *old* and the *new* values of the modified tuples (e.g., to check that salaries have not been changed by more than 5%). We postpone the discussion of these issues until Chapter 7, where many more examples of triggers will be given. In particular, we will discuss how general triggers can be used to maintain inclusion dependencies in the presence of updates (analogous to how ON DELETE and ON UPDATE triggers are used to maintain foreign-key constraints).

3.3.9 Database Views

In Section 3.1, we discussed the three levels of abstraction in databases: the physical level, the conceptual level, and the external level. We have already shown how the conceptual layer is defined in SQL. We now discuss the external (or view) layer of SQL. The physical layer will be discussed in detail in Chapter 9.

In SQL, the external schema is defined using the CREATE VIEW statement. In many respects, a view is like an ordinary table: you can query it, modify it, or control access to it. However, in several important ways a view is not a table. For one thing, the rows of a view are derived from tables (and other views) of the database. Thus, in reality a view repackages information stored elsewhere. Furthermore, the contents of a view do not physically exist in the database. Instead, a recipe for *constructing* the contents on the fly from other database tables is stored in the system catalog. As will be seen shortly, the view definition is a hybrid of the CREATE TABLE statement and the SELECT statement introduced in Chapter 2. Because of this, views are often called **virtual tables**.

To illustrate, consider the following view, which tells which professors have taught which students (a professor is said to have taught a student if the student took a course in the semester in which the professor offered it).

```
CREATE VIEW     PROFSTUD (Prof, Stud)  AS
SELECT TEACHING.ProfId, TRANSCRIPT.StudId
FROM TRANSCRIPT, TEACHING
WHERE TRANSCRIPT.CrsCode = TEACHING.CrsCode
        AND TRANSCRIPT.Semester = TEACHING.Semester
```

3.5

The first line defines the name of the view and its attributes. The rest is just an SQL query that tells how to obtain the contents of the view. These contents, with respect to the database instance of Figure 3.5, are shown in Figure 3.9. To help you understand where the tuples in the view come from, each tuple is annotated with a "justification." (A justification for a tuple $\langle p, s \rangle$ is a course code together with the semester in which student s took that course from professor p.)

The view PROFSTUD might be part of the external schema that helps the university keep in touch with its alumni since establishing the relationship between students and professors through courses might be an important and frequent operation in such an application. So, instead of this relationship being reinvented by every single application, it can be defined once and for all in the form of a view. Once it is defined, all applications can refer to the view as if it were an ordinary table. The rows of the view are constructed at the time it is accessed, so the contents change as the underlying relations are updated by transactions.

PROFSTUD	Prof	Stud	Justification
	009406321	666666666	MGT123,F1994
	121232343	666666666	EE101,S1991
	900120450	666666666	MAT123,F1997
	555666777	987654321	CS305,F1995
	009406321	987654321	MGT123,F1994
	101202303	123454321	CS315,S1997; CS305,S1996
	900120450	123454321	MAT123,S1996
	121232343	023456789	EE101,F1995
	101202303	023456789	CS305,S1996
	900120450	111111111	MAT123,F1997
	783432188	111111111	MGT123,F1997

FIGURE 3.9 Contents of the view defined by SQL statement (3.5).

In Chapter 5, we will expand our discussion of the view mechanism and show how views can be used to modularize the construction of complex queries. The authorization mechanism is another important use of views. In Section 3.3.12, we will see that views can be treated as ordinary tables for the purpose of granting selective access rights to the information stored in the database.

3.3.10 Modifying Existing Definitions

Although database schemas are not supposed to change frequently, they do evolve. Occasionally, new fields are added to relations or existing fields are dropped; new constraints and domains are created, or old ones become invalid (perhaps because business rules change). Of course, we can always copy the old contents of a relation to a temporary space, erase the old relation and its schema, and then create a new relation schema with the old name. However, this process is tedious and error-prone. To simplify schema maintenance, SQL provides the ALTER statement, which in its simplest form looks like this.

```
ALTER TABLE  STUDENT
    ADD COLUMN Gpa INTEGER DEFAULT 0
ALTER TABLE  TEACHING
    ADD COLUMN Time TIME DEFAULT NULL
```

This first command adds a new field to the STUDENT relation and initializes the field's value in each tuple to 0. The second command adds a new field to TEACHING and initializes it to NULL. You can also use DROP COLUMN to remove a column from a relation and add or drop constraints. For instance,

```
ALTER TABLE  STUDENT
    ADD CONSTRAINT GPARANGE CHECK (Gpa >= 0 AND Gpa <= 4)
ALTER TABLE  TEACHING
    ADD CONSTRAINT TEACHKEY UNIQUE(ProfId, Semester, Time)
```

If the current instance of STUDENT violates the new constraint GPARANGE, or if TEACHING violates TEACHKEY, the newly added constraints are rejected.

In order for a constraint to be "droppable" from a table definition, the constraint must be named at the time when it is defined—an option we have not used until now. We make up for this by naming every constraint in a revised definition of TRANSCRIPT.

```
CREATE TABLE  TRANSCRIPT  (
  StudId      INTEGER,
  CrsCode     CHAR(6),
  Semester    CHAR(6),
  Grade       GRADES,
  CONSTRAINT TRKEY PRIMARY KEY (StudId, CrsCode, Semester),
  CONSTRAINT STUDFK FOREIGN KEY (StudId) REFERENCES STUDENT,
  CONSTRAINT CRSFK FOREIGN KEY (CrsCode) REFERENCES COURSE,
  CONSTRAINT IDRANGE CHECK ( StudId > 0 AND
                             StudId < 1000000000 ))
```

Now we can alter the above definition by dropping any one of the specified integrity constraints. For example,

```
ALTER TABLE  TRANSCRIPT DROP CONSTRAINT TRKEY
```

When a table is no longer needed, its definition can be erased from the catalog. In this case, the schema of the table and its instance are *both* lost. Previously defined assertions and domains can also be dropped. For example,

```
DROP TABLE  EMPLOYEE  RESTRICT
DROP ASSERTION THOUSHALTNOTFIREEVERYONE
DROP DOMAIN GRADES
```

Brain Teaser: What should happen to the foreign key CrsCode in TRANSCRIPT if we drop COURSE?

The DROP TABLE command has two options: RESTRICT and CASCADE. With the RESTRICT option, the DROP statement would refuse to delete a table if it is used in some other definition, such as integrity constraint. For instance, the constraint THOUSHALTNOTFIREEVERYONE would prevent deletion of EMPLOYEE in the above case. The CASCADE option, in contrast, deletes a table definition along with any other definition that uses this table. So, for example, if we used CASCADE in the above DROP TABLE command, the assertion THOUSHALTNOTFIREEVERYONE would be deleted along with the EMPLOYEE table (and with the constraint WATCHADMIN-COSTS). In this case, the above DROP ASSERTION statement would be redundant.

The DROP DOMAIN command has its own quirks. For instance, deleting the domain GRADES above will *not* leave the attribute Grade of TRANSCRIPT in limbo. Instead, the CHECK clause that defines GRADES is copied over and is attached to all tables where this domain is used. Only after the orphaned attributes are taken care of will the GRADE domain be erased from the system catalog.

> *Brain Teaser:* Can a relation instance become invalid after execution of an ADD CONSTRAINT statement? What about DROP CONSTRAINT? DROP DOMAIN?

3.3.11 SQL-Schemas

The structure of a database is described in the system catalog. A catalog is SQL's version of a directory, in which elements are schema objects, such as tables and domains. Thus, for example, Figure 3.8 on page 47 is a simplified version of a part of the catalog for the Student Registration System. SQL partitions the catalog into SQL-schemas. An **SQL-schema**[4] is a description of a portion of a database that is under the control of a single user who has the authorization to create and access the objects within it. For example,

```
CREATE SCHEMA SRS_STUDINFO AUTHORIZATION JohnDoe
```

creates the SQL-schema SRS_STUDINFO describing the part of the Student Registration System database that contains information about students. The AUTHORIZATION clause specifies the user (JohnDoe in our case) who controls the permissions for accessing tables and other objects defined in that SQL-schema.

The naming mechanism used in conjunction with SQL-schemas is similar to that used for directories in operating systems. For example, if JohnDoe wants to create a STUDENT table in the SRS_STUDINFO SQL-schema, he refers to it as SRS_STUDINFO.STUDENT. To refer to the STUDFK constraint, he uses SRS_STUDINFO.STUDFK. Thus, an SQL-schema also serves as a kind of namespace mechanism that allows use of the same name for different relations (domains, constraints, etc.) by putting them under the scope of different schemas.

As with every CREATE statement, there is a matching DROP SCHEMA statement. For instance, JohnDoe can delete the above schema (and the entire portion of the database under it) using the following statement:

[4] Note that this use of the word "schema" is different than our previous use to describe a relation schema or database schema. We use the term "SQL-schema" to refer to the SQL usage.

```
DROP SCHEMA SRS_STUDINFO
```

SQL does not specify the format in which the information in an SQL-schema must be stored, but it does require that each system catalog contains one particular schema, named INFORMATION_SCHEMA, whose contents are precisely specified. INFORMATION_SCHEMA contains a set of SQL tables that repeat, in a precisely defined way, all the definitions from all other SQL-schemas in the catalog. The information in INFORMATION_SCHEMA can be accessed by any authorized user.

Finally, we note that SQL defines a **cluster** as a set of catalogs. A cluster describes the set of databases that can be accessed by a single SQL program. Thus, our university might define a cluster describing all of the databases it maintains that can be accessed by a single transaction.

3.3.12 Access Control

Databases often contain sensitive information. Therefore, the system must ensure that only those authenticated users who are authorized to access the database are allowed to and that they are only allowed to access information that has been specifically made available to them. Many transaction processing systems provide extensive authentication and authorization mechanisms. Authentication occurs prior to access. It might be the result of providing a password to the DBMS, or it can be a more elaborate scheme involving a separate security server. In any case, once authentication has been completed, the user is assumed to be (correctly) associated with an *authorization Id* and access to the database can begin. In SQL, **authorization Ids** are tokens that denote sets of privileges. Several database users can have the same authorization Id, in which case they would all have the same privileges.

The creator of a table or other object is assumed to own that object and has all privileges with respect to it. The owner can grant other users certain specific privileges with respect to that object by using the GRANT statement

```
GRANT { privilege-list | All PRIVILEGES }
      ON object
      TO { user-list | PUBLIC } [ WITH GRANT OPTION ]
```

where WITH GRANT OPTION means that the recipient can subsequently grant to others the privileges she has been granted.

If the object is a table or a view, *privilege-list* can include

```
SELECT
DELETE
INSERT     [(column-comma-list)]
UPDATE     [(column-comma-list)]
REFERENCES  [(column-comma-list)]
```

The first four options grant the privilege of performing the specified statement. The options that include (*column-comma-list*) grant the privilege only for the specified columns. For example, if the INSERT privilege has been granted, only the values of the attributes named in *comma-list* can be specified in the inserted tuple. All *comma-lists* are optional, as indicated by the square brackets.

REFERENCES grants the privilege of referring to the table or column using a foreign key. It might seem strange to control this type of access, but security is not complete if foreign-key constraints are not controlled. Two problems arise if foreign-key constraints can be set up arbitrarily. Suppose that a student is permitted to create the table

```
CREATE TABLE  DONTDISMISSME  (
        Id    INTEGER,
        FOREIGN KEY (Id) REFERENCES STUDENT)
```

If she inserts a single row in DONTDISMISSME containing her Id, the registrar will not be able to dismiss the student—that is, delete the student's row from STUDENT—because a deletion would cause a violation of referential integrity and hence be rejected by the DBMS.

Unrestricted access to foreign keys can also create certain information leaks. Suppose that, in the interest of protecting student information, SELECT access to STUDENT is granted only to university employees in the registrar's office. If however, an intruder were allowed to create the above table (perhaps with the name PROBEPROTECTEDINFO), this restriction could be circumvented. If the intruder inserted the Id of a particular individual in the table and the insertion were permitted by the DBMS, the intruder could conclude that a row for that individual existed in STUDENT (since referential integrity would otherwise be violated). Similarly, if the insertion were denied, the intruder could conclude that the individual was not a student. Hence, even though the intruder did not have permission to access the table through a SELECT statement, he was able to extract some information.

Example 3.3.1 (Grant Statement). The following GRANT statement gives John Smyth and Mary Doe the permission to read a row and to update the ProfId column of the TEACHING relation.

```
GRANT SELECT, UPDATE (ProfId) ON STUDREGSYSTEM.TEACHING
      TO JohnSmyth, MaryDoe WITH GRANT OPTION
```

It also gives them permission to pass on the same privileges to other users. Note, however, that these users are not allowed to delete tuples from that relation. Nor can they change other columns. However, they can see the information stored in all columns of the relation. ■

Example 3.3.2 (Authorization through Views). SQL allows control of not only direct access to databases but also indirect access through views. For instance, the following statement gives all users who are classified as alumni unrestricted query access to the PROFSTUD view defined in statement (3.5) on page 59.

```
GRANT SELECT ON ProfStud TO Alumnus
```

However, this GRANT statement does not permit the alumni to pass their query rights to others, and they cannot update the view. What is more interesting is that these users do not even have the rights to access TRANSCRIPT and TEACHING—the two relations that supply the contents for the PROFSTUD view. Their access is *indirect* and only to the parts of these relations that are visible through the view. ■

It would have been convenient to use views to selectively grant UPDATE, INSERT, or DELETE privileges. For example, one might want to grant prof_smith the right to update the Grade column of the TRANSCRIPT table, but only on the rows corresponding to courses he has taught. Unfortunately, not every view is updatable, and so it is not always possible to use views in this way. Chapter 5 will have further discussion on this subject.

Privileges can also be granted for objects other than tables (for example, domains). We omit the details.

Privileges, or the grant option for privileges, can be revoked using the REVOKE statement.

```
REVOKE [ GRANT OPTION FOR ] privilege-list
    ON object
    FROM user-list {CASCADE | RESTRICT}
```

CASCADE means that if some user, U_1, whose user name appears on the list *user-list*, has granted those privileges to another user, U_2, the privileges granted to U_2 are also revoked. If U_2 has granted those privileges to still another user, those privileges are revoked as well, and so on. The option RESTRICT means that if any such dependent privileges exist, the REVOKE statement is rejected.

In many applications, granting privileges at the level of database operations, such as SELECT or UPDATE, is not adequate. For example, only a depositor can deposit in a bank account and only a bank official can add interest to the account, but both the deposit and interest transactions might use the same UPDATE statement. For such applications, it is more appropriate to grant privileges at the level of subroutines or transactions. Many transaction processing systems control access at this level.

BIBLIOGRAPHIC NOTES

The relational data model was introduced in [Codd 1970, 1990]. Later on [Codd 1979] proposed various extensions to the original model in order to capture more semantic information.

These ideas were extended and implemented in the two pioneering relational systems: System R [Astrahan et al. 1981] and INGRES [Stonebraker 1986]. Eventually, System R became DB2, a commercial product from IBM, and INGRES became a commercial product under the same name (currently sold by Computer Associates, Intl.).

A rich body of theory has been developed for relational databases, much of which found its way into research prototypes and commercial products. More in-depth discussion as well as additional topics not covered in this book can be found in [Maier 1983; Atzeni and Antonellis 1993; Abiteboul et al. 1995].

EXERCISES

3.1 Define data atomicity as it relates to the definition of relational databases. Contrast data atomicity with transaction atomicity as used in a transaction processing system.

3.2 Prove that every relation has a key.

3.3 Define the following concepts:

a. Key
b. Candidate key
c. Primary key
d. Superkey

3.4 Define

a. Integrity constraint
b. Static, as compared with dynamic, integrity constraint
c. Referential integrity
d. Reactive constraint
e. Inclusion dependency
f. Foreign-key constraint

3.5 Looking at the data that happens to be stored in the tables for a particular application at some particular time, explain whether or not you can tell

a. What the key constraints for the tables are
b. Whether or not a particular attribute forms a key for a particular table
c. What the integrity constraints for the application are
d. Whether or not a particular set of integrity constraints is satisfied

3.6 We state in the book that once constraints have been specified in the schema, it is the responsibility of the DBMS to make sure that they are not violated by the execution of any transactions. SQL allows the application to control when each constraint is checked. If a constraint is in *immediate mode*, it is checked immediately after the execution of any SQL statement in a transaction that might make it false. If it is in *deferred mode*, it is not checked until the transaction requests to commit. Give an example where it is necessary for a constraint to be in deferred mode.

3.7 Suppose we do not require that all attributes in the primary key are non-null and instead request that, in every tuple, at least one key (primary or candidate) does not have nulls in it. (Tuples can have nulls in other places and the non-null key can be different for different tuples.) Give an example of a relational instance that has two distinct tuples that *might* become one once the values for all nulls become known (that is, are replaced with real values). Explain why this is not possible when one key (such as the primary key) is designated to be non-null for all tuples in the relation.

3.8 Use SQL DDL to specify the schema of the Student Registration System fragment shown in Figure 3.4, including the constraints in Figure 3.6 and Example 3.2.2. Specify SQL domains for attributes with small numbers of values, such as `DeptId` and `Grade`.

3.9 Consider a database schema with four relations: SUPPLIER, PRODUCT, CUSTOMER, and CONTRACTS. Both the SUPPLIER and the CUSTOMER relations have the attributes `Id`, `Name`, and `Address`. An `Id` is a nine-digit number. PRODUCT has `PartNumber` (an integer between 1 and 999999) and `Name`. Each tuple in the CONTRACTS relation corresponds to a contract between a supplier and a customer for a specific product in a certain quantity for a given price.

a. Use SQL DDL to specify the schema of these relations, including the appropriate integrity constraints (primary, candidate, and foreign key) and SQL domains.

b. Specify the following constraint as an SQL assertion: *there must be more contracts than suppliers.*

3.10 You have been hired by a video store to create a database for tracking DVDs and videocassettes, customers, and who rented what. The database includes these relations: RENTALITEM, CUSTOMER, and RENTALS. Use SQL DDL to specify the schema for this database, including all the applicable constraints. You are free to choose reasonable attributes for the first two relations. The relation RENTALS is intended to describe who rented what and should have these attributes: `CustomerId`, `ItemId`, `RentedFrom`, `RentedUntil`, and `DateReturned`.

3.11 You are in a real estate business renting apartments to customers. Your job is to define an appropriate schema using SQL DDL. The relations are PROPERTY(`Id`, `Address`, `NumberOfUnits`), UNIT(`ApartmentNumber`, `PropertyId`, `RentalPrice`, `Size`), CUSTOMER (choose appropriate attributes), RENTALS (choose attributes; this relation should describe who rents what, since when, and until when), and PAYMENTS (should describe who paid for which unit, how much, and when). Assume that a customer can rent more than one unit (in the same or different properties) and that the same unit can be co-rented by several customers.

3.12 You love movies and decided to create a personal database to help you with trivia questions. You chose to have the following relations: ACTOR, STUDIO, MOVIE, and PLAYEDIN (which actor played in which movie). The attributes of MOVIE are `Name`, `Year`, `Studio`, and `Budget`. The attributes of PLAYEDIN are `Movie` and `Actor`. You are free to choose the attributes for the other relations as appropriate. Use SQL DDL to design the schema and all the applicable constraints.

3.13 You want to get rich by operating an auction Web site, similar to eBay, at which students can register used textbooks that they want to sell and other students can bid on purchasing those books. The site is to use the same proxy bidding system used by eBay (*http://www.ebay.com*).

Design a schema for the database required for the site. In the initial version of the system, the database must contain the following information:

1. For each book being auctioned: name, authors, edition, ISBN number, bookId (unique), condition, initial offering price, current bid, current maximum bid, auction start date and time, auction end date and time, userId of the seller, userId of the current high bidder, and an indication that the auction is either currently active or complete
2. For each registered user: name, userId (unique), password, and e-mail address

3.14 You want to design a room-scheduling system that can be used by the faculty and staff of your department to schedule rooms for events, meetings, classes, etc. Design a schema for the database required for the system. The database must contain the following information:

1. For each registered user: name, userId (unique), password, and e-mail address
2. For each room: room number, start date of the event, start time of the event, duration of the event, repetition of the event (once, daily, weekly, monthly, mon-wed-fri, or tues-thurs), and end date of repetitive event

3.15 Design the schema for a library system. The following data should either be contained directly in the system or it should be possible to calculate it from stored information:

1. About each patron: name, password, address, Id, unpaid fines, identity of each book the patron has currently withdrawn, and each book's due date
2. About each book: ISBN number, title, author(s), year of publication, shelfId, publisher, and status (on-shelf, on-loan, on-hold, or on-loan-and-on-hold). For books on-loan the database shall contain the Id of the patron involved and the due date. For books on hold the database shall contain a list of Ids of patrons who have requested the book.
3. About each shelf: shelfId and capacity (in number of books)
4. About each author: year of birth

The system should enforce the following integrity constraints. You should decide whether a particular constraint will be embedded in the schema, and, if so, show how this is done or will be enforced in the code of a transaction.

1. The number of books on a shelf cannot exceed its capacity.
2. A patron cannot withdraw more than two books at a time.
3. A patron cannot withdraw a book if his/her unpaid fines exceed $5. Assume that a book becomes overdue after two weeks and that it accumulates a fine at the rate of $.10 a day.

3.16 Suppose that the fragment of the Student Registration System shown in Figure 3.4 has two user accounts: `Student` and `Administrator`. Specify the permissions appropriate for these user categories using the SQL GRANT statement.

3.17 Suppose that the video store of Exercise 3.10 has the following accounts: `Owner`, `Employee`, and `User`. Specify GRANT statements appropriate for each account.

3.18 Explain why the REFERENCES privilege is necessary. Give an example of how it is possible to obtain partial information about the contents of a relation by creating foreign-key constraints referencing that relation.

4

Conceptual Modeling of Databases with Entity-Relationship Diagrams and the Unified Modeling Language

We have interviewed the users of the proposed Student Registration System, understood the requirements, and prepared a detailed Specification Document. That document has been approved by the university registrar, and we are ready to begin designing the database portion of the system. Ultimately this means coming up with a set of appropriate CREATE statements that declare the database schema—tables, indices, domains, assertions, and so forth.

The main issue in database design is to provide an accurate model of a large enterprise in the form of a relational database that can be efficiently accessed by concurrently executing transactions. As in other engineering disciplines, the complexity of the task requires that the design process be performed according to a well-defined methodology and be evaluated according to a set of objective criteria.

In this chapter, we present two design methodologies for relational databases: the *entity-relationship (E-R) approach* [Chen 1976] and *UML class diagrams* [Booch et al. 1999]. While the E-R approach is the more established of the two, UML is quickly gaining in popularity due to its rich feature set and because—unlike the many E-R notations—it has been standardized by the Object Management Group (*http://www.omg.org/*).

Database design is typically a two-stage process. The initial phase is based on the E-R or UML methodology, which we will learn about in this chapter. The result of this phase is then refined using the *relational normalization theory*, which provides objective criteria for evaluating alternative designs. This theory is discussed in Chapter 6.

A typical database design involves many dozens of relations, hundreds of attributes, and dozens of constraints—a task of daunting complexity. The good news is that many of the mechanisms underlying the E-R approach, UML, and the relational normalization theory have been captured in design software, which relieves humans of the most arduous, routine work. Still, database design requires a good deal of creativity, experience, technical expertise, and understanding of the fundamental principles. You will make significant headway toward the last two requirements by the time you finish reading this chapter.

4.1 Conceptual Modeling with the E-R Approach

First, keep in mind that the E-R approach is *not* a relative, a derivative, or a generalization of the relational data model. In fact, it is not a data model at all but a *design methodology*, which can be applied (but is not limited) to the relational model. The term "relationship" refers to one of the two main components of the methodology rather than to the relational data model.

The two main components of the E-R approach are the concepts of *entity* and *relationship*. Entities model the objects that are involved in an enterprise—for example, the students, professors, and courses in a university. Relationships model the connections among the entities—for example, professors *teach* courses. In addition, *integrity constraints* on the entities and relationships form an important part of an E-R specification, much as they do in the relational model. For example, a professor can teach only one course at a given time on a given day.

An **entity-relationship (E-R) diagram** (peek ahead at Figure 4.1, page 72, and Figure 4.2, page 74) is a graphical representation of the entities, relationships, and constraints that make up a given design. As in other visually oriented design methodologies, it provides a graphical summary of the database structure, which is extremely useful to the designer—not only in validating the correctness of the design but also in discussing it with colleagues and in explaining it to the programmers who will be using it. Unfortunately, there is no standard drawing convention for E-R diagrams, and hence there is a good deal of variation among database texts in many aspects of this approach.

Once the enterprise is represented by a set of E-R diagrams, there are standard ways of converting the diagrams into sets of CREATE TABLE statements. Unfortunately, not all aspects of an E-R diagram can be adequately captured with CREATE statements. These and related issues will be discussed in Section 4.5.

The creative part of the E-R methodology consists in deciding what entities, relationships, and constraints to use in modeling the enterprise. Some examples included in this and other texts might make these decisions look easy, but in practice designers must combine a detailed understanding of the workings of the enterprise with a considerable amount of technical knowledge and experience.

An important advantage of the methodology is that the designer can focus on complete and accurate modeling of the enterprise, without (initially) worrying about efficiently executing the required queries and updates against the final database. Later, when the E-R diagrams are to be converted to CREATE TABLE statements, the designer can add efficiency considerations to the final table designs using the normalization theory (Chapter 6) and tuning techniques to be discussed in Chapter 10.

4.2 Entities and Entity Types

The first step in the E-R approach is to select the entities that will be used to model the enterprise. An **entity** (or **entity instance**) is quite similar to an *object*, except that an entity does not have methods, that is, operations that take arguments and either return values or change the entity in some way. An entity can be a concrete object in the real world, such as John Doe, the Cadillac parked at 123 Main Street, or the

Empire State Building. Or it might be an abstract object, such as the Citibank account `123456789`, the database course `CS305`, or the Computer Science Department at Stony Brook.

Similar entities are aggregated into **entity types**. For instance, John Doe, Mary Doe, Joe Blow, and Ann White might be aggregated into the entity type PERSON based on the fact that these entities represent humans. John Doe and Joe Blow might also belong to the entity type STUDENT because in our sample database of Chapter 3 these objects represented students. Similarly, Mary Doe and Ann White might be classified as members of the entity type PROFESSOR.

Other examples of entity types include

- `CS305`, `MGT315`, and `EE101`—entities of type COURSE
- `Alf` and `E.T.`—entities of type SPACEALIEN
- `CIA`, `FBI`, and `IRS`—entities of type GOVERNMENTAGENCY

Attributes. Like relations and objects, entities are described using attributes. Every attribute of an entity specifies a particular property of that entity. For instance, the `Name` attribute of a PERSON entity normally specifies a string of characters that denotes the real-world name of the person represented by that database entity. Similarly, the `Age` attribute specifies the number of times the earth had circled around the sun since the moment that a particular person was born. As in the relational model, the **domain** of an attribute specifies the set from which its values are drawn.

In principle, it is possible for two different entities of the same type to have identical values in all of their attributes. This is one important difference with tuples in the relational model. However, in practice it is not advisable to introduce entity types that can have entities that cannot be distinguished by their attributes.

In all of our examples, each particular entity type included only semantically related entities. Indeed, it is usually pointless to classify people, cars, and paper clips in one entity type because they have little in common in a typical enterprise. It is more useful to classify semantically similar entities in one entity type, since they are likely to have common attributes that describe them. For example, in any enterprise, people have many common attributes, such as `Name`, `Age`, and `Address`. Classification into entity types allows us to associate these attributes with the entity type instead of with the individual entities.

Of course, different entity types will generally have different sets of attributes. For instance, the PAPERCLIP entity type might have attributes `Size` and `Price`, while COURSE might have attributes `CrsName`, `CrsCode`, `Credits`, and `Description`.

> *Brain Teaser:* Is it possible for an entity type not to have attributes?

Unlike the relational model, E-R attributes can be **set-valued**. This means that the value of an attribute can be a set of values from the corresponding domain rather than a single value. For example, an entity type PERSON might have set-valued attributes `ChildrenNames` and `Hobbies`.

The inability to express set-valued attributes conveniently was one of the major criticisms of the relational data model that motivated the development of the object-oriented data model. However, the use of set-valued attributes in the E-R model is just a matter of convenience. Relations (as defined in Chapter 3) can be used to model entities with set-valued attributes with some extra effort.

Keys. As with the relational model, it is useful to introduce key constraints associated with entity types. A **key constraint** on an entity type, $\mathcal{S}$, is a set of attributes, $\overline{A}$, of $\mathcal{S}$ such that

1. No two entities in $\mathcal{S}$ have the same value for each of the attributes in $\overline{A}$ (for instance, two different COMPANY entities cannot have the same value in both the `Name` and the `Address` attributes).
2. No proper subset of the attributes in $\overline{A}$ has property 1 (i.e., the set $\overline{A}$ is *minimal* with respect to property 1).

Brain Teaser: Does an entity type necessarily have to have a key?

Entity keys are analogous to candidate keys in the relational model. One subtle difference is that attributes in the E-R approach can be set-valued and such an attribute can be part of a key. However, in practice set-valued attributes that occur in keys are not very natural and are often indicative of poor design.

Schema. As in the relational model, we define the **schema** of an entity type to consist of the name of the type, the collection of its attributes (with their associated domains and the indicator of whether each attribute is set-valued or single-valued), and the key constraints.

E-R diagram representation. Entity types are represented in E-R diagrams as rectangles, and their attributes are represented as ovals. Set-valued attributes are represented as double ovals. Underlined attributes are keys. Figure 4.1 depicts one possible representation of the PERSON entity type.

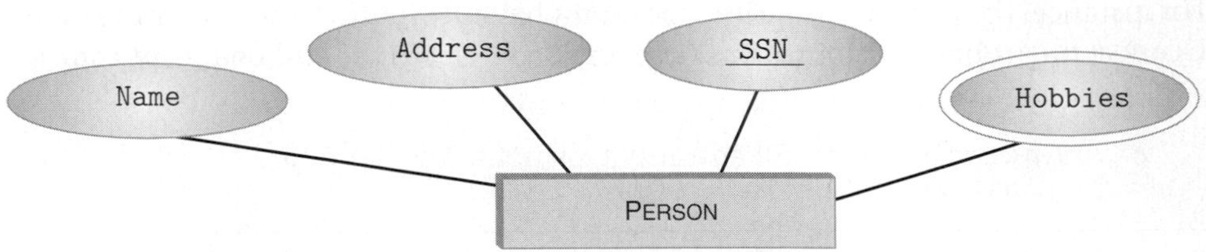

FIGURE 4.1 Fragment of the E-R diagram for the entity type PERSON. Here `Hobbies` is a set-valued attribute, and `SSN` is underlined to indicate that it is a key.

4.3 Relationships and Relationship Types

The E-R approach makes sharp distinction between the entities themselves and the mechanism that relates them to each other. This mechanism is called **relationship** (or **relationship instance**). Just as entities are classified into entity types, relationships that relate the same types of entities and that have the same meaning are grouped into **relationship types**.

For instance, STUDENT entities are related to PROGRAM entities via relationships of type MAJORSIN. Thus two instances of MAJORSIN might be the relationships between John Doe and computer science and Joe Blow and economics. Likewise, PROFESSOR entities are related to the departments they work for via relationships of type WORKSIN.

The concept of a *relationship* in the E-R approach is distinct from the concept of a *relation* (i.e., table) in the relational data model. Along with entities, relationships are modeling primitives in the arsenal of the E-R approach, and they are not tied to a particular data model. For instance, in a relational DBMS, both entity and relationship types are typically represented as relations. In an object-oriented database, they are typically modeled as classes. We will see, however, that in some cases relationship types are represented not as tables or classes, but rather as attributes and constraints.

Attributes and roles. Like entities, relationships can have attributes. For instance, the relationship MAJORSIN might have an attribute `Since`, which indicates the date the student was admitted into the corresponding major. The WORKSIN relationship might have the attribute `Since` to indicate the start date of employment.

Attributes do not provide a complete description of relationships. Consider the entity type EMPLOYEE and the relationship REPORTSTO, which relates employees to other employees. The first type of employee is the subordinate while the second is the boss. Thus, if we just say that ⟨`John`, `Bill`⟩ is a relationship, of type REPORTSTO, we still do not know who reports to whom.

Splitting the EMPLOYEE entity type into SUBORDINATE and SUPERVISOR does not help, because REPORTSTO might represent the entire chain of reporting in a corporate hierarchy, making some employees subordinates and supervisors at the same time.

The solution is to recognize that the various entity types participating in a relationship type play different roles in that relationship. For each entity type participating in a relationship type we define a **role** and give that role a name. For example, `Subordinate` and `Supervisor` are two roles that connect a relationship instance of REPORTSTO to the two entity instances that it relates in EMPLOYEE. Thus, a role is similar to an attribute, but instead of specifying some property of a relationship, it specifies in what way an entity type participates in the relationship. Both roles and attributes are part of the schema of the relationship type.

For example, the relationship type WORKSIN has two roles, `Professor` and `Department`. The `Professor` role identifies the PROFESSOR entity involved in a WORKSIN relationship, and the `Department` role identifies the corresponding

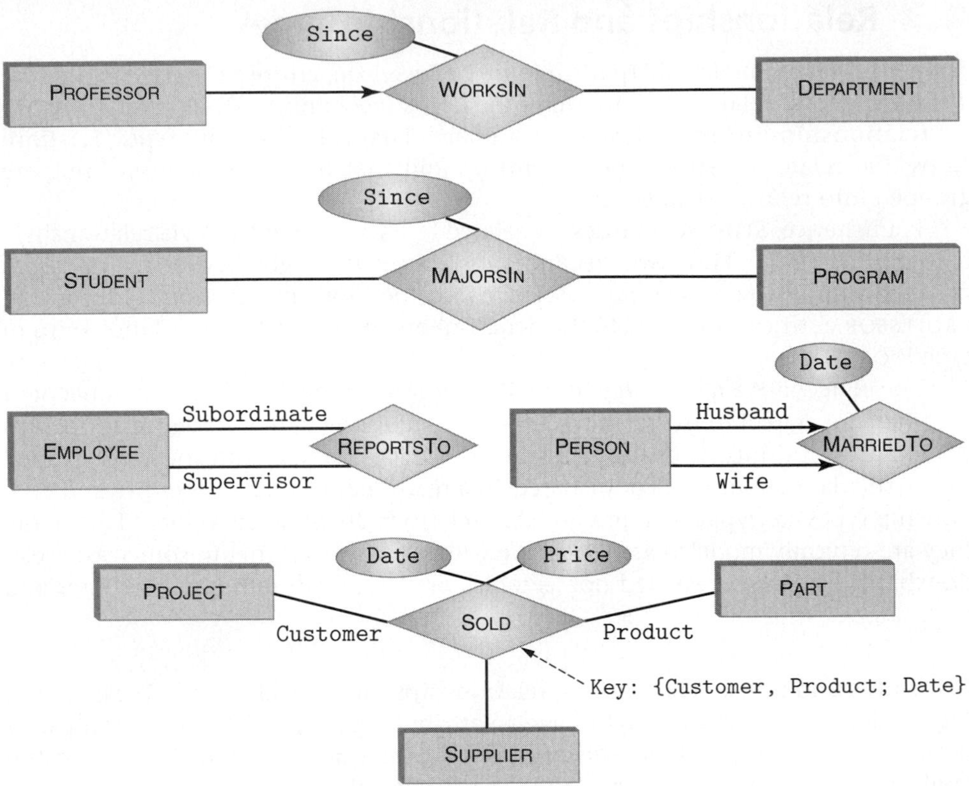

FIGURE 4.2 E-R diagrams for several relationship types.

DEPARTMENT entity in the relationship. Similarly, the relationship type MAJORSIN has two roles, `Student` and `Program`.

When all of the entities involved in a relationship belong to distinct entity types (as in WORKSIN and MAJORSIN), it is not necessary to explicitly indicate the roles, because we can always adopt some convention, such as naming the roles after the corresponding entity types (which is typical in practice).[1] Thus, the roles of WORKSIN are `Professor` and `Department`. This simplifying convention is not possible when some of the entities involved are drawn from the same entity type, as is the case with the REPORTSTO relationship. Here, we have to explicitly indicate the roles, `Subordinate` and `Supervisor`. In other situations (e.g., the relationship SOLD), naming the roles explicitly can help understand the intent behind the particular entity type. Figure 4.2 shows several examples of relationships, including those where roles are named explicitly.

[1] When confusion might arise, we will use different fonts to distinguish entity types from the roles they play in various relationships.

To summarize, the **schema of a relationship type** includes

- A list of attributes along with their corresponding domains. An attribute can be single-valued or set-valued.
- A list of roles along with their corresponding entity types. Unlike attributes, roles are always single-valued.
- A set of constraints. In Figure 4.2, some constraints are represented as arrows. This will be explained later.

The number of roles engaged in a relationship type is called the **degree** of the type.

We can now define the concept of a relationship more precisely. A relationship type **R** of degree n is defined by its attributes $A_1, \ldots, A_k$ and roles $R_1, \ldots, R_n$. The relationships populating **R** are defined to be tuples of the form

$$\langle \mathbf{e}_1, \mathbf{e}_2, \ldots, \mathbf{e}_n; a_1, a_2, \ldots, a_k \rangle$$

where $\mathbf{e}_1, \ldots, \mathbf{e}_n$ are entities involved in the relationship in roles $R_1, \ldots, R_n$, respectively, and $a_1, a_2, \ldots, a_k$ are values of the attributes $A_1, \ldots, A_k$, respectively. We assume that all of the values of the attributes in the relationship are in their respective domains, as defined in the relationship type, and all of the entities are of the correct entity types, as defined in their respective roles.

For instance, the relationship type MAJORSIN can have the schema

⟨`Student`, `Program`; `Since`⟩

where `Student` and `Program` are roles and `Since` is an attribute. One instance in this relationship type might be

⟨ `'Homer Simpson'`, `EE`; `1994`⟩

This relationship states that the entity `Homer Simpson` is a student who has been enrolled since 1994 in the program represented by the entity `EE`. The first two components in the tuple are entities; the last is a constant from the domain of years.

> *Brain Teaser:* Is it possible for a relationship type not to have attributes? Roles?

E-R diagram representation. In E-R diagrams, relationship types are represented as diamonds and roles are represented as edges that connect relationship types with the appropriate entity types. If a role must be named explicitly, the name is included in the diagram. Figure 4.2 shows the E-R diagram for several of the relationships we have been discussing (we omitted the attributes of all entities to reduce clutter). The first three relationships in the figure are **binary** because they each relate two entity types. The last relationship is **ternary** because it relates three entity types. This last diagram also illustrates the point that sometimes the semantics of a diagram can be easier to convey if default role names, such as `Project` and `Part` are renamed into something more appropriate, such as `Customer` and `Product`, respectively.

Keys. The key of a relationship enables the designer to express many constraints naturally and uniformly. In the case of the entity types, a key is just a set of attributes that uniquely identifies each entity. However, attributes alone do not fully characterize relationships. Roles must also be taken into account, so we define the **key of a relationship type**, **R**, to be a minimal set of roles and attributes of **R** whose values uniquely identify the relationship instances in that relationship type.

In other words, let $R_1, \ldots, R_k$ be a subset of the set of all roles of **R**, and $A_1, \ldots, A_s$ be a subset of the attributes of **R**. Then the set $\{R_1, \ldots, R_k; A_1, \ldots, A_s\}$ is a key of **R** if the following holds:

1. *Uniqueness*. **R** does not have a pair of distinct relationship instances that have the same values for every role and attribute in $\{R_1, \ldots, R_k; A_1, \ldots, A_s\}$.
2. *Minimality*. No subset of $\{R_1, \ldots, R_k; A_1, \ldots, A_s\}$ has property 1.

In some cases, the key of a relationship takes a special form. Consider the relationship WORKSIN between entities of type PROFESSOR and type DEPARTMENT. It is reasonable to assume that each department has several professors but that each professor works for at most one department. Because any given PROFESSOR entity can occur in at most one relationship of type WORKSIN, the role `Professor` is a key of WORKSIN. While there is no universally accepted representation for relationship keys in E-R diagrams, a relationship key that consists of just one role (a **single-role key**) can be conveniently expressed by drawing this role as an arrow pointing in the direction of the relationship's diamond. Observe that there can be several roles each of which forms a key, and so an E-R diagram can have several arrows pointing toward the same diamond. For instance, in Figure 4.2 both {`Husband`} and {`Wife`} are keys of the relationship type MARRIEDTO, so each of these roles is represented as an arrow.

Keys that consist of more than one role or attribute are usually represented textually, next to the diamonds that represent the corresponding relationship type. When representing such keys, we first list the roles and then the attributes. For example, in the last diagram of Figure 4.2 one key could be {`Customer`, `Product`; `Date`}. If such a key is declared, it would signify that there can be at most one sales transaction involving a given customer entity and a given product entity on a given date.

In many situations, however, the relationship has only one key that is the set of all roles. In such a case, we do not specify the key in the diagram.

> *Brain Teaser:* Is it possible to have two distinct relationships of the same type that relate the same entities in the same roles and have the same values of attributes?

Cardinality constraints. Single-role key constraints, which are drawn as arrows, can be generalized using the notion of a *cardinality constraint*.

Let **C** be an entity type and **A** be a relationship type that is connected to **C** via a role, *R*. A **cardinality constraint** on the role *R* is a statement of the form `min..max` attached to *R*; it restricts the number of relationship instances of type **A** in which

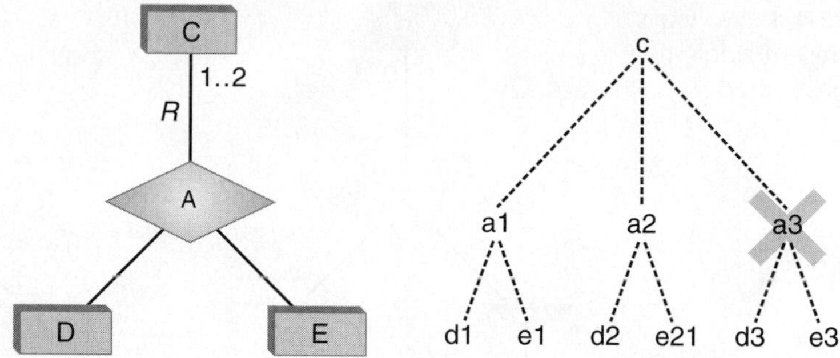

FIGURE 4.3 Cardinality in the E-R model.

a single entity of type **C** can participate in role *R* to be a number in the interval `min..max` (with end points included).

Figure 4.3 shows a diagram with a cardinality constraint on role *R*. On the right side it shows a valid instance of this diagram where the entity **c** participates in two relationships of type **A**. The relationship **a3** is crossed out because it would violate the cardinality bounds 1..2 on the role *R*.

More generally, the E-R model supports cardinality constraints of the form `min..max`, where `min` is a number greater than or equal to 0, `max` is a number greater than 0, and `min` ≤ `max`. In addition, `max` can be the * symbol, which represents infinity. Thus, a constraint of the form `3..*` on a role *R* that connects an entity type, **C**, with a relationship type, **A**, means that every entity of type **C** *must* participate in role *R* in *at least* three relationships of type **A** (with no upper limit). A constraint of the form `1..3` means that every such entity must participate in at least one but no more than three relationships. A constraint of the form `0..2` means that an entity does not have to participate in any relationship of type **A** in role *R*. However, if it does, then it must not participate in more than two relationships. Finally, we note that cardinality constraints of the form `N..N` (where `min` = `max`) are often abbreviated to just `N`, and that * stands for `0..*`.

Brain Teaser: What does the constraint `0..*` mean?

Cardinality constraints generalize the notion of a single-role key, which we earlier represented using arrows. Indeed, representing a role, *R*, using an arrow is tantamount to giving it a cardinality constraint `0..1`, as shown in Figure 4.4. Database designers also find it useful to talk about one-to-one, many-to-one, one-to-many, and many-to-many correspondences. These concepts refer to the correspondences between pairs of entity types *implied* by relationships of higher degree. Figure 4.5 illustrates these notions using a relationship type, **B**, of degree 4. The type of the relationship is determined by the cardinality constraints on the roles of the relationship. For instance, the relationship **B** implies a **one-to-one** correspondence between the entity types **C** and **D**. This means that an entity of type **C** can be associated

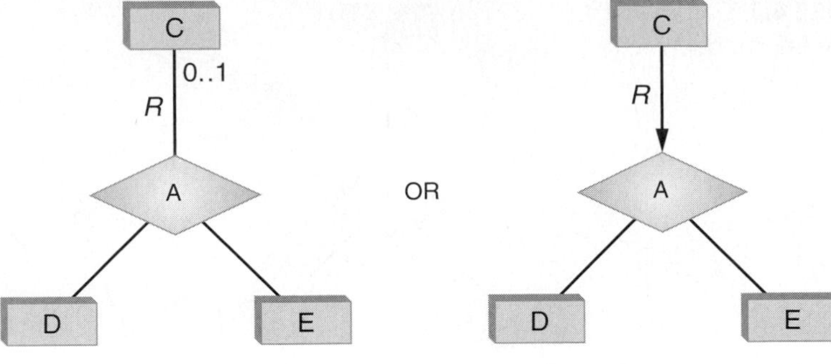

FIGURE 4.4 Two ways to represent single-role key constraints.

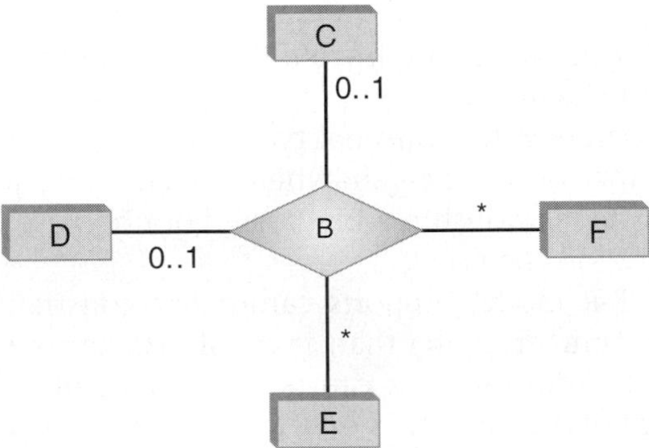

FIGURE 4.5 Many-to-one, one-to-one, and many-to-many correspondences.

with at most one entity of type **D**, and vice versa. At the same time, **B** implies **one-to-many** correspondences of **E** to **C** and **D** (and of **F** to **C** and **D**). This means that an entity of type **E** can be associated with any number (including zero) of entities of types **C** and **D**, but, for example, an entity of type **C** can be associated with at most one **E**-entity. Note that the one-to-many correspondence is not symmetric; the inverse correspondence (for example, the correspondence of **C** to **E**) is called **many-to-one**. Finally, the correspondence between **E** and **F** is said to be **many-to-many**, meaning that an **E**-entity can be associated with any number of **F**-entities, and vice versa.

4.4 Advanced Features in Conceptual Data Modeling

In this section we introduce a number of more advanced modeling concepts, such as type hierarchies, participation constraints, and the part-of relationship.

4.4.1 Entity Type Hierarchies

When modeling an enterprise with the E-R approach, you may find that some entity types are subtypes of others. For instance, every entity of type STUDENT is also a member of the type PERSON. Therefore, all of the attributes of the PERSON type are applicable to student entities. Students can also have attributes that are not applicable to a typical PERSON entity (e.g., `Major`, `StartDate`, `GPA`). In this case, we say that the entity type STUDENT is a subtype of the entity type PERSON.

Formally, a statement that an entity type **R** is a **subtype** of the entity type **R′** is a constraint with the following meaning:

1. Every entity instance in **R** is also an entity instance in **R′**.
2. Every attribute in **R′** is also an attribute in **R**.

One important consequence of this definition is that any key of a supertype is also a key of all of its subtypes.

Subtyping is not only a constraint but also a relationship between the supertype and its subtype with roles `Sub`(type) and `Super`(type). It is often called the **ISA relationship**. For instance, in the ISA relationship type that relates STUDENT and PERSON, the role `Sub` refers to STUDENT and the role `Super` refers to PERSON. A particular instance of this relationship type could be ⟨`Homer Simpson`, `Homer Simpson`⟩, which states that Homer Simpson is an element of both STUDENT *and* PERSON. Note that the two entities involved in an ISA relationship are always identical (although the entity types are different), and the names of the roles are fixed.

So what is so special about the ISA relationship? The answer lies in the fact that subtype constraints introduce a **classification hierarchy** in the conceptual model. For instance, FRESHMAN is a subtype of STUDENT, which in turn is a subtype of PERSON. This property is *transitive*, which means that FRESHMAN is also a subtype of PERSON. The transitive property gives us a way to draw diagrams in a more concise and readable manner. Because of property 2 of subtyping, every attribute of PERSON is also an attribute of STUDENT and, by transitivity, is also an attribute of FRESHMAN. This phenomenon is often expressed by saying that STUDENT **inherits** attributes from PERSON and that FRESHMAN inherits attributes from both PERSON and STUDENT.

Note that the inherited attributes (`SSN`, `Name`, etc.) are not shown explicitly in Figure 4.6 for the entity types STUDENT and FRESHMAN, and yet they are considered valid attributes because of the ISA relationship. In addition to the inherited attributes, STUDENT and FRESHMAN might have attributes of their own, which their corresponding supertypes might not have. Figure 4.6 illustrates this idea. As STUDENT is a subtype of PERSON, this entity type inherits all of the attributes specified for PERSON, and so there is no need to repeat the attributes `Name` and `D.O.B.` (date of birth) for the STUDENT type. Similarly, FRESHMAN, SOPHOMORE, and so forth, are subtypes of STUDENT, and so we do not need to copy the attributes of STUDENT and PERSON over to these subtypes. The EMPLOYEE branch of the ISA tree provides another example of attribute inheritance. Every EMPLOYEE entity has attributes `Department` and `Salary`. The relationship EMPLOYEE ISA PERSON says that, in addition, every EMPLOYEE entity is also a PERSON entity and, as such, has the attributes `Name`, `SSN`, and so forth.

Note that each ISA triangle in Figure 4.6 represents several relationship types. For instance, the upper triangle represents the relationship types STUDENT ISA PERSON

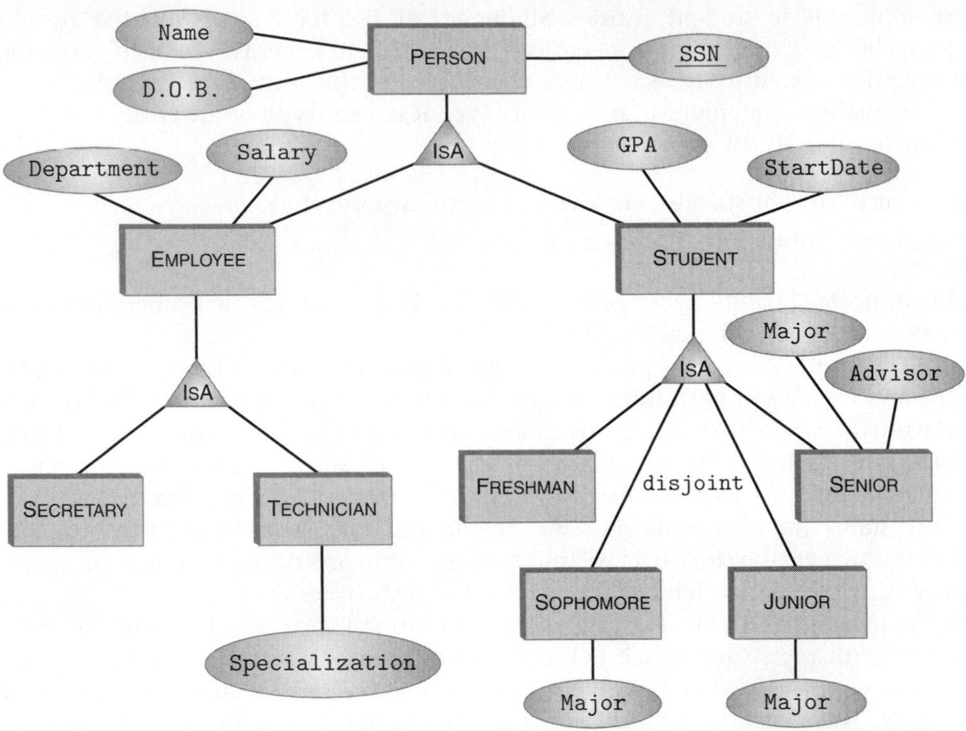

FIGURE 4.6 Example of an E-R diagram with an IsA hierarchy.

and Employee IsA Person. Although this notation makes the representation of the IsA relationship different from the representation of other kinds of relationships, it is used because there are a number of constraints associated with entity type hierarchies that can be naturally expressed using such notation.

For instance, the union of the entities that belong to the entity types Freshman, Sophomore, Junior, and Senior might be equal to the set of entities of type Student (for example, in a four-year college). This constraint, called the *covering constraint*, can be associated with the lower right IsA triangle. In addition, these entity types might always be disjoint (they are in most American universities), and such a *disjointness constraint* can also be associated with the lower right triangle. There is no universally accepted way of representing covering and disjointness constraints in the E-R diagrams—the most straightforward way is to write the word "`disjoint`" directly on the diagram.

Formally, a group of IsA relationships, C_1 IsA C; . . . ; C_k IsA C, satisfies the **disjointness constraint** if the sets of entity instances of $C_1, \ldots, C_k$ are disjoint. This group satisfies the **covering constraint** if the union of the sets of instances of $C_1, \ldots, C_k$ equals the set of instances of C.

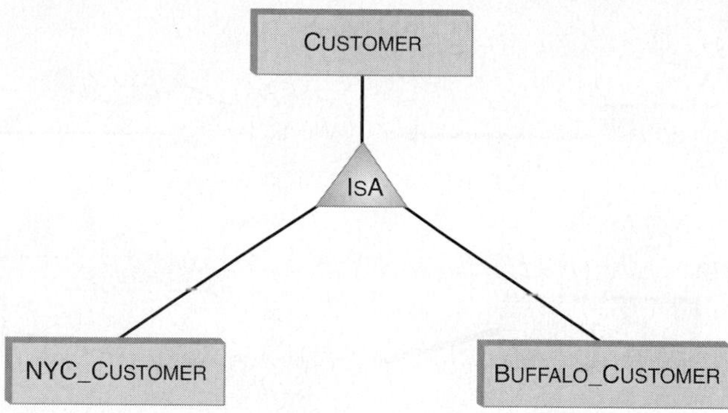

FIGURE 4.7 Using IsA for data partitioning.

Entity type hierarchies and data partitioning. While discussing the IsA relationship, we have been focusing on conceptual organization and attribute inheritance. However, these hierarchies are also a good way to approach the issue of physical **data partitioning**. The need for data partitioning often arises in distributed environments, where multiple geographically diverse entities must access a common database. Banking is a typical example because banks often have many branches in different cities.

The problem that arises in such distributed enterprises is that of network delay: accessing a database in New York City from a bank branch in Buffalo can be prohibitive for frequently running transactions. However, the bulk of the data needed by a local bank branch is likely to be of mostly local interest, and it might be a good idea to distribute fragments of such information among databases maintained at the individual branches. This approach is taken in distributed databases.

To see how data partitioning can be addressed at the database design stage, consider an entity type, CUSTOMER, which represents the information about all customers of a bank. For each branch, we can create subtypes, such as NYC_CUSTOMER or BUFFALO_CUSTOMER, that are related to CUSTOMER as described in Figure 4.7.

Observe that the constraints associated with type hierarchies provide considerable expressive power in specifying how data might be partitioned. For instance, Figure 4.7 could be interpreted as a requirement that the New York City and Buffalo data must be stored locally. It does not say that the New York City database and the Buffalo customer database must be disjoint, but this can be specified using the disjointness constraint introduced earlier. In addition, we can add the covering constraint to specify that the combined customer information at the branches includes all customers.

4.4.2 Participation Constraints

Suppose that while developing an E-R diagram for your university you have introduced a relationship type, WORKSIN, between the entity types PROFESSOR and DEPARTMENT. Each department has several professors but each professor is a member of a single department, so the role `Professor` is a key of WORKSIN.

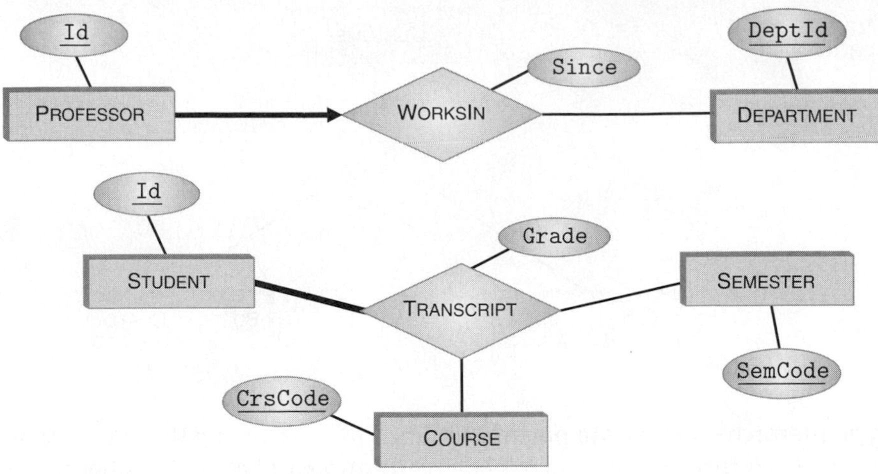

FIGURE 4.8 Participation constraints.

This key constraint ensures that no professor can occur in more than one relationship of type WORKSIN. However, it does not guarantee that each professor occurs in *some* relationship of this type. In other words, the key constraint does not rule out professors who do not work for any department (and possibly get away without teaching any courses!). To close this loophole, the designer can use *participation constraints*.

Given an entity type, **E**, a relationship type, **R**, and a role, *R*, a **participation constraint** of **E** in **R** in role *R* states that for every entity instance **e** in **E**, there is a relationship **r** in **R** such that **e** participates in **r** in role *R*.

Clearly, requiring that the entity type PROFESSOR participates in the relationship type WORKSIN in role `Professor` ensures that every professor works in some department.

For another example, we may want to ensure that every student takes at least one course. To this end, we can assume that there is a ternary relationship type, TRANSCRIPT, which relates STUDENT, COURSE, and SEMESTER. Our goal can be achieved by imposing a participation constraint on the `Student` role that connects the STUDENT entity type to the relationship TRANSCRIPT.

One common way of representing participation constraints in an E-R diagram is to draw a thick line for the role that connects the participating entity with the corresponding relationship, as in Figure 4.8. The thick arrow connecting PROFESSOR to WORKSIN indicates both that each professor participates in at least one relationship (denoted by the thick line) and that each professor can participate in at most one relationship (denoted by the arrow). Hence, a one-to-one mapping between PROFESSOR entities and WORKSIN relationships exists.

Alternatively, participation constraints can be represented using cardinality constraints. Participation of an entity type, **E**, in a relationship type, **R**, in role *R*

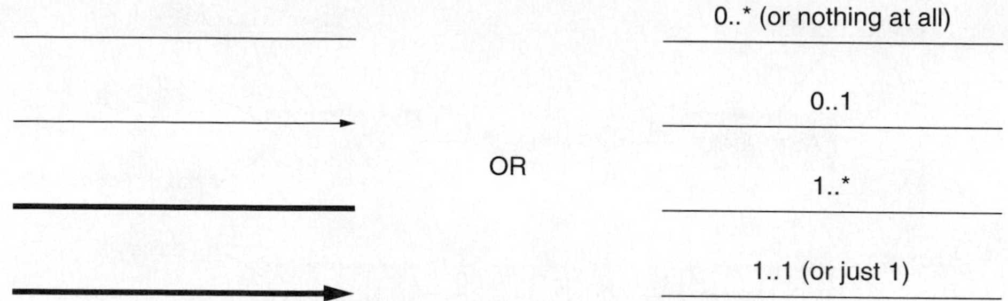

FIGURE 4.9 Line-based representation vs. cardinality constraints.

can be represented using the constraint of the form 1..* placed on the role *R*. A participation constraint combined with the single-role key (represented using a thick arrow) can be expressed as a cardinality constraint of the form `1..1` (or simply 1). Figure 4.9 summarizes the correspondence between the two representations.

4.4.3 The Part-of Relationship

The collective experience of database design suggests that, alongside the IsA, **part-of** is a useful kind of relationship. For example, a wheel entity can be part of an automobile entity.

There are two kinds of part-of relationships. In one, the subpart of the whole can exist independently even if the whole is destroyed. This type of part-of relationship is **non-exclusive**. A good example of a non-exclusive part-of relationship is the relationship between an automobile entity and the entities representing its parts. When it is no longer feasible to keep repairing an automobile, it might be brought to a junk yard and taken apart. The automobile no longer exists, but its wheels, transmission, and camshaft may continue their independent existence and even find new life as part of another automobile. In certain cases, the same entity can even be part of several other objects. For instance, the same course may be an integral part of two or more programs of study in a university curriculum.

Another kind of part-of relationship is when the subpart has no existence outside of the whole: when the whole object is destroyed, the subpart goes as well. It is usually further assumed that the subpart cannot be shared, that is, it can belong to *exactly one* whole. For instance, PROGRAM of study (biology, physics, etc.) is part of UNIVERSITY. If a university is dissolved, its programs no longer exist. Similarly, in a payroll database, DEPENDENT can be part of the information associated with the EMPLOYEE entity type. When an employee leaves, the information about his dependents is also erased. This type of part-of relationship is **exclusive**.

Non-exclusive part-of relationships do not have special representation in the E-R model. They are treated as regular relationships, and cardinality constraints are used to state whatever is appropriate in each particular situation. In a non-exclusive relationship, a subpart (e.g., an automobile wheel) can exist without

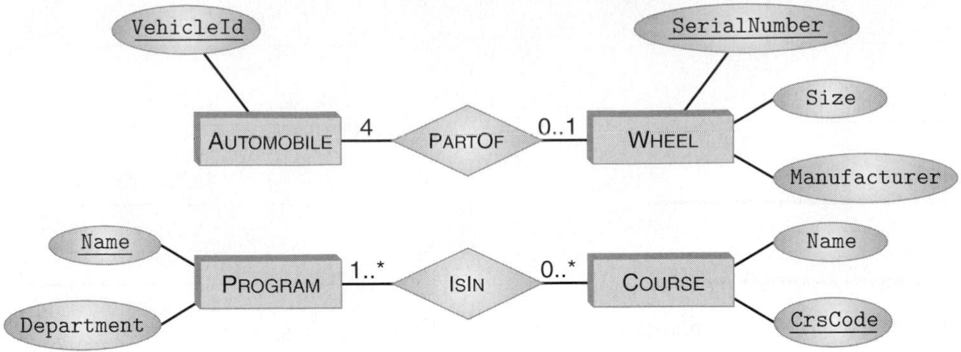

FIGURE 4.10 Non-exclusive part-of relationship in E-R.

being part of a concrete automobile. Therefore, there need not be a participation constraint between subparts and parts. Likewise, there need not be a many-to-one correspondence between the subpart entity type and the type of the whole part, because the same subpart (e.g., course) can be part of several different wholes (e.g., programs of study). Figure 4.10 shows examples of E-R diagrams representing non-exclusive part-of relationships. This is indicated by the minimum cardinality of 0 for entity types WHEEL and COURSE.

In contrast to non-exclusive part-of relationships, the exclusive ones are represented within the E-R approach using the special machinery of **weak entity types** and **identifying relationships**. Weak entities represent subparts and identifying relationships are the corresponding exclusive part-of relationships. In our examples, PROGRAM and DEPENDENT are weak entity types that are related through identifying relationships to their *master* entity types (which represent whole entities), UNIVERSITY and EMPLOYEE. In E-R diagrams, weak entities and their identifying relationships are represented using double boxes and double diamonds, respectively.

Observe that weak entities always participate in their identifying relationships and that each such entity is related to a single master object. Thus, there is always a thick arrow going from a weak entity to its identifying relationship, as shown in Figure 4.11.

Sometimes designers choose to strip weak entity types of their key attributes and have the entities identified through their relationship with the master entity. For example, the DEPENDENT entity might have the `Name` attribute, but not the `SSN` attribute. To find a dependent entity, one would have to first find the corresponding master (an EMPLOYEE entity) and then follow the identifying relationship.

Note that the identifying relationship is not the only kind of relationship in which a weak entity can take part. For instance, PROGRAM in Figure 4.11 can be related to another entity type, EMPLOYEE, via the relationship PROGRAMDIRECTOR. This relationship would not be identifying for PROGRAM (since a program might not have a director), and thus it would be represented using a single diamond. It is also conceivable (although not common) that a weak entity type can participate

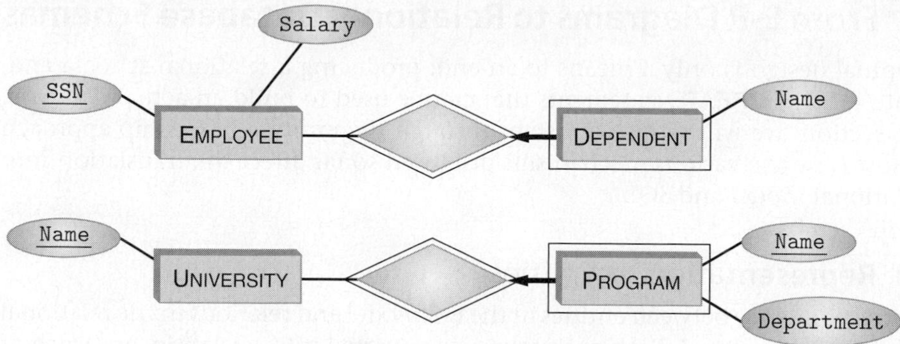

FIGURE 4.11 Exclusive part-of relationship in E-R: weak entities.

in a *ternary* (or higher-degree) relationship type with several master entity types. For instance, certain educational programs might be jointly run by universities and companies. In this case, PROGRAM takes part in a ternary identifying relationship with entities of the types UNIVERSITY and COMPANY, and destruction of either of these entities implies the destruction of the program entity.

Figure 4.12 summarizes the notation used in E-R diagrams.

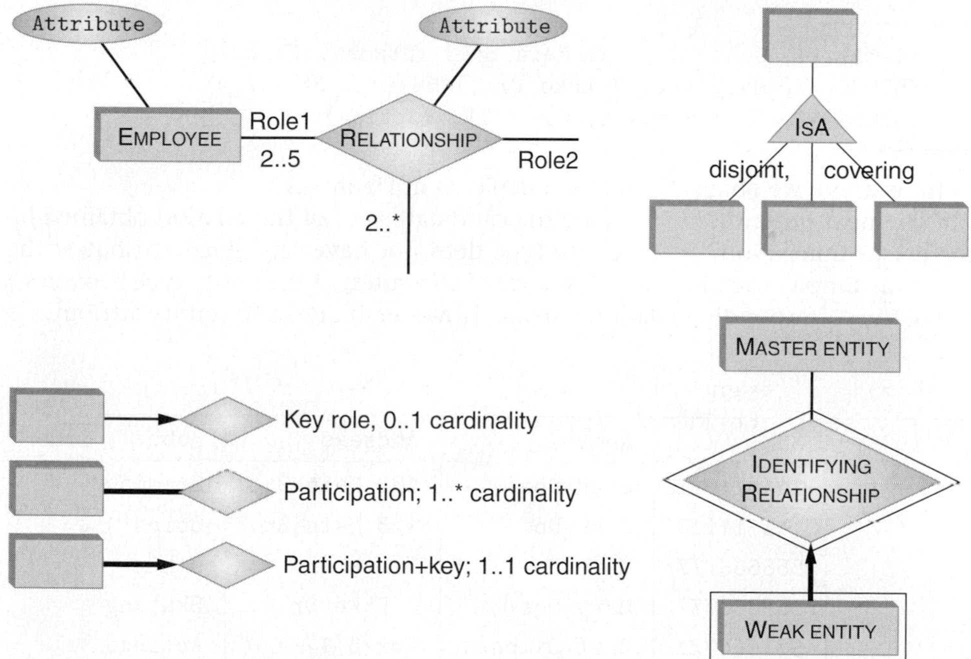

FIGURE 4.12 Summary of the E-R notation.

4.5 From E-R Diagrams to Relational Database Schemas

Conceptual design is only a means to an end: producing a relational schema and, ultimately, SQL's CREATE statements that can be used to build an actual database. In this section, we will retrace our steps through the entity-relationship approach and show how the various mechanisms discussed so far affect the translation into the relational model and SQL.

4.5.1 Representation of Entities

The correspondence between entities in the E-R model and relations in the relational model is straightforward. Each entity type is converted into a relation, and each of its attributes is converted into an attribute of the relation.

This simple set of rules might seem suspicious in view of the fact that entities can have set-valued attributes while relations cannot. How can a set-valued attribute of an entity be turned into a single-valued attribute of the corresponding relation without violating the property of data atomicity (defined in Section 3.2) of the relational model?

The answer is that, although each set-valued attribute of an entity type is represented as a single-valued attribute in the resulting relation, each entity instance is represented in the translation by a *set* of tuples—one for each member in the set of the attribute's values. To illustrate, suppose that the entity type PERSON of Figure 4.1 is populated by the following entities:

```
⟨111111111, John Doe, 123 Main St., {Stamps, Coins}⟩
⟨555666777, Mary Doe, 7 Lake Dr., {Hiking, Skating}⟩
⟨987654321, Bart Simpson, Fox 5 TV, {Acting}⟩
```

In translation, we obtain the relation depicted in Figure 4.13.

The next question is, What are the candidate keys of the relation obtained by the above translation? If the entity type does not have set-valued attributes, the answer is simple. Each key (which is a set of attributes) of the entity type becomes a key of the corresponding relation schema. However, if one of the entity attributes is

PERSON	SSN	Name	Address	Hobby
	111111111	John Doe	123 Main St.	Stamps
	111111111	John Doe	123 Main St.	Coins
	555666777	Mary Doe	7 Lake Dr.	Hiking
	555666777	Mary Doe	7 Lake Dr.	Skating
	987654321	Bart Simpson	Fox 5 TV	Acting

FIGURE 4.13 Translation of entity type PERSON into a relation.

set-valued, determining the keys is a bit more involved. In the entity type PERSON, the attribute SSN is a key because no two PERSON entities can have the same Social Security number. However, in the PERSON relation of Figure 4.13, both John Doe and Mary Doe are represented by a pair of tuples, and their Social Security numbers occur twice. Therefore, SSN is not a key of that relation. What is the problem here?

Clearly, the set-valued attribute Hobby is the troublemaker: to obtain a key of the relation in question, we must include this attribute. Thus, the key of the PERSON relation in Figure 4.13 is {SSN, Hobby}.

The following CREATE TABLE statement defines the schema for the PERSON relation.

```
CREATE TABLE  PERSON  (
      SSN       INTEGER,
      Name      CHAR(20),
      Address   CHAR(50),
      Hobby     CHAR(10),
      PRIMARY KEY (SSN, Hobby) )
```

4.1

Even though we have identified a key, a careful examination of the above table leaves us uneasy. It does not seem right that the Hobby attribute should have anything to do with identifying tuples in the PERSON relation. Furthermore, in the original entity type PERSON, any concrete value of SSN is known to uniquely identify the value of Name and Address. In the translation of Figure 4.13, we see that this property still holds, but it is not captured by the primary-key constraint, which states that in order to uniquely determine a tuple, we must specify the value of *both* SSN and Hobby. In contrast, in the entity type PERSON the value of Hobby is not required to determine the value of Name and Address. This important constraint has been lost in the translation!

The preceding example is the first indication that the E-R approach alone does not guarantee good relational design. Chapter 6 will provide a host of objective criteria that can help database designers evaluate the relational schema obtained by converting E-R diagrams into relations. In particular, the problem with the relation in Figure 4.13 is that it is not in a certain *normal form*. Chapter 6 proceeds to develop algorithms that can automatically rectify the problem by splitting the offending relations into smaller relations that are in a desired normal form. For instance, in our case, the PERSON relation would be split into two: one with the attributes SSN, Name, and Address, and another with the attributes SSN and Hobby.

Algorithm for converting entities into relations. We can now summarize the algorithm for translating entity types into the relational schema:

- Each entity type becomes a relation.
- Each attribute of the entity becomes an attribute of that relation.

- If attributes $K_1, K_2, \ldots, K_n$ form a key of the entity, then the attributes $K_1, K_2, \ldots, K_n, S_1, \ldots, S_k$ form a candidate key of the relation. Here $S_1, \ldots, S_k$ is a list of all set-valued attributes of the entity.

4.5.2 Representation of Relationships

The algorithm that maps relationship types into relation schemas can be summarized as follows:

1. Determine the attributes of the relation schema for the relationship type.
2. Determine the candidate keys of the schema.
3. Determine the foreign-key constraints.

We discuss each step of the algorithm in turn.

1. *Attributes of the relation schema derived from a relationship type* **R**. The attributes of the relation schema are
   (a) The attributes of **R** itself.
   (b) For each role in **R**, the primary key of the associated entity type. These attributes will become foreign keys referencing the corresponding entity types (as explained below).
   (c) Each attribute in these primary keys must be declared as NOT NULL unless this is already implied by the PRIMARY KEY constraint.

   Note that in (b) we use the primary key of the entity type—not the primary key of the relation schema constructed out of that entity type—because the goal is to uniquely identify the entity involved in the relationship. Thus, for example, in the case of a role associated with the entity type PERSON we use `SSN` and omit `Hobby`.

   Also, spend a moment to contemplate the reason for the NOT NULL requirement in step (c): By definition, a relationship, for example, of degree four must have exactly four entities involved and none of them can be missing—otherwise, it will not be a relationship of degree four. Therefore, a relationship must provide references to all of its participating entities, and none of the corresponding attributes can be NULL.

   While this sounds simple enough, there are two small problems: the primary keys of different roles can have identically named attributes that mean different things or different attributes that mean the same thing. For example, in the MARRIAGE relationship, the primary key of each of the roles, `Husband` and `Wife`, could be ⟨`FirstName`, `FamilyName`⟩. Assuming that couples use the same family name, the relation schema derived from this relationship will have two pairs of identically named attributes. In the first pair, the two occurrences of `FirstName` mean different things and must be renamed (e.g., to `HusbandFirstName` and `WifeFirstName`). In the second pair, the two occurrences of `FamilyName` mean the same thing—the family name of a married couple. In this case we can simply delete the second occurrence. We can also imagine situations where the keys can have differently named attributes that mean the same thing. In this case we can also delete duplicate occurrences of such attributes.

2. *Candidate keys of the relation schema.* In most cases, the keys of the relation schema are obtained by direct translation from the keys of **R** itself. That is, if a role, *R*, of **R** belongs to the key of **R**, then the attributes of the primary key, $\mathcal{K}$, of the entity type associated with *R* must belong to the candidate key of the relation schema derived from **R**.

   A slight problem arises when **R** has set-valued attributes. In that case, we resort to an earlier trick that was used for converting entity keys into relation keys: all set-valued attributes must be included in the candidate key of the relation (see the PERSON entity-to-relation translation in (4.1)). Note that roles are always single-valued, so this special treatment of set-valued attributes does not apply to roles.

3. *Foreign-key constraints of the relation schema.* Because, in the E-R model, a role always refers to some entity (which is mapped to a relation), roles translate into foreign-key constraints. The foreign keys of the relation schema derived from **R** are constructed as follows.

   > Let *R* be a role in **R** that connects **R** to an entity type, **E**. We use `rel(`**R**`)` and `rel(`**E**`)` to denote the relational schemas derived from **R** and **E**, respectively.
   >
   > For each such role, the primary key, $\mathcal{K}$, of **E** (which, by construction, is included among the attributes of `rel(`**R**`)`) becomes a foreign key of the schema `rel(`**R**`)` that references `rel(`**E**`)`, *provided that* $\mathcal{K}$ is also the primary key of `rel(`**E**`)`.

   The reason for the caveat in this definition is that, as we have seen, the primary key of an entity type need not be the primary key of the corresponding relational schema. For instance, in the case of the PERSON entity type, `SSN` is the primary key of the entity type, but not of the corresponding relation schema (which has `{SSN, Hobby}` as its primary key). This type of problem is eliminated by the relational normalization theory, to be discussed in Chapter 6.

Figure 4.14 shows the CREATE TABLE commands that define the schemas corresponding to some of the relationships in Figure 4.2 on page 74. Observe that, in the MARRIEDTO relation, we did not define the foreign-key constraint: although `SSNhusband` and `SSNwife` clearly reference the `SSN` attribute of the PERSON relation, `SSN` is not a candidate key for that relation, as explained earlier. The UNIQUE constraint in the schema guarantees that `SSNwife` is a candidate key. The NOT NULL constraints in WORKSIN and MARRIEDTO comes from step 1(c) of the above algorithm: it ensures that each relationship has both of its entities present.

Note that when E-R diagrams are translated into tables, some of these tables describe entities and others describe relationships. Thus, the first E-R diagram of Figure 4.2 would translate into three tables: one to describe the entity type PROFESSOR, one to describe the entity type DEPARTMENT, and one to describe the relationship type that links professors to departments.

FIGURE 4.14 Translations of some relationships.

```
CREATE TABLE  WORKSIN  (
    Since        DATE,
    ProfId       INTEGER,
    DeptId       CHAR(4)  NOT NULL,
    PRIMARY KEY (ProfId),
    FOREIGN KEY (ProfId) REFERENCES PROFESSOR (Id),
    FOREIGN KEY (DeptId) REFERENCES DEPARTMENT )
CREATE TABLE  MARRIEDTO  (
    Date         DATE,
    SSNhusband   INTEGER,
    SSNwife      INTEGER  NOT NULL,
    PRIMARY KEY (SSNhusband),
    UNIQUE (SSNwife) )
CREATE TABLE  SOLD  (
    Price        INTEGER,
    Date         DATE,
    ProjId       INTEGER,
    SupplierId   INTEGER,
    PartNumber   INTEGER,
    PRIMARY KEY (ProjId, PartNumber, Date),
    FOREIGN KEY (ProjId) REFERENCES PROJECT,
    FOREIGN KEY (SupplierId) REFERENCES SUPPLIER (Id),
    FOREIGN KEY (PartNumber) REFERENCES PART (Number) )
```

4.5.3 Representing IsA Hierarchies in the Relational Model

There are several ways to represent the IsA relationship using relational tables. First we present a general way of dealing with IsA in the relational model, and then we show two other techniques, which may have advantages in certain situations.

1. *General representation.* Choose a candidate key for all entity types related by the IsA hierarchy. Add the attributes of this key to each entity type in the hierarchy, and then convert the resulting entities into relations, as discussed in Section 4.5.1. The choice of such a key is possible because, as was observed in Section 4.4.1, a key of a supertype is also a key of each subtype. Therefore, the required key is the key of the top entity type in the hierarchy.

   For instance, in Figure 4.6 we can choose {SSN} as the common key of all entity types in the hierarchy, so SSN will be added to STUDENT, EMPLOYEE, etc. The next step in the translation process will yield the following relation schemas.

   PERSON(SSN, Name, D.O.B.)
   STUDENT(SSN, StartDate, GPA)
   FRESHMAN(SSN)
   SOPHOMORE(SSN, Major)
   JUNIOR(SSN, Major)

SENIOR(SSN, Major, Advisor)
EMPLOYEE(SSN, Department, Salary)
SECRETARY(SSN)
TECHNICIAN(SSN, Specialization)

In addition, inclusion dependencies pointing from sub-entity types to parent entity types are needed. This ensures that every entity in a subtype also belongs to the supertype. In our particular case, since SSN is a key in the supertypes, the inclusion dependencies can be specified as foreign-key constraints. For instance, the relations STUDENT and EMPLOYEE will have the constraint

```
FOREIGN KEY (SSN) REFERENCES PERSON
```

Similarly, the relations corresponding to the sub-entity types FRESHMAN, . . . , SENIOR will have the constraint

```
FOREIGN KEY (SSN) REFERENCES STUDENT
```

Finally, the relations SECRETARY and TECHNICIAN will have the constraint

```
FOREIGN KEY (SSN) REFERENCES EMPLOYEE
```

2. *Representation for disjoint* ISA *relationships.* If a group of ISA relationships, C_1 ISA C; . . . ; C_k ISA C, satisfies the disjointness constraint, then the following representation can be used. All entities that participate in the relationship are stored in a single relation whose attribute set is the union of the attribute sets of all entity types involved (i.e., attributes(C) $\cup_{i=1}^{k}$ attributes(C_i)). One extra attribute is added to indicate the original entity type of each tuple in the relation. We should also add the common key inherited from the top type in the ISA hierarchy, as in the general translation algorithm discussed earlier. Tuples that come from the entity types that do not have certain attributes are padded with NULLs over such attributes. (For instance, tuples from C that are not in any of the C_is are likely to have such NULLs.)

   As an example, consider the part of the hierarchy below the STUDENT entity type. We can create a single relation schema with the attributes SSN, GPA, StartDate, Major, Advisor (SSN is the key attribute inherited from the supertype Person) plus the new attribute Status with the domain {Freshman, Sophomore, Junior, Senior}. This attribute is used to indicate the original entity type of every tuple. For instance, a FRESHMAN entity will be represented by a tuple that has normal values in the attributes SSN, GPA, StartDate, and Status, and NULL in the attributes Major and Advisor. A student who does not belong to any of the four subtypes of STUDENT will have a NULL also in the Status attribute.

> *Brain Teaser:* Name one advantage and one disadvantage of this representation compared to the general representation for the ISA relationship.

3. *Representation for covering* ISA *relationships*. If a group of ISA relationships, C_1 ISA C; . . . ; C_k ISA C, satisfies the covering constraint, we can use the following translation: create one relation schema per each subtype of the ISA relationship. The attribute set of the relation associated with a subtype, C_i, is the union of the attribute sets for the subtype and the supertype (i.e., attributes(C_i) ∪ attributes(C)) plus the key inherited from the top entity in the hierarchy, which was used in all previous translations.

   For instance, assuming that the only people described in our database are employees and students, the ISA relationship that connects EMPLOYEE and STUDENT to their supertype PERSON satisfies the covering constraint and can be represented by the following pair of relation schemes:

```
EMPLREL(SSN,Name,D.O.B.,Department,Salary)
STUDREL(SSN,Name,D.O.B.,GPA,StartDate)
```

   An advantage of this representation over the general one is that attributes such as `Name` and `Salary` are in the same relation and thus queries of the form "What is John's salary?" can be answered more efficiently. On the other hand, this representation causes redundant information to be stored if, for example, John is both an employee and a student. In that case, John's name, date of birth, and SSN will be stored both in the tuple that represents John in the EMPLREL relation and in the tuple for John in STUDREL.

4.5.4 Representation of Participation Constraints

Conceptually, representing participation constraints in the relational model is easy. We have already seen, in Figure 4.14 on page 90, the CREATE TABLE statement for the WORKSIN relationship. So all it takes to enforce the participation constraint of PROFESSORS in WORKSIN is to specify an inclusion dependency (refer back to Section 3.2.2 for the definition) that states

```
PROFESSOR(Id) references WORKSIN(ProfId)
```

Since `Id` is a foreign key (because `ProfId` is a key of WORKSIN), we can state the participation constraint in SQL by simply declaring the `Id` attribute of PROFESSOR as a foreign key.

```
CREATE TABLE  PROFESSOR  (
     Id         INTEGER,
     Name       CHAR(20),
     PRIMARY KEY (Id),
     FOREIGN KEY (Id) REFERENCES WORKSIN (ProfId) )
```

Note that the foreign-key constraint does not rule out the possibility that `Id` can be NULL, which means that in general a NOT NULL constraint for `Id` would be in order. However, in our case, `Id` is declared as a primary key of PROFESSOR, so the NOT NULL constraint is implicit. Also observe that the DeptId attribute is missing (in contrast to Figure 3.5). It was not included because the above schema for PROFESSOR was derived from the E-R diagram in Figure 4.8, and DeptId is not one of the attributes of the PROFESSOR entity type there. Instead, the connection between professors and departments is represented by the WORKSIN relation.

We can do a better translation by noticing that Id is a key of PROFESSOR and also of WORKSIN (indirectly, through the foreign-key constraint). Thus, we can merge the attributes of WORKSIN into the PROFESSOR relation and identify the attribute ProfId with Id. This is possible because the common key of these tables guarantees that each PROFESSOR tuple has *exactly* one corresponding WORKSIN tuple, so no redundancy is created by concatenating such related tuples. This yields the table PROFESSORMERGEDWITHWORKSIN.

```
CREATE TABLE  PROFESSORMERGEDWITHWORKSIN  (
    Id        INTEGER,
    Name      CHAR(20),
    DeptId    CHAR(4) NOT NULL,
    Since     DATE,
    PRIMARY KEY (Id)
    FOREIGN KEY DeptId REFERENCES DEPARTMENT )
```

Note one subtle point about this merge—the NOT NULL clause in the DeptId attribute. One might conjecture that DeptId simply inherited NOT NULL from the WORKSIN relation during the merge. However, this is not a sufficient reason, for if professors could exist in the database without working for any department, then the DeptId attribute in PROFESSORMERGEDWITHWORKSIN should be allowed to accept a null value. In reality, the NOT NULL specification follows from two facts: the NOT NULL clause in the DeptId attribute on WORKSIN *and* the participation constraint by PROFESSOR in WORKSIN, which ensures that professors cannot exist outside of a department.

Although conceptually the representation of participation constraints in the relational model amounts to nothing more than specifying an inclusion dependency, the actual representation in SQL is not always as simple as the previous examples might suggest. The reason is that not all inclusion dependencies are foreign-key constraints (see Section 3.2.2), and expressing such constraints in SQL requires the heavier machinery of assertions or triggers, which can negatively affect the performance.

An example of this situation is the constraint on the participation of STUDENT entity type in the TRANSCRIPT relationship, depicted in Figure 4.8. The translation of TRANSCRIPT to SQL is

```
CREATE TABLE  TRANSCRIPT  (
    StudId   INTEGER,
    CrsCode  CHAR(6),
    Semester CHAR(6),
    Grade    CHAR(1),
```

```
    PRIMARY KEY (StudId, CrsCode, Semester),
    FOREIGN KEY (StudId) REFERENCES STUDENT (Id),
    FOREIGN KEY (CrsCode) REFERENCES COURSE (CrsCode),
    FOREIGN KEY (Semester) REFERENCES SEMESTERS (SemCode))
```

As before, the foreign-key constraints specified for the TRANSCRIPT table do not guarantee that every student takes a course. To ensure that every student participates in some TRANSCRIPT relationship, the STUDENT relation must have an inclusion dependency of the form

```
STUDENT(Id) references TRANSCRIPT(StudId)
```

However, since StudId is not a candidate key in TRANSCRIPT, this inclusion dependency is not a foreign-key constraint. In Chapter 3, we illustrated how inclusion dependencies can be defined using the CREATE ASSERTION statement (see (3.4) on page 52).

Unfortunately, verifying general assertions is often significantly more costly than verifying foreign-key constraints, so the use of constraints such as (3.4) should be carefully weighed against the potential overhead. For instance, if it is determined that including such an assertion slows down crucial database operations, the designer might opt for checking the inclusion dependency as part of a separate, periodically run transaction and forgo the real-time check.

4.5.5 Representation of the Part-of Relationship

We distinguish three cases: two deal with various forms of non-exclusive part-of relationships and one with the exclusive case.

- *Non-exclusive part-of: subpart can exist independently and be shared between different wholes.* In this case, translation into the relational model is done as if part-of were a regular relationship with no special properties, that is, it translates into a separate relation.
- *Non-exclusive part-of: subpart can exist independently but can be part of at most one whole.* This type of relationship would be represented by a diagram that has a thin arrow leading from the subpart entity to the part-of relationship (or an edge adorned with a cardinality constraint 0..1). Since every subpart can participate in at most one part-of relationship, we can represent both the subpart type and the relationship type using a single relation similarly to the merge of the relations PROFESSOR and WORKSIN into PROFESSORMERGEDWITHWORKSIN on page 93. A foreign key in the merged relation will reference the whole entity that contains the subpart and, in this way, the relationship between the subpart and the whole will be preserved.

  Since subparts do not need to be part of a whole, those that do not will have a null value in the fields of that foreign key. Therefore, the NOT NULL clause should *not* be attached to the attributes of that foreign key. For example, if AUTOMOBILE has {VehicleId} as its key and WHEEL has the attributes

SerialNumber, Size, and Manufacturer, then both the WHEEL entity type and the PARTOF relationship (see Figure 4.10) can be represented as

```
CREATE TABLE  WHEELMERGEDWITHPARTOF  (
    SerialNumber  INTEGER,
    Size          CHAR(10),
    Manufacturer  CHAR(20),
    VehicleId     CHAR(20)
    PRIMARY KEY (SerialNumber),
    FOREIGN KEY (VehicleId) REFERENCES AUTOMOBILE )
```

In line with the previous discussion, we did *not* declare VehicleId to be NOT NULL. So, if the car is disembodied and the wheel is sold separately, then VehicleId can be set to NULL.

- *Exclusive part-of.* In this case, the subpart is a weak entity and the part-of relationship is its identifying relationship. A weak entity participates in one and only one identifying relationship, and a thick arrow must exist between the subpart and the relationship. Therefore, this case is translated according to the rules for participation and key constraints. The main difference with respect to the previous case is that now the attributes of the foreign key that point to the master entity must have NOT NULL attached to them. An example of this kind of translation was given before (see PROFESSOR, WORKSIN, and PROFESSORMERGEDWITHWORKSIN).

4.6 UML: A New Kid on the Block

OPTIONAL

Unified Modeling Language (UML) [Booch et al. 1999] is a culmination of a long process, which led to unifying and generalizing a number of methodologies in software engineering, business modeling and management, database design, and others. The E-R approach was just one of the many inputs that have influenced the final product. Because UML designers tried to capture every known aspect of the design activity, the approach ended up with every complication a modeling language can possibly have. Nevertheless, perhaps actually *due* to its Swiss Army knife model, UML is gaining in popularity in many areas of design, including database design. In this section, we will introduce UML *class diagrams*—a subset of UML that is suitable for conceptual modeling of databases.

We should mention that other parts of UML are also useful for modeling various aspects of database applications. Thus, in Appendix B we employ UML **use case diagrams** to describe user interactions with the Student Registration System and UML **sequence diagrams** to model the dynamic aspects of those use cases. In C, we use UML **state diagrams** to describe the behavior of various objects in that system. In addition UML **activity diagrams** can be used to show how activities are coordinated, and **collaboration diagrams** can be used to describe interactions (i.e., message exchange) among the different objects that comprise a complex system. And then there are **component diagrams**, **deployment diagrams**, and more.

```
PERSON
-------------------------------------------
Name:              CHAR(20)
SSN:               INTEGER  <<PK>>
Address:           CHAR(50)
Hobbies[0..*]:     CHAR(10)
-------------------------------------------
ChangeAddr(NewAddr: CHAR(50))
AddHobby(Hobby: CHAR(10))
...    ...    ...
```

```
STUDENT
-------------------------------------------
Name:              CHAR(20)
Id:                INTEGER  <<PK>>
Address:           CHAR(50)
GPA:               DEC(2,1)
StartDate:         DATE
-------------------------------------------
ChangeAddr(NewAddr: CHAR(50))
SetStartDate(Date: DATE)
...    ...    ...
<<Invariant>> self.GPA > 2.0
```

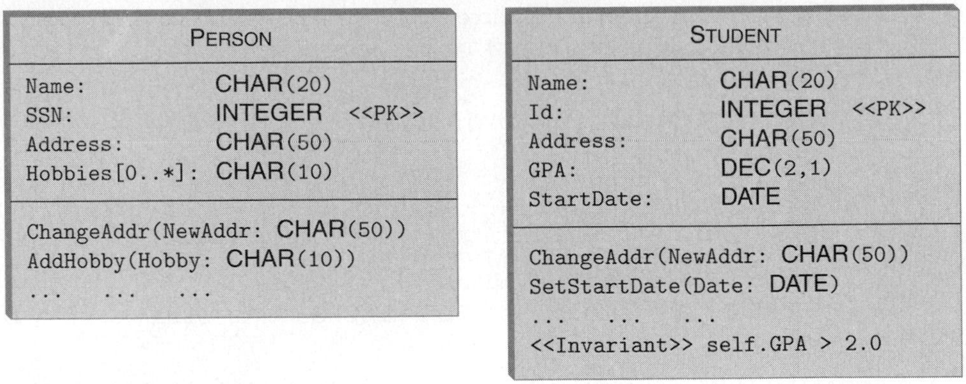

FIGURE 4.15 Examples of UML classes.

4.6.1 Representing Entities in UML

UML is an object-oriented modeling language, and, not surprisingly, entities are called **classes** there. Classes are depicted as boxes—as in the E-R case—and appear in UML **class diagrams**. The main visual difference between class diagrams and E-R diagrams is that entity attributes in E-R diagrams are shown inside ovals attached to the box, while in class diagrams attributes appear directly inside the box. UML classes corresponding to the entities PERSON and STUDENT are shown in Figure 4.15. Note that class attributes in UML can be set-valued, as in the E-R model. This is specified by means of a *multiplicity constraint* on the corresponding attribute. In the figure, the attribute `Hobbies` has the multiplicity `[0..*]`, meaning that it can have any number of values (including none). Other multiplicities, such as `[0..3]` or `[5..*]`, are also possible.

UML classes extend E-R entities in several ways. First, UML classes can include methods that operate on the objects (i.e., entities) that belong to these classes. Some methods that operate on STUDENT objects and on PEOPLE objects are shown in the bottom portion of Figure 4.15. The inclusion of methods allows the designer to specify operations that can be performed on entities that populate each class. This has a particular advantage for object-oriented databases (where the main building blocks are objects rather than relations), but even in relational databases we can use methods to represent transactions that are deemed to be closely associated with particular tables.

Second, UML 2.0 will include the **Object Constraint Language** (or OCL), which can be used to specify certain kinds of constraints directly in the UML diagrams. These constraints can impose restrictions on a single class or on several classes at once, and in this way they are analogous to CHECK and ASSERTION constraints of SQL.

Third, UML has extensibility mechanisms, which can be used to add additional features to the language and make it more suitable for database design. Unfortunately, database-specific extensions are not quite there yet. UML was designed to model software, not data, and it shows. For instance, while OCL is quite a complex language, it does not have the expressive power of assertions in SQL and thus it is lacking an important functionality required for data modeling. We therefore do not discuss OCL here and instead just show an example of a simple OCL constraint in Figure 4.15. This constraint, indicated with the `<<Invariant>>` flag, requires that all members of the STUDENT class have a grade point average higher than 2.

At present, UML is lacking even such basic data modeling features as standard ways for specifying primary keys. Not everything is lost, however, since the designers of UML provided for a way to extend the language with new features using *stereotypes*. A **stereotype** is a symbol enclosed in double-angled brackets, such as `<<PK>>` and `<<Invariant>>`—see Figure 4.15. Stereotypes have no set meaning within UML. Instead, their meaning is defined by conventions. For example, you and your coworkers may agree that expressions tagged with the stereotype `<<Invariant>>` represent constraints. Database designers, as a community, may agree that attributes tagged with the stereotype `<<PK>>` form a primary key of a class. Such sets of conventions within an organization or a community are called **UML profiles**. Clearly, a great deal of data semantics can be specified using stereotypes because one can put any phrase inside the double-angled brackets and then develop a set of conventions around the new stereotype. However, no universally agreed-upon data modeling profile has been adopted by the database community so far. (However, Rational Software [*http://www.rational.com/*], now a division of IBM, has put forward one proposal for a UML data modeling profile.)

4.6.2 Representing Relationships in UML

In UML, relationships are called **associations**, and relationship types are known as **association types**. In general, UML diagrams attach more semantics to associations than is normally found in E-R diagrams, and we will examine some of these mechanisms later in this and the next section.

Associations without attributes. As in the E-R approach, objects (i.e., entities) that are related to each other by associations (i.e., relationships) may play different roles in those associations. When ambiguity can arise or when greater clarity is desired, the roles can be given explicit names. For binary association types, UML simply uses a line to connect the classes involved in the association. When more than two classes are involved, UML uses a diamond, as in the E-R approach. Figure 4.16 shows the UML version of some of the relationship types previously depicted in Figure 4.2 using the E-R approach.

Association classes. Note that the relationships WORKSIN and SOLD have attributes, but the corresponding associations in Figure 4.16 do not, because UML does not offer this facility. Can a designer represent the information contained in those attributes? The answer is provided by **association classes**. An association class is like a regular class, but it is attached to an association in a special way (using a dashed line), which is intended to say that the attributes of the class are intended

OPTIONAL

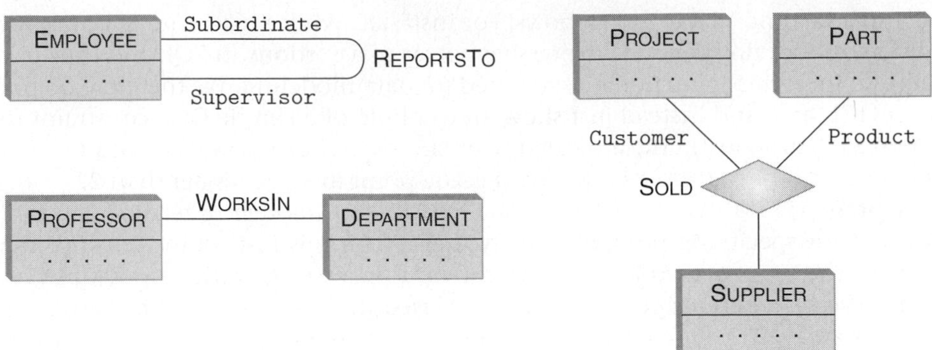

FIGURE 4.16 UML associations.

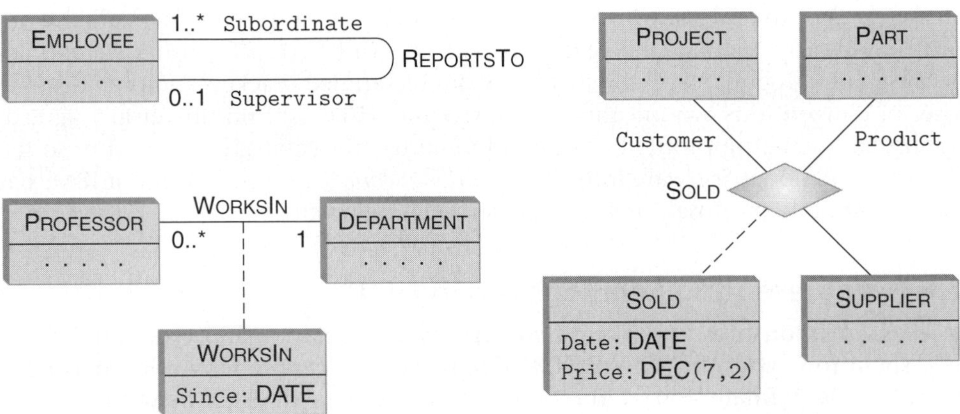

FIGURE 4.17 UML associations with association classes.

to describe the association. The relationships WORKSIN and SOLD with attached association classes are depicted in Figure 4.17.

Multiplicity constraints on roles. Recall that relationship keys can be specified in the E-R diagrams by drawing arrows (see Figure 4.2) or by explicitly writing down the attributes and roles that comprise those keys. In UML, arrows (and even more general constraints) are represented using *multiplicity constraints*.

A **multiplicity constraint** on a role, *R*, that connects an association type, **A**, with a class, **C**, is a range specification of the form `n..m` attached to *R*, where $\mathtt{n} \geq 0$ is a nonnegative integer and `m` is either the $*$ symbol or an integer $\geq n$. The range gives the lower and upper bounds on the number of objects of class **C** that can be connected by means of an association of type **A** to any given set of objects that are attached to the other ends of the association (one object for each end).

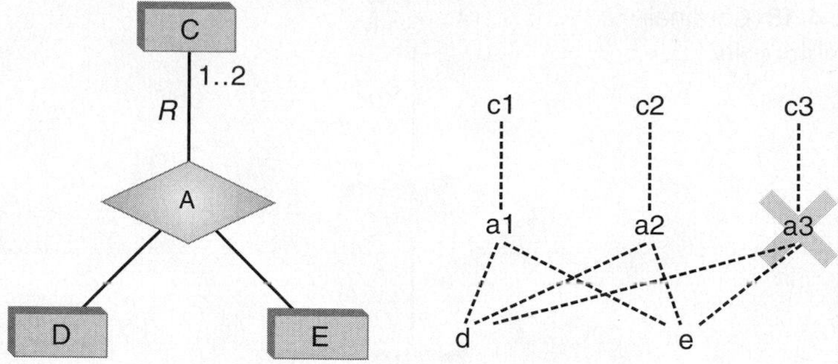

FIGURE 4.18 The meaning of the multiplicity constraint in UML.

To better understand this concept, take a look at Figure 4.18. In the picture, the class **C** is connected via the role *R* to the association type **A**, and other roles connect the association to classes **D** and **E**. The multiplicity constraint on *R* is 1..2. Therefore, each pair of objects, d ∈ **D** and e ∈ **E**, must be connected by associations of type **A** to at least one and at most two objects of class **C**. In the figure, having just two associations, a1 and a2, is legitimate. Adding a3 would violate the upper bound of the multiplicity constraint because this would allow three objects of type **C** to be connected to a particular pair of objects (d and e) of classes **D** and **E**, respectively. Likewise, it would be a violation of the lower bound of the constraint if d and e were not connected to *any* object of class **C** by an association of type **A**.

According to this semantics, the range 5..* attached to a role, *R*, which connects the association type **A** to class **C**, means that at least five **C**-objects (* means no upper limit) must participate in role *R* in associations of type **A** with each distinct set of objects attached to the other roles of these associations. The range * means 0..* and the range 3 means 3..3 (i.e., exactly 3). Figure 4.17 shows several uses of the multiplicity constraint in UML. The EMPLOYEE/REPORTSTO example illustrates the assignment of ranges to each role of an association. In this case each range is interpreted separately. The range on the Supervisor role says that an employee can have zero or one supervisor; the range on the Subordinate role says that a supervisor can supervise several employees (but at least one). The ranges in the PROFESSOR/WORKSIN example say that every professor works in exactly one department, but a department can have any number of professors including none.

UML multiplicity vs. E-R cardinality constraints. On the surface, the notion of multiplicity appears to be similar to cardinality constraints in the E-R approach. However, they are quite different. To see this, compare Figure 4.3 on page 77 with Figure 4.18. In these figures, the diagrams on the left are identical, but their interpretations are different. The valid instance of the UML diagram (on the right side of Figure 4.18) is nothing like the valid instance of the E-R diagram (on the right side of Figure 4.3).

In fact, it can be gleaned from Figures 4.18 and 4.3 that the multiplicity constraint in UML has, in a way, the opposite meaning to that of the cardinality

OPTIONAL

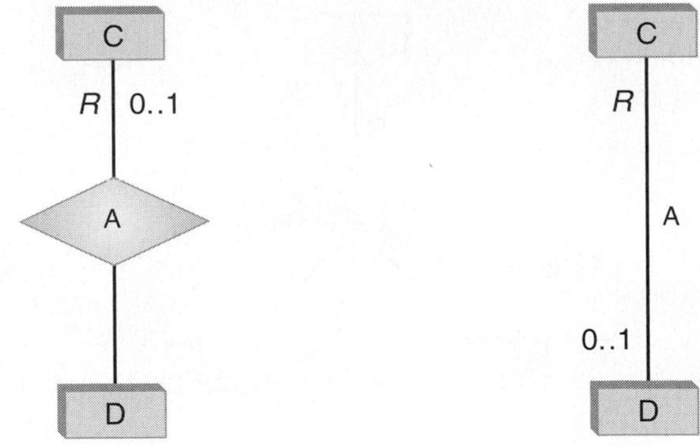

FIGURE 4.19 Cardinality vs. multiplicity.

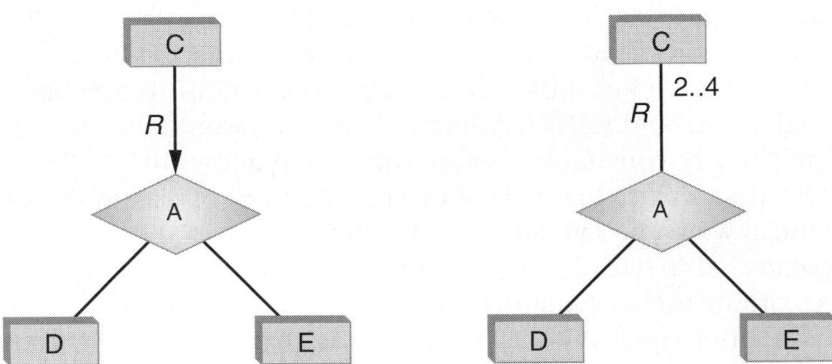

FIGURE 4.20 Cardinality constraints in E-R that cannot be represented using multiplicity in UML.

OPTIONAL

constraint in E-R. This is certainly true in the case of binary relationships and associations: Figure 4.19 shows an E-R diagram with a cardinality constraint on a binary relationship and an equivalent UML diagram with the corresponding multiplicity constraint. In both cases, the diagrams say that each entity of type **C** can be associated with at most one entity of type **D**. We see that the range specification in UML and E-R appear on the opposite ends of the association/relationship.

For binary relationships, multiplicity and cardinality constraints have equivalent expressive power, although their interpretations are exactly the opposite of each other. For ternary and higher-degree relationships, the difference is greater: the two types of constraints have different, incomparable expressive power. For instance, it is unclear how one can use multiplicity to express the constraints shown in the E-R diagrams in Figure 4.20.

The apparent similarity and the not-so-apparent differences between the notions of cardinality and multiplicity can be an endless source of confusion.

Key constraints in associations. Recall that in the E-R model, an arrow that leads from an entity type, **C**, to a relationship type, **A**, specifies a key constraint. It says that an element of **C** can participate in at most one relationship, and this implies that the primary key of the entity type is also a candidate key of the relationship. In UML, for *binary associations* the same constraint can be specified using multiplicity. If **A** is an association type connecting classes **C** and **D**, then placing the range 0..1 on the role that connects **A** with **D** enforces the same constraint: it says that each instance of **C** can be associated with at most one instance of **D**. This is illustrated in Figure 4.19. Figure 4.17 shows more examples of the use of multiplicity constraints to specify keys in association types.

As mentioned earlier, multiplicity cannot imitate certain constraints in ternary (and higher-degree) relationships, such as the ones in the E-R diagrams of Figure 4.20. General key constraints cannot be expressed using multiplicity constraints either. For example, a constraint on an association **A** relating classes **C**, **D**, and **E** that asserts that a particular pair of elements from **C** and **D** can participate in at most one association of type **A** cannot be expressed. However, UML allows just about any text to be placed inside curly braces on the diagram. Such text is intended to be understood as a UML constraint, but of course, it is up to the designer to interpret the meaning of such annotations. For instance, in Figure 4.21 we have annotated the association Sold with the constraint `{Key: Customer,Product; Date}`. By itself, this notation means nothing in UML, but the design team and the programming team might adopt internal conventions, which would make such notation meaningful.

Foreign-key constraints. As with primary keys, UML does not have a standard way of representing foreign keys. Typically, database designers use the stereotype <<FK>> for that purpose. Figure 4.21 shows examples of the use of this stereotype. This technique, although very common, requires that related attributes in different classes have the same name. Otherwise, it would not be possible to determine which primary keys are referred to by the foreign keys. To overcome this limitation, more expressive stereotypes are needed. For instance, if the identity of a professor is established via the `Id` attribute (as it has been in all previous examples), then the following stereotype (modeled after SQL) could be used in the WorksIn association class: <<FK Professor(Id)>> `ProfId: INT`. This means that the attribute `ProfId` in WorksIn refers to the `Id` attribute of Professor.

4.6.3 Advanced Modeling Concepts in UML

We will now discuss the UML representation of the advanced modeling concepts, which were studied in Section 4.4 in the context of the E-R approach.

Class hierarchies. In UML, the IsA relationship is called **generalization**. It is represented as a solid arrow with a large hollow head leading from a subclass to a superclass. An example of a generalization is shown in Figure 4.22.

As in E-R diagrams, several IsA/generalization relationships can be combined, as depicted on the right side of the figure. Covering and disjointness constraints

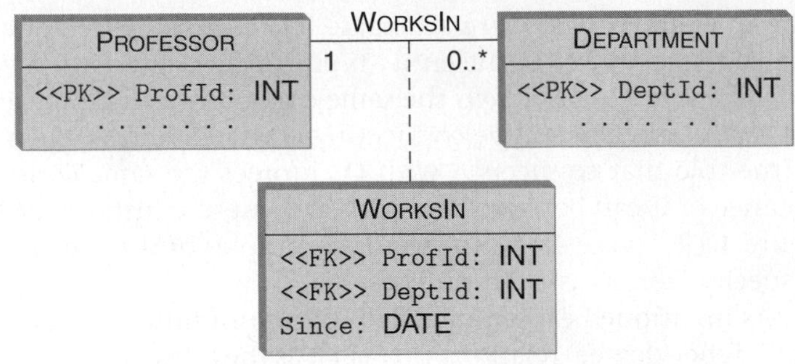

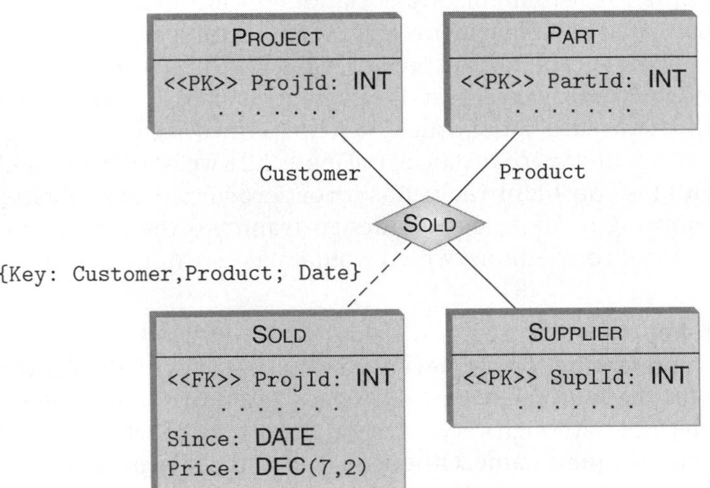

FIGURE 4.21 Foreign keys in UML.

OPTIONAL

are noted directly on the UML diagrams. In the figure, the covering constraint (which says that any student must belong to one of the four categories: FRESHMAN, SOPHOMORE, etc.) is indicated with the keyword "complete," and the disjointness constraint with the keyword "disjoint." They are written inside curly braces, as required by the UML conventions for constraints.

Participation constraints. It might seem natural to try to model participation constraints using multiplicity. However, it turns out that the problem is not so simple. Participation in binary association types can, indeed, be modeled using multiplicity constraints, but this cannot be done for associations of higher degree.

Recall the duality principle for binary relationships in E-R and UML shown in Figure 4.19. It says that any cardinality constraint, expressed as a range `n..m` on role *R* of the relationship **A** in E-R can be equivalently represented in UML by imposing the same range on the opposite end of the association **A**. Since participation constraints in E-R can be specified using the range `1..*`, as discussed earlier, expressing the same

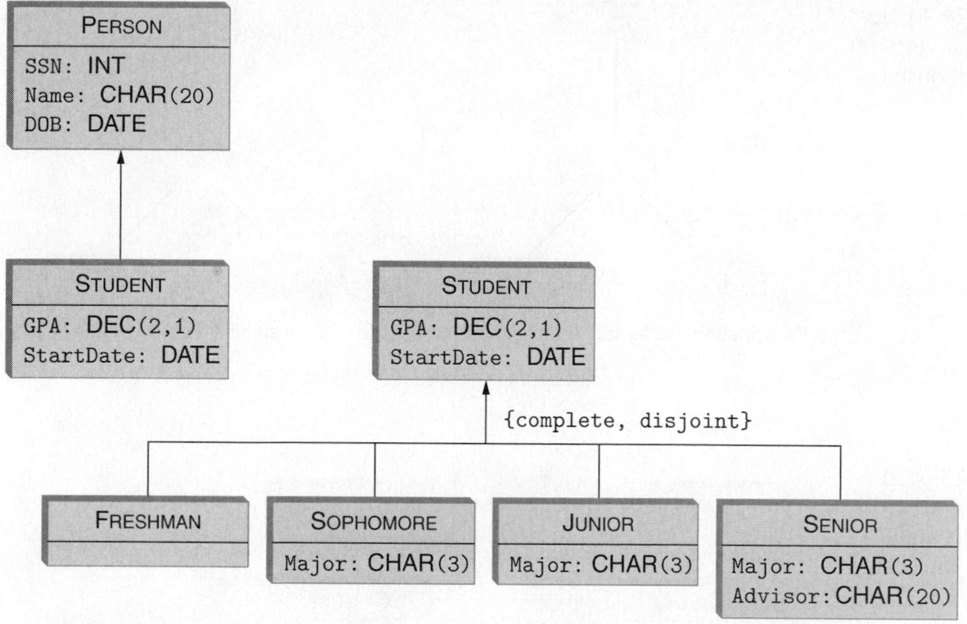

FIGURE 4.22 IsA (or generalization) hierarchies in UML.

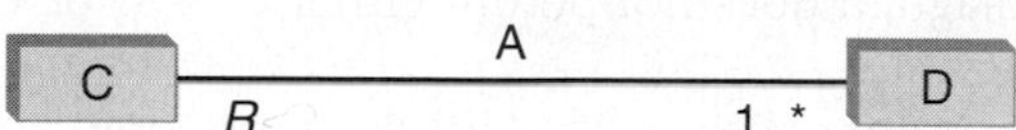

FIGURE 4.23 UML representation of the participation constraint for class C in binary association type A.

OPTIONAL

constraints in UML should be obvious. Figure 4.23 shows a UML diagram where class **C** participates in a binary association **A**.

For ternary and other associations, the issue is more involved. One might think that the duality principle can work here as well, and it should be possible to represent the participation constraint in E-R in Figure 4.24(a) using the multiplicity constraint in the UML diagram in Figure 4.24(b). However, the two constraints are not the same. The E-R participation constraint says: "For every entity c in **C** there are entities $d \in$ **D** and $e \in$ **E** that participate in a relationship $a \in$ **A** with c." In contrast, the (UML) multiplicity constraint says: "For every pair of objects $c \in$ **C** *and* $e \in$ **E** there is at least one object $d \in$ **D** that participates in a relationship $a \in$ **A** with c and e." The multiplicity constraint is stronger in some respects and weaker in others. Indeed, unless class **C** is empty, the multiplicity constraint implies that *every* E-object should be related to at least one **D** object. The participation constraint does not require this. On the other hand, if class **E** is empty, the multiplicity constraint is vacuously

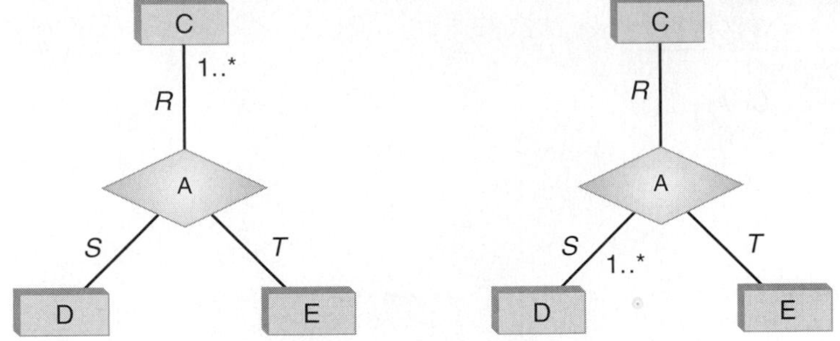

(a) Participation in a ternary relationship in E=R (b) Partial simulation of the same in UML

FIGURE 4.24 Participation constraints for ternary relationships.

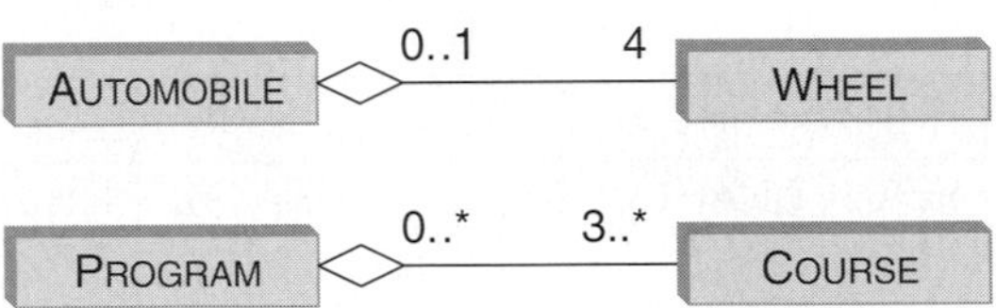

FIGURE 4.25 Aggregation: non-exclusive part-of association in UML.

OPTIONAL

satisfied, while the corresponding E-R diagram does not permit either class **D** or **E** to be empty.

Of course, since UML allows any constraint to be specified inside braces, one can simply attach the annotation `{participates}` to the role *R* in the UML diagram. However, this type of annotation requires that all parties to the design understand what this means since this annotation does not have any built-in semantics in UML.

Part-of relationship. In UML, the non-exclusive part-of relationship (where subparts can have independent existence) is called **aggregation**. UML aggregation has special notation—a line with a hollow diamond—as shown in Figure 4.25. (Recall that E-R does not use special notation for this kind of relationship.) Aggregation in UML is often accompanied by appropriate multiplicity constraints. For instance, the multiplicity constraints in Figure 4.25 indicate that each automobile must have four wheels and that a wheel can be part of at most one automobile. Similarly, the multiplicity constraints between programs in a university and courses indicate that a course can be associated with any number of programs (including none) but any particular program must include at least three courses.

The exclusive part-of relationship is called **composition** in UML; it is viewed as a special kind of aggregation. Compositions are represented using lines with filled diamonds at one end; Figure 4.26 shows two examples of composition analogous to

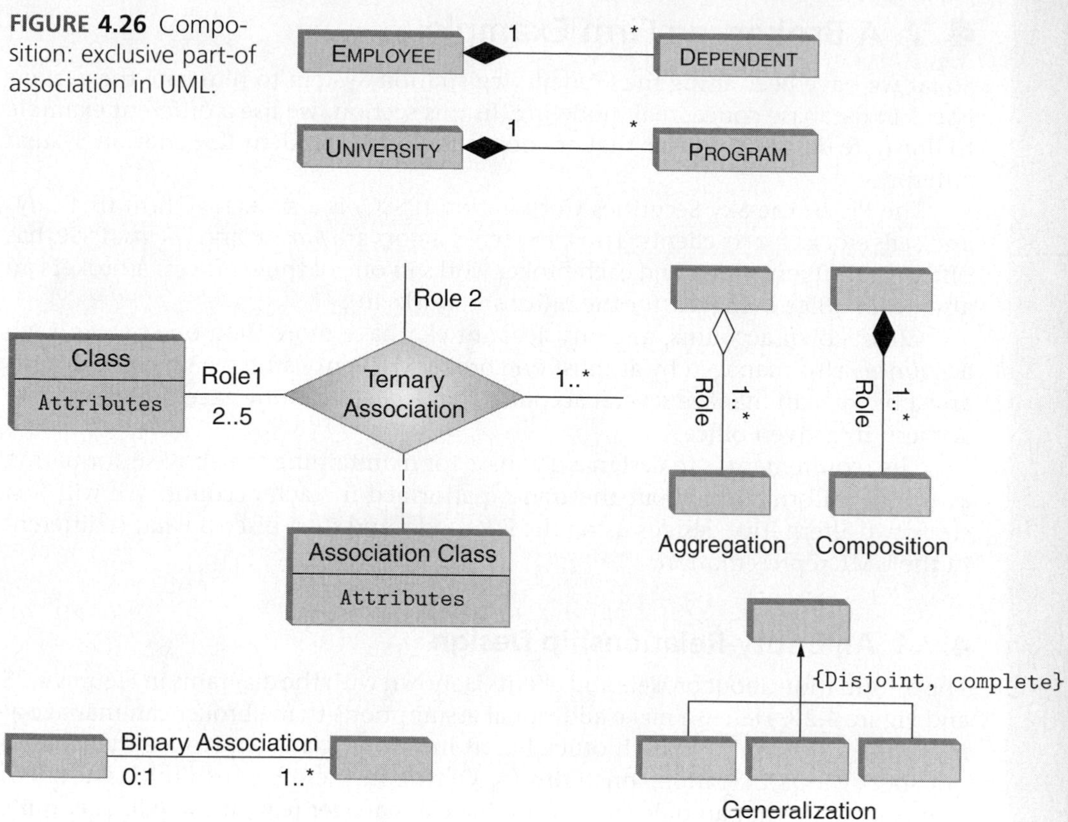

FIGURE 4.26 Composition: exclusive part-of association in UML.

FIGURE 4.27 Summary of the UML notation.

the examples of Figure 4.11 on page 85 for the E-R model. As in those examples, we assume that a PROGRAM object is destroyed if its master object of type UNIVERSITY is destroyed and that a DEPENDENT object is destroyed upon the destruction of the corresponding EMPLOYEE object.

Figure 4.27 summarizes the notation used in the UML diagrams.

4.6.4 Translation to SQL

Due to the close correspondence between the basic components of the E-R model and those of UML, translation of UML class diagrams into the relational model is done the same way as in the E-R case. The main problem is how to adequately translate the constraints that might exist in the diagram. In general, this is a complicated matter, which requires the use of CHECK and ASSERTION constraints. The following sections illustrate some of these issues.

4.7 A Brokerage Firm Example

So far we have been using the Student Registration System to illustrate the various issues in database conceptual modeling. In this section, we use a different example to illustrate design problems that are not found in the Student Registration System enterprise.

The Pie-in-the-Sky Securities Corporation (PSSC) is a brokerage firm that buys and sells stocks for its clients. Thus, the main actors are *brokers* and *clients*. PSSC has offices in different cities, and each broker works in one of these offices. A broker can also be an office manager (for the office she works in).

Clients own accounts, and any account can have more than one owner. Each account is also managed by at most one broker. A client can have several accounts and a broker can manage several accounts, but a client cannot have more than one account in a given office.

The requirement is to design a database for maintaining the above information as well as information about the trades performed in each account. We will first show two alternative designs using the E-R model and then discuss what is different in the UML representation.

4.7.1 An Entity-Relationship Design

The information about brokers and clients is shown with the diagrams in Figures 4.28 and Figure 4.29. Here we make additional assumptions that a broker can manage at most one office and that each office has at most one manager. Notice that we did not specify a participation constraint for OFFICE in the relationship MANAGEDBY, so it is possible that an office might not have a manager (e.g., if the manager quits and the position remains vacant). Since each account must be maintained in exactly one office and by at most one broker, Figure 4.29 shows a participation constraint of entity ACCOUNT in the relationship ISHANDLEDBY by the thick arrow leading

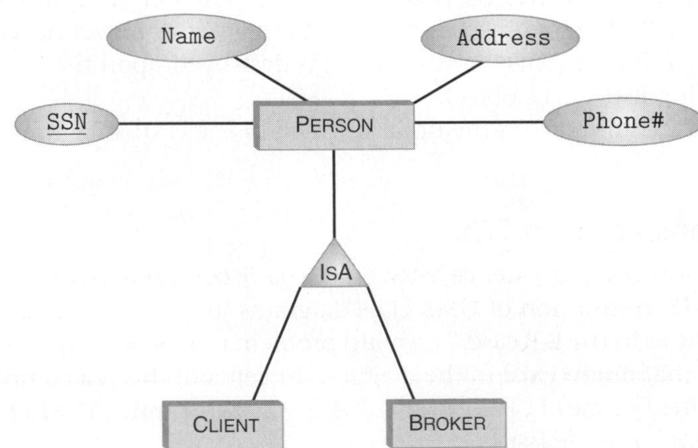

FIGURE 4.28 The IsA hierarchy of the PSSC enterprise.

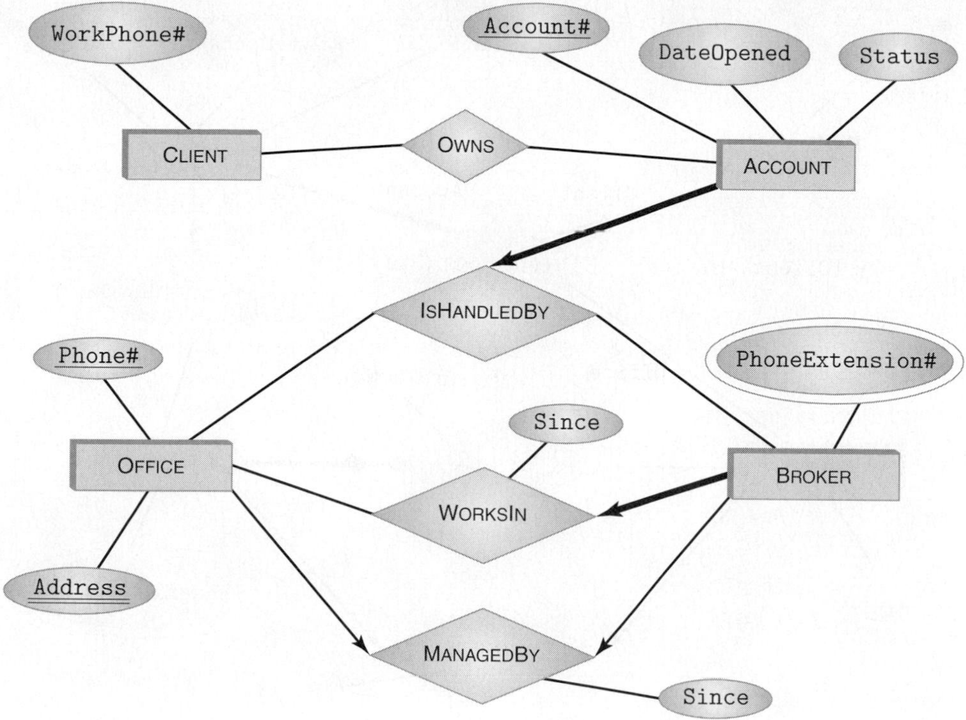

FIGURE 4.29 Client/broker information: first attempt.

from ACCOUNT to ISHANDLEDBY. Thus, {Account} is a key of ISHANDLEDBY. Notice that the attributes that form keys of entity types are underlined and different keys are underlined differently. Thus, for instance, OFFICE has two keys: {Phone#} and {Address}.

Unfortunately, the E-R diagram in Figure 4.29 has problems. First, it requires every account to have a broker. This was not part of our requirements. Second, the requirement that a client cannot have two separate accounts in the same office is not represented in the diagram.

We might try to rectify these problems using the diagram depicted in Figure 4.30. Here we take a slightly different approach and introduce a ternary relation HASACCOUNT with {Client, Office} as a key. Since BROKER is not involved in this relationship, it does not require that an account have a broker. The participation constraint on ACCOUNT says that each account has to be associated with at least one client-office pair and the key of HASACCOUNT guarantees that a client can have at most one account in a given office. In addition, we modify the relationship ISHANDLEDBY so that it involves accounts and brokers only; it does not require that every account has a broker.

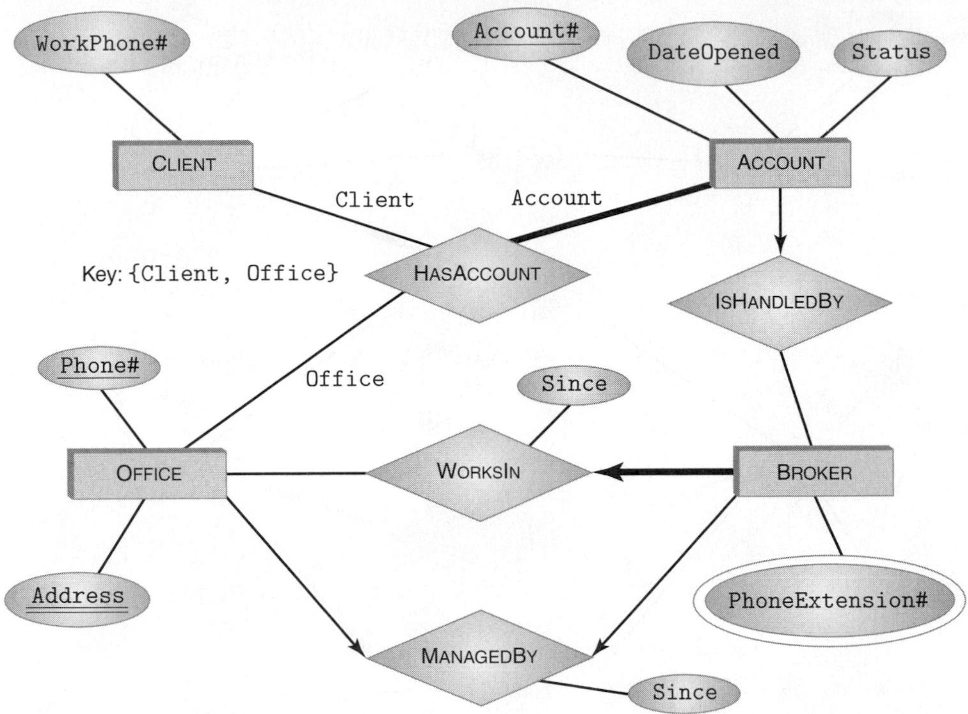

FIGURE 4.30 Client/broker information: second try.

Unfortunately, even this diagram has problems. First, notice that the edge that connects ACCOUNT and HASACCOUNT does not have an arrow. Such an arrow would have made the role `Account` a key of the relationship HASACCOUNT, which contradicts the requirement that an account can have multiple owners. However, our new design introduces a different problem: the constraint that each account is assigned to exactly one office is no longer represented in the diagram. The participation constraint of ACCOUNT in HASACCOUNT says that each account must be assigned to at least one office (and at least one customer), but nothing here says that such an office must be unique. Furthermore, we cannot solve this problem by adding an arrow to this participation constraint because this would imply that each account has at most one owner.

There is one more problem with our new design (which, in fact, was also present in our original design in Figure 4.29). Suppose that we have the following relationships:

⟨`Client1, Acct1, Office1` ⟩ ∈ HASACCOUNT

⟨`Acct1, Broker1`⟩ ∈ ISHANDLEDBY

⟨`Broker1, Office2`⟩ ∈ WORKSIN

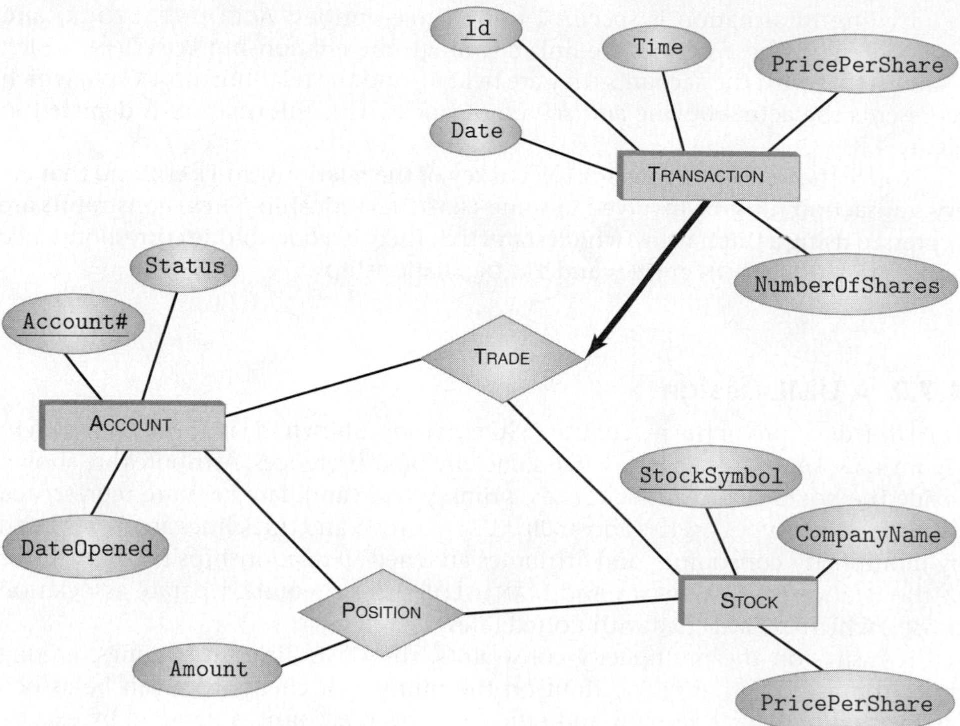

FIGURE 4.31 Trading information in the PSSC enterprise.

What is there to ensure that Office1 and Office2 are the same (i.e., Account1's office is the same as that of the broker who manages Account1)? This last problem is known as a **navigation trap**: starting with a given entity, Office1, and moving along the triangle formed by the three relationships HASACCOUNT, ISHANDLEDBY, and WORKSIN, we might end up with a different entity, Office2, of the same type. Navigation traps of this kind are particularly difficult to avoid in the E-R model because doing so requires the use of participation constraints in combination with *functional dependencies* (introduced in Section 6.3), but these constraints are supported by the E-R model only in a very limited way: as keys and participation constraints.

Note that we can avoid the navigation trap by removing the relationship HASACCOUNT completely and reintroducing the OWNS relationship between clients and accounts. However, this brings back the problem that the constraint that a client cannot have more than one account in any given office is no longer represented.

After these vain attempts to achieve a perfect design for this part of the database, we now turn our attention to the part that deals with stock trading. On a bigger canvas, Figures 4.30 and 4.31 would be connected through the entity type ACCOUNT.

Trading information is specified using three entities: Account, Stock, and Transaction. These entities are linked through the relationship Position, which relates stocks with the accounts they are held in, and the relationship Trade, which represents the actual buying and selling of stocks. This information is depicted in Figure 4.31.

Notice that the role Transaction is a key of the relationship Trade and that every transaction must be involved in some Trade relationship. These constraints are expressed using a thick arrow, which states that there is a one-to-one correspondence between Transaction entities and Trade relationships.

OPTIONAL

4.7.2 A UML Design

The UML diagram for the part of the PSSC enterprise shown in Figure 4.30 is given in Figure 4.32. Let us first acknowledge some obvious differences. Attributes are shown inside the boxes that describe classes, primary and candidate keys are represented using the stereotypes <<PK>> and <<UNIQUE>>, arrows and thick lines are represented by multiplicity constraints, and attributes attached to relationships (such as Since in the relationships WorksIn and ManagedBy) now require separate association classes, which are attached with dotted lines.

Focusing on the multiplicity constraints, the UML diagram specifies, among other things, that there is no limit on the number of clients that can be associated with a particular account and office, that each account is handled by exactly one broker, and that an arbitrary number of brokers can work in each office. The multiplicity constraint assigned to the Account role of HasAccount asserts that a particular client-office pair can be associated with an arbitrary number of accounts, but this problem is redeemed by the key attached to the association, which guarantees that any given client-office pair can be associated with at most one account through the HasAccount association.

Recall that the E-R representation in Figure 4.30 did not capture the intended semantics completely because the constraint that an account can be associated with exactly one office did not follow from that diagram. Instead, this constraint is approximated in Figure 4.30 by the participation constraint of Account in HasAccount, which says only that an account can be maintained in at least one office. Since, as we know, participation constraints on ternary relationships cannot be captured in UML, Figure 4.32 approximates the above participation constraint as suggested in Figure 4.24. Interestingly, this approximation brings us closer to expressing the original constraint (that each account is associated with exactly one office) than the participation constraint. Indeed, the multiplicity constraint on the Office role of HasAccount now says that any account object *together* with a client object uniquely determines the office. This constraint is weaker than what is required, because it allows the same account to be associated with different offices for different clients. However, the E-R diagram in Figure 4.30 does not capture even this much.

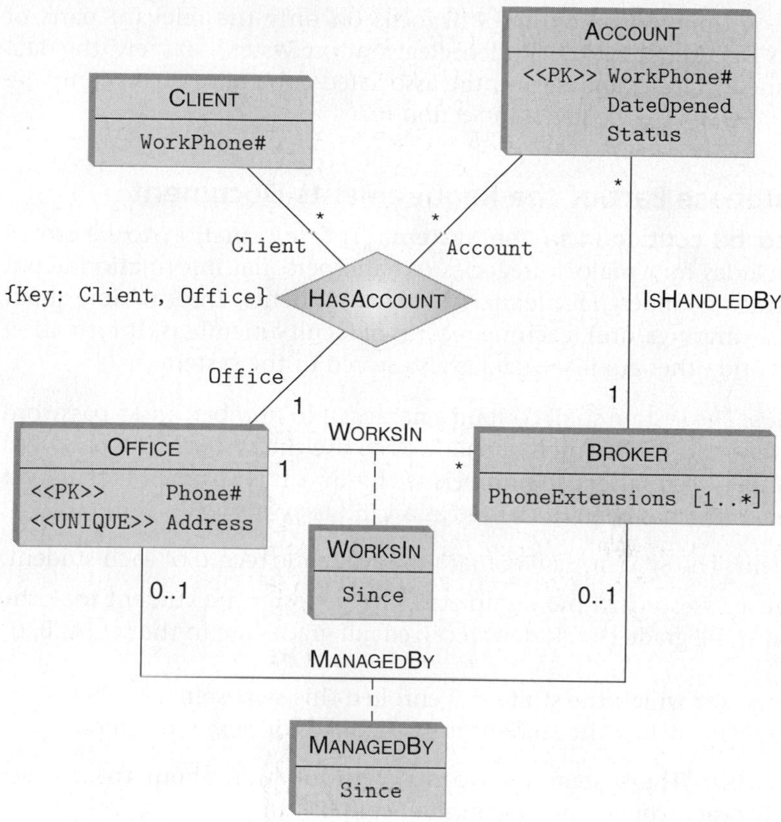

FIGURE 4.32 Client/broker information in UML.

4.8 Case Study: A Database Design for the Student Registration System

In this section, we carry out a conceptual design for the database part of the Student Registration System. The outcome of this design—an E-R or a UML diagram and a set of definitions for tables and constraints—is typically included in the Design Document for the entire application. The Design Document itself will be discussed in more detail in Section C.1.

Before we can start designing an application, we need to write down *precisely* what the system is supposed to do so that we know what it is that we want to design. The document that contains this description is called the **Requirements Document**. In this section, we are interested only in the conceptual design of the database part of our application, so we will focus on only the relevant parts of the Requirements Document for the Student Registration System: namely, the data items to be included in the database and the associated constraints. The complete Requirements Document will be given in Section B.2.

4.8.1 The Database Part of the Requirements Document

I. Information to be contained in the system. The information to be stored in the system includes four major categories of data: personal information about students and faculty members, academic records of students, information about courses and course offerings, and teaching records of faculty members. Information about classrooms and other auxiliary data is also stored in the system.

A. *Personal records*. The system shall contain a name, an Id number, and a password for each student and faculty member allowed to use the system. The password and the Id authenticates users. Id numbers are unique. It is assumed that at least one faculty member has been initialized as a valid user at startup time.

B. *Academic records*. The system shall contain the academic record of each student.
   1. Each course the student has completed, the semester the student took the course, and the grade the student received (all grades are in the set {A, B, C, D, F, I}).
   2. Each course for which the student is enrolled this semester.
   3. Each course for which the student has registered for next semester.

C. *Course information*. The system shall contain information about the courses offered, and for each course the system shall contain
   1. The course name, the course number (must be unique), the department offering the course, the textbook, and the credit hours.
   2. Whether the course is offered in spring, fall, or both.
   3. The prerequisite courses (there can be an arbitrary number of prerequisites for each course).
   4. The maximum allowed enrollment, the number of students who are enrolled (unspecified if the course is not offered this semester), and the number of students who have registered (unspecified if the course is not offered next semester).
   5. If the course is offered this semester, the days and times at which it is offered; if the course is offered next semester, the days and times at which it will be offered. The possible values shall be selected from a fixed list of weekly slots (e.g., MWF10).
   6. The Id of the instructor teaching the course this semester and next semester (Id unspecified if the course is not offered in the specified semester; it must be specified before the start of the semester in which the course is offered).
   7. The classroom assignment of the course for this semester and next semester (classroom assignment unspecified if the course is not offered in the speci-

fied semester; it must be specified before the start of the semester in which the course is offered).

D. *Teaching information.* The system shall contain a record of all courses that have been taught previously or are being taught currently, including the semester in which they were taught and the Id of the instructor.

E. *Classroom information.* The system shall contain a list of classroom identifiers and the corresponding number of seats. A classroom identifier is a unique three-digit integer.

F. *Auxiliary information.* The system shall contain the identity of the current semester and the next semester (e.g., F1997, S1998).

II. Integrity constraints. The database shall satisfy the following integrity constraints.

A. Id numbers are unique.

B. If in item I.B.2 (or I.B.3), a student is listed as enrolled (registered) for a course, that course must be indicated in item I.C.2 as offered this semester (or next semester).

C. In item I.C.4, the number of students registered or enrolled in a course cannot be larger than the maximum enrollment.

D. The count of students enrolled (registered) in a course in item I.B.2 (or I.B.3) must equal the current enrollment (registration) indicated in item I.C.4.

E. An instructor cannot be assigned to two courses taught at the same time in the same semester.

F. Two courses cannot be taught in the same room at the same time in a given semester.

G. If a student is enrolled in a course, the corresponding record must indicate that the student has completed all prerequisite courses with a grade of at least C.

H. A student cannot be registered (enrolled) in two courses taught at the same hour.

I. A student cannot be registered for more than 20 credits in a given semester.

J. The room assigned to a course must have at least as many seats as the maximum allowed enrollment for the course.

K. Once a letter grade of A, B, C, D, or F has been assigned for a course, that grade cannot later be changed to an I.

4.8.2 The Database Design

We will now present the conceptual design of the database and the corresponding relational representation.

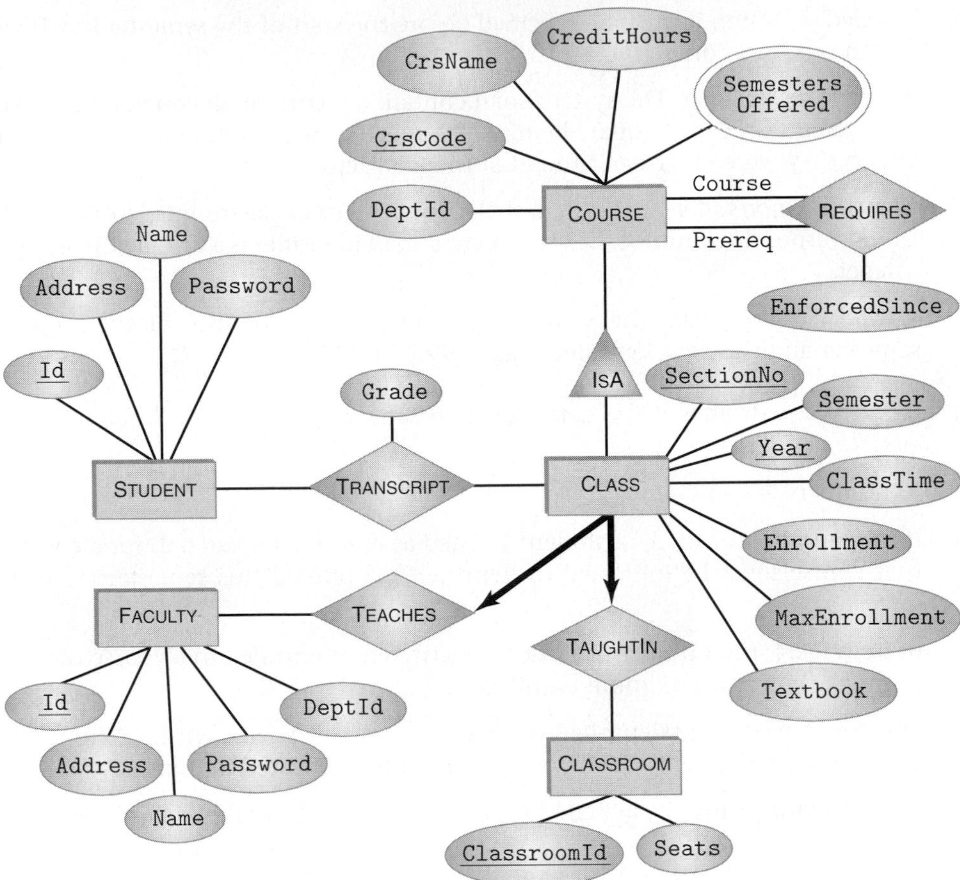

FIGURE 4.33 An E-R diagram for the Student Registration System.

A conceptual design diagram. The first step in the design process is to construct a diagram using the E-R approach or UML. The E-R diagram is shown in Figure 4.33. It is a model of the student registration enterprise as described in the sections of the Requirements Document that we just discussed. Note from the diagram that

- STUDENT is related to CLASS through TRANSCRIPT, which signifies that a student is registered, is enrolled, or has completed a class in some semester.
- FACULTY is related to CLASS through TEACHES, meaning that a faculty member teaches a class in some semester and every class is taught by exactly one faculty member.
- COURSE is related to itself through the relationship REQUIRES; that is, a course can be a prerequisite for another course in some semester. The attribute `EnforcedSince` specifies the date when the prerequisite was established.

- CLASS is related to CLASSROOM through TAUGHTIN; that is, a class is taught in a classroom in some semester.
- A class (i.e., a particular offering of a course) can use at most one textbook since the attribute `Textbook` is single-valued in the entity type CLASS.

UML representation. As far as UML is concerned, the Student Registration System does not introduce any new or interesting issues beyond what was shown in the E-R diagram. (Exercise 4.13 involves redrawing Figure 4.33 using UML conventions.)

Relational representation. On the basis of this E-R diagram and the list of integrity constraints given in the Requirements Document, the next step is to produce the schema shown in Figures 4.34 and 4.35. The translation was done in a straightforward manner using the techniques described in this chapter. Note that we did not create tables for the TEACHES and TAUGHTIN relationships: because of the participation and key constraints involving these relationships (i.e., a CLASS entity participates in exactly one TEACHES and one TAUGHTIN relationship), their corresponding tables can *both* be merged with the table for the entity CLASS, as explained in Section 4.5.2. The result of the merge is that the schema of the CLASS table includes the attributes `ClassroomId`, which identifies the room where the class is taught, and `InstructorId` of the faculty member who teaches it—see the corresponding CREATE TABLE statement in Figure 4.35.

Note that the simpler integrity constraints among those that are specified in the Requirements Document can and are defined within CREATE TABLE statements with the help of the CHECK clause (specifically the constraints that involve a single relation, such as constraints A, C, E, and F). In the complete schema design, other integrity constraints are defined as separate CREATE ASSERTION statements plus one trigger. However, this part of the design requires SQL constructs that we have not yet discussed, and so we will complete the schema design in Section C.7 after we cover these constructs.

We selected this particular design for inclusion in the book because it is straightforward. In practice, such a design might be a starting point for a number of enhancements whose goal is to capture more features and increase the efficiency of the final implementation.

Alternatives. Let us consider a few possible enhancements and alternatives. Consider course dependencies. One obvious omission in our schema is the *co-requisite* relationship and all of the constraints entailed by it. More subtly, university curricula change all the time: new courses are introduced, old courses are removed, and prerequisite dependencies between courses evolve in time. Thus, the REQUIRES relationship in Figure 4.33 might need two additional attributes, `Start` and `End`, to designate the period when the prerequisite relationship is effective. Even more interesting is the possibility that a particular prerequisite relationship might exist at different times. For instance, course A might be a prerequisite for course B between 1985 and 1990 and again between 1999 and the present. (Modeling this situation is left to Exercise 4.11.)

CASE STUDY

FIGURE 4.34 A schema for the Student Registration System—Part 1.

```
CREATE TABLE STUDENT (
    Id            CHAR(9),
    Name          CHAR(20) NOT NULL,
    Password      CHAR(10) NOT NULL,
    Address       CHAR(50),
    PRIMARY KEY (Id) )

CREATE TABLE FACULTY (
    Id            CHAR(9),
    Name          CHAR(20) NOT NULL,
    DeptId        CHAR(4) NOT NULL,
    Password      CHAR(10) NOT NULL,
    Address       CHAR(50),
    PRIMARY KEY (Id) )

CREATE TABLE COURSE (
    CrsCode       CHAR(6),
    DeptId        CHAR(4) NOT NULL,
    CrsName       CHAR(20) NOT NULL,
    CreditHours   INTEGER NOT NULL,
    PRIMARY KEY (CrsCode),
    UNIQUE (DeptId, CrsName) )

CREATE TABLE WHENOFFERED (
    CrsCode       CHAR(6),
    Semester      CHAR(6),
    PRIMARY KEY (CrsCode, Semester),
    CHECK (Semester IN ('Spring','Fall') ) )

CREATE TABLE CLASSROOM (
    ClassroomId   CHAR(3),
    Seats         INTEGER NOT NULL,
    PRIMARY KEY (ClassroomId) )
```

CASE STUDY

Another interesting enhancement is to account for the possibility that certain highly popular courses might be restricted to certain majors only. In this situation, the E-R diagram and the schema have to include information about the subjects in which each student is majoring, the majors allowed in a particular course (both are set-valued attributes), and a constraint to ensure that the restriction is enforced. (This enhancement is left to Exercise 4.12.)

Enhancements to express more complex requirements are one source of modifications to the proposed design. Another source is the vast range of possible alter-

FIGURE 4.35 A schema for the Student Registration System—Part 2.

```
CREATE TABLE REQUIRES (
    CrsCode        CHAR(6),
    PrereqCrsCode  CHAR(6),
    EnforcedSince  DATE        NOT NULL,
    PRIMARY KEY (CrsCode, PrereqCrsCode),
    FOREIGN KEY (CrsCode) REFERENCES COURSE(CrsCode),
    FOREIGN KEY (PrereqCrsCode) REFERENCES COURSE(CrsCode) )
CREATE TABLE CLASS (
    CrsCode        CHAR(6),
    SectionNo      INTEGER,
    Semester       CHAR(6),
    Year           INTEGER,
    Textbook       CHAR(50),
    ClassTime      CHAR(5),
    Enrollment     INTEGER,
    MaxEnrollment  INTEGER,
    ClassroomId    CHAR(3),            -- from TAUGHTIN
    InstructorId   CHAR(9),            -- from TEACHES
    PRIMARY KEY (CrsCode,SectionNo,Semester,Year),
    CONSTRAINT TIMECONFLICT
        UNIQUE (InstructorId,Semester,Year,ClassTime),
    CONSTRAINT CLASSROOMCONFLICT
        UNIQUE (ClassroomId,Semester,Year,ClassTime),
    CONSTRAINT ENROLLMENT
        CHECK (Enrollment <= MaxEnrollment AND Enrollment >= 0),
    FOREIGN KEY (CrsCode) REFERENCES COURSE(CrsCode),
    FOREIGN KEY (ClassroomId) REFERENCES CLASSROOM(ClassroomId),
    FOREIGN KEY (CrsCode, Semester)
        REFERENCES WHENOFFERED(CrsCode, Semester),
    FOREIGN KEY (InstructorId) REFERENCES FACULTY(Id) )
CREATE TABLE TRANSCRIPT (
    StudId         CHAR(9),
    CrsCode        CHAR(6),
    SectionNo      INTEGER,
    Semester       CHAR(6),
    Year           INTEGER,
    Grade          CHAR(1),
    PRIMARY KEY (StudId,CrsCode,SectionNo,Semester,Year),
    FOREIGN KEY (StudId) REFERENCES STUDENT(Id),
    FOREIGN KEY (CrsCode,SectionNo,Semester,Year)
        REFERENCES CLASS(CrsCode,SectionNo,Semester,Year),
    CHECK (Grade IN ('A','B','C','D','F','I') ),
    CHECK (Semester IN ('Spring','Fall') ) )
```

native designs, which might have implications for the overall performance of the system. We discuss one such alternative and its implications.

Consider the attribute SemestersOffered of entity COURSE in Figure 4.33. Because it is a set-valued attribute, we translate it using a separate table, WHENOFFERED. We chose this particular design because it makes it easy to express the constraint that the semester in which any particular class is taught must be one of the allowable semesters. For instance, it should not be possible for course CS305 to be offered only in spring semesters but for a certain class of this course to be taught in fall 2004. However, this should be allowed if CS305 is offered in both spring and fall semesters.

In our design, this requirement is expressed as a foreign-key constraint attached to table CLASS.

```
FOREIGN KEY (CrsCode, Semester)
            REFERENCES WHENOFFERED(CrsCode, Semester)
```

This constraint says that if a class of a course with code abc is offered during a semester, sem, then ⟨abc, sem⟩ should be a tuple in the relation WHENOFFERED; that is, sem must be one of the allowed semesters for the course.

Despite the simplicity of this design, one might feel that creating a separate relation for such a trivial purpose is unacceptable overhead. A separate relation requires an extra operation for certain queries and additional storage.[2] An alternative is to define a new SQL domain with three values in it:

```
CREATE DOMAIN   SEMESTERS CHAR(6)
    CHECK ( VALUE IN ('Spring', 'Fall', 'Both') )
```

The set-valued attribute SemestersOffered of the entity COURSE is now single-valued, but it ranges over the domain SEMESTERS. The advantage is that the translation into the relational model is more straightforward and there is no need for the extra relation WHENOFFERED. However, it is now more difficult to specify the constraint that a class can be taught only in the semesters when the corresponding course is offered. (Details are left to Exercise 4.14.)

Finally, let us consider the possible alternatives for representing the current and the next semesters, as required in item I.F. In fact, our design has no obvious place for this information. One simple way to tell which semester is current or next is to create a separate relation to store this information. However, this entails that any reference to the current or the next semester would require a database query—an expensive way to obtain such simple information. The right way to do this type of thing is to use the function CURRENT_DATE provided by SQL and the function EXTRACT to extract particular fields from that date. For instance, the following calls

[2] In our particular case, none of these disadvantages seems to apply: in all likelihood, the relation WHENOFFERED will be used to verify the above foreign-key constraint, and having a separate relation for course-semester pairs provides efficient support for such verification.

```
EXTRACT(YEAR FROM CURRENT_DATE)
EXTRACT(MONTHS FROM CURRENT_DATE)
```

return the numeric values of the current year and month. This should be sufficient to determine whether any given semester is current or next.

4.9 Limitations of Data Modeling Methodologies

We have now seen two case studies where the entity-relationship model and UML were used for conceptual database design. If conceptual design still is not completely clear to you, do not despair. Although we have discussed several concepts that might provide general guidance in organizing enterprise data, applying these concepts in any concrete situation requires a great deal of experience, intuition, and some black magic. There is considerable freedom in deciding whether a particular datum should be an entity (or class), a relationship (or association), or an attribute. Furthermore, even after these issues are settled, the various relationships that exist among entities can be expressed in different ways. This section discusses some of the dilemmas that are often faced by database designers. For concreteness, we use the E-R model in our examples, but the discussion equally applies to UML.

Entity or attribute? In Figure 4.8 on page 82, semesters are represented as entities. However, we could as well make TRANSCRIPT into a binary relation and turn SEMESTER into one of its attributes. The obvious question is which representation is best (and in which case).

To some extent, the decision about whether a particular datum should be represented as an entity or an attribute is a matter of taste. Beyond that, the representation might depend on whether the datum has an internal structure of its own. If the datum has no internal data structure, keeping it as a separate entity makes the E-R diagram more complex and, more important, adds an extra relation to your database schema when you convert the diagram into the relational model. On the other hand, if the datum has attributes of its own, it is possible that these attributes cannot be represented if the datum itself is demoted to the status of an attribute.

For instance, in Figure 4.8 the entity type SEMESTER does not have descriptive attributes apart from the identifying semester code, so representing the semester information as an entity appears to be an overkill. However, it is entirely possible that the Requirements Document might state that the following additional information must be available for each semester: `Start_date`, `End_date`, `Holidays`, `Enrollment` (which represents total enrollment in all courses during the semester). In such a case, the semester information cannot be an attribute of the TRANSCRIPT relationship as there would then be no place to specify the information about the key dates and the enrollment associated with semesters (e.g., the total enrollment in the university during a semester is not an attribute of any particular transcript relationship).

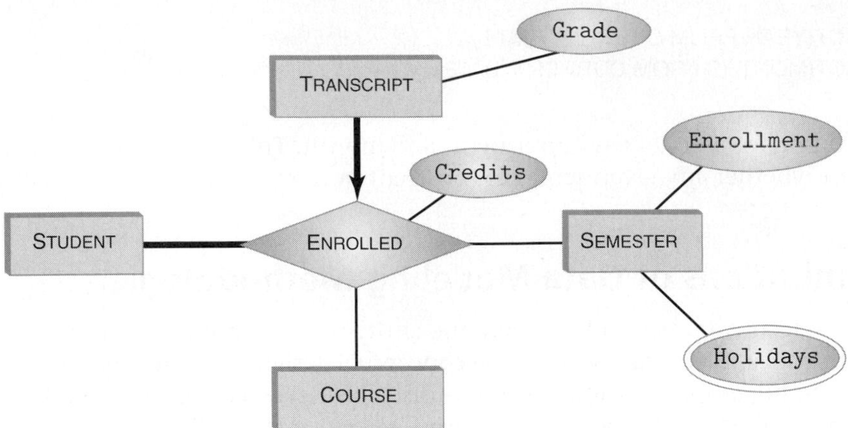

FIGURE 4.36 An alternative representation of the transcript information.

Entity or relationship? Consider once again the diagram in Figure 4.8 on page 82, where we treat transcript records as relationships between STUDENT, COURSE, and SEMESTER entities. An alternative to this design is to represent transcript records as entities and use a new relationship type, ENROLLED, to connect them. This alternative is shown in Figure 4.36. Here we incorporate some of the attributes for the entity SEMESTER, as discussed earlier. We also add an extra attribute, `Credits`, to the relationship ENROLLED, which means that the same course (e.g., thesis research) can be taken for a variable number of credits. Clearly, the two diagrams represent the same information (except for the extra attributes added to Figure 4.36), but which one is better?

As with the "entity vs. attribute" dilemma, the choice largely depends on your taste. However, a number of points are worth considering. For instance, it is a good idea to keep the total number of entities and relations as small as possible because it is directly related to the number of relations that will result when the E-R diagram is converted to the relational model. Generally, it is not too serious a problem if two relations are lumped together at this stage because the relational design theory presented in Chapter 6 will help identify the relation schemas that must be split. On the other hand, it is much harder to spot the opposite problem: needless decomposition of one relation into two or more.

Coming back to Figure 4.36, we notice that there is a participation constraint for the entity TRANSCRIPT in the relationship type ENROLLED. Moreover, the arrow leading from TRANSCRIPT to ENROLLED indicates that the `Transcript` role forms a key of the ENROLLED relationship. Therefore, there is a one-to-one correspondence between the relationships of type ENROLLED and the entities of type TRANSCRIPT. This means that relationships of type ENROLLED can be viewed as superfluous because TRANSCRIPT entities can be used instead to relate the entities of types STUDENT, COURSE, and SEMESTER. All that is required (in order not to lose information) is to

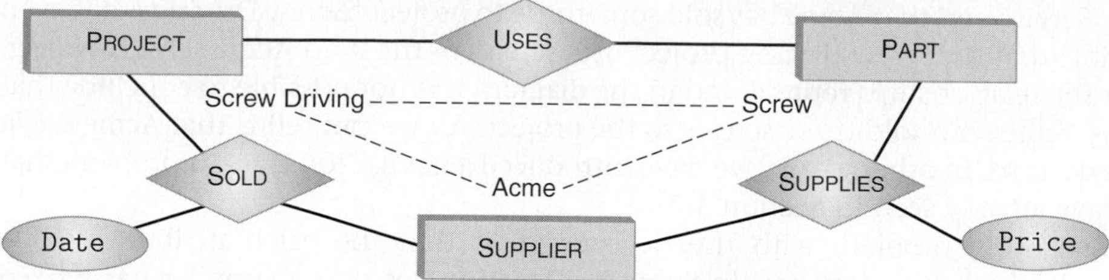

FIGURE 4.37 Replacing the ternary relationship SOLD of Figure 4.2 with three binary relationships.

transfer the descriptive attributes of ENROLLED to TRANSCRIPT after converting the latter into a relationship.

This discussion leads to the following rule:

> Consider a relationship type, **R**, that relates the entity types $\mathbf{E}_1, \ldots, \mathbf{E}_n$, and suppose that $\mathbf{E}_1$ is attached to **R** via a role that (by itself) forms a key of **R**, and that a participation constraint exists between $\mathbf{E}_1$ and **R**. Then it might be possible to collapse $\mathbf{E}_1$ and **R** into a new relationship type that relates the entity types $\mathbf{E}_2, \ldots, \mathbf{E}_n$.

Note that this rule is only an indication that $\mathbf{E}_1$ can be collapsed into **R**, not a guarantee that this is possible or natural. For instance, $\mathbf{E}_1$ might be involved in some other relationship, **R**′. In that case, collapsing $\mathbf{E}_1$ into **R** leaves an edge that connects two relationship types, **R** and **R**′, which is not allowed by the construction rules for E-R diagrams. Such is the situation of the BROKER and ACCOUNT entities in Figure 4.30: The above rule suggests that BROKER can be collapsed into WORKSIN, and ACCOUNT can be collapsed into ISHANDLEDBY. However, both BROKER and ACCOUNT are involved in two different relationships, and each such collapse leaves us with a diagram where two relationships, WORKSIN and ISHANDLEDBY or HASACCOUNT and ISHANDLEDBY, are directly connected by an edge. On the other hand, the TRANSACTION entity type in Figure 4.31 *can* be collapsed into the TRADE relationship type.

Information loss. We have seen examples where the degree of a relationship might change by demoting an entity to an attribute or by collapsing an entity into a relationship. In all of these cases, however, the transformations obviously preserve the information content of the diagrams. Now we are going to discuss some typical situations where seemingly innocuous transformations cause **information loss**; that is, they lead to diagrams with subtly changed information content.

Consider the PART/SUPPLIER/PROJECT diagram of Figure 4.2, page 74. Some designers do not like ternary relationships, preferring to deal with multiple binary relationships instead. Such a decision might lead to the diagram shown in Figure 4.37.

Although superficially the new diagram seems equivalent to the original, there are several subtle differences. First, the new design introduces a navigation trap of the kind we saw in the stock-trading example: It is possible that a supplier, Acme, sells "Screw" and that Acme has sold something to project "Screw Driving." It is even possible that the screw-driving project uses screws of the kind Acme sells. However, from the relationships represented in the diagram it is not possible to conclude that it was Acme who sold these screws to the project. All we can tell is that Acme *might* have done so. In other words, we have introduced a navigation trap—a problem that we have already seen in Section 4.7.

The other problem with the new design is that the price attribute is now associated with the relationship SUPPLIES. This implies that a supplier has a fixed price for each item regardless of the project to which that item is sold. In contrast, the original design in Figure 4.2 supports different pricing for different projects. Similarly, the new design allows only one transaction between a particular supplier and project on any given day because each sale is represented as a triple ⟨project, supplier; date⟩ in the SOLD relationship. So there is no way to represent different transactions between the same parties on the same day. The original design, on the other hand, allows several such deals, provided that different parts were involved.

Having realized the problem posed by navigation traps, one might become inclined to use higher-degree relationships whenever possible. For instance, in Figure 4.30 we might want to try eliminating the navigation trap caused by the relationships HASACCOUNT, WORKSIN, and ISHANDLEDBY by collapsing these three relationships into one. However, this transformation introduces more problems than it solves. For instance, if this transformation keeps the arrow that connects BROKER and WORKSIN, we unwittingly introduce the constraint that a broker can have at most one account and at most one client. If we do not keep this arrow, we lose the constraint that each broker is assigned to exactly one office. This transformation also makes it impossible to have brokers who have no accounts and accounts that have no brokers.

Conceptual design and object databases. Although we will not discuss object databases until Chapter 14, we briefly mention here that some of the difficult issues involved in translating the conceptual design diagrams into schemas become easier for object databases.

- In Section 4.2, we discussed the issues involved in representing entities with set-valued attributes in a relational database. The objects stored in an object database can have set-valued attributes, so the representation of such entities in the schema of the object database is considerably easier.
- In Section 4.4, we discussed the issues involved in representing the ISA relationship in a relational database. Object databases allow a direct representation of the ISA relationship within the schema, so, again, representation of such relationships is considerably easier.
- UML class diagrams allow methods to be specified along with attributes. These methods can be directly translated into the methods supported by object-oriented databases.

From these examples, it should be apparent that not only is it generally easier to go from conceptual design to object-oriented schemas, but for many applications, object databases support a much more intuitive model of the enterprise than do relational databases.

BIBLIOGRAPHIC NOTES

The entity-relationship approach was introduced in [Chen 1976]. Since then it has received considerable attention and various extensions have been proposed (see, for example, research papers in [Spaccapietra 1987]). Conceptual design using the E-R model has also been advanced significantly. The reader is referred to [Teorey 1999; Batini et al. 1992; Thalheim 1992] for comprehensive coverage.

The Unified Modeling Language [Booch et al. 1999] was a product of a long line of research on object-oriented modeling and design. Precursors of UML include OMT [Rumbaugh et al. 1991], the methods developed in [Booch 1994], and the methodology for modeling software through use cases [Jacobson 1992]. While UML was primarily motivated by the needs of software engineering, it borrows many ideas from the E-R model and extends it in the direction of object-oriented modeling. In particular, it provides means to model not only the structure of the data but also the behavioral aspects of programs and how large applications are to be deployed in complex computing environments. A succinct introduction to UML can be found in [Fowler and Scott 2003].

A number of tools exist to help the database designer with E-R and UML modeling. These tools guide the user through the process of specifying the diagrams, attributes, constraints, and so forth. When all is done, they map the conceptual model into relational tables. Such tools include *ERwin* from Computer Associates, *ER/Studio* from Embarcadero Technologies, and *Rational Rose* from Rational Software. In addition, DBMS vendors provide their own design tools, such as *Oracle Designer* from Oracle Corporation and *PowerDesigner* from Sybase.

EXERCISES

4.1 Suppose that you decide to convert IsA hierarchies into the relational model by adding a new attribute (such as `Status` in the case of STUDENT entities, as described on page 91—the second option for representing IsA hierarchies). What kind of problems exist if subentities are not disjoint (e.g., if a secretary can also be a technician)? What problems exist if the covering constraint does not hold (e.g., if some employees are not classified as either secretary or technician)?

4.2 Construct your own example of an E-R or UML diagram whose direct translation into the relational model has an anomaly similar to that of the PERSON entity (see the discussion regarding Figure 4.13 on page 86).

4.3 Represent the IsA hierarchy in Figure 4.6, page 80, in the relational model. For each IsA relationship discuss your choice of the representation technique Discuss the circumstances in which an alternative representation (to the one you have chosen) would be better.

4.4 Suppose, in Figure 4.8, the PROFESSOR entity did not participate in the relationship WORKSIN, but the arrow between them was still present. Would it make sense to merge PROFESSOR with WORKSIN during translation into the relational model? What kind of problems can arise here? Are they serious problems?

4.5 Translate the brokerage example of Section 4.7 into an SQL schema. Use the necessary SQL machinery to express all constraints specified in the E-R model.

4.6 Identify the navigation traps present in the diagram of Figure 4.29, page 107.

4.7 Consider the following database schema:

- SUPPLIER(`SName, ItemName, Price`)—supplier `SName` sells item `ItemName` at `Price`
- CUSTOMER(`CName, Address`)—customer `CName` lives at `Address`.
- ORDER(`CName, SName, ItemName, Qty`)—customer `CName` has ordered `Qty` of item `ItemName` from supplier `SName`.
- ITEM(`ItemName, Description`)—information about items.
  - (a) Draw the E-R diagram from which the above schema might have been derived. Specify the keys.
  - (b) Suppose now that you want to add the following constraint to this diagram: *Every item is supplied by some supplier*. Modify the diagram to accommodate this constraint. Also show how this new diagram can be translated back to the relational model.
  - (c) Repeat parts (a) and (b) in UML.

4.8 Perform conceptual design of the operations of your local community library. The library has books, CDs, tapes, and so forth, which are lent to library patrons. The latter have accounts, addresses, and so forth. If a loaned item is overdue, it accumulates penalty. Some patrons are minors, so they must have sponsoring patrons who are responsible for paying penalties (or replacing a book in case of a loss).

a. Use the E-R approach.
b. Use UML.

4.9 A real estate firm keeps track of the houses for sale and customers looking to buy houses. A house for sale can be *listed* with this firm or with a different one. Being "listed" with a firm means that the house owner has a contract with an agent who works for that firm. Each house on the market has price, address, owner, and a list of features, such as the number of bedrooms, bathrooms, type of heating, appliances, size of garage, and the like. This list can be different for different houses, and some features can be present in some houses but missing in others. Likewise, each customer has preferences that are expressed in the same terms (the number of bedrooms, bathrooms, etc.). Apart from these preferences, customers specify the price range of houses they are interested in. Perform conceptual design for this enterprise.

a. Use the E-R approach.
b. Use UML.

4.10 A supermarket chain is interested in building a decision support system with which they can analyze the sales of different products in different supermarkets at different times. Each supermarket is in a city, which is in a state, which is in a region. Time can be measured in days, months, quarters, and years. Products have names and categories (produce, canned goods, etc.).

a. Design an E-R diagram for this application.
b. Do the same in UML.

4.11 Modify the E-R diagram for the Student Registration System in Figure 4.33 on page 114 to include co-requisite and prerequisite relationships that exist over multiple periods of time. Each period begins in a certain semester and year and ends in a certain semester and year, or it continues into the present. Modify the translation into the relational model appropriately.

4.12 Modify the E-R diagram for the Student Registration System in Figure 4.33 on page 114 to include information about the student majors and the majors allowed in courses. A student can have several majors (which are codes of the various programs in the university, such as `CSE`, `ISE`, `MUS`, `ECO`). A course can also have several admissible majors, or the list of admissible majors can be empty. In the latter case, anyone is admitted into the course. Express the constraint that says that a course with restrictions on majors can have only those students who hold one of the allowed majors.

Alas, in full generality this constraint can be expressed only as an SQL assertion (introduced in Section 3.3) that uses features of Section 5.2 (which we have yet to study). However, it is possible to express this constraint under the following simplifying assumption: when a student registers for a course, she must declare the major toward which the course is going to be taken, and this declared major is checked against the admissible majors.

Modify the relation schema in Figures 4.34 and 4.35 to reflect this simplifying assumption and then express the aforesaid integrity constraint.

4.13 Redo the E-R diagram of the Student Registration System (Figure 4.33) in UML.

4.14 Make the necessary modifications to the schema of the Student Registration System to reflect the design that uses the SQL domain SEMESTERS, as discussed at the end of Section 4.8. Express the constraint that a class can be taught only during the semesters in which the corresponding course is offered. For instance, if the value of the attribute `SemestersOffered` for the course `CS305` is `Both`, then the corresponding classes can be taught in the spring and the fall semesters. However, if the value of that attribute is `Spring` then these classes can be taught only in the spring.

4.15 Design an E-R model for the following enterprise. Various organizations make business deals with various other organizations. (For simplicity, let us assume that there are only two parties to each deal.) When negotiating (and signing) a deal, each organization is represented by a lawyer. The same organization can have deals with many other organizations, and it might use different lawyers in each case. Lawyers and organizations have various attributes, like address and name. They also have their own unique attributes, such as specialization and fee, in the case of a lawyer, and budget, in the case of an organization.

Show how information loss can occur if a relationship of degree higher than two is split into a binary relationship. Discuss the assumption under which such a split does not lead to a loss of information.

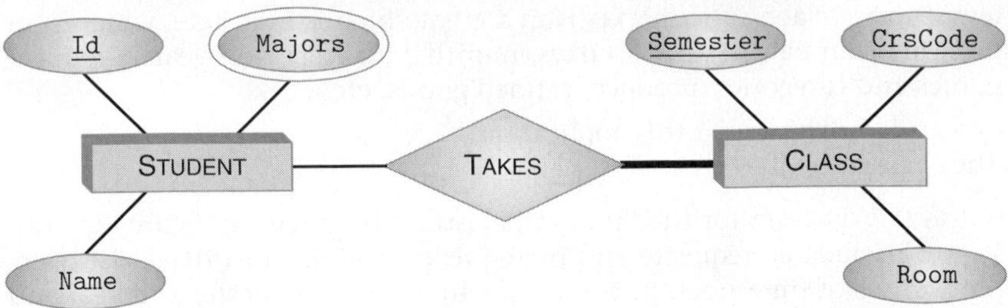

FIGURE 4.38 E-R diagram for Exercise 4.17.

4.16 Design an E-R model for the library system described in Exercise 3.15. Do the same with UML.

4.17 Consider the E-R diagram depicted in Figure 4.38. Write down the corresponding relational schema using SQL. Include all keys and other applicable constraints.

4.18 Consider the partial translation of an E-R participation constraint into UML (shown in Figure 4.24). Show that this is, indeed, an imprecise translation in that there are instances of the database (i.e., collections of objects and associations) that comply with the E-R constraint in Figure 4.24(b) such that it does not satisfy the multiplicity constraint in UML.

5

Relational Algebra and SQL

Now that we know how to create a database, the next step is to learn how to query it to retrieve the information needed for some particular application. Before relational databases, database querying was a dreadful task. To pose even a simple query (by today's standards), one would use a conventional programming language to write a program that could include multiple nested loops, error handling, and boundary condition checking. In addition, the programmer would deal with numerous details of the internal physical schema—in those days, data independence was only on the wish list.

A **database query language** is a special-purpose programming language designed for retrieving information stored in a database. The relational query language in which we are most interested is SQL (Structured Query Language). It is quite different from conventional programming languages. In SQL, you specify the properties of the information to be retrieved but not the detailed algorithm required for retrieval. For example, a query in the Student Registration System might specify retrieval of the names and Ids of all professors who have taught a particular course in a particular semester, but it would not provide a detailed procedure (involving while loops, if statements, pointer variables, etc.) to traverse the various database tables and retrieve the specified names. Thus, SQL is said to be *declarative*, as its queries "declare" what information the answer should contain, not how to compute it. Contrast this to conventional programming languages (e.g., C or Java), which are said to be *procedural* because programs written in them describe the exact actions to be performed to compute the answer.

As with other computer languages, a programmer can design simple queries after only a brief introduction to SQL, but the design of the complex queries needed in real applications requires a more detailed knowledge of the language and its semantics. Therefore, before we introduce SQL we study the *relational algebra*, which is another relational query language that is used by the DBMS as an intermediate language into which SQL statements are translated before they are optimized.

5.1 Relational Algebra: Under the Hood of SQL

Relational algebra is called an algebra because it is based on a small number of **operators**, which operate on relations (tables). Each operator operates on one or more relations and produces another relation as a result. A query is just an expression involving these operators. The result of the expression is a relation, which is the answer to the query.

While SQL is a declarative language, meaning that it does not specify the algorithm used to process queries, relational algebra is procedural. A relational expression can be viewed as a specification of such an algorithm (although at a much higher level than the algorithms specified using traditional programming languages).

Thus, even when programmers use SQL to specify their queries, DBMSs use relational algebra as an intermediate language for specifying query evaluation algorithms. The DBMS parses the SQL query and translates it into an expression in relational algebra, which usually leads to a rather simplistic, inefficient algorithm. The **query optimizer** then converts this algebraic expression into one that is *equivalent* but that (hopefully) takes less time to execute.[1] On the basis of the optimized algebraic expression it produced, the query optimizer prepares a **query execution plan**, which is then transformed into executable code by the code generator within the DBMS. Because algebraic expressions have precise mathematical semantics, the system can verify that the resulting "optimized" expression is equivalent to the original. The semantics also makes it possible to compare different proposed query evaluation plans. A schematic view of query processing is shown in Figure 5.1.

The relational algebra is the key to understanding the inner workings of a relational DBMS, which in turn is essential in designing SQL queries that can be processed efficiently.

5.1.1 Basic Operators

Relational algebra is based on five basic operators:

1. *Select*
2. *Project*
3. *Union*
4. *Set difference*
5. *Cartesian product* (also known as *cross product*)

each of which we consider in turn. In addition, there are three *derived* operators (i.e., they can be represented as expressions involving the basic operators): *intersection*, *division*, and *join*. We also discuss the *renaming* operator, which is useful in conjunction with Cartesian products and joins.

[1] Query optimizers do not really "optimize" (in the sense of producing the *most efficient* query evaluation algorithm) because this is generally an impossible task. Instead, they use heuristics known to produce equivalent expressions that are generally cheaper to evaluate.

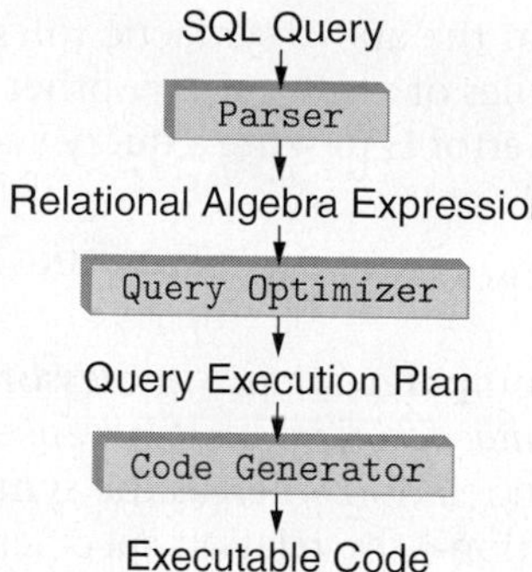

FIGURE 5.1 Schematic view of query processing.

Select operator. One of the most frequent operations performed on relations is **selection** of a subset of tuples (i.e., selection of some subset of the rows in a table). For instance, you might want a list of the professors in the CS department. Surely they are all listed in the PROFESSOR relation, but this relation might be large and a manual scan for the tuples of interest might be difficult. Using the select operator, this query can be expressed as

$$\sigma_{\texttt{DeptId = 'CS'}}(\text{PROFESSOR})$$

The query reads as "Select all tuples from the PROFESSOR relation that satisfy the condition `DeptId = 'CS'`."

The general syntax of the select operator is

$$\sigma_{\textit{selection-condition}}(\textit{relation-name})$$

We will see later that the argument of the select operator can be more general than simply a name that identifies a relation. It can also be an expression that evaluates to a relation.

The selection condition can have one of the following forms:

- *simple-selection-condition* (explained below)
- *selection-condition* AND *selection-condition*
- *selection-condition* OR *selection-condition*
- NOT (*selection-condition*)

A simple selection condition can be any one of the following:

- *relation-attribute* oper *constant*
- *relation-attribute* oper *relation-attribute*

where oper can be any one of the following comparison operators: $=$, $\neq$, $>$, $\geq$, $<$, and $\leq$. Each attribute that occurs in a comparison must be one of the attributes in the *relation-name* argument of the selection operator.

It is important to realize that the above syntactic rules *must be followed*, in the same way that you follow the rules of syntax in any other programming language. For instance, a common syntax error is to write a query such as

$$\sigma_{\texttt{ProfId=PROFESSOR.Id AND PROFESSOR.DeptId='CS'}}(\text{TEACHING})$$

to list all courses taught by computer science professors. However natural this expression might seem, it is *syntactically incorrect* because the selection condition uses attributes of the PROFESSOR relation whereas the syntax rules permit only the attributes of the TEACHING relation—the relation specified in the argument of the selection.

By itself, the expression $\sigma_{selection\text{-}condition}(\mathbf{R})$ is meaningless—it is just a string of characters. However, in a concrete database it can have a *value*, which represents the *meaning* of the expression in the context of that database. Thus, we always assume that we are working in the context of some concrete database, which associates a concrete relation instance with each relation name.

Suppose that **r** is such a relation instance associated with relation schema **R**. We define the *value* of the above expression with respect to **r**, denoted $\sigma_{selection\text{-}condition}(\mathbf{r})$, to be the relation that consists of the set of all tuples in **r** that satisfy *selection-condition*. Thus, the value of the select operator applied to a relation is another relation with the same set of attributes as the original.

For instance, the value of $\sigma_{\texttt{DeptId = 'CS'}}$ (PROFESSOR) with respect to the database of Figure 3.5 on page 39 is the relation CSPROF.

CSPROF	Id	Name	DeptId
	101202303	Smyth, John	CS
	555666777	Doe, Mary	CS

It should be clear what it means for a tuple in **r** to satisfy a selection condition. For instance, if the condition is $A > c$, where A is an attribute and c is a constant, a tuple, t, satisfies the condition if (and only if) the value of attribute A in t is greater than c.[2] When the selection condition is more complex (e.g., $cond_1$ AND $cond_2$), satisfaction is defined recursively. It is satisfied by t if and only if t satisfies both $cond_1$ and $cond_2$. The condition $cond_1$ OR $cond_2$ is similar, except that t needs to satisfy only one of the subconditions. Analogously, t satisfies NOT(*cond*) if t violates *cond*.

For instance, tuple 2 in the relation CSPROF satisfies the complex condition `Id` > 111222333 AND NOT (`DeptId` = `'EE'`) because it satisfies both of the following:

- `Id` > 111222333, since 555666777 > 111222333.
- NOT (`DeptId` = `'EE'`), since `'CS'` ≠ `'EE'` and thus the tuple violates the condition `DeptId` = `'EE'`.

2 We assume the existence of some ordering on the domain of A. In the case of numeric domains, the order is clear; in the case of domains of strings, we assume lexicographic order.

In contrast, tuple 1 in that relation violates the above complex condition because it violates the first term, Id > 111222333, of that condition (since 101202303 $\not>$ 111222333).

Here is a more complex selection:

$$\sigma_{\texttt{StudId}\neq\texttt{111111111 AND (Semester='S1991' OR Grade<'B')}}(\text{TRANSCRIPT})$$

where the comparison among strings (Grade < 'B') assumes lexicographic order in which 'A' < 'B', etc. The value of this expression in the context of the database of Figure 3.5 is the relation

SUBTRANSCRIPT	StudId	CrsCode	Semester	Grade
	666666666	MGT123	F1994	A
	666666666	EE101	S1991	B
	123454321	CS315	S1997	A
	123454321	CS305	S1996	A
	023456789	CS305	S1996	A

One obvious generalization of the selection condition is to allow conditions of the form *expression*$_1$ oper *expression*$_2$, where *expression* can be either an arithmetic expression that involves attributes (which act as variables) and constants, or a string expression (e.g., pattern matching, string concatenation).

Examples of such expressions are EmplSalary > (MngrSalary ∗ 2) and (DeptId + CrsNumber) LIKE CrsCode (here + denotes string concatenation and LIKE denotes pattern matching). The utility of such extended selections is obvious, and they are extensively used in database languages.

Project operator. When discussing selection, we often refer to values of certain attributes in a tuple. In relational algebra, such references are very common, so we introduce special notation for them. Let A denote an attribute of a relation, **r**, and let t be a tuple in **r**. Then $t.A$ denotes the component of tuple t that corresponds to the attribute A. For instance, if t denotes tuple 1 in relation SUBTRANSCRIPT, then t.CrsCode is MGT123.

Also, we often need to extract a *subtuple* from a tuple. A **subtuple**, t, is a sequence of values extracted from t in accordance with some list of attributes. It is denoted as

$$t.\{A_1, \ldots, A_n\}$$

where $A_1, \ldots, A_n$ are attributes.

For instance, if t is tuple 1 in SUBTRANSCRIPT, then t.{Semester, CrsCode} is the tuple ⟨ F1994, MGT123 ⟩. Note that the order of attributes here does not (and need not) follow the order in which these attributes are listed in the relation SUBTRANSCRIPT. Moreover, sometimes it is convenient to allow duplicate attributes in the list. Thus, t.{Semester, CrsCode, Semester} is ⟨F1994, MGT123, F1994⟩.

Now we are ready to define the **projection operator**, whose general syntax is

$$\pi_{\textit{attribute-list}}\ (\textit{relation-name})$$

For example, if **R** is a relation name and $A_1, \ldots, A_n$ are *some* (or all) of the attributes in **R**, then $\pi_{A_1,\ldots,A_n}(\mathbf{R})$ is called the **projection** of **R** on attributes $A_1, \ldots, A_n$. In other words, projection picks some subset of the columns in a table. (Sometimes it is convenient to view $A_1, \ldots, A_n$ as a list with possible repetition of attributes, but we will not need this generality here.)

As in the case of selection, the above expression can be assigned a value in the context of a concrete database. Suppose that **r** is a relation instance corresponding to **R** in such a database. Then the *value* of $\pi_{A_1,\ldots,A_n}(\mathbf{R})$, denoted $\pi_{A_1,\ldots,A_n}(\mathbf{r})$, is the set of *all* tuples of the form $t.\{A_1, \ldots, A_n\}$, where t ranges over all tuples in **r**.

For instance, $\pi_{\texttt{ProfId,CrsCode}}$ (TEACHING) is the relation

PROFCOURSES	ProfId	CrsCode
	009406321	MGT123
	121232343	EE101
	555666777	CS305
	101202303	CS315
	900120450	MAT123
	101202303	CS305
	783432188	MGT123

Observe that the original TEACHING relation of Figure 3.5 (page 40) has 9 tuples, while PROFCOURSES has only 7. What happened to the rest of the tuples? The answer becomes apparent if we examine the original relation more closely. It is easy to see that tuples 2 and 6 are identical in their ProfId and CrsCode attributes. The only difference between them is in the value of the Semester attribute. The same is true of tuples 5 and 8. Applying the projection operator to tuples 2 and 6 (and to tuples 5 and 8) yields identical tuples because the attribute Semester is eliminated. Relations are sets and thus have no duplicates; so, only one copy in each group of identical tuples is kept.

The purpose of the projection operator is to help us focus on the relationships of interest and ignore the attributes that are irrelevant to a particular query. For instance, suppose that we wish to know who taught which courses. The PROFCOURSES relation shows this information clearly without diluting the answer with data that we did not ask for (i.e., `Semester`). Projection also eliminates duplicates, which can save time on analyzing the answer.

Now that we have seen two relational operators, we can construct **relational expressions** out of them. This is not just an abstract mathematical exercise. Expressions are a general way of constructing queries in relational databases. For instance, the relation CSPROF, which contains the tuples corresponding to computer science professors, is the result of applying the selection operator to PROFESSOR. We could further request just the names of those professors using the projection operator: $\pi_{\texttt{Name}}$ (CSPROF). The advantage of the algebra is that operators can be combined just as in high-school algebra, so we write

$$\pi_{\texttt{Name}}(\sigma_{\texttt{DeptId = 'CS'}}(\text{PROFESSOR}))$$

without specifying the intermediate result, CSPROF, and without creating a temporary relation.

Set operations. The next two operators are the familiar set operators **union** and **set difference.** Clearly, since relations are sets, set operators are applicable to relations. The syntax is **R** ∪ **S** and **R** − **S**. If **r** and **s** are the relations corresponding to **R** and **S**, then

- The **value** of **R** ∪ **S** is **r** ∪ **s**, the set of all tuples that belong to either **r** or **s**.
- The **value** of **R** − **S** is **r** − **s**, the set of all tuples in **r** that *do not* belong to **s**.

We can also use the **intersection** operator, **R** ∩ **S** (whose value on **r** and **s** is, naturally, **r** ∩ **s**), but this operator is not independent of the rest. It can be represented as an expression built out of the basic five operators mentioned at the beginning of this section.

Unfortunately, we are not done yet. While the union of two sets is always a set, we cannot say the same about arbitrary relations. Consider the union of PROFESSOR with TRANSCRIPT. One problem is that relations are *tables* where all rows have the same number of items. However, the tuples in the PROFESSOR relation have three items each, while the tuples in the TRANSCRIPT relation have four. Since they have different arities, the collection of all of these tuples is a set (all right), but it does not constitute a relation.

Even when the arities are the same, in order for the union to be meaningful all items in the corresponding columns must belong to the same domain. Consider the set-theoretic union of PROFESSOR and TEACHING. If we match the columns, then `Id`, `Name`, and `DeptId` in PROFESSOR will correspond to `ProfId`, `CrsCode`, and `Semester`. In the union, the values in the first column are members of the same domain, so no problem there. However, the second and the third columns clearly do not belong to the same domain (e.g., people's names and course codes). Again, the union does not make sense.

CrsCode	Semester
CS305	F1995

$$\pi_{\texttt{CrsCode,Semester}}(\sigma_{\texttt{Grade='C'}}(\text{TRANSCRIPT})) - \pi_{\texttt{CrsCode,Semester}}(\sigma_{\texttt{CrsCode='MAT123'}}(\text{TEACHING}))$$

CrsCode	Semester
CS305	F1995
MAT123	S1996
MAT123	F1997

$$\pi_{\texttt{CrsCode,Semester}}(\sigma_{\texttt{Grade='C'}}(\text{TRANSCRIPT})) \cup \pi_{\texttt{CrsCode,Semester}}(\sigma_{\texttt{CrsCode='MAT123'}}(\text{TEACHING}))$$

CrsCode	Semester
MAT123	S1996

$$\pi_{\texttt{CrsCode,Semester}}(\sigma_{\texttt{Grade='C'}}(\text{TRANSCRIPT})) \cap \pi_{\texttt{CrsCode,Semester}}(\sigma_{\texttt{CrsCode='MAT123'}}(\text{TEACHING}))$$

FIGURE 5.2 Examples of relational expressions that involve set operators.

To overcome these problems, we limit the scope of the union operator and apply it only to *union-compatible* relations. Relations are **union-compatible** if their schemas satisfy the following rules:

- Both relations have the same number of columns.
- The names of the attributes are the same in both relations.
- Attributes with the same name in both relations have the same domain.

We also require union-compatibility for the difference and intersection operators.

Example 5.1.1 (Complex Relational Expressions). Figure 5.2 illustrates some non-trivial uses of set operators combined with select and project operators. The first query retrieves all course offerings *other than* MAT123, where some student received the grade C. The second query is a bit contrived but is a good illustration; it yields all course offerings where either somebody got a C or the offered course was MAT123. The third query lists all offerings of MAT123 where somebody got a C.

One interesting aspect of these examples is that the original relations, TRANSCRIPT and TEACHING, are not union-compatible. However, they become compatible after the incompatible attributes are projected out. All expressions in this figure are evaluated in the context of our running example of Figure 3.5 on page 39. ■

Id	Name
111223344	Smith, Mary
023456789	Simpson, Homer
987654321	Simpson, Bart

A subset of $\pi_{\texttt{Id,Name}}$(STUDENT)

Id	DeptId
555666777	CS
101202303	CS

A subset of $\pi_{\texttt{Id,DeptId}}$(PROFESSOR)

STUDENT.Id	Name	PROFESSOR.Id	DeptId
111223344	Smith, Mary	555666777	CS
111223344	Smith, Mary	101202303	CS
023456789	Simpson, Homer	555666777	CS
023456789	Simpson, Homer	101202303	CS
987654321	Simpson, Bart	555666777	CS
987654321	Simpson, Bart	101202303	CS

Their Cartesian product

FIGURE 5.3 Two relations and their Cartesian product.

The Cartesian product and renaming. The **Cartesian product** (also known as **cross product**), R × S, is close to the cross product operation on sets. If **r** and **s** are relational instances corresponding to **R** and **S**, respectively, the *value* of this expression, denoted **r** × **s**, is the set of all tuples, t, that can be obtained by concatenation of a tuple $r \in \mathbf{r}$ and a tuple $s \in \mathbf{s}$.[3]

Figure 5.3 shows a Cartesian product of a subset of $\pi_{\texttt{Id,Name}}$(STUDENT) and a subset of $\pi_{\texttt{Id,DeptId}}$(PROFESSOR). To make it clear which parts of each tuple in the product come from which relation, we have marked the boundary between the parts with a double line.

Brain Teaser: What is **r** × **s** when **s** is an empty relation?

[3] A slight difference between the usual set-theoretic cross product operation on relations and the relational cross product operation defined above is that in the former the result is a set of pairs of tuples of the form $(< a, b >, < c, d >)$ while in the latter it is a set of concatenated tuples (i.e., $< a, b, c, d >$).

We are now forced to address the problem of attribute naming in the results of the relational expressions, which so far we have conveniently ignored. The relations that are arguments to the algebraic expressions have their schema defined in the system catalog, so the names of their attributes are known. In contrast, the relations produced by evaluating the expressions are created on the fly, and their schema is not explicitly defined. For some operations, such as σ and π (when projection list does not include repeated attributes), this does not present a problem as we can simply reuse the schema of the argument relation. For $\cup$, $\cap$, and $-$, we do not have a naming problem either because the relations involved in these operations are union-compatible and so have the same schema, which, again, can be reused for the query answer.

The Cartesian product is the first time we must deal with the naming problem. Observe how some attributes in the product relation in Figure 5.3 have mysteriously changed names. This is because the relations involved in the operation, $\pi_{\texttt{Id,Name}}$ (STUDENT) and $\pi_{\texttt{Id,DeptId}}$ (PROFESSOR) have an identically named attribute, `Id`, which would otherwise appear twice in the product. The relational model does not allow different columns to have the same name within the same schema. To overcome this problem, we rename the attributes by prefixing them with the relation of their origin.

In this Cartesian product example, the problem of attribute name clashes was conveniently solved through a simple renaming convention, which we will continue to use in the future whenever possible. Unfortunately, this convention does not always work—for instance, it breaks down in the case of a cross product of two instances of the same PROFESSOR relation. Rather than trying to invent increasingly complex renaming schemes, we will place the burden on the programmer, who now becomes responsible for the renaming. To this end, we introduce the **renaming operator**, which does not belong to the core of the algebra and has no standard notation. We choose the following simple notation:

$$expression[A_1, \ldots, A_n]$$

where *expression* is an expression in relational algebra and $A_1, \ldots, A_n$ is a list of names to be used for the attributes in the result of that expression.

We assume that n represents the number of columns in the result of the expression. Moreover, we assume that there is some standard order of columns in the relation produced by evaluating the expression. For example, in the results of π, σ, $\cup$, $\cap$, and $-$, the order is the same as that in which the attributes are listed in the schema of the argument relations. For **R** $\times$ **S**, the attributes should be listed as in Figure 5.3. The attributes of **R** followed by the attributes of **S**. For instance,

$$(\pi_{\texttt{Id,Name}}(\text{STUDENT}) \times \pi_{\texttt{Id,DeptId}}(\text{PROFESSOR}))\,\texttt{[StudId,StudName,ProfId,ProfDept]}$$

renames the attributes of the product relation in Figure 5.3 to `StudId`, `StudName`, `ProfId`, `ProfDept` from left to right. In particular, the two occurrences of `Id` are renamed `StudId` and `ProfId`, respectively.

The renaming operator can also be applied to subexpressions. The following example is similar to the previous one except that we renamed the attributes of the PROFESSOR relation before applying other operators.

$$\pi_{\texttt{Id,Name}}(\text{STUDENT}) \times \pi_{\texttt{ProfId,ProfDept}}(\text{PROFESSOR } [\texttt{ProfId,ProfName, ProfDept}])$$

The result is the same as before, but the names of the attributes (from left to right) are now Id, Name, ProfId, ProfDept. Also note that we had to change the attributes in the rightmost π operator because the attributes in the argument relation were changed as a result of the renaming.

The Cartesian product holds the distinction of being the most computationally expensive operator in the whole of relational algebra. Consider **R** $\times$ **S**, and suppose that **R** has n tuples and **S** has m tuples. The Cartesian product has $n \times m$ tuples. In addition, each tuple in the product is larger in size. For concreteness, let both **R** and **S** have 1,000 tuples with 100 bytes per tuple. Then **R** $\times$ **S** has 1,000,000 tuples with 200 bytes per tuple. Thus, while the total size of the original relations is 200 kilobytes, the product has 200 megabytes. The cost of just writing out such a relation on disk can be prohibitive. This is just a small example. We will soon see that it is not uncommon for a query to involve three or more relations. Even in the case of four tiny relations of 100 tuples with 100 bytes per tuple, the Cartesian product has 100,000,000 tuples with 400 bytes per tuple—40 gigabytes of data!

In a course on analysis of algorithms, you might have been taught that algorithms with polynomial time complexity are acceptable as long as the degree of the polynomial is not too high. As you can see from the above example, in query processing even quadratic algorithms can be unacceptably expensive if they operate on large volumes of data. Because of the potentially huge costs, query optimizers attempt to avoid cross products if at all possible.

5.1.2 Derived Operators

Joins. A **join** of two relations, **R** and **S**, is an expression of the form

$$\mathbf{R} \bowtie_{\textit{join-condition}} \mathbf{S}$$

The *join condition* is a restricted form of the already familiar selection condition used in the σ operator:

$$\mathbf{R}.A_1 \ \ oper_1 \ \ \mathbf{S}.B_1 \text{ AND } \mathbf{R}.A_2 \ \ oper_2 \ \ \mathbf{S}.B_2 \text{ AND } \ldots \text{ AND } \mathbf{R}.A_n \ \ oper_n \ \ \mathbf{S}.B_n \qquad (5.1)$$

Here the list $A_1, \ldots, A_n$ is a subset of the attributes of **R**, and $B_1, \ldots, B_n$ is a subset of the attributes of **S**. Finally, $oper_1, \ldots, oper_n$ are the comparison operators $=$, $\neq$, $>$, and so forth.

These restrictions imply that join conditions can have only the AND connective (no ORs or NOTs) and that comparisons between attributes and constants are not allowed.

STUDENT.Id	Name	PROFESSOR.Id	DeptId
111223344	Smith, Mary	555666777	CS
023456789	Simpson, Homer	555666777	CS
023456789	Simpson, Homer	101202303	CS

$\pi_{\texttt{Id,Name}}(\text{STUDENT}) \bowtie_{\texttt{Id<Id}} \pi_{\texttt{Id,DeptId}}(\text{PROFESSOR})$

FIGURE 5.4 Join of relations in Figure 5.3.

Even though we use a new symbol to represent it, join is not a radically new operator. *By definition,* the above join is equivalent to

$$\sigma_{join\text{-}condition'}\ (\mathbf{R} \times \mathbf{S})$$

However, as joins occur frequently in database queries, they have earned the privilege of having their own symbol.

Notice one subtlety: we use *join-condition′* in $\sigma_{join\text{-}condition'}$ above rather than *join-condition,* which was used in $\bowtie_{join\text{-}condition}$ in the definition of the join. This is because **R** and **S** might have identically named attributes, which must be renamed as part of the Cartesian product operation. Thus, *join-condition′* is like *join-condition,* except that it uses the actual renamed attributes of **R** × **S** rather than the qualified attribute names in (5.1) above.

Example 5.1.2 (Join). Figure 5.4 is an example of a join of two relations. Note the simplified join condition Id < Id, which we use instead of STUDENT.Id < PROFESSOR.Id. It means that in order to qualify for the join, the value of the Id attribute in the STUDENT tuple must be less than the value of the Id attribute in the PROFESSOR tuple. We will continue to use such simplified join conditions when it is clear which attributes come from which relations. ■

Note that the definition of a join involves a Cartesian product as an intermediate step. Therefore, a join is a potentially expensive operation. However, the silver lining is that the Cartesian product is hidden inside the join. In fact, Cartesian products rarely occur on their own in typical database queries. Thus, even though the intermediate result (the product) can potentially be very large, the final result can be manageable, as only a small number of tuples in the product might satisfy the join condition.

For example, the result of the join in Figure 5.4 is half the size of the Cartesian product in Figure 5.3. It is not uncommon for the size of a join to be just a tiny fraction of the size of the corresponding cross product. The tricky part is to compute a join without having to compute the intermediate Cartesian product! This might sound like magic, but there are several ways to accomplish this feat, and query optimizers do so routinely. This subject is discussed in Chapter 10.

The general joins described above are sometimes called **theta-joins** because in antiquity the Greek letter θ was used to denote join conditions. While theta-joins are certainly common in query processing (the query *List all employees who earn more than their managers* involves a theta-join), the more common kind is one where all comparisons are equalities:

$$\mathbf{R}.A_1 = \mathbf{S}.B_1 \text{ AND } \ldots \text{ AND } \mathbf{R}.A_n = \mathbf{S}.B_n$$

Joins that utilize such conditions are called **equi-joins**.

Equi-joins are essentially what gives relational databases their "intelligence" because they tie together pieces of disparate information scattered throughout the database. Using equi-joins, programmers can uncover complex relationships hidden in the data with just a few lines of SQL code.

Example 5.1.3 (More Joins). Here is how one can find the names of professors who taught a course in the fall of 1994:

$$\pi_{\texttt{Name}} (\text{PROFESSOR} \bowtie_{\texttt{Id=ProfId}} \sigma_{\texttt{Semester='F1994'}} (\text{TEACHING}))$$

The inner join lines up the tuples in PROFESSOR against the tuples in TEACHING that describe courses taught by the respective professors in fall 1994. The final projection cuts off the uninteresting attributes. Finding the names of courses and the professors who taught them in the fall of 1995 is almost as easy:

$$\pi_{\texttt{CrsName,Name}} ((\text{PROFESSOR} \bowtie_{\texttt{Id=ProfId}} \sigma_{\texttt{Semester='F1995'}} (\text{TEACHING})) \bowtie_{\texttt{CrsCode=CrsCode}} \text{COURSE})$$

■

The second query in the above example involves two joins. We placed parentheses around the first join to indicate the order in which the joins are to be computed. However, this was not really necessary because join happens to be an *associative* operation, as can be proved using its definition:

$$\begin{aligned}
&\mathbf{R} \bowtie_{\texttt{cond}_1} (\mathbf{S} \bowtie_{\texttt{cond}_2} \mathbf{T}) \\
&= \sigma_{\texttt{cond}_1}(\mathbf{R} \times \sigma_{\texttt{cond}_2}(\mathbf{S} \times \mathbf{T})) && \text{by definition of } \bowtie \\
&= \sigma_{\texttt{cond}_1}(\sigma_{\texttt{cond}_2}(\mathbf{R} \times (\mathbf{S} \times \mathbf{T}))) && \text{because } \sigma \text{ and } \times \text{ commute (check!)} \\
&= \sigma_{\texttt{cond}_2}(\sigma_{\texttt{cond}_1}(\mathbf{R} \times (\mathbf{S} \times \mathbf{T}))) && \text{because two } \sigma\text{'s commute (check!)} \\
&= \sigma_{\texttt{cond}_2}(\sigma_{\texttt{cond}_1}((\mathbf{R} \times \mathbf{S}) \times \mathbf{T})) && \text{by associativity of } \times \text{ (check!)} \\
&= (\mathbf{R} \bowtie_{\texttt{cond}_1} \mathbf{S}) \bowtie_{\texttt{cond}_2} \mathbf{T} && \text{by definition of } \bowtie
\end{aligned}$$

The double-join query of Example 5.1.3 illustrates one additional point. Join conditions such as TEACHING.CrsCode = COURSE.CrsCode, which test for equality of attributes with the same name (but in different relations) are quite common. The main reason for this is that it is considered a good design practice to assign the same name to attributes that denote the same thing but belong to different relations. For instance, the semantics of `CrsCode` in COURSE, TEACHING, and TRANSCRIPT are the same (which is why we used the same name in all three cases!). Because finding hidden connections in the data often amounts to comparing similar attributes in different relations, the above design practice leads to equi-join conditions that equate identically named attributes.[4]

In fact, this design practice in which the join condition equates *only* identically named attributes yields equi-joins of a special variety. In recognition of their importance, such joins received their very own name: the **natural join**. A natural join actually is a little more than that. First, the join condition equates *all* identically named attributes in the two relations being joined. Second, as the equated attributes really denote the same thing in both relations (as indicated by the identity of their names), there is no reason to keep both of the columns. Thus, one copy is always projected out. In sum, the *natural join* of **R** and **S**, denoted $\mathbf{R} \bowtie \mathbf{S}$, is defined by the following relational expression:

$$\pi_{\textit{attr-list}}(\sigma_{\textit{join-cond}}(\mathbf{R} \times \mathbf{S}))$$

where

1. $\textit{attr-list} = \textit{attributes}(\mathbf{R}) \cup \textit{attributes}(\mathbf{S})$; that is, the attribute list used in the project operator contains all the attributes in the union of the argument relations *with duplicate attribute names removed*. Since duplicate attributes are deleted, there is no need to perform attribute renaming.
2. The join condition, *join-cond*, has the form

   $\mathbf{R}.A_1 = \mathbf{S}.A_1$ AND . . . AND $\mathbf{R}.A_n = \mathbf{S}.A_n$

   where $\{A_1, \ldots, A_n\} = \textit{attributes}(\mathbf{R}) \cap \textit{attributes}(\mathbf{S})$. That is, it is the list of all attributes that **R** and **S** have in common.

Note that the notation for natural joins *omits the join condition* because the condition is implicitly (and uniquely) determined by the names assigned to the attributes of the relations in the join.

A typical example of the use of natural joins is the following query:

$\pi_{\texttt{StudId,ProfId}}$ (TRANSCRIPT $\bowtie$ TEACHING)

[4] A natural question is, Why have we used different names for the Id attributes in STUDENT (`Id`) and TRANSCRIPT (`StudId`)—in clear violation of the design rule previously mentioned? We did it so that we could squeeze more examples out of a reasonably sized schema. In a well-designed database schema, `StudId` would be used in both places; likewise, `ProfId` would be used in both PROFESSOR and TEACHING; or, perhaps, `Id` would be used in all four places.

which lists all Ids of students who ever took a course along with the Ids of professors who taught them.

To further illustrate the difference between the natural join and the equi-join, it is instructive to compare the following two expressions:

```
TRANSCRIPT ⋈ TEACHING
TRANSCRIPT ⋈Cond TEACHING
```

where the equi-join condition `Cond` is TRANSCRIPT.`CrsCode`=TEACHING.`CrsCode` AND TRANSCRIPT.`Semester`=TEACHING.`Semester`. Both expressions are equi-joins, and both use the same join conditions (the natural join uses it implicitly). However, the resulting relations have different sets of attributes.

Natural join:

```
StudId, CrsCode, Semester, Grade, ProfId
```

Equi-join:

```
StudId, TRANSCRIPT.CrsCode, TEACHING.CrsCode,
        TRANSCRIPT.Semester, TEACHING.Semester, Grade, ProfId
```

The two expressions represent essentially the same information. However, the schema of the equi-join has two extra attributes (which are duplicates of other attributes), and the natural join benefits from a simpler attribute-naming convention.

Apart from finding hidden connections in the data, joins can be used for certain counting tasks. Here is how we can find all students who took at least two different courses:

$$
\begin{array}{l}
\pi_{\texttt{StudId}}\ (\\
\quad \sigma_{\texttt{CrsCode}\neq\texttt{CrsCode2}}\ (\\
\qquad \text{TRANSCRIPT} \bowtie \\
\qquad \text{TRANSCRIPT}[\texttt{StudId,CrsCode2,Semester2,Grade2}]\\
\quad))
\end{array}
$$

One obvious limitation of this technique is that if we want students who had taken fifteen courses, we have to join TRANSCRIPT with itself fifteen times. A better way is to extend the relational algebra with so-called *aggregate* functions, which include the counting operator. We do not pursue this possibility here, but we will return to aggregate functions in the context of SQL in Section 5.2.

The discussion of joins cannot be complete without mentioning that—rather unexpectedly—the intersection operator is a special case of a natural join. Suppose that **R** and **S** are union-compatible. It then follows directly from the definitions that $\mathbf{R} \cap \mathbf{S} = \mathbf{R} \bowtie \mathbf{S}$.

Brain Teaser: What is $\mathbf{R} \bowtie \mathbf{S}$, if **R** and **S** have not even one common attribute?

Outer joins. When two relations are joined, tuples that do not match fall by the wayside. The operators *outer join, left outer join,* and *right outer join* were introduced for the situations where this particular feature of joins is not wanted.

An **outer join** of two relations **r** and **s** with join condition *cond*, denoted $\mathbf{r} \bowtie^{outer}_{cond} \mathbf{s}$, is defined as follows. As before, it is a relation over the schema that contains the union of the (possibly renamed) attributes in **R** (the schema of **r**) and **S** (the schema of **s**). However, the tuples in $\mathbf{r} \bowtie^{outer}_{cond} \mathbf{s}$ consist of three categories:

1. The tuples that appear in the regular join of **r** and **s**, $\mathbf{r} \bowtie_{cond} \mathbf{s}$.
2. The tuples of **r** that do not join with any tuple in **s**. Since these tuples do not have values for the attributes that come from **S**, they are padded with NULL over these attributes.
3. The tuples of **s** that do not join with any tuple in **r**. Again, these tuples are padded with NULL over the attributes of **R**.

The outer join is sometimes also called **full outer join**. The **left outer join**, $\mathbf{r} \bowtie^{left}_{cond} \mathbf{s}$, is like the full outer join, except it does not include the third category of tuples (the tuples from **S** that are padded with NULL over **R**). The **right outer join**, $\mathbf{r} \bowtie^{right}_{cond} \mathbf{s}$, is like the full outer join, except that the second type of tuple is missing. Figure 5.5 illustrates these notions.

Note that the outer joins are not independent operators: they can be expressed using the other relational operators (see Exercise 5.9).

Example 5.1.4 (Left Outer Join). Outer joins are useful when the NULL-padded tuples still carry useful information for the task at hand. Suppose we need to compute the average grade for every student (let us assume, for the sake of this example, that the grades are numeric). We could join the STUDENT relation of Figure 3.3 on page 36 with the TRANSCRIPT relation of Figure 3.5 on page 39. Then we could group tuples corresponding to each student Id and compute the average (the relational algebra can be extended with operators that support such computation—see Exercise 5.11).

However, it is easy to see that the student with Id 111223344 has no TRANSCRIPT records. Therefore, we will have no information about the average grade of that student (which is 0). To rectify this problem, we could compute the left outer join instead of the regular join:

$$\text{STUDENT} \bowtie^{left}_{\texttt{Id=StudId}} \text{TRANSCRIPT}$$

SupplName	PartNumber
Acme Inc.	P120
Main St. Hardware	N30
Electronics 2000	RM130

SUPPLIER relation

PartNumber	PartName
N30	10'' screw
KCL12	2lb hammer
P120	10-ohm resistor

PARTS relation

SupplName	PartNumber	PartNumber2	PartName
Acme Inc.	P120	P120	10-ohm resistor
Main St. Hardware	N30	N30	10'' screw
Electronics 2000	RM130	NULL	NULL
NULL	NULL	KCL12	2lb hammer

Full outer join SUPPLIER $\bowtie^{outer}_{\texttt{PartNumber=PartNumber}}$ PARTS

SupplName	PartNumber	PartNumber2	PartName
Acme Inc.	P120	P120	10-ohm resistor
Main St. Hardware	N30	N30	10'' screw
Electronics 2000	RM130	NULL	NULL

Left outer join SUPPLIER $\bowtie^{left}_{\texttt{PartNumber=PartNumber}}$ PARTS

SupplName	PartNumber	PartNumber2	PartName
Acme Inc.	P120	P120	10-ohm resistor
Main St. Hardware	N30	N30	10'' screw
NULL	NULL	KCL12	2lb hammer

Right outer join SUPPLIER $\bowtie^{right}_{\texttt{PartNumber=PartNumber}}$ PARTS

FIGURE 5.5 Outer joins.

Now the tuple with Id 111223344 is part of the result and can take part in the computation of the average grade. In fact, we will see that, in practical languages like SQL, nulls are ignored during the computation of the average, which will give us the desired average grade for our student. ■

Division operator. While the join operator brings intelligence to query answering, the division operator holds the distinction of being the most difficult to understand and use correctly.

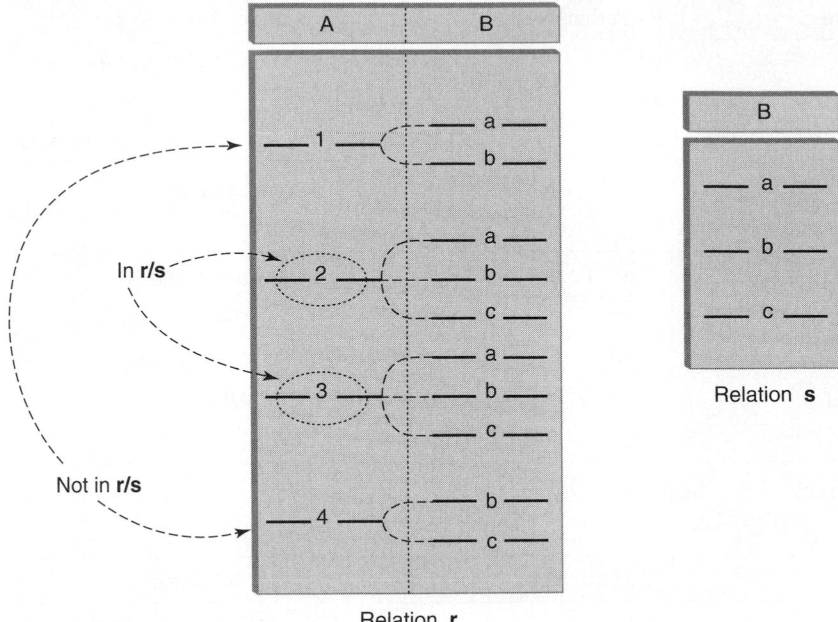

FIGURE 5.6 Division operator.

The **division operator** becomes useful when you feel the urge to find out *which professors taught* all *courses offered by the Computer Science Department* or *which students took a class from* every *professor in the Electrical Engineering Department*. The key here is that we are looking for tuples in one relation that match *all* tuples in another relation.

Here is a precise definition. Let **R** be a relation schema with attributes $A_1, \ldots, A_n, B_1, \ldots, B_m$ and let **S** be a relation schema with attributes $B_1, \ldots, B_m$. In other words, the set of attributes of **S** is a subset of the attributes of **R**. The **division** of **R** by **S** is an expression of the form **R/S**. If **r** and **s** are relation instances corresponding to **R** and **S** in our database, the **value** of **R/S**, denoted **r/s**, is a relation over the attributes $A_1, \ldots, A_n$ that consists of all tuples $\langle a \rangle$ such that, *for every* tuple $\langle b \rangle$ in **s**, the concatenated tuple $\langle a, b \rangle$ is in **r**. A schematic view of this definition is depicted in Figure 5.6.

An equivalent way to define division is

$$\langle a \rangle \in \mathbf{r}/\mathbf{s} \text{ if and only if } \{\langle a \rangle\} \times \mathbf{s} \subseteq \mathbf{r}$$

Here $\{\langle a \rangle\}$ denotes a relation that contains a single tuple, $\langle a \rangle$. Note that, if we view $\times$ as multiplication, we can view division as multiplication's inverse, which explains the name for this operation.

Brain Teaser: What is **r/s**, if **s** is empty?

Example 5.1.5 (Division). Consider the query *List all courses that have been taught by every computer science professor*. Here, by "every professor," we mean "every professor recorded in the database." That is, it is assumed that the database describes all we know about the situation. Not only does every tuple in the database assert a fact about the real-world enterprise being modeled, but there are no additional known facts that could be represented as tuples in the database relations. This is known as the **closed-world assumption** and is implicit in relational query processing.

Figure 5.7 shows three relations. The relation

$$\text{PROFCS} = \pi_{\texttt{Id}}(\sigma_{\texttt{DeptId='CS'}}(\text{PROFESSOR}))$$

contains the Ids of all known computer science professors. The relation

$$\text{PROFCOURSES} = (\pi_{\texttt{ProfId,CrsCode}}(\text{TEACHING}))\,[\texttt{Id,CrsCode}]$$

is a relationship between courses and professors who have taught them (at any time); it contains all known relationships of this kind. (Note that we have applied the renaming operator to make sure that the first attribute of PROFCOURSES has the same name as that of the attribute of PROFCS.) The third relation shows PROFCOURSES/PROFCS, the answer to the query. ■

Observe that before applying the division operator in the above example we carefully projected out some attributes (and renamed some others) to make the division operator applicable. The situation when projection must be applied to the operands of the division operator in order to make the division possible is quite typical. Here is another example.

Example 5.1.6 (Another Division). Consider the following query: *Retrieve all students who took a course from every professor who ever taught a course*. In the numerator we need a relation that associates students with professors who instructed them in some course. We can get this by taking the natural join of TRANSCRIPT and TEACHING:

$$\text{STUDPROF} = \text{TRANSCRIPT} \bowtie \text{TEACHING}$$

STUDPROF has attributes `StudId`, `CrsCode`, `Semester`, `Grade`, `ProfId`, which is more information than we want, so we eliminate unwanted columns using projection to get the numerator: $\pi_{\texttt{StudId,ProfId}}(\text{STUDPROF})$.

Because we are interested in students who took a course with *every professor*, we need a relation in the denominator that has a tuple for every professor. Professors

PROFCS	Id
	101202303
	555666777

All computer science professors: $\pi_{\texttt{Id}}(\sigma_{\texttt{DeptId='CS'}}(\text{PROFESSOR}))$

PROFCOURSES	Id	CrsCode
	009406321	MGT123
	121232343	EE101
	555666777	CS305
	101202303	CS315
	900120450	MAT123
	101202303	CS305
	783432188	MGT123

Who taught what: $(\pi_{\texttt{ProfId,CrsCode}}(\text{TEACHING}))[\texttt{Id,CrsCode}]$

CrsCode
CS305

The answer: `ProfCourses/ProfCS`

FIGURE 5.7 The anatomy of a query: *Courses taught by every computer science professor.*

who have taught a course have their Ids inside the tuples of the TEACHING relation. (We do not want to use PROFESSOR here as this would include tuples for professors who have not done any teaching.) Hence, the denominator is $\pi_{\texttt{ProfId}}(\text{TEACHING})$, and the answer to our query is

$$\pi_{\texttt{StudId,ProfId}}(\text{STUDPROF}) \;/\; \pi_{\texttt{ProfId}}\;(\text{TEACHING}) \quad \textbf{5.2}$$

■

Example 5.1.7 (Complex Division). *Find all students who took all courses that were taught by all computer science professors.* Here we need double division:

$$\begin{aligned}&(\pi_{\texttt{Id,Name}}(\text{STUDENT}))[\texttt{StudId,Name}] \bowtie \\ &\quad(\pi_{\texttt{StudId,CrsCode}}(\text{TRANSCRIPT}) \;/ \\ &\qquad((\pi_{\texttt{ProfId,CrsCode}}(\text{TEACHING}))[\texttt{Id,CrsCode}]/ \\ &\qquad\quad\pi_{\texttt{Id}}(\sigma_{\texttt{DeptId='CS'}}(\text{PROFESSOR}))))\end{aligned} \quad \textbf{5.3}$$

The second division above is our friend from Figure 5.7, which yields all courses taught by every computer science professor. Therefore, the last three lines in the expression define the Ids of all students who took all such courses. The natural join in the first line is then used to obtain the names of these students. We had to rename the attributes of the STUDENT relation before taking the join. ■

We conclude by showing how the division operator can be expressed using other relational operators: projection, set difference, and cross product. Let **R** be a relation with attributes *A* and *B*, and let **S** be a relation over a single attribute *B*. (The construction, below, works even if *A* and *B* are disjoint lists of attributes.) The expression **R/S** can then be computed without the use of division as follows:

$T_1 = \pi_A(\mathbf{R}) \times \mathbf{S}$	All possible associations between *A*-values in **R** and *B*-values in **S**.
$T_2 = \pi_A(T_1 - \mathbf{R})$	All those *A*-values in **R** that are **not** associated in **R** with every *B*-value in **S**. These are precisely those *A*-values that should **not** be in the answer. **5.4**
$T_3 = \pi_A(\mathbf{R}) - T_2$	*The answer:* All those *A*-values in **R** that are associated in **R** with all *B*-values in **S**.

5.2 The Query Sublanguage of SQL

SQL is the most widely used relational database language. An initial version was proposed in 1974, and it has been evolving ever since. A widely used version, generally referred to as SQL-92, is a standard of the American National Standards Institute (ANSI). The language continues to evolve and recently SQL:1999 and SQL:2003 have been completed. Like any rapidly changing language whose form is influenced by its many users, SQL has become surprisingly complex. The purpose of this section and the next is to introduce you to some of the complexity of the data manipulation sublanguage of SQL. However, you should be aware that a full treatment of this subject is well worth a book of its own. For example, [Melton and Simon 1992, Date and Darwen 1997] are more complete references to SQL-92; [Gulutzan and Pelzer 1999] describes SQL:1999. The unfortunate reality, however, is that commercial databases do not always adhere to the standards, and a vendor-specific reference is almost always a must for serious application development.

SQL can be used interactively by submitting an SQL statement directly to the DBMS from a terminal. However, particularly in transaction processing systems, SQL statements are usually embedded in a larger program that submits the statements to the DBMS at run time and processes the results. The special considerations that relate to such embedding will be discussed in Chapter 8.

5.2.1 Simple SQL Queries

Simple SQL queries are easy to design. Need a list of all professors in the Electrical Engineering (EE) Department? Happy to oblige:

```
SELECT   P.Name
FROM     PROFESSOR P                    5.5
WHERE    P.DeptId = 'EE'
```

Note the symbol P here, which is called a **tuple variable**. It ranges over the tuples of the relation PROFESSOR.[5] The tuple variable is actually unnecessary in this statement, and, if you recall, we tried to avoid its use in our brief introduction to SQL in Chapter 2. In simple queries, such as above, we could have referred to the attributes simply as `Name` and `DeptId` instead of `P.Name` and `P.DeptId`, since there is no ambiguity as to which relation the attributes come from. In some multi-table queries, we could have used PROFESSOR.`Name` and PROFESSOR.`DeptId` in case of ambiguity.

However, as we shall see shortly, in some situations the use of tuple variables is essential. In fact, *not* using tuple variables in SELECT statements is considered poor programming practice, which often leads to subtle mistakes. Therefore, from now on we will be pedantically declaring all tuple variables.

Although this statement is rather simple, it is important to understand operationally how a SELECT statement might be evaluated. SELECT statements can become very complex, and following an operational flow through the statement is often the only way to figure out what is going on. Of course, different DBMSs might adopt different strategies for evaluating the same statement, but since they all produce the same result it is useful to describe a particularly simple strategy.

An evaluation strategy for simple queries. The basic algorithm for evaluating SQL queries can be stated as follows:

Step 1. *The* FROM *clause is evaluated.* It produces a table that is the Cartesian product of the tables listed as its arguments. If a table occurs more than once in the FROM clause, as in query (5.11) on page 151, then this table occurs as many times in the product.

Step 2. *The* WHERE *clause is evaluated.* It takes the table produced in step 1 and processes each row individually. Attribute values from the row are substituted for the attribute names in the condition, and the condition is evaluated. The table produced by the WHERE clause contains exactly those rows for which the condition evaluates to true.

[5] Mastering SQL often means stuffing one's head with redundant terminology. For instance, SQL variables are also known as *table aliases*.

Step 3. *The* SELECT *clause is evaluated.* It takes the table produced in step 2 and retains only those columns that are listed as arguments. The resulting table is output by the SELECT statement.

As we discuss new features of the language, we will be adding additional steps to this strategy, but the basic idea remains the same. Each clause produces a table, which is the input to the next clause to be evaluated. Certain steps need not be present in a particular evaluation. For example, step 2 might not have to be evaluated because a SELECT statement does not have to have a WHERE clause. Other steps might be trivial. For example, although every SELECT statement must have a FROM clause, if the clause names only a single relation, the Cartesian product is not required and that relation is simply passed on to step 2.

In view of the above algorithm, the relational algebra equivalent of the SQL query (5.5) is

$$\pi_{\texttt{Name}}(\sigma_{\texttt{DeptId='EE'}}(\text{PROFESSOR}))$$

Join queries. Queries that express a join between two relations follow the same pattern as above. The following query, which returns the list of all professors who taught in fall 1994, involves a join.

```
SELECT   P.Name
FROM     PROFESSOR P, TEACHING T                              5.6
WHERE    P.Id = T.ProfId  AND  T.Semester = 'F1994'
```

Note that the tuple variables in this example clarify the meaning of the statement because they identify the table from which each attribute is drawn. In this particular case, however, there is no ambiguity as to where the attributes are coming from and so the use of these variables is just a matter of good practice. If, on the other hand, the Id attribute of PROFESSOR were called ProfId, then we would *have* to use tuple variables to distinguish the two references to Id.

Evaluation of the above statement follows the steps outlined above. In this example, in contrast to query (5.5), processing the FROM clause involves taking a Cartesian product. Take the time to convince yourself that query (5.6) is equivalent to the relational algebra expression

$$\pi_{\texttt{Name}}(\text{PROFESSOR} \bowtie_{\texttt{Id=ProfId}} \sigma_{\texttt{Semester='F1994'}}(\text{TEACHING})) \quad \textbf{5.7}$$

where we split the condition in the WHERE clause into a *join condition* and a *selection condition.* The join condition, Id = ProfId, ensures that related tuples in the two tables are combined. It makes no sense to combine a tuple from PROFESSOR that describes a particular professor with a tuple from TEACHING that describes a course taught by a different professor. Hence, the join condition eliminates garbage. The selection condition Semester = 'F1994', on the other hand, eliminates tuples that are not relevant to the query.

The relationship between SQL and relational algebra. The relational algebra expression

$$\pi_{\texttt{Name}}(\sigma_{\texttt{Id=ProfId AND Semester='F1994'}}(\text{PROFESSOR} \times \text{TEACHING}))$$

is equivalent to the expression (5.7) and to the SQL query (5.6). Although this expression leads to one of the least efficient ways of evaluating query (5.6), it is simple, uniform, and, from the syntactic point of view, reflects more closely the corresponding SQL statement. More generally, the query template

```
SELECT   TargetList
FROM     REL1 V1, ..., RELn Vn
WHERE    Condition
```
5.8

is roughly equivalent to the algebraic expression

$$\pi_{\mathit{TargetList}}\sigma_{\mathit{Condition}}(\text{REL}_1 \times \ldots \times \text{REL}_n) \quad \textbf{5.9}$$

"Roughly" means that we have to transform *Condition* into a relational algebra form. To be more concrete, consider the query *Find the names of the courses taught in fall 1995 together with the names of the professors who taught those courses.* In SQL we get

```
SELECT   C.CrsName, P.Name
FROM     PROFESSOR P, TEACHING T, COURSE C
WHERE    T.Semester = 'F1995' AND
         P.Id = T.ProfId AND T.CrsCode = C.CrsCode
```
5.10

The corresponding algebraic expression in the inefficient, but uniform, form described above is

$$\pi_{\texttt{CrsName,Name}}(\sigma_{\mathit{Condition}}(\text{PROFESSOR} \times \text{TEACHING} \times \text{COURSE}))$$

where *Condition* denotes the contents of the WHERE clause (modified to suit relational algebra):

```
Id = ProfId AND TEACHING.CrsCode = COURSE.CrsCode AND
    Semester = 'F1995'
```

Self-join queries. Let us return to the query that we considered earlier, *Find all students who took at least two courses.* We expressed this in relational algebra as

$$\pi_{\texttt{StudId}} (\sigma_{\texttt{CrsCode} \neq \texttt{CrsCode2}} (\text{TRANSCRIPT} \bowtie_{\texttt{StudId=StudId}} \text{TRANSCRIPT}[\texttt{StudId,CrsCode2,Semester2,Grade2}]))$$

Observe that we have joined the relation TRANSCRIPT with *itself.* To accomplish this in relational algebra, we have to apply the renaming operator to the second occurrence of TRANSCRIPT. In SQL, we must mention the TRANSCRIPT relation twice in the FROM clause and declare two different variables over this relation. Each variable is meant to represent a distinct occurrence of TRANSCRIPT in the join.

```
SELECT   T1.StudId
FROM     TRANSCRIPT T1, TRANSCRIPT T2                    5.11
WHERE    T1.CrsCode <> T2.CrsCode
             AND T1.StudId = T2.StudId
```

The symbol <> in this query is SQL's way of saying "not equal." Note that we do need *two distinct tuple variables* to range over TRANSCRIPT; if we were to use just one variable, T, the condition `T.CrsCode <> T.CrsCode` would never be satisfied, making the answer to the query the empty relation. Therefore, there is no obvious way to do this query without tuple variables.

Retrieving distinct answers. We already know from Chapter 3 that relations are sets, so no duplicate tuples are allowed. However, many relational operators can yield **multisets** (i.e., set-like objects that might contain multiple occurrences of identical elements) as an intermediate result of the computation. For instance, if we chop off the attribute `Semester` from the instance of the relation TEACHING depicted in Figure 3.5 (page 39), we get a list of tuples that contains duplicate occurrences of ⟨`009406321, MGT123`⟩ and of other tuples as well. As a consequence, in order for the SQL query

```
SELECT   T.ProfId, T.CrsCode
FROM     TEACHING  T                                     5.12
```

to return a relation (as required by the relational data model), the query processor must perform an additional scan of the query result in order to eliminate duplicates. In many cases, the application programmer is not willing to pay the price for duplicate elimination. Hence, the designers of SQL decided that, by default, duplicate tuples are not eliminated unless elimination is explicitly requested using the keyword DISTINCT.

```
SELECT   DISTINCT T.ProfId, T.CrsCode
FROM     TEACHING T                                    5.13
```

Note that this query is missing the WHERE clause, which is *optional* in SQL. When it is missing, the WHERE condition is assumed to be true regardless of the values of tuple variables in the FROM clause.

While the WHERE clause is optional, the SELECT and the FROM clauses are not.

Comments. As with every programming language, the programmer might wish to annotate queries with comments. In SQL, comments are strings that begin with the double minus sign, --, and end with a new line. For instance,

```
-- An example of SELECT DISTINCT
SELECT   DISTINCT T.ProfId, T.CrsCode                  5.14
FROM     TEACHING T    --Look, no WHERE clause!
```

Expressions in the WHERE clause. So far, the conditions in the WHERE clause have been comparisons of attributes against constants or other attributes. For numeric values, SQL provides the following comparison operators: = (equal), <> (not equal), > (greater than), >= (greater than or equal to), < (less than), and <= (less than or equal to).

All of these operators can be applied to numerals and character strings as well. (Strings can also be compared against patterns using the LIKE operator, which we will describe later.) Strings are compared character-wise, from left to right. For the purposes of this text, we limit our attention to ASCII symbols and assume that the ordering of characters in making comparisons between two strings is determined by the ASCII codes assigned to these characters.

The operands of these comparison operators can be **expressions**, not just single attributes or constants. For numeric values, expressions are composed of the usual operators, *, +, and the like. For strings, the concatenation operator, ||, can be used. Assume, for instance, an appropriate EMPLOYEE relation with the attributes SSN, BossSSN, LastName, FirstName, and Salary. Then the query

```
SELECT   E.SSN
FROM     EMPLOYEE E, EMPLOYEE M
WHERE    E.BossSSN = M.SSN AND E.Salary > 2 * M.Salary
         AND E.LastName = 'Mc' || E.FirstName
```

returns all employees whose salary is more than twice that of their bosses' and whose last names are a concatenation of "Mc" and the first name (e.g., Donald McDonald).

Expressions and special features in the SELECT clause. The SELECT clause has a number of special features. In Section 2.2, we noted that the asterisk (*) represents the list of all attributes of all relations in the FROM clause. Note that when it is used and a relation appears twice (or more) in the FROM clause, its attributes appear twice (or more) as well. For instance, the query

```
SELECT  *
FROM    EMPLOYEE  E, EMPLOYEE M
```

is the same as

```
SELECT  E.SSN, E.BossSSN, E.FirstName, E.LastName, E.Salary,
        M.SSN, M.BossSSN, M.FirstName, M.LastName, M.Salary
FROM    EMPLOYEE E, EMPLOYEE M
```

SQL permits expressions in the target list, not only in the WHERE clause (which we have seen so far). This feature is illustrated using the following example.

Example 5.2.1 (Expressions in Target List). Suppose that an audit office needs a report on salary gaps between employees and their immediate bosses. This can be accomplished with the following query:

```
SELECT  E.SSN, M.SSN, M.Salary - E.Salary
FROM    EMPLOYEE  E,  EMPLOYEE M
WHERE   E.BossSSN = M.SSN
```

The noteworthy feature here is an arithmetic expression in the last member of the target list. ■

If the above query is used interactively, most DBMSs would display a table where the first two columns are labeled SSN and the last column has no label at all. Obviously, this is not very satisfactory since it requires the user to remember the meaning of the items in the SELECT clause. To alleviate this problem, SQL allows the programmer to change attribute names and assign names where they do not exist. This is accomplished with the help of the keyword AS.

Example 5.2.2 (Naming Attributes in the Target List). For example, we can modify the previous query as follows.

```
SELECT  E.SSN AS EmplId,
        M.SSN AS MngrId,
        M.Salary - E.Salary AS SalaryGap
FROM    EMPLOYEE  E, EMPLOYEE M
WHERE   E.BossSSN = M.SSN
```

This query is identical to the previous one in all but the form of the output. While the result of the first query will have unnamed columns, the attributes of the last query will all be named and displayed as EmplId, MngrId, and SalaryGap. ■

Negation. Any condition in the WHERE clause can be negated with NOT. For instance, instead of T1.CrsCode <> T2.CrsCode in query (5.11), we could have written NOT (T1.CrsCode = T2.CrsCode). The negated condition need not be atomic—it can consist of an arbitrary number of subconditions connected with AND or OR, and it can even have nested applications of NOT, as in the following example.

```
NOT (E.BossSSN = M.SSN AND E.Salary > 2 * M.Salary
     AND NOT (E.LastName = 'Mc'|| E.FirstName))
```

5.2.2 Set Operations

SQL uses the set-theoretic operators from the relational algebra. Here is a simple query where set-theoretic operators can be used: *Find all professors who are working for the* CS *or* EE *departments.*

```
(SELECT  P.Name
 FROM    PROFESSOR P
 WHERE   P.DeptId = 'CS' )
UNION                                        5.15
(SELECT  P.Name
 FROM    PROFESSOR P
 WHERE   P.DeptId = 'EE' )
```

The query is self-explanatory. It consists of two subqueries: one retrieving all CS professors and the other retrieving all EE professors. The results are collected into a single relation using the UNION operator of the algebra. Note that UNION removes duplicates from the result.

While this example illustrates the basic use of set-theoretic operators in SQL, the benefits of using UNION here are small, since this query can be rewritten without UNION and in a more efficient way:

```
SELECT DISTINCT  P.Name
FROM     PROFESSOR P                         5.16
WHERE    P.DeptId = 'CS' OR P.DeptId = 'EE'
```

Note that DISTINCT is used here because UNION removes duplicate tuples.

Our next example, the query *Find all computer science professors and also all professors who ever taught a computer science course*, is more involved, and the advantages of set-theoretic operators there are more substantial.

Let us assume that all course codes in computer science begin with CS. In designing the query, we need to match patterns against strings (course codes). To verify whether a string matches a pattern, SQL provides the LIKE predicate. For instance, T.CrsCode LIKE 'CS%' verifies that the value of T.CrsCode matches the pattern that starts with CS and can have *zero or more* additional characters. SQL patterns are similar to wildcards in UNIX or DOS, although SQL's arsenal for building patterns is somewhat limited: besides %, there is _, a symbol that matches an arbitrary *single* character.[6]

Without the UNION operator, CS professors or those who taught a CS course can be found as follows:

```
SELECT  P.Name
FROM    PROFESSOR P, TEACHING T                              5.17
WHERE   (P.Id = T.ProfId AND T.CrsCode LIKE 'CS%')
        OR (P.DeptId = 'CS')
```

We see that, as the WHERE condition gets longer and more complicated, it becomes harder to read and understand. With the UNION operator, we can rewrite this query in the following way:

```
(SELECT  P.Name
 FROM    PROFESSOR P, TEACHING T
 WHERE   P.Id = T.ProfId AND T.CrsCode LIKE 'CS%')
UNION                                                        5.18
(SELECT  P.Name
 FROM    PROFESSOR P
 WHERE   P.DeptId = 'CS')
```

Although this is no more succinct than (5.17), it is more modular and easier to understand.

If we want to change our query so that it retrieves all professors who taught a CS course without being a CS professor, we can easily modify (5.18) by replacing UNION with EXCEPT—the SQL counterpart of the MINUS operator in relational algebra.

[6] Suppose that you need to construct a pattern where the special characters % and _ stand for themselves. For instance, suppose you need to match all strings that start with _%. This is possible, albeit cumbersome. You have to declare an escape character and then prefix it to the special character to let SQL know that you want these characters to stand for themselves. For instance, C.Descr LIKE '_\%__$' ESCAPE '\' compares the value of C.Descr with a pattern that matches all strings that begin with _%, followed by a pair of arbitrary characters, and terminated with the symbol $. Here \ is declared as an escape character via the ESCAPE clause and then used to "escape" % and _.

Changing (5.17) to answer the new query is more complex. The WHERE clause of (5.17) would have to be rewritten as

```
P.Id = T.ProfId AND T.CrsCode LIKE 'CS%' AND P.DeptId <> 'CS'
```

This is not as modular a change as in the case of (5.18).

Example 5.2.3 (Set Operators Help Simplify Queries). Suppose that we need to find all students who took both the transaction processing course, CS315, and the database systems course, CS305. As a first try, we might write the following query:

```
SELECT   S.Name
FROM     STUDENT S, TRANSCRIPT  T                                5.19
WHERE    S.StudId = T.StudId AND T.CrsCode = 'CS305'
         AND T.CrsCode = 'CS315'
```

On closer examination, however, we discover that this SQL query is not what we need because it requires that there be a tuple in TRANSCRIPT such that T.CrsCode is equal to both CS305 and CS315—an unsatisfiable condition. Thus, the formulation (5.19) illustrates one very common mistake—failure to recognize the need for an additional tuple variable. The correct formulation is

```
SELECT   S.Name
FROM     STUDENT S, TRANSCRIPT  T1, TRANSCRIPT T2
WHERE    S.StudId = T1.StudId AND T1.CrsCode = 'CS305'           5.20
         AND S.StudId = T2.StudId AND T2.CrsCode = 'CS315'
```

Observe that we used two distinct tuple variables over the relation TRANSCRIPT to express the fact that student S has taken two different courses.

What does this have to do with the original subject of set-theoretic operators of the relational algebra? It turns out that the INTERSECT operator lets us rewrite (5.20) in a more modular and less error-prone way:

```
(SELECT  S.Name
 FROM    STUDENT S, TRANSCRIPT  T
 WHERE   S.StudId = T.StudId  AND T.CrsCode = 'CS305')
INTERSECT                                                        5.21
(SELECT  S.Name
 FROM    STUDENT S, TRANSCRIPT  T
 WHERE   S.StudId = T.StudId AND T.CrsCode = 'CS315')
```

Notice that here we do not need multiple variables to range over the same relation, which somewhat reduces the risk of error. Instead, we write two simple, essentially similar queries and take the intersection of their results. ■

Set constructor. Finally, we mention one related feature, the constructor for building finite sets within SQL queries. The syntax of the set constructor is simple: (*set-elem*$_1$, *set-elem*$_2$, ..., *set-elem*$_n$). The operator IN lets us check if a particular element is within a set. For example, consider query (5.16), which, with the help of the set constructor, can be simplified to

```
SELECT  P.Name
FROM    PROFESSOR P                                    5.22
WHERE   P.DeptId  IN   ('CS','EE')
```

Note that if we take query (5.19) and replace its WHERE clause with

```
S.StudId = T.StudId  AND  T.CrsCode  IN ('CS305','CS315' )
```

we obtain a query with a meaning different from that of (5.19). This issue is further investigated in Exercise 5.13.

Negation and infix comparison operators. Earlier we discussed the NOT operator. For some infix operators, such as LIKE and IN, SQL provides two forms of negation: NOT (X LIKE Y) and, equivalently, X NOT LIKE Y. Similarly, one can write X NOT IN Y instead of the more cumbersome NOT(X IN Y).

5.2.3 Nested Queries

SQL would be only half as much fun if it offered only one way to do each task. Consider the query *Select all professors who taught in fall 1994*. One way to say this in SQL was given in (5.6) on page 149, but there is (at least) one other, radically different way. First compute the set of all professors who taught in fall 1994 using a **nested subquery**; then collect their names and produce the result.

```
SELECT   P.Name
FROM     PROFESSOR P
WHERE    P.Id IN
         -- A nested subquery
         (SELECT T.ProfId
          FROM TEACHING T
          WHERE T.Semester = 'F1994')
```

Note that in this example the nested subquery is evaluated only once, and then each row of PROFESSOR can be tested in the WHERE clause against the result of that evaluation.

The above example illustrates one way in which nested subqueries can be of help—*increased readability*. However, readability alone is not a sufficient reason for using this facility as most query processors cannot optimize nested subqueries well enough, and thus indulging in subqueries has a performance penalty. A much more important reason for the existence of nested subqueries is that they increase the expressive power of SQL—some queries simply cannot be formulated in a natural way without them.

Consider the query *List all students who did not take any courses*. In English this query sounds deceptively simple, but in SQL it cannot be done without the nested subquery facility (or the EXCEPT operator—try this alternative on your own).

```
SELECT   S.Name
FROM     STUDENT  S
WHERE    S.Id NOT IN                                          5.23
         -- Students who have taken a course
         (SELECT  T.StudId
          FROM    TRANSCRIPT T)
```

As a final example, a subquery can be used to extract a scalar value from a table. Suppose that you want to know which employees are paid a higher salary than you. Assuming that your Id is 111111111, you might use a subquery to return your salary from EMPLOYEE as follows:

```
SELECT   E.Id
FROM     EMPLOYEE  E
WHERE    E.Salary >                                           5.24
         (SELECT  E1.Salary
          FROM    EMPLOYEE E1
          WHERE   E1.Id = '111111111')
```

The overall query then finds all employees that earn more.

Correlated nested subqueries. Although nested subqueries can sometimes improve readability, on the whole they are one of the most complex, expensive, and error-prone features of SQL. To a large extent, this complexity is due to **query correlation**—the ability to define variables in the outer query and use them in the inner subquery. Nesting and correlation are akin to the notion of `begin`/`end` blocks in programming languages and the associated idea of the scope of a variable.

To illustrate, suppose that we need to find student assistants for professors who are scheduled to teach in a forthcoming semester (for definiteness, let us say in fall 2004). For each professor, we compute the set of all courses she will be teaching during that semester and then find students who have taken one of these courses (and so are eligible to assist with them). The list of courses taught by professors can be computed in a nested subquery, and associating professors with students can be done in an outer query. Here is a realization of this plan in SQL:

```
SELECT  R.StudId,  P.Id,  R.CrsCode
FROM    TRANSCRIPT R,  PROFESSOR P
WHERE   R.CrsCode  IN                                          5.25
        -- Courses taught by P.Id in F2004
        (SELECT T1.CrsCode
         FROM   TEACHING T1
         WHERE  T1.ProfId = P.Id AND T1.Semester = 'F2004' )
```

Here the scope of the variable T1 is limited to the subquery. In contrast, the variable P is visible in both the outer and inner queries. This variable parameterizes the inner query and correlates its result with the tuples of the outer query. For *each* value of P.Id, the inner query is computed independently *as if* P.Id *were a constant*. Each time an inner subquery is computed, the value of R.CrsCode is checked against the result returned. If this value belongs to the result, an output tuple is formed by the outer SELECT query.

Observe that, at a minimum, the inner query must be reevaluated for each row of PROFESSOR. This contrasts with uncorrelated nested queries and explains the expense associated with query correlation.

Even though nested queries are a challenge for query optimizers, inexperienced database programmers sometimes abuse them, substituting them for the much simpler ANDs, NOTs, and the like.

Example 5.2.4 (Abuse of Query Nesting). Here is an example of how *not* to write the previous query (even though it is semantically correct):

```
SELECT  R.StudId,  T.ProfId,  R.CrsCode
FROM    TRANSCRIPT R, TEACHING T
WHERE   R.CrsCode  IN
        -- Courses taught by T.ProfId in F2004
        (SELECT T1.CrsCode
         FROM   TEACHING T1
         WHERE  T1.ProfId = T.ProfId AND
        -- Bad style: unreadable and slow!
        T1.ProfId IN   (SELECT T2.ProfId
                        FROM   TEACHING T2
                        WHERE  T2.Semester = 'F2004' ) )
```

The third level of nesting can be avoided here. Not only is it a performance hit, but it is also much harder to understand compared to (5.25). ■

The EXISTS operator. It is often necessary to check if a nested subquery returns no answers. For instance, we might wish to *Find all students who never took a computer science course*. A way to approach this problem is to compute the set of all computer courses taken by a student and then list only those students for whom this set is empty. This can be done with the help of correlated nested subqueries and the EXISTS operator, which returns true if a set is non-empty.

Here is one SQL formulation of this query:

```
SELECT   S.Id
FROM     STUDENT S
WHERE    NOT EXISTS (
         -- All CS courses taken by S.Id                              5.26
         SELECT   T.CrsCode
         FROM     TRANSCRIPT T
         WHERE    T.CrsCode LIKE 'CS%'
                   AND   T.StudId = S.Id )
```

Once again, the variable S is global with respect to the inner subquery; this subquery is evaluated for each value of S.Id, which is treated as a constant during the evaluation. All values of S.Id for which the inner query has no answers constitute the answer to the outer query.

Expressing the division operator. We now show that query nesting can help in expressing the relational division operator. For concreteness, consider the query *List the students who have taken all computer science courses*. We can solve the problem by first computing a single-attribute relation that has a row for each CS course (this is the denominator of the division operator). Then, for each student, we check if the student's transcript contains all of these courses.

To make the idea easier to understand, we first realize our plan assuming the availability of a predicate, CONTAINS, which does not actually exist in SQL. As its name suggests, CONTAINS tests if one set contains another. Then we will show how this predicate is expressed using the SQL operators that do exist.

```
SELECT   S.Id
FROM     STUDENT S
WHERE    -- All courses taken by S.Id
         (SELECT  R.CrsCode
          FROM    TRANSCRIPT R
          WHERE   R.StudId = S.Id )
         CONTAINS
         -- All CS courses
         (SELECT  C.CrsCode
          FROM    COURSE C
          WHERE   C.CrsCode  LIKE 'CS%' )
```

Now, observe that A CONTAINS B is equivalent to NOT EXISTS (B EXCEPT A). Therefore, we can rewrite the above query as follows using only the available SQL operators. Clearly, the result is much harder to understand and construct than the query that involves the (alas nonexistent) operator CONTAINS.

```
SELECT   S.Id
FROM     STUDENT S
WHERE    NOT EXISTS (
         (SELECT  C.CrsCode
          FROM    COURSE C
          WHERE   C.CrsCode LIKE 'CS%' )
         EXCEPT
         (SELECT  R.CrsCode
          FROM    TRANSCRIPT R
          WHERE   R.StudId = S.Id ) )
```
5.27

The following is an example of an even harder query.

Example 5.2.5 (Complex Nested Query). Consider the query *Find the students who took a course from* every *professor in the* CS *department*. One possible SQL formulation of this query is

```
SELECT   S.Id
FROM     STUDENT S
WHERE
      NOT EXISTS (
      -- CS professors who did not teach S.Id
      (SELECT  P.Id -- All CS professors
       FROM    PROFESSOR P
       WHERE   P.Dept = 'CS')
      EXCEPT
      (SELECT  T.ProfId -- Professors who have taught S.Id
       FROM    TEACHING T, TRANSCRIPT R
       WHERE   T.CrsCode = R.CrsCode
               AND  T.Semester = R.Semester
               AND  S.Id = R.StudId) )
```
5.28

The variable S is global, and the subquery is evaluated for each value of S. The variable R ranges over all tuples in TRANSCRIPT. It is local to the second subquery where it is related to S through a condition in the WHERE clause. Therefore, the values of R.Semester and R.CrsCode correspond to all recorded enrollments of student S.Id. Similarly T.ProfId gets successively bound to all professors who ever taught S.Id.

To understand why this SQL expression represents the query at hand, recall that the combination NOT EXISTS/EXCEPT is nothing but the aforesaid CONTAINS predicate over sets. ■

Set comparison operators. Suppose that our STUDENT relation has one additional numeric attribute, GPA. We can ask the question *Is there a student in the university whose GPA is higher than that of* all *junior students?*

It turns out that nested queries are helpful here, too.

```
SELECT   S.Name, S.Id
FROM     STUDENT S
WHERE S.GPA >ALL  (SELECT  S.GPA
                   FROM    STUDENT S
                   WHERE   S.Status ='junior')
```
5.29

Here > ALL is a comparison operator, which returns true whenever its left argument is greater than *every* element of the set to the right. If we replace > ALL with >=ANY, we obtain a query about students whose GPA is greater than or equal to the GPA of *some* junior student.

One other point is worth noting about this query. The variable S is declared in both the outer and the inner queries. So which one is referred to in the WHERE clause of the inner query? The answer, as with **begin**/**end** blocks, is that the inner declaration is valid within the inner query. (However, excessive reuse of existing variable names in inner queries can be confusing.)

Nested subqueries in the FROM clause. As if query (5.28) were not complex enough, SQL has more up its sleeve: you can have nested subqueries in the FROM clause! This works as follows: You write a nested subquery (it must not be correlated and hence cannot use global variables). This subquery can be used in the FROM clause as if it were a relation name. You can use the keyword AS to attach a tuple variable to it. (Actually, AS is optional here but is highly recommended for readability.)

To illustrate, consider a query similar to (5.28) but without NOT EXISTS (i.e., the required answer would consist of all students who were *not* taught by at least one CS professor). We can formulate an equivalent query by moving the first nested subquery of (5.28) to the FROM clause as shown below. (Note that we cannot move the second subquery, because it is correlated.)

```
SELECT   S.Id
FROM     STUDENT S,
         (SELECT  P.Id -- All CS professors
          FROM PROFESSOR P
          WHERE P.Dept = 'CS') AS C
```
5.30

```
WHERE C.ProfId NOT IN
      (SELECT T.ProfId -- All S.Id's professors
       FROM TEACHING T, TRANSCRIPT R
       WHERE T.CrsCode = R.CrsCode
          AND T.Semester = R.Semester)
          AND S.Id = R.StudId )
```

The use of nested subqueries in the FROM clause should be avoided if at all possible as it tends to produce queries that are hard to understand and verify. A much better alternative is to use the view mechanism, which will be discussed in Section 5.2.8.

Apart from nested queries, SQL also permits explicit table joins in the FROM clause. However, we do not discuss this feature.

5.2.4 Quantified Predicates

Beginning with SQL:1999, the language supports a limited form of explicit universal and existential quantification. Although this new feature does not increase the expressive power of the language, it makes certain queries easier to understand. The basic idea is to include **quantified predicates** with the following general syntax:

```
FOR ALL table-name-or-query (condition)
FOR SOME table-name-or-query (condition)
```

A quantified predicate can be used in the WHERE clause like any other predicate. It is true if and only if every row (FOR ALL) or some rows (FOR SOME) in the set of tuples represented by *table-name-or-query* satisfy *condition*. The condition in a quantified predicate can be as complex as any WHERE-clause condition, and it can refer to the attributes of the tuples in *table-name-or-query*. To make this concrete, consider the following example of a quantified predicate:

```
FOR ALL PROFESSOR
    (Id IN (SELECT T.ProfId FROM TEACHING))
```

When it appears in a WHERE clause (e.g., as a conjunct along with other predicates), it verifies that every professor (identified through the Id attribute) is teaching something. For a more complex example, we show how quantified predicates can make expression of the division operator easier to understand.

Example 5.2.6 (Expressing Division Using Universal Quantification). Consider the query *List the students who have taken all computer science courses*, which was earlier represented in SQL in quite a convoluted way (see query (5.27)). The preceding discussion on page 160 made it clear that part of the reason for this complexity is the absence of the CONTAINS predicate in SQL. Fortunately, CONTAINS can be expressed as a quantified predicate much more naturally than with the NOT EXISTS/EXCEPT combination used in (5.27):

```
SELECT   S.Id
FROM     STUDENT S
WHERE
    FOR ALL   (SELECT  C.CrsCode
               FROM    COURSE C
               WHERE   C.CrsCode LIKE 'CS%' )
              (CrsCode IN
                  (SELECT  R.CrsCode
                   FROM    TRANSCRIPT R
                   WHERE   R.StudId = S.Id ) )
```

While this is not as simple as what would have been possible with CONTAINS, it comes close. ■

The explicit existential quantifier, FOR SOME, is less useful in SQL than the universal quantifier, but it is provided for symmetry. For instance, if we wanted to find out if any professor teaches CS305, we could use the following test in the WHERE clause:

```
FOR SOME PROFESSOR
     (Id IN  (SELECT T.ProfId FROM TEACHING
              WHERE T.CrsCode = CS305 ))
```

5.2.5 Aggregation over Data

In many instances, it is necessary to compute average salary, maximum GPA, number of employees per department, total cost of a purchase, and so forth. These tasks are performed with the help of **aggregate functions**, which operate on sets of tuples. SQL uses five aggregate functions that are described in Figure 5.8.

Aggregate functions cannot be expressed in pure relational algebra. However, the algebra can be extended to allow their use (these extensions are beyond the scope of this text).

To illustrate the use of aggregate functions, we assume that both STUDENT and PROFESSOR relations have the attribute Age and that the STUDENT relation also has the attribute GPA. We start with a few simple examples.

```
-- Average age of the student body
SELECT   AVG(S.Age)
FROM     STUDENT  S

-- Minimum age among professors in the Management Department
SELECT   MIN(P.Age)
```

```
FROM    PROFESSOR P
WHERE   P.DeptId = 'MGT'
```

The above queries find only the average and the minimum ages, not the actual people who have them. If we need to find the youngest professor(s) within the Management Department, we can use a nested subquery.

```
-- Youngest professor(s) in the Management Department
SELECT  P.Name, P.Age
FROM    PROFESSOR P
WHERE   P.DeptId = 'MGT'  AND
        P.Age = (SELECT  MIN(P1.Age)
                 FROM    PROFESSOR P1
                 WHERE   P1.DeptId = 'MGT'  )
```

The query (5.29) that returns the names and Ids of juniors with the highest GPA (previously written without aggregates) can be equivalently written with the use of MAX:

```
SELECT  S.Name, S.StudId
FROM    STUDENT  S
WHERE   S.GPA >= (SELECT  MAX(S1.GPA)                    5.31
                  FROM    STUDENT  S1
                  WHERE   S1.Status = 'Junior')
```

COUNT([DISTINCT] Attr)	Count the number of values in column Attr of the query result. The optional keyword DISTINCT indicates that each value should be counted only once, even if it occurs multiple times in different answer tuples.
SUM([DISTINCT] Attr)	Sum up the values in column Attr. DISTINCT means that each value should contribute to the sum only once, regardless of how often it occurs in column Attr.
AVG([DISTINCT] Attr)	Compute the average of the values in column Attr. Again, DISTINCT means that each value should be used only once.
MAX(Attr)	Compute the maximum value in column Attr. DISTINCT is not used with this function, as it would have no effect.
MIN(Attr)	Compute the minimum value in column Attr. Again, DISTINCT is not used with this function.

FIGURE 5.8 SQL aggregate functions.

The use of DISTINCT in aggregate functions can sometimes make subtle differences in the query semantics. For instance,

```
SELECT   COUNT(P.Name)
FROM     PROFESSOR P
WHERE    P.DeptId = 'MGT'
```
5.32

returns the number of professors in the Management Department. On the other hand,

```
SELECT   COUNT(DISTINCT P.Name)
FROM     PROFESSOR P
WHERE    P.DeptId = 'MGT'
```

returns the number of distinct *names* of professors in that department, which can be different from the number of professors. Similarly,

```
SELECT   AVG(P.Age)
FROM     PROFESSOR P
WHERE    P.DeptId = 'MGT'
```
5.33

returns the average age of professors in the Management Department. However, if we write AVG (DISTINCT P.Age) in the above SELECT clause, the query result is the average value among *distinct* ages—a statistically meaningless number.

Now that you have seen the good things you can do with aggregates, you should also keep in mind the things you cannot do. It makes no sense to mix an aggregate and an attribute in the SELECT list, as in

```
SELECT   COUNT(*), S.Id
FROM     STUDENT S
WHERE    S.Name  = 'JohnDoe'
```
5.34

This is because the aggregate produces a single value that pertains to the entire set of rows corresponding to John Doe, while the attribute S.Id produces a distinct value for each row (in our case there can be several people named John Doe). In some cases, however, such associations can be made meaningful with the help of the GROUP BY construct, to be defined shortly.

While associating aggregates with attributes in the SELECT clause is not normally very useful, having multiple aggregates does make sense. For instance,

```
SELECT   COUNT(*), AVG(P.Age)
FROM     STUDENT S                                     5.35
WHERE    S.Name = 'JohnDoe'
```

counts the number of John Does in the student relation and also computes their average age. One might also be tempted to rewrite statement (5.31) as

```
SELECT   S.Name, S.StudId
FROM     STUDENT  S
WHERE    S.GPA >= (MAX(SELECT  S1.GPA
                       FROM    STUDENT S1
                       WHERE   S1.Status = 'junior'))
```

but do not—it is an invalid construct! Aggregates cannot be applied to the result of a query.

Finally, we note that aggregate functions *cannot* be used in the WHERE clause. The reason for this will become clear in Section 5.2.6 after we explain how SQL evaluates queries that contain aggregate functions.

Aggregation and grouping. By now we know how to count professors in the Management Department. But what if we need this information for *each* department in the university? Of course, we could construct queries similar to (5.32) for each separate department. Each query would be the same, except that MGT in the WHERE condition would be replaced with other department codes. Clearly, this is not a practical solution, as even in a medium-sized enterprise the number of departments can reach several dozen. Furthermore, each time a new department is created, we have to construct a new query, and when departments change their name we have to do tedious maintenance.

A better solution is provided in the form of the GROUP BY clause, which can be included as a component of a SELECT statement. This clause lets the programmer partition a set of rows into groups whose membership is characterized by the fact that all of the rows in a single group agree on the values in some specified subset of columns. The aggregate function is then applied to each group and yields a single row for each such group, as shown in Figure 5.9. For example, if we group the instance of the relation TRANSCRIPT shown in Figure 3.5, page 39, based on the column StudId, five groups result. In any particular group, all rows have the same value in the StudId column but might differ in other columns.

For instance, the following query

```
SELECT     T.StudId, COUNT(*) AS NumCrs,
           AVG(T.Grade) AS CrsAvg
FROM       TRANSCRIPT T
GROUP BY   T.StudId
```

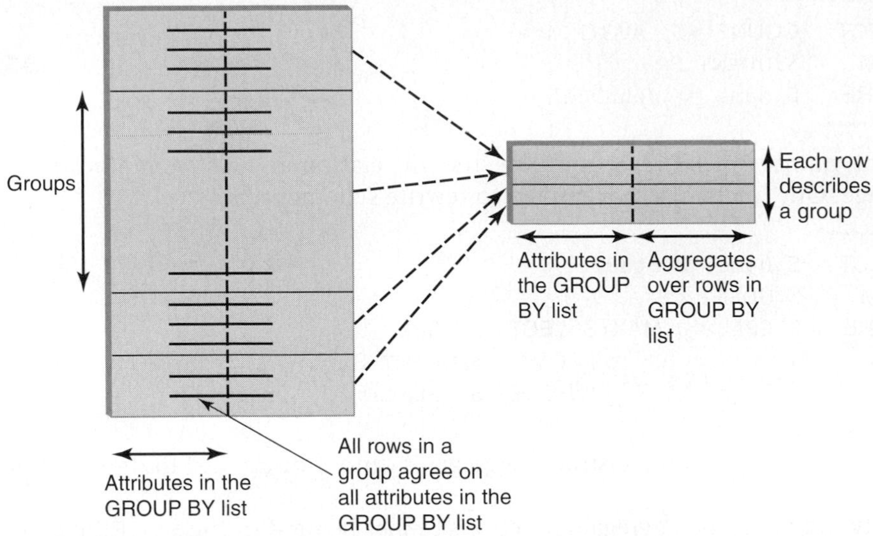

FIGURE 5.9 Effect of the GROUP BY clause.

produces the table

TRANSCRIPT	StudId	NumCrs	CrsAvg
	666666666	3	3.33
	987654321	2	2.5
	123454321	3	3.33
	023456789	2	3.5
	111111111	3	3.33

Here is how to determine the number of professors in each department and (why not?) their average age:

```
SELECT    P.DeptId, COUNT(P.Name) AS DeptSize,
          AVG(P.Age) AS AvgAge
FROM      PROFESSOR P
GROUP BY  P.DeptId
```

The important point to note in these two queries is that each column in the SELECT clause either must be named in the GROUP BY clause or must be the result of an aggregate function. Soon (on page 172) we will see why this is needed.

The HAVING clause. The HAVING clause is used in conjunction with GROUP BY. It lets the programmer specify a condition that restricts which groups (specified in the GROUP BY clause) are to be considered for the final query result. Groups that do not satisfy the condition are removed before the aggregates are applied. Suppose that we wish to know the number of professors and the average ages of professors by department, as in the previous query, but this time only if the department has more than 10 professors. This is accomplished as follows:

```
SELECT    P.DeptId, COUNT(*) AS DeptSize,
          AVG( P.Age) AS AvgAge
FROM      PROFESSOR P
GROUP BY  P.DeptId
HAVING    COUNT(*) > 10
```

The HAVING condition (unlike the WHERE condition) is applied to groups, *not* to individual tuples. So, for each group created by the GROUP BY clause, COUNT(∗) counts the number of tuples. Only the groups where this count exceeds 10 are passed on for further processing. In the end, the aggregate functions are applied to each group to yield a single tuple per group.

Observe that the above queries use AS to give names to columns produced by aggregate functions. Furthermore, ∗ is used with the COUNT function that appears in the HAVING clause. The ∗ is often convenient in conjunction with aggregate functions, and it can be used in both the SELECT list and the HAVING clause. However, it should be noted that, in the above example, there are several alternatives. We can use `P.Name` and even `P.DeptId` instead of ∗ because SQL will not eliminate duplicates without an explicit request (DISTINCT).

If we want to consider candidates for the dean's list on the basis of their grades for the 2003–2004 academic year, we might use

```
SELECT    T.StudId, AVG(T.Grade) AS CrsAvg
FROM      TRANSCRIPT T
WHERE     T.Semester IN ('F2003','S2004')
GROUP BY  T.StudId
HAVING    AVG(T.Grade) > 3.5
```

In general, the HAVING clause is just a syntactic convenience—the same result can always be achieved with the help of nested queries in the FROM clause. For example, the previous query can be replaced with the following query, which does not use HAVING:

```
SELECT   Stats.StudId, Stats.CrsAvg
FROM     (SELECT  T.StudId,
                  AVG(T.Grade) AS CrsAvg
          FROM    TRANSCRIPT T
          WHERE   T.Semester IN ('F2002', 'S2004')
          GROUP BY T.StudId) AS Stats
WHERE    Stats.CrsAvg > 3.5
```

However, the use of nested queries in the FROM clause should be avoided, as such queries are harder to understand and optimize.

The ORDER BY clause. Finally, the order of rows in the query result is generally not specified. If a particular ordering is desired, the ORDER BY clause can be used. For example, if we include the clause

```
ORDER BY CrsAvg
```

in the SELECT statement that produces the dean's list, rows of the query result will be in ascending order of the student's average grade. In general, the clause takes as an argument a list of column names of the query result. Rows are output in sorted order on the basis of the first column named in the list. In the case in which multiple rows have the same value in that column, the second column named in the list is used to decide the ordering, and so forth. For example, if we want to output the candidates for the dean's list ordered primarily by average grade and secondarily by student Id, we might use the following SELECT statement:

```
SELECT    T.StudId, AVG(T.Grade) AS CrsAvg
FROM      TRANSCRIPT T
WHERE     T.Semester IN ('F1997','S1998')
GROUP BY  T.StudId
HAVING    AVG(T.Grade) > 3.5
ORDER BY  CrsAvg, StudId
```

The attributes named in the ORDER BY clause must be the names of columns in the query result. Thus, we refer to the second element as StudId (not T.StudId) in this example since, by default, that is the column name in the query result. Similarly, we cannot order rows primarily by average grade without introducing the column alias CrsAvg in the SELECT clause because without the alias the column has no name.

Ascending order is used by default, but descending order can also be specified. If in the above example we had replaced the ORDER BY clause with

```
ORDER BY DESC CrsAvg, ASC StudId
```

the rows of the query result would have been presented in descending order of average grade and, for students with the same average grade, in ascending order of their Ids.

5.2.6 A Query Evaluation Algorithm for SQL with Aggregates

The overall query evaluation process in the presence of aggregates and grouping is illustrated in Figure 5.10.

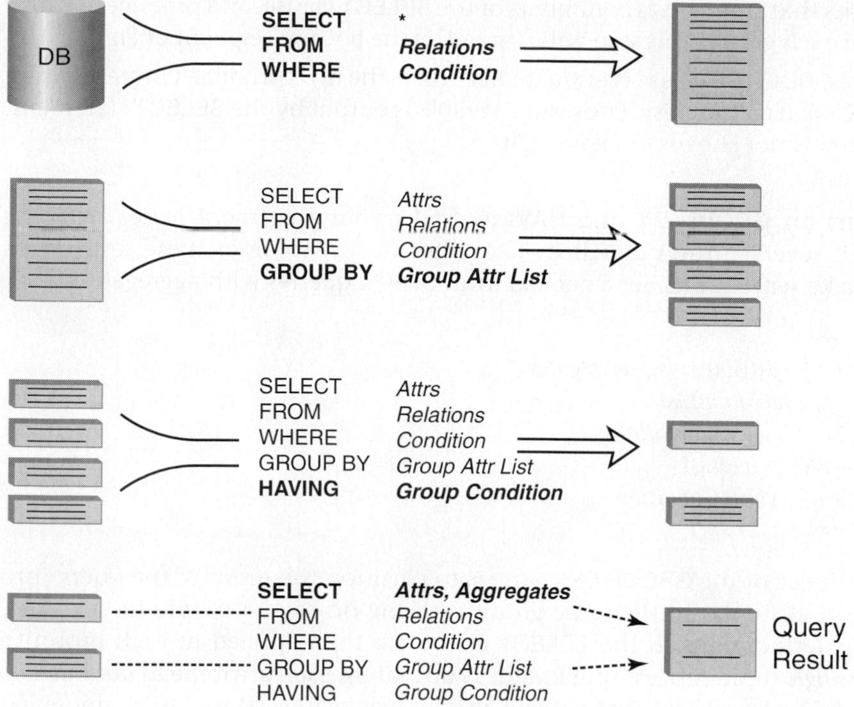

FIGURE 5.10 Query evaluation with aggregate functions.

Step 1. The FROM clause is evaluated. It produces a table that is the Cartesian product of the tables listed as its arguments.

Step 2. The WHERE clause is evaluated. It takes the table produced in step 1 and processes each row individually. Attribute values from the row are substituted for the attribute names in the condition, and the condition is evaluated. The table produced by the WHERE clause contains exactly those rows for which the condition evaluates to true. Note that since the WHERE clause is computed before the aggregate functions, aggregates cannot be used in this clause. Steps 1 and 2 are shown in the top segment of Figure 5.10.

Step 3. The GROUP BY clause is evaluated. It takes the table produced in step 2 and splits it into groups of tuples, where each group consists precisely of those tuples that agree on all attributes of the group attribute list. This step is shown in the second segment of Figure 5.10.

Step 4. The HAVING clause is evaluated. It takes the groups produced in step 3 and eliminates those that fail the group condition. This step is shown in the third segment of Figure 5.10.

Step 5. The SELECT clause is evaluated. It takes the groups produced in step 4, evaluates the aggregate functions in the target list for each group, retains those columns that are listed as arguments of the SELECT clause, and produces a single row for each group. This step is illustrated by the bottom segment of Figure 5.10.

Step 6. The ORDER BY clause is evaluated. It orders the rows produced in step 5 using the specified column list. The resulting table is output by the SELECT statement. This step is not shown in Figure 5.10.

Restrictions on GROUP BY and HAVING. Like your apartment lease, grouping comes with several strings attached. The difference is, some of these restrictions actually make sense! Consider a general form of SQL queries with aggregates:

```
SELECT    attributeList, aggregates
FROM      relationList
WHERE     whereCondition                         5.36
GROUP BY  groupList
HAVING    groupCondition
```

The purpose of the GROUP BY clause is to partition the result of the query into groups, with all tuples in the same group agreeing on each attribute in *groupList*. The aggregate functions in the SELECT clause are then applied to each group to produce a *single* tuple. Since a single value is output for each attribute in *attributeList* in the SELECT clause (and that value is not an aggregate), all tuples in any given group must agree on each attribute in the list. This property is achieved in SQL by requiring that *attributeList* be a subset of *groupList*, which is a sufficient condition to ensure that each group yields a single tuple. (The condition is not necessary but is good enough for most purposes.)

The second restriction concerns the HAVING condition. Intuitively, we need to ensure that *groupCondition* is either true or false for each group of tuples specified in GROUP BY. Generally, this condition consists of a number of comparisons of the form $expr_1$ op $expr_2$, which are tied together by the logical connectives AND, OR, and NOT. For an atomic comparison $expr_1$ op $expr_2$ to make sense, both $expr_1$ and $expr_2$ must evaluate to a single value for each group. In practice, this means that for every attribute mentioned in *groupCondition* either of the following must hold:

1. It is in *groupList* (and thus it has a single value per group).
2. It appears in *groupCondition* as an argument to an aggregate function (thus, the expression sees a single value when the aggregation is computed).

Most DBMSs enforce the above syntactic restrictions.

We should also note that the order of the clauses in (5.36) is important—for instance, the HAVING clause cannot precede the GROUP BY clause. However, the standard allows SQL statements that have the HAVING clause without the GROUP BY clause. In this case, the result of the SELECT-FROM-WHERE part of the query is treated as a single group and *groupCondition* in HAVING is applied to that group.

5.2.7 Join Expressions in the FROM Clause

In SQL terms, the objects that play the role of tables in the FROM clause are called **table expressions**. In most of the examples that we have seen so far, table expressions were simply table names. However, we have also seen that an entire SELECT query can be a table expression. But SQL does not stop there—it allows algebraic expressions to be table expressions as well. These expressions take the form of a join: natural, theta-join, and the three outer joins discussed on page 142. The syntax is as follows (we present only some of the options):

```
table1 [NATURAL] [INNER|FULL|LEFT|RIGHT] JOIN table2 [ON condition]
```

The term INNER refers to the normal join, and FULL, LEFT, and RIGHT refer to the three types of the outer join. The options NATURAL and ON are alternatives. If NATURAL is specified, then the join is performed on the common attributes of both tables; otherwise, the ON *condition* option must be given, where *condition* can be any legal condition in the WHERE clause. More commonly, however, these conditions take the form

```
table1.col1_1 op1 table2.col2_1 AND table1.col1_2 op2 table2.col2_2 AND...
```

where *op1*, *op2*, etc., are the usual comparisons =, >, and so on.

We illustrate this feature with an example of a left outer join, where the query computes the average grade for *every* student in the database. We assume that the grade attribute in the TRANSCRIPT relation is numeric.

```
SELECT    S.Name, AVG(S.Grade)
FROM      (STUDENT LEFT JOIN TRANSCRIPT                          5.37
               ON STUDENT.Id = TRANSCRIPT.StudId) AS S
GROUP BY  S.Id
```

Here students who never took a course will have their tuples padded with NULLs over the Grade attribute. The AVG function ignores NULL values, so the average grade for such students will be 0. Note that a regular join query such as

```
SELECT    S.Name, AVG(T.Grade)
FROM      STUDENT S, TRANSCRIPT T
WHERE     S.Id = T.StudId
GROUP BY  S.Id
```

would be incorrect. In our database, the STUDENT relation has tuples that do not match any record in the TRANSCRIPT relation and, therefore, the above regular join query will miss students who never took any course.

5.2.8 More on Views in SQL

The relations we have discussed up to this point are more technically referred to as **base relations**. They are the "normal" database relations. The contents of a base relation are physically stored on disk and are independent of the contents of other relations in the database.

As we already discussed in Chapter 3, a view is a relation whose contents are usually *not physically stored* in the database. Instead, it is defined as the query result of a SELECT statement. Each time the view is used, its contents are computed using the associated query. Hence, the *definition* of the view, that is, the query that determines the view's contents, is stored (in the system catalog) rather than the contents. Because each view is the result of executing a query, its contents depend on the contents of the base relations at the time the view is referenced.

The role of views in query languages is similar to that of *subroutines* in conventional programming languages. A view usually represents some meaningful query, which is used within several other, frequently asked queries, or it might have an independent interest. In either case, it makes sense to abstract the query and "pretend" that the database contains a relation whose contents precisely coincide with the query result.

Another important use of the view mechanism is to control user access to the data. Access control was discussed in Section 3.3.12; in the context of the views it is discussed later in this section.

Using views in queries. Once a view is defined, it can be used in SQL queries in the same way as any other table. Whenever it is used in a query, its definition is automatically substituted in the FROM clause, as illustrated in Figure 5.11.

Suppose that the university needs to find the department(s) where the average age of professors is the lowest. The application designer might determine that, in addition to the above query, a number of other queries compute the average age. In query processing, as in programming languages, this is a good enough reason to build a view for computing the average age.

FIGURE 5.11 Process of query modification by views.

```
SELECT   ... ... ...                              Query that uses
FROM     VIEW1 V                                  a view, VIEW1
WHERE    ... AND V.Attr = 'abc' AND ...

         becomes

SELECT   ... ... ...                              Query modified by
FROM     (definition of VIEW1) AS V               the view definition
WHERE    ... AND V.Attr = 'abc' AND...
```

```
CREATE VIEW AVGDEPTAGE(Dept,AvgAge) AS
    SELECT      P.DeptId, AVG(P.Age)
    FROM        PROFESSOR P
    GROUP BY    P.DeptId
```

Like a subroutine, this view allows us to solve part of a larger problem separately. For example, we can now find the departments with the minimum average age as follows:

```
SELECT  A.Dept
FROM    AVGDEPTAGE A                                          5.38
WHERE   A.AvgAge =   (SELECT MIN(A.AvgAge)
                      FROM AVGDEPTAGE A )
```

Views can make a complex SQL query easier to understand (and debug!). Consider query (5.28), page 161, which finds all students who have taken a course from each professor in the Department of Computer Science. The query uses two nested subqueries, one of which is correlated with the outer query. Because the issues of nesting and correlation are subtly intertwined, it might be hard to construct the right query the first time.

We can simplify the task with the help of views. The view

```
CREATE VIEW ALLCSPROFIDS(ProfId) AS
    SELECT  P.Id
    FROM    PROFESSOR P
    WHERE   P.DeptId = 'CS'
```

constructs the set of Ids of all computer science professors. Next, we define a view to represent the second correlated subquery of (5.28). This subquery has a target list with only one attribute, `ProfId`, but it also uses a global variable, `S`, which parameterizes the sets of answers returned by the query. Each query execution returns the set of all professors who have taught a particular student. Since SQL does not allow the creation of views parameterized by a global variable, we improvise by including the appropriate attributes in the target list of the view. More precisely, we include those attributes that are actually used in the subquery in conjunction with the global variable. In our case, the global variable is `S` and the additional attribute is `StudId`. The result turns out to be the already familiar view, PROFSTUD, defined in (3.5), page 59.

Unfortunately, we cannot subtract PROFSTUD from ALLCSPROFIDS yet, as they are not UNION-compatible. Furthermore, SQL allows the EXCEPT operator to be applied only to the results of subqueries—we cannot simply subtract one table from another. Therefore, we still must use nested subqueries. However, the subqueries are now much more manageable than in (5.28) since the views enable us to decompose a complex problem into smaller tasks.

```
SELECT   S.Id
FROM     STUDENT S
WHERE
         NOT EXISTS (
              (SELECT P.Id FROM ALLCSPROFIDS P)
              EXCEPT
              (SELECT P.Id FROM PROFSTUD P
               WHERE P.StudId = S.Id))
```

Although the CREATE VIEW statement is quite different from the CREATE TABLE statement used for base relations, the deletion of views and tables from the system catalog uses similar statements: DROP VIEW for views and DROP TABLE for base tables.

What if we want to drop a view or a base table but the database has other views that were defined through this view or this table? The problem here is that dropping such a view or table means that all of the views defined through them will become "abandoned" and there will be no way to use them. In such a case, SQL leaves the decision to the designer of the DROP statement. The general format of the statement is

```
DROP {TABLE | VIEW } table-or-view {RESTRICT | CASCADE}
```

If the RESTRICT option is used, the drop operation fails if some view is dependent on the table or view being dropped. With the CASCADE option, all dependent views are also dropped.

Access control and customization through views. Database views are used not only as a subroutine mechanism but also as a flexible device for controlling access to the data. Thus, we might allow certain users to access a view but not some of the tables that underlie it. For instance, students might not be allowed to query the PROFESSOR relation because of the Social Security information stored there. However, there is nothing wrong with giving students access to the AVGDEPTAGE view defined earlier. Thus, while the access to PROFESSOR might be restricted to administrators, we might let students query the view AVGDEPTAGE:

```
GRANT SELECT ON AVGDEPTAGE TO ALL
```

Note that by using views we can repair a deficiency in the GRANT statement. In granting UPDATE (or INSERT) permission, we are allowed to (optionally) specify a list of columns that can be updated (or into which values can be inserted), but in granting SELECT permission SQL provides no way to specify such a list. We can get the same effect, however, by simply creating a view of accessible columns and granting access to that view instead of to the base table.

The creator (and thus the owner) of a view need not also be the owner of the underlying base relations. All that is required is that the view creator have SELECT privileges on all of the underlying relations. For instance, if the PROFESSOR relation is owned by *Administrator*, who in turn grants the SELECT privilege on PROFESSOR to *Personnel*, *Personnel* can create the view AVGDEPTAGE and later issue the above GRANT statement.

What happens if *Administrator* decides to revoke the SELECT privilege from *Personnel*? Notice that if *Administrator* revokes the privilege, the view becomes "abandoned" and nobody can query it. The actual result depends on how the REVOKE statement is issued. If the administrator uses the RESTRICT option in the REVOKE statement, revocation fails. If the CASCADE option is used, the revocation proceeds *and the view itself is dropped* from the system catalog.

Yet another use of views is customization, which goes hand in hand with access control. A real production database might contain hundreds of relations, each with dozens of attributes. However, most users (both "naive" users and application developers) need to deal with only a small portion of the database schema, the part that is relevant to the particular task performed by the user or the application. There is no benefit in subjecting all users to the tortuous process of learning large parts of the database schema. A better strategy is to create views customized to the various user categories so that, for instance, AVGDEPTAGE can be one of the views customized for the statisticians. The advantages of this approach are threefold:

1. *Ease of use and learning.* This speeds up application development and might prevent bugs that occur as a result of misunderstanding parts of the database schema.
2. *Security.* Various users and applications can be granted access to specific views, thereby reducing the possible damage from human errors and malicious behavior.
3. *Logical data independence* (as discussed in Chapter 3). This benefit can result in huge savings in maintenance costs if later there is a need to change the database schema. Provided that schema reorganization does not lead to loss of information, none of the applications written against the views have to be changed—the only required change is in the view definitions themselves.

5.2.9 Materialized Views

If a view becomes popular with many queries, its contents might be stored in a cache. Cached views are often referred to as **materialized views**. View caching can dramatically improve the response time of queries defined in terms of such views, but update transactions must pay the price. If a view depends on a base relation and a transaction updates the base relation, the view cache might need to be updated as well.

Consider the view PROFSTUD in (3.5), page 59, and suppose that a transaction adds tuple ⟨023456789, CS315, S1997, B⟩ to TRANSCRIPT. This tuple joins with tuple ⟨101202303, CS315, S1997⟩ in TEACHING to produce a view tuple, ⟨101202303, 023456789⟩. But this latter tuple is already in the view (see Figure 3.9, page 60), so this update does not change the view. Had we added ⟨023456789, MGT123, F1997, A⟩

to TRANSCRIPT, the view would have acquired new tuples, ⟨783432188, 023456789⟩ and ⟨009406321, 023456789⟩.

Consider now what might happen when tuples are deleted from the base relations underlying a materialized view. If a transaction deletes tuple ⟨123454321, CS305, S1996, A⟩ from TRANSCRIPT, one might think that tuple ⟨101202303, 123454321⟩ should also be deleted from the view cache. This is not the case, however, because ⟨101202303, 123454321⟩ can still be derived through a join between ⟨123454321, CS315, S1997, A⟩ and ⟨101202303, CS315, S1997⟩. Observe that Figure 3.9 indicates *two* reasons for tuple ⟨101202303, 123454321⟩ to be in the view, and the deletion of ⟨123454321, CS305,S1996, A⟩ removes only one of the reasons! However, if the transaction deleted ⟨123454321, MAT123, S1996, C⟩ from TRANSCRIPT, the tuple ⟨900120450, 123454321⟩ should be removed from the view cache as well.

View cache maintenance is an algorithmically nontrivial task. Of course, a view can be simply recomputed anew each time a base table is changed, but this can be unacceptably expensive, especially if base tables change frequently. A number of algorithms have been proposed, which make it possible to recompute views *incrementally*, that is, by recomputing only those parts of the view that are directly related to the changes in the base tables (refer back to the earlier discussion of the view PROFSTUD). These advanced methods include [Gupta et al. 1993; Mohania et al. 1997; Gupta et al. 1995; Blakeley and Martin 1990; Chaudhuri et al. 1995; Staudt and Jarke 1996; Gupta and Mumick 1995], and more research is still being conducted on the topic. The main difference between the various approaches is how to determine which parts of the view might need to be recomputed (which affects the amount of work involved in a view update) and what type of views a particular method can handle.

Materialized views are especially important in *data warehousing*. A **data warehouse** is an (infrequently updated) database that typically consist of complex materialized views of the data stored in a *separate* production database. Data warehouses are commonly used for online analytical processing (OLAP), which was briefly discussed in Chapter 1. In contrast to most production databases, data warehouses are optimized for querying, not transaction processing, and they are the primary beneficiaries of the advanced query capabilities of SQL discussed in this chapter. (In many transaction processing applications, rapid response time and high throughput requirements preclude the use of the complex queries.)

As materialized views are becoming more and more important, commercial DBMSs are beginning to provide support for such views. Unfortunately, the SQL standard has not yet caught up with the idea, so we will illustrate the SQL extensions for supporting these views using Oracle as an example. Other implementations differ in detail but not substance.

Maintenance of materialized views involves the following main considerations:

- **Build method**. This concerns the time when the view is actually materialized, that is, when its contents are first computed based on the base tables. The build method can be IMMEDIATE or DEFERRED. When the build method is immediate, the view is populated right after the view is created. With the deferred build method, the view is populated using a utility that Oracle specifically provides for this purpose. The user must execute this utility manually.

- **Refresh mode**. This concerns the timing when the view is recomputed. Ideally, each materialized view should be refreshed each time a change is made to the underlying base tables. This refresh mode is known as ON COMMIT. However, if the changes happen frequently while the view access is infrequent, refreshing the view in this mode might consume computational resources for no apparent benefit. The ON DEMAND option allows the user to control when the refresh happens. In this case, the user must explicitly call a special routine to bring the view up to date. Yet another option is to refresh the view periodically (but automatically, without the user intervention). In this case, the user can tell when to perform the first refresh and how often to do it. This mode is especially useful in data warehousing applications where temporal discrepancy between views and the underlying base tables is not critical.
- **Refresh method**. This option tells the system how to refresh the view. One obvious way is to recompute the view from scratch, a COMPLETE refresh. Another possibility is a FAST refresh. This means that the system will try to use one of the advanced methods mentioned earlier, which try to update the view incrementally without recomputing it from scratch. Still, some complex views cannot be refreshed incrementally. If the user has difficulties determining whether a particular view can be refreshed using the FAST method, she can always specify the FORCE method. In this case, the system will try to determine if FAST is possible, and if not, it will use COMPLETE.
- **Query rewriting.** With a regular view, explicit references to the view cause the query to be rewritten to include the definition of the view, as explained in Figure 5.11. When a view is materialized, explicit references use the view cache instead. Using a cache instead of the view definition can have dramatic effects on performance. However, some queries might have been written without the mention of a materialized view even though the query can be equivalently rewritten into one that uses the view. This situation might occur for a number of reasons: the user might not have been aware of the view, the query could have been written before the view was added to the database, or the user might have failed to notice that the view can be used in a particular query. To illustrate the issue, consider the following query, which finds all students (just their Ids) who took a course from John Smyth.

```
SELECT R.StudId
FROM TRANSCRIPT R, TEACHING T, PROFESSOR P
WHERE T.ProfId = P.Id AND P.Name = 'John Smyth' AND
    R.CrsCode = T.CrsCode AND R.Semester = T.Semester
```

Notice that part of the WHERE clause, the condition R.CrsCode = T.CrsCode AND R.Semester = T.Semester, is equivalent to the one used to define the view

PROFSTUD in (3.5), page 59. Therefore, the above query can be rewritten in the following equivalent form:

```
SELECT S.Stud
FROM PROFSTUD S, PROFESSOR P
WHERE S.Prof = P.Id AND P.Name = 'John Smyth'
```

If the view PROFSTUD is materialized, such a rewriting might result in a significant performance gain. The option ENABLE QUERY REWRITE tells the query optimizer that it should try to rewrite queries using materialized views in a way similar to the above example.

Now we are ready to see examples of materialized views defined using Oracle's extensions of SQL.

```
CREATE MATERIALIZED VIEW PROFSTUD(Prof, Stud)
      BUILD IMMEDIATE
      REFRESH FAST ON COMMIT
      ENABLE QUERY REWRITE
AS
SELECT T.ProfId, R.StudId
FROM TRANSCRIPT R, TEACHING T
WHERE R.CrsCode = T.CrsCode AND R.Semester = T.Semester
```

This statement tells the system that the view should be filled in with data immediately and that it should be refreshed using an advanced algorithm for incremental view update. These refreshes should take place each time an update transaction commits changes to the underlying base tables. Finally, the query optimizer is told to attempt query rewriting using this view whenever possible. For the view AVGDEPTAGE, which was discussed in Section 5.2.8, we could choose different options:

```
CREATE MATERIALIZED VIEW AVGDEPTAGE(Dept, AvgAge)
      BUILD DEFERRED
      REFRESH COMPLETE
      START CURRENT_DATE + 1 NEXT CURRENT_DATE + 3
AS
   .
   .
   .
```

Here the view is said to be populated later on, when the user executes an appropriate system utility. View refreshing will be always done from scratch, and the first refresh should take place tomorrow. Subsequent refreshes should be done every other day regardless of the rate of changes to the base tables. No query rewriting should be attempted with this view.

5.2.10 The Null Value Quandary

In Chapter 3, we briefly discussed the concept of a *null value*. For instance, if we take the tuples in the TRANSCRIPT table to stand for courses taken in the past or those being taken in the current semester, some tuples might not have a valid value in the `Grade` attribute. NULL is a placeholder that SQL uses in such a case.

Null values are an unfortunately unavoidable headache in query processing. Indeed, what is the truth value of the condition `T.Grade = 'A'` if the value of `T` is a tuple that has NULL in the `Grade` attribute?

To account for this phenomenon, SQL uses so-called *3-valued logic*, where the truth values are *true*, *false*, and *unknown*, and where val_1 op val_2 (op being <, >, <>, =, etc.) is considered to be *unknown* whenever at least one of the values, val_1 or val_2, is NULL.

Nulls affect not only comparisons in the WHERE and CHECK clauses but also arithmetic expressions and aggregate functions. An arithmetic expression that encounters a NULL is itself evaluated to NULL. COUNT considers NULL to be a regular value (e.g., statement (5.32) on page 166 counts NULL as well as normal values in producing the number of professors in the Management Department). All other aggregates just throw NULLs away (e.g., statement (5.37) on page 173 ignores NULLs when computing the average). The following caveat holds, however: if such an aggregate function is applied to a column that has only NULLs, the result is a NULL.

If all this multitude of exceptions does not seem to be too bad—hang on: some vendors do not follow the standard and, for example, ignore NULL while counting.

Sadly, we have not reached the end of this confusing story. We also must decide what to do when a WHERE or a CHECK clause has the form $cond_1$ AND $cond_2$, $cond_1$ OR $cond_2$, or NOT *cond*, and one of the subconditions evaluates to *unknown* because of a pesky NULL hidden inside the subcondition. This issue is resolved by the truth tables in Figure 5.12, which shows the value of various Boolean functions depending on the values of subconditions.

$cond_1$	$cond_2$	$cond_1$ AND $cond_2$	$cond_1$ OR $cond_2$
true	*true*	*true*	*true*
true	*false*	*false*	*true*
true	*unknown*	*unknown*	*true*
false	*true*	*false*	*true*
false	*false*	*false*	*false*
false	*unknown*	*false*	*unknown*
unknown	*true*	*unknown*	*true*
unknown	*false*	*false*	*unknown*
unknown	*unknown*	*unknown*	*unknown*

cond	NOT *cond*
true	*false*
false	*true*
unknown	*unknown*

FIGURE 5.12 SQL's truth tables used to deal with the unknown.

If these tables seem bewildering, they should not be. The idea is very simple. Suppose that we need to compute the value of *true* AND *unknown*. Because *unknown* might turn out to be either *true* or *false*, the value of the entire expression can also be either *true* or *false* (that is, *unknown*). On the other hand, the expressions *false* AND *unknown* and *true* OR *unknown* evaluate to *false* and *true*, respectively, regardless of whether *unknown* turns out to be *true* or *false*. The table for NOT can be explained away similarly.

SQL introduces one additional predicate, IS NULL, which is specifically designed to test if some value is NULL. For instance, `T.Grade` IS NULL is true whenever the tuple assigned to `T` has a null value in the `Grade` attribute; it evaluates to false otherwise. Interestingly, this is the only true 2-valued predicate in SQL!

So what happens when the entire condition evaluates to *unknown*? The answer depends on whether this is a WHERE or a CHECK clause. If a WHERE clause evaluates to *unknown*, it is treated as *false* and the corresponding tuple is not added to the query answer. If a CHECK clause evaluates to *unknown*, the integrity constraint is considered to be observed (i.e., the result is treated as *true*). The difference in the way the unknown values are treated in queries and constraints can be given a rational explanation. It is assumed that the user expects the queries to return only the answers that are definitely *true*. On the other hand, a constraint of the form CHECK (*condition*) is viewed as a statement that the condition should *not* evaluate to *false*. Thus, the *unknown* truth value is considered acceptable.

We have presented only the general framework behind null values in SQL. Some details have been left out but can be found in most standard SQL references, such as [Date and Darwen 1997]. For instance, what is the impact of nulls on the LIKE condition, the IN condition, set comparisons (such as > ALL), the EXISTS feature, duplicate elimination (i.e., queries that use DISTINCT), and the like? Think of what might be reasonable in these cases and then compare your conclusions with those of [Date and Darwen 1997].

5.3 Modifying Relation Instances in SQL

So far we have been discussing the query sublanguage—by far the hardest part of SQL. However, databases exist not only for querying but also for entering and modifying the appropriate data. This section deals with the part of SQL that is used for data insertion, deletion, and modification.

5.3.1 Inserting Data

The INSERT statement has several forms, in the simplest of which the programmer specifies just the tuple to be inserted. The second version of this statement can insert multiple tuples and uses a query to tell which tuples to insert. To insert a single tuple, the programmer simply writes

```
INSERT INTO   PROFESSOR(DeptId,Id,Name)
VALUES ('MATH','100100100','Bob Parker')
```

The order of the attributes listed in the INTO clause need not correspond to the *default* order (i.e., the order in which they were listed in the CREATE TABLE statement). However, if you know the default attribute order, you can omit the attribute list in the INTO clause. Of course, the order of items in the VALUE clause must then correspond to the default attribute order. Despite the potential time-saving, omitting the attribute list in the INTO clause is error prone and is thus viewed as poor programming style (e.g., consider what might happen if the schema is later changed).

The second form of the INSERT statement enables bulk insertion of tuples into relations. The tuples to be inserted are the result of a query in the INSERT statement. Note that, even though a query is used to define the tuples to be inserted into a relation, this mechanism is fundamentally different from defining views via queries.

As an example, let us insert some tuples into a relation called HARDCLASS. A hard class[7] is one that is failed by more than 10% of the students. The attributes in HARDCLASS are course code, semester, and failure rate.

This query is actually quite complicated because expressing the failure rate in SQL requires some thought. We will tackle this query in steps and first define two views.

```
--Number of failures per class
CREATE VIEW CLASSFAILURES(CrsCode, Semester, Failed) AS
    SELECT    T.CrsCode, T.Semester, COUNT(*)
    FROM      TRANSCRIPT T
    WHERE     T.Grade = 'F'
    GROUP BY  T.CrsCode, T.Semester
```

Similarly, we can define the view CLASSENROLLMENT, which counts the number of students enrolled in each course.

```
--Number of enrolled students per class
CREATE VIEW CLASSENROLLMENT(CrsCode, Semester, Enrolled) AS
    SELECT    T.CrsCode, T.Semester, COUNT(*)
    FROM      TRANSCRIPT T
    GROUP BY  T.CrsCode, T.Semester
```

Now, HARDCLASS can be populated with tuples as follows:

```
INSERT INTO HARDCLASS(CrsCode, Semester, FailRate)
     SELECT   F.CrsCode, F.Semester, F.Failed/E.Enrolled          5.39
     FROM     CLASSFAILURES F, CLASSENROLLMENT E
     WHERE    F.CrsCode = E.CrsCode AND F.Semester = E.Semester
                   AND (F.Failed/E.Enrolled) > 0.1
```

[7] By "class" we mean a particular course offering in a given semester.

The final query looks simple, but imagine how complex it would have been if not for the views!

There are a few more subtleties we must mention. First, if an INSERT statement inserts a tuple that violates some integrity constraint, the entire operation is aborted and no tuple is inserted (assuming that constraint checking has not been DEFERRED, as will be described in Section 8.3).

Second, it is possible to omit a value in the list of values in the VALUE clause (and the corresponding attribute in the attribute list) and an attribute in the SELECT clause if the CREATE TABLE statement does not specify NOT NULL. If the CREATE TABLE statement specifies a default for the missing attribute, that default value is used. Instead of omitting values, a better style is to use the more informative keywords DEFAULT or NULL (whichever is appropriate) in place of the missing values (e.g., (100100100, NULL, DEFAULT)).

5.3.2 Deleting Data

Deletion of tuples is analogous to the second form of INSERT, except that now the keyword DELETE is used. For example, to delete the hard classes taught in the fall and spring of 2003 we use

```
DELETE FROM HARDCLASS
WHERE Semester IN ('S2003','F2003')
```

Note that the DELETE statement does not allow the use of tuple variables in the FROM clause.

Suppose that in order to improve teaching standards, the university decides to fire all professors with an excessively high failure rate in one of the courses. This turns out to be difficult (and not because of tenure!). The DELETE statement has a very limited form of the FROM clause. The programmer can specify just one relation, the one whose tuples are to be deleted. (What would it mean to delete rows from the Cartesian product of two relations?) However, in order to find out who to fire we need to look inside the HARDCLASS relation, but there is no room for this relation in the FROM clause. So what are we to do? Use nested subqueries!

```
DELETE FROM PROFESSOR
WHERE Id IN
        (SELECT  T.ProfId
         FROM    TEACHING T, HARDCLASS H                          5.40
         WHERE   T.CrsCode = H.CrsCode
                 AND T.Semester = H.Semester
                 AND H.FailRate > 0.5)
```

5.3.3 Updating Existing Data

Sometimes it is necessary to change the values of some attributes of existing tuples in a relation. For instance, the following statement changes the grade of student 666666666 for course EE101 from B to A:

```
UPDATE   TRANSCRIPT
SET      Grade ='A'
WHERE    StudId ='666666666' AND CrsCode = 'EE101'
```

Observe that, like DELETE, the UPDATE statement does not allow tuple variables and it uses only a limited form of the FROM clause (more precisely, UPDATE itself is a kind of FROM clause). As a result, some of the more complex updates require the use of nested subqueries. For instance, if instead of firing them we decide to transfer all poorly performing professors to administration, we use a subquery similar to the one in (5.40).

```
UPDATE   PROFESSOR
SET      DeptId = 'Adm'
WHERE    Id IN
           (SELECT T.ProfId
            FROM TEACHING T, HARDCLASS H                        5.41
            WHERE T.CrsCode = H.CrsCode
                  AND T.Semester = H.Semester
                  AND  H.FailRate > 0.5)
```

And, yes, here is our favorite again: *Raise the salary of all administrators by 10%*:

```
UPDATE   EMPLOYEE
SET      Salary = Salary * 1.1
WHERE    Department = 'Adm'
```

5.3.4 Updates on Views

Because views are often used as a customization device that shields users and programmers from the complexities of the conceptual database schema, it is only natural to let programmers update their views. Unfortunately, this is easier said than done because of the following three problems:

1. Suppose that we have a simple view over TRANSCRIPT—a projection on the attributes CrsCode, StudId, and Semester. If the programmer wants to insert a new tuple in such a view, the value for the Grade attribute will be missing. This problem is not serious. We can pad the missing attributes with null values if the CREATE TABLE statement for the underlying base relation permits this; if it does not, the insertion command can be rejected.

2. Consider a view, CSPROF, over the PROFESSOR relation, which is obtained by a simple selection on DeptId = 'CS'. Suppose that the programmer inserts ⟨121232343, 'Paul Schmidt','EE'⟩. If we propagate this insertion to the underlying base relation (i.e., PROFESSOR), we can observe the anomaly that querying the view *after* the insertion does not show any traces of the tuple we just inserted! Indeed, Paul Schmidt is not a CS professor, so he does not appear in the view defined through the selection DeptId = 'CS'!

   By default, SQL does not forbid such anomalies, but a careful database designer might include the clause WITH CHECK OPTION to ensure that the newly inserted or updated tuples in a view do, indeed, satisfy the view definition. In our example, we can write

```
CREATE VIEW CSPROF(Id,Name,DeptId) AS
    SELECT  P.Id, P.Name, P.DeptId
    FROM    PROFESSOR P
    WHERE   P.DeptId = 'CS'
    WITH CHECK OPTION
```

3. The following problem is much more involved. It turns out that some view updates might have several possible translations into the updates of the underlying base relations. This is potentially a very serious problem because the possibilities arising from a single view update might have drastically different consequences with respect to the underlying stored data.

   To illustrate this problem, consider the view PROFSTUD, discussed earlier.

```
CREATE VIEW PROFSTUD(ProfId,StudId) AS
    SELECT  T.ProfId, R.StudId
    FROM    TEACHING T, TRANSCRIPT R
    WHERE   T.CrsCode = R.CrsCode
                AND T.Semester = R.Semester
```

The contents of this view were depicted in Figure 3.9 on page 60. Suppose that we now decide to delete the tuple ⟨101202303, 123454321⟩ from that view. How should this update be propagated back to the base relations? There are four possibilities:

1. Delete ⟨101202303, CS315, S1997⟩ and ⟨101202303, CS305, S1996⟩ from the relation TEACHING.
2. Delete ⟨123454321, CS315, S1997, A⟩ and ⟨123454321, CS305, S1996, A⟩ from the relation TRANSCRIPT.
3. Delete ⟨101202303, CS315, S1997⟩ from TEACHING and ⟨123454321, CS305, S1996, A⟩ from TRANSCRIPT.
4. Delete ⟨101202303, CS305, S1996⟩ from TEACHING and ⟨123454321, CS315, S1997, A⟩ from TRANSCRIPT.

For each of these possibilities, the join implied by the view does not contain the tuple ⟨101202303, 123454321⟩. The only problem is, Which possibility should be used for the view update?

This example shows that, in the absence of additional information, it might not be possible to translate view updates into the updates of the underlying base relations uniquely. Much work has been done on defining heuristics aimed at disambiguating view updates, but none has emerged as an acceptable solution. SQL takes a simpleminded approach by defining only a very restricted class of views as updatable. The essence of these restrictions on the view definition is summarized here:

1. Exactly one table can be mentioned in the FROM clause (and only once). The FROM clause cannot have nested subqueries.
2. Aggregates, GROUP BY, or HAVING clauses and set operations, such as UNION and EXCEPT, are not allowed.
3. Nested subqueries in the WHERE clause of the view cannot refer to the (unique) table used in the FROM clause of the view definition. Moreover, a nested subquery cannot refer to this table, either explicitly, in the FROM clause, or implicitly, through a tuple variable defined in the outer query.
4. No expressions and no DISTINCT keyword in the SELECT clause are allowed.

Views satisfying these conditions (and some other rather obscure restrictions) are called **updatable** (in the SQL sense). Here is an example of an updatable view.

```
CREATE VIEW CanTeach(Professor, Course)
    SELECT   T.ProfId, T.CrsCode
    FROM     Teaching  T
```

Referring to the database of Figure 3.5, page 39, suppose that we delete ⟨09406321, MGT123⟩ from the view CanTeach. There are two tuples in the underlying base relation (Teaching) that give rise to the view tuple in question: ⟨09406321,MGT123, F1994⟩ and ⟨09406321, MGT123,F1997⟩. The translation of the view update into an update of Teaching must therefore delete both of these tuples.

BIBLIOGRAPHIC NOTES

Relational algebra was introduced in Codd's seminal papers [Codd 1972, 1970]. SQL was developed by IBM's System R research group [Astrahan et al. 1981]. [Melton and Simon 1992; Date and Darwen 1997] are references to SQL-92, and [Gulutzan and Pelzer 1999] describe the extensions provided in SQL:1999.

The view update problem received considerable attention in the past. The following is a partial list of works that propose various solutions: [Bancilhon and Spyratos 1981; Masunaga 1984; Cosmadakis and Papadimitriou 1983; Gottlob et al. 1988; Keller 1985; Langerak 1990; Chen et al. 1995]. The maintenance problem for materialized views has also been an active research area [Gupta et al. 1993; Mohania et al. 1997; Gupta et al. 1995; Blakeley and Martin 1990; Chaudhuri et al. 1995; Staudt and Jarke 1996; Gupta and Mumick 1995]. More research is being conducted because of the importance of materialized views in data warehousing.

EXERCISES

5.1 Assume that **R** and **S** are relations containing n_R and n_S tuples, respectively. What is the maximum and minimum number of tuples that can possibly be in the result of each of the following expressions (assuming appropriate union compatibilities)?

a. $\mathbf{R} \cup \mathbf{S}$
b. $\mathbf{R} \cap \mathbf{S}$
c. $\mathbf{R} - \mathbf{S}$
d. $\mathbf{R} \times \mathbf{S}$
e. $\mathbf{R} \bowtie \mathbf{S}$
f. $\mathbf{R} / \mathbf{S}$
g. $\sigma_{s=4}(\mathbf{R}) \times \pi_{s,t}(\mathbf{S})$

5.2 Assume that **R** and **S** are tables representing the relations of the previous exercise. Design SQL queries that will return the results of each of the expressions of that exercise.

5.3 Verify that the Cartesian product is an associative operator—that is,

$$\mathbf{r} \times (\mathbf{s} \times \mathbf{t}) = (\mathbf{r} \times \mathbf{s}) \times \mathbf{t}$$

for all relations **r**, **s**, and **t**.

5.4 Verify that selections commute—that is, for any relation **r** and any pair of selection conditions $cond_1$ and $cond_2$, $\sigma_{cond_1}(\sigma_{cond_2}(\mathbf{r})) = \sigma_{cond_2}(\sigma_{cond_1}(\mathbf{r}))$.

5.5 Verify that, for any pair of relations **r** and **s**, $\sigma_{cond}(\mathbf{r} \times \mathbf{s}) = \mathbf{r} \times \sigma_{cond}(\mathbf{s})$ if the selection condition *cond* involves *only* the attributes mentioned in the schema of relation **s**.

5.6 Prove that, if **r** and **s** are union-compatible, then $\mathbf{r} \cap \mathbf{s} = \mathbf{r} \bowtie \mathbf{s}$.

5.7 Using division, write a relational algebra expression that produces all students who have taken all courses offered in every semester (this implies that they might have taken the same course twice).

5.8 Using division, write a relational algebra expression that produces all students who have taken all courses that have been offered. (If a course has been offered more than once, they have to have taken it at least once.)

5.9 Construct a relational algebra query that produces the same result as the outer join $\mathbf{r} \bowtie^{outer}_{cond} \mathbf{s}$ using only these operators: union, difference, Cartesian product, projection, general join (not outer join). You can also use constant relations, that is, relations with fixed content (e.g., one that has tuples filled with nulls or other predefined constants).

5.10 Express each of the following queries in (*i*) relational algebra and (*ii*) SQL using the Student Registration System schema of Figure 3.4.

a. List all courses that are taught by professors who belong to the `EE` or `MGT` departments.

b. List the names of all students who took courses *both* in spring 1997 and fall 1998.

c. List the names of all students who took courses from at least two professors in different departments.

d. List all courses that are offered by the MGT Department and that have been taken by all students.

*e. Find every department that has a professor who taught all courses ever offered by that department.

5.11 Use the relational algebra to find the list of all "problematic" classes (i.e., course-semester pairs) where the failure rate is higher than 20%. (Assume, for simplicity, that grades are numbers between 1 and 4, and that a failing grade is anything less than 2.)

Because the relational algebra does not have aggregate operators, we must add them to be able to solve the above problem. The additional operator you should use is $count_{A/B}(\mathbf{r})$.

The meaning of this operator is as follows: A and B must be lists of attributes in $\mathbf{r}$. The *schema* of $count_{A/B}(\mathbf{r})$ consists of all attributes in B plus one additional attribute, which represents the counted value. The *contents* of $count_{A/B}(\mathbf{r})$ are defined as follows: for each tuple, $t \in \pi_B(\mathbf{r})$ (the projection on B), take $\pi_A(\sigma_{B=t}(\mathbf{r}))$ and count the number of tuples in the resulting relation (where $\sigma_{B=t}(\mathbf{r})$ stands for the set of all tuples in $\mathbf{r}$ whose value on the attributes in B is t). Let us denote this number by $c(t)$. Then the relation $count_{A/B}(\mathbf{r})$ is defined as $\{< t, c(t) > \mid t \in \pi_B(\mathbf{r})\}$.

You should be able to recognize the above construction as a straightforward adaptation of GROUP BY of SQL to the relational algebra.

5.12 State the English meaning of the following algebraic expressions (some of these queries are likely to yield empty results in a typical university, but this is beside the point):

a. $\pi_{\texttt{CrsCode,Semester}}(\text{TRANSCRIPT}) / \pi_{\texttt{CrsCode}}(\text{TRANSCRIPT})$

b. $\pi_{\texttt{CrsCode,Semester}}(\text{TRANSCRIPT}) / \pi_{\texttt{Semester}}(\text{TRANSCRIPT})$

c. $\pi_{\texttt{CrsCode,StudId}}(\text{TRANSCRIPT}) / (\pi_{\texttt{Id}}(\text{STUDENT}))[\texttt{StudId}]$

d. $\pi_{\texttt{CrsCode,Semester,StudId}}(\text{TRANSCRIPT}) / (\pi_{\texttt{Id}}(\text{STUDENT}))[\texttt{StudId}]$

5.13 Consider the following query:

```
SELECT  S.Name
FROM    STUDENT S, TRANSCRIPT T
WHERE   S.Id = T.StudId
        AND T.CrsCode IN ('CS305','CS315')
```

What does this query mean (express the meaning in one short English sentence)? Write an equivalent SQL query without using the IN operator and the set construct.

5.14 Explain the conceptual difference between views and bulk insertion of tuples into base relations using the INSERT statement with an attached query.

5.15 Explain why a view is like a subroutine.

5.16 Write query (5.38) on page 175 without the use of the views.

5.17 Express the following queries using SQL. Assume that the STUDENT table is augmented with an additional attribute, Age, and that the PROFESSOR table has additional attributes, Age and Salary.

a. Find the average age of students who received an A for *some* course.
b. Find the minimum age among straight A students *per course*.
c. Find the minimum age among straight A students per course among the students who have taken CS305 or MAT123. (Hint: a HAVING clause might help.)
d. Raise by 10% the salary of every professor who is now younger than 40 and who taught MAT123 in the spring 1997 or fall 1997 semester. (*Hint*: Try a nested subquery in the WHERE clause of the UPDATE statement.)
e. Find the professors whose salaries are at least 10% higher than the average salary of all professors. (*Hint*: Use views, as in the HARDCLASS example (5.39), page 183.)
f. Find all professors whose salaries are at least 10% higher than the average salary of all professors *in their departments*. (*Hint*: Use views, as in (5.39).)

5.18 Express the following queries in relational algebra.

a. (5.16), page 154
b. (5.20), page 156
c. (5.23), page 158

5.19 Write an equivalent expression in relational algebra for the following SQL query:

```
SELECT   P.Name, C.Name
FROM     PROFESSOR P, COURSE C, TAUGHT T
WHERE    P.Id = T.ProfId AND T.Semester = 'S2002'
              AND T.CrsCode = C.CrsCode
```

5.20 Consider the following schema:

```
TRANSCRIPT(StudId, CrsCode, Semester, Grade)
TEACHING(ProfId, CrsCode, Semester)
PROFESSOR(Id, ProfName, Dept)
```

Write the following query in relational algebra and in SQL: *Find all student Ids who have taken a course from* each *professor in the* MUS *Department*.

5.21 Define the above query as an SQL view and then use this view to answer the following query: *For each student who has taken a course from every professor in the* MUS *Department, show the number of courses taken, provided that this number is more than* 10.

5.22 Consider the following schema:

```
BROKER(Id, Name)    ACCOUNT(Acct#, BrokerId, Gain)
```

Write the following query in relational algebra and in SQL: *Find the names of all brokers who have made money in all accounts assigned to them (i.e.,* Gain > 0).

5.23 Write an SQL statement (for the database schema given in Exercise 5.22) to fire all brokers who lost money in at least 40% of their accounts. Assume that every broker has at least one account. (*Hint*: Define intermediate views to facilitate formulation of the query.)

5.24 Consider the following schema that represents houses for sale and customers who are looking to buy:

```
CUSTOMER(Id, Name, Address)
PREFERENCE(CustId, Feature)
AGENT(Id, AgentName)
HOUSE(Address, OwnerId, AgentId)
AMENITY(Address, Feature)
```

PREFERENCE is a relation that lists all features requested by the customers (one tuple per customer/feature; e.g., ⟨123, '5BR'⟩, ⟨123,'2BATH'⟩, ⟨432,'pool'⟩), and AMENITY is a relation that lists all features of each house (one tuple per house/feature).

A customer is *interested* in buying a house if the set of all features specified by the customer is a subset of the amenities the house has. A tuple in the HOUSE relation states who is the owner and who is the real estate agent listing the house. Write the following queries in SQL:

a. Find all customers who are interested in every house listed with the agent with Id 007.

b. Using the previous query as a view, retrieve a set of tuples of the form ⟨*feature*, *number_of_customers*⟩, where each tuple in the result shows a feature and the number of customers who want this feature such that
   - Only the customers who are interested in every house listed with Agent 007 are considered.
   - The number of customers interested in *feature* is greater than three. (If this number is not greater than three, the corresponding tuple ⟨*feature*, *number_of_customers*⟩ is not added to the result.)

5.25 Consider the schema PERSON(Id, Name, Age). Write an SQL query that finds the 100th oldest person in the relation. A 100th oldest person is one such that there are 99 people who are strictly older. (There can be several such people who might have the same age, or there can be none.)

5.26 The last section of this chapter presented four main rules that characterize updatable views in SQL. The third rule states that if the WHERE clause contains a nested subquery, none of the tables mentioned in that subquery (explicitly or implicitly) can be the table used in the FROM clause of the view definition.

Construct a view that violates condition 3 but satisfies conditions 1, 2, and 4 for updatability, such that there is an update to this view that has two different translations into the updates on the underlying base relation.

5.27 Using the relations TEACHING and PROFESSOR, create a view of TRANSCRIPT containing only rows corresponding to classes taught by John Smyth. Can this view be used in a GRANT statement whose purpose is to allow Smyth to update student grades, but only those he has assigned? Explain.

6

Database Design with the Relational Normalization Theory

Conceptual modeling using the E-R or UML approach is a good way to start dealing with the complexity of modeling a real-world enterprise. However, conceptual modeling is only a set of guidelines that requires considerable expertise and intuition to use successfully, and it can lead to several alternative designs for the same enterprise. Unfortunately, E-R and UML do not provide the criteria or tools to help evaluate alternative designs and suggest improvements. In this chapter, we present the **relational normalization theory**, which includes a set of concepts and algorithms that can help with the evaluation and refinement of the designs obtained through conceptual modeling.

The main tool used in normalization theory is the notion of *functional dependency* (and, to a lesser degree, *join dependency*). Functional dependency is a generalization of the key dependencies in the E-R and UML approaches whereas join dependency does not have a counterpart. Both types of dependency are used by designers to spot situations in which conceptual modeling unnaturally places attributes of two distinct entity types into the same relation schema. These situations are characterized in terms of *normal forms*, from which comes the term "normalization theory." Normalization theory forces relations into an appropriate normal form using *decompositions*, which break up schemas involving unhappy unions of attributes of unrelated entity types. Because of the central role that decompositions play in relational design, the techniques that we are about to discuss are sometimes also called **relational decomposition theory**.

6.1 The Problem of Redundancy

The best way to understand the potential problems with relational designs based on the E-R or UML approach is through an example. Consider the CREATE TABLE PERSON statement (4.1) on page 87. Recall that this relation schema was obtained by direct translation from the E-R diagram in Figure 4.1. The first indication of something wrong with this translation was the realization that SSN is not a key of the resulting PERSON relation. Instead, the key is a combination (SSN, Hobby). In other words, the attribute SSN does not uniquely identify the tuples in the PERSON relation even though it does uniquely identify the entities in the PERSON entity set.

Not only is this counterintuitive, but it also has a number of undesirable effects on the instances of the PERSON relation schema.

To see this, we take a closer look at the relation instance shown in Figure 4.13, page 86. Notice that John Doe and Mary Doe are both represented by multiple tuples and that their addresses, names, and Ids occur multiple times as well. Redundant storage of the same information is apparent here. However, wasted space is the least of the problems. The real issue is that when database updates occur, we must keep all the redundant copies of the same data consistent with each other, and we must do it efficiently. Specifically, we can identify the following problems:

- ***Update anomaly.*** If John Doe moves to 1 Hill Top Drive, updating the relation in Figure 4.13 requires changing the address in both tuples that describe the John Doe entity.
- ***Insertion anomaly.*** Suppose that we decide to add Homer Simpson to the PERSON relation, but Homer's information sheet does not specify any hobbies. One way around this problem might be to add the tuple ⟨`023456789, Homer Simpson, Fox 5 TV, NULL`⟩—that is, to fill in the missing field with `NULL`. However, `Hobby` is part of the primary key, and SQL does not allow null values in primary keys. Why? For one thing, DBMSs generally maintain an index on the primary key, and it is not clear how the index should refer to the null value. Assuming that this problem can be solved, suppose that a request is made to insert ⟨`023456789, Homer Simpson, Fox 5 TV, acting`⟩. Should this new tuple just be added, or should it replace the existing tuple ⟨`023456789, Homer Simpson, Fox 5 TV, NULL`⟩? A human will most likely choose to replace it, because humans do not normally think of hobbies as a defining characteristic of a person. However, how does a computer know that the tuples with primary key ⟨`111111111, NULL`⟩ and ⟨`111111111, acting`⟩ refer to the same entity? (Recall that the information about which tuple came from which entity is lost in the translation!) Redundancy is at the root of this ambiguity. If Homer were described by at most one tuple, only one course of action would be possible.
- ***Deletion anomaly.*** Suppose that Homer Simpson is no longer interested in acting. How are we to delete this hobby? We can, of course, delete the tuple that talks about Homer's acting hobby. However, since there is only one tuple that refers to Homer (see Figure 4.13), this throws out perfectly good information about Homer's Id and address. To avoid this loss of information, we can try to replace `acting` with `NULL`. Unfortunately, this again raises the issue of nulls in primary key attributes. Once again, redundancy is the culprit. If only one tuple could possibly describe Homer, the attribute `Hobby` would not be part of the key.

For convenience, we sometimes use the term "update anomalies" to refer to all of the above anomaly types.

6.2 Decompositions

The problems caused by redundancy—wasted storage and anomalies—can be fixed using the following simple technique. Instead of having one relation describe all that is known about persons, we can use two separate relation schemas.

```
PERSON1(SSN, Name, Address)
HOBBY(SSN, Hobby)
```
6.1

Projecting the relation in Figure 4.13 on each of these schemas yields the result shown in Figure 6.1. The new design has the following important properties:

1. Assuming for the moment that everyone has hobbies, the original relation of Figure 4.13 is exactly the natural join of the two relations in Figure 6.1. In fact, one can prove that this property is not an artifact of our particular choice of relation instances—if SSN uniquely determines the name and address of a person, then *every* relation, **r**, over the schema of Figure 4.13 equals the natural join of the projections of **r** on PERSON1 and HOBBY. This property, called *losslessness,* will be discussed in Section 6.6.1. This means that our decomposition preserves the original information represented by the PERSON relation.
2. We no longer have to accept the unnatural result that the Hobby attribute is part of a key. SSN is now the key of both relations. Whereas we could not describe people with no hobbies in PERSON, it is now not even necessary to use nulls for this purpose: we simply do not include rows for such people in the relation HOBBY. Thus, the removal of Bart Simpson's hobbies from the database does not delete the information about his address. The natural join of PERSON1 and HOBBY is no longer PERSON, but then we should not expect this to be the case since we are now describing a more diverse group of people.

SSN	Name	Address
111111111	John Doe	123 Main St.
555666777	Mary Doe	7 Lake Dr.
987654321	Bart Simpson	Fox 5 TV

(a) PERSON1

SSN	Hobby
111111111	stamps
111111111	hiking
111111111	coins
555666777	hiking
555666777	skating
987654321	acting

(b) HOBBY

FIGURE 6.1 Decomposition of the PERSON relation shown in Figure 4.13.

SSN
111111111
555666777
987654321

Name
John Doe
Mary Doe
Bart Simpson

Address
123 Main St.
7 Lake Dr.
Fox 5 TV

Hobby
stamps
hiking
coins
skating
acting

FIGURE 6.2 The "ultimate" decomposition.

3. The redundancy present in the original relation of Figure 4.13 is gone and so are the update anomalies. The only items that are stored more than once are SSNs, which are identifiers of entities of type PERSON. Thus, changes to addresses, names, or hobbies now affect only a single tuple. The insertion anomaly is also gone because we can now add people and hobbies independently.

Observe that the new design still has a certain amount of redundancy and that we might still need to use null values in certain cases. First, since we use SSNs as tuple identifiers, each SSN can occur multiple times and all of these occurrences must be kept consistent across the database. So consistency maintenance has not been eliminated completely. However, if the identifiers are not dynamic (for instance, SSNs do not change frequently), consistency maintenance is considerably simplified. Second, imagine a situation in which we add a person to our PERSON1 relation and the address is not known. Clearly, even with the new design, we have to insert `NULL` in the `Address` field for the corresponding tuple. However, `Address` is not part of a primary key, so the use of `NULL` here is not that bad (we will still have difficulties joining PERSON1 on the `Address` attribute, though).

It is important to realize that not all decompositions are created equal. In fact, most of them do not make any sense even though they might be doing a good job at eliminating redundancy. The decomposition

```
SSN(SSN)
NAME(Name)
ADDRESS(Address)                                    6.2
HOBBY(Hobby)
```

is the ultimate "redundancy eliminator." Projecting of the relation of Figure 4.13 on these schemas yields a database where each value appears exactly once, as shown in Figure 6.2. Unfortunately, this new database is completely devoid of any useful information; for instance, it is no longer possible to tell where John Doe lives or who collects stamps as a hobby. This situation is in sharp contrast with the decomposition of Figure 6.1, where we were able to completely restore the information represented by the original relation using a natural join.

The need for schema refinement. Translation of the PERSON entity type into the relational model indicates that one cannot rely solely on conceptual modeling for designing database schemas. Furthermore, the problems exhibited by the PERSON example are by no means rare or unique. Consider the relationship HASACCOUNT of Figure 4.30. A typical translation of the relationship HASACCOUNT of Figure 4.30, page 108, into the relational model might be

```
CREATE TABLE HASACCOUNT (
AccountNumber INTEGER NOT NULL,
ClientId      CHAR(20),
OfficeId      INTEGER,
PRIMARY KEY (ClientId, OfficeId),
FOREIGN KEY (OfficeId) REFERENCES OFFICE
... ... ... )
```

Recall that a client can have at most one account in an office, and hence (ClientId, OfficeId) is a key. Also, an account must be assigned to exactly one office. Careful analysis shows that this requirement leads to some of the same problems that we saw in the PERSON example. For example, a tuple that records the fact that a particular account is managed by a particular office cannot be added without also recording client information (since ClientId is part of the primary key), which is an insertion anomaly. This (and the dual deletion anomaly) is perhaps not a serious problem, because of the specifics of this particular application, but the update anomaly could present maintenance issues. Moving an account from one office to another involves changing OfficeId in every tuple corresponding to that account. If the account has multiple clients, this might be a problem.

We return to this example later in this chapter because HASACCOUNT exhibits certain interesting properties not found in the PERSON example. For instance, even though a decomposition of HASACCOUNT might still be desirable, it incurs additional maintenance overhead that the decomposition of PERSON does not.

The above discussion brings out two key points: (1) Decomposition of relation schemas can serve as a useful tool that complements the E-R approach by eliminating redundancy problems; (2) The criteria for choosing the right decomposition are not immediately obvious, especially when we have to deal with schemas that contain many attributes. For these reasons, the purpose of Sections 6.3 through 6.6 is to develop techniques and criteria for identifying relation schemas that are in need of decomposition as well as to understand what it means for a decomposition not to lose information.

The central tool in developing much of decomposition theory is **functional dependency**, which is a generalization of the idea of key constraints. Functional dependencies are used to define **normal forms**—a set of requirements on relational schemas that are desirable in update-intensive transaction systems. This is why the theory of decompositions is often also called **normalization theory**. Sections 6.7 through 6.9 develop algorithms for carrying out the normalization process.

6.3 Functional Dependencies

For the remainder of this chapter we use a special notation for representing attributes, which is common in relational normalization theory. Capital letters from the beginning of the alphabet (e.g., A, B, C, D) represent individual attributes; capital letters from the middle to the end of the alphabet with bars over them (e.g., $\overline{P}$, $\overline{V}$, $\overline{W}$, $\overline{X}$, $\overline{Y}$, $\overline{Z}$) represent *sets* of attributes. Also, strings of letters, such as $ABCD$, denote sets of the respective attributes ($\{A, B, C, D\}$ in our case); strings of letters with bars over them, (e.g., $\overline{X}\,\overline{Y}\,\overline{Z}$), stand for unions of these sets (i.e., $\overline{X} \cup \overline{Y} \cup \overline{Z}$). Although this notation requires some getting used to, it is very convenient and provides a succinct language, which we use in examples and definitions.

A **functional dependency** (FD) on a relation schema, **R**, is a constraint of the form $\overline{X} \rightarrow \overline{Y}$, where $\overline{X}$ and $\overline{Y}$ are sets of attributes used in **R**. If **r** is a relation instance of **R**, it is said to **satisfy** this functional dependency if

> For every pair of tuples, t and s, in **r**, if t and s agree on all attributes in $\overline{X}$, then t and s agree on all attributes in $\overline{Y}$.

Put another way, there must not be a pair of tuples in **r** such that they have the same values for every attribute in $\overline{X}$ but different values for some attribute in $\overline{Y}$.

Example 6.3.1 (Functional Dependencies). Consider the relations PERSONI and HOBBY in Figure 6.1. The FD `SSN` → `Name Address` is satisfied by the relation PERSONI. On the other hand, the FD `SSN` → `Hobby` is *not* satisfied by the relation HOBBY. Indeed, there are tuples that have the same value `111111111` in the attribute `SSN` but different values in the attribute `Hobby`. Similarly, `Hobby` → `SSN` is violated by the relation HOBBY: the two tuples that have the value `hiking` in the `Hobby` attribute differ in their `SSN` attribute. ■

Note that the key constraint, introduced in Section 3.2.2, is a special kind of FD. Suppose that `key`($\overline{K}$) is a key constraint on the relational schema **R** and that **r** is a relational instance over **R**. By definition, **r** satisfies `key`($\overline{K}$) if and only if there is no pair of distinct tuples, $t, s \in$ **r**, such that t and s agree on every attribute in `key`($\overline{K}$). Therefore, this key constraint is equivalent to the FD $\overline{K} \rightarrow \overline{R}$, where $\overline{K}$ is the set of attributes in the key constraint and $\overline{R}$ denotes the set of all attributes in the schema **R**.

Keep in mind that functional dependencies are associated with relation schemas, but when we consider whether or not a functional dependency is satisfied we must consider relation instances over those schemas. This is because FDs are *integrity constraints* on the schema (much like key constraints), which restrict the set of allowable relation instances to those that satisfy the given FDs. It is quite common for some instances of the schema to satisfy the FDs that are not part of that schema. Such satisfaction is considered *accidental* because it not sanctioned in the schema and thus is not guaranteed to hold in the future.

Example 6.3.2 (Schema Constraints vs. Accidental FDs). Consider again the relation PERSONI in Figure 6.1. In designing a real-life schema for a relation that is supposed to hold basic information about people, such as PERSON1, we will likely make the FD SSN → Name Address part of the schema but will leave out the FDs Name → Address and Address → SSN. Yet the relation in 6.1(a) *happens* to satisfy both of these FDs.

However, since we did not include these FDs into the schema for PERSON1, nothing precludes us from later adding another John Doe with a different SSN and a different address. Likewise, if we later find out that Mary Doe's child lives at 7 Lake Drive, we will be free to add this new person to the relation PERSON1 without the fear of violating a constraint. ■

To summarize, given a schema, **R** = ($\overline{R}$; *Constraints*), where $\overline{R}$ is a set of attributes and *Constraints* is a set of FDs, a **legal instance** of **R** is a relation with the attributes $\overline{R}$ that satisfies every FD in *Constraints*. We are interested in legal instances because only such relations can exist in a correct database state.

Brain Teaser: What does the FD $X \rightarrow Y$ mean, if X is an empty set of attributes?

Functional dependencies and update anomalies. Certain functional dependencies that exist in a relational schema can lead to redundancy in the corresponding relation instances. Consider the two examples discussed in Sections 6.1 and 6.2: the schemas PERSON and HASACCOUNT. Each has a primary key, as illustrated by the corresponding CREATE TABLE commands (4.1), page 87, and (6.3), page 197, respectively. Correspondingly, there are the following functional dependencies:

```
PERSON:      SSN Hobby → SSN Name Address Hobby
HASACCOUNT:  ClientId OfficeId → AccountNumber
                                 ClientId OfficeId
```
6.4

These are not the only FDs implied by the original specifications, however. For instance, both Name and Address are defined as single-valued attributes in the E-R diagram of Figure 4.1. This clearly implies that one PERSON entity (identified by its attribute SSN) can have at most one name and one address. Similarly, the business rules of PSSC (the brokerage firm discussed in Section 4.7) require that every account be assigned to exactly one office, which means that the following FDs must also hold for the corresponding relation schemas:

```
PERSON:      SSN → Name Address
HASACCOUNT:  AccountNumber → OfficeId
```
6.5

It is easy to see that the syntactic structure of the dependencies in (6.4) closely corresponds to the update anomalies that we identified for the corresponding relations. For instance, the problem with PERSON is that for any given SSN we cannot change the values for the attributes Name and Address independently of whether the corresponding person has hobbies: if the person has multiple hobbies, the change has to occur in multiple rows. Likewise with HASACCOUNT we cannot change the value of `OfficeId` (i.e., transfer an account to a different office) without having to look for all clients associated with this account. Since a number of clients might share the same account, there can be multiple rows in HASACCOUNT that refer to the same account, hence, multiple rows in which `OfficeId` must be changed.

Note that in both cases, the attributes involved in the update anomalies appear on the left-hand sides of an FD. We can see that update anomalies are associated with certain kinds of functional dependencies. Which dependencies are the bad guys? At the risk of giving away the store, we draw your attention to one major difference between the dependencies in (6.4) and (6.5): the former specify key constraints for their corresponding relations whereas the latter do not.

However, simply knowing which dependencies cause the anomalies is not enough—we must do something about them. We cannot just abolish the offending FDs, because they are part of the semantics of the enterprise being modeled by the database. They are implicitly or explicitly part of the Requirements Document and cannot be changed without an agreement with the customer. On the other hand, we saw that schema decomposition can be a useful tool. Even though a decomposition cannot abolish a functional dependency, it can make it behave. For instance, the decomposition shown in (6.1) on page 195 yields schemas in which the offending FD, `SSN` → `Name Address`, becomes a well-behaved key constraint.

6.4 Properties of Functional Dependencies

Before going any further, we need to learn some mathematical properties of functional dependencies and develop algorithms to test them. Since these properties and algorithms rely heavily on the notational conventions introduced at the beginning of Section 6.3, it might be a good idea to revisit these conventions.

The properties of FDs that we are going to study are based on *entailment*. Consider a set of attributes $\overline{R}$, a set, $\mathcal{F}$, of FDs over $\overline{R}$, and another FD, f, on $\overline{R}$. We say that $\mathcal{F}$ **entails** f if every relation **r** over the set of attributes $\overline{R}$ has the following property:

If **r** *satisfies every FD in* $\mathcal{F}$, *then* **r** *satisfies the FD* f.

Given a set of FDs, $\mathcal{F}$, the **closure** of $\mathcal{F}$, denoted $\mathcal{F}^+$, is the set of all FDs entailed by $\mathcal{F}$. Clearly, $\mathcal{F}^+$ contains $\mathcal{F}$ as a subset.[1]

If $\mathcal{F}$ and $\mathcal{G}$ are sets of FDs, we say that $\mathcal{F}$ **entails** $\mathcal{G}$ if $\mathcal{F}$ entails every individual FD in $\mathcal{G}$. $\mathcal{F}$ and $\mathcal{G}$ are said to be **equivalent** if $\mathcal{F}$ entails $\mathcal{G}$ and $\mathcal{G}$ entails $\mathcal{F}$.

Algorithm for computing a candidate key. Why should you care about entailment? For one, you will see that almost all design algorithms discussed in this section

[1] If $f \in \mathcal{F}$, then every relation that satisfies every FD in $\mathcal{F}$ obviously satisfies f. Therefore, by the definition of entailment, f is entailed by $\mathcal{F}$.

involve entailment in one way or another. Here is an immediate payoff, however—an algorithm for finding a candidate key in a relation schema. Let $\mathbf{R} = (\overline{R}, \mathcal{F})$ be a database schema with the set of attributes $\overline{R}$ and a set of FDs $\mathcal{F}$. Suppose that we know how to effectively check whether $\mathcal{F}$ entails an arbitrary FD (we will develop such an algorithm later). Then we can find a candidate key of **R** as follows: Pick up an arbitrary attribute, $A \in \overline{R}$, and check if $\mathcal{F}$ entails $(\overline{R} - A) \to \overline{R}$. If it does, we know that some candidate key hides inside $(\overline{R} - A)$. Remove another arbitrary attribute from what was left (let us denote the remaining set by X) and test that $X \to \overline{R}$ is still entailed by $\mathcal{F}$. If it does not, choose another attribute and test the same. Continue in this way trying to remove more and more attributes. The algorithm terminates when you cannot remove any attribute and still have $X \to \overline{R}$ entailed by $\mathcal{F}$. The remaining set of attributes must be a key.

The above algorithm works from the top down by eliminating attributes. There is also a bottom-up counterpart: start with an empty set of attributes and keep adding attributes until you find an X such that $X \to \overline{R}$ is entailed by $\mathcal{F}$. Can we find all keys in this way? The answer is yes, but not so quickly. There can be an exponential number of such keys, and insisting on finding all of them can cost you a lunch, dinner, and the next breakfast. One way, which is just slightly better than brute force, is to order all subsets of $\overline{R}$ by the amount of attributes in them and systematically apply the top-down algorithm or the bottom-up one until you cannot proceed any further. Each instance of the algorithm will discover some key. All the instances together will find all keys.

We now present several simple but important properties of entailment and later develop an algorithm for testing entailment.

Reflexivity. Some FDs are satisfied by every relation no matter what. These dependencies all have the form $\overline{X} \to \overline{Y}$, where $\overline{Y} \subseteq \overline{X}$, and are called **trivial** FDs.

- The reflexivity property states that, if $\overline{Y} \subseteq \overline{X}$, then $\overline{X} \to \overline{Y}$.

To see why trivial FDs are always satisfied, consider a relation, **r**, whose set of attributes includes all of the attributes mentioned in $\overline{X}$. Suppose that $t, s \in \mathbf{r}$ are tuples that agree on $\overline{X}$. But, since $\overline{Y} \subseteq \overline{X}$, this means that t and s agree on $\overline{Y}$ as well. Thus, **r** satisfies $\overline{X} \to \overline{Y}$.

We can now relate trivial FDs and entailment. Because a trivial FD is satisfied by every relation, it is entailed by every set of FDs (even the empty set)! In particular, $\mathcal{F}^+$ contains every trivial FD.

Augmentation. Consider an FD, $\overline{X} \to \overline{Y}$, and another set of attributes, $\overline{Z}$. Let $\overline{R}$ contain $\overline{X} \cup \overline{Y} \cup \overline{Z}$. Then $\overline{X} \to \overline{Y}$ entails $\overline{X}\,\overline{Z} \to \overline{Y}\,\overline{Z}$. In other words, every relation **r** over $\overline{R}$ that satisfies $\overline{X} \to \overline{Y}$ must also satisfy the FD $\overline{X}\,\overline{Z} \to \overline{Y}\,\overline{Z}$.

- The augmentation property states that, if $\overline{X} \to \overline{Y}$, then $\overline{X}\,\overline{Z} \to \overline{Y}\,\overline{Z}$.

To see why this is true, observe that if tuples $t, s \in \mathbf{r}$ agree on every attribute of $\overline{X}\,\overline{Z}$ then in particular they agree on $\overline{X}$. Since **r** satisfies $\overline{X} \to \overline{Y}$, t and s must also agree on $\overline{Y}$. They also agree on $\overline{Z}$, since we have assumed that they agree on a bigger set of attributes, $\overline{X}\,\overline{Z}$. Thus, if s, t agree on every attribute in $\overline{X}\,\overline{Z}$, they must agree on $\overline{Y}\,\overline{Z}$. As this is an arbitrarily chosen pair of tuples in **r**, it follows that **r** satisfies $\overline{X}\,\overline{Z} \rightarrow \overline{Y}\,\overline{Z}$.

Transitivity. The set of FDs $\{\overline{X} \rightarrow \overline{Y},\ \overline{Y} \rightarrow \overline{Z}\}$ entails the FD $\overline{X} \rightarrow \overline{Z}$.

- The transitivity property states that, if $\overline{X} \rightarrow \overline{Y}$ and $\overline{Y} \rightarrow \overline{Z}$, then $\overline{X} \rightarrow \overline{Z}$.

This property can be established similarly to the previous two (see the exercises at the end of the chapter).

These three properties of FDs are known as **Armstrong's axioms**; they are typically used as *inference rules* in the proofs of correctness of various database design algorithms. However, they are also a powerful tool used by (real, breathing, human) database designers because they can help spot problematic FDs in relational schemas. We now show how Armstrong's axioms are used to derive new FDs.

Union of FDs. Any relation, **r**, that satisfies $\overline{X} \rightarrow \overline{Y}$ and $\overline{X} \rightarrow \overline{Z}$ must also satisfy $\overline{X} \rightarrow \overline{Y}\,\overline{Z}$. To show this, we can derive $\overline{X} \rightarrow \overline{Y}\,\overline{Z}$ from $\overline{X} \rightarrow \overline{Y}$ and $\overline{X} \rightarrow \overline{Z}$ using simple syntactic manipulations defined by Armstrong's axioms. Such manipulations can be easily programmed on a computer, unlike the tuple-based considerations we used to establish the axioms themselves. Here is how it is done:

(a) $\overline{X} \rightarrow \overline{Y}$ Given
(b) $\overline{X} \rightarrow \overline{Z}$ Given
(c) $\overline{X} \rightarrow \overline{Y}\,\overline{X}$ Adding $\overline{X}$ to both sides of (a): Armstrong's augmentation rule
(d) $\overline{Y}\,\overline{X} \rightarrow \overline{Y}\,\overline{Z}$ Adding $\overline{Y}$ to both sides of (b): Armstrong's augmentation rule
(e) $\overline{X} \rightarrow \overline{Y}\,\overline{Z}$ By Armstrong's transitivity rule, applied to (c) and (d)

Decomposition of FDs. In a similar way, we can prove the following rule: every relation that satisfies $\overline{X} \rightarrow \overline{Y}\,\overline{Z}$ must also satisfy the FDs $\overline{X} \rightarrow \overline{Y}$ and $\overline{X} \rightarrow \overline{Z}$. This is accomplished by the following simple steps:

(a) $\overline{X} \rightarrow \overline{Y}\,\overline{Z}$ Given
(b) $\overline{Y}\,\overline{Z} \rightarrow \overline{Y}$ By Armstrong's reflexivity rule, since $\overline{Y} \subseteq \overline{Y}\,\overline{Z}$
(c) $\overline{X} \rightarrow \overline{Y}$ By transitivity from (a) and (b)

Derivation of $\overline{X} \rightarrow \overline{Z}$ is similar.

> *Brain Teaser:* What kind of FD is $X \rightarrow Y$, if Y is an empty set of attributes?

Armstrong's axioms are obviously *sound*. By **sound** we mean that any expression of the form $\overline{X} \rightarrow \overline{Y}$ derived using the axioms from a set of FDs $\mathcal{F}$ is actually a functional dependency that holds in any relation that satisfies every FD in $\mathcal{F}$. Soundness follows from the fact that we have proved that these inference rules are valid for every relation. It is much less obvious, however, that they are also **complete**—that is, if a set of FDs, $\mathcal{F}$, entails another FD, f, then f can be derived from $\mathcal{F}$ by a sequence of steps, similar to the ones above, that rely solely on Armstrong's axioms! For the curious, we provide a proof of this fact at the end of this section.

Note that the definition of entailment of FDs on page 200 does not even hint at an algorithm for checking entailment (i.e., for testing whether $f \in \mathcal{F}^+$). The definition is completely *semantic* in nature and, according to the definition, testing $f \in \mathcal{F}^+$ involves perusing an infinite number of relations. In contrast, Armstrong's axioms provide *syntactic* manipulations that can be carried out by a computer.

Of course, not all syntactic manipulations make sense. For instance, deleting attribute A from every FD does not. However, if the manipulations are sound and complete, then using them is *correct* and is *equivalent* to using the definition of entailment. Thus, soundness and completeness of Armstrong's axioms is not just a theoretical curiosity—this result has considerable practical value because it guarantees that entailment of FDs can be verified by a computer program. We are now going to develop one such algorithm (and a better one later).

Naive algorithm for checking entailment. An obvious way to verify entailment of an FD, f, by a set of FDs, $\mathcal{F}$, is to instruct the computer to apply Armstrong's axioms to $\mathcal{F}$ in all possible ways. Since the number of attributes mentioned in $\mathcal{F}$ and f is finite, this derivation process cannot go on forever. When we are satisfied that all possible derivations have been made, we can simply check whether f is among the FDs derived by this process. Completeness of Armstrong's axioms guarantees that $f \in \mathcal{F}^+$ if and only if f is one of the FDs thus derived.

Example 6.4.1 (Entailment Checking with Armstrong's Axioms). To see how this process works, consider the following sets of FDs: $\mathcal{F} = \{AC \rightarrow B,\ A \rightarrow C,\ D \rightarrow A\}$ and $\mathcal{G} = \{A \rightarrow B, A \rightarrow C, D \rightarrow A, D \rightarrow B\}$. We can use Armstrong's axioms to prove that these two sets are equivalent, that is, that every FD in $\mathcal{G}$ is entailed by $\mathcal{F}$, and vice versa. For instance, to prove that $A \rightarrow B$ is implied by $\mathcal{F}$, we can apply Armstrong's axioms in all possible ways. Most of these attempts will not lead anywhere, but a few will. For instance, the following derivation establishes the desired entailment:

(a) $A \rightarrow C$ An FD in $\mathcal{F}$

(b) $A \rightarrow AC$ From (a) and Armstrong's augmentation axiom

(c) $A \rightarrow B$ From (b), $AC \rightarrow B \in \mathcal{F}$, and Armstrong's transitivity axiom

The FDs $A \rightarrow C$ and $D \rightarrow A$ belong to both $\mathcal{F}$ and $\mathcal{G}$, so the derivation is trivial. For $D \rightarrow B$ in $\mathcal{G}$, the computer can try to apply Armstrong's axioms until this FD is derived. After awhile, it will stumble upon this valid derivation:

(a) $D \rightarrow A$ an FD in $\mathcal{F}$

(b) $A \rightarrow B$ derived previously

(c) $D \rightarrow B$ from (a), (b), and Armstrong's transitivity axiom

This shows that every FD in $\mathcal{F}$ entailed by $\mathcal{G}$ is done similarly. ■

Although the simplicity of checking entailment by blindly applying Armstrong's axioms is attractive, it is not very efficient. In fact, the size of $\mathcal{F}^+$ can be exponential in the size of $\mathcal{F}$, so for large database schemas it can take a very long time before the designer ever sees the result. We are therefore going to develop a more efficient algorithm, which is also based on Armstrong's axioms but which applies them much more judiciously.

Checking entailment of FDs using attribute closure. The idea of the new algorithm for verifying entailment is based on the concept of *attribute closure*.

Given a set of FDs, $\mathcal{F}$, and a set of attributes, $\overline{X}$, we define the **attribute closure** of $\overline{X}$ with respect to $\mathcal{F}$, denoted $\overline{X}^+_{\mathcal{F}}$, as follows:

$$\overline{X}^+_{\mathcal{F}} = \{A \mid \overline{X} \to A \in \mathcal{F}^+\}$$

In other words, $\overline{X}^+_{\mathcal{F}}$ is a set of all those attributes, A, such that $\overline{X} \to A$ is entailed by $\mathcal{F}$. Note that $\overline{X} \subseteq \overline{X}^+_{\mathcal{F}}$ because, if $A \in \overline{X}$, then, by Armstrong's reflexivity axiom, $\overline{X} \to A$ is a trivial FD that is entailed by every set of FDs, including $\mathcal{F}$.

It is important to keep in mind that the closure of $\mathcal{F}$ (i.e., $\mathcal{F}^+$) and the closure of $\overline{X}$ (i.e., $\overline{X}^+_{\mathcal{F}}$) are related but *very different* notions: $\mathcal{F}^+$ is a set of functional dependencies, whereas $\overline{X}^+_{\mathcal{F}}$ is a set of attributes.

Always true: $\overline{X} \subseteq \overline{X}^+_{\mathcal{F}}$ and $\mathcal{F} \subseteq \mathcal{F}^+$

Example 6.4.2 (Attribute Closure). Let $\mathcal{F} = \{B \to E, C \to F, BD \to G\}$. Then the attribute closure of ABC with respect to $\mathcal{F}$ is $ABCEF$.

To see this, you can verify by direct inspection that $\mathcal{F}$ entails $ABC \to x$, where x is A, B, C, E, or F. You can also verify that $\mathcal{F}$ does *not* entail $ABC \to y$, where y is any other attribute. A standard method to prove such a negative result is to construct a counterexample relation, such as the following:

```
 A B C E F  D G  ... y ...
---------------------------
 0 0 0 0 0  0 0  ... 0 ... 0
 0 0 0 0 0  1 1  ... 1 ... 1
```

It obviously does not satisfy $ABC \to y$, but it does satisfy every FD in $\mathcal{F}$. Therefore $\mathcal{F}$ does not entail $ABC \to y$. ■

If we knew how to compute attribute closure efficiently, we could check FD entailment using the following algorithm: Given a set of FDs, $\mathcal{F}$, and an FD, $\overline{X} \to \overline{Y}$, check whether $\overline{Y} \subseteq \overline{X}^+_{\mathcal{F}}$. If this is so, then $\mathcal{F}$ entails $\overline{X} \to \overline{Y}$. Otherwise, if $\overline{Y} \not\subseteq \overline{X}^+_{\mathcal{F}}$, then $\mathcal{F}$ does not entail $\overline{X} \to \overline{Y}$.

The correctness of this algorithm follows from Armstrong's axioms. If $\overline{Y} \subseteq \overline{X}^+_{\mathcal{F}}$, then $\overline{X} \to A \in \mathcal{F}^+$ for every $A \in \overline{Y}$ (by the definition of $\overline{X}^+_{\mathcal{F}}$). By the union rule for FDs,

FIGURE 6.3 Computation of attribute closure $\overline{X}^+_{\mathcal{F}}$.

```
closure := X̄
repeat
        old := closure
        if there is an FD Z̄ → V̄ ∈ ℱ such that Z̄ ⊆ closure and V̄ ⊄ closure then
                closure := closure ∪ V̄
until old = closure
return closure
```

it follows that $\mathcal{F}$ entails $\overline{X} \to \overline{Y}$. Conversely, if $\overline{Y} \not\subseteq \overline{X}^+_{\mathcal{F}}$, then there is $B \in \overline{Y}$ such that $B \notin \overline{X}^+_{\mathcal{F}}$. Hence, $\overline{X} \to B$ is not entailed by $\mathcal{F}$. But then $\mathcal{F}$ cannot entail $\overline{X} \to \overline{Y}$. If it did, it would have to entail $\overline{X} \to B$ as well, by the decomposition rule for FDs.

The heart of the above algorithm is a check of whether a set of attributes belongs to $\overline{X}^+_{\mathcal{F}}$. Therefore, we are not done yet. We need an algorithm for computing the closure of $\overline{X}$, which we present in Figure 6.3. The idea behind the algorithm is to enlarge the set of attributes known to belong to $\overline{X}^+_{\mathcal{F}}$ by applying the FDs in $\mathcal{F}$. The closure is initialized to $\overline{X}$, since we know that $\overline{X}$ is always a subset of $\overline{X}^+_{\mathcal{F}}$.

The soundness of the algorithm can be proved by induction. Initially, *closure* is $\overline{X}$, so $\overline{X} \to$ *closure* is in $\mathcal{F}^+$. Then, assuming that $\overline{X} \to$ *closure* $\in \mathcal{F}^+$ at some intermediate step in the **repeat** loop of Figure 6.3, and given an FD $\overline{Z} \to \overline{V} \in \mathcal{F}$ such that $\overline{Z} \subset$ *closure*, we can use the *generalized transitivity rule* (see Exercise 6.10) to infer that $\mathcal{F}$ entails $\overline{X} \to$ *closure* $\cup \overline{V}$. Thus, if $A \in$ *closure* at the end of the computation, then $A \in \overline{X}^+_{\mathcal{F}}$. The converse is also true: if $A \in \overline{X}^+_{\mathcal{F}}$, then at the end of the computation $A \in$ *closure* (see Exercise 6.11).

Unlike the simple-minded algorithm that uses Armstrong's axioms indiscriminately, the run-time complexity of the algorithm in Figure 6.3 is quadratic in the size of $\mathcal{F}$. In fact, an algorithm for computing $\overline{X}^+_{\mathcal{F}}$ that is *linear* in the size of $\mathcal{F}$ is given in [Beeri and Bernstein 1979]. This algorithm is better suited for a computer program, but its inner workings are more complex.

Example 6.4.3 (Checking Entailment). Consider a relational schema, $\mathbf{R} = (\overline{R};\ \mathcal{F})$, where $\overline{R} = ABCDEFGHIJ$, and the set of FDs, $\mathcal{F}$, which contains the following FDs: $AB \to C$, $D \to E$, $AE \to G$, $GD \to H$, $ID \to J$. We wish to check whether $\mathcal{F}$ entails $ABD \to GH$ and $ABD \to HJ$.

First, let us compute $ABD^+_{\mathcal{F}}$. We begin with *closure* = ABD. Two FDs can be used in the first iteration of the loop in Figure 6.3. For definiteness, let us use $AB \to C$, which makes *closure* = $ABDC$. In the second iteration, we can use $D \to E$, which makes *closure* = $ABDCE$. Now it becomes possible to use the FD $AE \to G$ in the third iteration, yielding *closure* = $ABDCEG$. This in turn allows $GD \to H$ to be applied in the fourth iteration, which results in *closure* = $ABDCEGH$. In the fifth iteration, we cannot apply any new FDs, so *closure* does not change and the loop terminates. Thus, $ABD^+_{\mathcal{F}} = ABDCEGH$.

FIGURE 6.4 Testing equivalence of sets of FDs.

Input: $\mathcal{F}$, $\mathcal{G}$ – FD sets
Output: *true*, if $\mathcal{F}$ is equivalent to $\mathcal{G}$; *false* otherwise
for each $f \in \mathcal{F}$ **do**
    if $\mathcal{G}$ does not entail f **then return** *false*
for each $g \in \mathcal{G}$ **do**
    if $\mathcal{F}$ does not entail g **then return** *false*
return *true*

Since $GH \subseteq ABDCEGH$, we conclude that $\mathcal{F}$ entails $ABD \rightarrow GH$. On the other hand, $HJ \not\subseteq ABDCEGH$, so we conclude that $ABD \rightarrow HJ$ is not entailed by $\mathcal{F}$. Note, however, that $\mathcal{F}$ does entail $ABD \rightarrow H$. ■

The above algorithm for testing entailment leads to a simple test for equivalence between a pair of sets of FDs. Let $\mathcal{F}$ and $\mathcal{G}$ be such sets. To check that they are equivalent, we must check that every FD in $\mathcal{G}$ is entailed by $\mathcal{F}$, and vice versa. The algorithm is depicted in Figure 6.4.

OPTIONAL

Proof of completeness of Armstrong's axioms. Suppose that an FD $f : \overline{X} \rightarrow A$ is entailed by a set of FDs $\mathcal{F}$, but there is no derivation of f from $\mathcal{F}$ based on Armstrong's axioms. We will show that then there must be a relation, **r**, that satisfies every FD in $\mathcal{F}$, but not f. This would be a contradiction since we assumed that f is entailed by $\mathcal{F}$.

Let the relation **r** consist of just two tuples, t_0 and t_1, where t_0 has 0 in every position and t_1 has 0 for every attribute in the set

$$\widehat{X} = \{B \mid \overline{X} \rightarrow B \text{ can be derived from } \mathcal{F} \text{ using Armstrong's axioms}\}$$

and 1 everywhere else:

	$\widehat{X}$	*other attributes*
t_0:	0 0 0 0 0	0 0 0 0 0 0 . . .
t_1:	0 0 0 0 0	1 1 1 1 1 1 . . .

Note that the set $\widehat{X}$ is similar to the attribute closure $\overline{X}^+_{\mathcal{F}}$ except that instead of using every $\overline{X} \rightarrow B$ that is *entailed* by $\mathcal{F}$ we consider only those that are *derivable* from $\mathcal{F}$. Because of the soundness of Armstrong's axioms, every derivable FD is entailed by $\mathcal{F}$, so $\widehat{X} \subseteq \overline{X}^+_{\mathcal{F}}$. In fact, the two sets are equal, but we do not know this yet because we have not proved the completeness of the axioms.

Let us note a few simple properties of $\widehat{X}$. First, $\overline{X} \subseteq \widehat{X}$, because $\overline{X} \rightarrow B$ is Armstrong's reflexivity axiom for every $B \in \overline{X}$. Second, since we assumed that $f : X \rightarrow A$ is not derivable from $\mathcal{F}$, the attribute A is not in $\widehat{X}$. Therefore, t_0 and t_1 have different values over A and so f is violated in **r**. Thus, if we show that every FD in $\mathcal{F}$ holds in **r**, then we will arrive at a contradiction with the assumption that $\mathcal{F}$ entails f.

So, let us prove that every $g : \overline{Y} \rightarrow C \in \mathcal{F}$ holds in **r**.

- If $\overline{Y} \subseteq \widehat{X}$ then C must be in $\widehat{X}$. Indeed, $\overline{Y} \subseteq \widehat{X}$ implies that the FD $\overline{X} \rightarrow \overline{Y}$ is derivable from $\mathcal{F}$ using Armstrong's axioms. (Proving this is left as a simple exercise.) Therefore, $\overline{X} \rightarrow C$ can be derived from $\overline{X} \rightarrow \overline{Y}$ and g by Armstrong's transitivity rule. By the definition of $\widehat{X}$, C must be in $\widehat{X}$; and since t_0 and t_1 have the same value 0 over all attributes of $\widehat{X}$, it follows that the FD g is satisfied in **r**.
- If $\overline{Y} \not\subseteq \widehat{X}$ then the tuples t_0 and t_1 have different values over some attributes in $\overline{Y}$, so they do not have to agree over C. In this case, g is satisfied in **r** in a trivial manner.

Since g was chosen arbitrarily, the above establishes that every FD in $\mathcal{F}$ is satisfied by **r**, which completes the proof.

6.5 Normal Forms

To eliminate redundancy and potential update anomalies, database theory identifies several *normal forms* for relational schemas such that, if a schema is in one of the normal forms, it has certain predictable properties. Each normal form is characterized by a set of restrictions. Thus, for a schema to be in a normal form it must satisfy the restrictions associated with that form. Originally, [Codd 1970] proposed three normal forms, each successively imposing more restrictions and eliminating more and more anomalies and redundancies than the previous one.

The **first normal form** (1NF), as introduced by Codd, is equivalent to the definition of the relational data model. In particular, the value of an attribute must be atomic. It cannot be anything that has structure, such as a record (with multiple fields) or a set. The **second normal form** (2NF) says that a schema must not have an FD, $X \rightarrow Y$, where X is a strict subset of that schema's key and Y has attributes that do not occur in any of the schema's keys. This normal form is of no practical use, and we do not discuss it any further.

The **third normal form** (3NF) was initially thought to be the "ultimate" normal form. However, Boyce and Codd soon realized that 3NF can still harbor undesirable combinations of functional dependencies, so they introduced the **Boyce-Codd normal form** (BCNF). Unfortunately, there is rarely a free lunch in computational sciences. Even though BCNF is more desirable, it is not always achievable without paying a price elsewhere. In this section, we define both BCNF and 3NF. Subsequent sections in this chapter develop algorithms for automatically converting relational schemas that possess various bad properties into sets of schemas in 3NF and BCNF. We also study the trade-offs associated with such conversions.

In Section 6.9, we show that certain types of redundancy are caused by dependencies other than the FDs. To deal with this problem, we introduce the **fourth normal form** (4NF), which further extends BCNF.

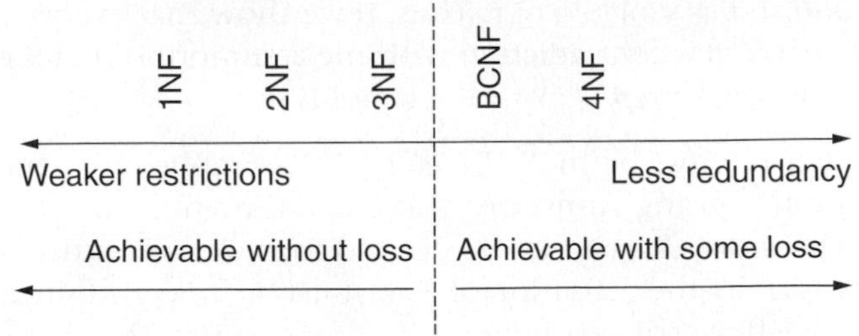

FIGURE 6.5 Relationship among normal forms.

The relationship between the different normal forms is depicted in Figure 6.5. The higher normal forms (to the right) impose more restrictions on relational schemas, and this ensures that the corresponding relations have less redundant information. Note that as we go to the left, restrictions become weaker, and thus any relation schema that satisfies the conditions of a higher normal form also satisfies the conditions of the lower. The figure also shows that the lower normal forms can always be achieved, while the higher ones can be achieved only at a certain price. You will learn what all this means in the remainder of this chapter.

6.5.1 The Boyce-Codd Normal Form

A relational schema, $\mathbf{R} = (\overline{R};\ \mathcal{F})$, where $\overline{R}$ is the set of attributes of **R** and $\mathcal{F}$ is the set of functional dependencies associated with **R**, is in Boyce-Codd normal form if, for every FD $\overline{X} \rightarrow \overline{Y} \in \mathcal{F}$, either of the following is true:

- $\overline{Y} \subseteq \overline{X}$ (i.e., this is a trivial FD).
- $\overline{X}$ is a superkey of **R**.

In other words, the only nontrivial FDs are those in which a key functionally determines one or more attributes.

Examples. It is easy to see that PERSON1 and HOBBY, the relational schemas given in (6.1), are in BCNF, because the only nontrivial FD is `SSN` → `Name Address`. It applies to PERSON1, which has `SSN` as a key.

On the other hand, consider the schema PERSON defined by the CREATE TABLE statement (4.1), page 87, and the schema HASACCOUNT defined by the SQL statement (6.3), page 197. As discussed earlier, these statements fail to capture some important relationships, which are represented by the FDs in (6.5), page 199. Each of these FDs is in violation of the requirement to be in BCNF. They are not trivial, and their left-hand sides—`SSN` and `AccountNumber`—are not keys of their respective schemas.

Properties of BCNF. Note that a BCNF schema can have more than one key. For instance, $\mathbf{R} = (ABCD;\ \mathcal{F})$, where $\mathcal{F} = \{AB \rightarrow CD,\ AC \rightarrow BD\}$ has two keys, AB and AC. And yet it is in BCNF because the left-hand side of each of the two FDs in $\mathcal{F}$ is a key.

Observe that we defined BCNF by looking only at the set of FDs in $\mathcal{F}$, not $\mathcal{F}^+$. One might wonder, therefore, whether $\mathcal{F}^+ - \mathcal{F}$ might have any FDs that violate BCNF, in which case this normal form will not make much sense. Fortunately, the above situation cannot occur. To see this, consider an arbitrary FD $\overline{X} \rightarrow A \in (\mathcal{F}^+ - \mathcal{F})$ such that $A \notin \overline{X}$. As we know, it must be the case that $A \in \overline{X}^+_{\mathcal{F}}$ and $\overline{X}^+_{\mathcal{F}}$ should be computable by the attribute closure algorithm in Figure 6.3. Recall that the main step in that algorithm hinges on being able to find an FD $\overline{Z} \rightarrow \overline{V} \in \mathcal{F}$ such that $\overline{Z} \subseteq closure$. Since initially $closure = \overline{X}$, there must be an FD in $\mathcal{F}$ whose left-hand side, $\overline{Z}$, is a subset of $\overline{X}$. But since the schema is in BCNF, $\overline{Z}$ must be a superkey. Hence, so must be $\overline{X}$, that is, the FD $\overline{X} \rightarrow A$ does not violate the BCNF conditions.

Nonredundancy of BCNF. An important property of BCNF schemas is that their instances do not contain redundant information that arises due to FDs. Since we have been illustrating redundancy problems only through concrete examples, the above statement might seem vague. Exactly what is redundant information? For instance, does the abstract relation

A	*B*	*C*	*D*
1	1	3	4
2	1	3	4

over the above-mentioned BCNF schema **R** store redundant information?

Superficially it might seem so because the two tuples agree on all but one attribute. However, having identical values in some attributes of different tuples does not necessarily imply that the tuples are storing redundant information. Redundancy arises when the values of some set of attributes, $\overline{X}$, necessarily implies the value that must exist in another attribute, *A*—a functional dependency. If two distinct tuples have the same values in $\overline{X}$, they must have the same value of *A*. This means that an association between *A* and the attributes in $\overline{X}$ is stored multiple times. Redundancy is eliminated if we store such an association only once (in a separate relation) instead of repeating it in all tuples of an instance of the schema **R** that agree on $\overline{X}$. Since **R** does not have FDs over the attributes *BCD*, no redundant information is stored. The fact that the tuples in the relation coincide over *BCD* is coincidental. For instance, the value of attribute *D* in the first tuple can be changed from 4 to 5 without regard for the second tuple.

A DBMS automatically eliminates one type of redundancy. Two tuples with the same values in the key fields are prohibited in any instance of a schema. This is a special case. The key identifies an entity and so determines the values of all attributes describing that entity. As the definition of BCNF precludes associations that do not contain keys, the relations over BCNF schemas do not store redundant information. As a result, deletion and update anomalies do not arise in BCNF relations.

Relations with more than one key still can have insertion anomalies. To see this, suppose that associations over *ABD* and over *ACD* are added to our relation as shown:

A	*B*	*C*	*D*
1	1	3	4
2	1	3	4
3	4	NULL	5
3	NULL	2	5

Because the value over the attribute *C* in the first association and over *B* in the second is unknown, we fill in the missing information with `NULL`. However, now we cannot tell if the two newly added tuples are the same—it all depends on the real values for the nulls. A practical solution to this problem, as adopted by the SQL standard, is to designate one key as *primary* and to prohibit null values in its attributes. Under this restriction, every tuple is defined over the attributes of the primary key and, in particular, the above situation with newly added tuples is impossible.

6.5.2 The Third Normal Form

A relational schema, $\mathbf{R} = (\overline{R};\ \mathcal{F})$, where $\overline{R}$ is the set of attributes of **R** and $\mathcal{F}$ is the set of functional dependencies associated with **R**, is in **third normal form** if, for every FD $\overline{X} \rightarrow \overline{Y} \in \mathcal{F}$, any of the following conditions are true:

- $\overline{Y} \subseteq \overline{X}$ (i.e., this is a trivial FD).
- $\overline{X}$ is a superkey of **R**.
- Each attribute in $A \in \overline{Y} - \overline{X}$ belongs to some candidate key of **R**.

Observe that the first two conditions in the definition of 3NF are identical to the conditions that define BCNF. Thus, 3NF is a relaxation of BCNF's requirements. Every schema that is in BCNF must also be in 3NF, but the converse is not true in general. For instance, the relation HASACCOUNT (6.3) on page 197 is in 3NF because the only FD that is not based on a key constraint is `AccountNumber` → `OfficeId`, and `OfficeId` is part of the key. However, this relation is not in BCNF, as shown previously.[2]

If you are wondering about the intrinsic merit of the third condition in the definition of 3NF, the answer is that there is none. In a way, 3NF was discovered by accident—in the search for what we now call BCNF! The reason for the remarkable survival of 3NF is that it was later found to have some very desirable algorithmic properties, which BCNF does not possess. We discuss these issues in subsequent sections.

[2] In fact, HASACCOUNT is the *smallest* possible example of a 3NF relation that is not in BCNF (see Exercise 6.5).

Brain Teaser: Find a 2NF relation that is not in 3NF.

Redundancy in 3NF. Recall from Section 6.2 that relation instances over HASACCOUNT might store redundant information. Now we can see that this redundancy arises because of the functional dependency that relates `AccountNumber` and `OfficeId` and that is not implied by key constraints.

For another example, consider the schema PERSON discussed earlier. This schema violates the 3NF requirements because, for example, the FD `SSN` $\rightarrow$ `Name` is not based on a key constraint (`SSN` is not a superkey) and `Name` does not belong to a key of PERSON. However, the decomposition of this schema into PERSON1 and HOBBY in (6.1), page 195, yields a pair of schemas that are in both 3NF and BCNF.

We can ask the same question as in the case of BCNF: is it possible that some FD in $\mathcal{F}^+ - \mathcal{F}$ violates the 3NF conditions, thereby making this normal form ill-defined? It is easy to guess that the answer is "no," for, otherwise, 3NF would not be worth including in a textbook. However, proving this is a notch harder than in the case of BCNF, so we leave it to Exercise 6.25.

6.6 Properties of Decompositions

Since there is no redundancy in BCNF schemas and redundancy in 3NF is limited, we are interested in decomposing a given schema into a collection of schemas, each of which is in one of these normal forms.

The main thrust of the discussion in the previous section was that 3NF does not completely solve the redundancy problem. Therefore, at first glance, there appears to be no justification to consider 3NF as a goal for database design. It turns out, however, that the maintenance problems associated with redundancy do not show the whole picture. As we will see, maintenance is also associated with integrity constraints,[3] and 3NF decompositions sometimes have better properties in this regard than do BCNF decompositions. Our first step is to define these properties.

Recall from Section 6.2 that not all decompositions are created equal. For instance, the decomposition of PERSON shown in (6.1) is considered good while the one in (6.2) makes no sense. Is there an objective way to tell which decompositions make sense and which do not, and can this objective way be explained to a computer? The answer to both questions is "yes." The decompositions that make sense are called *lossless*. Before tackling this notion, we need to be more precise about what we mean by a decomposition in the first place.

A **decomposition of a schema**, $\mathbf{R} = (\overline{R};\ \mathcal{F})$, where $\overline{R}$ is a set of attributes of the schema and $\mathcal{F}$ is its set of functional dependencies, is a collection of schemas

$$\mathbf{R}_1 = (\overline{R}_1; \mathcal{F}_1),\ \mathbf{R}_2 = (\overline{R}_2; \mathcal{F}_2),\ \ldots,\ \mathbf{R}_n = (\overline{R}_n; \mathcal{F}_n)$$

[3] For example, a particular integrity constraint in the original table might be checkable in the decomposed tables only by taking the join of these tables—which results in significant overhead at run time.

such that the following conditions hold:

1. $R_i \neq R_j$, if $i \neq j$
2. $\overline{R} = \cup_{i=1}^{n} \overline{R}_i$
3. $\mathcal{F}$ entails $\mathcal{F}_i$ for every $i = 1, \ldots, n$.

The second condition in the definition is clear: a decomposition should not introduce new attributes, and it should not drop attributes found in the original schema. The third condition in the definition says that a decomposition should not introduce new functional dependencies (but may drop some). We discuss this latter requirement in more detail later.

The decomposition of a schema naturally leads to decomposition of relations over it. A **decomposition of a relation**, **r**, defined over schema **R**, relative to a schema decomposition $\mathbf{R}_1 = (\overline{R}_1; \mathcal{F}_1), \ldots, \mathbf{R}_n = (\overline{R}_n; \mathcal{F}_n)$ is a set of relations

$$\mathbf{r}_1 = \pi_{\overline{R}_1}(\mathbf{r}), \mathbf{r}_2 = \pi_{\overline{R}_2}(\mathbf{r}), \ldots, \mathbf{r}_n = \pi_{\overline{R}_n}(\mathbf{r})$$

where π is the projection operator. It can be shown (see Exercise 6.12) that, if **r** is a valid instance of **R**, then each $\mathbf{r}_i$ satisfies all FDs in $\mathcal{F}_i$ and thus each $\mathbf{r}_i$ is a valid relation instance over the schema $\mathbf{R}_i$. The purpose of a decomposition is to replace the original relation, **r**, with a set of relations $\mathbf{r}_1, \ldots, \mathbf{r}_n$ over the schemas that constitute the decomposed schema.

In view of the above definitions, it is important to realize that *schema decomposition* and *relation instance decomposition* are two different (but related) notions—the former is a set of relation schemas, while the latter is a set of relation instances.

Example 6.6.1 (Decomposition). Applying the above definitions to our running example, we see that splitting PERSON into PERSON1 and HOBBY (see (6.1) and Figure 6.1 on page 195 yields a decomposition. Splitting PERSON as shown in (6.2) and Figure 6.2 is also a decomposition in the above sense. It clearly satisfies the first requirement for being a decomposition. It also satisfies the second since only trivial FDs hold in (6.2), and these are entailed by every set of dependencies. ■

This last example shows that the above definition of a decomposition does not capture all of the desirable properties of a decomposition because, as you may recall from Section 6.2, the decomposition in (6.2) makes no sense. In the following section, we introduce additional desirable properties of decompositions.

6.6.1 Lossless and Lossy Decompositions

Consider a relation, **r**, and its decomposition, $\mathbf{r}_1, \ldots, \mathbf{r}_n$, as defined above. Since after the decomposition the database no longer stores the relation **r** and instead maintains its projections $\mathbf{r}_1, \ldots, \mathbf{r}_n$, the database must be able to reconstruct the original relation **r** from these projections. Not being able to reconstruct **r** means that the decomposition does not represent the same information as does the original database (imagine a bank losing the information about who owns which account or, worse, associating those accounts with the wrong owners!).

In principle, one can use any computational method that guarantees reconstruction of **r** from its projections. However, the natural and, in most cases, practical method is the natural join. We thus assume that **r** is reconstructible if and only if

$$\mathbf{r} = \mathbf{r}_1 \bowtie \mathbf{r}_2 \bowtie \cdots \bowtie \mathbf{r}_n$$

Reconstructibility must be a property of schema decomposition and not of a particular instance over this schema. At the database design stage, the designer manipulates schemas, not relations, and any transformation performed on a schema must guarantee that reconstructibility holds for all of its valid relation instances.

This discussion leads to the following notion. A decomposition of schema $\mathbf{R} = (\overline{R};\ \mathcal{F})$ into a collection of schemas

$$\mathbf{R}_1 = (\overline{R}_1; \mathcal{F}_1), \mathbf{R}_2 = (\overline{R}_2; \mathcal{F}_2), \ldots, \mathbf{R}_n = (\overline{R}_n; \mathcal{F}_n)$$

is **lossless** if, for *every* valid instance **r** of schema **R**,

$$\mathbf{r} = \mathbf{r}_1 \bowtie \mathbf{r}_2 \bowtie \cdots \bowtie \mathbf{r}_n$$

where

$$\mathbf{r}_1 = \pi_{\overline{R}_1}(\mathbf{r}), \mathbf{r}_2 = \pi_{\overline{R}_2}(\mathbf{r}), \ldots, \mathbf{r}_n = \pi_{\overline{R}_n}(\mathbf{r})$$

A decomposition is **lossy** otherwise.

In plain terms, a lossless schema decomposition is one that guarantees that any valid instance of the original schema can be reconstructed from its projections on the individual schemas of the decomposition. Note that

$$\mathbf{r} \subseteq \mathbf{r}_1 \bowtie \mathbf{r}_2 \bowtie \cdots \bowtie \mathbf{r}_n$$

holds for *any* decomposition whatsoever (Exercise 6.13), so losslessness really just asserts the opposite inclusion:

$$\mathbf{r} \supseteq \mathbf{r}_1 \bowtie \mathbf{r}_1 \bowtie \cdots \bowtie \mathbf{r}_n$$

The fact that

$$\mathbf{r} \subseteq \mathbf{r}_1 \bowtie \mathbf{r}_2 \bowtie \cdots \bowtie \mathbf{r}_n$$

holds, no matter what, may seem confusing at first. If we can get more tuples by joining the projections of **r**, why is such a decomposition called lossy? After all, we gained more tuples—not less! To clarify this issue, observe that what we might lose here are not tuples but rather information about *which tuples are the right ones*. Consider, for instance, the decomposition (6.2) of schema PERSON on page 196. Figure 6.2 presents the corresponding decomposition of a valid relation instance over PERSON shown in Figure 4.13. However, if we now compute a natural join of the relations in the decomposition (which becomes a Cartesian product since these relations do not share attributes), we will not be able to tell who lives where and who has what hobbies. The relationship among names and SSNs is also lost. In other words, when reconstructing the original relation, getting more tuples is as bad as getting fewer—we must get *exactly* the set of tuples in the original relation.

Now that we are convinced of the importance of losslessness, we need an algorithm that a computer can use to verify this property since the definition of lossless joins does not provide an effective test but only tells us to try every possible relation. This is neither feasible nor efficient.

A general test of whether a decomposition into n schemas is lossless exists but is somewhat complex. It can be found in [Beeri et al. 1981]. However, there is a much simpler test that works for binary decompositions, that is, decompositions into a pair of schemas. This test can establish losslessness of a decomposition into more than two schemas provided that this decomposition was obtained by a series of binary decompositions. Since most decompositions are obtained in this way, the simple binary test introduced below is sufficient for most practical purposes.

Testing the losslessness of a binary decomposition. Let $\mathbf{R} = (\overline{R};\ \mathcal{F})$ be a schema and $\mathbf{R}_1 = (\overline{R}_1;\ \mathcal{F}_1)$, $\mathbf{R}_2 = (\overline{R}_2;\ \mathcal{F}_2)$ be a binary decomposition of $\mathbf{R}$. This decomposition is lossless if and only if either of the following is true:

- $(\overline{R}_1 \cap \overline{R}_2) \rightarrow \overline{R}_1 \in \mathcal{F}^+$.
- $(\overline{R}_1 \cap \overline{R}_2) \rightarrow \overline{R}_2 \in \mathcal{F}^+$.

To see why this is so, suppose that $(\overline{R}_1 \cap \overline{R}_2) \rightarrow \overline{R}_2 \in \mathcal{F}^+$. Then $\overline{R}_1$ is a superkey of $\mathbf{R}$ since, by augmentation with $\overline{R}_1$, we can derive $\overline{R}_1 \rightarrow \overline{R}_1 \cup \overline{R}_2$, and $\overline{R} = \overline{R}_1 \cup \overline{R}_2$. Let $\mathbf{r}$ be a valid relation instance for $\mathbf{R}$. Since $\overline{R}_1$ is a superkey of $\overline{R}$ every tuple in $\mathbf{r}_1 = \pi_{\overline{R}_1}(\mathbf{r})$ extends to exactly one tuple in $\mathbf{r}$. Thus, as depicted in Figure 6.6, the cardinality (the number of tuples) in $\mathbf{r}_1$ equals the cardinality of $\mathbf{r}$, and every tuple in $\mathbf{r}_1$ joins with exactly one tuple in $\mathbf{r}_2 = \pi_{\overline{R}_2}(\mathbf{r})$ (if more than one tuple in $\mathbf{r}_2$ joined with a tuple in $\mathbf{r}_1$, the FD $(\overline{R}_1 \cap \overline{R}_2) \rightarrow \overline{R}_2$ would not be satisfied in $\mathbf{r}_2$). Therefore, the cardinality of $\mathbf{r}_1 \bowtie \mathbf{r}_2$ equals the cardinality of $\mathbf{r}_1$, which in turn equals the cardinality of $\mathbf{r}$. Since $\mathbf{r}$ must be a subset of $\mathbf{r}_1 \bowtie \mathbf{r}_2$, it follows that $\mathbf{r} = \mathbf{r}_1 \bowtie \mathbf{r}_2$. Conversely, if neither of the above FDs holds, it is easy to construct a relation $\mathbf{r}$ such that $\mathbf{r} \subset \mathbf{r}_1 \bowtie \mathbf{r}_2$. Details of this construction are left to Exercise 6.14.

The above test can now be used to substantiate our intuition that the decomposition (6.1) of PERSON into PERSON1 and HOBBY is a good one. The intersection of the attributes of HOBBY and PERSON1 is {SSN}, and SSN is a key of PERSON1. Thus, this decomposition is lossless.

Note that this test can be used to verify losslessness of certain decompositions into three or more schemas. Indeed, it is easy to verify that if we take a lossless decomposition and losslessly decompose one of its member schemas into a pair of subschemas, then the result is lossless as well (Exercise 6.15). Therefore, any decomposition that can be derived by a sequence of binary lossless decompositions is itself lossless.

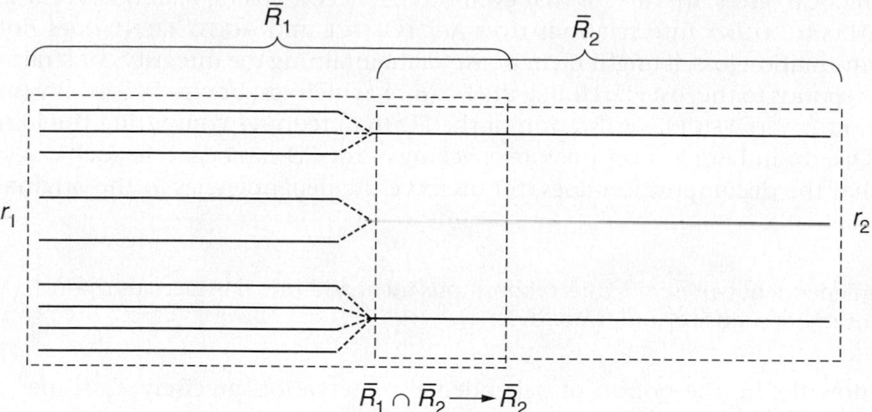

FIGURE 6.6 Tuple structure in a lossless binary decomposition: a row of $\mathbf{r}_1$ combines with exactly one row of $\mathbf{r}_2$.

A general algorithm for testing losslessness of an arbitrary n-ary decomposition exists but is outside of the scope of this book. A curious reader is referred to [Maier 1983].

6.6.2 Dependency-Preserving Decompositions

Consider the schema HASACCOUNT once again. Recall that it has attributes `AccountNumber`, `ClientId`, `OfficeId`, and its FDs are

```
ClientId OfficeId → AccountNumber                                    6.6
AccountNumber → OfficeId                                             6.7
```

According to the losslessness test, the following decomposition is lossless:

```
ACCTOFFICE = (AccountNumber, OfficeId;
                        {AccountNumber → OfficeId})                  6.8
ACCTCLIENT = (AccountNumber, ClientId; { })
```

because `AccountNumber` (the intersection of the two attribute sets) is a key of the first schema, ACCTOFFICE.

Even though decomposition (6.8) is lossless, something seems to have fallen through the cracks. ACCTOFFICE hosts the FD (6.7), but ACCTCLIENT's associated set of FDs is empty. This leaves the FD (6.6), which exists in the original schema, homeless. Neither of the two schemas in the decomposition has all of the attributes needed to house this FD; furthermore, the FD cannot be derived from the FDs that belong to the schemas ACCTOFFICE and ACCTCLIENT.

In practical terms, this means that even though decomposing relations over the schema HASACCOUNT into relations over ACCTOFFICE and ACCTCLIENT does not lead to information loss, it might incur a cost for maintaining the integrity constraint that corresponds to the lost FD. Unlike the FD (6.7), which can be checked locally (in the relation ACCTOFFICE), verification of the FD (6.6) requires computing the join of ACCTOFFICE and ACCTCLIENT before checking of the FD can begin. In such cases, we say that the decomposition does not preserve the dependencies in the original schema.

> Non-dependency-preserving decompositions incur additional overhead of constraint maintenance at run time.

We now define the notion of dependency preservation precisely. Consider a schema, $\mathbf{R} = (\overline{R};\ \mathcal{F})$, and suppose that

$$\mathbf{R}_1 = (\overline{R}_1; \mathcal{F}_1),\ \mathbf{R}_2 = (\overline{R}_2; \mathcal{F}_2),\ \ldots,\ \mathbf{R}_n = (\overline{R}_n; \mathcal{F}_n)$$

is a decomposition. $\mathcal{F}$ entails each $\mathcal{F}_i$ by definition, so $\mathcal{F}$ entails $\cup_{i=1}^{n}\mathcal{F}_i$. However, this definition does not require that the two sets of dependencies be equivalent—that is, that $\cup_{i=1}^{n}\mathcal{F}_i$ must also entail $\mathcal{F}$. This reverse entailment is what is missing in the above example. The FD set of HASACCOUNT, which consists of dependencies (6.6) and (6.7), is not entailed by the union of the dependencies in decomposition (6.8), which consists of only a single dependency `AccountNumber` → `OfficeId`. Because of this, (6.8) is not a dependency-preserving decomposition.

Formally,

$$\mathbf{R}_1 = (\overline{R}_1;\ \mathcal{F}_1),\ \mathbf{R}_2 = (\overline{R}_2;\ \mathcal{F}_2),\ \ldots,\ \mathbf{R}_n = (\overline{R}_n;\ \mathcal{F}_n)$$

is said to be a **dependency-preserving decomposition** of $\mathbf{R} = (\overline{R};\ \mathcal{F})$ if and only if it is a decomposition of **R** and the sets of FDs $\mathcal{F}$ and $\cup_{i=1}^{n}\mathcal{F}_i$ are equivalent.

Example 6.6.2 (Dependency-Preserving Decomposition). Consider a schema with the attributes `SSN`, `EmplId`, and `DeptId`, and the FDs $\mathcal{F} = \{f_1 : \texttt{SSN} \rightarrow \texttt{EmplId},\ f_2 : \texttt{EmplId} \rightarrow \texttt{SSN},\ f_3 : \texttt{SSN} \rightarrow \texttt{DeptId}\}$. Its decomposition into $\mathbf{R}_1 = (\texttt{SSN EmplId}; \mathcal{F}_1 = \{f_1, f_2\})$ and $\mathbf{R}_2 = (\texttt{EmplId, DeptId}; \mathcal{F}_2 = \{f_4 : \texttt{EmplId} \rightarrow \texttt{DeptId}\})$ is dependency preserving.

Note that the FD $f_3 \in \mathcal{F}$ is not in $\mathcal{F}_1 \cup \mathcal{F}_2 = \{f_1, f_2, f_4\}$, but nonetheless $\mathcal{F}^+ = (\mathcal{F}_1 \cup \mathcal{F}_2)^+$ because f_3 can be derived from f_1 and f_4; and f_4 from f_2 and f_3. ■

The above example shows that even if some FD, $f \in \mathcal{F}$, is not found in any of the $\mathcal{F}_i$s this does *not* mean that the decomposition is not dependency preserving, since f might be entailed by $\cup_{i=1}^{n}\mathcal{F}_i$. In this case, maintaining f as a functional dependency requires no extra effort. If the FDs in $\cup_{i=1}^{n}\mathcal{F}_i$ are maintained, f will be also. It is only when f is not entailed by $\cup_{i=1}^{n}\mathcal{F}_i$ that the decomposition is not dependency preserving and so maintenance of f requires a join.

Example 6.6.3 (Nonpreserving Decomposition). The decomposition (6.8) of HASACCOUNT is not dependency preserving, and this is precisely what is wrong. The

AccountNumber	ClientId	OfficeId
B123	111111111	SB01
A908	123456789	MN08

HASACCOUNT

AccountNumber	OfficeId
B123	SB01
A908	MN08

ACCTOFFICE

AccountNumber	ClientId
B123	111111111
A908	123456789

ACCTCLIENT

FIGURE 6.7 Decomposition of the HASACCOUNT relation.

dependencies that exist in the original schema but are lost in the decomposition become interrelational constraints that cannot be maintained locally. Each time a relation in the decomposition is changed, satisfaction of the interrelational constraints can be checked only after the reconstruction of the original relation. To illustrate, consider the decomposition of HASACCOUNT in Figure 6.7.

If we now add the tuple ⟨B567, SB01⟩ to the relation ACCTOFFICE and the tuple ⟨B567, 111111111⟩ to ACCTCLIENT, the two relations will still satisfy their local FDs (in fact, we see from (6.8) that only ACCTOFFICE has a dependency to satisfy). In contrast, the interrelational FD (6.6) is not satisfied after these updates, but this is not immediately apparent. To verify this, we must join the two relations, as depicted in Figure 6.8. We now see that constraint (6.6) is violated by the first two tuples in the updated HASACCOUNT relation. ■

AccountNumber	ClientId	OfficeId
B123	111111111	SB01
B567	111111111	SB01
A908	123456789	MN08

HASACCOUNT

AccountNumber	OfficeId
B123	SB01
B567	SB01
A908	MN08

ACCTOFFICE

AccountNumber	ClientId
B123	111111111
B567	111111111
A908	123456789

ACCTCLIENT

FIGURE 6.8 HASACCOUNT and its decomposition after the insertion of several rows.

The next question to ask is how hard it is to check whether a decomposition is dependency preserving. If we already *have* a decomposition $(\overline{R}_1;\ \mathcal{F}_1)$, ..., $(\overline{R}_n;\ \mathcal{F}_n)$ of $(\overline{R};\ \mathcal{F})$ and know the sets of functional dependencies (the $\mathcal{F}_i$s) attached to every subschema, then dependency preservation can be checked in polynomial time. We simply need to verify that each FD in the original set, $\mathcal{F}$, is entailed by $\cup_{i=1}^{n}\mathcal{F}_i$. For each such test, we can use the quadratic attribute closure algorithm discussed in Section 6.4.

In practice, the situation is more involved. Typically, we (and computer algorithms) must first decide *how* to split the attribute set in order to form the decomposition, and only then attach FDs to those attribute sets. Intuitively, an FD $\overline{X} \to \overline{Y}$ is applicable to an attribute set $\overline{S}$ if $\overline{X} \cup \overline{Y} \subseteq \overline{S}$. We state this more formally as follows.

Consider a schema, $\mathbf{R} = (\overline{R};\ \mathcal{F})$, a relation, **r**, over **R**, and a set of attributes, $\overline{S}$, such that $\overline{S} \subseteq \overline{R}$. If $\overline{S}$ is one of the schemas in a decomposition of **R**, the only FDs that are guaranteed to hold over $\pi_{\overline{S}}(\mathbf{r})$ are $\overline{X} \to \overline{Y} \in \mathcal{F}^+$ such that $\overline{X}\,\overline{Y} \subseteq \overline{S}$ (see Exercise 6.36). This leads to the following notion:

$$\pi_{\overline{S}}(\mathcal{F}) \;=\; \{\overline{X} \to \overline{Y} \mid \overline{X} \to \overline{Y} \in \mathcal{F}^+ \text{ and } \overline{X} \cup \overline{Y} \subseteq \overline{S}\}$$

which is called the **projection of the set $\mathcal{F}$ of FDs** onto the set of attributes $\overline{S}$.

Note that to compute $\pi_{\overline{S}}(\mathcal{F})$ we must look at all the FDs in $\mathcal{F}^+$—not just in $\mathcal{F}$. For instance, if $\mathcal{F} = \{A \to B,\ B \to C\}$ and $\overline{S}$ is AC then $\pi_{\overline{S}}(\mathcal{F}) = \{A \to C\}$. If in the above definition we were looking at $\mathcal{F}$ only then the projection would have been empty!

The notion of projection for FDs opens a way to construct decompositions knowing only how to split the attribute set of the original schema. If $\mathbf{R} = (\overline{R};\ \mathcal{F})$ is a schema and $\overline{R}_1, \ldots, \overline{R}_n$ are subsets of attributes such that $\overline{R} = \cup_{i=1}^{n}\overline{R}_i$, then the collection of schemas $(\overline{R}_1; \pi_{\overline{R}_1}(\mathcal{F})), \ldots, (\overline{R}_n; \pi_{\overline{R}_n}(\mathcal{F}))$ is a decomposition. In a sense, such a decomposition preserves as many dependencies from the original set $\mathcal{F}$ as possible.

From now on we will consider only decompositions of this kind, that is, those where $\mathcal{F}_i$ is equivalent to $\pi_{\overline{R}_i}(\mathcal{F})$. Since, given an attribute set in a decomposition, it is now possible to uniquely determine the corresponding set of FDs by taking a projection, it is customary to omit the FDs when specifying schema decompositions.

Constructing decompositions thus requires computing projections of FDs. This computation involves calculating the closure of $\mathcal{F}$,[4] which, in the worst case, can take time exponential in the size of $\mathcal{F}$. If the cost of this computation is factored into the cost of checking for dependency preservation, this checking is exponential as well. In this regard, it is interesting that, in order to test a decomposition for losslessness, one does not need to compute the projections $\pi_{\overline{R}_i}(\mathcal{F})$). The test presented earlier uses the original set $\mathcal{F}$ of FDs and is polynomial in the size of $\mathcal{F}$.

To summarize, we considered two important properties of schema decomposition: losslessness and dependency preservation. We also saw an example of a relation (HASACCOUNT) that has a lossless but not dependency-preserving decomposition

[4] There is a way to avoid computing the entire closure $\mathcal{F}^+$, but the worst-case complexity is the same.

into BCNF (and which, as we shall see, does not have a BCNF decomposition that has both properties). Which of these two properties is more important? The answer is that losslessness is mandatory while dependency preservation, though very desirable, is optional. The reason is that lossy decompositions lose information contained in the original database, and this is not acceptable. In contrast, decompositions that do not preserve FDs only lead to computational overhead when the database is changed and interrelational constraints need to be checked.

6.7 An Algorithm for BCNF Decomposition

We are now ready to present our first decomposition algorithm. Let $\mathbf{R} = (\overline{R};\ \mathcal{F})$ be a relational schema that is not in BCNF. The algorithm in Figure 6.9 constructs a new decomposition by repeatedly splitting **R** into smaller subschemas so that at each step the new database schema has strictly fewer FDs that violate BCNF than does the schema in the previous iteration (see Exercise 6.16). Thus, the algorithm always terminates and all schemas in the result are in BCNF.

To see how the BCNF decomposition algorithm works, consider the HASACCOUNT example once again. This schema is not in BCNF, because of the FD `AccountNumber` → `OfficeId` whose left-hand side is not a superkey. Therefore, we can use this FD to split HASACCOUNT in the **while** loop of Figure 6.9. The result is, not surprisingly, the decomposition we saw in (6.8).

The next example is more involved and also much more abstract.

Example 6.7.1 (BCNF Decomposition). Consider a relation schema, $\mathbf{R}=(\overline{R};\ \mathcal{F})$, where $\overline{R} = ABCDEFGH$ (recall that A, B, etc., denote attribute names), and let the set $\mathcal{F}$ of FDs be

$$
\begin{aligned}
ABH &\rightarrow C\\
A &\rightarrow DE\\
BGH &\rightarrow F\\
F &\rightarrow ADH\\
BH &\rightarrow GE
\end{aligned}
$$

FIGURE 6.9 Lossless decomposition into BCNF.

Input: $\mathbf{R} = (\overline{R};\ \mathcal{F})$
Output: A lossless decomposition of **R** where each schema is in BCNF.

Decomposition := {**R**} /* Initially *Decomposition* consists of only one schema */
while there is a schema $\mathbf{S} = (\overline{S};\ \mathcal{F}')$ in *Decomposition* that is not in BCNF **do**
  /* Let $\overline{X} \rightarrow \overline{Y}$ be an FD in $\mathcal{F}$ such that $\overline{X}\,\overline{Y} \subseteq \overline{S}$ and
   it violates BCNF in **S**. Decompose using this FD */
  Replace **S** in *Decomposition* with schemas $\mathbf{S}_1 = (\overline{X}\,\overline{Y};\ \mathcal{F}_1')$ and
  $\mathbf{S}_2 = ((\overline{S} - \overline{Y}) \cup \overline{X};\ \mathcal{F}_2')$, where $\mathcal{F}_1' = \pi_{\overline{X}\,\overline{Y}}(\mathcal{F}')$ and $\mathcal{F}_2' = \pi_{(\overline{S}-\overline{Y})\cup\overline{X}}(\mathcal{F}')$
end
return *Decomposition*

At the start, *Decomposition* in the algorithm contains only one schema, **R**, so, in the first iteration of the **while** loop, **S** denotes **R**. The algorithm first identifies the FDs that violate BCNF—the FDs whose left-hand side is not a superkey in **R**. We can see that the first FD is *not* one of the violators because the attribute closure $(ABH)^+$ (computed with the algorithm in Figure 6.3) contains all schema attributes, so ABH is a superkey. However, the second FD, $A \rightarrow DE$, does violate BCNF. The attribute closure of A is ADE, and so A is not a superkey. We can thus split **R** using this FD:

$$\mathbf{R}_1 = (ADE; \{A \rightarrow DE\})$$
$$\mathbf{R}_2 = (ABCFGH; \{ABH \rightarrow C, BGH \rightarrow F, F \rightarrow AH, BH \rightarrow G\})$$

(Since, in the first iteration of the **while** loop, **S** denotes **R**, it follows that $\mathbf{S}_1$ and $\mathbf{S}_2$ in the algorithm denote $\mathbf{R}_1$ and $\mathbf{R}_2$, respectively.) Notice that we separated $F \rightarrow ADH$ into $\{F \rightarrow AH,\ F \rightarrow D\}$ and $BH \rightarrow GE$ into $\{BH \rightarrow G,\ BH \rightarrow E\}$ and that some FDs fell by the wayside: $F \rightarrow D$ and $BH \rightarrow E$ no longer have a home since none of the new schemas contains all the attributes used by these FDs. However, things are still looking bright since the FD $F \rightarrow D$ can be derived from other FDs embedded in the new schemas $\mathbf{R}_1$ and $\mathbf{R}_2$: $F \rightarrow AH$ and $A \rightarrow DE$. Similarly, $BH \rightarrow E$ can still be derived because the attribute closure of BH with respect to the FDs embedded in $\mathbf{R}_1$ and $\mathbf{R}_2$, contains E. (Verify this claim using the algorithm in Figure 6.3!) The above decomposition is therefore dependency preserving.

In the second iteration of the loop in Figure 6.9, *Decomposition* = $\{\mathbf{R}_1, \mathbf{R}_2\}$, and we must check if any of these schemas violates BCNF. It is easy to see that $\mathbf{R}_1$ is in BCNF. Although $A \rightarrow DE$ violates BCNF in **R**, it does not violate BCNF in $\mathbf{R}_1$ since, by construction, A is a key of $\mathbf{R}_1$. Note that it will always be true that the offending FD, f, in **R** that is used as the basis for the decomposition is converted to a nonoffending FD in $\mathbf{R}_1$. In general, however, you cannot assume that $\mathbf{R}_1$ will always be in BCNF since it can have other FDs that violate BCNF.

What about $\mathbf{R}_2$? The FDs $ABH \rightarrow C$ and $BGH \rightarrow F$ did not violate BCNF in **R** since both ABH and BGH are superkeys. As a result, they do not violate BCNF in $\mathbf{R}_2$ (which has only a subset of the attributes of **R**). The FD that violates BCNF here is $F \rightarrow AH$, so in the second iteration of the algorithm **S** is $\mathbf{R}_2$. The algorithm then splits $\mathbf{R}_2$ as follows:

$$\mathbf{R}_{21} = (FAH; \{F \rightarrow AH\})$$
$$\mathbf{R}_{22} = (FBCG; \{FB \rightarrow CG\})$$

(Note that the FD $FB \rightarrow CG$ is not in $\mathcal{F}$ but is derivable from it.)

Now both schemas, $\mathbf{R}_{21}$ and $\mathbf{R}_{22}$, are in BCNF. However, the price is that the FDs $ABH \rightarrow C$, $BGH \rightarrow F$, and $BH \rightarrow G$ that were present in $\mathbf{R}_2$ are now homeless. Furthermore, none of these FDs can be derived using the FDs that are still embedded in $\mathbf{R}_1$, $\mathbf{R}_{21}$, and $\mathbf{R}_{22}$. For instance, computing $(ABH)^+$ with respect to this set of FDs yields $ABHDE$, which does not contain C, so $ABH \rightarrow C$ is not derivable. Thus, we obtain a *non-preserving* decomposition of **R** into three BCNF schemas: $\mathbf{R}_1$, $\mathbf{R}_{21}$, and $\mathbf{R}_{22}$.

This decomposition is by no means unique. For instance, if our algorithm had picked up $F \rightarrow ADH$ at the very first iteration, the first decomposition would have been

$$\mathbf{R}'_1 = (FADH; \{F \rightarrow ADH, A \rightarrow D\})$$
$$\mathbf{R}'_2 = (FBCEG; \{F \rightarrow E, FB \rightarrow CG\})$$

Observe that none of these schemas is in BCNF ($A \rightarrow D$ violates the BCNF requirements in the first schema and $F \rightarrow E$ in the second) and need to be decomposed further. This is not the end of the differences, however: some FDs that were present in the decomposition into $\mathbf{R}_1$, $\mathbf{R}_{21}$, $\mathbf{R}_{22}$ are no longer embedded in the new decomposition (e.g., $A \rightarrow E$). ■

Properties of the BCNF decomposition algorithm. First and foremost, the BCNF decomposition algorithm in Figure 6.9 always yields a lossless decomposition. To see this, consider the two schemas involving attribute sets $\overline{X}\,\overline{Y}$ and $(\overline{S} - \overline{Y}) \cup \overline{X}$ that replace the schema $\mathbf{S} = (\overline{S}, \mathcal{F}')$ in the algorithm. Notice that $\overline{X}\,\overline{Y} \cap ((\overline{S} - \overline{Y}) \cup \overline{X}) = \overline{X}$ and thus $\overline{X}\,\overline{Y} \cap ((\overline{S} - \overline{Y}) \cup \overline{X}) \rightarrow \overline{X}\,\overline{Y}$ since $\overline{X} \rightarrow \overline{Y} \in \mathcal{F}$. Therefore, according to the losslessness test for binary decompositions on page 214, $\{\overline{X}\,\overline{Y},\ (\overline{S} - \overline{Y}) \cup \overline{X}\}$ is a lossless decomposition of $\mathbf{S}$. This means that at every step in our algorithm we replace one schema by its lossless decomposition. Thus, by Exercise 6.15, the final decomposition produced by this algorithm is also lossless.

Are the decompositions produced by the BCNF algorithm always dependency preserving? We have seen that this is not the case. Decomposition (6.8) of HASACCOUNT is not dependency preserving. Moreover, it is easy to see that no BCNF decomposition of HASACCOUNT (not only those produced by this particular algorithm) is both lossless and dependency preserving. Indeed, there are just three decompositions to try, and we can simply check them all.

The BCNF decomposition algorithm is nondeterministic.

Finally, Example 6.7.1 shows that the BCNF decomposition algorithm is nondeterministic. The final result depends on the order in which FDs are selected in the **while** loop. The decomposition chosen by the database designer can be a matter of taste, or it can be based on objective criteria. For instance, some decompositions might be dependency preserving, others not; some might lead to fewer FDs left out as interrelational constraints (e.g., the decomposition $\mathbf{R}_1$, $\mathbf{R}_{21}$, $\mathbf{R}_{22}$ in Example 6.7.1 is better in this sense than the decomposition $\mathbf{R}'_1$, $\mathbf{R}'_2$). Some attribute sets might be more likely to be queried together so they better not be separated in the decomposition. The next section describes one common approach that can help in choosing one BCNF decomposition over another.

6.8 Synthesis of 3NF Schemas

We have seen that some schemas (such as HASACCOUNT, in Figure 6.8) cannot be decomposed into BCNF so that the result is also dependency preserving. However, if we agree to settle for 3NF instead of BCNF, dependency-preserving decompositions are always possible (but recall that 3NF schemas might contain redundancies—see page 211).

Before we present a 3NF decomposition algorithm, we need to introduce the concept of *minimal cover*, which is really very simple. We know that sets of FDs might look completely different but nonetheless be logically equivalent. Figure 6.4 presented one fairly straightforward way of testing equivalence. Since there might be many sets of FDs equivalent to any given set, we question whether there is a set of FDs that can be viewed as canonical. It turns out that defining a unique canonical set is not an easy task, but the notion of minimal cover comes close.

6.8.1 Minimal Cover

Let $\mathcal{F}$ be a set of FDs. A **minimal cover** of $\mathcal{F}$ is a set of FDs, $\mathcal{G}$, that has the following properties:

1. $\mathcal{G}$ is equivalent to $\mathcal{F}$ (but, possibly, different from $\mathcal{F}$).
2. All FDs in $\mathcal{G}$ have the form $\overline{X} \rightarrow A$, where A is a single attribute.
3. It is not possible to make $\mathcal{G}$ "smaller" (and still satisfy the first two properties) by either of the following:
   (a) Deleting an FD
   (b) Deleting an attribute from an FD

An FD, f, that can be deleted from a set, $\mathcal{F}$, while preserving the equivalence (i.e., when $\mathcal{F} - f$ is equivalent to $\mathcal{F}$) is said to be a **redundant FD**. An attribute, A, in f that can be deleted while preserving the equivalence (i.e., if $\mathcal{F}$ and $\mathcal{F} - \{f\} \cup \{f'\}$ are equivalent, where f' is f with A deleted) is said to be a **redundant attribute**. Thus, a minimal cover has neither redundant FDs nor redundant attributes.

Clearly, because of Armstrong's rule of decomposition for functional dependencies, it is easy to convert $\mathcal{F}$ into an equivalent set of FDs where the right-hand sides are singleton attributes. However, property 3 is more subtle. Before presenting an algorithm for comput ng minimal covers, we illustrate it with a concrete example.

Example 6.8.1 (Minimal Cover). Consider the attribute set $ABCDEFGH$ and the following set, $\mathcal{F}$, of FDs:

$ABH \rightarrow C$ $F \rightarrow AD$
$A \rightarrow D$ $E \rightarrow F$
$C \rightarrow E$ $BH \rightarrow E$
$BGH \rightarrow F$

Since not all right-hand sides are single attributes, we can use the decomposition rule to obtain an FD set that satisfies the first two properties of minimal covers.

$$\begin{array}{ll} ABH \rightarrow C & F \rightarrow A \\ A \rightarrow D & F \rightarrow D \\ C \rightarrow E & E \rightarrow F \\ BGH \rightarrow F & BH \rightarrow E \end{array} \tag{6.9}$$

We can see that $BGH \rightarrow F$ is entailed by $BH \rightarrow E$ and $E \rightarrow F$, and that $F \rightarrow D$ is entailed by $F \rightarrow A$ and $A \rightarrow D$. Thus, we are left with

$$\begin{array}{ll} ABH \rightarrow C & F \rightarrow A \\ A \rightarrow D & E \rightarrow F \\ C \rightarrow E & BH \rightarrow E \end{array} \tag{6.10}$$

It is easy to check by computing attribute closures that none of these FDs is redundant; that is, one cannot simply throw out an FD from this set without sacrificing equivalence to the original set $\mathcal{F}$. However, is the resulting set a minimal cover of $\mathcal{F}$? The answer turns out to be *no* because it is possible to delete the attribute A from the first FD, since $BH \rightarrow C$ is entailed by the set (6.10) (verify this by computing the attribute closure of BH) and $ABH \rightarrow C$ is obviously entailed by $BH \rightarrow C$. Thus, we get

$$\begin{array}{ll} BH \rightarrow C & F \rightarrow A \\ A \rightarrow D & E \rightarrow F \\ C \rightarrow E & BH \rightarrow E \end{array} \tag{6.11}$$

Interestingly, the latter set of FDs is still not minimal because the FD $BH \rightarrow E$ is redundant. Removing this FD yields a minimal cover at last. ■

The algorithm for computing minimal covers is presented in Figure 6.10. **Step 1** is performed by a simple splitting of the FDs according to their right-hand sides. For instance, $\overline{X} \rightarrow AB$ turns into $\overline{X} \rightarrow A$ and $\overline{X} \rightarrow B$.

Step 2 is performed by checking every left-hand attribute in $\mathcal{G}$ for redundancy. That is, for every FD $\overline{X} \rightarrow A \in \mathcal{G}$ and every attribute $B \in \overline{X}$, we have to check if $(\overline{X} - B) \rightarrow A$ is entailed by $\mathcal{G}$—very tedious work if done manually. In the above example, we performed this step when we checked that $BH \rightarrow C$ is entailed by the FD set (6.10), which allowed us to get rid of the redundant attribute A in $ABH \rightarrow C$. **Step 3** is accomplished by another tedious algorithm: for every $g \in \mathcal{G}$, check that the FD g is entailed by $\mathcal{G} - \{g\}$.

Nonuniqueness of minimal covers. Observe that the outcome of steps 2 and 3 in the algorithm in Figure 6.10 may depend on the particular order in which we test the candidates for removal (both attributes and FDs). This suggests that a set of FDs can

FIGURE 6.10 Computation of a minimal cover.

Input: a set of FDs $\mathcal{F}$
Output: $\mathcal{G}$, a minimal cover of $\mathcal{F}$

Step 1: $\mathcal{G} := \mathcal{F}$, where all FDs are converted to use singleton attributes on the right-hand side.
Step 2: Remove all redundant attributes from the left-hand sides of FDs in $\mathcal{G}$.
Step 3: Remove all redundant FDs from $\mathcal{G}$.

return $\mathcal{G}$

---

have several minimal covers. For instance, $\{A \to B, B \to C, C \to A, A \to C, C \to B, B \to A\}$ has two minimal covers: $\{A \to B, B \to C, C \to A\}$ and $\{A \to C, C \to B, B \to A\}$.

Noninterchangeability of steps 2 and 3. An important observation about the algorithm in Figure 6.10 is that steps 2 and 3 *cannot* be done in a different order. Performing step 3 before 2 will not always return a minimal cover. In fact, we have already seen this phenomenon in Example 6.8.1. We obtained set (6.10) by removing redundant FDs from (6.9); then we obtained set (6.11) by deleting redundant attributes. Nevertheless, the result still had a redundant FD, $BH \to E$. On the other hand, if we first remove the redundant attributes from (6.9), we get

$$
\begin{array}{ll}
BH \to C & F \to A \\
A \to D & F \to D \\
C \to E & E \to F \\
BH \to F & BH \to E
\end{array}
$$

Then removing the redundant FDs $BH \to F$, $F \to D$, and $BH \to E$ yields the following minimal cover:

$$
\begin{array}{ll}
BH \to C & F \to A \\
A \to D & E \to F \\
C \to E &
\end{array}
\quad (6.12)
$$

6.8.2 3NF Decomposition through Schema Synthesis

The algorithm for constructing dependency-preserving 3NF decompositions works very differently from its BCNF counterpart. Instead of starting with one big schema and successively splitting it, the 3NF algorithm starts with individual attributes and groups them into schemas. For this reason, it is called **3NF synthesis**. Given a schema, $\mathbf{R} = (\overline{R}; \mathcal{F})$, where $\overline{R}$ is a set of attributes and $\mathcal{F}$ is a set of FDs, the algorithm for synthesizing a 3NF decomposition of **R** carries out four steps:

1. Find a minimal cover, $\mathcal{G}$, for $\mathcal{F}$.
2. Partition $\mathcal{G}$ into FD sets $\mathcal{G}_1, \ldots, \mathcal{G}_n$, such that each $\mathcal{G}_i$ consists of all FDs in $\mathcal{G}$ that share the same left-hand side. (It is not necessary to assume that different $\mathcal{G}_i$s have different left-hand sides, but it is usually a good idea to merge sets whose left-hand sides are the same.)
3. For each $\mathcal{G}_i$, form a relation schema, $\mathbf{R}_i = (\overline{R}_i; \mathcal{G}_i)$, where $\overline{R}_i$ is the set of all attributes mentioned in $\mathcal{G}_i$.
4. If one of the $\overline{R}_i$s, is a superkey of $\mathbf{R}$ (i.e., $(\overline{R}_i)^+_{\mathcal{F}} = \overline{R}$), we are done—$\mathbf{R}_1, \ldots, \mathbf{R}_n$ is the desired decomposition. If no $\overline{R}_i$ is a superkey of $\mathbf{R}$, let $\overline{R}_0$ be some key of $\mathbf{R}$, and let $\mathbf{R}_0 = (\overline{R}_0;\ \{\})$ be a new schema. Then $\mathbf{R}_0, \mathbf{R}_1, \ldots, \mathbf{R}_n$ is the desired decomposition.

   Note that the collection of schemas obtained after step 3 might not even be a decomposition because some attributes of **R** might be missing (see Example 6.8.2 below). However, any such missing attributes will be recaptured in step 4, because these attributes must be part of the key of **R** (Exercise 6.28).

Is it dependency preserving? This is easy to see: By construction, every FD in $\mathcal{G}$ has a home, so $\mathcal{G} = \cup\mathcal{G}_i$. By definition of minimal covers, $\mathcal{G}^+ = \mathcal{F}^+$, so $\mathcal{F}$ is preserved.

Checking for BCNF—pitfalls. It might seem that each $\mathbf{R}_i$ is in BCNF, because every FD in $\mathcal{G}_i$ is superkey-based. However, do not fall for this argument so easily. The FDs in $\mathcal{G}_i$ might not be the only ones that hold in $\mathbf{R}_i$. This is because the full set of FDs that is guaranteed to hold in $\mathbf{R}_i$ is the projection $\pi_{\overline{R}_i}(\mathcal{G})$. Although this projection always entails $\mathcal{G}_i$, the opposite may not be true: $\mathcal{G}^+$ might have FDs that are not entailed by $\mathcal{G}_i$, but their attribute sets may be entirely contained within $\overline{R}_i$. To see this, consider a slight modification of our tried-and-true schema HASACCOUNT. Here $\overline{R}$ consists of the attributes `AccountNumber`, `ClientId`, `OfficeId`, `DateOpened`, and $\mathcal{F}$ consists of the FDs `ClientId OfficeId` → `AccountNumber` and `AccountNumber` → `OfficeId DateOpened`. The above algorithm then produces two schemas:

```
R1 = ({ClientId,OfficeId,AccountNumber},
           {ClientId OfficeId → AccountNumber})
R2 = ({AccountNumber,OfficeId,DateOpened},
           {AccountNumber → OfficeId DateOpened})
```

A careful examination shows that, even though `AccountNumber` → `OfficeId` is not explicitly specified for $\mathbf{R}_1$, it must nonetheless hold over the attributes of that schema because this FD is entailed by the original set of FDs (and is even present in the decomposed schema $\mathbf{R}_2$).

To get a better intuition for why the FDs of $\mathbf{R}_2$ must be taken into account when considering $\mathbf{R}_1$, observe that the pair of attributes `AccountNumber`, `OfficeId` represents the same real-world relationship in both $\mathbf{R}_1$ and $\mathbf{R}_2$. So it is an inconsistency if the tuples in $\mathbf{R}_2$ obey a constraint over this pair of attributes while the tuples in $\mathbf{R}_1$ do not.

Thus, in general, to check which of the schemas $\mathbf{R}_i$ obtained by the 3NF synthesis are in BCNF, it is not enough to look for violators of BCNF among the FDs in $\mathcal{G}_i$. Instead, it is necessary to compute the projections $\pi_{\overline{R_i}}(\mathcal{G})$ and look for the violators there. As explained earlier, this is rather tiresome to do manually (except for small examples) because computing projections of FDs is exponentially hard. This exponential complexity is the primary reason why the 3NF algorithm does not explicitly include all of $\pi_{\overline{R_i}}(\mathcal{G})$ into the FD set of $\mathbf{R}_i$ (thereby creating a source for potential misunderstanding of which FDs are *really* part of the $\mathbf{R}_i$s).

> The full set of FDs that belong to $\mathbf{R}_i$ is $\pi_{\overline{R_i}}(\mathcal{G})$ — not just $\mathcal{G}_i$.

Is it really 3NF? It seems obvious that each $\mathbf{R}_i$ is a 3NF schema, because the only FDs associated with $\mathbf{R}_i$ are those in $\mathcal{G}_i$ and they all share the same left-hand side (which is thus a superkey of $\mathbf{R}_i$). However, the above argument regarding BCNF shows that schemas produced by the synthesis algorithm might have FDs with different left-hand sides and thus conformance to 3NF is not at all obvious. Nevertheless, it can be *proved* that the above algorithm always yields 3NF decompositions (see Exercise 6.17).

Is it lossless? The final question is whether the synthesis algorithm yields lossless decompositions of the input schema. The answer is yes, but proving this is more difficult than proving the 3NF property. Although it might not be obvious, achieving losslessness is in fact the only purpose of step 4 in that algorithm. This is illustrated in the following example.

Example 6.8.2 (3NF Synthesis Where Step 4 Is Essential). Consider the schema with FDs depicted in (6.9) on page 223. A minimal cover for this set is shown in (6.12). Since no two FDs here share the same left-hand side, we end up with the following schemas: $(BHC;\ BH \rightarrow C)$ $(AD;\ A \rightarrow D)$, $(CE;\ C \rightarrow E)$, $(FA;\ F \rightarrow A)$, and $(EF;\ E \rightarrow F)$. Notice that none of these schemas forms the superkey for the entire set of attributes. For instance, the attribute closure of BHC does not contain G. In fact, the attribute G is not even included in any of the schemas! So, according to our remark about the purpose of step 4, this decomposition is not lossless (in fact, it is not even a decomposition!) To make it lossless, we perform step 4 and add the schema $(BGH;\ \{\,\})$. ■

> *Brain Teaser:* Does 3NF synthesis always produce a unique result?

6.8.3 BCNF Decomposition through 3NF Synthesis

So, how can 3NF synthesis help design BCNF database schemas? The answer is simple. To decompose a schema into BCNF relations, do *not* use the BCNF algorithm first. Instead, use 3NF synthesis, which is lossless and guaranteed to preserve dependencies. If the resulting schemas are already in BCNF (as in Example 6.8.2), no further action is necessary. If, however, some schema in the result is not in BCNF, use the BCNF algorithm to split it until no violation of BCNF remains. Repeat this step for each non-BCNF schema produced by the 3NF synthesis.

The advantage of this approach is that, if a lossless and dependency-preserving decomposition exists, 3NF synthesis is likely to find it. If some schemas are not in BCNF after the first stage, loss of some FDs is inevitable (Exercise 6.34). But at least we tried hard. Here is a complete example that illustrates the above approach.

Example 6.8.3 (Combining Schema Synthesis and Decomposition). Let the attribute set be St (student), C (course), Sem (semester), P (professor), T (time), and R (room) with the following FDs:

```
St C Sem → P            P Sem T → C R
P Sem → C               P Sem C T → R
C Sem T → P             P Sem T → C
```

These functional dependencies apply at a university in which multiple sections of the same course might be taught in the same semester (in which case providing the name of a course and a semester does not uniquely identify a professor) and a professor teaches only one course a semester (in which case providing the name of a professor and a semester uniquely identifies a course) and all the sections of a course are taught at different times.

We begin by finding a minimal cover for the above set. The first step is to split the right-hand sides of the set of FDs into singleton attributes.

```
St C Sem → P            P Sem T → C
P Sem → C               P Sem T → R
C Sem T → P             P Sem C T → R
                        P Sem T → C
```

Let $\mathcal{F}$ denote this set of FDs. The last FD is a duplicate, so we delete it from the set. Next we reduce the left-hand sides by eliminating redundant attributes. For instance, to check the left-hand side St C Sem, we must compute several attribute closures—$(\texttt{St Sem})^+_{\mathcal{F}}$ = {St, Sem}; $(\texttt{St C})^+_{\mathcal{F}}$ = {St, C}; $(\texttt{C Sem})^+_{\mathcal{F}}$ = {C, Sem}—which show that there are no redundant attributes in the first FD. Similarly, P Sem, C Sem T, and P Sem T cannot be reduced. However, checking P Sem C T brings a reward: $(\texttt{P Sem T})^+_{\mathcal{F}}$ = P Sem T C R, so C can be deleted.

The outcome from this stage is the following set of FDs, which we number for convenient reference.

```
FD1. St C Sem -> P
FD2. P Sem -> C
FD3. C Sem T -> P
FD4. P Sem T -> C
FD5. P Sem T -> R
```

The next step is to get rid of the redundant FDs, which are detected with the help of attribute closure, as usual. Since $(\texttt{St C Sem})^+_{\{\mathcal{F}-\text{FD1}\}}$ = `St C Sem`, FD1 cannot be eliminated. Nor can FDs 2, 3, and 5. However, FD4 is redundant (because of FD2), so it can be eliminated. Thus, the minimal cover is

```
St C Sem -> P
P Sem -> C
C Sem T -> P
P Sem T -> R
```

This leads to the following dependency-preserving 3NF decomposition:

```
(St C Sem P; St C Sem -> P)
(P Sem C; P Sem -> C)
(C Sem T P; C Sem T -> P)
(P Sem T R; P Sem T -> R)
```

It is easy to verify that none of the above schemas forms a superkey for the original schema; therefore, to make the decomposition lossless we also need to add a schema whose attribute closure contains all the original attributes. The schema `(St T Sem P; { })` is one possibility here.

If you trust that the 3NF synthesis algorithm is correct and that we did not make mistakes applying it, no checking for 3NF is necessary. However, a quick look reveals that the first and the third schemas are not in BCNF because of the FD `P Sem` → `C` embedded in the second schema. (Recall the discussion on page 225, *Checking for BCNF*, which explains that to determine whether a subschema, $\mathbf{R}_i$, is in BCNF one must consider all the dependencies over the attributes of $\mathbf{R}_i$ that are implied by the original set of dependencies $\mathcal{G}$ — namely, all the dependencies in $\pi_{\overline{R}_i}(\mathcal{G})$. `P Sem` → `C` is one such FD.)

Further decomposition of the first schema with respect to `P Sem` → `C` yields `(P Sem C; P Sem` → `C)` and `(P Sem St; { })`—a lossless decomposition but one in which the FD `St C Sem` → `P` is not preserved.

Decomposition of the third schema with respect to `P Sem` → `C` yields `(P Sem C; P Sem` → `C)` and `(P Sem T; {})`—another lossless decomposition, which, alas, does not preserve `C Sem T` → `P`.

So, the final BCNF decomposition is

```
(P Sem C; P Sem → C)
(P Sem St)
(P Sem T)
(P Sem T R; P Sem T → R)
(St T Sem P)
```

This decomposition is lossless because we first obtained a lossless 3NF decomposition and then applied the BCNF algorithm, which preserves losslessness. It is not dependency preserving, however, since St C Sem → P and C Sem T → P are not represented in the above schemas. ■

6.9 The Fourth Normal Form

OPTIONAL

Not all of the world's problems are due to bad FDs. Consider the following schema:

PERSON(SSN, PhoneN, ChildSSN) **6.13**

where we assume that a person can have several phone numbers and several children. Here is one possible relation instance.

SSN	PhoneN	ChildSSN
111-22-3333	516-123-4567	222-33-4444
111-22-3333	516-345-6789	222-33-4444
111-22-3333	516-123-4567	333-44-5555
111-22-3333	516-345-6789	333-44-5555
222-33-4444	212-987-6543	444-55-6666
222-33-4444	212-987-1111	555-66-7777
222-33-4444	212-987-6543	555-66-7777
222-33-4444	212-987-1111	444-55-6666

6.14

As there are no nontrivial functional dependencies (we assume that most children in the database have two parents and so the FD ChildSSN → SSN does not hold), this schema is in 3NF and even BCNF. Nonetheless, it is clearly not a good design as it exhibits a great deal of redundancy. There is no particular association between phone numbers and children, except through the SSN, so every child item related to a given SSN must occur in one tuple with every PhoneN related to the same SSN. Thus, whenever a phone number is added or deleted, several tuples might need to be added or deleted as well. If a person gives up all phone numbers, the information about her children will be lost (or NULL values will have to be used).

It might seem that a compression technique can help here. For instance, we might decide to store only some tuples as long as there is a way to reconstruct the original information.

SSN	PhoneN	ChildSSN
111-22-3333	516-123-4567	222-33-4444
111-22-3333	516-345-6789	333-44-5555
222-33-4444	212-987-6543	444-55-6666
222-33-4444	212-987-1111	555-66-7777

Still, although this is more efficient, it solves none of the aforesaid anomalies. Also, it imposes an additional burden on the applications, which now must be aware of the compression schema.

In our discussion of BCNF, we concluded that redundancy arises when a particular semantic relationship among attribute values is stored more than once. In Figure 4.13 on page 86, the fact that the person with SSN 111111111 lives at 123 Main Street is an example of that—it is stored two times. In that case, the problem was traced back to the functional dependency that relates SSN and Address and the fact that SSN is not a key (and hence there can be several rows with the same SSN value). The redundant storage of a semantic relationship, however, is not limited to this situation. In the relation **r** shown in (6.14), the relationships SSN-PhoneN and SSN-ChildSSN are stored multiple times and there are no FDs involved. The problem arises here because there are several attributes—in this case PhoneN and ChildSSN—that have the property that their sets of values are associated with a single value of another attribute—in this case SSN. A relationship between a particular SSN value and a particular PhoneN value is stored as many times as there are children of the person with that SSN. Note that the relation satisfies the following property:

$$\mathbf{r} = \pi_{\texttt{SSN,PhoneN}}(\mathbf{r}) \bowtie \pi_{\texttt{SSN,ChildSSN}}(\mathbf{r}) \quad \textbf{6.15}$$

Join dependencies. When (6.15) is required of all legal instances of a schema, this property is known as *join dependency*. A join dependency can arise when characteristics of an enterprise are described by sets of values. With the E-R approach to database design, we saw that such characteristics are represented as set-valued attributes and that translating them into attributes in the relational model is awkward. In particular, when an entity type or a relationship type has several set-valued attributes, a join dependency results.

Condition (6.15) should look familiar to you. It guarantees that a decomposition of **r** into the two tables $\pi_{\texttt{SSN,PhoneN}}(\mathbf{r})$ and $\pi_{\texttt{SSN,ChildSSN}}(\mathbf{r})$ will be lossless. That is certainly true in this case, but it is not our immediate concern. The condition also tells us something about **r**: a join dependency indicates that semantic relationships can be stored redundantly in an instance of **r**.

OPTIONAL

Formally, let $\overline{R}$ be a set of attributes. A **join dependency** (JD) is a constraint of the form

$$\overline{R} = \overline{R}_1 \bowtie \cdots \bowtie \overline{R}_n$$

where $\overline{R_1}, \ldots, \overline{R}_n$ are attribute sets that represent a decomposition of $\overline{R}$. Note that here the $\overline{R}_i$'s are sets of attributes and $\bowtie$ is just a symbol—we are not actually joining any relations. However, this expression *is* related to a join. Recall that earlier (on page 198) we defined the notion of satisfaction of FDs by relational instances. We now define the same notion for JDs: a relation instance, **r**, over $\overline{R}$ **satisfies** the above join dependency if

$$\mathbf{r} = \pi_{\overline{R}_1}(\mathbf{r}) \bowtie \cdots \bowtie \pi_{\overline{R}_n}(\mathbf{r})$$

It is easy to see from the definition that the existence of a JD is really another way of saying that there is a lossless decomposition of the schema. Why are we defining the same thing twice? The answer is that previously we used FDs to state that such a decomposition exists, but now we find that a lossless decomposition cannot always be indicated by the presence of certain kinds of FDs. Therefore, we need a new kind of syntactic constraint—join dependencies—which we can attach to a database schema to indicate the presence of a lossless decomposition. In fact, as we will soon see, an FD always implies some sort of a JD, and this is precisely the reason why lossless decompositions are possible with respect to FDs. For instance, consider the schema PERSON2(`SSN`, `Name`, `ChildSSN`) with the FD `SSN`→`Name`. It is easy to see from the conditions for losslessness on page 214 that this FD implies the JD

$$(\texttt{SSN Name ChildSSN}) = (\texttt{SSN Name}) \bowtie (\texttt{SSN ChildSSN})$$

Moreover, due to the one-to-many relationship between `SSN` and `ChildSSN`, a typical relational instance over PERSON2 will have similar redundancy to that of relation (6.14) above.

Let $\mathbf{R} = (\overline{R};\ Constraints)$ be a relational schema, where $\overline{R}$ is a set of attributes and *Constraints* is a set of FDs and JDs. As in the case of FDs alone, a relation over the set of attributes $\overline{R}$ is a **legal instance** of **R** if and only if it satisfies all constraints in *Constraints*.

Multivalued dependencies and 4NF. Of particular interest are **binary join dependencies**, also known as **multivalued dependencies** (*MVD*). These are JDs of the form $\overline{R} = \overline{R}_1 \bowtie \overline{R}_2$. The redundancy exhibited by the relation schema PERSON (6.13) was caused by this particular type of join dependency. The *fourth normal form*, introduced in [Fagin 1977], is designed to prevent redundancies of this type.

MVDs constrain instances of a relation in the same way that FDs do, so a description of a relation schema must include both. As a result, we describe a relation schema, **R**, as $(\overline{R}; \mathcal{D})$, where $\mathcal{D}$ is now a set of FDs and MVDs. **Entailment** of JDs is defined in the same way as entailment of FDs. Let $\mathcal{S}$ be a set of JDs (and possibly FDs)

OPTIONAL

and d be a JD (or an FD). Then $\mathcal{S}$ **entails** d if every relation instance **r** that satisfies all dependencies in $\mathcal{S}$ also satisfies d. In Section 6.10.1, we show how an MVD can be entailed by a set of MVDs. With this in mind, a relation schema, $\mathbf{R} = (\overline{R}; \mathcal{D})$, is said to be in **fourth normal form** (4NF) if, for every MVD $\overline{R} = \overline{X} \bowtie \overline{Y}$ that is entailed by $\mathcal{D}$, either of the following is true:

- $\overline{X} \subseteq \overline{Y}$ or $\overline{Y} \subseteq \overline{X}$ (i.e., the MVD is trivial).
- $\overline{X} \cap \overline{Y}$ is a superkey of $\overline{R}$ (i.e., $(\overline{X} \cap \overline{Y}) \rightarrow \overline{R}$ is entailed by $\mathcal{D}$).

It is easy to see that PERSON is *not* a 4NF schema, because the MVD PERSON = (`SSN PhoneN`) $\bowtie$ (`SSN ChildSSN`) holds whereas `SSN` = {`SSN, PhoneN`} $\cap$ {`SSN, ChildSSN`} is not a superkey. What is the intuition here? If `SSN` were a superkey, then for each value of `SSN` there would be at most one value of `PhoneN` and one value of `ChildSSN` and hence no redundancy. This not being the case, PERSON has redundancy. However, splitting PERSON into a relation over the attributes (`SSN, PhoneN`) and another one over the attributes (`SSN, ChildSSN`) yields a lossless decomposition where every relation is in 4NF and no redundant information is stored.

OPTIONAL

4NF and BCNF. As it turns out, 4NF schemas are also BCNF schemas (i.e., 4NF closes the loopholes that BCNF leaves behind). To see this, suppose that $\mathbf{R} = (\overline{R}; \mathcal{D})$ is a 4NF schema and $\overline{X} \rightarrow \overline{Y}$ is a nontrivial functional dependency that holds in **R**. To show that 4NF schemas are also BCNF schemas we must demonstrate that $\overline{X}$ is a superkey of **R**. For simplicity, assume that $\overline{X}$ and $\overline{Y}$ are disjoint. Then $\overline{R}_1 = \overline{X}\,\overline{Y}$, $\overline{R}_2 = \overline{R} - \overline{Y}$ is a lossless decomposition of **R**. This follows directly from the test for losslessness of binary schema decompositions presented in Section 6.6.1 on page 214. Thus, $\overline{R} = \overline{R}_1 \bowtie \overline{R}_2$ is a binary join dependency, that is, an MVD that holds in **R**. But by the definition of 4NF it follows that either $\overline{X}\,\overline{Y} = \overline{R}_1 \subseteq \overline{R}_2 = \overline{R} - \overline{Y}$ (an impossibility) or $\overline{R} - \overline{Y} = \overline{R}_2 \subseteq \overline{R}_1 = \overline{X}\,\overline{Y}$ (which implies that $\overline{R} = \overline{X}\,\overline{Y}$ and $\overline{X}$ is a superkey) or that $\overline{R}_1 \cap \overline{R}_2$ $(= \overline{X})$ is a superkey. This means that every nontrivial FD in **R** satisfies the BCNF requirements.

It can also be shown (but it is harder to do) that if $\mathbf{R} = (\overline{R};\ \mathcal{D})$ is such that $\mathcal{D}$ consists only of FDs, then **R** is in 4NF if and only if it is in BCNF (see [Fagin 1977]). In other words, 4NF is an extension of the requirements for BCNF to design environments where MVDs, in addition to FDs, must be specified.

Brain Teaser: Can a 4NF schema not be in BCNF if FDs are the only dependencies?

Designing 4NF schemas. Because 4NF implies BCNF, we cannot hope to find a general algorithm for constructing a dependency-preserving and lossless decomposition of an arbitrary relation into relations in 4NF. However, as with BCNF, a lossless decomposition into 4NF can always be achieved. Such an algorithm is very similar to that for BCNF. It is an iterative process that starts with the original schema and at each stage yields decompositions that have fewer MVDs that violate 4NF: if $\mathbf{R}_i = (\overline{R}_i;\ \mathcal{D}_i)$ is such an intermediate schema and $\mathcal{D}_i$ entails an MVD of the form

FIGURE 6.11 Lossless decomposition into 4NF.

Input: $\mathbf{R} = (\overline{R};\ \mathcal{D})$ /* $\mathcal{D}$ is a set of FDs and MVDs; FDs are treated as MVDs */
Output: A lossless decomposition of **R** where each schema is in 4NF.

Decomposition := {**R**} /* Initially decomposition consists of only one schema */
while there is a schema $\mathbf{S} = (\overline{S};\ \mathcal{D}')$ in *Decomposition* that is not in 4NF **do**
/* Let $\overline{X} \bowtie \overline{Y}$ be an MVD in $\mathcal{D}^+$ such that $\overline{X}\,\overline{Y} \subseteq \overline{S}$ and
it violates 4NF in **S**. Decompose using this MVD */
Replace **S** in *Decomposition* with schemas $\mathbf{S}_1 = (\overline{X}\,\overline{Y};\ \mathcal{D}'_1)$ and
$\mathbf{S}_2 = ((\overline{S} - \overline{Y}) \cup \overline{X};\ \mathcal{D}'_2)$, where $\mathcal{D}'_1 = \pi_{\overline{X}\,\overline{Y}}(\mathcal{D}')$ and $\mathcal{D}'_2 = \pi_{(\overline{S}-\overline{Y})\cup\overline{X}}(\mathcal{D}')$
end
return *Decomposition*

$\overline{R}_i = \overline{X} \bowtie \overline{Y}$, which violates 4NF, then the algorithm replaces $\mathbf{R}_i$ with a pair of schemas $(\overline{X};\ \mathcal{D}_{i,1})$ and $(\overline{Y};\ \mathcal{D}_{i,2})$. The new schemas do not have the offending MVD. Eventually, there will be no MVDs left that violate the requirements for 4NF. The algorithm is described more precisely in Figure 6.11.

Two important points regarding this algorithm need to be emphasized. First, if $\mathbf{R}_i = (\overline{R}_i;\ \mathcal{D}_i)$ is a schema and $\overline{S} \rightarrow \overline{T} \in \mathcal{D}$ (for simplicity, assume that $\overline{S}$ and $\overline{T}$ are disjoint), then this FD implies the MVD $R_i = \overline{S}\,\overline{T} \bowtie (\overline{R}_i - \overline{T})$. Thus, the 4NF decomposition algorithm can treat FDs as MVDs. The other nonobvious issue in the 4NF decomposition algorithm has to do with determining the set of dependencies that hold in the decomposition. That is, if $\mathbf{R}_i = (\overline{R}_i;\ \mathcal{D}_i)$ is decomposed with respect to the MVD $\overline{R}_i = \overline{X} \bowtie \overline{Y}$, what is the set of dependencies that is expected to hold over the attributes $\overline{X}$ and $\overline{Y}$ in the resulting decomposition? The answer is $\pi_{\overline{X}}(\mathcal{D}_i^+)$ and $\pi_{\overline{Y}}(\mathcal{D}_i^+)$—the *projections* of $\mathcal{D}_i^+$ on $\overline{X}$ and $\overline{Y}$. Here $\mathcal{D}_i^+$ is the **closure** of $\mathcal{D}_i$, that is, the set of all FDs and MVDs entailed by $\mathcal{D}_i$ (the optional Section 6.10 provides a set of inference rules for MVD entailment).

Projection of an FD on a set of attributes has been defined in Section 6.6.2. **Projection of an MVD,** $\overline{R}_i = \overline{V} \bowtie \overline{W}$, on a set of attributes $\overline{X}$, denoted $\pi_{\overline{X}}(\overline{R}_i = \overline{V} \bowtie \overline{W})$, is and MVD over the attributes of $\overline{X}$. It is defined as $\overline{X} = (\overline{X} \cap \overline{V}) \bowtie (\overline{X} \cap \overline{W})$, if $\overline{V} \cap \overline{W} \subseteq \overline{X}$, and is undefined otherwise. It follows directly from the definitions that the projection rule for MVDs is sound, that is, if an MVD, m, holds in a relation **r** then $\pi_{\overline{X}}(m)$ holds in $\pi_{\overline{X}}(\mathbf{r})$ (see Exercise 6.31). **Projection of a set of MVDs,** $\pi_{\overline{X}}(\mathcal{D})$, is a set that consists of all the MVDs of the form $\pi_{\overline{X}}(m)$, where $m \in \mathcal{D}$ and is such that $\pi_{\overline{X}}(m)$ is defined.

Example 6.9.1 (4NF Decomposition). Consider a schema with attributes $ABCD$ and the MVDs $ABCD = AB \bowtie BCD$, $ABCD = ACD \bowtie BD$, and $ABCD = ABC \bowtie BCD$. Applying the first MVD, we obtain the following decomposition: AB, BCD. Projection of the remaining MVDs on AB is undefined. Projection of the second MVD on BCD is $BCD = CD \bowtie BD$, and projection of the third MVD on BCD is

OPTIONAL

$BCD = BC \bowtie BCD$, which is a trivial MVD. Thus, we can decompose BCD with respect to this last MVD, which yields the following final result: AB, BD, CD. Note that if we first decomposed $ABCD$ with respect to the third MVD, the final result would be different: AB, BC, BD, CD. ■

The design theory for 4NF is not as well developed as that for 3NF and BCNF, and very few algorithms are known. The basic recommendation is to start with a decomposition into 3NF and then proceed with the above algorithm and further decompose the offending (non-4NF) schemas. On a more sophisticated level, the work reported in [Beeri and Kifer 1986a, 1986b, 1987], among others, develops a design theory and the corresponding algorithms that can rectify design problems by synthesizing *new*(!) attributes. These advanced issues are briefly surveyed in Section 6.10.

Example 6.9.2 (Combining 3NF Synthesis with 4NF Decomposition). Consider the schema **R** over the attributes ABCDEFG with the following functional dependencies:

$$AB \rightarrow C$$
$$C \rightarrow B$$
$$BC \rightarrow DE$$
$$E \rightarrow FG$$

and the following multivalued dependencies:

$$\mathbf{R} = BC \bowtie ABDEFG$$
$$\mathbf{R} = EF \bowtie FGABCD$$

We begin with 3NF synthesis using the FDs only. This step is already familiar to us, so we present only the final result:

$$\mathbf{R}_1 = (ABC;\ \{AB \rightarrow C, C \rightarrow B\})$$
$$\mathbf{R}_2 = (CBDE;\ \{C \rightarrow BDE\})$$
$$\mathbf{R}_3 = (EFG;\ \{E \rightarrow FG\})$$

The first schema, $\mathbf{R}_1$, is not in BCNF due to the FD $C \rightarrow B$ (this FD must hold in $\mathbf{R}_1$ because it is in the original set of FDs and its attributes are contained within $\mathbf{R}_1$). So, we follow the BCNF decomposition algorithm and decompose $\mathbf{R}_1$ further using $C \rightarrow B$: $\mathbf{R}_{11} = (AC;\ \{A \rightarrow C\})$ and $\mathbf{R}_{12} = (BC;\ \{C \rightarrow B\})$.

Now we still have two MVDs left. Note that $\mathbf{R} = BC \bowtie ABDEFG$ projects onto $\mathbf{R}_2$ as $\mathbf{R}_2 = BC \bowtie BDE$, and it violates 4NF there because $B = BC \cap BDE$ is not a superkey of $\mathbf{R}_2$. So, we can use this MVD to decompose $\mathbf{R}_2$ into $(BC;\ \{C \rightarrow B\})$ and $(BDE;\ \{\ \})$. Similarly, $\mathbf{R} = EF \bowtie FGABCD$ projects onto $\mathbf{R}_3$ as $\mathbf{R}_3 = EF \bowtie FG$. This makes $\mathbf{R}_3$ violate 4NF, and we decompose it into $(EF;\ \{E \rightarrow F\})$ and $(FG;\ \{\ \})$.

The resulting decomposition is not dependency preserving. For instance, the FD $A \rightarrow B$, which was present in the original schema, is now not derivable from the FDs that are attached to the schemas in the decomposition. ■

OPTIONAL

The fifth normal form. We are not going to cover the fifth normal form in this book. Suffice it to say that it exists but that the database designer usually need not be concerned with it. 5NF is similar to 4NF in that it is based on join dependencies, but unlike 4NF it seeks to preclude all nontrivial JDs (not just the binary ones) that are not entailed by a superkey.

6.10 Advanced 4NF Design

The 4NF design algorithm outlined in Section 6.9 was intended to familiarize you with MVDs and 4NF, but it only scratches the surface of the 4NF design process. In this section, we provide more in-depth information, explain the main difficulties in designing database schemas in the presence of both FDs and MVDs, and outline the solutions. In particular, we explain why the 4NF decomposition algorithm does not truly solve the redundancy problem and why BCNF might be inadequate in the presence of MVDs. We refer you to the literature for more details.

6.10.1 MVDs and Their Properties

Multivalued dependencies are binary join dependencies. However, unlike general join dependencies they have a number of nice algebraic properties similar to those of FDs. In particular, a set of syntactic rules, analogous to Armstrong's axioms for FDs, exists for finding MVDs entailed by a given MVD set. These rules have a particularly simple form when we use a special notation for MVDs: It is customary to represent the multivalued dependency of the form $\overline{R} = \overline{V} \bowtie \overline{W}$ over a relation schema $\mathbf{R} = (\overline{R}, \mathcal{D})$ as $\overline{X} \twoheadrightarrow \overline{Y}$, where $\overline{X} = \overline{V} \cap \overline{W}$ and $\overline{X} \cup \overline{Y} = \overline{V}$ or $\overline{X} \cup \overline{Y} = \overline{W}$. Hence, $\overline{X} \twoheadrightarrow \overline{Y}$ is synonymous with $\overline{R} = \overline{X}\,\overline{Y} \bowtie \overline{X}(\overline{R} - \overline{Y})$.

Take a moment to understand the intuition behind this notation. An MVD arises when a single value of one attribute, for example, A, is related to a set of values of attribute B and a set of values of attribute C. Attribute A, contained in $\overline{X}$, can be thought of as an independent variable whose value determines (hence the symbol $\twoheadrightarrow$) the associated sets of values of both B and C, one of which is contained in $\overline{Y}$ and the other in the complement of $\overline{X}\,\overline{Y}$. For example, the MVD in the PERSON relation (6.13), `SSN PhoneN` $\bowtie$ `SSN ChildSSN`, can be expressed as `SSN` $\twoheadrightarrow$ `PhoneN` or `SSN` $\twoheadrightarrow$ `ChildSSN`.

In addition, it is often convenient to combine MVDs that share the same left-hand side. For example, $\overline{X} \twoheadrightarrow \overline{Y}$ and $\overline{X} \twoheadrightarrow \overline{Z}$ can be represented as $\overline{X} \twoheadrightarrow \overline{Y} \mid \overline{Z}$. It is simple to show that such a pair of MVDs is equivalent to a join dependency of the form $\overline{X}\,\overline{Y} \bowtie \overline{X}\,\overline{Z} \bowtie \overline{X}(\overline{R} - \overline{Y}\,\overline{Z})$. The representation $\overline{X} \twoheadrightarrow \overline{Y} \mid \overline{Z}$ is convenient not only for the inference system but also as a device that shows where the redundancy is: if the attributes of $\overline{X}$, $\overline{Y}$, and $\overline{Z}$ are contained within one relational schema, the associations between $\overline{Y}$ and $\overline{Z}$ are likely to be stored redundantly. We saw this problem in the context of the PERSON relation on page 229 and will come back to it later.

With this notation, we now present an inference system that can be used to decide entailment for *both* FDs and MVDs. The extended system contains Armstrong's axioms for FDs plus the following rules.

FD-MVD glue. These rules mix FDs and MVDs.

- *Replication.* $\overline{X} \rightarrow \overline{Y}$ entails $\overline{X} \twoheadrightarrow \overline{Y}$.
- *Coalescence.* If $\overline{W} \subset \overline{Y}$ and $\overline{Y} \cap \overline{Z} = \emptyset$, then $\overline{X} \twoheadrightarrow \overline{Y}$ and $\overline{Z} \rightarrow \overline{W}$ entail $\overline{X} \rightarrow \overline{W}$.

MVD-only rules. Some of these rules are similar to rules for FDs; some are new.

- *Reflexivity.* $\overline{X} \twoheadrightarrow \overline{X}$ holds in every relation.
- *Augmentation.* $\overline{X} \twoheadrightarrow \overline{Y}$ entails $\overline{X}\,\overline{Z} \twoheadrightarrow \overline{Y}$.
- *Additivity.* $\overline{X} \twoheadrightarrow \overline{Y}$ and $\overline{X} \twoheadrightarrow \overline{Z}$ entail $\overline{X} \twoheadrightarrow \overline{Y}\,\overline{Z}$.
- *Projectivity.* $\overline{X} \twoheadrightarrow \overline{Y}$ and $\overline{X} \twoheadrightarrow \overline{Z}$ entail $\overline{X} \twoheadrightarrow \overline{Y} \cap \overline{Z}$ and $\overline{X} \twoheadrightarrow \overline{Y} - \overline{Z}$.
- *Transitivity.* $\overline{X} \twoheadrightarrow \overline{Y}$ and $\overline{Y} \twoheadrightarrow \overline{Z}$ entail $\overline{X} \twoheadrightarrow \overline{Z} - \overline{Y}$.
- *Pseudotransitivity.* $\overline{X} \twoheadrightarrow \overline{Y}$ and $\overline{Y}\,\overline{W} \twoheadrightarrow \overline{Z}$ entail $\overline{X}\,\overline{W} \twoheadrightarrow \overline{Z} - (\overline{Y}\,\overline{W})$.
- *Complementation.* $\overline{X} \twoheadrightarrow \overline{Y}$ entails $\overline{X} \twoheadrightarrow \overline{R} - \overline{X}\,\overline{Y}$, where $\overline{R}$ is the set of all attributes in the schema.

These rules first appeared in [Beeri et al. 1977], but [Maier 1983] provides a more systematic and accessible introduction to the subject. The rules are *sound* in the sense that in any relation where a rule premise holds, the consequent of the rule holds as well. For example, replication follows using the same reasoning that we used for losslessness: if $\overline{X} \rightarrow \overline{Y}$ then the decomposition of $\overline{R}$ into $\overline{R_1} = \overline{X}\,\overline{Y}$ and $\overline{R_2} = \overline{X}(\overline{R} - \overline{Y})$ is lossless; hence, $\overline{R} = \overline{X}\,\overline{Y} \bowtie \overline{X}(\overline{R} - \overline{Y})$ and so $\overline{X} \twoheadrightarrow \overline{Y}$.

A remarkable fact, however, is that given a set, $\mathcal{S}$, that consists of MVDs and FDs and a dependency, *d* (which can be either an FD or an MVD), $\mathcal{S}$ entails *d* if and only if *d* can be derived by a purely syntactic application of the above rules (plus Armstrong's axioms) to the dependencies in $\mathcal{S}$. A similar property for FDs alone was earlier called *completeness*. Proving the soundness of the above inference rules is a good exercise (see Exercise 6.24). Completeness is much harder to prove. The interested reader is referred to [Beeri et al. 1977; Maier 1983].

6.10.2 The Difficulty of Designing for 4NF

The inference rules for MVDs are useful because they can help eliminate redundant MVDs and FDs. Also, as in the case of FDs alone, using nonredundant dependency sets can improve the design produced by the 4NF decomposition algorithm described on page 232. However, even in the absence of redundant dependencies, things can go awry. We illustrate some of the problems on a number of examples. Three issues are considered: loss of dependencies, redundancy, and design using both FDs and MVDs.

A contracts example. Consider the schema

CONTRACTS(Buyer, Vendor, Product, Currency)

where a tuple of the form ⟨John Doe, Acme, Paper Clips, USD⟩ means that buyer John Doe has a contract to buy paper clips from Acme, Inc., using U.S. currency. Suppose that our relation represents contracts of an international network of buyers and companies. Although the contract was consummated in dollars, if Acme sells some of its products in Euros (perhaps it is a European company), it may be convenient to store the contract in two tuples: one with the financial information expressed in USD, the other with information expressed in Euros. In general, CONTRACTS satisfies the rule that, if a company accepts several currencies, each contract is described in each one. This can be expressed using the following combined MVD:

Buyer Vendor $\twoheadrightarrow$ Product | Currency **6.16**

To be explicit, this MVD means

CONTRACTS = (Buyer Vendor Product) $\bowtie$ (Buyer Vendor Currency)

The second rule of our international network example is that if two vendors supply a certain product, both accept a certain currency, and a buyer of that product has a contract to buy that product with one of the two vendors, then this buyer must have a contract for purchasing that product with the other vendor as well. For example, if, in addition to the above tuple, CONTRACTS contained ⟨Mary Smith, OfficeMin, Paper Clips, USD⟩, then it must also contain the tuples ⟨John Doe, OfficeMin, Paper Clips, USD⟩ and ⟨Mary Smith, Acme, Paper Clips, USD⟩. This type of constraint is expressed using the following MVD:

Product Currency $\twoheadrightarrow$ Buyer | Vendor **6.17**

Let us now attempt a design using the 4NF decomposition algorithm. If we first decompose using the dependency (6.16), we get the following lossless decomposition:

(Buyer, Vendor, Product)
(Buyer, Vendor, Currency) **6.18**

Observe that once this decomposition is done, the second MVD can no longer be applied because no join dependency holds in either one of the above schemas.[5] The

[5] This may not be obvious because we have not discussed the tools for verifying such facts. However, in this particular example, our claim can be checked directly using the definition of the natural join. We again recommend [Maier 1983] as a good reference for learning about such techniques.

OPTIONAL

situation here is very similar to the problem we faced with the BCNF decomposition algorithm. Some dependencies might get lost in the process. In our case, it is the dependency (6.17). The same problem exists if we first decompose using the second dependency above, but in this case we lose (6.16).

Unlike losing FDs during BCNF decomposition, losing MVDs is potentially a more serious problem because the result might still harbor redundancy even if every relation in the decomposition is in 4NF! To see this, consider the following relation for the CONTRACTS schema:

Buyer	Vendor	Product	Currency
B_1	V_1	P	C
B_2	V_2	P	C
B_1	V_2	P	C
B_2	V_1	P	C

It is easy to check that this relation satisfies MVDs (6.16) and (6.17). For instance, to verify (6.16) take the projections on decomposition schema (6.18).

Buyer	Vendor	Product
B_1	V_1	P
B_2	V_2	P
B_1	V_2	P
B_2	V_1	P

Buyer	Vendor	Currency
B_1	V_1	C
B_2	V_2	C
B_1	V_2	C
B_2	V_1	C

Joining these two relations (using the natural join) clearly yields the original relation for CONTRACTS. A closer look shows that the above relations still contain a great deal of redundancy. For instance, the first relation twice says that product P is supplied by vendors V_1 and V_2. Furthermore, it twice says that P is wanted by buyers B_1 and B_2. The first relation seems to beg for further decomposition into (Buyer, Vendor) and (Vendor, Product), and the second relation begs to be decomposed into (Buyer, Currency) and (Vendor, Currency). Alas, none of these wishes can be granted because none of these decompositions is lossless (for example, Vendor is not a key of the first relation). As a result, decomposition (6.18) suffers from the usual update anomalies even though each relation is in 4NF! Furthermore, since 4NF implies BCNF, even BCNF does not guarantee complete elimination of redundancy in the presence of MVDs!

A dictionary example. For another example, consider a multilingual dictionary relation, DICTIONARY(English, French, German), which provides translations from one language to another. As expected, every term has a translation (possibly more than one) into every language, and the translations are independent of each other. These constraints are easily captured using MVDs.

OPTIONAL

```
English ->> French | German
French ->> English | German                                   6.19
German ->> English | French
```

The problem, as before, is that applying any one of these MVDs in the 4NF decomposition algorithm loses the other two dependencies, and the resulting decomposition exhibits the usual update anomalies.

A multilingual thesaurus example. Let us enhance the previous example so that every term is now associated with a unique concept and each concept has an associated description. For the purpose of this example, ignore the language used for the description. The corresponding schema becomes DICTIONARY(Concept, Description, English, French, German) and the dependencies are

```
English -> Concept
French -> Concept
German -> Concept                                             6.20
Concept -> Description
Concept ->> English | French | German
```

An example of a concept is A5329 with description "homo sapiens" and translations {human, man}, {homme}, and {Mensch, Mann}.

The 4NF decomposition algorithm suggests that we start by picking up an MVD that violates 4NF and then use it in the decomposition process. Since every FD is also an MVD, we might choose English → Concept first, which yields the schema (English, Concept) and (English, French, German, Description). Using the transitivity rule for MVDs, we can derive the MVD English ↠ French | German | Description and further decompose the second relation into (English, French), (English, German), and (English, Description).

The resulting schema has two drawbacks. First, it is lopsided toward English whereas the original schema was completely symmetric. Second, every one of the bilingual relations, such as (English, French), redundantly lists all possible translations from English to French and back. For example, if a and b are English synonyms, c and d are French synonyms, and a translates into c, then the English-French dictionary (English, French) has all four tuples: $\langle a, c\rangle$, $\langle a, d\rangle$, $\langle b, c\rangle$, and $\langle b, d\rangle$.

A better way to use the 4NF decomposition algorithm is to compute the attribute closure (defined on page 204) of the left-hand side of the MVD in (6.20) with respect to functional dependencies in (6.20) and derive the following MVD by the augmentation rule:

```
Concept Description ->> English | French | German
```

We can then apply the 4NF decomposition algorithm using this MVD, which yields the decomposition (Concept, Description, English), (Concept, Description,

French), and (Concept, Description, German). We can further decompose each of these relations into BCNF using the FDs alone, splitting off (Concept Description). Not only do we end up with a decomposition into 4NF, but also all dependencies are preserved.

6.10.3 A 4NF Decomposition How-To

The above examples make it clear that designing for 4NF is not a straightforward process. In fact, this problem was an active area of research until the early 1980s [Beeri et al. 1978; Zaniolo and Melkanoff 1981; Sciore 1983]. Eventually, all of this work was integrated into a uniform framework in [Beeri and Kifer 1986b]. While we cannot go into the details of this approach, its highlights can be explained with our three examples: contracts, dictionary, and thesaurus.

1. *The anomaly of split left-hand sides*. It is indicative of a design problem when one MVD *splits the left-hand side* of another, as in our contracts example. We say that an MVD $X \twoheadrightarrow V \mid W$ **splits the left-hand side** of the MVD $Y \twoheadrightarrow K \mid L$ if $Y \cap V$, and $Y \cap W$ are both non-empty sets of attributes. For instance, the MVD (6.17) splits the left-hand side, (Buyer, Vendor), of (6.16), which indicates that Buyer and Vendor are unrelated attributes (every buyer is associated in some tuple with every vendor) and thus should not be in the same relation. This is precisely the reason for the redundancy that we observed in the decomposition of the CONTRACTS relation into (Buyer, Vendor, Product) and (Buyer, Vendor, Currency).

   One reason for the problem with this schema might be the incorrectly specified dependencies. Instead of the MVDs given in the CONTRACT schema, the join dependency

   ```
   Buyer Product ⋈ Vendor Product
             ⋈ Vendor Currency ⋈ Buyer Currency
   ```

   seems more appropriate. It simply says that each buyer needs certain products, each vendor sells certain products, a vendor can accept certain currencies, and a buyer can pay in certain currencies. As long as a buyer and a vendor can match on a product and a currency, a deal can be struck. This English-language description matches the requirements in the description of the contracts example, and the designer might simply have failed to recognize that the above JD is all that is needed.

2. *Intersection anomaly*. An **intersection anomaly** is one in which a schema has a pair of MVDs of the form $\overline{X} \twoheadrightarrow \overline{Z}$ and $\overline{Y} \twoheadrightarrow \overline{Z}$ but there is no MVD $\overline{X} \cap \overline{Y} \twoheadrightarrow \overline{Z}$. Notice that our dictionary example has precisely this sort of anomaly: there are MVDs English $\twoheadrightarrow$ French and German $\twoheadrightarrow$ French, but there is no dependency $\emptyset \twoheadrightarrow$ French. [Beeri and Kifer 1986b] argue that this is a design problem that can be rectified by inventing new attributes. In our case, the attribute Concept is missing. In fact, the thesaurus example was constructed out of the dictionary

OPTIONAL

example by adding this very attribute[6] plus the dependencies that relate it to the old attributes. Perhaps somewhat unexpectedly, this type of anomaly can be corrected completely automatically—the new attribute and the associated dependencies can be invented by a well-defined algorithm [Beeri and Kifer 1986a, 1987].

3. *Design strategy*. Assuming that the anomaly of split left-hand sides does not arise,[7] a dependency-preserving decomposition of the schema $\mathbf{R} = (\overline{R}; \mathcal{D})$ into fourth normal form can be achieved in five steps:
   (a) Compute attribute closure, X^+, of the left-hand side of every MVD $X \twoheadrightarrow Y$ using the FDs entailed by $\mathcal{D}$. Replace every $X \twoheadrightarrow Y$ with $X^+ \twoheadrightarrow Y$.
   (b) Find the minimal cover of the resulting set of MVDs. It turns out that such a cover is unique if $\mathcal{D}$ does not exhibit the anomaly of split left-hand sides.
   (c) Use the algorithm of [Beeri and Kifer 1986a, 1987] to eliminate intersection anomalies by adding new attributes.
   (d) Apply the 4NF decomposition algorithm using MVDs only.
   (e) Apply the BCNF design algorithm within each resulting schema using FDs only.

Every relation in the resulting decomposition is in 4NF and no MVD is lost on the way, which guarantees that no redundancy is present in the resulting schemas. Moreover, if the decompositions in the last stage are dependency preserving, so is the overall five-step process.

The transition from the dictionary example to the thesaurus example and then to the final decomposition of the thesaurus example is an illustration of this five-step process. Let us enhance the dictionary slightly by adding the `Description` attribute and the FDs `English` → `Description`, `German` → `Description`, and `French` → `Description` (so the dictionary example now contains four attributes). Then we can obtain a BCNF decomposition as follows:

- Apply steps (a) and (b). (Step (b) applies vacuously, as the set of MVDs is already minimal.) The resulting MVDs are `English Description` ↠ `French | German`, etc.
- Apply step (c). According to the algorithm in [Beeri and Kifer 1986a], this introduces a new attribute, `Concept`, with the exact set of dependencies depicted in the thesaurus example (6.20), except that the last MVD has a closed left-hand side: `Concept Description` ↠ `English | French | German`. (Of course, the algorithm does not propose the name for the newly invented attribute — this is a job for the database designer.)
- Apply step (d)—perform the 4NF decomposition with respect to the above MVD and then step (e)—apply the BCNF design process within each of the resulting schemas.

[6] The other attribute, `Description`, was added to illustrate a different point. Ignore it for the moment.

[7] Any such anomaly means that the dependencies are incorrect or incomplete.

The result has four schemas, as explained in the thesaurus example: (`Concept`, `English`), (`Concept`, `French`), (`Concept`, `German`), and (`Concept`, `Description`), where `English`, `French`, and `German` are keys in the first three schemas and `Concept` in the last.

6.11 Summary of Normal Form Decomposition

We summarize some of the properties of the normal form decomposition algorithms discussed.

- *Third normal form* schemas might have some redundancy. The decomposition algorithm that we discussed generates 3NF schemas that are lossless and dependency preserving. It does not take multivalued dependencies into account.
- *Boyce-Codd* decompositions do not have redundancy if only FDs are considered. The decomposition algorithm we discussed generates BCNF schemas that are lossless but that might not be dependency preserving. (As we have shown, some schemas do not have Boyce-Codd decompositions that are both lossless and dependency preserving.) It does not take multivalued dependencies into account, so redundancy due to such dependencies is possible.
- *Fourth normal form* decompositions do not have any nontrivial multivalued dependencies. The algorithm we sketched generates 4NF schemas that are lossless but that might not be dependency preserving. It attempts to eliminate redundancies associated with MVDs, but it does not guarantee that all such redundancies will go away.

Note that none of these decompositions produces schemas that have all of the properties we want.

CASE STUDY

6.12 Case Study: Schema Refinement for the Student Registration System

Having spent all that effort studying the relational normalization theory, we will now put the new knowledge to good use and verify our design for the Student Registration System as outlined in Section 4.8. The good news is that we did a pretty good job of converting the E-R diagram in Figure 4.33, page 114, into the relations in Figures 4.34 and 4.35, so most of the relations turn out to be in Boyce-Codd normal form. However, you did not struggle through this chapter in vain—read on!

To determine whether a schema is in a normal form we need to collect all FDs relevant to it. One source is the PRIMARY KEY and the UNIQUE constraints. However, there might be additional dependencies that are not captured by these constraints or the E-R diagram. They can be uncovered only by careful examination of the schema and of the specifications of the application, a process that requires much care and concentration. If no new dependencies are found, all FDs in the schema are the primary and the candidate keys (or the FDs entailed by them), so the schema is in

BCNF. If additional FDs are uncovered, we must check if the schema is in a desirable normal form and, if not, make appropriate changes.

In our case, we can verify that all relation schemas in Figure 4.35, except CLASS, are in BCNF, as they have no FDs that are not entailed by the keys. This verification is not particularly hard because these schemas have six or fewer attributes. It is harder in the case of CLASS, which has ten.

We illustrate the process using the CLASS schema. Along the way, we uncover a missing functional dependency and then normalize CLASS. First, let us list the key constraints specified in the CREATE TABLE statement for that relation.

1. CrsCode SectionNo Semester Year → ClassTime
2. CrsCode SectionNo Semester Year → Textbook
3. CrsCode SectionNo Semester Year → Enrollment
4. CrsCode SectionNo Semester Year → MaxEnrollment
5. CrsCode SectionNo Semester Year → ClassroomId
6. CrsCode SectionNo Semester Year → InstructorId
7. Semester Year ClassTime InstructorId → CrsCode
8. Semester Year ClassTime InstructorId → Textbook
9. Semester Year ClassTime InstructorId → SectionNo
10. Semester Year ClassTime InstructorId → Enrollment
11. Semester Year ClassTime InstructorId → MaxEnrollment
12. Semester Year ClassTime InstructorId → ClassroomId
13. Semester Year ClassTime ClassroomId → CrsCode
14. Semester Year ClassTime ClassroomId → Textbook
15. Semester Year ClassTime ClassroomId → SectionNo
16. Semester Year ClassTime ClassroomId → Enrollment
17. Semester Year ClassTime ClassroomId → MaxEnrollment
18. Semester Year ClassTime ClassroomId → InstructorId

Verifying that additional dependencies hold in a large schema can be difficult: one has to consider every subset of the attributes of CLASS that is not a superkey and check if it functionally determines some other attribute. This "check" is not based on any concrete algorithm. The decision that a certain FD does or does not hold in a relation is strictly a matter of how the designer understands the semantics of the corresponding entity in the real-world enterprise that is being modeled by the database, and it is inherently error prone. However, research is being conducted to help with the problem. For instance, FDEXPERT [Ram 1995] is an expert system that helps database designers discover FDs using knowledge about typical enterprises and their design patterns.

Unfortunately, we do not have an expert system handy, so we do the analysis the hard way. Consider the following candidate FD:

```
ClassTime ClassroomId InstructorId → CrsCode
```

It is easy to see why this FD does not apply: different courses can be taught by the same instructor in the same room at the same time—if all this happens in different semesters and years. Many other FDs can be rejected through a similar argument. However, since in Section 4.8 we assumed that at most one textbook can be used in any particular course, the following FD is an appropriate addition to the set of constraints previously specified for CLASS:

```
CsrCode Semester Year → Textbook                          6.21
```

Although the textbook used in a course can vary from semester to semester, if a certain course is offered in a particular semester and is split in several sections because of large enrollment, all sections use the same textbook.[8]

It is now easy to see the problem with the design of CLASS: the left-hand side of the above dependency is not a key, and `Textbook` does not belong to any key either. For these reasons, CLASS is not in 3NF. The 3NF synthesis algorithm on page 224 suggests that the situation can be rectified by splitting the original schema into the following pair:

- CLASS1, with all the attributes of CLASS, except `Textbook`, and FDs 1, 3–7, 9–13, 15–18 (these numbers refer to the numbered list of FDs on page 243.)
- TEXTBOOKS(`CrsCode`, `Semester`, `Year`, `Textbook`), with the single FD `CrsCode Semester Year → Textbook`

Both of these schemas are in BCNF—we can verify by direct inspection that all of their FDs are entailed by key constraints. The 3NF synthesis algorithm also guarantees that the above decomposition is lossless and dependency preserving.

Let us now consider a more realistic situation in which classes can have more than one recommended textbook and all sections of the class in a particular semester use the same set of textbooks. In this case, FD (6.21) does not hold, of course. Observe that the textbooks used in any particular class are independent of meeting time, instructor, enrollment, and so forth. This situation is similar to the one in Section 6.9 relative to the PERSON relation shown in (6.14): here, the independence of the attribute `Textbook` from the attributes `ClassTime`, `InstructorId`, and so forth, is formally represented through the following multivalued dependency:

```
(CrsCode Semester Year ClassTime SectionNo
     InstructorId Enrollment MaxEnrollment ClassroomId)
          ⋈ (CrsCode Semester Year Textbook)
```

[8] This rule might not be true of all universities, but it is certainly true of many.

Like the schema of the PERSON relation, CLASS is in BCNF; even so, it contains redundancy because of the above multivalued dependency. The solution to the problem is to try for a higher normal form—4NF—and, fortunately, this is easy using the algorithm in Section 6.9 on page 232. We simply need to decompose CLASS using the above dependency, which yields the following lossless decomposition (losslessness is guaranteed by the 4NF decomposition algorithm):

- CLASS1(`CrsCode, Semester, Year, ClassTime, SectionNo, InstructorId, Enrollment, MaxEnrollment, ClassroomId`) with the FDs 1, 3–7, 9–13, 15–18
- TEXTBOOKS(`CrsCode, Semester, Year, Textbook`) with no FDs

Note that the only difference between this schema and the one obtained earlier under the one-textbook-per-class assumption is the absence, in the second schema, of the FD

```
CrsCode Semester Year → Textbook
```

The result of applying relational normalization theory to the preliminary design for the Student Registration System developed in Section 4.8 is a lossless decomposition where every relation is in 4NF (and thus in BCNF as well). Luckily, this decomposition is dependency preserving, since every FD specified for the schema is embedded in one of the relations in the decomposition—something that is not always achievable with 4NF and BCNF design.

6.13 Tuning Issues: To Decompose or Not to Decompose?

In this chapter, we have learned a great deal about the schema decomposition theory. However, this theory was motivated by concerns that redundancy leads to consistency-maintenance problems in the presence of frequent database updates. What if most of the transactions are read-only queries? Schema decomposition seems to make query answering harder because associations that existed in one relation before the decomposition might be broken into separate relations afterward.

For instance, finding the average number of hobbies per address is more efficient using the monolithic relation of Figure 4.13 rather than the pair of relations of Figure 6.1 because the latter requires a join before the aggregates can be computed. This is an example of the classic time/space trade-off. Adding redundancy can improve query performance. Such a trade-off has to be evaluated in the context of a particular application if the performance of a frequently executed query is found wanting. The term **denormalization** describes situations in which achieving certain normal forms incurs a punishing performance penalty, and thus perhaps there should be no decomposition.

In general, no one recommendation works in all cases. Sometimes, simulation can help resolve the issue. Here is an incomplete list of conflicting guidelines that need to be evaluated against each particular mix of transactions:

1. Decomposition generally makes answering complex queries less efficient because additional joins must be performed during query evaluation.
2. Decomposition can make answering simple queries more efficient because such queries usually involve a small number of attributes that belong to the same relation. Since decomposed relations have fewer tuples, the tuples that need to be scanned during the evaluation of a simple query are likely to be fewer.
3. Decomposition generally makes simple update transactions more efficient. However, this may not be true for complex update transactions (such as *Raise the salary of all professors who taught every course required for computer science majors*) since they might involve complex queries (and thus might require complex joins).
4. Decomposition can lower the demand for storage space since it usually eliminates redundant data.
5. Decomposition can increase storage requirements if the degree of redundancy is low. For instance, in the PERSON relation of (6.14), suppose that, with few exceptions, most people have just one phone number and one child. In this situation, schema decomposition can actually increase storage requirements without bringing tangible benefits. The same applies to the decomposition of HASACCOUNT in Figure 6.7, which can increase the overhead for update transactions. The reason is that verification of the FD

   ```
   ClientId OfficeId → AccountNumber
   ```

   after an update requires a join because the attributes `ClientId` and `OfficeId` belong to different relations in the decomposition.

BIBLIOGRAPHIC NOTES

Relational normal forms and functional dependencies were introduced in [Codd 1970]. Armstrong's axioms and the proof of their soundness and completeness first appeared in [Armstrong 1974], although more accessible exposition can be found in [Ullman 1988; Maier 1983]. An efficient algorithm for entailment of FDs first appeared in [Beeri and Bernstein 1979]. A general test for lossless decompositions was first developed in [Beeri et al. 1981]. The algorithm for synthesizing the third normal form is due to [Bernstein 1976].

The fourth normal form was introduced in [Fagin 1977], which also presents a naive decomposition algorithm and explores the relationship between 4NF and BCNF. The fifth normal form is discussed in [Beeri et al. 1977], but we recommend [Maier 1983] as a more systematic introduction to the subject. The survey in [Kanellakis 1990] is also a good starting point. Other papers on 4NF are [Beeri et al. 1978; Zaniolo and Melkanoff 1981; Sciore 1983]. Eventually, all of this work on designing 4NF schemas in the presence of FDs and MVDs was extended and integrated into a uniform framework in [Beeri and Kifer 1986a, 1986b, 1987]. More recent works on 4NF are [Vincent and Srinivasan 1993; Vincent 1999].

In-depth coverage of the relational design theory is provided in texts such as [Mannila and Raäihä 1992; Atzeni and Antonellis 1993].

As illustrated in Section 6.12, one of the most difficult obstacles to applying the results discussed in this chapter to database design is finding the right set of dependencies to use in the schema normalization process. We mentioned the FDEXPERT system [Ram 1995], which helps discover functional dependencies using knowledge about various types of enterprises. Extensive work has also been done on the algorithms for discovering FDs, MVDs, and inclusion dependencies using the techniques from *machine learning* and *data mining* [Huhtala et al. 1999; Kantola et al. 1992; Mannila and Raäihä 1994; Flach and Savnik 1999; Savnik and Flach 1993].

EXERCISES

6.1 The definition of functional dependencies does not preclude the case in which the left-hand side is empty—that is, it allows FDs of the form $\{\} \rightarrow A$. Explain the meaning of such dependencies.

6.2 Give an example of a schema that is not in 3NF and has just two attributes.

6.3 What is the smallest number of attributes a relation key can have?

6.4 A table, ABC, has attributes A, B, and C, and a functional dependency $A \rightarrow BC$. Write an SQL CREATE ASSERTION statement that prevents a violation of this functional dependency.

6.5 Prove that every 3NF relation schema with just two attributes is also in BCNF. Prove that every schema that has *at most* one nontrivial FD is in BCNF.

6.6 If the functional dependency $X \rightarrow Y$ is a key constraint, what are X and Y?

6.7 Can a key be the set of all attributes if there is at least one nontrivial FD in a schema?

6.8 The following is an instance of a relation schema. Can you tell whether the schema includes the functional dependencies $A \rightarrow B$ and $BC \rightarrow A$?

A	B	C
1	2	3
2	2	2
1	3	2
4	2	3

6.9 Prove that Armstrong's transitivity axiom is sound—that is, every relation that satisfies the FDs $\overline{X} \rightarrow \overline{Y}$ and $\overline{Y} \rightarrow \overline{Z}$ must also satisfy the FD $\overline{X} \rightarrow \overline{Z}$.

6.10 Prove the following *generalized transitivity rule*: If $\overline{Z} \subseteq \overline{Y}$, then $\overline{X} \rightarrow \overline{Y}$ and $\overline{Z} \rightarrow \overline{W}$ entail $\overline{X} \rightarrow \overline{W}$. Try to prove this rule in two ways:

- Using the argument that directly appeals to the definition of FDs, as in Section 6.4
- By deriving $\overline{X} \rightarrow \overline{W}$ from $\overline{X} \rightarrow \overline{Y}$ and $\overline{Z} \rightarrow \overline{W}$ via a series of steps using Armstrong's axioms

*6.11 We have shown the *soundness* of the algorithm in Figure 6.3—that if $A \in closure$ then $A \in \overline{X}^+_{\mathcal{F}}$. Prove the *completeness* of this algorithm; that is, if $A \in \overline{X}^+_{\mathcal{F}}$, then $A \in closure$ at the end of the computation. *Hint:* Use induction on the length of derivation of $X \rightarrow A$ by Armstrong's axioms.

6.12 Suppose that $\mathbf{R} = (\overline{R}, \mathcal{F})$ is a relation schema and $\mathbf{R}_1 = (\overline{R}_1; \mathcal{F}_1), \ldots, \mathbf{R}_n = (\overline{R}_n; \mathcal{F}_n)$ is its decomposition. Let $\mathbf{r}$ be a valid relation instance over $\mathbf{R}$ and $\mathbf{r}_i = \pi_{\overline{R}_i}(\mathbf{r})$. Show that $\mathbf{r}_i$ satisfies the set of FDs $\mathcal{F}_i$ and is therefore a valid relation instance over the schema $\mathbf{R}_i$.

6.13 Let $\overline{R}_1$ and $\overline{R}_2$ be sets of attributes and $\overline{R} = \overline{R}_1 \cup \overline{R}_2$. Let $\mathbf{r}$ be a relation on $\overline{R}$. Prove that $\mathbf{r} \subseteq \pi_{\overline{R}_1}(\mathbf{r}) \bowtie \pi_{\overline{R}_2}(\mathbf{r})$. Generalize this result to decompositions of $\overline{R}$ into $n > 2$ schemas.

6.14 Suppose that $\mathbf{R} = (\overline{R}; \mathcal{F})$ is a schema and that $\mathbf{R}_1 = (\overline{R}_1; \mathcal{F}_1)$, $\mathbf{R}_2 = (\overline{R}_2; \mathcal{F}_2)$ is a binary decomposition such that neither $(\overline{R}_1 \cap \overline{R}_2) \rightarrow \overline{R}_1$ nor $(\overline{R}_1 \cap \overline{R}_2) \rightarrow \overline{R}_2$ is implied by $\mathcal{F}$. Construct a relation, $\mathbf{r}$, such that $\mathbf{r} \subset \pi_{\overline{R}_1}(\mathbf{r}) \bowtie \pi_{\overline{R}_2}(\mathbf{r})$, where $\subset$ denotes strict subset. (This relation, therefore, shows that at least one of these FDs is necessary for the decomposition of $\mathbf{R}$ to be lossless.)

6.15 Suppose that $\mathbf{R}_1, \ldots, \mathbf{R}_n$ is a decomposition of schema $\mathbf{R}$ obtained by a sequence of binary lossless decompositions (beginning with a decomposition of $\mathbf{R}$). Prove that $\mathbf{R}_1, \ldots, \mathbf{R}_n$ is a lossless decomposition of $\mathbf{R}$.

6.16 Prove that the loop in the BCNF decomposition algorithm of Figure 6.9 has the property that the database schema at each subsequent iteration has strictly fewer FDs that violate BCNF than has the schema in the previous iteration.

*6.17 Prove that the algorithm for synthesizing 3NF decompositions in Section 6.8.2 yields schemas that satisfy the conditions of 3NF. (*Hint*: Use the proof-by-contradiction technique. Assume that some FD violates 3NF and then show that this contradicts the fact that the algorithm synthesized schemas out of a minimal cover.)

6.18 Consider a database schema with attributes A, B, C, D, and E and functional dependencies $B \rightarrow E$, $E \rightarrow A$, $A \rightarrow D$, and $D \rightarrow E$. Prove that the decomposition of this schema into AB, BCD, and ADE is lossless. Is it dependency preserving?

6.19 Consider a relation schema with attributes $ABCGWXYZ$ and the set of dependencies $\mathcal{F} = \{XZ \rightarrow ZYB,\ YA \rightarrow CG,\ C \rightarrow W,\ B \rightarrow G,\ XZ \rightarrow G\}$. Solve the following problems using the appropriate algorithms.

a. Find a minimal cover for $\mathcal{F}$.
b. Is the dependency $XZA \rightarrow YB$ implied by $\mathcal{F}$?
c. Is the decomposition into $XZYAB$ and $YABCGW$ lossless?
d. Is the above decomposition dependency preserving?

6.20 Consider the following functional dependencies over the attribute set $ABCDEFGH$:

$$A \rightarrow E \qquad BE \rightarrow D$$
$$AD \rightarrow BE \qquad BDH \rightarrow E$$
$$AC \rightarrow E \qquad F \rightarrow A$$
$$E \rightarrow B \qquad D \rightarrow H$$
$$BG \rightarrow F \qquad CD \rightarrow A$$

Find a minimal cover, then decompose into lossless 3NF. After that, check if all the resulting relations are in BCNF. If you find a schema that is not, decompose it into a lossless BCNF. Explain all steps.

6.21 Find a projection of the following set of dependencies on the attributes AFE:

$$A \to BC \qquad E \to HG$$
$$C \to FG \qquad G \to A$$

6.22 Consider the schema with the attribute set $ABCDEFH$ and the FDs depicted in (6.12), page 224. Prove that the decomposition $(AD;\ A \to D)$, $(CE;\ C \to E)$, $(FA;\ F \to A)$, $(EF;\ E \to F)$, $(BHE;\ BH \to E)$ is not lossless by providing a concrete relation instance over $ABCDEFH$ that exhibits the loss of information when projected on this schema.

6.23 Consider the schema $BCDFGH$ with the following FDs: $BG \to CD$, $G \to F$, $CD \to GH$, $C \to FG$, $F \to D$. Use the 3NF synthesis algorithm to obtain a lossless, dependency-preserving decomposition into 3NF. If any of the resulting schemas is not in BCNF, proceed to decompose them into BCNF.

***6.24** Prove that all rules for inferring FDs and MVDs given in Section 6.10 are sound. In other words, for every relation, **r**, which satisfies the dependencies in the premise of any rule, R, the conclusion of R is also satisfied by **r** (e.g., for the augmentation rule, prove that if $\overline{X} \twoheadrightarrow \overline{Y}$ holds in **r** then $\overline{X}\,\overline{Z} \twoheadrightarrow \overline{Y}$ also holds in **r**).

6.25 Prove that if a schema, $\mathbf{S} = (\overline{S}, \mathcal{F})$, is in 3NF, then every FD in $\mathcal{F}^+$ (not only those that are in $\mathcal{F}$) satisfies the 3NF requirements.

6.26 If $X = \{A, B\}$ and $F = \{A \to D,\ BC \to EJ,\ BD \to AE,\ EJ \to G,\ ADE \to H,\ HD \to J\}$, what is X_F^+? Are the FDs $AB \to C$ and $AE \to G$ entailed by F?

6.27 Using only Armstrong's axioms and the FDs

(a) $AB \to C$
(b) $A \to BE$
(c) $C \to D$

give a complete derivation of the FD $A \to D$.

6.28 Consider a decomposition $\mathbf{R}_1, \ldots, \mathbf{R}_n$ of $\mathbf{R}$ obtained via steps 1, 2, and 3 (but not step 4) of the 3NF synthesis algorithm on page 225. Suppose there is an attribute A in $\mathbf{R}$ that does not belong to any of the $\mathbf{R}_i$, $i = 1, \ldots, n$. Prove that A must be part of every key of $\mathbf{R}$.

6.29 Consider the schema $\mathbf{R} = (ABCDEFGH, \{BE \to GH,\ G \to FA,\ D \to C,\ F \to B\})$.

a. Can there be a key that does not contain D? Explain.
b. Is the schema in BCNF? Explain.
c. Use one cycle of the BCNF algorithm to decompose **R** into two subrelations. Are the subrelations in BCNF?
d. Show that your decomposition is lossless.
e. Is your decomposition dependency preserving? Explain.

6.30 Find a minimal cover of the following set of FDs: $AB \to CD$, $BC \to FG$, $A \to G$, $G \to B$, $C \to G$. Is the decomposition of $ABCDFG$ into $ABCD$ and $ACFG$ lossless? Explain.

6.31 Let $\overline{X}, \overline{Y}, \overline{S}, \overline{R}$ be sets of attributes such that $\overline{S} \subseteq \overline{R}$ and $\overline{X} \cup \overline{Y} = R$. Let **r** be a relation over $\overline{R}$ that satisfies the nontrivial MVD $\overline{R} = \overline{X} \bowtie \overline{Y}$ (i.e., neither set $\overline{X}$ or $\overline{Y}$ is a subset of the other).

a. Prove that if $\overline{X} \cap \overline{Y} \subseteq \overline{S}$, then the relation $\pi_{\overline{S}}(\mathbf{r})$ satisfies the MVD $\overline{S} = (\overline{S} \cap \overline{X}) \bowtie (\overline{S} \cap \overline{Y})$.

b. Suppose $\overline{X}, \overline{Y}, \overline{S}$, and $\overline{R}$ satisfy all the above conditions, except that $\overline{X} \cap \overline{Y} \not\subseteq \overline{S}$. Give an example of **r** that satisfies $\overline{R} = \overline{X} \bowtie \overline{Y}$ but does not satisfy $\overline{S} = (\overline{S} \cap \overline{X}) \bowtie (\overline{S} \cap \overline{Y})$.

6.32 Consider a relation schema over the attributes *ABCDEFG* and the following MVDs:

$ABCD \bowtie DEFG$
$CD \bowtie ABCEFG$
$DFG \bowtie ABCDEG$

Find a lossless decomposition into 4NF.

6.33 For the attribute set *ABCDEFG*, let the MVDs be:

$ABCD \bowtie DEFG$
$ABCE \bowtie ABDFG$
$ABD \bowtie CDEFG$

Find a lossless decomposition into 4NF. Is it unique?

6.34 Consider a decomposition $\mathbf{R}_1, \ldots, \mathbf{R}_n$ of **R** obtained through 3NF synthesis. Suppose that $\mathbf{R}_i$ is *not* in BCNF and let $X \rightarrow A$ be a violating FD in $\mathbf{R}_i$. Prove that $\mathbf{R}_i$ must have another FD, $Y \rightarrow B$, which will be lost if $\mathbf{R}_i$ is further decomposed with respect to $X \rightarrow A$.

***6.35** This exercise relies on a technique explained in the optional Section 6.10. Consider a relation schema over the attributes *ABCDEFGHI* and the following MVDs and FDs:

$D \rightarrow AH$	$D \twoheadrightarrow BC$
$G \rightarrow I$	$C \twoheadrightarrow B$
	$G \twoheadrightarrow ABCE$

Find a lossless and dependency-preserving decomposition into 4NF.

6.36 Let $\mathbf{R} = (\overline{R}; \mathcal{F})$ be a schema and $\overline{S}$ a set of attributes, such that $\overline{S} \subseteq \overline{R}$. Let $\overline{X} \rightarrow \overline{Y}$ be an FD such that $\overline{X}, \overline{Y} \subseteq S$. Prove that

1. If $\overline{X} \rightarrow \overline{Y} \in \mathcal{F}^+$ then for *every* legal instance **r** of **R** its projection $\pi_{\overline{S}}(\mathbf{r})$ satisfies $\overline{X} \rightarrow \overline{Y}$.
2. Conversely, if $\overline{X} \rightarrow \overline{Y} \notin \mathcal{F}^+$ then there is a legal instance **r** of **R** such that $\pi_{\overline{S}}(\mathbf{r})$ violates $\overline{X} \rightarrow \overline{Y}$.

7

Triggers and Active Databases

In Chapter 3, we discussed triggers in the context of reactive constraints in databases. However, triggers have other uses as well. For example, they arise naturally in applications that require **active databases**—databases that must react to various external events. In these applications, the general classes of possible external events are known but their exact timings are not. This is what makes triggers a good paradigm for these applications.

Although triggers were not a part of the SQL-92 standard, a number of database vendors include (proprietary, nonstandard) support for triggers in their products. As of 1999, triggers are a part of the SQL standard, and we discuss that part of the standard in this chapter. More information on triggers in SQL can be found in [Gulutzan and Pelzer 1999].

7.1 What Is a Trigger?

A **trigger** is an element of the database schema that has the following structure:

ON *event* IF *precondition* THEN *action*

where **event** is a request for the execution of a particular database operation (e.g., insert a row in a table whose rows represent students registered for a course), **precondition** is an expression that evaluates to true or false (e.g., the class is full), and **action** is a statement of what needs to be done when the trigger is **fired**, that is, when the event occurs and the precondition is true (e.g., delete something from the database or send e-mail to the administrator). Because triggers are built out of the above three ingredients, they are also called **event-condition-action**, or **ECA**, rules.

Triggers fill a number of roles in database processing, including

1. *Constraint maintenance*. In Section 3.3.8, we discussed triggers that are used to maintain the foreign-key and semantic constraints. The most common form of a trigger of this kind uses the ON DELETE and ON UPDATE clauses, which are attached to foreign keys. In the same section we saw an example of a

trigger intended to enforce a semantic constraint, which prevents dropping of a course after the grade is given. More generally, triggers can be used to maintain ASSERTION constraints of SQL.

2. *Business rules*. A business rule is a concise formal statement of a basic principle that underlies a business process in an enterprise. For instance, a business rule encoded as a database trigger could state that if an international money transfer is made into a client's account then an e-mail message should be sent to the client. Thus, insertion of a tuple of type "international money transfer" would trigger the action of insertion of an appropriate message into an e-mail queue (which might also be a relation in the same database).
3. *Monitoring*. Complex physical objects, such as power plants, spaceships, aircraft, etc., are monitored by sensor networks, which record their measurements in a database. Since insertion of each new record in the database is an event, triggers can be used, indirectly, to monitor the state of such physical objects. For instance, if a sensor records an elevated level of carbon monoxide, then the ventilation system should be turned on and the record of this secondary event inserted into the log.
4. *Maintenance of auxiliary cached data*. Materialized views, discussed in Section 5.2.9, is one example of such a use. A trigger can update a materialized view each time a change is made to the base tables on which the trigger depends.
5. *Simplified application design*. Separating core program logic from exception handling can drastically simplify certain applications. In cases where exceptions can be modeled as update operations on a database, triggers are an ideal vehicle for such separation.

7.2 Semantic Issues in Trigger Handling

Surprisingly, a number of complex issues lurk behind the conceptual simplicity of the notion of a trigger. First, several types of triggers are possible, each of which might be useful for different applications. Second, we will soon discover many nuances in how and when triggers are applied. Third, at any given point in time several triggers might be activated—how should a DBMS decide which to apply and in what order? Different choices can lead to different executions.

Finally, execution of a trigger might enable other triggers. Therefore, a single event can cause a chain reaction of trigger firing, and there is no guarantee that the process will ever stop. Chain reaction may be indicative of a design problem if it cannot be shown to always terminate. To prevent infinite executions, each DBMS has a limit on the depth of such chain reactions; for instance, if the depth exceeds 32, an exception is raised, the chain reaction stops, and all of the changes made by the original update statement and the triggers are rolled back. However, this limit is a safety valve, not a feature, and trigger systems should not be designed to rely on it. Some techniques for preventing chain reaction will be discussed in Section 7.4.

Trigger consideration. A trigger is **activated** when the triggering event is requested. The **consideration** of a trigger refers to when, after activation, the precondition specified in the trigger is checked. To see why consideration is an issue, assume that when the triggering event is requested, the triggering precondition is true and so the trigger can fire. However, moments later the precondition might become false (because of updates made by this or other transactions). If the precondition is not checked immediately, the trigger will not fire.

Consider the following trigger, whose purpose is to ensure that student registration does not exceed course capacity:

ON *inserting a row in course registration table*
IF *over course capacity*
THEN *abort registration transaction*

When a student attempts to insert her name in the course registration table, the course might be full. Thus, if the precondition is checked when the registration attempt is made, the student's request will be rejected. However, at about the same time another student might execute a transaction to drop the course (or the registrar might have increased the course capacity), and this second transaction might commit before the first one. Therefore, if the trigger precondition is checked at the time the registration transaction commits, rather than at the event time, our student will happily register for the course. In this example, deferring the consideration of trigger preconditions might be a suitable policy.

However, if our database is monitoring a nuclear power plant and the triggering event is a pressure increase while the precondition is that the pressure not exceed a certain limit, then in all likelihood the immediate consideration of the trigger precondition is a better idea.

In summary, there are at least two useful strategies: a trigger can be considered **immediately** when the triggering event is requested, or consideration can be **deferred** until the transaction commits.

Trigger consideration is actually a little more subtle. Suppose that a trigger, T, is activated by an event, **e**, that affects the relation R, and let C be the condition associated with T. Many systems (SQL included) make it possible for C to take into account the state of R immediately *before* **e** takes place and also immediately *after* **e** has been executed. Therefore, if C uses only these two states of R and does not refer to any other relation in the database, the immediate and the deferred considerations of T yield the same result. Moreover, if C refers only to the *before state* of R, we can say that C is evaluated before **e** takes place! But if C does take into account database relations other than R, the two consideration modes might yield different results.

Trigger execution. If trigger consideration is deferred, trigger execution is necessarily also deferred until the end of the triggering transaction. However, when triggers are considered immediately we have at least two options. We can execute the trigger immediately after its consideration, or we can defer execution until the end of the triggering transaction. Again, for a nuclear reactor database, immediate execution might be the way to go, but in less critical situations deferred execution might be a better option.

> *Brain Teaser:* What would immediate execution under deferred consideration mean?

With immediate execution, there are the following further possibilities. The trigger can be executed *after* the triggering event (an **after trigger**), *before* it (a **before trigger**), or *instead* of it (an **instead-of trigger**). At first glance, the last two possibilities seem quite strange. How can an action caused by a real-life event execute before or instead of that event? The answer lies in the fact that the event is a request to the DBMS issued by a transaction, so it is quite possible for the DBMS to ignore the request and execute the trigger instead. Or the system might execute the trigger first and then allow the requested action to occur.

The SQL standard supports only before and after triggers, but some vendors (e.g., Oracle) support instead-of triggers as well. These triggers can be useful in a number of scenarios, the most common being maintenance of views. In this scenario, the events of insertion, deletion, and update on a view can be monitored by triggers. When, say, a tuple is inserted into a view, the trigger is activated and performs appropriate insertions into the base tables of the view *instead of* inserting the tuple directly into the view. (Recall from Section 5.3.4 that in most cases direct update of a view is not even feasible because such operation is ambiguous.) Example 7.3.5 illustrates this type of trigger.

> *Brain Teaser:* Do before triggers make any sense under deferred execution?

Trigger granularity. The issue here is what constitutes an event. **Row-level granularity** assumes that a change to a single row is an event, and changes to different rows are viewed as separate events that might cause the trigger to be executed multiple times. In contrast, **statement-level granularity** assumes that events are statements, such as INSERT, DELETE, and UPDATE, *not* the individual tuple-level changes they make. Thus, for instance, an UPDATE statement that makes no changes (because the condition in its WHERE clause affects no tuples currently in the database) is an event that can cause a trigger to execute!

At row-level granularity, a trigger might need to know the old and the new values of the affected tuple so it can test the precondition properly. In the case of a salary increase, for example, the old tuple contains the old salary and the new one contains the new salary. If both values are available, the trigger can verify that the increase does not exceed 10% or can apply corrective actions as appropriate. Row-level triggers usually provide access to the old and the new values of the affected tuple through special variables.

At statement-level granularity, updates are collected in temporary structures, such as OLD TABLE and NEW TABLE. This allows the trigger to query both tables and act on the basis of the results.

Trigger conflicts. It is possible for an event to activate several triggers at once. For instance, when a student registers for a course, the following two triggers might be considered:

ON *inserting a row in course registration table*
IF *over course capacity*
THEN *notify registrar about unmet demands*

ON *inserting a row in course registration table*
IF *over course capacity*
THEN *put on waiting list*

In such situations, an important question is which trigger should be considered first. Two alternatives exist.

- *Ordered conflict resolution.* Evaluate trigger preconditions in turn. When a condition is evaluated and found to be true, the corresponding trigger is executed; when that execution is complete, the next trigger is considered. In our case, the student might accept one of the alternative courses and abandon the request to add the course that is full. Therefore, by the time the second trigger is considered, its precondition is no longer true, and the trigger will not fire. One common way to order triggers is according to the times when their enabling events occur.
- *Group conflict resolution.* Evaluate all trigger preconditions at once and then schedule for execution all those whose preconditions are true. In this case, all scheduled triggers will be executed (one after another or concurrently), even if the preconditions attached to some triggers might become false shortly after their evaluation.

With the first option, the system can decide on trigger ordering or it can pick triggers at random. With the second option, trigger ordering is not necessary since all triggers can be scheduled to run concurrently, although most DBMSs do order triggers anyway.

Triggers and integrity constraints. In Chapter 3, we discussed the possibility of updates to the database that might violate referential integrity constraints. We saw that SQL has a way of specifying compensating actions (such as ON DELETE CASCADE) that the DBMS should take to restore integrity. These actions can be viewed as special triggers with very strict semantics. At the end of the execution, the integrity of the database must be restored. The situation is complicated by the fact that a compensating action might activate other triggers that can cause violations of referential integrity. In this case, the scheduling of all of these triggers must have the goal of ultimately restoring the integrity constraint. The problem of trigger scheduling does not have an obvious solution. We will discuss how this issue is resolved in SQL in the next section.

7.3 Triggers in SQL

Triggers were added to SQL as part of the SQL:1999 update. Convergence of an agreeable syntax and semantics for triggers in the current SQL standard involved a rather long and painful process. First, the various database vendors already had triggers in their systems, so the standard had to offer sufficient benefits to convince the vendors to change their implementations. Second, as we have seen, the semantic issues associated with triggers are not trivial, and the standard would not have been accepted unless it offered reasonable solutions to the problems discussed earlier.

Armed with a new understanding of the issues associated with trigger handling, we can now approach the SQL standard systematically:

- *Triggering events.* An event can be the execution of an SQL INSERT, DELETE, and UPDATE statement as a whole or a change to individual rows made by such statements.
- *Trigger precondition.* Any condition allowed in the WHERE clause of SQL.
- *Trigger action.* An SQL query, a DELETE, INSERT, UPDATE, ROLLBACK, or SIGNAL statement, or a program written in the language of SQL's *persistent stored modules* (*SQL/PSM*), which smoothly integrates procedural control statements with SQL query and update statements. We discuss SQL/PSM in Chapter 8.
- *Trigger conflict resolution.* Ordered—SQL assumes that all triggers are ordered and executed in some implementation-specific way. Since the order is likely to be different from one database product to another, applications must be designed so that they do not rely on trigger ordering.
- *Trigger consideration.* Immediate—the preconditions of all triggers activated by an event are checked immediately when the event is requested.
- *Trigger execution.* Immediate—execution can be specified to be before or after the triggering event.
- *Trigger granularity.* Row-level and statement-level granularities are both available.

Here is the general syntax of SQL triggers. Constructs in square brackets are optional; clauses in curly brackets specify a choice of one of the constructs separated by vertical lines.

```
CREATE TRIGGER trigger-name
    {BEFORE | AFTER}
        {INSERT | DELETE | UPDATE [ OF column-name-list ]}
    ON table-name
        [ REFERENCING [ OLD AS var-to-refer-to-old-tuple ]
                      [ NEW AS var-to-refer-to-new-tuple ] ]
```

```
                    [ OLD TABLE AS name-to-refer-to-old-table ] ]
                    [ NEW TABLE AS name-to-refer-to-new-table ] ]
    [ FOR EACH { ROW | STATEMENT } ]
    [ WHEN (precondition) ]
        statement-list
```

The syntax of SQL triggers closely follows the model discussed in Section 7.2. A trigger has a name; it is activated by certain events (specified by the INSERT-DELETE-UPDATE clause); it can be defined as a BEFORE or an AFTER trigger (indicating whether the precondition is to be checked in the state that exists before or after the event); and it can have a precondition (specified by the WHEN clause). The clauses FOR EACH ROW and FOR EACH STATEMENT specify the trigger granularity. If FOR EACH ROW is specified, the trigger is activated by the changes to every individual tuple in the table watched by that trigger. If FOR EACH STATEMENT is specified (which is the default), the trigger is activated once per execution of an INSERT, DELETE, or UPDATE statement on the table being monitored, regardless of the number of tuples changed by that execution (it will be activated even if no changes occurred).

The *statement list* following the WHEN clause defines the actions to be executed when the trigger is fired. Usually, these actions are SQL statements (that insert, delete, or modify tuples), but in general they can be statements written in SQL/PSM, which can include SQL statements intermixed with if-then-else statements, loops, local variables, and so forth. We discuss SQL/PSM in Chapter 8.

The REFERENCING *clause* is the means of referring to the pre-update and the post-update contents of the relation *table name*. This information can be used both in the WHEN condition and in the statement list that follows.

There are two types of references, depending on the granularity of the trigger. If the trigger has row-level granularity, we can use the clauses OLD AS and NEW AS, which define tuple variables to be used to refer to the old and the new value of the tuple that caused trigger activation. If the event is an INSERT, OLD is not applicable; if it is a DELETE, NEW is not applicable. If the trigger has statement-level granularity, SQL provides access to the old and the new values of the table affected by the triggering statement. Thus, the clause OLD TABLE names the table that contains the old state of the tuples affected by the update whereas the clause NEW TABLE defines the name under which the new state of these tuples can be accessed.

Note. NEW AS and OLD AS specify tuple variables that range *only over the tuples affected by the update*. That is, in tuple insertion, NEW AS refers to the inserted tuple. In tuple modification, it refers to the new state of the modified tuple. OLD AS refers to deleted tuples or to the old states of modified tuples.

Likewise, OLD TABLE and NEW TABLE contain *only the tuples affected by the update*, not the entire old and new states of the table. If **r** was the state of a table before the update, the state after the update is (**r** – *old table*) ∪ *new table*.

Finally, SQL imposes certain restrictions on what BEFORE and AFTER triggers can do.

BEFORE triggers. All BEFORE triggers execute entirely before the triggering events. They are not allowed to modify the database, but can only test the precondition specified in the WHEN clause and either accept or abort the triggering transaction. Since BEFORE triggers cannot modify the database, they cannot activate other triggers.

A typical use of BEFORE triggers is to preserve application-specific data integrity. For instance, the following trigger makes sure that course enrollment limits are never exceeded.

Example 7.3.1 (Business Rule Enforced with a* BEFORE *Trigger). Let us assume that, in addition to the already familiar relation TRANSCRIPT, the database includes a relation CRSLIMITS with the attributes CrsCode, Semester, and Limit (with their usual meanings). The following is a trigger that enforces course enrollment limits by monitoring tuple insertions into the TRANSCRIPT relation.

```
CREATE TRIGGER RoomCapacityCheck
    BEFORE INSERT ON Transcript
      REFERENCING NEW AS N
    FOR EACH ROW
    WHEN
      ((SELECT COUNT(T.StudId) FROM Transcript T
        WHERE T.CrsCode = N.CrsCode AND T.Semester = N.Semester)
      >=
      (SELECT L.Limit FROM CrsLimits L
       WHERE L.CrsCode = N.CrsCode AND L.Semester = N.Semester))
    ROLLBACK
```

Observe that an INSERT statement can insert several tuples involving different courses. The trigger specifies row granularity, so each insertion is treated as a separate event. If the course is filled to capacity, the insertion is rejected. ■

Note that the first SQL statement in the WHEN clause refers simultaneously to the new TRANSCRIPT tuples (through the tuple variable N) and to all tuples in the relation TRANSCRIPT (through the variable T). What state of the relation TRANSCRIPT is assumed while checking the validity of the WHEN condition? In the case of tuples referenced by N, the answer is clear. It must be the new state for each referenced tuple. However, it is less obvious what state is referenced by T. The answer is that BEFORE triggers assume that all referenced tables are in their old state while AFTER triggers assume the new state for each relation.

AFTER triggers. AFTER triggers execute entirely after the triggering event has applied its changes to the database. They are allowed to make changes to the database and thus can activate other triggers (which can cause a chain reaction, as explained earlier). In this way, AFTER triggers serve as an extension of the application logic. They can take care of various events automatically, thereby relieving application programmers of the need to code all of these event handlers in each application.

Example 7.3.2 (Business Rule Enforced with an* AFTER *Trigger). The following trigger enforces a dynamic constraint that caps any salary raises performed by a single transaction at 5%. We assume that the database has a relation called EMPLOYEE with an attribute named Salary.

```
CREATE TRIGGER LIMITSALARYRAISE
    AFTER UPDATE OF Salary ON EMPLOYEE
    REFERENCING OLD AS O
                NEW AS N
    FOR EACH ROW
    WHEN (N.Salary - O.Salary > 0.05 * O.Salary)
        UPDATE EMPLOYEE
        SET Salary = 1.05 * O.Salary
        WHERE Id = O.Id
```

Whenever the Salary attribute in an EMPLOYEE tuple is updated, the trigger causes the DBMS to compare its old and new values and, if the raise exceeds the cap, to adjust the salary increase to just 5%. If the raise does not exceed the cap or if the update is a salary decrease, the trigger does not fire. Note that the tuple variables O and N in the above statement always *refer to the same tuple* that was affected by the database update that activated the trigger. The difference is that O refers to the old state of that tuple and N refers to the new state. ■

Notice that when the trigger LIMITSALARYRAISE fires, its action overrides the effect of the original event that triggered LIMITSALARYRAISE. Furthermore, execution of the action is itself a triggering event for LIMITSALARYRAISE! However, the new event does not lead to a chain reaction. When the trigger is checked the second time, the salary actually decreases (to become exactly 5% above the original). Thus, the WHEN condition is false, and the trigger does not fire a second time.

We have seen several examples of triggers that have the granularity of a single row. However, some applications require that a trigger be fired only once per statement, after all updates specified in the statement have been processed. We illustrate the use of statement-level triggers with the following examples.

Example 7.3.3 (Statement-Level Trigger). Suppose that after each salary raise we want to record the new average salary for all employees. We can achieve this with the help of the following trigger:

```
CREATE TRIGGER RECORDNEWAVERAGE
    AFTER UPDATE OF Salary ON EMPLOYEE
    FOR EACH STATEMENT
        INSERT INTO LOG
        VALUES (CURRENT_DATE,
                (SELECT AVG(Salary) FROM EMPLOYEE))
```

When the trigger is executed, it inserts a record into the table LOG that gives the new average salary. The record also indicates the date on which the average was calculated (CURRENT_DATE is a built-in SQL function that returns the current date). Since it does not make sense to compute a new average after every individual salary change, statement-level granularity is better suited here than is row-level granularity. ■

The next example illustrates the use of statement-level triggers for maintaining inclusion dependencies. We discussed inclusion dependencies in Chapter 3 as a useful generalization of foreign-key constraints, which occur frequently in practical settings. One such dependency, *No professor can be scheduled to teach a course that has no registered students*, was given in (3.1) on page 45. It is a referential integrity constraint that is *not* based on foreign keys, and its representation in SQL requires the use of assertions (see (3.4) on page 52). We now show how AFTER triggers can help maintain this constraint in the presence of updates.[1]

Example 7.3.4 (Maintenance of Inclusion Dependencies). The key idea is to construct an SQL view, IDLETEACHING, that includes precisely those tuples from the TEACHING relation that describe course offerings with no corresponding tuples in the TRANSCRIPT relation. In other words, the view contains precisely the tuples that violate the inclusion dependency. Designing such a view definition is left as an exercise.

The trigger works as follows: after one or more students drop a class (or several classes), the trigger deletes all tuples found in IDLETEACHING from TEACHING.

```
CREATE TRIGGER MAINTAINCOURSESNONEMPTY
    AFTER DELETE,UPDATE OF CrsCode,Semester ON TRANSCRIPT
    FOR EACH STATEMENT
        DELETE FROM TEACHING
        WHERE EXISTS (SELECT *                                    7.1
                      FROM IDLETEACHING T
                      WHERE Semester = T.Semester
                          AND CrsCode = T.CrsCode)
```

Similarly, we can construct a trigger to maintain the inclusion dependency when tuples are added to the TEACHING relation. This trigger should abort any transaction that tries to insert a tuple into TEACHING if there is no corresponding tuple in TRANSCRIPT. ■

Note that the above trigger might cause a chicken-and-egg problem. We cannot assign a course to a professor until somebody registers for it. However, in most schools the course schedule for the next semester is published before any student registers for any course, so some triggers might need to be created and then

[1] The same technique can be used to emulate the ON DELETE and ON UPDATE clauses of foreign-key constraints in systems that are not SQL-92 compliant.

destroyed. The above trigger, for instance, might need to be in effect *only* between the deadline for adding courses and the deadline for dropping them.

Example 7.3.5* (INSTEAD OF *Triggers). Although INSTEAD OF triggers are not part of the SQL standard, this advanced feature is included in a number of database products. In this example we illustrate the approach used in the Oracle DBMS. Consider the following view:

```
CREATE VIEW WorksIn(ProfId,DeptName) AS
        SELECT   P.Id, D.Name
        FROM     Professor P, Department D
        WHERE    P.DeptId = D.DeptId
```

and suppose that the following operation is performed on the view:

```
DELETE FROM WorksIn
WHERE Id = 111111111
```

Since the contents of a view is not stored in the database, such an operation must be translated into appropriate operations on the base tables of the view, Professor and Department. However, in general, there may be several translations: we could delete the department where the professor with Id 111111111 works; we can delete the professor; or we can set the DeptId field in the professor's tuple to NULL. There is no way to automatically decide which of these three possibilities is the right one. However, INSTEAD OF triggers offer a way for the application designer to specify the appropriate course of action. For instance,

```
CREATE TRIGGER WorksInTrig1
    INSTEAD OF DELETE ON WorksIn
    REFERENCING OLD AS O
    FOR EACH ROW
        UPDATE Professor
        SET DeptId = NULL
        WHERE Id = O.ProfId
```

is a trigger that directs the DBMS to set the DeptId field to NULL whenever a deletion operation on the view WorksIn is performed. ■

Summary of the trigger evaluation procedure. Suppose that an event, **e**, occurs during the execution of a database update statement, $\mathcal{S}$, and this event activates a set of triggers, $\mathbf{T} = \{T_1, \ldots, T_k\}$. Then we can summarize the procedure for trigger processing as follows:

1. Put the newly activated triggers on the trigger queue, **Q**.
2. Suspend the execution of $\mathcal{S}$.

3. Compute OLD and NEW if row-level granularity is used, or OLD TABLE and NEW TABLE if statement-level granularity is used.
4. Consider all BEFORE triggers in **T**. Execute those whose preconditions are true, and place all AFTER triggers whose preconditions are true on **Q**.
5. Apply the updates specified in $\mathcal{S}$ to the database.
6. Consider each AFTER trigger on **Q** according to the (implementation-dependent) priority, and execute it immediately if the triggering condition is true. If the execution of a trigger activates new triggers, execute this algorithm recursively, starting with step 1.
7. Resume the execution of statement $\mathcal{S}$.

Triggers and foreign-key constraints. When the event that activates a trigger is invoked on a relation that has foreign-key constraints with ON DELETE and ON UPDATE clauses, the compensating actions specified in these clauses are likely to cause updates of their own. As a result, the exact semantics of the system becomes quite complicated. In fact, it took several iterations for the designers of the SQL:1999 standard to find a satisfactory solution.

One might ask why the actions attached to foreign-key constraints are not treated as regular triggers. The answer is that these constraints *are* triggers, but they have special semantics—they are intended to rectify states that violate foreign-key constraints, and it is desirable to capture this semantics in the trigger-evaluation procedure. To do so, we modify step 5:

5′. Apply the updates specified in $\mathcal{S}$ to the database (as before). For each FOREIGN KEY statement violated by the current (new) state, let **act** denote the associated compensating action (i.e., CASCADE, SET DEFAULT, SET NULL, or NO ACTION). Note that **act** is an event that can in turn activate other triggers, which we denote as $\mathbf{S} = \{S_1, \ldots, S_n\}$. Then

(a) Consider all triggers in **S**. Execute the BEFORE triggers whose preconditions are true, and place on **Q** all AFTER triggers whose preconditions are true.
(b) Apply the updates specified in **act**.

Note that in step 5′(b), we did not say whether the unprocessed triggers in **S** should be placed in front of **Q** or appended to it. The reason for this is that SQL processes triggers according to their implementation-dependent priority.

Observe that execution of AFTER triggers in step 6 can activate other triggers and also cause violation of foreign-key constraints. In this case, steps 1 through 6 are invoked recursively.

The above algorithm is designed to handle very complex interactions of triggers and foreign-key constraints—interactions that might involve dozens of triggers. We illustrate the algorithm on a simple example that involves just two triggers and one foreign-key constraint.

Example 7.3.6 (Interaction of Triggers and Foreign-Key Constraints). Let us assume that courses mentioned in the TRANSCRIPT relation must also be listed in the COURSE relation. Both of these relations are described in Figure 3.4 on page 38. The foreign-key constraint between these relations, which we call CHECKCOURSEVALIDITY, can be expressed as follows:

```
CREATE TABLE TRANSCRIPT (
    StudId   INTEGER,
    CrsCode  CHAR(6),
    Semester CHAR(6),
    Grade    grades,
    PRIMARY KEY (StudId, CrsCode, Semester),
    CONSTRAINT CHECKCOURSEVALIDITY
        FOREIGN KEY (CrsCode) REFERENCES COURSE (CrsCode)
            ON DELETE CASCADE
            ON UPDATE CASCADE )
```

CHECKCOURSEVALIDITY deletes or updates all TRANSCRIPT tuples if the corresponding COURSE tuple is deleted or updated.

Suppose, in addition, that there is an AFTER trigger, WATCHCOURSEHISTORY, that records all changes to the tuples in the COURSE relation. We leave it to Exercise 7.5 to define this trigger in SQL. Finally, the trigger MAINTAINCOURSESNONEMPTY (7.1) is also part of the database scheme. Note that in this example we do not consider other foreign-key constraints (in particular, those associated with the TEACHING relation—including such constraints would make a much more complex example).

Suppose now that some course code is changed in the relation COURSE, specifically CS305 becomes CS405 beginning with fall 2000. This change activates the trigger WATCHCOURSEHISTORY and the CHECKCOURSEVALIDITY foreign-key constraint. Because WATCHCOURSEHISTORY is an AFTER trigger, it is placed on Q, and the trigger-processing algorithm handles the foreign-key constraint first as required in step 5′(b). Therefore, all tuples in the TRANSCRIPT relation that have CS305 in them are changed to refer to CS405.

This change activates the second trigger, MAINTAINCOURSESNONEMPTY. Since CS305 has been changed to CS405, the professor who is listed as teaching CS305 in fall 2000 is left without a class. In other words, CS305 is listed in TEACHING for the fall 2000 semester, but TRANSCRIPT does not have any corresponding tuples. Therefore, the WHEN condition in MAINTAINCOURSESNONEMPTY is true, and the trigger can be executed.

Because MAINTAINCOURSESNONEMPTY is an AFTER trigger, it is put on Q (step 5′(b)), which already contains WATCHCOURSEHISTORY. The order in which these two triggers in the queue are actually fired depends on the implementation of the particular DBMS being used and cannot be predicted.[2] When all triggers eventually

[2] Most vendors use scheduling strategies based on timestamps that reflect the time of trigger consideration. In our case, such timestamp ordering favors WATCHCOURSEHISTORY.

fire, the record about the course change goes into the history log and the teaching assignment for CS305 is deleted.

Note that the interaction of the two triggers and the foreign-key constraint described above might not yield the intended result in this example. For instance, it might be more reasonable to update the teaching assignment of CS305 to a teaching assignment of CS405. ■

7.4 Avoiding a Chain Reaction

The possibility of a never-ending chain reaction in trigger execution is a serious concern. As mentioned earlier, commercial DBMSs impose an a priori upper limit on the length of chain reactions. However, relying on this upper limit is not a good idea since it is hard to predict the final outcome.

Trigger systems in which chain firing terminates in all cases are called **safe**. Unfortunately, there is no algorithm that can tell whether any given set of triggers is safe. However, there are conditions that are sufficient to guarantee safety (i.e., if the conditions are satisfied, the triggers are safe), but they are not necessary (i.e., a set of triggers might be safe but not satisfy the conditions). The fact that there is no algorithm to test safety implies that there can be no verifiable necessary *and* sufficient condition for safety.

In view of this sorry state of affairs, we present one condition that is sufficient to guarantee safety but that rejects many perfectly safe trigger systems. A **triggering graph** is a graph whose nodes are triggers (or foreign-key constraints as a special case). An arc goes from trigger T to trigger T' if and only if execution of T is an event that can activate T'.

It is easy to see that one can use a simple syntactic analysis to determine whether one trigger might activate another trigger. Indeed, the events that enable a trigger are listed in the BEFORE/AFTER clause in the trigger definition (or in the ON DELETE/UPDATE clause in foreign-key constraint definitions); the events *caused* by the triggers can be determined from the statements in the trigger body. Figure 7.1 shows the triggering graph for some of the triggers discussed in this chapter.

Clearly, if the trigger graph is *acyclic*, it is not possible for the triggers to invoke each other in a nonterminating manner. By this criterion, the triggers WATCHCOURSEHISTORY, MAINTAINCOURSESNONEMPTY, and CHECKCOURSEVALIDITY cannot be involved in a chain reaction.

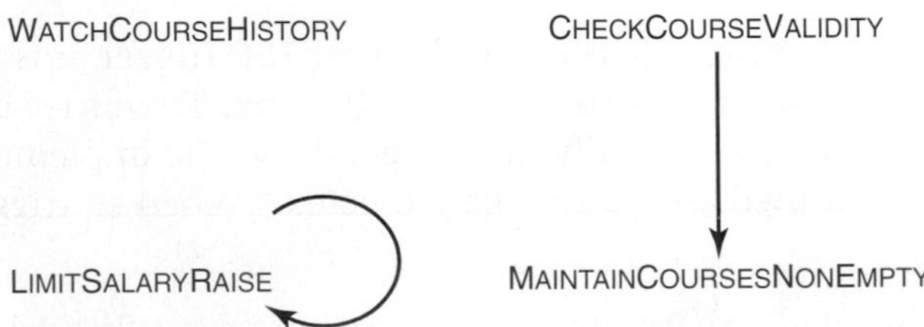

FIGURE 7.1 Cyclic trigger graph. The cycle does not cause a chain reaction.

Even though this method can certify the safety of some systems, it fails in many cases. Indeed, the part of our triggering graph that involves LIMITSALARYRAISE is cyclic because syntactic analysis shows that its execution activates this very trigger again. However, this trigger will fire only once because its WHEN condition will be false on the second invocation. This analysis exposes a major weakness of the triggering graph method. It does not take into account the semantics of the triggering conditions associated with the triggers. For example, if one can verify that no cycle in the triggering graph can be traversed infinitely many times (as in our example), the trigger system is safe.

There are a number of enhancements to the triggering graph methods, but they are outside of the scope of this book.

BIBLIOGRAPHIC NOTES

The main concepts underlying triggers in databases are described in [Paton et al. 1993]. The algorithm for integration of triggers with foreign-key constraints originates in [Cochrane et al. 1996]. The syntax of SQL:1999 triggers is described in recent guides to SQL, such as [Gulutzan and Pelzer 1999].

There is a vast body of literature on active databases; the information on SQL triggers provided here is only the tip of an iceberg. The interested reader is referred to [Widom and Ceri 1996] for a comprehensive study.

EXERCISES

7.1 Explain the semantics of the triggers that are available in the DBMS that is used for your course project. Describe the syntax for defining these triggers.

7.2 Give the exact syntactic rules for constructing the triggering graphs from the sets of SQL triggers and foreign-key constraints.

7.3 Design a trigger that complements the trigger MAINTAINCOURSESNONEMPTY (see (7.1) on page 260) by precluding the insertion of tuples into the relation TEACHING when there are no corresponding tuples in the TRANSCRIPT relation.

7.4 Design a trigger that works like MAINTAINCOURSESNONEMPTY but is a row-level trigger.

7.5 Define the trigger WATCHCOURSEHISTORY that uses a table LOG to record all changes that transactions make to the various courses in the COURSE relation.

7.6 Define triggers that fire when a student drops a course, changes her major, or when her grade average drops below a certain threshold. (For simplicity, assume that there is a function, `grade_avg()`, which takes a student `Id` and returns the student average grade.)

7.7 Consider the IsA relationship between STUDENT(`Id`,`Major`) and PERSON(`Id`, `Name`). Write the triggers appropriate for maintaining this relationship: when a tuple is deleted from PERSON, the tuple with the same Id must be deleted from STUDENT;

when a tuple is inserted into STUDENT, check whether a corresponding tuple exists in PERSON and abort if not. (Do not use the ON DELETE and ON INSERT clauses provided by the FOREIGN KEY statement.)

7.8 Consider a brokerage firm database with relations HOLDINGS(`AccountId`, `StockSymbol`, `CurrentPrice`, `Quantity`) and BALANCE(`AccountId`, `Balance`). Write the triggers for maintaining the correctness of the account balance when stock is bought (a tuple is added to HOLDINGS or `Quantity` is incremented), sold (a tuple is deleted from HOLDINGS or `Quantity` is decremented), or a price change occurs.

Solve the problem using both row-level and statement-level triggers. Give an example of a situation when row-level triggers are more appropriate for the above problem and when statement-level triggers are more appropriate.

7.9 Consider an enterprise in which different projects use parts supplied by various suppliers. Define the appropriate tables along with the corresponding foreign-key constraints. Define triggers that fire when a project changes a supplier for a part; when a supplier discontinues a part; or when a project stops using a part.

7.10 Consider triggers with immediate consideration and deferred execution. What do OLD AS and NEW AS refer to during consideration and during execution?

7.11 Give an example of an application where SQL triggers could be used for a purpose other than just maintaining integrity constraints.

8

Using SQL in an Application

In the previous chapters, we discussed SQL as an interactive language. You type in a query, anxiously listen to your hard drive, and then see the results appear on your screen (or more likely scroll by on the screen too quickly to be read). This mode of execution, called **direct execution**, was part of the original vision of SQL.

In most transaction processing applications, however, SQL statements are part of an application program written in some conventional language, such as C, Cobol, Java, or Visual Basic, and the program executes on a computer different from the one on which the database server resides. In this chapter, we discuss some advanced features of SQL that address the issues involved in this type of execution. Our goal is to present the basic concepts involved, not to cover all the syntactic options.

8.1 What Are the Issues Involved?

We are interested in creating programs that involve a mixture of SQL statements and statements from a conventional language. The SQL statements enable the program to access a database. The conventional language, called the **host language**, supplies features that are unavailable in SQL. These features include control mechanisms, such as the **if** and **while** statements, assignment statements, and error handling.

In our discussion of how SQL statements can be included in a host language, we must deal with two issues, discussed here:

1. Prior to executing an SQL statement, a **preparation** step is performed. Preparation involves parsing the statement and then making a *query execution plan*, which determines the sequence of steps necessary for statement execution. In what order will tables be joined? Should the tables be sorted first? What indices will be used? What constraints will be checked? Because the execution of a single SQL statement can involve considerable computational and I/O resources, it is essential that it be carefully planned. The query execution plan is designed by the DBMS using the database schema and the structure of the statement: the statement type (e.g., SELECT, INSERT), the tables and columns accessed, and the column domains. Factors such as the number of rows in a table might also

be taken into account in query optimization. The SQL statement is executed according to the sequence of steps outlined in the plan.

2. SQL constructs can be included in an application program in two different ways:

(a) **Statement-level interface (SLI).** The SQL constructs appear as new statement types in the program. The program is then a mixture of statements in two languages: the host language and the new statement types. Before the program can be compiled by the host language compiler, the SQL constructs must be processed by a **precompiler**, which translates the constructs into calls to host language procedures. The entire program can then be compiled by the host language compiler. At run time, these procedures communicate with the DBMS, which takes the actions necessary to cause the SQL statements to be executed.

The SQL constructs can take two forms. In the first, referred to as **embedded SQL**, they are ordinary SQL statements (e.g., SELECT, INSERT). In the second, they are directives for preparing and executing SQL statements, but the SQL statements *appear in the program as the values of string variables that are constructed by the host language portion of the program at run time*. Since in this case the actual SQL statements to be executed might not be known at compile time, this form is referred to as **dynamic SQL**. This is in contrast to embedded SQL, where the SQL statements are known at compile time and are written directly into the program. Hence, embedded SQL is also referred to as **static SQL**. SQL-92 defines a standard for embedded SQL. We also discuss SQLJ—a version of SLI designed specifically for Java—which was standardized in SQL:2003.

(b) **Call-level interface (CLI).** Here, unlike static and dynamic SQL, the application program is written entirely in the host language. As with dynamic SQL, SQL statements are the values of string variables constructed at run time. These variables are passed as arguments to host language procedures provided by the CLI. Since no special syntax is used, no precompiler is needed.

We discuss two CLIs in this chapter: **JDBC** (Java DataBase Connectivity), which is specifically designed for the Java language, and **ODBC** (Open DataBase Connectivity), which can be used with many languages. JDBC was standardized in SQL:2003 and has an interface very similar to ODBC in SQL:1999.

8.2 Embedded SQL

Embedded SQL is a statement-level interface that allows SQL statements to be embedded in a host language program. The schema of the database to be accessed by the program must be known at the time the program is written so that the SQL statements can be constructed. For example, the programmer must know the names of tables and the names and domains of columns.

Before the compilation of the program by the host language compiler, a precompiler (usually supplied by the vendor of the DBMS) scans the application program and locates the embedded SQL statements. These statements are not part of the host language, so they cannot be processed by the host language compiler. Instead they are set off by a special syntax so that the precompiler can recognize them. The precompiler translates each statement into a sequence of subroutine calls in the host language to a run-time library, which can be processed by the host language compiler at the next stage. Later, when the program is run and the SQL statement is to be executed, the subroutines are called and they send the SQL statement (that was originally embedded in the application) to the DBMS, which prepares and executes it.

It would be reasonable for the precompiler to check the form of each SQL statement and prepare a query execution plan since that would eliminate a significant source of run-time overhead. However, most precompilers do not do this. Preparation requires the precompiler to communicate with the DBMS (to determine the schema of the database that the statement is accessing), and this communication might not be possible at compile time. Furthermore, since the query execution plan might depend on the size of tables, the closer in time the preparation is to the execution, the better.

In the best of all possible worlds, the embedded SQL constructs would be written in some standardized version of SQL (e.g., SQL-92 or SQL:1999), and the precompiler for each DBMS would perform any necessary translation to the dialect of SQL recognized by that DBMS. In the real world, however, most precompilers do not perform such translations, and the SQL constructs must be written in the exact dialect of the DBMS being accessed. In practice, then, the DBMS, as well as the database schema, must be known at the time the program is written.

Requiring the application program to use the exact dialect of the DBMS can be a disadvantage if, at some later time, it becomes necessary to change to a different DBMS with a different dialect. In some situations, however, using the dialect of the DBMS can be an advantage. Many DBMSs contain proprietary extensions to SQL. If the SQL embedded in the host language is exactly SQL-92, those extensions are not available to the programmer. Of course, if the proprietary extensions supported by a particular DBMS are used in an application, the difficulty of changing to a different DBMS at a later time increases.

The SQL standard requires that all implementations of embedded SQL provide precompilers for at least seven host languages: Ada, C, COBOL, Fortran, M (formerly known as MUMPS), Pascal, and PL/1. In practice, precompilers are available for other languages as well.

Figure 8.1 is a fragment of a C program with embedded SQL statements. Each embedded SQL statement is preceded by the words EXEC SQL, so it can be located by the precompiler. We use the syntax of SQL-92, but be aware that many database vendors use their own dialect of SQL.

All examples in this chapter come from the following two schemas:

CLASS(CrsCode:CHAR(6), Semester:CHAR(6),
          Enrollment:INTEGER, ProfId:CHAR(9), Room:CHAR(10))
The Key of CLASS: {CrsCode, Semester}
TRANSCRIPT(StudId:INTEGER, CrsCode:CHAR(6), Semester:CHAR(6),
          Grade:CHAR(1))
The Key of TRANSCRIPT: {StudId, CrsCode, Semester}

FIGURE 8.1 Fragment of an embedded SQL program written in C.

```
EXEC SQL BEGIN DECLARE SECTION;
        unsigned long num_enrolled;
        char *crs_code, *semester;
        :
EXEC SQL END DECLARE SECTION;
     :  other host language declarations and statements
     :  statements to set the variables semester and crs_code

EXEC SQL SELECT C.Enrollment
        INTO :num_enrolled
        FROM CLASS C
        WHERE C.CrsCode = :crs_code
                AND C.Semester = :semester;
     :  the rest of the host language program
```

The domains of the attributes CrsCode, Semester, and Grade are the same as in Figure 3.5, page 39. That is, course codes are strings of the form MAT123 or CS305, semesters are strings of the form F1999 or S2000, and grades are letters, such as A or B.

For the application program as a whole to communicate with the database, host language statements and SQL statements must be able to access common variables. In that way, results computed by the host language portion of the program can be stored in the database, and data extracted from the database can be processed by host language statements.

The first group of statements in the fragment of Figure 8.1 declares variables of the host program, or **host variables**, that are used for that purpose. The declarations are included between EXEC SQL BEGIN DECLARE SECTION and EXEC SQL END DECLARE SECTION so that they can be easily found and processed by the precompiler. However, the declarations themselves are *not* preceded by EXEC SQL. In this way, the declarations can be processed by both the precompiler and the host language compiler.

Host variables are used in the SELECT statement shown in Figure 8.1. Note the colon that precedes each use of a host variable in the SELECT statement to differentiate it from the table and column names of the database schema. The value of Enrollment is returned in the host variable num_enrolled and can be accessed by host language statements in the normal way after the SELECT statement has been executed.

Since CrsCode and Semester together form the primary key of CLASS, the SELECT statement returns a *single* row. This is an important point. If the SELECT statement returned more than one row, which one would be used to provide the value for the variable num_enrolled? For this reason, it is an error for a SELECT INTO statement to return more than one row. We address the case in which the result consists of multiple rows in Section 8.2.4.

We can think of the host language variables as parameterizing the SQL statement. They are used to communicate scalar values, not table or column names or structured data. Host language variables that occur in WHERE clauses correspond to **in parameters**, while those used in INTO clauses correspond to **out parameters**. When the statement is executed, the values of the *in* parameters are used to form a complete SQL statement that can be executed by the database manager. Note, however, that the SQL statement can be prepared before the values of the in parameters are determined because, for example, table and column names are known (they cannot be parameters). Therefore, the query execution plan used when the statement is first executed can be saved for subsequent executions of the same statement (since only the parameter values differ on each execution). This is an important advantage of embedded SQL. One function of the precompiler is to select routines that, at run time, move values into and out of host language variables and to handle formatting for communication with the DBMS.

8.2.1 Status Processing

In the real world, things do not always proceed smoothly. For example, when you attempt to connect to a database on a distant server, the server might be down or it might reject the connection. Or an INSERT statement that you attempt to execute might be rejected by the DBMS because it would cause a constraint violation. You might categorize these as error situations since the requested action did not occur. In other situations, an SQL statement might execute correctly and return information describing the outcome of the execution. For example, the DELETE statement returns the number of rows deleted. SQL provides two mechanisms for returning information describing such situations to the host program: a five-character string SQLSTATE and a **diagnostics area**.

In Figure 8.2, we have added status processing to the fragment shown in Figure 8.1. SQLSTATE is declared within the declaration section since it is used for communication between the DBMS and the host language portion of the application. (It is declared as a six-character string when SQL is embedded in C, to account for the additional null character that terminates strings in C.) Note that SQLSTATE is not preceded by a colon when used in SQL statements because it is recognized by the preprocessor as a special keyword.

This declaration is required in all embedded SQL programs. (Earlier versions of SQL use a slightly different technique. Status is communicated through an integer variable, SQLCODE.) The DBMS sends information to be stored in that string after each SQL statement is executed. The statement can then be followed by a (host language) conditional statement that checks the value of SQLSTATE. If that value is 00000, the last SQL statement executed successfully. If not, the particular exception situation can be determined, and appropriate action can be taken. In Figure 8.2, a status message is printed.

FIGURE 8.2 Adding some status processing.

```
#define OK "00000"
EXEC SQL BEGIN DECLARE SECTION;
    char SQLSTATE[6];
    unsigned long num_enrolled;
    char *crs_code, *semester;
EXEC SQL END DECLARE SECTION;
    :  other statements; get the values for crs_code, semester
    :
EXEC SQL SELECT C.Enrollment
    INTO :num_enrolled
    FROM CLASS C
    WHERE C.CrsCode = :crs_code
        AND C.Semester = :semester;
if (strcmp(SQLSTATE,OK) != 0)
    printf("SELECT statement failed\n");
```

Instead of checking status after each SQL statement, we can include a single WHENEVER statement anywhere before the first SQL statement is executed.

```
EXEC SQL WHENEVER SQLERROR GOTO label;
```

Then any nonzero status in a subsequently executed statement causes a transfer of control to `label`. The WHENEVER statement remains in effect until another WHENEVER statement is executed.

More detailed information on the outcome of the last executed SQL statement can be retrieved from the diagnostics area using a GET DIAGNOSTICS statement. A single SQL statement can raise several exceptions. The diagnostics area records information about all exceptions raised.

Before this becomes a problem, we should mention one confusing issue: the difference in string notation in SQL (including all of its components, such as embedded SQL) and many of the host languages, such as C and Java. In SQL, strings are set in single quotes, while in C and Java they are set in double quotes. Thus, a C program with embedded SQL can have both kinds of notation. For instance, in

```
semester = "F2000";
EXEC SQL SELECT C.Enrollment
    INTO :num_enrolled
    FROM CLASS C
    WHERE C.CrsCode = 'CS305'
        AND C.Semester = :semester;
```

the string F2000 appears in a regular assignment statement and is processed by the C compiler, while CS305 occurs in an SQL statement and is handled by the SQL preprocessor.

8.2.2 Sessions, Connections, and Transactions

We introduce some terminology from the SQL standard. Before an application program that includes SQL statements can perform any database operations, it must establish an **SQL connection** to an **SQL server**. That connection initiates an **SQL session** on the server. Once an SQL session has been established, the application program can execute any number of **SQL transactions**, until it disconnects from the server, breaking the SQL connection and ending the SQL session.

SQL connections are established by executing a CONNECT statement (possibly implicitly), the general form of which is

```
CONNECT TO {DEFAULT | db-name-string}
    [AS connection-name-string] [USER user-id-string]
```

Phrases in square brackets are optional. Phrases in curly brackets refer to alternatives: one of the enclosed phrases separated by a vertical line must be chosen.

The option *db-name-string* is the name of the data source, *connection-name-string* is the name that *you* give to the connection, and *user-id-string* is the name of a user account; it is used by the data source for authorization. The format used to specify a data source depends on the vendor. It can be a string that identifies the database by name on a local machine or something like

```
tcp:postgresql://db.xyz.edu:100/studregDB
```

on a remote machine.

A program can execute additional CONNECT statements to different servers, after which the new connection and the new session become current and the previous connection and session become dormant. The program can switch to a dormant connection and session by executing

```
SET CONNECTION TO {DEFAULT | connection-name-string}
```

SQL connections and SQL sessions are terminated by executing (possibly implicitly)

```
DISCONNECT {DEFAULT | db-name-string}
```

8.2.3 Executing Transactions

There is no explicit SQL-92 statement that initiates a transaction. A transaction is initiated automatically when the first SQL statement that accesses the database is executed within a session.

In SQL:1999, transactions can also be initiated by using a START TRANSACTION statement that initiates a transaction and specifies certain of its characteristics similarly to the SET TRANSACTION statement, described below, in this section.

In SQL-92, transactions can be terminated with either COMMIT or ROLLBACK. The next SQL statement (after COMMIT or ROLLBACK) immediately starts a new transaction. This is referred to as **chaining**.

SQL:1999 also has COMMIT AND CHAIN and ROLLBACK AND CHAIN statements, which start a new transaction immediately after the commit or rollback completes without waiting until the start of the next SQL statement.

The default mode of execution for transactions is READ/WRITE, meaning that the transaction can both read and make changes to the database. Alternatively, it can be restricted to READ ONLY access to protect the database from unauthorized changes.

In Section 2.3, we pointed out that, although only serializable schedules guarantee correct execution for all applications, less demanding levels of isolation can often be used for a particular application to improve performance. Hence, the default isolation level is SERIALIZABLE, but other levels are offered as well. We discuss these levels at some length in Appendix A.

If a mode of execution other than the default mode is wanted, the SET TRANSACTION statement can be used. For example,

```
SET TRANSACTION READ ONLY
        ISOLATION LEVEL READ COMMITTED
        DIAGNOSTICS SIZE 6;
```

sets the mode to READ ONLY and the isolation level to READ COMMITTED. The following isolation levels are defined:

```
READ UNCOMMITTED
READ COMMITTED
REPEATABLE READ
SERIALIZABLE
```

The DIAGNOSTICS SIZE clause determines the number of exception conditions (caused by the last executed SQL statement) that can be described at one time in the diagnostics area.

Figure 8.3 illustrates the use of connection and transaction statements as well as status processing. After the declarations, the next set of statements makes a connection to the server. The program does not use explicit statements for beginning

FIGURE 8.3 The use of connection and transaction statements in a C program with embedded SQL statements whose purpose is to deregister a student from a course.

```
#define OK  "00000"
EXEC SQL BEGIN DECLARE SECTION;
     unsigned long stud_id;
     char *crs_code, *semester;
     char SQLSTATE[6];
     char *dbName;
     char *connectName;
     char *userId;
EXEC SQL END DECLARE SECTION;

// Get values for dbName, connectName, userId
dbName = "studregDB";
connectName = "conn1";
userId = "ji21";

      .
      :  other statements
      .

EXEC SQL CONNECT TO :dbName AS :connectName USER :userId;
if (strcmp(SQLSTATE,OK) != 0)
     exit(1);

 .
 :  get the values for stud_id, crs_code, etc.
 .

EXEC SQL DELETE FROM TRANSCRIPT
     WHERE StudId = :stud_id
          AND Semester = :semester
          AND CrsCode = :crs_code;

if (strcmp(SQLSTATE,OK) != 0)
     EXEC SQL ROLLBACK;
else {
     EXEC  SQL  UPDATE  CLASS
          SET Enrollment = (Enrollment - 1)
          WHERE CrsCode = :crs_code
                    AND Semester = :semester;

     if (strcmp(SQLSTATE,OK) != 0)
          EXEC SQL ROLLBACK;
     else
          EXEC SQL COMMIT;
}
EXEC SQL DISCONNECT :connectName;
```

a transaction; instead, a transaction is implicitly started once the connection is established.

The figure shows a fragment of the program that deregisters a student from a course. We assume that the host language variable `semester` contains the current semester, which can be determined through a call to the operating system, such as `time()`. The program makes two modifications to the database state: deleting the row of TRANSCRIPT that indicates that the student is registered in the course, and decrementing the `Enrollment` attribute of the course's tuple in CLASS. If either the DELETE statement or the UPDATE statement fails (and hence the value of `SQLSTATE` is not `"00000"` when the statement completes), the ROLLBACK command is executed. Otherwise, the COMMIT command is executed. Then the transaction disconnects.

If the DELETE statement fails, no modification has been made to the database, which might lead us to think that the ROLLBACK command is not needed. However, the system must be notified that the transaction has completed so that, for example, an appropriate entry can be made in the system log and any locks acquired by the transaction can be released. The log is part of the mechanism the system uses to ensure transaction atomicity.

When an application executes either EXEC SQL COMMIT or EXEC SQL ROLLBACK, it is requesting that the database server, *S*, to which the application has a current connection, commit or roll back any changes it has made to the database at *S*. However, the application program might be executing a transaction that does more than just access a single database server. For example, by establishing several connections and switching among them, it might be accessing several database servers, or it might be putting the results of its computation into a local file system. The COMMIT and ROLLBACK statements are sent over the connection to *S* and therefore do not apply to these tasks.

If the program is connected to more than one database, the transactions at each can be separately committed or rolled back. However, the global transaction consisting of all of the separate transactions might not be atomic (for example if the transaction at one database commits and the transaction at another database is rolled back).

8.2.4 Cursors

One of the advantages of SQL as a database language is that its statements can deal with entire tables. Thus, a SELECT statement might return a table, which we refer to as the **query result** or **result set**. When the statement is executed in direct or interactive mode rather than embedded in an application program, the result set scrolls out on the screen. The following SELECT statement, for example, returns the Ids and grades of all students enrolled in a particular course in a given semester.

```
EXEC SQL SELECT T.StudId, T.Grade
     FROM TRANSCRIPT T
     WHERE T.Semester = :semester
          AND T.CrsCode = :crs_code;
```

Suppose that we want to include such a statement in a host language program. The number of rows in the result set is not known until the statement is executed, so we face the problem of allocating storage within the program for an unknown number of rows. For example, if an array is to be used, how large should the array be?

This problem points up a fundamental difference between SQL and the host language. The fundamental unit dealt with by an SQL statement is a set of tuples, whereas the fundamental unit dealt with by a statement in the host language is a variable. This difference is often called an **impedance mismatch**.

The SQL mechanism for solving this problem is the **cursor**, which allows the application program to deal with one row in a result set at a time. Think of a cursor as a pointer to a row in the result set. A FETCH statement fetches the row pointed to by the cursor and assigns the attribute values in the row to host language variables in the program. In this way, variables need be allocated only for a single row. From the database schema, we know the types of the values in each row and so can declare variables of the appropriate type.

Figure 8.4 is a fragment of an embedded SQL program that uses cursors. The DECLARE CURSOR statement declares the name of the cursor as GETENROLLED, specifies it as INSENSITIVE (a qualification we discuss shortly), and associates it with a particular SELECT statement. It does not, however, cause that statement to be executed. The statement is executed when the OPEN statement is executed.

In the example, the associated SELECT statement is parameterized. Only tuples whose attributes `CrsCode` and `Semester` match the values stored in the host variables `crs_code` and `semester` are selected. When the OPEN statement is executed, parameter substitution takes place and then the SELECT statement is executed. Hence, changes to the values of the parameters made after the cursor is opened have no effect on the tuples that are retrieved through it. OPEN positions the cursor prior to the first row in the result set.

When the FETCH statement is executed, the cursor is advanced. Thus, the FETCH statement in Figure 8.4 points the cursor to the first row in the result set, and the values in that row are fetched and stored in the host language variables `stud_id` and `grade`. The CLOSE statement closes the cursor. (In this example, only the first row of the result set is retrieved—clearly an artificial situation. The next example is more realistic.)

Each of the SQL statements in the program has a number of options. The general form of the DECLARE CURSOR statement is

---

DECLARE *cursor-name* [INSENSITIVE] [SCROLL] CURSOR FOR
    table-expression
    [ORDER BY *order-item-comma-list*]
    [FOR { READ ONLY | UPDATE [OF *column-commalist*] }]

---

where *table-expression* is generally a table, view, or SELECT statement.

The option INSENSITIVE means that the execution of OPEN will effectively create a copy of the rows in the result set and all accesses through the cursor will be to that copy. The SQL standard uses the word "effectively" to mean that the standard

FIGURE 8.4 Using cursors.

```
#define OK  "00000"
EXEC SQL BEGIN DECLARE SECTION;
    unsigned long stud_id;
    char grade[1];
    char *crs_code, *semester;
    char SQLSTATE[6];
EXEC SQL END DECLARE SECTION;
  .
  :  input values for crs_code, semester, etc.
  .

EXEC SQL DECLARE GETENROLLED INSENSITIVE CURSOR FOR
    SELECT T.StudId, T.Grade
        FROM TRANSCRIPT T
        WHERE T.CrsCode = :crs_code
            AND T.Semester = :semester;

EXEC SQL OPEN GETENROLLED;
if (strcmp(SQLSTATE,OK) != 0) {
    printf("Cannot open cursor\n");
    exit(1);
}
EXEC SQL FETCH GETENROLLED INTO :stud_id, :grade;
if (strcmp(SQLSTATE,OK) != 0){
    printf("Cannot fetch\n");
    exit(1);
}
EXEC SQL CLOSE GETENROLLED;
```

---

does not specify how the INSENSITIVE option must be implemented, but whatever implementation is used must have the same effect as if a separate copy had been made. This type of returned data is sometimes called a **snapshot**.

INSENSITIVE cursors have very intuitive semantics. The selection over the base tables implied by the SELECT statement is performed when OPEN is executed, and the result set is computed and stored. This copy can then be browsed at a later time using the cursor. The situation is shown in Figure 8.5 for the cursor of Figure 8.4, where semester = 'F1997' and crs_code = 'CS315'.

Because an INSENSITIVE cursor accesses a copy of the result set, any modifications to the base tables by other statements in the same transaction made (not through this cursor) after the cursor has been opened will not be seen through the cursor. For example, the transaction might execute

```
INSERT INTO TRANSCRIPT
VALUES ('656565656', 'CS315', 'F1997', 'C');
```

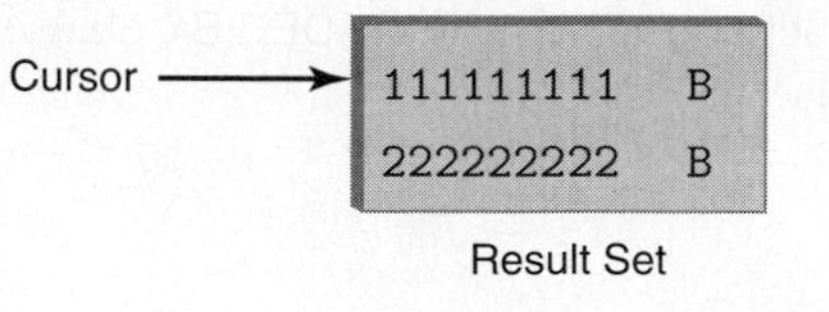

111111111	CS315	F1996	F
111111111	CS315	F1997	B
111111111	CS306	F1997	A
222222222	CS315	F1997	B
333333333	CS303	S1997	C

Transcript

FIGURE 8.5 With an insensitive cursor, the result set is effectively calculated when the cursor is opened and the underlying table is not accessed when rows are fetched.

after opening the cursor, thus inserting a new tuple directly (not through the cursor) into TRANSCRIPT. Although `crs_code = 'CS315'` and `semester = 'F1997'` at the time GETENROLLED is opened, the cursor will not retrieve values from the above newly inserted row. This is true even if the transaction executes an UPDATE statement that changes the attributes in one of the tuples in the result set after the cursor has been opened. Similarly, modifications of the base tables by concurrently executing transactions after the cursor has been opened will not be seen through the cursor.

The SQL standard does not specify what effects should be observed when changes are made to the base tables and the INSENSITIVE option has not been selected. Every database vendor is free to implement whatever it deems appropriate. Many vendors use the semantics called KEYSET_DRIVEN, which is part of ODBC and is described in Section 8.6.

If INSENSITIVE is not specified, the cursor has not been declared READ ONLY, and the SQL query in the cursor declaration satisfies the conditions for an updatable view (see Section 5.3), then the current row of the base table can be updated or deleted through the cursor, and the cursor is said to be "updatable." UPDATE or DELETE statements are used for this purpose, but the WHERE clause is replaced by WHERE CURRENT OF *cursor-name*. Thus, the general syntax is

```
UPDATE table-name
SET assignment-comma-list
WHERE CURRENT OF cursor-name
```

and

```
DELETE
FROM table-name
WHERE CURRENT OF cursor-name
```

Because an INSENSITIVE cursor points to a copy of the result set, UPDATE and DELETE statements would have no effect on tables from which the result set was calculated. Hence, to avoid confusion, these operations cannot be performed through an INSENSITIVE cursor.

If a particular ordering of rows in the result set is desired, the ORDER BY clause can be used. If, for example, we include the clause

```
ORDER BY Grade
```

in the declaration of GETENROLLED, rows of the result set will be in ascending order of Grade.

The general form of the FETCH statement is

```
FETCH [ [ row-selector ] FROM ] cursor-name
INTO target-commalist
```

where *target-commalist* is a list of host language variables that must match in number and type the list of attributes of the cursor's result set. The *row-selector* determines how the cursor is to be moved over the result set before the next row is fetched. The options are

```
FIRST
NEXT
PRIOR
LAST
ABSOLUTE n
RELATIVE n
```

If the row selector is NEXT, the cursor is moved to the next row of the result set and that row is fetched into the variables named in *target-commalist*. If the row selector is PRIOR, the cursor is moved to the preceding row and that row is fetched. Similarly, the FIRST row selector causes the cursor to be moved to the first row, and the LAST row selector causes the cursor to be moved to the last row. Finally, ABSOLUTE *n* refers to the *n*th row in the table, and RELATIVE *n* refers to the *n*th row before or after the row to which the cursor is pointing (as determined by a negative or positive *n*). If *row-selector* is omitted, NEXT is assumed. In that case, if the above ORDER BY clause is used in GETENROLLED, rows are fetched in ascending grade order.

The option SCROLL in the declaration of the cursor means that all forms of the FETCH statement are allowable. If SCROLL is not specified, only NEXT is allowable.

In Figure 8.6, we extend the example of Figure 8.4 so that all of the students enrolled in a particular course can be processed. The FETCH statement is now in a loop that terminates when the status returned indicates that execution was unsuccessful. The conditional statement following the loop checks for a "no data" condition (SQLSTATE has value "02000"), indicating that the result set has been completely scanned. It calls an error-handling routine if this is not the case.

FIGURE 8.6 Using a cursor to scan a table.

```
#define OK "00000"
#define EndOfScan "02000"
EXEC SQL BEGIN DECLARE SECTION;
    unsigned long stud_id;
    char grade[1];
    char *crs_code;
    char *semester;
    char SQLSTATE[6];
EXEC SQL END DECLARE SECTION;

EXEC SQL DECLARE GETENROLLED INSENSITIVE CURSOR FOR
    SELECT T.StudId, T.Grade
        FROM TRANSCRIPT T
        WHERE T.CrsCode = :crs_code
            AND T.Semester = :semester
    FOR READ ONLY;

  :
  :  get values for crs_code, semester
  :

EXEC SQL OPEN GETENROLLED;
if (strcmp(SQLSTATE,OK) != 0) {
    printf("Cannot open cursor\n");
    exit(1);
}

EXEC SQL FETCH GETENROLLED INTO :stud_id, :grade;
while (strcmp(SQLSTATE,OK) == 0) {
        :
        :  process the values in stud_id and grade
        :
    EXEC SQL FETCH GETENROLLED INTO :stud_id, :grade;
}

if (strcmp(SQLSTATE,EndOfScan) != 0) {
    printf("Something fishy: error before end-of-scan\n");
    exit(1);
}

EXEC SQL CLOSE GETENROLLED;
```

8.2.5 Stored Procedures on the Server

Many DBMS vendors allow **stored procedures** to be included as elements of the database schema. These procedures can then be invoked by an application at a client site and executed at the server site. Among the advantages of stored procedures are the following:

- Since the procedure executes at the server, only its results need be transmitted from the server back to the application program. For example, a stored procedure might use a cursor to scan a large result set and analyze the rows to produce a single value that is returned to the application program. By contrast, if the cursor is used from within the application program, the entire result set must be returned to the application program for analysis, thereby increasing communication costs and response time.
- The SQL statements within a stored procedure can be prepared before the application is executed since the procedure is part of the schema stored at the server. By contrast, preparation of embedded SQL statements is generally done at run time. Hence, even if a stored procedure contains only a single SQL statement, that statement will execute more efficiently in the procedure than if it had been embedded directly in the application.

  This advantage can become a disadvantage because query plans tend to go stale when there are significant database changes after the preparation has been computed. Thus, "old" stored procedures might avoid the overhead of query preparation but incur run-time overhead due to out-of-date query plans. Some vendors (e.g., Sybase) provide an option, WITH RECOMPILE, that can be specified at the time of the procedure call. The application can thus periodically recompile stored procedures and keep query execution plans up to date.
- Authorization can be checked by the DBMS at the level of the stored procedure using the GRANT EXECUTE statement, which extends the GRANT statement introduced in Section 3.3. Thus, even the users who are not authorized to access particular relations in the database might be authorized to execute certain procedures that contain statements that access those relations. For example, both the registration and grade-changing transactions might invoke stored procedures that use a SELECT statement to access the same tuples in a particular table, but one stored procedure can be executed only by students and the other only by faculty.

  In addition, a stored procedure can control what the user can do beyond the capabilities of the SQL GRANT statement. For example, the code within the stored procedure can enforce the requirement that only the student can execute a transaction to register himself.
- The application programmer need not know the details of the database schema since all database accesses can be encapsulated within the procedure body. For example, the registrar's office might supply the procedure body for the registration transaction. The application programmer need only know how to call it.

- Maintenance of the system is simplified since only one copy of the procedure, stored on the server, need be maintained and updated. By contrast, if the code contained in a procedure is part of a number of application programs, all of those copies have to be maintained and updated.
- The physical security of the code for the procedure is enhanced because the code is stored on the server rather than with the application program.

The original SQL-92 standard did not support stored procedures, but this support was added retroactively in 1996. We illustrate the language of stored procedures through an example.

Figure 8.7 shows the DDL declaration of a stored procedure for the transaction that deregisters a student from a course. We assume that the application program will connect to the DBMS before calling the procedure and will disconnect after the procedure returns.

The procedure body is written in the **SQL Persistent Stored Modules** language (**SQL/PSM**), as specified by the expanded SQL-92 standard.[1] The standard also provides for stored procedures written in other languages, such as C. Note that in this context SQL/PSM is simply another host language in which SQL statements are embedded. The procedure in the example has three *in* parameters, indicated by the keyword IN, and two *out* parameters, indicated by the keyword OUT. The standard also allows parameters that can be used both ways (INOUT).

The body of the procedure is enclosed in a BEGIN/END block. The option ATOMIC ensures that the entire block executes as a single atomic unit (i.e., it either executes to completion or the partial results of the execution are rolled back). Next follows a series of variable declarations, which are given initial value using the DEFAULT statement (which is optional). Note that neither the parameters nor the host variables (i.e., PSM variables declared within the stored procedure) have the colon (:) prefix. This is because SQL/PSM is a unified language whose compiler understands the host variable declarations, the control statements, and the SQL query and update statements. Our example illustrates the use of the variables both within and outside of the query and update statements. In particular, their value can be changed with the SET clause, and they can be part of arithmetic and string expressions.

PSM is a powerful, full-blown programming language that is well integrated with the rest of SQL. In our brief discussion, we omit many features, such as the looping constructs, the case statement, and cursors. A detailed treatment of PSM and stored procedures appears in [Melton 1997]; here we only touch upon error handling in PSM, which is somewhat different from that in embedded SQL.

Rather than have the program check the variable SQLSTATE after each update statement (or using the WHENEVER statement), in SQL/PSM, **condition handlers** are declared for different values of SQLSTATE. A condition handler is a program that gets executed when an SQL statement terminates with a value for SQLSTATE that

[1] Other vendors provide similar languages that precede SQL/PSM and differ from it in various ways. Oracle has PL/SQL, Microsoft and Sybase offer Transact-SQL, and Informix has the SPL language.

FIGURE 8.7 A stored procedure that deregisters a student from a course.

```
CREATE PROCEDURE Deregister( IN   crs_code CHAR(6),
                             IN   semester CHAR(6),
                             IN   student_id INTEGER,
                             OUT  status INTEGER,
                             OUT  statusMsg CHAR VARYING(100))
BEGIN ATOMIC
    DECLARE message CHAR VARYING(50)
        DEFAULT 'Houston, we have a problem: ';
    DECLARE Success INTEGER DEFAULT 0;
    DECLARE Failure INTEGER DEFAULT -1;

    IF 1 <> (SELECT COUNT(*) FROM CLASS C
            WHERE C.Semester = semester AND C.CrsCode = crs_code)
    THEN
        SET statusMsg = 'Course not offered';
        SET status = Failure;
    ELSE
        BEGIN   -- Block limits the scope of error handler
            DECLARE UNDO HANDLER FOR SQLEXCEPTION
                BEGIN
                    SET statusMsg = message || 'cannot delete';
                    SET status = Failure;
                END
            DELETE FROM TRANSCRIPT
               WHERE StudId = student_id
                    AND Semester = semester
                    AND CrsCode = crs_code;
        END
        BEGIN -- Block limits the scope of error handler
            DECLARE UNDO HANDLER FOR SQLEXCEPTION
                BEGIN
                    SET statusMsg = message || 'cannot update';
                    SET status = Failure;
                END
            UPDATE CLASS
               SET Enrollment = (Enrollment - 1)
               WHERE Semester = semester
                    AND CrsCode = crs_code;
        END
        -- Normal termination
        SET status = Success;
        SET statusMsg = 'OK';
    END IF;
END;
```

matches one of the values associated with that condition handler. In our case, we have two handlers associated with SQLEXCEPTION, which is a condition that matches any *error code* (an SQLSTATE value that does *not* begin with 00, 01, or 02). Each handler's scope is delimited by a BEGIN/END block, which allows us to associate different handlers with different SQL statements. Both handlers are UNDO handlers, which means that the DBMS will roll back the effects of the stored procedure and exit after the execution of the handler. UNDO handlers can occur only inside BEGIN ATOMIC blocks. If we specify CONTINUE handlers instead, the execution proceeds after the handler has been executed as if no error occurred. We can specify EXIT instead of UNDO, in which case the procedure will exit after the execution of the condition handler but the changes made by the procedure will *not* be rolled back.

In direct (interactive) SQL (and inside another stored procedure), a stored procedure can be executed using the SQL statement

```
CALL procedure_name(argument-commalist);
```

In a host program with embedded SQL, a CALL statement is preceded by EXEC SQL. In that case, the procedure arguments are host language variables preceded by a colon (:). For example, to execute the stored procedure Deregister(), we might use

```
EXEC SQL CALL Deregister(:crs_code,:semester,:stud_id);
```

where crs_code, semester, and stud_id are host variables.

8.3 More on Integrity Constraints

A consistent transaction moves the database from an initial to a final state, both of which satisfy all integrity constraints. However, a constraint might be false in an intermediate state during transaction execution; for example, in the case of referential integrity, if the reference to a row is added before the row itself. Similarly, the state produced by the DELETE statement in the procedure Deregister (Figure 8.7) violates the integrity constraint that the number of students listed as enrolled in a course in TRANSCRIPT be equal to the NumEnrolled attribute value for the course in CLASS. If the DBMS checks constraints immediately after each statement is executed, the DELETE would be rejected.

To deal with this situation, SQL allows the application to control the mode of each constraint. If a constraint is in **immediate mode**, it is checked immediately after the execution of any SQL statement in the transaction that might make it false. If it is in **deferred mode**, it is not checked until the transaction requests to commit.

- If constraint checking for a particular constraint is immediate and an SQL statement causes the constraint to become false, the offending SQL statement is rolled back and an appropriate error code is returned through SQLSTATE. The transaction can retrieve the name of the violated constraint from the diagnostics area.

- If constraint checking for a particular constraint is deferred, the constraint is not checked until the transaction requests to commit. If the constraint is found to be false at that time, the transaction is aborted and an appropriate error code returned. Deferred constraint checking is obviously preferable to immediate checking if integrity constraints are violated in intermediate transaction states.

When a constraint is initially defined, it can be specified with options. For example, a table constraint conforms to the rule

```
[ CONSTRAINT constraint-name ] CHECK conditional-expression
        [ { INITIALLY DEFERRED | INITIALLY IMMEDIATE } ]
        [ { DEFERRABLE | NOT DEFERRABLE } ]
```

The first option gives the initial mode of the constraint. Thus, if INITIALLY DEFERRED is specified, the constraint is checked in the deferred mode until the mode is changed by an explicit SET CONSTRAINTS statement. The second option tells whether or not the constraint can be deferred by a subsequent SET CONSTRAINTS statement. The options NOT DEFERRABLE and INITIALLY DEFERRED are considered contradictory and cannot be specified together.

A DEFERRABLE constraint can be in IMMEDIATE or DEFERRED mode at different times. The mode switch is performed with the following statement:

```
SET CONSTRAINTS { constraint-list | ALL } { DEFERRED | IMMEDIATE }
```

where *constraint-list* is a list of constraint names, given in CONSTRAINT statements.

8.4 Dynamic SQL

With static SQL, an SQL statement to be executed is designed and embedded in the application program at the time the program is written. All of the details of the statement (e.g., whether it is SELECT or INSERT), schema information (e.g., attribute and table names referred to in the statement), and host language variables used as *in* or *out* parameters are known at compile time.

In some applications, not all of this information is known when the program is written. To handle this situation, SQL defines a syntax for including **directives** in a host language program to construct, prepare, and execute an SQL statement. The statement is constructed by the host language portion of the program at run time. The directives are collectively referred to as *dynamic SQL* to distinguish them from static SQL and to indicate that SQL statements can be (dynamically) constructed at run time. Since, as with static SQL, the directives use a syntax that sets them apart from the host language, dynamic SQL is also a statement-level interface. Static and dynamic SQL use the same syntax, so they can be processed by the same precompiler. An application program can include both static and dynamic SQL constructs.

The constructed SQL statement appears in the program as the value of a host language variable of type string and is passed to the DBMS at run time as the argument of a dynamic SQL directive for preparation. Once prepared, the statement can be executed. As with static SQL, the statement must be constructed in the dialect understood by the target DBMS.

Suppose that, for example, your university has a single student registration system that allows a student to register for any course at any of its campuses. Assume that each campus has its own course database with its own table- and attribute-naming conventions. When a student executes the registration interaction, the application program might construct, at run time, the appropriate SQL statements to perform the registration at the specified campus. For example, it might have string representations of the appropriate SELECT statements for each campus stored in a file. The correct string is retrieved from the file at run time, assigned to a host language variable, and then prepared and executed. Or the program might use a skeleton of an appropriate SQL statement, which was prepared in advance, and then fill in appropriate table and attribute names at run time.

In the above example, there might be some commonality among the schemas and the SQL statements that must be executed to register a student at all campuses. Hence, the application program might know something about the SQL statements that it is executing. As another example, consider an application that monitors a terminal and allows the user to input an arbitrary SQL statement for execution at some database manager. The application now has no advance information about the SQL statements that it is sending to the database but must simply take the string that has been input to a variable and send it to the DBMS for processing. Similarly, consider an application in which a spreadsheet is connected to a database. At run time, the user might specify that the value of a particular entry in the spreadsheet is some expression involving database items that must be retrieved with queries. The queries might be expressed by the user in some graphical notation, but the application translates this notation into SELECT statements. Again, it has no advance information about the SQL statement to be executed and, possibly, none about the schema of the database the statement is accessing.

This lack of information can create a problem since the domains of the *in* and *out* parameters of the SQL statement must be known so that host language variables of the appropriate type can be used for parameter passing. For situations in which this information is not available to the application program at compile time, dynamic SQL provides directives that allow the program to query the DBMS at run time to obtain schema information.

8.4.1 Statement Preparation in Dynamic SQL

We illustrate the idea of dynamically constructed SQL statements with the following example:[2]

[2] For readers who need help with C, the function `scanf()` reads user input and puts the result in the variable `column`. The function `sprintf()` substitutes the value of the variable `column` for the format symbol `%s` and puts the result in the variable `my_sql_stmt`. The backslash in the SELECT clause indicates that the string continues on the following line.

```
printf("Which column of CLASS would you like to see?");
scanf("%s", column); // get user input (Enrollment or Room)
// Incorporate user input into SQL statement
sprintf(my_sql_stmt,
        "SELECT C.%s FROM CLASS C \
             WHERE C.CrsCode = ? AND  C.Semester = ?",
        column);
EXEC SQL PREPARE st1 FROM :my_sql_stmt;
EXEC SQL EXECUTE st1
     INTO :some_string_var
     USING :crs_code, :semester;
```

Here, in addition to the fact that the values of CrsCode and Semester are not known at compile time, the exact form of the SELECT statement is also not known at that time since the column to be retrieved by the query depends on what the user inputs at run time. The PREPARE statement sends the query string (in the variable my_sql_stmt) to the database manager for preparation and assigns the name st1 to the prepared statement. Note that st1 here is an SQL variable (used only in SQL statements), not a host language variable, so it is not preceded with a colon (:).

The EXECUTE statement causes the statement named st1 to be executed. The string has two *in* parameters marked with ?. The host language variables whose values are to be substituted for these parameters are named in the USING clause. In addition, the host variable to receive the result is named in the INTO clause. The ? marker is called a **dynamic parameter**, or **placeholder**, and can be used in SELECT, INSERT, UPDATE, and DELETE statements. Once prepared, st1 can be executed many times with different host language variables as arguments. The query execution plan created by the PREPARE statement is used for all subsequent executions during the current session.

Note that, just like SELECT INTO, EXECUTE INTO requires that the query result be a single row. If the result has more than one row, a cursor must be used instead of EXECUTE INTO. We describe cursors over dynamic SQL statements in Section 8.4.3.

Parameter passing in dynamic SQL is different from that in static SQL. Placeholders, instead of the names of host language variables, are used in the string to be prepared, and the INTO clause is now attached to the EXECUTE statement instead of the SELECT statement. Why is parameter passing different in this case?

- With static SQL, the names of the host language variables serving as parameters are provided to the precompiler in the WHERE and INTO clauses of the SQL statements. The precompiler parses these clauses at compile time. The variables are described in the compiler's symbol table that is used to translate variable names to addresses (recall that declarations in the DECLARE SECTION are processed by both the precompiler and the host language compiler). The symbol table entries contain the mapping between variable names and addresses plus the type information needed by the precompiler to generate the code for converting data items from the database representation to these variables and back. This code is executed in the host language program at the time the SQL statement is executed.

- With dynamic SQL, as in the above example, the SQL statement might not be available to the precompiler. Thus, if host language variables to be used as parameters were embedded in the statement, they could not be processed using information contained in the symbol table. To make parameter information available at compile time, it is supplied in one of two ways: through the *SQLDA* mechanism, explained on page 291, and by supplying the input and output variables in the clauses USING and INTO, as in our example. In the latter case, the precompiler generates the code for fetching and storing the argument values from and to these variables for communication with the DBMS.

Applications should be designed using static SQL whenever possible since dynamic SQL is generally less efficient. The separation of preparation and execution implies added communication and processing costs—although, if the statement is executed multiple times, the added cost can be prorated over the executions because preparation need be done only once. Moreover, this cost can be eliminated in some cases. With certain SQL statement to be executed only once, we can combine preparation and execution using the EXECUTE IMMEDIATE directive:

```
EXEC SQL EXECUTE IMMEDIATE
    'INSERT INTO TRANSCRIPT '
    || 'VALUES (''656565656'', ''CS315'', ''F1999'', ''C'') ';
```

Note the treatment of strings. INSERT INTO is part of the dynamic SQL statement, so we are using single quotes to denote strings. Since the statement is long, it is split into two strings, which are concatenated with the usual SQL concatenation operator, ||. To include a quote symbol in a string, it must be doubled, as in the case of `''656565656''`. This enables the SQL parser to parse the string correctly. In the result, each occurrence of `''` is replaced with a single quote, thus producing a valid SQL statement.

More generally, as with EXECUTE, the SQL statement can be constructed in a host language string variable, in which case the EXECUTE IMMEDIATE statement takes the form

```
EXEC SQL EXECUTE IMMEDIATE :my_sql_stmt;
```

Note the : prepended to the variable `my_sql_stmt`. As before, it indicates that `my_sql_stmt` is a host language variable rather than an SQL variable.

EXECUTE IMMEDIATE is merely a shortcut that combines the PREPARE and EXECUTE statements into one and does not preserve the execution plan after the statement has been executed. This shortcut imposes additional syntactic restrictions, some logical and some not. For instance, it does not allow an associated INTO clause.

Therefore, the statement to be executed cannot have any *out* parameters (i.e., it cannot retrieve any data) and so cannot be a SELECT statement.

EXECUTE IMMEDIATE also does not allow an associated USING clause, but this is not a serious limitation. The need for USING in the EXECUTE statement comes from the fact that the statement is prepared once, with dynamic *in* parameters marked as `?`, and then is executed many times with different arguments. Since EXECUTE IMMEDIATE does preparation and execution in one step (and the prepared statement is not saved for posterity), the special dynamic parameters are not needed. We can simply *plug* the appropriate parameter values into the SQL statement (represented as a string in the host language) using the host language facilities and then pass the fully constructed statement to EXECUTE IMMEDIATE.

As in static SQL, `SQLSTATE` is used to return the status of PREPARE, EXECUTE, EXECUTE IMMEDIATE, and all other dynamic SQL statements.

OPTIONAL

8.4.2 Prepared Statements and the Descriptor Area

Even though the query in the example of Section 8.4.1 on page 288 is constructed at run time and the name of the output column is not known at compile time, the example is still fairly simple because the application knows that the query target list contains exactly one attribute name and that the WHERE clause has exactly two dynamic parameters. Knowing the number of outputs and inputs thus allows us to use the EXECUTE statement and provide concrete variable names for the USING and INTO clauses. The precompiler can then supply such niceties as automatic format conversion. For example, if the user inputs `Enrollment`, which is an integer, conversion to the string format is automatic: the precompiler determines that the INTO variable is of type string. Since the DBMS provides, at run time, the type of the value returned by the SELECT statement, the nature of the conversion can be determined at that time.

Suppose now that, at run time, the application allows the user to specify the number of attributes in the target list and the condition in the WHERE clause. In this case we do not know the number of inputs and outputs at design time and will not be able to use the form of the EXECUTE statement described in Section 8.4.1 since we do not know how many variables to supply in the INTO and USING clauses at the time of writing the program.

To deal with this situation, dynamic SQL provides a run-time mechanism that the application program can use to request from the DBMS information describing the parameters of a statement. For example, suppose that an application allows the user to query any 1-tuple relation in the database:[3]

```
printf("Which table would you like to inspect?");
scanf("%s", table); // get user input (e.g., Class or Transcript)
// Incorporate user input into SQL statement
```

[3] Our example uses the EXECUTE statement, which can handle only 1-tuple queries. For the general case, a cursor and the FETCH statement are needed. We discuss the use of cursors in dynamic SQL in Section 8.4.3.

```
sprintf(my_sql_stmt,
        "SELECT * FROM %s WHERE COUNT(*)=1",
        table);
```

This statement has no input parameters but has an indeterminate number of output parameters because the table to be used in the FROM clause is not known in advance. Thus, it is not known how many table attributes (i.e., *out* parameters) are represented by the * in the SELECT clause. Although the application knows nothing about these parameters, once the statement has been prepared, the DBMS knows all there is to know about them and can provide this information to the application. It does this through a descriptor area. The application first requests that the DBMS allocate a **descriptor area**, sometimes called an **SQLDA**, in which parameter information can be stored. After the statement has been prepared, the application can then request that the DBMS populate the descriptor with the parameter information. For the above example, we populate the descriptor area as follows:

```
EXEC SQL PREPARE st FROM :my_sql_stmt;
EXEC SQL ALLOCATE DESCRIPTOR 'st_output' WITH MAX 21;
EXEC SQL DESCRIBE OUTPUT st
     USING SQL DESCRIPTOR 'st_output';
```

Here st_output is an SQL variable that references the descriptor area that has been allocated. The ALLOCATE DESCRIPTOR statement creates space in the database manager, which must be sufficient to describe at most 21 parameters of the statement (as specified by the WITH MAX clause). The descriptor can be thought of as a one-dimensional array with an entry for each parameter, together with a count of the *actual* number of parameters. Each entry has a fixed structure consisting of components that describe a particular parameter, such as its name, type, and value. All fields are initially undefined. The DESCRIBE statement causes the DBMS to populate the *i*th entry of the descriptor st_output with meta-information about the *i*th *out* parameter of the prepared statement st (which includes name, type, and length of the parameter). It also stores the number of these parameters in the descriptor.

Returning to our example, the application causes the prepared statement st to be executed using the directive

```
EXEC SQL EXECUTE st
     INTO SQL DESCRIPTOR 'st_output';
```

Execution causes the value of the ith attribute of the row returned to be stored in the *value field* of the ith entry in st_output. To retrieve the meta-information about the attributes as well as their values, the application can use the GET DESCRIPTOR statement. Typically this is done in a loop that inspects each column in the retrieved row, as illustrated in Figure 8.8. In the end, the program calls DEALLOCATE DESCRIPTOR to free the space occupied by the descriptor st_output.

OPTIONAL

FIGURE 8.8 Example of using GET DESCRIPTOR.

```
int collength, coltype, colcount;
char colname[255];
// Arrange variables for different types of data
char stringdata[1024];
int intdata;
float floatdata;
:
:  variable declarations for other types
:
// Store the number of columns in colcount
EXEC SQL GET DESCRIPTOR 'st_output' :colcount = COUNT;
for (i=0; i < colcount; i++) {
  // Get meta-information about the ith attribute
  // Note: type is represented by an integer constant, such as
  // SQL_CHAR, SQL_INTEGER, SQL_FLOAT, defined in a header file
  EXEC SQL GET DESCRIPTOR 'st_output' VALUE :i
    :coltype = TYPE,
    :collength = LENGTH,
    :colname = NAME;
  printf("Column %s has value: ", colname);
  switch (coltype) {
  case SQL_CHAR:
    EXEC SQL GET DESCRIPTOR 'st_output' VALUE :i :stringdata = DATA;
      printf("%s\n", stringdata); // print string value
      break;
  case SQL_INTEGER:
      EXEC SQL GET DESCRIPTOR 'st_output' VALUE :i :intdata = DATA;
      printf("%d\n", intdata); // print integer value
      break;
  case SQL_FLOAT:
      EXEC SQL GET DESCRIPTOR 'st_output' VALUE :i :floatdata = DATA;
    printf("%f\n", floatdata); // print floating point value
    break;
  :
  :  other cases
  :
  } // switch
} // for loop
```

Situations in which the SQL statement to be executed contains an unknown number of input parameters are rare. When they do occur, the application can use ALLOCATE and DESCRIBE INPUT to set up a descriptor area for the *in* parameters specified as ? placeholders. As before, this descriptor is essentially an array with an entry for each placeholder. The application then uses the DESCRIBE INPUT statement

OPTIONAL

to request that the DBMS populate the descriptor area with the information about each *in* parameter: for example, its type, length, and name. In this case the value has to be supplied by the application using the SET DESCRIPTOR statement. We do not discuss the details of this procedure and refer the reader to SQL manuals such as [Date and Darwen 1997; Melton and Simon 1992].

8.4.3 Cursors

Like SELECT INTO, EXECUTE INTO has the problem that the result of the query must be a single tuple. A more likely situation is that the result of a query is a relation and the cursor mechanism is needed to scan it. Fortunately, cursors can be defined for prepared statements in dynamic SQL as they are in static SQL, although the syntax is slightly different. For instance, the following is equivalent to the program in Figure 8.4 in static SQL (for brevity we have not shown the status checks in this case):

```
my_sql_stmt = "SELECT T.StudId, T.Grade \
                FROM Transcript T \
                WHERE T.CrsCode = ? \
                AND T.Semester = ?";
EXEC SQL PREPARE st2 FROM :my_sql_stmt;
EXEC SQL DECLARE GETENROLL INSENSITIVE CURSOR FOR st2;
EXEC SQL OPEN GETENROLL USING :crs_code, :semester;
EXEC SQL FETCH GETENROLL INTO :stud_id, :grade;
EXEC SQL CLOSE GETENROLL;
```

As with static SQL, the DECLARE CURSOR statement has the options INSENSITIVE and SCROLL, while the FETCH statement has the option that allows a row selector (FIRST, NEXT, PRIOR, etc.) to be specified for scrollable cursors. UPDATE and DELETE statements can also be performed through a dynamic cursor that is not insensitive.

8.4.4 Stored Procedures on the Server

Some DBMSs allow stored procedures to be called using dynamic SQL. To call the stored procedure of Figure 8.7, we might use

```
my_sql_stmt = "CALL Deregister(?,?,?)";
EXEC SQL PREPARE st3 FROM :my_sql_stmt;
EXEC SQL EXECUTE st3
    USING :crs_code, :semester, :stud_id;
```

The PREPARE statement prepares the call to the `Deregister` procedure. The EXEC SQL EXECUTE statement calls the procedure and supplies the values of host language variables as arguments.

8.5 JDBC and SQLJ

JDBC[4] is an API to the database manager that provides a call-level interface for the execution of SQL statements from a Java language program. As in dynamic SQL, an SQL statement can be constructed at run time as the value of a string variable. JDBC was developed by Sun Microsystems and is an integral part of the Java language.

In contrast, SQLJ is a statement-level interface to Java, analogous to static embedded SQL. Unlike JDBC, it was developed by a consortium of companies and has become a separate ANSI standard. In the end, both JDBC and SQLJ were included as part of SQL:2003.

Both JDBC and SQLJ are designed to access databases over the Internet and are much more portable than the various implementations of embedded and dynamic SQL. As part of SQL:2003, JDBC and SQLJ are described in the document titled *Object Language Bindings*.

8.5.1 JDBC Basics

Recall that, in dynamic and static SQL, the target DBMS must be known at compile time since the SQL statements must use the target's dialect. With dynamic SQL, the schema need not be known at compile time. By contrast, in JDBC neither the DBMS nor the schema need be known at compile time. Applications can use core SQL dialect that all JDBC drivers are required to support, and, as with dynamic SQL, JDBC supplies features that allow the application to request information about the schema from the DBMS at run time.

The mechanism that allows JDBC programs to deal with different DBMSs at run time is shown in Figure 8.9. The application communicates with a DBMS through a JDBC module called a **driver manager**. When the application first connects to a particular DBMS, the driver manager chooses another JDBC module, called a **driver**, to pass SQL statements specified in the JDBC calls to that DBMS. JDBC maintains a separate driver for most commonly used DBMSs. The manager chooses the one corresponding to the particular DBMS being accessed. When an SQL statement is to be executed, the application program sends a string representation of the statement to the appropriate driver, which performs any necessary reformatting and then sends the statement to the DBMS, where it is prepared and executed.

The software architecture of JDBC consists of a set of predefined object classes, such as `DriverManager` and `Statement`. The methods of these object classes provide the call-level interface to the database. A JDBC program must first load these predefined object classes, then create appropriate instances of the object types, and then use the appropriate methods to access the database. The general structure of JDBC calls within a Java program is shown in Figure 8.10. We explain each statement as it appears:

- `import java.sql.*` imports all of the classes in the package `java.sql` and hence makes the JDBC API available within the Java program. The classes

[4] JDBC is a trademark of Sun Microsystems, which claims that it is not an acronym. Nevertheless, it is often assumed to stand for "Java DataBase Connectivity."

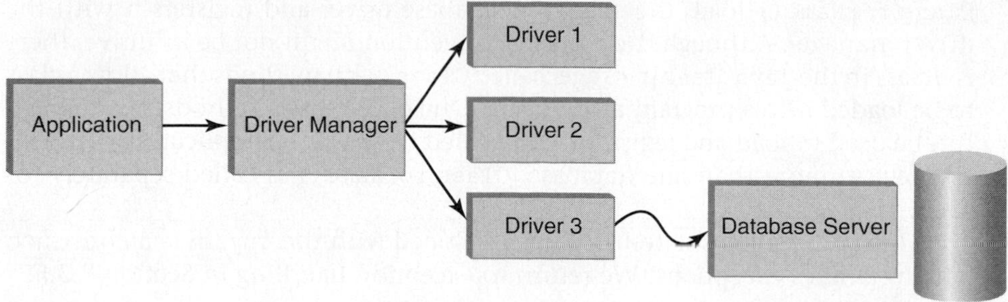

FIGURE 8.9 Connecting to a database through JDBC.

FIGURE 8.10 Skeleton of procedure calls needed for JDBC.

```
import java.sql.*;
  .
  .
  .
   String  url,userId,password;
   Connection  con1;
   .
   .
   .
   try {
      // Use the right driver for your database
      Class.forName("sun.jdbc.odbc.JdbcOdbcDriver"); // load the driver
      con1 = DriverManager.getConnection(url, userId, password);
   } catch (ClassNotFoundException e) {
      System.err.println("Cannot load driver\n");
      System.exit(1);
   } catch (SQLException e) {
      System.err.println("Cannot connect\n");
      System.exit(1);
   }
   Statement stat1 = con1.createStatement(); // create a statement object
   String myQuery = ... some SELECT statement ...
   ResultSet res1 = stat1.executeQuery(myQuery);
         .
         :  process results
         .
   stat1.close(); // free up the statement object
   con1.close();  // close connection
```

Connection, Statement, DriverManager, and ResultSet that occur in the figure are all in this package, as are PreparedStatement, CallableStatement, ResultSetMetadata, and SQLException. (CallableStatement is a subclass of PreparedStatement, which in turn is a subclass of Statement.)

- `Class.forName()` loads the specified database driver and registers it with the driver manager. Although the naming convention might not be intuitive, there is a class in the `java.lang` package, called `Class`, with methods that allow a class to be loaded into a program at run time. One of its static methods, `forName()`, can be used to load and register the specified driver. If the application wants to connect to more than one database, `Class.forName()` is called separately for each.

  This and the next statement are enveloped with the `try/catch` construct, which handles exceptions. We return to exception handling in Section 8.5.5.

- `DriverManager.getConnection()` uses the static method `getConnection()` of the class `DriverManager` to connect to the DBMS at the given address. The method tests each of the database drivers that have been loaded to see if any are capable of establishing a connection to that DBMS. If so, it

  1. Establishes the connection using the specified user Id and password
  2. Creates a `Connection` object and assigns it to the variable `con1`, declared earlier

  The parameter `url` contains the URL (uniform resource locator) of the target DBMS. This URL is obtained from the database administrator and looks something like

  ```
  jdbc:odbc:http://server.xyz.edu/sturegDB:8000
  ```

  The prefix `jdbc` specifies the main protocol for connecting to the database (JDBC, not surprisingly). The second component, `odbc`, specifies the subprotocol (which is vendor and driver specific). Next comes the address of the database server, followed by the communication port number on which the server is listening.

- `con1.createStatement()` uses the `createStatement()` method of the `Connection` object `con1` to create a `Statement` object and assign it to the `Statement` variable `stat1`.

- `stat1.executeQuery()` prepares and executes the SELECT statement provided as an argument, using the `Statement` object `stat1`. The SQL statement can have no *in* parameters, and the result set it returns is stored in the `ResultSet` object `res1`, which is created by the `executeQuery()` method. This method is analogous to the EXECUTE IMMEDIATE directive in dynamic SQL since it combines both preparation and execution. A major difference is that the JDBC method creates an object for returning data, which EXECUTE IMMEDIATE cannot do. We discuss the `ResultSet` class in Section 8.5.3.

  To execute an UPDATE, DELETE, or INSERT statement (or a DDL statement), the appropriate form is

  ```
  stat1.executeUpdate(... some SQL statement ...);
  ```

This function returns an integer denoting how many rows are affected (or 0 for a DDL statement, such as CREATE).

- stat1.close() and con1.close() deallocate the Statement object and close the connection (deallocating the Connection object), respectively. After a statement has been executed, the Statement object that supported it need not be closed but can be reused to support another statement.

8.5.2 Prepared Statements

The call to executeQuery() in Figure 8.10 both prepares and executes the specified statement. To prepare a statement and then execute it separately, the appropriate calls are

```
PreparedStatement ps1 =
      con1.prepareStatement(... SQL preparable statement ...);
```

which returns a PreparedStatement object that is assigned to ps1, followed by either

```
ResultSet res1 = ps1.executeQuery();
```

or in the case of an update statement,

```
int n = ps1.executeUpdate();
```

where executeUpdate() returns an integer denoting how many rows were updated.

PreparedStatement is a subclass of the class Statement. Note that both classes have methods with the names executeQuery() and executeUpdate(), but that the methods for PreparedStatement have no arguments (because a prepared statement knows which query it is).

As in dynamic SQL, the string argument of prepareStatement() can contain dynamic *in* parameters marked with the ? placeholders. Also as with dynamic SQL, the placeholders must be given concrete values before execution. This is done using the setXXX() methods. For instance,

```
ps1.setInt(1, someIntVar);
```

replaces the first ? placeholder with the value stored in the host language variable someIntVar. PreparedStatement has a number of setXXX() methods, where XXX specifies the type (e.g., Int, Long, String) to supply *in* arguments of different types.

8.5.3 Result Sets and Cursors

The execution of a query statement stores its result (the *out* arguments) in the specified ResultSet object. The rows in that result set are retrieved using a cursor.

FIGURE 8.11 Fragment of JDBC program using a cursor.

```
import java.sql.*;
      :
      :
    Connection con2;
    try {
      // Use appropriate URL and JDBC driver
      String url = "jdbc:odbc:http://server.xyz.edu/sturegDB:800";
      Class.forName("sun.jdbc.odbc.JdbcOdbcDriver");
      con2 = DriverManager.getConnection(url, "pml", "36.ty");
    } catch ...   // catch exceptions

    // Use the "+" operator, for readability
    String query2 = "SELECT T.StudId, T.Grade " +
                    "FROM TRANSCRIPT T " +
                    "WHERE T.CrsCode = ? " +
                     "AND T.Semester = ?";

    PreparedStatement ps2 = con2.prepareStatement(query2);
    ps2.setString(1, "CS308");
    ps2.setString(2, "F2000");
    ResultSet res2 = ps2.executeQuery();

    long studId;
    String grade;
    while (res2.next()) {
      studId = res2.getLong("StudId");
      grade = res2.getString("Grade");
      :
      :  process the values in studId and grade
      :
    }

ps2.close();
con2.close();
```

A JDBC cursor is implemented using the `next()` method of class `ResultSet`. When invoked on a `ResultSet` object, it scans the entire set tuple by tuple. In Figure 8.11, the result set object is stored in the variable `res2`, and `res2.next()` advances the cursor to the next row.

The program prepares the query, supplies arguments, and then executes the query. It then uses a while loop to retrieve all of the rows of the result set. The method `next()` moves the cursor and returns `false` when there are no more rows to return. In each iteration of the while loop, the result tuples are retrieved using calls to `getLong()` and `getString()`, which come in two forms: those that take attribute names as a parameter and those that take positional arguments. Thus, we can use getLong(1) to obtain the student Id (since StudId is the first attribute in the result set res2) and getString(2) to obtain the grade (since Grade is the second attribute). The class ResultSet has getXXX() methods for all primitive types supported by Java.

JDBC defines three result set types. They differ in their support of scrolling and sensitivity.

1. A *forward-only* result set, as its name implies, is not scrollable (the cursor can move only in the forward direction). It uses the default cursor type (INSENSITIVE or non-INSENSITIVE) of the underlying DBMS.
2. A *scroll-insensitive* result set is scrollable and uses an INSENSITIVE cursor of the specified DBMS so that changes made to the underlying tables after the result set is computed (either by the transaction that created the result set or by other transactions) are not seen in the result set.
3. A *scroll-sensitive* result set is scrollable and uses a non-INSENSITIVE cursor. As we discussed in Section 8.2.4, the SQL standard does not define any required behavior when the INSENSITIVE option has not been selected. Database vendors are free to implement whatever semantics they deem appropriate, and JDBC generally provides the semantics supported in the DBMS it is accessing. Many vendors have implemented the semantics called KEYSET_DRIVEN, which is part of the ODBC specification and is described in Section 8.6. In that semantics, row updates and deletes made after the result set is created are visible but inserts are not. JDBC provides a variety of methods for querying the driver to determine what to expect.

If the target DBMS does not support the scrolling or sensitivity properties requested by an application, a warning is issued.

A result set can be read-only or updatable. With an updatable result set, the SQL query on which the result set is based must satisfy the conditions for updatable views (see Section 5.3). For example, the following variant of createStatement() creates an instance s3 of the class Statement:

```
Statement s3 =
    con1.createStatement(ResultSet.TYPE_SCROLL_SENSITIVE,
                         ResultSet.CONCUR_UPDATABLE);
```

If the executeQuery() method of s3 is later invoked, the result set that will be created will be updatable and scroll-sensitive. Consult the description of classes ResultSet and Connection in your JDK documentation to see other options.

The current row of an updatable result set, res, produced by a SELECT statement that returns the value of a string attribute, Name, might be updated by assigning the value Smith to Name using

```
res.updateString("Name", "Smith");
```

As with the methods setXXX() and getXXX(), there is an updateXXX() method for every primitive type.

When the new value of the row has been completely constructed, the underlying table is updated by the execution of

```
res.updateRow();
```

Not only can rows in an updatable result set be updated and deleted but, in contrast to cursors in static and dynamic SQL, new rows can be inserted through the result set as well. The column values of the row to be inserted are first assembled in a buffer associated with the result set. The method `res.insertRow()` is then called to insert the buffered row in the result set `res` and in the database simultaneously.

8.5.4 Obtaining Information about a Result Set

As with dynamic SQL, information about a result set might not be known when the program is written. JDBC provides mechanisms for querying the DBMS to obtain such information. For example, JDBC provides a class `ResultSetMetaData`, whose methods can be used for this purpose. Thus

```
ResultSet rs3 = stmt3.executeQuery("SELECT * FROM TABLE3");
ResultSetMetaData rsm3 = rs3.getMetaData();
```

creates a `ResultSetMetaData` object, `rsm3`, and populates it with information about the result set `rs3`. This object can then be queried with such methods as

```
int numberOfColumns = rsm3.getColumnCount();
String columnName = rsm3.getColumnName(1);
String typeName = rsm3.getColumnTypeName(1);
```

The first method returns the number of columns in the result set, and the last two return the name and type of column 1. Using these methods, even without knowing the schema of a result set, one can iterate over the columns of each row in a loop, examine their types, and fetch the data. For instance, if `rsm3.getColumnTypeName(2)` returns `"Integer"`, the program can call `rs3.getInt(2)` to obtain the value stored in the second column of the current row.

JDBC also has a class, `DatabaseMetaData`, which can be queried for information about the schema and other database information.

8.5.5 Status Processing

Status processing in JDBC uses the standard exception-handling mechanism of Java. The basic format is

```
try {
      .
      .  code that might cause an exception goes here
      .
}
```

```
catch (SQLException e) {
      System.err.println("Bad things have happened:\n");
      System.err.println("Message: " + e.getMessage());
      System.err.println("SQLState: " + e.getSQLState());
      System.err.println("ErrorCode: " + e.getErrorCode());
};
```

In fact, in our examples, all calls to `executeQuery()`, `prepareStatement()`, and the like should have been enveloped with such a `try` statement.

The system *tries* to execute the statements within the `try` clause. Each such statement can contain method calls for Java or JDBC objects, and the declaration of each method can specify that, if certain errors occur during method execution, one or more named exceptions are **thrown**, where the name of the exception denotes the type of error that occurred. For example, the JDBC method `executeQuery()` throws the exception `SQLException` if the DBMS returns an access error during query execution. An access error occurs whenever there is an unsuccessful or incomplete execution of an SQL statement—more precisely, an execution for which `SQLSTATE` has any value other than successful completion (of the form `"00XXX"`), warning (of the form `"01XXX"`), or no data (`"02000"`).

If such an exception is thrown within the `try` clause, it is **caught** by the corresponding `catch` clause, which is then executed. In the example, an `SQLException` object, `e`, is created, whose methods can be used to print out an error message, return the value of `SQLSTATE`, or return any vendor-specific error code. When the `catch` clause completes, execution continues with the next statement following the clause.

8.5.6 Executing Transactions

By default, the database is in **autocommit mode** when a connection is created. Each SQL statement is treated as a separate transaction, which is committed when that statement is (successfully) completed. To allow two or more statements to be grouped into a transaction, autocommit mode is disabled using

```
con4.setAutoCommit(false);
```

where `con4` is a `Connection` object.

Initially, each transaction uses the default isolation level of the database manager. The level can be changed with a call such as

```
con4.setTransactionIsolation(Connection.TRANSACTION_SERIALIZABLE);
```

Serialization levels `TRANSACTION_SERIALIZABLE`, `TRANSACTION_REPEATABLE_READ`, and the like are constants (static integers) defined in class `Connection`.

Transactions can be committed or aborted using the `commit()` or `rollback()` methods of class `Connection`.

```
con4.commit();
con4.rollback();
```

After a transaction is committed or rolled back, a new one starts when the next SQL statement is executed (or, in the case of the first SQL statement in the program, when that statement is executed). This way of structuring transactions is called *chaining*.

If the program is connected to more than one DBMS, the transactions at each can be separately committed or rolled back. JDBC does not support a commit protocol that ensures that the set of transactions will be globally atomic. However, a Java package, JTS (Java Transaction Service), includes a TP monitor (and an appropriate API, called JTA [Java Transaction API]), which does guarantee an atomic commit of distributed transactions using JDBC. Also J2EE (Java 2 Enterprise Edition) provides transaction services based on JDBC and JTS.

8.5.7 Stored Procedures on the Server

JDBC can be used to call a stored procedure if the DBMS supports this feature. For example, to call the stored procedure defined in Figure 8.7 on page 284 we might use the program fragment

```
CallableStatement cs5 =
      con5.prepareCall("{call Deregister(?,?,?,?,?)}");
cs5.setString(1, crs_code);
cs5.setString(2, semester);
cs5.setInt(3, stud_id);
cs5.getInt(4, status);
cs5.setString(5, message);
cs5.executeUpdate();
```

where `con5` is a `Connection` object.

The first statement declares a `CallableStatement` object with the name `cs5` and assigns to it the stored procedure `Deregister()`. The braces around the construct `{call Deregister(?,?,?,?,?)}` denote that the construct is part of the **SQL escape syntax** and signals the driver that the code within the braces should be handled in a special way. The values of the three *in* parameters of `Deregister()`, obtained from the Java variables `crs_code`, `semester`, and `stud_Id`, are specified with setXXX() method calls. (We omit the details of *out* parameters and return values, which are handled somewhat differently.) The final statement executes the call.

The DBMS might allow a stored procedure to return a result set, perhaps in addition to updating the database. A call to such a procedure is viewed as a query, in which case the last statement in the above program fragment is replaced by

```
ResultSet rs5 = cs5.executeQuery();
```

JDBC also has facilities for creating a stored procedure (as a string) and sending it to the DBMS.

8.5.8 An Example

Figure 8.12 is a fragment of a Java program containing calls to the JDBC API. The program performs roughly the same transaction as that of Figure 8.3, except that, for simplicity, it uses constants in the SQL statements instead of the ? placeholders.

8.5.9 SQLJ: Statement-Level Interface to Java

Although call-level interfaces, such as JDBC, can be used in static transaction processing applications (where the database schema and the format of the SQL statements are known at compile time), they are fundamentally less efficient at run time than statement-level interfaces, such as static SQL, because preparation and execution generally involve separate communication with the DBMS. For this reason, a consortium of companies developed a statement-level SQL interface to Java, called **SQLJ**, which is now an ANSI standard. An important goal of SQLJ is to obtain some of the run-time efficiency of embedded SQL for (static) Java applications while retaining the advantage of accessing DBMSs through JDBC.

SQLJ is analogous to embedded SQL but was designed specifically to be embedded in Java programs. Such programs are translated by a precompiler into standard Java, and the embedded SQLJ constructs are replaced by calls to an SQLJ run-time package, which accesses a database using calls to a JDBC driver. An SQLJ program can connect to multiple DBMSs using different JDBC drivers in this way. As with embedded SQL, the precompiler can also check SQL syntax and the number and types of arguments and results.

We do not discuss the syntax of SQLJ in detail but highlight some of the differences between SQLJ, embedded SQL, and JDBC:

- In contrast to embedded SQL, in which each DBMS vendor supports its own proprietary version of SQL, SQLJ supports a core sublanguage of SQL-92 and is much more portable across vendors. (DBMS vendors can provide proprietary extensions, however.)
- SQL statements appear in a Java program as part of an **SQLJ clause**, which begins with #SQL (instead of EXEC SQL, as in embedded SQL) and can contain an SQL

FIGURE 8.12 A fragment of a Java program using JDBC.

```
import java.sql.*;
    .
    .
    .
    try {
        // Use the right JDBC driver here
        Class.forName("sun.jdbc.odbc.JdbcOdbcDriver");
    } catch (ClassNotFoundException e) {
        return(-1);  // Cannot load driver
    }
    Connection con6 = null;
    try {
        String url = "jdbc:odbc:http://server.xyz.edu/sturegDB:8000";
        con6 = DriverManager.getConnection(url,"john","ji21");
    } catch (SQLException e) {
        return(-2);  // Cannot connect
    }
    con6.setAutoCommit(false);
    Statement stat6 = con6.createStatement();
    try {
        stat6.executeUpdate("DELETE FROM TRANSCRIPT " +
                            "WHERE StudId = 123456789 " +
                              "AND Semester = 'F2000'  " +
                              "AND CrsCode = 'CS308'" );
    } catch (SQLException e) {
        con6.rollback();
        stat6.close();
        con6.close();
        return(-3);  // Cannot execute
    }
    try {
        stat6.executeUpdate("UPDATE CLASS " +
                            "SET Enrollment = (Enrollment - 1) " +
                              "AND Semester = 'F2000' " +
                              "WHERE CrsCode = 'CS308'");
    } catch (SQLException e) {
        con6.rollback();
        stat6.close();
        con6.close();
        return(-4);  // Cannot update
    }

    con6.commit();
    stat6.close();
    con6.close();
    return(0);  // Success!
```

FIGURE 8.13 Use of an iterator in SQLJ.

```
import java.sql.*
    :
    #SQL iterator GetEnrolledIter(int studentId, String studGrade);
    GetEnrolledIter iter1;
    #SQL iter1 = { SELECT T.StudId AS "studentId",
                          T.Grade AS "studGrade"
                   FROM TRANSCRIPT T
                   WHERE T.CrsCode = :crsCode
                          AND T.Semester = :semester };
    int id;
    String grade;
    while (iter1.next()) {
        id = iter1.studentId();
        grade = iter1.studGrade();
        :   process the values in id and grade
    }
    iter1.close();
```

statement inside curly braces. For example, the SELECT statement of Figure 8.1 becomes in SQLJ:

```
#SQL {SELECT C.Enrollment
        INTO :numEnrolled
        FROM CLASS C
        WHERE C.CrsCode = :crsCode
           AND C.Semester = :semester};
```

- Any Java variable can be included as a parameter in an SQL statement prefixed with :, as in static SQL. This method of passing parameters into an SQL construct (which, you will recall, is done at compile time) is considerably more efficient during run time than the method used in JDBC, in which the value of each argument must be bound to a ? parameter at run time.
- In SQLJ, a query returns an **SQLJ iterator** object instead of a `ResultSet` object. SQLJ iterators are similar to result sets in that they provide a cursor mechanism. In fact, both the SQLJ iterator object and the `ResultSet` object implement the same Java interface `java.util.Iterator`. (SQLJ iterators can be converted into result sets, and vice versa.) An iterator object stores an entire result set and provides methods, such as `next()`, to scan through the rows in the set. Figure 8.13 shows an SQLJ version of the program fragment in Figure 8.6.

The first statement in the figure tells the SQLJ preprocessor to generate Java statements that define a class, GetEnrolledIter, which implements the interface sqlj.runtime.NamedIterator. This is an interface that extends the standard Java interface, java.util.Iterator, and provides the venerable next() method. The class GetEnrolledIter can be used to store result sets in which each row has two columns: an integer and a string. The declaration gives a Java name to these columns, studentId and studGrade, and (implicitly) defines the **column accessor** methods, studentId() and studGrade(), which can be used to return data stored in the corresponding columns.

The second statement declares an object, iter1, in the class GetEnrolled-Iter.

The third statement executes SELECT and places the result set in iter1. Note that the AS clause is used to associate the SQL attribute names in the result set with the column names in the iterator. These names do not have to be the same, but the sequence of columns in the result set and the iterator must correspond in number and type.

The while statement fetches the results one at a time into the host variables id and grade and processes them.

- SQLJ has its own mechanism, which we do not discuss, for defining connection objects and for connecting to a database. A program can have several such connections active at the same time. Unlike in embedded SQL, each individual SQLJ statement can optionally designate a specific database connection to which that clause is to be applied. For example, the SELECT statement on page 305 can be rewritten as

```
#SQL [db1] {SELECT C.Enrollment
            INTO :num_enrolled
            FROM CLASS C
            WHERE C.CrsCode = :crs_code
              AND C.Semester = :semester};
```

  to specify that it is to be applied to the (previously defined) database connection named db1. If this option is not used, all SQL statements are applied to a default database connection, as in embedded SQL. Recall that, in JDBC, each SQL statement is always associated with a specific database connection *explicitly*, through its Statement object. In contrast, in embedded SQL, connection is set in a rather awkward and inflexible way via the SET CONNECTION statement.
- Just as static and dynamic embedded SQL statements can be included in the same host language program, SQLJ statements and JDBC calls can be included in the same Java program.

8.6 ODBC

ODBC (Open DataBase Connectivity) is an API to the DBMS that provides a call-level interface for SQL statement execution. Our presentation is based on the ODBC specification developed by Microsoft, but be aware that some vendors do not support all of the features.

It should also be noted that the SQL standardization body has for quite a long time been working on a specification for a call-level interface, known as **SQL/CLI**, to replace the bulky dynamic SQL. ODBC is a branch of an earlier version of this specification, and it has much in common with the recently finalized release of SQL/CLI, which is included in SQL:1999. Microsoft has pledged to align ODBC with this newly adopted standard.

The software architecture of an ODBC application is similar to that of JDBC in that it uses a driver manager and a separate driver for each DBMS to be accessed. ODBC is not object oriented, however, and its interface to the DBMS is at a much lower level. For example, in ODBC an application must specifically allocate and deallocate the storage it needs within the driver manager and the driver, whereas in JDBC that storage is automatically allocated when the appropriate objects are created, and deallocated when these objects are no longer needed. Thus, before an ODBC application calls the function `SQLConnect()` to request a connection to a database manager, it must first call the function `SQLAllocConnect()` to request that the driver manager allocate storage for that connection. Later, after the application calls `SQLDisconnect()` to disconnect from the database manager, it must call `SQLFreeConnect()` to deallocate this storage. As a result, ODBC applications are prone to **memory leaks**—an accumulation of garbage memory blocks that occurs when a program fails to free up ODBC structures that are no longer in use.

Figure 8.14 shows the structure of one version of the required function calls as they might appear in a C program.[5] Each function returns a value that denotes success or failure.

- `SQLAllocEnv()` allocates and initializes storage within the driver manager for use as ODBC's interface to the application. It returns an identifying *handle*, `henv`. A **handle** is simply a mechanism the application can use to refer to this data structure. In C, a handle is implemented as a pointer, but other host languages might implement it differently. The environment area is used internally by the ODBC driver manager to store run-time information.
- `SQLAllocConnect()` allocates memory within the driver manager for the connection and returns a connection handle, `hdbc`.

[5] We have simplified the syntax in this and subsequent examples to emphasize the semantics of the ODBC interaction. For example, in reality, string parameters, such as `database_name`, are passed with an accompanying length field.

OPTIONAL

FIGURE 8.14 Skeleton of procedure calls needed for ODBC in a C program.

```
SQLAllocEnv(&henv);
SQLAllocConnect(henv, &hdbc);
SQLConnect(hdbc,database_name,userId, password);
SQLAllocStmt(hdbc, &hstmt);
SQLExecDirect(hstmt, ... SQL statement ...);
:  process results
SQLFreeStmt(hstmt, fOption);
SQLDisconnect(hdbc);
SQLFreeConnect(hdbc);
SQLFreeEnv(henv);
```

OPTIONAL

- `SQLConnect()` loads the appropriate database driver and then connects to the DBMS server using previously allocated connection, `hdbc`, the database name, user Id, and password.

  If the application wants to connect to more than one database manager, `SQLAllocConnect()` and `SQLConnect()` are called separately for each manager. The drivers (there might be more than one in this case) maintain separate transactions for each such connection.
- `SQLAllocStmt()` allocates storage within the driver for an SQL statement and returns a handle, `hstmt`, for that statement.
- `SQLExecDirect()` takes a statement handle previously allocated using `SQL-AllocStmt()` and a string variable containing an SQL statement and asks the DBMS to prepare and execute the statement. The same handle can be used multiple times to execute different SQL statements.

  The SQL statement can be a data-manipulation statement, such as SELECT or UPDATE, as well as a DDL statement, such as CREATE or GRANT. It cannot contain an embedded reference to a host variable, since variable names can be translated to memory addresses only at compile time. Note that `SQL-ExecDirect()` is related to but is more versatile than EXECUTE IMMEDIATE in dynamic SQL. Whereas EXECUTE IMMEDIATE cannot return data to the application (see Section 8.4.1), `SQLExecDirect()` can produce a result set using a SELECT statement, and this set can then be accessed through a cursor (see Section 8.6.2).
- `SQLDisconnect()` disconnects from the server. This function takes the connection handle as an argument.
- `SQLFreeStmt()`, `SQLFreeConnect()`, and `SQLFreeEnv()` release the handles and free up the corresponding storage space allocated by the corresponding `Alloc` functions.

8.6.1 Prepared Statements

Instead of calling SQLExecDirect(), the application program can call

```
SQLPrepare(hstmt, ... SQL statement ...);
```

to prepare the statement and then

```
SQLExecute(hstmt);
```

to execute it.

As in dynamic SQL, the statement argument of SQLPrepare() can contain the ? placeholders. Arguments can be supplied to those parameters using the SQLBindParameters() function. For example, the call

```
SQLBindParameters(hstmt, 1, SQL_PARAMETER_INPUT,
                  SQL_C_SSHORT, SQL_SMALLINT, &int1);
```

binds the first parameter of the statement hstmt, which is an *in* parameter, to the host language variable int1, where int1 is of type short in the C language. The parameter's value replaces the first ? placeholder in hstmt when SQLBindParameters() is executed. SQLBindParameters() performs the conversion from type short in C to type SMALLINT in SQL.[6] Since the procedure call is compiled by the host language compiler, references to host language variable int1 in the parameter list can be resolved at compile time. This contrasts with the use of SQLExecDirect(), where references to host variables are not allowed.

8.6.2 Cursors

The execution of a SELECT statement using SQLExecDirect() or SQLExecute() does not return any data to the application. Instead, data is returned through a cursor, which is maintained within the ODBC driver and referred to by the statement handle, hstmt, returned by SQLAllocStmt(). Additional ODBC functions must be called to bring the data into the application.

The program can optionally call SQLBindCol(), which binds a particular column of the result set to a specific host variable in the program. For example, we might use the following call to bind the first column to the integer variable int2.

```
SQLBindCol(hstmt, 1, SQL_C_SSHORT, &int2);
```

[6] In a number of ODBC constructs, as in this one, the programmer must specify the desired conversion between the SQL data types used within the DBMS and the C language data types used within the application program.

OPTIONAL

When SQLFetch(hstmt) is then called, the cursor is advanced and the values in the columns of the current row that had been bound to host variables are stored in those variables. If a column has not been bound to a designated host variable, the program can call SQLGetData() to retrieve and store its value. For example, to store the value of the second column of the current row in the integer variable int3 we might use the call

```
SQLGetData(hstmt, 2, SQL_C_SSHORT, &int3);
```

Before executing the SELECT statement, the application can use SQLSetStmtOption() to specify one of the following three types for the cursor:

1. STATIC. As with the INSENSITIVE option for cursors in embedded SQL, when the SELECT statement is executed, the driver effectively calculates the result set and stores it separately from the base table. A call to SQLFetch() fetches a row from the result set. The situation is shown in Figure 8.5, page 279. This type of returned data is called a *snapshot*.
2. KEYSET_DRIVEN. When the SELECT statement is executed, the driver effectively constructs a set of pointers to the rows in the base table that satisfy the WHERE clause. A call to SQLFetch() follows the pointer and fetches the row from the base table. The situation is shown in Figure 8.15. Note the difference between this figure and Figure 8.5, where the result set is calculated at the time the SELECT statement is executed and rows are fetched from the result set. This type of returned data is sometimes called a **dynaset**.

   Since rows are obtained from the base table, any change to the base table will be seen through the pointers. For example, if a statement in this or a concurrent transaction *modifies* or *deletes* a row that is the target of a pointer, the change will be seen in a subsequent call to SQLFetch(). Furthermore, if a statement in this or a concurrent transaction *inserts* a row that satisfies the WHERE clause, the new row will not be seen by subsequent calls to SQLFetch() (since a pointer to the row is not in the set). Unfortunately, that is not the only anomaly that can occur. A change of an attribute value in a row that previously satisfied the WHERE clause can cause the row to no longer satisfy the clause. However, the row will still be visible through the cursor.
3. DYNAMIC. The data in the result set is completely dynamic. A statement in this or some other concurrently executing transaction can change, delete, *and* insert a row into the result set after the SELECT statement is executed. Those changes will be seen in subsequent calls to SQLFetch().

The ODBC specification calls for the implementation of all of these cursor types. However, the mechanisms made available to ODBC by a particular DBMS might make the implementation of a particular cursor type difficult, so a driver for that DBMS might support only a subset of cursor types. Clearly, DYNAMIC cursors are the most difficult to implement, and many drivers do not implement them.

OPTIONAL

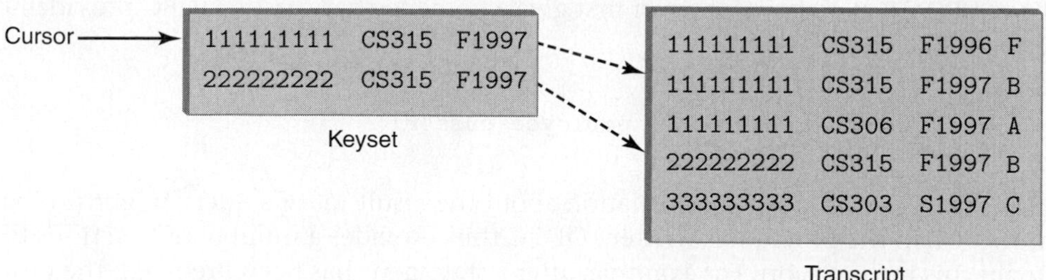

FIGURE 8.15 Effect of using a KEYSET_DRIVEN cursor to retrieve records from TRANSCRIPT.

The statement `SQLSetStmtOption()` is used to request a cursor type as follows:

```
SQLSetStmtOption(hstmt,SQL_CURSOR_TYPE, Option);
```

where *Option* is one of the constants `SQL_CURSOR_STATIC`, `SQL_CURSOR_DYNAMIC`, or `SQL_CURSOR_KEYSET_DRIVEN`.

ODBC also supports positioned updates through a non-STATIC cursor. For such an update, the SELECT statement must be defined with a FOR UPDATE clause. For example,

```
SQLExecDirect(hstmt1,  "SELECT * \
                        FROM EMPLOYEE \
                        FOR UPDATE OF Salary");
```

uses a previously allocated statement handle, `hstmt1`, to prepare a query whose cursor will allow updates to the EMPLOYEE relation through the `Salary` attribute.

Now, suppose we have executed a number of `SQLFetch(hstmt1)` statements and the cursor is now positioned at the employee named Joe Public. To raise Joe's salary by $1000, we might execute the following statement (where `hstmt2` is a previously allocated statement handle):

```
SQLExecDirect(hstmt2,  "UPDATE EMPLOYEE \
                        SET Salary = Salary + 1000\
                        WHERE CURRENT OF employee_cursor");
```

The only problem with the above statement is that the cursor name, `employee_cursor`, required by the WHERE CURRENT OF clause, comes out of the blue. In particular, it is not connected in any way to the cursor associated with the `hstmt1` handle that we used to execute the SELECT statement. Thus, before executing the

OPTIONAL

above UPDATE statement we must first give a name to that cursor. ODBC provides a special call to do just this:

```
SQLSetCursorName(hstmt1, employee_cursor);
```

As with dynamic SQL, information about the result set of a query might not be known when the program is written. ODBC thus provides a number of functions to obtain this information. For example, after a statement has been prepared, the program can call the function `SQLNumResultCols()`, to obtain the number of columns in a result set, and the functions `SQLColAttributes()` and `SQLDescribeCol()`, to provide information about a specific column in a result set.

ODBC also has a number of functions, called **catalog functions**, which return information about the database schema. For example, `SQLTables()` returns, in a result set, the names of all tables, and `SQLColumns()` returns column names.

8.6.3 Status Processing

The ODBC procedures we have been discussing are actually functions, which return a value, of type RETCODE, indicating whether or not the specified action was successful. Thus, we might have

```
RETCODE retcode1;
.
.
.
retcode1 = SQLConnect(...);
if (retcode1 != SQL_SUCCESS)   {
        .
        : do something
        .
}
```

Additional information about the error can be found by calling `SQLError()`.

8.6.4 Executing Transactions

By default, the database is in autocommit mode when a connection is created. To allow two or more statements to be grouped into a transaction, autocommit mode is disabled using

```
SQLSetConnectionOption(hdbc,
                        SQL_AUTOCOMMIT,
                        SQL_AUTOCOMMIT_OFF);
```

where `hdbc` is a connection handle. Initially, each transaction uses the default isolation level of the database manager. This can be changed with a call such as

OPTIONAL

```
SQLSetConnectionOption(hdbc,
                       SQL_TXN_ISOLATION,
                       SQL_TXN_REPEATABLE_READ);
```

Transactions can be committed or rolled back using

```
SQLTransact(henv, hdbc, Action);
```

where Action is either SQL_COMMIT or SQL_ABORT.

After a transaction is committed or rolled back, a new transaction starts when the next SQL statement is executed (or, in the case of the first SQL statement in the program, when that statement is executed).

If the program is connected to more than one database, the transactions at each database can be separately committed or rolled back. ODBC does not support a commit protocol that ensures that the set of transactions will be globally atomic. However, Microsoft has introduced a new TP monitor, MTS (Microsoft Transaction Server), that includes a transaction manager (and an appropriate API) guaranteeing an atomic commit of distributed transactions using ODBC.

OPTIONAL

8.6.5 Stored Procedures on the Server

ODBC can be used to call a stored procedure if the DBMS supports this feature. For example, to call the stored procedure of Figure 8.7 on page 284 we might begin with the statement

```
SQLPrepare(hstmt, "{call Deregister(?,?,?,?,?)}");
```

which prepares the call statement. The braces around the call to Deregister() denote the SQL escape syntax discussed in Section 8.5.7. The parameters of Deregister() can be bound to host variables with SQLBindParameter() functions. Then the procedure call can be executed with

```
SQLExecute(hstmt);
```

As with embedded SQL, if the DBMS allows a stored procedure to return a result set, the application program can retrieve data from the result set using a cursor.

8.6.6 An Example

Figure 8.16 is a fragment of a C program containing ODBC procedure calls. It executes the same transaction as that in Figure 8.12. The constant SQL_NTS, when supplied as an argument to a procedure (SQLConnect() and SQLExecDirect() in this example) indicates that the preceding argument is a null-terminated string.

FIGURE 8.16 A fragment of an ODBC program written in C.

```
HENV henv;
HDBC hdbc;
HSTMT hstmt;
RETCODE retcode;
SQLAllocEnv(&henv);
SQLAllocConnect(henv, &hdbc);
retcode = SQLConnect(hdbc, dbName, SQL_NTS, "john", SQL_NTS, "j121",
                      SQL_NTS);
if (retcode != SQL_SUCCESS){
    SQLFreeEnv(henv);
    return(-1);
}
SQLSetConnectionOption(hdbc, SQL_AUTOCOMMIT, SQL_AUTOCOMMIT_OFF);
SQLAllocStmt(hdbc, &hstmt);
retcode = SQLExecDirect(hstmt,
                         "DELETE FROM TRANSCRIPT \
                           WHERE StudId = 123456789 \
                                 AND Semester = 'F2000' \
                                 AND CrsCode = 'CS308'",
                         SQL_NTS);
if (retcode != SQL_SUCCESS) {
    SQLTransact(henv, hdbc, SQL_ABORT);
    SQLFreeStmt(hstmt, SQL_DROP);
    SQLDisconnect(hdbc);
    SQLFreeConnect(hdbc);
    SQLFreeEnv(henv);
    return(-2);
}
retcode = SQLExecDirect(hstmt,
                         "UPDATE CLASS \
                           SET Enrollment = (Enrollment - 1) \
                           WHERE CrsCode = 'CS308'",
                         SQL_NTS);
if (retcode != SQL_SUCCESS)   {
    SQLTransact(henv, hdbc, SQL_ABORT);
    SQLFreeStmt(hstmt, SQL_DROP);
    SQLDisconnect(hdbc);
    SQLFreeConnect(hdbc);
    SQLFreeEnv(henv);
    return(-3);
}
SQLTransact(henv, hdbc, SQL_COMMIT);
SQLFreeStmt(hstmt, SQL_DROP);
SQLDisconnect(hdbc);
SQLFreeConnect(hdbc);
SQLFreeEnv(henv);
```

OPTIONAL

8.7 Comparison

We have discussed a variety of techniques for creating programs that can access a database—each has its own advantages and disadvantages. Here we summarize some of the issues involved:

- In some cases, the program contains SQL statements that use a special syntax (static SQL, SQLJ); in others, the statements are values of variables (dynamic SQL, JDBC, ODBC). An advantage of the former is its simplicity, but a disadvantage is that the interaction with the database is fixed at compile time. In some applications, the statement to be executed cannot be determined until run time; in such cases, it is important that the application be able to construct SQL statements dynamically.
- In some cases, the application must use the SQL dialect supported by the particular DBMS to which it is connected, making it difficult to port the application to a different vendor's product. In other cases (ODBC, JDBC), a single dialect or a common core is used in the application, and modules are provided to translate it to each vendor's dialect. Portability is thus enhanced, but the application might not have access to the proprietary features supported by a particular vendor's product.
- A number of factors are involved in assessing the run-time overhead incurred by each technique. These include the cost of communication, preparation, and parameter passing. In some cases, the cost depends on how a technique is implemented, but certain general observations can be made.

  With a statement-level interface, the SQL statement has embedded parameter names that can be processed at compile time to generate parameter-passing code. At run time, the statement can be passed to the server for both preparation and execution, so a single communication is sufficient. With a call-level interface and with dynamic SQL, parameter names are not included in the statement because the statement is not available at compile time when parameter names can be mapped to addresses using the symbol table. Instead, they are provided separately so that they can be dealt with at compile time. Except in special cases (e.g., EXECUTE IMMEDIATE), therefore, one communication is used to send the statement for preparation and one additional communication is needed for requesting execution. This issue is important, since communication is expensive and time consuming.

  Preparation must take place at run time if the SQL statement is constructed dynamically (dynamic SQL, JDBC, and ODBC). However, even with static SQL, preparation is generally done at run time when the statement is submitted for execution. In all of these cases, if the statement is executed many times, the preparation cost can be prorated over each execution and might not be a major factor. The most effective way to avoid run-time preparation is to use stored procedures, in which case the DBMS can be instructed to create and store a query execution plan prior to execution of the application. Often, this is simply a separate plan for each SQL statement in the procedure. More sophisticated systems create an optimized plan for the procedure as a whole, since the sequence of SQL statements is known. Data structures created for one statement might be preserved for use by the next.

BIBLIOGRAPHIC NOTES

Embedded and dynamic SQL date back to prehistoric times, and every SQL manual covers them to some degree. The following references are good places to look: [Date and Darwen 1997; Melton and Simon 1992; Gulutzan and Pelzer 1999].

There is vast literature on ODBC. Microsoft publishes an authoritative guide [Microsoft 1997], but there are more accessible books, such as [Signore et al. 1995]. The history and principles behind SQL/CLI, the new SQL standard analogous to (and designed to replace) ODBC, are discussed in [Venkatrao and Pizzo 1995]. SQL stored procedures are discussed in [Eisenberg 1996; Melton 1997]. Information on JDBC and SQLJ is readily available on the Web at [Sun 2000] and [SQLJ 2000], but published references, such as [Reese 2000; Melton et al. 2000], are better places to learn these technologies.

EXERCISES

8.1 Explain why a precompiler is needed for embedded SQL and SQLJ but not for ODBC and JDBC.

8.2 Since the precompiler for embedded SQL translates SQL statements into procedure calls, explain the difference between embedded SQL and call-level interfaces, such as ODBC and JDBC, where SQL statements are specified as the arguments of procedure calls.

8.3 Explain why constraint checking is usually deferred in transaction processing applications.

8.4 Give an example where immediate constraint checking is undesirable in a transaction processing application.

8.5 Explain the advantages and disadvantages of using stored procedures in transaction processing applications.

8.6 Write transaction programs in

a. Embedded SQL
b. JDBC
c. ODBC
d. SQLJ

that implement the registration transaction in the Student Registration System. Use the database schema from Figures 4.34 and 4.35.

8.7 Write transaction programs in

a. Embedded SQL
b. JDBC

c. ODBC
d. SQLJ

that use a cursor to print out a student's transcript in the Student Registration System. Use the database schema from Figures 4.34 and 4.35.

8.8 Explain the following:

a. Why do embedded SQL and SQLJ use host language variables as parameters, whereas dynamic SQL, JDBC, and ODBC use the ? placeholders?
b. What are the advantages of using host language variables as parameters in embedded SQL compared with ? placeholders?

8.9 Explain the advantages and disadvantages of using dynamic SQL compared with ODBC and JDBC.

8.10 Write a transaction program in

a. Embedded SQL
b. JDBC
c. ODBC
d. SQLJ

that transfers the rows of a table between two DBMSs. Is your transaction globally atomic?

8.11 Write a Java program that executes in your local browser, uses JDBC to connect to your local DBMS, and makes a simple query against a table you have created.

8.12 Suppose that, at compile time, the application programmer knows all of the details of the SQL statements to be executed, the DBMS to be used, and the database schema. Explain the advantages and disadvantages of using embedded SQL as compared with JDBC or ODBC as the basis for the implementation.

8.13 Section 8.6 discusses KEYSET_DRIVEN cursors.

a. Explain the difference between STATIC and KEYSET_DRIVEN cursors.
b. Give an example of a schedule in which these cursors give different results even when the transaction is executing in isolation.
c. Explain why updates and deletes can be made through KEYSET_DRIVEN cursors.

8.14 Give an example of a transaction program that contains a cursor, such that the value returned by one of its FETCH statements depends on whether or not the cursor was defined to be INSENSITIVE. Assume that this transaction is the only one executing. We are not concerned about any effect that a concurrently executing transaction might have.

8.15 Compare the advantages and disadvantages of the exception handling mechanisms in embedded SQL, SQL/PSM, JDBC, SQLJ, and ODBC.

PART THREE

Optimizing DBMS Performance

In this part we will discuss various issues related to optimizing the performance of a database application. This subject is very important in the real world because it consumes a significant amount of the effort of database practitioners.

In Chapter 9 we will discuss the physical organization of databases, including various indexing mechanisms.

In Chapters 10 and 11 we will present the basic ideas of query processing and query optimization.

Chapter 12 discusses various aspects of database tuning, including the choice of indices, cache tuning, and methods for tuning the schema.

9

Physical Data Organization and Indexing

One important advantage of SQL is that it is declarative. An SQL statement describes a query about information stored in a database, but it does not specify the technique the system should use in executing it. The DBMS itself decides that.

Such techniques are intimately associated with **storage structures**, **indices**, and **access paths**. A table is stored in a file, and the term "storage structure" is used to describe the way the rows are organized in the file. An index is an auxiliary data structure, perhaps stored in a separate file, that supports fast access to the rows of a table. An access path refers to a particular technique for accessing a set of rows. It uses an algorithm based on the storage structure of the table and on a choice among the available indices for that table.

An important aspect of the relational model is that the result of executing a particular SQL statement (i.e., the statement's effect on the database and the information returned by it) is not affected by the storage structure used to store the table that is accessed, the indices that have been created for that table, or the access path that the DBMS chooses to use to access the table. Thus, when designing the query, the programmer does not have to be aware of these issues.

Although the choice of an access path does not affect the result produced by a statement, it does have a major impact on performance. Depending on the access path used, execution time might vary from seconds to hours, particularly when the statement refers to large tables involving thousands, and perhaps hundreds of thousands, of rows. Furthermore, different access paths are appropriate for different SQL statements used to query the same table.

Because execution time is sensitive to access paths, most database systems allow the database designer and system administrator to determine which access paths should be provided for each table. Generally, this decision is based on the nature of the SQL statements used to access the table and the frequency with which these statements are executed.

In this chapter, we describe a variety of access paths and compare their performance when used in the execution of different SQL statements. We continue this discussion in Chapter 12.

9.1 Disk Organization

For the following reasons, databases are generally stored on mass storage devices rather than in main memory:

- **Size.** Databases describing large enterprises frequently contain a huge amount of information. Databases in the gigabyte range are not uncommon, and those in the terabyte range already exist. Such databases cannot be accommodated in the main memory of current machines or of machines that are likely to be available in the near future.
- **Cost.** Even in situations in which the database can be accommodated in main memory (e.g., when its size is in the megabyte range), it is generally stored on mass storage.[1] The argument here is one of economy. The cost per byte of storage in main memory is on the order of one hundred times that of storage on disk.
- **Volatility.** We introduced the notion of durability in Chapter 2 in connection with the ACID properties of transactions. The argument for durability goes beyond transactions, however. It is an important property of any database system. The information describing an enterprise must be preserved in spite of system failures. Unfortunately, most implementations of main memory are **volatile**: the information stored in main memory can be lost during power failures and crashes. Hence, main memory does not naturally support database system requirements. Mass storage, on the other hand, is **nonvolatile** since the stored information survives failures. Hence, mass storage forms the basis of most database systems.

Since data on mass storage devices is not directly accessible to the system processors, accessing an item in the database involves first reading it from the mass storage device into a buffer in main memory—at which point a copy exists on both devices—and then accessing it from the buffer. If the access involves changing the item, the copy on mass storage becomes obsolete and the buffer copy must be used to overwrite it.

The most commonly used form of mass storage is a disk. Since the strategy used to enhance the performance of a database system is based on the physical characteristics of a disk, it is important to review how a disk works in order to understand performance issues.

A disk unit contains one or more circular **platters** attached to a rotating spindle, as shown in Figure 9.1. One, and sometimes both, surfaces of each platter are coated with magnetic material, and the direction of magnetism at a particular spot determines whether that spot records a one or a zero. Since information is stored magnetically, it is durable in spite of power failures.

Each platter (or surface) is accessed through an associated **read/write head** that is capable of either detecting or setting the direction of magnetism on the spot over which it is positioned. The head is attached to an arm, which is capable of moving

[1] In applications requiring very rapid response times, the database is often stored in main memory. Such systems are referred to as **main memory database systems**.

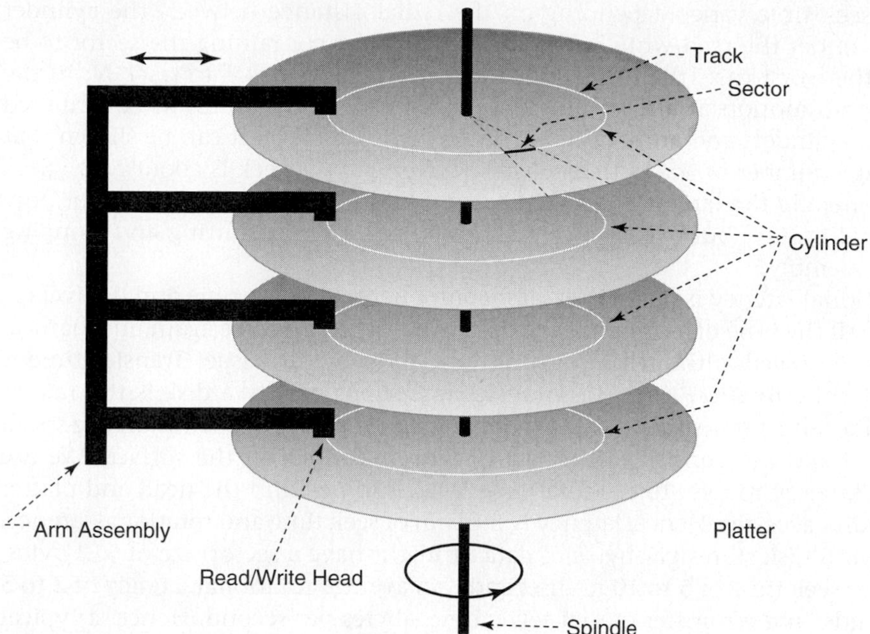

FIGURE 9.1 Physical organization of a disk storage unit.

radially toward either the center or the circumference of the platter. Since platters rotate, this movement enables the head to be positioned over an arbitrary spot on the platter's surface.

As a practical matter, data is stored in **tracks**, which are concentric circles on the surface of the platter. Each platter has the same fixed number, N, of tracks, and the storage area consisting of the ith track on all platters is called an ith **cylinder**. Since there is a head for each platter, the disk unit as a whole has an array of heads, and the arm assembly moves all heads in unison. Thus, at any given time all read/write heads are positioned over a particular cylinder. It would seem reasonable to be able to read or write all tracks on the current cylinder simultaneously, but engineering limitations generally allow only a single head to be active at a time. Finally, each track is divided into **sectors**, which are the smallest units of transfer allowed by the hardware.

Before a particular sector can be accessed, the head must be positioned over the beginning of the sector. Hence, the time to access a sector, S, can be divided into three components:

1. **Seek time.** The time to position the arm assembly over the cylinder containing S
2. **Rotational latency.** The additional time it takes, after the arm assembly is over the cylinder, for the platters to rotate to the angular position at which S is under the read/write head
3. **Transfer time.** The time it takes for the platter to rotate through the angle subtended by S

The seek time varies depending on the radial distance between the cylinder currently under the read/write heads and the cylinder containing the sector to be read. In the worst case, the heads must be moved from track 1 to track N; in the best case, no motion at all is required. If disk requests are uniformly distributed across the cylinders and are serviced in the order they arrive, it can be shown that the average number of tracks that must be traversed by a seek is about $N/3$.[2] Seek time is generally the largest of the three components because it involves not only mechanical motion but overcoming the inertia involved in starting and stopping the arm assembly.

Rotational latency is the next-largest component of access time and on average is about half the time of a complete rotation of the platters. Once again, mechanical motion is involved, although in this case inertia is not an issue. Transfer time is also limited by rotation time. The transfer rate supported by a disk is the rate at which data can be transferred once the head is in position; it depends on the speed of rotation and the density with which bits are recorded on the surface. We use the term **latency** to refer to the total time it takes to position the head and platter between disk accesses. Hence, latency is the sum of seek time and rotational latency.

A typical disk stores gigabytes of data. It might have a sector size of 512 bytes, an average seek time of 5 to 10 milliseconds, an average rotational latency of 2 to 5 milliseconds, and a transfer rate of several megabytes per second. Hence, a typical access time for a sector is on the order of 10 milliseconds.

The physical characteristics of a disk lead to the concept of the distance between two sectors, which is a measure of the latency between accesses to them. The distance is smallest if the sectors are adjacent on the same track since latency is zero if they are read in succession. After that, in order of increasing distance, sectors are closest if they are on the same track, on the same cylinder, or on different cylinders. In the last case, sectors on tracks n_1 and n_2 are closer than sectors on tracks n_3 and n_4 if $| n_1 - n_2 | < | n_3 - n_4 |$.

Several conclusions can be drawn from the physical characteristics of a disk unit:

- Most important, disks are extremely slow devices compared to CPUs. A CPU can execute hundreds of thousands of instructions in the time it takes to access a disk sector. Hence, in attempting to optimize the performance of a database system, it is necessary to optimize the flow of information between main memory and disk. While the database system should use efficient algorithms in processing data, the payoff in improved performance pales in comparison with that obtained from optimizing disk traffic. In recognition of this fact, in our discussion of access paths later in this chapter we estimate performance by counting I/O operations and ignoring processor time.
- In applications in which after accessing record A_1, the next access will, with high probability, be to record A_2, latency can be reduced if the distance between the

[2] The problem can be stated mathematically: suppose that we have an interval and we place two marks at random somewhere in the interval; how far apart are the marks on average?

sectors containing A_1 and A_2 is small. Thus the performance of the application is affected by the way the data is physically stored on the disk. For example, a sequential scan through a table can be performed efficiently if the table is stored on a single track or cylinder.

- To simplify buffer management, database systems transfer the same number of bytes with each I/O operation. How many bytes should that be? Using the typical numbers quoted earlier, it is apparent that the transfer time for a sector is small compared with the average latency. This is true even if more than one sector is transferred with each I/O operation. Thus, even though from a physical standpoint the natural unit of transfer is the data in a single sector, it might be more efficient if the system transfers data in larger units.

  The term **page** generally denotes the unit of data transferred with each I/O operation. A page is stored on the disk in a **disk block**, or simply a block, which is a sequence of adjacent sectors on a track such that the page size is equal to the block size. A page can be transferred in a single I/O operation, with a single latency to position the head at the start of the containing block since there is no need to reposition either the arm or the platter in moving from one sector of the block to the next.

  A trade-off is involved in choosing the number of sectors in a block (i.e., the page size). If, when a particular application accesses a record, A, in a table, there is a reasonable probability that it will soon access another record, B, in the table that is close to A (this would be the case if the table was frequently scanned), the page size should be large enough so that A and B are stored in the same page. This avoids a subsequent I/O operation when B is actually accessed. On the other hand, transfer time grows with page size, and larger pages require larger buffers in main memory. Hence, too large a page size cannot be justified, since it is far from certain that B will actually be accessed. With considerations such as these in mind, a typical page size is 4096 bytes (4 kilobytes).

  A checksum is generally computed each time the data in a page is modified and stored with the data in the block. Each time the page is read a checksum over the data is computed and compared with the stored checksum. If the page has been corrupted on the disk it is very unlikely that the two values will be equal, and hence storage failures can be readily detected.

The system keeps an array of page-size buffers, called a **cache**, in main memory. With page I/O, the following sequence of events occurs when an application requests access to a particular record, A, of a table. We assume that each table is stored in a **data file**. First, the database system determines which of the file's pages contains A. Then it initiates the transfer of the page from mass storage into one of the buffers in the cache (we modify this part of the description in a moment). At some later time (generally signaled by an interrupt from the mass storage device), the system recognizes that the transfer has completed and copies A from the page in the buffer to the application.

The system attempts to keep the cache filled with pages that are likely to be referenced in the future. Then, if an application refers to an item contained

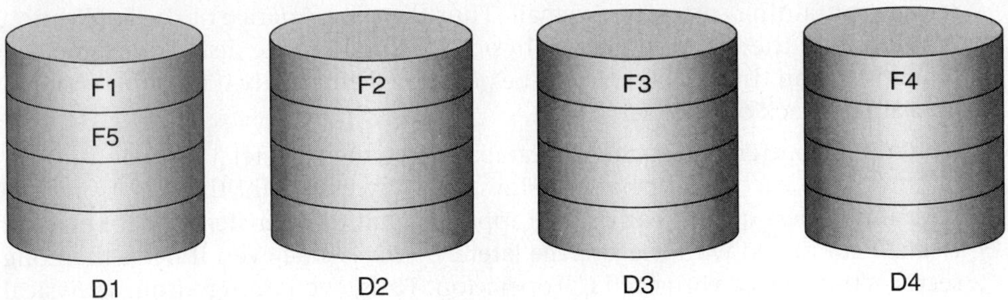

FIGURE 9.2 The striping of a file across four disks.

in a page in the cache, an I/O operation can be avoided and a **hit** is said to have occurred. Hence, proper cache management can greatly improve performance. Cache management is treated in more detail in Section 12.1.

9.1.1 RAID Systems

At various points in the book we will discuss a number of techniques that are made available to the application programmer or are provided within the DBMS to overcome the performance bottleneck caused by disk I/O: indices, query optimization, caches, and prefetching. A **RAID** (**Redundant Array of Independent Disks**) system is another, lower-level, approach to the problem. It consists of an array of disks configured to operate like a single disk. In particular, the RAID system responds to the usual operating system commands of read, write, and so on.

A RAID system has the potential for providing better throughput than a single disk of similar capacity since the individual disks of a RAID can function independently. There are two dimensions to this. If multiple requests access data on different disks of the RAID, they can be handled concurrently. Thus, a RAID involving n disks has the potential of improving throughput by a factor of n. The performance of a single request involving a large block of data can also be improved. If the data is spread over several disks, it can be transferred in parallel, reducing the transfer time. Thus, if it is spread over n disks, the transfer time can be reduced by a factor of n.

Data that is spread across an array of disks is said to be **striped**. The data is divided into **chunks** for this purpose, where the size of a chunk is configurable and might be a byte, a block, or some multiple of the block size. For example, if a file is striped over four disks, its first chunk, F1, would be stored on the first disk, D1, the second chunk, F2, on the second disk, D2, the third, F3, on D3, and the fourth, F4, on D4. The four chunks are referred to as a stripe. The fifth chunk, F5, is stored on D1 and successive chunks are laid out on the next stripe. The situation is shown in Figure 9.2. Then, if the entire file is to be read, data can be transferred from all four disks simultaneously.

In addition to increasing throughput, an important objective of RAID systems is to use redundant storage to increase the availability of the data by reducing downtime due to disk failure. Such failures are magnified when an array of disks is used since the mean time to failure of at least one disk in an array of n is (approximately) the mean time to failure of one disk divided by n. For example, if a single disk has a mean time to failure of 10 years, the mean time to failure of at least one disk in an array of 50 is about two months—an unacceptable failure rate for most applications. To address this issue, five RAID levels have been defined, with different types of redundancy.

Level 0. Level 0 uses striping to increase throughput but does not use any redundancy. The bad news is that if all files are striped, the failure of a single disk destroys them all. Some people would say that Level 0 is not really RAID at all since there is no redundancy—the R in RAID.

Level 1. Level 1 does not perform striping but involves **mirroring**. In this case the disks in the array are paired, and the data stored on both elements of a pair is identical. Hence, a write to one (automatically) results in a write to the other, and as long as one disk in each pair is operational, all the data stored in the RAID can be accessed. Note that, assuming both disks in a pair are operational, the pair has twice the read rate of a single disk since both disks can be independently read at the same time (perhaps by different transactions). Although it might seem that doubling the number of required disks would be too expensive for many applications, the sharply decreased prices of disks have made mirroring increasingly attractive. Many transaction processing systems use mirrored disks to store their log, which has a very high requirement for durability.

Level 3. The higher levels of RAID perform striping and, in addition, store various types of redundant information to increase availability. In Level 3, the chunks are bytes (the striping is at the byte level), and in addition to the n disks on which the data is stored, the stripe includes an $(n+1)$st disk that stores the *exclusive or* (XOR) of the corresponding bytes on the other n disks. It follows that if $x_{i,j}$ is the jth bit on disk i then

$$x_{1,j} \; XOR \; x_{2,j} \; XOR \; \cdots \; XOR \; x_{n+1,j} = 0$$

Thus, whenever a chunk is written on any one of the n disks, its XOR with the other $n-1$ chunks in the stripe is computed and stored as a byte on the $(n+1)$st disk. This disk is sometimes called the **parity disk** since taking the XOR of a set of bytes is called "computing their parity." In contrast to Level 1, instead of dedicating half of the capacity of the RAID to parity data, only $1/n+1$ of the capacity is used in this way.

For example, consider a RAID containing six disks and assume that parity is stored on the sixth disk. If the first bit of each byte on the first five disks is 1 0 1 0 0, then the first bit of the corresponding byte on disk six is 0. Observe that setting the bit on the parity disk equal to the XOR of the bits on the others also makes the bit on *each* disk the XOR of the bits on the others. Thus, if any disk fails, its information can be reconstructed as the XOR of the bits on the other disks. (Note that this reconstruction method requires knowledge of which disk has failed, but this information can be supplied by the controller for that disk.)

With byte-level striping, a large data segment can be read at a very high transfer rate. This is important in a number of applications. For example, multimedia data must be transferred at a rate that is sufficient to keep up with real-time requirements. Level 3 is particularly useful for such single-user, high-transfer-rate applications.

Writes, however, can be a bottleneck since not only must new data be written to one of the n disks, but the new value of the parity must be computed and written to the parity disk. Its value is given by

$$new\_parity\_bit = (old\_data\_bit \ XOR \ new\_data\_bit) \ XOR \ old\_parity\_bit$$

Thus, four disk accesses are required to write a single byte: the old value of the byte to be overwritten and the old value of the parity byte must be read, and then the new data byte and the new parity byte must be written. Furthermore, since each write request to the RAID involves a write to the parity disk, that disk can become a bottleneck.

Level 5. Level 5 also involves striping and storing parity information, but it differs from Level 3 in two ways:

1. The chunks are disk blocks (or multiples of disk blocks), which is more efficient for some applications. For example, if there are many concurrent transactions, each of which wants to read a chunk of data, their requests can be satisfied in parallel. Thus, Level 5 can be viewed as an efficient way to distribute data over multiple disks to support parallel access.
2. The parity information is itself striped and is stored, in turn, on each of the disks, which eliminates the bottleneck caused by a single parity disk. Thus, in the above example, in the first stripe, the data blocks might be stored on the first five disks and the parity block on the sixth; in the second stripe, the data blocks might be stored on disks 1, 2, 3, 4, and 6 and the parity block on the fifth disk; in the third stripe, the parity block might be stored on the fourth disk, and so on.

Level 10. Many hardware vendors provide hybrid RAID levels combining some of the features of the basic RAID levels. One interesting hybrid is Level 10, which combines the disk striping of Level 0 with the mirroring of Level 1. It uses a striped array of n disks (as in Level 0), in which each of the n disks is mirrored (as in Level 1), making a total of $2n$ disks. In other words, it consists of a striped array of n mirrored disks. Level 10 has the performance benefits of disk striping with the disk redundancy of mirroring. It provides the best performance of all RAID levels, but, as with Level 1, it requires doubling the number of required disks.

Controller cache. To further improve the performance of a RAID system, a **controller cache** can be included. This is a buffer in the main memory of the disk controller that can speed up both reading and writing.

- When reading, the RAID system can transfer a larger portion of data than was requested into the cache. If the program that made the request subsequently requests the additional data, it is immediately available in the buffer—no I/O has to be performed. For example, if a transaction is scanning a table, it will access all the pages in sequence. If *n* successive pages are stored in a stripe, and the entire stripe is retrieved when the first page is requested, I/O operations for subsequent pages in the stripe are eliminated. This is an example of prefetching, to which we will return in Chapter 12.
- In a **write-back cache** the RAID reports back that the write is complete as soon as the data is in the cache, before it has actually been written to the disk. Thus, the effective write time appears to be very fast. To implement a write-back cache, there must be some means of protecting the data in case of failures in the cache system. Some write-back caches are mirrored and/or have battery backup in case of electrical failure.
- The overhead of writing to a Level 5 RAID can be alleviated with a cache if all the blocks in a stripe are to be updated. In that case the parity block can be computed in the cache, and then all the blocks can be written to the disks in parallel: no extra disk reads are required. When used in this way the cache is referred to as a **write-gathering cache**.

Of all the RAID levels, Level 5, with a controller cache, is the one most often recommended for high-performance transaction processing applications.

9.2 Heap Files

We assume that each table is stored in a separate file, in accordance with some storage structure. The simplest storage structure is a **heap file**. With a heap file, rows are effectively appended to the end of the file as they are created. Thus the ordering of rows in the file is arbitrary. No rule dictates where a particular row should be placed. Figure 9.3 shows table TRANSCRIPT stored as a heap file. Recall that the table has four columns: `StudId`, `CrsCode`, `Semester`, and `Grade`. We have modified the schema so that grades are stored as real numbers, and we have assumed that four rows fit in a single page.

The important characteristic of a heap file, as far as we are concerned, is the fact that its rows are unordered. We ignore a number of significant issues since they are internal to the workings of the database system and the programmer generally has no control over them. Still, you should be aware of what these issues are. For example, we have assumed in Figure 9.3 that all rows are of the same length, and hence exactly the same number of rows fit in each page. This is not always the case. If, for example, the domain associated with a column is VARCHAR (3000), the number of bytes necessary to store a particular column value varies from 1 to 3000. Thus, the number of rows that will fit in a page is not fixed. This significantly complicates storage allocation. Furthermore, whether rows are of fixed or variable length, each page must be formatted with a certain amount of header information that keeps

666666666	MGT123	F1994	4.0	
123454321	CS305	S1996	4.0	page 0
987654321	CS305	F1995	2.0	
111111111	MGT123	F1997	3.0	
123454321	CS315	S1997	4.0	
666666666	EE101	S1991	3.0	page 1
123454321	MAT123	S1996	2.0	
234567890	EE101	F1995	3.0	
234567890	CS305	S1996	4.0	
111111111	EE101	F1997	4.0	page 2
111111111	MAT123	F1997	3.0	
987654321	MGT123	F1994	3.0	
425360777	CS305	S1996	3.0	
666666666	MAT123	F1997	3.0	page 3

FIGURE 9.3 TRANSCRIPT table stored as a heap file. At most four rows can be fit in a page.

track of the starting point of each row in the page and that locates unused regions of the page. We assume that the logical address of a row in a data file is given by a **row Id** (*rid*) that consists of a **page number** within the file and a **slot number** identifying the row within the page. The actual location of the row is obtained by interpreting the slot number using the page's header information. The situation is further complicated if a row is too large to fit in a page.

The good thing about a heap file is its simplicity. Rows are inserted by appending them to the end of the file, and they are deleted by declaring the slot that they occupy as empty in the header information of the page in which they are stored. Figure 9.4 shows the file of Figure 9.3 after the records for the student with Id 111111111 were deleted and the student with Id 666666666 completed CS305 in the spring of 1998. Note that deletion leaves gaps in the file and eventually a significant amount of storage is wasted. These gaps cause searches through the file to take longer because more pages have to be examined. Eventually, the gaps become so extensive that the file must be compacted. Compaction can be a time-consuming process if the file is large since every page must be read and the pages of the compacted version written out.

Access cost. We can compare the efficiency of accessing a heap file with other storage structures, which we discuss later, by counting the number of I/O operations required to do various operations. Let F denote the number of pages in the file. First

666666666	MGT123	F1994	4.0	
123454321	CS305	S1996	4.0	page 0
987654321	CS305	F1995	2.0	
123454321	CS315	S1997	4.0	
666666666	EE101	S1991	3.0	page 1
123454321	MAT123	S1996	2.0	
234567890	EE101	F1995	3.0	
234567890	CS305	S1996	4.0	
				page 2
987654321	MGT123	F1994	3.0	
425360777	CS305	S1996	3.0	
666666666	MAT123	F1997	3.0	page 3
666666666	CS305	S1998	3.0	

FIGURE 9.4 TRANSCRIPT table of Figure 9.3 after insertion and deletion of some rows.

consider insertion. Before a row, A, can be inserted, we must ensure that A's key does not duplicate the key of a row already in the table. Hence, the file must be scanned. If a duplicate exists, it will be discovered in $F/2$ page reads on average, and at that point the insertion is abandoned. The entire file has to be read in order to conclude that no duplicate is present, and then the last page (with A inserted) has to be rewritten, yielding a total cost of $F + 1$ page transfers in this case.

A similar situation exists for deletion. If a tuple, A, with a specified key is present, it will be discovered in $F/2$ page reads on average, and then the page (with A deleted) will be rewritten, yielding a cost of $F/2 + 1$. If no such tuple is present, the cost is F. If the condition specifying the tuples to be deleted does not involve a key, the entire file must be scanned since an arbitrary number of rows satisfying the condition can exist in the table.

A heap file is an efficient storage structure if queries on the table involve accessing all rows and if the order in which the rows are accessed is not important. For example, the query

```
SELECT  *
FROM    TRANSCRIPT
```

returns the entire table. With a heap storage structure, the cost is F, which is clearly optimal. Of course, if we want the rows printed out in some specific order, the cost is much greater since the rows have to be sorted before being output. An example of such a query is

```
SELECT   *
FROM     TRANSCRIPT T
ORDER BY T.StudId
```

As another example, consider the query

```
SELECT   AVG(T.Grade)
FROM     TRANSCRIPT T
```

which returns the average grade assigned in all courses. All rows of the table must be read to extract the grades no matter how the table is stored, and the averaging computation is not sensitive to the order in which reading occurs. Again, the cost, F, is optimal.

Suppose, however, a query requests the grade received by the student with Id 234567890 in CS305 in the spring of 1996.

```
SELECT   T.Grade
FROM     TRANSCRIPT T                                          9.1
WHERE    T.StudId = '234567890' AND
         T.CrsCode = 'CS305' AND T.Semester = 'S1996'
```

Since {StudId, CrsCode, Semester} is the key of TRANSCRIPT, at most one grade will be returned. If TRANSCRIPT has the value shown in Figure 9.3, exactly one grade (namely, 4.0) will be returned. The database system must scan the file pages looking for a row with the specified key and return the corresponding grade. In this case, it must read three pages. Generally, an average of $F/2$ pages must be read, but if a row with the specified key is not in the table, all F pages must be read. In either case, the cost is high considering the small amount of information actually requested.

Finally, consider the following queries. The first returns the course, semester, and grade for all courses taken by the student with Id 234567890, and the second returns the Ids of all students who received grades between 2.0 and 4.0 in some course. Since, in both cases, the WHERE clause does not specify a candidate key, an arbitrary number of rows might be returned. Therefore, the entire table must be searched at a cost of F.

```
SELECT   T.Course, T.Semester, T.Grade
FROM     TRANSCRIPT T                                          9.2
WHERE    T.StudId = '234567890'
```

```
SELECT   T.StudId
FROM     TRANSCRIPT                                    9.3
WHERE    T.Grade BETWEEN '2.0' AND '4.0'
```

The conditions in the WHERE clauses of statements (9.1) and (9.2) are equality conditions since the tuples requested must have the specified attribute values. A search for a tuple satisfying an equality condition is referred to as an **equality search**. The condition in the WHERE clause of statement (9.3) is a **range condition**. It involves an attribute whose domain is ordered and requests that all rows with attribute values in the specified range be retrieved. The actual value of the attribute in a requested tuple is not specified in the range condition. A search for a tuple satisfying a range condition is referred to as a **range search**.

9.3 Sorted Files

The last examples ((9.1), (9.2), and (9.3)) illustrate the weakness of heap storage. Even though information is requested about only a subset of rows, the entire table (or half the table) must be searched since without scanning a page we cannot be sure that it does not contain a row in the subset. These examples motivate the need for more sophisticated storage structures, one of which we consider in this section.

Suppose that, instead of storing the rows of a table in arbitrary order, we sort them based on the value of some attribute(s) of the table. We refer to such a structure as a **sorted file**. For example, we might store TRANSCRIPT in a sorted file in which the rows of the table are ordered on StudId, as shown in Figure 9.5. An immediate advantage of this is that if we are using a scan to locate rows having a particular value of StudId, we can stop the scan at the point in the file at which those rows must be located. But beyond that, we can now use a binary search. We explore these possibilities next.

Access cost. A naive way to search for the data records satisfying (9.2) is to scan the records in order until the first record having the value 234567890 in the StudId column is encountered. All records having this value would be stored consecutively, and access to them requires a minimum of additional I/O. In particular, if successive pages are stored contiguously on the disk, seek time can be minimized. In the figure, the rows describing courses taken by student 234567890 are stored on a single page. Once the first of these rows is made available in the cache, all others satisfying query (9.2) can be quickly retrieved. If the data file consists of F pages, an average of $F/2$ page I/O operations is needed to locate the records—a significant improvement over the case in which TRANSCRIPT is stored in a heap file. Note that the same approach works for query (9.1).

In some cases, it is more efficient to locate the record with a **binary search** technique. The middle page is retrieved first, and its Id values are compared to 234567890. If the target value is found in the page, the record has been located; if the target value is less than (or greater than) the page values, the process is repeated

111111111	MGT123	F1997	3.0	
111111111	EE101	F1997	4.0	page 0
111111111	MAT123	F1997	3.0	
123454321	CS305	S1996	4.0	
123454321	CS315	S1997	4.0	page 1
123454321	MAT123	S1996	2.0	
234567890	EE101	F1995	3.0	
234567890	CS305	S1996	4.0	page 2
425360777	CS305	S1996	3.0	
666666666	MGT123	F1994	4.0	
666666666	MAT123	F1997	3.0	page 3
666666666	EE101	S1991	3.0	
987654321	MGT123	F1994	3.0	
987654321	CS305	F1995	2.0	page 4

FIGURE 9.5 TRANSCRIPT table stored as a sorted file. At most four rows fit in a page.

recursively on the first half (or last half) of the data file. With this approach, the worst-case number of page transfers needed to locate the record with a particular student Id is approximately $log_2 F$.

Unfortunately, the number of page transfers is not always the most accurate way of measuring the cost of searching a sorted file since it does not take into account the seek latency incurred. While doing a binary search, we might have to visit pages located on different disk cylinders, and this might involve considerable seek-latency costs. In fact, under certain circumstances the seek latency might be more important than the number of page transfers. Consider a sorted file that occupies N consecutive cylinders and in which successive pages are stored in adjacent blocks. A binary search might cause the disk head to move across $N/2$, $N/4$, then $N/8$ cylinders, and so on. Hence, the total number of cylinders traversed by the disk head will be about N, and the total cost of binary search will be

$$N \times seek\ time + log_2 F \times transfer\ time$$

On the other hand, if we do a simple sequential search through the file, the average number of cylinders canvassed by the disk head will be $N/2$ and the total cost

$$N/2 \times seek\ time + F/2 \times transfer\ time$$

Since seek time dominates transfer time, binary search is justified only if F is much larger than N.[3] In view of these results, neither sequential search nor binary search is considered a good option for equality searches in sorted files. A much more common approach is to augment sorted files with an index (see Section 9.4) and use binary search within the index. Since the index is designed to fit in main memory, a binary search over the index is very efficient and does not suffer from the disk-latency overhead described earlier.

Sorted files support range searches if the file is sorted on the same attribute as the requested range. Thus, the TRANSCRIPT file of Figure 9.5 supports a query requesting information about every student whose Id is between 100000000 and 199999999. An equality search for Id 100000000 locates the first tuple in the range (which might have Id 100000000 or, if such a tuple does not exist, will be the tuple with the smallest Id greater than this value). Subsequent tuples in the range occupy consecutive slots, and cache hits are likely to result as they are retrieved. If B is the number of rows stored in a page and R is the number of rows in a particular range, the number of I/O operations needed to retrieve all pages of the data file containing rows in the range (once the first row has been located) is roughly R/B.

Contrast these numbers with a heap file in which each row in the range can be on a different page and it is necessary to scan the entire file to ensure that all of them have been located. If the data file has F pages, the number of I/O operations is F. Similarly, a sorted file supports the retrieval of tuples that satisfy query (9.3), although in this case the table must be sorted on `Grade` instead. It cannot be sorted on both search keys at the same time.

Maintaining sorted order. In practice, it is difficult to maintain rows in sorted order if the table is dynamic. A heavy I/O price must be paid if, whenever a new row is inserted, all of the following rows have to be moved down one slot in the data file (that is, on average, half the pages have to be updated). One (partial) solution to this problem is to leave empty slots in each page when a data file is created to accommodate subsequent insertions between rows. The term **fillfactor** refers to the percentage of slots in a page that are initially filled. For example, the fillfactor for a heap file is 100%. In Figure 9.5 the fillfactor is 75% because three out of the four slots on a page are filled.

Empty slots do not provide a complete solution, however, since they can be exhausted as rows are inserted, and the problem then reappears for a subsequent insert. An **overflow page** might be used in this case, which Figure 9.6 illustrates using the TRANSCRIPT table. We have assumed that the initial state of the data file is as shown in Figure 9.5. Each page has a pointer field containing the page number of an overflow page (if it exists). In the figure, two new rows have been added to

[3] We have ignored the rotational delay, which strongly favors sequential over binary search.

111111111	MGT123	F1997	3.0	
111111111	EE101	F1997	4.0	page 0
111111111	MAT123	F1997	3.0	

123454321	CS305	S1996	4.0	
123454321	CS315	S1997	4.0	page 1
123454321	MAT123	S1996	2.0	

Overflow: 5				
234567890	EE101	F1995	3.0	
234567890	CS305	S1996	4.0	page 2
234567890	LIT203	F1997	3.0	
425360777	CS305	S1996	3.0	

666666666	MGT123	F1994	4.0	
666666666	EE101	S1991	3.0	page 3
666666666	MAT123	F1997	3.0	

987654321	MGT123	F1994	3.0	
987654321	CS305	F1995	2.0	page 4

313131313	CS306	F1997	4.0	page 5

FIGURE 9.6 The TRANSCRIPT table (augmented with overflow pointers) stored as a sorted file after the addition of several rows.

page 2 since the file was created. If an overflow page itself overflows, we can create an **overflow chain**: a linked list of overflow pages. Note that it is generally not the case that rows in the overflow chain are sorted. The problem of keeping the overflow chain sorted is the same as the problem of keeping the original file sorted.

While the use of overflow chains helps keep files **logically sorted**, we lose the advantage of the sorted files being stored in contiguous space on disk because an overflow page can be distant from the page that links to it. This causes additional latency during a sequential scan that reads records in order, and the number of I/O operations necessary to transfer records in a range is no longer R/B. If performance of sequential scan is an important issue (and it usually is), the data file must be reorganized periodically to ensure that all of its records are stored in contiguous disk space. The lesson here is that maintaining a data file in sorted order can be expensive if the file is dynamic.

9.4 Indices

Suppose that you have set up a database for an application and given it to a set of users. However, instead of receiving a check in the mail for your work, you start getting angry phone calls complaining that the system is too slow. Some users claim that they have to wait a long time to get a response to their queries. Others claim that throughput is unacceptable. Queries are being submitted to the system at a rate greater than that at which the system is capable of processing them.

Indices can be used to improve this situation. An index over a table is analogous to a book index or a library card catalog. In the case of a book, certain terms that are of interest to readers are selected and made into index entries. In this case, each **index entry** contains a term (e.g., "gas turbines") and a pointer (e.g., "p. 348") to the location(s) in the book where the term appears. The entries are then sorted on the term to construct a table, called an **index**, for easy reference. Instead of having to scan the entire book for the locations at which a particular term is discussed, we can access the index efficiently and go directly to those locations.

The analogy is even closer in the case of a card catalogue. In this case, there might be several indices based on different properties of books: author, title, and subject. In each index, the entries are sorted on that property's value and each entry points to a book in the collection. Thus, an entry in an author index contains an author's name and a pointer (e.g., section, shelf) to a book that she has written.

Similarly, an index on a database table provides a convenient mechanism for locating a row (data record) without scanning the entire table and thus greatly reduces the time it takes to process a query. The property to be located is a column (or columns) of the indexed table called a **search key**. Do not confuse a search key of an index on a table with a candidate key of the table. Remember that a candidate key is a set of one or more columns having the property that no two rows in any instance of the table can have the same values in these columns. A search key does not have this restriction, so, for example, TRANSCRIPT has more than one row for the student with Id `111111111`, which means that the index on `StudId` will have several index entries with the search-key value `111111111`.

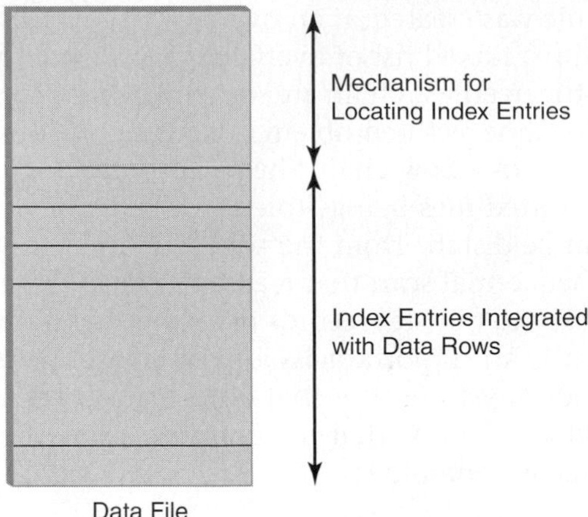

FIGURE 9.7 A storage structure in which an index is integrated with the data records.

As with a candidate key, a search key can involve several columns. For example, the search key might include both the student Id and the semester. However, in contrast to a candidate key, the order of columns in a search key makes a difference, so you should think of a search key as a sequence (as contrasted with a set) of columns of the indexed table. You will see a context in which the ordering is important when we discuss partial-key searches.

An index consists of a set of index entries together with a mechanism for locating a particular entry efficiently based on a search-key value. With some indices, such as an ISAM index or a B^+ tree, the location mechanism relies on the fact that the index entries are sorted on the search key. A hash index takes a different approach. In either case, the data structure that supports the location mechanism, together with the index entries, can be integrated into the data file containing the table itself, as shown in Figure 9.7. This integrated data file is regarded as a new storage structure and is called an **integrated index**. Later in this chapter we discuss ISAM, B^+ trees, and hash storage structures as alternatives to heap and sorted storage structures. With an integrated storage structure, each index entry actually *contains* a row of the table (no pointer is needed).

Alternatively, the index might not be integrated, but instead stored in a separate file, called an **index file**, in which each index entry contains a search-key value and a rid.[4] This organization is shown in Figure 9.8. For example, the table TRANSCRIPT of

[4] With some indices, only the page Id field of the rid is stored. Since the major cost of accessing the data file is the cost of transferring a page, storing only the page Id in the index entry makes it possible to locate the correct page. Once the page has been retrieved, the record within it with the target search-key value can be located using a linear search. The added computational time for this search is generally small compared to the time to transfer a page and might be justified by the saving of space in each index entry. With smaller index entries, the index can fit in fewer pages, and hence less page I/O is needed to access it. In some index organizations, a single index entry can contain several pointers. Since this feature only complicates the discussion without adding any new concepts, we do not consider it further.

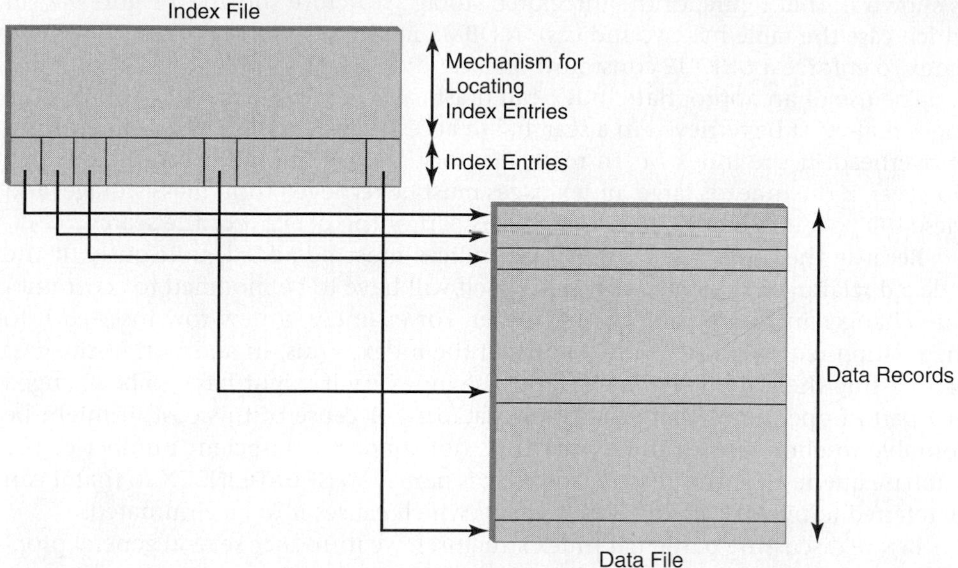

FIGURE 9.8 A clustered index that references a separate data file.

Figure 9.3 on page 330 might have an index on `StudId`. Each index entry contains a value that appears in the `StudId` column in some row of the table and the rid of that row in the data file. Thus, the entry `(425360777, (3,1))` is present in the index.

Integration saves space since no pointer is needed and the search key does not have to be stored in both the index entry and the data record containing the corresponding row.

The SQL standard does not provide for the creation or deletion of indices. However, indices are an essential part of the database systems provided by most vendors. In some, for example, an index with a search key equal to the primary key is automatically created when a table is created. Such indices are often integrated storage structures that make it possible to efficiently guarantee that the primary key is unique when a row is added or modified (and to support the efficient execution of queries that involve the primary key). Heap storage structures result when no primary key is declared.

In addition to indices that are automatically created, database systems generally provide a statement (in their own dialect) that explicitly creates an index. For example,

```
CREATE INDEX TRANSGRD ON TRANSCRIPT (Grade)
```

creates an index named TRANSGRD on the table TRANSCRIPT with `Grade` as a search key. If CREATE INDEX does not provide an option to specify the type of index, a B^+ tree is generally the result. In any case, the index created might be stored in an index file, as shown in Figure 9.8. The index might reference a heap or sorted file, as shown in that figure, or the integrated storage structure shown in Figure 9.7 (in which case the table has two indices). A DBMS might automatically create such an index to enforce a UNIQUE constraint on a candidate key.

The use of an appropriate index can drastically reduce the number of data file pages that must be retrieved in a search, but accessing the index itself is a new form of overhead. If the index fits in main memory, this additional overhead is small. However, if the index is large, index pages must be retrieved from mass storage, and these I/O operations must be considered as part of the net cost of the search.

Because they require maintenance, indices must be added judiciously. If the indexed relation is dynamic, the index itself will have to be modified to accommodate changes in the relation as they occur. For example, a new row inserted into the relation requires a new index entry in the index. Thus, in addition to the cost of accessing the index used in a search, the index itself might have to be changed as a part of operations that modify the database. Because of this cost, it might be desirable to eliminate an index that does not support a sufficient number of the database queries. For this reason, an index is named in CREATE INDEX so that it can be referred to by a DROP INDEX statement, which causes it to be eliminated.

Before discussing particular index structures, we introduce several general properties for categorizing indices.

9.4.1 Clustered versus Unclustered Indices

In a *clustered* index, the physical proximity of index entries in the index implies some degree of proximity among the corresponding data records in the data file. Such indices enable certain queries to be executed more efficiently than with unclustered indices. Query optimizers can use the fact that an index is clustered to improve the execution strategy. (Chapters 10 and 11 explain how clustering information is used by the query optimizer.) Clustering takes different forms depending on whether index entries are sorted (as in ISAM and B^+ trees) or not (as in hash indices). A sorted index is **clustered** if the index entries and the data records are sorted on the same search key; otherwise, it is said to be **unclustered**. Clustered hash indices will be defined in Section 9.6.1. These definitions imply that, if the index is structured so that its entries are integrated with data records (the entries contain the records), it *must* be clustered. The index shown in Figure 9.8 is an example of a clustered index in which the index and the table are stored in separate files (and therefore the data records are not contained in the index entries). The regular pattern of the pointers from the index entries to the records in the data file is meant to reflect the fact that both index entries and data records are sorted on the same columns. The index shown in Figure 9.9 is unclustered.

A clustered index is often called a **main index**; an unclustered index is often called a **secondary index**.[5] There can be at most a single clustered index (since the

[5] Clustered indices are also sometimes called **primary indices**. We avoid this terminology because of a potential confusion regarding the connection between primary indices and the primary keys of relations. A primary index is *not* necessarily an index on the primary key of a relation. For instance, the PROFESSOR relation could be sorted on the `Department` attribute (which is not even a key) and

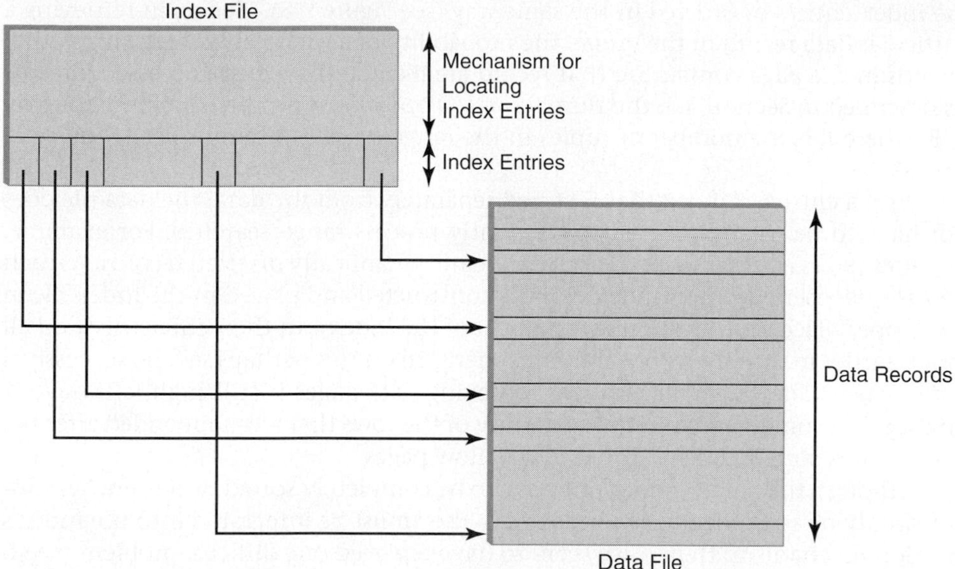

FIGURE 9.9 An unclustered index over a data file.

data file can be sorted on at most one search key), but there can be several secondary indices. An index created by a CREATE TABLE statement is often clustered. With some database systems, a clustered index is always integrated into the data file as a storage structure. In this case, index entries contain data records, as shown in Figure 9.7. An index created by CREATE INDEX is generally a secondary, unclustered index stored in a separate index file (although some database systems allow the programmer to request the creation of a clustered index, which involves reorganizing the storage structure). The search key of the main index might be the primary key of the table, but this is not necessarily so.

A file is said to be **inverted** on a column if a secondary index exists with that column as a search key. It is **fully inverted** if a secondary index exists on all columns that are not contained in the primary key.

A clustered index with a search key, *sk*, is particularly effective for range searches involving *sk*. Its location mechanism efficiently locates the index entry whose search-key value is at one end of the range, and, since entries are ordered on *sk*, subsequent entries in the range are in the same index page (or in successive pages—we discuss this situation in Section 9.5). The data records can be retrieved using these entries.

The beauty of a clustered index is that the data records are themselves grouped together (instead of scattered throughout the data file). They are either contained in

a clustered index could be built, while the index on the `Id` attribute of that relation (which is also its primary key) will be unclustered because rows will not be sorted on that attribute.

the index entries or ordered in the same way (see Figure 9.8). Hence, in retrieving a particular data record in the range, the probability of a cache hit is high since other records in the page containing that record are likely to have been accessed already. As described in Section 9.3, the number of I/O operations on the data file is roughly R/B, where R is the number of tuples in the range and B is the number of tuples in a page.

With a clustered index that is stored separately from the data, the data file does not have to be totally ordered to efficiently process range searches. For example, overflow pages might be used to accommodate dynamically inserted records. As each new row is inserted, a new index entry is constructed and placed in the index file in the proper place. The location mechanism of the index can then efficiently find all index entries in the range since they are ordered in one (or perhaps several successive) index pages. The cache-hit ratio for retrieving data pages is still high, although it might suffer somewhat from the scattering of the rows that were appended after the data file was sorted and are stored in overflow pages.

Although the data file does not have to be completely sorted, index entries cannot simply be appended to the index file—they must be integrated into the index's location mechanism. Hence, we seem to have replaced one difficult problem (keeping the data file sorted) with another (keeping the index file properly organized). However, the latter problem is not as difficult as it appears. For one thing, index entries are generally much smaller than data records, so the index file is much smaller than the data file and therefore index reorganization requires less I/O. Furthermore, as we will see, the algorithms associated with a B^+ tree index are designed to accommodate the efficient addition and deletion of index entries.

The algorithm for locating the index entries containing search-key values in a range is the same for clustered or unclustered indices. The problem with an unclustered index is that, instead of finding the corresponding data records in the index entries or grouped together in the data file, the records might be scattered throughout the data file. Thus, if there are R entries in the range, as many as R separate I/O operations might be necessary to retrieve the data records (we will discuss a technique for optimizing this number in a later section).

For example, a data file might contain 10,000 pages, but there might be only 100 records in the range of a particular query. If an unclustered index on the attributes of the WHERE clause of that query is available, at most 100 I/O operations will be needed to retrieve the pages of the data file (as compared with 10,000 I/O operations if the data is stored in a heap file with no index). If the index is clustered and each data file page contains an average of 20 data records, approximately five data pages will have to be retrieved. We have ignored the I/O operations on the index file in this comparison. We deal with index I/O in the individual discussions of different index structures later in this chapter.

9.4.2 Sparse versus Dense Indices

We have been assuming that indices are dense. A **dense index** is one whose entries are in a one-to-one correspondence with the records in the data file. A secondary,

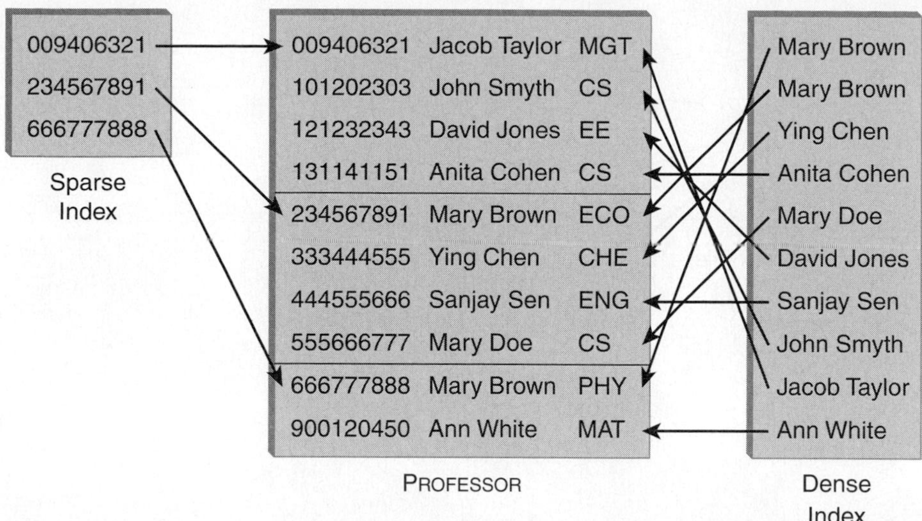

FIGURE 9.10 The index entries of (left) a sparse index with search key `Id` and (right) a dense index with search key `Name`. Both refer to the table PROFESSOR stored in a file sorted on `Id`.

unclustered index must be dense, but a clustered index need not be. A **sparse index** over a sorted file is one in which there is a one-to-one correspondence between index entries and pages of the data file. The entry contains a value that is less than or equal to all values in the page it refers to. The difference between a sparse and a dense index is illustrated using the table PROFESSOR in Figure 9.10. To simplify the figure we do not show overflow pages in the data file and assume that all slots are filled. The data file is indexed by two separate index files. Only the index entries are shown in the index files, not the location mechanisms. Once again, we assume four slots per page. The `Id` attribute is the primary key of this table and is also the search key for the sparse index shown at the left of the figure. The `Name` attribute is the search key for the dense index at the right.

To retrieve the record for the faculty member with Id 333444555, we can use the sparse index to locate the index entry containing the largest value that is smaller than the target Id. In our case, the entry contains the value 234567891 and points to the second page of the data file. Once that page has been retrieved, the target record can be found by searching forward in the page. With a sparse index, it is essential that the data file be ordered on the same key as the index since it is the ordering of the data file that allows us to locate a record not referenced by an index entry. Hence, the sparse index must be clustered.

An important point concerning sparse indices is that the search key should be a candidate key of the table since, if several records exist in the data file with the same search key value and they are spread over several pages, the records in the first of those pages might be missed. The problem is illustrated in Figure 9.11. The search key of the sparse index is the first column of the table, which is not a candidate key.

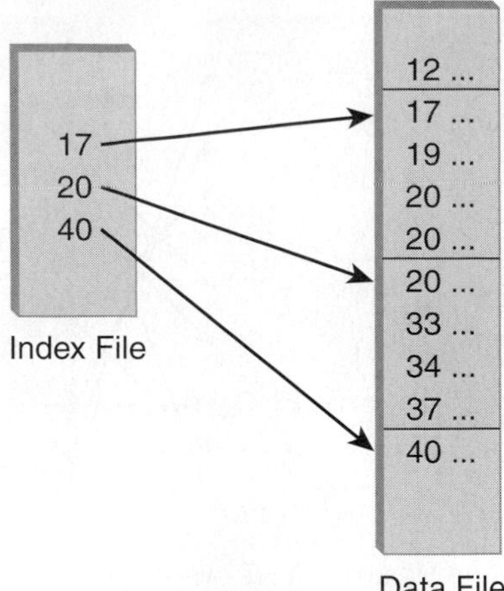

FIGURE 9.11 Sparse index with a problem: the search key is not a candidate key.

A search through the index for records having a search-key value of 20 follows the pointer in the index having a search-key value 20. Searching forward in the target page yields a single record with search-key value 20 and misses the records with that value in the previous page of the data file.

Several techniques can be used to correct this problem. The simplest is to start the search through the data file at the prior page when the target value is equal to the value in the sparse index. Another approach is to create an index entry for each *distinct search-key value* in the table (as opposed to one index entry per page). In that case, there might be several entries that point to the same page, but if there is considerable duplication of search-key values in the rows of the table, this index will still be considerably smaller than a dense index.

Unclustered indices are dense. The index on the right in Figure 9.10 is unclustered and, since an index entry exists for each record, the search key need not be a candidate key of the table. Therefore, several index entries can have the same search-key value (as shown in the figure).

9.4.3 Search Keys Containing Multiple Attributes

Search keys can contain multiple attributes. For example, we might construct an index on PROFESSOR by executing the statement

```
CREATE INDEX NAMEDEPT ON PROFESSOR (Name, DeptId)
```

Such an index is useful if clients of the supported application frequently request information about professors they identify by name and department Id. With such an index, the system can directly retrieve the required record. Not only is a scan of the entire table avoided, but records of professors with the same name in different departments are not retrieved (there might be two professors having the same name in a particular department, but this is unlikely).

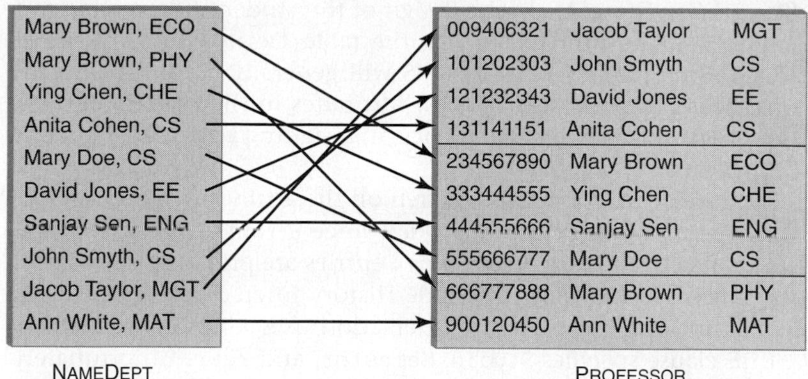

FIGURE 9.12 Dense index on PROFESSOR with search key `Name, DeptId`.

A dense, unclustered index that results from this statement is shown in Figure 9.12. The index entries are lexicographically ordered on `Name, DeptId` (notice that the order of the two entries for `Mary Brown` is now reversed from their position in the dense index of Figure 9.10).

One advantage of using multiple attributes in a search key is that the resulting index supports a finer granularity search. NAMEDEPT allows us to quickly retrieve the information about the professor named Mary Brown in the Economics Department; the dense index of Figure 9.10 requires that we examine two data records.

A second advantage of multiple attributes arises if the index entries are sorted (as with an ISAM or B^+ tree index but not a hash index) since then a variety of range searches can be supported. For example, we can not only retrieve the records of all professors named Mary Brown in a particular department (an equality search), but in addition we can retrieve the records of all professors named Mary Brown in any department with a name alphabetized between economics and sociology, or all professors named Mary Brown in all departments, or any professor whose name is alphabetized between Mary Brown and David Jones in all departments. All of these are examples of range searches. In each case, the search is supported because index entries are sorted first on `Name` and second on `DeptId`. Hence, the target index entries are (logically) consecutive in the index file, and we are able to limit the range of entries to be scanned. The last two searches are examples of **partial-key searches**—that is, the values for some of the attributes in the search key are not specified.

Note that a range search that is not supported by NAMEDEPT is one in which a value for `Name` is not supplied (e.g, retrieve the records of all professors in the Computer Science Department) since in that case the desired index entries are not consecutive in the index file. This is precisely the reason that, in distinguishing a search key from a candidate key, we said that the ordering of attributes in a search key is important whereas it is not important for a candidate key. With partial-key searches, values for a *prefix* of the search key can be used in the index search, while searching on a proper suffix of the key is not supported by the index.

Example 9.4.1 (Partial-Key Search). In the design of the Student Registration System given in Section 4.8, the primary key for the table TRANSCRIPT is (`StudId, CrsCode, SectionNo, Semester, Year`). A DBMS will generally automatically create an index whose search key consists of these attributes in the given order. The Student Grade interaction can use this index since, in assigning a grade to a student, all of this information must be supplied.

The Class Roster interaction performs a search on the attributes `CrsCode, SectionNo, Semester, Year`. It cannot use the index since a value of `StudId` is not provided, and this is the attribute on which index entries are primarily sorted.

However, the index is helpful for the Grade History interaction since `StudId` is supplied, but it is not optimal since the interaction uses a SELECT statement in which the WHERE clause specifies `StudId`, `Semester`, and `Year`. Unfortunately, the index does not support the use of `Semester` and `Year` unless `CrsCode` and `SectionNo` are also supplied. Reversing the order of the attributes in the primary key specification allows it to support the Grade History interaction optimally and also the Student Grade interaction. An additional index is needed for the Class Roster interaction. ■

In general, a tree index on table **R** with search key K supports a search of the form

$$\sigma_{attr_1 \mathrm{op}_1 val_1 \wedge \ldots \wedge attr_n \mathrm{op}_n val_n}(\mathbf{R}) \qquad \textbf{9.4}$$

if some prefix of K is a subset of $\{attr_1, attr_2, \ldots, attr_n\}$. For example, if s attributes of (9.4), $s \leq n$, are a prefix of K (assume for simplicity that these are the first s attributes), the search locates the smallest index entry satisfying $attr_1 = val_1 \wedge \ldots \wedge attr_s = val_s$ and scans forward from that point to locate all entries satisfying (9.4). Thus, a particular index can be used in different ways to support a variety of searches and can therefore be used in a variety of access paths to **R**.

Finally, since an index can have a search key with multiple attributes, it can contain an arbitrary fraction of the information in the indexed table. In particular, a dense unclustered index has an index entry for each row, r, and that entry contains r's values of the search-key attributes. The implication is that, for some queries, it is possible to find all the requested information in the index itself, *without accessing the table*. Thus, for example, the result of executing the query

```
SELECT  P.Name
FROM    PROFESSOR P
WHERE   P.DeptId = 'EE'
```

can be obtained from the index NAMEDEPT, without accessing PROFESSOR, by scanning the index entries. Such a scan is less costly than a scan of PROFESSOR, since the index is stored in fewer pages than is the table. The use of an index in this way is referred to as an *index-only strategy* and is discussed in Section 12.2.1.

9.5 Multilevel Indexing

In previous sections, we discussed the index entries but not the location mechanism used to find them. In this section we discuss the location mechanism used in tree indices and then describe its use more specifically in the *index-sequential access method* (*ISAM*) and in *B^+ trees*.

To understand how the location mechanism for a tree index works, consider the dense index on the table PROFESSOR shown in Figure 9.10. Since the search key is `Name`, the index entries are ordered on that field, and since the data records are ordered differently in the data file, the index is unclustered. We assume that the list of index entries is stored in a sequence of pages of the index file. A naive location mechanism for the index is a binary search over the entries. Thus, to locate the data record describing Sanjay Sen, we enter the list of index entries at its midpoint and compare the value `Sanjay Sen` with the search-key values found in that page. If the target value is found in the page, the index entry has been located; if it is less (or greater) than the values in the page, the process is repeated recursively on the first half (or, respectively, the last half) of the list. Once the index entry is located, the data page containing the record can be retrieved with one additional I/O operation.

It is important to note that a binary search on the list of index entries is a major improvement over a binary search on a sorted data file, as described in Section 9.3, since data records are generally much larger than index entries. Thus, if Q is the number of pages containing the index entries of a dense tree index and F is the number of pages in the data file, Q is much less than F. The number of I/O operations needed to locate a particular index entry using binary search can be no larger than approximately $log_2 Q$.

We can further reduce the cost of locating the index entry by indexing the list of index entries itself. We construct a sparse index, using the same search key, on the index entries (a sparse index is possible because the index entries are sorted on that key) and do a binary search on that index. The entries in this second-level index serve as separators that guide the search toward the index entries of the first-level index. We thus use **leaf entry** to refer to the index entries (the entries that reside in the lowest level of the tree) and **separator entry** to refer to the entries that reside at higher levels.

The technique is illustrated in Figure 9.13, which shows a two-level index. To keep the figure concise, we assume a table with a candidate key having an integer domain, and we use that key as a search key for the index. We assume that a page of the index file can accommodate four index entries. Of course, in real systems one index page accommodates many more (e.g., 100), and the size of the index is relatively insignificant compared to the size of the data file.

In this and subsequent figures, we do not explicitly show the data records. The figures can be interpreted in two ways: (1) the leaf entries contain pointers to the data records in a separate data file; (2) the leaf entries contain the data records (the index is clustered in this case), and the figure represents a storage structure. In interpretation 1, the index file contains both leaf entries and the second-level index, and one additional I/O operation is required to access the data record in the

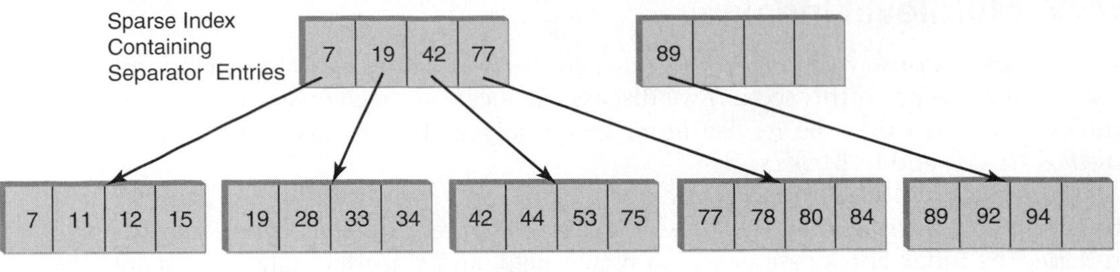

FIGURE 9.13 A two-level index. At most four entries fit in a page.

data file. In interpretation 2, retrieving a leaf entry also retrieves the corresponding data record, and no additional I/O is required. Our discussion of multilevel indices applies to both interpretations.

Finally, although in the figure the separators in the second-level index look identical to leaf entries, this is not always the case. In interpretation 2, only leaves, not separator entries, contain data records, and thus they are considerably larger than the separator entries. In interpretation 1, separators and leaf entries look identical, except that separators in the second level point to the nodes of the first level whereas leaf entries point to the records in the actual data file. The formats of these pointers will be different.

With a two-level index, we replace the binary search of the leaves by a two-step process. If we are looking for a data record with search-key value k, then we first do a binary search of the top-level sparse index to find the appropriate separator entry. The ith separator entry, with search-key value k_i, points to a page containing index entries with search-key values greater than or equal to k_i. It will be the appropriate entry if $k_i \leq k < k_{i+1}$. In this case we next retrieve that page to find the index entry (if it exists). Thus, if we are looking for a search-key value of 33, we first do a binary search of the upper index to locate the rightmost separator with a value less than or equal to 33, which in this case is the separator containing 19. We then follow the pointer to the second page of index leaves and do a linear search in that page to find the desired index entry. If the target search-key value were 32, we would perform the same steps and conclude that no row in the indexed table had value 32 in the candidate-key field.

What have we achieved by introducing the second-level index? Since the upper-level index is sparse, it has fewer separator entries than there are leaf entries at the first level. If we assume separate data and index files, separator and leaf entries in the index are roughly the same size. Moreover, if we assume 100 entries in an index page, the second-level index occupies $Q/100$ pages (where Q is the number of leaf pages) and the maximum cost of accessing a leaf entry using a binary search of the second-level index is roughly $log_2(Q/100)$ page I/Os plus 1 (for the page containing the index leaf). This compares to $log_2 Q$ for a binary search over the index's leaf entries and represents a major savings if Q is large.

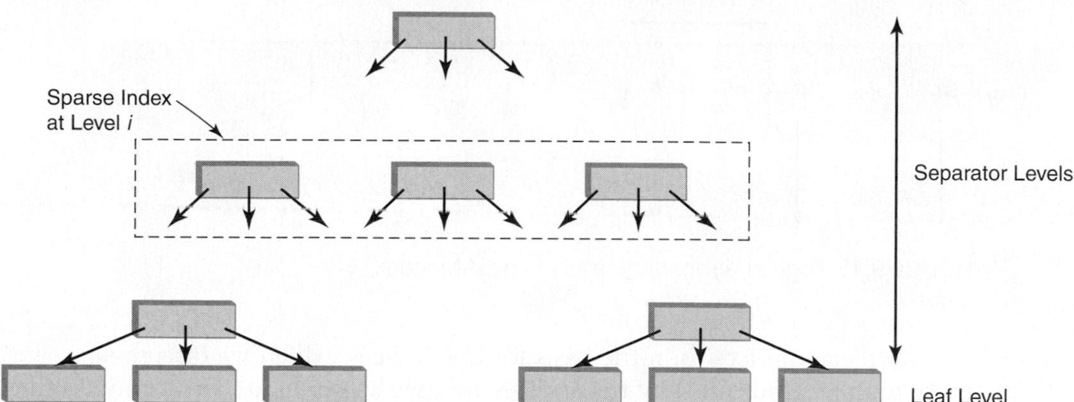

FIGURE 9.14 Schematic view of a multilevel index.

These considerations lead us to a multilevel index. If a two-level index is good, why not a multilevel index? Each index level is indexed by a higher-level sparse index of a smaller size, until we get to the point where the index is contained in a single page. The I/O cost of searching that index is 1, and so the total cost of locating the target leaf entry equals the number of index levels.

A multilevel index is shown schematically in Figure 9.14. Each shaded rectangular box represents a page. The lowest level of the tree contains the leaf entries and is referred to as the **leaf level**. If we concatenate all of the pages at this level in the order shown, the leaf entries form an ordered list. The upper levels contain separators and are referred to as **separator levels**. This is the location mechanism of a tree index. If we concatenate all of the pages at a particular separator level in the order shown, we get a sparse index on the level below. The root of the tree (the top separator level) is a sparse index contained in a single page of the index file. If the leaf entries contain data records, the figure shows the storage structure of a tree-indexed file.

We use the term **index level** to refer to any level of an index tree, leaf or separator. We use the term **fan-out** to refer to the number of index separators in a page. The fan-out controls the number of levels in the tree: the smaller it is, the more levels the tree has. The number of levels equals the number of I/O operations needed to fetch a leaf entry. If the fan-out is denoted by Φ, the number of I/O operations necessary to retrieve a leaf entry is $log_{\Phi}Q + 1$.

If, for example, there are 10,000 pages at the leaf level and the fan-out is 100 (10^6 rows in the data file assuming that leaf and separator entries are the same size), three page I/Os are necessary to retrieve a particular leaf. Thus, with a large fan-out, traversal of the index, even for a large data file, can be reduced to a few I/O operations. Since the root index occupies only a single page, it can often be kept in main memory, further reducing the cost. It might be practical to keep even the second-level index, which in this case occupies 100 pages, in main memory.

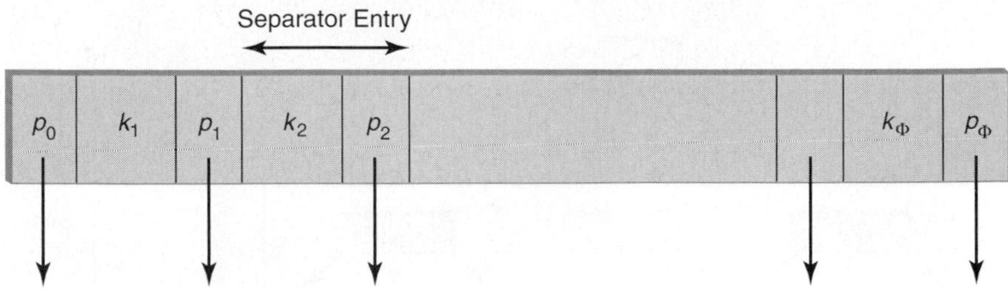

FIGURE 9.15 Page at a separator level in an ISAM index.

Multilevel indices form the basis for tree indices, which we discuss next, and these numbers indicate why tree indices are used so frequently. Not only do they provide efficient access to the data file, but, as we will see, they also support range queries.

9.5.1 Index-Sequential Access

The **index-sequential access method** (**ISAM**)[6] is based on the multilevel index. An ISAM index is a main index, and hence it is a clustered index over records that are ordered on the search key of the index. Generally, the records are contained in the leaf level, so ISAM is a storage structure for the data file.

The format of a page at a separator level is shown in Figure 9.15. Each separator level is effectively a sparse index over the next level below. Each separator entry consists of a search-key value, k_i, and a pointer, p_i, to another page in the storage structure. This page might be in the next, lower separator level, or it might be a page at the leaf levels. The separators are sorted in the page, and we assume that a page contains a maximum of Φ separators.

Each search-key value, k_i, separates the set of search-key values in the two subtrees pointed to by the adjacent pointers, p_{i-1} and p_i. If a search-key value, k, is found in the subtree referred to by p_{i-1}, it satisfies $k < k_i$; if it is found in the subtree referred to by p_i, it satisfies $k \geq k_i$ (hence the term "separator"). It appears as if an ISAM index page contains an extra pointer, p_0, if we compare it with a page of a sparse index in a multilevel index.[7] Actually, a better way to compare a page of an ISAM index to an index page at the separator level is that the latter contains an extra search-key value: the smallest search-key value in the page, k_0, is actually unnecessary.

Example 9.5.1 (ISAM Index). Figure 9.16 is an example of an ISAM index. In it, the tree has two separator levels and a leaf level. Search-key values are the names

[6] The term "access method" is often used interchangeably with the term "access path." We prefer **access path** since it conforms more closely to the concept.

[7] Note that the fan-out is now $\Phi + 1$. Since Φ is generally much greater than 1, we ignore the difference between Φ and $\Phi + 1$ in cost calculations.

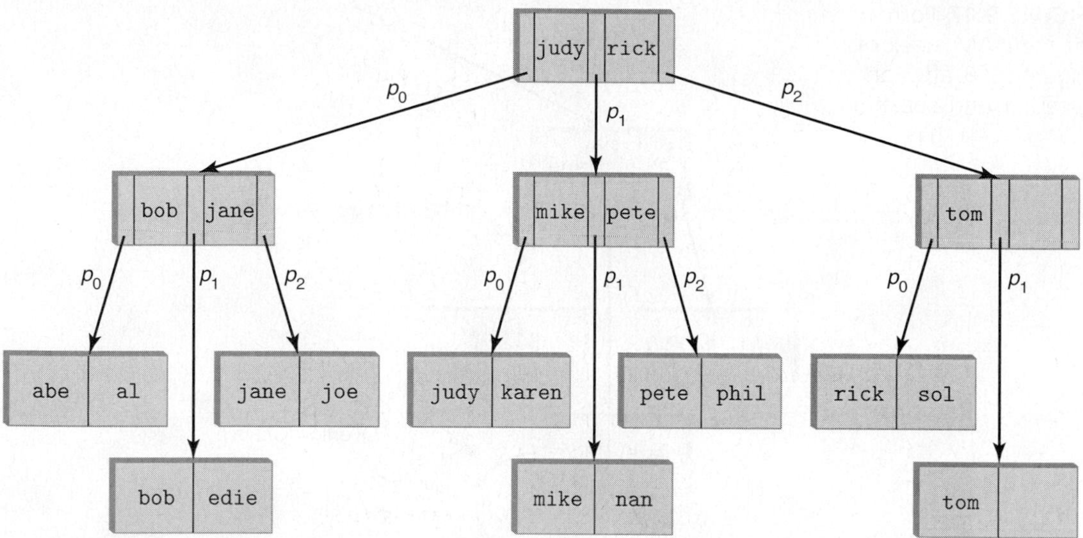

FIGURE 9.16 An example of an ISAM index.

of students, and the ordering is lexicographic. All search-key values in the leftmost subtree (the subtree referred to by p_0 in the root page) are less than `judy`, and all search-key values in the middle subtree (the subtree referred to by p_1 in the root page) are greater than or equal to `judy`.

A search for the data record containing the search-key value `karen` starts at the root, determines that the target value is between `judy` and `rick`, and follows p_1 to the middle page at the next index level. From that page, it determines that `karen` is less than `mike` and follows p_0 to the leaf page that must contain the index entry for `karen` (if it exists). If the goal were to retrieve all data records with search-key values between `karen` and `pete`, we would locate the index entry with the largest search-key value less than or equal to `karen` and then scan the leaf level until the first entry with search-key value greater than `pete` is encountered. Because pages at the leaf level are stored sequentially in sorted order, the desired entries are consecutive in the file. ■

Example 9.5.1 illustrates the use of an ISAM index in supporting a range search. In addition the index supports keys with multiple attributes and partial-key searches.

An ISAM file is built by first allocating pages sequentially in the storage structure for the leaf pages (containing the data rows) and then constructing the separator levels from the bottom up: the root is the topmost index built. Therefore, the ISAM index initially has the property that all search-key values that appear at a separator level also appear at the leaf level.

The separator levels of an ISAM index never change once they have been constructed. It is for this reason that an ISAM index is referred to as a static index. Although the contents of leaf-level pages might change, the pages themselves are

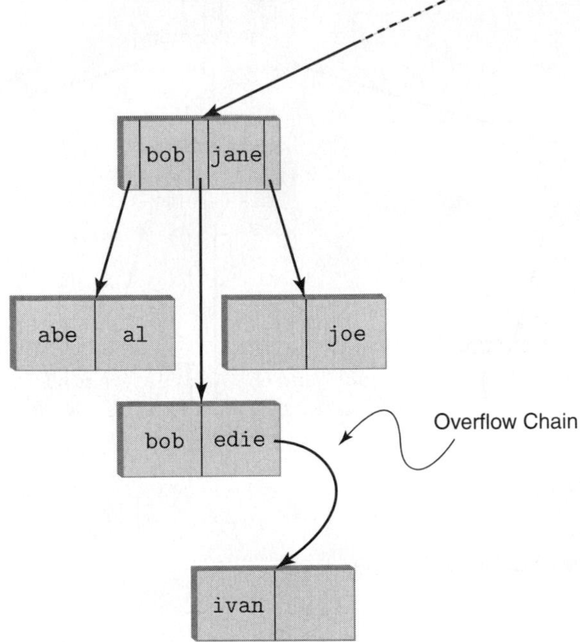

FIGURE 9.17 Portion of the ISAM index of Figure 9.16 after an insertion and a deletion.

not allocated or deallocated and hence their position in the file is fixed. If a row of the table is deleted, the corresponding leaf entry is deleted from the leaf-level page but no changes are made to the separator levels. Such a deletion can create a situation in which a search-key value in a separator entry has no corresponding value in a leaf entry. This would happen, for example, if `jane`'s row were deleted from Figure 9.16: the entry for Jane at the leaf level would be removed, but the entry at the separator level would remain. Such an index might seem strange, but it still functions correctly and does not represent a serious problem (other than a potential waste of space where the deallocated leaf entry resided).

Some systems take advantage of the static nature of an ISAM storage structure by placing pages on the disk so that the access time for a scan of the leaf level is minimized. The time to perform a range search can be minimized in this case.

A more serious problem arises when a new row is added since a new leaf entry must be created and the appropriate leaf page might be full. This can be avoided by using a fillfactor less than 1 (a fillfactor of .75 is reasonable for an ISAM file), but overflow pages might ultimately be necessary. For example, if a row for `ivan` were inserted (and the row for `jane` deleted), the leftmost subtree of the resulting index would be as shown in Figure 9.17. Note that the new page is an overflow of a leaf-level page, *not* a new level or even a new leaf-level page. If a table is dynamic, with frequent insertions, overflow chains can become long and, as a result, the index structure becomes less and less efficient because the overflow chains must be searched to satisfy queries. The entries on the chains might not be ordered, and the

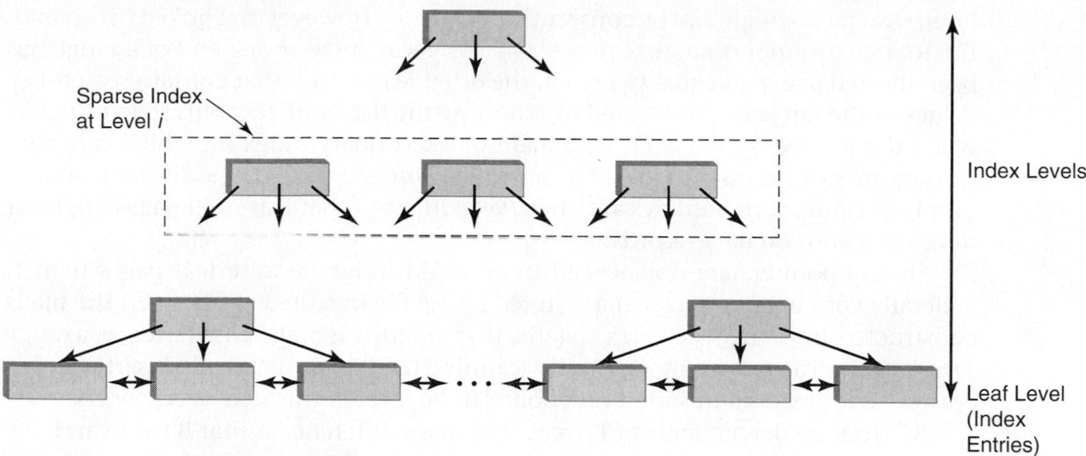

FIGURE 9.18 Schematic view of a B$^+$ tree.

overflow pages might not be physically close to one another on the mass storage device. The index can be reconstructed periodically to eliminate the chains, but this is expensive. For this reason, although an ISAM index can be effective for a relatively static table, it is generally not used when the table is dynamic.

9.5.2 B$^+$ Trees

A **B$^+$ tree** is the most commonly used index structure. Indeed, in some database systems it is the only one available. As with an ISAM index, the B$^+$ tree structure is based on the multilevel index and supports equality, range, and partial-key searches. Leaf pages might contain data records, in which case the B$^+$ tree acts not only as an index but as a storage structure that organizes the placement of records in the data file. Or the tree might be stored in an index file in which the leaf pages contain pointers to the data records. In the first case, the B$^+$ tree is a main index similar to an ISAM index since it is clustered. In the second case, it might be a main or a secondary index, and the data file need not be sorted on its search key.

Searching the tree. Figure 9.18 shows a schematic diagram of a B$^+$ tree in which each page contains a sorted set of entries. Each separator page has the form shown in Figure 9.14, and a search through the separator levels is conducted using the technique described for an ISAM index: if we are searching for a record with search-key value k, we choose the ith separator entry, where $k_i \leq k < k_{i+1}$.

The only difference between Figure 9.18 and Figure 9.14 is the addition of **sibling pointers**, which link pages at the leaf level in such a way that the linked list contains the search-key values of the data records of the table in sorted order. In contrast to an ISAM index, the B$^+$ tree itself changes dynamically. As records are added and deleted, leaf and separator pages have to be modified, added, and/or deleted, and hence leaf pages might not be consecutive in the file. However, the linked list enables the B^+ tree to support range searches. Once the leaf entry at one end of a range has been located using an equality search, the other leaf entries that contain search-key values in the range can be located by scanning the list. Note that this scheme works when the B^+ tree is used as either a main or a secondary index (in which case data records are not necessarily sorted in search-key order). With the addition of sibling pointers, Figure 9.16 becomes a B^+ tree (keep in mind that leaf-level pages might or might not contain data records).

Sibling pointers are not needed in an ISAM index because leaf pages (which generally contain data records) are stored in the file in sorted order when the file is constructed and, since the index is static, that ordering is maintained. Hence, a range search can be carried out by physically scanning the file. Dynamically inserted index entries are not stored in sorted order but can be located through overflow chains.

B^+ trees are descendants of **B trees**. The main difference is that B trees can have pointers to the records in the data file *at any level*—not just at the leaf level. Thus, each index page can have a mixture of separator and leaf entries. This implies that a particular search-key value appears exactly once in the tree. A B^+ tree does not possess this property. Therefore, a B tree can be smaller than the corresponding B^+ tree and searching in a B tree can be a little faster. However, it is harder to organize pointers to the data records in a sorted fashion in such a tree since not all such pointers are stored in the leaves (note that adding sibling pointers to a B tree will be of little help here). Therefore, performing range searches in a B tree is trickier.

Access cost. The second difference between a B^+ tree and an ISAM index is that a B^+ tree is a **balanced tree**. This means that, despite the insertion of new records and the deletion of old records, any path from the root to a leaf page has the same length as any other. This is an important property. If the tree is unbalanced, then it is possible that the path from the root to a leaf page becomes very long, the I/O cost of accessing index entries in that page is large, and the index becomes the problem rather than the solution.

With a balanced tree the I/O cost of retrieving a particular leaf page is the same for all leaves. We have seen that, for multilevel indices with a reasonable fan-out, this cost can be surprisingly small. Φ is the maximum number of separator entries that can be fit in an index page. If we assume that the algorithms for inserting and deleting entries (to be described shortly) ensure that the minimum number of separators stored in a page is $\Phi/2$ (i.e., $\Phi/2$ is the minimum fan-out),[8] then the maximum cost of a search through a B^+ tree having Q leaf pages is $log_{\Phi/2}Q + 1$. (In general, the root node can have fewer than $\Phi/2$ separators, which affects this formula slightly.) Contrast this with an ISAM index with overflow chains. Because the length of a chain is unbounded, the cost of retrieving a leaf page at the end of a chain is also unbounded.

[8] In case Φ is odd, the minimum number of separators should really be $\lceil \Phi/2 \rceil$—the smallest integer greater than $\Phi/2$.

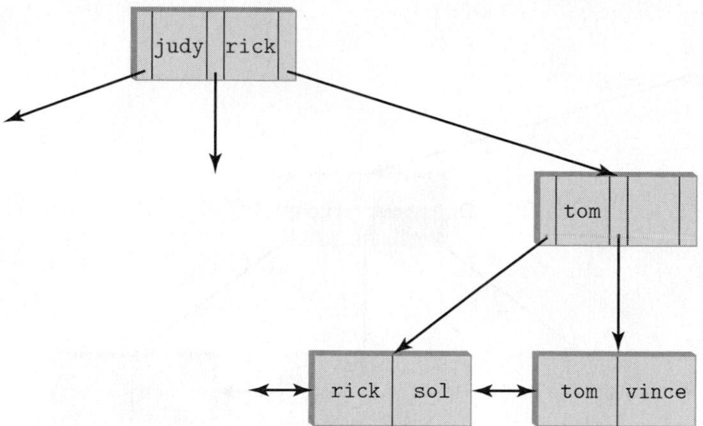

FIGURE 9.19 Portion of the index of Figure 9.16 after insertion of an entry for `vince`.

Inserting new entries. A major advantage of the B^+ tree over an ISAM index is its adaptation to dynamically changing tables. Instead of creating an overflow chain when a new record is added, we modify the tree structure so that it remains balanced. As the structure changes, entries are added to and deleted from pages and the number of separators in a page varies between $\Phi/2$ and Φ.

Example 9.5.2 (B^+ Tree). Let us trace a sequence of insertions into the index of Figure 9.16, viewing that index as a B^+ tree. In this case, $\Phi = 2$. Figure 9.19 shows the rightmost subtree after a record for `vince` has been added. Since `vince` follows `tom` in search-key order and there is room for an additional leaf entry in the rightmost leaf page, no modification to the B^+ tree structure is required.

Suppose that the next insertion is `vera`, which follows `tom`. Since the rightmost leaf page is now full, a new page is needed, but instead of creating an overflow page (as in an ISAM index), we create a new leaf page. This requires modifying the structure of the index, which sets the B^+ tree solution apart from the ISAM solution. Because the ordering of search-key values at the leaf level must be preserved, `vera` must be inserted between `tom` and `vince`. Hence, it is not sufficient simply to create a new rightmost leaf page containing `vera`. Instead, we must allocate a new leaf page and split the search-key values in sorted order between the existing leaf page and the new page so that roughly half are stored in each. The result is shown in Figure 9.20. The smallest entry in the new leaf page, labeled C in the figure, is `vince`, so `vince` becomes a new separator in index page D (all entries in leaf page B are less than `vince`), which fortunately has enough room for that entry. In general, when a (full) leaf page containing Φ entries is split to accommodate an insertion, we create two leaf pages—one containing $\Phi/2 + 1$ entries and the other containing $\Phi/2$ entries—and we insert a separator at the next index level up. We refer to this as Rule 1. Note that we have both a separator and a leaf entry for `vince`.

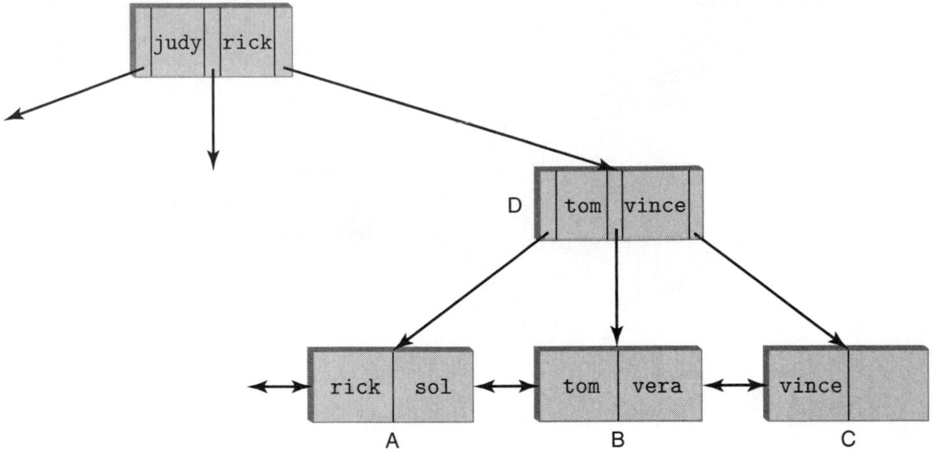

FIGURE 9.20 Index subtree of Figure 9.19 after the insertion of `vera` has caused the split of a leaf page.

If the next insertion is `rob`, the problem is more severe. The new index entry must lie between `rick` and `sol`, requiring a split of page A, and four pointers are needed at the separator level (to refer to the two pages that follow from the split as well as B and C) in page D. Unfortunately, a separator page can accommodate only three pointers, and therefore we must split D as well. Furthermore, following Rule 1, the new separator value is `sol` (since it will be the smallest search-key value in the new leaf page). In the general case, an index page is split when it has to store $\Phi + 1$ separators (in this case `sol`, `tom`, and `vince`) and thus $\Phi + 2$ pointers to index pages at the next lower level. Each page that results from the split contains $\Phi/2 + 1$ pointers and $\Phi/2$ separators. It might seem that we have misplaced a separator, but we are not done yet.

The situation after the split of page A into A1 and A2 and page D into D1 and D2 is shown in Figure 9.21. Note that the total number of separator entries in pages D1 and D2—two—is the same as in page D, although the values are different: `sol` has replaced `tom`. This number seems strange, since the number of separators required to separate the pages at the leaf level is three (`sol`, `tom`, and `vince`). The explanation is that `tom`, the separator that separates the values contained in the two subtrees rooted at D1 and D2, becomes a separator at a higher level. In general, in splitting a page at the separator level to accommodate $\Phi + 1$ separators, the middle separator in the separator sequence is not stored in either of the two separator pages resulting from the split, but instead is *pushed up* the tree. We refer to this pushing as Rule 2.

Hence, we are not finished. The separator has to be pushed and a reference has to be made to the new separator page (D2) at the next-higher index level. In other words, the process has to be repeated. In general, the process has to be repeated until an index level is reached that can accommodate a new separator without requiring

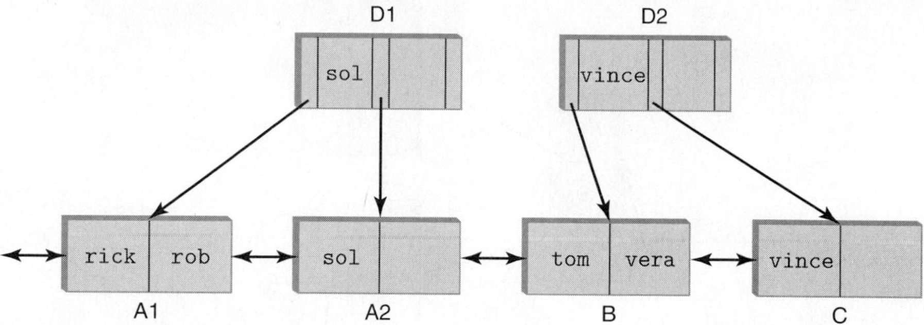

FIGURE 9.21 Index subtree of Figure 9.20 after the insertion of `rob` has caused the split of a leaf page and of a separator page.

a split. In our example, the next index level is the root page, and since it cannot accommodate another separator, it will have to be split. In this case, the sequence of separators that we are dealing with is `judy`, `rick`, and `tom`. Using Rule 2, `rick` must be pushed up to be stored in a new root page.

This completes the process and yields the B^+ tree shown in Figure 9.22. Note that the number of levels has increased by 1 but that the tree remains balanced. Four I/O operations are now required to access any leaf page. If the table is accessed frequently, the number of I/O operations might be reduced by keeping one or more of the upper levels of the tree in main memory. Also note that, in splitting A, the sibling pointer in B must be updated, which requires an additional I/O operation. ■

The above example explains the main points of the process of inserting an entry into a B^+ tree. The algorithm is summarized in pseudocode in Figure 9.23.

A node split incurs overhead and should be avoided, if possible. One way to do this is to use a fillfactor that is less than 1 when the B^+ tree is created. A fillfactor of .75 is reasonable (however, if a table is read-only the fillfactor should be 1). Of course, this might increase the number of levels in the tree. One variation of the insertion algorithm that attempts to avoid a split involves redistributing index entries in the leaf-level pages. For example, if we insert a leaf entry for `tony`, in Figure 9.20 we might make room in page B by moving the entry for `vera` to page C (and replacing `vince` with `vera` as the separator in page D). Redistribution is generally done at the leaf level between neighboring pages that have the same immediate parent. Such pages are referred to as **siblings**.

Deleting entries. Deletion presents a different problem. When pages become sparsely occupied, the tree can become deeper than necessary, increasing the cost of each search down the tree and each scan across the leaf level. To avoid such situations, pages can be compacted. A minimum occupancy requirement of $\Phi/2$ entries

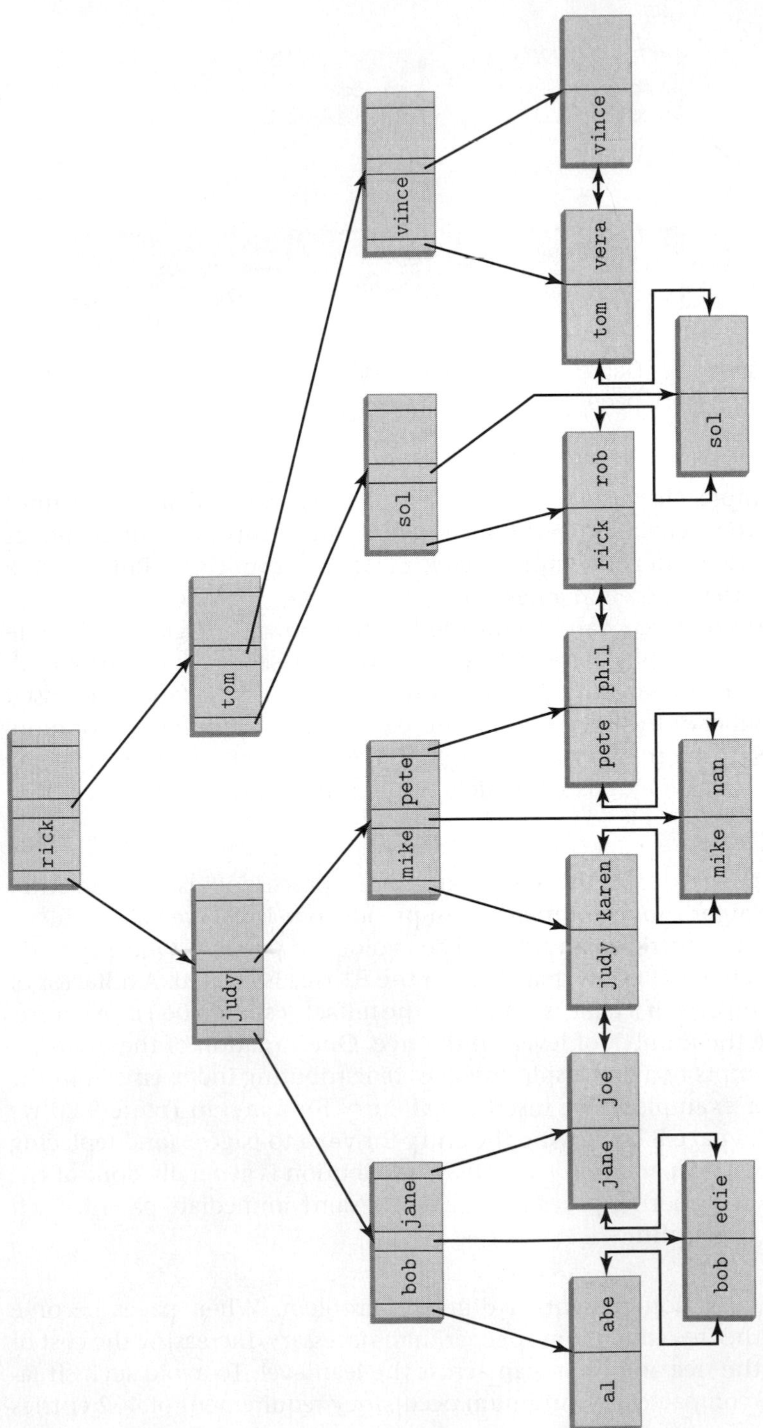

FIGURE 9.22 B^+ tree that results from the insertion of `vince`, `vera`, and `rob` into the index of Figure 9.16.

FIGURE 9.23 A pseudocode rendering of the B+ tree insertion algorithm. An entry in the index has the form $< k, P >$ where k is a search-key value and P is a pointer, and the tree nodes have the form $(P_0, < k_1, P_1 >, < k_2, P_2 >, ..., < k_{n-1}, P_{n-1} >, < k_n, P_n >)$. In the figure, `*ptr` denotes dereferencing (i.e., the actual tree nodes pointed to by the pointer `ptr`) and `&node` denotes the address of `node`.

```
proc insert(subtree, new, pushup)
// Insert entry *new into subtree with root page *subtree (new and subtree are pointers to nodes).
The maximum number of separators in a page is Φ (assumed to be even). pushup is null initially
and upon return unless the node pointed to by subtree is split. In the latter case it contains a pointer
to the entry that must be pushed up the tree. If the number of levels in the tree increases, *subtree
is the new root page when the outer level of recursion returns.

  if *subtree is a non-leaf node
        (let's denote it N = (P0, <k1, P1>, ..., <kn, Pn>)) then
    let n be the number of separators in N
    let i be such that ki ≤ (search-key value of *new) < ki+1
        or i = 0 if (search-key value of *new) < k1
        or i = n if kn ≤ (search-key value of *new);
    insert(Pi, new, pushup);
    if pushup is null return;
    else       // then *pushup has the form <key,ptr>
      if N has fewer that Φ entries then // recall: N = *subtree
        insert *pushup in N in sorted order;
        pushup := null,
        return;
      else       // N has Φ entries
        add *pushup to a list of the entries in N in sorted order
        split N: first Φ/2 + 1 entries stay in N,
          last Φ/2 entries are placed in new page, N';
        pushup := &(<smallest key value in N', &(N')>);
        if N was the root of the entire B+ tree then
          create a new root-page N'' containing <&(N), *pushup>;
          subtree := &(N'');
        return;
  if *subtree is a leaf page (denoted L) then
    if L has fewer than Φ entries then
      insert *new in L in sorted order;
      pushup := null;
      return;
    else   // L has Φ entires
      add *new to a list of the entries in L in sorted order
      split L: first (Φ/2) + 1 entries stay in L;
                the remaining Φ/2 entries placed in a new page, L';
      pushup := &(<smallest key value in L', &(L')>);
      set sibling pointers in L, L', and in the leaf page following L';
      return;
endproc
```

FIGURE 9.24 A pseudocode rendering of the first part of the B^+ tree deletion algorithm. An entry in the index has the form $< k, P >$ where k is a search-key value and P is a pointer, and the tree nodes have the form $(P_0, < k_1, P_1 >, < k_2, P_2 >, ..., < k_{n-1}, P_{n-1} >, < k_n, P_n >)$. In the figure, `*ptr` denotes dereferencing of `ptr` and `&node` denotes the address of `node`.

```
proc delete(parentptr, subtree, oldkey, removedptr)
// Delete oldkey from subtree with root *subtree.
// The minimum number of separators in a page is Φ/2 (Φ is assumed to be even).
// parentptr is null initially,
// but contains a pointer to the current index page of the caller thereafter.
// removedptr is null initially and upon return, unless a child page has been
// deleted. In that case, removedptr is a pointer to that deleted child.
// On return, *subtree is the (possibly new) root of the tree.

  if *subtree is a non-leaf node
        (henceforth denoted N = (P_0, <k_1, P_1>, ..., <k_n, P_n>)) then
    let n be the number of separators in N;
    let i be such that k_i ≤ oldkey < k_{i+1}
        or i = 0 if oldkey < k_1 or i = n if k_n ≤ oldkey;
    delete(subtree, P_i, oldkey, removedptr);
    if removedptr is null then return;   // no pages deleted in the process
    else   // a child page has been deleted
      remove separator containing removedptr from N;
      if N is the root of the entire B+ tree then
        if N is not empty then return;
        else    // delete root node
          discard N;
          subtree := P_i;
          return;
```

per page is set for this purpose. When a deletion is made from a page, p, with $\Phi/2$ entries, an attempt is first made to redistribute entries from one of p's siblings. This is not possible if both siblings also have $\Phi/2$ entries. In this case p is merged with a sibling: p and its sibling are deleted and replaced with a new page containing the $\Phi - 1$ entries previously stored in the deleted pages. Furthermore, a separator entry is deleted from the parent node in the next-higher level of the tree (recall that siblings have a common parent). Just as the effect of a split can propagate up the tree, so too can the effect of a merge. The deletion can cause the parent page to fall below the threshold level, requiring separators to be redistributed or pages to be merged. If the effect propagates up to the root and the last separator in the root is deleted, the depth of the tree is reduced by 1.

The deletion algorithm is summarized in pseudocode in Figures 9.24 and 9.25. The algorithm calls procedures `redistributeleft` and `redistributeright` to

FIGURE 9.24 (continued)

```
// N is not the root
if (number of entries in N) ≥ Φ/2 then
  removedptr := null;
  return;
else      // N has fewer than Φ/2 entries
  use parentptr to locate siblings of N;
  if N has a sibling, S, with more than Φ/2 entries then
    if S is a right sibling of N then
      redistributeleft(parentptr, subtree, &(S)); // recall that here *subtree = N
      removedptr := null;
      return;
    else    // S is a left sibling of N
      redistributeright(parentptr, &(S), subtree); // recall that here *subtree = N
      removedptr := null;
      return;
  else      // merge N and a sibling S
    choose a sibling, S;
    let M1 be the leftmost of the nodes N and S, and M2 the rightmost;
    removedptr := &(M2);
    move all entries from M2 to M1;
    discard M2;
    return;
```

move an entry from a sibling to a page whose occupancy has fallen below $\Phi/2$. `redistributeleft` is shown in Figure 9.26. `redistributeright` is similar (see Exercise 9.13).

Since tables tend to grow over time, some database systems do not enforce the minimum occupancy requirement but simply delete pages when they become empty. If necessary, a tree can be completely reconstructed to eliminate pages that do not meet the minimum occupancy requirement.

Multiple identical search-key values. Although we ignored this possibility in our previous discussion, when the search key is not a candidate key of the table, multiple rows might have the same search-key value. Suppose, for example, that a record for another student named `vince` is added to the B^+ tree of Figure 9.19. Using Rule 1, the rightmost leaf node must then be split to accommodate a second index entry with search-key value `vince`, and a new separator must be created, as shown in Figure 9.27. The first thing to note is that the search-key values in page B are no longer strictly less than the value `vince` in the separator entry in D. The second is that a search for `vince` terminates in leaf page C and therefore does not find the

FIGURE 9.25 A continuation of the pseudocode from Figure 9.24 for the procedure `delete()`.

```
if *subtree is a leaf node (denoted L) then
  if oldkey is not in L then return;
  if (number of entries in L) > Φ/2 then
    delete entry containing oldkey from L;
    removedptr := null;
    return;
  else    // L has Φ/2 entries
    delete entry containing oldkey from L;
    use sibling pointers to locate siblings of L;
    if L has a sibling, S, with more than Φ/2 entries then
        if S is a right sibling of L then
          redistributeleft(parentptr, subtree, &(S)); // here *subtree = L
          removedptr := null;
          return;
        else  // S is a left sibling of L
          redistributeright(parentptr, &(S), subtree); // here *subtree = L
          removedptr := null;
          return;
    else       // merge L and a sibling S
      choose a sibling, S;
      let M1 be the leftmost of the nodes L and S, and M2 the rightmost;
      removedptr := &(M2);
      move all entries from M2 to M1;
      discard M2;
      adjust sibling pointers;
      return;
endproc
```

---

index entry for the other `vince` in B. Finally, if rows for additional students named `vince` are inserted, there will be several separators for `vince` at the lowest (and perhaps a higher) separator level. One way of handling duplicates is thus to modify the search algorithm to accommodate these differences. We leave the details of the modification to an exercise.

Another approach to handling the insertion of a duplicate is simply to create an overflow page if the leaf is full. In this way, the search algorithm does not have to be modified, although overflow chains can grow large and the cost estimates for using the tree described earlier will no longer apply.

FIGURE 9.26 A pseudocode for the procedure `redistributeleft()` called by the procedure `delete()` in Figure 9.24. The procedure moves a key from $*rightptr$ to $*parentptr$ and from $*parentprt$ to $*leftptr$.

```
proc redistributeleft(parentptr, leftptr, rightptr)
//Let e1 be entry in *parentptr containing rightptr: e1 = < k1, rightptr >
//Let e2 be smallest entry in *rightptr: e2 = < k2, ptr >
//Let P0 be the leftmost pointer in *rightptr
  add < k1, P0 > to *leftptr;
  delete e1 from *parentptr;
  add < k2, rightptr > to *parentptr;
  delete e2 from *rightptr;
  set the leftmost pointer in *rightptr to ptr;
endproc
```

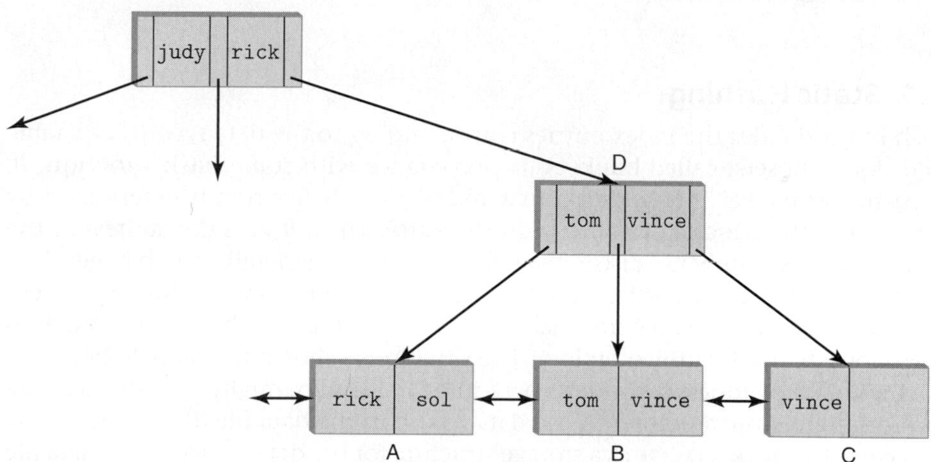

FIGURE 9.27 Index subtree of Figure 9.19 after the insertion of a duplicate entry for `vince` has caused the split of a leaf page.

9.6 Hash Indexing

Hashing is an important search algorithm in many computer applications. In this section, we discuss its use for indexing database relations, looking at both **static hashing**, where the size of the hash table stays constant, and **dynamic hashing**, where the table may grow or shrink. The first technique is superior when the contents of a relation are more or less stable; the second is superior when indexing relations that are subject to frequent inserts and deletes.

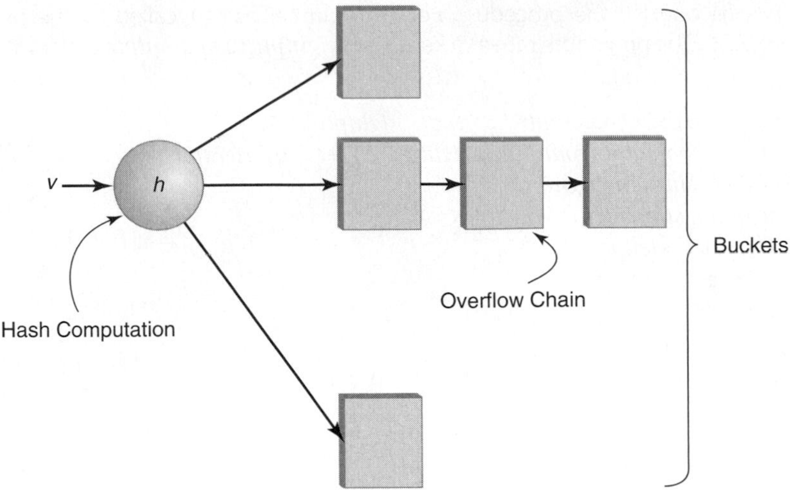

FIGURE 9.28 Schematic depiction of a hash index.

9.6.1 Static Hashing

A hash index divides the index entries corresponding to the data records of a table into disjoint subsets, called **buckets**, in accordance with some **hash function**, *h*. The particular bucket into which a new index entry is inserted is determined by applying *h* to the search-key value, *v*, in the entry. Thus, *h*(*v*) is the address of the bucket. Since the number of distinct search-key values is generally much larger than the number of buckets, a particular bucket will contain entries with different search-key values. Each bucket is generally stored in a page (which might be extended with an overflow chain), identified by *h*(*v*). The situation is shown in Figure 9.28.

As with a tree index, an index entry in a hash index might contain the data record or might store a pointer to the data record in the data file. If it contains the data record, the buckets serve as a storage structure for the data file itself: the data file is a sequence of buckets. If it contains a pointer to the record, the index entries are stored as a sequence of buckets in an index file and the records in the data file can be stored in arbitrary order. In this case, the hash index is secondary and unclustered. If the data records referred to by the index entries in a particular bucket are grouped together in the data file, the hash index is clustered. This implies that data records with the same value of the search key are physically close to each other on mass storage.

Hash search. An equality search for index entries with search key *v* is carried out by computing *h*(*v*), retrieving the bucket stored in the referenced page, and then scanning its contents to locate the index entries (if any) containing *v*. Since no other bucket can possibly contain entries with that key value, if the entry is not found in the bucket, it is not in the file. Thus, without having to maintain an index structure analogous to a tree, the target index entry of an equality search can be retrieved with a single I/O operation (assuming no overflow chain).

A properly designed hash index can perform an equality search more efficiently than a tree index can, since, with a tree index, several index-level pages must be retrieved before the leaf level is reached. If a succession of equality searches must be performed, however, a tree index might be preferable. Suppose, for example, that it is necessary to retrieve the records with search-key values $k_0, k_1, \ldots, k_l$, that the sequence is ordered on the search key (i.e., $k_i < k_{i+1}$), and that the sequence represents the order in which records are to be retrieved. Because the index leaves of a tree index are sorted on the key, the likelihood of cache hits when retrieving index entries is great. But with a hash index, each search-key value might hash to a different bucket, so the retrieval of successive index entries in the sequence might not generate cache hits. The example shows that, in evaluating which index might improve an application's performance, the entire application should be considered.

Despite the apparent advantage that hash indices have for equality searches, tree indices are generally preferable because they are more versatile: hash indices cannot support range or partial-key searches. A partial-key search is not supported because the hash function must be applied to the entire key. To understand why a range search cannot be supported efficiently, consider the student table discussed earlier. Suppose that we want to use a hash index to retrieve the records of all individuals in the file with names between `paul` and `tom`. Hashing can determine that there are no individuals with the name `paul`, and it can retrieve the index entry for `tom`, but it is of no help in locating index entries for individuals with names inside the range because we have no recourse but to apply the hash function to every *possible* value in the range—only a few of which are likely to appear in the database. Successive entries in the range are spread randomly through the buckets, so the cost of evaluating such a range query is proportional to the number of entries in the range. In the worst case (when the number of such entries exceeds the number of pages in the file), the cost associated with the use of the index might exceed the cost of simply scanning the entire file!

In contrast, with a clustered ISAM or B^+ tree index the data records in the range can be located by using the index to find the first record and then using a simple scan. A simple scan is possible because data records in the file are maintained in search-key order. The cost of this search is proportional to the number of pages in the range plus the cost of searching the index. The important difference is that the I/O cost of a B^+ tree search depends on the number of *leaf pages* in the range, while the cost of a hash index search depends on the number of *records* in the range, which is much larger.

Hash functions. Hash functions are chosen with the goal of randomizing the index entries over the buckets in such a way that, for an average instance of the indexed table, the number of index entries in each bucket is roughly the same. For example, h might be defined as

$$h(v) = (a * v + b) \bmod M$$

where a and b are constants chosen to optimize the way the function randomizes over the search-key values, M is the number of buckets, and v is a search-key value treated as a binary number in the calculation of the hash value. Note that, with some applications, no matter how clever the hash function, it might be impossible to keep the population of a bucket close to the average: if the search key is not a candidate key a large fraction of the rows might have the same search-key value and hence will necessarily reside in the same bucket. For simplicity, we assume M to be a power of 2 in all of the algorithms that follow (but in practice it is usually a large prime number).

The indexing scheme we have just described is referred to as a static hash because M is fixed when the index is created. With static hashing, the location mechanism is the hash function—no data structures are involved in this case. The efficiency of static hashing depends on the assumption that all entries in each bucket fit in a single page. The number of entries in a bucket is inversely proportional to M: if fewer buckets are used, the average bucket occupancy is larger. The larger the average occupancy, the more unlikely it is that a bucket will fit in a page and so overflow pages will be needed. The choice of M is thus crucial to the index's efficient operation.

If Φ is the maximum number of index entries that can fit in a page and L is the total number of index entries, choosing M to be L/Φ leads to buckets that overflow a single page. For one thing, h does not generally divide entries exactly evenly over the buckets, so we can expect that more than Φ entries will be assigned to some buckets. For another, bucket overflow results if the table grows over time. One way to deal with this growth is to use a fillfactor less than 1 and enlarge the number of buckets. The average bucket occupancy is chosen to be $\Phi * \mathit{fillfactor}$ so that buckets with larger than average populations can be accommodated in a single page. M then becomes $L/(\Phi * \mathit{fillfactor})$. Fillfactors as low as .5 are not unreasonable. The disadvantage of enlarging M is that space requirements increase because some buckets have few entries.

This technique reduces, but does not solve, the overflow problem, particularly since the growth of some tables cannot be predicted in advance. Therefore, bucket overflow must be dealt with, and this can be done with overflow chains as shown in Figure 9.28. Unfortunately, as with an ISAM index, overflow chains can be inefficient. Because an entire bucket must be scanned with each equality search, a search through a bucket stored in n pages costs n I/O operations. This multiplies the cost of a search by n over the ideal case. Fortunately, studies have shown that $n = 1.2$ for a good hash function.

OPTIONAL

9.6.2 Dynamic Hashing Algorithms

Just as B^+ trees are adapted from tree indices to deal with dynamic tables, dynamic hashing schemes are adapted from static hashing to deal with the same problem. The goal of dynamic hashing is to change the number of buckets dynamically in order to reduce or eliminate overflow chains as rows are added and deleted. Two dynamic hashing algorithms that have received the most attention are *extendable hashing* and *linear hashing*. We briefly discuss them here.

Static hashing uses a fixed hash function, h, to partition the set of all possible search-key values into subsets, S_i, $1 \le i \le M$, and maps each subset to a bucket, B_i. Each element, v, of S_i has the property that $h(v)$ identifies B_i. Dynamic hashing schemes allow S_i to be partitioned at run time into disjoint subsets, S_i' and S_i'', and B_i to be split into B_i' and B_i'', such that the elements of S_i' are mapped to B_i' and the elements of S_i'' are mapped to B_i''. By reducing the number of values that map to a bucket, a split has the potential of replacing one overflowing bucket with two that are not full. A change in the mapping implies a change in the hash function that takes into account the split of a single bucket (or the merge of two buckets). Extendable and linear hashing do this mapping in different ways.

Extendable hashing. **Extendable hashing** uses a sequence of hash functions, $h_0, h_1, \ldots, h_b$, based on a single hash function, h, which hashes a search-key value into a b-bit integer. For each k, $0 \le k \le b$, $h_k(v)$ is the integer formed by the last k bits of $h(v)$. Stated mathematically,

$$h_k(v) = h(v) \bmod 2^k$$

Thus, the number of elements in the range of each function, h_k, is twice that of its predecessor, h_{k-1}. At any given time, a particular function in the sequence, h_k, directs all searches.

Unlike static hashing, dynamic hashing uses a second stage of mapping to determine the bucket associated with some search-key value, v. This mapping uses a level of indirection implemented through a directory, as shown in Figure 9.29. The value produced by $h_k(v)$ serves as an index into the directory, and the pointer in the directory entry refers to the bucket associated with v. The key point is that distinct entries in the directory might refer to the same bucket, so $v1$ and $v2$ might be mapped to the same bucket even though $h_k(v1)$ and $h_k(v2)$ are distinct. Example 9.6.1 shows how this situation might arise.

Example 9.6.1 (Extendable Hashing). Consider an extendable hash index of student names as shown in Figure 9.29, and suppose that the range of h is the set of integers between 0 and $2^{10} - 1$. We assume that a bucket page can hold two index entries. The figure depicts the algorithm at a point at which h_2 is used to hash search-key values (and, thus, the directory contains $2^2 = 4$ entries). Since h_2 uses only the last two bits of the values in the range of h, the figure could be produced by the following function h:

v	$h(v)$
pete	1001111010
mary	0100000000
jane	1100011110
bill	0100000000
john	0001101001

OPTIONAL

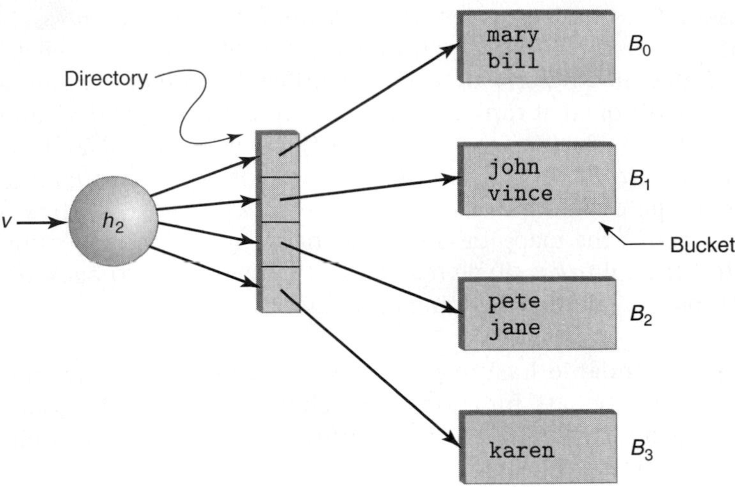

FIGURE 9.29 With extendable hashing, the hash result is mapped to a bucket through a directory.

OPTIONAL

```
vince 1101110101
karen 0000110111
```

Thus, h hashes `pete` to `1001111010`. Since h_2 uses only the last two bits (10), it indicates that the third directory entry refers to the bucket, B_2, that contains `pete`.

Suppose that we now insert a record for `sol` into the table and that h(`sol`) = 0001010001. h_2 maps `john`, `vince`, and `sol` to B_1, causing an overflow. Rather than create an overflow chain, extendable hashing splits B_1 so that a new bucket, B_5, is created, as shown in Figure 9.30. To accommodate five buckets, it is necessary to use a hash function whose range contains more than four values, so the index replaces h_2 with h_3. Since the high-order bit of h_3(`john`), 0, and h_3(`vince`), 1, differ (whereas the two low-order bits, 01, are the same), h_3 avoids overflow by mapping `john` and `vince` to different buckets (h_2 does not do this). In Figure 9.30, note that if both $v1$ and $v2$ are elements of B_1 (or B_5), $h(v1)$ and $h(v2)$ agree in their last three bits.

The directory is needed to compensate for the fact that only B_1 has been split. Indeed, h_3 not only distinguishes between `john` and `vince`, but also produces different values for `pete` (`010`) and `jane` (`110`). Hence, without a directory it would be necessary to split B_2 as well when h_2 is replaced by h_3. By interposing a directory between the hash computation and the buckets, we can map both `pete` and `jane` to B_2, which we do by storing a pointer to B_2 in both the third (`010`) and seventh (`110`) directory entries. As a result, in contrast to B_1 and B_5, if $v1$ and $v2$ are elements of B_2, the values of the third bit of $h(v1)$ and $h(v2)$ might differ (but the values of the first two bits must be 10). ■

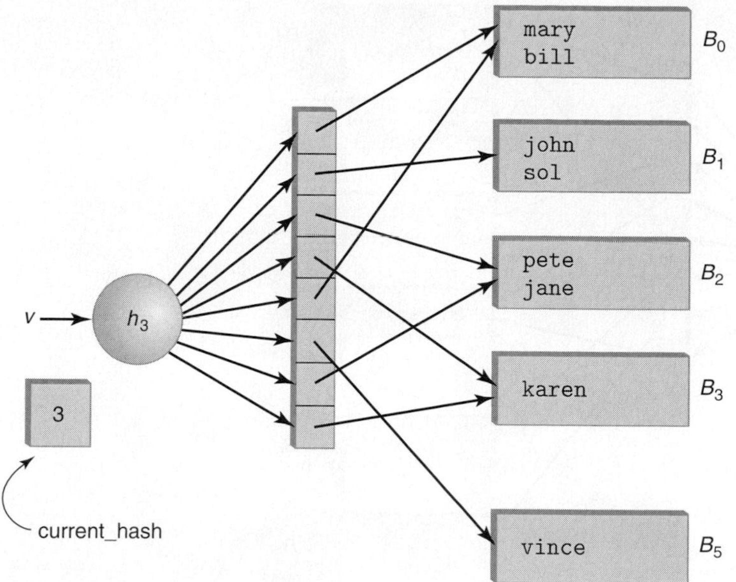

FIGURE 9.30 Bucket B_1 of Figure 9.29 has been split using extendable hashing.

The algorithm used in moving from Figure 9.29 to Figure 9.30 is quite simple.

1. A new bucket, B', is allocated and the contents of the overflowing bucket, B, are split between B and B' using the next hash function in the sequence.
2. A new directory is created by concatenating a copy of the old directory with itself.
3. The pointer to B in the copy is replaced by a pointer to B'.

Thus, the two halves of the directory in Figure 9.30 are identical except for the pointers in the second and sixth entry (which are the two halves of the bucket that has been split).

To give a complete description of the algorithm, we must deal with a few additional issues. First of all, how do we know which hash function in the sequence to use when a search has to be performed? That's easy. We simply store the index of the current hash function along with the directory. We assume a variable *current_hash* for this purpose, which is initialized to 0 (with only a single directory entry). In general, the number of directory entries is $2^{current\_hash}$. The value of *current_hash* is 2 in Figure 9.29 (not shown) and 3 in Figure 9.30.

A more subtle problem arises when an overflow occurs, but the current hash function can handle the new bucket that must be created. The situation is illustrated in Example 9.6.2, which extends Example 9.6.1.

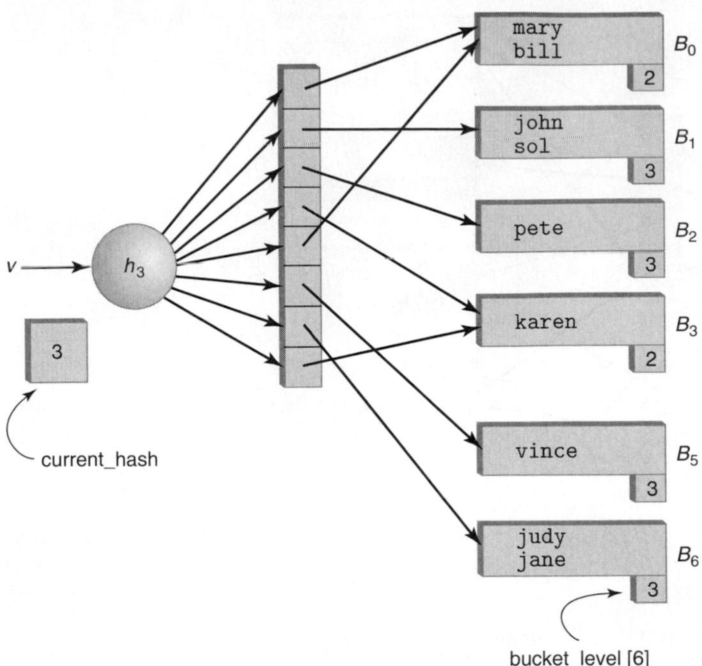

FIGURE 9.31 Bucket B_2 of Figure 9.30 is split, without enlargement of the directory.

Example 9.6.2 (Extendable Hashing, continued). Suppose a row for `judy` is inserted into the hash table shown in Figure 9.30 and $h($`judy`$) = 1110000110$. `judy` is mapped to B_2 in Figure 9.30, causing the bucket to overflow and requiring it to be split. However, this situation is different from the one that caused us to replace h_2 with h_3, since h_3 itself is capable of distinguishing among index entries that are mapped to B_2 (recall that the hash values of the index entries in B_2 agree in only their last two bits). In the example, h_3 distinguishes `judy` and `jane` (`110`) from `pete` (`010`), so, instead of moving to a new hash function to deal with the overflow, we need only create a new bucket for `judy` and `jane` and update the appropriate pointer in the directory to refer to it. This is shown in Figure 9.31, in which the new bucket is labeled B_6. ■

There is a reason that the directory does not have to be enlarged this time. Each time it is enlarged, it becomes capable of storing pointers to accommodate the split of *every* bucket that exists at that time, whereas, in fact, only *one* bucket is actually split. Thus, when a directory is extended, all but one of the pointers in its new portion simply point back to an existing bucket. The directory in Figure 9.30 was created to accommodate the split of B_1, so only entry `101` in the new portion of that directory refers to a new bucket. Since entries `010` and `110` both point to B_2, the directory can accommodate a split of B_2 without further enlargement.

We can detect this case by storing, along with each bucket, the number of times it has been split. We refer to this value as the *bucket level* and associate a variable, *bucket_level*[i] to store it. Initially *bucket_level*[0] is 0 and, when B_i is split, we use *bucket_level*[i] + 1 as the bucket level of both B_i and the newly created bucket. Because each time the directory is enlarged without splitting B_i, we double the number of pointers in the directory that refer to B_i, $2^{current\_hash-(bucket\_level[i])}$ is the number of pointers that point to B_i in the directory. Furthermore, when a bucket is split, the index entries are divided between the two resulting buckets so that, if $v1$ and $v2$ are both elements of B_i, then $h(v1)$ and $h(v2)$ agree in their last *bucket_level*[i] bits.

bucket_level[1] is 3 in both Figure 9.30 (not shown) and Figure 9.31, whereas *bucket_level*[2] is 2 in Figure 9.30 and is incremented to 3 in Figure 9.31.

The merge of two buckets can be handled using the inverse of the split algorithm. If the deletion of an index entry causes a bucket, B', to become empty, and B' and B'' were created when B was split, B' can be released by redirecting the pointer to B' in the directory so that it points to B'' and decrementing the bucket level of B''. In addition, when merging creates a state in which the upper and lower halves of the directory are identical, one half can be released and *current_hash* decremented. Merging is often not implemented since it is assumed that, although a table might temporarily shrink, it is likely to grow in the long term, and therefore a merge will ultimately be followed by a split.

Extendable hashing eliminates most of the overflow chains that develop with static hashing when the number of index entries grows. Unfortunately, though, it has several deficiencies. One is that additional space is required to store the directory. The other is that the indirection through the directory to locate the buffer requires additional time. If the directory is small, it can be kept in main memory, so neither of these deficiencies is major. In that case, directory access does not impose the cost of an additional I/O operation. Nevertheless, a directory can grow quite large and, if it cannot be kept in main memory, the I/O cost of extendable hashing is twice that of static hashing. Finally, splitting a bucket does not necessarily divide its contents and eliminate the overflow. For example, when the overflow is caused by multiple entries with the same search-key value, splitting cannot remove the overflow.

Linear hashing. Because the deficiencies of extendable hashing are associated with the introduction of a directory, it is natural to search for a dynamic hashing scheme for which a directory is not required. A directory is needed with extendable hashing because, when a bucket is split, it might be necessary to switch to a hash function with a larger range: search keys stored in different buckets must hash to different values. Thus, the range of h_{i+1} contains twice as many elements as the range of h_i, and therefore $h_i(v)$ and $h_{i+1}(v)$ might not be the same. However, if v is an element of a bucket that is not being split, the index must direct the search to that bucket before and after the split. The directory overcomes this problem.

Can this problem be overcome in a way that does not involve a directory? One possible way uses the same sequence of hash functions, $h_0, h_1, \ldots, h_b$, as extendable hashing does, but differently. h_i and h_{i+1} are used concurrently: h_i for values belonging in buckets that have not been split and h_{i+1} for values belonging in

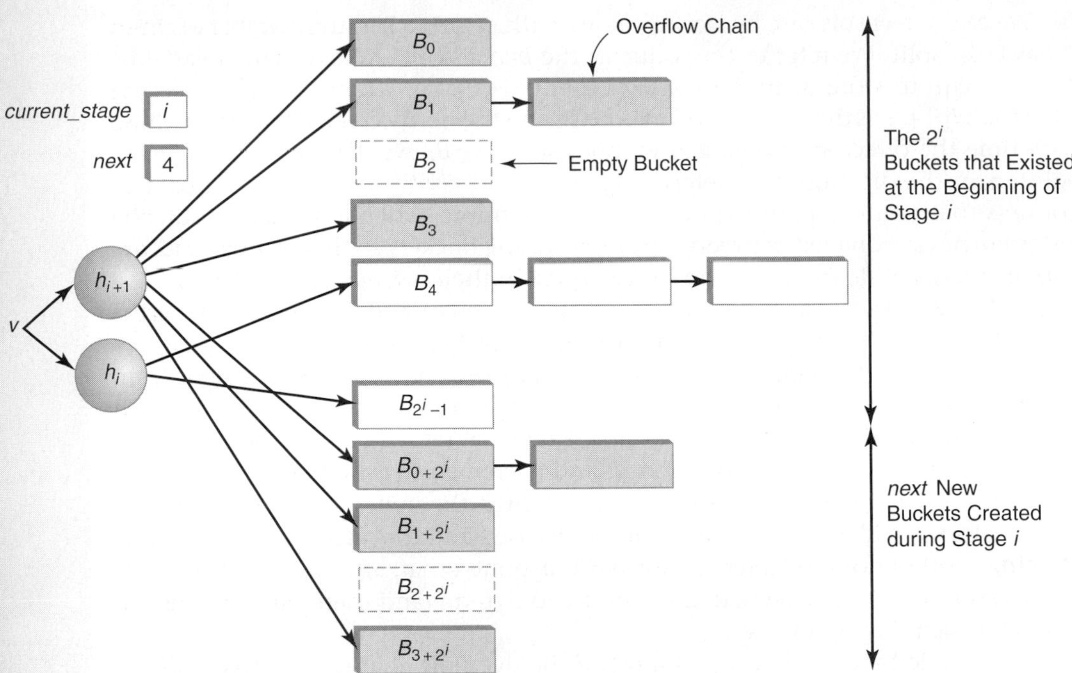

FIGURE 9.32 Linear hashing splits buckets consecutively. The shaded buckets are accessed through h_{i+1}.

OPTIONAL

buckets that have. This approach has the advantage of providing the same mapping before and after the split for search keys that belong in buckets not involved in the split. The trick is to be able to tell, when initiating a search through the index, which hash function to use.

With **linear hashing**, bucket splitting is divided into stages. The buckets that exist at the start of a stage are split consecutively during the stage so that there are twice as many buckets at the end of the stage as there were in the beginning. The situation is shown in Figure 9.32. Stages are numbered, and the number of the current stage is stored in the variable *current_stage*. Initially *current_stage* is 0 and there is a single bucket. The variable *next* indicates the next bucket in the sequence to be split during the current stage.

In Figure 9.32 *current_stage* has value i, indicating that it is in stage i. When stage i started there were 2^i buckets and *next* was initialized to 0, indicating that no buckets have yet been split in this stage. Since no buckets have yet been split, h_i, with range $\{0 \ldots 2^i - 1\}$, is used to hash search-key values for an index search. Once the algorithm starts splitting buckets during the stage, both h_i and h_{i+1} are used.

A decision is made periodically to split a bucket (we return to this point shortly), and the value of *next* is used to determine which bucket, among those that existed at the beginning of the stage, is to be split. *next* is incremented when the split occurs.

Hence, buckets are split consecutively and *next* distinguishes those that have been split in the current stage from those that have not. Since *next* refers to the next bucket to be split, buckets with index less than *next* have been split in this stage. (Split buckets and their images are shaded in the figure.) Stage i is complete when the 2^i buckets that existed when the stage began have been split.

The new bucket created when B_{next} is split has index $next + 2^i$. Elements of B_{next} are divided using h_{i+1}: if v was an element of B_{next}, it remains in that bucket if $h_{i+1}(v) = h_i(v)$ and is moved to B_{next+2^i} otherwise. When the value of *next* reaches 2^i, a new stage is started by resetting *next* to 0 and incrementing *current_stage*.

When a search is to be performed on search key v, $h_i(v)$ is calculated. If $next \leq h_i(v) < 2^i$, the bucket indicated by $h_i(v)$ is scanned for v. If $0 \leq h_i(v) < next$, the bucket indicated by $h_i(v)$ has been split and $h_i(v)$ does not provide enough information to determine whether $B_{h_i(v)}$ or $B_{h_i(v)+2^i}$ should be scanned for v. However, since h_{i+1} was used to divide the elements when the split was made, we can decide which bucket to search using $h_{i+1}(v)$. Hence, v is rehashed using h_{i+1}.

The important point to note about linear hashing is that the bucket that is split has not necessarily overflowed. We might decide to perform a split when a bucket, B_j, overflows, but the bucket that is split is B_{next}, and the value of *next* might be different from j. Note that in Figure 9.32 $next = 4$, which means that B_0, B_1, B_2, and B_3 have been split. In particular, B_2 was split when it was empty and, hence, had certainly not overflowed. Thus, linear hashing does not eliminate overflow chains (in this case, an overflow page must be created for B_j). Ultimately, however, B_j will be split because every bucket that exists at the start of the current stage is split before the stage completes. So, although an overflow chain might be created for a bucket, B, it tends to be short and is normally eliminated the next time B is split. The average lifetime of an overflow page can be decreased by splitting more frequently, although the price for doing that is lower space utilization since buckets that have not overflowed are split during each stage.

OPTIONAL

Example 9.6.3 (Linear Hashing). Given the assumption that a split occurs each time an overflow page is created, Figure 9.33 shows the sequence of states that a linear index goes through when it starts in the same state as shown for extendable hashing in Figure 9.29 and experiences the same subsequent insertions. In Figure 9.33(a) we have assumed that the index has just entered stage 2. Figure 9.33(b) shows the result of inserting `sol` into B_1. Although B_1 has overflowed, B_0 is split since *next* has value 0. Note that, since both `mary` and `bill` are hashed to B_0 by h_3, B_4 is empty. Figure 9.33(c) shows the result of inserting `judy` into B_2. B_1 is now split, eliminating its overflow chain, but a new overflow chain is created for B_2. ■

It might seem that linear hashing splits the wrong bucket, but this is the price that is paid for avoiding the directory. Splitting buckets in sequence makes it easy to distinguish the buckets that have been split from those that have not. Although overflow chains exist with linear hashing, there is no additional cost for fetching the directory.

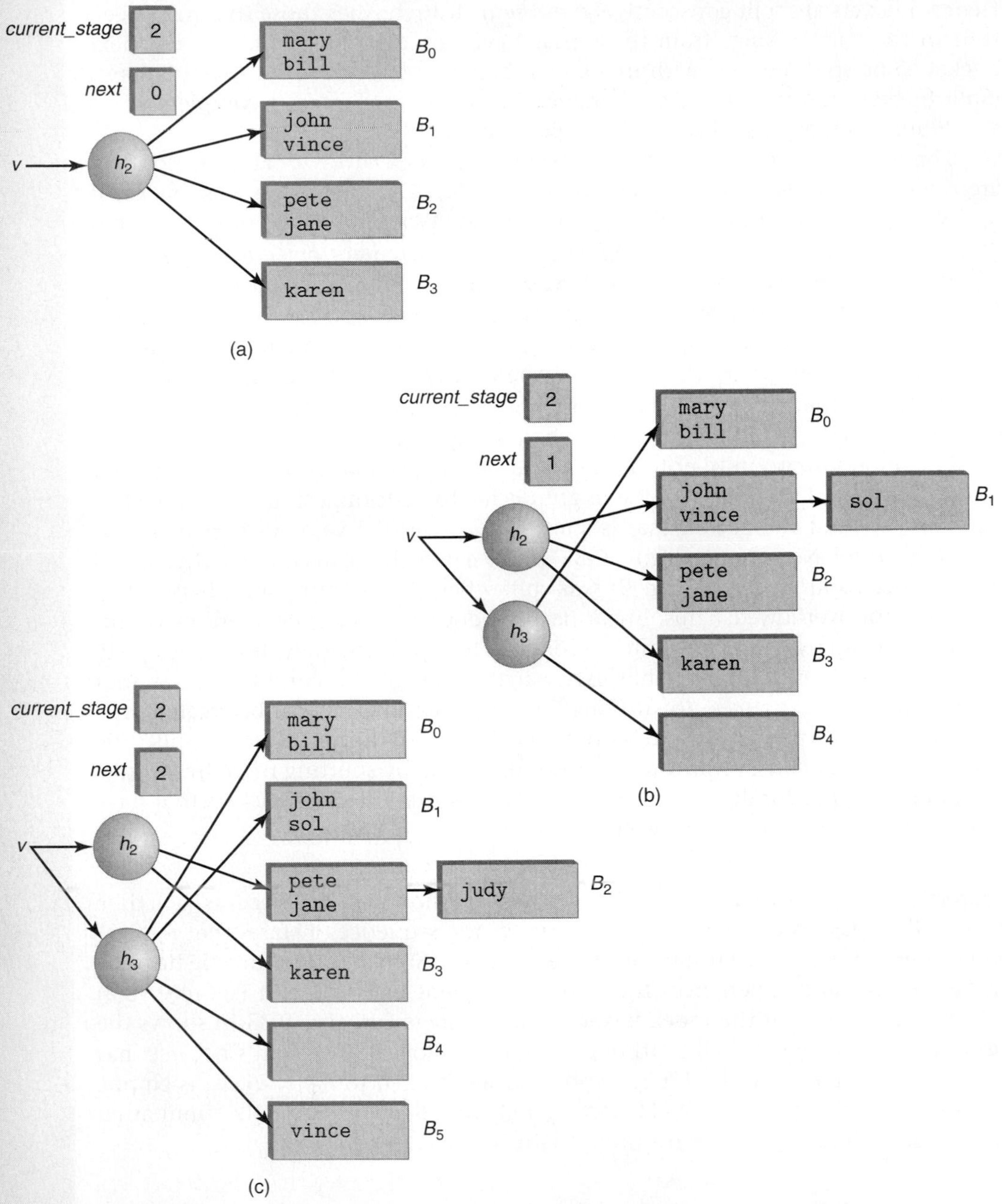

FIGURE 9.33 (a) State of a linear hash index at the beginning of a stage; (b) state after insertion of `sol`; (c) state after insertion of `judy`.

9.7 Special-Purpose Indices

The index structures introduced so far can be used in a variety of situations. However, there are a number of index structures that are applicable in only very special cases but can yield large savings in storage space and processing time. We consider two such techniques: bitmap and join indices.

9.7.1 Bitmap Indices

A **bitmap index** [O'Neil 1987] is implemented as one or more bit vectors. It is particularly appropriate for attributes that can take on only a small number of values—for example, the `Sex` attribute of the PERSON relation, which can take only two values: `Male` and `Female`. Suppose that PERSON has a total of 40,000 rows. A bitmap index on PERSON contains two bit vectors, one for each possible value of `Sex`, and each bit vector contains 40,000 bits, one for each row in PERSON. Thus, the *i*th bit in the `Male` bit vector is 1 if, in the *i*th row of PERSON, the `Sex` attribute has value `Male`. As a result, we can identify the row numbers of males by scanning the `Male` bit vector. Given the row number, we can calculate the offset from the beginning of the data file and find the desired row on disk by direct access.

Note that the space to store the index in our example is just 80,000 bits, or 10K bytes, which can fit handily in main memory. Because searching such an index is done entirely in main memory, it can be carried out quickly using sequential scan.

You may have noticed that bitmap indices seem to waste more space than they need to. Indeed, to encode the `Sex` attribute we use *two* bits, while only one bit suffices to encode all of its possible values. The reason for this is that bitmap indices are designed to trade space for efficiency, especially the efficiency of selecting on two or more attributes. To illustrate, suppose that our PERSON relation represents the result of a health survey and that there is an attribute `Smoker` and an attribute `HasHeartDisease`, both accepting just two values, `Yes` and `No`. One query might request the number of males in a certain age group who smoke but do not have heart disease. As part of this query, we have a selection with the following condition:

```
Sex = 'Male' AND Smoker = 'Yes' AND HasHeartDisease = 'No'
```

If all three attributes have bit indices, we can easily find rids of all tuples that satisfy this condition: take the logical AND of the bit strings that correspond to the `Male` value of the `Sex` attribute, the `Yes` value of the `Smoker` attribute, and the `No` value of the `HasHeartDisease` attribute. The rids of the tuples that satisfy the condition correspond to the positions that have 1 in the resulting bit string.

More generally, bitmap indices can handle selection conditions that contain OR and NOT—all we have to do is compute an appropriate Boolean combination of the corresponding bit strings. For instance, suppose that the `Age` attribute has a bitmap index with 120 bit strings with a cost of 120 bits per PERSON record. This is quite

OPTIONAL

acceptable, as a regular index will take at least 8 bytes (64 bits) per PERSON record anyway. Now we should be able to efficiently find all smoking males between the ages of 50 and 80 who never suffered from heart disease as follows: First compute the logical AND of the three bit strings as described above. Then compute the logical OR of the bit strings corresponding to ages 50 to 80 in the bitmap index for the Age attribute. Finally, compute the logical AND of the two results. Again, the 1s in the final bit string give us the Ids of the records we need to answer the query.

Bitmap indices play an important role in data mining and OLAP (online analytical processing) applications. The reason for their popularity is that such applications typically deal with queries that select on low-cardinality attributes, such as sex, age, company locations, financial periods, and the like. It also has to do with the fact that these applications operate on data that is fairly static, and bitmap indices are expensive to maintain if the underlying data changes frequently (think of what it takes to update a bitmap index if records are inserted or deleted in the data file).

In conclusion, we note that with a little more thought it is possible to devise a schema where only $n - 1$ bit vectors would be needed to index an attribute that can take n different values. In particular, for Boolean attributes, such as Sex, only one bit vector is needed. We leave the development of such a schema to Exercise 9.25.

OPTIONAL

9.7.2 Join Indices

Suppose we want to speed up an equi-join of two relations, such as $\mathbf{p} \bowtie_{A=B} \mathbf{q}$. A **join index** [Valduriez 1987] is a collection that consists of all pairs of the form $\langle p, q \rangle$, where p is a rid of a tuple, t, in **p** and q is a rid of a tuple, s, in **q**, such that $t.A = s.B$ (i.e., the two tuples join).

A join index is typically sorted lexicographically in ascending order of rids. Thus, the pair $\langle 3, 3 \rangle$ precedes the pair $\langle 4, 2 \rangle$. Such an index can also be organized as a B^+ tree or as a hash table. The values of the search key in the entries of a B^+ tree are the rids of the rows in **p**. To find the rids of all rows of **q** that join with a row of **p** having rid p, one searches the tree using p. The pointers in the leaf entries (if they exist) with search-key value p are the requested rids. Similarly, a hash index hashes on p to find the bucket containing the entries for that rid. Those entries contain the rids of the rows in **q** that join with the row in **p** at rid p.

A join index can be thought of as a precomputed join that is stored in compact form. Although its computation might require that a regular join be performed first, its advantage (apart from its compact size) is that it can be maintained incrementally: when new tuples are added to **p** or **q**, new index entries can be added to the join index without the entire join having to be recomputed from scratch (Exercise 9.24).

Given a join index, $\mathcal{J}$, the system can compute $\mathbf{p} \bowtie_{A=B} \mathbf{q}$ simply by scanning $\mathcal{J}$ and finding the rids of **p** and **q** that match. Note that, if $\mathcal{J}$ is sorted on its **p** field, the rids corresponding to the tuples in **p** appear in ascending order. Therefore, the join is computed in one scan of the index and of **p**. For each rid of a tuple in **q**, one access to **q** is also needed.

Worth mentioning is one other variation on the join index, called a **bitmapped join index** [O'Neil and Graefe 1995]. Recall that a join index is typically organized as a sorted file, a hash table, or a B^+ tree in a way that makes it easy to find the rids of all rows of **q** that join with the row of **p** at rid p. We can combine these rids in **q** in the following (at first, unusual) way: for each rid p in **p**, replace all tuples of the form $\langle p, q \rangle$ in $\mathcal{J}$ with a single tuple of the form

$$\langle p, \textit{ bitmap for matching tuples in } \mathbf{q} \rangle$$

The bitmap here has 1 in the ith position if and only if the ith tuple in **q** joins with the tuple in **p** at the rid p. Attaching a bitmap might seem like a huge waste of space, because each bitmap has as many bits as there are tuples in **q**. However, bitmaps are easily compressed, so this is not a major issue.

9.8 Tuning Issues: Choosing Indices for an Application

Each type of index is capable of improving the performance of a particular group of queries. Hence, in choosing the indices to support a particular application it is important to know the queries that are likely to be executed and their approximate frequency. Creating an index to improve the performance of a rarely executed query is probably not wise since each index carries with it added overhead, particularly for operations that update the database.

For example, if query (9.2) on page 332, with the value of `StudId` specified as a parameter, is executed frequently, an index to ensure fast response might be called for. The search key for such an index is chosen from among the columns named in the WHERE clause (*not* the SELECT clause) because these are the columns that direct the search. In this case, an index on TRANSCRIPT with search key `StudId` is useful. Instead of scanning the entire table for rows in which the value of `StudId` is `111111111`, the location mechanism finds the index entries containing the search-key value. Each entry contains either the record or the rid of the record. Thus, while a scan requires that the system retrieve (on average) half the pages in the data file, access through the index requires only a single retrieval. On the other hand, an index on `StudId` is of no use in the execution of query (9.3) on page 333.

Suppose, however, that we need to support the query

```
SELECT   T.Grade
FROM     TRANSCRIPT T                                              9.5
WHERE    T.StudId = '111111111' AND T.Semester = 'F1997'
```

We might choose to create a multiattribute index on `StudId` and `Semester`. If, however, we choose to limit ourselves to an index on a single attribute (perhaps to support other queries and avoid too many indices), which attribute should be its search key? Generally, the attribute that is most selective is chosen. If an index on `StudId` is created, the database system uses it to fetch all rows for the target student and then scans the result, retaining those rows for the target semester. This is more efficient than fetching all rows for the target semester since there are likely to be many more rows for a given semester than for a given student. In general, columns that have only a few values in their domain (for example, Sex) are not likely to be very selective.

The following points provide some guidance in the choice of a search key:

1. A column used in a join condition might be indexed.
2. A clustered B^+ tree index on a column that is used in an ORDER BY clause makes it possible to retrieve rows in the specified order.
3. An index on a column that is a candidate key makes it possible to enforce the unique constraint efficiently.
4. A clustered B^+ tree index on a column used in a range search allows elements in a particular range to be quickly retrieved.

A more complete discussion of tuning can be found in Chapter 12.

BIBLIOGRAPHIC NOTES

B trees were introduced in [Bayer and McCreight 1972], and B^+ trees first appeared in [Knuth 1973]. The latest edition of that book, [Knuth 1998], contains much information on the material covered in this chapter. Hashing as a data structure was first discussed in [Peterson 1957]. Linear hashing was proposed in [Litwin 1980]; extendable hashing in [Fagin et al. 1979]. Index sequential files were analyzed in [Larson 1981].

Join indices were first proposed in [Valduriez 1987], and bitmap indices were first described in [O'Neil 1987]. Bitmapped join indices were introduced in [O'Neil and Graefe 1995].

EXERCISES

9.1 State the storage capacity, sector size, page size, seek time, rotational latency, and transfer time of the disk

a. On your local PC
b. On the server provided by your university

9.2 Explain the difference between an equality search and a range search.

9.3 a. Give an upper bound on the number of pages that must be fetched to perform a binary search for a particular name in the phone book for your city or town.
b. By how much is this number reduced if an index is prepared giving the name of the first entry on each page of the phone book? (Does that index fit on one page of the phone book?)
c. Conduct an experiment using your usual (informal) method to search for the name "John Lewis" in your local phone book, and compare the number of pages you look at with the number in Exercise 3(a).

9.4 Explain why a file can have only one clustered index.

9.5 Explain why a secondary, unclustered index must be dense.

9.6 Does the final structure of a B$^+$ tree depend on the order in which the items are added to it? Explain your answer and give an example.

9.7 Starting with an empty B$^+$ tree with up to two keys per node; show how the tree grows when the following keys are inserted one after another:

18, 10, 7, 14, 8, 9, 21

9.8 Consider the partially specified B$^+$ tree in Figure 9.34.

a. Fill in the internal nodes without adding new keys.
b. Add the key bbb. Show how the tree changes.
c. Delete the key abc from the result of (b). Show how the tree changes.

9.9 Consider the B$^+$ tree in Figure 9.35. Suppose that it was obtained by inserting a key into a leaf node of some other tree, *causing a node split*. What was the original tree and the inserted key? Is the solution unique? Explain your answer.

9.10 Describe a search algorithm for a B$^+$ tree in which the search key is not a candidate key. Assume that overflow pages are not used to handle duplicates.

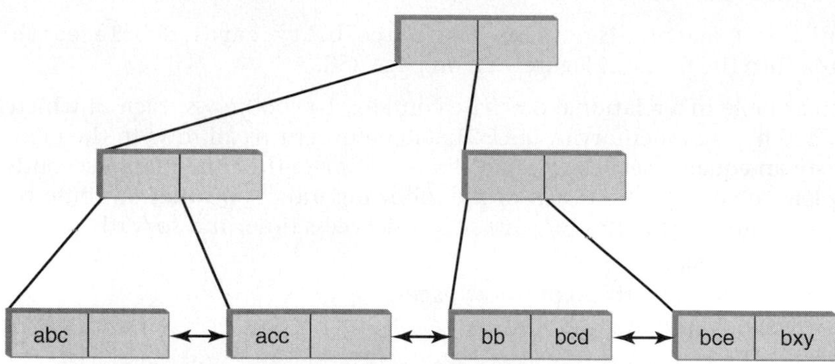

FIGURE 9.34 Partially specified B$^+$ tree.

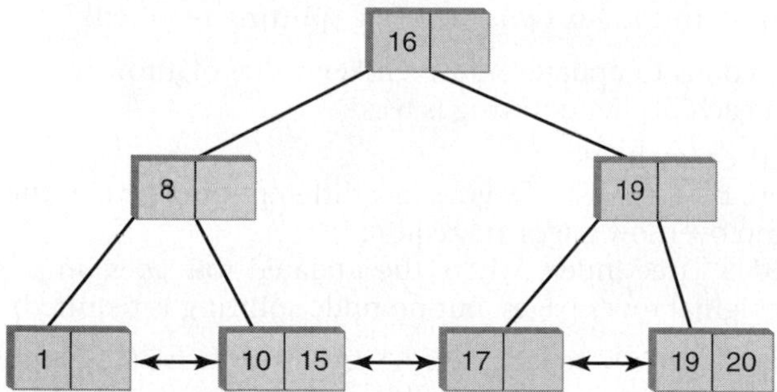

FIGURE 9.35 B$^+$ tree.

9.11 Consider a hash function, h, that takes as an argument a value of a composite search key that is a sequence of r attributes, $a_1, a_2, \ldots, a_r$. If h has the form

$$h(a_1 \circ a_2 \circ \ldots \circ a_r) = h_1(a_1) \circ h_2(a_2) \circ \ldots \circ h_r(a_r)$$

where h_i is a hash of attribute a_i and $\circ$ is the concatenation operator, h is referred to as a **partitioned hash function**. Describe the advantages of such a function with respect to equality, partial-key, and range searches.

9.12 Starting with the B^+ tree shown in Figure 9.22 show the successive B^+ trees that result from deleting `pete`, `phil`, `mike` and `nan`.

9.13 Give the pseudocode for the procedure `redistributeright` called by the procedure `delete` shown in Figure 9.24.

9.14 Express the algorithm for insertion and deletion of index entries in the extendable hashing schema using pseudocode.

9.15 Give examples of select statements that are

a. Speeded up due to the addition of the B^+ tree index shown in Figure 9.22 on page 358.
b. Slowed down due to the addition of the B^+ tree index shown in that figure.

9.16 Draw the B^+ tree that results from inserting `alice`, `betty`, `carol`, `debbie`, `edith`, and `zelda` into the index of Figure 9.22 on page 358.

9.17 A particular table in a relational database contains 100,000 rows, each of which requires 200 bytes of memory. A SELECT statement returns all rows in the table that satisfy an equality search on an attribute. Estimate the time in milliseconds to complete the query when each of the following indices on that attribute is used. Make realistic estimates for page size, disk access time, and so forth.

a. No index (heap file)
b. A static hash index (with no overflow pages)
c. A clustered, unintegrated B^+ tree index

9.18 Estimate the time in milliseconds to insert a new row into the table of Exercise 9.17 when each of the following indices is used:

a. No index (file sorted on the search key)
b. A static hash index (with no overflow pages)
c. A clustered, unintegrated B^+ tree index (with no node splitting required)

9.19 Estimate the time in milliseconds to update the search-key value of a row in the table of Exercise 9.17 when each of the following is used:

a. No index (file sorted on the search key)
b. A static hash index (where the updated row goes in a different bucket than the original row's page, but no overflow pages are required)
c. A clustered, unintegrated B^+ tree index (where the updated row goes on a different page than the original row's pages, but no node splitting is required)

9.20 Estimate the amount of space required to store the B^+ tree of Exercise 9.17 and compare that with the space required to store the table.

9.21 Explain what index types are supported by your local DBMS. Give the commands used to create each type.

9.22 Design the indices for the tables in the Student Registration System. Give the rationale for all design decisions (including those not to use indices in certain cases where they might be expected).

9.23 Explain the rationale for using fillfactors less than 1 in

a. Sorted files
b. ISAM indices
c. B^+ tree indices
d. Hash indices

9.24 Design an algorithm for maintaining join indices incrementally—that is, so that the addition of new tuples to the relations involved in the join do not require the entire join to be recomputed from scratch.

***9.25** Propose an improvement that permits bitmap indices to maintain only $n - 1$ bit vectors in order to represent attributes that can take n different values. Discuss the change that is needed to perform selection, especially in case of a multiattribute selection that requires a Boolean operation on multiple bit vectors.

10

The Basics of Query Processing

An application designer must understand the principles and methods of query processing in order to produce better systems. In this chapter, we examine the methods used to evaluate the basic relational operators and discuss their impact on physical database design. Chapter 11 will deal with a more advanced aspect of query processing: query optimization.

10.1 Overview of Query Processing

SQL queries submitted by the user are first parsed by the DBMS parser. The parser verifies the syntax of the query and, using the system catalogue, determines if the attribute references are correct. For instance, TRANSCRIPT.Student is not a correct reference because the relation TRANSCRIPT does not have Student as an attribute. Likewise, applying the AVG operator to the CrsCode attribute violates the type of that attribute.

Since an SQL query is declarative rather than procedural, it does not suggest any specific implementation. Thus, parsed queries must first be converted into relational algebra expressions. For instance, a query

```
SELECT S.Name
FROM TRANSCRIPT T, STUDENT S
WHERE T.Semester='F2004' AND S.Id=T.StudId AND S.Name='John Doe'
```

might be translated into the following expression:

$$\pi_{\text{Name}}(\sigma_{\text{Semester = 'F2004' AND StudId=Id AND Name = 'John Doe'}}(\text{TRANSCRIPT} \times \text{STUDENT}))$$

A naive way to evaluate this expression would be to compute the results of the relational operators directly as specified. If we did so on a large university database, we would quickly realize that it takes awhile to get an answer. The problem is that the expression involves the Cartesian product, and the intermediate result of the computation can become very large only to be reduced to a few bytes in the end.

To improve performance, a DBMS will play around with the above expression before trying to evaluate it. First, it might convert it to an equivalent expression of the following (or similar) form:

$$\pi_{\texttt{Name}}(\sigma_{\texttt{Semester='F2004'}}(\text{TRANSCRIPT} \bowtie_{\texttt{StudId=Id}} \sigma_{\texttt{Name = 'John Doe'}}(\text{STUDENT})))$$

This transformation is based on a heuristic that believes that joins are better than Cartesian products and that joining smaller relations is better than joining larger ones. Next, the system would choose the appropriate algorithms to compute each operator mentioned in the query. It will make these decisions based on a set of heuristics for estimating the cost of the different algorithms.

This complex series of transformations and estimates, which result in a **query execution plan**, are performed by a DBMS module called a **query optimizer**. A simplified view of query processing in a typical DBMS is depicted in Figure 5.1 on page 129.

We will study the workings of a query optimizer in the next chapter. But before we can do this, we need to familiarize ourselves with the repertoire of algorithms that a query optimizer has at its disposal, and we need to learn to estimate the cost of the alternative ways of computing the relational operators. These algorithms are the subject of this chapter.

10.2 External Sorting

Sorting is an important part of many algorithms used in computer programming and is at the very core of the algorithms that support relational operations. For instance, sorting is one of the most efficient ways to get rid of duplicate tuples and is also the basis of some join algorithms. The sorting algorithms used to process queries in relational DBMSs are not the ones you might have studied in a basic course on algorithms. The latter are designed to perform sorting when all data is stored in main memory, which usually cannot be assumed in the database context. When files are large and are kept in external storage, such as a disk, we use what is called **external sorting**.

The main idea behind external sorting is to bring portions of the file into main memory, sort them using one of the known in-memory algorithms (e.g., Quicksort), and then dump the result back to disk. This creates sorted file segments, which must be merged in order to create a single sorted file. Because the time to execute an I/O operation is several orders of magnitude greater than the time to execute an instruction, it is assumed that the cost of I/O dominates the cost of in-memory sorting. Hence, the computational complexity of external sorting is often measured only in the number of disk reads and writes. More specifically, we will measure the complexity in terms of the number of pages that need to be transfered between the main memory and the disk. A typical external sorting algorithm consists of two stages: *partial sorting* and *merging*.

Partial sorting. The partial sorting stage is very simple. Suppose that we have a buffer in main memory that can accommodate M pages available for sorting and

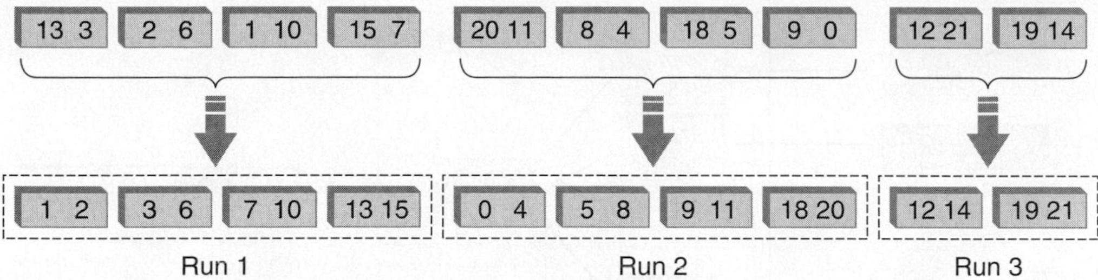

FIGURE 10.1 Partial sorting of a file, $M = 4$, $F = 10$.

that the file has F pages. F is typically much larger than M. The first stage of the algorithm is as follows:

```
do {
    read M pages from disk into main memory
    sort them in memory with one of the known methods.
        (Assume that, apart from the M-page buffer, additional memory
        is available to enable the in-memory sorting algorithm to run)
    dump the sorted file segment into a new file
} until (end-of-file)
```

We use the term **run** to refer to a sorted file segment produced by one iteration of the above loop. The size of a run is the number of pages in the segment. Thus, the first stage produces $\lceil F/M \rceil$ sorted runs at the cost of $2F$ disk I/O operations (for simplicity, we assume that each I/O operation transfers exactly one page to or from main memory). (The symbol $\lceil\ \rceil$ here denotes the operation of rounding up to the nearest integer that is greater than or equal to F/M.) The partial sorting stage is illustrated in Figure 10.1, in which we assume that each disk block contains two file records.

***k*-way merging.** The next stage of the algorithm takes the sorted runs and merges them into larger sorted runs. This process can be repeated until we end up with just one sorted run, which is our final goal: the sorted version of the original file. A k-way merge algorithm takes k sorted runs of size R pages and produces one run of size kR, as illustrated in Figure 10.2. The actual algorithm works as follows:

```
while (there are nonempty input runs) {
    choose a smallest tuple (with respect to the sort key) in each
        run, and output the smallest among these
    delete the chosen tuple from the respective input run
}
```

Because each run is sorted, the choice step is simple since the smallest remaining element in a run is always its current head element. Figure 10.3 illustrates repeated

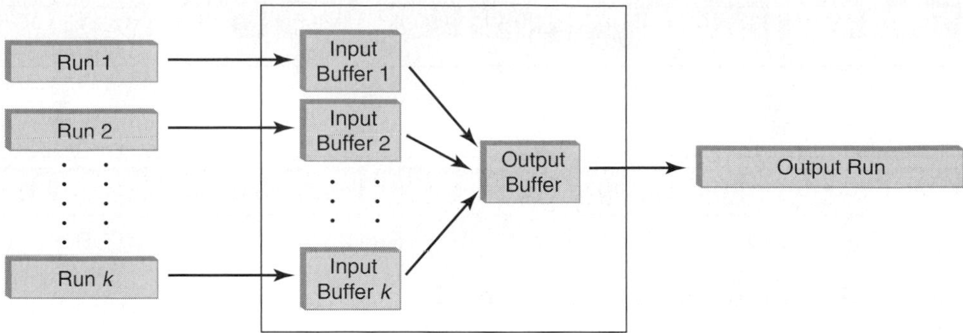

FIGURE 10.2 *k*-way merge.

application of the 2-way merge step; Figure 10.4 shows a 3-way merge. In each case we need to have a buffer with enough pages to perform the merge—three for the 2-way merge and four for the 3-way merge. The buffer size in the figures ($M = 4$) can accommodate both 2-way and 3-way merges.

What is the cost of a k-way merge of k runs of size R pages? Clearly, each run must be scanned once and then the entire output must be written back on disk. The cost is thus $2kR$. Since we might start with more than k runs, we divide them into groups of k and apply the k-way merge separately to each group. If we refer to this process as a step and if we start with N runs, we have $\lceil N/k \rceil$ groups, and the upper bound on the total cost of the merge step is $2RN$. Note that this value does not depend on k. Moreover, since at the next merge step we start with $\lceil N/k \rceil$ runs, each with a maximum size kR, the cost of the merge again does not exceed $2RN$, and we are left with $\lceil N/k^2 \rceil$ runs. In fact, it is easy to show by induction that this upper bound on the I/O cost holds for every step of the merge algorithm.

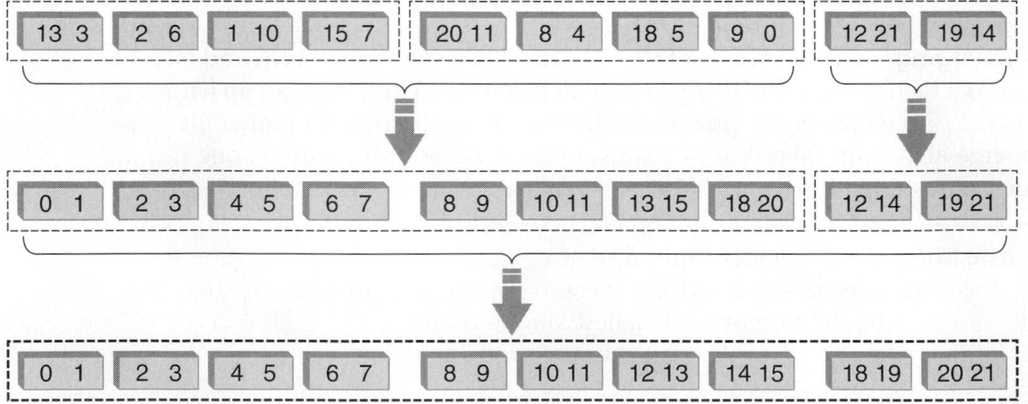

FIGURE 10.3 Merging sorted runs in a 2-way merge, $M = 4$, $F = 10$.

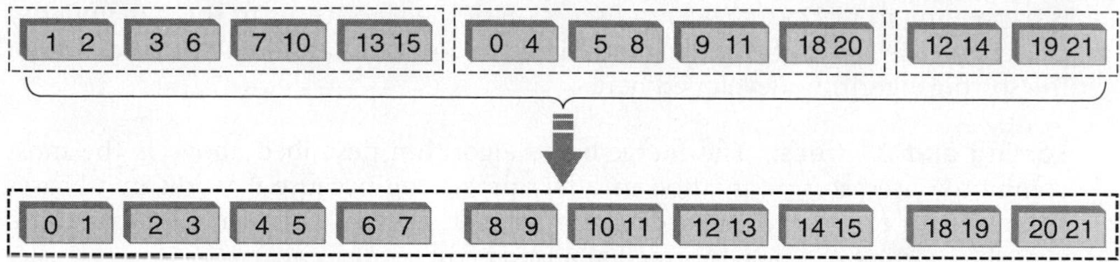

FIGURE 10.4 Merging sorted runs in a 3-way merge, $M = 4$, $F = 10$.

The next question is what the value of k should be at the merging stage in an external sort algorithm. If we start with N runs and perform a k-way merge at each step, the number of steps is $\lceil log_k N \rceil$. Thus, the cost of the entire merging stage of the algorithm is bound by $2RN * log_k N$, where R is the initial size of a sorted run. Since, in our case, $R = M$ (i.e., we can use the entire buffer to produce the largest possible initial runs) and consequently $N = \lceil F/M \rceil$, we conclude that the cost is bounded by $2F * log_k \lceil F/M \rceil$.

Thus, it appears that the larger k is, the smaller is the cost of external sorting. Why, then, should we not take k to be the maximum possible—that is, the number of initial sorted runs? The answer is that we are limited by the size M of the main memory buffer allocated for the external sort procedure. This reasoning suggests that we should utilize this memory in such a way as to make k as large as possible. Since we must allocate at least one page to collect the output (which is periodically flushed to disk) during the merge, the maximum value of k is $M - 1$. By substituting this value into the earlier cost estimate, we obtain the following estimate:

$$2F\ (log_{(M-1)} F - log_{(M-1)} M) \approx 2F(log_{(M-1)} F - 1)$$

Finally, by combining this cost with the cost of the partial sorting stage, we obtain an estimate for the entire procedure of external sorting:

$$2F * log_{(M-1)} F \qquad \textbf{10.1}$$

In commercial DBMSs, the external sorting algorithms are highly optimized. They take into account not only the cost of in-memory sorting of the initial runs but also the fact that transferring multiple pages in one I/O operation might be more cost-effective than performing several I/O operations that transfer one page at a time. For instance, if we have a buffer that holds 12 pages, we can either perform an 11-way merge reading one page at a time or a 3-way merge reading three pages at a time. Since reading (and writing) three pages takes almost the same time as reading one, it is reasonable to consider such a 3-way merge as an alternative. Another consideration has to do with delays when the output buffer is being flushed to disk during the merge operation. Techniques such as double or triple buffering might be used to reduce such delays. Despite all of these simplifications, however, the algorithm and the cost estimate developed in this section provide a good approximation for what is happening in real systems. Our discussion of the algorithms in the remainder of this chapter relies on the understanding of the cost estimates and on the details of the sorting algorithm developed here.

Sorting and B$^+$ trees. The merge-based algorithm described above is the most commonly used sorting method in query processing because it works in all cases and does not require auxiliary data structures. However, when such structures are available, sorting can be performed at a lower cost.

For instance, suppose that a secondary B$^+$ tree index on the sort key is available. Traversal of the leaf entries of the tree produces a sorted list of the record Ids (rids) for the actual data file. In principle, then, we can simply follow the pointers and retrieve the records in the data file in the order of the search key. Surprisingly, this might not always beat the merge-based algorithm!

The main consideration in deciding whether a B$^+$ tree index is worth considering for sorting a file is whether the index is clustered or unclustered. The short answer is, if the index is clustered, using a B$^+$ tree index is a good idea; otherwise, it might be a bad idea. If the index is clustered, the data file must already be almost sorted (by definition), so there is nothing we need to do. However, if the index is unclustered, traversing the leaves of a B$^+$ tree and following the data record pointers retrieves pages of the main file in random order. In the worst case, this might mean that we must transfer one page for each *record* in the index leaf (recall that our previous analysis was based on the number of *pages* in the file—typically a much smaller number than the number of records). Exercise 10.1 deals with estimating the cost of using unclustered B$^+$ trees for external sorting.

10.3 Computing Projection, Union, and Set Difference

At first glance, computing the projection, union, and set difference operators is easy. With projection, for instance, we can just scan the relation and delete the unwanted columns. However, the situation is more complicated if the user query has the DISTINCT directive. The problem here is that duplicate tuples, which might arise as a result of the projection operation, must be eliminated. For instance, if we project out the attributes `StudId` and `Grade` of the relation TRANSCRIPT in Figure 3.5 on page 39, the tuple ⟨`MGT123, F1994`⟩ will appear twice in the result. Thus, we must find efficient ways of eliminating duplicate tuples.

The same problem with duplicates can arise in the computation of the union of two relations. In the case of the difference of two relations, $\mathbf{r} - \mathbf{s}$, duplicates cannot arise unless the relation **r** had them all along. Nevertheless, the problem we are facing is similar: to identify the tuples in **r** that are equal to tuples in **s**.

There are two techniques for finding identical tuples: sorting (which we discussed in Section 10.2) and hashing. We first apply these techniques to the projection operator and then discuss the modifications needed for union and set difference operators.

Sort-based projection. This technique scans the original relation, removes the tuple components that are to be projected out, and writes the result back on disk.

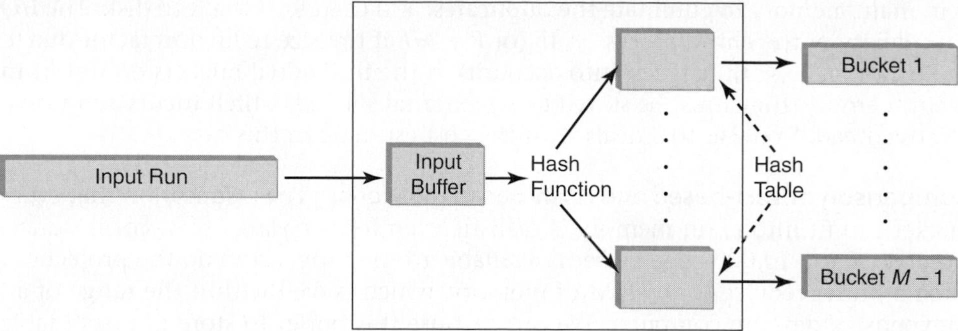

FIGURE 10.5 Hashing input relation into buckets.

(We assume that there is not enough memory to store the result.) The cost of this operation is of the order $2F$, where F is the number of pages in the relation. Then the result is sorted at the cost of $2F * log_{(M-1)} F$, where M is the number of main memory pages available for sorting. Finally, we scan the result again (at the cost of $2F$), and, since identical tuples are right next to each other (because the relation is sorted), we can easily delete the duplicates.

In fact, we can do better than that if we combine sorting and scanning. First, we delete the unwanted components from the tuples during the partial sorting stage of the sorting algorithm. At that stage, we have to scan the original relation anyway, so removal of the tuple components comes at no additional cost in terms of disk I/O. Second, we eliminate the final scan needed to remove the duplicates by combining duplicate elimination with the steps in which sorted runs are output to the disk. Since each such step writes out blocks of sorted tuples, duplicate elimination can be done in main memory, at no additional I/O cost.

Thus, the cost of the sort-based projection is $2F * log_{(M-1)} F$. Furthermore, if we take into account that the first scan is likely to produce a smaller relation (of size αF, where $\alpha < 1$ is the reduction factor), the cost of projection is even lower (see Exercise 10.2).

Hash-based projection. Another way to quickly identify the duplicates is to use a hash function. Suppose that a hash function yields integers in the range of 1 to $M - 1$ and that there are M buffer pages in main memory, which includes an $(M - 1)$-page hash table and an input buffer. The algorithm works as follows. In the first phase, the original relation is scanned. During the scan, we chop off the tuple components that are to be projected out, and the rest of the tuple is hashed on the remaining attributes. Whenever a page of the hash table becomes full, it is flushed to the corresponding bucket on disk. This step is illustrated in Figure 10.5.

Clearly, duplicate tuples are always hashed into the same bucket, so we can eliminate duplicates in each bucket separately. This elimination is done in the second phase of the algorithm. Assuming that each bucket fits into the main memory, the second phase can be carried out by simply reading each bucket in its entirety, sorting it in main memory to eliminate the duplicates, and then flushing it to disk. The I/O complexity of the entire process is $4F$ (or $F + 3\alpha F$ if the size reduction factor due to projection, α ($\alpha < 1$), is taken into account). If the individual buckets do not fit in main memory, they must be sorted using external sorting, which incurs additional I/O overhead. Exercise 10.3 deals with the cost estimate in this case.

Comparison of sort-based and hash-based methods. The assumption that every bucket can fit into main memory is realistic even for very large files. For instance, suppose that a 10,000-page buffer is available to the program to do the projection. Such a buffer requires only 40M of memory, which is well within the range of an inexpensive desktop computer. We can first use this buffer to store the hash table and then use it to read in the buckets. Let us assume that each hash bucket fits into our buffer and suppose we have a $10{,}000 \times 10{,}000 = 10^8$-page file (400G) to process. According to the above discussion, projection of such a file can be computed at the cost of just under 4×10^8 page transfers. Does the sort-based projection algorithm fare better? In this case, the sort-based algorithm costs a bit more: $2 \times 10^8 \; log_{10^4-1} 10^8$ page transfers.

The possibility that we might have to externally sort an average-size hash bucket is fairly remote. A much bigger risk is that the hash function we use will not distribute tuples to the buckets evenly. In this case, although the average bucket might fit in main memory, other buckets will not. In the worst case (which is unlikely), all tuples might fall into the same buffer, which will require external sorting. The cost will then be $2F$ to scan the original relation and copy it into the single bucket plus $2F \; log_{(M-1)} F$ to sort the bucket and eliminate the duplicates—a waste of $2F$ page transfers compared to sort-based projection.

Computing union and set difference. Computing the union and set difference of two relations is similar to computing projection, except that we do not need to chop off unwanted attributes. For example, to compute a set difference, **r** – **s**, we sort both **r** and **s** and then scan them in parallel, similar to the merging process. However, instead of merging tuples, whenever we discover that a tuple, t, of **r** is also in **s**, we do not add it to the result. Furthermore, we can combine this step with the final merges of the sorted runs of **r** and of **s**, which are part of the sorting algorithm. Details of this combination are left to Exercise 10.9. Since the final scan of **r** and **s** comes for free, the cost of union and difference operations is the cost of sorting of these two relations.

In hash-based set difference computation, we can hash **r** and **s** into buckets as described earlier. However, in each bucket we must keep the distinction between tuples that came from **r** and those that came from **s**. In the second stage, the set difference operation must be applied to each bucket separately.

10.4 Computing Selection

Computing the selection operator can be much more complex than computing projection and computing the set operations, and a wider variety of techniques can be used. The choice of a technique for a particular selection operator can depend on the type of the selection condition and on the physical organization of the relation in question. Typically, the DBMS decides automatically on the technique it will use based on the heuristics that we describe in the following subsections. However, understanding these heuristics gives the programmer an opportunity to request the physical organization that is most favorable to the selection types that occur most frequently in a particular application.

We first consider simple selection conditions of the form *attr* op *value* (where op is one of the comparisons =, >, <, and the like) and then generalize our techniques to complex conditions that involve Boolean operators.

Database queries usually lead to two distinct kinds of selection: those based on equality ($attr = val$) and those based on inequality (such as $attr < val$). The latter are called **range queries** because they usually come in pairs that specify a range of values, for example, $\sigma_{c_1 < attr \leq c_2}(\mathbf{r})$.

Our discussion of the techniques for implementing the selection operator focuses on the cost of retrieving the requisite tuples and ignores the cost of outputting the result. The reason is that the cost of the output is the same in all cases and thus is irrelevant for comparing the different techniques. Section 11.4 presents some heuristics for estimating this cost.

10.4.1 Selections with Simple Conditions

One obvious way of evaluating a selection, $\sigma_{attr\ \mathrm{op}\ value}(\mathbf{r})$, is to scan the relation **r** and check the selection condition for each tuple, outputting those that satisfy it. However, if only a small number of tuples satisfies the condition, the price of scanning an entire relation seems too high. In situations where more information is available about the structure of **r**, a complete scan is not needed. We consider three cases: (1) when no index is available on *attr*; (2) when there is a B^+ tree index on *attr*; and (3) when there is a hash index on *attr*. In case 3, only the equality selections (where op is =) can be handled efficiently. In case 2, both equality selections and range queries can be handled efficiently, although case 3 is generally better for equality selection. In case 1, complete scan of **r** is the only option unless the relation **r** is already sorted on *attr*. In this case, both equality and range conditions can be handled, although not as efficiently as when a B^+ tree index is available.

No index. In general, we might have no choice but to scan the entire relation **r** at the cost of F page transfers (the number of disk blocks in **r**). However, if **r** is sorted on *attr*, we can use binary search to find the pages of **r** that house the first tuple where $attr = value$ holds. We can then scan the file in the appropriate direction to retrieve all of the tuples that satisfy *attr* op *value*.

The cost of such a binary search is proportional to $log_2 F$. To this, we must add the cost of scanning the blocks that contain the qualifying tuples. For instance, if **r** has 500 pages, the cost of the search is $\lceil log_2 500 \rceil$, that is, 9 page transfers (plus the number of disk blocks that contain the qualifying entries).

B^+ tree index. With a B^+ tree index on *attr*, the algorithm is similar to that for a sorted file. However, instead of the binary search, we use the index to find the first tuple of **r** where *attr* = *value*. More precisely, we find the leaf node of the B^+ tree that contains or points to the first row satisfying the condition. From there, we scan the leaves of the B^+ tree index to find all of the index entries that point to the pages that hold the tuples that satisfy *attr* op *value*.

The cost of finding the first qualifying leaf node of the index equals the depth of the B^+ tree. As before, we also have to add the cost of scanning the leaves of the index to identify all of the qualifying entries. Of course, this cost depends on the number of qualifying entries, which depends on the selection condition as well as on the actual data in the relation.

This is not the whole story, however. So far we have described only the process of getting the index entries. The cost of getting the actual tuples depends on whether or not the index is clustered. If the index is clustered, all of the tuples of interest are stored in one page or in several adjacent pages (this is true whether or not the index is integrated into the storage structure). For instance, if there are 1000 qualifying tuples and each disk block stores 100 tuples, getting all these tuples (assuming that we already had found the appropriate index nodes) requires 10 page transfers. On the other hand, if the index is unclustered, each qualifying tuple might be in a separate block, so retrieving all qualifying tuples might take 1000 page transfers!

This raises the unhappy prospect of having to perform as many page transfers as the number of qualifying tuples in the selection, which can handily beat the number of pages in the entire relation **r**. Fortunately, with a little thought, we can do better than that. Let us first sort the record Ids of the qualifying tuples that we obtained from the index. Then we can retrieve the data pages from the relation in the ascending order of qualifying record Ids, which guarantees that every data page will be retrieved at most once. Thus, even with an unclustered index, the cost is proportional to the number of pages that contain qualifying tuples (plus the cost of searching the index and sorting the record Ids). In the worst case, this cost can be as high as the number of pages in the original relation (but not as large as the number of tuples there!). This is because the qualifying tuples are not packed into the retrieved pages as they would be with a clustered index: a retrieved page might only contain a single qualifying tuple. Hence, a clustered index is still greatly preferred.

Hash index. In this case, we can use the hash function to find the bucket that has the tuples where *attr* = *value* holds. Since two tuples that differ only slightly in *value* can hash to different buckets, this method cannot be efficiently used with range conditions, such as *attr* < *value*.

Generally, the cost of finding the right bucket is constant (close to 1.2 for a good hash function). However, the actual cost of tuple retrieval depends on the number of qualifying tuples. If this number is larger than one, then, as in the case of B^+ tree indices, the actual cost depends on whether or not the index is clustered. In the clustered case, all qualifying tuples are packed into a few adjacent pages and the cost of retrieval is just the cost of scanning these pages. In the unclustered case, tuples are scattered through the data file and we face the same problem as with unclustered B^+ trees—sorting the record Ids results in a cost proportional to the number of pages that contain qualifying tuples.

10.4.2 Access Paths

The above algorithms for implementing the relational operators all assume that certain auxiliary data structures (indices) are available (or unavailable) for the relations being processed. These data structures, along with the algorithms that use them, are called **access paths**. So far, we have seen several examples of access paths that can be used to process a particular query: a *file scan* can always be used; a *binary search* can be used on files that are sorted on attributes specified in the query; a *hash index* or a B^+ tree can be used if the index has a search key that involves those attributes.

Example 10.4.1 (Access Paths). Consider the TRANSCRIPT relation of Figure 3.5, page 39, and suppose that we have a hash index on the search key ⟨`StudId`, `Semester`⟩. The index is useful in computing $\pi_{\texttt{StudId,Semester}}$(TRANSCRIPT), since we can be certain that any duplicates created as a result of the projection originate from tuples that were stored in the same bucket. This greatly simplifies duplicate elimination since the search for duplicates can be done one bucket at a time. If we compute $\pi_{\texttt{StudId,CrsCode}}$(TRANSCRIPT), on the other hand, the index is of no help in eliminating duplicates. Although the projections of tuples t_1 and t_2 on ⟨`StudId`, `CrsCode`⟩ might be identical, t_1 and t_2 might be hashed to different buckets since the values of their `Semester` attribute can differ. In order to use hashing for duplicate elimination, the entire search key of the hash index must be contained in the set of attributes that survive the projection (see Exercise 10.4).

At the same time, the above hash index can be very useful for computing the query $\sigma_{\texttt{StudId=666666666} \wedge \texttt{Grade='A'} \wedge \texttt{Semester='F1994'}}$(TRANSCRIPT). We can use the hash index to retrieve the tuples that satisfy the partial condition `StudId=666666666` ∧ `Semester='F1994'` and then scan the result (which presumably will be small) to find the tuples that additionally satisfy `Grade='A'`. On the other hand, the same index is of no help in evaluating the expression $\sigma_{\texttt{StudId=666666666}}$(TRANSCRIPT) since we cannot hash on a partial-search key and tuples satisfying this condition can be scattered over different buckets.

Finally, a hash index on ⟨`Grade`, `StudId`⟩ is not helpful for computing the query $\sigma_{\texttt{Grade>'C'}}$(TRANSCRIPT), but a B^+ tree index on the search key ⟨`Grade`, `StudId`⟩ can help (although a B^+ tree with search key ⟨`StudId`, `Grade`⟩ cannot). To use the hash function, we have to supply all possible values for `StudId` and all values for `Grade` above `'C'`, which is impractical. In contrast, since `Grade` is a *prefix* of the B^+ tree search key, we can use this tree to efficiently find all of the index entries with the search key ⟨`g`, `id`⟩, where g is higher than `'C'`. ■

Example 10.4.1 leads to the notion of when an access path *covers* the use of a particular relational operator. We define this notion precisely only for a selection operator whose selection condition is a conjunction of terms of the form *attr* op *value*. Projection and set difference operators are left to Exercise 10.6.

Covering relates access paths to relational expressions that can be evaluated using those paths. Consider a relational expression of the form

$$\sigma_{attr_1 \; \texttt{op}_1 \; val_1 \wedge \ldots \wedge attr_n \; \texttt{op}_n \; val_n}(\text{R}) \quad \textbf{10.2}$$

where **R** is a relation schema. This expression is **covered** by an access path if and only if one of the following conditions holds:

- The access path is a file scan. (A file scan can obviously be used to compute any expression.)
- The access path is a hash index whose search key is a subset of the attributes $attr_1, \ldots, attr_n$ *and* all $\mathtt{op}_i$ in this subset are equality operators. (We can use the hash index to identify the tuples that satisfy some of the conjuncts in the selection condition and then scan the result to verify the conjuncts that remain.)
- The access path is a B^+ tree index with the search key $sk_1, \ldots, sk_m$ such that some prefix $sk_1, \ldots, sk_i$ of that search key is a *subset* of $attr_1, \ldots, attr_n$. (Section 9.4.3 explained how to use B^+ trees for partial-key searches. This can help us find the tuples that satisfy some of the conjuncts in the selection. The rest of the conjuncts can be verified by a sequential scan of the result.)
- The access path is a binary search, and the relation instance corresponding to **R** is sorted on the attributes $sk_1, \ldots, sk_m$. The definition of covering in this case is the same as for B^+ tree indices.

Note that access paths based on hashing can be used only if all comparisons that correspond to the attributes in the search key are =. The other access paths can be used even if these comparisons involve inequalities, such as $\leq$, $<$, $>$, and $\geq$. If the comparison operator is $\neq$, the only applicable access path is a file scan since no index is effective in enumerating all the qualifying tuples in this case.

Example 10.4.2 (Covering Complex Selection). Consider the expression $\sigma_{a_1 \geq 5 \wedge a_2 = 3.0 \wedge a_3 = 'a'}(\mathbf{R})$, and assume that there is a B^+ tree with search key a_2, a_1, a_4 on **R**. This access path covers the expression, which can be computed as follows. Use the index to find the leaf entry, *e*, in which a_2 has value 3.0 and a_1 has value 5 or, if such an entry is not present, the first entry in the index that would follow *e*. Then scan the leaf entries from that point on to find all those tuples in which, in addition, a_3 has value *a*. ■

One more notion before we proceed: the **selectivity** of an access path is the number of pages that will be retrieved if we use the evaluation method corresponding to that path. The smaller the selectivity, the better the access path. Selectivity is closely related to the cost of evaluating a query, although the query cost might involve other factors. For example, multiple access paths might be used (see Section 10.4.3) or it might be necessary to sort the result before output (if an ORDER BY clause is used). Clearly, for any given relational expression, access path selectivity depends on the size of the result of that expression and is always greater than or equal to the number of pages that hold the tuples in that result. However, some access paths have selectivity that is closer to the theoretical minimum, while others are closer to the cost of the entire file scan. The notion of when an access path covers an expression helps in identifying access paths whose selectivity seems "reasonable" for the given type of expression.

10.4.3 Selections with Complex Conditions

We are now ready to discuss the methods used to evaluate arbitrary selection.

Selections with conjunctive conditions. These are the expressions of the form (10.2) considered on page 393. We have two choices:

1. *Use the most selective access path to retrieve the corresponding tuples.* Such an access path tries to form a prefix of the search key by using as many of the attributes mentioned in the selection condition as possible. In this way, it retrieves the smallest possible superset of the required tuples, and we can scan the result to find the tuples that satisfy the entire selection condition. For instance, suppose that we need to evaluate

$$\sigma_{\texttt{Grade>'C'}\wedge\texttt{Semester='F1994'}}(\text{TRANSCRIPT})$$

and there is a B^+ tree index with the search key ⟨`Grade, StudId`⟩. Since this access path covers the selection condition `Grade>'C'`, we can use it to compute $\sigma_{\texttt{Grade>'C'}}(\text{TRANSCRIPT})$. Then we can scan the result to identify the transcript records that correspond to the fall 1994 semester. If we had a B^+ tree index with the search key ⟨`Semester, Grade`⟩, we could use *it* as an access path, because this path covers both selection conditions.

2. *Use several access paths that cover the expression.* For instance, we might have two secondary indices whose selectivity is less than that of the plain file scan. We can then use both access paths to find the rids of the tuples that might belong to the query result and then compute the intersection of those sets of rids. Finally, we can retrieve the selected tuples and test them for the remaining selection conditions. For instance, consider the expression

$$\sigma_{\texttt{StudId=666666666}\wedge\texttt{Grade='A'}\wedge\texttt{Semester='F1994'}}(\text{TRANSCRIPT})$$

and suppose that there are two hash indices: on `Semester` and on `Grade`. Using the first access path, we can find the rids of the transcript records for the fall 1994 semester. Then we can use the second access path to find the rids for the records with grade `'A'`. Finally, we can find the rids that belong to both sets and retrieve the corresponding pages. As we scan the tuples, we can further select those that correspond to the student Id 666666666.

Selections with disjunctive conditions. When selection conditions contain disjunctions, we must first convert them into *disjunctive normal form.* A condition is in **disjunctive normal form** if it has the form $C_1 \vee \ldots \vee C_n$, where each C_i is a conjunction of comparison terms (as in expression (10.2)).

It is known from elementary predicate calculus that every condition has an equivalent disjunctive normal form. For instance, for the condition

```
(Grade='A'  ∨ Grade='B') ∧ (Semester='F1994'  ∨ Semester='F1995')
```

the corresponding disjunctive normal form is

```
(Grade='A' ∧ Semester='F1994') ∨ (Grade='A' ∧ Semester='F1995')
∨ (Grade='B' ∧ Semester='F1994') ∨ (Grade='B' ∧ Semester='F1995')
```

For conditions in disjunctive normal form, the query processor must examine the available access paths for the individual disjuncts and choose the appropriate strategy. Here are some possibilities:

- *One of the disjuncts, C_i, must be evaluated using a file scan.* In this situation, we might as well evaluate the entire selection expression during that scan.
- *Each C_i has an access path that is better than the plain file scan.* We have two subcases here:
  1. The sum of the selectivities of all of these paths is close to the selectivity of the file scan. In this case, we should prefer the file scan because the overhead of the index search and other factors are likely to outweigh the small potential gain due to the use of more sophisticated access paths.
  2. The combined selectivity of the access paths for all disjuncts is much smaller than the selectivity of the file scan. In this case, we should compute $\sigma_{C_i}(\mathbf{R})$ separately, using the appropriate access paths, and then take the union of the results.

10.5 Computing Joins

The methods for computing projections, selections, and the like, are nothing but a prelude to a more difficult problem: evaluation of relational joins. With all of the attention given to the comparison of different access paths, the worst that can happen during the computation of a projection or selection is that we might have to scan or sort the entire relation. The result of such an expression is also well behaved: it cannot be larger than the original relation.

Compare this to relational joins, where both the number of pages to be scanned and the size of the result can be *quadratic* in the size of the input. While "quadratic" might not seem too bad in applications in which some algorithms have exponential complexity, it is prohibitive in database query evaluation because of the large amounts of data and the relative slowness of disk I/O. For example, joining two files that span a mere 1000 pages can require 10^6 I/O operations, which might be unacceptable even for batch jobs. And joining just three such relations would fetch 10^9 I/Os. For these reasons, joins are given special attention in database query processing.

Consider a join expression $\mathbf{r} \bowtie_{A=B} \mathbf{s}$, where A is an attribute of $\mathbf{r}$ and B is an attribute of $\mathbf{s}$. There are three main methods for computing joins: nested loops (with and without the help of indices), sort-merge, and hash-based joins. We consider them in this order.

10.5.1 Computing Joins Using Simple Nested Loops

One obvious way to evaluate the join $\mathbf{r} \bowtie_{A=B} \mathbf{s}$ is to use the following loop:

```
foreach t ∈ r do
    foreach t' ∈ s do
        if t.A = t'.B then output ⟨t, t'⟩
```

The cost of this procedure can be estimated as follows. Let $F_\mathbf{r}$ and $F_\mathbf{s}$ be the number of pages in **r** and **s**, and let $\tau_\mathbf{r}$ and $\tau_\mathbf{s}$ be the number of tuples in **r** and **s**, respectively. It is easy to see that the relation **s** must be scanned from start to end for each tuple in **r**, resulting in $\tau_\mathbf{r} F_\mathbf{s}$ page transfers. In addition, **r** must be scanned once in the outer loop. All in all, there are $F_\mathbf{r} + \tau_\mathbf{r} F_\mathbf{s}$ page transfers. (In all cost estimates for the join operation, we ignore the cost of writing the final result to disk because this step is the same for all methods and also because the estimate at this stage depends on the actual size of the result. Trying to estimate this size takes us away from the main topic and is a distraction at this stage.)

The above cost estimate teaches us two lessons:

1. *It involves a lot of page transfers!* Let $F_\mathbf{r} = 1000$, $F_\mathbf{s} = 100$, and $\tau_\mathbf{r} = 10{,}000$. Our cost estimate says that the computation might require $1000 + 10{,}000 \times 100 = 1{,}001{,}000$ page transfers—too much to join such relatively small tables (about 166 minutes if one page I/O takes 10 ms).
2. *The order of the loops matters.* Suppose that instead of scanning **r** in the outer loop, we scan **s** in the outer loop and **r** in the inner loop. Suppose that $\tau_\mathbf{s} = 1000$. Switching **r** and **s** in the cost estimate yields: $100 + 1000 \times 1000 = 1{,}000{,}100$. Although, in this example, the reduction in operations is minimal (a whopping nine seconds!), it is clear that the order of scans matters.

Simple nested loops are actually never used for computing joins, because it is a hugely wasteful method. We will now consider a related, but much better technique.

Block-nested loops join. The complexity of the nested loops join can be reduced considerably if, instead of scanning **s** once per tuple of **r**, we scan it once per page of **r**. This will reduce the cost estimate to $F_\mathbf{r} + F_\mathbf{r} F_\mathbf{s}$—a reduction of an order of magnitude from the above example. The way to achieve this feat is to output the result of the join for all tuples in the page of **r** that is currently in memory.

```
foreach page p_r of r do
    foreach page p_s of s do
            output p_r ⋈_{A=B} p_s
```

If we can reduce the number of scans of **s** to one per page of **r**, can we further reduce this number to one per group of pages? The answer is yes—if we can use a little more memory. Suppose that the query processor has an M-page main memory buffer to do the join. We can allocate $M - 2$ of these pages for the outer loop relation

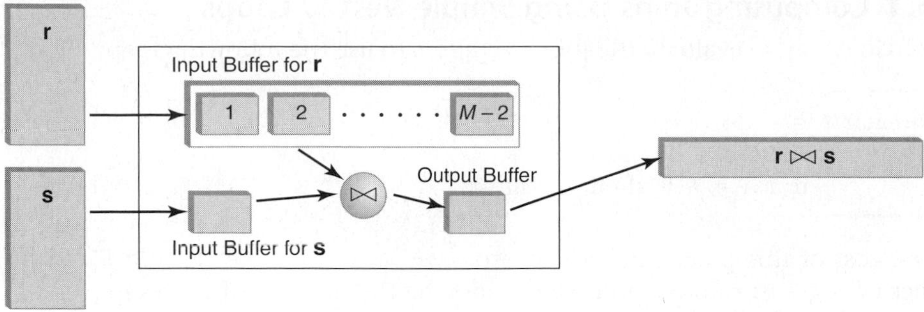

FIGURE 10.6 Block-nested loops join.

r and one page for the inner loop relation s, leaving the last page reserved for the output buffer. This process is depicted in Figure 10.6.

The cost of a block-nested loops join can be estimated similarly to our previous examples: the outer relation r is scanned once at the cost of $F_{\mathbf{r}}$ page transfers; the relation s is scanned once per group of $M - 2$ pages of r, that is, $\lceil \frac{F_{\mathbf{r}}}{M-2} \rceil$. Thus, the cost (excluding the cost of writing the output to disk) is

$$F_{\mathbf{r}} + F_{\mathbf{s}} \lceil \frac{F_{\mathbf{r}}}{M-2} \rceil \qquad \mathbf{10.3}$$

Example 10.5.1 (An Estimate of a Block-Nested Loops Join). In our example, if $M = 102$, the cost will go down to $1000 + 100 \times 10 = 2000$. And, if the smaller relation, s, is scanned in the outer loop, the cost will be even lower: $100 + 100 \times 10 = 1100$ (or 11 seconds, assuming 10 ms per page I/O)—quite a reduction from 10^6, the cost of the original, naive implementation. ■

This example shows again that the order of the loops matters. Looking at the general formula (10.3) we can observe that $F_{\mathbf{s}} \lceil \frac{F_{\mathbf{r}}}{M-2} \rceil$ and $F_{\mathbf{r}} \lceil \frac{F_{\mathbf{s}}}{M-2} \rceil$ are approximately the same. Therefore, if $F_{\mathbf{r}} > F_{\mathbf{s}}$ then $F_{\mathbf{r}} + F_{\mathbf{s}} \lceil \frac{F_{\mathbf{r}}}{M-2} \rceil > F_{\mathbf{s}} + F_{\mathbf{r}} \lceil \frac{F_{\mathbf{s}}}{M-2} \rceil$.

It is always cheaper to scan the smaller relation in the outer loop.

Index-nested loops join. The next idea is to use indices. This technique achieves particularly good results if the number of tuples in r and s that match on the attributes A and B is small compared to the size of the file.

Suppose that relation s has an index on attribute B. Then, instead of scanning s in the inner loop, we can use the index to find the matching tuples:

```
foreach t ∈ r do {
    Use the index on B to find all tuples t′ ∈ s such that t.A = t′.B
    Output ⟨t, t′⟩ for each such t′
}
```

To estimate the cost of this method, we have to take into account the type of index and whether it is clustered or not. The number of matching tuples in **s** also matters.

If the index is a B^+ tree, the cost of finding the first leaf node for the matching tuple in **s** is 2 to 4 I/O operations, depending on the size of the relation. In a hash-based index, it is about 1.2, if the hash function is well chosen. The next question is how many I/O operations are required to fetch the matching tuples in **s**, and the answer depends on the number of matching tuples and whether the index is clustered or unclustered.

If the index is unclustered, the number of I/Os needed to retrieve all matching tuples can be as high as the number of pages in **s** (this cost is bounded both by the number of pages in **s** and the number of matching tuples). So unclustered indices are not very useful for index-nested loops joins, *unless* the number of matching tuples is small (for instance, if B is a candidate key of **s**). For clustered indices, all matching tuples are likely to be in the same or adjacent disk blocks, so the number of I/Os needed to retrieve them is typically 1 or 2. Thus, in case of the clustered index the cost estimate is

$$F_{\mathbf{r}} + (\rho + 1) \times \tau_{\mathbf{r}}$$

where ρ is the number of I/Os needed to retrieve the leaf node of a B^+ tree index or to find the correct bucket of a hash index (we assume that the index is not integrated with the data file and that all matching tuples fit in one page, which is where the 1 comes from). In case of an unclustered index, the cost is

$$F_{\mathbf{r}} + (\rho + \mu) \times \tau_{\mathbf{r}}$$

where μ is the average number of matching tuples in **s** per tuple in **r**.[1]

Example 10.5.2 (An Estimate of an Index-Nested Loops Join). Let us return to our example and compare this cost with the cost of block-nested loops joins. Assuming that ρ is 2 (our relations are fairly small), we obtain $1000 + 3 \times 10{,}000 = 31{,}000$ in the case of a clustered index—much higher than in the case of block-nested loops. However, if we switch **r** and **s** in the nested loop, the costs of index- and block-nested loops are much closer: $100 + 3 \times 1000 = 3100$ versus 1100. ■

Still, in this example indices seem to be losing to block-nested loops by a large margin. Why consider indices at all? It turns out that indexed loops have one remarkable property: the cost is not significantly affected by the size of the inner relation, as can be seen from the above formulas. So, for example, if we use **s** in the inner loop and its size grows to 10,000 pages (100,000 tuples), the cost of block-nested loops joins grows to $1000 + 10{,}000 \times 10 = 101{,}000$ page transfers. In contrast, the cost of index-nested loops joins increases much more conservatively: $1000 + 3 \times 10{,}000 = 31{,}000$. Thus, indexed joins tend to work better when relations in the join are fairly large and one is much larger than the other.

[1] Assuming that the number of matching tuples in **s** per tuple in **r** is always less than the number of pages in **s**, which is typically the case.

FIGURE 10.7 The merge step of the sort-merge join algorithm.

```
Input: relation r sorted on attribute A;
       relation s sorted on attribute B
Output: r ⋈_{A=B} s

Result := {}                                  // initialize Result
t_r := getFirst(r)                            // get first tuple
t_s := getFirst(s)
while !eof(r) and !eof(s) do {
    while !eof(r) && t_r.A < t_s.B do
        t_r := getNext(r)                     // get next tuple
    while !eof(s) and t_r.A > t_s.B do
        t_s := getNext(s)
    if t_r.A = t_s.B = c then {               // for some constant c
        Result := (σ_{A=c}(r) × σ_{B=c}(s)) ∪ Result;
        t_r := the next tuple t ∈ r where t.A > c;
    }
}
return Result;
```

10.5.2 Sort-Merge Join

The idea behind sort-merge is first to sort each relation on the join attributes and then to find matching tuples using a variation of the merge procedure, that is, scanning both relations simultaneously and comparing the join attributes. When a match is found, the joined tuple is added to the result.

The algorithm for this merge step is shown in Figure 10.7. The algorithm scans the relations **r** and **s** until a match on the attributes A and B is found. When this happens, all possible combinations (the Cartesian product) of the matching tuples are added to the result and the scan resumes.

Let us now estimate the cost of the sort-merge join in terms of the number of page transfers. Obviously, we must pay the usual price to sort the relations **r** and **s**: $2F_{\mathbf{r}}\lceil log_{M-1}F_{\mathbf{r}}\rceil + 2F_{\mathbf{s}}\lceil log_{M-1}F_{\mathbf{s}}\rceil$ (assuming that M buffers are available).

The cost of the merging step consists of the cost of scanning **r** and **s**, which is $F_{\mathbf{r}} + F_{\mathbf{s}}$ I/Os, plus the cost of computing $\sigma_{A=c}(\mathbf{r}) \times \sigma_{B=c}(\mathbf{s})$ for each match between **r** and **s**. At first, it seems that $\sigma_{A=c}(\mathbf{r}) \times \sigma_{B=c}(\mathbf{s})$ can be computed during the scan of **r** and **s** in Figure 10.7. However, if $\sigma_{A=c}(\mathbf{r})$ does not fit in main memory, computing the Cartesian product might require additional scans of $\sigma_{B=c}(\mathbf{s})$. The best way to compute this product would then be the block-nested loops join algorithm. The actual number of page transfers here depends on the sizes of $\sigma_{A=c}(\mathbf{r})$ and $\sigma_{B=c}(\mathbf{s})$, and on the amount of available memory. Typically, however, these subrelations are small and can fit in the available buffer, so the additional scans of $\sigma_{B=c}(\mathbf{s})$ can be avoided.

In this lucky case, the I/O cost of $\sigma_{A=c}(\mathbf{r}) \times \sigma_{B=c}(\mathbf{s})$ is zero and the entire sort-merge join takes $2F_{\mathbf{r}}\lceil log_{M-1}F_{\mathbf{r}}\rceil + 2F_{\mathbf{s}}\lceil log_{M-1}F_{\mathbf{s}}\rceil + F_{\mathbf{r}} + F_{\mathbf{s}}$ + cost of outputting the result.

> *Brain Teaser:* What is the maximum size of $\sigma_{A=c}(\mathbf{r}) \times \sigma_{B=c}(\mathbf{s})$ in terms of the sizes of **r** and **s**?

An optimization. A more careful analysis of the sort-merge algorithm shows that one can save the cost of one scan of **r** and **s**. The idea is to combine the scan needed for the merging step with the final stage of sorting **r** and **s**—analogously to the optimization for the union and difference operators discussed earlier. This can be accomplished as follows.

First, **r** and **s** are sorted in parallel, each using $\frac{M}{2}$ buffer pages. (We could split the buffer into unequal chunks depending on the relative sizes of the files, but we will ignore this possible enhancement.) The final stage of sorting **r** consists of merging all the remaining sorted runs of **r** into one final sorted relation. Similarly, the final stage of sorting **s** merges the remaining sorted runs of **s**. Instead of performing these final steps, we can modify the algorithm in Figure 10.7 to perform a generalized merge of the set of final sorted runs of **r** with the set of final sorted runs of **s**. Since the number of runs in each file is $\leq (\frac{M}{2} - 1)$, we can use one buffer page for scanning each run of **r** and **s**. One more page will be used for the output of the merge.

The new merge algorithm looks like the old one except that **r** is now understood as being a set of final runs of the first relation to be joined and **s** is viewed as a set of final runs of the second relation. The operation `getNext` is changed so that it will return the tuple with the lowest value of the join attributes in **r** and **s**, respectively. Details are left to Exercise 10.10.

The overall cost of the optimized algorithm is: $2F_{\mathbf{r}}\lceil log_{\frac{M}{2}-1}F_{\mathbf{r}}\rceil + 2F_{\mathbf{s}}\lceil log_{\frac{M}{2}-1}F_{\mathbf{s}}\rceil$ (to sort and merge) plus the cost of outputting the final result (which is the same as before). Note that for large M and F, $log_{\frac{M}{2}-1}F = (log_{M-1}F) \times log_{\frac{M}{2}-1}(M-1) \approx log_{M-1}F$, which means that we have eliminated the cost of one scan of **r** and **s**.

Example 10.5.3 (An Estimate of a Sort-Merge). For our running example, we have the following relation sizes in blocks—$F_{\mathbf{r}} = 1000$, $F_{\mathbf{s}} = 100$—and the buffer dedicated to our join operation has 102 pages. This means **s** can be sorted in 200 page transfers and **r** in $2 \times 1000 \times \lceil log_{101}1000\rceil = 4000$ page transfers. Assuming that during the merge step of the join the matching tuples all fit in $M - 1$ pages, this step can be done without the need for an additional scan of **r** and **s** (by combining this step with the final merge performed while sorting **r** and **s**, as explained earlier). Thus, the whole join will take 4200 page transfers. ■

It may seem that the block-nested loops algorithm is better than sort-merge in this particular case. However, just as with the index-nested loops method, the asymptotic behavior of sort-merge is better than that of block-nested loops. When the sizes of **r** and **s** grow, the cost of block-nested loops grows quadratically—$O(F_{\mathbf{r}}F_{\mathbf{s}})$—while the cost of sort-merge join increases much more slowly (assuming that $\sigma_{A=c}(\mathbf{r})$ and $\sigma_{B=c}(\mathbf{s})$ are small, as discussed above)—$O(F_{\mathbf{r}}logF_{\mathbf{r}} + F_{\mathbf{s}}logF_{\mathbf{s}})$.

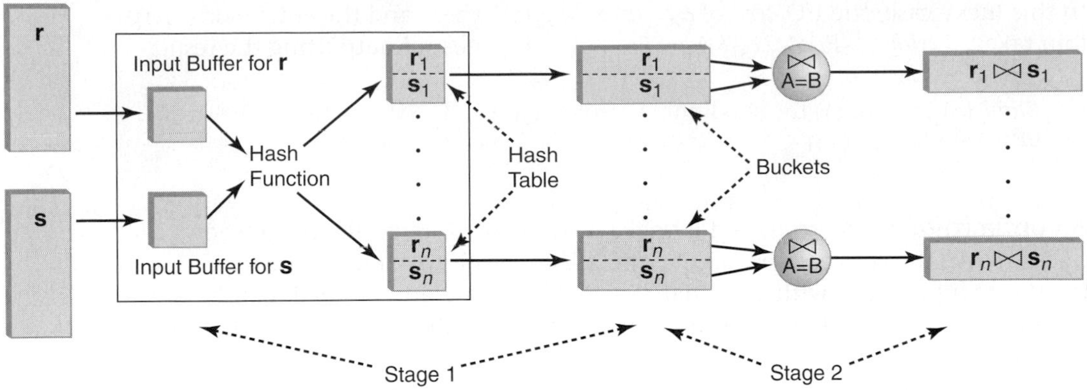

FIGURE 10.8 Hash join.

10.5.3 Hash Join

One way to compute a join, $\mathbf{r} \bowtie_{A=B} \mathbf{s}$, is to preprocess the relations **r** and **s** so that the tuples that possibly match will be placed on the same or adjacent pages. Such preprocessing eliminates the need for repeated scans of the inner-loop relation and is the basic idea behind the sort-merge technique described above. However, sorting is just one of the possible preprocessing techniques. Alternatively, we can use hashing to make sure that matching tuples are placed close to each other. We used this technique earlier, when we needed to place duplicate tuples (that arise due to projection or set-theoretic operations) close to each other. Clearly, the problem of identifying the duplicates is a special case of the problem we now face: identifying the tuples that have the same value for one or more attributes (e.g., A and B above). The idea is illustrated in Figure 10.8.

The hash-join method first hashes each input relation onto the hash table, where **r** is hashed on attribute A and **s** is hashed on attribute B. This has the effect that the tuples of **r** and **s** that can *possibly* match are put in the same bucket.

In the second stage, the **r** half and the **s** half of each bucket are joined to produce the final result. If both halves fit in main memory, all of these joins can be done at the cost of a single scan of **r** and **s**. If the buckets are too large for main memory, other join techniques can be tried. Typically in this case, the **r** portion of each bucket is further partitioned by hashing on the attribute A using a different hash function. Then the **s** portion of the corresponding bucket is scanned. In the process, each tuple of **s** is hashed on attribute B using the new hash function, and matching tuples in **r** are identified.

Assuming that each bucket fits in memory, we can join **r** and **s** at the cost of three I/Os per page of each relation: $3(F_{\mathbf{r}} + F_{\mathbf{s}})$. First, **r** and **s** must be input and the resulting buckets output (2 I/Os per page). Then each bucket must be input to join the two parts of the bucket. This requires one additional scan for each relation (recall that we do not include the cost of dumping the final result of the join on disk). In our running example, the cost is 3300 page transfers, which is higher than the cost of block-nested loops but the asymptotic behavior of hash join is better. In fact, if each hash bucket produced at the first stage of the algorithm fits in main memory, the cost is linear in the size of **r** and **s**. This makes hash join the best among all of the methods considered so far. However, it is important to realize that hash-join heavily depends on the choice of hash function and can be easily subverted by an unfortunate data skew (what if all tuples are hashed into the same bucket?). In addition, hash joins can be used only for equi-joins and are inappropriate for more general join conditions, such as inequalities.

10.6 Multirelational Joins

OPTIONAL

In Section 9.7, we discussed join indices and their use in computing joins. The algorithm for computing a join of the form $\mathbf{p} \bowtie_{A=B} \mathbf{q}$ works by scanning the join index and fetching the tuples whose rids are found in the index entries.

The actual computation is essentially similar to the indexed loop join, with **p** scanned in the outer loop, except that we use the join index to locate the tuples of **q** instead of a general-purpose index on attribute B of **q**. The advantage of the join index over other index types in this case is that it does not need to be searched: since all matching tuples are already associated with each other, the index can simply be scanned, the pairs or rids of the matching tuples fetched, and the tuples joined.

The idea underlying join indices can be extended to multirelational joins, where an index can be created to relate rids of more than two tuples. For instance, in a 3-way join, $\mathbf{p} \bowtie \mathbf{q} \bowtie \mathbf{r}$, a join index consists of triples of the form $\langle p, q, r \rangle$, where p is a rid of a tuple in relation **p**, q is a rid of a matching tuple in **q**, and r is a rid of a matching tuple in **r**. The triples are sorted in ascending order of rids beginning with the first column of the index, then the second, and then the third (the index can also be a B^+ tree).

With such an index, the join can be computed with a simple loop that scans the join index. For each triple $\langle p, q, r \rangle$ in the index, the tuples corresponding to the rids p, q, and r are fetched. Since the index is sorted on column 1 first, the join is performed in a single scan of the index and of the relation **p**. However, the relations **q** and **r** might have to be accessed many times. Indeed, if N is the average number of matching tuples in **q** per tuple in **p** and M is the average number of matching tuples in **r** per tuple in **p**, then, to compute the join, $\mid \mathbf{p} \mid \times N$ pages of **q** and $\mid \mathbf{p} \mid \times M$ pages of **r** might have to be retrieved.

Multiway join indices are especially popular for speeding up **star joins**—a common type of join used in online analytical processing.

A **star join** is a multiway join of the form $\mathbf{r} \bowtie_{cond_1} \mathbf{r}_1 \bowtie_{cond_2} \mathbf{r}_2 \bowtie_{cond_3} \ldots$, where each $cond_i$ is a join condition that involves the attributes of **r** and $\mathbf{r}_i$ only. In other words, there are no conditions that relate the tuples of $\mathbf{r}_i$ and $\mathbf{r}_j$ directly, and all matching is done through the tuples of **r**. An example of a star join is shown in

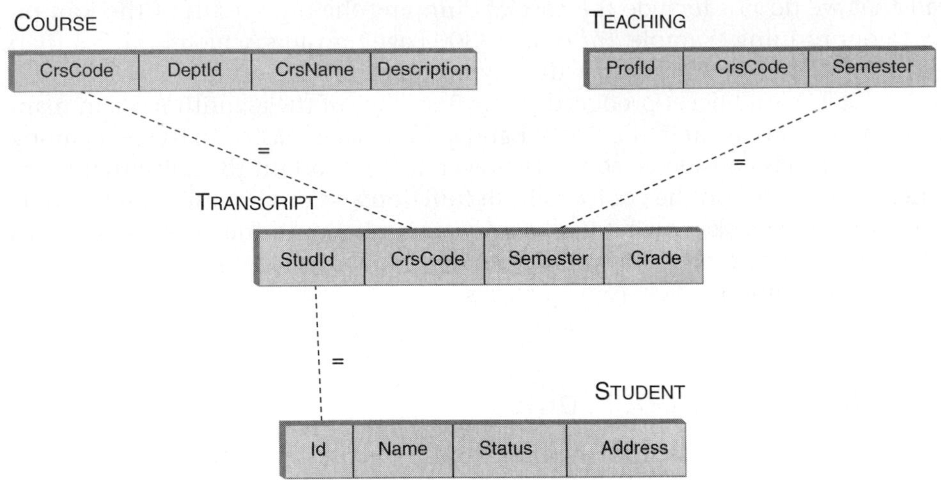

FIGURE 10.9 Star join.

OPTIONAL

Figure 10.9, where the "satellite" relations COURSE, TEACHING, and STUDENT are joined with the "star" relation TRANSCRIPT using equi-join conditions that match the attributes of the satellite relations only to the attributes of the star relation.

One reason that multiway join indices are good for computing star joins is that the join index of a star join is easier to maintain than the join index of a general multiway join (Exercise 10.14). Furthermore, computing a general multiway join using a join index can be expensive. Consider a join, $\mathbf{r} \bowtie \mathbf{r}_1 \bowtie \mathbf{r}_2 \bowtie \ldots \bowtie \mathbf{r}_n$, and suppose that N is the average number of matching tuples in $\mathbf{r}_i$ per tuple in $\mathbf{r}$. Then, using analysis similar to that for 3-way joins, a join index computation might need to access $\mid \mathbf{r} \mid \times N \times n$ pages.

Fortunately, star joins have more promising methods. One, described in [O'Neil and Graefe 1995], takes advantage of bitmapped join indices, introduced in Section 9.7.2. Instead of one join index that involves n relations, we can use one bitmapped join index, $\mathcal{J}_i$, for each partial join $\mathbf{r}_i \bowtie \mathbf{r}$. Each $\mathcal{J}_i$ is a collection of pairs $\langle v, \mathit{bitmap} \rangle$, where v is a rid of a tuple in $\mathbf{r}_i$ and *bitmap* has 1 in the kth position if and only if the kth tuple in $\mathbf{r}$ joins with the $\mathbf{r}_i$'s tuple represented by v. We can then scan $\mathcal{J}_i$ and logically OR all of the bitmaps. This will give us the rids of all tuples in $\mathbf{r}$ that can join with *some* tuple in $\mathbf{r}_i$. After obtaining such an ORed bitmap for each satellite relation $\mathbf{r}_i$, where $i = 1, \ldots, n$, we can logically AND these bitmaps to obtain the rids of all tuples in $\mathbf{r}$ that join with some tuple in each $\mathbf{r}_i$. In other words, this procedure prunes away all tuples in $\mathbf{r}$ that *do not* participate in the star join. The rationale is that there will be only a small number of tuples left, so the join can be computed inexpensively by a brute-force technique like nested loops.

Join indices and star join optimization are supported by the recent versions of commercial DBMSs from the major vendors, such as IBM's DB/2, Oracle, and Microsoft's SQL Server.

10.7 Computing Aggregate Functions

Generally, computing aggregate functions (such as AVG or COUNT) in a query involves a complete scan of the query output. The only issue here is the computation of aggregates in the presence of the GROUP BY *attrs* statement. Once again, the problem reduces to finding efficient techniques for partitioning the tuples according to the values of certain attributes. We have identified three such techniques so far:

1. Sorting
2. Hashing
3. Indexing

All three techniques provide efficient ways to access the groups of tuples specified by the GROUP BY clause. All that remains is to apply the aggregate functions to the member tuples of these groups.

BIBLIOGRAPHIC NOTES

Sort-based evaluation techniques for relational operators are discussed in [Blasgen and Eswaran 1977]; hash-based techniques are covered in [DeWitt et al. 1984; Kitsuregawa et al. 1983]. Good surveys of techniques for evaluating relational operators and additional references can be found in [Graefe 1993; Chaudhuri 1998]. The use of join indices for computing multirelational joins is studied in [Valduriez 1987], and techniques for computing various relational operators with the help of bitmap indices are discussed in [O'Neil and Graefe 1995; O'Neil and Quass 1997].

EXERCISES

10.1 Consider the use of unclustered B^+ trees for external sorting. Let R denote the number of data records per disk block, and let F be the number of blocks in the data file. Estimate the cost of such a sorting procedure as a function of R and F. Compare this cost to merge-based external sorting. Consider the cases of $R = 1$, 10, and 100.

10.2 Estimate the cost of the sort-based projection assuming that, during the initial scan (where tuple components are deleted), the size of the original relation shrinks by the factor $\alpha < 1$.

10.3 Consider hash-based evaluation of the projection operator. Assume that all buckets are about the same size but do not fit in main memory. Let N be the size of the hash table measured in memory pages, F be the size of the original relation measured in pages, and $\alpha < 1$ be the reduction factor due to projection. Estimate the number of page transfers to and from the disk needed to compute the projection.

10.4 Give an example of an instance of the TRANSCRIPT relation (Figure 3.5) and a hash function on the attribute sequence ⟨StudId, Grade⟩ that sends two identical tuples in $\pi_{\texttt{StudId,Semester}}$(TRANSCRIPT) into *different* hash buckets. (This shows that such a hash-based access path cannot be used to compute the projection.)

10.5 Clearly, the theoretical minimum for the selectivity of an access path is the number of pages that hold the output of the relational operator involved. What is the best theoretical upper bound on the selectivity of an access path when selection or projection operators are involved?

10.6 Based on the discussion in Section 10.4.2, give a precise definition of when an access path covers the use of projection, union, and set-difference operators.

10.7 Consider the expression

$$\sigma_{\texttt{StudId=666666666} \wedge \texttt{Semester='F1995'} \wedge \texttt{Grade='A'}}(\text{TRANSCRIPT})$$

Suppose the following access paths are available:

- An unclustered hash index on `StudId`
- An unclustered hash index on `Semester`
- An unclustered hash index on `Grade`

Which of these access paths has the best selectivity, and which has the worst? Compare the selectivity of the worst access path (among the above three) to the selectivity of the file scan.

10.8 Compute the cost of $\mathbf{r} \bowtie_{\texttt{A=B}} \mathbf{s}$ using the following methods:

- Nested loops
- Block-nested loops
- Index-nested loops with a hash index on B in **s** (consider both clustered and unclustered index)

where **r** occupies 2000 pages, 20 tuples per page; **s** occupies 5000 pages, 5 tuples per page; and the amount of main memory available for a block-nested loops join is 402 pages. Assume that at most 5 tuples of **s** match each tuple in **r**.

10.9 In sort-based union and difference algorithms, the final scan—where the actual union or difference is computed—can be performed at no cost in I/O because this step can be combined with the last merge step during sorting of the relations involved. Work out the details of this algorithm.

*** 10.10** In the sort-merge join of $\mathbf{r} \bowtie \mathbf{s}$, the scan in the algorithm of Figure 10.7 can be performed at no cost in I/O because it can be combined with the final merging step of sorting **r** and **s**. Work out the details of such an algorithm.

10.11 Estimate the number of page transfers needed to compute $\mathbf{r} \bowtie_{\texttt{A=B}} \mathbf{s}$ using a sort-merge join, assuming the following:

- The size of **r** is 1000 pages, 10 tuples per page; the size of **s** is 500 pages, 20 tuples per page.
- The size of the main memory buffer for this join computation is 10 pages.
- The Cartesian product of matching tuples in **r** and **s** (see Figure 10.7) is computed using a block-nested loops join.
- `r.A` has 100 distinct values and `s.B` has 50 distinct values. These values are spread around the files more or less evenly, so the size of $\sigma_{\texttt{A}=c}(\mathbf{r})$, where $c \in$ `r.A`, does not vary much with c.

10.12 The methods for computing joins discussed in Section 10.5 all deal with equi-joins. Discuss their applicability to the problem of computing inequality joins, such as $\mathbf{r} \bowtie_{\texttt{A<B}} \mathbf{s}$.

10.13 Consider a relation schema, **R**(A, B), with the following characteristics:

- Total number of tuples: 1,000,000
- 10 tuples per page
- Attribute A is a candidate key; range is 1 to 1,000,000
- Clustered B^+ tree index of depth 4 on A
- Attribute B has 100,000 distinct values
- Hash index on B

Estimate the number of page transfers needed to evaluate each of the following queries for each of the proposed methods:

- $\sigma_{A<3000}$: sequential scan; index on A
- $\sigma_{A>3000 \wedge A<3200 \wedge B=5}$: index on A; index on B
- $\sigma_{A \neq 22 \wedge B \neq 66}$: sequential scan; index on A; index on B

10.14 Design an algorithm for incremental maintenance of a join index for a multiway star join.

10.15 Design a join algorithm that uses a join index. Define the notion of a *clustered* join index (there are three possibilities in the case of a binary join!) and consider the effect of clustering on the join algorithm.

11

An Overview of Query Optimization

This chapter is an overview of relational query optimization techniques typically used in database management systems. Our goal here is not to prepare you for a career as a DBMS implementor but rather to make you a better application designer or database administrator. Just as the knowledge of the evaluation techniques used in relational algebra can help you make better physical design, an understanding of the principles of query optimization can help you formulate SQL queries that stand a better chance of being efficiently implemented by the query processor.

Relational query optimization is a fascinating example of tackling a problem of immense computational complexity with relatively simple heuristic search algorithms. A more extensive treatment of the subject can be found in [Garcia-Molina et al. 2000].

11.1 Query Processing Architecture

When the user submits a query, it is first parsed by the DBMS, which verifies the syntax and type correctness of the query. Being a declarative language, SQL does not suggest concrete ways to evaluate its queries. Therefore, a parsed query has to be converted into a relational algebra expression, which can be evaluated directly using the algorithms presented in Chapter 10. A typical SQL query such as

```
SELECT   DISTINCT TargetList
FROM     REL1 V1, ..., RELn Vn                    (11.1)
WHERE    Condition
```

is normally translated into the following relational algebraic expression:

$$\pi_{TargetList}(\sigma_{Condition'}(\text{REL}_1 \times \ldots \times \text{REL}_n))$$

where `Condition'` is `Condition` converted from SQL syntax to relational algebra form. Section 10.1 has an example of such a transformation from SQL to the relational algebra.

While the above algebraic expressions are straightforward and easy to produce, it might take ages to evaluate them. For one thing, they contain Cartesian products, so a join of four 100-block relations produces a 10^8-block intermediate relation, which, with a disk speed of 10 ms/page, takes about 50 hours just to write out. Even if we manage to convert the Cartesian product into equi-joins (as explained in Section 11.2), we might still have to grapple with the long turnaround time (dozens of minutes) for the above query. It is the job of the **query optimizer** to bring this time down to seconds (or, for very complex queries, a few minutes).

A typical **rule-based query optimizer** uses a set of rules (e.g., an access path based on an index is better than a table scan) to construct a **query execution plan**. A **cost-based query optimizer** estimates the cost of query plans based on statistics maintained by the DBMS and uses this information, in addition to the rules, to choose a plan. The two main components of a cost-based query optimizer are the **query execution plan generator** and the **plan cost estimator**. A query execution plan can be thought of as a relational expression with concrete evaluation methods (or *access paths*, as we called them in Chapter 10) attached to each occurrence of a relational operator in the expression. Thus, the main job of the optimizer is to propose a single plan that can evaluate the given relational expression at a "reasonably cheap" cost according to the cost estimator. This plan is then passed to the *query plan interpreter*, a software component directly responsible for query evaluation according to the given plan. The overall architecture of query processing is depicted in Figure 11.1.

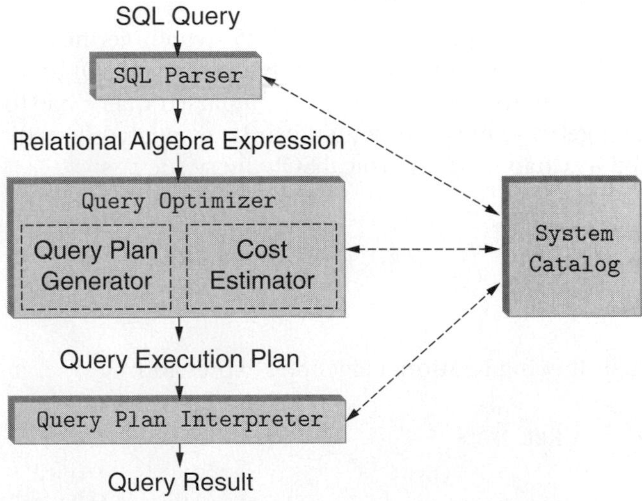

FIGURE 11.1 Typical architecture for DBMS query processing.

11.2 Heuristic Optimization Based on Algebraic Equivalences

The heuristics used in relational query evaluation are (for the most part) based on simple observations, such as that joining smaller relations is better than joining large ones, that performing an equi-join is better than computing a Cartesian product, and that computing several operations in just one relation scan is better than doing so in several scans. Most of these heuristics can be expressed in the form of relational algebra transformations, which take one expression and produce a different but equivalent expression. Not all transformations are optimizations by themselves. Sometimes they yield less efficient expressions. However, relational transformations are designed to work with other transformations to produce expressions that are better overall.

We now present a number of heuristic transformations used by the query optimizers.

Selection and projection-based transformations.

- $\sigma_{cond_1 \wedge cond_2}(\mathbf{R}) \equiv \sigma_{cond_1}(\sigma_{cond_2}(\mathbf{R}))$. This transformation is known as **cascading of selections**. It is not an optimization per se, but it is useful in conjunction with other transformations (see the discussion on page 412 of pushing selections and projections through joins).
- $\sigma_{cond_1}(\sigma_{cond_2}(\mathbf{R})) \equiv \sigma_{cond_2}(\sigma_{cond_1}(\mathbf{R}))$. This transformation is called **commutativity of selection**. Like cascading, it is useful in conjunction with other transformations.
- $\pi_{attr}(\mathbf{R}) \equiv \pi_{attr}(\pi_{attr'}(\mathbf{R}))$, if $attr \subseteq attr'$ and $attr'$ is a subset of the attributes of **R**. This equivalence is known as **cascading of projections** and is used primarily with other transformations.
- $\pi_{attr}(\sigma_{cond}(\mathbf{R})) \equiv \sigma_{cond}(\pi_{attr}(\mathbf{R}))$, if *attr* includes all attributes used in *cond*. This equivalence is known as the **commutativity of selection and projection**. It is usually used as a preparation step for pushing a selection or a projection through the join operator.

Cross product and join transformations. The transformations used for cross products and joins are the usual commutativity and associativity rules for these operators.

- $\mathbf{R} \bowtie \mathbf{S} \equiv \mathbf{S} \bowtie \mathbf{R}$
- $\mathbf{R} \bowtie (\mathbf{S} \bowtie \mathbf{T}) \equiv (\mathbf{R} \bowtie \mathbf{S}) \bowtie \mathbf{T}$
- $\mathbf{R} \times \mathbf{S} \equiv \mathbf{S} \times \mathbf{R}$
- $\mathbf{R} \times (\mathbf{S} \times \mathbf{T}) \equiv (\mathbf{R} \times \mathbf{S}) \times \mathbf{T}$

These rules can be useful in conjunction with the various nested loops evaluation strategies. As we saw in Chapter 10, it is generally better to scan the smaller relation in the outer loop, and the above rules can help maneuver the relations into the right positions. For instance, BIGGER $\bowtie$ SMALLER can be rewritten as SMALLER $\bowtie$ BIGGER, which intuitively corresponds to the query optimizer deciding to use SMALLER in the outer loop.

The commutativity and associativity rules (at least in the case of the join) can reduce the size of the intermediate relation in the computation of a multirelational join. For instance, $\mathbf{S} \bowtie \mathbf{T}$ can be much smaller than $\mathbf{R} \bowtie \mathbf{S}$, in which case the computation of $(\mathbf{S} \bowtie \mathbf{T}) \bowtie \mathbf{R}$ might take fewer I/O operations than the computation of $(\mathbf{R} \bowtie \mathbf{S}) \bowtie \mathbf{T}$. The associativity and commutativity rules can be used to transform the latter expression into the former.

In fact, the commutativity and associativity rules are largely responsible for the many alternative evaluation plans that might exist for the same query. A query that involves the join of N relations can have $T(N) \times N!$ query plans just to handle the join, where $T(N)$ is the number of different binary trees with N leaf nodes. ($N!$ is the number of permutations of N relations, and $T(N)$ is the number of ways a particular permutation can be parenthesized.) This number grows very rapidly and is huge even for very small N.[1] A similar result holds for other commutative and associative operations (e.g., union), but our main focus is on join because it is the most expensive operation to compute.

The job of the query optimizer is to estimate the cost of these plans (which can vary widely) and to choose one "good" plan. Because the number of plans is large, it can take longer to find a good plan than to evaluate the query by brute force. (It is faster to perform 10^6 I/Os than 15! in-memory operations.) To make query optimization practical, an optimizer typically looks at only a small subset of all possible plans, and its cost estimates are approximate at best. Therefore, query optimizers are very likely to miss the optimal plan and are actually designed only to find one that is "reasonable." In other words, the "optimization" in "query optimizer" should always be taken with a grain of salt since it does not adequately describe what is being done by that component of the DBMS architecture.

Pushing selections and projections through joins and Cartesian products.

- $\sigma_{cond}(\mathbf{R} \times \mathbf{S}) \equiv \mathbf{R} \bowtie_{cond} \mathbf{S}$. This rule is used when *cond* relates the attributes of both **R** and **S**. The basis for this heuristic is the belief that Cartesian products should never be materialized. Instead, selections must always be combined with Cartesian products and the techniques for computing joins should be used. By applying the selection condition as soon as a row of $\mathbf{R} \times \mathbf{S}$ is created, we can save one scan and avoid storing a large intermediate relation.
- $\sigma_{cond}(\mathbf{R} \times \mathbf{S}) \equiv \sigma_{cond}(\mathbf{R}) \times \mathbf{S}$, if the attributes used in *cond* all belong to **R**. This heuristic is based on the idea that if we absolutely must compute a Cartesian product, we should make the relations involved as small as possible. By pushing the selection down to **R**, we hope to reduce the size of **R** *before* it is used in the cross product.

[1] When $N = 4$, $T(4)$ is 5, and the number of all plans is 120. When $N = 5$, $T(5) = 14$, and the number of all plans is 1680.

- $\sigma_{cond}(\mathbf{R} \bowtie_{cond'} \mathbf{S}) \equiv \sigma_{cond}(\mathbf{R}) \bowtie_{cond'} \mathbf{S}$, if the attributes in *cond* all belong to **R**. The rationale here is the same as for Cartesian products. Computing a join can be very expensive, and we must try to reduce the size of the relations involved. Note that if *cond* is a conjunction of comparison conditions, we can push each conjunct separately to either **R** or **S** as long as the attributes named in the conjunct belong to only one relation.
- $\pi_{attr}(\mathbf{R} \times \mathbf{S}) \equiv \pi_{attr}(\pi_{attr'}(\mathbf{R}) \times \mathbf{S})$, if $attributes(\mathbf{R}) \supseteq attr' \supseteq (attr \cap attributes(\mathbf{R}))$, where $attributes(\mathbf{R})$ denotes the set of all the attributes of **R**. The rationale for this rule is that, by pushing the projection inside the Cartesian product, we reduce the size of one of its operands. In Chapter 10, we saw that the I/O complexity of the join operation (of which $\times$ is a special case) is proportional to the number of pages in the relations involved. Thus, by applying the projection early we might reduce the number of page transfers needed to evaluate the cross product.
- $\pi_{attr}(\mathbf{R} \bowtie_{cond} \mathbf{S}) \equiv \pi_{attr}(\pi_{attr'}(\mathbf{R}) \bowtie_{cond} \mathbf{S})$, if $attr' \subseteq attributes(\mathbf{R})$ is such that it contains all the attributes that **R** has in common with either *attr* or *cond*. The potential benefit here is the same as for the cross product. The important additional requirement is that *attr′* must include those attributes of **R** that are mentioned in *cond*. If some of these attributes are projected out, the expression $\pi_{attr'}(\mathbf{R}) \bowtie_{cond} \mathbf{S}$ will not be syntactically correct. This requirement is unnecessary in the case of the Cartesian product since no join condition is involved.

The rules for pushing selections and projections through joins and cross products are especially useful when combined with the rules for cascading σ and π. For instance, consider the expression $\sigma_{c_1 \wedge c_2 \wedge c_3}(\mathbf{R} \times \mathbf{S})$, where c_1 involves the attributes of both **R** and **S**, c_2 involves only the attributes of **R**, and c_3 involves only the attributes of **S**. We can transform this expression into one that can be evaluated more efficiently by first cascading the selections, then pushing them down and finally eliminating the Cartesian product:

$$\sigma_{c_1 \wedge c_2 \wedge c_3}(\mathbf{R} \times \mathbf{S}) \equiv \sigma_{c_1}(\sigma_{c_2}(\sigma_{c_3}(\mathbf{R} \times \mathbf{S}))) \equiv \sigma_{c_1}(\sigma_{c_2}(\mathbf{R}) \times \sigma_{c_3}(\mathbf{S})) \equiv \sigma_{c_2}(\mathbf{R}) \bowtie_{c_1} \sigma_{c_3}(\mathbf{S})$$

We can optimize the expressions that involve projections in a similar way. Consider, for instance, $\pi_{attr}(\mathbf{R} \bowtie_{cond} \mathbf{S})$. Suppose that $attr_1$ is a subset of the attributes in **R** such that $attr_1 \supseteq attr \cap attributes(\mathbf{R})$ and such that $attr_1$ contains all the attributes in *cond*. Let $attr_2$ be a similar set for **S**. Then

$$\begin{aligned} \pi_{attr}(\mathbf{R} \bowtie_{cond} \mathbf{S}) &\equiv \pi_{attr}(\pi_{attr_1}(\mathbf{R} \bowtie_{cond} \mathbf{S})) \equiv \pi_{attr}(\pi_{attr_1}(\mathbf{R}) \bowtie_{cond} \mathbf{S}) \\ &\equiv \pi_{attr}(\pi_{attr_2}(\pi_{attr_1}(\mathbf{R}) \bowtie_{cond} \mathbf{S})) \equiv \pi_{attr}(\pi_{attr_1}(\mathbf{R}) \bowtie_{cond} \pi_{attr_2}(\mathbf{S})) \end{aligned}$$

The resulting expression can be more efficient because it joins smaller relations.

Using the algebraic equivalence rules. Typically, the above algebraic rules are used to transform queries expressed in relational algebra into expressions that are believed to be better than the original. The word "better" here should not be understood literally because the criteria used to guide the transformation are heuristic. In fact, in the next section we will see that following through with all the suggested transformations might not yield the best result. Thus, the outcome of the algebraic transformation step should yield a set of candidate queries, which must then be further examined using cost-estimation techniques discussed in Section 11.3. Here is a typical heuristic algorithm for applying algebraic equivalences:

1. Use the cascading rule for selection to break up the conjunctions in selection conditions. The result is a single selection transformed into a sequence of selection operators, each of which can be applied separately.
2. The previous step leads to greater freedom in pushing selections through joins and Cartesian products. We can now use the rules for commutativity of selection and for pushing selections through joins to propagate the selections as far inside the query as possible.
3. Combine the Cartesian product operations with selections to form joins. As we saw in Chapter 10, there are efficient techniques for computing joins, but little can be done to improve the computation of a Cartesian product. Thus, converting these products into joins is a potential time and space saver.
4. Use the associativity rules for joins and Cartesian products to rearrange the order of join operations. The purpose here is to come up with the order that produces the smallest intermediate relations. (Note that the size of the intermediate relations directly contributes to overhead, so reducing these sizes speeds up query processing.) Techniques for the estimation of the size of intermediate relations are discussed in Section 11.3.
5. Use the rules for cascading projections and for pushing them into queries to propagate projections as far into the query as possible. This can potentially speed up the computation of joins by reducing the size of the operands.
6. Identify the operations that can be processed in the same pass to save time writing the intermediate results to disk. This technique is called *pipelining* and is illustrated in Section 11.3.

11.3 Estimating the Cost of a Query Execution Plan

As defined earlier, a query execution plan is more or less a relational expression with concrete evaluation methods (access paths) attached to each operation. In this section, we take a closer look at this concept and discuss ways to evaluate the cost of a plan to compute query results.

For discussion purposes, it is convenient to represent queries as trees. In a **query tree** each inner node is labeled with a relational operator and each leaf is labeled with a relation name. Unary relational operators have only one child; binary operators have two. Figure 11.2 presents four query trees corresponding to the following equivalent relational expressions, respectively:

$$\pi_{\texttt{Name}}(\sigma_{\texttt{DeptId='CS'} \wedge \texttt{Semester='F1994'}}(\text{PROFESSOR} \bowtie_{\text{Id=ProfId}} \text{TEACHING})) \quad \textbf{11.2}$$

$$\pi_{\texttt{Name}}(\sigma_{\texttt{DeptId='CS'}}(\text{PROFESSOR}) \bowtie_{\text{Id=ProfId}} \sigma_{\texttt{Semester='F1994'}}(\text{TEACHING})) \quad \textbf{11.3}$$

$$\pi_{\texttt{Name}}(\sigma_{\texttt{Semester='F1994'}}(\sigma_{\texttt{DeptId='CS'}}(\text{PROFESSOR}) \bowtie_{\text{Id=ProfId}} \text{TEACHING})) \quad \textbf{11.4}$$

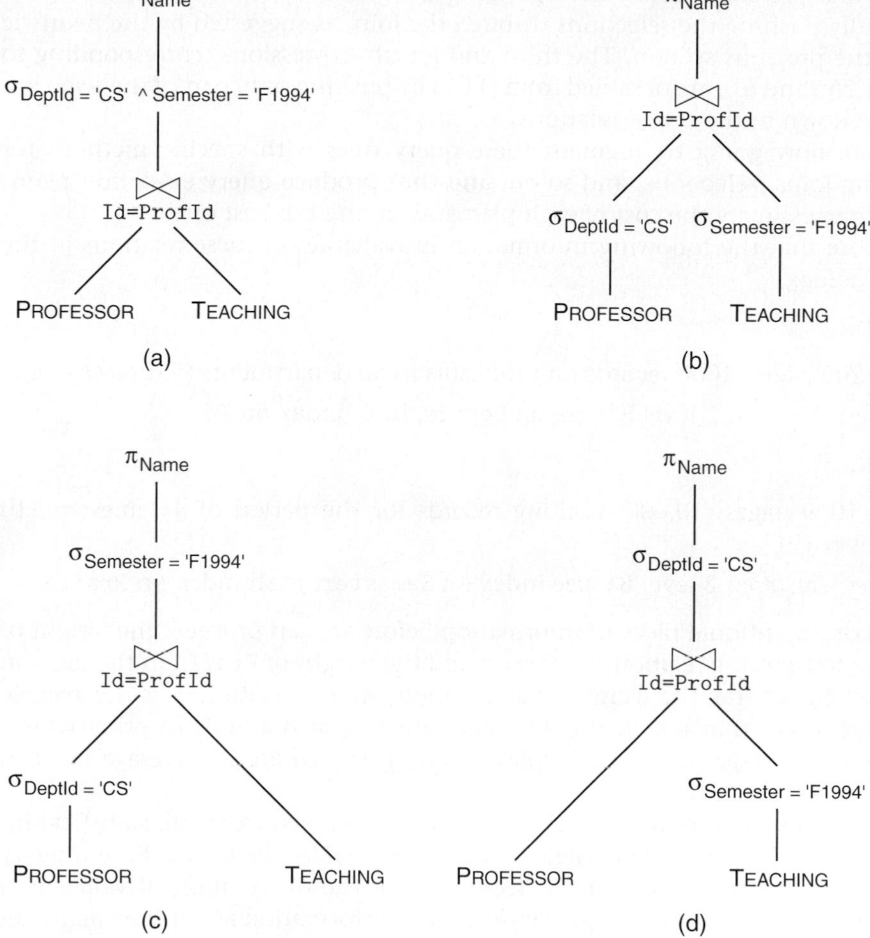

FIGURE 11.2 Query trees for relational expressions (11.2) through (11.5).

$$\pi_{Name}(\sigma_{\texttt{DeptId='CS'}}(\text{PROFESSOR} \bowtie_{\texttt{Id=ProfId}} \sigma_{\texttt{Semester='F1994'}}(\text{TEACHING}))) \qquad \textbf{11.5}$$

The relations PROFESSOR and TEACHING were described in Figure 3.5, page 39.

Expression (11.2), corresponding to Figure 11.2(a), is what a query processor might initially generate from the SQL query (after combining the selection `Id = ProfId` with the cross product)

```
SELECT   P.Name
FROM     PROFESSOR P, TEACHING T                              11.6
WHERE    P.Id = T.ProfId AND T.Semester = 'F1994'
         AND P.DeptId = 'CS'
```

The second expression, (11.3), corresponding to Figure 11.2(b), is obtained from the first by fully pushing the selections through the join, as suggested by the heuristic rules in the previous section. The third and fourth expressions, corresponding to Figure 11.2(c) and (d), are obtained from (11.2) by pushing only part of the selection condition down to the actual relations.

We are now going to augment these query trees with specific methods for computing joins, selections, and so on, and thus produce query execution plans. We will then estimate the cost of each plan and choose the best one.

Suppose that the following information is available on these relations in the system catalog:

PROFESSOR

Size: 200 pages, 1000 records on professors in 50 departments (5 tuples/page).

Indices: clustered 2-level B^+ tree on `DeptId`, hash index on `Id`.

TEACHING

Size: 1000 pages, 10,000 teaching records for the period of 4 semesters (10 tuples/page).

Indices: clustered 2-level B^+ tree index on `Semester`, hash index on `ProfId`

We need one additional piece of information before we can proceed: the weight of the attribute `Id` in the relation PROFESSOR and the weight of `ProfId` in the relation TEACHING. In general, the **weight** of an attribute, *A*, in a relation, **r**, is the average number of tuples that match the different values of attribute *A*. In other words, weight is the average number of tuples in $\sigma_{A=value}(\mathbf{r})$, where the average is taken over all values of *A* in **r**.

The weights for various attributes are typically derived from the statistical information stored in the system catalog and maintained by the DBMS. Recent query optimizers go as far as maintaining *histograms* for the distribution of values in a particular attribute. Histograms give more precise information about how many tuples are likely to be selected for a given value of the attribute. Attribute weights are needed to estimate the cost of computing the join using index-based techniques, as well as to estimate the size of the result of all of the operations in our examples. Since intermediate results of the various operations might later be used as input to other operators, knowing the sizes is important for estimating the cost of each concrete plan. Section 12.6 discusses statistics and size estimation in more detail.

Returning to our example, we first need to find realistic weights for the attributes `Id` and `ProfId`. For the `Id` attribute of PROFESSOR, the weight must be 1, since `Id` is a key. For the weight of `ProfId` in TEACHING, let us assume that each professor is likely to have been teaching the same number of courses. Since there are 1000 professors and 10,000 teaching records, the weight of `ProfId` must be about 10. Let us now consider the four cases in Figure 11.2. In all of them, we assume that a 52-page buffer is available for evaluating the join and that there is a small amount of additional memory to hold some index blocks and other auxiliary information (the exact amount will be specified when necessary).

Case a: selection not pushed. One possibility to evaluate the join is the index-nested loops method. For instance, we can use the smaller relation, PROFESSOR, in the outer loop. Since the indices on Id and ProfId are not clustered *and* because each tuple in PROFESSOR is likely to match some tuple in TEACHING (generally, every professor teaches something), the cost can be estimated as follows.

- *To scan the* PROFESSOR *relation*: 200 page transfers.
- *To find matching tuples in* TEACHING: We can use 50 pages of the buffer to hold the pages of the PROFESSOR relation. Since there are 5 PROFESSOR tuples in each such page, and since each tuple matches 10 TEACHING tuples, the 50-page chunk of the PROFESSOR relation can, on average, match $50 \times 5 \times 10 = 2500$ tuples of TEACHING. The index on the ProfId attribute of TEACHING is not clustered, so record Ids retrieved from it will not be sorted. As a result, the cost of fetching the matching rows of the data file (leaving aside for the moment the cost of fetching the Ids from the index), can be as much as 2500 page transfers. By sorting the record Ids of these matching tuples first, however (a technique described in Section 10.4.1), we can guarantee that the tuples will be fetched in no more than 1000 page transfers (the size of the TEACHING relation).[2] Since this trick must be performed four times (for each 50-page chunk of PROFESSOR), the total number of page transfers to fetch the matching tuples of TEACHING is 4000.
- *To search the index*: Since TEACHING has a hash index on ProfId, we can assume 1.2 I/Os per index search. For each ProfId, the search finds the bucket that contains the record Ids of all matching tuples (10 on average). These Ids can be retrieved in one I/O operation. Thus, the 10,000 matching record Ids of tuples in TEACHING can be retrieved 10 tuples per I/O—1000 I/Os in total. The total cost of the index search for all tuples is therefore 1200.
- *Combined cost*: $200 + 4000 + 1200 = 5400$ page transfers.

Alternatively, we can use a block-nested loops join or a sort-merge join. For a block-nested loops join that utilizes a 52-page buffer of main memory, the inner relation, TEACHING, must be scanned 4 times. This leads to a smaller number of page transfers: $200 + 4 \times 1000 = 4200$. Note, however, that if the weight of ProfId in TEACHING is lower, the comparison between the index-nested and block-nested techniques can be very different (Exercise 11.4) since the index may become more effective in reducing the number of I/Os.

The result of the join is going to have 10,000 tuples (because Id is a key for PROFESSOR and every PROFESSOR tuple matches roughly 10 TEACHING tuples). Since every PROFESSOR tuple is twice the size of a TEACHING tuple, the resulting file will be three times the size of TEACHING—3000 pages.

Next we need to apply the selection and the projection operators. As the result of the join does not have any indices, we choose the file scan access path. Moreover, we can apply selection and projection during the same scan. Examining each tuple

[2] Note that we need extra space for sorting the record Ids. Since we have rids for 2500 tuples and each rid is typically 8 bytes long, we need about five 4K pages to hold all these rids in main memory.

in turn, we discard it if it does not satisfy the selection condition; if it does, we discard the attributes not named in the SELECT clause and output the result.

We could treat the join phase and the select/project phase separately, outputting the result of the join to an intermediate file and then inputting the file to do the select/project, but there is a better way. By interleaving the two phases, we can eliminate the I/O operations associated with creating and accessing the intermediate file. With this technique, called **pipelining**, join and select/project operate as coroutines. The join phase is executed until the available buffers in memory are filled, and then select/project takes over, emptying the buffers and outputting the result. The join phase is then resumed, filling the buffers, and the process continues until select/project outputs the last tuple. In pipelining, the output of one relational operator is "piped" to the input of the next relational operator—without saving the intermediate result on disk.

The resulting query execution plan is depicted in Figure 11.3(a). All in all, using the block-nested loops strategy, evaluating this plan takes $4200 + \alpha \times 3000$ page I/Os, where 3000 is the size of the join (computed earlier) and α, a number between 0 and 1, is the reduction factor due to selection and projection. We study the techniques for estimating this reduction factor in Section 11.4. The last component, $\alpha \times 3000$, represents the cost of writing the query result out on disk. Since this cost is the same for all plans, (a) through (d), we will ignore it in our further analysis.

Case b: selection fully pushed. The query tree in Figure 11.2(b) suggests a number of alternative query execution plans. First, if we push selections down to the leaf nodes of the tree (the relations PROFESSOR and TEACHING), then we can compute the relations $\sigma_{\texttt{DeptId='CS'}}$(PROFESSOR) and $\sigma_{\texttt{Semester='F1994'}}$(TEACHING) using the existing B$^+$ tree indices on `DeptId` and `Semester`. However, the resulting relations will not have any indices (unless the DBMS decides that it is worth building them, which incurs additional cost). In particular, we cannot make use of the hash indices on PROFESSOR.`Id` and TEACHING.`ProfId`. Thus, we must use block-nested loops or sort-merge to compute the join. The projection is then applied to the result of the join on the fly, while it is being written out to disk. In other words, we again use pipelining to minimize the overhead of applying the projection operator.

We estimate the cost of the plan, depicted in Figure 11.3(b), where the join is performed using block-nested loops. Since there are 1000 professors in 50 departments, the weight of `DeptId` in the PROFESSOR relation is 20; hence, the size of $\sigma_{\texttt{DeptId='CS'}}$(PROFESSOR) is about 20 tuples, or 4 pages. The weight of `Semester` in TEACHING is 10,000/4 = 2500 tuples, or 250 pages. Because the indices on `DeptId` and `Semester` are clustered, computing the selection will require the following I/Os: 4 (to access the two indices) + 4 (to access the qualifying tuples in PROFESSOR) + 250 (to access the qualifying tuples in TEACHING).

The results of the two selections do not need to be written out on disk. Instead, we can pipe $\sigma_{\texttt{DeptId='CS'}}$(PROFESSOR) and $\sigma_{\texttt{Semester='F1994'}}$(TEACHING) into the join operation, which is computed using block-nested loops. Since the first relation is only 4 pages long, we will keep it entirely in main memory. As we compute the second relation, we join the results with the 4-page $\sigma_{\texttt{DeptId='CS'}}$(PROFESSOR) relation and pipe the result further into the operation $\pi_{\texttt{Name}}$. After the entire selection of

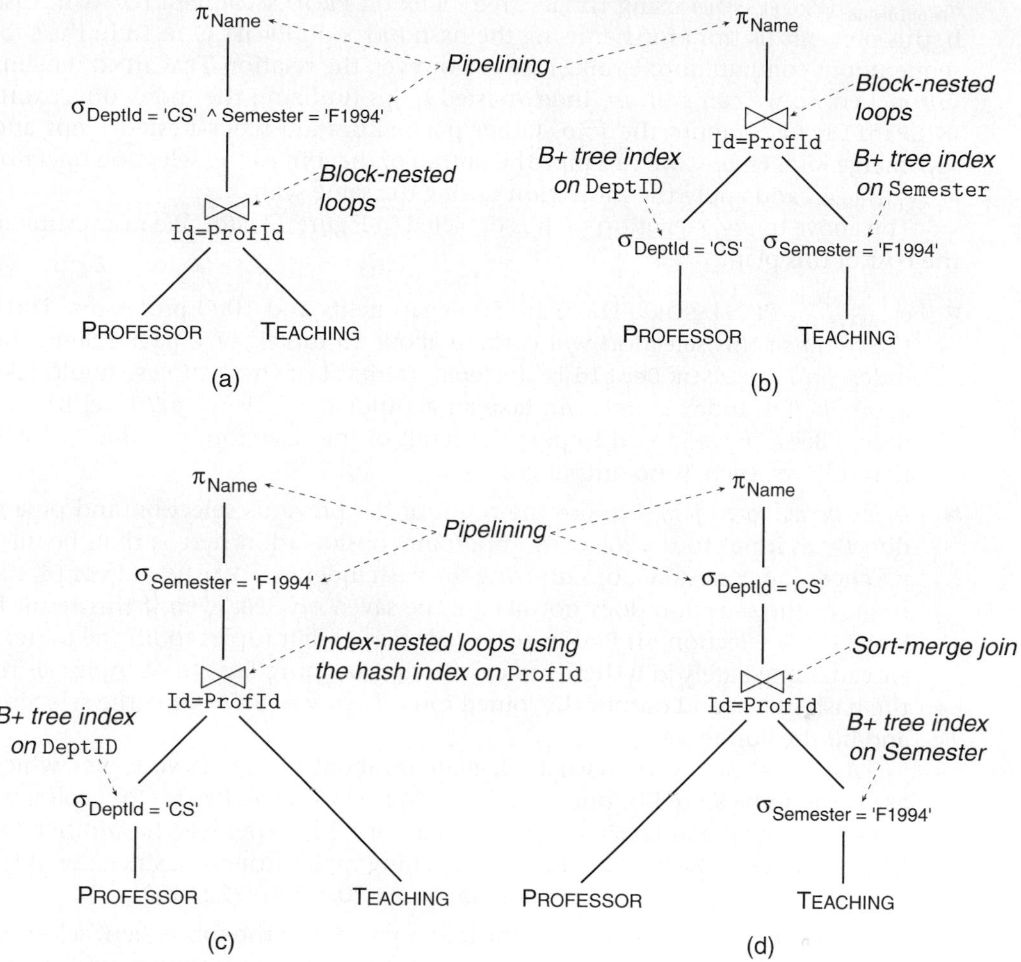

FIGURE 11.3 Query execution plans for relational expressions (11.2) through (11.5).

TEACHING is computed, the join will also be finished with no extra I/O. Thus, the total cost is $4 + 4 + 250 = 258$.

Note that if $\sigma_{\texttt{DeptId='CS'}}$(PROFESSOR) were too big to fit in the buffer, then it would not be feasible to compute the join without writing $\sigma_{\texttt{Semester='F1994'}}$(TEACHING) on disk. Indeed, scanning of $\sigma_{\texttt{DeptId='CS'}}$(PROFESSOR) and the initial scan of $\sigma_{\texttt{Semester='F1994'}}$(TEACHING) could still be done through pipelining but now $\sigma_{\texttt{Semester='F1994'}}$(TEACHING) would have to be scanned multiple times, once for each chunk of $\sigma_{\texttt{DeptId='CS'}}$(PROFESSOR). To enable this, $\sigma_{\texttt{Semester='F1994'}}$(TEACHING) would have to be written out on disk after the first scan.

Case c: selection pushed to the PROFESSOR **relation.** For the query tree in Figure 11.2(c), a query execution plan can be constructed as follows. First, compute

$\sigma_{\texttt{DeptId='CS'}}$(PROFESSOR) using the B^+ tree index on PROFESSOR.DeptId. As in case b, this prevents us from further using the hash index on PROFESSOR.Id in the subsequent join computation. Unlike case b, however, the relation TEACHING remains untouched, so we can still use index-nested loops (utilizing the index on TEACHING.ProfId) to compute the join. Other possibilities are block-nested loops and sort-merge join. Finally, we can pipe the output of the join to the selection operator $\sigma_{\texttt{DeptId='F1994'}}$ and apply the projection during the same scan.

The above query execution plan is depicted in Figure 11.3(c). We now estimate the cost of this plan.

- $\sigma_{\texttt{DeptId='CS'}}$(PROFESSOR). There are 50 departments and 1000 professors. Thus, the result of this selection will contain about 20 tuples, or 4 pages. Since the index on PROFESSOR.DeptId is clustered, retrieval of these tuples should take about 4 I/Os. Index search will take an additional 2 I/Os for a 2-level B^+ tree index. Because we intend to pipe the result of the selection into the join step that follows, there is no output cost.
- *Index-nested loops join.* We use the result of the previous selection and pipe it directly as input to the join. An important consideration here is that, because we chose index-nested loops utilizing the hash index on TEACHING.ProfId, the result of the selection does not need to be saved on disk even if this result is large. Once selection on PROFESSOR produces enough tuples to fill the buffers, we can immediately join these tuples with the matching TEACHING tuples, using the hash index, and output the joined rows. Then we can resume the selection and fill the buffers again.

  As before, each PROFESSOR tuple matches about 10 TEACHING tuples, which are going to be stored in one bucket. So, to find the matches for 20 tuples, we have to search the index 20 times at the cost of 1.2 I/Os per search. Another 200 I/Os are needed to actually fetch the matching tuples from disk since the index is unclustered. All in all, this should take $1.2 * 20 + 200 = 224$ I/Os.
- *Combined cost.* Since the result of the join is piped into the subsequent selection and projection, these latter operations do not cost anything in terms of I/O. Thus, the total cost is: $4 + 2 + 224 = 230$ I/Os.

Case d: selection pushed to the TEACHING relation. This case is similar to case c, except that selection is now applied to TEACHING rather than to PROFESSOR. Since the indices on TEACHING are lost after applying the selection, we cannot use this relation in the inner loop of the index-nested loops join. However, we can use it in the outer loop of the index-nested loops join that utilizes the hash index on PROFESSOR.Id in the inner loop. This join can also be computed using block-nested loops and sort-merge. For this example, we select sort-merge. The subsequent application of selection and projection to the result can be done using pipelining, as in earlier examples. The resulting query plan is depicted in Figure 11.3(d).

- *Join: the sorting stage.* The first step is to sort PROFESSOR on Id and $\sigma_{\texttt{Semester='F1994'}}$ (TEACHING) on ProfId.

- To sort PROFESSOR, we must first scan it and create sorted runs. Since PROFESSOR fits in 200 blocks, there will be $\lceil 200/50 \rceil = 4$ sorted runs. Thus, creation of the 4 sorted runs and storing them back on disk takes $2 \times 200 = 400$ I/Os. These runs can then be merged in just one more pass, but we postpone this merge and combine it with the merging stage of the sort-merge join. (See below.)
- To sort $\sigma_{\texttt{Semester='F1994'}}$(TEACHING), we must first compute this relation. Since TEACHING holds information for about 4 semesters, the size of the selection is about 10,000/4 = 2500 tuples. The index is clustered, so the tuples are stored consecutively in the file in 250 blocks. The cost of the selection is therefore about 252 I/O operations, which includes 2 I/O operations for searching the index.

  The result of the selection is not written to disk. Instead, each time the 50-page buffer in main memory is filled, it is immediately sorted to create a run and then written to disk. In this way we create $\lceil 250/50 \rceil = 5$ sorted runs. This takes 250 I/Os.

  The 5 sorted runs of $\sigma_{\texttt{Semester='F1994'}}$(TEACHING) can be merged in one pass. However, instead of doing this separately, we combine this step with the merging step of the join (and the merging step of sorting PROFESSOR, which was postponed earlier).

- *Join: the merging stage.* Rather than merging the 4 sorted runs of PROFESSOR and the sorted runs of $\sigma_{\texttt{Semester='F1994'}}$(TEACHING) into two sorted relations, the runs are piped directly into the merge stage of the sort-merge join without writing the intermediate sorted results on disk. In this way, we combine the final merge steps in sorting these relations with the merge step of the join.

  The combined merge uses 4 input buffers for each of the sorted runs of PROFESSOR, 5 input buffers for each sorted run of $\sigma_{\texttt{Semester='F1994'}}$ (TEACHING), and one output buffer for the result of the join. The tuple p with the lowest value of p.Id among the heads of the 4 PROFESSOR's runs is selected and matched against the tuple t with the lowest value of t.ProfId among the tuples in the head of the 5 runs corresponding to $\sigma_{\texttt{Semester='F1994'}}$(TEACHING). If p.Id=t.ProfId, t is removed from the corresponding run and the joined tuple is placed in the output buffer (we remove t and not p because the same PROFESSOR tuple can match several TEACHING tuples). If p.Id< t.ProfId, p is discarded; otherwise, t is discarded. The process then repeats itself until all the input runs are exhausted.

  The combined merge can be done at a cost of reading the sorted runs of the two relations: 200 I/Os for the runs of PROFESSOR and 250 I/Os for $\sigma_{\texttt{Semester='F1994'}}$ (TEACHING), respectively.
- *The rest.* The result of the join is then piped directly to the subsequent selection (on DeptId) and projection (on Name) operators. Since no intermediate results are written to disk, the I/O cost of these stages is zero.
- *Combined cost.* Summing up the costs of the individual operations, we get: $400 + 252 + 250 + 200 + 250 = 1352$.

And the winner is . . . . Tallying up the results, we can see that the best plan (among those considered—only a small portion of all possible plans) is plan (c) from Figure 11.3. The interesting observation here is that this plan is better than plan (b), even though plan (b) joins smaller relations (because the selections are fully pushed). The reason for this apparent paradox is the loss of an index when selection is pushed down to the TEACHING relation. This illustrates once again that the heuristic rules of Section 11.2 are just that—heuristics. While they are likely to lead to better query execution plans, they must be evaluated within a more general cost model.

11.4 Estimating the Size of the Output

The examples in Section 11.3 illustrate the importance of accurate estimates of the output size of various relational expressions. The result of one expression serves as input to the next, and the input size has a direct effect on the cost of the computation. To give a better idea of how such estimates can be done, we present a simple technique based on the assumption that all values have an equal chance of occurring in a relation.

The system catalog can contain the following set of statistics for each relation name **R**:

- *Blocks*(**R**). The number of blocks occupied by the instance of table **R**
- *Tuples*(**R**). The number of tuples in the instance of **R**
- *Values*(**R**.*A*). The number of distinct values of attribute *A* in the instance of **R**
- *MaxVal*(**R**.*A*). The maximum value of attribute *A* in the instance of **R**
- *MinVal*(**R**.*A*). The minimum value of attribute *A* in the instance of **R**.

Earlier we introduced the notion of attribute weight and used it to estimate sizes of selection and equi-join. We now define a more general notion, the *reduction factor*. Consider the following general query:

```
SELECT  TargetList
FROM    R1 V1, ..., Rn Vn
WHERE   Condition
```

The **reduction factor** of this query is the ratio

$$\frac{Blocks(\text{the result set})}{Blocks(\mathbf{R}_1) \times \cdots \times Blocks(\mathbf{R}_n)}$$

At first, this definition seems cyclic: to find out the size of the result we need to know the reduction factor, but for this we need to know the size of the result set. However, the reduction factor can be *estimated* by induction on the query structure without knowing the size of the query result.

We assume that reduction factors associated with different parts of the query are independent of each other. Thus,

$$reduction(Query) = reduction(TargetList) \times reduction(Condition)$$

where *reduction(TargetList)* is the size reduction due to projection of rows on the attributes in the SELECT clause and *reduction(Condition)* is the size reduction due to the elimination of rows that do not satisfy *Condition*.

We also assume that if $Condition = Condition_1$ AND $Condition_2$ then

$$reduction(Condition) = reduction(Condition_1) \times reduction(Condition_2)$$

and if $Condition = Condition_1$ OR $Condition_2$, then

$$reduction(Condition) = min(1,\ reduction(Condition_1) + reduction(Condition_2))$$

Thus, the size reduction due to a complex condition can be estimated in terms of the size reduction due to the components of that condition.

It remains to estimate the reduction factors due to projection in the SELECT clause and due to atomic conditions in the WHERE clause. We ignore nested subqueries and aggregates in this discussion.

- $reduction(\mathbf{R}_i.A = value) = \frac{1}{Values(\mathbf{R}_i.A)}$, where $\mathbf{R}_i$ is a relation name and A is an attribute in $\mathbf{R}_i$. This estimate is based on the uniformity assumption—all values are equally probable.
- $reduction(\mathbf{R}_i.A = \mathbf{R}_j.B) = \frac{1}{\mathtt{max}(Values(\mathbf{R}_i.A), Values(\mathbf{R}_j.A))}$, where $\mathbf{R}_i$ and $\mathbf{R}_j$ are relations and A and B are attributes. Using the uniformity assumption, we can decompose $\mathbf{R}_i$ (respectively, $\mathbf{R}_j$) into subsets with the property that all elements of a subset have the same value of $\mathbf{R}_i.A$ (respectively, $\mathbf{R}_j.B$). If we assume that there are $N_{\mathbf{R}_i}$ tuples in $\mathbf{R}_i$ and $N_{\mathbf{R}_j}$ tuples in $\mathbf{R}_j$ and that every element of $\mathbf{R}_i$ matches an element of $\mathbf{R}_j$, then we can conclude that the number of tuples that satisfy the condition is $Values(\mathbf{R}_i.A) \times (N_{\mathbf{R}_i}/Values(\mathbf{R}_i.A)) \times (N_{\mathbf{R}_j}/Values(\mathbf{R}_j.B))$. In general, the reduction factor is calculated assuming (unrealistically) that each value in the smaller range always matches a value in the larger range. Assuming that $\mathbf{R}_i A$ is the smaller range, and dividing this expression by $N_{\mathbf{R}_i} \times N_{\mathbf{R}_j}$, yields the above reduction factor.
- $reduction(\mathbf{R}_i.A > value) = \frac{MaxVal(\mathbf{R}_i.A) - value}{MaxVal(\mathbf{R}_i.A) - MinVal(\mathbf{R}_i.A)}$. The reduction factor for $\mathbf{R}_i.A < value$ is defined similarly. These estimates are also based on the assumption that all values are distributed uniformly.
- $reduction(TargetList) = \frac{\text{number-of-attributes}(TargetList)}{\Sigma_i \text{ number-of-attributes}(\mathbf{R}_i)}$. Here, for simplicity, we assume that all attributes contribute equally to the tuple size.

The weight of an attribute, which we used in Section 11.3, can now be estimated using the notion of reduction factor:

$$weight(\mathbf{R}_i.A) = Tuples(\mathbf{R}_i) \times reduction(\mathbf{R}_i.A = value)$$

For instance, the reduction factor of the query PROFESSOR.`DeptId` = *value* is 1/50, since there are 50 departments. As the number of tuples in PROFESSOR is 1000, the weight of the attribute `DeptId` in PROFESSOR is 20.

11.5 Choosing a Plan

In Section 11.3 we looked at some query execution plans and showed how to estimate their cost. However, we did not discuss how to *produce* candidate plans. Unfortunately, the number of possible plans can be quite large, so we need an efficient way of choosing a relatively small, promising subset. We can then estimate the cost of each and choose the best. There are at least three major issues involved in this process:

1. Choosing a logical plan
2. Reducing the search space
3. Choosing a heuristic search algorithm

We discuss each of these issues in turn.

Choosing a logical plan. We defined a query execution plan as a query tree with the relational implementation methods attached to each inner node. Thus, constructing such a plan involves two tasks: choosing a tree and choosing the implementation methods. Choosing the right tree is the more difficult job because of the number of trees involved, which, in turn, is caused by the fact that the binary associative and commutative operators, such as join, cross product, union, and the like, can be processed in so many different ways. We mentioned in Section 11.2 that the subtree of a query tree in which N relations are combined by such an operator can be formed in $T(N) \times N!$ ways. We want to deal with this kind of exponential complexity separately, so we first focus on **logical query execution plans**, which avoid the problem by grouping consecutive binary operators of the same kind into one node, as shown in Figure 11.4.

The different logical query execution plans are created from the "master plan" (as in Figure 11.2(a) on page 415) by pushing selections and projections down and by combining selections and Cartesian products into joins. Only a few of all possible logical plans are retained for further consideration. Typically, the ones selected are fully pushed trees (because they are expected to produce the smallest intermediate results) plus all the "nearly" fully pushed trees. The reason for the latter should be clear from the discussion and examples in Section 11.3: Pushing selection or projection down to a leaf node of a query tree might eliminate the option of using an index in the join computation.

According to this heuristic, the query tree in Figure 11.2(a) will not be selected since nothing has been pushed. The remaining trees include the one in Figure 11.3(c), which has the least estimated cost and which is superior to the fully pushed query plan in Figure 11.3(b). In this example, all joins are binary, so the transformation shown in Figure 11.4 does not pertain.

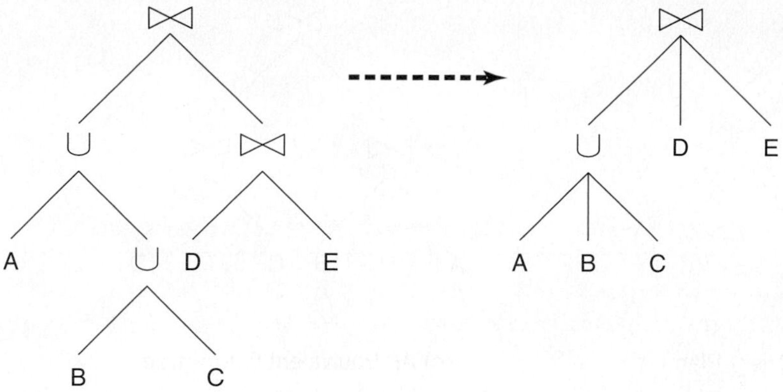

FIGURE 11.4 Transforming a query tree into a logical query execution plan.

Reducing the search space. Having selected candidate logical query execution plans, the query optimizer must decide how to evaluate the expressions that involve the commutative and associative operators. For instance, Figure 11.5 shows several alternative but equivalent ways of converting a commutative and associative node of a logical plan that combines multiple relations (a) into query trees (b), (c), and (d).

The space of all possible equivalent query (sub)trees that correspond to a node in a logical query plan is two-dimensional. First, we must choose the desired *shape* of the tree (by ignoring the labels on the nodes). For instance, the trees in Figure 11.5 have different shapes, with (d) being the simplest. Trees of such a shape are called **left-deep query trees**. A tree shape corresponds to a particular parenthesizing of a relational subexpression that involves an associative and commutative operator. Thus, the logical query execution plan in Figure 11.5(a) corresponds to the expression $\mathbf{A} \bowtie \mathbf{B} \bowtie \mathbf{C} \bowtie \mathbf{D}$, while the query trees (b), (c), and (d) correspond to the expressions $(\mathbf{A} \bowtie \mathbf{B}) \bowtie (\mathbf{C} \bowtie \mathbf{D})$, $\mathbf{A} \bowtie ((\mathbf{B} \bowtie \mathbf{C}) \bowtie \mathbf{D})$, and $((\mathbf{A} \bowtie \mathbf{B}) \bowtie \mathbf{C}) \bowtie \mathbf{D}$, respectively. A left-deep query tree always corresponds to an algebraic expression of the form $(\ldots((E_{i_1} \bowtie E_{i_2}) \bowtie E_{i_3}) \bowtie \ldots) \bowtie E_{i_N}$.

Query optimizers usually settle on one particular shape for the query tree: left-deep. This is because, even with a fixed tree shape, query optimizers have plenty of work to do. Indeed, given the left-deep tree of Figure 11.5(d), there are still 4! possible ways to order the joins. For instance, $((\mathbf{B} \bowtie \mathbf{D}) \bowtie \mathbf{C}) \bowtie \mathbf{A}$ is another ordering of the join of Figure 11.5(d) that leads to a different left-deep query execution plan. So, if computing cost estimates for 4! query execution plans does not sound like a lot, think of what it would take to estimate the cost of 10! or 12! or 16! plans. Incidentally, all commercial query optimizers give up at around 16 joins.

Apart from the general need to reduce the search space, there is another good reason to choose left-deep trees over the trees of the form Figure 11.5(b): pipelining. For instance, in Figure 11.5(d) we can first compute $\mathbf{A} \bowtie \mathbf{B}$ and pipe the result to the next join with **C**. The result of this second join can also be piped up the tree

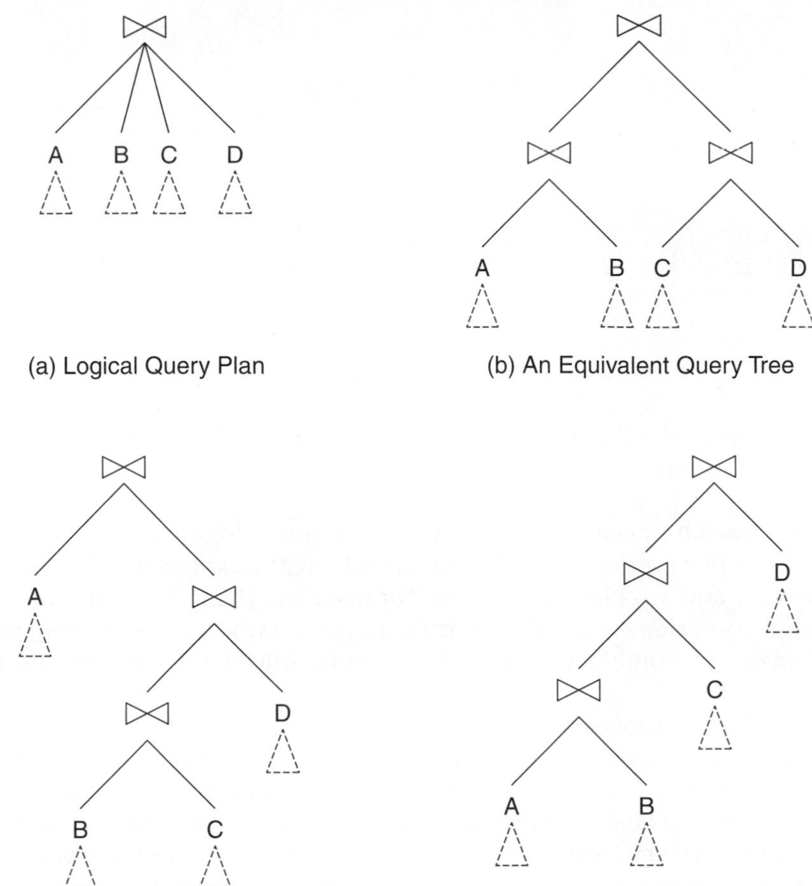

FIGURE 11.5 Logical plan and three equivalent query trees.

without materializing the intermediate relation on disk. The ability to do this is very important for large relations because the intermediate output from a join can be very large. For instance, if the size of the relations **A**, **B**, and **C** is 1000 pages, the intermediate relation can reach 10^9 pages just to shrink back to a few pages after joining with **D**. The overhead of storing such intermediate results on disk can be huge.

Note that the tree of Figure 11.5(b) does not lend itself to pipelining. For example, an attempt to pipe the result of $\mathbf{A} \bowtie \mathbf{B}$ and the result of $\mathbf{C} \bowtie \mathbf{D}$ to a module, M, that will join the two does not work. A row, t, of $\mathbf{A} \bowtie \mathbf{B}$ must be compared to every row of $\mathbf{C} \bowtie \mathbf{D}$ in order to compute the total join. That means that when t arrives, M must have received and stored all of $\mathbf{C} \bowtie \mathbf{D}$, which is exactly what we are trying to avoid. The alternative of storing one piece of $\mathbf{C} \bowtie \mathbf{D}$ at a time is unsatisfactory since

FIGURE 11.6 Heuristic search of the query execution plan space.

Input: *A logical plan* $E_1 \bowtie \cdots \bowtie E_N$
Output: *A "good" left-deep plan* $(\ldots((E_{i_1} \bowtie E_{i_2}) \bowtie E_{i_3}) \bowtie \ldots) \bowtie E_{i_N}$

```
1-Plans := all 1-relation plans
Best := all 1-relation plans with lowest cost
for (i := 1; i < N; i++) do
    // Below, ⋈meth denotes join marked with an implementation method, meth*
    Plans := { best ⋈meth 1-plan | best ∈ Best; 1-plan ∈ 1-Plans, where
                               1-plan is a plan for some Ej that has not
                               been used so far in best }
        Best := { plan | plan ∈ Plans, where plan has the lowest cost }
end
return Best;
```

it implies that t has to be re-sent to M each time a new piece arrives. Observe that the tree (c) in that figure is *equivalent* to a left-deep tree but is not one of them. This means that even though the query optimizer limits the search to left-deep trees, the search space actually covers a much larger domain, which includes all the trees that are equivalent to the left-deep ones.

A heuristic search algorithm. The choice of left-deep trees has reduced the size of the search space from immense to huge. Next we must assign relations to the leaf nodes of the left-deep tree. There are $N!$ such assignments, so estimating the cost of all is still a hopelessly intractable problem. Therefore, a heuristic search algorithm is needed to find a reasonable plan by looking at only a tiny portion of the overall search space. One such algorithm is based on *dynamic programming* and is used (with variations) in a number of commercial systems (e.g., DB2). We explain the main idea below; details are given in [Griffiths-Selinger et al. 1979]. A different heuristic search algorithm, described in [Wong and Youssefi 1976], is used in Ingres, another DBMS that was influential in the olden days.

A simplified version of the dynamic programming heuristic search algorithm is described in Figure 11.6. It builds a left-deep query tree by first evaluating the cost of all plans for computing each argument of an N-way join, $E_1 \bowtie \cdots \bowtie E_N$, where each E_j is a 1-relation expression. These are referred to as *1-relation plans*. Note that each E_j can have several such plans (due to different possible access paths; e.g., one might use a scan and another an index), so the number of 1-relation plans can be N or larger. The *best* among all these plans (i.e., those with lowest cost) are expanded into 2-relation plans, then 3-relation plans, etc., as follows. To expand a best 1-relation plan, p (for definiteness, assume that p is a plan for E_{i_1}) into a 2-relation plan, p is joined with every 1-relation plan, excluding the plans for E_{i_1} (because we already selected p as *the* plan for E_{i_1}). We then evaluate the cost of all such plans and retain the best 2-relation plans. Each best 2-relation plan, q (let us assume that it is a plan for $E_{i_1} \bowtie E_{i_2}$), is expanded into a set of 3-relation plans by joining q with every 1-relation plan, except the plans for E_{i_1} and E_{i_2} (since the latter are already accounted for in q). Again, only the lowest-cost plans are retained for the next stage. The process continues until a left-deep expression corresponding to the logical plan $E_1 \bowtie \cdots \bowtie E_N$ is fully constructed.

Example 11.5.1 (Choosing the Best Plan). We illustrate the overall process using our running example, query (11.6). First, the query processor generates a number of plausible logical plans—in our case, most likely the fully pushed tree of Figure 11.2(b) on page 415 plus the two partially pushed trees (c) and (d).

The shape of the trees depicted in Figure 11.2 are left-deep, but there are two query execution plans corresponding to each such tree: they differ in the order of relations in the join. Let us consider the query execution plans generated using the algorithm of Figure 11.6 starting with the logical plan of Figure 11.2(c).

The 1-relation plans for $\sigma_{\text{DeptId='CS'}}$(PROFESSOR) can use the following access paths: a scan, the clustered index on PROFESSOR.DeptId, or a binary search (because PROFESSOR is sorted on DeptId). The best plan uses the index, so it is retained. For the expression TEACHING, scan is all that can be done. We now have two 1-relation plans. In the next iteration, the algorithm expands the chosen 1-relation plans to 2-relation plans. This amounts to generating the two expressions $\sigma_{\texttt{DeptId= 'CS'}}$(PROFESSOR) $\bowtie_{\texttt{Id=ProfId}}$ TEACHING and TEACHING $\bowtie_{\texttt{ProfId=Id}}$ $\sigma_{\texttt{DeptId= 'CS'}}$(PROFESSOR) and deciding on the evaluation strategy to use for the join in each. We estimated the different plans for the former expression in Section 11.3 and concluded that the index-nested loops join is the best. The second expression cannot be evaluated in the same way because the order of the arguments indicates that the relation TEACHING is scanned first. This expression can be evaluated using sort-merge or block-nested loops. Both methods are more expensive, so they are discarded.

Once the best plan for evaluating the join is selected, we can consider the result of the join as a 1-relation expression, E, and we now have to find a plan for $\pi_{\texttt{Name}}(\sigma_{\texttt{Semester='F1994'}}(E))$. Since the result of E is not sorted or indexed and since duplicate elimination is not requested, we choose a sequential scan access path to compute both selection and projection. Also, since E generates the result in main memory, we choose pipelining to avoid saving the intermediate result on disk. ■

The dynamic programming algorithm is likely to miss some good plans because it focuses on what is best at the current moment without trying to look ahead. One improvement here is to retain not only the best plans but also certain "interesting" plans. A plan might be considered interesting if its output relation is sorted or if it has an index, even if the cost of the plan is not minimal. This heuristic recognizes the fact that a sorted relation can significantly reduce the cost of subsequent operations, such as sort-merge join, duplicate elimination, and grouping. Likewise, an indexed relation can reduce the cost of subsequent joins.

BIBLIOGRAPHIC NOTES

An extensive textbook treatment of query optimization can be found in [Garcia-Molina et al. 2000]. Heuristic search algorithms are described in [Griffiths-Selinger et al. 1979; Wong and Youssefi 1976].

For further reading on the latest query optimization techniques as well as additional references, see [Ioannidis 1996; Chaudhuri 1998].

EXERCISES

11.1 Is there a *commutativity* transformation for the projection operator? Explain.

11.2 Write down the sequence of steps needed to transform $\pi_A((\mathbf{R} \bowtie_{B=C} \mathbf{S}) \bowtie_{D=E} \mathbf{T})$ into $\pi_A((\pi_E(\mathbf{T}) \bowtie_{E=D} \pi_{ACD}(\mathbf{S})) \bowtie_{C=B} \mathbf{R})$. List the attributes that each of the schemas **R**, **S**, and **T** *must* have and the attributes that each (or some) of these schemas must *not* have in order for the above transformation to be correct.

11.3 Under what conditions can the expression $\pi_A((\mathbf{R} \bowtie_{cond_1} \mathbf{S}) \bowtie_{cond_2} \mathbf{T})$ be transformed into $\pi_A(\pi_B(\mathbf{R} \bowtie_{cond_1} \pi_C(\mathbf{S})) \bowtie_{cond_2} \pi_D(\mathbf{T}))$ using the heuristic rules given in Section 11.2?

11.4 Consider the join PROFESSOR $\bowtie_{\texttt{Id=ProfId}}$ TEACHING used in the running example of Section 11.3. Let us change the statistics slightly and assume that the number of distinct values for TEACHING.ProfId is 10,000 (which translates into lower weight for this attribute).

a. What is the cardinality of the PROFESSOR relation?

b. Let there be an unclustered hash index on ProfId and assume that, as before, 5 PROFESSOR tuples fit in one page, 10 TEACHING tuples fit in one page, and the cardinality of TEACHING is 10,000. Estimate the cost of computing the above join using index-nested loops and block-nested loops with a 51-page buffer.

11.5 Consider the following query:

```
SELECT DISTINCT E.Ename
FROM    EMPLOYEE E
WHERE   E.Title = 'Programmer' AND E.Dept = 'Production'
```

Assume that

- 10% of employees are programmers
- 5% of employees are programmers who work for the production department
- There are 10 departments
- The EMPLOYEE relation has 1000 pages with 10 tuples per page
- There is a 51-page buffer that can be used to process the query

Find the best query execution plan for each of the following cases:

a. The only index is on Title, and it is a clustered 2-level B^+ tree.

b. The only index is on the attribute sequence Dept, Title, Ename; it is clustered and has two levels.

c. The only index is on `Dept`, `Ename`, `Title`; it is a clustered 3-level B+ tree.
d. There is an unclustered hash index on `Dept` and a 2-level clustered tree index on `Ename`.

11.6 Consider the following schema, where the keys are underlined:

```
EMPLOYEE(SSN, Name,Dept)
PROJECT(SSN,PID,Name,Budget)
```

The `SSN` attribute in PROJECT is the Id of the employee working on the project, and `PID` is the Id of the project. There can be several employees per project, but the functional dependency `PID` → `Name,Budget` holds (so the relation is not normalized). Consider the query

```
SELECT   P.Budget, P.Name, E.Name
FROM     EMPLOYEE E, PROJECT P
WHERE    E.SSN = P.SSN AND
         P.Budget > 99 AND
         E.Name = 'John'
ORDER BY P.Budget
```

Assume the following statistical information:

- 10,000 tuples in EMPLOYEE relation
- 20,000 tuples in PROJECT relation
- 40 tuples per page in each relation
- 10-page buffer
- 1000 different values for `E.Name`
- The domain of `Budget` consists of integers in the range of 1 to 100
- Indices
  - EMPLOYEE relation
    - On `Name`: Unclustered, hash
    - On `SSN`: Clustered, 3-level B+ tree
  - PROJECT relation
    - On `SSN`: Unclustered, hash
    - On `Budget`: Clustered, 2-level B+ tree

a. Draw the *fully pushed* query tree.
b. Find the "best" execution plan and the second-best plan. What is the cost of each? Explain how you arrived at your costs.

11.7 Consider the following schema, where the keys are underlined (different keys are underlined differently):

```
PROFESSOR(Id, Name, Department)
COURSE(CrsCode, Department, CrsName)
TEACHING(ProfId, CrsCode, Semester)
```

Consider the following query:

```
SELECT   C.CrsName, P.Name
FROM     PROFESSOR P, TEACHING T, COURSE C
WHERE    T.Semester='F1995' AND P.Department='CS'
         AND P.Id = T.ProfId AND T.CrsCode=C.CrsCode
```

Assume the following statistical information:

- 1000 tuples with 10 tuples per page in PROFESSOR relation
- 20,000 tuples with 10 tuples per page in TEACHING relation
- 2000 tuples, 5 tuples per page, in COURSE
- 5-page buffer
- 50 different values for Department
- 200 different values for Semester
- Indices
  - PROFESSOR relation
    - On Department: Clustered, 2-level B^+ tree
    - On Id: Unclustered, hash
  - COURSE relation
    - On CrsCode: Sorted (no index)
    - On CrsName: Hash, unclustered
  - TEACHING relation
    - On ProfId: Clustered, 2-level B^+-tree
    - On Semester, CrsCode: Unclustered, 2-level B^+ tree

a. First, show the *unoptimized* relational algebra expression that corresponds to the above SQL query. Then *draw* the corresponding *fully pushed* query tree.

b. Find the best execution plan and its cost. Explain how you arrived at your costs.

11.8 Consider the following relations that represent part of a real estate database:

```
AGENT(Id, AgentName)
HOUSE(Address, OwnerId, AgentId)
AMENITY(Address, Feature)
```

The AGENT relation keeps information on real estate agents, the HOUSE relation has information on who is selling the house and the agent involved, and the AMENITY relation provides information on the features of each house. Each relation has its keys underlined. Consider the following query:

```
SELECT   H.OwnerId, A.AgentName
FROM     HOUSE H, AGENT A, AMENITY Y
WHERE    H.Address=Y.Address AND A.Id = H.AgentId
              AND Y.Feature = '5BR' AND H.AgentId = '007'
```

Assume that the buffer space available for this query has 5 pages and that the following statistics and indices are available:

- AMENITY
  10,000 records on 1000 houses, 5 records per page
  Clustered 2-level B^+ tree index on `Address`
  Unclustered hash index on `Feature`, 50 features
- AGENT
  200 agents with 10 tuples per page
  Unclustered hash index on `Id`
- HOUSE
  1000 houses with 4 records per page
  Unclustered hash index on `AgentId`
  Clustered 2-level B^+ tree index on `Address`

Answer the following questions (and explain how you arrived at your solutions).

a. Draw a fully pushed query tree corresponding to the above query.
b. Find the best query plan to evaluate the above query and estimate its cost.
c. Find the next-best plan and estimate its cost.

11.9 None of the query execution plans in Figure 11.3 for queries (11.2)–(11.5) does duplicate elimination. To account for this, let us add one more relational operator, δ, which denotes the operation of duplicate elimination. Modify the plans in Figure 11.3 by adding δ in appropriate places so as to minimize the cost of the computation. Estimate the cost of each new plan.

11.10 Build a database for the scenario in Exercise 11.5 using the DBMS of your choice. Use the EXPLAIN PLAN statement (or an equivalent provided by your DBMS) to compare the best plan that you found manually with the plan actually generated by the DBMS.

11.11 Follow Exercise 11.10, but use the scenario in Exercise 11.6.

11.12 Follow Exercise 11.10, but use the scenario in Exercise 11.7.

11.13 Consider the query execution plans in Figure 11.3. Show how each of these plans can be *enhanced* by pushing the projection operator past the join *without altering the strategies used for computing the join.*

11.14 Using the result of Exercise 11.13, show which of the enhanced plans can be further enhanced by adding the duplicate elimination operator δ introduced in Exercise 11.9.

12

Database Tuning

Tuning is the process of modifying an application and adjusting the parameters of the underlying DBMS to improve performance. Performance is measured in terms of the response time seen by a user (the time it takes to perform a task—for example, to execute an SQL statement) and throughput (the amount of work completed in a unit of time). It is important to realize that tuning does not affect the semantics of the system: the tuned and the original systems return the same information to the user and are left in the same final state when subjected to the same sequence of requests.

The first step in tuning a system is to determine where the bottlenecks are. If the system spends only 2% of its time executing a particular (hardware or software) module, then no matter how inefficient it is, revising or replacing it can improve performance by at most 2%.

An application and DBMS, taken together, form an exceedingly complicated system, and many different aspects of it are subject to tuning. The SQL code and schema are at the highest level. Tuning at this level is concerned with such issues as how queries should be expressed and what indices should be created. These are application-related questions and, since this is an "application-oriented" text, it is the level to which we pay the most attention. You might have wondered why the material in Chapters 10 and 11 was included in an application-oriented text since those chapters describe algorithms internal to the DBMS. The reason lies in this chapter. While Chapters 10 and 11 described a number of different techniques that a DBMS can use to process the SQL statements that your application submits, this chapter discusses methods that you can use to encourage the DBMS to use the technique that performs the best for the particular application you are implementing.

The DBMS occupies the next level. Examples of performance issues at this level are the physical placement of data on secondary storage and how the DBMS manages its buffers. Decisions in this area are largely under the control of the database administrator, and hence the application programmer can influence them indirectly. As a result we spend some time in this chapter discussing tuning at the DBMS level.

The lowest tuning level is the hardware level. In order to perform well the system must be supported by a sufficient amount of main memory, a sufficient number of

CPUs and secondary storage devices, and adequate communication facilities. The specification of these resources is generally beyond the control of the application programmer, and we do not discuss these issues.

12.1 Disk Caches

In Chapter 9 we discussed the huge difference between the speed of the CPU and the time to transfer a page between the CPU and mass store. In recognition of this, the cost of a query plan is measured as the estimated number of page transfers it incurs, and the job of the query optimizer is to find the plan that minimizes this number. While that plan is generally a good one, its cost is often still significant, and other measures are necessary to make query processing efficient. One of the most significant of these is the cache. A *cache* is a main memory buffer in the DBMS in which recently accessed database pages are stored. When a transaction accesses a database item, the DBMS brings the database page(s) on disk that contain that item into the cache and then copies the value of the item from the cache into the application's buffer. The page is generally retained in the cache under the assumption that there is a high probability that the application will either update the item or read another item in the same page at a later time. Or another application might concurrently reference an item in the page. In either case, a disk access will have been avoided since the page will be directly accessible in the cache. For example, an index page has a high probability of being accessed frequently.

Although it is natural to think of the database item as a page of a table or an index, it can also be the execution plan for an SQL statement or a stored procedure. In fact, some DBMSs maintain a separate **procedure cache** for this purpose. Although I/O cost is the major limitation on the performance of an application, the CPU cost of building an appropriate execution plan is also substantial. Hence, once an execution plan has been determined, it is saved since it might be possible to reuse it. Prior to preparing a new execution plan, existing plans are scanned to see if any are usable.

If a database item is to be updated, the database page containing the item must first be brought into the cache (if it is not already there), and it is the cache copy of the page that is modified (not the original copy in the database).

Eventually the cache becomes full, and any new page fetched from the database must overwrite a page, p, in the cache. If p has not been updated since arriving in the cache, its contents are identical to the corresponding page in the database, and hence it can simply be overwritten by the new page. However, if p has been updated since arriving in the cache, it must be written back to the database before the space it occupies in the cache can be freed. In order to distinguish between these two cases, the DBMS marks pages that have been updated as **dirty** and those that have not as **clean**.

Decisions concerning which pages should be kept in the cache and which can be overwritten when a new page is to be fetched are made by a **page replacement algorithm** whose goal is to maximize the number of database accesses that can be satisfied by pages in the cache. A least recently used (LRU) algorithm, for example, selects the least recently used page in the cache as the one to be replaced. It concludes that since no application has accessed the page recently it is no longer useful. Hence it tends to keep actively used pages in the cache.

A more sophisticated algorithm takes into account the circumstances under which a page was brought into the cache. For example, if the page was brought in as part of a table scan (which is typical, for example, when sorts are performed), once the rows in the page have been accessed it is not likely that the application will reference the page again. In this case a most recently used algorithm (MRU) is preferable. Hence a page replacement policy might use a combination of an LRU and an MRU algorithm depending on what information is contained in the page (index or data) and in what context the page is referenced.

If a transaction's access request can be satisfied from the cache, a **hit** is said to have taken place; if it cannot be satisfied, then a **miss** has occurred. To obtain a high throughput, many designers consider it mandatory to obtain a hit rate of over 90% (90% of the accesses can be satisfied from the cache). To achieve such a hit rate, the cache size must often be a significant percentage of the size of the database. Cache sizes in the megabyte range are normal. In some large applications, the cache size is measured in tens of gigabytes.

12.1.1 Tuning the Cache

Now that you have an understanding of how the cache works, the question is, "What can the application programmer or the database administrator do to optimize the way the DBMS uses the cache to improve the performance of her application?" DBMSs generally offer several mechanisms that can be invoked for this purpose.

- Some DBMSs allow pieces to be carved out of the (default) cache to be managed as separate caches. The programmer can then bind a particular item (e.g., a table or an index) to a specific cache and in so doing cause all pages of that item to be buffered in that cache. For example, if tables T_1 and T_2 are bound to different caches, a page of T_1 can never overwrite a page of T_2. This approach might be useful if T_2 was not used very often but fast response time was required of the application that referenced it.
- Some DBMSs allow a particular cache to be subdivided into several distinct pools of buffers of different sizes. For example, while by default all buffers in a cache might have 2K bytes, it might be possible to reallocate the cache storage area so that several buffer pools are created with sizes 2K, 4K, 8K, etc. If a table is bound to such a cache, the query optimizer then has the option of choosing the I/O size that best suits a query plan that accesses that table. For example, the page size on secondary storage might be 2K bytes, and the DBMS might allocate disk space to a table in contiguous blocks of eight pages. It then follows that the time to retrieve an eight-page block is not much larger than the time to retrieve a single page since the seek time is the same in both cases. If the query plan calls

for a table scan, and the table is bound to a cache that has a 16K pool of buffers, the query optimizer can save time by retrieving eight pages with a single I/O operation.

Some query optimizers take this idea one step further by **prefetching** pages. Ordinarily, during the scan of a table or index, the next page is requested when the page fetched by the previous I/O operation has been scanned. The scan must then wait until the I/O operation for the next page completes. It is possible to improve on this in situations, such as scans, in which the optimizer can anticipate future requests. In such cases the optimizer can initiate the I/O operation for a page that has not yet been requested. Then, if the time to process a page is long enough, the next page will already be in the cache when it is requested.

By using both prefetching and a large I/O size, the time to do a table scan can be greatly reduced. This possible reduction has an impact on the query optimizer's choice between an access path that involves an index and an access path that uses a table scan for a particular query. It also raises the question of whether the application programmer should create an index for that query.

- Some DBMSs provide commands that allow the page replacement policy for a cache to be specified. This is particularly useful when multiple caches are used. A policy appropriate to the items bound to the cache can then be chosen.

In addition to configuring a data cache to best suit the application, the programmer can design the application to make the best use possible of a procedure cache. For example, performance can be improved by not using explicit constants in SQL statements. The execution plan for the statement

```
SELECT   P.Name
FROM     PROFESSOR P
WHERE    P.DeptId = 'EE'
```

is essentially the same as the execution plan for the statement with the constant EE replaced by CS. But since the two statements are different, the DBMS might miss this fact when it scans the procedure cache looking for an execution plan, and as a result the DBMS might create a separate execution plan for each statement. It is possible to eliminate this overhead by instead using the statement

```
SELECT   P.Name
FROM     PROFESSOR P
WHERE    P.DeptId = :deptid
```

where deptid is a host variable (see Chapter 8), and successively assigning EE and CS to that variable. Since the same statement is now executed twice, the execution plan created when the statement is first executed will be reused when it is executed for the second time.

12.2 Tuning the Schema

The schema you design for your database is at the heart of the application. If the schema is well designed, it is possible to write SQL statements that perform efficiently. Your strategy in tuning at the application level is to first design a normalized database as described in Chapter 6 and then estimate the sizes of the tables, the distribution of column values, and the nature and frequency of the queries and updates that will be addressed to the database. Adjustments to the normalized schema to facilitate the most frequent operations follow from these estimates. Adding indices is the most important of these adjustments, and we discuss it first. Another technique is denormalization, which involves adding redundancy so that items of information that are generally associated with one another through frequently executed queries can be found in one place. Finally, we discuss partitioning, which is a rather specialized technique for dealing with very large tables.

12.2.1 Indices

In Chapter 11 we showed that different query plans for a particular query might have wildly different costs and that in many cases the differences were a function of the indices used in the plan. For better or worse, the choice of plan is made by the optimizer based on the indices available to it at the time the query is prepared. It is the role of the application programmer to "encourage" a good choice by making sure that appropriate indices have been created. In this section our goal is to expose the reasoning a programmer might use in deciding what indices to create.

Indices might seem like the ultimate database tuning device. However, free computational lunches are rare. Each index carries an associated storage overhead. More importantly, extra indices might significantly increase the processing time of statements that *modify* the database since every index must be updated whenever the table it references is changed. Thus, you should think twice before creating an index on a table where rows are frequently inserted or deleted. Similarly, you should think twice before creating an index with a search key involving a frequently updated column. Will the performance gain realized in processing queries be sufficient to compensate for the added cost of processing statements that modify the table? To illustrate some of the considerations involved in the tuning process, consider the following examples (which make use of the schema shown in Figure 3.4 on page 38).

1. Consider the query

```
SELECT  P.DeptId
FROM    PROFESSOR P
WHERE   P.Name = :name
```

   Since the primary key of PROFESSOR is Id, we can expect that the DBMS has created a clustered index on that attribute. That index is no help for this query because we need a quick way to find all professors with a particular name. One possibility is to explicitly create an unclustered index on Name. Assuming that only a few professors have the same name, this index should speed things up. But suppose this is not the case: many professors have the same name. Then a better solution is to make the index on Name clustered and the index on Id unclustered. As a result, rows with the same name will be grouped together and can be retrieved in a single (or a few) I/O operations. The index could be a B^+ tree or a hash (since the condition on Name involves equality).

The lesson here is that since a table can have only one clustered index, it is pointless to waste it on an attribute that cannot take advantage of clustering. DBMSs generally create a clustered index on the primary key, but you should not be intimidated by this. An unclustered index on the primary-key attribute is sufficient to guarantee the key's uniqueness, and since at most one row can have a particular key value, clustering cannot be justified as a means of grouping rows with the same value of the attribute. So, if we are unlikely to want to order rows based on the primary key (as is the case with PROFESSOR), there is no reason to use a clustered index for this purpose.

Keep in mind that replacing one clustered index with another is a time-consuming operation since it implies a complete reorganization of the storage structure. You certainly do not want to create a new clustered index each time you execute a query. You should analyze your application in advance, considering the kinds of queries you expect and their frequency, create the clustered index that will do the most good, and stick with it until performance considerations indicate that the system needs a tune-up.

2. Consider the query

```
SELECT  T.Name, T.CrsCode
FROM    TRANSCRIPT T
WHERE   T.Grade = :grade
```

One is tempted to cluster the rows around Grade since we want to retrieve all rows with the same grade, but suppose that our first priority is to speed the response to a different query, a request for a class roster, and for that purpose we use a clustered index on the primary key ⟨CrsCode, Semester, StudId⟩. We could create an unclustered index on Grade, but using such an index might not be a good idea. In most cases the number of rows with a particular grade is a large fraction of the total number of rows (since the domain of Grade is small). In those cases we can expect that a large fraction of the table's pages will be fetched, one by one, in random order, through the unclustered index.[1] Unfortunately, the optimizer does not know what grade will be supplied at run time, and even if it did, it would not know which ones produced small result sets (we will correct this inadequacy shortly). Hence a table scan might be a better solution.

[1] If 10% of the rows are randomly fetched and each page contained 20 rows, then the probability that a particular page contains no rows in the result set is $(.9)^{20}$, which is approximately .12.

A number of lessons can be drawn from this example. First, an unclustered index is appropriate if only a few rows of a table are to be retrieved, and a full table scan is appropriate if a large fraction of the rows are to be retrieved. Determining a reasonable break-even point is not easy. One vendor states that a table scan is appropriate if more than 20% of the rows of the table are to be accessed. A more cautious approach would be to simulate the workload if more than a few rows are to be accessed to determine if building an index is a good idea. Second, do not create an index on a column with a small domain if attribute values tend to be evenly distributed over the domain. The query optimizer is *unlikely* to choose such an index since it will recognize that the selectivity of the access path through this index is large for any value of search key. Finally, do not create indices indiscriminately: they are costly to maintain, and, with the techniques described in Section 12.1, table scans can be quite fast.

3. Suppose that the most frequent access path to TRANSCRIPT selects rows based on a condition involving both `StudId` and `CrsCode`. A less frequently used path selects rows based on a condition on `Semester`. If we build one index on ⟨`StudId,CrsCode`⟩ (actually an index on the primary key ⟨`StudId,CrsCode, Semester`⟩ would work fine) and another on `Semester`, which should be clustered? At first glance, it might seem that the index on ⟨`StudId,CrsCode`⟩ should be clustered because it is the main access path. However, even though ⟨`StudId, CrsCode`⟩ is *not* a candidate key, the number of TRANSCRIPT rows that agree on both of these attributes will be one in almost all cases—only when a student retakes a course can this number be larger than one. Therefore, clustering around ⟨`StudId, CrsCode`⟩ will not yield significant benefits. Also, it is not likely that range queries will be asked against this pair of attributes, so the overhead of a B^+ tree index does not seem justified—a hash index is probably the best solution here. On the other hand, a clustered B^+ tree index on `Semester` can greatly improve the efficiency of selections and joins on that attribute and makes an excellent choice for a secondary access path.

   The lesson here is that clustering is useful to group together rows that might be output in a result set. These rows might be grouped because they all agree on the value of an attribute(s) or because they fall within a range of values of that attribute(s). In either case, when a choice has to be made as to what attribute to cluster on, you should make the choice based on the size of the result sets you expect in your application.

4. Assume the PROFESSOR table has the additional attribute `Salary`, and suppose we want to optimize the performance of the range query:

```
SELECT  P.Name
FROM    PROFESSOR P
WHERE   P.Salary BETWEEN :lower AND :upper
```

The analysis here is similar to that of example 1 with the exception that we now want a clustered index on `Salary` and it must be a B^+ tree.

5. If two different queries would benefit from two different clustered indices on the same table, we have a problem since only one clustered index is possible. One solution is to make it possible for the optimizer to use an **index-only strategy**. For example, suppose that TEACHING already has a clustered B^+ tree index on `Semester`, but another important query would benefit from a clustered index on `ProfId` in order to quickly access the course codes associated with a given professor. We can sidestep the problem by creating an *unclustered* B^+ tree index with search key ⟨`ProfId, CrsCode`⟩. Then all the information required by the query is contained in the index (and the index is often referred to as a **covering index**), and TEACHING does not have to be accessed at all! We simply search down the index using `ProfId` to the leaf level. Since the values of `CrsCode` at that level are clustered around `ProfId`, we can scan forward from that point at the leaf level of the index to get the required result set using only the index entries. This approach produces the same effect as that of a clustered index with search key ⟨`ProfId, CrsCode`⟩ on TEACHING (in fact, it is more efficient because the index is smaller and hence scanning a section of the leaf level requires fewer I/O operations than scanning a section of TEACHING).

   Index-only query processing comes in two varieties. In this example we searched the index using `ProfId` to quickly locate the associated course codes. Suppose, however, another query required that we find the `ProfId`s of all professors who had taught a particular course. Unfortunately, although all the information we need is in the index, it cannot be searched because `CrsCode` is not the first attribute of the search key. But all is not lost. Another way to produce the desired result set is to scan the entire leaf level of the index. This is not as efficient as a search, but it might be better than having to scan the entire data file (the index is smaller!) or create and use an unclustered index on `CrsCode`.

6. The ability to nest queries is one of the most powerful features of SQL. Unfortunately, however, nested queries are very difficult to optimize. Consider the query

```
SELECT  P.Name, C.CrsName
FROM    PROFESSOR P, COURSE C
WHERE   P.Department = 'CS' AND C.DeptId = 'MAT' AND
        C.CrsCode IN                                          12.1
          (SELECT T.CrsCode
           FROM TEACHING T
           WHERE T.Semester = 'S2003' AND T.ProfId = P.Id)
```

that returns a set of rows in which the value of the first attribute is the name of a CS professor who has taught a course in the Math Department in the spring of 2003 and the value of the second is the name of one such course.

Typically, a query optimizer splits this query into two separate parts. The inner query is considered as an independently optimized unit. The outer query is also optimized independently (with the result set of the inner SELECT statement viewed as a database relation). In this case, the subquery is correlated, so it is crucial that it be executed efficiently since it will be executed many times. For example, a clustered index on TEACHING with search key ⟨ProfId, Semester⟩ would permit quick retrieval of all courses taught by a particular professor in a semester (and hopefully this is a small set). If possible (as in this example), the search key should involve all the attributes of the WHERE clause to avoid retrieving rows unnecessarily.

However, there is another point to note here. Because the two queries are optimized separately, certain alternatives might not be considered by the optimizer. For instance, the use of a clustered index on TEACHING with search key CrsCode would *not* be considered since the correlated nested subquery produces a set of course codes for each value of P.Id that is supplied and CrsCode is not even mentioned in the WHERE clause of that subquery. On the other hand, it is easy to see that the above query is equivalent to

```
SELECT   C.CrsName, P.Name
FROM     PROFESSOR P, TEACHING T, COURSE C
WHERE    T.Semester='S2003' AND P.Department='CS'
         AND C.DeptId = 'MAT'
         AND P.Id = T.ProfId AND T.CrsCode=C.CrsCode
```

and the use of that index *would be* considered in optimizing this query. One strategy that can take advantage of this index corresponds to the following expression:[2]

$$\sigma_{\texttt{Department= 'CS'}}(\text{PROFESSOR}) \bowtie_{\texttt{Id=ProfId}} \sigma_{\texttt{Semester= 'S2003'}}(\text{TEACHING} \bowtie_{\texttt{CrsCode=CrsCode}} \sigma_{\texttt{DeptId= 'MAT'}}(\text{COURSE})) \quad \textbf{12.2}$$

After computing $\sigma_{\texttt{DeptId='MAT'}}(\text{COURSE})$, the index for CrsCode in TEACHING can be used to compute the join $\bowtie_{\texttt{CrsCode=CrsCode}}$ in the index-nested loops algorithm.

It should be remarked that some query optimizers do, in fact, try to eliminate nested subqueries and take other steps to reduce the cost of processing them. However, it is still a good idea to avoid query nesting whenever possible.

[2] This strategy may or may not be the best for this query depending on the sizes of the relations, selectivity of the attributes, and other parameters.

7. Consider the query

```
SELECT   T.Semester, COUNT(*)
FROM     TRANSCRIPT T
WHERE    T.Grade <= :grade
GROUP BY T.Semester
```

Our first inclination is to create a clustered B^+ tree on Grade since a range is indicated. Our intention is to influence the optimizer to first retrieve all rows satisfying the condition, sort them on Semester (which brings all the members of a group together), and then count the size of each group. But this is not necessarily a good idea. The condition is not selective, so we will have to sort a large intermediate table.

Suppose instead we reverse the order of operations: we do the sort before the selection. In fact, if we choose a clustered index on Semester, the table is sorted before the query is executed. Since the grouping is already done, all we have to do is scan the table and count all the qualifying rows in each group—clearly a better plan when the condition is not selective. Note that the index can be either a B^+ tree or a hash. In both cases the rows in a group will be together.

The lesson here is that an index is not simply an access path to data; it is a way of storing the data. In this example, the query plan does not actually use the index to find a particular row but simply takes advantage of the way the rows are stored.

8. Consider the query

```
SELECT   S.Name
FROM     STUDENT S, TRANSCRIPT T
WHERE    S.Id = T.StudId AND T.CrsCode = 'CS305'
```

If appropriate indices are not present, the optimizer might choose a block-nested loops join or a sort-merge join as the basis of a query plan. These choices are likely to be inefficient, since the size of the result set that we expect is considerably smaller than the size of the tables involved. As a general rule of thumb, you should investigate the possibility of an index-nested loops join when you expect a small result set, reserving other methods for large result sets.

So how can we encourage the optimizer to consider an index-nested approach? If we create a clustered index on TRANSCRIPT with search key CrsCode, the optimizer has a way of quickly finding, as part of the outer loop of the join, all students who have taken CS305. We can easily ensure that such an index exists since CrsCode is an attribute in the primary key of the table: all we have to do is make sure that it is declared as the first attribute of the key. The DBMS will generally oblige by creating a B^+ tree on the primary key.

For the inner loop of the join we need an index on STUDENT with search key Id. This is no problem at all since Id is the primary key. The DBMS will create an index, and we do not care whether it is clustered or unclustered, B^+ tree or hash, since Id is unique.

9. Consider the query

```
SELECT  Te.ProfId, Tr.StudId
FROM    TEACHING Te, TRANSCRIPT Tr
WHERE   Te.Semester = Tr.Semester AND Te.CrsCode = Tr.CrsCode
```

We expect the size of the result set to be much larger than the size of either table. Hence, a sort-merge algorithm is likely to be efficient in performing the join. We can make such an algorithm attractive to the optimizer by using clustered B^+ indices on the tables involved. For example, if such an index (with search key ⟨Semester, CrsCode⟩) is created on TRANSCRIPT, the relation will already be sorted on the join attributes and a significant part of the sorting step of the algorithm comes for free. Since these two attributes are a part of the primary key of the table, the DBMS has already created such an index—all we need to do is make sure that the ordering of primary-key attributes is ⟨Semester, CrsCode, StudId⟩.

10. Consider a database with two tables: PROJECTPART(ProjId, PartId), which relates a project to each part that it uses, and PARTSUPPLIER(PartId, SupplId), which relates a part to each supplier that sells that part. The query

```
SELECT  P.ProjId, S.SupplId
FROM    PROJECTPART P, PARTSUPPLIER S
WHERE   P.PartId = S.PartId
```

produces a (ProjId, SupplId) pair for each project that uses a part that the supplier sells. An index-nested loops join could scan PROJECTPART and use an index with search key PartId on PARTSUPPLIER to find the rows of that table that match each scanned row. Encouraging the use of such an algorithm, however, is probably a bad idea since many rows of PARTSUPPLIER join with each row of PROJECTPART. Reversing the tables so that PARTSUPPLIER is scanned produces the same result. Hence a sort-merge or hash join might be less expensive. The lesson here is that it is not a good idea to create an index unless you are sure it is going to be of use. In this case it might lead to the wrong query plan and result in added overhead when the indexed table is updated.

Miscellaneous considerations. A foreign-key constraint can be essential in supporting the integrity of your database but introduces a hidden cost since it must be checked when certain modifications are made to the tables that it relates. Suppose such a constraint is declared on attribute $A1$ of table T1 referring to attribute $A2$ of table T2. When a row, $t1$, is inserted in T1, the DBMS must ensure that there is a row in T2 in which the value of $A2$ matches the value of $A1$ in $t1$. Fortunately, this is not a problem since $A2$ must be a key of T2 and hence there is an index with search key *A2* that can be used to make the check quickly. Unfortunately, this approach does not work in reverse. If a row, *t2*, of T2 is deleted, the DBMS must check that there does not exist a row of T1 that refers to it. Since *A1* is not a key of T1, T1 might not have an index with search key *A1*, and if not, a table scan will be required to check the foreign-key constraint. If T1 is large and rows of T2 are deleted or updated frequently, this table scan can be a significant source of overhead. In that case, an index on T1 with search key *A1* should be created.

A common query is one that counts the rows in a table using COUNT. Such a query can result in a table scan if a proper index is not available. The table scan can be replaced by an index scan if the index is over a column that has a NOT NULL constraint because a row in which that attribute is null would not be indexed. The I/O cost of an index scan can be substantially less since the leaf level of the index can be packed into fewer pages than the table. Note that even if the DBMS has created statistics describing the table, the values will generally not be current and so cannot be used.

12.2.2 Denormalization

In Chapter 6, we learned a great deal about schema decomposition. That discussion was motivated by concerns that redundancy leads to consistency-maintenance problems in the presence of frequent database updates. What if most of the transactions are read-only queries? Schema decomposition seems to make query answering harder because associations between columns that existed in one relation before the decomposition might be broken into separate relations afterward.

For instance, finding the hobbies of the person with a particular `SSN` is more efficient using the monolithic relation of Figure 4.13 than the pair of relations of Figure 6.1 because the latter requires a join. This is an example of the classic time/space trade-off: the redundancy present in the monolithic relation improves query performance and argues against decomposing the relation. Such a trade-off has to be evaluated in a particular application if the performance of a frequently executed query is found wanting.

Denormalization refers to situations in which an attempt is made to improve performance of read-only queries by adding redundant information to a table. It reverses the normalization process and results in a violation of normal form conditions.

Denormalization often takes the form of adding a redundant column. For example, in order to print a class roster that lists student names, a join is required between the tables STUDENT and TRANSCRIPT. The join can be avoided by adding a `Name` column to TRANSCRIPT. In contrast to the previous example, STUDENT contains other information (e.g., `Address`), so denormalization does not eliminate the need to retain STUDENT.

As another example, a join involving the tables STUDENT and TRANSCRIPT is needed to produce a result set that associates a student's name with her cumulative grade point average. If the query is performed frequently, we might improve performance by adding a `GPA` column to the STUDENT table. Although prior to the modification the GPA was not stored in the database, redundancy has been added since the GPA can be computed from TRANSCRIPT. This is a particularly attractive example of denormalization because the additional storage requirements are nominal.

But do not get carried away with denormalization. In addition to the extra storage required, a price has to be paid to maintain consistency. In this case, every time a grade is changed or a new row added to TRANSCRIPT, `GPA` has to be updated. This might be done by the transaction doing the modification, adding to its complication and degrading its performance. A better alternative is to add a trigger that updates STUDENT when the modification takes place. Although the performance penalty is not avoided, complication is reduced and the possibility that transactions do not properly maintain consistency is avoided.

There is no general rule on when to denormalize. Here is an incomplete list of conflicting guidelines that need to be evaluated against each particular mix of transactions:

1. Normalization can lower the demand for storage space since it usually eliminates redundant data and null values. Tables and rows are smaller, reducing the amount of I/O that must be performed and allowing more rows to fit into the cache.
2. Denormalization increases storage requirements since redundant data is added. When the degree of redundancy is low, however, normalization can also increase storage requirements. For instance, in the PERSON relation of (6.14) on page 229, suppose that most people have just one phone number and one child. In this case, schema decomposition actually increases storage requirements (since `SSN` must be repeated in each table) without bringing tangible benefits. The same applies to the decomposition of HASACCOUNT in Figure 6.7, which can increase the overhead for update transactions. The reason is that verification of the FD

   ```
   ClientId OfficeId → AccountNumber
   ```

   after an update requires a join because the attributes `ClientId` and `OfficeId` belong to different relations in the decomposition.
3. Normalization generally makes answering complex queries (for example, in OLAP systems) less efficient because joins must be performed during query evaluation.
4. Normalization can make answering simple queries (for example, in OLTP systems) more efficient because such queries often involve a small number of attributes that belong to the same relation. Since decomposed relations have fewer tuples, the tuples that need to be scanned during the evaluation of a simple query are likely to be fewer.
5. Normalization generally makes simple update transactions more efficient since it tends to reduce the number of indices per table.
6. Normalization might make complex update transactions (such as *Raise the salary of all professors who taught every course required for computer science majors*) less

efficient since they might involve complex queries (and thus might require complex joins).

7. Normalization results in more tables, and hence more clustered indices, which translates into more flexibility when tuning queries.

12.2.3 Repeating Groups

In some situations the same information can be stored in either columns or rows, and the choice can be based on performance considerations. For example, suppose one wanted to store the total sales of each salesperson in each sales region of the country. One possible solution is to store the data for each salesperson in separate rows:

```
CREATE TABLE  SALES  (
    Id            INTEGER,
    Region        CHAR(6),
    TotalSales    DECIMAL )
```

The pair (`Region, TotalSales`) is referred to as a repeating group. Unfortunately, this requires retrieving multiple rows to access information about a single salesperson. Alternatively, the information describing a salesperson could be compacted into a single row. Assuming three regions, we could store the data using this table:

```
CREATE TABLE  SALES  (
    Id          INTEGER,
    Region1Sales  DECIMAL,
    Region2Sales  DECIMAL,
    Region3Sales  DECIMAL )
```

This schema has the limitation that only a fixed number of sales regions can be accommodated, but if it is generally the case that all of the information about a salesperson is retrieved at the same time, it might yield performance benefits.

12.2.4 Partitioning

The I/O cost of accessing a very large table can be reduced by explicitly splitting the table (in the schema) into partitions. One reason for doing this is to separate frequently accessed data in the table from data that is rarely referenced. By packing data that is frequently accessed into fewer pages, the number of I/O operations can be reduced and it is less likely that pages in the cache contain data that is not being referenced. A second reason is to make it possible to access different parts of the table concurrently, and we discuss this in Section 12.5.

With horizontal partitioning, all partitions have the same set of columns and each contains a subset of the rows. The partitioning of the rows is based on a natural criterion that populates the partitions with disjoint subsets. For example, the table STUDENT might be partitioned into two partitions. Rows describing inactive students, those who have graduated, might be in a partition named ALUMNI. Rows describing active students, the current undergraduates, might be in a partition called CURRENT_STUDENTS. A page of CURRENT_STUDENTS in the cache is more likely to be referenced again than a page of ALUMNI since most references are to active students and a page of CURRENT_STUDENTS contains only those students. This reduces the number of I/O operations. Similarly, the cost of a scan to retrieve undergraduate information is greatly reduced.

With vertical partitioning, subsets of the columns of a table form the partitions. This can be useful when a table has many columns, and hence long rows, and some of the columns are infrequently referenced. Once again, without partitioning, performance is degraded by the need to transfer inactive data from the disk when active data is referenced. By storing the infrequently accessed columns in a separate partition, this problem can be alleviated. Oracle, for example, effectively separates infrequently accessed columns without requiring explicit partitioning. These columns are designated in the CREATE TABLE statement of a table that has an integrated, clustered index. In this case the infrequently accessed columns are not stored in the leaf level of the index but instead are stored in overflow pages linked to leaf pages. Scans involving only frequently accessed columns can skip the overflow pages.

An astute reader must have noticed that vertical partitioning is conceptually the same as schema decomposition, discussed in Chapter 6. In particular, partitions must form a lossless decomposition of the original relation, which can be ensured by, for example, including a key of the relation in all partitions. However, partitioning is typically driven not by the need to normalize the schema but by other considerations. For instance, if in a STUDENT table the attributes `Address` and `Phone` are accessed infrequently, they (and the student Id) might be separated into a different partition even though the STUDENT table is already in BCNF. With this secondary information split off, the main partition of the STUDENT table becomes smaller and thus queries involving this table run faster.

Partitioning involves a trade-off, and in this case the price that must be paid is the additional complexity of managing and accessing multiple tables. Hence, it should be used only when the performance benefits are clear.

12.3 Tuning the Data Manipulation Language

A modification of the schema of a particular table can have a global impact: it can affect (hopefully improve) the performance of all the SQL statements that access the table. A modification to a query or a statement of the DBMS has a local impact: it affects the performance of only that statement. There are many nuggets of wisdom that we could include here. We have chosen just a few based on what we think offers interesting insights into SQL and the way it is processed by a DBMS.

Avoid sorts. Sorting is expensive and should be avoided if possible. You need to be aware of the kinds of queries that might cause an optimizer to introduce a sort into the query plan and avoid those queries if possible. In addition to the sort-merge join, duplicate elimination involves sorting. Hence, do not use DISTINCT unless it is important in the application. Set operators like UNION and EXCEPT also involve a sort to find duplicates, but their use may be unavoidable (however, some DBMSs provide the UNION ALL operator, which does not eliminate duplicates and hence does not involve a sort).

A sort is necessary to process an ORDER BY clause (so you should carefully consider whether an ordering on the output is necessary), and a GROUP BY clause will also frequently involve a sort. If sorting is unavoidable, consider presorting by using a clustered index (as in example 6 on page 440).

Do not scan unnecessarily. Use of "not equals" in a WHERE condition is likely to result in a scan. For example, the optimizer might not use an index on `CreditHours` when evaluating the condition `CreditHours` $\neq$ 3. This is unfortunate since it is likely that the vast majority of courses carry three credits. Accessing the few that do not through an index would therefore be appropriate. If a histogram showing the distribution of values (see Section 12.6) were available to the optimizer, it might consider using the index if the condition were rewritten as `CreditHours` IN (1,2,4) or

```
CreditHours = 1 OR CreditHours = 2 OR CreditHours = 4
```

Similarly, a table scan will be used to resolve a condition of the form WHERE `Name` LIKE `'%son'` since a prefix of the search-key value is not provided.

An index on a column will not contain an entry for a row if the column value is null, so if you want to search for nulls you cannot use the index. A better way to handle the situation in that case is to use a default value (e.g., `unknown`) instead of null, and search for the default.

Minimize communication. Client/server communication is generally very expensive, so eliminate it where you can. A major culprit is the cursor, which invokes communication for every row fetched. Hence, if you are updating a table, try to use UPDATE statements instead of fetching the row, modifying it, and then writing it back. For example, an application might adjust the salary of employees based on the department in which they work. This might be done using a cursor in which the fetch is followed by a case statement with a branch for each department. The body of the branch for a particular department then makes the adjustment appropriate for that department. Alternatively, the application might use a sequence of UPDATE statements in which the WHERE clause of each statement in the sequence referred to a different department, and the SET clause performed the update appropriate to that department. The second approach involves far less communication, and this might compensate for any extra index searches or table scans.

If you are retrieving aggregate information, consider computing the aggregate in a stored procedure and then return only the result to the client. If you must analyze each row in the application code, see if your DBMS allows the fetch statement to retrieve multiple rows (some DBMSs support an array fetch).

Be careful with views. In Section 5.2.8 we discussed the fact that a query that names a view in its FROM clause is equivalent to a query with the view definition replacing the view name in the clause (and that it is the latter query that is analyzed by the DBMS). From this you can conclude that you are not going to get any performance gain by using a view since there is always an equivalent query that does not involve the view that will give exactly the same performance. This might seem like old news, but the really bad news is that the use of a view might actually impact performance negatively.

Consider the following view defined over the tables COURSE and CLASS of Section 4.8.

```
CREATE VIEW   CLASSES (C.CrsCode, C.DeptId, C.CrsName
                         CL.Enrollment, CL.MaxEnrollment) AS
SELECT    C.CrsCode, C.DeptId, C.CrsName,
               CL.Enrollment, CL.MaxEnrollment
FROM      COURSE C, CLASS CL
WHERE     C.CrsCode = CL.CrsCode
```

The query

```
SELECT    C.CrsCode, C.CrsName
FROM      CLASSES
```

pays the price of a join, whereas the query

```
SELECT    C.CrsCode, C.CrsName
FROM      COURSE
```

achieves the same result without a join because the columns in the result set are all derived from the columns of a single base table.

Some optimizers, however, can recognize that a join is unnecessary and can eliminate the overhead.

Consider restructuring the query. There are often several different ways to formulate a complex query. The cost of each formulation will depend on the state of the tables involved and the indices available, and there is no easy rule that you can use to decide which formulation is best. For example, we could express the query that returns the Ids of all professors who taught a course in the spring 2003 semester in the following three ways:

1.
```
SELECT    *
FROM      PROFESSOR P
WHERE EXISTS
            (SELECT *
             FROM TEACHING T
             WHERE T.Semester = 'S2003' AND T.ProfId = P.Id)
```

2.
```
SELECT    *
FROM      PROFESSOR P
WHERE     P.Id IN
            (SELECT T.ProfId
             FROM TEACHING T
             WHERE T.Semester = 'S2003')
```

3.
```
SELECT DISTINCT     P.Id, P.Name, P.DeptId
FROM      PROFESSOR P, TEACHING T
WHERE     P.Id = T.ProfId AND T.Semester = 'S2003'
```

The first formulation has a correlated subquery, so it looks bad. However, with an index on ⟨ProfId, Semester⟩, the subquery can be executed efficiently since only a few rows match the condition. In the second formulation, the subquery is only executed once so even if no usable index were available and a table scan were necessary, the cost might not be excessive. The cost of the third formulation is difficult to predict without knowing more about the state of the relations involved, and so would also have to be investigated.

Although a sort is generally unavoidable in the plan for a query with a GROUP BY clause, you should attempt to minimize its cost by making the relation to be sorted as small as possible. One way to do this is to strengthen the WHERE clause. For example, the query

```
SELECT    P.DeptId, MAX(P.Salary)
FROM      PROFESSOR P
GROUP BY  P.DeptId
HAVING    P.DeptId IN('CS', 'EE', 'Math')
```

produces the same result as

```
SELECT    P.DeptId, MAX(P.Salary)
FROM      PROFESSOR P
WHERE     P.DeptId IN ('CS', 'EE', 'Math')
GROUP BY  P.DeptId
```

but the second formulation has lower cost since nonparticipating rows are eliminated earlier.

12.4 Tools

DBMS vendors usually provide a variety of tools to help with tuning. The use of these tools normally requires creation of a mock-up database in which the different plans can be tried out. A typical tool in most DBMSs is the EXPLAIN PLAN statement, which lets the user see the query plans the DBMS generates. This statement is not part of the SQL standard, so the syntax varies among vendors. The basic idea is first to execute a statement of the form

```
EXPLAIN PLAN SET queryno=123 FOR
        SELECT  P.Name
        FROM    PROFESSOR P, TEACHING T
        WHERE   P.Id = T.ProfId AND T.Semester = 'F1994'
                AND T.Semester = 'CS'
```

which causes the DBMS to generate a query execution plan and store it as a set of tuples in a relation called PLAN_TABLE. queryno is one attribute of that table. Some DBMSs use a different attribute name, for example, id. The plan can then be retrieved by querying PLAN_TABLE as follows:

```
SELECT * FROM PLAN_TABLE WHERE queryno=123
```

Text-based facilities for examining query plans are extremely powerful, but these days they are used mostly by people who enjoy fixing their own cars. A busy database administrator uses text-based facilities only as a last resort because many vendors provide flashy graphical interfaces to their tuning tools. For instance, IBM has Visual Explain for DB/2, Oracle supplies Oracle Diagnostics Pack, and SQL Server from Microsoft has Query Analyzer. These tools not only show query plans, but they can also suggest indices that can speed up various queries.

By examining the query plan, you are in a position to determine whether or not the DBMS has chosen to ignore the hints you have provided (see page 454) and the indices you have so carefully created. If you are dissatisfied, you can try other strategies. More importantly, many DBMSs provide trace tools that allow you to trace the execution of a query as well as output the CPU and I/O resources used and the number of rows processed by each step. With a trace tool available, your strategy should be to coax the DBMS into using a variety of query plans and to evaluate the performance of each.

12.5 Managing Physical Resources

The physical resources—CPUs, I/O devices, etc.—available to the DBMS are an important factor in the performance of an application, but the application programmer is generally not in a position to control these resources. Some DBMSs, however, provide the programmer or database administrator, with mechanisms for controlling how the existing physical resources should be used.

A disk unit has a single doorway through which each read or write request for a table or index must pass in sequence. Hence, if many heavily used items are placed on the disk, a queue of waiting requests will form and response time will suffer. The lesson here is that many small disks can perform better than a single large disk because items can be spread across the disks and I/O can be performed concurrently on different disks. The discussion of RAID (Section 9.1.1) has already made this point. Since the assignment of items to disks can have a major impact on performance, DBMSs provide mechanisms that allow the user to specify the disk on which a particular item is placed.

In addition to spreading *different* tables across the available disks, concurrent access to a *single* table can be achieved by partitioning it and distributing the partitions on different disks. For example, the STUDENT table might be split into FRESH_STUDENT, SOPH_STUDENTS, JUN_STUDENTS, and SEN_STUDENTS. Note that in this case all partitions contain rows that are frequently referenced. If the partitions are placed on different disks, performance can be improved since multiple I/O requests for information about students can be performed concurrently.

Beyond distributing files across disks, the next point to note is that reading a file sequentially (e.g., a table scan) is generally more efficient than reading data randomly. This follows from the fact that DBMSs attempt to keep the pages of a file together, and as a result the seek time between the reads of two successive pages can be eliminated. But it is not so easy to take advantage of sequential I/O since, in general, a disk will store multiple files. Since requests for the files from different processes will be interleaved, the disk assembly will move from one cylinder to another. Thus, even though a process accesses a file sequentially, two successive requests from the process will pay a seek price since requests from other processes will be interleaved between them. Note that this is true even if *all* files on the disk are accessed sequentially. The lesson here is that if you want to take advantage of the fact that a file is accessed sequentially, place it on its own private disk. A good example of such a file is the log file maintained by a database system to implement atomicity.

In addition to influencing the way I/O devices are employed in an application, the programmer can influence the way CPUs are used. Generally, a single process (or thread) is assigned to execute the query plan for a particular SQL statement. Processes are sequential—they do one thing at a time. Either they require the services of a CPU to execute some code or they request an I/O transfer and wait until the operation completes. Hence, they make use of one physical device at a time. As a result, in an OLAP environment with only a few concurrent users, throughput may suffer because resource utilization is low. In an OLTP environment with many concurrent users, resource utilization will be high, but the response time possible when only a single process is assigned to execute a query plan can be unacceptable.

The response time of a query can often be improved using **parallel query processing** in which multiple concurrent processes are assigned to execute different components of the query plan. Improvement is likely when the system has multiple CPUs (so the processes can execute simultaneously), the query plan involves table scans, the query accesses very large tables (so considerable I/O is required), and the data is spread across multiple disks (so the processes can be using the disks simultaneously). DBMSs provide mechanisms, called *hints* (discussed on page 454), that the application programmer can use to request parallel query processing.

12.6 Influencing the Optimizer

In Chapters 10 and 11 we discussed algorithms used by the DBMS to create an efficient query execution plan. The plan selected depends on first identifying promising alternatives and then choosing from among those alternatives the plan that seems best. The application programmer is in a position to affect this process in two ways: he can modify the schema—primarily by creating appropriate indices—to create new alternatives that the DBMS might find promising, and he can influence the choice among the alternatives. We discussed schema modification earlier. In this section we will discuss mechanisms for influencing choice.

Statistics. In Section 11.1 we discussed the fact that cost-based query optimizers use statistics to predict the size of the output produced by various relational expressions in order to estimate the cost of a query plan. These statistics describe not only tables but the indices that can be used to access the tables (for example, the depth, number of leaf pages, number of distinct search-key values at the leaf level, etc.). Optimizers that use this information are referred to as **cost-based optimizers**. They contrast with **rule-based optimizers** that make decisions using rules based on the structure of the SQL statement and the availability of indices but do not attempt to evaluate the costs involved. The trend in DBMS design is toward cost-based optimization.

If some statistics are good, more statistics might be even better. Additional statistics take the form of histograms describing the distribution of values in particular columns. Advanced query optimizers can make use of such information in certain cases. For example, an employee table might have an integer-valued column `Children` that gives the number of children of each employee. Without a histogram the optimizer might be able to determine from the available statistics that the maximum value in the column is 9 and that there are 10,000 rows in the table. It can then conclude that on average, for each value between 0 and 9 there are 1000 employees with that many children. As a result, a query whose result set contains the rows satisfying the WHERE condition `E.Children = 9` might use a table scan for the access path rather than an unclustered index on `Children`. (For example, if there were 500 pages in the table then it is likely that at least one row describing a fertile employee is contained in most pages.)

With a histogram the optimizer can do much better. Since the histogram contains the number of rows having each column value, the optimizer is in a position to determine that only two employees have nine children and, as a result, an access path that uses the index on `Children` is far superior to a table scan.

Maintaining a histogram is a time-consuming process. Hence, DBMSs that make use of histograms provide the programmer with a mechanism to specify the columns over which histograms are to be constructed.

If you have been reading carefully, you probably have noticed that we are describing an approach here that contradicts what was said in Section 12.1. There we argued that it was desirable to use host variables instead of literals so that query plans could be reused. Here we have made the point that literals are preferable since they allow the optimizer to use histograms. The choice of which to use has to be made for each specific application.

Care and feeding. Although a system might function efficiently when it is initially configured, you might discover that, over time, performance degrades even though the load is unchanged. This might be due to changes in the state of the database. Even though the size of tables might remain roughly the same, as rows are added and deleted the organization of the tables and indices might deteriorate. For example, although the pages of a B^+ tree might initially be full, the steady state situation might be one in which the occupancy of pages might be low. Although this might not cause the tree to be deeper, it might substantially increase the number of leaf pages, and hence the cost of scans at the leaf level. Similarly, the space created by deleted rows in a heap file is often not recovered since rows are added at the end. As a result, the cost of table scans is increased. Each DBMS has its own quirks in the way it stores information that may result in similar inefficiencies. Check your manual.

Maintaining statistics is time consuming, and hence statistics are not normally updated each time the value of a table changes. Instead, the DBMS supports a command that causes it to reevaluate statistics. It can be invoked by the programmer at a time when the state of the table has substantially changed since the last time the statistics were evaluated. The use of outdated statistics can lead to poor query plans. Furthermore, since the query plans of stored procedures might be saved, stored procedures that access dynamically changing tables should be recompiled frequently. Similarly, if indices of tables referred to by a stored procedure change, the procedure should be recompiled.

Hints. Some DBMSs allow the programmer to insert suggestions, called **hints**, into an SQL statement that the query optimizer can use in constructing a query plan. For example, we saw in Chapter 11 that there are $N!$ different orders in which N tables can be joined, and that the optimizer cannot explore all possibilities even when N is small. A major problem in joining tables is the I/O and storage costs of manipulating large intermediate tables. The wrong order can result in huge intermediate tables, which are reduced to just a few rows in the final step. Promising orders are those in which the first table to be joined is one in which the WHERE clause includes a selective condition that eliminates many rows that cannot possibly play a role in forming a row in the result set. Eliminating such rows early prevents them from producing useless rows at intermediate stages.

Unfortunately, it might be difficult for the optimizer to detect that a condition is selective. For example, although a condition such as `T.Model = 'Rolls Royce'` on a table containing the inventory of Slippery Joe's Used Cars might be very selective, the optimizer might have no way of knowing that. Even if a histogram were maintained on the attributes of the table, the optimizer would be stymied if 'Rolls Royce' were replaced by a host variable :model. Although the optimizer might not have enough information, the programmer probably does. He can list the tables in the FROM clause in the desired join order and provide a hint to the effect that the optimizer should use that order in the query plan.

Hints can cover many issues. For example, different databases allow you to specify the join methodology to use (hash, sort-merge, etc.), the index to use, whether parallel query execution should be considered, and whether to optimize a query plan so that it retrieves the first row of a result set quickly (for fast response time for an interactive query) or whether it should minimize the time for retrieving the entire result set (for batch queries).

BIBLIOGRAPHIC NOTES

A complete discussion of the principles and practices involved in tuning a DBMS (which is not specialized to any particular product) can be found in the book by [Shasha and Bonnet 2003]. The trade books and product manuals describing the measures taken in particular systems are also very informative: for SQL Server [Whalen et al 2001], for Oracle [Harrison 2001], for Sybase [Sybase 1999].

EXERCISES

12.1 Choose an index for each of the following SELECT statements. Specify whether your choice is clustered or unclustered and whether it is a hash index or a B^+ tree.

a.
```
SELECT  S.Name
FROM    STUDENT S
WHERE   S.Id = '111111111'
```

b.
```
SELECT  S.Name
FROM    STUDENT S
WHERE   S.Status = 'Freshman'
```

c.
```
SELECT  T.StudId
FROM    TRANSCRIPT T
WHERE   T.Grade = 'B' AND T.CrsCode = 'CS305'
```

d.
```
SELECT  P.Name
FROM    PROFESSOR P
WHERE   P.Salary BETWEEN 20000 AND 150000
```

e.
```
SELECT  T.ProfId
FROM    TEACHING T
WHERE   T.CrsCode LIKE 'CS%' AND T.Semester = 'F2000'
```

f.
```
SELECT  C.CrsName
FROM    COURSE C, TEACHING T
WHERE   C.CrsCode = T.CrsCode AND T.Semester = 'F2002'
```

12.2 Suppose both queries (e) and (f) from the previous exercise need to be supported. What indices should be chosen for TEACHING and COURSE?

12.3 The table FACULTY has 60,000 rows, each row occupies 100 bytes, and the database page size is 4^k bytes. Assuming pages in the index and data files are 100% occupied, estimate the number of page transfers required for the following SELECT statement in each of the cases listed below.

```
SELECT   F.DeptId
FROM     FACULTY F
WHERE    F.Id = '111111111'
```

a. The table has no index.
b. The table has a clustered B^+ tree index on Id. Assume a (nonleaf) index entry has 20 characters.
c. The table has an unclustered B^+ tree index on Id. Assume a (nonleaf) index entry has 20 characters.
d. The table has an unclustered B^+ tree index on (Id, DeptId). Assume that an index entry now has 25 characters.
e. The table has an unclustered B^+ tree index on (DeptId, Id). Assume that an index entry now has 25 characters.

12.4 The table FACULTY has 60,000 rows, each row occupies 100 bytes, and the database page size is 4^k bytes. The table contains an attribute City, indicating the city in which a professor lives, there are 50 cities with names city10 ... city50, and professors are randomly distributed over the cities. Assuming that pages in the index and data files are 100% occupied, estimate the number of page transfers required for the following SELECT statement in each of the cases listed below.

```
SELECT   F.Id
FROM     FACULTY F
WHERE    F.City > 'city10' AND F.City < 'city21'
```

a. The table has no index.
b. The table has a clustered B^+ tree index on City. Assume a (nonleaf) index entry has 25 characters.
c. The table has an unclustered B^+ tree index on City. Assume an index entry has 25 characters.
d. The table has an unclustered B^+ tree index on (City, Id). Assume an index entry has 40 characters.
e. The table has an unclustered B^+ tree index on (Id, City). Assume an index entry has 40 characters.

12.5 Choose indices for the following SELECT statement. Specify whether your choices are clustered or unclustered, hash index or B^+ tree.

```
SELECT   C.CrsName, COUNT(*)
FROM     COURSE C, TRANSCRIPT T
WHERE    T.CrsCode = C.CrsCode AND T.Semester = :sem
```

```
GROUP BY T.CrsCode, C.CrsName
HAVING COUNT(*) ≥ 100
```

12.6 Consider the following query:

```
SELECT   T.CrsCode, T.Grade
FROM     TRANSCRIPT T, STUDENT S
WHERE    T.StudId = S.Id AND S.Name = 'Joe'
```

Assume that Id is the primary key of STUDENT, (CrsCode, Semester, StudId) is the primary key of TRANSCRIPT, and that Name is not unique. Set up a database containing these two tables on the DBMS available to you. Initialize the tables with a large number of rows. Write a program that measures the query execution time by reading the clock before and after submitting the query. Be sure to flush the cache between successive measurements (perhaps by executing a query that randomly reads a sufficient number of rows of a large dummy table).

a. Test your understanding by making an educated guess of what query plan will be chosen by the DBMS assuming that there are no indices other than those for the primary keys. Run the query, output the query plan, and check your guess. Measure the response time.

b. Now assume that an unclustered index on StudId on TRANSCRIPT is added. What query plan would you expect? Run the query, check your answer, and measure the response time. Try the query under two conditions: Joe has taken very few courses; Joe has taken many courses.

c. In addition to the index added in (b), assume that an unclustered index on STUDENT on Name has been added and repeat the experiment.

12.7 Consider the table AUTHORS with attributes Name, Publ, Title, and YearPub. Assume that Name is the primary key (authors' names are unique) and hence one would expect that the DBMS would automatically create a clustered index on that attribute. Consider the statement

```
SELECT    A.Publ, COUNT(*)
FROM      AUTHORS A
WHERE     . . . range predicate on YearPub . . .
GROUP BY  A.Publ
```

a. Assume that the statement is generally executed with a very narrow range specified in the WHERE clause (the publication year of only a few books will fall within the range). What indices would you create for the table and what query plan would you hope the query optimizer would use (include any changes you might make to the index on Name).

b. Repeat (a) assuming that a very broad range is generally specified.

12.8 Give the trigger that maintains the consistency of the database when a GPA column is added to the table STUDENT, as described in Section 12.2.2.

12.9 In applications that cannot tolerate duplicates it may be necessary to use DISTINCT. However, the query plan needed to support DISTINCT requires a sort, which is expensive. Therefore you should only use DISTINCT when duplicates are possible in the result set. Using the schema of Section 4.8, check the following queries to see if duplicates are possible. Explain your answer in each case.

a.
```
SELECT   S.Name
FROM     STUDENT S
WHERE    S.Id LIKE '1'
```

b.
```
SELECT   S.Id
FROM     STUDENT S, FACULTY F
WHERE    S.Address = F.Address
```

c.
```
SELECT   C.CrsCode, COUNT(*)
FROM     TRANSCRIPT T
GROUP BY T.CrsCode
```

d.
```
SELECT   F.Name, F.DeptId, C.ClassTime, C.CrsCode,
         C.Semester, C.Year
FROM     FACULTY, CLASS C
WHERE F.Id = C.InstructorId
```

e.
```
SELECT   S.Name, F.Name, T.Semester, T.Year
FROM     FACULTY, CLASS C, TRANSCRIPT T, STUDENT S
WHERE F.Id = C.InstructorId AND S.Id = T.StudId AND
         C.CrsCode = T.CrsCode AND
         C.SectionNo = T.SectNo AND
         C.Year = T.Year AND C.Semester = T.Semester
```

12.10 A particular query can have several formulations, and a query optimizer may produce different query plans with different costs for each.

a. Assume that the Computer Science Department teaches only three 100-level courses: CS110, CS113, and CS114. Write an SQL statement whose result set contains the course codes of all courses that have these as prerequisites in three ways: using OR, UNION, and a nested subquery involving LIKE.

b. Write an SQL statement whose result set contains the names of all computer science courses that are prerequisites to other courses in three ways: using a join, a nested subquery involving EXISTS, and a nested subquery involving IN.

12.11 On page 440 we discussed the choice of indexes to optimize the execution of the nested query (12.1) and pointed out that a clustered index on TEACHING with search key CrsCode would not be considered. It might, however, be used in optimizing the execution of the equivalent, non-nested query

```
SELECT   C.CrsName, P.Name
FROM     PROFESSOR P, TEACHING T, COURSE C
WHERE    T.Semester='S2003' AND P.Department='CS'
         AND C.DeptId = 'MAT'
         AND P.Id = T.ProfId AND T.CrsCode=C.CrsCode
```

Under what conditions might such an index be used?

PART FOUR

Advanced Topics in Databases

In this part we will discuss a number of more-advanced topics: relational calculus, deductive databases, object-oriented databases, semistructured data and XML databases, distributed databases, online analytical processing, and data mining.

Relational calculus is a theoretical tool that underlies SQL and visual database languages, such as Microsoft Access. The aim of the field of deductive databases is to develop declarative query languages that are more expressive and are easier to use than SQL. Deductive databases have also influenced SQL itself, and the mechanism of recursive queries was added to SQL in 1999. All these topics will be discussed in Chapter 16.

Object databases are beginning to find their way into the mainstream both independently and as extensions to existing relational products. In Chapter 14, we will study the principles underlying the object data model and the corresponding query languages, as well as the embodiment of these principles in existing standards.

XML databases represent an emerging field that is expected to become important once the underlying standards and tools are developed. In Chapter 15, we will discuss some of these emerging standards and their applications.

Like object databases, distributed databases are becoming increasingly important for many applications. In Chapter 16, we will discuss distributed database design, query design, and query optimization.

Additional applications of database technology are data warehousing, online analytical processing (OLAP), and data mining. A data warehouse is a database optimized for complex read-only queries typical in decision-support applications (e.g., aggregate company sales by region and period). In Chapter 17, we will discuss the data structures, language constructs, and algorithms that simplify such queries and improve system performance.

13

Relational Calculus, Visual Query Languages, and Deductive Databases

Relational algebra was used in Chapter 5 to explain how SQL queries are evaluated. In fact, DBMSs often use the relational algebra as a high-level intermediate code into which SQL queries are translated before being optimized. Conceptually and syntactically, however, SQL is based on a completely different formal query language, called **relational calculus**. The relational calculus is a subset of classical predicate logic, a subject that had been well researched long before the relational model was born. One of the major insights of E. F. Codd was the realization that this tool could become the basis for a powerful database query language.

There are two relational calculi. In the next section, we introduce the basics of **tuple relational calculus (TRC)**, which was introduced by Codd in [Codd 1972]. TRC is important for proper understanding of the query sublanguage of SQL. Indeed, as we shall see, SQL can be viewed as TRC with some of the mathematical symbols replaced with English words. For instance, [Date 1992] showed how TRC can be effectively used as an intermediate language for constructing complex SQL queries.

Then we sketch **domain relational calculus (DRC)** and discuss the visual query languages built around it. If you have studied the elements of the usual predicate logic, DRC should look familiar as it is essentially a subset of that logic. It was proposed as a language for database queries in [Lacroix and Pirotte 1977].

At the end of this chapter we introduce the field of **deductive databases**. This section is divided into two subjects: the recursive extensions of SQL, introduced in SQL:1999, and Datalog—a more convenient language for writing recursive queries, which is used in research and also commercially.

13.1 Tuple Relational Calculus

Queries in TRC all have the form

$$\{T \mid Condition\}$$

The part of the query to the left of the bar | is called the query **target**; the part to the right is the query **condition** (or the **body** of the query).

The target consists of a **tuple variable**, *T*, which is just like the usual variables in high-school algebra except that it ranges over *tuples of values* (such as relational tuples) rather than individual values (such as numbers and strings).

The query condition must be such that

- It uses the variable *T* and possibly some other variables.
- If a *concrete tuple* of values is substituted for each occurrence of *T* in *Condition*, the condition evaluates to a Boolean value of *true* or *false*.

Here is a simple example: *Find all teaching records for the courses offered in the fall of 1997.*

```
{T | TEACHING(T) AND T.Semester = 'F1997'}
```

The term TEACHING(T) is a test of whether tuple T belongs to the relation instance of TEACHING. `T.Semester = 'F1997'` is another test. It is easy to see that this TRC query corresponds to the SQL query

```
SELECT  *
FROM    TEACHING T
WHERE   T.Semester = 'F1997'
```

It should now be clear why we said earlier that SQL is essentially a syntactic variant of TRC. The target of a TRC query corresponds to the SELECT list of an SQL query. The query condition in TRC is split between two clauses in SQL: the FROM clause, which holds conditions of the form *Relation*(*Variable*) (which restrict particular variables to range over tuples of particular relations); and the WHERE clause, which holds all other conditions.

The easiest way to understand the meaning of TRC queries is to think of them *declaratively*, with no particular query evaluation algorithm in mind. You can consider this process as enumerating all possible choices for the target tuple variable T and then checking which choices turn the query condition into a true statement about the given database instance. This interpretation leads to the following definition:

> The *result* of a TRC query with respect to a given database is the set of all choices of values for the variable T that make the query condition a true statement about the database.

In fact, this definition is also a correct way to think about SQL queries (and sometimes the only sure way to verify that an SQL query does what the programmer intended).

Let us see how this definition works in more detail. Suppose that we choose ⟨009406321, MGT123, F1980⟩ as a possible answer for T in the above example. Substituting this for T yields

```
TEACHING(009406321, MGT123, F1980) AND 'F1980' = 'F1997'
```

Wrong guess. This tuple does not belong to the relation instance of TEACHING (check Figure 3.5 (continued) on page 40), and 'F1980' = 'F1997' is also false. So this choice is discarded.

Here's another try: ⟨009406321, MGT123, F1994⟩. Substituting this for T yields

```
TEACHING(009406321, MGT123, F1994) AND 'F1994' = 'F1997'
```

A better choice but still a wrong guess. Although ⟨009406321, MGT123, F1994⟩ belongs to the instance of relation TEACHING (so that part of the query condition is true), the proposition 'F1994' = 'F1997' is still false.

Our third choice, ⟨009406321, MGT123, F1997⟩, yields

```
TEACHING(009406321, MGT123, F1997) AND 'F1997' = 'F1997'
```

which is a true statement about the current state of our database, so the last tuple belongs to the query result. In fact, only three tuples satisfy this query: ⟨009406321, MGT123, F1997⟩, ⟨783432188, MGT123, F1997⟩, and ⟨900120450, MAT123, S1997⟩, as can be verified by an exhaustive search of all possible elements of all domains.

Of course, DBMSs do not necessarily perform an exhaustive search. Instead, they use much more sophisticated algorithms (which are different for different DBMSs). However, we present the semantics of the language using exhaustive search as a teaching device because it is easy to understand and it can serve as a yardstick of correctness for more sophisticated query evaluation algorithms.

In addition, the exhaustive search semantics can be very helpful in verifying that a particular formulation of an SQL query does what we expect it to do—when writing complex SQL queries, we have seen how unreliable human intuition can be.

We are now ready for the nuts and bolts of TRC. It may surprise you that we have already presented most of the underlying ideas. Only two things remain to be explained:

- The syntax of query conditions
- What it means for a condition to be true after substituting a guess-tuple for the tuple variable in the query target

Syntax of query conditions. The basic building blocks used in query conditions have one of these forms:

- **P**(T), where **P** is a relation name and T is a tuple variable. Intuitively, **P**(T) is a test of whether tuple T belongs to the relation instance of **P** (of course, the test makes sense only after we choose a value for T). Example: STUDENT(T).
- $T.A$ oper $S.B$, where oper is a comparison operator ($=$, $>$, $\geq$, $\neq$, etc.), T and S are tuple variables, and A and B are attributes. The term "$T.A$" denotes the

component of T corresponding to the attribute A. The intended meaning here is a comparison of one component of a tuple against another. Example: `T.StudId` $\geq$ `S.ProfId`.

- $T.A$ oper *const*. This is similar to the previous form, except that the comparison is with a constant rather than with a component of a tuple. Example: `T.Semester` = `'F1994'`.

These basic building blocks are called **atomic conditions**. More complex query conditions are constructed recursively as follows:

- C is a query condition if it is an atomic condition.
- If C_1 and C_2 are query conditions, then C_1 AND C_2, C_1 OR C_2, and NOT C_1 are also query conditions.
- If C is a query condition, **R** is a relation name, and T is a tuple variable, then $\forall T \in \mathbf{R}\ (C)$ and $\exists T \in \mathbf{R}\ (C)$ are query conditions.

The symbol $\forall$ stands for "for all," and the symbol $\exists$ stands for "there exists." They are called the **universal quantifier** and the **existential quantifier**, respectively.

The intended meaning of the atomic conditions has been explained. The intended meaning of conditions in the second group should be obvious. For instance, C_1 AND C_2 is a condition that evaluates to true if and only if *both* C_1 and C_2 evaluate to true. The condition C_1 OR C_2 is true if and only if at least one of C_1 and C_2 evaluates to true. NOT C_1 is true if and only if C_1 is false.

The meaning of the quantified formulas can be read directly from the formulas. Let **r** be the relation instance of **R**. Then $\forall T \in \mathbf{R}\ (C)$ stands for: *For every tuple t* $\in$ **r**, *condition C becomes true if t is substituted for the variable T*. Similarly, $\exists T \in \mathbf{R}\ (C)$ stands for: *There exists a tuple t* $\in$ **r**, *such that C becomes true after t is substituted for T*.

One more notion and we are done with the syntax. In the formulas $\forall T \in \mathbf{R}\ (C)$ and $\exists T \in \mathbf{R}\ (C)$, the variable T is said to be **bound** by the quantifier. Any variable that is not explicitly bound in this way is said to be **free**. For instance, in `T.Name = S.Name` both `T` and `S` are free, but in ∀`S` ∈ STUDENT (`T.Name = S.Name`) the variable `S` is bound and `T` is free.

What do all of these free and bound variables have to do with the semantics of queries? Consider the sentence "It rained on day X." Here X is a free variable, and hence the phrase has no truth value until we make X concrete—that is, substitute a particular value for it. For comparison, consider the sentence "For all days $X \in$ July, it rained on day X." The English statement might sound awkward, but that is how you say it in logic (thereby eliminating possible ambiguity). Observe that we still have a variable in the second phrase, but now we intuitively feel that the phrase is either true or false (assuming that the context makes it clear which July and which location is meant). The main difference between the two sentences is that X is free in the first and bound in the second.

The implication of this discussion is that bound variables are used to make assertions about tuples in the database whereas free variables are used to specify the tuples to be returned by the query. Free variables can be used only in the query target.

This is because the query answer is determined by substituting concrete values for the target variables and, after a substitution, the query condition is not supposed to have any free variables left (or else we are unable to tell whether a particular choice of values for the target variables makes the query condition true). Therefore, revisiting the definition of a TRC query {*T* | *Condition*}, we should add the following restriction:

> *T* must be the *only* free variable in *Condition*.

Evaluation of query conditions. So, how do we decide if a particular choice of a tuple satisfies a query condition? Let us look at a concrete example.

```
{ E | COURSE(E) AND
      ∀S ∈ STUDENT (∃T ∈ TRANSCRIPT(
      T.StudId = S.Id AND T.CrsCode = E.CrsCode))}          13.1
```

This query returns *courses that have been taken by every student*.

Let us see if a particular choice for E satisfies the query condition. Because we know that a correct choice must be a tuple in COURSES, we choose a concrete tuple that belongs to this relation, which is depicted in Figure 3.5 on page 39: ⟨MGT123, MGT, Market Analysis, Get rich quick⟩. After substituting this tuple for E, the query condition has no free variables but is still rather complex.

```
COURSE(MGT123, MGT, Market Analysis, Get rich quick) AND
    ∀S ∈ STUDENT (∃T ∈ TRANSCRIPT(
        T.StudId = S.Id AND T.CrsCode = 'MGT123'))          13.2
```

To find out if this condition is true in our database, we evaluate it recursively by chipping off pieces of syntax in the order opposite to that in which the expression was built up from the atomic conditions. Since the first component of (13.2) is true in our database (the tuple ⟨MGT123, MGT, Market Analysis, Get rich quick⟩ does describe an existing course), we need only check if the second component is true.

The topmost piece in the second component is ∀*S* ∈ STUDENT. The purpose of this quantifier is to say that for every concrete tuple *s* ∈ STUDENT, if we replace the variable S with tuple s, the subcondition

```
∃T ∈ TRANSCRIPT (T.StudId = s.Id AND T.CrsCode = 'MGT123')          13.3
```

must be true. If this is the case, the expression (13.2) evaluates to true. If the subcondition (13.3) is false even for just one tuple in STUDENT, the whole condition (13.2) evaluates to false.

Since we need to test (13.3) for all students, let us try the tuple from Figure 3.2 that describes John Doe (page 36). Because its Id component is 111111111, we have to evaluate (13.3) with *s*.Id replaced by 111111111. The topmost construct in (13.3) is ∃T ∈ TRANSCRIPT, so (13.3) evaluates to true if we can find a tuple *t* ∈ TRANSCRIPT such that, after substituting *t* for T, the condition

```
t.StudId = 111111111 AND t.CrsCode = 'MGT123'
```

becomes true. Incidentally, John Doe took MGT123 in fall 1997 and received a B, as evidenced by a tuple in TRANSCRIPT. So, substituting this tuple for T, we get

```
111111111 = 111111111 AND 'MGT123' = 'MGT123'
```

which is true in our database because each subcondition is true.

Are we done proving that our original choice, ⟨MGT123, MGT, Market Analysis, Get rich quick⟩, is an answer to the query? No! We have to verify that (13.3) is true for *every* tuple *s* ∈ STUDENT. So far, we have established only that this condition is true when *s* is the tuple describing John Doe.

Now let *s* be the tuple that describes Homer Simpson, Id 023456789. In order for *s* to satisfy (13.3), we need to verify that there is a tuple in TRANSCRIPT such that, if we substitute it for T, the following will be true in the database:

```
T.StudId = 023456789 AND T.CrsCode = 'MGT123'
```

We can try each tuple in TRANSCRIPT in turn, but we will save time by verifying that this relation has no tuple where the StudId attribute is 023456789 and the CrsCode attribute is MGT123. Therefore, substitution of Homer Simpson's tuple in (13.3) creates a condition that is false in our database, and thus (13.3) is *not* true for *every* student in our database. This means that (13.2) is false and so our original guess (of a tuple for COURSE) is *not* an answer to query (13.1).

If you have time, you can check that no choice satisfies the query condition in (13.1), so the answer is empty. But this need not necessarily be so. If we were to add appropriate transcript records for MGT123 so that all students in our database would have taken this course, the COURSE tuple that describes MGT123 would belong to the query result.

The above process, although tedious, is essentially what an expert might use to verify that a choice belongs to the query answer. With some experience, you will develop various shortcuts and time-saving devices ("optimizations"), but the above process will still serve as a "yardstick of correctness." A query designer might use some similar process to validate that a particular query design satisfies its intended requirements.

The above procedure for verifying TRC queries is admittedly tedious, but you do not need to perform it each time you design a query (just as you do not execute a Java program manually for every record in a file to make sure that the program is correct). In most cases, queries can be verified by reading them in English, provided that you exercise rigor in their translation from TRC to English. This approach works well in many cases because humans have a certain inbred feeling for logical correctness. However, sometimes the English interpretation can get too complicated for complex queries, and this is where the above verification procedure may help.[1]

Select, project, join queries in TRC. To get a better feel for TRC, we consider some queries that ordinarily require join, project, and select in relational algebra. In TRC, such queries require ∃ and AND. To simplify our queries, we slightly extend the syntax to allow more than one tuple variable in the target and to allow mixing of terms of the form *T.attribute* for different tuple variables. For example,

```
{S.Name, T.CrsCode | STUDENT(S) AND TRANSCRIPT(T) AND...}
```

This extension is just a notational convenience, as we could have written the same query in the old, more restrictive syntax by introducing a new tuple variable, R, with attributes Name and CrsCode as follows:

```
{R |∃S ∈ STUDENT (∃T ∈ TRANSCRIPT (
    R.Name = S.Name AND R.CrsCode = T.CrsCode AND...))}
```

With this extended notation, the query *List the names of all professors who have taught* MGT123 is expressed as

```
{P.Name | PROFESSOR(P) AND                                        13.4
  ∃T ∈ TEACHING (P.Id = T.ProfId AND T.CRSCODE = 'MGT123')}
```

Note that this query would involve the selection, projection, and join operators if we tried to express it in relational algebra. The corresponding SQL query is just a syntactic variant.

```
SELECT   P.Name
FROM     PROFESSOR P, TEACHING T
WHERE    P.Id = T.ProfId AND T.CrsCode = 'MGT123'
```

If we wanted the names of professors who had the distinction of teaching Homer Simpson, we would write

```
{P.Name | PROFESSOR(P) AND
    ∃T ∈ TRANSCRIPT (∃S ∈ STUDENT (∃E ∈ TEACHING(
```

[1] It is interesting to compare verifying TRC (or SQL) queries with verification of a Java program. In TRC, programs are short but individual statements are quite powerful. The difficulty is thus in verifying the combined meaning of a small number of powerful statements. In contrast, in Java, each individual command is easy to check, but programs are large. It is thus hard to see all the consequences of executing a large number of simple statements.

```
        P.Id = E.ProfId AND T.StudId = S.Id AND                    13.5
        E.CrsCode = T.CrsCode AND E.Semester = T.Semester
        AND S.Name = 'Homer Simpson'))}
```

The following query finds the Id numbers of all students who have taken the same course twice (but in different semesters):

```
{T.StudId | TRANSCRIPT(T) AND
    ∃T1 ∈ TRANSCRIPT(
        T.StudId = T1.StudId AND T.CrsCode = T1.CrsCode
        AND T.Semester ≠ T1.Semester)}
```

Notice that in this query we are using two tuple variables, one free and one bound, both ranging over TRANSCRIPT. In relational algebra, we would have joined TRANSCRIPT with itself using the above join condition.

Division in TRC. Let us look at some queries that require the division operator in relational algebra. We have already discussed one such query in detail, query (13.1), which produces a *list of all those courses that have been taken by every student*. In discussing the division operator, we constructed query (5.2), on page 146, which yielded *the list of all students who took a course from every professor who ever taught a course*. In TRC, this query is expressed as

```
{S.Id | STUDENT(S) AND
    ∀T ∈ TEACHING ∃T1 ∈ TEACHING ∃R ∈ TRANSCRIPT (
        S.Id = R.StudId AND                                        13.6
        T.ProfId = T1.ProfId AND T1.CrsCode = R.CrsCode
        AND T1.Semester = R.Semester)}
```

An explanation is in order here. A particular value of T.ProfId identifies a professor who taught a course. A particular student, with Id S.Id, took a course with that professor if there exists a tuple, T1, in TEACHING that states that the professor has taught a course (i.e., T.ProfId = T1.ProfId) and a tuple, R, in TRANSCRIPT that states that the student took that course (i.e., S.Id = R.StudId AND T1.CrsCode = R.CrsCode AND T1.Semester = R.Semester). The student S.Id must be in the query result if he took a course with all such professors (∀T ∈ TEACHING).

This query appears to be slightly more complex than the equivalent algebraic query (5.2). However, in TRC we do not need to introduce special operators to handle such queries (try to write query (5.2) without the division operator!), and the TRC query is more versatile. For instance, if we want to list student names rather than Id numbers, all we have to do is replace S.Id with S.Name. In contrast, in algebra, this would require one extra join with the COURSE relation.

Note that, if we omit the existentially quantified variable T1 and replace it with T in the rest of the query, we get all students who took all course offerings in the university (as opposed to a course from every professor). It is a useful exercise to go over this query and understand how it is different from query (13.6).

The SQL query corresponding to (13.6) is much harder to write because SQL designers considered universal quantifiers hard to use correctly, so these quantifiers were mostly eliminated from the language.[2] To compensate for this, SQL was given a number of features, such as nested subqueries and the EXISTS operator, that are even harder to use. Thus, the significant syntactic differences in expressing the above query in SQL have to do with the need to translate the universal quantifier into an equivalent statement that uses a nested subquery.

Rules of quantification. There are a few issues about quantification that are important to keep in mind. First, adjacent existential quantifiers commute (as do universal quantifiers). Indeed, it does not matter whether we write

$$\exists \mathrm{R} \in \mathrm{TRANSCRIPT}\ (\exists \mathrm{T1} \in \mathrm{TEACHING}\ (\ldots))$$

or

$$\exists \mathrm{T1} \in \mathrm{TRANSCRIPT}\ (\exists \mathrm{R} \in \mathrm{TEACHING}\ (\ldots))$$

This can be verified using the method for evaluating query conditions given earlier.

Second, universal and existential quantifiers *do not* commute. A moment's reflection should convince us that saying "For every TEACHING tuple there is a TRANSCRIPT tuple such that statement *St* is true" is not the same as saying "There is a TRANSCRIPT tuple such that for all TEACHING tuples *St* is true."

Third, in relational calculus, quantifiers are analogous to **begin/end** blocks in that they define the scope of variables. For instance,

$$\forall T \in \mathbf{R}_1 \left(U(T) \text{ AND } \exists T \in \mathbf{R}_2\ (V(T))\right)$$

is legal. The two occurrences of the variable T appear under the scope of different quantifiers. Therefore, as is the case with identically named variables that occur in nested **begin/end** blocks, these two occurrences are completely independent and the above expression is equivalent to

$$\forall T \in \mathbf{R}_1 \left(U(T) \quad \text{AND} \quad \exists S \in \mathbf{R}_2\ (V(S))\right)$$

where S is some other, new variable.

Views in TRC. Now, suppose that we want to modify query (13.6) just slightly. Instead of listing students who took a course from *every* professor who ever taught a course, we might want to see the students who took a course from *every computer science* professor. This seemingly minor change appears to cause serious difficulties for TRC (but not for the algebra!). The SQL formulation of this query was given in query (5.28), page 161.

[2] Recall that SQL:1999 introduced a *limited* form of universal and existential quantification, the FOR ALL and FOR SOME operators described in Section 5.2.4.

Intuitively, the easiest way to modify (13.6) to handle such a query is to replace ∀T ∈ TEACHING with ∀C ∈ CSPROF and replacing `T.ProfId` with `C.Id`, where CSPROF is a subset of PROFESSOR that corresponds to professors in the Computer Science Department. This change would have been correct *if* we had such a relation. Since CSPROF does not exist in our database, we *define* it as a view:

```
CSPROF = {P.Id | PROFESSOR(P) AND P.DeptId = 'CS' }
```

We can now use CSPROF as a database view (or a "subroutine") in a larger query:

```
{S.Id | STUDENT(S) AND ∀C ∈ CSPROF (
          ∃T ∈ TEACHING ∃R ∈ TRANSCRIPT(R) (                     13.7
            S.Id = R.StudId AND C.Id = T.ProfId AND
             T.CrsCode = R.CrsCode AND T.Semester = R.Semester))}
```

A purist might want to avoid the use of a view and instead try to modify the query (13.6) to fit our needs. One common mistake here is to add

```
AND ∃P ∈ PROFESSOR (P.DeptId = 'CS' AND P.Id = T.ProfId)         13.8
```

to the query condition (inside the innermost parentheses). The problem with this change is that T ranges over the entire TEACHING relation, so this additional piece of formula must be true for all values of `T.ProfId` in TEACHING. This is possible only if *every* teaching professor in the database is working in the Computer Science Department, which is unlikely to be the case. The correct query is more complex. It requires the "if-then" implication, →, and takes some patience to understand. We discuss this problem in the next subsection.

OPTIONAL

Using if-then in queries. Query (13.7) above makes a point that some complex queries can be simplified using views and that some "obvious" ways of avoiding views may not work. The correct formulation that does not use a view must use the if-then connective →.

```
{S.Id | STUDENT(S) AND
   ∀P ∈ PROFESSOR( P.DeptId = 'CS'
     → ∃T ∈ TEACHING ∃R ∈ TRANSCRIPT (                           13.9
          S.Id = R.StudId AND P.Id = T.ProfId AND
          T.CrsCode = R.CrsCode AND T.Semester = R.Semester))}
```

The condition in the query says that `S.Id` is in the result of the query if and only if for every professor, P: *If* P is in the CS department, *then* there must be a teaching record T and a transcript record R, which correspond to professor P and student S such that T and R refer to the same course offering (i.e., S took a course from P).

A careful examination of query (13.9) shows that it can be obtained from query (13.7) by substituting into it the definition of the view CSPROF. The fact that the resulting query is more complex is not really surprising—think what would happen to a Java program if all subroutines were substituted in!

Many people tend to confuse if-then with AND and make mistakes such as the one illustrated at the end of the previous subsection. Using views in such queries is often a saving grace. Unfortunately, for more complex queries, it is sometimes easier to use → directly than trying to find an appropriate view. Consider the query *Find all students who received an A in every course they took*. Paraphrasing, we can say that we are looking for each student, *S*, such that for every course, *C*, if *S* took *C*, then the grade was A. This latter query translates directly to TRC:

```
{S.Name | STUDENT(S) AND ∀C ∈ COURSE (
          ∃T ∈ TRANSCRIPT (
               (T.StudId = S.Id AND T.CrsCode = C.CrsCode)
                                       → T.Grade = 'A')) }
```

Observe that, as in query (13.9) earlier, it is not correct to use AND instead of →. If we wrote T.StudId = S.Id AND T.CrsCode = C.CrsCode AND T.Grade = 'A', then the TRC expression would represent the query *Find all students such that for every course in the university there is a transcript record stating that the student took that course and received an A*. In particular, any students in the result set of this query must have taken every course offered by the university, and it is unlikely that such students exist.

Try to find a view that would allow a reformulation of the above query without the use of if-then and see if this is simpler than writing the original query.

A condition of the form *all objects of type* **T** *have property* **P** is written as $\forall O(\mathrm{T}(O) \rightarrow \mathrm{P}(O))$ and ***not*** as $\forall O(\mathrm{T}(O) \wedge \mathrm{P}(O))$.

OPTIONAL

13.2 Understanding SQL through Tuple Relational Calculus

We have seen that SQL is essentially the language of tuple relational calculus, generously sprinkled with noise words whose intention is to hide the relationship to predicate logic.[3]

Apart from the pedigree, TRC is important for SQL because understanding it can help in writing complex SQL queries. Some SQL books rely on relational algebra to provide meaning to general SQL queries (as we did in Chapter 5). Unfortunately, the algebraic expressions are neither more intuitive than the equivalent TRC queries

[3] Back in the 1970s, when the first relational systems were being designed in research labs, there was belief that a language based on relational calculus might be able to offer a sufficiently high level of programming that even nontechnical users, such as a company CEO, might be able to use them. Needless to say, even twenty years later this vision has not been fulfilled, while SQL keeps getting more and more complex with every new release.

nor helpful with more advanced SQL. Indeed, translating the SQL queries of Section 5.2.3, which have nested subqueries, into algebra is not a straightforward task. More important, relational algebra is not a good vehicle to help translate SQL database queries into English to verify that they will function as intended.

Although an English description is not as formal as a mathematical specification, it has the advantage that both the customer and the programmer can easily understand it and hence confirm together that it corresponds to their intentions. The question then arises as to whether a given SQL query satisfies its English specification. We can reason as follows. An SQL query satisfies its English specification if and only if

1. For every tuple, t, that must be in the query result according to the English formulation, there is a way to assign tuples to the variables mentioned in the FROM clause so that this assignment makes the WHERE condition true and turns the target list into t.
2. Every tuple produced by the SQL query is in the result of the English formulation.

The main difficulty in applying these conditions is determining what it means for a particular assignment of tuples to variables to satisfy a WHERE condition. One can rely on intuition in simple cases, but this becomes increasingly error prone for more complex SQL queries, such as (5.28) on page 161.

Fortunately, this difficulty is resolvable because of the close correspondence between SQL and TRC. Given an SQL query, the idea is to first construct an equivalent TRC query that is then translated into English. As TRC is much closer to SQL than to English, there is a better chance to do the first step correctly. The next step, the translation of TRC to English, is actually a well-defined process (explained in many textbooks on predicate logic), which can be performed even by a computer.

In this way, the problem of verifying SQL queries is reduced to the problem of translating SQL into TRC. For simple cases, this translation is easy, as illustrated earlier. We now illustrate the idea with a more complex example of an SQL query with a nested subquery. Consider the following query template, where, for definiteness, we assume that the attributes of REL1 are A, B; the attributes of REL2 are C, D; and that REL3 and REL4 have the attributes E, F and G, H, respectively.

```
SELECT   R1.A, R2.C
FROM     REL1 R1, REL2 R2
WHERE    Condition1(R1, R2) AND                              13.10
    R1.B IN (SELECT R3.E
             FROM REL3 R3, REL4 R4
             WHERE Condition2(R2,R3,R4))
```

In this template, the variables R3 and R4 are local to the subquery and the variables R1 and R2 are global. In addition, the WHERE condition in the subquery uses the variables R2,R3,R4 (which is what the notation *Condition2*(R2,R3,R4) is supposed to convey). Because R2 is a global variable used by *Condition2*, it parameterizes the inner subquery.

We assume that *Condition1* is of the form acceptable to TRC (i.e., it is a legal selection condition in relational algebra). However, the nested subquery is obviously not of the form TRC understands. Nevertheless, the translation into TRC is straightforward. To see this, recall the discussion of relational views on page 469.

Let us represent the inner subquery in (13.10) as a view—that is, a named virtual relation (call it TEMP)—whose contents are not stored but rather computed by a query. One subtlety needs to be taken care of here: what is the right set of attributes to use with TEMP? We cannot take only the attributes from the target list of the inner subquery (i.e., E), because the inner subquery (and hence its result) is *parameterized* by the global variable R2. Recall that the free variables in the condition are those named in the target list (since the condition must evaluate to true or false once values of the target variables have been substituted). R2 must be free because it is assigned a value in the outer query. Therefore, the proper set of attributes for TEMP must include the attributes of REL2 (C and D) in addition to the attributes of the inner subquery's target list (i.e., E).[4] This reasoning leads to the following view definition for TEMP:

```
TEMP = {R3.E, R2.C, R2.D | REL2(R2) AND REL3(R3)
            AND ∃R4∈REL4 (Condition2(R2,R3,R4))}          13.11
```

The variables R2 and R3 are free here, but R4 must be quantified because it does not occur in the query target list.

Now the translation from (13.10) to TRC is

```
{R1.A, R2.C | REL1(R1) AND REL2(R2) AND Condition1(R1, R2)
            AND ∃R∈TEMP (R.E = R1.B AND R.C = R2.C          13.12
            AND R.D = R2.D)}
```

How does this TRC query express the condition R1.B IN (SELECT R3.E . . .)? Through the equality R.E = R1.B. Indeed, the assignment of tuple ⟨a,b⟩ to R1 and of tuple ⟨c,d⟩ to R2 satisfies the condition in (13.12) if and only if these tuples belong to the relations REL1 and REL2, respectively, and ⟨b,c,d⟩ is a tuple in TEMP—the relation representing the inner subquery in (13.10). But b is the value of R1.B, which means that b must be in the result of the inner subquery.

As another example, consider the more complex query (5.28) on page 161 that returns the Ids of all students who have taken a course from every professor in the Computer Science Department. Here we have to construct two views, one for each subquery of (5.28). The first view, CSPROF, is straightforward:

[4] As a matter of fact, we need to include only those attributes of REL2 that are *actually used* in *Condition2*. That is, if *Condition2* uses R2.C but not R2.D, then R2.D need not be included in the attribute set of TEMP (but including it does no harm).

```
CSPROF = {P.ProfId | PROFESSOR(P) AND P.Dept ='CS'}
```

The result of this view is the set of Ids of all professors in the Computer Science Department. The second subquery of (5.28) returns the set of Ids of all professors who have taught a course taken by the student with Id `R.StudId`, where `R` is a variable that parameterizes the subquery. As explained earlier, the TRC view that corresponds to such a subquery must include `R` in the target list:

```
PROFSTUD = {T.ProfId, R.StudId | TEACHING(T) AND TRANSCRIPT(R) AND
            ∃R1∈TRANSCRIPT (T.CrsCode = R1.CrsCode AND
                           T.Semester = R1.Semester AND
                           R.StudId = R1.StudId)}
```

Finally, the whole of query (5.28) can be rephrased as follows: we are looking for those students, `s`, such that there does not exist professor `c` in CSPROF for whom the tuple ⟨`c,s`⟩ is not in PROFSTUD. Expressing this query in TRC is a bit cumbersome.

```
{S.StudId | STUDENT(S) AND NOT (∃C∈CSPROF (NOT(∃P∈PROFSTUD
            (P.ProfId = C.ProfId AND P.StudId = S.StudId))))}
```

This expression can be simplified if we recall that in the standard logic NOT $\exists X$ NOT is equivalent to $\forall X$:

```
{S.StudId | STUDENT(S) AND ∀C∈CSPROF ∃P∈PROFSTUD
                (P.ProfId = C.ProfId AND P.StudId = S.StudId)}
```

In English this statement reads as follows: *a student Id,* `s`*, is in the result of this query if and only if, for every computer science professor,* `c`*, the tuple* ⟨`c,s`⟩ *is in the view* PROFSTUD*; that is,* `c` *has taught* `s`.

Now compare this with the original English formulation of (5.28): *find all students who took a course from every professor in the* CS *department.* These two sentences have exactly the same meaning, which means that our complex SQL query has been validated.

13.3 Domain Relational Calculus and Visual Query Languages

Tuple relational calculus has become the basis of textual database query languages such as SQL. The other flavor of relational calculus, **domain relational calculus** (DRC), has become the basis of visual query languages such as IBM Query-By-Example and languages for PC databases such as Microsoft Access.

DRC is quite similar to TRC. The main difference is that it uses **domain variables** rather than tuple variables in its queries. Recall that a tuple consists of a set of named attributes, each taking its values from some domain. A domain variable takes its values from the domain of some attribute. For example, a TEACHING relation might have an attribute named `ProfId`, with a domain consisting of valid Id numbers. Then `Pid` might be a domain variable, which takes its values from the domain of valid Id numbers.

As in TRC, the output of a DRC query is a relation, and the general form of a DRC query is

$$\{X_1, \ldots, X_n \mid \textit{Condition}\}$$

where $X_1, \ldots, X_n$ is a list of (not necessarily distinct) domain variables, which form the **target** part of the query, and *Condition* is the query condition, which looks much the same as in TRC. Here is an example:

```
{Pid, Code | TEACHING(Pid,Code,F1997)}
```

This is essentially the same as the TRC query

```
{T | TEACHING(T) AND T.Semester = 'F1997'}
```

(except that one returns a table with two columns and the other a table with three), but it is simpler because we can put the constant `F1997` directly into the condition TEACHING(`Pid, Code, F1997`), thereby eliminating the need for the conjunct `T.Semester = 'F1997'`. Such substitution often makes DRC queries more compact and easier to understand than their TRC equivalents.

Because DRC and TRC are so close, many of the features and techniques they employ are either identical or very similar. Therefore, we do not discuss DRC at the same level of detail as we did TRC.

Syntax of DRC query conditions. The general syntax of query conditions in DRC follows the outline of TRC. The basic building blocks have one of the following forms:

- $\mathbf{P}(X_1, \ldots, X_n)$, where **P** is a relation name and $X_1, \ldots, X_n$ are domain variables. Intuitively, $\mathbf{P}(X_1, \ldots, X_n)$ is a test of whether the tuple $\langle X_1, \ldots, X_n \rangle$ belongs to the relation instance of **P** (as in TRC, this expression is evaluated under a particular choice of values for $X_1, \ldots, X_n$). Example: STUDENT(`Sid, N, A, S`).
- X oper Y, where oper is a comparison operator ($=$, $>$, $\geq$, $\neq$, etc.) and X and Y are domain variables. The intended meaning here is a comparison of the value of X against the value of Y. Example: `Sid` $\geq$ `Pid`. Note that since domain variables represent tuple components directly, we do not need to use the dot-notation of TRC (for example, `A.Sid = B.Pid`).
- X oper *const*, which is similar to the previous form, but here the comparison is with a constant rather than a variable. Example: X = `'F1994'`.

These basic building blocks are called **atomic conditions**. More complex query conditions are constructed recursively as follows:

- C is a query condition if it is an atomic condition.
- If C_1 and C_2 are query conditions, C_1 AND C_2, C_1 OR C_2, and NOT C_1 are also query conditions.
- If C is a query condition, **R** is a relation name, and X is a domain variable, then $\forall X \in \mathbf{R}.A\,(C)$ and $\exists X \in \mathbf{R}.A\,(C)$ are query conditions.

  The quantifiers here are similar to those in TRC with one difference: the expression $\mathbf{R}.A$ denotes column A of relation **R**, and the variable X ranges over the values that occur in that column. In other words, $\forall X \in \mathbf{R}.A\,(C)$ says that *for all* values that occur in column A of relation **R** (in the current database instance), the condition C must be true. The expression $\exists X \in \mathbf{R}.A\,(C)$ says that there is *at least one* value, x, in column $\mathbf{R}.A$ such that C becomes true if x is substituted for all occurrences of X.

The rules for free and bound variables are the same as in TRC, and, as in TRC, the target variables are the only ones allowed to occur free in the query condition. To make the rules a bit more flexible, we allow constants to occur in the target as well. To summarize, in

$$\{X_1, \ldots, X_n \mid Condition\} \qquad \textbf{13.13}$$

each X_i, for $i = 1, \ldots, n$, is either a free variable that occurs in *Condition* or a constant. No other variable occurs free in *Condition*.

The *result* of query (13.13) on a given database is defined similarly to the result of a TRC query: it is the set of *all* choices of tuples $\langle x_1, \ldots, x_n \rangle$ such that when x_1 is substituted for X_1, x_2 for X_2, and so on, *Condition* evaluates to true. If some X_i is a constant, no substitution occurs—the query result has this constant in the ith position in all tuples.

Examples. To illustrate the use of DRC and to highlight the differences between it and TRC, we use the same suite of queries as that used to illustrate relational algebra and TRC.

DRC queries often use more variables than do their TRC counterparts because DRC variables range over simple values, whereas TRC variables range over tuples. Thus, one TRC variable effectively stands for several DRC variables. However, the DRC notation can be made more succinct in several ways. One is to introduce the **universal domain**, $\mathcal{U}$, which contains all values in all domains, and instead of writing $\exists X \in \mathcal{U}$ (*Condition*), use a shorthand, $\exists X$ (*Condition*).

One reason why the universal domain is useful is that any expression of the form $\exists X \in \mathbf{R}.A_i(\mathbf{R}(\ldots, X, \ldots) \ldots)$, where A_i is the attribute of **R** that corresponds to the occurrence of X, is equivalent to $\exists X(\mathbf{R}(\ldots, X, \ldots) \ldots)$. In other words, we can replace the domain $\mathbf{R}.A_i$ with the universal domain $\mathcal{U}$ (and then omit it). Certainly, $\mathcal{U}$ contains $\mathbf{R}.A_i$, but it can be much larger. However, any choice, x, for X that is outside of $\mathbf{R}.A_i$ cannot make $\exists X(\mathbf{R}(\ldots, X, \ldots) \ldots)$ into a true statement since in order for

R(..., *x*, ...) to be true, *x* must be the value of A_i in some tuple in an instance of **R** and hence, *x* must belong to the column **R**.A_i, for some *i*.

Let us now turn to the example queries of Section 13.1. The DRC equivalent of the query *List all names of professors who taught* MGT123 (TRC query (13.4)) is

```
{N |∃I∈PROFESSOR.Id ∃D∈PROFESSOR.DeptId (
        PROFESSOR(I,N,D) AND
        ∃S∈TEACHING.Semester (TEACHING(I, MGT123, S)))}
```

A cursory look at this query makes the utility of the universal domain apparent: dropping the long domain names would make this query much shorter. We take advantage of this property in the following examples.

The next query returns the names of all professors who had the honor to teach Homer Simpson (TRC query (13.5)).

```
{Pname | ∃Pid ∃Dept (PROFESSOR(Pid, Pname, Dept) AND
        ∃Grd ∃Crs ∃Sem ∃Sid ∃Addr ∃Stat (TEACHING(Pid, Crs, Sem)
            AND TRANSCRIPT(Sid, Crs, Sem, Grd)                    13.14
            AND STUDENT(Sid, 'Homer Simpson', Addr, Stat)))}
```

Note that DRC queries typically require more quantified variables than their TRC counterparts but fewer components of the form $\mathbf{R}_1.Attr_1 = \mathbf{R}_2.Attr_2$. (Compare, for example, the above two queries with (13.4) and (13.5).)

Any discussion of a query language would be incomplete without an example that illustrates a division operator-like capability. We therefore use DRC to express the venerable query *Find all students who took a course from every professor*.

```
{Sid | ∀Pid∈TEACHING.ProfId (∃Crs ∃Sem ∃Grd (
        TEACHING(Pid, Crs, Sem) AND                               13.15
        TRANSCRIPT(Sid, Crs, Sem, Grd)))}
```

This DRC query is substantially simpler than the corresponding SQL query (5.28), page 161, and the TRC query (13.6) on page 468. In particular, it is not necessary to have TEACHING mentioned twice. (Recall that in TRC, TEACHING must occur twice for a nonobvious reason.) Note that in (13.15) we use ∃ explicitly, to avoid the ambiguity that arises when ∀ and ∃ occur in the same query.

One additional point is worth mentioning: we *cannot* replace the domain TEACHING.ProfId of the variable Pid with the universal domain $\mathcal{U}$. In general, $\forall X \in \mathbf{R}.A_i\ (\mathbf{R}(\ldots, X, \ldots))$ is *not* equivalent to $\forall X(\mathbf{R}(\ldots, X, \ldots))$. Using $\mathcal{U}$ instead of TEACHING.ProfId in (13.15) means that, in order for a particular value, sid, to be in the result of the query, the condition TEACHING(pid, crs, sem) AND TRANSCRIPT(sid, crs, sem, grd) must be true for *all* pid $\in \mathcal{U}$ and for some crs, sem, and grd. This is clearly impossible if pid is chosen to be a constant that does not correspond to any actual professor Id. ($\mathcal{U}$ must have such a constant since TEACHING.ProfId is a proper subset of $\mathcal{U}$.) However, as discussed earlier, in $\exists X \in \mathbf{R}.A_i$ the domain $\mathbf{R}.A_i$ *can* be replaced with $\mathcal{U}$.

Implicit quantification. Commercial database languages built on top of DRC and TRC do not use quantifiers explicitly. Instead, all variables that *do not occur explicitly* in the target list of the query are assumed to be *implicitly quantified* with ∃ and range over the universal domain. Using this convention, all quantifiers in some DRC queries can be dropped. For example, the query (13.14) becomes

```
{Pname | PROFESSOR(Pid, Pname, Dept)
         AND TEACHING(Pid,Crs,Sem)
         AND TRANSCRIPT(Sid, Crs, Sem, Grd)
         AND STUDENT(Sid, Homer Simpson, Addr, Stat)}
```

In contrast, TRC quantifiers cannot be dropped without further adjustments to the query because in some cases we might lose useful information about the corresponding quantified variables. To illustrate, let us revisit the TRC query (13.4) about professors who taught MGT123.

```
{P.Name | PROFESSOR(P) AND
    ∃T∈TEACHING (P.Id = T.ProfId AND T.CrsCode = 'MGT123')}
```

Here, dropping ∃T ∈ TEACHING would leave T "undeclared," in the terminology of programming languages, because we lose the information that the range of T is TEACHING. Range information is not lost in DRC because undeclared variables are assumed to range over the universal domain, which we do not have in TRC. However, there is a way to drop existential quantifiers in TRC and yet preserve the information about ranges. Notice that ∃T ∈ TEACHING (...) is equivalent to ∃T ∈ TEACHING (TEACHING(T) AND ...). Therefore, we can rewrite the query as

```
{P.Name | PROFESSOR(P) AND
    TEACHING(T) AND P.Id = T.ProfId AND T.CrsCode = 'MGT123'}
```

without losing the information about the range of T. This reformulation is correct if we adopt the convention that the nontarget variable T is implicitly quantified with ∃.

When existential quantifiers are dropped in either DRC or TRC there is potential ambiguity if ∃ and ∀ both occur in the same query. For example, consider ∀Y(LIKES(X,Y)), where LIKES(X,Y) means that X likes Y. The convention that X is implicitly quantified with ∃ still leaves us with a dilemma: does this expression mean ∀Y∃X (LIKES)(X,Y) or ∃X∀YLIKES(X,Y)? A moment's reflection shows that these two expressions correspond to two very different English sentences: "every Y is liked by some X" and "some X likes every Y." Hence, in some cases quantification cannot be dropped. This ambiguity does not arise in SQL, as it does not allow the use of ∀. The tradeoff, as we have seen, is the difficulty in formulating queries that involve division. Techniques for overcoming this deficiency of SQL were studied in Section 5.2.

13.4 Visual Query Languages: QBE and PC Databases

QBE (Query-by-Example) was the first widely acclaimed visual query language. Like SQL it was developed at IBM and at about the same time [Zloof 1975]. QBE is part of IBM's DB2 relational database product, and several other vendors have developed QBE clones. However, the greatest success of visual query languages came with the advent of PC databases, such as Microsoft Access.

In this section, we review QBE. Our goal here is to emphasize concepts, not to provide an exhaustive reference. At the end of the section, we briefly discuss Microsoft Access, whose interface is also based on domain calculus but more loosely than is QBE.

The basics of QBE. QBE is one of the best illustrations of how a purely theoretical tool, the domain calculus, can be put to practical use. The main idea behind QBE is that the user (who is not necessarily a programmer) specifies a query by choosing relation templates from a menu and then filling these templates with "example tuples" that specify the desired answer. The example tuples in QBE consist of variables and constants, but even variables are made to look like examples of constants—QBE avoids programming notation as much as possible.[5]

Suppose that you want to find all professors in the MGT department. In QBE, you select a template corresponding to the PROFESSOR relation and then fill in the example tuple as follows:

PROFESSOR	Id	Name	DeptId
		P._John	MGT

It should be apparent that this QBE query is just a different, visual representation for the textual DRC query {Name | ∃I PROFESSOR(I, Name, MGT)}. The symbol _John is a domain variable in disguise, while MGT is a constant. Even though these two symbols might look similar to an unsuspecting user, the prefix _ betrays the special status of _John as a glorified variable. Furthermore, the operator **P.** (meaning *print*) indicates that _John is a target variable in the sense of relational calculus since it is output by the print command. QBE uses several operators, usually represented by a keyword followed with a period, but in this overview we use mainly **P.**—the mother of all QBE operators, which separates target variables from the rest.

[5] QBE goes out of its way to hide any semblance of programming terminology. It calls constants "example values" and variables "example elements."

Earlier we mentioned that commercial query languages do not quantify variables explicitly, and, surely, we do not find quantifiers in QBE queries. Instead, all non-target variables are assumed to be implicitly quantified with ∃. However, QBE goes one step further: some nontarget variables, such as `I` in the DRC version of the above query, can be omitted. When this happens, the system invents a unique variable name and automatically substitutes it in.

In fact, even the variable `_John` is not necessary, and we could drop it without affecting the final result. In that case the `Name` column contains just **P.** Thus, **P.** can occur in a query as a stand-alone operator. If the query result must be a relation with two or more attributes, we can put **P.** in several places in the query. If all attributes of a relation are to be output, we can put **P.** directly under the relation name instead of in each column.

PROFESSOR	Id	Name	DeptId
P.			MGT

Joins and advanced queries. The above query does not explicitly mention *any* variable. However, in general we cannot get away without using variables. If a variable needs to be mentioned twice or more in a query, it represents an equality between attributes in the same or different tuples and therefore cannot be omitted. This situation arises most often in specifying an equi-join. The following is a QBE version of the familiar query, *List all names of professors who taught* `MGT123`:

PROFESSOR	Id	Name	DeptId
	_123456789	P. _John	

TEACHING	ProfId	CrsCode	Semester
	_123456789	MGT123	

Here, `_John` is a target variable, as before, and `_123456789` is a variable that is implicitly quantified with ∃. It is used in the query to specify an equi-join of two tables and therefore cannot be omitted. (In contrast, `_John` can be omitted, as before.)

We have seen that QBE lets the user specify simple selections by simply putting appropriate constants in the templates. QBE goes one step further by allowing the following syntax, which finds all professor names with Ids greater than the specified constant.

PROFESSOR	Id	Name	DeptId
	> 123456789	P.	

(Note the difference between the constant 123456789 and the variable _123456789.) However, more complex selections or join conditions cannot be specified in this way, so QBE provides a special template, called a **conditions box**, in which the user can write arbitrarily complex selection and join conditions using a syntax similar to that of relational algebra. For instance, to obtain the Ids of all students who have taken CS305 and received A or B, we can write

TRANSCRIPT	StudId	CrsCode	Semester	Grade
	P.	CS305		_G

CONDITIONS
_G = A OR _G = B

Since the result of a QBE query is a relation, there are certain restrictions on where the **P.** operator can occur. In particular, to avoid the possibility that **P.** is placed under two identically named attributes in different relational templates, QBE requires that all occurrences of **P.** must be in the same template.[6] How, then, can we specify the query *Find all professors together with the students they taught*? Since professors and students are stored in different relations, it does not appear possible to answer this query if all occurrences of **P.** are to appear in just one of the templates.

One solution is to allow users to construct *new* templates so that they will not be restricted to just the templates of the relations that already exist in the database. To answer the above query, a user uses the menu system to define a new template, HASTAUGHT, as follows:

HASTAUGHT	Prof	Stud
I.	_123456789	_987654321

TRANSCRIPT	StudId	CrsCode	Semester	Grade
	_987654321	_CS305	_F1996	

TEACHING	ProfId	CrsCode	Semester
	_123456789	_CS305	_F1996

The operator **I.** (meaning *insert*) in the template HASTAUGHT specifies the tuples that should populate the corresponding table. The user can then query HASTAUGHT using the **P.** operator as follows:

HASTAUGHT	Prof	Stud
P.		

[6] This is a fairly serious restriction introduced to solve a relatively minor problem.

The price of a free lunch. The earlier examples showed that the right choice of visual primitives and conventions can make the domain relational calculus accessible even to a nonspecialist. Unfortunately, as often happens in language design, features that make some things easy make other things hard. In the case of database query languages, the price is usually the expressive power—that is, the inability to specify certain types of queries—or the awkwardness associated with doing so. In the case of QBE (and, in fact, SQL as well), the price is paid when one needs to ask queries that involve the division operator, such as *Find all courses taken by every student known to the database*. We will return to this query shortly.

Since QBE does not provide the universal quantifier ∀, it uses the *negation* operator to construct ¬∃¬, which is the same thing. To illustrate, let us consider the query *List all professors who did not teach any course in fall 1995*. In DRC this query can be stated either as

```
{Name|PROFESSOR (Id, Name, DeptId)
          AND ∀CrsCode (NOT(TEACHING (Id, CrsCode, F1995)))}
```

or as

```
{Name|PROFESSOR (Id, Name, DeptId)
          AND NOT (∃CrsCode (TEACHING (Id, CrsCode, F1995)))}
```

In both cases we have assumed that Id and DeptId are existentially quantified. QBE chooses the second formulation, which appears as

PROFESSOR	Id	Name	DeptId
	_123456789	**P.**	

TEACHING	ProfId	CrsCode	Semester
¬	_123456789		F1995

The symbol ¬ denotes the negation operator, and it occurs in the TEACHING template since we are requiring that there be no rows in TEACHING that match a particular Id in PROFESSOR. This negation roughly corresponds to set difference. The first template produces the names of all professors in the PROFESSOR relation and the second removes from that set those professors who taught a course in fall 1995. This query looks innocent enough, but there are pitfalls. Previously, we said that all variables in QBE are implicitly quantified with ∃ and that the blank columns in the templates are really filled with system-generated variables (which are also implicitly quantified with ∃). Not so with negated example tuples! Indeed, if the system-generated variable (for example, _Crs123) that implicitly occurs in the column CrsCode were existentially quantified, we would have the following query:

```
{Name | ∃Id ∃DeptId ∃CrsCode(
        PROFESSOR(Id, Name, DeptId) AND
        NOT TEACHING(Id, CrsCode, 'F1995'))}
```

This query returns an Id, say, 111111111, if there is a course, for example, MGT123, such that the row ⟨111111111, MGT123, F1995⟩ is *not* in TEACHING. That is, it returns the Ids of all professors who did not teach *some* course in F1995—a different query than the one we posed! A correct formulation is

```
{Name | ∃Id ∃DeptId ∀CrsCode(
        PROFESSOR(Id, Name, DeptId) AND                    13.16
        NOT TEACHING(Id, CrsCode, 'F1995'))}
```

That is, the desired quantification of _Crs123 is universal.

The uncertainty of proper quantification of variables in negated tuples was an early source of semantic problems in QBE. Eventually, it was decided to assume all system-generated variables in negated tuples to be implicitly quantified with ∀. The reasoning behind this decision was the belief that, as in the previous example, universal quantification is what the user wants in most cases.

Unfortunately, this simple convention still does not completely resolve the issue because, as we already know, ∃ and ∀ do not commute. So there is a question of the order in which to arrange the quantification prefix. For instance, in (13.16) we could have ordered the quantifiers differently and obtained a different query:

```
{Name | ∀CrsCode ∃Id ∃DeptId(
        PROFESSOR(Id, Name, DeptId) AND                    13.17
        NOT TEACHING(Id, CrsCode, 'F1995'))}
```

It finds all professor names with the following property: for every course, there is a professor with that name who did not teach that particular course.

In the end, the semantics of QBE was resolved so that the quantification prefix is ordered in such a way that the existential quantifiers go first. Thus, the previous QBE query must be interpreted as (13.16).

> Variables that occur *only* in negated tables are implicitly quantified with ∀. All other variables are implicitly quantified with ∃. All existential quantifiers precede the universal quantifiers.

Now that we understand negation in QBE, the query about the courses taken by every student can be expressed as follows. First, we need to find courses that have not been taken by at least one student. The relation containing all such courses, which we call NOTANSWER, is constructed as follows:

NOTANSWER	CrsCode
I.	_MGT111

COURSE	CrsCode	CrsName	Descr
	_MGT111		

STUDENT	Id	Name	Status	Address
	_123456789			

TRANSCRIPT	StudId	CrsCode	Semester	Grade
¬	_123456789	_MGT111		

Again, we used the insert operator to specify the tuples we wanted inserted into the relation NOTANSWER. Thus, the contents of NOTANSWER are described by the DRC query

```
{CrsCode | ∃CrsName ∃Descr ∃Id ∃Name ∃Status ∃Address
     ∀Semester ∀Grade(
          COURSE(CrsCode, CrsName, Descr) AND                    13.18
               STUDENT(Id, Name, Status, Address) AND
               NOT TRANSCRIPT(Id, CrsCode, Semester, Grade))}
```

Finally, to obtain the answer to the original query we need to subtract NOTANSWER from COURSE.

NOTANSWER	CrsCode
¬	_MGT111

COURSE	CrsCode	CrsName	Descr
	_MGT111	P.	

Although we have covered most of its features, QBE has several aspects that we did not discuss (or mentioned only briefly). For instance, it has a very convenient data definition sublanguage, whose visual appearance is consistent with the query sublanguage. It also supports aggregate functions, such as counting, and averages, which are provided to the user in the form of operators (COUNT, AVG., etc.). Aggregate functions were discussed in detail in Section 5.2, although the focus there was on SQL, not QBE. Finally, we have seen the operator **I.**, which is a part of the data manipulation sublanguage of QBE. Similar operators are used to delete and modify tuples.

PC databases. Conceptually, if you have seen one visual query language, you have seen them all. The main difference between QBE and Microsoft Access lies in the

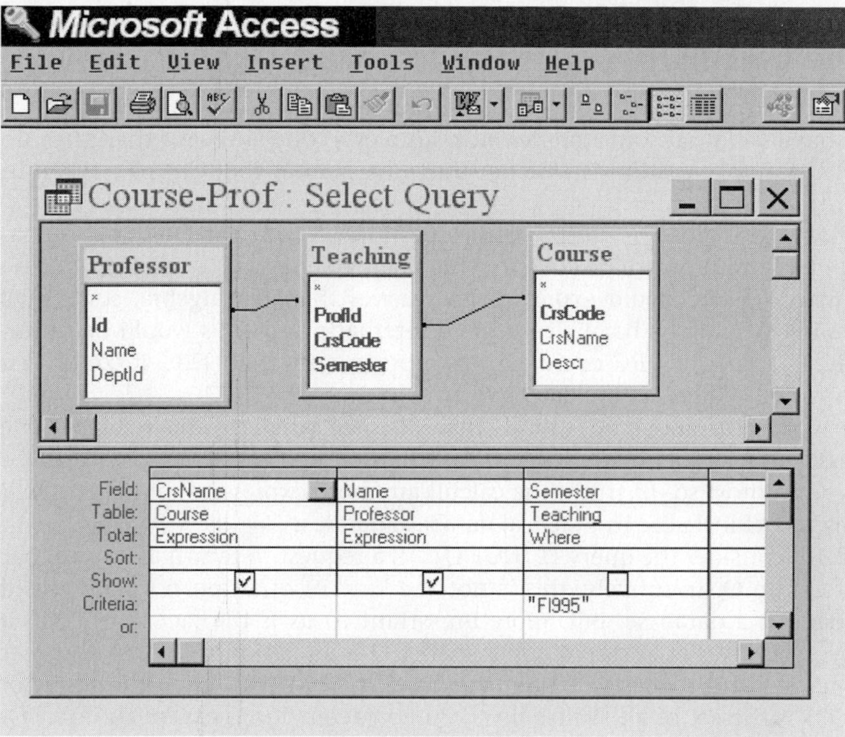

FIGURE 13.1 A visual query in Microsoft Access.

details of the graphical interface. Figure 13.1 depicts a query specified in the Access "design mode." The query returns all courses offered in fall 1995 along with the names of the professors who taught them.

Access tries hard to hide its relational calculus origins. To specify an equi-join, instead of using variables, the user drags one attribute into another, creating the graphical links seen in the figure, which represent join conditions (e.g., PROFESSOR.Id = TEACHING.ProfId). Access has an analog of QBE's conditions box (e.g., the criterion that TEACHING.Semester = 'F1995'). This box is used much more heavily than in QBE, particularly to specify things that QBE does with the help of operators, such as **P.** (See the line labeled "Show:" in Figure 13.1.)

All in all, QBE is more flexible than Access and generally more intuitive to database specialists who are familiar with relational languages. However, for the drag-and-drop generation, Access design mode is easier to use, at least for simple queries.

13.5 The Relationship between Relational Algebra and the Calculi

We have presented a detailed overview of relational algebra and the two relational calculi. We have seen that some queries look simpler in one language than they do in another. A natural question is whether there are queries that can be written in only one of the languages.

Note that this is not an idle theoretic question. Recall that DBMSs use relational algebra as an intermediate code to which SQL queries are translated in order to be optimized. If TRC could express more queries than the algebra, some SQL queries possibly would not have algebraic counterparts and thus would be unimplementable. Similarly, if DRC could express more queries than TRC, it could be a better platform on which to base database languages.

The answer to the above question is that all three languages have exactly the same expressive power: queries that can be asked in one language can also be asked in another—or almost so. In truth, the calculi are more expressive, but this added expressiveness is of little use in practical database queries.

To explain, consider the query {T | NOT **Q**(T)}, a request to return all tuples that are *not* in relation **Q**. Intuitively, this is not the kind of question normally asked about the data in a database. But, more important to us is the fact that it has a very strange property. For example, suppose that **Q** is a relation that contains a set of student names and that the domain of names is CHAR(20). Then the result of {T | NOT **Q**(T)} is the set of all strings up to 20 characters long, except those in **Q**. Now, suppose that the domain of names is later changed to become the set of all strings up to 30 characters long. Then the answer to the above query changes, even though the database instance does not!

Another situation where the answer to a query depends on the domain might arise when the query condition contains a disjunction. For instance, {T | ∃S(**Q**(T) OR **R**(S))} returns the set of all tuples in **Q** if **R** is an empty relation. However, if **R** contains even one tuple, the answer to this query is the set of all possible tuples (because ∃S(**R**(S)) is true and so the query condition is true regardless of **Q**(T)). In this case, then, the query answer depends on the universal domain.

Database queries whose result *does not* change when their domains change are called **domain-independent**. Exercise 13.6 shows that the queries expressed using relational algebra are always domain-independent. However, we have just seen that it is possible to use relational calculus to express a domain-dependent query. Even so, it turns out that

> Every domain-independent query in TRC and DRC has a translation into an equivalent query written in relational algebra, and vice versa.

The first part of this statement is not exactly obvious. A proof appears in [Ullman 1988]. However, the other direction, a translation from algebra into calculus, is an easy and worthwhile exercise because it shows how the operators of relational algebra relate to the constructs in the relational calculi.

- *Selection*

  Algebra. $\sigma_{Condition}(\mathbf{R})$
  TRC. {T | **R**(T) AND *Condition*$_1$}
  DRC. {$X_1, \ldots, X_n$ | **R**($X_1, \ldots, X_n$) AND *Condition*$_2$}

  In TRC, *Condition*$_1$ is obtained from *Condition* by replacing attributes with the appropriate components of T. For instance, if *Condition* is A = B AND C = d, where A, B, C are attributes and d is a constant, then *Condition*$_1$ is T.A = T.B AND T.C = d.

  In DRC, *Condition*$_2$ is obtained by replacing the attributes that occur in *Condition* with appropriate variables. For instance, if A is the first attribute of **R**, B is the second, and C is the third, then *Condition*$_2$ is $X_1 = X_2$ AND $X_3 = d$.

- *Projection*

  Algebra. $\pi_{A,B,C}(\mathbf{R})$
  TRC. {T.A, T.B, T.C | **R**(T)}
  DRC. {X, Y, Z | ∃V∃W(**R**(X, Y, Z, V, W))}.
  Here we assume that **R** has five attributes and that A, B, C are the first three.

- *Cartesian product*

  Algebra. **R** × **S**
  TRC. {T.A, T.B, T.C, V.D, V.E | **R**(T) AND **S**(V)}.
  We assume, for definiteness, that **R** has attributes A, B, C and that **S** has attributes D, E.
  DRC. {X, Y, Z, V, W | **R**(X, Y, Z) AND **S**(V, W)}

- *Union*

  Algebra. **R** ∪ **S**
  TRC. {T | **R**(T) OR **S**(T)}
  DRC. {$X_1, \ldots, X_n$ | **R**($X_1, \ldots, X_n$) OR **S**($X_1, \ldots, X_n$)}
  Note that since **R** and **S** must be union-compatible for the ∪ operator to make sense, the two relation schemas must have the same arity.

- *Set difference*

  Algebra. **R** − **S**
  TRC. {T | **R**(T) AND (NOT **S**(T))}
  DRC. Exercise 13.8

- No discussion of relational algebra is complete without saying something about the division operator.

  Algebra. **R/S**, where **R** has attributes A, B, and **S** has only B.
  TRC. {T.A | **R**(T) AND ∀X ∈ **S** (∃Y ∈ **R** (Y.B = X.B AND Y.A = T.A))}
  DRC. Exercise 13.8.

It turns out that domain independence is undecidable, that is, there is no algorithm that, for any given query in TRC or DRC, can tell whether that query is domain-independent or not [Di Paola 1969]. However, it is possible to develop a set of syntactic restrictions on the form of the calculus queries that guarantee domain independence. In view of the above undecidability result, such restrictions are only sufficient conditions, which might rule out some perfectly good queries. Nevertheless, such restrictions can be made sufficiently general for all practical purposes. In essense, SQL is based on one set of such restrictions, and this is why SQL queries can always be translated into the relational algebra.

OPTIONAL

13.6 Deductive Databases

The field of **deductive databases** (see [Ramakrishnan and Ullman 1995; Minker 1997] for surveys) was born out of recognition of the limitations of the expressive power of SQL. As it turned out, SQL cannot express even such unquestionably basic database queries as finding all prerequisites of a course, determining a sequence of flights that are required for traveling between a pair of cities, or computing the cost of an assembly that consists of subparts, which in turn have subparts of their own. In an acknowledgment of these limitations, SQL:1999 introduced a number of extensions designed to deal with so called *recursive* queries. These extensions are discussed in Section 13.6.2. Finally, Section 13.6.3 introduces a language called **Datalog**—the subject of most studies in deductive databases.

13.6.1 Limitations of Relational Query Languages

Numerous examples in this and preceding chapters illustrate the vast expressive power of relational query languages. Yet these languages are not expressive enough to allow the programmer to write complete applications in SQL. Surprisingly, SQL cannot even be used to express some very common queries, such as whether one course is a (possibly indirect) prerequisite of another.

To illustrate the problem, consider the relation PREREQ in Figure 13.2. Suppose that we want to find out if `CS113` is a prerequisite course for `CS632`. With relational algebra, we can try to approach the problem as follows. Let $\text{PREREQ}_2(\texttt{Crs, PreCrs})$ denote the expression

$$\pi_{\texttt{Crs,PreCrs}}((\text{PREREQ} \bowtie_{\texttt{PreCrs=Crs}} \text{PREREQ})[\texttt{Crs,P1,C2,PreCrs}]) \cup \text{PREREQ}$$

where, as before, [Crs,P1,C2,PreCrs] denotes attribute renaming. We can now compute the expression $\sigma_{\texttt{Crs='CS632' AND PreCrs='CS113'}}(\text{PREREQ}_2)$ and see if the result is nonempty. If it is, `CS113` is a prerequisite of `CS632`, twice removed. However, it is easy to verify that in our concrete case the above expression evaluates to an empty relation, so we are not done yet.

We can try to see if `CS113` is three prerequisites removed from `CS632` by evaluating the following expression, which we denote $\text{PREREQ}_3(\texttt{Crs, PreCrs})$.

$$\pi_{\texttt{Crs,PreCrs}}((\text{PREREQ} \bowtie_{\texttt{PreCrs=Crs}} \text{PREREQ}_2)[\texttt{Crs,P1,C2,PreCrs}]) \cup \text{PREREQ}_2$$

PREREQ	Crs	PreCrs
	CS632	CS532
	CS505	CS213
	CS532	CS305
	CS305	CS213
	CS305	CS214
	CS214	CS114
	CS114	CS113
	CS305	CS220

FIGURE 13.2 A list of prerequisites.

If $\sigma_{Crs='CS632' \text{ AND } PreCrs='CS113'}$ (PREREQ$_3$) is nonempty, our hypothesis is confirmed. Again, however, this expression is empty so we have not yet established the indirect prerequisite relationship between the two courses. If we give the relation PREREQ the alias PREREQ$_1$, we start seeing the pattern that each iteration in the above process has the form

$$\text{PREREQ}_{i+1} = \pi_{\texttt{Crs,PreCrs}}((\text{PREREQ} \bowtie_{\texttt{PreCrs=Crs}} \text{PREREQ}_i)\,[\texttt{Crs,P1,C2,PreCrs}]) \cup \text{PREREQ}_i \qquad \textbf{13.19}$$

Continuing in this vein, we create PREREQ$_4$, PREREQ$_5$, and so on. It is easy to verify by direct inspection that $\sigma_{\texttt{Crs='CS632' AND PreCrs='CS113'}}$(PREREQ$_5$) is nonempty, and thus the two courses are five prerequisites removed.

Note that the above process can be used to provide negative answers as well. For instance, to verify that CS220 is *not* a direct or indirect prerequisite of CS505, we can compute PREREQ$_2$, PREREQ$_3$, and so on, and see that applying the selection $\sigma_{\texttt{Crs='CS505' AND PreCrs='CS220'}}$ yields an empty result in each case. How do we know that, for example, $\sigma_{\texttt{Crs='CS505' AND PreCrs='CS220'}}$(PREREQ$_{1000}$) is empty? Simple: PREREQ$_5$, PREREQ$_6$, and so on, are all equal because the join operation used in constructing these relations stops producing new tuples after several joins.

In view of the above discussion, it might seem that indirect prerequisites for courses can be found using the relational algebra alone. In our example, all we have to do is to check the contents of PREREQ$_5$. However, after more careful consideration things turn out to be more complex. What if, instead of the tuple ⟨CS305,CS214⟩, our PREREQ relation had the tuple ⟨CS220,CS214⟩? In this case, it would take one more iteration to establish the indirect prerequisite relation between CS632 and CS113; that is, $\sigma_{\texttt{Crs='CS632' AND PreCrs='CS113'}}$(PREREQ$_5$) would still be empty, but $\sigma_{\texttt{Crs='CS632' AND PreCrs='CS113'}}$(PREREQ$_6$) would not.

OPTIONAL

In other words, the number of iterations of the expression (13.19) needed to reach a stable state (where subsequent joins do not make a difference) is *data-dependent* and cannot be predicted in advance. Because of this, it is not easy to point to a single expression, such as $\sigma_{\texttt{Crs='CS632'} \text{ AND } \texttt{PreCrs='CS113'}}(\text{PREREQ}_5)$, as one that will tell us whether or not CS113 is an indirect prerequisite of CS632 for all legal contents of the relation PREREQ. In fact, it is shown in [Aho and Ullman 1979] that *no relational expression can provide such an answer*! This result means that relational languages, such as relational algebra, calculus, and SQL, have limited expressive power. In fact, as follows from Exercise 13.17, checking prerequisites has polynomial time complexity, which implies that SQL cannot express even certain polynomial time queries. The immediate practical consequence of this theoretical result is that it is not possible to write even simple database applications entirely in SQL. This is one reason why, in the real world, SQL is used from within a host language, such as C or Java, which provides the general application logic. (Chapter 8 explains how this is done.)

Equation (13.19) is called **recurrent**, and queries expressed as recurrent equations are called **recursive**. A recursive query is computed by applying the recurrence equation repeatedly, starting with some known initial value (PREREQ in our case), until a stable state is reached, that is, until PREREQ_{N+1} equals PREREQ_N for some N. In other words, the answer to our query about the prerequisites is the *stable state* of the recurrence equation (13.19). Thus, another interpretation of the aforesaid result in [Aho and Ullman 1979] is that the stable state of a recurrence equation cannot, in general, be represented as an expression in relational algebra.

OPTIONAL

> The number of iterations needed to reach a stable state of a recursive query can vary with the contents of the relations. Such queries require different numbers of joins for different database content, so they cannot be represented as relational algebra expressions since each such expression would have a fixed number of operators.

13.6.2 Recursive Queries in SQL

User demand has led database vendors to recognize the need for processing recursive queries, and some products (e.g., Oracle) have provided partial support based on a home-grown solution to the problem. A much better solution was provided by SQL:1999, which extended SQL with support for recursive queries based on the vast body of prior research in deductive databases. We discuss these extensions next.

SQL does *not* use recurrent equations such as (13.19) to define recursive queries because these equations correspond to the procedural view of *how* such queries are evaluated. Faithful to its original philosophy, SQL specifies what is to be retrieved *declaratively* rather than procedurally. Nevertheless, the connection between recurrence equations and the way SQL expresses recursive queries is clearly seen from the syntax, especially the syntax of recursive views. For instance, the following view specifies all course-prerequisite pairs.

```
CREATE RECURSIVE VIEW IndirectPrereqView(Crs, PreCrs) AS
      ( (SELECT * FROM Prereq)
        UNION
        (SELECT P.Crs, I.PreCrs                                    13.20
         FROM Prereq P, IndirectPrereqView I
         WHERE P.PreCrs = I.Crs) )
```

The difference between a regular view and a recursive view is that the definition of a recursive view consists of two distinct parts.

- *The nonrecursive subquery.* In our example, it is the first SELECT statement (above the UNION operator). It cannot contain references to the view relation being defined.
- *The recursive part.* This part consists of the subquery that appears below the UNION operator. Unlike the nonrecursive subquery, it references the relation IndirectPrereqView—the very view that is being defined by the Create Recursive View statement.

It should now be clear why such views are called recursive: their definitions appear to be cyclic.

The contents of recursive views are defined using the recurrence equations mentioned earlier. The purpose of the nonrecursive subquery in a recursive view definition is to specify the initial contents for the recursive relation used in the recurrence equation. In our case, this subquery states that the initial contents of IndirectPrereqView are the contents of the relation Prereq. Let us denote these contents as $\text{IndirectPrereqView}_1$.

The recursive part specifies the actual recurrence equation. It says that, to obtain the next approximation of the contents of IndirectPrereqView, one must evaluate this query assuming the current approximation. In other words, $\text{IndirectPrereqView}_2$ is the relation computed by forming the union of $\text{IndirectPrereqView}_1$ with the result of the query

```
SELECT P.Crs, I.PreCrs
FROM Prereq P, IndirectPrereqView1 I
WHERE P.PreCrs = I.Crs
```

where we use the previous approximation, $\text{IndirectPrereqView}_1$, to compute the value of $\text{IndirectPrereqView}_2$. The stable state of this recurrence equation is considered to be the contents of the recursive view. In our case, a stable state is reached when joining of the current contents of IndirectPrereqView with the

OPTIONAL

original relation PREREQ no longer yields new course-prerequisite pairs, that is, when the result of the query

```
SELECT P.Crs, I.PreCrs
FROM PREREQ P, INDIRECTPREREQVIEW_N I
WHERE P.PreCrs = I.Crs
```

is contained in INDIRECTPREREQVIEW$_N$ for some $N > 0$.

Having defined a recursive view, we can now query it using a regular SELECT statement. For instance, to find out if CS113 is an indirect prerequisite of CS632, we can write

```
SELECT *
FROM INDIRECTPREREQVIEW I                                    13.21
WHERE I.PreCrs = 'CS113' AND I.Crs = 'CS632'
```

SQL also provides a syntax for recursive queries that does not rely on views. The overall idea is similar: a recursive query consists of two parts—the definition of a recursive relation and the query against this relation. The syntax of the first part is very close to the recursive view definition that we saw earlier, and the syntax of the second part is a regular SQL (nonrecursive) query. For instance, the query about the indirect prerequisite relationship between CS113 and CS632 can be expressed as follows:

```
WITH RECURSIVE INDIRECTPREREQQUERY(Crs, PreCrs) AS
        ((SELECT * FROM PREREQ)
         UNION
         (SELECT P.Crs, I.PreCrs
          FROM PREREQ P, INDIRECTPREREQQUERY I
          WHERE P.PreCrs = I.Crs))
SELECT *
FROM INDIRECTPREREQQUERY I
WHERE I.PreCrs = 'CS113' AND I.Crs = 'CS632'
```

Note that the top portion of this query is almost identical to the definition of the recursive view INDIRECTPREREQVIEW. The only essential difference is that a view definition is saved in the system catalog and can later be reused in other queries whereas the definition of the query INDIRECTPREREQQUERY is discarded by the system right after processing. The bottom portion of the above query corresponds to query (13.21) against the view INDIRECTPREREQVIEW.

Mutually recursive queries. The transitive closure recursive queries considered so far do not illustrate the full power of the recursive query facility in SQL:1999. For

OPTIONAL

a more complex example, consider that (out of sheer curiosity) we want to find prerequisite courses that are removed by an odd number of prerequisites. We can express this query by defining a relation, ODDPREREQ, that is **mutually recursive** with another relation, EVENPREREQ (i.e., each relation is defined in terms of the other). Mutual recursion can be expressed with the help of the WITH statement as follows:

```
WITH RECURSIVE OddPrereq(Crs, PreCrs) AS
        ((SELECT * FROM Prereq)
         UNION
         (SELECT P.Crs, E.PreCrs
          FROM Prereq P, EvenPrereq E
          WHERE P.PreCrs = E.Crs)),                    13.22
    RECURSIVE EvenPrereq(Crs, PreCrs) AS
         (SELECT  P.Crs, O.PreCrs
          FROM Prereq P, OddPrereq O
          WHERE P.PreCrs = O.Crs)
SELECT * FROM OddPrereq
```

In this query, the WITH statement defines two temporary relations, ODDPREREQ and EVENPREREQ. The first relation has a nonrecursive subquery that says that every direct prerequisite is also an odd prerequisite. The recursive part of the definition of ODDPREREQ says that the rest of the odd prerequisites are obtained by joining the PREREQ relation with the relation EVENPREREQ that contains all of the even prerequisites. This latter relation is defined using the second recursive query. This query does not have a nonrecursive part, which means that the initial value of EVENPREREQ is the empty relation. Subsequent approximations to EVENPREREQ are obtained by joining PREREQ with ODDPREREQ. Thus, ODDPREREQ and EVENPREREQ depend on each other.

Brain Teaser: What is the result of a recursive query that has no nonrecursive part?

Restrictions on the use of negation. SQL:1999 has a number of restrictions on the use of recursion that seem to exist solely to give vendors a way out of having to implement some of the more esoteric features. However, some restrictions are motivated by technical considerations and the desire to simplify query evaluation. The most important restriction in this category has to do with negation, which is expressed using the keywords EXCEPT and NOT. To illustrate, suppose that we want to find all *truly odd* prerequisites, that is, those that are not even. (It is possible for a prerequisite to be both odd and even because any pair of courses can be connected by more than one chain of prerequisites and the chains can have different lengths.) We can *try* to express this query as follows:

OPTIONAL

```
WITH RECURSIVE ODDPREREQ(Crs, PreCrs) AS
        ( (SELECT * FROM PREREQ)
          UNION
          ( (SELECT P.Crs, E.PreCrs
              FROM PREREQ P, EVENPREREQ E
              WHERE P.PreCrs = E.Crs)
           EXCEPT
           (SELECT * FROM EVENPREREQ) ) ),
    RECURSIVE EVENPREREQ(Crs, PreCrs) AS
        (SELECT P.Crs, O.PreCrs
         FROM PREREQ P, ODDPREREQ O
         WHERE P.PreCrs = O.Crs )
SELECT * FROM ODDPREREQ
```
(13.23)

The problem with this query has to do with subtraction of EVENPREREQ within the recursive part of the definition of ODDPREREQ. Since these two relations are dependent on each other, it seems that in order to know which tuples are *in* ODDPREREQ, we need to know which tuples are *not in* EVENPREREQ. This, in turn, requires knowing which tuples *are* in EVENPREREQ. But to compute EVENPREREQ we need to compute ODDPREREQ first—back to square one.

A commonly accepted solution to this problem (and the one adopted in SQL:1999) is to require the use of negation (namely, of the operators EXCEPT and NOT) to be **stratified**. That is, if the definition of a relation, **P**, depends on knowing the *complement* of a relation, **Q**, then the definition of **Q** must *not* depend on **P** (or on its complement). In particular, **P** cannot depend on its own complement. Note (Exercise 13.18) that every use of negation in a nonrecursive query is stratified, so stratification is automatically satisfied by all SQL-92 queries.

The use of negation in query (13.23) is not stratified, so it is not legal in SQL. To construct a legal query for retrieving all truly odd prerequisites, we must break mutual recursion in the definition of ODDPREREQ and EVENPREREQ.

```
WITH RECURSIVE ODDPREREQ(Crs, PreCrs) AS
        ( (SELECT * FROM PREREQ)
          UNION
          ( (SELECT P.Crs, E.PreCrs
              FROM PREREQ P, PREREQ P1, ODDPREREQ O
              WHERE P.PreCrs = P1.Crs AND P1.PreCrs = O.Crs)
           EXCEPT
           (SELECT * FROM EVENPREREQ) ) ),
    RECURSIVE EVENPREREQ(Crs, PreCrs) AS
        ((SELECT P.Crs, P1.PreCrs
          FROM PREREQ P, PREREQ P1
          WHERE P.PreCrs = P1.Crs
         UNION
```

```
        (SELECT P.Crs, E.PreCrs
         FROM PREREQ P, PREREQ P1, EVENPREREQ E
         WHERE P.PreCrs=P1.Crs AND P1.PreCrs = E.Crs))
SELECT * FROM ODDPREREQ
```

In this query, the two relations ODDPREREQ and EVENPREREQ are still recursive but not mutually so. ODDPREREQ depends on the complement of EVENPREREQ (because of the EXCEPT clause in its definition), but EVENPREREQ does not depend on ODDPREREQ. Therefore, the use of negation in this query is stratified and thus allowed.

Restrictions on the use of aggregation. Recursion through aggregation poses the same problems as does recursion through negation. To illustrate the problem, we extend our earlier INDIRECTPREREQVIEW example. Suppose you are planning your academic career and need to know how many semesters are necessary in order to complete the prerequisites for a certain course. Since courses might have multiple simultaneous prerequisites, we basically need to find the *longest* path of prerequisites to your course of interest.

The main part in such a query is building a view, LONGESTPREREQCHAIN(Crs, Prereq,Distance), which determines the longest distance between Crs and Prereq in the chain of prerequisites to Crs. To create such a view, our first thought is to modify the well-known shortest-path algorithm and compute the *longest* path between Prereq and Crs as follows: first compute the longest path between Prereq to every immediate prerequisite, Crs1, of Crs; then find the longest prerequisite chain over all such prerequisites, and add 1. This procedure is clearly recursive, which is reflected in our view definition:

```
CREATE RECURSIVE VIEW LONGESTPREREQCHAIN(Crs, Prereq, Distance) AS
    ( (SELECT P.Crs, P.PreCrs, 1
       FROM PREREQ P)
      UNION
      (SELECT P.Crs, L.Prereq, MAX(L.Distance)+1
       FROM PREREQ P, LONGESTPREREQCHAIN L
       WHERE L.Crs = P.PreCrs
       GROUP BY P.Crs, L.Prereq) )
```

Unfortunately, SQL:1999 does not support this kind of use of aggregation with recursion. The problem is that in order to compute MAX in the second SELECT clause, one needs to know the *entire* relation LONGESTPREREQCHAIN (or so it seems). But since this clause is part of the definition of LONGESTPREREQCHAIN, this relation is not known in its entirety when we iterate, using the second select clause, to find the stable database state for this query. In syntactic terms, the above query has **recursion though aggregation**, which leads to circular reasoning of the kind that we just saw.

OPTIONAL

In truth, "circular reasoning" in this view definition exists only at a rather superficial level, and deeper analysis can give a perfectly good semantics (and computation) to such views [Van Gelder 1992]. However, SQL outlaws recursion through aggregates anyway. To solve the career-planning problem in a legal way, we would have to use a less efficient query, but one that has no recursion through aggregate functions, and thus would be allowed in SQL. In this solution, we first compute prerequisite distances without trying to maximize them and apply MAX only when all distances have been computed.

```
WITH RECURSIVE PREREQCHAINDIST(Crs, Prereq, Distance) AS
     ( (SELECT P.Crs, P.PreCrs, 1
        FROM PREREQ P )
       UNION
       (SELECT P.Crs, L.Prereq, L.Distance+1
        FROM PREREQ P, PREREQCHAINDIST L
        WHERE L.Crs = P.PreCrs) )
SELECT L.Crs, L.Prereq, MAX(L.Distance)
FROM PREREQCHAINDIST L
GROUP BY L.Crs, L.Prereq
```

OPTIONAL

The difference between this query and LONGESTPREREQCHAIN is that here we are computing all chains between courses and are not pruning the space by retaining only the longest chains. As a result, the relation PREREQCHAINDIST can be potentially much larger than LONGESTPREREQCHAIN, as it can have the same course-prerequisite pair listed with different distances among them.

Is the problem solved? The extensions described above close the expressivity gap that previously made it impossible to use SQL for recursive queries such as finding of course prerequisites or planning of multistep trips. However, from the practical point of view, the use of the recursive extensions of SQL is limited by the verbose nature of the language. We have seen that even simple recursive queries lead to fairly complex SQL statements because all queries that involve mutually recursive relations must be part of the same SQL statement. Queries that involve three or four mutually recursive relations quickly lead to a blow-up in the size of the corresponding SQL statements, and it becomes increasingly hard to write such statements by hand correctly. A good way to harness this complexity is provided by *Datalog,* a modular and concise language that does not have the above drawbacks.

13.6.3 Datalog

Datalog is the language of choice in the study of recursive queries in deductive databases. It is closely related to the recursive extensions of SQL and to domain relational calculus. It is related to recursion in SQL because SQL recursion is just an adaptation of a similar mechanism in Datalog to the rather awkward syntax of SQL. It is related to domain relational calculus because Datalog simplifies and extends DRC at the same time. Datalog-based systems typically work with their own database format or serve as front ends to commercial, relational databases. In this latter case, a Datalog query is translated into a series of SQL queries that are executed by the relational DBMS, and the results are put together by the Datalog engine.

Apart from influencing SQL, Datalog has not yet made it into the mainstream of database processing despite being a better language. However, it is widely used in research and in advanced experimental information-processing applications. Datalog is supported, in part, by commercial offerings, such as JRules from ILOG, Inc. [JRules 2003], and by popular open-source rule-based systems such as CLIPS [CLIPS 2003] and Jess [Jess 2003]. Another open-source system, XSB [Sagonas et al. 1994; XSB 2003], provides a complete implementation of Datalog as part of a much richer language environment. The emerging field of Semantic Web (see *http://semanticweb.org*) brings new opportunities for Datalog in the areas of processing meta-data, information integration, and more. In recognition of the emergence of Datalog and related languages as important tools for dealing with semantic information on the Web, a number of efforts have sprung up to standardize such languages (see *http://ruleml.org, http://www.daml.org/rules/*).

Basic syntax and semantics. Datalog has only two main types of constructs: *rules* and *queries*. A **rule** is of the form

```
head :- body.
```

and a query has the form

```
?- body.
```

The **body of a rule** can be any expression in domain relational calculus, except that quantifiers, ∀ and ∃, are not allowed. The AND connective is often written as "," and OR as ";". The **head of a rule** is a DRC expression of the form $\mathbf{R}(X_1, \ldots, X_n)$, where **R** is a relation name and $X_1, \ldots, X_n$ are domain variables or constants. The **body of a query** has the same syntax as the body of a rule. Here is an example of a rule and a query:

```
PROFNAMESEM(?Name,?Semester) :-
    PROFESSOR(?Id,?Name,?Dept), TEACHING(?Id,'MGT123',?Semester).
?- PROFNAMESEM(?Name,?Semester).
```

The first statement is a rule that defines a new relation, PROFNAMESEM; it contains the names of all professors who ever taught MGT123 and the semesters in which they taught this course. Datalog rules are like view definitions. Relations that appear in the head of a rule are called **derived relations**; they correspond to views in SQL. Like views, derived relations can appear in the body of another rule and thus take part in defining other derived relations. Relations that occur in the rule bodies

OPTIONAL

but never in their heads are called **base relations**; they correspond to the relations whose contents are physically stored in the database.

The second statement is a query; it simply asks to retrieve all tuples in the corresponding relation. If we wanted to find out who taught MGT123 in fall of 2003, we could ask a different query using the same view:

```
?- ProfNameSem(?Name,'F2003').
```

In this and other examples of Datalog, we will be using the ?–mark to denote variables. Thus, ?Id and ?Semester are variables. Other symbols that occur in argument positions, such as MGT123 and F2003, are constants. As in the relational calculi, the actual names of the variables are unimportant. For instance, consistent replacement of all occurrences of the variable ?Name with ?N and of ?Id with ?I in the definition of ProfNameSem leads to an equivalent definition.

The semantics of the above Datalog definition of ProfNameSem is given by the following DRC view definition:

```
ProfNameSem = {Name,Sem | ∃Id ∃Dept ( Professor(Id,Name,Dept)
                                   AND Teaching(Id,'MGT123',Sem) )}
```

Compared to DRC, Datalog shuns explicit quantification of variables and instead uses a convention similar to what we have seen in SQL and QBE: the variables in the rule body that do not occur in the rule head are considered to be implicitly quantified with ∃; the rest of the variables in the body must also occur in the rule head.

A more general way of understanding Datalog rules is to read the symbol :- as an implication. In our example, the rule states: If there are values id, name, dept, and sem, such that the tuple ⟨id,name,dept⟩ is in relation Professor and the tuple ⟨id,'MGT123',sem⟩ is in Teaching, then the tuple ⟨name,sem⟩ must be in ProfNameSem. Moreover, the contents of ProfNameSem are assumed to consist of *all* the tuples derived in this way from the formula in the rule body, and nothing else.

Such a semantics for Datalog rules seems natural enough, but there are issues to be dealt with. Let us extend the definition of ProfNameSem to also include professors who taught CS305. In Datalog, this would be expressed as

```
ProfNameSem(?Name,?Semester) :-
    Professor(?Id,?Name,?Dept), Teaching(?Id,'MGT123',?Semester).
ProfNameSem(?Name,?Semester) :-
    Professor(?Id,?Name,?Dept), Teaching(?Id,'CS305',?Semester).
```

When a view relation is defined via multiple rules, our semantics needs an adjustment. The contents of ProfNameSem is now said to consist of all (and only) those tuples that can be derived via *either* of the two rules. In our example, using

OPTIONAL

the database in Figure 3.5 on page 39, Mary Doe is a professor at the CS department and her Id is 555666777. Hence, PROFESSOR(555666777,'Mary Doe','CS') is true. In addition, Mary Doe taught CS305 in fall 1995, which makes TEACHING(555666777,'CS305','F1995') true as well. Therefore, by the second rule, we can derive PROFNAMESEM('Mary Doe','F1995'). By a similar argument, the tuple ⟨'John Smyth','S1996'⟩ must be in PROFNAMESEM. The first rule above can derive an additional four tuples: ⟨'Jacob Tailor','F1994'⟩, ⟨'Jacob Tailor','F1997'⟩, ⟨'Qi Chen','F1994'⟩, and ⟨'Adrian Jones','F1997'⟩. No other tuple can be derived using either rule, so we conclude that these six tuples constitute the entire content of the derived relation PROFNAMESEM.

A moment's reflection shows that in DRC the above extended view PROFNAMESEM can be defined as follows:

```
PROFNAMESEM =
    {Name,Sem | ∃Id ∃Dept ( PROFESSOR(Id,Name,Dept) AND
                            (TEACHING(Id,'MGT123',Sem) OR
                               TEACHING(Id,'CS305',Sem)) )}
```

Although this looks different from the two Datalog rules that define the same relation, keep in mind that the Datalog version can be written as one rule using Datalog's disjunction operator ";", which matches the above DRC definition of PROFNAMESEM.

```
PROFNAMESEM(?Name,?Sem) :- PROFESSOR(?Id,?Name,?Dept),
                             ( TEACHING(?Id,'MGT123',?Sem)
                               ; TEACHING(?Id,'CS305',?Sem) ).
```

This representation is equivalent to the earlier two-rule definition due to the well known logical tautology (A, (B; C)) ≡ ((A, B); (A, C)) (distributivity of AND through OR) and the fact that a rule of the form H : −(B; C) is equivalent to the pair of rules H : −B and H : −C.

Brain Teaser: Prove that the single rule *H* : −*A*, (*B*; *C*) is equivalent to the pair of rules *H* : −*A*, *B* and *H* : −*A*, *C* using the above two tautologies.

Recursion. Our examples of Datalog so far were not very different from DRC, both syntactically and semantically. The important difference, however, is that derived relations can be defined *recursively*—something that is not possible in DRC. In Section 13.6.2, we have already described how recursion increases the expressive power of SQL and enables queries such as finding all course prerequisites. Here is a Datalog version of that query:

```
INDIRECTPREREQ(?Crs,?Prereq) :- PREREQ(?Crs,?Prereq).
```

OPTIONAL

```
INDIRECTPREREQ(?Crs,?Prereq) :-                                   13.24
           PREREQ(?Crs,?Intermediate),
           INDIRECTPREREQ(?Intermediate,?Prereq).
```

Although conceptually it is the same as the corresponding SQL query (13.20), the Datalog version is much cleaner and more elegant. The difference becomes even more pronounced when more rules are involved. For instance, compare the SQL query (13.22) to its Datalog version:

```
ODDPREREQ(?Crs,?PreCrs) :- PREREQ(?Crs,?PreCrs).
ODDPREREQ(?Crs,?PreCrs) :-
         PREREQ(?Crs,?MidCrs), EVENPREREQ(?MidCrs,?PreCrs).
EVENPREREQ(?Crs,?PreCrs) :-
         PREREQ(?Crs,?MidCrs), ODDPREREQ(?MidCrs,?PreCrs).
```

Here the definitions of ODDPREREQ and EVENPREREQ are cleanly separated, and joins are indicated by placing the same variable in different argument positions (`MidCrs` in our case). The first two rules can be further combined into one using the disjunction operator ";", as in SQL's version (13.22), making the entire specification even shorter. (However, this shorter formulation might be perceived as less clear.)

OPTIONAL

Semantics of Datalog without negation. We will now describe the semantics of recursive (and, as a special case, nonrecursive) queries in a more precise fashion than we were able to in Section 13.6.1.

We first consider Datalog queries without negated relations in the rule body. Since disjunction in a rule body, such as `H :- (B; C)`, can be eliminated by replacing the rule with `H :- B` and `H :- C`, we can assume that rule bodies do not have disjunction either. We will call such rules **positive**. In view of these restrictions and the previous discussion about the relationship between rules and DRC expressions, we can conclude that any positive Datalog rule can be represented using the following DRC expression:

$$HeadRelation = \{\, HeadVars \mid \exists BodyOnlyVars\ (RuleBody)\,\} \qquad \textbf{13.25}$$

Here *RuleBody* is a DRC condition that combines relational tests, such as $\mathbf{P}(X_1, \ldots, X_n)$, with simple comparisons, such as `X>Y`, using the AND operator. *BodyOnlyVars* is a list of variables that occur in the body of the rule but not in its head. As discussed previously, such variables are assumed to be implicitly quantified with ∃. *HeadVars* are the variables that occur in the head and in the body. A major difference with DRC is that (13.25) can be recursive and *HeadRelation* can occur as one of the relation names in *RuleBody*. Even if it does not, recursion can span several rules as in the case of odd and even prerequisites. In this case, *RuleBody* can contain a relation, *Rel*, which is defined by another DRC expression of the form *Rel*={...|... *RuleBody2*}, where *HeadRelation* occurs in *RuleBody2*.

The semantics of Datalog queries that are defined by a set of positive rules can be described in several ways, including a completely declarative way that does not appeal to any algorithm. However, we will instead use a simple algorithmic definition, which will also serve us later when we allow queries to have negation. The algorithm computes the stable state of a set of possibly recursive or mutually recursive Datalog rules. A database state in Datalog consists of instances for all relations, both base and derived ones. The *initial state* of the computation assigns empty instances to all derived relations; the base relations get the instances that they have in the current database. Computation of the instances for the derived relations then proceeds as follows:

Algorithm (Computing recursive queries with no negation in the rule body)

1. Set the variable *CurrentState* to the initial state as described above.
2. For each derived relation, **R**, let $r_1, \ldots, r_n$ be all the rules that have **R** in the head. Evaluate the DRC query that corresponds to each rule r_i and take the union of the results. Assign this union as the new relation instance for **R**.

   Let *NewState* denote the new database state obtained as a result of the replacement of the old instances of the derived relations with the new instances computed in this step. The instances of the base relations remain unchanged.
3. **If** *CurrentState* = *NewState*
   Then Stop: *NewState* is the stable state for the given set of Datalog rules.
   Else Set *CurrentState* := *NewState* and repeat step 2.

This algorithm always terminates (in fact, in polynomial time in the size of the database). Before proving this fact, we illustrate the workings of this algorithm using the set of Datalog rules given in (13.24). The DRC query that would be repeatedly evaluated by this algorithm is

```
{Crs, Prereq | PREREQ(Crs,Prereq) OR
               ∃Intermediate (PREREQ(Crs,Intermediate) AND
                              INDIRECTPREREQ(Intermediate,Prereq))}
```

Initially, INDIRECTPREREQ is empty and PREREQ's state is determined by the current database instance. The first iteration derives *NewState* = {INDIRECTPREREQ = PREREQ}. In the second iteration, INDIRECTPREREQ is initially equal to PREREQ. *NewState* is then computed to be as follows: the contents of PREREQ do not change, but the contents of INDIRECTPREREQ become the union of PREREQ and a join of PREREQ with the old contents of INDIRECTPREREQ (once- and twice-removed prerequisites). In the third iteration, these newly computed contents of INDIRECTPREREQ are used as the "old" contents and the new contents are computed by a join with PREREQ, and so on. You may have noticed the similarity between this process and the one described in Section 13.6.1. In fact, it is the same process: take a moment to convince yourself that any iteration over the above DRC query is tantamount to an iteration over the relational expression (13.19), which was used in that section.

OPTIONAL

Properties of the algorithm for recursive queries without negation. The proof of termination rests on the following lemma, which will be proven shortly:

CurrentState $\subseteq$ *NewState*

It says that, after each iteration over step 2, for each relation, **R**, in the database, its relation instance in *CurrentState* is contained in the relation instance of **R** in *NewState*. This means that *CurrentState* and *NewState* grow monotonically. The key observation is that the values of these variables cannot grow indefinitely. Indeed, Datalog rules do not generate new constants (assuming that the rules do not use arithmetic operators that create new numbers), and the initial database state can contain only a finite number of constants. Since relations have fixed arity, there can be only a finite number of tuples that can possibly be generated from a given finite set of constants. Therefore, the monotonic growth of *CurrentState* and *NewState* will eventually stop. At this point, *CurrentState* will equal *NewState*, and the algorithm will terminate.

We can show that termination will take place after a polynomial number of steps in the size of the database using the following estimate (which is very rough; optimization can reduce the cost by orders of magnitude). Let D be the number of constants in the database and N be the sum of arities of all relations used in the query. Then, each iteration of the algorithm cannot take more than D^N number of steps—the cost of producing the Cartesian product of all the attribute domains involved in the query. Since each iteration must produce at least one new tuple and there cannot be more than D^N tuples in the result, the computation must stop after D^N iterations. Thus, the number of steps is bounded by $D^N \times D^N$. If we fix the query, then N is constant. Therefore, only D depends on the size of the database. Hence, the number of steps is polynomial in the size of the database.

We will now prove the lemma that *CurrentState* $\subseteq$ *NewState*. Observe that the positive DRC queries of the form (13.25) have the following interesting *monotonicity* property: the more tuples we feed into *RuleBody*, the more answers the query produces. In other words, if **db** and **db**′ are sets of relation instances for the relations used in *RuleBody* and **db** $\subseteq$ **db**′, then the query will produce more answers if it is evaluated with the instances in **db**′ than if it is evaluated with **db**. (We will prove this fact shortly.)

The rest follows from the monotonicity property: we can view each iteration of the algorithm as a computation of the function T_Q, where Q denotes the set of DRC queries. T_Q takes a set of relation instances, *CurrentState*, and produces another set of relation instances, *NewState*. As we have just shown, T_Q is a monotonic function, that is, if $\mathbf{db} \subseteq \mathbf{db}'$, then $T_Q(\mathbf{db}) \subseteq T_Q(\mathbf{db}')$.

Recall that we started with a set of relational instances, $\mathbf{db}_0$, where derived relations have empty instances. After the first iteration, we computed $\mathbf{db}_1$. The important observation here is that $\mathbf{db}_0 \subseteq \mathbf{db}_1$ because the base relations have the same instances in both $\mathbf{db}_0$ and $\mathbf{db}_1$, while derived relations have the same or

OPTIONAL

larger instances (one cannot have a smaller instance than the empty set!). Due to monotonicity, we obtain the following inclusions:

$$\mathbf{db}_0 \subseteq \mathbf{db}_1 = T_Q(\mathbf{db}_0) \subseteq T_Q(\mathbf{db}_1) = \mathbf{db}_2 .$$

Thus, $\mathbf{db}_1 \subseteq \mathbf{db}_2$. Continuing this argument by induction, we can conclude that $\mathit{CurrentState} = \mathbf{db}_i \subseteq \mathbf{db}_{i+1} = \mathit{NewState}$ for all $i \geq 0$.

Proof of the monotonicity of T_Q. A crucial assumption in the proof of the monotonicity is that all DRC queries in Q have the form (13.25). In particular, the condition part of each such DRC query has neither NOT nor the universal quantifier ∀. If negation (the next subsection) or ∀ are allowed, then the monotonicity property no longer holds.

One easy way to prove that T_Q is monotonic is by induction of the structure of *RuleBody* in the DRC expression of the form (13.25). Recall that *RuleBody* is a conjunction of simple conditions, which are either relation tests, like $\mathbf{P}(X_1, \ldots, X_n)$, where **P** is a relation, or comparisons that involve =, <, etc. (e.g., $X \geq Y$ or $X = c$).

If $N = 1$, *RuleBody* is a comparison or a relation test. Clearly, in this case, the larger is the database instance—the larger is the answer to the query. So let us assume that monotonicity holds when *RuleBody* has more than 1 but less than N conjuncts.

For the inductive step, suppose that *RuleBody* has N conjuncts. Then it can be represented as $\mathit{RuleBody}_1 \wedge \mathit{Conjunct}$, where $\mathit{RuleBody}_1$ has $N - 1$ conjuncts and *Conjunct* is either a comparison or a relation test of the form $\mathbf{P}(X_1, \ldots, X_n)$. By the inductive assumption, $\mathit{RuleBody}_1$ is monotonic. If *Conjunct* is a comparison, then a result produced by *RuleBody* is obtained from the result of $\mathit{RuleBody}_1$ via a selection operator, which is monotonic. If $\mathit{RuleBody} \equiv (\mathit{RuleBody}_1$ AND $\mathbf{P}(X_1, \ldots, X_n))$, then the result produced by *RuleBody* is a join of the result of $\mathit{RuleBody}_1$ and the relation **P**. Since both $\mathit{RuleBody}_1$ and **P** are monotonic queries and join is a monotonic operation, we conclude that *RuleBody* must be monotonic as well.

Negation in Datalog. Section 13.6.2 gave a preview of the problems posed by the presence of EXCEPT and NOT in SQL queries. A similar problem arises in Datalog when relations are negated with the **not** operator.

The most common use of negation in Datalog is when a query involves a division operator of relational algebra, that is, when it is necessary to find all tuples in one relation that join with *every* tuple in another relation. Recall that in DRC such queries require universal quantification. Since Datalog does not permit universal quantifiers, one can expect difficulties similar to those in SQL. Consider the query *Find all students who took a course from every professor*. In Datalog, this is expressed in the following (slightly roundabout) way:

```
ANSWER(?Sid) :- STUDENT(?Sid,?Name,?Addr),
                not DIDNTTAKECOURSEFROMSOMEPROF(?Sid).
DIDNTTAKECOURSEFROMSOMEPROF(?Sid) :-
                PROFESSOR(?Pid,?Pname,?Dept),
```

OPTIONAL

```
                        STUDENT(?Sid,?Name,?Addr),
                        not HASTAUGHT(?Pid,?Sid).
HASTAUGHT(?Pid,?Sid) :-
                        TEACHING(?Pid,?Crs,?Sem),
                        TRANSCRIPT(?Sid,?Crs,?Sem,?Grd).
?- ANSWER(?Sid).
```

Although not as straightforward as in DRC, the formulation of this query is fairly logical and can be read directly by interpreting the Datalog rules: the answer to the query consists of all students for whom it is not true that they did not take a course from some professor. Then we define what it means to be a tuple in DIDNTTAKECOURSEFROMSOMEPROF: $\langle s \rangle$ is such a tuple if s is an Id of a student such that there is a professor with Id p and $\langle p, s \rangle$ is not in HASTAUGHT. The final rule states that a professor is considered to have taught a student if the student took a course from that professor.

So far so good. The use of negation in Datalog is not free of pitfalls, however. It might be tempting to reformulate the above query as

```
ANSWER(?Sid) :- STUDENT(?Sid,?Name,?Addr),
                        PROFESSOR(?Pid,?Pname,?Dept),
                        not PROFWHODIDNTTEACHSTUD(?Pid,?Sid).
PROFWHODIDNTTEACHSTUD(?Pid,?Sid) :-
                        PROFESSOR(?Pid,?Pname,?Dept),
                        STUDENT(?Sid,?Name,?Addr),
                        not HASTAUGHT(?Pid,?Sid).
HASTAUGHT(?Pid,?Sis) :- ...
```

Here the tuple $\langle p, s \rangle$ is in PROFWHODIDNTTEACHSTUD if p is a professor's Id, s is an Id of a student, and $\langle p, s \rangle$ is not in HASTAUGHT. Note that the only difference between PROFWHODIDNTTEACHSTUD and DIDNTTAKECOURSEFROMSOMEPROF is that the former has an extra variable, ?Pid. This seemingly natural definition has a logical flaw in the first rule—the negation of PROFWHODIDNTTEACHSTUD. Remember that all variables that do not appear in the rule head are assumed to be quantified existentially, therefore, the first rule is really

```
ANSWER(?Sid) :- ∃?Pid ∃?Name ...(
                            STUDENT(?Sid,?Name,?Addr),
                            PROFESSOR(?Pid,?Pname,?Dept),
                            not PROFWHODIDNTTEACHSTUD(?Pid,?Sid) ).
```

In other words, student s will be in the answer set if there *exists* a professor who taught s. But we wanted s to be in the answer only if *every* professor taught s. So, the second formulation of the query gets the quantification wrong.

OPTIONAL

Negation and recursion. The second problem with negation arises when one relation recursively depends on the negation of another (or negation of itself). This problem was illustrated in the context of SQL in query (13.23), where ODDPREREQ is not only mutually recursive with EVENPREREQ but also depends on knowing the complement to the relation EVENPREREQ. The goal is to find all odd prerequisites that are not even prerequisites at the same time. (It is possible that there are chains of odd and even length between the same pair of prerequisites; we do not want such results to be returned.) The Datalog version of this query is

```
OddPrereq(?X,?Y) :- Prereq(?X,?Y).
OddPrereq(?X,?Y) :- Prereq(?X,?Z), EvenPrereq(?Z,?Y),
                      not EvenPrereq(?X,?Y).                13.26
EvenPrereq(?X,?Y) :- Prereq(?X,?Z), OddPrereq(?Z,?Y).
?- OddPrereq(?X,?Y).
```

The difficulty in assigning a meaning to this query is that the computation ODD PREREQ requires knowing the complement of EVENPREREQ, which requires knowing the entire contents of the relation EVENPREREQ. However, to compute the latter requires at least some knowledge of ODDPREREQ—a circular reasoning argument.

Note that the algorithm for positive recursive queries, which was discussed earlier, is inapplicable when rule bodies have negation. For termination, that algorithm relied on the fact that the DRC queries, which were used at each iteration, define a monotonic mapping. But with negation in the rule body, the mapping is no longer monotonic. For instance, consider the DRC query that returns students who did not take MAT123 in fall of 2004:

```
{Id,Name | ∃Addr ∃Grade ( Student(Id,Name,Addr) AND
                NOT Transcript(Id,'MAT123','F2004',Grade) ) }
```

It is easy to see that assigning a larger relation instance to STUDENT makes the query answer larger, but assigning a larger instance to TRANSCRIPT makes the answer smaller. If both relations get larger instances, then whether the answer will increase or not is a toss-up.

ODDPREREQ was an example of a query with negation, the semantics of which are dubious. The following query is an example of a recursive query with "well-behaved" negation. Consider a problem of scholarship maintenance in the Financial Aid Department at XYZ University. The department has a database of students who receive tuition scholarships, and this needs to be updated every year. The Financial Aid Department hired an IT firm that is aware of the deductive database technology. To reduce the need for manual data entry, the firm proposes to formulate the scholarship rules as a *policy*, which is supposed to eliminate much of the routine associated with updating of the scholarship rosters. The English description of the policy is *Once awarded, scholarship continues in subsequent years unless the student becomes ineligible. The student is ineligible if the scholarship is rescinded for some reason.*

OPTIONAL

An ineligible student continues to be ineligible in subsequent years unless the scholarship is explicitly reinstated. The IT firm quickly realized that Datalog is ideal for expressing this type of policy in a concise and clear manner:

```
SCHOLARSHIP(?Sid,?Year) :- AWARDED(?Sid,?Year).
SCHOLARSHIP(?Sid,?Year) :-
        SCHOLARSHIP(?Sid,?Year-1), not INELIGIBLE(?Sid,?Year).
INELIGIBLE(?Sid,?Year) :- RESCINDED(?Sid,?Year).                    13.27
INELIGIBLE(?Sid,?Year) :-
        INELIGIBLE(?Sid,?Year-1), not REINSTATED(?Sid,?Year).
```

These rules correspond to the scholarship policy statements almost one to one. The first rule says that a student has a scholarship in a certain year if the scholarship was awarded in that year. The next rule says that the scholarship continues in year Y if it was in place in year Y-1 and the student did not become ineligible in year Y. The third rule says that a student becomes ineligible if the scholarship was rescinded, and the last rule says that ineligibility continues until scholarship is reinstated. In this example, AWARDED, RESCINDED, and REINSTATED are base relations, while SCHOLARSHIP and INELIGIBLE are derived.

The benefit realized by this representation is that maintenance of the scholarship information is much simplified. The information needs to be updated only when a new award is made and, in subsequent years, only when something exceptional happens (such as when a student becomes ineligible or is reinstated). Since these exceptions are rare, very little additional data entry is required.

Let us now examine these rules from the technical point of view. As before, we see that SCHOLARSHIP and INELIGIBLE are recursive relations, and both depend on the complement of another relation. However, there is no circular reasoning in this case. To compute SCHOLARSHIP we need to know the complement of INELIGIBLE. Although INELIGIBLE is recursive, it does not depend on SCHOLARSHIP, so we can try to compute INELIGIBLE first. To do so, we need to know the complement of REINSTATED, which we can compute since REINSTATED is a base relation. (To sidestep the question of how to deal with the fact that the complement of REINSTATED is infinite, let us assume that the domain of the attribute Year is finite.) Therefore, the query ?- SCHOLARSHIP(?X,?Y) can be computed as follows:

1. First compute the complement of REINSTATED. Make this complement into the contents of a new relation, call it NOTREINSTATED, and use this instead of **not** REINSTATED in the last rule of (13.27).
2. Compute INELIGIBLE using the rules

```
INELIGIBLE(?Sid,?Year) :- RESCINDED(?Sid,?Year).
INELIGIBLE(?Sid,?Year) :-
        INELIGIBLE(?Sid,?Year-1), NOTREINSTATED(?Sid,?Year).
```

OPTIONAL

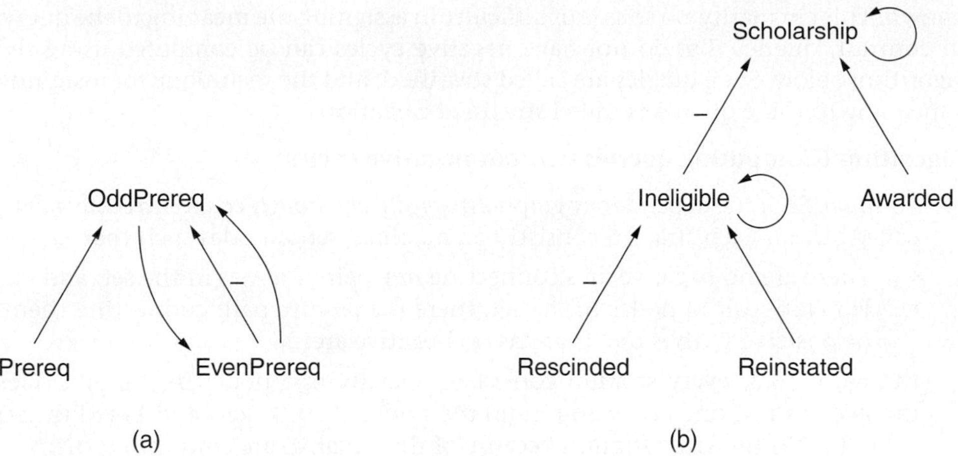

FIGURE 13.3 Dependency graphs for queries (13.26) and (13.27).

3. Compute the complement of INELIGIBLE and make it into the contents of a new relation, NOTINELIGIBLE.
4. Now compute SCHOLARSHIP using the first two rules in (13.27) where **not** INELIGIBLE is replaced with NOTINELIGIBLE.

To explain the difference between the SCHOLARSHIP query (13.27) and the ODD PREREQ query (13.26), we introduce the notion of a **dependency graph**. The nodes of the graph are the names of the relations; the arcs are defined as follows:

- If relation **P** occurs in the head and **Q** in the body of the same rule then the graph has an arc leading from **Q** to **P**.
- If, furthermore, **Q** occurs under the scope of a **not** in that rule body, then the arc is also labeled with the "–" sign—a **negative arc**. Otherwise, the arc is unlabeled and is called **positive**.

The dependency graphs for queries (13.26) and (13.27) are shown in Figures 13.3(a) and (b), respectively. In part (a), we see that the graph has a cycle in which one of the arcs is negative. Part (b) also has negative arcs, but none of these arcs is involved in a cycle (although there are other cycles). It is easy to see that an arc from **Q** to **P** in the dependency graph signifies that computing some tuples in **P** requires computing some tuples in **Q** first. (It does *not* mean that *all* of **Q** must be computed first—otherwise computing recursive queries would not be possible!) If, in addition, an arc is labeled with a "–", then computing **P** requires knowing some tuples in the complement of **Q**. Note that in order to know if a tuple belongs to the complement of **Q**, the *entire* relation **Q** must be computed first.

Thus, if a dependency graph has a cycle with at least one negative arc (a **negative cycle**), as in Figure 13.3(a), then we have a circular argument on our hands: to compute **P**, all of **Q** must be known, and to compute **Q** at least some of **P** must be

OPTIONAL

known. This circularity is a source of difficulty in assigning the meaning to the query. In contrast, queries that do not have negative cycles can be computed using the algorithm below. Such queries are called **stratified**, and the technique for assigning a meaning to these queries is called **stratified negation**.

Algorithm (Computing queries without negative cycles)

1. *Partition*. Split the dependency graph into *positively strongly connected components*, called **strata**. Each stratum consists of a maximal set of nodes such that
   - There are no negative arcs connecting *any* pair of nodes in the set; and
   - For *every* pair of nodes in the set, there is a *positive* path connecting them. (A **positive path** is one that has no negative arcs.)

   In Figure 13.3, every stratum consists of exactly one node: In (b), all cycles involve at most one node, and in (a) the nodes ODDPREREQ and EVENPREREQ cannot be in the same stratum because of the negative arc connecting them.

   > *Brain Teaser:* Suppose a stratum contains a base relation. How many relations can this stratum have?

2. *Stratify*. Order the strata in such a way that if there is a path from some node in a stratum, π, to a node in another stratum, σ, then π must precede σ in that ordering. If there is no path connecting π and σ, then the two strata can be ordered arbitrarily. We will prove later that if the dependency graph has no negative cycles then the above rules define a partial order among the strata. Any *total* ordering among the strata that is consistent with this partial order is called a **stratification**.

   In Figure 13.3(a), no total ordering exists, due to the negative cycle in the graph, which induces a cycle among the strata ODDPREREQ and EVENPREREQ. In 13.3(b), one stratification is REINSTATED, RESCINDED, INELIGIBLE, AWARDED, SCHOLARSHIP. Other stratifications can be obtained by swapping RESCINDED and REINSTATED, AWARDED and REINSTATED, and so on.

3. *Evaluate*. Evaluate the strata in the order of stratification. Evaluation of each stratum is done using the algorithm for computing positive recursive queries (on page 501).

The last step calls for a clarification. The algorithm on page 501 deals with rules that do not have the **not** operator in their bodies; this is not true in our case. However, we can rely on the trick that was used for the scholarship example above. We explain this trick for a general Datalog query.

Let Q denote the set of Datalog rules involved in the query and let $\pi_1, \ldots, \pi_n$ be a stratification of that query. We can partition Q into subsets $Q_1, \ldots, Q_n$, where each Q_i consists precisely of the rules from Q whose heads are relations that belong to π_i. Clearly, if π_i consists only of base relations then Q_i is empty.

> *Brain Teaser:* How many rules can Q_1 have?

OPTIONAL

Next, we evaluate the rule sets $Q_1, \ldots, Q_n$ in that order using a modified algorithm of page 501. One has to deal with the following cases in the process:

- Q_i is empty. This means that π_i contains a single base relation, so there is nothing to compute—the relation is stored in the database.
- The rules in Q_i do not have negation in their bodies. Then the relations in the body of the rules in Q_i can be either in π_i or they might belong to the strata with sequence numbers less than i. In the latter case, these relations will be computed while evaluating the Q_js with $j < i$, and we can treat these relations as if they were base relations. The relations in the stratum π_i can therefore be computed using the algorithm on page 501 directly.
- Some rules in Q_i have occurrences of **not** $\mathbf{R}_1, \ldots,$ **not** $\mathbf{R}_k$ in their bodies. In this case, $\mathbf{R}_1, \ldots, \mathbf{R}_k$, belong to the strata lower than π_i and thus, again, their instances $\mathbf{r}_1, \ldots, \mathbf{r}_k$, must have been computed earlier. Let Q_i' be the set of rules obtained from Q_i by replacing each occurrence of **not** $\mathbf{R}_i$, where $i = 1, \ldots, k$, with a new relation, $\mathbf{NotR}_i$. We treat $\mathbf{NotR}_i$ as a base relation whose contents are the complement to $\mathbf{r}_i$. Since Q_i' does not have negated relations in the body, we can use the algorithm on page 501 to compute the instances of all the relations in the stratum π_i.

After evaluating Q_n, we will know the relation instances for all the derived relations in Q. One of these relations will be the query relation, and its instance is the answer to our query.

Note that the stratification order is not unique, because strata that do not depend on each other can be ordered arbitrarily. The question then is whether all stratifications yield the same final result (i.e., that the same instances are computed for the derived relations regardless of stratification). Fortunately, the answer is affirmative (see [Apt et al. 1988]), which reassures us that the semantics that we have adopted for stratified queries has intrinsic merit.

For completeness, we should mention that the circular argument that arises when dependency graphs have negative cycles can be resolved, and semantics that extend the realm of meaningful queries beyond stratification do exist [Przymusinski 1988; Van Gelder et al. 1991]. However, the treatment of these advanced topics is beyond the scope of this text.

Existence of a stratification. We will now prove that some stratification must exist if the dependency graph has no negative cycles. We first prove that there are no cycles among strata, that is, there can be no path from a node in one stratum, π, to a node in another stratum, π', and from a node in π' back to a node in π. Suppose, to the contrary, that the dependency graph has a path from node $n \in \pi$ to a node $n' \in \pi'$ and back, from a node $m' \in \pi'$ to $m \in \pi$. Since n and m belong to the same stratum, there must be a path from m to n. Similarly, there must be a path from n' to m'. Therefore, there is a cycle involving these four nodes. Since there are no negative cycles, this cycle must be positive. But then, by the definition of the strata, all the

OPTIONAL

nodes in $\pi \cup \pi'$ must be in the *same* stratum—contrary to the assumption that π and π' are different strata.

Let $\pi < \pi'$ mean that the dependency graph has a path from a node in π to a node in π'. The absence of cycles among strata means that $<$ is a partial order. It is a well-known fact in the theory of algorithms that every partial order can be extended into a total order. Since any total order among the strata is a stratification, we have shown that there always exists some stratification provided that the dependency graph has no negative cycles.

BIBLIOGRAPHIC NOTES

Tuple relational calculus was introduced in [Codd 1972] as a theoretical tool in the study of the expressiveness of relational algebra as a query language. [Date 1992] shows how TRC can be effectively used as an intermediate language for constructing complex SQL queries. Domain relational calculus was proposed as a language for database queries in [Lacroix and Pirotte 1977]. Query-by-example was introduced in [Zloof 1975]. A proof of the equivalence of domain-independent queries in either of the calculi with the relational algebra is due to Codd and can be found in [Ullman 1988]. Domain independence and related issues were studied in [Di Paola 1969; Van Gelder and Topor 1991; Kifer 1988; Topor and Sonenberg 1988; Avron and Hirshfeld 1994] and others.

The proof that the transitive closure query cannot be expressed using relational algebra is due to [Aho and Ullman 1979]. Deductive databases and Datalog are extensively covered in [Ullman 1988; Abiteboul et al. 1995], and a number of research prototypes of deductive database systems are described in [Ramakrishnan et al. 1994; Sagonas et al. 1994; Vaghani et al. 1994]. Stratified negation was introduced in [Apt et al. 1988], and extensions that support more general queries with negation are described in [Przymusinski 1988; Van Gelder et al. 1991]. Recursion through aggregation was studied in [Van Gelder 1992].

EXERCISES

13.1 a. Explain why tuple relational calculus is said to be declarative whereas relational algebra is said to be procedural.

b. Explain why, even though SQL is declarative, the query optimizer in a relational DBMS translates SQL statements into relational algebra, which is procedural.

13.2 Express in words the meaning of each of the following expressions (where TOOK(s, c) means "student s took course c"). For example, the meaning of one of these expressions is "Every student has taken at least one course."

a. ∃S ∈ STUDENT (∀C ∈ COURSE TOOK(S, C))
b. ∀S ∈ STUDENT (∃C ∈ COURSE TOOK(S, C))
c. ∃C ∈ COURSE (∀S ∈ STUDENT TOOK(S, C))
d. ∀C ∈ COURSE (∃S ∈ STUDENT TOOK(S, C))

13.3 Write the query that finds all students who took some course from Professor Joe Public; use TRC and DRC.

13.4 Write a query that finds all students who took MAT123 from Professor Ann White but did not take MAT321 from her.

** 13.5 Prove that any query in tuple relational calculus has an equivalent query in domain relational calculus, and vice versa.

* 13.6 Prove that relational algebra queries are domain-independent. *Hint:* Use induction on the structure of the relational algebra expression.

13.7 Consider the relation schema corresponding to the IsA hierarchy in Figure 4.6. Assume that this schema has one relation per entity. (Consult Section 4.4 to refresh your memory about translation of IsA hierarchies into the relational model.) Write the following queries both in tuple and domain relational calculus:

a. Find the names of all sophomores in the computer science major.
b. Find the names of all students in the computer science major.
c. Find all departments where some technician has every specialization that any other technician (in the same or another department) has.

13.8 Write a domain relational calculus query that is equivalent to the following algebraic expressions:

a. **R** – **S**
b. **R**/**S**, where relation **R** has attributes *A*, *B* and **S** has only one attribute, *B*.

13.9 Express each of the following queries in tuple relational calculus, domain relational calculus, and QBE using the schema of Figure 3.4, page 38.

a. Find all courses that are taught by professors who belong to either of the departments `EE` and `MGT`. (Assume that certain courses that are listed in one department can be taught by professors from other departments.)
b. List the names of all students who took courses in spring 1997 and fall 1998.
c. List the names of all students who took courses from at least two professors in different departments.
d. Find all courses in department `MGT` that were taken by all students.
*e. Find every department that has a professor who has taught all courses ever offered by that department.

Compare the two calculi, QBE, and SQL with respect to the ease of their use for formulating the above queries.

13.10 If you have a copy of MS Access or of a similar DBMS, design the above queries using the visual languages that come with them.

* 13.11 Write the query of Exercise 5.20 using TRC and DRC.

* 13.12 Write the query of Exercise 5.22 using TRC and DRC.

** 13.13 Consider the relation schema of Exercise 5.24. Write the following queries using TRC and DRC.

a. Find all customers who are interested in every house listed with Agent "007".
b. Using the previous query as a view, retrieve a set of tuples of the form $\langle$*feature*, *customer*$\rangle$ where each tuple in the result shows a feature and a customer who wants it such that

- Only the customers who are interested in every house listed with Agent "007" are considered; and
- The number of customers interested in "feature" is greater than 2. (If this number is 2 or less, the corresponding tuple ⟨*feature*, *customer*⟩ is not added to the result.)

This part of the query cannot be *conveniently* expressed by TRC or DRC because they lack the counting operator. However it is possible nevertheless (and is not hard).

13.14 Write SQL query (5.10), page 150, and query (5.11), page 151, using TRC and DRC.

13.15 Investigate the logical relationship between the SQL operator EXISTS and the TRC quantifier ∃. For concreteness, express query (5.26), page 160, using TRC.

13.16 Consider the following relational schema:

```
SUPPLIER(Name,Part)
PROJECT(Name,Part)
```

A tuple, ⟨n,p⟩, in the first relation means that supplier n has part p. A tuple ⟨n,p⟩ in the second relation means that the project named n uses part p. Write the following query in tuple and domain relational calculi: *Find the names of suppliers who have a part, that is used by every project*.

*** 13.17** Show that the iterative process of computing the transitive closure of PREREQ terminates after a finite number of steps. Show that this process can compute the transitive closure in polynomial time.

13.18 Show that in SQL-92 the use of negation in every query is stratified.

13.19 Consider a relation DIRECTFLIGHT(StartCity, DestinationCity) that lists all direct flights among cities. Use the recursion facility of SQL:1999 to write a query that finds all pairs ⟨$city_1$, $city_2$⟩ such that there is an *indirect* flight from $city_1$ to $city_2$ with at least two stops in between.

13.20 Use the recursion facility of SQL:1999 to express a so-called "same generation" query: *Given a* PARENT *relation, find all pairs of people who have the same ancestor and are removed from her by equal number of generations*. (For example, a child is removed from her parent by one generation and from grandparent by two.)

*** 13.21** Consider the following bill of materials problem: the database has a relation SUBPART(Part, Subpart, Quantity), which tells which direct subparts are needed for each part and in what quantity. For instance, SUBPART(mounting_assembly, screw, 4) means that the mounting assembly includes four screws. For simplicity, let us assume that parts that do not have subparts (the *atomic* parts) are represented as having NULL as the only subpart (for instance, SUBPART(screw, NULL,0)). Write a recursive query to produce a list of all parts and for each part the number of primitive subparts it has.

13.22 Consider the following relational schema:

```
DIRECTFLIGHT(From,To,Distance)
```

Write a recursive SQL query that returns tuples of the form ⟨`From,To,Distance`⟩, which represent direct or indirect flights (i.e., flights composed of one or more segments) and the aggregate distance over all segments for each such flight. (If there are several ways to reach `B` from `A` and the total distance is different in each case, then the output would have several tuples such as ⟨`A,B,1000`⟩, ⟨`A,B,1500`⟩, etc.) The exact query is: *Find all tuples of the above form provided that the distance is less than 10,000*.

13.23 Using Datalog, write the query that finds all students who took some course from Professor Joe Public.

13.24 Use Datalog to find all students who took all classes ever offered by Professor Joe Public.

13.25 Show how to express the relational operators of projection, selection, Cartesian product, natural join, union, and set-difference using Datalog.

13.26 Express the query of Exercise 13.19 in Datalog.

13.27 Use Datalog to express the query of Exercise 13.21.

13.28 Using Datalog, express the “bill of materials” query described in Exercise 13.21.

13.29 Express the query of Exercise 13.22 in Datalog.

14

Object Databases

In this chapter, we introduce the concept of a *database object* and define *object databases*. First we discuss the limitations of the relational data model that motivate the need for a richer data model. Unlike relational databases, object databases have a number of standards, which makes the relationships among the different technologies difficult to understand. To navigate the field, we start by introducing a conceptual data model for object databases without reference to any particular standard or language. Then we present the two main standards in the field: ODMG and the object-relational extensions of SQL, SQL:1999, and SQL:2003, explaining their features in terms of the conceptual object model. In the last part of the chapter, we introduce CORBA—a standard promoted by the Object Management Group to facilitate the development of distributed client/server applications. Although CORBA is not a database standard per se, it can be used as a framework for developing distributed object data services, which makes it relevant to this chapter.

Issues that are closely related to object databases include the XML data model and XML query languages. Of particular interest are XML Schema, XQuery, and SQL/XML. We discuss these subjects at length in Chapter 15.

14.1 Limitations of the Relational Data Model

Relational DBMSs swept the database market in the 1980s because of the simplicity of their underlying relational model and because tables turned out to be just the right representation for much of the data used in business applications. Encouraged by this success, attempts were made to use relational databases in other application domains for which the relational model was not specifically designed—for example, computer-aided design (CAD) and geographical data. It soon became obvious that relational databases are not appropriate for such "nontraditional" applications. Even in their core application area, relational databases have certain limitations. In this section, we use a series of simple examples to illustrate some of the problems with the relational data model.

Set-valued attributes. Consider the following relational schema that describes people by their Social Security number, name, phone numbers, and children:

```
PERSON (SSN: String, Name: String, PhoneN: String, Child: String)
```

We assume that a person can have several phone numbers and several children, and that Child is a foreign key to the relation PERSON. Thus, the key of this schema consists of the attributes SSN, PhoneN, and Child. Here is one possible relation instance of this schema:[1]

SSN	Name	PhoneN	Child
111-22-3333	Joe Public	516-123-4567	222-33-4444
111-22-3333	Joe Public	516-345-6789	222-33-4444
111-22-3333	Joe Public	516-123-4567	333-44-5555
111-22-3333	Joe Public	516-345-6789	333-44-5555
222-33-4444	Bob Public	212-987-6543	444-55-6666
222-33-4444	Bob Public	212-987-1111	555-66-7777
222-33-4444	Bob Public	212-987-6543	555-66-7777
222-33-4444	Bob Public	212-987-1111	444-55-6666

This schema is *not* in the third normal form because of the functional dependency

$$\text{SSN} \rightarrow \text{Name}$$

since SSN is not a key and Name is not one of the attributes in a key. Furthermore, it is easy to verify that if we first decompose this relation into its projections onto SSN,Name,PhoneN and SSN,Name,Child and then join the projections, we get the original relation back. Thus, according to Section 6.9, this relation satisfies the following join dependency:

$$\text{PERSON} = (\text{SSN Name PhoneN}) \bowtie (\text{SSN Name Child})$$

In Section 6.9, we argued that relations that satisfy nontrivial join dependencies might contain a great deal of redundant information (in fact, much more than the amount of redundancy caused by the FDs). Since information redundancy is a cause of update anomalies, the relational design theory suggests that we should decompose the original relation into the following three:

PERSON	SSN	Name
	111-22-3333	Joe Public
	222-33-4444	Bob Public

[1] For brevity, we omit some tuples needed to satisfy the foreign-key constraint.

PHONE	SSN	PhoneN
	111-22-3333	516-345-6789
	111-22-3333	516-123-4567
	222-33-4444	212-987-6543
	222-33-4444	212-135-7924

CHILDOF	SSN	Child
	111-22-3333	222-33-4444
	111-22-3333	333-44-5555
	222-33-4444	444-55-6666
	222-33-4444	555-66-7777

While this decomposition certainly removes update anomalies, there are still difficulties. Consider the query *Get the phone numbers of all of Joe's grandchildren.* The SQL statement

```
SELECT  G.PhoneN
FROM    PERSON P, PERSON C, PERSON G
WHERE   P.Name = 'Joe Public' AND                         14.1
        P.Child = C.SSN AND
        C.Child = G.SSN
```

performs the query for the original schema, while the statement

```
SELECT  N.PhoneN
FROM    CHILDOF C, CHILDOF G,
        PERSON P, PHONE N
WHERE   P.Name = 'Joe Public' AND                         14.2
        P.SSN = C.SSN AND
        C.Child = G.SSN AND
        G.SSN = N.SSN
```

does the same for the decomposed schema. Both of these SQL expressions seem rather cumbersome implementations of the simple query we just stated in English.

One problem is that the redundancy in the original schema for PERSON is solely due to the inability of the relational data model to handle set-valued attributes in a natural way. A much more appropriate schema for the original table would be

```
PERSON(SSN: String, Name: String,
       PhoneN: {String}, Child: {String})
```

where the braces {} represent set-valued attributes. For instance, Child: {String} says that the value of the attribute Child in a tuple is a *set* of elements of type String. The rows in such a table might look as follows (note the set-valued components):

```
(111-22-3333, Joe Public,
    {516-123-4567, 516-345-6789}, {222-33-4444, 333-44-5555})
(222-33-4444, Bob Public,
    {212-987-1111, 212-987-6543}, {444-55-6666, 555-66-7777})
```

The second problem with the example above is the awkwardness with which SQL handles queries (14.1) and (14.2).

Suppose that the type of the attribute Child were {PERSON} rather than {String} and that SQL could treat the value of the Child attribute as a set of PERSON tuples (rather than just a set of strings that represent SSNs). It would then be possible to formulate the query much more concisely and naturally because the expression P.Child.Child can be given precise meaning: the set of all tuples corresponding to the children of the children of P. This would allow us to write the above query in the following elegant way:

```
SELECT  P.Child.Child.PhoneN
FROM    PERSON P                                    14.3
WHERE   P.Name = 'Joe Public'
```

Expressions of the form P.Child.Child.PhoneN are called **path expressions**.

IsA hierarchies. Suppose that some but not all people in our database are students. Since a student is a person, we can represent this fact by drawing arrows in the corresponding E-R or UML diagrams. Since the relational model does not support the concept of IsA hierarchies, we would simulate it by factoring out the general information pertinent to all persons and have the schema for STUDENT contain only the information specific to students (see Section 4.5.3 for a discussion of the representation techniques for IsA):

```
STUDENT(SSN: String, Major: String)
```

Then we reason that since a STUDENT is also a PERSON, every student has a Name attribute. Consider the query *Get the names of all computer science majors*, which we can *try* to write in SQL as follows:

```
SELECT  S.Name
FROM    STUDENT S
WHERE   S.Major = 'CS'
```

Unfortunately, SQL-92 would reject the above query because the attribute `Name` is not explicitly included in the schema of STUDENT. However, if the system *knew* about the ISA relationship between students and persons, it could infer that STUDENT inherits `Name` from PERSON.

Although ISA hierarchies exist in the E-R and UML models, these models do not come with their own query languages. We are thus compelled to use the relational model and standard SQL, which forces us to write the following, more complex query:

```
SELECT   P.Name
FROM     PERSON P, STUDENT S
WHERE    P.SSN = S.SSN AND S.Major = 'CS'
```

In essence, this query simulates the effects of inheritance, and this complication arises in SQL-92 each time the ISA relationship is invoked.

Blobs. The term "blob" means **binary large object**. Virtually all relational DBMSs allow relations to have attributes of type `blob`. For example, a database of movies can have this schema:

```
MOVIE (Name: String, Director: PERSON, Video: blob)        14.4
```

The attribute `Video` might hold a video stream, which can contain gigabytes of data. From the relational point of view, a video stream is a large, unstructured sequence of bits.

Although blobs can be useful for storing large data items, this method is less than elegant when the DBMS needs to be able to look inside the data item and understand its internal structure. Consider the query

```
SELECT   M.Director
FROM     MOVIE M
WHERE    M.Name = 'The Simpsons'
```

Some systems might drag the entire tuple containing the blob from disk into main memory to evaluate the WHERE clause. This is a huge overhead. Even when a DBMS is optimized to handle blobs, its options are limited. Suppose that we need only the frames in the range 20,000 to 50,000. We cannot obtain this information if we stay within the traditional relational model. To handle such a query, we need a special routine, `frameRange(from, to)`, perhaps implemented as a stored procedure, which, for a given video blob, returns frames in the specified range.

Would it make sense to add `frameRange()` as an operator to the relational data model? While this addition would enable anyone to play with video blobs, it would not help with blobs that store DNA sequences or VLSI chip designs. Thus, rather than burdening the data model with all kinds of specialized operations, a general mechanism is needed to let users define such operations separately for each type of blob.

Impedance mismatch in database languages. Since it is impossible to write complete applications entirely in SQL, database applications are typically written in a host language, such as C or Java, and they access databases by executing SQL queries embedded in a host program. Chapter 8 discussed a number of mechanisms for accessing databases from host languages.

One problem with this approach is that SQL is set oriented, meaning that its queries return sets of tuples. In contrast, host languages do not understand relations and do not support high-level operations on them. Apart from this mismatch of types, there is a sharp difference between the declarative nature of SQL (which specifies *what* has to be done) and the procedural nature of host languages (in which the programmer must specify *how* things are to be done). This phenomenon has been dubbed the **impedance mismatch** between the data access language and the host language; the cursor mechanism (Section 8.2.4) was invented to serve as an adaptor between procedural host languages and SQL.

The impedance mismatch was one of the important reasons that drove the development of object databases in the early days. The basic idea is simple and elegant: take a typical object-oriented language (C++ and Smalltalk were the primary candidates in those days; Java was added in the 1990s), and use *it* as a data manipulation language. Since objects underly both object languages and object databases, no impedance mismatch occurs.

This vision seemed attractive at the time, but there are a number of difficulties. First, there was still a need for a powerful, declarative query language, such as SQL, to support complex data querying. Since C++ or Java could not be easily extended to a declarative query language, the impedance mismatch remained.[2]

Another difficulty was that, instead of just one data manipulation language, SQL (even if mismatched to the host language), we now had as many data manipulation languages as there were host languages. This was not bad in itself since none of these host languages was new and most programmers were presumably familiar with them. The problem was that the different object languages had somewhat different object models. Thus, if certain objects were created using an application in one host language, accessing them using applications written in other host languages could be problematic.

The two main object database standards discussed in this chapter, SQL (1999 and 2003) and ODMG 3.0, offer very different views of the significance of impedance mismatch. Partly because of the above difficulties and partly because of a different design philosophy, SQL does not address the problem of the impedance mismatch. In contrast, ODMG sees elimination of this mismatch as a major (even if still somewhat elusive) goal.

[2] In this context, we should mention the ongoing work on the **Java Data Objects Specification**, which is aiming at (among other things) the development of a query language that better blends into the Java syntax.

14.2 Object Databases versus Relational Databases

The limitations of SQL, which we just discussed, led to the idea of databases that can store and retrieve objects. An object consists of a set of attributes and a set of methods that can access those attributes, together with an associated inheritance hierarchy.

Attribute values can be instances of complex data types or other objects. For example, the attributes of a person object might include a complex data type representing the person's address and an object representing her spouse.

Since the value of an attribute can be an instance of an object, the operations defined for the object can be used in queries. Thus, a video object might have a method, `frameRange()`, which can be used as follows:

```
SELECT  M.frameRange(20000,50000)
FROM    MOVIE M
WHERE   M.Name = 'The Simpsons'
```

We can begin to see the broad outlines of the object model and how it relates to the relational model.

- A relational database consists of relations, which are sets of tuples, while an object database consists of classes, which are sets of objects. Thus, a relational database might contain a relation, called PERSON, with tuples containing information about each person, whereas an object database might contain a class, called PERSON, with objects containing information about each person. A particular relational database can be implemented within the object model by defining a class for each relation. The attributes of a particular class are the attributes of the corresponding relation, and each object instantiated from the class corresponds to a tuple.
- In a relational database, the components of a tuple must be primitive types (strings, integers, etc.); in an object database, the components of an object can, in addition, be complex types (sets, tuples, objects, etc.).
- Object databases have certain properties for which there is no analogy in relational databases:
  - Objects can be organized into an inheritance hierarchy, which allows objects of a lower type to inherit the attributes and methods from objects of a higher type. This helps reduce clutter in type specifications and leads to more concise queries.
  - Objects can have methods, which can be invoked from within queries. For instance, the specification of the class MOVIE mentioned earlier might contain a method, `frameRange`, with a declaration of the form

```
list(VIDEOFRAME)   frameRange(Integer,Integer);
```

which states that `frameRange` takes two integer arguments and returns a list of video frames. Such declarations are made using a special object definition language, which is similar to the data definition sublanguage of SQL.

- Method implementations are written in advance using a standard host language and stored on the server. In this respect, methods are similar to stored procedures in SQL databases (Section 8.2.5). However, stored procedures are not associated with any particular relation, while a stored method is an integral part of the respective class and is inherited along the object type hierarchy in a manner similar to that for methods in object-oriented programming languages.
- In some object database systems, the data manipulation language and the host language are the same.

Before concluding this section, we will outline two key ideas that motivated much of the work on object databases: *nested relations* and *persistent objects*.

Nested relations. The **nested relational model** [Makinouchi 1977; Arisawa et al. 1983; Roth and Korth 1987; Jaeschke and Schek 1982; Ozsoyoglu and Yuan 1985] was an early approach to dealing with some of the limitations of the relational data model mentioned in Section 14.1. In a nested relation, attributes can be of type `relation`. For instance, in the following table

SSN	Name	PhoneN	Child	
111-22-3333	Joe Public	516-345-6789	222-33-4444	Bob Public
		516-123-4567	333-44-5555	Sally Public
222-33-4444	Bob Public	212-987-6543	444-55-6666	Maggie Public
		212-987-1111	555-66-7777	Mary Public

each tuple has four components. The first two are atomic values, as in the traditional relational model. However, the values of the third and fourth attributes are not atomic: they are unary and binary relations, respectively, a clear violation of the requirements for the first normal form. Hence, this model is also known as the **non-1NF** data model. The unary relation in the third component of the first tuple represents the list of phone numbers of Joe Public, while the fourth component in this tuple is a relation that describes Joe's children (via the Social Security number and name).

Experience has shown that the nested relational model is too limited, and its query languages and schema design theory are too complex.

Persistent objects. The ideas underlying persistent objects come from programming languages and trace back to the late 1960s. The early object database systems were, conceptually, nothing more than persistent C++ or Smalltalk [Copeland and Maier 1984]. The basic idea is simple and elegant.

1. The user declares certain C++ or Smalltalk objects as **persistent**.
2. When an application program refers to a persistent object, the system checks if the object is in a main memory buffer. If not, an **object fault** occurs and the system brings the object into main memory transparently to the user program.
3. When the program completes, if any persistent object was changed in main memory, the system ensures that the new version of that object is returned to the mass storage—again transparently to the user.

Programming languages that support persistent objects eliminate the mismatch between database types and the data types of the host language. However, they do not provide a mechanism for high-level declarative querying similar to the SELECT statement in SQL. As a result, all queries must be programmed procedurally using the constructs available in the host language. We will see, in Section 14.5.5, that the ODMG standard trades some degree of impedance mismatch for the luxury of declarative query language support.

14.3 The Conceptual Object Data Model

Let us begin with understanding the basic concepts first and, following the example of relational databases, develop a conceptual data model suitable for object databases. This model, called the **Conceptual Object Data Model** (or CODM), is derived from the work of the research team behind O_2 [Bancilhon et al. 1990], an object DBMS that has had significant influence on the ODMG standard. In fact, CODM is close to ODMG. However, it is not burdened with some of the nitty-gritty details and low-level implementation concerns motivated by the need for compatibility with existing products. In addition, the object-relational extensions of SQL can be conveniently explained in terms of CODM, which makes the relationship between the two standards easier to understand.

In CODM, every object has a unique and immutable identity, called the **object Id** (**oid**), which is independent of the actual value of the object. The oid is assigned by the system when the object is created and does not change during the object's lifetime. Note the distinction between oids and the primary keys of relations. Like an oid, a primary key uniquely identifies the object. However, unlike an oid, the value of a primary key might change (a person might change her Social Security number). In addition, oids are normally hidden, while primary keys are visible and can be explicitly used in queries.

14.3.1 Objects and Values

An object that describes a person, Joe Public, might look as follows:

```
(#32, [  SSN: 111-22-3333,
         Name: Joe Public,
         PhoneN: {"516-123-4567", "516-345-6789"},
         Child: {#445, #73}] )
```

14.5

The symbol #32 is the oid of the data object that describes a real-world Joe Public. The rest specifies the *value* part of the object. The oid identifies this object among other objects, and the value provides the actual information about Joe. Observe that the value of the Child attribute is a set of oids that (presumably) describe Joe's children.

Formally, an **object** is a pair of the form (*oid*, *val*), where *oid* is an object Id and *val* is a value. The **value** part, *val*, can take one of the following forms:

- *Primitive value.* A member of an Integer, String, Float, or Boolean data type; example: "516-123-4567"

  Primitive values are not new to CODM—they also exist in the relational model.
- *Reference value.* An oid of an object; example: #445

  Reference values do not exist in the relational model since it does not have a representation for complex objects.
- *Tuple value.* Of the form $[A_1 : v_1, \ldots, A_n : v_n]$, where the $A_1, \ldots, A_n$ are distinct attribute names and the $v_1, \ldots, v_n$ are values; example: the entire value part (inside the brackets) of object #32 in (14.5). Note that each v_i is a value that takes one of the four forms introduced in this definition: a primitive value, a reference value, a tuple value, or a set value.

  Tuple values exist in the relational model also. However, they can occur only at the top level, as rows of relations. In CODM, tuple values can appear at any level. For instance, they can occur as components of top-level rows.
- *Set value.* Of the form $\{v_1, \ldots, v_n\}$, where the $v_1, \ldots, v_n$ are values; examples: {"516-123-4567", "516-345-6789"} or {#445,#73}. Each v_i here can have one of the four forms mentioned in this definition.

  Set values do not exist in the relational model except in the sense that relations are sets.

Thus, in addition to the objects of the form (14.5), other (perhaps less obvious) examples of objects are (#38, "Joe Average")—because "Joe Average" is a primitive value, (#77, #534)—because #534 is a reference value, and (#47, {#987,#34})—because {#987,#34} is a set value.

Reference, tuple, and set values are called **complex values** to distinguish them from primitive values. The actual ODMG data model includes additional complex value types, such as bags (sets that can have multiple copies of the same element), lists, structures, enumerated types, and arrays. However, we do not consider these here because they add nothing new to the overall conceptual picture.

Note that the oid part of an object cannot change (if it did, it would indicate a different object). In contrast, the value part of an object can be replaced by another value as a result of an update. For example, if one of Joe Public's phone numbers should change, the value of the PhoneN attribute is replaced by a new value, but the object retains the same oid and is considered to be the same object.

> The oid of an object cannot change, but the value can.

14.3.2 Classes

In object-oriented systems, semantically similar objects are organized into **classes**. For instance, all objects representing persons are grouped into class PERSON.

Classes play the same role in CODM that relations play in relational databases. Whereas in SQL-92 a database is a set of relations and each relation is a set of tuples, in CODM a database is a set of classes and each class is a set of objects. Thus, in SQL-92 we might have a relation called PERSON with tuples containing information about each person, and in CODM we might have a class called PERSON with objects containing information about each person. Note that we can always convert a relational database into an object database by attaching a unique oid to each tuple.

Classes help organize objects into categories. A class has a **type**, which describes the common structure of all objects in the class (e.g., all objects in a class might be sets of tuples), and **method signatures**, which are declarations of the operations that can be applied to the class objects. We discuss these notions in more detail below. Only method signatures are part of CODM—method implementations are *not*. A method implementation is a procedure, written in a host language, that is stored on the database server. An ODBMS must provide a mechanism to invoke the appropriate implementation whenever the method is used in the program.

In the relational data model, two tables can be related to each other by means of an interrelational constraint (e.g., a foreign-key constraint). In the object data model, one additional relationship—the *IsA relationship*—enjoys a special status. Suppose that, in addition to the PERSON class, which groups together all objects representing persons, we have a STUDENT class, which groups together all objects representing students. Naturally, every student is a person, so the set of objects that constitute class STUDENT must be a subset of the set of objects that constitute class PERSON. This is an example of the **subclass relationship**, in which STUDENT is a subclass of PERSON. The subclass relationship is also called the **IsA relationship**.

The set of all objects assigned to a class is called the **extent** of the class. To adequately reflect our intuition about the subclass relationship, extents must satisfy the following property:

If C_1 is a subclass of C_2, the extent of C_2 contains the extent of C_1.

For example, since STUDENT is a subclass of PERSON, the set of all students is a subset of the set of all persons.

The query language and the data manipulation languages are aware of the subclass relationship. For example, if a query is supposed to return all PERSON objects that have a certain property and if some STUDENT object has that property, the query will return the STUDENT object in the query result since every student is also a person.

To summarize, a class has a type (which describes the structure of all the objects in the class), method signatures (which are often considered part of the type), and an extent (which lists all objects that belong to the class). Thus

> Class, type, and extent are related but distinct notions.

14.3.3 Types

An important requirement of any data model is that the data must be properly structured. Because of the simplicity of the structure of tuples in the relational model, typing is not a big issue in relational databases. It is more complex in object databases. Consider, for example, the object in (14.5). We can say that its type is represented by the following expression:

```
[SSN: String, Name: String, PhoneN: {String}, Child: {PERSON}]
```
14.6

This type definition states that the attributes `SSN` and `Name` draw their values from the primitive domain `String`; the attribute `PhoneN` must have values that are sets of strings; and the values of the attribute `Child` are sets of objects that belong to class PERSON.

Intuitively, the type of an object is just the collection of the types of its components. More precisely, complex types suitable for structuring objects can be defined as follows:

- *Basic types*. `String`, `Float`, `Integer`, and so forth
- *Reference types*. User-defined class names, such as PERSON and STUDENT
- *Tuple types*. Expressions of the form $[A_1 : T_1, \ldots, A_n : T_n]$, where each A_i is a distinct attribute name and T_i is a type. The type given in (14.6) is an example of a tuple type.
- *Set types*. Expressions of the form $\{T\}$, where T is a type. For example, {`String`} is a set type.

Note that (14.6) describes a type in which complex structures are nested within other structures. For instance, the values of `PhoneN` are sets of primitive values, while the values of `Child` are sets of objects drawn from the class PERSON.

What does it mean for an object to conform to a type? Given the recursive structure of objects and the presence of the ISA hierarchy, the answer to this question is not straightforward. We develop this concept in the following paragraphs.

Subtyping. In addition to grouping objects structurally, the type system can tell which types have "more structure" than others. For instance, suppose the type of the objects in class PERSON is PERSONTYPE and is defined as follows:

```
[SSN: String, Name: String,
    Address: [StNumber: Integer, StName: String]]
```

This is a tuple type in which the first two components have a basic type and the third has a tuple type.

Consider now the objects that populate the class STUDENT. Clearly, students have names, addresses, and everything else that PERSON objects have. However, students have additional attributes, so an appropriate type might be

```
[SSN: String, Name: String,
 Address: [StNumber: Integer, StName: String],
 Majors: {String}, Enrolled: {COURSE}]
```

Intuition suggests that this type—let us call it STUDENTTYPE—has more structure than the type PERSONTYPE because

1. it has all the attributes of PERSONTYPE,
2. the values of these attributes have at least as much structure as the corresponding attributes in PERSONTYPE, and
3. STUDENTTYPE has attributes not present in PERSONTYPE.

This intuition leads to the notions of **subtype** and **supertype**—Type T is a *subtype* of (supertype) T' if $T \neq T'$, and one of the following conditions holds:

- T and T' are reference types, and T is a subclass of T'.
- $T = [A_1 : T_1, \ldots, A_n : T_n, A_{n+1} : T_{n+1}, \ldots, A_m : T_m]$ and $T' = [A_1 : T'_1, \ldots, A_n : T'_n]$ are tuple types (note that T includes all attributes of T', that is, $m \geq n$), and either $T_i = T'_i$ or T_i is a subtype of T'_i, for each $i = 1, \ldots, n$.
- $T = \{T_0\}$ and $T' = \{T'_0\}$ are set types, and T_0 is a subtype of T'_0.

According to this definition, STUDENTTYPE is a subtype of PERSONTYPE because it contains all of the structure of PERSONTYPE and has additional attributes of its own. Note, however, that having additional attributes is not necessary for a type to be a subtype. For instance,

```
[SSN: String, Name: String,
 Address: [StNumber: Integer, StName: String, POBox: String]      14.7
]
```

is still a subtype of PERSONTYPE even though (14.7) has no attributes that are not found also in PERSONTYPE. Instead, the attribute `Address` in (14.7) has more structure than the same attribute in PERSONTYPE.

Domain of a type. The **domain** of a type is a set of all values that conform to that type. Intuitively the domain of a type, T, denoted *domain*(T), is the appropriate combination of the domains of the components of T. More precisely,

- The domain of a basic type, such as `Integer` or `String`, is just what we would expect—the set of all integers or strings, respectively.
- The domain of a reference type, T, is the extent of T, that is, the set of all Ids of objects in class T. For instance, if T is PERSONTYPE, the domain is the set of all oids of objects in class PERSON.

- The domain of a tuple type, $[A_1 : T_1, \ldots, A_n : T_n]$, is

$$\{[A_1 : w_1, \ldots, A_n : w_n] \mid w_i \in \mathit{domain}(T_i)\}$$

  that is, the set of all tuple values whose components conform to the corresponding types of attributes. For instance, the domain of type shown in (14.6) is the set of all values of the form (14.5).
- The domain of a set type, $\{T\}$, is

$$\{\{w_1, \ldots, w_k\} \mid w_i \in \mathit{domain}(T)\}$$

  That is, it consists of *finite* sets of values that conform to the given type T. For instance, the domain of type {COURSE} is the set whose members are finite sets of oids for COURSE objects.

> *Brain Teaser:* Is it useful to allow infinite sets as elements of the domain for a set type?

It is easy to see that domains are defined in such a way that the domain of a subtype, S, is (in a sense) a subset of the domain of a supertype, S'. More precisely, for any given object, o, in S, either o is already in S' or we can use o to obtain another object, o', in S', by throwing out some components of o or of sub-objects included in o. For instance, an object of type PERSONTYPE can be obtained from an object of type STUDENTTYPE by throwing out the components corresponding to the `Majors` and `Enrolled` attributes. Similarly, a PERSON object can be obtained from an object of type (14.7) by throwing out the `POBox` component from the nested address.

> *Brain Teaser:* What is the domain of the tuple type `[ ]`, which has no attributes?

Database schema and instance. In object databases, the **schema** contains the specification for each class of objects that can be stored in the database. For each class, C, it includes

- The *type* associated with C. This type determines the structure of each object of C.
- The *method signatures* of C. A **method signature** specifies the method name, the type and order for the allowed method arguments, and the type of the result produced by the method. For instance, the method `enroll()` in class COURSE might have the following signature:

```
Boolean enroll (STUDENT);
```

  and the method `enrolled()` in class STUDENT might have the signature

```
{COURSE} enrolled ();
```

The signature of `enroll()` says that in order to enroll a student in a course, one must invoke the method `enroll()` on the COURSE-object and supply the STUDENT-object as a parameter. The method returns a Boolean value that indicates the outcome of the operation. The signature of `enrolled()` says that, to check the enrollment of a student, one can invoke the method `enrolled()` in the context of the STUDENT-object corresponding to that student, and the result will be a set of COURSE-objects corresponding to courses in which the student is enrolled.

- The *subclass-of* relationship, which identifies the superclasses of *C*
- The *integrity constraints*, such as key constraints, referential constraints, or more general assertions, which are similar to constraints in relational databases

An **instance** of the database is a set of objects for the classes specified in the schema. The objects must satisfy all of the constraints implied by the schema, which includes type constraints. Thus, the value of each object must belong to the domain of the type associated with the object's class. Each object must also have a unique oid.

> *Brain Teaser:* What domains must an object belong to if it is a member of several classes?

This completes the definition of the conceptual object model. As you can see, most of the notions used in CODM are extensions of familiar concepts from the relational model, but they require considerably more care because of the richness of the underlying data model.

14.3.4 Object-Relational Databases

This breed of DBMS arrived in the early 1990s when a number of vendors began advocating object-relational DBMS (instead of full-blown object databases) as a safer migration path from relational DBMS. The main selling point was that such databases could be implemented as conservative extensions to the existing relational DBMSs. After long deliberation, the SQL:1999 working group finally adopted a subset of the object-relational data model. SQL:2003 gave support for the full object-relational submodel of CODM.

An **object-relational database** consists of a set of top-level classes, which are populated by *tuple objects.* A **tuple object** is of the form (*oid*, *val*), where *oid* is an object Id and *val* is a tuple value whose components can be *arbitrary* values (i.e., primitive values, sets, tuples, and references to other objects).

Since the top-level structure of the top-level classes is a tuple, these classes are called *relations,* which explains the term "object-relational."

The main difference between the object-relational and CODM models is that in the former, the top-level structure of each object instance is always a tuple while in the latter, the top-level structure can be an arbitrary value. However, this restriction on object-relational DBMSs does not significantly decrease the ability to model real-world enterprises.

What differentiates object-relational and traditional relational models is that the tuple components must be primitive values in the relational model whereas they can be arbitrary values in the object-relational model. Thus, the relational model can be viewed as a subset of the object-relational model (and hence of CODM).

We discuss the object-relational model underlying SQL:1999/2003 in the next section.

14.4 Objects in SQL:1999 and SQL:2003

Object-oriented extensions in SQL have gone through many revisions. The final result is a reasonably clean version of the object-relational model. It was a difficult standardization process, given the requirement to preserve backward compatibility with SQL-92—a language *not* designed with objects in mind.

The goals of this backward compatibility were that SQL:1999/2003 could be used in any of the following ways:

- To work with standard SQL-92 relations
- To work with relations that are similar to those in SQL-92 except that attributes can have values of complex user-defined types (such as sets or tuples)

In this section, we survey the new object-relational extensions of SQL:1999 and 2003. SQL:1999 is described in [Gulutzan and Pelzer 1999]. SQL:2003 is available through the standards organizations, such as ISO (*http://www.iso.org/*).

An SQL:1999/2003 database consists of a set of relations. Each relation is either a set of tuples or a set of objects. An **SQL object** is a pair of the form (o, v), where o is an oid and v is an SQL tuple value. An SQL **tuple value** has the form $[A_1 : v_1, \ldots, A_n : v_n]$, where $A_1, \ldots, A_n$ are distinct attribute names and each v_i takes one of the following values (using the terms introduced in Section 14.3.1):

- *Primitive value.* Constants of the usual SQL primitive types, such as CHAR(18), INTEGER, DECIMAL, and BOOLEAN
- *Reference value.* Object Ids
- *Tuple value.* Of the form $[A_1 : v_1, \ldots, A_n : v_n]$, where each A_i is a distinct attribute name and each v_i is a value
- *A multiset value.* Created using the MULTISET construct. It is the only major object-oriented addition introduced by SQL:2003. (SQL:1999 also provides the ARRAY construct, but it is only of marginal interest to us and will not be discussed in this book.)

As expected of an object-relational data model, the top-level value of every object in SQL:1999/2003 is a tuple. Tuples and sets can be nested, however.

14.4.1 Row Types

The simplest way to construct a tuple type is with the ROW **type constructor.** For instance, we can define the relation PERSON as follows:

```
CREATE TABLE PERSON (
    Name CHAR(20),
    Address ROW(Number INTEGER, Street CHAR(20), ZIP CHAR(5)) )
```

We reference the components of a row type using the usual mechanism of path expressions.

```
SELECT P.Name
FROM PERSON P
WHERE P.Address.ZIP = '11794'
```

A table with row types can be populated with the help of the ROW **value constructor** as follows:

```
INSERT INTO PERSON(Name, Address)
VALUES ('John Doe', ROW(666, 'Hollow Rd.', '66666'))
```

Updating tables that have attributes of type ROW is also straightforward.

```
UPDATE PERSON
SET Address.ZIP = '12345'
WHERE Address.ZIP = '66666'
```

When John Doe moves, we can change the entire address as follows:

```
UPDATE PERSON
SET Address = ROW(21, 'Main St.', '12345')
WHERE Address = ROW(666, 'Hollow Rd.', '66666')
        AND Name = 'John Doe'
```

14.4.2 User-Defined Types

Recall from Section 14.3.3 that a type (in CODM) is a set of rules for structuring data. The set of objects that conform to these rules is the type's domain. A class consists of a schema (which includes the type and method signatures) and an extent—a subset of the domain of the type. When we add method bodies to the signatures associated with a type, we get an **abstract data type.** In SQL:1999/2003, abstract data types are called **user-defined types** (or UDT). The following are examples of UDT definitions:

```
CREATE TYPE PersonType AS (
    Name CHAR(20),
    Address ROW(Number INTEGER, Street CHAR(20), ZIP CHAR(5)) );
CREATE TYPE StudentType UNDER PersonType AS (
    Id INTEGER,
    Status CHAR(2) )
METHOD award_degree() RETURNS BOOLEAN;
CREATE METHOD award_degree() FOR StudentType
LANGUAGE C
EXTERNAL NAME 'file:/home/admin/award_degree';
```

The first CREATE TYPE statement is syntactically similar to the earlier definition of table PERSON, except that now we define a type rather than a table. This type does not have any explicitly defined methods, but we will soon see that the DBMS automatically creates a number of methods for us.

The second statement is more interesting. It defines STUDENTTYPE as a subtype of PERSONTYPE, which is indicated with the clause UNDER. As such, it inherits the attributes of PERSONTYPE. In addition, STUDENTTYPE is defined to have attributes of its own plus a method, `award_degree()`. The type definition includes only the signature of the method. The actual definition is done using the CREATE METHOD statement (which is associated with STUDENTTYPE through the FOR clause). The statement says that the method body is written in the C language (so that the DBMS knows how to link with this procedure) and tells where its executable can be found. If we specified LANGUAGE SQL instead, we could have defined the method code inside an attached BEGIN/END block using SQL/PSM, the language of stored procedures (see Chapter 8).

User-defined types can appear in two main contexts. First, they can be used to specify the domain of an attribute in a table, just like the primitive types of integers or character strings:

```
CREATE TABLE Transcript (
    Student StudentType, -- a previously defined UDT
    CrsCode CHAR(6),                                          14.8
    Semester CHAR(6),
    Grade CHAR(1) )
```

Here we are using the CREATE TABLE statement with the only difference that some attributes (`Student`) have complex types (STUDENTTYPE).

Second, a UDT can be used to specify the type of an entire table. This is done through a new kind of CREATE TABLE statement, which, instead of enumerating the columns of a table, simply provides a UDT. This means that all rows of the table must have the structure specified by the UDT. For instance, we can define the following table based on the previously defined UDT STUDENTTYPE:

```
CREATE TABLE STUDENT OF STUDENTTYPE;                                    14.9
```

Tables constructed via the CREATE TABLE ... OF statement, as in (14.9), are called **typed tables**. The rows of a typed table are considered to be **objects**. Thus the rows of the table in (14.9) are objects, while the values of the Student attribute in (14.8) are *not*—even though the same UDT is used in both cases. These two distinct uses of UDTs are discussed next.

14.4.3 Objects

The only way to create an object in SQL is to insert a row into a typed table. In other words, every row in such a table is treated as an object with its own oid. The table itself is then viewed as a class (as defined in CODM), and its set of rows corresponds to the extent of the class.

It is instructive to compare (14.9) with the following declaration:

```
CREATE TABLE STUDENT1 (
    Name CHAR(20),
    Address ROW(Number INTEGER, Street CHAR(20), ZIP CHAR(5)),
    Id INTEGER,
    Status CHAR(2) )
```

Note that STUDENT1 contains exactly the same attributes as STUDENT—both names and types. However, STUDENT is a typed table whereas STUDENT1 is not, which means that SQL considers the tuples of STUDENT—but not the tuples of STUDENT1—to be objects. This disparity (one may even say inconsistency) between the two ways of constructing tables is solely due to the need to stay backward-compatible with SQL-92. Note also the difference in the use of STUDENTTYPE in (14.8) and (14.9). Instances of STUDENTTYPE in (14.8) are *not* objects, while they *are* objects in (14.9).

The next question concerns how we refer to an object. To understand the issue, let us come back to the TRANSCRIPT table in (14.8) and consider the attribute Student. Since the same student is likely to have taken several courses, he has several tuples in TRANSCRIPT. The trouble is that the declaration

```
Student STUDENTTYPE
```

means that the value of this attribute in a row of TRANSCRIPT is *not* a reference to a STUDENTTYPE object. Thus, information about every student (name, address, etc.) must be duplicated in each transcript record for that student. Clearly, this is the same redundancy we tried to eliminate in Chapter 6 using the relational normalization theory. SQL solves the problem by introducing the explicit **reference type**, denoted REF(STUDENTTYPE), which we will discuss further in Section 14.4.6. For now, we have to remember that the domain of a reference type is a set of oids. To reference an object in SQL, we need to obtain its oid, and so we have to look at the mechanism provided for this purpose.

The SQL:1999/2003 standard says that every typed table, such as (14.9), has a **self-referencing column**. For each tuple, this column holds the oids of that tuple (hence the name "self-referencing"). The oid is generated automatically when the tuple is created. However, to gain access to the oids stored in the self-referencing column, we have to give the column a name explicitly. The declaration of STUDENT-TYPE above does not name the self-referencing column, thus there is no way to refer to the oids of the objects in that table.

Here is a way to take care of the self-referencing column:

```
CREATE TABLE STUDENT2 OF STUDENTTYPE                    14.10
REF IS stud_oid;
```

The REF IS clause gives an explicit name, stud_oid, to the self-referencing column. (Note that this column also exists in (14.9) but is unnamed and hence cannot be referenced.) For most purposes, stud_oid is an attribute like any other. In particular, we can use it in queries (in both SELECT and WHERE clauses), but we cannot change its value because oids are assigned by the system and are immutable.

The distinction between objects and their references, as manifested by the reference types and self-referencing columns, is one of the muddier aspects of the object-relational extensions of SQL. This complication exists thanks to the undue influence of the C and C++ languages and also because the object extensions were tacked onto SQL as an afterthought. Note that such a distinction does not exist in Java, which is a true object-oriented language, or in the ODMG standard, which is discussed in Section 14.5.

14.4.4 Querying User-Defined Types

Querying UDTs does not present any new problems. We can simply use path expressions to descend into the objects and extract the needed information. For instance,

```
SELECT T.Student.Name, T.Grade
FROM TRANSCRIPT T                                       14.11
WHERE T.Student.Address.Street = 'Hollow Rd.'
```

queries the TRANSCRIPT relation and returns the names and grades of the students who live on Hollow Road. Note that T.Student returns complex values of type STUDENTTYPE, and inheritance from PERSONTYPE allows us to access the Name and Address attributes defined for it.

Note also that although STUDENT and STUDENT1 are defined differently, queries concerning students look identical in both cases. Thus,

```
SELECT S.Address.Street
FROM X S
WHERE S.Id = '111111111'
```

returns the street name of a student with Id 111111111 regardless of whether X is STUDENT or STUDENT1.

14.4.5 Updating User-Defined Types

Having discussed the data definition aspects of UDTs, we turn to the issue of populating relations based on these UDTs. We have already seen in Section 14.4.1 how to insert tuples into the PERSON table, which contains a ROW type. By analogy, we can use the same method to insert tuples into the tables STUDENT and STUDENT2, which contain UDTs. The fact that these relations contain objects (and the extra self-referencing attribute) does not matter because the oids are generated by the system. We have to worry about only the actual attributes. We might try a similar INSERT statement to populate the relation TRANSCRIPT:

```
INSERT INTO TRANSCRIPT(Student, Course, Semester, Grade)
VALUES (????, 'CS308', '2000', 'A')
```

But what should appear as the first component of the VALUES clause? There are two answers to this question. One will be discussed shortly and the other in Section 14.4.6.

Insertion is further complicated by the fact that a UDT is considered to be **encapsulated**, that is, its components can be accessed only through the methods provided by the type. Although we did not define any methods for STUDENTTYPE, the DBMS did it for us. Namely, for each attribute the system provides an **observer method** (which can be used to query the attribute value) and a **mutator method** (which is used to change that value). Both the observer and the mutator have the same name as the attribute. In the case of STUDENTTYPE, the system provides the following observer methods:

- `Id: ()` ⟶ INTEGER. This method returns an integer and, like all observers, it does not take any arguments.[3]
- `Name` and `Status`: These methods have the types () ⟶ CHAR(20) and () ⟶ CHAR(2), respectively.
- `Address: ()` ⟶ `ROW(INTEGER, CHAR(20), CHAR(5))`.

Looking back at query (14.11) we can now say that it uses the observer methods `Name` and `Address`. On the other hand, the `Grade` attribute of the table TRANSCRIPT used in that same query is not part of a UDT, so it does not use an observer method. However, the difference is conceptual and not syntactic—syntactically we reference `Grade` in the same way we do `Name`.

The mutator methods are called in the context of a STUDENTTYPE object and return this same object. For instance, the mutator for an attribute, say, `Id`, takes

[3] The notation () indicates that the method takes no arguments.

a value for Id and returns the original object with the changed value of the Id attribute.

- Id: INTEGER ⟶ STUDENTTYPE. This method takes an integer and replaces the value of Id of the object with that integer. In other words, this mutator method changes the student Id and returns the modified object.
- Name: CHAR(20) ⟶ STUDENTTYPE. This method takes a string and replaces the value of the Name attribute in the student object. It returns the updated student object. The mutator for Status is similar.
- Address: ROW(INTEGER, CHAR(20), CHAR(5)) ⟶ STUDENTTYPE. This method takes a row that represents an address and replaces the student address with it.

Brain Teaser: Why does a mutator, such as Id(), return the entire object rather than just the new value for the Id attribute?

Note that SQL does not have the public and private specifiers of C++ and Java to control access to methods. Instead, access is controlled through the EXECUTE privilege and the usual GRANT/REVOKE mechanism introduced in Section 3.3.12.

We are now ready for our first insertion into a UDT:

```
INSERT INTO TRANSCRIPT(Student, Course, Semester, Grade)
VALUES (NEW StudentType()
            .Id(666666666)
            .Status('G5')
            .Name('Vlad Dracula')
            .Address(ROW(666,'Transylvania Ave.','66666')),
        'HIS666',
        'F1462',
        'D')
```
14.12

Two things should be noted here. A blank student object in the first component of the inserted tuple is created by a call to StudentType()—a default constructor that the DBMS creates for every UDT. Then the mutator methods are invoked one by one on the newly created object to fill it in with data.[4]

If the student's address, name, and grade are to be changed, we can use the following update statement:

```
UPDATE TRANSCRIPT
SET Student = Student
                  .Address(ROW(21,'Main St.','12345'))
                  .Name('John Smith'),
```

[4] Note that the syntax above is just an indented and more readable form of NEW StudentType().Id(...).Status(...).Name(...).Address(...).

```
        Grade = 'A'
    WHERE Student.Id = 666666666
            AND CrsCode = 'HIS666' AND Semester = 'F1462'
```

To change the value of the student object, we use the mutator methods for STUDENTTYPE, which are generated for us by the DBMS. First, we apply the `Address()` mutator to change the address and then the `Name()` mutator. In contrast, since the type of the `Grade` attribute is primitive, the grade is changed by a direct assignment.

You have certainly noticed that inserting new tuples into relations that involve UDTs is rather cumbersome. However, the ability to associate methods with complex data types can simplify this to some extent. Namely, we can define a special constructor method that takes only scalar values. In this way, a complex object can be created in one call to the constructor.

We illustrate the idea using the language of SQL stored procedures. First, we need to add the following declaration to our earlier definition of STUDENTTYPE:

```
ALTER TYPE StudentType
ADD METHOD StudentConstr(name CHAR(20), id INTEGER,
                         streetNumber INTEGER,
                         streetName CHAR(20),
                         zip CHAR(5), status CHAR(2))
RETURNS STUDENTTYPE;
```

Then we define the body of the method as follows:

```
CREATE METHOD StudentConstr(name CHAR(20), id INTEGER,
                            streetNumber INTEGER,
                            streetName CHAR(20),
                            zip CHAR(5), status CHAR(2))
FOR STUDENTTYPE
RETURNS STUDENTTYPE
LANGUAGE SQL
    BEGIN
        RETURN NEW STUDENTTYPE()
                .Name(name)
                .Id(id)
                .Status(status)
                .Address(ROW(streetNumber,streetName,zip));
    END;
```

With this new constructor, the insertion of a new tuple into the TRANSCRIPT relation corresponding to (14.12) becomes less of a chore:

```
INSERT INTO TRANSCRIPT(Student, Course, Semester, Grade)
VALUES (StudentConstr('Vlad Dracula', 666666666, 666,
                      'Transylvania Ave.', '66666', 'G5'),
        'HIS666',
        'F1462',
        'D')
```

14.4.6 Reference Types

In schema (14.8) for the TRANSCRIPT relation, the attribute Student has the type STUDENTTYPE. As explained in Section 14.4.3, this prevents sharing of student objects because every student object is physically stored inside the corresponding transcript tuple. To enable object sharing, SQL uses **reference data types**. A reference is an oid, and the domain of a type of the form REF(*SomeUDT*) consists of all of the oids of objects of type *SomeUDT*. With this feature, we can rewrite our definition of TRANSCRIPT in (14.8) as follows:

```
CREATE TABLE TRANSCRIPT1 (
        Student REF(STUDENTTYPE) SCOPE STUDENT2,
        CrsCode CHAR(6),                                  14.13
        Semester CHAR(6),
        Grade CHAR(1) )
```

The type of the Student attribute needs more explanation. First, the type REF(STUDENTTYPE) means that the value of Student must be an oid of an object of type STUDENTTYPE. However, we can create many different tables and associate them with STUDENTTYPE. Each such table can contain all kinds of students. We might not want Student to refer to just *any* student. Instead, we want some kind of referential integrity that ensures that this attribute refers to students described by a *particular* table. The clause SCOPE achieves just that by requiring that the value of Student be not just any oid of type STUDENTTYPE but one that belongs to an existing object in the table STUDENT2. To be consistent, the scope, such as the STUDENT2 relation, must have the type mentioned in REF. In our example, STUDENT2 is of type STUDENTTYPE, which is consistent with the type REF(STUDENTTYPE) of the attribute Student.

Note: the use of STUDENT2 rather than STUDENT in (14.10) is not accidental—we will come back to discuss this issue shortly.

Querying reference types. "Misfeatures" often come on the heels of new features. Here is how query (14.11) looks when we use table TRANSCRIPT1, defined in (14.13), instead of TRANSCRIPT:

```
SELECT T.Student->Name, T.Grade
FROM TRANSCRIPT1 T
WHERE T.Student->Address.Street = 'Hollow Rd.'
```

Recall that `T.Student` returns the Id of an object of type STUDENTTYPE. Observe the use of the symbol -> to refer to the attributes of that type. This means that the syntax for accessing the attributes of an object depends on whether the object is given by its oid or its value. The unfortunate distinction between references by . and -> is the disease that SQL contracted from C and C++. Such a distinction is not necessary in an object-oriented language, and it does not exist in Java or in ODMG databases.

The rule for deciding whether to use . or -> is the same as in C and C++. If an attribute has a reference type, then -> is used in path expressions; if it has an object type, then . is used. In our case, `T.Student` has a reference type, REF(STUDENTTYPE), so we use `T.Student -> Address` to access the attributes of the student object. In contrast, the earlier query (14.11) uses `T.Student.Address` because, there, `T.Student` has the type STUDENTTYPE, which is not a reference type.

Creating tuples that contain reference types. The next important question is how to populate the table TRANSCRIPT1. In Section 14.4.5, we saw examples of tuple insertion into complex types. However, in those cases we did not deal with object references. In order to insert a tuple into TRANSCRIPT1, we must find a way to access oids of student objects and assign them to the attribute `Student`. This is where the self-referencing column, introduced in Section 14.4.3, comes in handy. Recall that table STUDENT2 defined in that section has a self-referencing column, called `stud_oid`.[5] Recall also that the table STUDENT in (14.9) has the same type as STUDENT2, except that its self-referencing column is unnamed. Thus, we cannot obtain oids of the tuples in STUDENT and assign them as values of the `Student` attribute in the table TRANSCRIPT1. Because of this handicap, we have to use STUDENT2 instead of STUDENT in the definition of TRANSCRIPT1.

Assuming that the `Id` attribute in STUDENT2 is a key, we can now insert a student into TRANSCRIPT1 as follows:

```
INSERT INTO TRANSCRIPT1(Student, Course, Semester, Grade)
SELECT S.stud_oid, 'HIS666', 'F1462', 'D'
FROM STUDENT2 S
WHERE S.Id = '666666666'
```

Observe that we use the SELECT statement to retrieve the oid of the desired student object (`S.stud_oid`). This oid becomes the value for the `Student` attribute. The

[5] Note that the self-referencing attribute `stud_oid` has nothing to do with the attribute `Id`. The latter is a regular attribute of STUDENTTYPE whose value is set explicitly by the programmer.

values for the attributes Course, Semester, and Grade are simply tacked onto the target list of the SELECT statement.

14.4.7 Inheritance

Recall that STUDENTTYPE was defined in Section 14.4.2 as being UNDER (i.e., as a subtype) of PERSONTYPE. This means that although the attributes of PERSONTYPE, Name, and Address are not explicitly defined in STUDENTTYPE, they are nevertheless applicable to the rows of the tables that have the type STUDENTTYPE.

Let STUDENT be a table of type STUDENTTYPE and PERSON a table of type PERSONTYPE. Suppose we insert a tuple into the STUDENT table as follows:

```
INSERT INTO STUDENT(Name, Address, Id, Status)
VALUES ('John Jones', ROW(123,'Main St.',11733), 111222333, 'G2')
```

Will this tuple automatically show up in the relation PERSON? The answer is *no*. The reason is actually quite logical: one can define several tables using the same UDT PERSONTYPE. Should the above STUDENT tuple show up in all such tables or only in some? The designers of SQL decided that it should show up in only some tables—those that the user explicitly marked as **supertables** (by analogy with superclasses) of the table STUDENT. Supertables are specified with the same keyword, UNDER, but this time it applies to tables rather than types:

```
CREATE TABLE STUDENT OF STUDENTTYPE UNDER PERSON
```

With this declaration, PERSON becomes a supertable of the table STUDENT, and all tuples inserted into STUDENT will automatically show up in PERSON (with the attributes that do not belong to PERSONTYPE removed).

To summarize, in order for a table, *T1*, to be a subtable of another table, *T2*, the following must hold:

1. The UDT of *T1* must be a subtype of (defined as being UNDER) the UDT of *T2*; and
2. The table *T1* must be defined as being UNDER the table *T2*.

> *Brain Teaser:* What will the value of the attributes Name and Address be if we insert a tuple into STUDENT using only the proper attributes of the STUDENTTYPE data type: INSERT INTO STUDENT(Id, Status) VALUES (111222333, 'G2')?

14.4.8 Collection Types

SQL:2003 introduced the MULTISET collection type, thereby making the SQL data model fully object-relational. A **multiset** collection type is like a set except that the same element can occur in the collection more than once. This is in accordance with the default SQL strategy of retaining duplicate tuples, which makes query results into multisets (see Section 5.2.1). To illustrate the new collection type, we will add a new set-valued attribute, Enrolled, to STUDENTTYPE:

```
CREATE TYPE StudentType UNDER PersonType AS (
    Id INTEGER,
    Status CHAR(2),
    Enrolled REF(CourseType) MULTISET
)
```

In this example, the value of the attribute Enrolled must be a (multi)set of oids of tuples of the type COURSETYPE. We assume that COURSETYPE is a new data type that has attributes CrsCode, Name, and Description.

With multiset collection types, a new kind of query becomes possible in which multiset-valued path expressions can act as table expressions in the FROM clause. This is analogous to SELECT statements in the FROM clause, which is permitted in SQL-92. We illustrate the use of multisets with a query that returns all tuples of the form $\langle i, n \rangle$, where the student with Id i took the course with name n.

```
SELECT S.Id, C.Name
FROM Student S, Course C
WHERE C.CrsCode IN
        ( SELECT E ->TmpCrsCode
          FROM UNNEST(S.Enrolled) AS TmpCourse(TmpCrsCode) E)
```

We assume that the relation STUDENT is of type STUDENTTYPE and COURSES of type COURSETYPE. The WHERE clause tests each course object for whether student S is enrolled in it. The condition uses a nested SELECT statement to produce the set of course codes of the courses taken by student S.

The new feature here appears in the FROM clause of the nested SELECT statement. The range of the variable E is the set of references to courses specified by a path expression, S.Enrolled. It lists the courses in which S is enrolled. This set is not a table, however, since the elements of this set are object Ids, not tuples. The UNNEST function converts multisets into one-column tables. This conversion is shown in Figure 14.1.

The UNNEST function can also specify a temporary relation name and its attributes, which can be used to refer to the table produced by unnesting. In our example, this relation is TMPCOURSES(TmpCrsCode).

Note that since E ranges over object references, we must access the attributes of the individual objects using the -> operator.

SQL:2003 also supports conversion in the opposite direction, from one-column tables to multisets. This is done with the help of the MULTISET function. In the following example, we use this function to add a new tuple to the STUDENT table. To

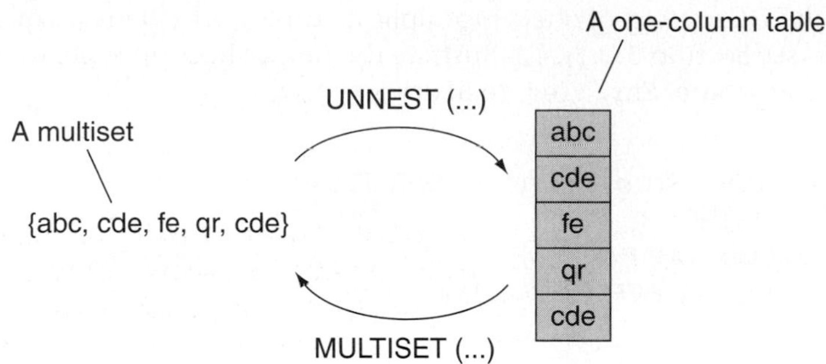

FIGURE 14.1 Conversion between multisets and one-column tables.

create such a tuple, we need to construct a multiset of type CourseType and assign it to the attribute `Enrolled`. Let us assume that transcripts reside in the following relation:

```
CREATE TABLE TRANSCRIPTI (
     Student REF(STUDENTTYPE),
     Course REF(COURSETYPE),
     Semester CHAR(6),
     Grade CHAR(1) )
```

We can now insert a new record into Student as follows:

```
INSERT INTO STUDENT(Id, Status, Enrolled)
VALUES(123987564, 'G2', MULTISET(SELECT T.Course
                                 FROM TRANSCRIPTI T
                                 WHERE TRANSCRIPTI->Id=123987564)
     )
```

The last component of the inserted tuple corresponds to the attribute `Enrolled` and thus must be a multiset of references to objects of type CourseType. The nested query returns a one-column table that includes the desired references; the MULTISET function converts this column into a multiset.

SQL:2003 introduces a number of additional functions and predicates to facilitate working with multisets:

- SET(*multiset*)—function. Eliminates duplicates from *multiset*
- CARDINALITY(*multiset*)—function. Returns the cardinality of *multiset*
- *multiset1* INTERSECT *multiset2*, *multiset1* EXCEPT *multiset2*, etc.—functions. Return the results of the corresponding set-theoretic operations on multisets
- *multiset* IS [NOT] A SET—predicate. Tests if *multiset* is (or is not) a set

- *multiset1* [NOT] SUBMULTISET OF *multiset2*—predicate. Tests if *multiset1* is (or is not) a submultiset of *multiset2*
- *element* [NOT] MEMBER OF *multiset*—predicate. Tests if *element* is (or is not) a member of *multiset*

Here is a modification of a previous query that uses some of these functions and predicates:

```
SELECT S.Id, C.Name
FROM STUDENT S, COURSE C
WHERE C.CrsCode IN
          ( SELECT E -> Code
            FROM UNNEST(S.Enrolled) AS TEMPCOURSES(Code) E
            WHERE CARDINALITY(SET(S.Enrolled)) < 3
                     AND S.Enrolled IS NOT A SET   )
```

This query will return student-course name pairs for only those students who are enrolled in fewer than three distinct courses (CARDINALITY(SET(S.Enrolled)) < 3) and in at least one course, two or more times (S.Enrolled IS NOT A SET). (This situation is possible if a student is enrolled in different sections of the same course, such as Independent Study, which permit this kind of enrollment).

14.5 The ODMG Standard

We now turn our attention to the ODMG standard, which was developed by the Object Database Management Group. It covers object database systems and (as a special case) object-relational database systems. ODMG 3.0 is fully described in [Cattell and Barry 2000]. Commercial systems that support this standard include GemStone (*http://www.gemstone.com*), ObjectStore (*http://www.odi.com*), and Poet (*http://www.poet.com*). We will discuss the following subjects:

- *The data model*. What kinds of objects can be stored in an ODMG database?
- *The Object Definition Language (ODL)*. How are these objects described to the database management system?
- *The Object Query Language (OQL)*. How is the database queried?
- *The transaction mechanisms*. How are transaction boundaries specified?
- *Language bindings*. How are ODMG databases used in the "real world"?

The data model underlying ODMG is very close to CODM, although we briefly discuss a few differences in Section 14.5.1. After that, we present ODL, the Object Definition Language of ODMG—a concrete syntax for describing classes and their types and then, in Section 14.5.2, discuss the ODMG query language, OQL.

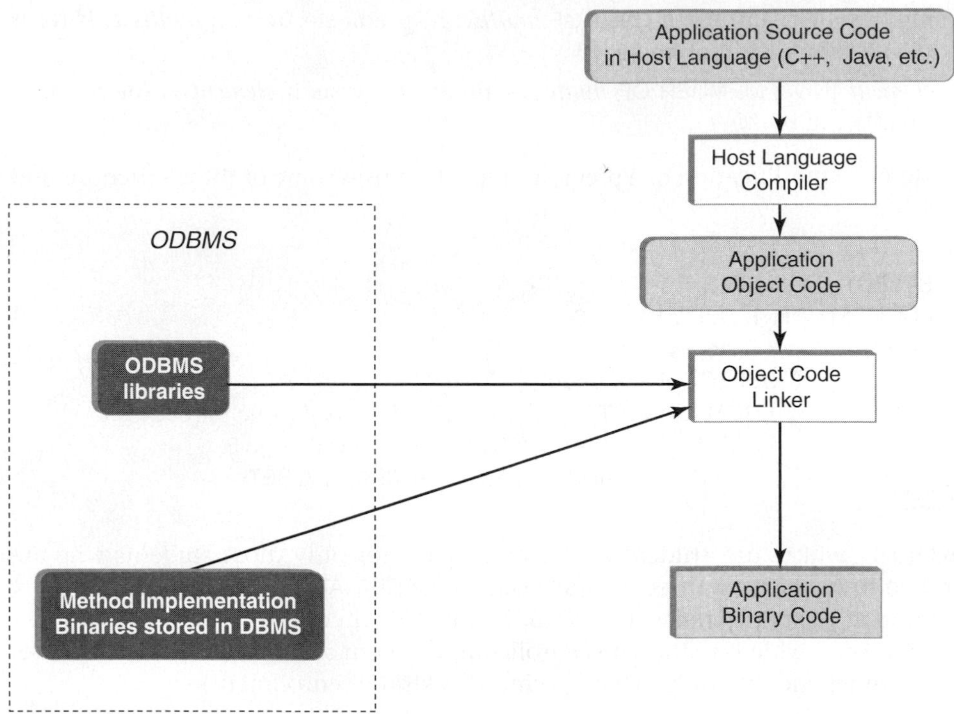

FIGURE 14.2 Structure of ODMG applications.

The architecture of an ODMG database. The overall architecture of an ODMG database is depicted in Figures 14.2 and 14.3. As with relational databases, an application that uses an ODMG database is written in a host language, such as C++. In order to access the database, the application must be linked with the ODBMS libraries and with the code that implements its class methods. In object databases, much of the code that manipulates objects is part of the database itself: each class comes with the set of methods allowed for the objects in the class. The code for these methods is stored on the database server, and the method signatures are specified as part of the schema using ODL. The ODBMS is responsible for the invocation of the appropriate code whenever a method is called. In principle, methods can execute either at the server or at the client site. However, to execute a method at the client site requires that the ODBMS provide infrastructure for shipping method code to client machines. Because of the difficulty in implementing such infrastructure, commercial ODBMS typically execute methods at the server. The introduction of Java makes code shipping much easier, and we might see more client-side method invocation in future products.

Storing code on the server is reminiscent of stored procedures in relational databases (see Section 8.2.5). However, the important difference is that a method

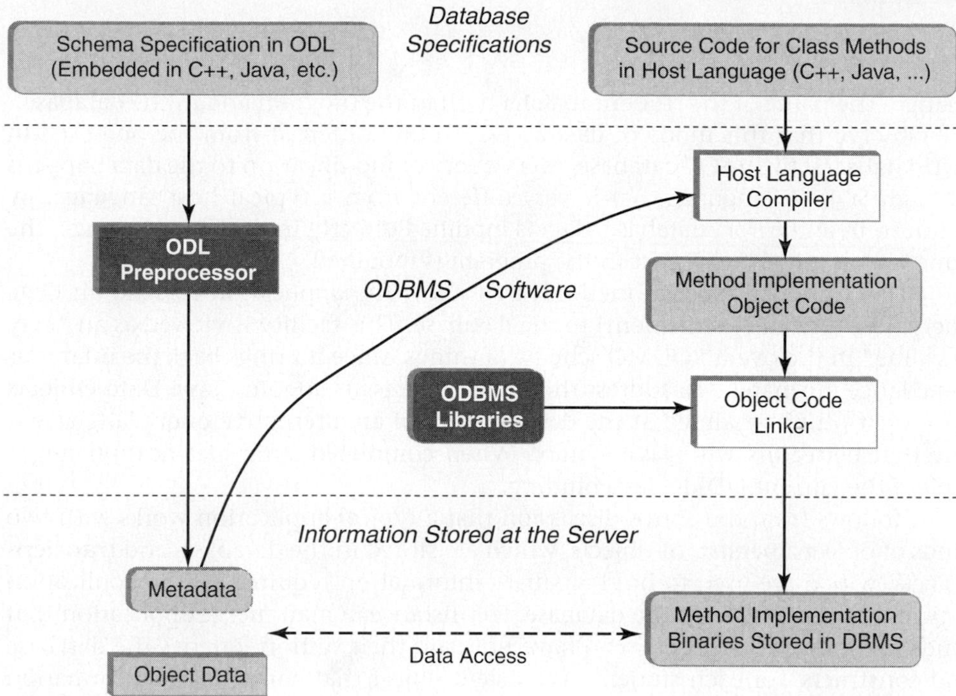

FIGURE 14.3 Architecture of an ODMG database.

implementation is integral to an object, whereas a stored procedure is an external application routine stored in the database for performance and security reasons.

Elimination of impedance mismatch between the data access language and the host language is one of the most important design goals of ODMG. The immediate practical implication of this goal is that the host language also serves as the data manipulation language. This is achieved using **language bindings**—a set of APIs (one per host language) that define how object definitions in C++, Java, and Smalltalk are mapped to database objects. This mapping allows the host program to manipulate database objects *directly* through regular host language statements (assignment, increment, etc.) or by executing methods defined for the corresponding classes. Once such an interaction occurs, the ODBMS is responsible for making sure that resulting changes are made durable when the transaction commits.

Typically, an application finds an object or set of objects in the database using an OQL query. Then the application manipulates and updates those objects with programming language statements and the objects' methods. No special SQL-style update statements are needed since any updates of an object within the program cause corresponding updates to the copy of the object in the database. For instance, if the host language variable `Stud` contains the oid of a persistent STUDENT object, the following statement in C++ or Java

```
Stud.Name = "John";
```

changes the name of the student to John both in the program and in the database.[6]

Observe that this mode of data access is quite different from the one used in SQL databases. In an SQL database, every query or modification to the data happens through SQL—a language that is very different from a typical host language. By contrast, in an ODMG database, data is modified directly in the host language, the same way as any other object in the program is modified.

ODMG provides special methods that allow the application to send an OQL query (i.e., a SELECT statement) to the database. This facility is viewed as an "ugly duckling" in the overall ODMG scheme of things, since it brings back the infamous impedance mismatch. To address this issue, there is an ongoing **Java Data Objects Specification** effort aimed at the development of an alternative query language—one that better fits with Java syntax. When completed, this specification might replace the current ODMG Java binding.

It follows from the above discussion that a typical application works with two kinds of objects: **persistent** objects, which are stored in the database, and **transient** objects, which are used to hold auxiliary information required by the application logic but are not saved in the database. For instance, a mail-merge application that sends reminders to students who have not paid their tuition, queries the database and constructs, for each student, a transient object that contains the information that must be included in the reminder (e.g., name, address, amount of tuition, deadline). Such an object is useful only while the application is active and does not need to be saved. On the other hand, the STUDENT objects might need to be updated and saved to reflect the fact that a tuition notice had been sent. The exact syntax for specifying object persistence is part of the language binding specification, which is discussed in Section 14.5.5.

14.5.1 ODL—The ODMG Object Definition Language

The ODMG Object Definition Language (ODL) is analogous to the data definition sublanguage of SQL. It is used to describe the schema of an object database. As in SQL, schema information defined using ODL is stored in the system catalog and is used at run time to evaluate queries and perform database updates.

ODL in the grand schema of things. In SQL, the role of the data definition language is very clear—it is the only way to describe data to the database. The role of ODL in ODMG is less obvious. Language bindings allow the programmer to declare database objects and classes directly in the host program using the syntax of the host language (for example, Java), so ODL need not be used for this purpose. This is very different from the mechanism used by embedded SQL, SQLJ, ODBC, or JDBC, where

[6] Note that ODMG, like C++ and Java, uses double quotes to represent strings. In contrast, strings are usually set in single quotes in SQL.

the database schema is defined in a separate language (the DDL subset of SQL) and is joined to the host language using a call- or statement-level interface. To further complicate matters, very few ODMG vendors have actually implemented ODL in their systems. Why, then, do we bother discussing it?

The role of ODL becomes more clear if we recall that complete elimination of the impedance mismatch is problematic. The idea of using the same language for programming applications and database access sounded very appealing back in the days when people believed that C++ was the only respectable way to program. Objects would be declared uniformly in the host language—independently of whether they were persistent (and intended to reside in the database) or transient (and intended to be deallocated when the application terminated). However, the arrival of Java made things more complicated. The problem is that Java's object definition facilities are not as extensive as those of C++. Even before Java, Smalltalk (with its own limitations) had a sizable following in the ODBMS application development community, so the question is: how can all of these languages, with their dissimilar object definition facilities, access the same object store? Can a Java application manipulate objects created by a C++ application? Which is the ODMG data model—the one defined by the C++ language binding or the one defined by the Java binding?

These questions are not an issue in SQL databases precisely because there is a single data definition language separate from all host languages. In ODMG, because of the crusade against the impedance mismatch, forcing (the same) ODL on each host language is difficult. Nevertheless, ODL is still useful as a way of specifying a reference data model and as a target language for the three language bindings defined by ODMG. So, while ODL might not exist as a software package, it plays an important role in holding the ODMG standard together by providing it with a unifying conceptual foundation. In particular, ODMG specifies that an object created in one language can be accessed by an application written in another language if the object definition belongs to the subset of ODL common to both.

ODL and the ODMG data model. The terminology used in ODL differs in some respects from that used in CODM, and we highlight the differences as we go.

ODL describes the attributes and methods of each object type, including its inheritance properties. A method is specified by its **signature**, which consists of the method's name; the names, order, and types of its arguments; the type of its return value; and the names of any exceptions it can raise (errors and special conditions).

ODL is an extension of the **Interface Definition Language (IDL)** that is used to specify objects in the CORBA standard (Section 14.6). Following Java, ODL distinguishes between two kinds of classes. The first is called an *interface*, the second a *class*. To avoid confusion with CODM classes, we call these **ODMG interfaces** and **ODMG classes**, respectively.

In terms of CODM, ODMG interface and class definitions specify

- A class name (in the CODM sense) along with the relevant part of the inheritance hierarchy
- A type associated with the class

A collection of such definitions specifies the entire ODMG database schema. The main differences between ODMG interfaces and ODMG classes follow:

- An ODMG interface cannot include code for methods; only method signatures are allowed (which is why it is called an interface). ODMG classes do include the code for the methods of the class. The signature and the code can be either explicitly specified using a host language or it can be inherited from a class higher up in the hierarchy.
- An ODMG interface cannot have its own member objects; that is, object instances of the interface cannot be created. In contrast, an ODMG class can (and usually does) have member objects. Thus, the extent of an ODMG interface consists of the objects that belong to its ODMG subclasses.
- An ODMG interface cannot inherit from an ODMG class but only from another ODMG interface.
- An ODMG class can inherit from multiple ODMG interfaces, but it can have at most one immediate ODMG superclass.

The distinction between classes and interfaces exists for two reasons. First, it makes ODL a superset of CORBA's IDL, thereby providing a degree of compatibility with this important standard for distributed systems. Second, it enables ODL to sidestep some of the problems associated with multiple inheritance that arise when a class inherits two different definitions for the same method from different superclasses.

Similarly to CODM, ODMG distinguishes between objects and values. Values are called **literals** in the ODMG terminology. Objects are pairs (*oid*, *val*), as in CODM. Literals, on the other hand, might have complex internal states, but they do not have oids, and they do not have any associated methods. In ODL, objects are created as instances of an ODMG class, while literals are instances of types specified using the struct keyword.

The following example shows a definition of an interface, PERSONINTERFACE; a class, PERSON, which inherits from the interface; and a literal, ADDRESS.

```
// An interface.
// Note: Object is the top interface in ODMG, but is a class in Java.
interface PERSONINTERFACE: Object
{    attribute String Name;
     attribute String SSN;
     Integer Age();
}
// An ODMG class
// PERSON inherits from PERSONINTERFACE, but has no ODMG superclass
class PERSON: PERSONINTERFACE
(    extent PERSONEXT
     keys SSN, (Name, PhoneN) ): PERSISTENT;
// properties of the instances of the type
```

```
{   attribute ADDRESS Address;
    attribute Set<String> PhoneN;
    attribute date DateOfBirth;
    attribute enum Gender {m,f} Sex;
// relationships among instances of the type
    relationship PERSON Spouse;
    relationship Set<PERSON> Child;
// methods of instances of the type
    void add_phone_number(in String phone);
}
```

```
// A literal type
struct ADDRESS
{   String StNumber;
    String StName;
}
```

In the example, the clause PERSONINTERFACE: Object states that PERSONINTERFACE is a child of Object in the inheritance hierarchy. Object is a built-in interface definition that provides signatures for methods that are common to all objects, such as delete(), copy(), and same_as(). (One object is same_as another if and only if the two have the same oid.) Similarly, PERSON : PERSONINTERFACE states that the class PERSON inherits from the interface PERSONINTERFACE. In our example PERSON is not a child of any ODMG class.

The clauses that begin with extent and keys specify the properties of the class PERSON as a whole. The keyword extent gives a name to the set of all PERSON objects. This distinction between the class name and the extent name in a Data Definition language is quite unusual from the point of view of relational DBMSs. It is similar to giving one name to the relation schema (i.e., the symbol used in the CREATE TABLE statement) and a different name to the actual relation instance over that schema. From both conceptual and practical viewpoints, the value of the extent clause is questionable.

The keys clause specifies that the extent has two distinct candidate keys: SSN and ⟨Name, PhoneN⟩. In other words, this type cannot have distinct objects with the same SSN or with the same combination of name and phone number.

The rest of the specification defines the type (in the CODM sense) associated with the interface PERSONINTERFACE, the class PERSON, and the literal type ADDRESS. Every instance of these types is allowed to have several methods and attributes. The attributes Name and SSN of PERSONINTERFACE have primitive type String. The method Age() of PERSONINTERFACE is a method that returns values of type Integer.

The Address attribute of the class PERSON has the user-defined type ADDRESS, which is the literal type found right under the definition for PERSON. The PhoneN attribute has a set type, where each member of the set is a string. This type is represented using the ODMG interface set. Finally, the attribute Sex has the enumeration type with possible values m and f. Note that, unlike Java, ODMG interfaces can specify attributes (Name, SSN) and methods (Age()). They can even have relationships (explained next).

ODMG distinguishes between *attributes* and *relationships*. The value of an **attribute** is a literal (not an object) that is stored within the given object. A **relationship** refers to some other object stored in the database; it specifies how that object is related to the given object. The PERSON definition includes two relationships. Spouse refers to another PERSON object (stored separately) that corresponds to the object's spouse. Child refers to the set of PERSON objects (also stored separately), that lists all children of the given person.

Unfortunately, the use of the ODMG term "relationship" clashes with the use of this term in the E-R model. ODMG relationships and attributes are quite similar except that relationships involve objects rather than values. In contrast, E-R relationships are similar to objects and have their own internal structure, which is represented using attributes and roles. In fact, it is the E-R notion of role that corresponds to the ODMG notion of relationship because a role is essentially an attribute whose domain is a set of entities (instead of primitive types, such as integers and strings).

In addition to specifying attributes and relationships, the class definition can also have method signatures (recall that method implementations are provided separately, in the host language). In our example, the signature for the method add_phone_number() has been specified. The keyword in in the parameter list of the method specifies the **parameter passing mode**; here it says that the parameter phone is an input parameter. This feature is borrowed from the CORBA Interface Definition Language (we also saw it in SQL/PSM in Chapter 8). Other parameter-passing keywords are out and inout (for output parameters and parameters that can be used for both input and output).

The ADDRESS specification above defines an ODMG literal type (whose instances are "values" in CODM terminology). For this definition, ODMG uses the keyword struct instead of class. Literals have only attributes and no relationships, so the keywords attribute or relationship are not needed in a literal definition.

We continue to develop the above example by (partially) defining another ODMG class, STUDENT:

```
class STUDENT extends PERSON {
    (extent STUDENTEXT)
     . . .
    attribute Set<String> Major;
    relationship Set<COURSE> Enrolled;
     . . .
}
```

The clause STUDENT extends PERSON makes STUDENT a subclass of the class PERSON. Note that ODMG uses the : construct to denote inheritance from an interface and the extends keyword to denote inheritance from a class. Inheritance from a class definition implies inheritance of the method implementations in addition to that of the attributes and method signatures. Furthermore, the extent of STUDENT becomes a subset of the extent of PERSON.

ODMG's inheritance model resembles Java's. An ODMG class can extend only one other ODMG class but can inherit method signatures from several ODMG interfaces. However, ODMG prohibits *name overloading*: a method with a given name cannot be inherited from more than one class or interface. For example, if LIBRARIAN is defined as a subclass of both FACULTY and STAFF, then FACULTY and STAFF cannot have identically named methods, such as `weeklyPay`. (Note that, in the case of LIBRARIAN, since multiple inheritance from classes is not permitted, either FACULTY or STAFF or both must be interfaces.)

The relationship `Enrolled` in the STUDENT definition states that the student is enrolled in a set of courses, where COURSE is an object defined (and stored) separately. The definition of COURSE might be

```
class COURSE : Object {
    (extent COURSEEXT)
    attribute Integer CrsCode;
    attribute String Department;
    relationship Set<STUDENT> Enrollment;
     . . .
}
```

which defines the relationship `Enrollment` that relates a course to the students enrolled in it.

These relationship declarations automate the enforcement of referential integrity as we know it from SQL. For instance, if a course object is deleted from the database, it is automatically removed from the set of courses that can be returned by the attribute `Enrolled` of STUDENT objects. Similarly, when a STUDENT object is deleted, it is removed from the set of students enrolled in the appropriate courses.

The ODMG standard does not provide a mechanism, similar to the ON DELETE CASCADE clause in SQL, to react to such deletions. However, almost the same functionality can be obtained with the ODMG *exception* mechanism (which we do not discuss here).

ODL also provides for automatic maintenance of consistency between the values returned by the relationships `Enrolled` and `Enrollment`. If `john` is an object in class STUDENT and `john.Enrolled` contains the course `CS532`, but the value of `CS532.Enrollment` does not include `john`, the database is inconsistent. To prevent this, the database designer can indicate that the `Enrollment` relationship is the inverse of the `Enrolled` relationship, and vice versa.

```
class STUDENT extends PERSON {
    (extent STUDENTEXT)
    . . .
    attribute Set<String> Major;                                   14.14
    relationship Set<COURSE> Enrolled
                 inverse COURSE::Enrollment;
    . . .
}
class COURSE : Object {
    . . .
    relationship Set<STUDENT> Enrollment
                 inverse STUDENT::Enrolled;
    . . .
}
```

Here, the statement relationship Set<COURSE> `Enrolled` inverse COURSE::`Enrollment` says that, if a COURSE object, *c*, is in the set *s*.`Enrolled`, where *s* is a STUDENT object, then *s* must be in the set *c*.`Enrollment`. The clause relationship Set< STUDENT> `Enrollment` inverse STUDENT::`Enrolled` states the opposite inclusion. Note that this constraint is stronger than referential integrity, which can only guarantee that no student is registered for a bogus course and that course rosters do not contain phantom students.

14.5.2 OQL—The ODMG Object Query Language

Although objects can be queried directly through their methods and attributes, ODMG provides a powerful declarative query language to access an object database. As in relational databases, ODMG queries can be issued interactively or embedded in applications. However, as many vendors do not support the interactive mode, embedded queries are usually used in the real world. The syntax for embedding queries depends on the host language. Section 14.5.5 illustrates how this is done in Java. In this section, we discuss the query language itself, independent of the mode.

The ODMG Object Query Language (OQL) is similar in many respects to the query language subset of SQL. For example, the query

```
SELECT DISTINCT S.Address
FROM PERSONEXT S
WHERE S.Name = "Smith"
```

returns the set of addresses of all persons named `Smith`. More precisely, it returns a value of type Set<ADDRESS>. The set type comes with built-in methods that give the programmer access to the elements of the set to obtain the functionality provided by cursors in SQL.

Recall that ODMG makes a clear distinction between the name of a class and the name of the class extent. It is the name of the extent, not of the class, that is used in the FROM clause. Thus, the above example uses the symbol PERSONEXT, which represents the extent (i.e., the collection of all objects) of class PERSON.

If, in the above query, the keyword DISTINCT is omitted from the SELECT statement, the query will return a value of type Bag<ADDRESS>, a bag of addresses (a bag is similar to a set but can have duplicate elements).

Methods can also be invoked in a SELECT statement. Using the example of a MOVIE object, defined in (14.4) on page 519, we can write

```
SELECT M.frameRange(100,1000)
FROM MOVIE M
WHERE M.Name = "The Simpsons"
```

The SELECT clause invokes the frameRange() method, which returns a set of frame range objects, one for each movie with the title "The Simpsons." If frameRange() has been redefined in the inheritance hierarchy, the system will select the correct implementation of the method based on the inheritance rules. Methods, with or without parameters, can be used anywhere in the query.[7]

SELECT statements that invoke methods can have side effects. For instance, if class PERSON has a method for updating the set of personal telephone numbers, we can write the following OQL query, where an update method is invoked in the SELECT clause:

```
SELECT S.add_phone_number("555-1212")
FROM PERSONEXT S                                    14.15
WHERE S.SSN = "123-45-6789"
```

This query changes the database but does not return anything to the caller.

The ability to call update methods in the OQL SELECT statement blurs the boundary between the data manipulation and query languages.

The syntax of the SELECT statement also includes complex WHERE predicates, joins, aggregates, group-by, order-by, and so forth, as in SQL.

Path expressions. Path expressions are a key part of OQL; they allow the query to go inside a complex attribute and execute object methods. As noted in Section 14.1, this technique can significantly simplify query formulation. For example,

```
SELECT DISTINCT S.Address.StName
FROM PERSONEXT S
WHERE S.Name = "Smith"
```

returns the set of strings (a value of type Set<String>) corresponding to the street names in the addresses of all persons named Smith.

[7] There might be typing restrictions if, for example, the result of a method is used in some other expression, for example, X.age() = Y.frameRange(100,1000) is a type error.

Relationships can be used in SELECT statements wherever an attribute is allowed. For example, in the following query we are using a relationship, Spouse, instead of an attribute, Address.

```
SELECT S.Spouse.Name()
FROM PERSONEXT S
WHERE S.Name = "Smith"
```

The query returns the set of names (a value of type Set<String>) corresponding to the spouses of persons named Smith (there can be several Smiths in the database).

Formally, a **path expression** is of the form

$$P.name_1.name_2. \ldots . name_n$$

where P can be an object or a variable that ranges over objects and each $name_i$ can be an attribute name, method invocation (with arguments), or a relationship name. We have seen path expressions that involve attributes. In contrast, the following expression involves methods: M.frameRange(100,1000).play().

A path expression must be **type consistent**. In an earlier example, we used

```
S.Address.StName
```

to return the street names in the addresses of all people named Smith. This expression is type consistent for the following reasons:

- The variable S refers to an object of type PERSON.
- The type PERSON has an Address attribute.
- The subexpression S.Address returns a value of type ADDRESS.
- The type ADDRESS has the attribute StName.

In (14.3) on page 518, we used the path expression

```
P.Child.Child.PhoneN                                                    14.16
```

which was intended to represent the set of phone numbers of all grandchildren of the object P. In OQL, this path expression has an unexpected twist. A person can have more than one child, so the issue here is the nature of the result returned by the subexpression P.Child. Is it a *set of objects*, each of which is of type PERSON, or is it a single *set object* of type Set<PERSON>?

In some object-oriented query languages (e.g., XSQL [Kifer et al. 1992]) P.Child is a set of objects. Thus, in XSQL we can continue to apply Child and later PhoneN to each individual child. In the end, we get the set of all phone numbers of P's grandchildren. However, in OQL P.Child returns a single set object of type Set<PERSON>.

Since this set object is *not* of type PERSON, the attribute Child is not defined for it. As far as OQL is concerned, then, expression (14.16) has a type error!

OQL introduces a special operator, flatten, whose purpose is to break up set objects and other aggregate objects, such as lists. For instance, flatten(Set<1,2,3>) is a set of objects {1,2,3}, not a single set object. So, while in XSQL the expression (14.16) is correct, the corresponding expression in OQL is more cumbersome:

```
flatten(flatten(P.Child).Child).PhoneN
```

Nested queries in OQL. As in SQL, some OQL queries require the nested subquery mechanism. Recall that in SQL, nested subqueries occur in two places:

- In the FROM clause, to specify a virtual range for a tuple variable (e.g., query (5.30), page 162)
- In the WHERE clause, to specify complex query conditions (e.g., query (5.24), page 158)

Nested subqueries can occur in OQL in the FROM and WHERE clauses for the same reasons that they can in SQL. However, OQL queries can also have nested subqueries in the SELECT clause if there is a need to construct a set object and return it as a result. Clearly, this situation is unique to object-oriented query languages, because set objects cannot occur as components of a tuple in the relational model.

To illustrate, suppose that we need to obtain the list of all students along with the computer science courses they are taking. We want the outcome to be a set of tuples where the first attribute is of primitive type String but the second is of type Set<COURSE>.

```
SELECT struct{name:    S.Name,
              courses: (SELECT E
                        FROM S.Enrolled E                    14.17
                        WHERE E.Department="CS")
             }
FROM STUDENTEXT S
```

Note that we are using the C-style struct construct to tell OQL that the output of the query is to be treated as a set of complex values. A nested query in the SELECT clause constructs a set to be assigned to the attribute courses, which creates a complex nested structure—something that cannot happen in the relational model (and thus is not allowed in SQL, except for subqueries that return a single scalar value). We would like to highlight another interesting feature of the nested query—the expression S.Enrolled in the FROM clause, which appears in the position of a class extent. This expression represents a collection, a set of COURSE objects, and the variable E gets bound to the individual objects of that collection. No flattening of the set-object represented by S.Enrolled is needed.

Aggregation and grouping. OQL provides the usual aggregate functions such as sum, count, avg, and so forth. From Section 5.2.5, we know that aggregation is interesting mainly when it is used together with grouping. In SQL, grouping requires a special clause, GROUP BY. Interestingly, OQL grouping can be achieved through nested subqueries in the SELECT clause, and no special grouping clause is required.

To make this concrete, consider query (14.17). Its output is a set of tuples where the first component is a student name and the second is a set of courses in which the student is enrolled. Thus, the output is *already grouped*. With a small change (adding the count operator), we can convert the above example into one that produces a list of students along with the total number of computer science courses in which each student is enrolled. The result is similar to an SQL statement that uses a GROUP BY clause.

```
SELECT  name:   S.Name,
        count:  count(SELECT E.CrsCode
                      FROM   S.Enrolled E
                      WHERE  E.Department="CS")
FROM StudentExt S
```

Even though GROUP BY is not necessary in OQL, it is provided along with the HAVING clause. However, it exists not to increase the expressive power of the language or to serve as syntactic sugar—the expressive power does not change, and in most cases GROUP BY does not simplify query formulation. Instead, it is useful as a *hint* to the query optimizer, which uses it to build a better query execution plan.

To explain, consider how a query processor might execute the above query. To answer this query efficiently, the query processor should organize course objects into groups, where each group represents the enrollment course list for a particular student. However, it is unlikely that the query optimizer would figure out on its own that there is a need to group courses around each student, so the probable plan will be to scan StudentExt and execute the subquery for each value of S. On the other hand, the optimizer might process the following query differently:

```
SELECT S.Name, count: count(E.CrsCode)
FROM StudentExt S, S.Enrolled E
WHERE E.Department = "CS"
GROUP BY S.SSN
```

In this query, the FROM clause produces a sequence of oid pairs, $< s, e >$, where e is the oid of a course in which the student with oid s is enrolled.

Because of the GROUP BY clause, the optimizer now knows that courses must be grouped around the students who take them, so it might join the classes Student and Course using the method that leaves the resulting tuples correctly grouped. One way to do this is to scan the instances of class Course and, for each course, c, hash it on the oid of every student who takes c. As a result, the course oids will be placed in buckets in such a way that all courses taken by the same student end up in the same bucket. Therefore, we can compute the join and count the courses taken by each student during the same bucket scan.

14.5.3 Transactions in ODMG

Before a transaction can be initiated, a **database object**, which references the database the transaction is to access, must be open. Creating, opening, and closing database objects is performed through a built-in interface called `DatabaseFactory`. Thus, the call

```
db1 = DatabaseFactory.new();
```

creates a new database object and returns a reference, `db1`, to it. That reference can then be used in the calls

```
db1.open(in String database_name);
```

which opens the database with name *database_name*, and

```
db1.close();
```

which closes it. Only one database can be open at a time.

ODMG has a built-in interface called `TransactionFactory`, which can be used to create new transaction objects to access the currently open database. Thus, the call

```
trans1 = TransactionFactory.new();
```

creates a new transaction object and returns a reference, `trans1`, to it. That reference can then be used in calls such as

```
trans1.begin();
trans1.commit();
trans1.abort();
```

to perform the indicated operations. ODMG assumes that vendors will provide classes that implement the `DatabaseFactory` and `TransactionFactory` interfaces.

14.5.4 Object Manipulation in ODMG

An object manipulation language deals with object creation, deletion, and updating. However, ODMG databases typically do not support a separate data manipulation language because the host language serves that purpose. ODMG language bindings (discussed next) specify how object manipulation is done using the native syntax of the host language. For instance, to create a new database object, the new constructor is used in C++ and Java. Deletion and modification of an object is done in the host language simply by invoking the methods defined for the corresponding classes.

Another way to update objects is to invoke a method in the SELECT clause, as in (14.15). This technique can be used to update sets of objects that satisfy certain conditions.

14.5.5 Language Bindings

One of the goals of ODMG is to encourage vendors to implement commercial object DBMSs based on the ODMG data model. As with relational databases, most applications of object databases are written in a host language. An important goal of ODMG is to provide uniform ways for such programs to access databases, particularly in C++, Smalltalk, and Java. All of these languages are object oriented and include facilities to specify and create objects similar to those in ODL. To allow these languages to access ODMG databases, **language bindings** have been defined for each. A language binding addresses a number of issues.

- *Mapping ODL object definitions to the native syntax of the host language*. To better understand this problem, recall that Java, C++, and other host languages do not understand ODL syntax. So how can we use such languages to define ODMG schema? One way is to use a statement-level interface so that ODL statements can be inserted directly into host language programs. The preprocessor then converts these statements into calls to the appropriate database library routines. This is the approach taken by embedded SQL, as discussed in Section 8.2. However, ODMG took a different approach. Instead of modifying the host language, it defines a series of classes and interfaces in the host language, which represent the corresponding concepts in ODL. DBMS libraries then must ensure that operations on instances of such classes in the host language are correctly reflected in the corresponding database objects.
- *Accessing and querying objects from within the host language*. One way to access the database is by binding a run-time object (defined through the regular mechanisms of the host language) to a database object. Then the database object can be queried and modified by applying the methods supplied with the database object's class to that run-time object. A more powerful way is to access objects by sending OQL queries (i.e., SELECT statements) to the server in a way that is conceptually similar to how this is done in JDBC and ODBC (discussed in Sections 8.5 and 8.6). ODMG bindings use both approaches.

For instance, consider the following class in Java:

```
public class STUDENT extends PERSON {
    public DSet Major;
    // Plus, possibly, other attributes
}
```

Here DSet is an ODMG-defined Java interface that corresponds to the ODL interface Set. DSet is defined because the existing Java interfaces do not provide all of the functionality of Set in ODL. To add a major to a student, we can call a native Java method on a STUDENT object as follows:

```
STUDENT X;
 . . .
X.Major.add("CS");
 . . . . .
```

where add is a method that applies to DSet objects. The main design principle behind all language bindings is that the regular host language facilities should be used, with minimal changes, on ODMG objects, thereby eliminating the impedance mismatch. However, a number of facilities needed to implement the standard do not exist in some or all of the host languages. As a result, ODMG language bindings lack syntactic (and sometimes conceptual) unity, and their details vary widely from one host language to another. To get a glimpse of the difficulties, consider the following:

- *How does the language binding distinguish persistent from transient objects of a particular class*? For instance, an application that enables data entry into the database has both persistent and transient objects. Persistent objects are bound directly to the database objects to be updated. Transient objects do not directly correspond to the information stored in the database, but they are used by the application logic (e.g., to display forms or to hold intermediate results of the computation).

  Each host language has its own solution to this problem. First, a class must be declared **persistence capable** (which is done differently in each of the three languages). Second, any object of a persistence-capable class that needs to be automatically saved in the database must be made persistent explicitly. In the C++ binding, a special form of the new() method is used for this purpose. In the Java binding, an object becomes persistent via a special method, called makePersistent(), defined in the interface Database, or if it is referenced by an already persistent object. From then on, it is the database's responsibility to make sure that the object is saved in the database.
- *How do the bindings represent and implement relationships*? None of the three languages, in their original forms, implement relationships. The current version of the Java binding does not support them, and the bindings for C++ and Smalltalk implement relationships with specially defined classes and methods.
- *How are ODMG literals represented*? In C++, literals can be represented using the struct keyword, but in Smalltalk and Java they cannot be represented directly and must be mapped into objects.
- *How are OQL queries executed*? Again, each language has its own implementation, but they all basically rely on a mechanism similar to that used in JDBC

(Section 8.5): a query object is instantiated, and the OQL query is supplied to that object as a parameterized string. The parameters in the query can be instantiated to specific objects using special methods. Then the query is executed with the `execute()` method of the query object.

- *How are databases opened and closed, and how are transactions executed?* Each language has predefined classes corresponding to the `database` and `transaction` objects of ODL, with appropriate methods for executing the required operations.

A Java binding example. To make the above discussion more concrete, we discuss how OQL queries can be executed using the Java binding.

The ODMG host language bindings provide two complementary mechanisms for querying objects: OQL queries, using the `OQLQuery` class, and the methods defined by the DCollection interface. The first extracts sets of objects from the database and assigns them to Java variables; the second queries collections of objects previously retrieved from the database, using the first mechanism, and stored in some Java variables. We illustrate both mechanisms below.[8]

To use the `OQLQuery` approach, a query object must first be created using the constructor method of class `OQLQuery`. Some of the methods in this class are

```
class OQLQuery {
     public OQLQuery(String query); // query constructor
     public bind(Object parameter); // supplies arguments
     public Object execute();       // executes queries
      . . .  . . . .  . . .
}
```

The `OQLQuery()` constructor takes as input a string containing an OQL query (a SELECT statement) and creates a query object. The OQL query itself can be parameterized using **placeholders**—`$1`, `$2`, and so forth—which correspond to the ? placeholders in dynamic SQL, JDBC, and ODBC (Chapter 8). These arguments can be replaced with actual Java objects via the method `bind()`. After all placeholders in the query object are bound, we can execute the query via the method `execute()`.

As an example, the following program fragment computes the set of all courses taken exclusively by computer science students in the spring 2004 semester:

```
DSet students, courses;
String semester;
OQLQuery query1, query2;
```

[8] Note that this design has a certain amount of impedance mismatch since it uses a separate language, OQL, to retrieve objects from the database. We discussed this problem on page 546 and mentioned that the forthcoming Java Data Object Specification is intended to overcome this problem.

```
query1 = new OQLQuery("SELECT S FROM STUDENT S "
                      + "WHERE \"CS\" IN S.Major");
students = (DSet) query1.execute();
query2 = new OQLQuery("SELECT T FROM COURSE T "
                      + "WHERE T.Enrollment.subsetOf($1) "
                      + "AND T.Semester = $2" );
semester = new String("S2004");
query2.bind(students); // bind $1 to the value of students
query2.bind(semester); // bind $2 to the value of semester
courses = (DSet) query2.execute();
```

The variables students and courses are declared to be of type DSet—a Java interface that corresponds to the Set interface of ODL. Conceptually, one can imagine that the Java binding *maps* the interface DSet to the ODL's interface Set.

Next, the variable students is assigned a set-object that includes all objects that represent students in the Computer Science Department. This set-object is obtained first by creating an OQL query object and then by invoking the method execute() on it.

Note that the target list of the first OQL query consists of just one variable of type DSet. The query returns a set of oids, and assigning the result to a DSet variable makes it possible to access the corresponding objects and apply methods to them. Actually, the signature of execute() says that this method returns a member of class Object, so we have to cast the result to class DSet.

The next step creates another query object and saves it in the variable query2. The method subsetOf() returns the value true or false depending on whether the set T.Enrollment is a subset of the set provided as the parameter $1. The second query is not completely specified—it is a *query template* since it contains two placeholders. The first, $1, is then bound by the call query2.bind(students) to the object saved in the variable students (which now represents the set of all computer science students). The second placeholder, $2, is bound by the second invocation of bind() to the String object supplied by the variable semester.[9] At this point, the query is fully specified and can be executed using the method execute(). The Object returned as a result of this execution is cast to type DSet before being assigned to courses.

Having obtained the desired collection of courses, we might want to further select a subset of these objects, check the existence of an object with given properties, or process the objects one by one using a cursor-like mechanism. All of this is provided through the interface DCollection, which is a supertype of the interface DSet. Like DSet, DCollection is part of ODMG Java binding. We show a fragment of the interface DCollection:

[9] Note that the order of the statements query2.bind() matters.

```
public interface DCollection extends java.util.Collection {
     public DCollection query(String condition);
     public Object selectElement(String condition);
     public Boolean existsElement(String condition);
     public java.util.Iterator select(String condition);
}
```

The most interesting methods here are `query()` and `select()`. The `query()` method is similar to, but more general than, the selection operator in relational algebra. For instance, the `condition` argument in the above methods might contain the quantifiers `forall` and `exists`. The `select()` method of `DCollection` creates a collection specified by the condition supplied as an argument plus an **iterator** object for that collection. An iterator is the embodiment of the familiar notion of a cursor. The Java `Iterator` interface defines methods that allow the host program to process individual objects in a collection one by one.

Returning to our example, we can take the collection `courses` computed by the second query and further select those courses that have fewer than three credits:

```
DSet seminars;
seminars = (DSet) courses.query("this.Credits < 3")
```

Here `this` is a variable that ranges over the elements of the collection to which `query()` is applied. We also assume that the class COURSE has the attribute `Credits`. Of course, the new collection, `seminars`, could have been computed by an OQL query directly. However, if we need to compute different subcollections of the collection saved in the variable `courses`, it might be more efficient first to compute the larger collection and then to use the `DCollection` interface to further query the result.

The other methods specified by the interface `DCollection` work in similar ways. For instance, `selectElement()` selects some member of the collection that satisfies the condition passed as a parameter. The method `existsElement()` tests if the subcollection determined by `condition` is nonempty.

OPTIONAL

14.6 Common Object Request Broker Architecture

CORBA is designed for an environment in which clients need to access objects residing on servers. One way in which a client can obtain such services is through **remote procedure call** (**RPC**) [Birrell and Nelson 1984]: the client process executes a procedure call that causes the procedure body to be executed within the server process, which might be on a different computer.

The Object Management Group (OMG) has proposed a new middleware standard, the **Common Object Request Broker Architecture** (**CORBA**). Like RPC, CORBA enables clients to access objects that reside on servers, but it is more general and flexible. Even so, it is not a replacement for RPC or similar mechanisms. In fact, CORBA often is implemented on top of RPC.

CORBA is also like RPC in that it provides **location transparency** for distributed computational resources. This means that clients access resources in a location-independent way, and a change in the location of a resource does not affect the clients. Unlike RPC, which is designed to specify remote resources as collections of unrelated procedures, CORBA specifies resources as objects in which related operations are grouped together. It also provides mechanisms for client applications to discover and use remote services that were not available (or even planned) at the time the application was written.

Included in CORBA is a layer called *CORBAservices*, which provides infrastructure for persistence, query, and transactional services—the issues of particular interest to us in this section. CORBA has also become a platform for various application frameworks in areas such as manufacturing, electronic commerce, banking, and healthcare. These frameworks are part of the architectural layer known as *CORBA-facilities*. We do not discuss this layer here, but an introduction to this topic can be found in [Pope 1998].

14.6.1 CORBA Basics

Each server specifies the interfaces to the objects it hosts using a generic **Interface Definition Language** (**IDL**). IDL is a subset of ODMG's Object Definition Language, ODL, discussed in Section 14.5.1. Like ODL, IDL is used to specify classes and the signatures of their methods. However, IDL classes have no extents and they are called "interfaces" (in agreement with ODL terminology). IDL is also missing constraints and collection types (such as sets), which are present in ODL.

To illustrate the idea, consider a public library server, which provides an interface that allows searching of the library's holdings. Client applications can use these search facilities to enhance the user experience.

```
/* File: Library.idl */
module Library {
  interface myTownLibrary {
    string searchByKeywords(in string keywords);
    string searchByAuthorTitle(in string author, in string title);
  }
}
```

Interfaces are often grouped into modules, which serve several purposes. One important advantage of modules is that they avoid name clashes among interfaces built by different organizations or different units within the same organization. This is

OPTIONAL

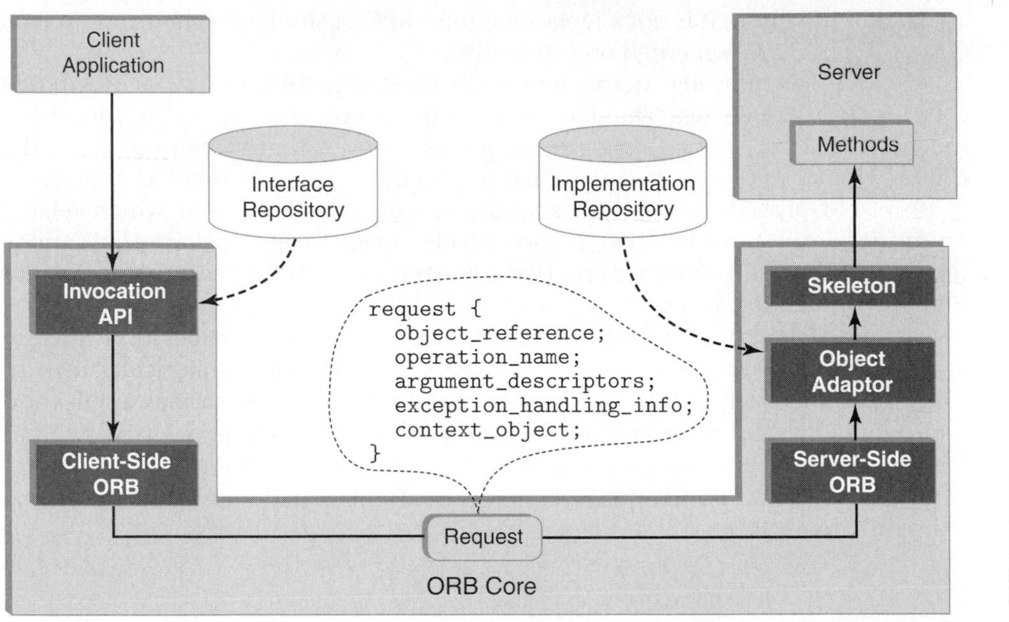

FIGURE 14.4 CORBA architecture.

OPTIONAL

possible because the module name is always prefixed to the method names. Thus, the client application refers to a method such as `searchByKeywords()` as follows:

```
Library_myTownLibrary_searchByKeywords( . . . )
```

How does a request from an application on a client machine cause the execution of code on the server? This is a matter for the object request broker, discussed next.

Object request brokers. The new component in the CORBA architecture is the **object request broker (ORB)** that sits between the client and the various servers, as shown in Figure 14.4. When the client executes a method call based on the IDL description, the call goes to the ORB. The ORB is responsible for locating a server that hosts the object and then for making any necessary translations between the client's method call and the method call required by that server's class definition. In other words, the ORB *maps* the IDL description into the language in which the object is implemented. The CORBA standard defines IDL mappings for C, C++, Java, Cobol, Smalltalk, and Ada.

The details of a remote call to a server object are as follows.[10] At the time the server is deployed, the IDL definition, `Library.idl`, is compiled by the IDL compiler

[10] We describe the overall process. Some aspects might be specific to a particular CORBA implementation.

supplied by a CORBA vendor. The result of the compilation is a pair of files, `Library-stubs.c` and `Library-skeleton.c`. In addition, the method signatures defined by the interface and related IDL information are stored in the **interface repository**.

The file `Library-skeleton.c` contains a **server skeleton**. This is code that maps client requests specified in an operating-system and language-independent form into concrete (operating-system and language-specific) calls to the methods `searchByKeywords()` and `searchByAuthorTitle()` on our library server. The skeleton is compiled and linked with the server before the server is deployed. When a server starts, it registers itself with the **object adaptor**, which is part of the ORB that resides on the server. By registering, the server informs the ORB that it can handle calls to certain methods in certain interfaces that are described in the interface repository.[11]

Interestingly, several different implementations can be registered to handle the same method call (in the same interface), and it is a job of the object adaptor to choose one. For instance, if the library's catalog is distributed, the object adaptor might satisfy the requests of the library patrons with an implementation that searches local cached copies of the catalog. On the other hand, staff requests might be satisfied with an implementation that performs distributed search. The object adaptor can decide which implementation to use based on the **context object** that the client includes with the request.[12] The ORB maintains the **implementation repository** to keep track of the available implementations for the different methods on the server.

On the client side, method invocation can proceed in one of the following ways. If the client application knows how to call the server methods (i.e., the name of the method and the types of its arguments), it can use **static invocation**, in which the client is compiled and linked with the **client stub**. In our example, the client stub is stored in `Library-stubs.c`—one of the files produced by the IDL compiler. With static invocation, the client calls the remote method as if it were a call to a local subroutine. The stub contains code that converts such a call (whose internal format can be OS- and language-specific) into an OS- and language-independent remote method invocation request that the ORB transmits over the network. Recall that the skeleton on the server then converts this request back into an OS- and language-specific call to a server procedure. The important point here is that the server and the client might execute under different operating systems and can be written in different languages.

Conversion of method calls into a machine-independent format primarily involves the process of **marshaling the arguments**. This is needed because different machines and languages often use different encodings for the data. For instance,

[11] Different methods in the same interface can, in principle, be handled by different servers. Likewise, methods in different interfaces can be handled by the same server.

[12] CORBA defines an interface, `Context`, which provides methods for setting arbitrary property name/value pairs. The context object carries with it the collection of all such pairs set by the client. The server can use the `Context` interface to examine the properties available in the context object and act accordingly. In this way, context objects can be used by the client to supply the server with meta information about the request.

OPTIONAL

some machines use so-called big-endian representation, some little-endian; some machines use 32-bit words, some 64-bit; some computer languages terminate character strings with a null byte, and some do not.

As you can see, sending data "as is" will likely make it unusable for the receiving computer. In CORBA, both client and server follow an agreed-upon protocol for data encoding and decoding. In particular, a method invocation request contains a **descriptor** for each method argument (or method result), which includes the value of the argument and its type and length. Moreover, all of these data items are encoded in a machine-independent network format. It should be clear, however, that the programmer does not deal with this conversion directly. Instead, it is carried out through CORBA library routines that are called (indirectly) by the stub. The overall structure of a method invocation request in CORBA is shown in Figure 14.4 on page 564.

In some cases, the client does not know how to call methods on the server. This at first might sound like an impossible situation; however, there are very real examples when it might occur and even be useful. Let us come back to the library search application, but now assume that it provides the user with search capabilities in a number of different catalogs that belong to different libraries. One possibility is that we force all library servers to use the same interface, `myTownLibrary`, but this might be unrealistic since the libraries are likely to have their own legacy systems, which are expensive to change. Different libraries can also provide different search capabilities—for instance, some might provide search using patterns and wildcards.

If the libraries participating in the search had remained the same, we could have coded all of the different interfaces into our client application and the problem would have gone away. However, we want our application to continue to work when new libraries join or leave the system, and when a new library joins we want it to be searchable by our program. For instance, if `yourTownLibrary` joins the system, we modify our `Library` IDL module as follows:

```
/* File: Library.idl */
module Library {
  interface myTownLibrary {
    string searchByKeywords(in string keywords);
    string searchByAuthorTitle(in string author, in string title);
  }
  interface yourTownLibrary {
    void searchByTitle(in string title, out string result);
    void searchByWildcard(in string wildcard, out string result);
  }
}
```

Not only are the method names and the invocation sequences different in the interface to `yourTownLibrary`, but the result is returned in a different way—as an out

OPTIONAL

parameter instead of the function result. After compiling `Library.idl` and linking the skeleton with `yourTownLibrary`'s server, we expect the client search application to be able to search both libraries.

To achieve these goals, we design the client application in such a way that it displays a general form to be filled out by the user that contains a number of optional fields, such as book ISBN, author, keywords, and wildcards. The client application then analyzes all interfaces defined in `Library.idl` and, based on the names of the arguments, constructs appropriate calls to the server. For example, if the user fills out the fields for the author, keywords, and wildcards, the client application might then choose `searchByKeywords()` in the interface `myTownLibrary` and `searchByWildcard()` in `yourTownLibrary`. If the user enters a title and a wildcard, it might not choose `myTownLibrary` (because it does not have the right arguments) but `searchByTitle()` in `yourTownLibrary`. To make this invocation strategy possible, we can require that the member libraries choose argument names from a fixed vocabulary when they write IDL descriptions of their interfaces. This requirement does not necessitate any changes to the legacy server but merely instills some discipline in the design of the interfaces.

How can we implement such a flexible method invocation strategy? This is where the interface repository comes in. Instead of using the stub, the client application can use a special **dynamic invocation API**, provided by CORBA, to query the interface repository. This API allows the application to determine all interfaces available in module `Library`, the methods defined in each interface, the argument names and types for each method, and the method's return value type. Based on the names of the arguments, our search application decides which methods to call and which arguments to provide. It then constructs appropriate request objects using the API call `CORBA_Object_create_request()`. A request object includes the name of the method to be called, the names and types of its arguments, and the type of the result it returns. A fully constructed request can be used as a parameter to a CORBA API subroutine, `CORBA_Request_invoke()`, to perform the actual invocation of the method on the server. This request has a machine-independent format, and the above API subroutine transmits it over the network to the server side of the ORB. The latter uses the server skeleton to convert the request into a concrete call to the server method.

It should be noted that static invocation performs the same actions in constructing a request for the ORB. However, since the exact calling sequence of the server method is known in advance, the required sequence of operations is generated automatically by the IDL compiler and constitutes the core of the client stub.

In our discussion of client-side method invocation, we have omitted one ingredient: the actual object on which the client asks the server to perform its operations. An **object reference** that identifies the object in question is part of the client's request for the ORB. How does the client obtain such a reference?

One possible way is to have client and server designers agree on some protocol. For instance, the server might publish object references as strings in some well-known location on the network. In our example, all references to the participating objects can be published in some agreed-upon document on the Web. The string

OPTIONAL

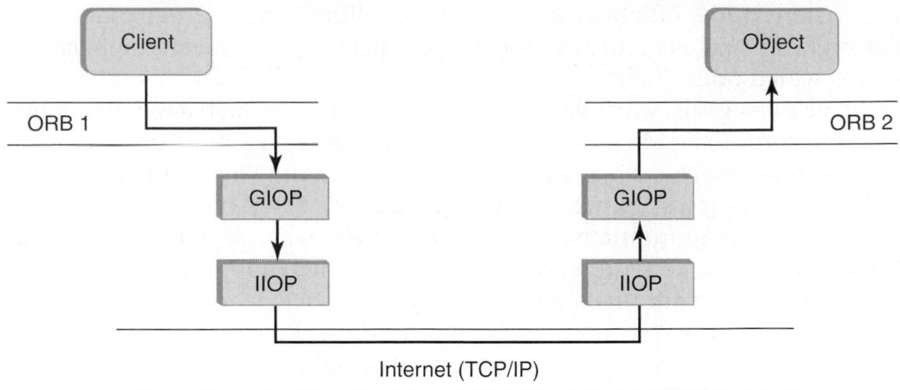

FIGURE 14.5 Inter-ORB architecture.

format of a reference can then be converted into an internal binary format used within CORBA via the API call to `CORBA_ORB_string_to_object()`.

A more portable way to obtain object references is to use the *naming service* discussed in Section 14.6.2.

Interoperability within CORBA. If there were only one ORB in the world, every object would be able to talk to every other object. In reality, different organizations and companies are likely to deploy their own ORBs, which bind together the objects that implement their business processes. If a group of companies collaborates on a project, they might deploy another ORB specifically for that project. The question is how to communicate with objects that are controlled by different ORBs. An ORB can deliver requests to the objects it controls. However, if an object belongs to a different ORB, a protocol is needed to pass the request to it.

Fortunately, CORBA has a general answer to this question—a **general inter-ORB protocol** (**GIOP**). GIOP is essentially a special message format that makes it possible for one ORB to send requests to objects under the scope of another ORB and to receive replies. Since these messages must somehow be delivered using real-world networks, it is necessary to map them into a message format of an existing network, one obvious candidate being the Internet. The **Internet inter-ORB protocol** (**IIOP**) specifies how GIOP messages are translated into TCP/IP messages so that they can be delivered via the Internet, as illustrated in Figure 14.5.

Similar translation protocols exist for other popular network protocols, such as *Point-to-Point Protocol* (*PPP*), which is often used to connect to the Internet using a modem, and other middleware standards, such as the *Distributed Computing Environment* (*DCE*).

14.6.2 CORBA and Databases

CORBA has outgrown its initial modest goals and is rapidly becoming a ubiquitous standard for distributed computing. Originally CORBA's purpose was to allow client programs to access objects residing on server computers. However, since objects are persistent, the possibility exists that collections of such objects can be used as a database. To achieve the full functionality of a database system, additional CORBA services beyond those originally provided are necessary. These services are now available through an architectural layer, called *CORBAservices*, which lives above the basic ORB mechanism. Using CORBAservices, it is possible to use ORBs to build a functional database out of disparate objects scattered around the Internet or other networks.

Conceptually, CORBAservices is a set of APIs designed to accomplish specific services, which include event notification services, licensing services (to control the use of certain objects or to charge users for accessing these objects), and life cycle services (to allow copying, moving and deletion of objects). The services that are of particular interest in the database context are

- *Persistence services*
- *Naming services*
- *Object query services*
- *Transaction services*
- *Concurrency control services*

through which CORBA allows a set of objects, perhaps located at different, geographically separated servers, to act as a database and to be accessed transactionally with the full set of ACID properties enforced.[13]

As an example of a CORBA application using persistent objects, a group of companies might get together to design a new product (a so-called *virtual company*). Each company keeps its part of the design (diagrams, parts lists, documentation, etc.) as persistent objects on its local computer and might implement its objects in a different language and under a different operating system. Using an ORB, an engineer at any one company can access the design objects of any of the other companies and perhaps incorporate them into local documents. The engineer can access any particular design object by name, without knowing on what company's computer it is stored. Query services allow the users to query the entire collection of objects in our virtual company, ORBs allow users to invoke methods on the objects, and transaction and concurrency control services make it possible to write applications that require transactional properties.

Persistence state services. CORBA provides a mechanism that an application can use to interact with remote objects that have made IDL interfaces available to clients.

[13] Observe that there is no need for a separate "object update service" because objects change state when clients invoke methods on them. Such invocations are provided by the ORBs, which are below the CORBA services layer.

OPTIONAL

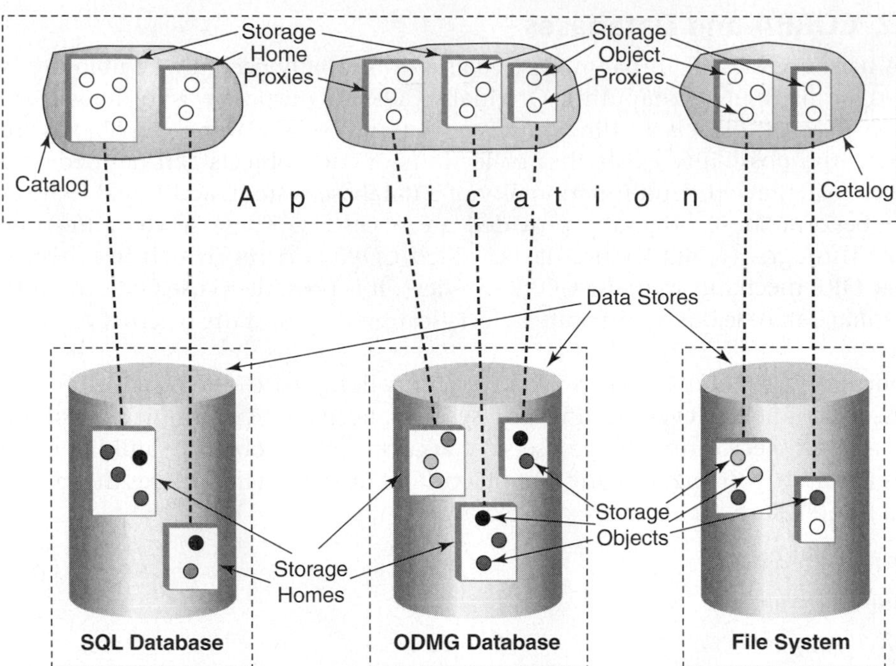

FIGURE 14.6 Architecture of CORBA persistent state services.

OPTIONAL

What is lacking, however, is a standard way for a data source, such as an ODMG database, to export interfaces to its data objects and to allow CORBA clients to manipulate them. Furthermore, there is no standard way for CORBA clients to create or delete objects in a data source. Of course, clients could go outside of CORBA and use, for example, ODBC to talk to databases, but this detracts from the stated goal of CORBA, namely, to provide a unified object-based interface for building distributed applications. CORBA **persistent state services** (**PSS**) fills these gaps.

The overall architecture of CORBA persistent state services is shown in Figure 14.6. The basic idea is that persistent objects on the server side are organized into **storage homes**, collections of which are organized into **data stores**. A data store can be anything that provides nonvolatile storage, such as a database or a file system.

On the application side, a program can work with several different data stores simultaneously, as shown in Figure 14.6. To start using a data store, an application must connect to the store using a special method call. Different mechanisms are used to gain access to a storage home, depending on the programming language. In an object-oriented language, such as Java or C++, a storage home corresponds to a public class. To *access* a storage home, the application must have a public class with the same name as the storage home, which we call the **storage home proxy**.[14] To *create* a storage home, the programmer must supply a class definition that includes the access methods (both signature and code). The class must then be compiled on the server and registered with the PSS.

The objects that populate a storage home proxy act as proxies of the storage objects on the server. The client application manipulates the proxies directly in the host language by invoking their methods. These methods might directly access a cached copy of a storage object or they might communicate with the server. It is the responsibility of PSS to ensure that any changes to the proxies are reflected on the actual storage objects.

It is easy to see that the design of PSS is influenced by the ODMG architecture and its drive to reduce or eliminate impedance mismatch. Indeed, by manipulating the proxies, the client program has the illusion that it operates on the persistent CORBA objects *directly*, as if they are local objects in the program—it does not use any special API to send query and update requests to the remote objects.

Naming services. Naming services provide a convenient way for programs to refer to (persistent) objects using a well-defined naming mechanism. This mechanism is similar to the way files are named in an operating system. The CORBA namespace is a directed acyclic graph in which each arc is labeled by a simple name. The full object name is the concatenation of all names found on a path from the root of the graph to the object. An object can have more than one full name (depending on the paths followed).

In our library example, instead of using the previously described homegrown protocol for exporting object references (page 567), the server might decide to use the naming service of the ORB, which is defined via the CORBA interface `NamingContext`. The two important methods here are

- `void bind(in Name n, in Object o);`
- `Object resolve(in Name n);`

The first method is used by the server to bind a particular external name[15] (such as `/Library/myTownLibrary/search`) to the concrete object created by the server. The second method is used by the client who passes the published name of an object as an argument to the method and obtains the internal CORBA object reference.

Object query services. Object query services (OQS) enable applications to query persistent CORBA objects. OQS draws heavily on the ODMG and SQL standards and provides OQL- and SQL-style querying capabilities to object stores that do not support these query languages.

[14] In the current version of PSS, this class is called an "instance" of the storage home. We avoid this confusing terminology because, in the object-oriented setting, an instance is an object that belongs to a class, not a class that is designed somehow to represent another class.

[15] The data structure `Name` is defined by CORBA and includes the published object's string name.

OPTIONAL

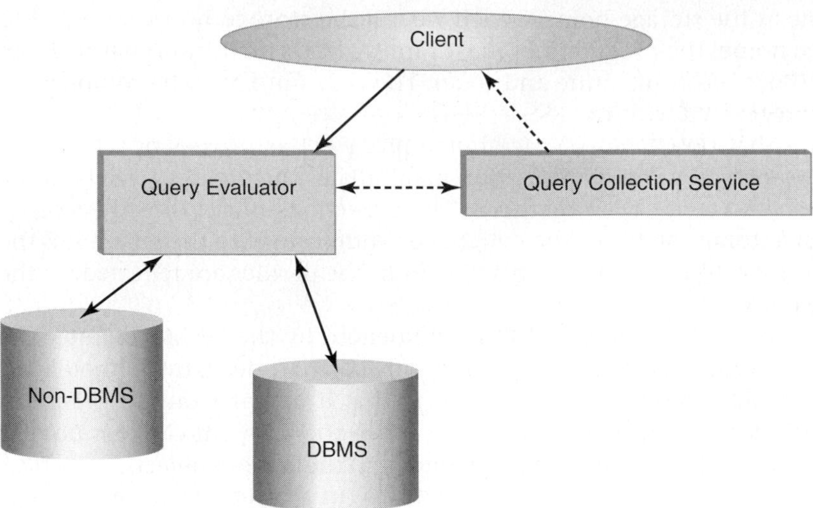

FIGURE 14.7 Architecture of object query services.

OPTIONAL

The overall OQS architecture is depicted in Figure 14.7. A client application passes a query to the query evaluator, whose role is somewhat similar to that of ODBC. It can pass the query to a DBMS with minimal changes, or it might have to break the query into a sequence of requests and manage the query evaluation process. Such query management is required when the DBMS in question does not support all features in the query, if the query evaluator acts as a front end to a non-DBMS data store (e.g., a store of spreadsheets), or if multiple data stores are involved.

In addition, the query evaluator creates an object of type *collection*, whose members are references to the server objects that belong to the query result. The collection object is then passed to the client application for further processing.

Earlier we discussed the collection interface used in the ODMG Java binding (Section 14.5.5) and SQLJ (Section 8.5.9). The CORBA collection interface is similar. It includes the methods for inserting objects into and deleting them from the collection, plus an **iterator method**, which provides cursor-like functionality and allows the application to process the collection one object at a time.

Note that, even though the collection object that represents the query result is usually created by the query evaluator at the client site, the objects that are members of that collection remain in their data stores. When the client invokes the methods of the query result object, the ORB transmits these requests to the member objects at their servers. Such server-side processing of all requests is common in CORBA. In this case, an ORB serves only as a smart communication channel among objects, but the objects themselves stay on the server.

Transaction and concurrency control services. In Section A.3.1, we introduced a *transaction manager* module, which orchestrates the execution of a transaction that accesses a number of different databases, perhaps widely distributed geographically, and guarantees that the transaction is atomic. CORBA provides a similar capability through its **transaction services** (also known as **object transaction services** or OTS) for transactions that access a number of different persistent objects or databases, as in Figure 14.6.

Transaction services allow applications to turn a thread of execution into a transaction. A thread can call the `begin()` method on a special transaction object, after which a transaction context is created for this thread. This context is maintained by the transaction service for the duration of the transaction. The thread can then invoke `commit()` and `rollback()` to perform the corresponding transactional operations.

CORBA objects modified by such a transaction must be declared as *transactional* and *recoverable*, which means that they can respond correctly to the `commit` and `rollback` commands. Transactional and recoverable objects must reside on **transactional** and **recoverable servers**, which provide the logging and other services (see Section A.2) needed to implement the `commit` and `rollback` commands.

CORBA also provides **concurrency control services**, which allow applications to request and release locks on CORBA objects and to implement the *two-phase locking* protocol (see Section A.1.2), which ensures transaction isolation. Note that CORBA-level locking is independent of, and layered on top of, the locking that might be happening in a DBMS that is accessed through CORBA.

Transaction services use the two-phase commit protocol (Section A.3.1) to guarantee global atomicity of the entire transaction, which might access multiple objects, including persistent objects stored in databases (see Figure 14.6). Any object that is accessed in this way must support a particular API, called X/Open standard API, which includes commands to commit and rollback databases.

Keep in mind that CORBA only *supports* concurrency and transactional semantics—it does not enforce it. In other words, it does not prevent nontransactional CORBA applications from accessing objects nor does it prevent applications that do not use CORBA from accessing those objects. Thus, all applications must agree to use transaction and concurrency control services in order for a CORBA object's semantics to have ACID properties.

OPTIONAL

BIBLIOGRAPHIC NOTES

The emergence of object-oriented databases was preceded by many developments—in particular, the growing popularity of object-oriented languages and the realization of the limitations of the relational data model. The idea of using an existing object-oriented language as a data manipulation language first appeared in [Copeland and Maier 1984]. Nested relations, which represent early attempts to enrich the relational data model, are discussed in [Makinouchi 1977; Arisawa et al. 1983; Roth and Korth 1987; Jaeschke and Schek 1982; Ozsoyoglu and Yuan 1985; Mok et al. 1996].

POSTGRES [Stonebreaker and Kemnitz 1991] was an early proposal for enriching relational databases with abstract data types. Now known as PostgreSQL, this system is a powerful open-source object-relational DBMS that is freely available at [PostgreSQL 2000]. The object database O_2, which strongly influenced the ODMG data model and its query language, is described in [Bancilhon et al. 1990]. The latest version of the ODMG standard can be found in [Cattell and Barry 2000]. A number of problems with the design of the ODMG standard (and some possible solutions) are discussed in [Alagic 1999].

The Conceptual Object Data Model, presented in Section 14.3, and related issues, are discussed more fully in [Abiteboul et al. 1995]. Logical foundations of object-oriented database query languages have been developed in [Kifer et al. 1995].

The use of path expressions for querying object-like structures first appeared in the GEM system [Zaniolo 1983]. Path expressions were later incorporated in all major proposals for querying objects, including OQL and the various object-oriented extensions of SQL, such as XSQL, discussed in [Kifer et al. 1992].

The early databases that supported the object-relational data model were UniSQL, POSTGRES, and O_2. Currently, most major relational database vendors (such as Oracle, Informix, and IBM) provide object-relational extensions to their products. Many ideas underlying the design of these systems found their way into the SQL:1999 and SQL:2003 standards. Further details on the SQL:1999 object-relational extensions can be found in [Gulutzan and Pelzer 1999], while at the time of this writing SQL:2003 is available only through the standards organizations, such as ISO (*http://www.iso.org/*).

Since SQL:1999/2003 object extensions are rather new, there are no products that fully conform to this standard. However, IBM's DB/2 and Oracle 9i come close in terms of syntax and supported features.

A comprehensive guide to CORBA with examples in the C language can be found in [Pope 1998]. Good guides to CORBA for Java and C++ programmers are [Orfali and Harkey 1998; Henning and Vinoski 1999].

This chapter omitted discussion of the database design issues associated with object-oriented databases, which would correspond to the material developed in Chapters 4 and 6 for relational databases. For further discussion see [Biskup et al. 1996a; Biskup et al. 1996b; Gogola et al. 1993; Missaoui et al. 1995]. The approach to object-oriented database design that is growing in popularity is the **Unified Modeling Language (UML)** [Booch et al. 1999; Fowler and Scott 2003]. We described the basics of conceptual database design using UML (and applied it to the relational model) in Chapter 4.

While object-oriented E-R style modeling is currently well developed, the corresponding normalization theory has turned out to be much harder to develop than in the relational case. Beginnings of such a theory can be found in [Weddell 1992; Ito and Weddell 1994; Biskup and Polle 2000a; Biskup and Polle 2000b].

EXERCISES

14.1 Give examples from the Student Registration System where

a. It would be convenient to use a set-valued attribute.
b. It would be convenient to express a relationship (in the ODMG style) between two objects.
c. It would be convenient to use inheritance.

14.2 Specify an appropriate set of classes for the Student Registration System. Do this using first UDTs of SQL:2003 and then the ODL language of ODMG.

14.3 Explain the difference between the object id in an object database and the primary key of a relation in a relational database.

14.4 Explain the different senses in which the objects in an object database can be considered equal.

14.5 A relational database might have a table called ACCOUNTS with tuples for each account and might support stored procedures `deposit()` and `withdraw()`. An object database might have a class (a UDT) called ACCOUNTS with an object for each account and methods `deposit()` and `withdraw()`. Explain the advantages and disadvantages of each approach.

14.6 Consider the following type in CODM: `[Name: STRING, Members: {PERSON}, Address: [Building: INTEGER, Room: INTEGER]]`. Give three examples of subtype for this type. In one example, add more structure to the attribute `Members`; in another, add structure to the attribute `Address`; and in the third, add structure by introducing new attributes.

14.7 Give an example of an object that belongs to the domain of the type `[Name: STRING, Children: {PERSON}, Cars: {[Make: STRING, Model: STRING, Year: STRING]}]`. Consider a supertype `[Name: STRING, Cars: {[Make: STRING, Model: STRING]}]` of that type. Show how one can obtain an object of the second type from the object of the first type, which you constructed earlier.

14.8 Consider the following type, which describes projects: `[Name: STRING, Members: {PERSON}, Address: [Building: INTEGER, Room: INTEGER]]`. Use SQL:1999/2003 to specify the UDT corresponding to this type.

14.9 Use the UDT constructed in Exercise 14.8 to answer the following query: *List the names of all projects that have more than five members.*

14.10 Suppose that the ACCOUNTS class in the object database of the previous example has child classes SAVINGSACCOUNTS and CHECKINGACCOUNTS and that CHECKINGACCOUNTS has a child class ECONOMYCHECKINGACCOUNTS. Explain how the semantics of inheritance affects the retrieval of objects in each class. (For example, what classes need to be accessed to retrieve all checking account objects that satisfy a particular predicate?)

14.11 Use SQL:2003 (with the MULTISET construct, if necessary) to complete the schema partially defined in Section 14.4. Include UDTs for the following tables: PERSON, STUDENT, COURSE, PROFESSOR, TEACHING, and TRANSCRIPT. Your solution should follow the object-oriented design methodology. Repeating the statements from Chapters 3 and 4, which use SQL-92, is *not* acceptable.

14.12 Use the schema defined for the previous problem to answer the following queries:

a. Find all students who have taken more than five classes in the Mathematics Department.

b. Represent grades as a UDT, called GRADETYPE, with a method, `value()`, that returns the grade's numeric value.

c. Write a method that, for each student, computes the average grade. This method requires the `value()` method that you constructed for the previous problem.

14.13 Use SQL:2003 and its MULTISET construct to represent a bank database with UDTs for accounts, customers, and transactions.

14.14 Use SQL:1999/2003 and the schema constructed for the previous exercise to answer the following queries:

a. Find all accounts of customers living at the postal ZIP code 12345.

b. Find the set of all customers satisfying the property that for each the total value of his or her accounts is at least $1,000,000.

14.15 Explain the difference between a set object and a set of objects.

14.16 a. Explain the difference between ODMG attributes and relationships.

b. Explain the difference between ODMG relationships and E-R relationships.

14.17 Explain the concept of type consistency of a path expression.

14.18 Add the appropriate inverse to the `Spouse` relationship in the PERSON definition given in Section 14.5.1 on page 546.

14.19 Section 14.5.1 on page 546 has an ODL description of a PERSON object with the relationship `Spouse`.

a. How would you express in ODL that a person has a spouse?

b. Give an OQL query that returns the name of a particular person's spouse.

14.20 Consider an ACCOUNT class and a TRANSACTIONACTIVITY class in a banking system.

a. Posit ODMG ODL class definitions for them. The ACCOUNT class must include a relationship to the set of objects in the TRANSACTIONACTIVITY class corresponding to the deposit and withdraw transactions executed against that account.

b. Give an example of a database instance satisfying that description.

c. Write an OQL query against that database that will return the account numbers of all accounts for which there was at least one withdrawal of more than $10,000.

14.21 Give an OQL query that returns the names of all spouses of all grandchildren of the person with SSN `123-45-6789` in the PERSON definition given in Section 14.5.1 on page 546.

14.22 Consider the class PERSON with an additional attribute, `age`. Write an OQL query that, for each age, produces a count of people of this age. Use two methods: with the GROUP BY clause and without it (using a nested query in SELECT). Describe a plausible query evaluation strategy in each case and explain which query will run faster.

14.23 Write an OQL query that, for each major, computes the number of students who have that major. Use the STUDENT class defined in (14.14) on page 552.

14.24 E-R diagrams can be used for designing class definitions for object databases. Design ODMG class definitions for the E-R diagrams in Figure 4.1, Figure 4.6, and Figure 4.36.

14.25 Consider the following ODL definitions:

```
class PERSON : OBJECT
      ( extent PERSONEXT ) : PERSISTENT;
{
  attribute String Name;
  ... ... ...
}
class STUDENT extends PERSON
      ( extent STUDENTEXT ) : PERSISTENT;
{
  attribute Integer Id;
  attribute Set<TRANSCRIPTRECORD> Transcript;
  ... ... ...
}
struct TRANSCRIPTRECORD {
   String CrsCode;
   float  Grade;
   String Semester;
}
```

Write the following query with and without the GROUP BY clause: *List all students with their corresponding average grade.*

15

XML and Web Data

The Web opens a new frontier in information technology and presents new challenges to the existing database framework. Unlike traditional databases, data sources on the Web do not typically conform to any well-known structure, such as a relation or object schema. Thus, traditional database storage and manipulation techniques are inadequate to deal with such data sources. This creates a need to extend existing database technologies to support new Web-based applications in electronic information delivery and exchange.

15.1 Semistructured Data

At first sight, the information on the Web bears no resemblance to the information stored in traditional databases. However, certain of its characteristics make it possible to apply many of the techniques developed in databases and information retrieval. First note that much of the Web data is presented in a somewhat structured form. For example, Figure 15.1 shows a student list as a tree encoded in Hypertext Markup Language (HTML), in which different data elements are set out using HTML tags.

To the human eye—albeit not quite so to the machine—the information on this HTML page appears to be a completely structured list of students, which, as shown in Figure 15.2, can be represented using the Conceptual Object Data Model (CODM) of Section 14.3. The actual object appears at the top of the figure. (We represent this object as an oid-value pair, as in Chapter 14.) The schema corresponding to the student list appears at the bottom of the figure.

How did we get from Figure 15.1, where the structure is implicit and intermixed with the data, to Figure 15.2, where the structure is represented separately from the data? Fortunately, the designer of the Web page was conscious of the need to make the structure easily understandable to a human and so made the data **self-describing** by including the names of the attributes (e.g., `Name`) along with the values (e.g., `John Doe`) within the data fields (e.g., `Name: John Doe`). In contrast, the object contains only the values, and the schema contains only the attributes and their types. The label PERSONLIST has been added as the name of the type described by the schema.

Suppose now that the same information is delivered over the Web to a machine (rather than a human) for processing. Unlike the human reader, the machine is less

FIGURE 15.1 A student list in HTML.

```
<html>
  <head><Title>Student List</Title></head>
  <body>
      <h1>ListName: Students</h1>
      <b>Contents:</b>
      <dl>
        <dt>Name: John Doe
          <dd>Id: 111111111
          <dd>Address:
              <ul>
              <li>Number: 123
              <li>Street: Main St
              </ul>
        <dt>Name: Joe Public
          <dd>Id: 666666666
          <dd>Address:
              <ul>
              <li>Number: 666
              <li>Street: Hollow Rd
              </ul>
      </dl>
  </body>
</html>
```

FIGURE 15.2 Student list in object form.

Object :

```
(#12345, ["Students",
          { ["John Doe", "111111111", [123,"Main St"] ],
            ["Joe Public", "666666666", [666,"Hollow Rd"] ] }
])
```

Schema :

```
PERSONLIST [ ListName: STRING,
             Contents: {
                 [Name: STRING,
                  Id: STRING,
                  Address: [Number: INTEGER, Street: STRING] ] }
             ]
```

likely to make an intelligent guess about the intended structure of the data received since it cannot distinguish attributes from values in Figure 15.1. Furthermore, the schema might not even be well defined, as some students on the list might have additional attributes, such as a phone number, or some addresses might have a variable structure (e.g., post office box instead of street address). Therefore, to facilitate machine-to-machine exchange of information, it is advantageous to agree on a format that makes the data self-describing by distinguishing the attribute names from values within the data.

In sum, Web data *created for machine consumption* is likely to have the following characteristics:

- It is *objectlike*; that is, it can be represented as a collection of objects of the form described by the conceptual data model introduced in Section 14.3.
- It is *schemaless*; that is, it is not guaranteed to conform to any type structure, unlike the objects discussed in Section 14.3.
- It is *self-describing*.

Data with the above characteristics has been dubbed **semistructured**. The "self-describing" property may be somewhat misleading since it can imply that the meaning of the data is carried along with the data itself. In reality, semistructured data carries only the names of the attributes and has a lower degree of organization than the data in databases. In particular, since the schema is absent, there is no guarantee that all objects have the same attributes and that the same attribute in different objects has the same meaning.

In view of our observations, Figure 15.2 is not a completely adequate representation of the original data depicted in Figure 15.1 because neither the object notation nor the schema notation of CODM was designed for self-describing data representation. However, an appropriate notation can be developed by combining elements from both the object and the schema notation of CODM. With the new notation, our student list can be represented as schemaless but self-describing as follows:

```
(#12345,
  [ListName:"Students",
   Contents:{ [Name:"John Doe",
                Id: "111111111",
                Address:[Number:123, Street:"Main St"]],
              [Name:"Joe Public",
                Id: "666666666",
                Address:[Number:666, Street:"Hollow Rd"]] }
])
```

15.1

Like the specification in Figure 15.2 (and unlike that in Figure 15.1), this syntax for self-describing objects is precise, machine understandable, and conforms to the best of database practices. However, this is not the format chosen for data exchange on the Web. The winner is called the **Extensible Markup Language** (XML)—a standard adopted in 1998 by the World Wide Web Consortium (W3C).

From the data modeling standpoint, XML is a format for semistructured data.

Since its introduction, XML has been steadily gaining momentum and is on the way to becoming the main format for the information intended for both human and machine consumption. Section 15.2 introduces the various components of the language and provides examples of its use.

Although at its core, XML data is schemaless, schema-compliant data is always more useful. In particular, the needs of electronic data exchange require stricter enforcement of the formats for transmission than that provided by semistructured data. To help, XML has *optional* mechanisms for specifying document structure. We discuss two such mechanisms: the **document type definition** language (**DTD**), which is part of the XML standard itself, and the **XML Schema**, which is a more recent specification built on top of XML. In Section 15.4, we introduce four query languages for XML: a lightweight language called **XPath**, a document transformation language called **XSLT**, a full-blown language called **XQuery**, and an extension of SQL, called SQL/XML, which is designed to provide interoperability between the relational world and the world of XML.

15.2 Overview of XML

XML is not a solution to all of the world's problems. It is not a revolutionary or even a new idea. Why, then, is it causing a revolution? In a nutshell, XML is a human- and machine-readable data format that can be easily parsed by an application and thus considerably simplifies data exchange. Formats for data exchange were proposed in the past, but either they were nonopen, proprietary standards or they did not have enough momentum. XML happened to be in the right place at the right time. People saw what the Web and open standards were doing for communication, education, publishing, and commerce, and they recognized the need to simplify data exchange among software agents. It also helped that a trusted standards body, the W3C, was in place and not affiliated with any particular industry group or government. For the first time a simple, open, and widely accepted data standard emerged, and this gave a boost to a wide range of Web applications.

XML is an HTML-like language with an arbitrary number of user-defined tags and no a priori tag semantics. To better understand what this means, consider HTML, a document format in which various pieces of text are marked with tags that affect the rendering of that text by a Web browser. Important points are that the number of tags in HTML is *fixed* by the HTML definition and each tag has its own well-defined semantics. The browser displays an HTML document by implementing the semantics of each tag. For instance, any text between the tags `<table>` and `</table>` is supposed to be rendered by the browser as a table, and the tag <p> tells the browser to start a new paragraph. In contrast, the repertoire of tags in XML is not set in advance, and the user is free to introduce new tag names. Furthermore, there is no set semantics for any XML tag.

The lack of semantics in XML might seem like a step backward. How does the receiver of an XML document know what to do with the documents it receives? The answer is that each category of applications will supply its own semantic layer on top of XML. Browser rendering is just one type of application. A browser renders an XML document using a **stylesheet**—a transformation that converts the XML document into an HTML document (which the browser already knows how to present). In this way, a stylesheet supplies a "visualization semantics" to XML documents. We discuss stylesheets in Section 15.4.2. Most XML documents, however, are not intended for visual display. Instead, they are exchanged by applications and are processed without human intervention (for example, invoices, payments, and purchase orders). As with browsers, the application infers the semantics by interpreting XML tags appropriate to the application domain. For example, a retail application might interpret the tag `<price>` to be the price of a product. At this time, whole industries are developing semantic layers for representing information in application domains such as catalogs, commerce, engineering, and other fields. All these efforts have the same common need: the ability to define schema. We discuss the structuring mechanisms available in XML in Sections 15.2.4 and 15.3, although it should be noted that, despite the schema, XML data remains semistructured. Compliance with the schema remains optional, and applications are free to ignore part or all of it.

For concreteness, consider the document in Figure 15.3, which is one possible XML representation of the student list from Figure 15.1. The first line is a mandatory statement that tells the program receiving the document (any such program is called **XML processor**) that it is dealing with XML version 1.0. The rest is structured like an HTML document except for the following important points:

- The document contains a large assortment of tags chosen by the document author. In contrast, the only valid tags in HTML are those sanctioned by the official specification of the language; other tags are ignored by the browser.
- Every opening tag *must* have a matching closing tag, and the tags must be properly nested (i.e., sequences such as `<a><b></a></b>` are not allowed). In contrast, some HTML tags are not required to be closed (e.g., `<p>`), and browsers are forgiving even when closing tags are missing.
- The document has a **root element**—the element that contains all other elements. In Figure 15.3, the root element is `PersonList`.

Any properly nested piece of text of the form `<sometag>...</sometag>` is called an **XML element**, and `sometag` is the **name** of that element. The text between the opening and closing tag is called the **content** of the element. Elements directly nested within other elements are called **children**. For instance, in our example `Name`, `Id`, and `Address` are children of `Person`, which is a child of `Contents`, which is a child of the top-level element, `PersonList`. Conversely, `PersonList` is said to be the **parent** of the elements `Contents` and `Title`, and `Contents` is a parent of `Person`.

FIGURE 15.3 XML representation of the student list.

```
<?xml version="1.0" ?>
<PersonList Type="Student" Date="2000-12-12">
    <Title Value="Student List"/>
    <Contents>
        <Person>
            <Name>John Doe</Name>
            <Id>111111111</Id>
            <Address>
                <Number>123</Number>
                <Street>Main St</Street>
            </Address>
        </Person>
        <Person>
            <Name>Joe Public</Name>
            <Id>666666666</Id>
            <Address>
                <Number>666</Number>
                <Street>Hollow Rd</Street>
            </Address>
        </Person>
    </Contents>
</PersonList>
```

XML also defines the **ancestor/descendant** relationships among elements, which are important for querying XML documents and will be revisited in Section 15.4. These relationships have their natural meaning: an ancestor is a parent, a grandparent, and so on, and a descendant is a child, a grandchild, and so on. For instance, PersonList is an ancestor of Person and Address, and Address is a descendent of PersonList.

An opening tag can have **attributes**. In the tag <PersonList Type="Student"> of Figure 15.3, Type is the name of an attribute that belongs to the element PersonList, and Student is the attribute value. Unlike HTML, all attribute values must be quoted, as shown in the figure, but text strings between tags are not. Also note the element <Title Value="Student List"/>, which contains an attribute. This element does not have a closing tag but instead is enclosed in <.../> and is called an **empty element** because it has no content. In XML, this is a shorthand notation for the combination <Title Value="Student List"> </Title>.

Apart from elements and attributes, XML allows **processing instructions** and **comments**. A processing instruction is a statement of the form

```
<?my-command go bring coffee?>
```

and can contain pretty much anything the document author might want to communicate to the XML processor (in the hope that the processor knows what to do with this information). Processing instructions are used fairly rarely. We will see one use in Section 15.4.2 in conjunction with XML stylesheets.

A comment takes the following form:

```
<!-- A comment -->
```

It is allowed to occur everywhere except inside the **markups**, that is, between the symbols < and >, which open or close tags. Perhaps surprisingly, a comment is an integral part of the document—the sender is *not* supposed to delete comments prior to transmission, and the receiver is permitted to look inside the comments and use what it finds. Although such treatment of comments goes against prevailing practice in programming and database languages, it is not unheard of in document processing. For instance, JavaScript programs are often placed as comments in HTML documents, and an HTML browser is not supposed to ignore them. Instead, it executes JavaScript programs found inside the comments, unless the JavaScript feature is turned off.

Another feature of XML that is worth a brief mention is the `CDATA` construct, which serves as a quotation mechanism. Suppose we use XML to write a structured guide to Web publishing. We might want to include the following text:

> Web browsers attempt to correct publishers' errors, such as improperly nested tags. For instance, `<b><i>Attention!</b></i>` would be displayed properly by most browsers.

Because of the XML tags included in this text, its inclusion would result in an ill-formed document rejected by every XML-compliant processor. Fortunately, *any* text can be included inside `<![CDATA[...]]>` brackets. For instance, the following is correct XML:

```
<![CDATA[<b><i>Attention!</b></i>]]>
```

Finally, a document can have an optional **document type definition** (or DTD), which determines document structure. We discuss DTDs in Section 15.2.4.

15.2.1 XML Elements and Database Objects

Let us now evaluate the XML document of Figure 15.3 as a format for sending semistructured data over the Web. It is easy to see that the element names effectively serve as attribute names for the object (XML attribute names can serve the same purpose), so this document is essentially yet another, equivalent textual representation for the self-describing object depicted in (15.1).

Conversion of XML elements into objects. A moment's reflection should convince us that the nested tag structure of XML is well suited to represent tree-structured self-describing objects. Each element in an XML document can be viewed as an object. The tag names of the children elements then correspond to the object's attributes, and the child elements themselves are the attribute values. For instance, the first `Person` element in Figure 15.3 can be partially mapped back to an object as follows (where #6543 is some object Id):

```
{#6543, [Name: "John Doe",
         Id: "111111111",
         Address: <Address>
                      <Number>123</Number>
                      <Street>Main St</Street>
                  </Address>
         ]
}
```

The conversion process is recursive. Simple elements such as `Name` and `Id` are converted immediately by directly extracting their contents. The element `Address` is left unchanged because it has a complex internal structure, which can be broken further by applying the same conversion procedure recursively. This results in a creation of a new address object:

```
{#098686, [Number: "123",
           Street: "Main St" ]
}
```

Differences between XML elements and objects. Despite the apparent close correspondence between XML elements and structured database objects, there are several fundamental differences. First, XML evolved from and was greatly influenced by Standard Generalized Markup Language (SGML) [SGML 1986], which is a *document* markup language rather than a *database* language. For instance, XML allows documents of the form

```
<Address>
     Sally lives on
     <Street>Main St</Street>
     house number
     <Number>123</Number>
     in the beautiful Anytown, USA.
</Address>
```

This mixture of text and child elements, allowed in XML, is a hindrance when it comes to automated data processing since the mixture complicates the document.

Second, XML elements are *ordered*, while the attributes of an object in a database are not. Thus, the following two objects are considered the same:

```
{#098686, [Number: "123",              {#098686, [Street: "Main St",
           Street: "Main St" ]                    Number: "123" ]
}                                      }
```

whereas the following two XML documents are different:

```
<Address>                              <Address>
    <Number>123</Number>                   <Street>Main St</Street>
    <Street>Main St</Street>               <Number>123</Number>
</Address>                             </Address>
```

Third, XML has only one primitive type, a string, and very weak facilities for specifying constraints. Fortunately, many of these weaknesses are addressed by the XML Schema specification in Section 15.3.

15.2.2 XML Attributes

We saw the use of XML attributes such as `Type` and `Value` in Figure 15.3. An element can have any number of user-defined attributes. However, considering the expressive power of XML elements illustrated earlier, we are left to wonder about the role of XML attributes as a tool for data representation. That is, are they useful in data representation, and do they offer anything beyond what elements can offer?

The answer is that XML attributes are sometimes convenient for representing data, but almost everything they can do can also be done with elements. Still, attributes are widely used in XML-based specifications, such as XML Schema, which we introduce in Section 15.3. We also use attributes extensively in the examples to illustrate the various features of XML and because this often leads to more concise representation.

In document processing, attributes are used to annotate pieces of text enclosed between a pair of tags with values that are *not* part of that text but are related to it. In the following dialog,

```
<Act Number="5">
    <Scene Number="1" Place="Mantua. A street.">
         .
         .
         .
         <Apothecary Voice="scared">
              Such mortal drugs I have; but Mantua's law
              Is death to any he that utters them.
         </Apothecary>
```

```
          <Romeo Voice="persistent">
              Art thou so bare and full of wretchedness,
              And fear'st to die?
              .
              .
              .
          </Romeo>
          .
          .
          .
      </Scene>
  </Act>
```

we use attributes to annotate the text with meta-information that is not part of the dialog per se but is still relevant. They are convenient to use here because they do not disrupt the dialog flow. In data processing, on the other hand, text flow is a minor concern since computers are unlikely to start appreciating this type of prose in the near future. The concern here is that XML attributes represent yet another, unnecessary dimension in data representation that database programmers have to worry about.

In addition, attribute values can only be strings, which severely limits their usefulness, while XML elements can have child elements, which makes them much more versatile.

Having made these unflattering remarks, we should mention some advantages of attributes. First, the order of attributes in an element does not matter. Thus, the documents

```
<thing price="2" color="yellow">foobar</thing>
```

and

```
<thing color="yellow" price="2">foobar</thing>
```

are considered the same—much as they are in databases. Second, an attribute can occur at most once (i.e., `<thing price="2" price="2">` is not allowed), while elements with the same tag can be repeated, as in Figure 15.3. This constraint can be handy in the right circumstances. Third, attributes can lead to more succinct representation. For instance, `<thing price="2" color="yellow"/>` is much shorter than `<thing><price>2</price><color>yellow</color></thing>`.

Useful features of an XML attribute are that it can be declared to have a unique value and it can also be used to enforce a limited kind of referential integrity. This cannot be done with elements alone in plain XML. (However, this and much more can be done with the help of XML Schema, discussed in Section 15.3.) After we discuss document type definitions (DTDs) in Section 15.2.4, we will see that an attribute can be declared to be of type `ID`, `IDREF`, or `IDREFS`.

An attribute of type `ID` must have a unique value throughout the document. This means that if `attr1` and `attr2` are of type `ID`, it is illegal for both `<elt1`

attr1="abc"> and <elt2 attr2="abc"> to occur in the same document (regardless of whether elt1 and elt2 are the same tag, or whether attr1 and attr2 are the same attribute). In a sense, ID is a poor cousin of a *key* in relational databases. An attribute of type IDREF must refer to a valid Id declared in the same document. That is, its value must occur somewhere in the document as a value of another attribute of type ID. Thus, IDREF is a poor cousin of a *foreign key*.

To illustrate, we consider the report document in Figure 15.4. An attribute of type IDREFS represents a space-separated list of strings, which are references to valid Ids. In our document, we can declare the attribute StudId of the element Student and the attribute CrsCode of the element Course to be of type ID; the attribute CrsCode of the element CrsTaken to be of type IDREF; and the attribute Members of the element ClassRoster of type IDREFS. As a result, any compliant XML processor will verify that no student or course is declared twice and that referential integrity holds—that is, that a course referenced in a CrsTaken element does exist and that all students mentioned in the Members lists are also present in the document.

You might be wondering why we have changed the Ids of students in Figure 15.4 from purely numerical to Ids that start with a letter. The answer is that XML requires that the values of attributes of type ID (and thus of IDREF as well) start with a letter.

We can now define an important correctness requirement. An XML document is **well formed** if the following conditions hold:

- It has a root element.
- Every opening tag is followed by a matching closing tag, and the elements are properly nested inside each other.
- Any attribute can occur at most once in a given opening tag; its value must be provided, as discussed above; and this value must be quoted.

Note that the restrictions on ID, IDREF, and IDREFS are not part of the definition of "well formed" because these attribute types are specified using DTDs, which well-formedness completely ignores.

15.2.3 Namespaces

Namespaces were not part of the original XML specification and were added as an afterthought. However, they have become central to many important standards built on top of XML, so we consider them to be an integral XML feature for all practical purposes.

The driving force behind the introduction of namespaces was the realization that different communities will be building vocabularies of terms appropriate for the various domains (e.g., education, finance, and electronics) and will use them as XML tags. In this situation, naming conflicts between different vocabularies are inevitable, and the integration of information obtained from different sources becomes very hard. For instance, the term Name might have different meanings and structure depending on whether we are talking about people or companies, as we see in these two document fragments:

```
<Name><First>John</First> <Last>Doe</Last></Name>
<Name>IBM</Name>
```

So it will become harder for an application to process documents that are built out of vocabularies that contain conflicting tag names.

To overcome this problem, it has been decided that the name of every XML tag must have two parts: the **namespace** and the **local name**, with the general structure *namespace:local-name*. Local names have the same form as regular XML tags except that they cannot have a : in them. A namespace is represented by a string in the form of a **uniform resource identifier** (**URI**), which can be an abstract identifier (a general string of characters serving as a unique identifier) or a **uniform resource locator** (**URL**) (a Web page address).

The overall idea seems simple enough: different authors use different namespace identifiers for different domains, and thus terminological clashes are avoided. The strategy generally followed since the introduction of namespaces is that authors choose as namespace identifiers the URLs that are under their control. For instance, if Joe Public authors a vocabulary for the school supplies marketed by Acme, Inc., he uses a namespace such as

```
http://www.acmeinc.com/jp#supplies
```

and for toys the namespace could be

```
http://www.acmeinc.com/jp#toys
```

Note that these URLs need not refer to actual documents.

Namespace declarations. The W3C recommendation[1] for incorporating namespaces into XML [Bray et al. 1999] goes beyond a simple two-part naming schema—it also fixes a particular syntax for declaring namespaces, their use, and scoping rules. Here is an example:

```
<item xmlns="http://www.acmeinc.com/jp#supplies"
     xmlns:toy="http://www.acmeinc.com/jp#toys">
    <name>backpack</name>
    <feature>
        <toy:item>
            <toy:name>cyberpet</toy:name>
        </toy:item>
    </feature>
</item>
```

[1] The final documents produced by W3C are modestly called "recommendations," but in reality they are as good as standards.

FIGURE 15.4 A report document with cross-references.

```
<?xml version="1.0" ?>
<Report Date="2000-12-12">
  <Students>
    <Student StudId="s111111111">
      <Name><First>John</First><Last>Doe</Last></Name>
      <Status>U2</Status>
      <CrsTaken CrsCode="CS308" Semester="F1997"/>
      <CrsTaken CrsCode="MAT123" Semester="F1997"/>
    </Student>
    <Student StudId="s666666666">
      <Name><First>Joe</First><Last>Public</Last></Name>
      <Status>U3</Status>
      <CrsTaken CrsCode="CS308" Semester="F1994"/>
      <CrsTaken CrsCode="MAT123" Semester="F1997"/>
    </Student>
    <Student StudId="s987654321">
      <Name><First>Bart</First><Last>Simpson</Last></Name>
      <Status>U4</Status>
      <CrsTaken CrsCode="CS308" Semester="F1994"/>
    </Student>
  </Students>
  <Classes>
    <Class>
      <CrsCode>CS308</CrsCode><Semester>F1994</Semester>
      <ClassRoster Members="s666666666 s987654321"/>
    </Class>
    <Class>
      <CrsCode>CS308</CrsCode><Semester>F1997</Semester>
      <ClassRoster Members="s111111111"/>
    </Class>
    <Class>
      <CrsCode>MAT123</CrsCode><Semester>F1997</Semester>
      <ClassRoster Members="s111111111 s666666666"/>
    </Class>
  </Classes>
  <Courses>
    <Course CrsCode="CS308">
      <CrsName>Software Engineering</CrsName>
    </Course>
    <Course CrsCode="MAT123">
      <CrsName>Algebra</CrsName>
    </Course>
  </Courses>
</Report>
```

Namespaces are defined using the attribute `xmlns`, which is a reserved word. In fact, W3C has advised that all names starting with `xml` be considered as reserved for the W3C's use. In our example, we declare two namespaces in the scope of the element `item`. The first one is declared using the syntax `xmlns=` and is called the **default namespace**. Naturally, there can be only one default namespace declaration per opening tag (this follows not only because of the semantics but also because XML does not permit multiple occurrences of the same attribute within the same opening tag). The second namespace is defined with the `xmlns:toy=` declaration. The **prefix** `toy` serves as a shorthand for the full namespace string `http://www.acmeinc.com/jp#toys`. One can declare several prefixed namespaces as long as the prefixes are distinct.[2]

Tags belonging to the namespace `http://www.acmeinc.com/jp#toys` should be prefixed with `toy:`. In our example, they are the inner tags `toy:item` and `toy:name`. Tags without any prefix (the outer `item`, `name`, and `feature`) are assumed to belong to the default namespace.

Namespace declarations have scope, which can be nested like a program block. To illustrate, we consider the following example:

```
<item xmlns="http://www.acmeinc.com/jp#supplies"
      xmlns:toy="http://www.acmeinc.com/jp#toys">
    <name>backpack</name>
    <feature>
        <toy:item>
            <toy:name>cyberpet</toy:name>
        </toy:item>
    </feature>
    <item xmlns="http://www.acmeinc.com/jp#supplies2"
          xmlns:toy="http://www.acmeinc.com/jp#toys2">
        <name>notebook</name>
        <toy:name>sticker</toy:name>
    </item>
</item>
```

Here we added one more child element to the outermost `item` element. The child is also called `item`, but it has its own default namespace and a redeclared namespace prefix, `toy`. Thus, the outermost `item` tag belongs to the default namespace

```
http://www.acmeinc.com/jp#supplies
```

[2] Nevertheless, two tags are assumed to belong to the same namespace, even if they have different prefixes, if and only if their prefixes refer to the same URI ("same" meaning that the URIs are equal as character strings).

The inner unprefixed `item` tag and its unprefixed child tag, `name`, are both in the scope of the default namespace

```
http://www.acmeinc.com/jp#supplies2
```

Similarly, the tags `toy:item` and `toy:name` inside the `feature` element belong to the namespace

```
http://www.acmeinc.com/jp#toys
```

The occurrence of `toy:name` at the end of the document belongs to the namespace

```
http://www.acmeinc.com/jp#toys2
```

Observe that, just as the innermost declaration of the default namespace overshadows the outermost declaration, the innermost declaration of the prefix `toy` overshadows the outermost declaration for the same prefix. A namespace-aware XML processor is supposed to understand these subtleties and, in particular, to recognize that the two unprefixed occurrences of `item` are *different tags* since they belong to different namespaces. Similarly, the unprefixed occurrences of `name` are different tags, and so are the prefixed versions of `name`. An XML processor that is *unaware* of namespaces will still be able to parse the above document. However, it will think that all unprefixed versions of `item` and `name` are the same and that all occurrences of the prefixed tag `toy:name` are the same. It will just wonder why the name has that weird : inside.

> Scoping rules for namespaces are similar to the scoping rules for variables in traditional block-structured languages (e.g., Java).

Even though the idea of a namespace seems like motherhood and apple pie—who could possibly be against it—it has been one of the least understood recommendations coming out of W3C [Bourret 2000]. Everyone agrees that tag names should come in two parts, but people have been trying to read between the lines of the recommendation and find things that are not there. One of the most confusing issues is the use of URLs as namespace identifiers. In our everyday experience, a URL points to some Web resource, and if a URL is used for a namespace, one tends to assume that it is a real address that contains some kind of schema describing the corresponding set of names. In reality, the name of a namespace is just a string that happens to be a URL, and it can be a big disappointment when pointing the browser toward such a URL brings up an unattractive error message.

Namespaces are nothing more than a mechanism for disambiguating tag names. An XML processor that reads a document encoded with namespaces should "know" how to parse it—that is, how to find its schema (represented as a DTD or an XML Schema—the specification languages described later). The information on the schema location can be provided in a special attribute, or it can be part of the convention used in a particular enterprise or community. For example, the toy industry might agree that all toy-related documents should be parsed using the DTD at a particular URL. One convention taking hold right now is that certain vocabularies (such as those used in the XML Schema specification—see Section 15.3) be identified using certain "well-known" namespaces, which prescribe the document schema uniquely.

15.2.4 Document Type Definitions

There are fixed rules that an author must follow in order to create an HTML document that can be properly rendered by the browser. For instance, the `table` element cannot occur inside the `form` element. XML, on the other hand, is intended for a variety of application domains (e.g., retail, healthcare, and education), and each has its own idea of a properly structured document. Therefore, XML includes a language for specifying the document structure.

A set of rules for structuring an XML document is called a **document type definition (DTD)**. A DTD can be specified as part of the document itself, or the document can give a URL where its DTD can be found. A document that conforms to its DTD is said to be **valid**. The XML specification does not require processors to check each document for conformance to its DTD because some applications might not care if the document is valid. In some cases, the processor does not check validity, instead relying on the guarantee of the sender for this (e.g., in electronic billing, where both sides use software guaranteed to produce valid documents). XML does not even require that the document have a DTD, but it does require that all documents be well formed. (The conditions for well-formedness—proper element nesting and restrictions on the attributes—have been discussed in Section 15.2.2.)

These two notions of correctness can lead to significant simplification and speedup for XML processors. An HTML browser usually tries to correct bugs in the HTML documents and to display as much of a buggy document as possible. In contrast, an XML processor is expected to simply reject documents that are not well formed. A processor that expects valid documents would reject invalid ones (those that do not comply with the DTD) even if they are well formed.

For those who are familiar with formal languages, a DTD is a *grammar* that specifies a valid XML document, based on the tags used in the document and their attributes. For instance, the following DTD is consistent with the document in Figure 15.3 on page 584:

```
<!DOCTYPE PersonList [
     <!ELEMENT PersonList (Title,Contents)>
     <!ELEMENT Title EMPTY>
     <!ELEMENT Contents (Person*)>
     <!ELEMENT Person (Name,Id,Address)>
     <!ELEMENT Name (#PCDATA)>
```

```
        <!ELEMENT Id (#PCDATA)>
        <!ELEMENT Address (Number,Street)>
        <!ELEMENT Number (#PCDATA)>
        <!ELEMENT Street (#PCDATA)>
        <!ATTLIST PersonList Type CDATA #IMPLIED
                             Date CDATA #IMPLIED>
        <!ATTLIST Title Value CDATA #REQUIRED>
    ]>
```

This example illustrates the most common DTD components: a **name** (PersonList in the example) and a set of ELEMENT and ATTLIST statements. The name of a DTD must coincide with the tag name of the root element of the document that conforms to that DTD. One ELEMENT statement exists for each allowed tag, including the root tag. Furthermore, for each tag that can have attributes, the ATTLIST statement specifies the allowed attributes and their type.

In our example, the first ELEMENT statement says that the element PersonList consists of a Title element followed by a Contents element. A Title element (the second ELEMENT statement) does not contain any elements (it is an empty element). The * in the definition of the Contents element indicates that there are zero or more elements of type Person. If we use + instead of "*", it would mean that at least one Person element must be present. The elements Name, Id, Number, and Street are declared to be of type #PCDATA, that is, a character string.[3] Element content can also be specified as ANY, meaning that the element can have any content.

Following the element list, a DTD contains the description of allowed element attributes. In our case, PersonList is permitted to have the attributes Type and Date, while Title can only have the attribute Value. Other elements are not allowed to have attributes. Moreover, both attributes of PersonList are *optional*, as specified by the keyword #IMPLIED, while the Value attribute of Title is mandatory. All three attributes have the type CDATA, which is, again, a character string. (Note that different syntax is used to declare character string types for elements and attributes.)

Observe that our document in Figure 15.3 is valid with respect to the above DTD, but if, for example, we delete some Address elements from it, it will become invalid because the DTD says that each person must have an address. On the other hand, if the DTD has

```
    <!ELEMENT Person (Name,Id,Address?)>
```

the address field becomes optional since ? indicates zero or one occurrences of the Address element.

[3] PCDATA stands for *parsed character data*.

It is also possible to state that the order of elements in a person's description does not matter, using the connective |, which represents alternatives:

```
<!ELEMENT Person
     ((Name,Id,Address)|(Name,Address,Id)|(Id,Address,Name)
       |(Id,Name,Address)|(Address,Id,Name)|(Address,Name,Id))>
```

You can see that it becomes rather awkward, however.

DTDs allow the author to specify several types for an attribute. We have seen CDATA. The other frequently used types are ID, IDREF, and IDREFS, mentioned on page 588 in connection with the report document in Figure 15.4. We pointed out that a document of this type needs a mechanism for enforcing referential integrity—much as in the database examples of Chapter 3.

Specifically, we want to make sure that the values of the attributes StudId in Student and CrsCode in Course are distinct throughout the document, that the attribute CrsCode in CrsTaken represents a reference to a course mentioned in this document (that there is a Course element with a matching value in its CrsCode attribute), and that the members in a list indicated by Members in ClassRoster refer to student records mentioned in the document (for each such member there is a Student element with the matching value of its StudId attribute). This can be enforced with the DTD shown in Figure 15.5, in which we omit some easily reconstructible parts.

A compliant XML processor that insists on document validity is obliged by this DTD to make sure that no two Student elements have the same value in their StudId attribute (similarly for Course elements). This is because StudId is declared to have the type ID. In fact, no pair of attributes of type ID (with the same or different names) can have the same value in a valid XML document.

Referential integrity is maintained using the IDREF and IDREFS declarations. Because the attribute CrsCode of the element CrsTaken is declared as IDREF, referential integrity for course codes is preserved. The attribute Members in ClassRoster is declared as IDREFS, which represents *lists* of values of type IDREF. This secures the integrity of references to student Ids.

There are also constraints in the document that beg to be noticed, but they cannot be enforced using DTDs. We discuss these issues in the next section.

15.2.5 Inadequacy of DTDs as a Data Definition Language

XML was conceived as a simplified, streamlined version of SGML [SGML 1986], which was standardized years before the work on XML began. SGML was created for specifying documents that can be exchanged and automatically processed by software agents, and this was the original goal of XML as well. DTDs and the rationale behind their use were borrowed from SGML. Their technical underpinnings come from the theory of formal languages, and general-purpose parsers that can validate any document against any DTD are well known. Such validation has important implications for document-processing software. For instance, if an XML processor

FIGURE 15.5 A DTD for the report document in Figure 15.4.

```
<!DOCTYPE Report [
    <!ELEMENT Report (Students,Classes,Courses)>
    <!ELEMENT Students (Student*)>
    <!ELEMENT Classes (Class*)>
    <!ELEMENT Courses (Course*)>
    <!ELEMENT Student (Name,Status,CrsTaken*)>
    <!ELEMENT Name (First,Last)>
    <!ELEMENT First (#PCDATA)>
    .
    .
    .
    <!ELEMENT CrsTaken EMPTY>
    <!ELEMENT Class (CrsCode,Semester,ClassRoster)>
    <!ELEMENT Course (CrsName)>
    .
    .
    .
    <!ELEMENT ClassRoster EMPTY>
    <!ATTLIST Report Date CDATA #IMPLIED>
    <!ATTLIST Student StudId ID #REQUIRED>
    <!ATTLIST Course CrsCode ID #REQUIRED>
    <!ATTLIST CrsTaken CrsCode IDREF #REQUIRED
                       Semester CDATA #REQUIRED>
    <!ATTLIST ClassRoster Members IDREFS #IMPLIED>
]>
```

can expect that the documents it receives have been validated and will conform to the DTD `Report` shown in Figure 15.5, it does not need to take care of special cases and exceptions, such as the possibility that a student might have taken a nonexistent course or that a street address is missing.

During the development of XML, new ideas started to emerge. In particular, XML introduced the possibility of treating Web documents as data sources that can be queried (as with database relations) and that can be related to each other through semantically meaningful links (as with foreign-key constraints). It was at this point that XML began to outgrow its SGML heritage. One of the first enhancements, which came too late to be included in XML 1.0, was namespaces, discussed earlier. A much more significant enhancement is the development of the XML Schema specification (Section 15.3), which is designed to rectify many of the limitations of DTD as a data definition language. These limitations include the following:

- DTDs are not designed with namespaces in mind. A DTD views `xmlns` as just another attribute with no special meaning. It is not hard to extend them to include namespaces, but there is a problem of backward compatibility and, in view of other limitations of DTDs, such enhancement is probably a futile exercise.

- DTDs use syntax that is quite different from that of XML documents. While this is not a fatal drawback, it is not the most elegant feature of XML 1.0 either.
- DTDs have a very limited repertoire of basic types (essentially just glorified strings).
- DTDs provide only limited means for expressing data-consistency constraints. They do not have keys (except for the very limited `ID` type), and the mechanism for specifying referential integrity is very weak. The only way to reference something is through the `IDREF` and `IDREFS` attributes, and even these are based on only one primitive type, a string. In particular, it is not possible to type the references. One cannot require that the attribute `CrsCode` of the element `CrsTaken` in the report document of Figure 15.4 references only `Course` elements. Thus, it is possible for John Doe to have a child element

```
<CrsTaken CrsCode="s666666666" Semester="F1999"/>
```

  which refers to the student Id of Joe Public instead of to a course, and no XML 1.0–compliant processor can detect this problem. DTDs have ways of enforcing referential integrity for attributes but no corresponding feature for elements. For example, the content of the element `Class` includes the elements `CrsCode` and `Semester` (not to be confused with similarly named attributes of the tag `CrsTaken`). Clearly, we want the content of the element `CrsCode` to refer to a valid course and match a value of the attribute `CrsCode` in some `Course` element. Furthermore, for each pair of values of the attributes in the element `CrsTaken`, there must be a corresponding pair of values of `CrsCode`/`Semester` tags in some `Class` element. These constraints cannot be enforced using DTDs.
- XML data is ordered; database data is unordered (e.g., the order of tuples does not matter). Also, the order of the attributes in a database relation or an object does not matter; the order of elements in XML matters. We already saw that DTDs allow us to specify alternatives, and through them we can state that the order of elements is immaterial (as in the earlier example of the `Name`, `Address`, and `Id` children of the element `Person`). However, this becomes extremely awkward as the number of attributes grows. For instance, to state that the order among N children elements is immaterial, a DTD must specify $N!$ alternatives.
- Element definitions are global to the entire document. If a DTD specifies that, for example, `Name` consists of children elements `First` and `Last`, then it is not possible to have a *differently structured* `Name` element anywhere else in the document. This happens because a DTD can have only one `ELEMENT` clause per element name. There is no way to localize it with respect to a parent element so that different definitions would apply to different occurrences of `Name`, depending on where it is nested.

15.3 XML Schema

XML Schema, a data definition language for XML documents, became a recommendation of W3C in 2001. It was developed in response to the aforesaid limitations of the DTD mechanism and has the following main features:

- It uses the same syntax as that used for ordinary XML documents.
- It is integrated with the namespace mechanism. In particular, different schemas can be imported from different namespaces and integrated into one schema.
- It provides a number of built-in types, such as string, integer, and time—similar to SQL.
- It provides the means to define complex types based on simpler ones.
- It allows the same element name to be defined as having different types depending on where the element is nested.
- It supports key and referential integrity constraints.
- It provides a better mechanism for specifying documents where the order of element types does not matter.

The downside is that XML Schema is an order of magnitude more complex than the DTDs, and the DTDs are still widely used for simpler kinds of XML processing, those where the advanced features just described are not required.

An XML document that conforms to a given schema is said to be **schema valid** and is called an **instance** document of the schema. As with DTDs, the XML Schema specification does not require an XML processor to actually use the document schema. It is free to ignore the schema or to use a different one. For instance, the XML processor might want to consider only the documents that satisfy stricter integrity constraints than those given in the schema, or it might decide to enforce only part of the schema. This liberal attitude should be contrasted with databases, where *all* data must comply with the schema. In this sense, XML data as a whole should be considered semistructured (Section 15.1) despite the fact that a schema might partially describe it.

15.3.1 XML Schema and Namespaces

An XML Schema document (like a DTD) describes the structure of other (instance) XML documents. It begins with a declaration of the namespaces to be used in the schema, three of which are particularly important:

- `http://www.w3.org/2001/XMLSchema`—The namespace that identifies names of tags and attributes used *in the schema*. These names are not related to, nor do they appear in, any particular instance document. Instead, they are used in schema documents to describe structural properties of instance documents. Hence, this namespace is part of schema documents but is not used in instance documents. Among the names associated with this namespace are `schema`, `attribute`, and `element`.

- `http://www.w3.org/2001/XMLSchema-instance`—Another namespace used in conjunction with `http://www.w3.org/2001/XMLSchema`. It identifies a small number of special names, which are also defined in the XML Schema specification but are used in the instance documents rather than in their schema (whence the name `XMLSchema-instance`). One such name, `schemaLocation`, specifies the location of the schema for the document. Another defines the special null value when it appears in a document. We will discuss these features in due time. This namespace is part of the specification of instance documents since it defines tags used in those documents.
- The **target namespace**—Identifies the set of names *defined* by a particular schema document, in other words, the user-defined names that are to be used in the instance documents of that particular schema. For instance, in the schema document for Figure 15.4, the names `CrsTaken`, `Student`, `Status`, and so forth, would be associated with the target namespace. (We will soon start developing the various parts of that schema.) The target namespace is declared using the attribute `targetNameSpace` of the opening tag of the `schema` element—the root tag of every schema document.

The integration with namespaces is one of the important items missing in DTDs: a DTD can define any number of tags, but there is no way to associate those tags with a namespace.

We now begin to develop a schema for the report document of Figure 15.4. Our first example simply declares the namespaces to be used in the schema we are creating.

```
<schema xmlns="http://www.w3.org/2001/XMLSchema"
        targetNameSpace="http://xyz.edu/Admin">

    <!-- Nothing here yet -->
</schema>
```

The first namespace declared in this example makes the standard `XMLSchema` namespace the default. This is handy because in creating the schema, we are likely to use many special tags defined by the XML Schema specification, and making `XMLSchema` the default namespace will obviate the need for namespace prefixes for them. If, however, we want a different namespace to be the default, we can use

```
xmlns:xs="http://www.w3.org/2001/XMLSchema"
```

By convention, `xs` is the prefix for names in the standard `XMLSchema` namespace. In this case, we have to use `xs` whenever a name associated with the XML Schema's namespace is used:

```
<xs:schema xmlns:xs="http://www.w3.org/2001/XMLSchema"
        xs:targetNameSpace="http://xyz.edu/Admin">

    <!-- Nothing here yet -->
</xs:schema>
```

The first attribute here says that `xs` is the prefix for names associated with the `XMLSchema` namespace. The second attribute says that the new tags and attributes defined by the above schema document are considered to be part of the `http://xyz.edu/Admin` namespace. Note that since `targetNameSpace` is a name defined by the XML Schema specification, its use is prefixed with `xs`.

Suppose now that we have filled in all the blanks in the above schema. How does the fact that we now have a schema for the instance document in Figure 15.4 change this document? We need to add three things to the instance: the declaration of the default namespace it uses (in our case, `http://xyz.edu/Admin`), the location of its schema, and the `XMLSchema-instance` namespace. The latter is needed because the attribute `schemaLocation`, which specifies the schema location, occurs in instance documents and is part of the `XMLSchema-instance` namespace. To better understand the relationship among the schema, the actual instance document, and the various namespaces, we show the report document and its schema together in Figure 15.6.

Note in the figure that the default namespace in the instance document is `http://xyz.edu/Admin`—the namespace defined in the `targetNameSpace` attribute

FIGURE 15.6 Schema and an instance document.

```
<!-- An XML schema document; located at http://xyz.edu/Admin.xsd -->
<schema xmlns="http://www.w3.org/2001/XMLSchema"
        targetNameSpace="http://xyz.edu/Admin">

    <!-- Nothing here yet -->
</schema>

<!-- An instance document conforming to the above schema;
     it uses the target namespace defined in that schema -->
<?xml version="1.0" ?>
<Report xmlns="http://xyz.edu/Admin">
        xmlns:xsi="http://www.w3.org/2001/XMLSchema-instance"
        xsi:schemaLocation="http://xyz.edu/Admin
        http://xyz.edu/Admin.xsd">

<!-- Same content as in the report document of Figure 15.4 -->
</Report>
```

of the schema document.[4] There need not be anything at this URL because a namespace is just an identifier that is used to disambiguate the names of document tags and attributes. This namespace is chosen as a default in order to minimize the number of namespace prefixes that need to be used in the document. Because the document in Figure 15.6 is supposed to have the same content as in the report in Figure 15.4, most of the tag and attribute names belong to this default namespace.

The attribute `xsi:schemaLocation` is part of the XML Schema specification and belongs to the namespace

```
http://www.w3.org/2001/XMLSchema-instance
```

The value of the attribute is a namespace-URL pair, and it says that the schema for the namespace `http://xyz.edu/Admin` can be found in an XML Schema document at the URL `http://xyz.edu/Admin.xsd`. However, as mentioned earlier, XML processors are not bound by these hints. They can choose to ignore the schema or to use a different one.

Before plunging into the specifics of defining the actual schema, we mention one other important detail, the `include` statement. It is easy to see from Figure 15.4 that our report has three distinct components: a student list, a class list, and a course list. Since these components have very different structures, it is reasonable to assume that they might well occur separately in other contexts and that they might have their own schemas. Given this, it is unreasonable for us to copy those schemas over in order to create the schema for the report document. Instead, we can use the `include` statement in the schema document as follows:

```
<schema xmlns="http://www.w3.org/2001/XMLSchema"
        targetNameSpace="http://xyz.edu/Admin">

  <include schemaLocation="http://xyz.edu/StudentTypes.xsd"/>
  <include schemaLocation="http://xyz.edu/ClassTypes.xsd"/>
  <include schemaLocation="http://xyz.edu/CourseTypes.xsd"/>

  <!-- Nothing here yet -->
</schema>
```

The effect of the `include` statement is to include the schemas at the specified address in the given document. This technique allows for greater flexibility and modularity of XML schemas. Included schemas must have the same target namespace as the including schema since the include statement effectively integrates them into the including schema document. Observe one possibly confusing detail in the above example: we have used the attribute `schemaLocation` without prefixing it with `xsi`,

[4] Most namespaces and document locations used in the examples have been changed to protect the innocent. However, the `XMLSchema` and `XMLSchema-instance` namespaces are real.

and, unlike the previous example, we did not include the XMLSchema-instance namespace. This discrepancy has a rational explanation. The schemaLocation attribute of the tag include belongs to the standard XMLSchema namespace (like the include tag itself); that is, this attribute is different from the similarly named attribute in the report document above. Since, unlike the report document, our schema does not use any names from the XMLSchema-instance namespace, this namespace was not declared.

15.3.2 Simple Types

First we define simple types—types whose members have little or no internal structure.

Primitive types. The dearth of primitive types is one of the criticisms leveled against DTDs. The XML Schema specification rectifies the problem by adding many useful primitive types, such as decimal, integer, float, boolean, and date, in addition to string, ID, IDREF, and IDREFS. More important, it provides type constructors, such as *list* and *union*, and a mechanism to derive new primitive types from the basic ones. This mechanism is similar to the CREATE DOMAIN statement of SQL (see Section 3.3.6).

Deriving simple types using the list and union constructors. As in DTDs, IDREFS is one of the primitive types in the XML Schema specification. However, it can also be derived using the list constructor:[5]

```
<simpleType name="myIdrefs">
    <list itemType="IDREF"/>
</simpleType>
```

Here the name attribute is used to give a name, myIdrefs, to the newly defined type whose instances are lists of IDREF items. This and any other name introduced by the name attribute in a schema document belongs to the target namespace of that document.

The union type can be useful when there is a need for two or more ways to enter data. For instance, in the United States a telephone number can be seven or ten digits long, which can be expressed as follows:

```
<simpleType name="phoneNumber">
    <union memberTypes="phone7digits phone10digits"/>
</simpleType>
```

We will see the definitions of the types phone7digits and phone10digits shortly.

[5] Unless stated otherwise, all examples of XML schemas assume the standard http://www.w3.org/2000/10/XMLSchema namespace as a default.

Deriving simple types by restriction. A more interesting way of deriving new types is via the **restriction** mechanism, which allows us to constrain a basic type using one or more constraints from a fixed repertoire defined by the XML Schema specification. This is how we are going to define the type phone7digits:

```
<simpleType name="phone7digits">
    <restriction base="integer">
        <minInclusive value="1000000"/>
        <maxInclusive value="9999999"/>
    </restriction>
</simpleType>
```

The 10-digit number type is defined similarly. In the definition of phone7digits, we used the tags maxInclusive and minInclusive to define the range of acceptable numbers. XML Schema provides a large number of built-in constraints to play with, such as minInclusive/maxInclusive [XMLSchema 2000a; XMLSchema 2000b]. Here we mention just a few of the more interesting ones. Suppose that, in addition, we let the user specify phone numbers in the XXX-YYYY format. This can be done in several ways, one being

```
<simpleType name="phone7digitsAndDash">
    <restriction base="string">
        <pattern value="[0-9]{3}-[0-9]{4}"/>
    </restriction>
</simpleType>
```

Here we use the pattern tag to restrict the set of all strings to those that match the given pattern. The language for constructing patterns is similar to that used in the Perl programming language, but the basics should be familiar to anyone with a working knowledge of text editors such as Vi or Emacs. In the above example, [0-9] means "any digit between 0 and 9" and {3} is a pattern modifier that says that only a sequence of exactly three digits is allowed.

Other ways to derive simple types from the basic string type include the following:

- <length value="7"/>—Restricts the domain to strings of length seven.
- <minLength value="7"/>—Restricts the domain to strings of length *at least* seven.
- <maxLength value="14"/>—Restricts the domain to strings of length *at most* 14.
- <enumeration value="ABC"/>—Specifies one value in an enumerated set.

The above constraints are not limited to strings, and enumeration is applicable to virtually any base type. Here is an example:

```
<simpleType name="emergencyNumbers">
    <restriction base="integer">
        <enumeration value="911"/>
        <enumeration value="333"/>
        <enumeration value="5431234"/>
    </restriction>
</simpleType>
```

Simple types for the report document. We now define some simple types for our report document of Figure 15.4 on page 591. We will later attach these types to the appropriate attributes in the document schema. For easy reference, we summarize all student-related types in Figure 15.9 on page 618 and all course-related types in Figure 15.10 on page 619.

```
<simpleType name="studentId">
    <restriction base="ID">
        <pattern value="s[0-9]{9}"/>
    </restriction>
</simpleType>
<simpleType name="studentRef">
    <restriction base="IDREF"
        <pattern value="s[0-9]{9}"/>
    </restriction>
</simpleType>
<simpleType name="studentIds">
    <list itemType="adm:studentRef"/>
</simpleType>
<simpleType name="courseCode">
    <restriction base="ID">
        <pattern value="[A-Z]{3}[0-9]{3}"/>
    </restriction>
</simpleType>
<simpleType name="courseRef">
    <restriction base="IDREF">
        <pattern value="[A-Z]{3}[0-9]{3}"/>
    </restriction>
</simpleType>
```

The first type, `studentId`, defines student Ids as strings that consist of the letter `s` followed by nine digits; it will be used to specify the domain of values for `studId` in the report. Recall that XML requires the strings of type `ID` to start with a letter, which is why the pattern indicates that all `ID`s start with letter `s`. The second `simpleType` expression defines the type of *references* to student Ids; the third defines *lists* of references to student Ids; the fourth defines course codes as strings of three uppercase letters followed by three digits; and the fifth is the type for course references. Note also that we have used ID and IDREF as base types. They have the same semantics as they do in DTDs, so uniqueness and referential integrity are guaranteed. The definition of the type studentIds uses a previously defined type studentRef. Note that the reference to that type is tagged with a namespace prefix adm, which is here assumed to be associated with the target namespace of the schema document. The need for this prefix will be explained shortly.

Observe that we are already doing better than in the case of the Report DTD shown in Figure 15.5 on page 597. It is impossible for a DTD to say that the attribute Members returns a list of references to students rather than to courses or to impose a similar restriction on the attribute CrsCode of the tag CrsTaken. In contrast, the above simple types prevent such meaningless references because the type courseRef is disjoint from the domain of studentId and the domain of studentRef is disjoint from that of courseCode.

Type declarations for simple elements and attributes. So far, we have been talking about types without attaching them to elements and attributes. Here are some simple cases of type declaration for tags in our report document, which will later become part of the schema document for this report.

```
<element name="CrsName" type="string"/>                        15.2
<element name="Status" type="adm:studentStatus"/>
```

The first declaration states that the element CrsName has a simple content of type string. The last declaration is fancier: it associates the Status tag with a derived type, studentStatus, defined as an enumeration of strings U1, U2, U3, U4, G1, G2, G3, G4, and G5, which represent the various status codes for undergraduate and graduate students.

```
<simpleType name="studentStatus">
     <restriction base="string">
          <enumeration value="U1"/>
          <enumeration value="U2"/>
          .
          .
          .
          <enumeration value="G5"/>
     </restriction>
</simpleType>
```

A subtle but very important point in this example is the prefix adm attached to studentStatus in (15.2)—a consequence of the namespace consideration. To understand this better, let us consider the context in which the above statements appear:

```
<schema xmlns="http://www.w3.org/2001/XMLSchema"
      xmlns:adm="http://xyz.edu/Admin"
      targetNameSpace="http://xyz.edu/Admin">
   :
   <element name="CrsName" type="string"/>
   <!-- reference to StudentStatus -->
   <element name="Status" type="adm:studentStatus"/>
   :
   <!-- definition of StudentStatus -->
   <simpleType name="studentStatus">
      :
   </simpleType>
   :
</schema>
```

In a schema document the default is typically the standard XMLSchema namespace. This enables us to use frequently occurring symbols, such as element, simpleType, name, and type, without a prefix. In addition, a schema document defines a number of types (e.g., studentStatus), elements (e.g., Status), and attributes (see Section 15.3.3) that belong to a target namespace (http://xyz.edu/Admin in our case). When we define a new element or type, we use it without a prefix (for example, name="Status" and name="studentStatus") because these names are newly defined and hence cannot be part of the default namespace; they are automatically placed in the target namespace. However, how do we *refer* to the names defined within the same schema (for example, our reference to studentStatus in the type attribute)? If we do not use any prefix, the XML processor is supposed to assume that the name belongs to the default namespace. This is precisely what happens with the string type of the element CrsName. Since string is not prefixed, it is assumed to be taken out of the standard XMLSchema namespace, which is correct. In contrast, using studentStatus without a prefix causes the XML processor to assume that this symbol also comes from the default namespace, which is an error since XML Schema does not define studentStatus. Therefore, we need to define a namespace prefix for the target namespace and use it with every reference to a component of the target schema. The purpose of the second occurrence of the xmlns attribute of the schema element in the above example is thus to associate the prefix adm to the target namespace. From now on, we assume that the target namespace has the prefix adm, and we will use it with defined types without mention.

Next, consider how one specifies the types of some attributes in our document:

```
<attribute name="Date" type="date"/>
<attribute name="StudId" type="adm:studentId"/>
<attribute name="Members" type="adm:studentIds"/>
<attribute name="CrsCode" type="adm:courseCode"/>
```

Notice that these declarations do not associate attributes with elements, so they are not very meaningful at this point. We cannot make the association here because elements that have attributes are considered to have *complex types* (even if they have empty content, such as CrsTaken), so we need to familiarize ourselves with such types first.

15.3.3 Complex Types

Complex types are suitable for defining the structure of elements in an XML document.

Basic example. So far we have seen how to define *simple types*—the only types allowed in attributes and the types of elements that do not have attributes or children. The fragment of a schema in Figure 15.7 defines a complex type suitable for the Student element in the report document.

This example contains two type declarations and many new features. First, the tag complexType is used instead of simpleType to warn the XML processor of things to come. Second, the sequence tag is used to specify that the elements Name, Status, and CrsTaken must occur in the given order. Third, the CrsTaken element (whose

FIGURE 15.7 Definition of the complex type studentType.

```
<complexType name="studentType">
    <sequence>
        <element name="Name" type="adm:personNameType"/>
        <element name="Status" type="adm:studentStatus"/>
        <element name="CrsTaken" type="adm:courseTakenType"
            minOccurs="0" maxOccurs="unbounded"/>
    </sequence>
    <attribute name="StudId" type="adm:studentId"/>
</complexType>
<complexType name="personNameType">
    <sequence>
        <element name="First" type="string"/>
        <element name="Last" type="string"/>
    </sequence>
</complexType>
```

type will be defined shortly) is said to occur zero, one, or more times. In general, we can specify any number as a value of `minOccurs` and `maxOccurs`. Doing the same with DTDs is possible but extremely awkward since one must use alternatives (specified using |), which leads to unwieldy schemas. For other elements, we did not specify `minOccurs` and `maxOccurs` because they both default to one occurrence (which we want anyway). Finally, the attribute declaration at the end of the complex type definition associates `StudId` with the type `studentId` (Figure 15.9 on page 618), and, because it occurs in the scope of the definition of `studentType`, it means that every element of type `studentType` must have this attribute (and no other).

The second type declaration in Figure 15.7 supplies the type for the `Name` element used in the definition of `studentType`. This declaration does not introduce new features.

Associating a complex type with an element is no different from associating a simple type with an element. The following statement associates the `Student` element with the complex type `studentType`:

```
<element name="Student" type="adm:studentType"/>
```

Special cases. The simple picture just described is complicated by two special cases: how do we define the type of an element that has both a simple content (just text with no children elements) *and* attributes, and how can we define the type of an element that has attributes but *no* content (defined as `EMPTY` in the DTD)? We have seen the first kind of element in the dialog between Romeo and Apothecary on page 587; the second kind is represented by the element `CrsTaken` of Figure 15.4, page 591.

Defining the first type of element is a little awkward, and we skip this topic since it rarely occurs in data representation using XML.[6] On the other hand, defining the type for elements such as `CrsTaken` is easy:

```
<complexType name="courseTakenType">
    <attribute name="CrsCode" type="adm:courseRef"/>
    <attribute name="Semester" type="string"/>
</complexType>
```

Combining elements into groups. The example of `studentType` in Figure 15.7 shows how to combine elements into an ordered group using `sequence`. Tags such as `sequence`, which describe how elements can be combined into groups, are called **compositors**; they are required when an element has **complex content**, that is, when the element has at least one child element. XML Schema defines several

[6] Defining an element whose content is just text (no children elements) and which has attributes is done with the help of the `simpleContent` tag defined by XML Schema; see, for example, the XML Schema Primer [XMLSchema 2000a].

compositors; one provides a way to combine elements into *unordered* sets. Note that the lack of a practical way to specify unordered collections of elements was one of the criticisms of DTDs in Section 15.2.5.

Suppose that we want to allow the street name, number, and city name to appear in any order in an address. We can specify this using the compositor all:

```
<complexType name="addressType">
    <all>
        <element name="StreetName" type="string"/>
        <element name="StreetNumber" type="string"/>
        <element name="City" type="string"/>
    </all>
</complexType>
```

Unfortunately, there are a number of restrictions on all that make it hard to use in many cases. First, all must appear directly below complexType, so the following is illegal:

```
<complexType name="studentType2">
    <sequence>
        <all>
            <element name="Name" type="adm:personNameType"/>
            <element name="Status" type="adm:studentStatus"/>
        </all>
        <element name="CrsTaken" type="adm:courseTakenType"
                minOccurs="0" maxOccurs="unbounded"/>
    </sequence>
    <attribute name="StudId" type="adm:studentId"/>
</complexType>
```

Second, no element within it can be repeated. In other words, maxOccurs must be one for every child of all, so the following is also not allowed:

```
<complexType name="studentType3">
    <all>
        <element name="Name" type="adm:personNameType"/>
        <element name="Status" type="adm:studentStatus"/>
        <element name="CrsTaken" type="adm:courseTakenType"
                minOccurs="0" maxOccurs="unbounded"/>
    </all>
    <attribute name="StudId" type="adm:studentId"/>
</complexType>
```

In addition to sequence and all, the third grouping construct of XML Schema is the choice compositor, which plays the same role for complex types as union does for simple types. For instance, in the following example,

```
<complexType name="addressType">
    <sequence>
        <choice>
            <element name="POBox" type="string"/>
            <sequence>
                <element name="Name" type="string"/>
                <element name="Number" type="string"/>
            </sequence>
        </choice>
        <element name="City" type="string"/>
    </sequence>
</complexType>
```

choice lets us substitute the post office box for the street address. That is, a valid address must have precisely one of the two possibilities: a post office box or a street address.

Note that a content descriptor, such as a compositor, is required even if the type contains only one child element. For instance,

```
<complexType name="foo">
    <element name="bar" type="integer"/>
</complexType>
```

is illegal, but

```
<complexType name="foo">
    <sequence>
        <element name="bar" type="integer"/>
    </sequence>
</complexType>
```

is correct.

Local element names. In DTDs, all element declarations are global because only one ELEMENT statement per element name is allowed. Thus, it is not possible to define a valid report document (with respect to *any* DTD) where both Student and Course have a Name child element with different types. Indeed, this is the case in Figure 15.4 on page 591, where a course name is a string while a student name has complex type personNameType. Since the types are different, we could not use Name as the element name for both. Instead, we had to use CrsName to identify course names.

For the same reason, DTDs do not let us use the element name `Course` instead of the name `CrsCode` for the child element of `Class`: the `Course` child inside the element `Courses` has a different structure than the `CrsCode` element inside `Class`. Thus, if we replace the tag name `CrsCode` with `Course`, the DTD must have two different `ELEMENT` statements for `Course`, which is impossible.

The XML Schema specification corrects this problem by providing local scope to element declarations. This is done as in any programming language. A declaration of an element type is considered local to the nearest containing `<complexType ... > ... </complexType>` block. In the report document, this local scoping allows us to rename the `CrsName` tag to `Name` and define the following schema:

```
<complexType name="studentType">
    <sequence>
        <element name="Name" type="adm:personNameType"/>
        <element name="Status" type="adm:studentStatus"/>
        <element name="CrsTaken" type="adm:courseTakenType"
            minOccurs="0" maxOccurs="unbounded"/>
    </sequence>
    <attribute name="StudId" type="adm:studentId"/>
</complexType>
<complexType name="courseType">
    <sequence>
        <element name="Name" type="string"/>
    </sequence>
    <attribute name="CrsCode" type="adm:courseCode"/>
</complexType>
```

Here both `studentType` and `courseType` include a child element, `Name`. In the first case, this element has a complex type `personNameType`, which includes two elements: `First` and `Last`. In the second case, it has a simple type, `string`. However, unlike in a DTD, the two declarations have a different scope and thus their definitions do not clash.

> *Brain Teaser:* Can there be a DTD for an instance document with the above schema?

Importing schemas. In Section 15.3.1, we illustrated the use of the `include` instruction for constructing a schema out of separate components that reside in different files. This facility supports modular construction of complex XML Schemas by small teams of collaborating programmers. Therefore, it requires that the target namespace of an included schema be the same as the target namespace of the containing schema.

At the same time, the designers of the XML Schema specification understood that the true potential of the Web can be realized only if people can pull together schemas constructed by different groups or organizations. This is the goal of the `import` statement. As with the `include` statement, the `schemaLocation` attribute is provided, but it is optional for `import`. The only required attribute is `namespace` because it is possible to import a schema whose target namespace is different from the target namespace of the importing schema. In the absence of `schemaLocation`, the XML processor is supposed to find the schema on its own, possibly deriving it from the namespace using some convention. Even when `schemaLocation` is provided, the processor is allowed to ignore it or to use a different schema. The only thing that the processor must not ignore is the namespace. Thus, the `namespace` attribute of the `import` statement determines the target namespace of the imported schema.

In the following example, we use `import` instead of `include`:

```
<schema xmlns="http://www.w3.org/2001/XMLSchema"
        targetNameSpace="http://xyz.edu/Admin"
        xmlns:reg = "http://xyz.edu/Registrar"
        xmlns:crs = "http://xyz.edu/Courses">
  <import namespace="http://xyz.edu/Registrar"
       schemaLocation="http://xyz.edu/Registrar/StudentTypes.xsd"/>
  <import namespace="http://xyz.edu/Courses"/>
  .
  .
  .
</schema>
```

Here we assume that the schemas describing students and courses use different target namespaces and that the report-processing software knows where to find the schema that describes courses. Therefore, the `schemaLocation` attribute is not provided in the second `import` statement (but it is in the first). The first `import` statement imports a schema with target namespace `http://xyz.edu/Registrar`. This namespace is assigned the prefix `reg` so that any part of the imported schema, for example, `x`, could be referred to as `reg:x`.

Deriving new complex types by extension and restriction. In some cases, the user might need to modify parts of the included or imported schema. This is easy with inclusion because all documents are assumed to be under the author's control. With importing, however, the control is usually with an external entity and the importer might not be allowed to copy the schema, or this might not be desirable. For example, in many cases, the importer just wants to have a "view" of the original schema so that the importer's schema would change along with that original.

XML Schema provides two mechanisms for modifying imported schema: **extension** and **restriction**. Both are special cases of the notion of *subtype* defined in Section 14.3.3. **Extending** a schema means adding new elements or attributes to it. **Restricting** a schema means tightening its definition in order to exclude some instance documents.

Suppose that `foo.edu` decides to follow the example of `xyz.edu` and "XML-ize" their registration system. Overall they like the schema of `xyz.edu` but want to add a short course syllabus to every course record. Because `xyz.edu` is constantly improving its XML student registration tools, `foo.edu` decides that it can take advantage of these improvements by importing and *extending* the schema rather than copying it over. Specifically, `foo.edu` wants to extend the type `courseType` (Figure 15.10, page 619) with an additional element, `syllabus`. To this end, they create the following schema document:

```
<schema xmlns="http://www.w3.org/2001/XMLSchema"
        xmlns:xyzCrs="http://xyz.edu/Admin"
        xmlns:fooAdm="http://foo.edu/Admin"
        targetNameSpace="http://foo.edu/Admin">
    <!-- fooAdm is the prefix to be used for references
        to the target namespace within this schema -->
    <import namespace="http://xyz.edu/Admin"/>

    <complexType name="courseType">
        <complexContent>
            <extension base="xyzCrs:courseType">
                <element name="syllabus" type="string"/>
            </extension>
        </complexContent>
    </complexType>
    <!-- Now define a Course element for the target namespace
        and associate it with the derived type -->
    <element name="Course" type="fooAdm:courseType"/>
    .
    .
    .
</schema>
```

Notice that the target namespace is now `http://foo.edu/Admin`—that of the client university—and we associate the prefix `fooAdm` with it. The document uses the import statement to obtain the schema of `xyz.edu` to use as a basis for constructing a new schema. We assume that the important schema has the namespace `http://xyz.edu/Admin`. Since the new schema refers to the names defined in `xyz.edu`'s namespace (such as `courseType`), we need to associate a prefix with the imported namespace of `xyz.edu`. We choose `xyzCrs`.

After defining the namespaces, we define a new type, `courseType`, using a similar type in the imported schema. The newly defined type is not prefixed because we want it to belong to the target namespace. However, the base type imported from `xyz.edu` is prefixed and is referred to as `xyzCrs:courseType`. To signal the XML processor that a complex type is to be defined by modifying another type, the XML Schema specification requires the `<complexContent> ... </complexContent>` tag pair. Inside this pair, either an `extension` or a `restriction` clause is specified. We use `extension` in the above example, which means that the specified element, `syllabus`, is to be added to the content of the type `xyzCrs:courseType` to form the new type `courseType` (in the target namespace `http://foo.edu/Admin`).

> Extending an imported schema means that the new attributes are *appended* after the attributes inherited from the imported schema.

`foo.edu` might need to make other changes to the schema. For instance, they might generally like the type `studentType` defined in the namespace `http://xyz.edu/Admin` (Figure 15.9, page 618), but not that it allows students to take any number of courses (because of `maxOccurs="unbounded"`). Thus, `foo.edu` decides to limit this number to 63 by *restricting* the original schema:

```
<schema xmlns="http://www.w3.org/2001/XMLSchema"
    xmlns:xyzCrs="http://xyz.edu/Admin"
    xmlns:fooAdm="http://foo.edu/Admin">
    targetNameSpace="http://foo.edu/Admin">

  <import namespace="http://xyz.edu/Admin"/>
  .
  .
  .
  <complexType name="studentType">
    <complexContent>
      <restriction base="xyzCrs:studentType">
        <sequence>
          <element name="Name" type="xyzCrs:personNameType"/>
          <element name="Status" type="xyzCrs:studentStatus"/>
          <element name="CrsTaken" type="xyzCrs:courseTakenType"
                   minOccurs="0" maxOccurs="63"/>
        </sequence>
        <attribute name="StudId" type="xyzCrs:studentId"/>
      </restriction>
    </complexContent>
  </complexType>
  <!-- Now define a Student element for the target namespace
       and associate it with the derived type -->
  <element name="Student" type="fooAdm:studentType"/>
  .
  .
  .
</schema>
```

Analogously to the type extension mechanism, we use the tag `restriction` inside the `complexContent` block. The important difference, however, is that, when restricting a complex type, we must repeat all the element and attribute declarations from the base type. At the same time, we can impose restrictions on the components of the base type, for instance, by replacing `maxOccurs="unbounded"` with the more restrictive `maxOccurs="63"`. Thus, a restriction of a complex base type has exactly the same overall structure as the base type except that some elements and attributes comprising the restriction may be subsets of the corresponding ranges of the base type.

> *Brain Teaser:* Why is it necessary to repeat all the attributes of the base schema in order to specify a restriction? What ambiguities might arise otherwise?

15.3.4 Putting It Together

We have now defined a large number of simple and complex types, and we are ready to put them together to form a complete schema, which can describe document instances such as the report in Figure 15.4 on page 591. Such a schema requires a number of type definitions and at least one declaration of a **global element**. One of these global elements typically serves as the root element of the document instances described by the schema (e.g., the `Report` element in Figure 15.8). The others can be elements that are used in the definition of the type of the root. We will discuss global elements more fully on page 620. In our example, a single global declaration associates the root element, called `Report`, with its type, `adm:reportType`. This complex type contains declarations of other elements and attributes together with their types. Starting with the root element, then, we can descend into its type and find all of its elements and attributes. Repeating this recursively, we can find the elements and attributes at any depth in the document structure. A complete schema for our example (whose parts are defined elsewhere and inserted using the `include` statement) is shown in Figure 15.8.

We omit the definition of the lower-level types `classOfferings` and `courseCatalog`, which are defined similarly to `studentList`. Like `studentList`, these types are defined in terms of the types shown in Figures 15.9 and 15.10, which are the targets of the `include` statement in Figure 15.8.

As before, we must be careful about the namespaces, so we define `adm` as a prefix for the target namespace and use it in all references to the names defined in this schema (except in the statements that define these names using the attribute `name`). Recall that the including and included schemas are required to have the same namespace, so one prefix, `adm`, suffices to refer both to the names defined by the including schema (e.g., `adm:courseCatalog`) and the names defined in the included schemas (e.g., `adm:studentType`).

15.3.5 Shortcuts: Anonymous Types and Element References

We will now present two constructs that can help reduce the size and complexity of a schema document.

FIGURE 15.8 A complete schema.

```
<schema xmlns="http://www.w3.org/2001/XMLSchema"
    xmlns:adm="http://xyz.edu/Admin"
    targetNameSpace="http://xyz.edu/Admin">

  <!-- The following schemas are shown in Figures 15.9, 15.10, and 15.11 -->
  <include schemaLocation="http://xyz.edu/StudentTypes.xsd"/>
  <include schemaLocation="http://xyz.edu/CourseTypes.xsd"/>
  <include schemaLocation="http://xyz.edu/ClassTypes.xsd"/>

  <element name="Report" type="adm:reportType"/>

  <complexType name="reportType">
    <sequence>
      <element name="Students" type="adm:studentList"/>
      <element name="Courses" type="adm:courseCatalog"/>
      <element name="Classes" type="adm:classOfferings"/>
    </sequence>
  </complexType>
  <complexType name="studentList">
    <sequence>
      <element name="Student" type="adm:studentType"
               minOccurs="0" maxOccurs="unbounded"/>
    </sequence>
  </complexType>

  <!-- Plus the definition of classOfferings, courseCatalog -->
  <!-- The definition of studentType is in the included schema
       http://xyz.edu/studentTypes.xsd -->
</schema>
```

Anonymous types. All types defined so far were **named types** because each type definition had an associated name, and every element was explicitly associated with a named type. Naming is useful when we expect to share the same type among several definitions of elements or attributes. In many cases, however, a type might be one of a kind and not expected to be reused. For instance, in the above combined schema for the report document, the type `reportType` (as well as several other types such as `studentList` and `classOfferings`) is not shared. In this case, **anonymous types** can be a convenient shortcut.

Anonymous types are defined similarly to named types, except that the `name` attribute is not used and the type definition must be attached to the appropriate `element` or `attribute` definition that uses it. These definitions with attached anonymous types are also slightly different from definitions of named types. First, they do

FIGURE 15.9 Student types at `http://xyz.edu/StudentTypes.xsd`.

```
<schema xmlns="http://www.w3.org/2001/XMLSchema"
          xmlns:adm="http://xyz.edu/Admin"
          targetNameSpace="http://xyz.edu/Admin">

    <complexType name="studentType">
        <sequence>
            <element name="Name" type="adm:personNameType"/>
            <element name="Status" type="adm:studentStatus"/>
            <!-- courseTakenType is defined in Figure 15.10 -->
            <element name="CrsTaken" type="adm:courseTakenType"
                     minOccurs="0" maxOccurs="unbounded"/>
        </sequence>
        <attribute name="StudId" type="adm:studentId"/>
    </complexType>
    <complexType name="personNameType">
        <sequence>
            <element name="First" type="string"/>
            <element name="Last" type="string"/>
        </sequence>
    </complexType>
    <simpleType name="studentStatus">
        <restriction base="string">
            <enumeration value="U1"/>
            <enumeration value="U2"/>
            .
            .
            .
            <enumeration value="G5"/>
        </restriction>
    </simpleType>

    <simpleType name="studentId">
        <restriction base="ID">
            <pattern value="s[0-9]{9}"/>
        </restriction>
    </simpleType>
    <simpleType name="studentIds">
        <list itemType="adm:studentRef"/>
    </simpleType>
    <simpleType name="studentRef">
        <restriction base="IDREF">
            <pattern value="s[0-9]{9}"/>
        </restriction>
    </simpleType>
</schema>
```

FIGURE 15.10 Course types at `http://xyz.edu/CourseTypes.xsd`.

```
<schema xmlns="http://www.w3.org/2001/XMLSchema"
            xmlns:adm="http://xyz.edu/Admin"
            targetNameSpace="http://xyz.edu/Admin">

    <complexType name="courseTakenType">
        <attribute name="CrsCode" type="adm:courseRef"/>
        <attribute name="Semester" type="string"/>
    </complexType>
    <complexType name="courseType">
        <sequence>
            <element name="Name" type="string"/>
        </sequence>
        <attribute name="CrsCode" type="adm:courseCode"/>
    </complexType>

    <simpleType name="courseCode">
        <restriction base="ID">
            <pattern value="[A-Z]{3}[0-9]{3}"/>
        </restriction>
    </simpleType>
    <simpleType name="courseRef">
        <restriction base="IDREF">
            <pattern value="[A-Z]{3}[0-9]{3}"/>
        </restriction>
    </simpleType>
</schema>
```

not use the type attribute to introduce the anonymous type. Second, instead of the empty tags `<element ... />` and `<attribute ... />`, they use tag pairs, and the definition of the anonymous type is physically enclosed by the opening and closing tag. Thus, we can change the definition of the element Report in our schema to use an anonymous type as follows:

```
<element name="Report">
  <complexType>
    <sequence>
      <element name="Students" type="adm:studentList"/>
      <element name="Courses" type="adm:courseCatalog"/>
      <element name="Classes" type="adm:classOfferings"/>
    </sequence>
  </complexType>
</element>
```

Similarly, we can change the definitions of the elements Students, Classes, and Courses to use anonymous types. In this case, the content of the corresponding type definitions would be physically included in the above schema.

Referencing global elements. We conclude the discussion of the facilities for type definition in XML Schema with a mention of yet another shortcut, **global element referencing**, which is frequently used in schema definitions.

The overall scenario in which element referencing is used is as follows. First, a global element is defined as usual. A **global element** definition is one that appears as a direct child of the schema tag (not inside of any type definition). For instance, the element Report in Figure 15.8 is global. The ref attribute of an element tag allows us to include any global element in any type definition.

To illustrate, suppose that we want to use the element Comment, defined as

```
<element name="Comment" type="string"/>                                    15.3
```

in several parts of the schema in Figure 15.8 (for instance, both in reportType and studentList types). To do so, we would place (15.3) as a child of schema (for example, right after the definition of the element Report) and then place

```
<element ref="Comment"/>                                                   15.4
```

in each place where a comment element is to appear. For instance, the following modification of our previous definition includes Comment as part of reportType:

```
<complexType name="reportType">
  <sequence>
    <element ref="Comment"/>
    <element name="Students" type="adm:studentList"/>
    <element name="Courses" type="adm:courseCatalog"/>
    <element name="Classes" type="adm:classOfferings"/>
  </sequence>
</complexType>
```

One can say that we have not achieved a great deal of savings through the use of the reference facility since (15.4) is not much shorter than the full definition (15.3). Nevertheless, if the Comment element needs to be inserted in many places, the referencing facility can provide a degree of consistency.

15.3.6 Integrity Constraints

In Section 15.3.2 we touched upon the issue of referential integrity in XML documents and showed how the XML Schema specification improves upon DTDs in this regard. Even in XML Schema, however, we still used the special types ID and

IDREF that are inherited from DTDs. In XML Schema, the types ID and IDREF can be given to elements as well as attributes, which is already an improvement over DTDs. Still, these types are inadequate for representing integrity constraints. First, ID values must be globally unique. More importantly, the ID type cannot represent multiattribute keys. To illustrate, consider Figure 15.11, which shows a definition for the type classType.

If a student claims to have taken a course using a CrsTaken element (of type CrsTakenType declared in Figure 15.10), the corresponding course should have been offered in the specified semester. Such offerings are described by Class elements in the instance document. Given an element such as

```
<CrsTaken CrsCode="CS308" Semester="F1997"/>
```

there must exist an element of the form

```
<Class>
  <CrsCode>CS308</CrsCode><Semester>F1997</Semester>
    .
    .
    .
</Class>
```

The problem is that neither CrsCode nor Semester alone uniquely determines the Class element, so the ID/IDREF mechanism is inapplicable.

XML keys. To address the above problems, the XML Schema specification allows general multiattribute keys and foreign-key constraints in a way that resembles SQL. There is a slight complication, however. SQL deals with flat relations, so to

FIGURE 15.11 http://xyz.edu/ClassTypes.xsd: type for the element Class in Figure 15.4, page 591.

```
<element name="Class" type="adm:classType"/>
<complexType name="classType">
  <sequence>
    <!-- courseCode type is defined in Figure 15.10 -->
    <element name="CrsCode" type="adm:courseCode"/>
    <element name="Semester" type="string"/>
    <element name="ClassRoster" type="adm:classListType"/>
  </sequence>
</complexType>
<complexType name="classListType">
  <!-- studentIds is defined in Figure 15.9 -->
  <attribute name="Members" type="adm:studentIds"/>
</complexType>
```

specify a key we simply list the attributes that belong to that key. Similarly, to specify a foreign-key constraint in SQL we simply specify a sequence of attributes in both the referencing and the referenced relation. In XML, we are dealing with complex structures, and the notion of a key is more involved. Indeed, a key might be composed of a sequence of values located at different depths inside an element.

Assuming that the frame of reference is the parent element of the Class elements, we can say that the key of the collection of Class elements is composed of values reachable using the pair of path expressions Class/CrsCode and Class/Semester. The idea of path expressions is familiar to us from Chapter 14, but in XML they take a more elaborate form. In fact, XML path expressions are part of another specification, called **XPath**, which we study in Section 15.4.1.

To see how complicated a key specification can be, let us expand the definition of Class in the schema by adding sections and splitting the season from the year in semester names. Then, in an instance document we might have the following class:

```
<Class>
  <CrsCode Section="2" Number="CS308"/>
  <Semester><Term>Fall</Term><Year>1997</Year></Semester>
  .
  .
  .
</Class>
```

Here the set of values that uniquely determines the class is scattered in different places (in attributes and in element content) and at different levels (in the attributes of the tag CrsCode and in the Term and Year children of the Semester element). The path expressions needed to reach each of these components are specified in XPath as follows:

```
CrsCode/@Section
CrsCode/@Number
Semester/Term
Semester/Year
```

All of these path expressions are relative to Class elements in the report document. The first selects the value of the attribute Section of the tag CrsCode, which must be a child of the current element (assumed to be Class). The second selects the value of the attribute Number of the CrsCode element. The third and fourth select the content of the elements Term and Year, respectively, which must be children of the element Semester, which in turn must be a child of the current element.

XML Schema provides two ways to specify a key. One uses the tag unique and is similar to the UNIQUE constraint in SQL; it specifies *candidate keys*, in the terminology of Chapter 3. The other uses the tag key and corresponds to the PRIMARY KEY constraint in SQL. The only difference between unique and key is that keys cannot have *null values*. (In XML, the value of an element of the form

<footag></footag> is an empty string and not necessarily a null.) For footag to have a null value (called a **nil** in the XML Schema) the following is used:

```
<footag xsi:nil="true"></footag>
```

Here nil is a symbol defined in the namespace

```
http://www.w3.org/2001/XMLSchema-instance
```

(and we assume that xsi is a prefix that has been defined to refer to that namespace).

Next is an example of a primary-key declaration for the report document. Declaring candidate keys is similar except that the tag unique is used instead of the tag key. Referring to the type classType of Figure 15.11 (not the more elaborate type with section numbers that we just discussed), we want to specify that the pair of values of tags CrsCode and Semester uniquely identifies the Class element within the document. To show how this is done we elaborate on the earlier schema in Figure 15.8 on page 617.

```
<schema xmlns="http://www.w3.org/2001/XMLSchema"
        xmlns:adm="http://xyz.edu/Admin"
        targetNameSpace="http://xyz.edu/Admin">

  <include schemaLocation="http://xyz.edu/StudentTypes.xsd"/>
  <include schemaLocation="http://xyz.edu/CourseTypes.xsd"/>
  <include schemaLocation="http://xyz.edu/ClassTypes.xsd"/>

  <element name="Report" type="adm:reportType"/>

  <complexType name="reportType">
    <sequence>
      <element name="Students" type="adm:studentList"/>
      <element name="Classes">
        <!-- Replacing adm:classOfferings with anonymous type -->
        <complexType>
          <sequence>
            <!-- adm:classType is defined in Figure 15.11 and
                 included with http://xyz.edu/ClassTypes.xsd -->
            <element name="Class" type="adm:classType"
                     minOccurs="0" maxOccurs="unbounded"/>
          </sequence>
        </complexType>

        <key name="PrimaryKeyForClass">
          <selector xpath="Class"/>
```

```
          <field xpath="CrsCode"/>
          <field xpath="Semester"/>
        </key>
      </element>
      <element name="Courses" type="adm:courseCatalog"/>
    </sequence>
  </complexType>
   .
   .
   .
</schema>
```

The above schema lists the relevant type definitions for our report document. The namespace declarations and the include statements have already been discussed. The type `reportType` is used for the root element, `Report`. It is a sequence of three elements: `Students`, `Classes`, and `Courses`. Their types were defined in Figures 15.9, 15.11, and 15.10 on pages 618, 621, and 619, respectively. The definition of `courseCatalog`, the type for the element `Courses`, is an easy exercise.

The most interesting feature here is the key declaration specified with a `key` tag; it is named `PrimaryKeyForClass` using the attribute `name`. Declaration of a key is always part of an element specification. However, observe that `PrimaryKeyForClass` appears in the definition of the element `Classes` rather than of `Class`, even though the key involves only the components of type `classType` and refers to `Class` elements only. This is intentional, to illustrate the point that XML key declarations are associated with collections of objects (which typically are sets of elements) and that these objects can be identified using XPath expressions regardless of where the key definition occurs. The `xpath` attribute of the `selector` tag specifies a path expression (relative to the element that contains the key declaration), which identifies the collection of objects to which the key declaration applies. In our case, the selecting path expression is `Class`; it is relative to the element `Classes` because the key declaration appears as a child of this element declaration. The collection identified by the selector is simply the set of all `Class` elements in the document.

Having identified the appropriate collection of objects, we use the subsequent `field` elements to specify the fields that constitute the key. As explained earlier, these fields can come from different places in an object and can be nested in complex ways. In our case, however, things are simple: the first field in the key is the content of the child element `CrsCode` of the element `Class`, and the second field is the content of the child element `Semester`. (Path expressions specified in the `xpath` attribute of the `field` clause are relative to the collection of the objects determined by the selector. This is why, for example, the first path expression is simply `CrsCode` rather than `Class/CrsCode`.) Note that, for a path expression to make sense as a specification of a field in a key, it must return precisely one value for each object to which it applies. For instance, the path expression `CrsCode` returns precisely one value for any given `Class` element, so the field specification

```
<selector xpath="Class"/>
<field xpath="CrsCode"/>
    .
    .
    .
```

is allowed. In contrast, the path expression CrsTaken/@CrsCode within the scope of a Student element can return a set of courses taken by the student (refer to studentType defined in Figure 15.9 on page 618), so the field specification

```
<selector xpath="Student"/>
<field xpath="CrsTaken/@CrsCode"/>
    .
    .
    .
```

is not allowed within the scope of the element Students.

Foreign-key constraints in XML. Next, we want to be able to state that every element CrsTaken in a student record refers to an actual class element in the same report. This is akin to a foreign-key constraint and is defined using the keyref element, as depicted in Figure 15.12.

A foreign-key constraint has a name, a reference identifier, a selector, and a list of fields. The name of a foreign key is of little importance. The reference is defined using the attribute refer, and its value must match the name of a key or unique constraint. In our case, it matches the key constraint, PrimaryKeyForClass, defined within the scope of the element Classes. In SQL, this corresponds to the REFERENCES *relation-name* part of a foreign-key constraint. Next comes the selector. As in the case of the key constraint, it identifies a **source collection** of elements through its xpath attribute. In our case, the collection in question consists of all CrsTaken elements. Each of these is supposed to reference the key of an object from the **target collection** specified in the key constraint PrimaryKeyForClass.

Finally, we have to specify the foreign key itself, that is, the fields inside the CrsTaken elements (the source collection) that actually reference the fields in the target collection (specified in the key constraint). We do this using the already familiar field tag. As before, this tag provides a path expression (relative to the selected collection of objects) that leads to a value. We want the attributes CrsCode and Semester of the source collection of CrsTaken elements to refer to the fields that constitute the key of the target collection of Class elements. In XPath, we use the path expressions @CrsCode and @Semester to identify these attributes. As with the fields that form a key, each path expression in a foreign key (@CrsCode and @Semester in our case) must yield a single value when applied to an object in the source collection.

In a similar way, we can specify other key and foreign-key constraints in the report document (see Exercises 15.5 and 15.7).

FIGURE 15.12 Part of a schema with a key and a foreign-key constraint.

```
<schema xmlns="http://www.w3.org/2001/XMLSchema"
    xmlns:adm="http://xyz.edu/Admin"
    targetNameSpace="http://xyz.edu/Admin">

  <complexType name="courseTakenType">
    <attribute name="CrsCode" type="adm:courseRef"/>
    <attribute name="Semester" type="string"/>
  </complexType>
  <complexType name="classType">
    <sequence>
      <element name="CrsCode" type="adm:courseCode"/>
      <element name="Semester" type="string"/>
      <element name="ClassRoster" type="adm:classListType"/>
    </sequence>
  </complexType>

  <complexType name="reportType">
    <sequence>
      <element name="Students" type="adm:studentList">
        <keyref name="NoEmptyClasses" refer="adm:PrimaryKeyForClass">
          <selector xpath="Student/CrsTaken"/>
          <field xpath="@CrsCode"/>
          <field xpath="@Semester"/>
        </keyref>
      </element>
      <element name="Classes" type="adm:classOfferings">
        <key name="PrimaryKeyForClass">
          <selector xpath="Class"/>
          <field xpath="CrsCode"/>
          <field xpath="Semester"/>
        </key>
      </element>
      <element name="Courses" type="adm:courseCatalog"/>
    </sequence>
  </complexType>
</schema>
```

We should note that it is not clear how to specify IDREFS-style referential integrity with the help of the key and keyref tags. For instance, the attribute Members in ClassListType (Figure 15.11) has the type studentIds, which is a list of values of type studentRef. Since studentRef is derived by restriction from the base type IDREF (see Figure 15.9 on page 618), studentIds can be seen as a specialized version of IDREFS. We can *try* to specify the desired referential integrity using something like this:

```
<keyref name="RosterToStudIdRef" refer="adm:studentKey">
  <selector xpath="Class"/>
  <field xpath="ClassRoster/@Members"/>
</keyref>
```

where studentKey is an appropriately defined key constraint for Student elements:

```
<key name="studentKey">
  <selector xpath="Student"/>
  <field xpath="@StudId"/>
</key>
```

The problem here is that the value of the attribute Members is a *list* while the value of the key attribute StudId in the Student tag is a *single* item. Unfortunately, it is not possible in XPath to create a reference from the individual components of a list data type (represented by the Members attribute) to other entities in the document (i.e., student Ids defined in the Student elements). The only solution is to use a representation where student Ids are not in a list but occur as individual elements (Exercise 15.9).

15.4 XML Query Languages

Why would you want to query an XML document? Will databases soon begin storing XML and will they speak it fluently?

Storing XML documents in a database specifically designed for this kind of data is one possibility—methods exist for efficient storage and retrieval of tree-structured objects, including XML documents [Deutsch et al. 1999; Zhao and Joseph 2000]—and major relational database vendors are beginning to offer an option for native storage for XML documents. Native storage is also supported by SQL/XML, a forthcoming standard for interoperability between SQL databases and XML (see Section 15.4.4). In this capacity, SQL/XML can be seen as an alternative way of storing objects in a database (the other alternative being the SQL object-relational extensions).

XML documents can also be stored by mapping them to the relational or object-oriented format. Utilities that perform such mapping automatically are widely available and are part of most major database products. Such databases can receive XML documents and convert them into relations or objects; they also provide tools for generating XML from the data already stored in the database. Once generated, an XML document is transmitted to another machine, which either presents it to the user or processes it automatically. To help with this task, the W3C has developed the **document object model** (DOM) for XML [DOM 2000], which standardizes the

API by which a client application can access various parts of an XML document and thereby simplifies the task of writing such applications.

What does a query language have to do with all this? First, if XML documents are stored natively in a database, one needs a way to query them. The second possibility is even more intriguing. Imagine that you are preparing your next semester's schedule and need to find all courses offered in that semester between 3 PM and 7 PM. If the university database server lets you pose such a query, you are in good shape, but more likely it provides a fixed interface that supports only a limited set of queries. In this case, finding what you want might require a tedious process of filling out a series of forms and eyeballing the results, and you might also have to use low-tech instruments, such as pen and paper, to record the needed information.

An alternative is to ask the server for an XML document containing the list of all courses offered this semester and have a client application find the desired information. As mentioned, DOM simplifies this task considerably. Still, it provides only a low-level interface to XML. If your query requires joining information stored in different parts of the document or in separate documents, you might end up writing a fairly large program (and the semester will be over by the time you debug it). An analogy here is using nested loops and IF-statements to replace a complex SQL query. We will see how a powerful, high-level query language can simplify this task, enabling a new class of client applications capable of processing information in an intelligent and custom-tailored way.

In the remainder of Section 15.4, we discuss four query languages for XML: **XPath** [XPath 2003], **XSLT** [XSLT 1999], **XQuery** [XQuery 2004], and **SQL/XML**. The first three are official W3C recommendations, and the last is going to be part of a future release of the SQL standard.

XPath is intended to be simple and efficient. It is based on the idea of path expressions, with which we became familiar in Chapter 14, and is designed so that queries are compact and can be incorporated into URLs. Combined URL/XPath expressions became part of the **XPointer** specification [XPointer 2000], which we also introduce briefly. XSLT, on the other hand, is a full-blown programming language with powerful (albeit still limited) query capabilities. XQuery is an SQL-style query language designed in the database tradition. It has the most powerful and elegant query capabilities among the languages presented in this section. Finally, SQL/XML is an extension of SQL designed to provide interoperability between data stored in relational databases and XML documents.

15.4.1 XPath: A Lightweight XML Query Language

In an object-oriented language, such as OQL (Section 14.5.2), a path expression is a sequence of object attributes that provides the exact route to a data element nested deep within the object structure. The requirement to provide an exact route is not a problem when the schema of the database is known to the programmer and is not likely to change. However, when the schema is not known and the structure of data needs to be explored (which is often the case in Web applications), merely adopting path expressions from object-oriented languages is not enough.

XPath extends path expressions with query facilities by allowing the programmer to replace parts of the route to data elements with search conditions. By then examining the data, the XPath interpreter is supposed to find the missing parts of the route at run time. The idea of augmenting path expressions with queries is not new. It appeared in [Kifer and Lausen 1989; Kifer et al. 1992; Frohn et al. 1994] in the context of object-oriented databases and was further developed in works on semistructured data, such as [Buneman et al. 1996; Abiteboul et al. 1997; Deutsch et al. 1998; Abiteboul et al. 2000]. XPath was built on these ideas and became an important basis for many XML extensions.

The XPath data model. XPath views XML documents as trees, and it views elements, attributes, comments, and text as nodes of those trees. There is a special **root node** in the tree, which should not be confused with the root element of an XML document. This is illustrated in Figures 15.13 and 15.14. The XML instance document in Figure 15.13 (itself a fragment of the report document in Figure 15.4, page 591) is the basis for the XPath document tree in Figure 15.14.

Note that the root node of the XPath tree is different from the node that corresponds to `Students`, which is the root element of the document. The need for the special root node is apparent from Figure 15.14: it serves as a gathering point for all of the document components, including the comments that are allowed to occur outside the scope of the root element.

As usual in a tree, every node except the root node has a parent. A node, P, immediately above another node, C, is the **parent** of that node, and C is a **child** of P. However, the XPath specification has an important and sometimes confusing exception: an attribute is *not considered a child of its parent node*. That is, if C corresponds to an attribute of P, then P is a parent of C, but C is not a child of P. Because of the potential confusion due to the peculiar XPath terminology, we use the standard terminology for tree data structures and do regard attributes as children of their parents. To avoid ambiguity, we sometimes talk about ***e*-children**, ***a*-children**, and ***t*-children** when we want to restrict attention to the particular type of children: elements, attributes, or text. For example, `Name` is an *e*-child of `Student`, `StudId` is an *a*-child of `Student`, and `John` is a *t*-child of `First`. When we want to include both element children and text children, we refer to ***et*-children**. Similarly, ***ta*-children** refers to text and attribute children, and so on.

Another peculiarity of the XPath data model is that text that occurs inside XML elements (e.g., `John`, `U4`) is represented by a node in the tree. However, text that represents attribute values (e.g., the value `s987654321` of the attribute `StudId`) is not deemed to be worthy of a tree node of its own.

The XPath data model provides operators for navigating the document and accessing its various components. These operators include accessing the root of the XPath tree, the parent of a node, its children, the content of an element, the value of an attribute, and the like.

We saw some of these operators when we discussed constraints in XML Schemas. The basic syntax is that of the UNIX file-naming schema: the symbol "`/`" represents the root of the XPath tree, "`.`" represents the current node, and "`..`" represents the

FIGURE 15.13 Fragment of the report document in Figure 15.4, page 591.

```
<?xml version="1.0" ?>
<!-- Some comment -->
<Students>
    <Student StudId="s111111111">
        <Name><First>John</First><Last>Doe</Last></Name>
        <Status>U4</Status>
        <CrsTaken CrsCode="CS308" Semester="F1997"/>
        <CrsTaken CrsCode="MAT123" Semester="F1997"/>
    </Student>
    <Student StudId="s987654321">
        <Name><First>Bart</First><Last>Simpson</Last></Name>
        <Status>U4</Status>
        <CrsTaken CrsCode="CS308" Semester="F1994"/>
    </Student>
</Students>
<!-- Some other comment -->
```

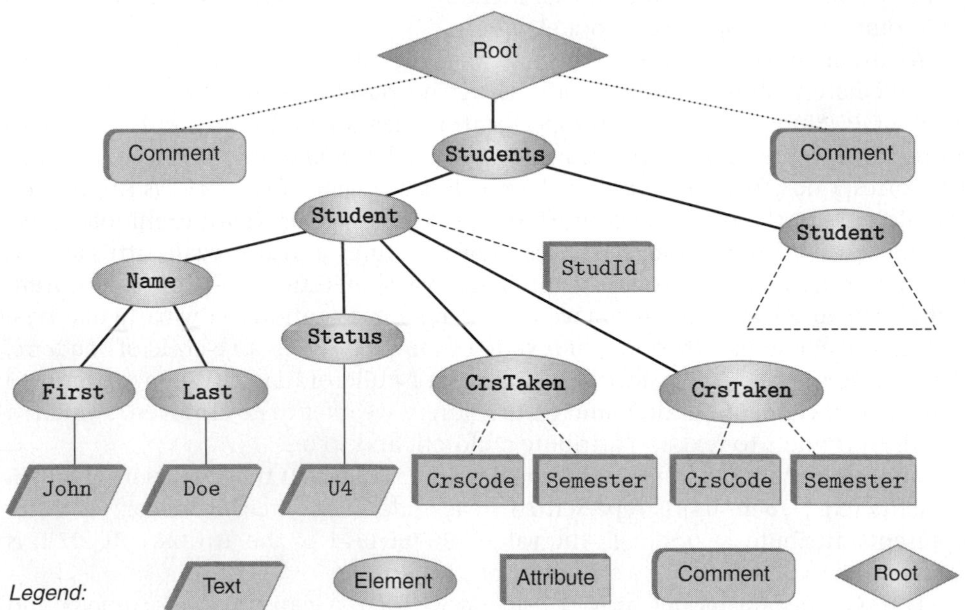

FIGURE 15.14 XPath document tree corresponding to document in Figure 15.13.

parent node of the current node. An XPath expression takes a document tree and returns a list of nodes in the tree. The path expression `/Students/Student/CrsTaken` is **absolute**; it returns the set of nodes that correspond to the elements `CrsTaken`, that are reachable from the root through a `Students` child and a `Student` grandchild. Our tree has three such `CrsTaken` nodes (one is not shown in Figure 15.14). If the current node corresponds to the element `Name`, then `First` and `./First` both refer to the same child element. If the current node corresponds to the element `First`, then `../Last` is the sibling node corresponding to the element `Last`. These are **relative path expressions** since their departure point for navigation is the *current node* rather than the root.

Many uses of XPath provide some notion of a context in which one of the nodes in the document tree is the **current node**. We have already seen this in the way XPath is used in XML Schema. For instance, in Figure 15.12 on page 626 we used relative path expressions in the definition of the primary key `PrimaryKeyForClass` and of the foreign key `NoEmptyClasses`. The primary key is defined as part of the XML type `reportType`, and in this context the current node corresponds to the `Report` element. A relative XPath expression `Classes/Class` is applied to that node to yield the set of all `Class` nodes that are grandchildren of `Report`. The two relative XPath expressions `CrsCode` and `Semester` are applied in the context of the `Class` nodes returned by the aforesaid expression `Classes/Class`. Here the current node can be any of these `Class` nodes, and the `CrsCode` expression returns the `CrsCode` child of that node; similarly the `Semester` expression returns the `Semester` child.

To access an attribute, the symbol `@` is used. For instance, the list of attribute nodes that correspond to `CrsCode` in the document of Figure 15.13 is obtained using the path expression `/Students/Student/CrsTaken/@CrsCode`. In our case, this list consists of three nodes because the `CrsCode` attribute occurs three times: with the values `CS308`, `MAT123`, and `CS308` (note the repetition due to the fact that the same value occurs more than once in different attribute nodes). Text nodes are accessed using the `text()` function. For instance, `/Students/Student/Name/First/text()` represents the collection of nodes, each representing the text content of an element of type `First`. We have two such nodes in our document; one corresponds to John and the other to Bart. If you were wondering, the two comment nodes in Figure 15.13 can be selected using the expression `/comment()`.

Advanced navigation in XPath. The more advanced features of XPath navigation include facilities to select specific nodes of an XML document as well as facilities to jump through an indeterminate number of children. For instance, to select the second course taken by John Doe, we use the expression `/Students/Student[1]/CrsTaken[2]`. Here, `/Students/Student[1]` selects the first of the two `Student` nodes in the document tree. The expression `CrsTaken[2]` then selects the second `CrsTaken` *e*-child in that first `Student` node. Another example of selection of a particular node is `/Students/Student/CrsTaken[last()]`. This is similar to the above except that the prefix `/Students/Student` selects all nodes that correspond to `Student` and `CrsTaken[last()]` then chooses the last `CrsTaken` node under each selected `Student` node. In our case, the above expression returns

```
<CrsTaken CrsCode="MAT123" Semester="F1997"/>
<CrsTaken CrsCode="CS308" Semester="F1994"/>
```

At times, we might not know the exact structure of the document, or specifying the exact navigation path might be cumbersome, so XPath provides several wildcard facilities. One is the *descendant-or-self* operation, `//`, illustrated by the expression `//CrsTaken`, which is an absolute path expression that starts at the root and selects all `CrsTaken` elements in the entire tree. In our particular case, the effect is the same as that produced by `/Students/Student/CrsTaken`. However, if the document contains elements `CrsTaken` nested under different types of elements and at different depths, then selecting all such elements without a wildcard is hard and unwieldy. Similarly, `/Students//CrsTaken` selects all `CrsTaken` elements that are descendants of `Students` nodes regardless of the nesting level.

The descendant operation can be used in relative expressions as well. For instance, `.//CrsTaken` searches through all descendants (or self) of the current node to find the `CrsTaken` elements. Observe that `./CrsTaken` and `CrsTaken` are the same. However, `.//CrsTaken`, `CrsTaken`, and `//CrsTaken` are all different: the first expression returns all `CrsTaken` descendants at the current node (or the current node itself, if it is a `CrsTaken` element); the second expression returns only the `CrsTaken` children at the current node; and the third, all `CrsTaken` elements found anywhere in the document.

XPath also allows searching through all ancestors (parent, grandparent, etc.) of any given node, but we omit this wildcard.

The third wildcard, `*`, lets us collect all *e*-children of a node, irrespective of type. For instance, `Student/*` selects all *e*-children of the `Student` children of the current node. (If the current node is the [only] `Students` node, the wildcard selects the two `Name` nodes, the two `Status` nodes, and the three `CrsTaken` nodes.) The expression `/*//*` selects all *e*-children of the root and their *e*-descendants (since `//` is descendant-or-self, the set of nodes `/*//*` includes the set of children nodes of the root, `/*`).

The `*` wildcard can also be applied to attributes. For instance, `CrsTaken/@*` selects all attribute values of the `CrsTaken` nodes that sit below the current node. Note that `*` does not include the text nodes that could possibly exist among the children of the `Student` element. To select those, the expression `Student/text()` is used.

XPath semantics. The general form of an XPath query is

```
locationStep1/locationStep2/...   or   /locationStep1/locationStep2/...
```

where each location step is of the form *axis*`::`*nodeSelector*`[`*selectionCondition*`]`. The term *axis* refers to the **navigation axis**, which indicates the direction along which navigation is taking place in the corresponding location step. The available axes are *child* (i.e., go to a child node), *parent*, *descendant* (i.e., child, grandchild, etc.), *descendant-or-self*, etc. The node selector is either the name of the node (e.g., the name of an element or attribute); a selector for an unnamed node, such as `text()` or `comment()`; or a wildcard, such as "*" or "@*". For instance, `child::Student` is a simple location step that directs navigation from the current node down to a child element named `Student`; `descendant-or-self::@Semester` directs navigation from the current node to a `Semester` attribute in either the current node or in a descendant of that node. Because the full syntax of XPath is so verbose, most axes have convenient abbreviations, and this is what we have been using up until now (and will continue using). For instance, `child::Student` abbreviates as `Student`, the relative expression `descendant-or-self::@Semester` abbreviates as `.//@Semester`, and the absolute expression `/descendant-or-self::@Semester` as `//@Semester`. The optional `selectionCondition` in a location step selects a subset of nodes reachable by the location step. We will see examples of such conditions shortly.

The value of a location step `axis::nodeSelector[selectionCondition]` on an instance document is the set of all nodes of the form `nodeSelector` that are reachable by the navigation `axis` and that satisfy `selectionCondition`. For instance, `.//@Semester` specifies the set of attribute nodes called `Semester` that are reachable from the current node by the axis `descendant-or-self`. In plain English this is the set of all `Semester` attributes that appear in either the current node or in one of its descendants.

For a path expression $\texttt{locationStep}_1$/$\texttt{locationStep}_2$/. . ., the value on a source document is the set of all document nodes computed as follows: From the current node, find all nodes reachable by $\texttt{locationStep}_1$. For each such node, *N*, find the set of all nodes that are reachable from *N* via $\texttt{locationStep}_2$. Take the union of all node sets reachable by $\texttt{locationStep}_2$. Apply $\texttt{locationStep}_3$ to each node in the union, etc., until the last location step is reached. The value of the path expression is the set of nodes obtained at this last step.

> *Brain Teaser:* With the full syntax for XPath, location steps can go back and forth in the document tree. Is it possible to write an XPath expression that returns an infinite number of nodes?

XPath queries. We are particularly interested in the features of XPath that give it the ability to select nodes using a query facility. XPath queries can include selection conditions at any step in the navigation process. To give meaningful examples of XPath expressions with queries, we go back to our report document in Figure 15.4, page 591.

Here is a simple example of a path expression that selects all student nodes where the student has taken a course in fall 1994:

```
//Student[CrsTaken/@Semester = "F1994"]
```

Here we have a wildcard expression, //Student, that selects all Student nodes under the root node. The expression inside the square brackets is a **selection condition** that eliminates the nodes that do not satisfy the condition by selecting a Student node only if the path expression CrsTaken/@Semester can be applied at this node and if it returns a set that *includes* F1994.[7] To select elements based on the content of an element rather than of an attribute, we use the following expression:

```
//Student[Status = "U3" and starts-with(.//Last, "P")
          and not(.//Last = .//First)]
```

This example introduces several important features:

1. Selection conditions can be combined using and, or, and not.
2. To select an element based on the content of one of its children or descendants, we simply equate the appropriate path expression with another such expression or a constant. Strictly speaking, we should have written Status/text() = "U3" instead of Status = "U3", but since Status does not have subelements, XPath allows us to be less pedantic in this case. This is possible because, in order to evaluate a comparison such as the one above, XPath converts every node returned by the path expression into its **string value** and then compares strings. For simple element nodes such as those returned by //Student/Status or //Student//Last, the string value is simply the text inside the element. For attribute nodes, such as those returned by //Student/CrsTaken/@Semester the string value is the value of the attribute. A full set of rules that defines string values for the various nodes in an XPath tree is given in [XPath 2003].
3. XPath has a rich repertoire of functions that greatly increase its expressive power. For the full list of these functions, we refer you to the XPath specification [XPath 2003].

In the above example, we use the built-in predicate starts-with() to select only those students whose last names start with P. To summarize the above query, it selects all students who have the status U3, whose last names start with P, and whose last and first names are different. The other string manipulation functions allow us to check for containment, perform concatenation, determine length, and so forth. For instance, the following query can be used to search for students who have "van" as part of their name:

```
//Student[contains(concat(Name//text()), "van")]
```

Here Name//text() returns the set of all text nodes that are descendants of the Name element, and the concatenation function makes one string out of those nodes—in

[7] Note that if a Student node has several CrsTaken children, then the path expression CrsTaken/@Semester returns a *set* of nodes.

this case the student's first and last names. Then we check if the result contains van as a substring.

Aggregate functions available in XPath include sum() and count(). For example, the following selects the students who have taken at least five courses:

```
//Student[count(CrsTaken) &gt;= 5]
```

In this expression, CrsTaken returns the set of all *e*-children of type CrsTaken for the current node (which must be a Student node). Thus, Count(CrsTaken) returns the number of these children, which is compared with "5". The obscure >= contraption, stands for >=. This complication is due to the fact that the symbols < and > must be encoded as < and > because < and > are reserved for tag delimiters.

It should be noted that selection conditions can be applied at different levels and multiple times in a path expression. Thus, the following is legal:

```
//Student[Status="U4"]/CrsTaken[@CrsCode="CS305"]
```

This expression selects all the CrsTaken elements in the document that occur in Student elements with status U4 and whose CrsCode attribute has the value CS305.

Multiple selection conditions can also be applied at the same level in a path expression, as shown in the following expression that selects all Student elements having the property that the student took (among other courses) MAT123 in fall 1994:

```
//Student/CrsTaken[@CrsCode="MAT123"][@Semester="F1994"]
```

The same expression can be written as

```
//Student/CrsTaken[@CrsCode="MAT123" and @Semester="F1994"]
```

Note that this expression is different from

```
//Student[CrsTaken/@CrsCode="MAT123" and CrsTaken/Semester="F1994"]
```

which selects students who took MAT123 during some semester and also took a course (possibly a different one) in the fall of 1994. The reason for this difference in the interpretation is that nothing in the latter expression tells us that the two occurrences of the CrsTaken expression select the same element node. The "or" connective—for example, CrsTaken/@CrsCode="MAT123" or CrsTaken/@Semester="F1994"—is also allowed.

There is one other interesting form of selection condition, one where a path expression is used as a predicate rather than as an argument to a predicate. Suppose that Grade is an optional attribute of CrsTaken. Then

```
//Student[CrsTaken/@Grade]
```

selects all student elements that have a CrsTaken child element with an explicitly specified Grade attribute (regardless of its value). Likewise,

```
//Student[Name/First or CrsTaken]
```

selects all Student elements that have either the element First as a grandchild or the element CrsTaken as a child.

Finally, recall that SQL allows the use of algebraic query operators, such as UNION and EXCEPT. XPath, being a frugal language, allows only the union operator, which is denoted by the symbol |, as in the expression

```
//CrsTaken[@Semester="F1994"] | //Class[Semester="F1994"]
```

The set of nodes selected by this query is a union of elements of different types: the CrsTaken elements that pertain to the fall 1994 semester and the Class elements that describe fall 1994 course offerings. This illustrates how a path expression can return a set containing elements of different types.

XPointer—A Smarter URL. With all of its interesting features, XPath is not an expressive query language. It cannot express joins and is basically suitable only for navigation within tree-structured documents. However, it is precisely this narrow scope that makes XPath suitable as a plug-in component for many XML applications. In Section 15.3.6, we used XPath to express constraints in XML schemas. Its other popular application is to enhance URLs with a simple query facility. A number of extensions to XPath have been developed to facilitate such applications and are going to be standardized in a forthcoming XPointer recommendation from W3C.

XPointer mutated out of the union of URLs and XPath. To understand how XPointer is used, suppose that we need to create a hyperlink from one document to a particular place in another document. Such links are routine in today's HTML documents—a typical example is a table of contents, where clicking on a particular link inside the table takes the user to the corresponding section. In HTML, linking into the middle of a document is done by marking a particular place with an anchor,[8] for example, interesting-place, and then referencing it with the URL syntax *document-url#interesting-place*. The problem is that it is possible to create such a link only if the document author has created the appropriate anchors in advance—an outside viewer of a document cannot arbitrarily bookmark places of interest in a document.

This is where XPath comes in. The idea is to allow the user to concatenate a URL and a path expression. The browser then retrieves the document using the URL

[8] In HTML, this is specified using the tag <A name="...">.

and finds the desired places using the path expression. This is precisely what an `xpointer` is; more specifically, it is an expression of the form:

```
someURL#xpointer(XPathExpr1)xpointer(XPathExpr2)...
```

which is processed as follows: first the document at URL *someURL* is found. Then $XPathExpr_1$ is evaluated against it. If a nonempty set of document nodes is returned, we are done. Otherwise, $XPathExpr_2$ is tried. If it fails to return a nonempty set, the next path expression is tried, and so on. For instance, assuming that the document in Figure 15.4, page 591, is at URL *http://www.foo.edu/Report.xml*, we can link directly to the second student transcript as follows:

```
http://www.foo.edu/Report.xml#xpointer(//Student[2])
```

XPointer would not be so useful if it were not for the ability of XPath to select document nodes based on queries. For instance, we can easily extract the fall 1994 class of `MAT123`:

```
http://www.foo.edu/Report.xml#
        xpointer(//Student[CrsTaken/@CrsCode="MAT123"
                           and CrsTaken/@Semester="F1994"])
```

(This expression should be written in one line; it occupies several lines in the text because of formatting limitations.)

To conclude, we mention that XPointer defines a number of extensions to XPath, such as ranges of document nodes, which we do not discuss here. The interested reader is referred to [XPointer 2000].

15.4.2 XSLT: A Transformation Language for XML

XSL Transformation (XSLT) is a transformation language that is part of **XSL**, the **Extensible Stylesheet Language** of XML. Its original intent was to be a language for converting XML documents into HTML in order to display them with ordinary browsers. However, it is a general transformation language that can produce any type of document (HTML, XML, plaintext) from an XML source. In this capacity, XSLT can be used to query XML documents, in a way that goes far beyond stylesheets.

As a query language, XSLT is different from what we have seen so far in this book. Relational algebra, described in Chapter 5, is an **imperative** language, where queries are constructed by specifying the exact sequence of operations that must be performed to obtain the answer. SQL and *Query-By-Example* (QBE), discussed in Chapters 5 and 13, are based on relational calculus, which is a subset of predicate logic, and thus belong to the **declarative** group of languages. OQL, the object-oriented query language of ODMG discussed in Chapter 14, belongs to the same category.

OPTIONAL

In these languages, the user specifies the information to be retrieved and its relationship to the database sources, from which the system must then obtain that information. XSLT, on the other hand, is a **functional** programming language that uses the syntax of XML. As with SQL (and unlike relational algebra), the user specifies the required result indirectly. But instead of logic, XSLT specifies the result using recursive functions. Query languages based on functional programming are almost as old as those based on algebra and logic [Shipman 1981]. However, prior to XSLT they had difficulty gaining a foothold in the database world.

XSLT is only one of the two components of XSL. The other is a *formatting* language, which specifies the look of a document when it is rendered in a browser or on paper. The overall process of rendering an XML document consists of transforming it into another document that augments the original document with rendering instructions. The result might lose some of the original content (e.g., to make it usable in a handheld device, such as a Palm Pilot) or it might gain extra content (e.g., a table of contents). When XSL formatting is used, the output document will be in XML format, which can be displayed by some browsers or word processors. Alternatively, XSLT can be used alone to transform XML documents provided as input into a completely different format, such as HTML (to be rendered by an ordinary browser) or LaTeX (for high-quality paper documents).

Formatting is not the subject of this section. Instead, we concentrate on XSLT and, especially, on its use as a query language. Furthermore, we focus on the most interesting of XSLT query capabilities—pattern-based document transformations—and refer the reader to [Kay 2000; XSLT 1999] for full details on XSLT.

OPTIONAL

XSLT basics. An XSLT program (usually called a **stylesheet**) specifies a transformation of one type of document into another type. As before, we illustrate its various features using the tried-and-true `report` document in Figure 15.4, page 591. To process a document, an XML processor needs to know the location of the corresponding stylesheet. This is specified using the `xml-stylesheet` processing instruction, which must occur in the document **preamble**, between the initial `<?xml ... ?>` instruction and the first XML tag. For instance, to supply a stylesheet for our report, the document should start as follows:

```
<?xml version="1.0" ?>
<?xml-stylesheet type="text/xsl"
                 href="http://xyz.edu/Report/report.xsl" ?>
<Report Date="2000-12-12">
.
.
.
</Report>
```

The `type` attribute in the `xml-stylesheet` instruction says that the stylesheet is a text XSL document, so the XML processor can choose the appropriate parser.

The href attribute specifies the stylesheet location. The processor then fetches the stylesheet from the specified site and transforms the document accordingly.

Here is an example of a stylesheet that takes a report (such as the one in Figure 15.4) and extracts the list of all students:

```
<?xml version="1.0" ?>
<StudentList xmlns:xsl="http://www.w3.org/1999/XSL/Transform"
            xsl:version="1.0">
     <xsl:copy-of select="//Student/Name"/>
</StudentList>
```

The effect of the transformation defined by this stylesheet on our report is the following document:

```
<StudentList>
     <Name><First>John</First><Last>Doe</Last></Name>
     <Name><First>Joe</First><Last>Public</Last></Name>
     <Name><First>Bart</First><Last>Simpson</Last></Name>
</StudentList>
```

A stylesheet consists of "examples," which are tags defined in the stylesheet (such as StudentList in our case) and **XSLT instructions** (such as copy-of). The examples are simply copied to the result document, while the instructions extract data items from the source document and place them in the result document. Observe that when viewed as an XML document, our stylesheet has StudentList as its root tag. Thus, like most XML documents, the root tag of a stylesheet contains the declaration of a namespace. StudentList also contains the version attribute required by XSLT. (The XSLT-mandated attributes and the namespace declaration are not copied to the result document.)

The xmlns declaration associates the prefix xsl—a conventional prefix used with XSLT—with the standard namespace that defines the XSLT vocabulary. This vocabulary includes copy-of and other XSLT instructions that we will see shortly. For a rather subtle reason, we cannot use http://www.w3.org/1999/XSL/Transform as a default namespace. If we did, StudentList would belong to it (according to the scoping rules for namespace declarations). However, StudentList does not exist in this namespace and, in fact, was invented just for this example to serve as a top-level tag of the result document.

The copy-of statement is an XSLT instruction that simply copies the elements selected by the XPath expression specified in the select attribute. In our example, the path expression selects all the Name elements that are children of Student, which produces the list of Name elements shown above.

XSLT includes a number of conditional and looping instructions, such as if (an "if-then" without the "else"), choose (an enhanced version of the switch statement in C/C++ and Java), and for-each. Figure 15.15 is an example that uses some of these

OPTIONAL

FIGURE 15.15 Nonrecursive stylesheet.

```
<?xml version="1.0" ?>
<StudentList xmlns:xsl="http://www.w3.org/1999/XSL/Transform"
             xsl:version="1.0">

   <xsl:for-each select="//Student">
     <xsl:if test="count(CrsTaken) &gt; 1">
       <FullName>
         <!-- Last is two levels below Student; use * to skip one level -->
         <xsl:value-of select="*/Last"/>,
         <xsl:value-of select="*/First"/>
       </FullName>
     </xsl:if>
   </xsl:for-each>
</StudentList>
```

OPTIONAL

features. The result of applying this transformation to our document in Figure 15.4, page 591, is as follows:

```
<StudentList>
   <FullName>
     Doe, John
   </FullName>
   <FullName>
     Public, Joe
   </FullName>
</StudentList>
```

The `for-each` statement selects the nodes specified by the corresponding path expression (the set of all `Student` elements in our case) and then applies the statements that appear inside the `for-each` element. For each student, this program first checks if the student has taken more than one course. (As discussed before, we must encode > using its XML notation, `>`.) Our document has only two students who satisfy this condition: John Doe and Joe Public, for each of whom a block of example tags, `<FullName> ... </FullName>`, is copied from the stylesheet to the result document.

Next, we break the structure of the `Name` element in our report and extract the last and first names, discarding the tags. The student names are then displayed in an unstructured textual form. Extraction of the textual content of an element is achieved using the XSLT instruction `value-of`, which works similarly to `copy-of` except that it extracts the content of an element rather than the element itself. Had we used `copy-of` instead, the result would have been different:

```
<StudentList>
   <FullName>
     <Last>Doe</Last>, <First>John</First>
   </FullName>
   <FullName>
     <Last>Public</Last>, <First>Joe</First>
   </FullName>
</StudentList>
```

XSLT templates. The procedural features of XSLT seem powerful, but they are not adequate for dealing with all XML documents. The problem is that the `for-each` instruction can iterate over elements selected by a path expression, but it cannot recursively descend into these elements and transform the document on the way. Since XML documents can be arbitrarily deep, recursive traversal of their structure is essential to extract the desired information. The traversal of XML trees is provided by **pattern-based templates**. The `StudentList` stylesheet (described earlier) uses a simplified syntax that is a shorthand for the following template:

```
<?xml version="1.0" ?>
<xsl:stylesheet xmlns:xsl="http://www.w3.org/1999/XSL/Transform"
                xsl:version="1.0">
     <xsl:template match="/">
          <StudentList>
               <xsl:for-each select="//Student">
                . . . . . . . . .
               </xsl:for-each>
          </StudentList>
     </xsl:template>
</xsl:stylesheet>
```

Essentially, the old stylesheet is wrapped here with the `<xsl:template match="/"> ... </xsl:template>` tag pair, which says that the example part and the instructions in the body of the stylesheet should be applied in the context of the root node of the document. We can therefore assume that *every* stylesheet is a collection of templates.

An XSLT template is a transformation function, which is usually recursively defined in terms of other templates. Inside, a template can use the procedural features we have seen already (`copy-of`, `for-each`, etc.) or it can call other templates. The interesting aspect of such a call is that typically a template is not called directly but is invoked when the XPath expression that is the value of its match attribute matches the current node in the document tree. Figure 15.16 shows a template program that achieves the same result as that of the stylesheet of Figure 15.15, which we formulated with the help of the `for-each` statement. Although the new

OPTIONAL

FIGURE 15.16 Recursive stylesheet that produces the same result as that of Figure 15.15.

```
<?xml version="1.0" ?>
<xsl:stylesheet xmlns:xsl="http://www.w3.org/1999/XSL/Transform"
                xsl:version="1.0">
  <xsl:template match="/">
    <StudentList>
      <xsl:apply-templates/>
    </StudentList>
  </xsl:template>
  <xsl:template match="//Student">
    <xsl:if test="count(CrsTaken) &gt; 1">
      <FullName>
        <xsl:value-of select="*/Last"/>,
        <xsl:value-of select="*/First"/>
      </FullName>
    </xsl:if>
  </xsl:template>
  <xsl:template match="text()">
    <!-- Empty template -->
  </xsl:template>
</xsl:stylesheet>
```

OPTIONAL

stylesheet is more complex than the earlier one, it is simple enough and illustrates the main ideas.

For simplicity, we first describe the effect of this template on the simplified report document presented in Figure 15.14, page 630. Then we consider a more complex document. The evaluation starts by matching the root node of the XPath tree in Figure 15.14 to a path expression specified in the `match` attribute of one of the templates. In our case, the only expression that matches the root is / in the first template. This template emits the `StudentList` tag pair, sets the *current* node to the root of the XPath tree, and recursively calls other templates using the `apply-templates` instruction. The result of this call will be inserted between the `StudentList` tag pair.

The `apply-templates` instruction drives the recursive traversal of the document tree. It constructs the set of all *et*-children (i.e., *it ignores the attributes*) of the current node and applies a matching template to each child.[9]

The only *et*-child of the root node of the XPath tree is the `Students` element, and, since our stylesheet does not appear to have a template that matches this node, we seem to be at a dead end. To get out of this complication, we can specify the following template:

[9] These templates are applied independently of each other, but the results are output in the order in which the children appear in the XML tree.

```
<xsl:template match="*|/">
    <xsl:apply-templates/>
</xsl:template>
```

15.5

which matches any e-node (because of *) or the root node (because of /) and so is applicable. Fortunately, this template is the *default* that XSLT applies when no other template matches the current element node, so we do not have to specify it explicitly (the default for text and attribute nodes is different, as explained below). The above default template does not emit anything and simply continues to apply templates to the *et*-children of `Students`—the two `Student` nodes that describe John Doe and Bart Simpson. Fortunately, we have an explicit template that matches this time—the second template in the stylesheet. (The actual transformation performed by this template was discussed in connection with the earlier stylesheet, which used the `for-each` instruction.)

To make this example more illustrative, let us assume that in addition to `Students`, the root of the XPath tree has another *e*-child, `Classes`, which looks exactly as in the report document of Figure 15.4. In this case the `apply-templates` instruction of the first template of Figure 15.16 will consider the branch of the XPath tree that corresponds to `Classes` in addition to the branch corresponding to `Students`, which we have already discussed. Since no template matches `Classes` explicitly, XSLT applies the default template, which in turn uses the `apply-templates` instruction on the *et*-children of `Classes`. Note that the default template ignores attributes and text nodes; however, when it is applied to an element of type `CrsCode` or `Semester` (which are descendants of `Classes`), their *t*-children (for example CS308) are affected by the `apply-templates` statement since XSLT has another default template that applies to attribute and text nodes:

```
<xsl:template match="text()|@*">
    <xsl:value-of select="."/>
</xsl:template>
```

This means that when this template matches an attribute or a text node, the value of the attribute or the text is copied by the processor to the result document. Unfortunately, in our case this produces spurious text that represents semesters and course codes that are of no interest (recall that we want to see student names only).

The third template in the stylesheet in Figure 15.16 was added precisely to address this problem. This empty template matches only the text nodes and emits nothing. (We do not need to worry about the attributes here since `<xsl:apply-templates>` ignores *a*-children of the current node.) Since we have an explicit rule that matches text nodes, the default rule for these nodes is suppressed.

The algorithm for applying stylesheets to documents is very complicated because of the large number of features available in XSLT. Even the official W3C recommendation [XSLT 1999] does not describe it adequately. Here we provide an outline of the evaluation process for simplified pattern-based templates—those that

OPTIONAL

can add at most one element node to the result document and, possibly, invoke apply-templates. In particular, we exclude the for-each loop.

1. Transformation begins by creating a root for the result document. The process then copies the root of the source document to the result tree and makes it a child of the result document's root node. The source document's root is set to be the *current node* (*CN*), and the *current node list* (*CNL*) is initially set to contain only the source root node.
2. *CNL* maintains the collection of nodes in the source document to which templates are to be applied. During the algorithm, *CN* is always the first node in *CNL*. Also, whenever a node, *N*, is placed in *CNL*, its copy (which we denote N^R) is placed in the result document tree. The node N^R can later be deleted or replaced by the application of a template, but such nodes play the role of markers that indicate where changes to the result tree might subsequently occur.
3. The process finds the **best-matching template** for *CN* and applies it to *CN*. The best-matching template is one whose path expression returns the smallest set of source document nodes (by set inclusion) that contains the current node.[10] If there is no template whose path expression returns a set that includes the current node, the appropriate default template is used.
4. Application of a template can lead to the following changes:
   (a) CN^R in the result document tree can be replaced by a subtree. For instance, suppose *CN* is the Students node in Figure 15.14. Suppose also that the stylesheet of Figure 15.16 uses the following template (which thus becomes best matching) instead of the initial template (the one with the matching path expression "/"):

```
<xsl:template match="//Students">
    <StudentList>
        <xsl:apply-templates/>
    </StudentList>
</xsl:template>
```

   In this case, CN^R is replaced with the StudentList *e*-node and each *et*-child of *CN* in the source tree (each of the two Student nodes) is copied over to the result tree and becomes a child of StudentList. This transformation is shown in Figure 15.17, case (a).
   (b) CN^R in the result document tree can be deleted, and its parent might acquire additional children. For instance, the default rule in the stylesheet of Figure 15.16

[10] If there are several such templates, other rules are used to find the best match among them; see [XSLT 1999].

OPTIONAL

```
<xsl:template match="*|/">
    <xsl:apply-templates/>
</xsl:template>
```

deletes CN^R when applied to any node. The *et*-children of *CN* in the source tree are copied over to the result tree and become children of the parent of CN^R. This transformation is shown in Figure 15.17, case (b).

In both cases, if *CN* has no *et*-children, *CNL* will become shorter as a result of the template application. Otherwise (if it does have such children), *CNL* might grow because *CN* is replaced in *CNL* with the list of its *et*-children. The order in which these children are placed in the result tree and in *CNL* is the same as their order in the source tree. In particular, the first node in *CNL* becomes the new *CN*.

In general, the apply-templates instruction can have a select attribute:

```
<xsl:apply-templates select="some path expression"/>
```
15.6

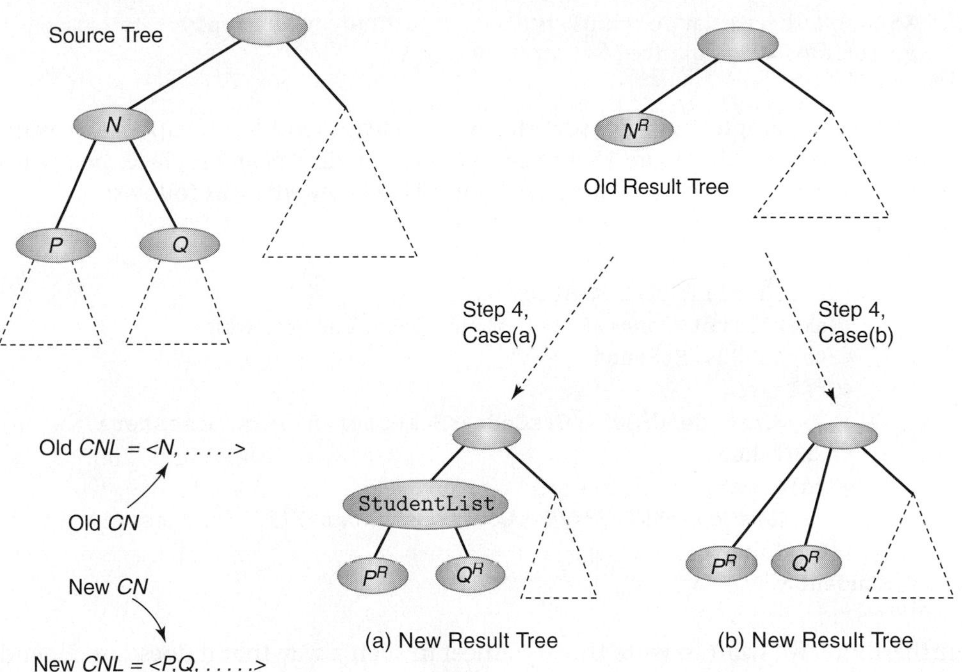

FIGURE 15.17 Effect of apply-templates on the document tree.

In fact, `<xsl:apply-templates/>` is simply a shorthand for `<xsl:apply-templates select="node()"/>`, where `node()` is an XPath function that returns the set of *et*-children of the given element node. For instance, `<xsl:apply-templates select="@*|text()"/>` applies to attributes (because of the wildcard `@*`) and text nodes (because of the function `text()`), but not to elements.

In general, the transformation (15.6) replaces *CN* with the nodes specified by the `select` attribute—not necessarily the *et*-children of *CN* as in the default case. These nodes are also copied to the result tree, as explained in cases (a) and (b). The algorithm then proceeds with step 3.

5. The algorithm terminates when *CNL* becomes empty. In general, however, it might not terminate, and it is the responsibility of the stylesheet author to make sure that it does. For instance, if the path expression in the `select` attribute of `apply-templates` is "`.`" (i.e., it refers to the current node), then `apply-templates` will obviously loop forever. A general path expression can refer to parents, ancestors, or siblings of the current node, which makes termination analysis difficult. A simple condition that ensures termination is to require that all path expressions in the `select` attribute search only the subtree of the current node. Therefore, at some point *CNL* will start shrinking and eventually become empty.

XSLT stylesheets that do not use the `select` attribute in the `apply-templates` instructions are guaranteed to terminate.

OPTIONAL

Our next example illustrates several advanced features of XSLT. Suppose we want to rewrite the report in Figure 15.4 to get rid of the attributes and replace them with elements so that the record dealing with John Doe is rewritten as follows:

```
<Student>
    <StudId>s111111111</StudId>
    <Name><First>John</First><Last>Doe</Last></Name>
    <Status>U2</Status>
    <CrsTaken>
        <CrsCode>CS308</CrsCode><Semester>F1997</Semester>
    </CrsTaken>
    <CrsTaken>
        <CrsCode>MAT123</CrsCode><Semester>F1997</Semester>
    </CrsTaken>
</Student>
```

Furthermore, we want to write this stylesheet in such a way that it does not depend on knowledge of the actual attribute names used in the source document. Thus, if the `Grade` attribute is added to the `CrsTaken` element in the future, our program should still work and transform `<CrsTaken ... Grade="A"/>` into

```
<CrsTaken> ... <Grade>A</Grade></CrsTaken>
```

To accomplish this feat, the stylesheet must be able to emit an element whose name is not known in advance but is computed on the fly, based on the attributes found at run time in the source document. Two new features of XSLT make this possible.

- The `element` instruction tells the stylesheet to copy an element with a given name to the result document. For instance,

  ```
  <xsl:element name="name(current())">
        I do not know where I am
  </xsl:element>
  ```

  will copy different elements during evaluation, depending on the current nodes in which it is evaluated. For instance, if during the evaluation, the current node is an attribute named `foo`, the instruction will copy the following element to the result:

  ```
  <foo>
       I do not know where I am
  </foo>
  ```

  In this stylesheet, `current()` is an XSLT function that at any particular point during execution returns the current node. The function `name()` is an XPath function that returns the name[11] of the first node in the node set that is passed to the function as an argument. In our case, the argument is always the current node in the evaluation process, so the function returns the name of the current node.

- The `copy` instruction always outputs the node that is *current* at that particular point in the evaluation process. This feature should not be confused with the `copy-of` instruction, introduced earlier, which outputs the node set returned by its `select` attribute.

  Moreover, while the `copy-of` instruction copies nodes together with all of their belongings (attributes, child elements, etc.), the `copy` instruction strips the current node of its attributes and other children.[12] This feature is important to us since it provides a degree of control over what is to be output and, in particular, enables the stylesheet to intercept attribute nodes and emit them as elements.

  The `copy` instruction is also different from the `current()` function: `current()` is not an XSLT instruction, so it does not copy anything to the result

OPTIONAL

[11] For an element node, the node name is the name of the tag. For an attribute node, it is the name of the attribute.

[12] If the current node is a text node or an attribute, there is nothing to strip and the node is copied in its entirety.

FIGURE 15.18 XSLT stylesheet that converts attributes into elements.

```
<?xml version="1.0" ?>
<xsl:stylesheet xmlns:xsl="http://www.w3.org/1999/XSL/Transform"
              xsl:version="1.0">
    <xsl:template match="node()">
        <xsl:copy>
            <xsl:apply-templates select="@*"/>
            <xsl:apply-templates/>
        </xsl:copy>
    </xsl:template>
    <xsl:template match="@*">
        <xsl:element name="name(current())">
            <xsl:value-of select="."/>
        </xsl:element>
    </xsl:template>
</xsl:stylesheet>
```

OPTIONAL

document. Instead, as a function, it returns the current node (with everything in it), and the returned result can be used by XSLT instructions.

One possible solution to our problem (of finding a stylesheet that converts attributes into elements) is shown in Figure 15.18. This stylesheet has two templates. Processing of the source document starts, as usual, with the root. Since none of the explicit templates matches the root, the appropriate default template is used. As seen earlier, the default template (15.5) on page 643 replaces *CN* on *CNL* with the list of its *e*-children and tells the processor to apply matching templates to the list. In the document in Figure 15.14 on page 630, the only child of the root node is the element `Students`, so the processor tries to find a matching template for it.

Only the first template in our style sheet matches: the XPath function `node()` matches every node in the document tree *except* the root and attribute nodes. (The second template selects the document nodes that match the path expression `@*`, which matches every attribute of the current node.)

The first template copies the current node, *N*, to the result. Recall that the `copy` instruction strips the children and the attributes, so only the bare-bones *N* is copied. Processing the attributes and the *et*-children of *N* is performed by the two `apply-templates` instructions within the `copy` instruction.

The first `apply-templates` instruction adds the attributes of *N* (which is the current node) to the beginning of *CNL*. The first node in *CNL* becomes the new current node, *CN*. Assuming that *N* had attributes, only the second template matches *CN*, so it is used. It outputs the element that has the same name as the current attribute (since the template applies only to attributes and thus `current()` must return an attribute node) and then makes the value of the current attribute the content of that element. (For instance, `Attr="something"` is transformed into `<Attr>something</Attr>`.)

The second `apply-templates` inside the `copy` instruction is already familiar to us. It applies templates to every *et*-child of the current node but not to attribute nodes. As before, only the first template matches such nodes, so they are copied, their attributes are converted into elements, and the process recurs.

Limitations of XSLT. XSLT has a number of features that give it the qualities of a database query language: it can extract sets of nodes from a document, rearrange them, and apply transformations by recursively traversing the document tree. However, XSLT is lacking in certain important ways, which limits its use as a query language.

The most important problem has to do with joining documents or parts of the same document, analogously to the join operation in relational databases. As a simple example, consider taking the report in Figure 15.4 and producing a list of student records where every course taken by the student has the course name attached. To do this, we have to relate `CrsTaken` elements to `Course` elements that have the same course code.

It turns out that formulating such a join-query in XSLT is rather cumbersome. One way is to descend into the `Student` elements and, for each `CrsTaken`, use `apply-templates` with the `select` attribute pointing to the corresponding `Course` element. Such an approach is possible, although not very natural, with the help of XSLT variables—a mechanism not discussed in this section. Another way is to use nested `for-each` loops and XSLT variables that hold sets of document nodes. This method is similar to querying databases by explicitly coding joins as nested loops in embedded SQL.

Fortunately, XSLT is not the last word in XML querying, and a number of other XML query languages have been proposed.

OPTIONAL

15.4.3 XQuery: A Full-Featured Query Language for XML

XPath and XSLT provide certain query facilities for XML documents. However, we have seen that XPath was designed to be lightweight and so can express only simple queries. XSLT has much greater expressive power but was not designed as a query language; as a result, it has difficulty formulating complex queries.

Among the many languages specifically designed for querying XML, XQL and XML-QL deserve special mention. XQL [Robie et al. 1998] is an extension of XPath; XML-QL [Deutsch et al. 1998; Florescu et al. 1999] is an SQL-style query language, which also builds on ideas borrowed from languages such as OQL (Section 14.5.2) and Lorel [Abiteboul et al. 1997]. More recently, the best features of XQL and XML-QL were combined in a language called **XQuery** [XQuery 2004]. Like XSLT, XQuery uses XPath as a syntax for its path expressions. However, XQuery is generally more succinct and transparent than XSLT when it comes to querying. This section introduces the main features of XQuery.

Selections and joins. Unlike XSLT, XQuery does not use the verbose syntax of XML, as there is no good reason for any query language to do so (at least, for human consumption). Instead, XQuery statements have some similarity with SQL:

```
FOR     variable declarations
WHERE   condition
RETURN  result
```

The FOR clause plays the same role as the FROM clause in SQL, and the WHERE clause is borrowed from SQL with the same functionality. The RETURN clause is analogous to SELECT: in SQL, it defines the template for the result relation; in XQuery, it specifies the template for the result document.

At a deeper level, XQuery is strongly influenced by OQL, the object-oriented query language for ODMG databases (Section 14.5.2). This connection will be apparent from the examples. We start with simple queries against the document shown in Figure 15.19, which resides at the URL `http://xyz.edu/transcripts.xml`.

The first query retrieves all students who have ever taken `MAT123`.

```
(: Students who took MAT123 :)
FOR $t IN doc("http://xyz.edu/transcripts.xml")//Transcript
WHERE $t/CrsTaken/@CrsCode = "MAT123"
RETURN $t/Student
```

The text between `(:` and `:)` is a comment and can be ignored. The FOR clause declares a variable, `$t`, and its range—a set of document nodes. This set is specified using the XPath expression `//Transcript`, which is applied to the document obtained using the function `doc()`. This function, borrowed from XSLT, returns the root of the document specified by the URL. Hence `$t` ranges over all `Transcript` nodes in the document. To navigate within document trees, XQuery relies on XPath expressions, which are extended with variables. Thus, `$t/CrsTaken/@CrsCode` and `$t/Student` are extended XPath expressions. When `$t` is bound to a `Transcript` node in the document tree, the first expression returns the nodes corresponding to the `CrsCode` attribute of the `CrsTaken` *e*-children of that node. The second expression returns `Student` *e*-children of the node.

The condition `$t/CrsTaken/@CrsCode = "MAT123"` in the WHERE clause has a subtlety that illustrates one very important aspect of the XQuery semantics. Note that `$t/CrsTaken/@CrsCode` is a *set-valued* expression that contains all `CrsCode` attribute nodes listed in a transcript, `$t`. On the other hand, `"MAT123"` is a *single* constant. What does it mean to equate a set and a constant? More generally, what does it mean to compare two set-valued XPath expressions, `pathexpr1 op pathexpr2`? In XQuery, such a condition is true if and only if there is an element `e1` in the set `pathexpr1` and an element `e2` in the set `pathexpr2` such that `e1 op e2` is true. Thus, the WHERE condition in the above query selects a subset of the

FIGURE 15.19 Transcripts at `http://xyz.edu/transcripts.xml`.

```
<?xml version="1.0" ?>
<Transcripts>
    <Transcript>
        <Student StudId="s111111111" Name="John Doe"/>
        <CrsTaken CrsCode="CS308" Semester="F1997" Grade="B"/>
        <CrsTaken CrsCode="MAT123" Semester="F1997" Grade="B"/>
        <CrsTaken CrsCode="EE101" Semester"F1997" Grade="A"/>
        <CrsTaken CrsCode="CS305" Semester="F1995" Grade="A"/>
    </Transcript>
    <Transcript>
        <Student StudId="s987654321" Name="Bart Simpson"/>
        <CrsTaken CrsCode="CS305" Semester="F1995" Grade="C"/>
        <CrsTaken CrsCode="CS308" Semester="F1994" Grade="B"/>
    </Transcript>
    <Transcript>
        <Student StudId="s123454321" Name="Joe Blow"/>
        <CrsTaken CrsCode="CS315" Semester="S1997" Grade="A"/>
        <CrsTaken CrsCode="CS305" Semester="S1996" Grade="A"/>
        <CrsTaken CrsCode="MAT123" Semester="S1996" Grade="C"/>
    </Transcript>
    <Transcript>
        <Student StudId="s023456789" Name="Homer Simpson"/>
        <CrsTaken CrsCode="EE101" Semester="F1995" Grade="B"/>
        <CrsTaken CrsCode="CS305" Semester="S1996" Grade="A"/>
    </Transcript>
</Transcripts>
```

Transcript nodes, where each node has at least one CrsTaken element with MAT123 as the value of the CrsCode attribute.

The variable $t is successively bound to each Transcript node that satisfies the WHERE clause, and the RETURN clause is executed for each such binding of $t. Each execution of the RETURN clause outputs a fragment of the result document, which in our case is the Student element contained within the Transcript node that constitutes the current value of $t. In the example, the following is output:

```
<Student StudId="s111111111" Name="John Doe"/>
<Student StudId="s123454321" Name="Joe Blow"/>
```

One problem with this output is that it is not a well-formed XML document. It produces a list of Student elements, which is not contained within a single parent element. This problem is easy to fix by embedding the above query between a pair of tags.

```
<StudentList>
{
    FOR $t IN doc("http://xyz.edu/transcripts.xml")
                              //Transcript
    WHERE $t/CrsTaken/@CrsCode = "MAT123"
    RETURN $t/Student
}
</StudentList>
```

The result is that the FOR clause outputs Student elements one by one and places them as children of StudentList. In this context, the StudentList tag pair is called **direct element constructor**. The curly braces indicate that the text inside is an expression that is to be evaluated to become the content of the element denoted by the element constructor. In the following examples, we will omit the outermost element constructor.

The previous example has shown the convenience of using set-valued XPath expressions in the WHERE clause. Before proceeding to more complex queries, a word of caution is in order: set-valued comparisons can let subtle mistakes creep in. One frequent problem is illustrated in the following example. Suppose in the previous example we wanted only those students who took MAT123 in a particular semester as, for instance, in

```
$t/CrsTaken/@CrsCode = "MAT123" and $t/CrsTaken/@Semester = "F2002"
```

While this condition seems natural, it is incorrect. The correct one is

```
$t/CrsTaken[@CrsCode = "MAT123" and @Semester = "F2002"]
```

The problem with the former expression is that it selects those Transcript nodes that contain a record for MAT123 and a record that refers to a course for fall 2002. The two records do not need to be the same, however. The second expression avoids this ambiguity.

The next example illustrates the restructuring capabilities of XQuery. The Transcripts document in Figure 15.19 groups course records around the students who took them. However, the user reading this document might want to reconstruct class lists for each course. In other words, for each course offering in a particular semester, she might want to obtain the list of students who took that course. In XQuery, this can be done directly from the transcripts.xml document, as shown in Figure 15.20. In that query, the variable $c ranges over the set of all distinct CrsTaken nodes in the document transcripts.xml. For each such node, a fragment of the result document is constructed as described in the RETURN clause.

The query in Figure 15.20 is almost correct, but it has a flaw that we will explain after discussing the new features it exhibits. First, observe that the query is nested. The interesting point, however, is that the nesting occurs in the RETURN clause, which corresponds to the SELECT clause in SQL. The SQL specification bans nested

FIGURE 15.20 Construction of class rosters from transcripts: first try.

```
FOR $c IN distinct-values(doc("http://xyz.edu/transcripts.xml")
                                    //CrsTaken)
RETURN <ClassRoster CrsCode={$c/@CrsCode} Semester={$c/@Semester}>
    {
        FOR $t IN doc("http://xyz.edu/transcripts.xml")
                                    //Transcript
        WHERE $t/CrsTaken[@CrsCode = $c/@CrsCode and
                         @Semester = $c/@Semester]
        RETURN
                $t/Student
                ORDER BY $t/Student/@StudId
    }
</ClassRoster>
ORDER BY $c/@CrsCode
```

queries in the SELECT clause because they do not make sense in the relational model.[13] Indeed, a nested query typically returns a set of tuples whereas the target list of a SELECT clause in SQL is a template for a single tuple. In contrast, nested queries in the RETURN clause make perfect sense for an XML query language because the purpose here is to construct a document that can have an arbitrarily complex nested structure. In our case, nesting serves the purpose of embedding student lists into class rosters. We have already encountered the use of nested queries in the target list of a query: this is allowed in the object-oriented query language OQL (see query (14.17) on page 555). Nesting is used there for the same reason it is used in XQuery.

Let us look more closely at the RETURN clause in the query in Figure 15.20, which is executed for each value of the variable `$c`. First, it constructs the `ClassRoster` element with the appropriate values for the attributes `CrsCode` and `Semester`. Then the nested subquery is invoked to construct the *sorted* list of students who took this class (i.e., the given course in the given semester). In it, `$t` ranges over `Transcript` elements and the WHERE clause selects those that have a `CrsTaken` element that matches the semester and course specified in `$c`. The output consists of elements such as

```
<ClassRoster CrsCode="CS305" Semester="F1995">
    <Student StudId="s111111111" Name="John Doe"/>
    <Student StudId="s987654321" Name="Bart Simpson"/>
</ClassRoster>
```

which are themselves sorted by the `CrsCode` attribute that occurs in each roster.

[13] SQL allows nested queries in SELECT only if they return a single scalar value, such as an integer or a string.

So far so good, except for one thing: John Doe and Bart Simpson received different grades for CS305 in fall 1995, so the FOR clause binds $c to two different CrsTaken elements for that class:

```
<CrsTaken CrsCode="CS305" Semester="F1995" Grade="A"/>
<CrsTaken CrsCode="CS305" Semester="F1995" Grade="C"/>
```

This means that the above ClassRoster element will be output twice. In general, each roster will be output once for every distinct grade received in the corresponding class. Note that the function distinct-values in the FOR clause, which eliminates textually equivalent elements in the range of the variable $c, does not take care of this problem because the above CrsTaken elements are distinct.

One way to overcome this problem is to create a new document that contains a list of all classes and then bind $c to the elements of that list. This can be easily done by selecting all CrsTaken elements from the transcripts document and then stripping off the Grade attribute from each new one.

We will revisit this idea later, but for now we avoid this problem by assuming that the document in Figure 15.21, which resides at the URL *http://xyz.edu/classes.xml*, already exists. The following query is a reformulation of the faulty query of Figure 15.20 with slight enhancements intended to illustrate the join operation in XQuery:

```
FOR $c IN doc("http://xyz.edu/classes.xml")//Class
RETURN
    <ClassRoster CrsCode={$c/@CrsCode} Semester={$c/@Semester}>
        {
            $c/CrsName,
            $c/Instructor,
            FOR $t IN doc("http://xyz.edu/transcripts.xml")
                                   //Transcript
            WHERE $t/CrsTaken[@CrsCode = $c/@CrsCode and
                              @Semester = $c/@Semester]
            RETURN
            $t/Student
            ORDER BY $t/Student/@StudId
        }
</ClassRoster>
ORDER BY $c/@CrsCode
```

The change in this new query is that the variable $c ranges over the set of all Class nodes of the document in Figure 15.21. Since classes do not occur multiple times there, we no longer have the problem of outputting multiple instances of the same roster (and we do not even need to apply the function distinct-values()). The result of the new query is enriched by including the course name ($c/CrsName)

FIGURE 15.21 Classes at `http://xyz.edu/classes.xml`.

```
<?xml version="1.0" ?>
<Classes>
    <Class CrsCode="CS308" Semester="F1997">
        <CrsName>Software Engineering</CrsName>
        <Instructor>Adrian Jones</Instructor>
    </Class>
    <Class CrsCode="EE101" Semester="F1995">
        <CrsName>Electronic Circuits</CrsName>
        <Instructor>David Jones</Instructor>
    </Class>
    <Class CrsCode="CS305" Semester="F1995">
        <CrsName>Database Systems</CrsName>
        <Instructor>Mary Doe</Instructor>
    </Class>
    <Class CrsCode="CS315" Semester="S1997">
        <CrsName>Transaction Processing</CrsName>
        <Instructor>John Smyth</Instructor>
    </Class>
    <Class CrsCode="MAT123" Semester="F1997">
        <CrsName>Algebra</CrsName>
        <Instructor>Ann White</Instructor>
    </Class>
</Classes>
```

and the instructor (`$c/Instructor`) as child elements in each roster. They are conjoined to the nested `FOR`-expression using the **concatenation operator** "," to output elements such as

```
<ClassRoster CrsCode="..." Semester="...">
   <CrsName>...</CrsName>
   <Instructor>...</Instructor>
   <Student ... />
   <Student ... />
   ... ... ...
</ClassRoster>
```

Thus, this query computes a kind of *equi-join* on the attributes `CrsCode` and `Semester` between the `Transcript` elements of the document in Figure 15.19 and the `Class` elements of the document in Figure 15.21. As remarked at the end of Section 15.4.2, it is difficult to formulate this kind of transformation in XSLT.

Note that in the above query, even if some class has no students, the corresponding element `ClassRoster` will still appear in the result with `CrsName` and

Instructor present, but with no Student elements. This is different from the join operation in relational databases, where a tuple in a CLASS relation with no matching tuples in the TRANSCRIPT relation will not be considered in an equi-join on the attributes CrsCode and Semester. The kind of join produced by the above XQuery example is known in relational databases as an **outer join** (see Section 5.1.2, page 142). Nevertheless, it is easy to reformulate the query and make it perform a "real" join by adding an appropriate WHERE clause to the outermost FOR statement:

```
FOR $c IN doc("http://xyz.edu/classes.xml")//Class
WHERE doc("http://xyz.edu/transcripts.xml")
                    //CrsTaken[@CrsCode = $c/@CrsCode
                              and @Semester = $c/@Semester]
RETURN
    <ClassRoster CrsCode={$c/@CrsCode} Semester={$c/@Semester}>
        {
            $c/CrsName,
            $c/Instructor,
            FOR $t IN doc("http://xyz.edu/transcripts.xml")
                                    //Transcript
            WHERE $t/CrsTaken[@CrsCode = $c/@CrsCode and
                              @Semester = $c/@Semester]
            RETURN
                  $t/Student
                  ORDER BY $t/Student/@StudId
        }
    </ClassRoster>
ORDER BY $c/@CrsCode
```

The purpose of the new WHERE clause is to test whether the document at http://xyz.edu/transcripts.xml has CrsTaken elements that match the attributes CrsCode and Semester for the current value of the variable $c. This test is performed by the path expression //CrsTaken[...] in the first WHERE clause. Only if such elements exist is the corresponding ClassRoster element output. Thus, rosters for the classes with no students will not appear in the result.

We will add one final touch to this example before turning our attention to other features of XQuery. Note that doc("http://xyz.edu/transcripts.xml") occurs twice in the above query. In general, a complex expression that denotes a set of nodes can occur multiple times in the same query. It is therefore natural to introduce variables that can take node sets as values. This is what the LET construct lets you do. The rewritten query is shown in Figure 15.22. In this figure the use of LET is still just a syntactic sugar, but soon we will see more substantial uses of this construct.

FIGURE 15.22 Construction of class rosters: correct version.

```
LET $trs := doc("http://xyz.edu/transcripts.xml")
FOR $c IN doc("http://xyz.edu/classes.xml")//Class
WHERE $trs//CrsTaken[@CrsCode = $c/@CrsCode and
                     @Semester = $c/@Semester]
RETURN
    <ClassRoster CrsCode={$c/@CrsCode} Semester={$c/@Semester}>
        {
            $c/CrsName,
            $c/Instructor,
            FOR $t IN $trs//Transcript
            WHERE $t/CrsTaken[@CrsCode = $c/@CrsCode and
                              @Semester = $c/@Semester]
            RETURN
                  $t/Student
                  ORDER BY $t/Student/@StudId
        }
    </ClassRoster>
ORDER BY $c/@CrsCode
```

The semantics of XQuery. So far, we have discussed the various examples informally, without explaining how the actual query evaluation mechanism works. We are now going to clarify these issues.

The FOR clause has the following functions:

- To specify the documents to be used in the query.
- To declare variables. Multiple variables can be declared in the same FOR clause as follows: FOR $*var1* IN *expr1*, $*var2* IN *expr1*, ...
- To bind each variable to its range, which is a *list* of document nodes specified by an XQuery expression. Typically, this is an XPath expression, but it can also be a query or a function that returns a list of nodes.

The bindings produced by the FOR clause translate into an ordered list of tuples, each containing a concrete binding for every variable mentioned in the FOR clause. For instance, if the FOR clause declares the variables `$a` and `$b` and binds them to the document nodes `{v,w}` and `{x,y,z}`, respectively, then the following ordered list of tuples will be produced: `{v,x}`, `{v,y}`, `{v,z}`, `{w,x}`, `{w,y}`, `{w,z}`. Each tuple, such as `{w,x}`, provides a concrete binding—`$a/w`, `$b/x`—to our variables.

Next, the tuples of bindings are filtered through the WHERE condition. Thus, if the condition is `$a/CrsTaken/@CrsCode = $b/Class/@CrsCode` and the document nodes `w` and `x` are such that `w/CrsTaken/@CrsCode = x/Class/@CrsCode`, then the tuple `(w,x)` of bindings for `$a` and `$b` is retained; otherwise, it is discarded. The effect of the WHERE clause is thus a selection of an ordered sublist from the original list of tuples.

Finally, for each surviving tuple of bindings the RETURN expression is instantiated. The result is the creation of a fragment for the output document. The process repeats until all eligible tuple bindings are exhausted.

> *Brain Teaser:* With the features described so far, is it possible to write a non-terminating XQuery expression?

User-defined functions. XQuery provides a large number of built-in functions, which include all of the core functions available in XPath. It also provides some other useful functions, such as `distinct-values()` and `doc()`, and others that we will see later.

More interestingly, a query in XQuery can define a number of functions, which can then be called from within the main FOR-WHERE-RETURN query. Functions can call themselves recursively; they can take singleton nodes as well as collections of nodes as arguments; and they can return primitive types, document nodes, or collections of any of these types. The body of a function is an XQuery expression, which can be general (even queries are treated as expressions). An expression can evaluate to an integer, an element, a list of elements, and so on, and the function returns its result.

Here is an example of a function that counts the number of descendant element nodes in a document fragment rooted at node `$e`:

```
DECLARE FUNCTION countNodes($e AS element()) AS integer {
    RETURN
        IF empty($e/*) THEN 0
        ELSE sum(FOR $n IN $e/* RETURN countNodes($n))
            + count($e/*)
}
```

This function definition illustrates a great number of features.

- The declaration `$e` AS `element()` says that the argument to the function must be an element. (`element()` is a data type that accepts any element.) In particular, it cannot be an attribute or a text node, and it cannot be an integer. The function is said to return an integer. The argument cannot be a list either: lists are considered distinct data types and must be specified as such (e.g., `element()*` for lists of elements). We explain a bit later where such types come from.

  The body of an XQuery function is an **XQuery expression**, which evaluates to a value (an integer, a string, a document node, a list of nodes, etc.). The value of that expression is returned. XQuery expressions are explained next.

- The statement IF-THEN-ELSE is a conditional XQuery expression. The part between IF and THEN must be a Boolean expression—in our case `empty($e/*)`, which uses the built-in function `empty()` to check whether the path expression `$e/*` returns the empty set of document nodes.[14]

  The THEN and ELSE parts must be XQuery expressions. We do not define the full syntax of XQuery expressions here—see [XQuery 2004]. Typically they are path expressions (which return a set of document nodes), function calls (which can return a primitive type such as `integer` or `string`, a document node, or a set of nodes in the case of user-defined functions), arithmetic expressions, concatenations of lists of nodes, IF-THEN-ELSE conditionals, or full-blown queries (which can return a single document or a list of document fragments).

  In our case, the THEN expression is just a constant and the ELSE part is an arithmetic expression that makes calls to the aggregate functions `sum()` and `count()`. The function `sum()` applies to a collection of numeric values computed by recursive calls to `countNodes()`, and sums them up. The function `count()` counts the number of nodes returned by the path expression `$e/*`.

In the next example, we come back to the "nearly correct" query in Figure 15.20. Recall that the problem was that a class roster might appear multiple times in the result if at least two students in that class receive different grades. One solution that we came up with was to join transcripts with the document in Figure 15.21. XQuery functions make it possible to create an intermediate document similar to that of Figure 15.21 and join it with `Transcripts` in the same query, without relying on the existence of another, external document. The solution is shown in Figure 15.23.

The first part of the query defines the function `extractClasses()`. This function accepts a single element and returns a list of elements. The return type is specified as `element()*` using the already familiar type `element()` and the sequence indicator "*". The result of the function is obtained by evaluating a simple query, which iterates through all `CrsTaken` descendants of the function argument, strips off the `Grade` attribute, and outputs the result as a list of `Class` elements.

The main query appears below the function definition. It returns a document with the top-level tag `Rosters`, which contains a list of individual elements tagged with `ClassRoster`. This query is almost identical to the one in Figure 15.20 except that the variable `$c` ranges over the result produced by the function `extractClasses()`. Also, the WHERE clause has been eliminated and replaced with a selection condition on the XPath expression that binds the variable `$t`. (Selection conditions in XPath expressions were introduced in Section 15.4.1.)

The last example of user-defined functions illustrates how XQuery can perform document transformations of the kind discussed in connection with XSLT. Specifically, we rewrite the XSLT stylesheet in Figure 15.18 on page 648, which traverses

[14] Recall that the wildcard "*" selects all *e*-children of the current node, so `$e/*` returns the set of all elements that are children of the node assigned to `$e`.

FIGURE 15.23 Class rosters constructed with user-defined functions.

```
DECLARE FUNCTION extractClasses($e AS element()) AS element()* {
  FOR $ct IN $e//CrsTaken
  RETURN <Class CrsCode=$ct/@CrsCode Semester=$ct/@Semester/>
}

<Rosters>
{
  LET $trs := doc("http://xyz.edu/transcripts.xml")
  FOR $c IN distinct-values(extractClasses($trs))
  RETURN
    <ClassRoster CrsCode={$c/@CrsCode} Semester={$c/@Semester}>
      {
        FOR $t IN  $trs//Transcript[CrsTaken/@CrsCode=$c/@CrsCode and
                                    CrsTaken/@Semester=$c/@Semester]
        RETURN $t/Student
        ORDER BY $t/Student/@StudId
      }
    </ClassRoster>
}
</Rosters>
```

an XML document and replaces attributes with elements that have the same name and content. The XQuery equivalent of that program is as follows:

```
DECLARE FUNCTION convertAttribute($a AS attribute()) AS element() {
  RETURN
    element {name($a)} {data($a)}
}
DECLARE FUNCTION convertElement($e AS element()) AS element(){
  RETURN
    element {name($e)}
    {
      {FOR $a IN $e/@* RETURN convertAttribute($a)},
      IF empty($e/*) THEN $e/text()
      ELSE {FOR $n IN $e/* RETURN convertElement($n)}
    }
}

RETURN convertElement(doc("...")/*)
```

The actual query consists of a single call to a previously defined function, `convertElement()`, which takes as an argument a single element node. In this case, the argument is the child node of the document root.[15] Note that since a well-formed XML document has exactly one topmost element, there is no need for an iteration construct, such as the FOR clause.

The first function, `convertAttribute()`, takes an attribute node as an argument and converts it into the element that has the same name (obtained via a call to the XPath function `name()`). The value of the attribute (obtained via the XQuery function `data()`) becomes the content of the element. The actual element is constructed using a **computed element constructor**, which is specified as `element` {*element name expression*} {*content expression*}.

The second function, `convertElement()`, does the bulk of the work. It is called to convert an element node into an attribute-less element with the same name. For a given element, `convertElement()` outputs an element with the same name (again, using a computed element and a call to `name()`), then converts the element's attributes (the FOR clause), and finally its *et*-children (the IF clause). The two parts are conjoined via the concatenation operator ",". The FOR-expression, which takes care of the element's attributes, repeatedly invokes `convertAttribute()` on each attribute.[16]

Having finished with attributes, `convertElement()` turns to text nodes and elements. If the element has no *e*-children (as determined by `empty()`),[17] the only child must be a text node (or nothing at all if the element is empty). In the first case, the function emits the text node if it exists; in the second case, it transforms the *e*-children of the current node by calling itself recursively in a FOR loop.

The above query does not perform quite the same transformation as the XSLT stylesheet in Figure 15.18, on page 648. For instance, if an element has mixed content—that is, its children include elements as well as text nodes (for example, `<foo>some text<bar>more text</bar>even more</foo>`)—the query ignores the text (because the XPath expression `$e/*` selects only *e*-children) and proceeds to convert the elements. We tackle this problem in the next example, after explaining the relationship between XQuery, namespaces, and XML schemas.

XQuery, namespaces, and data types. The previous queries showed the use of primitive types, such as `integer`, and the XQuery generic types, like `element()` and `attribute()`. However, XQuery goes much further by integrating smoothly with the XML Schema specification and by allowing the importation and use of the types defined in various XML schemas. In fact, the primitive type `integer` used earlier is not a native XQuery type but rather the one defined by the XML Schema specification, so it should be used in conjunction with the corresponding namespace.

[15] We ignore the possibility that there might be other children of the root, such as comments and processing instructions.
[16] Recall that "`@*`" is an XPath wildcard that returns all the attributes of an element. The XPath function `text()` returns all *t*-children of the current node.
[17] In this case, the element would have the form `<foo>some text</foo>`.

FIGURE 15.24 XQuery transformation that does the same work as the stylesheet in Figure 15.18.

```
IMPORT SCHEMA namespace aux = "http://types.r.us/auxiliary"
          AT "http://types.r.us/auxiliary/types.xsd";
DECLARE FUNCTION local:convertNode($n AS node()) AS node() {
     RETURN
          IF ($n NOT INSTANCE OF aux:ProtectedElement
               AND $n INSTANCE OF element()) THEN {
               element {fn:name($n)}
               {
                    {FOR $a IN $n/@* RETURN local:convertNode($a)},
                    {FOR $c IN $n/node() RETURN local:convertNode($c)}
               }
          } ELSE IF $n INSTANCE OF attribute() THEN {
               element {fn:name($n)} {fn:data($n)}
          } ELSE $n
}

RETURN local:convertNode(fn:doc("...")/*)
```

We will now illustrate the integration of XQuery with XML schemas and namespaces using a true XQuery equivalent of the XSLT stylesheet in Figure 15.18 on page 648. To make things more interesting, we will add a twist: only the elements that are not of type `ProtectedElement` will have their attributes converted into elements. Protected elements will be output as is. To this end, we assume that the type `ProtectedElements` is defined in a schema found in the document at the URL `http://types.r.us/auxiliary/types.xsd` with the target namespace `http://types.r.us/auxiliary`:

```
<schema xmlns="http://www.w3.org/2001/XMLSchema"
        targetNamespace="http://types.r.us/auxiliary">
    <complexType name="ProtectedElement">
        . . . . . . . . .
    </complexType>
</schema>
```

Figure 15.24 shows the XQuery expression we are looking for.

The clause IMPORT SCHEMA tells the XQuery processor the namespace associated with that schema (the URL preceding “at”) and where to find the schema used in the query (the URL following “at”). In our case, this schema contains the definition of the union type `ProtectedElement`, which we use inside the function `convertNode()`. This clause also introduces a namespace prefix, aux, for the namespace `http://types.r.us/auxiliary`, which is used in the query. This namespace identifies the schema where the type `ProtectedElement` is defined. Note that this namespace matches both the target namespace of the schema document that defines ProtectedElement and the namespace mentioned in the IMPORT SCHEMA clause.

Note that now we attach namespace prefixes to every built-in function mentioned in the document since XQuery actually requires that all functions must be associated with a namespace. The built-in functions that are available to users (such as name(), doc(), count(), or distinct-values()) typically come from the namespace http://www.w3.org/2004/07/xpath-functions and fn is understood by XQuery processors as a prefix denoting this namespace. Functions defined for the local use, such as convertNode() above, are assumed to come from the namespace http://www.w3.org/2004/07/xquery-local-functions, and XQuery predefines local to be a namespace prefix for that.

The function convertNode() takes an argument of type node and returns document nodes of type node. The built-in type node includes all nodes in the document tree and is specified as node().

The only other new feature in the query is the predicate INSTANCE OF, which tests whether a given node (the value of $n in our case) conforms to a given type. We use this test in the function convertNode() to determine whether the argument to the function is an attribute node or an element of type ProtectedElement.

The function convertNode() works analogously to convertElement(), which we discussed earlier. It first checks the argument type. If it is an unprotected element, the appropriate element is created. Its content is specified by two sequences of recursive calls to convertNode(). The first sequence converts the attributes of the current element into elements, and the second converts each *et*-child of the current node.[18] If the argument is an attribute, it is replaced with an element that has the same name as the attribute, and the attribute value becomes the content of that element. If the argument is neither an attribute nor an element, it must be a text node, in which case the node is simply copied to the result document.

In some cases, an XQuery expression may reference symbols defined in namespaces that do not come from imported schemas. Typically this is needed in order to specify the namespace of the elements *produced* by XQuery expressions. In this case, the DECLARE NAMESPACE clause is used. In the following example we declare a namespace with a prefix rep for the element Roster, which is output by the query.

```
IMPORT SCHEMA namespace adm = "http://xyz.edu/Admin"
              AT "http://xyz.edu/Admin.xsd";
DECLARE NAMESPACE rep = "http://xyz.edu/Report";
LET $trs := fn:doc("http://xyz.edu/transcripts.xml")
FOR $c IN fn:distinct-values($trs//adm:CrsTaken)
RETURN  <rep:Roster> { ... } </rep:Roster>
```

Grouping and aggregation. Unlike SQL, XQuery does not use a separate grouping operator; instead it relies on a more consistent mechanism that applies aggregate

[18] Recall that node() is an XPath function that returns all *et*-children of the current node.

functions to explicitly constructed collections of document nodes. This is achieved with the help of the already familiar LET clause, which declares a variable and initializes it with a collection of nodes specified by an XQuery expression. Interestingly, the use of LET outside of a FOR clause is just syntactic sugar, as we saw in Figure 15.22, but its use in thc scope of a FOR clause can be essential because grouping cannot be achieved in any other way.

To illustrate, the following query takes the `Transcripts` document in Figure 15.19 on page 651 and produces a document that lists students along with the number of courses each has taken so far.

```
FOR $t IN fn:doc("http://xyz.edu/transcripts.xml")//Transcript,
    $s IN $t/Student
LET $c := $t/CrsTaken
RETURN
  <StudentSummary StudId={$s/@StudId} Name={$s/@Name}
                  TotalCourses={fn:count(fn:distinct-values($c))}/>
ORDER BY StudentSummary/@TotalCourses
```

Recall that the FOR clause iterates by binding `$t` to every `Transcript` element of the document. For each such binding there is a unique `Student` element that gets bound to `$s`.[19] The trick here is that the variable `$c` is assigned a new list of `CrsTaken` elements each time `$t` is bound to a new element because LET occurs in the scope of the FOR clause that binds `$t`. In other words, for any `Transcript` binding for `$t`, `$c` is bound to the list of classes mentioned in that transcript element, and the subsequent call to `count()` simply counts the number of distinct elements on the list.

The similarity between the FOR and LET clauses might be deceiving. Both specify variable bindings as collections of document nodes, but FOR binds the variables to the *individual nodes* of a collection *in succession* while LET binds the variables to the *entire collection* of nodes *at once*.

> *Brain Teaser:* What is the purpose of the curly braces inside the element constructor in the RETURN statement of the previous query?

The next query is slightly more complicated as it involves a join of the `Transcripts` document in Figure 15.19 and the `Classes` document in Figure 15.21. It creates a list of classes along with the average grade in each. To obtain the numeric value for a grade, we use the function `numericGrade()`, which can be easily defined as an XQuery function (and is omitted). This example also illustrates another important feature: the binding for the variables in the LET clause (and, for that matter, in the FOR clause) does not need to be specified as an XPath expression, but can be

[19] If a `Transcript` element could have several `Student` children, then `$s` would bind to each in succession and the FOR clause would function as a nested loop.

any XQuery expression that returns a list of nodes. In particular, it can be a query as shown below:

```
FOR $c IN fn:doc("http://xyz.edu/classes.xml")//Class
(: $g gets the collection of all numeric grades in the class bound to $c :)
LET $g := {
           FOR $ct IN fn:doc("http://xyz.edu/transcripts.xml")
                                              //CrsTaken
           WHERE $ct/@CrsCode = $c/@CrsCode
                 AND $ct/@Semester = $c/@Semester
           RETURN local:numericGrade($ct/@Grade)
         }
RETURN
  <ClassSummary CrsCode = {$c/@CrsCode} Semester={$c/@Semester}
             CsrName = {$c/CrsName} Instructor={$c/Instructor}
             AvgGrade = {fn:avg($g)}/>
ORDER BY ClassSummary/@CrsCode
```

This is essentially the same query as the one on page 654, which constructs class rosters by joining the documents `transcripts.xml` and `classes.xml`. However, instead of listing all students in the class in the result document, we compute the list of all grades in the class and assign it to a variable, $g, using the LET clause. These grades are then averaged, and the result is assigned as a value of the attribute `AvgGrade`.

Note that, when the LET clause occurs in the scope of a FOR clause, it introduces a new issue as far as the query semantics is concerned. This happens because now variables are bound both by the FOR and LET clauses. The LET clause is incorporated into the evaluation mechanism as follows: For each tuple of bindings for the variables in the FOR clause, the bindings for the LET variables are determined. Unlike the bindings for the FOR variables, the LET clause bindings are to lists of nodes, which are typically used as arguments to aggregate functions. Thus, the binding for the LET variables is completely determined by the binding for the FOR variables.

The rest of the query evaluation procedure remains unchanged: the WHERE clause filters out tuples of bindings produced by the FOR clause. The only difference is that now the condition in WHERE might also use the variables bound by LET. Finally, for each tuple of bindings for the FOR variables, the RETURN clause generates a fragment for the result document.

Quantification. Suppose we want to extract the list of all students who took `MAT123`. In SQL, this requires the EXISTS operator (which is analogous to the XQuery function `empty()`). XQuery provides similar facilities through the quantifiers SOME and EVERY, which precisely correspond to the existential quantifier ∃ and the universal quantifier ∀ in relational calculus (Chapter 13). As shown in Chapter 13, explicit use of quantifiers greatly simplifies the formulation of certain queries as compared to their formulation in SQL.

The next query uses the SOME quantifier to return the list of all students who took MAT123.

```
FOR $t IN fn:doc("http://xyz.edu/transcripts.xml")//Transcript
WHERE SOME $ct IN $t/CrsTaken
        SATISFIES $ct/@CrsCode = "MAT123"
RETURN $t/Student
```

In many cases, the SOME quantifier can be eliminated from the query. For instance, assuming that a student cannot take the same course twice, the above query is equivalent to

```
FOR $t IN fn:doc("http://xyz.edu/transcripts.xml")//Transcript,
    $ct IN $t/CrsTaken
WHERE $ct/@CrsCode = "MAT123"
RETURN $t/Student
```

The analogy between SQL and XQuery should not be taken too far, however. Consider the following queries, which return the course names for classes that have at least one enrolled student: the SQL query

```
SELECT   C.CrsName
FROM     CLASS C, TRANSCRIPT T
WHERE    C.CrsCode = T.CrsCode AND C.Semester = T.Semester
```

and the XQuery query

```
FOR      $c IN fn:doc("http://xyz.edu/classes.xml")//Class,
         $ct IN fn:doc("http://xyz.edu/transcripts.xml")//CrsTaken
WHERE    $c/@CrsCode = $ct/@CrsCode AND $c/@Semester = $ct/@Semester
RETURN   $c/CrsName
```

Since T does not occur in the SELECT clause and $t does not occur in the RETURN clause, the two are assumed to be existentially quantified. In both cases, a course name is output even if just one matching transcript record is found. If more than one is found, an SQL query processor might or might not output duplicate course names, depending on the inner workings of the query optimizer. (Since SQL is a relational query language, its semantics imply that only one name per course should be output. The possibility of duplicates is an implementation detail.) In contrast, the semantics of the FOR clause in XQuery imply that a course name will be output for *every* matching transcript record. This is because FOR specifies a loop in which the RETURN clause is executed for each binding of $c and $t, and every binding for $c is likely to have multiple matching bindings for $t.

Note that, while SELECT DISTINCT in SQL guarantees that there are no duplicates, the distinct-values() function in XQuery does not easily achieve the same goal (see Exercise 15.31). One way to eliminate duplicates in our example is to use SOME. Unlike the previous example of students who took MAT123, however, SOME is essential and cannot be eliminated simply by moving variables from the WHERE to the FOR clause.

```
FOR    $c IN fn:doc("http://xyz.edu/classes.xml")//Class
WHERE
  SOME $ct IN fn:doc("http://xyz.edu/transcripts.xml")//CrsTaken
  SATISFIES $c/@CrsCode = $ct/@CrsCode AND $c/@Semester = $ct/@Semester
RETURN $c/CrsName
```

In contrast to the existential quantifier, the universal quantifier, EVERY, cannot be easily eliminated from most queries. As discussed in Chapter 13, the universal quantifier provides a natural way of expressing queries that involve the division operator in relational algebra. Such queries look rather awkward in SQL because SQL does not support universal quantification directly.[20] To illustrate, the following query retrieves all classes in which every enrolled student took MAT123:

```
FOR $c IN fn:doc("http://xyz.edu/classes.xml")//Class
(: $g gets bound to the set of all Transcript elements
    corresponding to the particular class that binds $c     :)
LET $g := {
    FOR $t IN fn:doc("http://xyz.edu/transcripts.xml")
                                   //Transcript
    WHERE $t/CrsTaken[@CrsCode = $c/@CrsCode and
                       @Semester = $c/@Semester]
    RETURN $t
         }
(: Take only those $g in which every transcript
    has a CrsTaken element for MAT123          :)
WHERE EVERY $tr IN $g
    SATISFIES NOT fn:empty($tr[CrsTaken/@CrsCode = "MAT123"])
RETURN $c ORDER BY $c/@CrsCode
```

Here, for every binding of $c to a Class element, $g is bound to the list of transcripts of students who took this class. The outer WHERE clause checks that every student transcript in $g indicates that the student has taken MAT123. (Recall that the XPath

[20] We saw in Section 5.2.3 that expressing universal quantification in SQL requires EXISTS, nested subqueries, and double negation (NOT and EXCEPT). However, Section 5.2.4 describes a limited form of universal quantification, which was introduced in SQL:1999. Although not sufficiently adequate, this new feature provides some relief for writing queries that involve the relational division operator.

expression `$tr[CrsTaken/@CrsCode = "MAT123"]` returns a nonempty set of nodes if and only if `$tr` is bound to a transcript element that includes a `CrsTaken` element for the course `MAT123`.)

15.4.4 SQL/XML

SQL is not called Intergalactic Dataspeak for nothing. When OQL-speaking aliens (see Chapter 14) descended on our galaxy, SQL was extended with object-relational constructs. SQL is now being extended with a new dialect, called SQL/XML. This extension can be viewed as yet another way to introduce object-relational data into SQL—see Section 14.4 for an earlier proposal, which became part of SQL:1999/2003. The major vendors have implemented most of the proposed extensions. When complete, it is expected that SQL/XML will become part of the SQL standard.

SQL/XML addresses the following practical needs:

- To publish the contents of SQL tables and even the contents of entire databases as XML documents. This requires the development of conventions for translation of the primitive SQL data types, such as CHAR(4), into XML Schema data types and back.
- More generally, to create XML documents out of SQL query results. This requires the addition of primitives to allow the creation of XML elements by SQL queries.
- To store XML documents in relational databases and to query them effectively using SQL. Since SQL is unable to deal with tree-like structures directly, XPath is used for that purpose.

In the remainder of this section, we review the current state of SQL/XML. Keep in mind, however, that the work on this standard is still ongoing, that some details will definitely change after this text is published, and that vendor implementations (e.g., from Oracle, IBM, and Microsoft) will vary in some ways from the SQL/XML proposal.

Encoding relations as XML documents. This part of the SQL/XML specification defines the conventions for converting relations into XML documents (and relation schemas into XML schemas). The main purpose is to provide a standard way of exchanging relations on the Internet. The current proposal does not include a built-in function that would take a table and return an XML document. However, it provides more general functions that make it possible to create arbitrary XML documents using the SELECT clause. We discuss these functions in the next subsection, on page 671.

There are many ways to encode relational data in XML (see Exercise 15.1). SQL/XML does this as follows:

- The entire relation is enclosed in a pair of tags named after the relation.
- Each row is enclosed within the `row` tag pair.
- Each attribute value is enclosed within a pair of tags named after that attribute.

For instance, the PROFESSOR relation in Figure 3.5 on page 39 will be represented as

```
<Professor>
  <row>
    <Id>101202303</Id>
    <Name>John Smyth</Name><DeptId>CS</DeptId>
  </row>
  <row>
    <Id>783432188</Id>                                         15.7
    <Name>Adrian Jones</Name><DeptId>MGT</DeptId>
  </row>
  <row>
    <Id>121232343</Id>
    <Name>David Jones</Name><DeptId>EE</DeptId>
  </row>
  .
  .
  .
</Professor>
```

Suppose the type of the Id attribute in the PROFESSOR relation is INTEGER and the types for Name and DeptId are CHAR(50) and CHAR(3), respectively. Defining an XML Schema document corresponding to the relational schema of the PROFESSOR relation is not hard. The only question is the representation of SQL types in XML Schema. In our particular case, this representation is easy:

```
<schema xmlns="http://www.w3.org/2001/XMLSchema"
        xmlns:tnc="http://xyz.edu/Admin"
        targetNameSpace="http://xyz.edu/Admin">
  <element name="Professor">
    <complexType>
      <sequence>
        <element name="row" minOccurs="0" maxOccurs="unbounded">
          <complexType>
            <sequence>
              <element name="Id"  type="integer"/>
              <element name="Name" type="CHAR_50"/>
              <element name="DeptId" type="CHAR_3"/>
            </sequence>
          </complexType>
        </element>
      </sequence>
    </complexType>
  </element>
</schema>
```

The types CHAR_50 and CHAR_3 are standard conventions within SQL/XML for the corresponding SQL CHAR(...) types. For example, CHAR_50 is defined by restricting the base XML Schema type string as follows:

```
<simpleType name="CHAR_50">
   <restriction base="string">
      <length value="50"/>
   </restriction>
</simpleType>
```

The real problem is that SQL has a large number of built-in types, such as INTERVAL, TIMESTAMP, MULTISET, etc., as well as user-defined types, which are created using the CREATE DOMAIN statement. All of these need to be painstakingly defined in XML, and much of the XML/SQL specification deals with this issue. We omit the gory details in this text.

Storing and publishing XML documents: The XML data type. Although an XML document could be stored inside a table as an attribute of type string, doing so would make querying the document extremely inefficient. For example, XPath would have to scan the entire string and parse it before an expression could be evaluated. Hence, SQL/XML envisions support for *native storage* of an XML document as a hierarchical tree structure, which facilitates navigation within the document. For example, the structure would make it easy to locate the children of each node. Fortunately, efficient storage and indexing techniques exist to support native storage of XML documents [Deutsch et al. 1999; Zhao and Joseph 2000], and a new data type, XML, was added to SQL for this purpose. For instance, we might decide to store transcripts in the native XML format along with the student information, as follows:

```
CREATE TABLE  StudentXML (
  Id         INTEGER,
  Details    XML )
```
15.8

The Details attribute is supposed to contain XML documents of the form

```
<Student>
    <Name><First>John</First><Last>Doe</Last></Name>
    <Status>U2</Status>
    <CrsTaken CrsCode="CS308" Semester="F1997"/>
    <CrsTaken CrsCode="MAT123" Semester="F1997"/>
</Student>
```
15.9

However, since we indicated that the type of Details is XML, such a document will be stored not as a string but in a special data structure, which supports efficient navigation and querying.

Using a CHECK constraint, we can even tell the DBMS to validate the above Student XML document against a suitable schema before allowing the document to be inserted:

```
CREATE TABLE STUDENTXML (
  Id        INTEGER,
  Details   XML,
  CHECK(Details
        IS VALID ACCORDING TO SCHEMA 'http://xyz.edu/student.xsd'))
```

Here we assume that the schema is stored at the URL http://xyz.edu/student.xsd. The predicate IS VALID ACCORDING TO SCHEMA ensures that the value of the Details attribute in every tuple is a valid XML document with respect to that schema. We will come back to this predicate on page 678.

The XMLELEMENT and XMLATTRIBUTES functions. Since SQL is a relational language, an SQL query does not produce an XML document directly. Instead, a query result can contain tuples in which the value in a particular column is an XML document. We already know that XML documents can be stored as values of an attribute. What is new here is the ability to construct such documents on the fly from data stored in tables. This process is often referred to as **publishing** database contents. The simplest way to do this is to use the XMLELEMENT function, which takes as parameters the name to be given to the element's tag and (optionally) the element's attributes and content. For instance, the following query produces a relation with a column that stores XML documents:

```
SELECT P.Id, XMLELEMENT(
                Name "Prof",                            -- The tag name
                XMLATTRIBUTES(P.DeptId AS "Dept"), -- The attribute(s)
                P.Name                                  -- The content
             ) AS Info
FROM   PROFESSOR P
```

The parameter that provides the element's tag is identified by the keyword Name, which in this case is Prof. The XMLATTRIBUTES function produces the element's attributes. In this case the element has the single attribute Dept. The remaining parameters specify the element's content. In this case the element has no *e*-children, and the content is simply the value of P.Name associated with P.Id. Using the PROFESSOR relation depicted in Figure 3.5, page 39, the query would produce the following tuples:

```
⟨ 101202303, <Prof Dept="CS">John Smyth</Prof> ⟩
⟨ 783432188, <Prof Dept="MGT">Adrian Jones</Prof> ⟩
  :
  :
```

The query maps each row of PROFESSOR into a row of the query result. The second component in each row is an XML element, and the column name is Info.

The XMLELEMENT constructs can be nested. This feature can be used to create arbitrarily complex XML elements. For instance, we could publish the PROFESSOR relation in the standard form defined by SQL/XML (see the document (15.7)) as follows:

```
SELECT  XMLELEMENT( Name "Professor",                   -- The tag name
                    XMLELEMENT(Name "Id", P.Id), -- Child elements
                    XMLELEMENT(Name "Name", P.Name),
                    XMLELEMENT(Name "DeptId", P.DeptId)
                  ) AS ProfElement
FROM    PROFESSOR P
```

The result of this query is not a set of XML elements but a table containing a single column with name ProfElement. Each row contains an XML element. The absence of an XMLATTRIBUTES parameter indicates that the element has no attributes. The remaining parameters of the outer XMLELEMENT define the content. In this case each element has exactly three child elements.

The XMLQUERY function. XMLQUERY provides functionality similar to XMLELEMENT in that it can be used to produce tables whose rows contain XML documents. However, XMLQUERY is more powerful and easier to use in complex situations. Its argument is composed of an XQuery expression and *parameter-passing statements*, which indicate how information is passed from the containing SQL statement to the embedded XQuery expression. The XQuery expression can contain *placeholder variables*, which have the usual XQuery syntax (e.g., $foo), and the parameter passing statement binds these variables to the values produced by the containing SQL statement. In addition, the XMLQUERY statement can indicate how the results are to be returned: as an object of type XML or as a string representation of that object. For instance, the previous query can be rewritten with the help of XMLQUERY as follows:

```
SELECT XMLQUERY( '<Professor>
                      <Id>{$I}</Id> , <Name>{$N}</Name> ,
                      <DeptId>{$D}</DeptId>
                  </Professor>'
                  PASSING BY VALUE
                      P.Id AS I,                              15.10
                      P.Name AS N,
                      P.DeptId AS D
                  RETURNING SEQUENCE
               ) AS ProfElement
FROM   PROFESSOR P
```

The first part of the argument to XMLQUERY (enclosed in quotes) is a simple form of an XQuery expression, a direct element constructor. The content of the element constructor Professor is defined by concatenating the direct element constructors Id, Name, and DeptId using the XQuery concatenation operator ",". Placeholder variables can occur in the position of XML elements and attributes, which provides great flexibility in the way XML documents can be constructed from relational data. The PASSING clause binds the value of the SQL expression P.Id to the XMLQUERY variable $I, the SQL expression P.Name to the XMLQUERY variable $N, etc. If the value of an SQL expression that binds an XQuery variable is an XML document retrieved from the database, then the parameter can be passed BY REF as opposed to BY VALUE. In this case, the variable would be bound to a reference to the document rather than to a copy of that document. The RETURNING SEQUENCE clause indicates that the result should be returned as an item of the special SQL's XML data type. An alternative is to return CONTENT, which means that the result should be returned as a plain string.

The expressions to be substituted for the placeholders in XMLQUERY are not limited to SQL variables, such as P.Id in the above example—they can be XML-generating expressions or even complete SELECT statements. For instance, we could rewrite the above query in the following way, where the expression to be substituted for $I generates an XML element of the form <Id>...</Id>:

```
SELECT XMLQUERY( '<Professor>
                     {$I} , <Name>{$N}</Name> ,
                     <DeptId>{$D}</DeptId>
                  </Professor>'
                  PASSING BY VALUE
                      XMLELEMENT(Name "Id", P.Id) AS I,
                      P.Name AS N,
                      P.DeptId AS D,
                  RETURNING CONTENT
              ) AS ProfElement
FROM   PROFESSOR P
```

This query also illustrates the use of the RETURNING CONTENT options, which requests that the query produce a relation with a single attribute of type string (as opposed to the XML type).

In general, the expression inside the XMLQUERY function can be a complete XQuery query with the FOR, WHERE, and RETURN clauses. For instance, suppose that the PROFESSOR relation has an additional attribute, Teaching, of type XML, which, for each tuple, lists all courses that were taught by the corresponding professor since the beginning of time. For concreteness, assume that this list has the same format as in Figure 15.21 on page 655, but without the Instructor subelement. Then we can extend the output of query (15.10) by enclosing the relevant lists of course names in each Professor element.

```
SELECT XMLQUERY( '<Professor>
                      <Id>{$I}</Id> , <Name>{$N}</Name> ,
                      <DeptId>{$D}</DeptId> ,
                      {
                        FOR $c IN $T
                        RETURN <Course>{$c//CrsName}</Course>
                      }
                  </Professor>'
                  PASSING BY VALUE
                        P.Id AS I,
                        P.Name AS N,
                        P.DeptId AS D,
                        P.Teaching AS T
                  RETURNING SEQUENCE
              ) AS ProfElement
FROM    PROFESSOR P
```

Grouping and XMLAGG. In SQL/XML, SELECT statements can be embedded inside XML constructors (such as XMLELEMENT) that appear in the SELECT clause of a parent query. As a result, it is possible to group elements as children of another element. The following example illustrates this facility with a query that returns student transcripts grouped inside Student elements, as shown in the document (15.9). For brevity, we omit student name and status from the output.

```
SELECT XMLELEMENT( Name "Student",
                   XMLATTRIBUTES(S.Id AS "Id"),
                   ( SELECT
                       XMLELEMENT(Name "CrsTaken",
                         XMLATTRIBUTES(T.CrsCode AS "CrsCode",
                                       T.Semester AS "Semester"))
                     FROM TRANSCRIPT T
                     WHERE S.Id = T.StudId ) )
FROM    STUDENT S
```

In this example, we assume that information is stored inside the relations STUDENT and TRANSCRIPT, as in Figures 3.2 and 3.5 on pages 36 and 39. The statement produces a table with a single column and a row corresponding to each row of STUDENT. The content of each row is an XML element describing a particular student. The element is produced by the outer XMLELEMENT function with tag Student and attribute Id. The nested SELECT clause creates the content of the Student element, which in this case is a list of CrsTaken child elements corresponding to that student. Each of these *e*-children has two attributes defined by the XMLATTRIBUTES function, but no other content. The result of this query will thus be a set of XML elements that look like Student elements at the top of Figure 15.4 on page 591 (with student name and status information omitted).

Note that, strictly speaking, the nested SELECT clause produces not a list of CrsTaken elements (despite what we said earlier), but a set of 1-tuples, each containing a CrsTaken element. At the time of this writing it is unclear whether such a set of tuples will be converted into a list of XML elements automatically or if a special function will be provided for this purpose.

Alternatively, we could express the same query using aggregation with the help of the XMLAGG function of SQL/XML. To understand how it works, consider the following example, which reformulates the previous query using XMLAGG.

```
SELECT   XMLELEMENT( Name "Student",
                   XMLATTRIBUTES(S.Id AS "Id"),
                   XMLAGG(
                     XMLELEMENT(Name "CrsTaken",
                       XMLATTRIBUTES(T.CrsCode AS "CrsCode",
                                     T.Semester AS "Semester"))
                     ORDER BY T.CrsCode )  )
FROM     STUDENT S,  TRANSCRIPT T
WHERE    S.Id = T.StudId
GROUP BY S.Id
```

XMLAGG provides the content of a Student element created by the outer XMLELEMENT function. Each Student element corresponds to a particular group produced by the GROUP BY clause, and each row in that group (selected from the set of tuples in the join of STUDENT and TRANSCRIPT, which have the same student Id) describes a course taken by a particular student. XMLAGG refers to that group through its use of the tuple variable T.

XMLAGG takes as an argument an XML construct, such as the nested XMLELEMENT invocation in the example, in which an SQL variable is a parameter—T in this case. The invocation of XMLAGG produces a *list* of elements—one for each legal value of the variable. Here the legal values are the rows of TRANSCRIPT that are joined with the particular row of STUDENT used to form the group. The list is nested within the Student element and is ordered by course codes using the optional ORDER BY clause of XMLAGG.

For instance, if a student, Bart Simpson, with Id 987654321 took CS305 in the fall of 1995 and MGT123 in the fall of 1994, then when S.Id is bound to 987654321, the GROUP BY clause will produce a group of two bindings for the variables S and T: one where S = ⟨987654321,Bart Simpson,...⟩ and T = ⟨987654321,CS305,F1995,C⟩, and another where S = ⟨987654321,Bart Simpson,...⟩ and T = ⟨987654321, MGT123,F1994,B⟩. For each binding of T, the XMLAGG operator will produce one

CrsTaken element. Thus, for this particular group of tuples the above query will construct the following element:

```
<Student Id="987654321">
   <CrsTaken CrsCode="CS305" Semester="F1995"/>
   <CrsTaken CrsCode="MGT123" Semester="F1994"/>
</Student>
```

You may find the reference to the word "aggregate" in the function name XMLAGG confusing. The aggregate here is the list—think of the above list of CrsTaken elements as a "sum" of the courses the student has taken.

Querying XML documents stored in tables. So far our main focus was on queries that take the relational data stored in SQL databases and publish it as XML documents. Although we discussed the new XML data type and its use for efficient storage of XML documents (see (15.8)), our queries never looked *inside* those documents and did not try to extract data from them. In SQL/XML, querying XML documents stored as members of the XML data type can be done with the help of the already familiar XMLQUERY construct in conjunction with the new predicate XMLEXISTS.

The predicate XMLEXISTS. The purpose of this predicate is to test whether the result of the XMLQUERY expression supplied as an argument to XMLEXISTS is an empty sequence of XML elements. The following example illustrates this feature using a query that lists all students who have at least one course in their transcript. Here we use the relation STUDENTXML defined in (15.8), which stores documents of the form (15.9).

```
SELECT  S.Id, XMLQUERY('$D//Name'
                          PASSING BY REF S.Details AS D
                          RETURNING SEQUENCE)
FROM    STUDENTXML S
WHERE   XMLEXISTS(XMLQUERY(                                15.11
          '$D//CrsTaken'
          PASSING BY REF S.Details as D
          RETURNING SEQUENCE))
```

Note that the query part of the XMLQUERY expression is an XPath statement, which is a special case of an expression in the XQuery language and is legal in XMLQUERY. However, using the full power of XQuery we can do more interesting querying of documents stored using the XML data type. The following query illustrates the idea; it returns the names and Ids of all honors students (who are listed in honors.xml using elements of the form <Honors Last="Doe" First="John"/>) who have status U3 and who took MAT123.

```
SELECT   S.Id, XMLQUERY('$D//Name'
                        PASSING BY REF S.Details as D
                        RETURNING SEQUENCE)
FROM     STUDENTXML S
WHERE    XMLEXISTS(XMLQUERY(
         'LET $H := fn:doc("honors.xml")
          WHERE $D//Status/text() = "U3"  AND
                $D//CrsTaken/@CrsCode = "MAT123" AND
                $H//Honors[@Last=$D//Last and @First=$D//First]
          RETURN $D'
         PASSING BY REF S.Details as D
         RETURNING SEQUENCE))
```

Note that in this query, application of the path expression `//Name` to any document in `S.Details` yields a single `Name` element, so the result of the query is a set of regular tuples (modulo the fact that the second tuple component is an XML element). In general, however, a path expression can yield a set. Will the result still be legal? The answer is yes: in this case XMLQUERY returns a sequence of elements as a *single* XML document.

Modifying data in SQL/XML. So far we have been focusing on schema and query-related issues pertaining to XML data stored in SQL databases. In this section we briefly review the support for updating such data.

XMLPARSE and IS VALID ACCORDING TO SCHEMA. We have seen some queries involving the table STUDENTXML defined in (15.8), which stores XML documents of the form (15.9) in the `Details` column. But how do you put XML documents into such a table in the first place?

Since an XML document can be viewed as a string of characters, we could, in principle, store it as a string data type. However, this misses an important point behind SQL/XML—the XML data type. XML documents are stored in columns of type XML, not as strings but rather using special tree structures. To produce such a structure, SQL/XML provides a special function, XMLPARSE, that converts an XML document represented as a string into the tree structures appropriate for the XML data type prior to storing it. This makes it possible to insert tuples into a relation that contains XML documents, as shown in the following example.

```
INSERT INTO STUDENTXML(Id, Details)
VALUES ( 123987456,
         XMLPARSE(
              '<Student>
                  <Name><First>John</First><Last>Doe</Last></Name>
                      <Status>U2</Status>
```

```
                    <CrsTaken CrsCode="CS310" Semester="F2003"/>
                    <CrsTaken CrsCode="CS305" Semester="F2003"/>
                </Student>' )
            )
```

The XMLPARSE function parses documents (to put them into the format appropriate to the XML data type) and checks for correctness, but it is not supposed to validate them—this is reserved for the IS VALID ACCORDING TO SCHEMA predicate as shown in the following modification of the above example:

```
INSERT INTO StudentXML(Id, Details)
VALUES ( 123987456,
         XMLPARSE(
             '<Student>
                <Name><First>John</First><Last>Doe</Last></Name>
                   <Status>U2</Status>
                   <CrsTaken CrsCode="CS310" Semester="F2003"/>
                   <CrsTaken CrsCode="CS305" Semester="F2003"/>
             </Student>'  )
         IS VALID ACCORDING TO SCHEMA http://xyz.edu/Student.xsd
       )
```

The result is the same as in the previous case, except that the XML document will be stored in the database only if it is validated against the given schema document.

It is expected that a future release of SQL/XML will include primitives for direct modification of documents stored using the XML data type.

The function XMLSERIALIZE. This function is less relevant to update operations, but it is appropriate to mention it here since it is the reverse of XMLPARSE. It takes a document of the XML data type and returns a string representation of that document.

One scenario in which this might be useful is when you want (for some reason) to store a copy of an XML document as a string. A more common case, however, is when SQL is embedded in a host language, such as C or C++, that does not understand XML. In this case, the embedded SQL query might need to convert the XML output into a string before the host program can deal with it. In the following example, we declare a cursor for a query that returns an XML data type in the second column and then transforms it into a string using the XMLSERIALIZE function.

```
EXEC SQL DECLARE GetProfessor CURSOR FOR
     SELECT P.Id, XMLSERIALIZE(XMLELEMENT(
                        Name "Prof",
                        P.Name
                    ))
     FROM   Professor P
```

Since the XML elements that are returned by the XMLELEMENT expression are now converted to strings, we can process each tuple in the result, one by one, using the following statement:

```
EXEC SQL FETCH GETPROFESSOR INTO :profId, :name;
```

Note that the XMLQUERY construct has an option, RETURNING CONTENT, which converts the result of the query to a string. Therefore, when we use XMLQUERY in the SELECT clause, XMLSERIALIZE becomes redundant.

BIBLIOGRAPHIC NOTES

The semistructured data model had an important influence on a number of developments in the XML arena, especially on XML query languages. A more in-depth study of semistructured data can be found in [Abiteboul et al. 2000].

XML came as a result of an effort to bring some order to Web information processing. Conceptually, it is a rewrite and a simplification of the well-established SGML standard [SGML 1986]. Version 1 was approved in 1998 and became a widely accepted standard [XML 1998]. As with every new hot topic, many publications appeared in a short period of time. There are too many to list here, so we mention just two recent ones, [Ray 2001; Bradley 2000a].

XML Schema is covered in a number of books, but, because it was a moving target until recently, we recommend the authoritative sources [XMLSchema 2000a; XMLSchema 2000b].

XPath, the XML path expression language, is described in most recent publications on XML. The official W3C recommendation can be found in [XPath 2003]. The original idea of path expressions comes from [Zaniolo 1983]. The idea of enhancing path expressions with query capability was developed by [Kifer and Lausen 1989; Kifer et al. 1992; Frohn et al. 1994; Abiteboul et al. 1997; Deutsch et al. 1998] and others.

XSLT became an official recommendation of W3C in 1999 [XSLT 1999], and the latest versions of major browsers, such as Internet Explorer, Mozilla, and Netscape, support it. This subject is covered in several publications, such as [Kay 2000; Bradley 2000b].

The XML query language XQuery is described in [XQuery 2004]. It is an eclectic language that builds on the ideas previously developed for SQL, OQL [Cattell and Barry 2000], XQL [Robie et al. 1998], XML-QL [Deutsch et al. 1998; Florescu et al. 1999], and Quilt [Robie et al. 2000; Chamberlin et al. 2000]. Full specification of the language is found at *http://www.w3.org/XML/Query*.

SQL/XML is a standard in the making. A number of relational vendors already support parts of this specification, but each vendor offers various extensions to the agreed-upon core. Details on the SQL/XML standardization activity and the current document drafts can be found at *http://www.sqlx.org/*.

EXERCISES

15.1 Use XML to represent the contents of the STUDENT relation in Figure 3.2, page 36. Specify a DTD appropriate for this document. Do *not* use the representation proposed by the SQL/XML specification discussed in Section 15.4.4.

15.2 Specify a DTD appropriate for a document that contains data from both the COURSE table in Figure 4.34, page 116, and the REQUIRES table in Figure 4.35, page 117. Try to reflect as many constraints as the DTDs allow. Give an example of a document that conforms to your DTD.

15.3 Restructure the document in Figure 15.4, page 591, so as to completely replace the elements `Name`, `Status`, `CrsCode`, `Semester`, and `CrsName` with attributes in the appropriate tags. Provide a DTD suitable for this document. Specify all applicable `ID` and `IDREF` constraints.

15.4 Define the following simple types:

a. A type whose domain consists of lists of strings, where each list consists of seven elements
b. A type whose domain consists of lists of strings, where each string is of length seven
c. A type whose domain is a set of lists of strings, where each string has between seven and ten characters and each list has between seven and ten elements
d. A type appropriate for the letter grades that students receive on completion of a course—A, A−, B+, B, B−, C+, C, C−, D, and F. Express this type in two different ways: as an enumeration and using the `pattern` tag of XML Schema.

15.5 Use the `key` statement of XML Schema to define the following key constraints for the document in Figure 15.4 on page 591:

a. The key for the collection of all `Student` elements
b. The key for the collection of all `Course` elements
c. The key for the collection of all `Class` elements

15.6 Assume that any student in the document of Figure 15.4 is uniquely identified by the last name and the status. Define this key constraint.

15.7 Use the `keyref` statement of XML Schema to define the following referential integrity for the document in Figure 15.4:

a. Every course code in a `CourseTaken` element must refer to a valid course.
b. Every course code in a `Class` element must refer to a valid course.

15.8 Express the following constraint on the document of Figure 15.4: no pair of `CourseTaken` elements within the same `Student` element can have identical values of the `CrsCode` attribute.

15.9 Rearrange the structure of the `Class` element in Figure 15.4 so that it becomes possible to define the following referential integrity: every student Id mentioned in a `Class` element references a student from the same document.

15.10 Write a unified XML schema that covers both documents in Figures 15.19 and 15.21. Provide the appropriate key and foreign-key constraints.

15.11 Use XML Schema to represent the fragment of the relational schema in Figure 3.6, page 43. Include all key and foreign-key constraints.

15.12 Write an XML Schema specification for a simple document that lists stockbrokers with the accounts that they handle and lists client accounts separately. The information about each broker includes the broker Id, name, and a list of accounts. The information about each account includes the account `Id`, the owner's name, and the account positions (i.e., stocks held in that account). To simplify matters, it suffices to list the stock symbol and quantity for each account position. Use `ID`, `IDREF`, and `IDREFS` to specify referential integrity.

15.13 Write a sample XML document, which contains

- A list of parts (part name and Id)
- A list of suppliers (supplier name and Id)
- A list of projects; for each project element, a nested list of subelements that represent the parts used in that project. Include the information on who supplies that part and in what quantity.

Write a DTD for this document and an XML schema. Express all key and referential constraints. Choose your representation in such a way as to maximize the number of possible key and referential constraints representable using DTDs.

15.14 Use XPath to express the following queries to the document in Figure 15.19:

a. Find all `Student` elements whose Ids end with 987 and who took `MAT123`.
b. Find all `Student` elements whose first names are Joe and who took fewer than three courses.
c. Find all `CrsTaken` elements that correspond to semester `S1996` and that belong to students whose names begin with `P`.

15.15 Formulate the following XPath queries for the document in Figure 15.21:

a. Find the names of all courses taught by Mary Doe in fall 1995.
b. Find the set of all document nodes that correspond to the course names taught in fall 1996 or all instructors who taught `MAT123`.
c. Find the set of all course codes taught by John Smyth in spring 1997.

15.16 Use XSLT to transform the document in Figure 15.19 into a well-formed XML document that contains the list of `Student` elements such that each student in the list took a course in spring 1996.

15.17 Use XSLT to transform the document in Figure 15.21 into a well-formed XML document that contains the list of courses that were taught by Ann White in fall 1997. *Do not* include the `Instructor` child element in the output, and discard the `Semester` attribute.

15.18 Write an XSLT stylesheet that traverses the document tree and, ignoring attributes, copies the elements and the text nodes. For instance, `<foo a="1"> the<best quality="S"/>bar</foo>` would be converted into `<foo>the <best/>bar</foo>`.

15.19 Write an XSLT stylesheet that traverses the document tree and, ignoring attributes, copies the elements and *doubles* the text nodes. For instance, `<foo a="1">the<best/>bar</foo>` would be converted into `<foo>thethe<best/> barbar</foo>`.

15.20 Write an XSLT stylesheet that traverses the document and preserves all elements, attributes, and text nodes, but discards the `CrsTaken` elements (with all their children). The stylesheet must not depend on the knowledge of where the CrsTaken elements reside in the source document.

15.21 Write a stylesheet that traverses the document tree and, while ignoring the attributes, preserves the other aspects of the tree (the parent–child relationships among the elements and the text nodes). However, when the stylesheet hits the foobar element, its attributes and the entire structure beneath are preserved and the element itself is repeated twice.

15.22 Write a stylesheet that traverses the document tree and preserves everything. However, when it hits the element foo it converts every *t*-child of foo into an element with the tag name text. For instance,

```
<foo a="1">the<best>bar<foo>in the</foo></best>world</foo>
```

would become

```
<foo a="1"><text>the</text><best>bar<foo> <text>in the</text>
</foo></best><text>world</text></foo>
```

15.23 Consider the relational schema in Figure 3.6, page 43. Assume that the Web server delivers the contents of these relations using the following XML format: the name of the relation is the top-level element, each tuple is represented as a tuple element, and each relation attribute is represented as an empty element that has a value attribute. For instance, the STUDENT relation would be represented as follows:

```
<Student>
     <tuple>
          <Id value="s111111111"/> <Name value="John Doe"/>
          <Address value="123 Main St."/> <Status value="U1"/>
     </tuple>
          .
          .
          .
</Student>
```

Formulate the following queries using XQuery:

a. Produce the list of all students who live on Main Street.

b. Find every course whose CrsCode value does not match the Id of the department that offers the course. (For instance, the course IS315 in information systems might be offered by the Computer Science (CS) Department.)

c. Create a list of all records from the TEACHING relation that correspond to courses taught in the fall semester.

15.24 Using the document structure described in Exercise 15.23, formulate the following queries in XQuery:

a. Create the list of all professors who ever taught MAT123. The information must include all attributes available from the PROFESSOR relation.

b. Create the list of all students (include student Id and name) who took a course from John Smyth and received an A.
c. Create the list of all courses in which Joe Public received an A.

15.25 Use the document structure described in Exercise 15.23 to formulate the following queries in XQuery:

a. Create an XML document that lists all students by name and, for each student, lists the student's transcript. The transcript records must include course code, semester, and grade.
b. Create a document that for each professor lists the name and classes taught. (A class is identified by a course code and semester.)
c. Create a document that lists every course and the professors who taught it. The course information must include the course name, and the professor information should include the professor's name.

15.26 Use the document structure described in Exercise 15.23 to formulate the following queries in XQuery:

a. List all students who took more than three courses.
b. List all students who received an A for more than three courses.
c. List all professors who gave an A to more than three students.
d. List all classes (identified by a course code and semester) where average grade is higher than B.
e. List all professors whose given grade (the average among all grades the professor ever assigned to any student) is B or higher. For this problem, you must write an XQuery function that computes numeric values of letter grades.
f. List all classes (identified by a course code and semester) where the average grade is less than the professor's given grade.

15.27 Use the document structure described in Exercise 15.23 to formulate the following queries in XQuery:

a. List all classes (identified by a course code and semester) where every student received a B or higher.
b. List all students who never received less than a B.

15.28 Write an XQuery function that traverses a document and computes the maximum branching factor of the document tree, that is, the maximal number of children (text or element nodes) of any element in the document.

15.29 Write an XQuery function that traverses a document and strips element tags. For instance,

```
<the>best<foo>bar</foo>in the world</the>
```

would become

```
<result>bestbarin the world</result>
```

15.30 Consider a document that contains a list of professors (name, Id, department Id) and a separate list of classes taught (professor Id, course code, semester). Use aggregate functions of XQuery to produce the following documents:

a. A list of professors (name, Id) with the number of different courses taught by each professor.
b. A list of departments (department Id) along with the number of different courses ever taught by the professors in them. (The same course taught in different semesters or a course taught in the same semester by different professors is counted as one.)

15.31 Consider the following query:

```
FOR     $c IN doc("http://xyz.edu/classes.xml")//Class,
        $t IN doc("http://xyz.edu/transcripts.xml")
             //CrsTaken
WHERE   $c/@CrsCode = $t/@CrsCode
AND     $c/@Semester = $t/@Semester
RETURN  $c/CrsName
```

Explain why every course name is likely to be output more than once. Can the use of the `distinct-values()` function (without any additional features) solve this problem with duplicates? Explain your answer.

15.32 Consider the relational schema in Figure 3.6, page 43. Assume that the contents of these relations are stored in a single XML column of a relation using the following XML format: the name of the relation is the top-level element, each tuple is represented as a `tuple` element, and each relation attribute is represented as an empty element that has a `value` attribute. For instance, the STUDENT relation would be represented as follows:

```
<Student>
    <tuple>
        <Id value="s111111111"/> <Name value="John Doe"/>
        <Address value="123 Main St."/> <Status value="U1"/>
    </tuple>
        .
        .
        .
</Student>
```

Formulate the following queries in SQL/XML:

a. Create the list of all professors who ever taught `MAT123`. The information must include all attributes available from the PROFESSOR relation.
b. Create the list of all courses in which Joe Public received an A.
c. Create the list of all students (include student Id and name) who took a course from John Smyth and received an A.

15.33 Consider an SQL/XML database schema that consists of two relations:

- The SUPPLIER relation has the following attributes:
  - `Id`, an integer
  - `Name`, a string
  - `Address`, an XML type appropriate for addresses

  - Parts, an XML type that represents the parts supplied by the supplier. Each part has Id, Name, and Price.
- The PROJECT relation has the following attributes:
  - Project Name, a string
  - Project Members, an appropriate XML type
  - Project Parts, an XML type. This attribute represents the list of parts used by the project and supplied by a supplier. Each part has an Id, a Name, and a SupplierId.

Use SQL/XML to define the database schema. Make sure that a CHECK constraint validates the XML documents inserted into the database using an appropriate XML Schema document. Then answer the following queries:

a. Find all projects that are supplied by Acme Inc. and that have Joe Public as a member.
b. Find all projects that are *not* supplied by Acme Inc., that is, none of the parts used by the project come from Acme Inc.
c. Find all project members who participate in every project.
d. Find the projects with the highest number of members.

15.34 Consider the database depicted in Figure 3.5 on page 39. Use SQL/XML to answer the following queries:

a. Based on the relation TRANSCRIPT, output the same information in a different format. The output should have two attributes: StudId and Courses, where Courses should be of type XML; it is similar to the type used throughout this chapter for the CourseTaken element (e.g., as in Figure 15.4).
b. Repeat the previous query, but use TEACHING instead. The output should have the attributes ProfId and Courses. The latter should be of type XML; it should describe the courses taught by the corresponding professor with the given ProfId.
c. Produce a list of professors (Id and Name) along with the list of courses that that professor teaches in spring 2004. The list of courses should have the XML type and should include CrsCode and DeptId as attributes of an element and CrsName as a text node.
d. For each course, produce a list of the professors who have ever taught it. The professor list should have the type XML. Choose your own schema.
e. Repeat the previous query, but output only the courses that have been taught by the largest number of professors.

16

Distributed Databases

An increasing number of applications require access to multiple databases located at different sites, perhaps widely separated geographically. These applications fall into two broad categories, each illustrated with an example.

- *Category 1.* An Internet grocer has established a nationwide network of warehouses to speed delivery of its products. Each warehouse has its own local database, and the merchant has a database at its headquarters. An application that determines the total inventory in all warehouses might execute at headquarters and access all warehouse databases.
- *Category 2.* When a customer makes a purchase from the Internet grocer, the transaction might involve both the merchant and a credit card company. Information about the purchase might have to be recorded in both the merchant's and the credit card company's databases.

Distributed data is involved in both of these applications. The difference lies in the way each accesses the databases at the individual sites. In category 1, the application is written in terms of a schema that allows it to access the sites at the level of SQL statements. Thus, it might send SELECT statements to each warehouse to obtain the desired information and then take the union of the returned tuples.

Applications in category 2 do not access data in this way. The merchant and the credit card company are separate enterprises, and their databases contain sensitive information that neither is willing to share. Furthermore, neither is willing to allow the other to (perhaps inadvertently) introduce inconsistencies into its database. Therefore, the credit card company provides a subroutine (perhaps a stored procedure executed as a transaction) that can be invoked to update its database to record the charges made to a customer's account. Since the credit card company creates the routine, it has more control over the security and integrity of its data.

In this chapter we discuss efficient strategies for accessing distributed data. Efficiency is affected by the location of the data items in the network and the algorithm used to manipulate the items (given that their location has been determined). Unfortunately, the techniques we discuss are not applicable to applications in category 2: the location of the data is determined by the individual companies, and the data is accessed by company-controlled routines. An application can be built that invokes these routines and manipulates the data they return, but it cannot access the databases directly, so the application programmer has little flexibility in designing an efficient strategy.

Hence, our focus is on applications in category 1. They access data directly and can employ database-oriented strategies to improve performance and availability. In this chapter, we discuss such strategies. For example,

- How should a distributed database be designed?
- At what site should individual data items or tables be stored?
- Which data items should be replicated, and at what sites should replicas be stored?
- How are queries that access multiple databases processed?
- What issues are involved in distributed query optimization?
- How do the techniques used for query optimization affect database design?

Why data might be distributed. Since distribution introduces new problems, why distribute data at all? Why not gather all of the data of a distributed enterprise into a single, central site? There are a number of (possibly conflicting) reasons why data might be distributed and, if so, for its locations.

- Data might be placed in such a way as to minimize communication costs and/or response time. This generally means that data is kept at the site that accesses it most often.
- Data might be distributed to equalize the workload so that individual sites are not overloaded to such a degree that throughput is impaired.
- Data might be kept at the site at which it was created so that its creators can maintain control and guarantee security.
- Certain data items might be replicated at multiple sites to increase their availability in the event of system crashes (if one replica becomes unavailable, an alternate can be accessed) or to increase throughput and reduce response time (since the data can be more quickly accessed using a local or nearby copy).

16.1 The Application Designer's View of the Database

An application that directly accesses a database submits SQL statements that have been constructed with some schema in mind. The schema describes the structure of the database seen by the application. We consider three kinds of schemas: multiple local, global, and restricted global.

Multiple local schemas. The distributed database looks to the application program like a collection of individual databases, each with its own schema, as shown in Figure 16.1(a). Such a system is an example of a **multidatabase**. If the individual DBMSs have been supplied by different vendors, the system is referred to as **heterogeneous**; if by the same vendor, it is referred to as **homogeneous**.

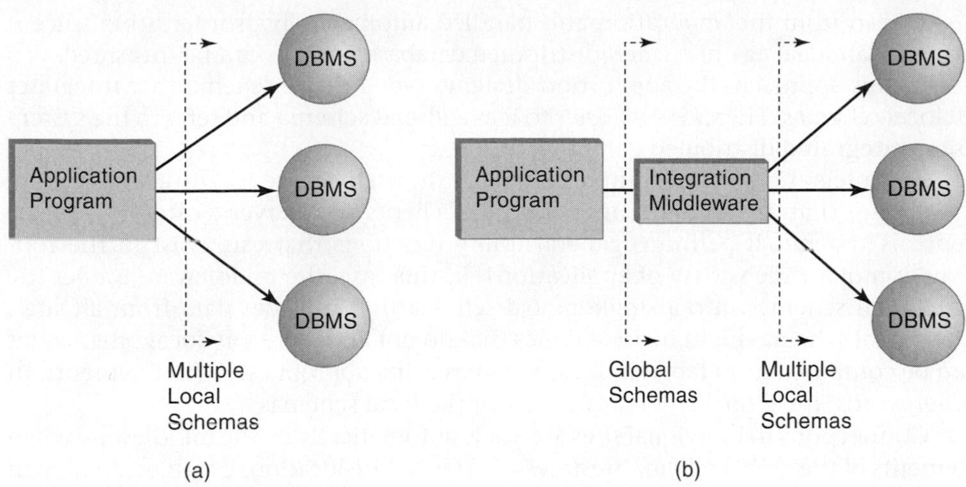

FIGURE 16.1 Views of a distributed database: (a) multidatabase with local schemas; (b) integrated distributed database supporting a global schema.

The application program must explicitly set up a connection to each site that contains data items to be accessed. After a connection has been established, the program can access the database using SQL statements constructed using the site's schema. If data items are moved from one site to another, the program must be changed.

A single SQL statement that refers to tables at different sites—for example, a global join—is not supported. If the application wants to join tables at different sites, it must read the tuples from each table into buffers at the application site (with separate SELECT statements) and explicitly test the join condition for each pair of tuples.

Data at different sites might be stored in different formats. For example, at one site an individual's last name might be stored first; at another it might be stored last. In addition, the types in the individual schema might be different. For example, at one site an Id might be stored as a sequence of characters; at another, as an integer. In these cases, the application must provide conversion routines that can be used at run time to integrate the data.

The application must manage replication. If a replicated item is being queried, the application must decide which replica should be accessed, and, if the item is being updated, it must ensure that the update occurs at all replicas.

The methods we discussed in Chapter 8 for accessing a distributed database using embedded SQL, JDBC, SQLJ, and ODBC all see a distributed database in this way.

Global schema. The local schema approach provides little support for the application programmer. All of the issues arising from the distributed nature of the database must be handled explicitly in the program. The opposite extreme, in which all issues are hidden from the application and handled automatically, is interesting since it provides an ideal against which distributed database systems can be measured.

In this approach, the application designer sees a single schema that integrates all local schemas. Therefore, we refer to it as a **global schema** and refer to the system as an **integrated** distributed database system.

The integration is done by middleware (as shown in Figure 16.1(b)). **Middleware** is software that supports the interaction of clients and servers, often in heterogeneous systems. It performs general utility functions that can assist in the construction of a wide variety of applications. In this case, the middleware unifies the individual schemas into a single global schema that includes data from all sites. The global schema might include tables that do not appear in any local schema but can be computed from tables in local schemas using appropriate SQL statements. In other words, the global schema is a view of the local schemas.

Connections to individual sites are made automatically by the middleware when elements of the global schema are accessed. Hence, the locations of tables are hidden from the application program (this is called **location transparency**). If data items are moved from one site to another, the global schema remains the same and the application program need not be changed. The mapping from global to local schema does need to be changed in the middleware, but doing so is easier than changing all the application programs that access the data.

As with local schemas, related data at different sites can be stored in different formats and types, which might not match those of the global schema. The middleware provides the conversion routines to integrate the systems under these circumstances.

A related problem is **semantic integration**, which involves at least the issues of value conversion and name conversion. Consider a distributed database that has sites in Europe, Japan, and the United States. Monetary values at all sites can be represented as double-precision numbers, so no format conversion is required. However, 1000 yen is different from 1000 euro, as 1000 euro is different from 1000 dollars. Thus, a request originating in Tokyo for a total sales figure might require currency conversion into yen, while the same request originating in Amsterdam might require conversion into euro. Attribute-name conversion has to deal with cultural differences and individual habits. Even ignoring the possibility that a site in Amsterdam might use a different language from one in New York, we still must deal with the possibility that two different U.S. sites refer to the same attribute as `item#` and `part#`.

Application programs execute SQL statements against the global schema. For example, the application might request the join of two tables, T_1 and T_2, in the global schema. If the tables are stored at the same site, the statement is passed on to that site for processing. If they are stored at different sites (a global join), the middleware must translate the join into a sequence of steps executed by the individual DBMSs and perform any other operations needed to compute the join. In a more complex case, both T_1 and T_2 can be views that are populated by the middleware using queries that join relations stored at different sites.

An important aspect of this is query optimization: the middleware attempts to choose a sequence of steps that constitutes a least-cost plan for evaluating the SQL statement submitted by the application. Cost is frequently measured in terms of the amount of data that must be transmitted between sites since this is generally the most time-consuming aspect of the plan. In this regard there is a significant difference between homogeneous and heterogeneous systems. With a heterogeneous system, each DBMS presents an SQL interface to the middleware, and hence a step performed by a DBMS is the execution of an SQL statement submitted by the middleware. As a result, data is transmitted between the middleware and each DBMS, but not directly between two DBMSs. Since the DBMSs of a homogeneous system are all produced by the same vendor, they can be built to support direct communication among themselves. Hence, the integration module shown in Figure 16.1(b) can be distributed among the individual DBMSs, and the opportunity to optimize the plan is much greater. We discuss some optimization techniques in Section 16.3.1.

The application designer might choose to replicate certain data items and designate the sites at which the replicas are to reside. However, replication is hidden from the application program. The program accesses a logical data item, and the middleware automatically manages the replication, supplying an appropriate replica to satisfy a query and updating all replicas when appropriate. This is referred to as **replication transparency** and is discussed in more detail in Section 16.2.3.

Restricted global schema. The application designer sees a single global schema, but the schema is the union (as contrasted with a view) of the schemas of individual databases. Thus, the restricted global schema consists of all the tables of the individual databases.

Restricted global schemas are supported by the vendors of some homogeneous systems. The database servers supplied by such a vendor cooperate directly, eliminating the need for middleware, but still function as shown in Figure 16.1(b).[1]

Applications use a naming convention to refer to the tables in each database. Thus, the location of the tables can be hidden from the application (location transparency). A connection to a site is made automatically when a table at that site is accessed.

The application can execute an SQL statement that refers to tables at different sites—for example, a global join. The system includes a global query optimizer to design efficient query plans and provides replication transparency.

16.2 Distributing Data among Different Databases

In many cases, the distribution of data among different sites is not under the control of the application designer. For example, certain data items might have to be stored at a particular site for security reasons. In other situations, the designer can participate in the decision as to where data is stored or replicated. In this section, we describe several issues related to data distribution.

[1] The view described here is similar to that supplied by Oracle except that the Oracle implementation supports a certain amount of heterogeneity by allowing limited access to databases from other vendors.

16.2.1 Partitioning

The simplest way to distribute data is to store individual tables at different sites. However, a table is not necessarily the best choice as the unit of distribution. Frequently a transaction accesses only a subset of the rows of a table, or a view of a table, rather than the table as a whole. If different transactions access different portions of the table and run at different sites, performance can be improved by storing a portion of the table at the site where the corresponding transaction is executed. When a table is decomposed in this way, we refer to the portions as **partitions**. For such applications, partitions are a better unit of data distribution than tables.

Distributing the partitions of a table has other potential advantages. For example, the time to process a single query over a large table can be reduced by distributing the execution over a number of sites at which partitions are stored. Consider, for example, the query that produces the names and grade point averages of all students at a university with multiple campuses. If the STUDENT and TRANSCRIPT tables are stored at the central administrative site, all processing takes place there. If, instead, the tables are partitioned and stored at individual campuses, the DBMSs at each campus can execute in parallel and together produce the result in less time. Furthermore, distributing partitions might make it possible to improve throughput, provided that a query executed at a site accesses the partition local to that site. Partitioning can be either horizontal or vertical.

Horizontal partitioning. A single table, T, is partitioned into several tables, called **partitions**

$T_1, T_2, \ldots, T_r$

where each partition contains a subset of the rows of T and each row of T is in exactly one partition. For example, the Internet grocer might have a relation

```
INVENTORY(StockNum, Amount, Price, Location)
```

to describe its inventory, together with the location of the warehouse where it is stored. The grocer might horizontally partition the relation by city so that, for example, it stores all the tuples satisfying

```
Location = 'Chicago'                                    16.1
```

in a partition named INVENTORY_CH at the Chicago warehouse, with the schema

```
INVENTORY_CH(StockNum, Amount, Price)
```

(The attribute Location is now redundant and so could be omitted.) Because each tuple is stored in some partition, horizontal partitioning is lossless. The table can be reconstructed by taking the union of its partitions.

More generally, each partition satisfies

$$T_i = \sigma_{C_i}(T)$$

where C_i is a selection condition and each tuple in T satisfies C_i for exactly one value of i and

$$T = \bigcup_i T_i$$

Expression (16.1) is an example of a selection condition.

Vertical partitioning. A table, T, is divided into partitions

$$T_1, T_2, \ldots, T_r$$

where each partition contains a subset of the columns of T. Each column must be included in at least one partition, and each partition must include the columns of a candidate key (the same for all partitions).

Thus, the Internet grocer might have a relation

```
EMPLOYEE(SSnum, Name, Salary, Title, Location)
```

to describe its employees at all warehouses. It might vertically partition EMPLOYEE as

```
EMP1 (SSnum, Name, Salary)
EMP2 (SSnum, Name, Title, Location)
```

where EMP1 is stored at the headquarters site (where the payroll is computed) and EMP2 is stored elsewhere. More generally

$$T_i = \pi_{attr\_list_i}(T)$$

Because each column must be in at least one partition and all partitions include the same candidate key, vertical partitioning is lossless: by taking the natural join of its partitions the original table can be reconstructed.

$$T = T_1 \bowtie T_2 \cdots \bowtie T_r$$

Because the candidate key is included in each partition, vertical partitioning involves replication. Other columns might be replicated as well. In our case, Name is included in both partitions because it is used by local applications at each site.

Note that the rationale behind vertical partitioning in the above case is very different from that behind relational normalization, which we discussed in Chapter 6.

Indeed, all three relations, EMPLOYEE, EMP1, and EMP2, are in Boyce-Codd normal form, so the algorithms proposed in Chapter 6 leave EMPLOYEE alone.

Mixed partitioning. Combinations of horizontal and vertical partitioning are also possible, but care must be taken to ensure that the original table can be reconstructed from its partitions. One approach is to do one type of partitioning and then the other. Thus, after our Internet grocer vertically partitions EMPLOYEE into EMP1 and EMP2, it might horizontally partition EMP2 by location. The partitions corresponding to the Chicago and Buffalo warehouses become

```
EMP2_CH (SSnum, Name, Title, Location)
EMP2_BU (SSnum, Name, Title, Location)
```

(Once again, the attribute `Location` might be omitted.) EMP1 is stored at the headquarters site, and EMP2_CH and EMP2_BU are stored at the corresponding warehouse sites.

Derived horizontal partitioning. In some situations, it might be desirable to horizontally partition a relation, but the information needed to decide which rows belong in which partition is not contained in the relation itself. Suppose, for example, that the Internet grocer has more than one warehouse in each city and each warehouse is identified by a warehouse number. Conceptually the database contains two tables:

```
INVENTORY(StockNum, Amount, Price, WarehouseNum)
WAREHOUSE(WarehouseNum, Capacity, Street-address, Location)
```

The grocer has one database site in each city and wants to horizontally partition INVENTORY so that a partition in a particular city contains information about all the items in all the warehouses in that city. The problem is that `Location`, which identifies the city in which a warehouse is located, is not an attribute of INVENTORY, and so it is not clear how the tuples are to be partitioned.

To solve this problem, we need to know the location of the warehouse that has been identified by a warehouse number. That information is contained in WAREHOUSE. Thus, we need to join the information in the two tables before we can do the partitioning. We use the *natural join* since the warehouse number is stored in the two tables using the same attribute name. The rows contained in the partition of INVENTORY describing Chicago, which we call INVENTORY_CH, are those that join with the rows of WAREHOUSE that satisfy the predicate `Location = 'Chicago'`. Hence,

$$\text{INVENTORY\_CH} = \pi_A(\text{INVENTORY} \bowtie (\sigma_{\texttt{Location='Chicago'}}(\text{WAREHOUSE})))$$

where A is the set of all attributes of INVENTORY. The join is used only to *locate* the rows of INVENTORY that we want to include in INVENTORY_CH. Because we do not want to retain any columns of WAREHOUSE, we project the result of the join on the attributes in A. Since

$$\sigma_{\texttt{Location = 'Chicago'}}(\text{WAREHOUSE})$$

is a partition of WAREHOUSE, the partitioning of INVENTORY is derived from a partitioning of WAREHOUSE, and we refer to this type of partitioning as **derived partitioning**. INVENTORY_CH is a *semi-join* of INVENTORY with a partition of WAREHOUSE. We discuss semi-joins in Section 16.3.1.

Horizontal partitioning is used when (most) applications at each site need to access only a *subset of the tuples* in a relation. Vertical partitioning is used when (most) applications at each site need to access only a *subset of the attributes* in a relation. We discuss methods for numerically comparing various possible database designs involving partitioning in Section 16.3.

Architectures based on the global schema can provide **partition transparency**. This means that the relation appears in its original unpartitioned form in the global schema and the middleware transforms any accesses to it into appropriate accesses to its partitions stored in different databases. In contrast, multidatabase systems do not provide partition transparency—each application program must be aware of the partitioning and use it appropriately in its queries.

> *Brain Teaser:* Can horizontal partitioning into disjoint sets of tuples decrease the overall storage requirements? Can it increase these requirements? How about the vertical partitioning of BCNF tables? Of 3NF tables?

16.2.2 Updates and Partitioning

Although our main interest has been in queries, we note that when relations are partitioned, update operations sometimes require tuples to be moved from one partition to another and hence from one database site to another. Suppose that an employee of the Internet grocer is transferred from the Chicago warehouse to the Buffalo warehouse. In the unpartitioned EMPLOYEE relation

```
EMPLOYEE (SSnum, Name, Salary, Title, Location)
```

the value of the `Location` attribute for that employee's tuple must be changed. If EMPLOYEE is partitioned into EMP2_CH and EMP2_BU, as described earlier, updating the `Location` attribute for that employee requires moving the corresponding tuple from the Chicago database to the Buffalo database.

The possibility that updates as well as queries might require moving data from one site to another must be taken into account when deciding where to place the data in a distributed database.

16.2.3 Replication

Replication is one of the most used, and most useful, mechanisms in distributed databases. Replicating data at several sites provides increased availability because the data can still be accessed if some of the sites fail. It also has the potential for improving performance: queries can be executed more efficiently because the data can be read from a local or nearby copy. However, updates are usually slower because all replicas of the data must be updated. Hence, performance is improved in applications in which updates occur substantially less often than queries. In this section, we discuss performance issues related to the execution of individual SQL statements.

Example 16.2.1 (Internet Grocer). To keep track of its customers, the Internet grocer might have a relation

```
CUSTOMER(CustNum, Address, Location)
```

where `Location` specifies an area serviced by a particular warehouse. The relation is queried by an application at the headquarters site that sends monthly mailings to all customers. An application at each warehouse site queries the relation to obtain information about deliveries in its area. The relation is updated by an application at the headquarters site when (1) a new customer registers with the company or (2) information about a particular customer changes (which happens infrequently). ■

Intuitively, it seems appropriate to horizontally partition the relation by `Location` so that a particular partition is stored both at the corresponding warehouse and at headquarters. Thus the relation would be replicated, with a complete copy at the headquarters site. We perform an analysis to evaluate that design choice compared to two others in which data is not replicated. The three choices are as follows:

1. Store the entire relation at the headquarters site and nothing at the warehouses.
2. Store all partitions at the warehouse sites with nothing at headquarters.
3. Replicate the partitions at both sites.

One way to compare the alternatives is to estimate the amount of information that must be transmitted between sites in each case when the specified applications are executed. To do this, we make the following assumptions about table sizes and the frequency with which each application is executed:

- The CUSTOMER relation has about 100,000 tuples.
- The mailing application at headquarters sends each customer one mailing each month.
- About 500 deliveries per day (over all warehouses) are performed, and a single tuple must be read for each delivery.
- The company gets about 100 new customers a day (and the number of changes to individual customers' information is negligible by comparison).

Now we can evaluate the three alternatives.

1. If we store the relation at the headquarters site, information must be transmitted from there to the appropriate warehouse site whenever a delivery is made—about 500 tuples per day.
2. If we store the partitions at the warehouse sites, information must be transmitted as follows:
   - From the warehouses to headquarters when the mailing application is executed—about 100,000 tuples per month or 3300 per day
   - From headquarters to the warehouses when a new customer registers—about 100 tuples per day

   In total, then, about 3400 tuples per day must be transmitted.
3. If we replicate the partitions at both headquarters and the warehouses, information must be sent from the headquarters site to the appropriate warehouse site when a new customer registers—about 100 tuples per day.

By this measure, replication appears to be the best alternative. We might also want to compare the alternatives using other measures, such as the response time of transactions.

1. If we store the relation at headquarters, the time to handle deliveries suffers because of the required remote access. This might not be viewed as important.
2. If we store the partitions at the warehouses and the monthly mailing is done by a single application, the 100,000 tuples that must be sent from the warehouses to headquarters might clog the communication system and slow down other applications. This can be avoided by running the mailing application late at night or over the weekend when few other applications are executing.
3. If we replicate the partitions, the time to register a new customer suffers because of the time required to update the tables at both the headquarters and the appropriate warehouse. This might be viewed as important because the customer is online when the update occurs and the time required to update the remote table might make the registration time unacceptably long. However, for this application the customer interaction can be considered complete when the headquarters database is updated. The update at the warehouse site can be performed later because the information is not needed there until some delivery transaction is executed. We discuss such **asynchronous-update replication** in Section A.3.3.

We see from this that replicating the partitions still seems to be the best alternative.

> Replication may reduce network traffic for queries, but it slows down updates. Potential benefits of replication must be evaluated on a case-by-case basis.

16.3 Query Planning Strategies

A multidatabase system is composed of a set of independent DBMSs. Typically, each DBMS exports an SQL interface, and an application is confronted with multiple local schemas. In order for the application to query information stored at multiple sites, it must decompose the query into a sequence of SQL statements, each of which is processed by a particular DBMS. On receiving an SQL statement, the query optimizer at the DBMS develops a query execution plan, the statement is executed, and results are returned to the application.

Systems that support a global schema contain a global query optimizer, which analyzes a query using the global schema and translates it into an appropriate sequence of steps to be executed at individual sites. Each step can be further optimized by the local query optimizer at a site and then executed. In this section we will assume a homogeneous distributed database. Since direct communication between individual DBMSs is supported in such systems, the query optimizer has a lot more flexibility and the difference between the cost of a good plan and a bad one can be substantial. Global query processing thus involves a distributed algorithm that involves the direct exchange of data between DBMSs.

In both cases, we are interested in executing the query efficiently. Since the cost of I/O is so much greater than that of computation, our measure of the efficiency of a query execution plan in Chapter 10 was an estimate of the number of I/O operations it requires. By similar reasoning, the cost of evaluating a query over a distributed database is based on the communication costs involved since communication is both expensive and time consuming. Communication costs will be measured by the number of bytes that have to be transmitted.

Our interest in query optimization is threefold. A familiarity with algorithms for global query optimization helps in designing

- Global queries that will execute efficiently for a given distribution of data
- Algorithms for efficiently evaluating global queries in multidatabase systems (Section 16.3.2)
- The distribution of data that will be accessed by global queries (Section 16.3.3)

16.3.1 Global Query Optimization

We will now discuss the techniques that are commonly used in optimizing distributed queries.

Planning with joins. Queries that involve a join of tables at different sites (a global join) are particularly expensive since information must be exchanged between sites in order to determine the tuples in the result. For example, suppose that an application at site A wants to join tables at sites B and C, with the result to be returned to site A. Two straightforward ways to execute the join that might be evaluated by a global query optimizer are

1. Transmit both tables to site A and execute the join there. The application program at site A then explicitly tests the join condition. This is the approach used in multidatabase systems that do not support global joins.
2. Transmit the smaller of the tables—for example, the table at site B, to site C, execute the join at site C, and then transmit the result to site A.

Example 16.3.1 (Distributed Student Database). To be more specific, we consider two tables, STUDENT(`Id`, `Major`) and TRANSCRIPT(`StudId`, `CrsCode`), where STUDENT records the major of each student and TRANSCRIPT records the courses in which a student is registered *this semester*. These tables are stored at sites B and C, respectively. Suppose that an application at site A wants to compute an equi-join with the join condition

$$\texttt{Id} = \texttt{StudId} \tag{16.2}$$

To compare alternative query plans, we must make certain assumptions about table sizes and, in some cases, about the relative frequency of operations on those tables. For this example, we assume that

- The lengths of the attributes are
  - `Id` and `StudId`: 9 bytes
  - `Major`: 3 bytes
  - `CrsCode`: 6 bytes
- STUDENT has about 15,000 tuples, each of length 12 bytes (9 + 3).
- Approximately 5000 students are registered for at least one course, and, on average, each student is registered for four courses. Thus, TRANSCRIPT has about 20,000 tuples, each of length 15 bytes (= 9 + 6). Note that 10,000 students are not registered for any course (this is the summer session).

The join then has about 20,000 tuples (each tuple in TRANSCRIPT corresponds to a tuple in the join), each of length 18 bytes (= 9 + 3 + 6).

Based on these assumptions, we can compare three alternative plans.

1. If we send both tables to site A to perform the join, we have to send 480,000 bytes ($= 15{,}000 * 12 + 20{,}000 * 15$).
2. If we send STUDENT to site C, compute the join there, and then send the result to site A, we have to send 540,000 bytes ($= 15{,}000 * 12 + 20{,}000 * 18$).
3. If we send TRANSCRIPT to site B, compute the join there, and then send the result to site A, we have to send 660,000 bytes ($= 20{,}000 * 15 + 20{,}000 * 18$).

Thus, we see that the best of the three is alternative (1). ■

Planning with semi-joins. Another, often more efficient approach that a global query optimizer might consider is to transmit from site B to site C only those tuples from STUDENT that will actually participate in the join, and then perform the join at site C between those tuples and TRANSCRIPT. This approach involves performing what is called a *semi-join*. The procedure involves three steps:

1. At site C, compute a table, **P**, that is the projection of TRANSCRIPT on `StudId`—the column involved in the join condition—and then send **P** to site B. Hence, **P** contains the Ids of students who are currently registered for at least one course. In this step we are sending $5000 * 9 = 45{,}000$ bytes.
2. At site B, form the join of STUDENT with **P** using join condition (16.2) and then send the resulting table, **Q**, to site C. **Q** contains all of the tuples in STUDENT that participate in the join. In the example, **Q** consists of all tuples in STUDENT that represent students who registered for at least one course. In this step we are sending $5000 * 12 = 60{,}000$ bytes.
3. At site C, join TRANSCRIPT with **Q** using the join condition. The result is the join of STUDENT and TRANSCRIPT, which is then sent to site A. Since the size of the join is 20,000 tuples $*$ 18 bytes, we are sending 360,000 bytes.

In total we are sending 465,000 bytes $(= 45{,}000 + 60{,}000 + 360{,}000)$. Hence, in terms of communication costs, this latest alternative is better than those we have investigated earlier. In fact, we can do even better. Instead of sending **Q** to C, we can send both **Q** and TRANSCRIPT to site A:

2′. At site B, form the join of STUDENT with **P** using join condition (16.2) and then send the resulting table, **Q**, to site A $(5000 * 12 = 60{,}000$ bytes).

3′. Send TRANSCRIPT to site A and join it there with **Q**. The communication cost of this operation is $20000 * 15 = 300{,}000$ bytes.

The total cost of the last plan is $45000 + 60000 + 300000 = 405{,}000$ bytes. This is the best among all the plans we have analyzed. Notice that the reason for the cost reduction in the last two cases is that we have managed to pare down STUDENT to only the subset of tuples that can possibly join with a tuple of TRANSCRIPT. In this way, we avoided the need to send STUDENT to site C (and TRANSCRIPT to site B) and instead sent only portions of these relations.

The result of step 2 (or step 2′), the relation **Q**, is called the *semi-join* of STUDENT with TRANSCRIPT. More generally, the **semi-join** $\mathbf{T}_1 \ltimes_{\textit{join-condition}} \mathbf{T}_2$ is defined to be the projection over the columns of $\mathbf{T}_1$ of the join of $\mathbf{T}_1$ and $\mathbf{T}_2$:

$$\pi_{\textit{attributes}(\mathrm{T}_1)} (\mathbf{T}_1 \bowtie_{\textit{join-condition}} \mathbf{T}_2)$$

Some tuples of $\mathbf{T}_1$ do not join with any tuple of $\mathbf{T}_2$ and hence are not a part of any tuple in $(\mathbf{T}_1 \bowtie_{\textit{join-condition}} \mathbf{T}_2)$. Hence, when the result of the join is projected on the attributes of $\mathbf{T}_1$, only a subset of the tuples of $\mathbf{T}_1$ are produced. In other words, the semi-join consists of the tuples of $\mathbf{T}_1$ that participate in the join with $\mathbf{T}_2$. Note that semi-join is not a symmetric operator: $\mathbf{P} \ltimes_{\textit{cond}} \mathbf{Q}$ is not equivalent to $\mathbf{Q} \ltimes_{\textit{cond}} \mathbf{P}$. One contains a subset of the tuples of **P** and the other a subset of the tuples of **Q**.

Armed with the concept of a semi-join, we can compute the join of the form

$$\mathbf{T}_1 \bowtie_{\textit{join-condition}} \mathbf{T}_2$$

by first computing a semi-join and then joining it with T_2:

$$(T_1 \ltimes_{join\text{-}condition} T_2) \bowtie_{join\text{-}condition} T_2$$

It is left to Exercise 16.10 to show that the above two expressions are equivalent.

Brain Teaser: We just saw that $(T_1 \ltimes T_2) \bowtie T_2 = T_1 \bowtie T_2$. What can you say about $T_1 \bowtie (T_1 \ltimes T_2)$?

It might seem that we have made a step backward by replacing one join with two. However, step 1 provides a clue—namely, the potential savings in performing a semi-join that lie in the following equivalence:

$$\begin{aligned} T_1 \ltimes_{join\text{-}condition} T_2 &= \pi_{attributes(T_1)} (T_1 \bowtie_{join\text{-}condition} T_2) \\ &= \pi_{attributes(T_1)} (T_1 \bowtie_{join\text{-}condition} \pi_{attributes(join\text{-}condition)}(T_2)) \end{aligned}$$

In other words, in computing a semi-join of T_1 and T_2 we can first take the projection of T_2 on the attributes mentioned in the join condition and then join the result with T_1 (using the same join condition). We leave the proof of this equivalence to Exercise 16.9. This first step potentially cuts communication costs because the projection of T_2 can be substantially smaller than T_2, so we avoid sending large chunks of data over the communication link. However, we do have to pay for performing the additional join between the result of the semi-join and T_2. If the savings in communication dominate the overhead of the extra join, we come out on top.

In our example, the three steps of the computation correspond to the following algebraic expression:

$$\begin{aligned} &\pi_{attributes(\text{STUDENT})} (\pi_{attributes(join\text{-}condition)}(\text{TRANSCRIPT}) \\ &\qquad\qquad \bowtie_{join\text{-}condition} \text{STUDENT}) \\ &\bowtie_{join\text{-}condition} \text{TRANSCRIPT} \end{aligned} \tag{16.3}$$

Step 1, computed at site C, corresponds to the table **P**:

$$\pi_{attributes(join\text{-}condition)}(\text{TRANSCRIPT})$$

This is sent to site B where it is used in step 2 in the computation

$$\pi_{attributes(\text{STUDENT})} (\mathbf{P} \bowtie_{join\text{-}condition} \text{STUDENT})$$

The result, **Q**, is sent back to site C and step 3, consisting of the computation

$$\mathbf{Q} \bowtie_{join\text{-}condition} \text{TRANSCRIPT}$$

is performed there. Query (16.3) can be expressed using the semi-join operator as

$$(\text{STUDENT} \ltimes_{join\text{-}condition} \text{TRANSCRIPT}) \bowtie_{join\text{-}condition} \text{TRANSCRIPT}$$

According to the previous discussion, this is equivalent to computing the join of STUDENT and TRANSCRIPT.

> Semi-joins may reduce network traffic, but this technique requires more locally performed joins. The overall benefits must be evaluated for each query plan.

Implementing global joins with replication. Still another way to implement a global join is to store a replica of one of the tables at the site of the other, thus turning the global join into a local join. In the example, we might store a replica of STUDENT at site C. We can then perform the join of STUDENT and TRANSCRIPT at site C and send the result, 360,000 bytes, to site A.

This approach speeds up the join operation but slows down updates of the replicated table. In the example, such updates might be rare because students seldom change their major.

Queries that involve joins and projections. Most queries involve not only joins but also other relational operators. In the above example, suppose that an application at site A executes a query that returns the majors and course codes of all students who are registered for at least one course. Thus, the row (`CS`, `CS305`) will be in the result table if there is at least one computer science (`CS`) student taking `CS305`. The query first takes the join of the two tables, STUDENT and TRANSCRIPT, and then projects on `Major` and `CrsCode` to obtain the result table, **R**. Our plan is to do the projection at the site at which the join is performed and then send **R** to site A.

In order to reevaluate the communication costs of the five alternatives we considered in the last section, we need to make one additional assumption—that **R** has 1000 tuples. Each tuple has a length of 9 bytes, so the size of **R** is 9000 bytes, making it much smaller than the joined table. That is common in real queries.

1. If we send both tables to site A and do all operations there, we have to send, as before, 480,000 bytes.
2. If we send the STUDENT table to site C, do the operations there, and then send **R** to site A, we have to send 189,000 bytes ($= 15{,}000 * 12 + 1000 * 9$).
3. If we send the TRANSCRIPT table to site B, do the operations there, and then send **R** to site A, we have to send 309,000 bytes ($= 20{,}000 * 15 + 1000 * 9$).
4. If we perform the semi-join at site B as previously described, we again have two options:
   (a) Send the result of the semi-join, **Q**, to site C; join it with STUDENT; project on `Major` and `CrsCode`; then send the result, **R**, to site A. The cost would be 114,000 bytes ($= 5000 * 9 + 5000 * 12 + 1000 * 9$).
   (b) Send both **Q**, and TRANSCRIPT to site A and complete the computation there. The cost of this is 405,000 bytes, as before.

Hence, the semi-join approach is still the best alternative, although now option (a) is better than option (b).

We can optimize this procedure by changing step 2 so that, after performing the semi-join to obtain Q, we do a projection on Q to retain only the columns of STUDENT needed for the query. Only those columns are sent from site B to site C. For example, suppose that STUDENT has additional attributes (such as `Address`, `Date_of_Birth`, `Entrance_date`,) and that, as before, the query requests the `Id`, `CrsCode`, and `Major` of students for each course in which a student is registered. Then, in step 2, we can project on those attributes named in the WHERE and SELECT clauses and send only those to site C.

This idea can be used in all of the approaches discussed so far. Before a table is sent from one site to another to perform a join, all unnecessary attributes can be eliminated.

Queries that involve joins and selections. A similar idea can be used when the query involves joins and selections. Suppose that there is only one warehouse in the Internet grocer application and that the EMPLOYEE relation is vertically partitioned as

```
EMP1 (SSnum, Name, Salary)
EMP2 (SSnum, Title, Location)
```
16.4

EMP1 is stored at site B (headquarters) and EMP2 is stored at site C (warehouse). Suppose that a query at a third site, A, requests the names of all employees with title "manager" whose salary is more than $20,000. (If we had assumed more than one warehouse, the reasoning would have been similar but the arithmetic would have been a bit more complex—see Exercise 16.14.)

A straightforward approach is to first perform the join of the tables (to regenerate the EMPLOYEE table) and then use the selection and projection operators on the result to obtain

$$\pi_{\texttt{Name}}(\sigma_{\texttt{Title='manager'}\ \text{AND}\ \texttt{Salary>'20000'}}\ (\text{EMP1} \bowtie \text{EMP2}))$$

Unfortunately, using the semi-join procedure to optimize the join will not reduce communication costs. This is because the two tables are the vertical partitions of the joined table, so EMP1 and EMP2 both contain `SSnum`, the key of EMPLOYEE. Hence all tuples of each table must be brought together to reconstruct EMPLOYEE.

Note, however, that the selection condition can be partitioned into selection conditions on the individual tables.

- Selection condition `Salary > '20000'` on EMP1
- Selection condition `Title = 'manager'` on EMP2

Now we can use the mathematical properties of the relational operators to change the order of the join and selection operators (recall the cascading and pushing rules for selection in Section 11.2):

$$\pi_{\text{NAME}}((\sigma_{\texttt{Salary>'20000'}}\ (\text{EMP1})) \bowtie (\sigma_{\texttt{Title='manager'}}\ (\text{EMP2})))$$

Specifically,

1. At site B, select all tuples from EMP1 for which the salary is more than \$20,000. Call the result $\mathbf{R_1}$.
2. At site C, select all tuples from EMP2 for which the title is manager. Call the result $\mathbf{R_2}$.
3. At some site (to be determined below), perform the join of $\mathbf{R_1}$ and $\mathbf{R_2}$ and project on the result using the `Name` attribute. Call the result $\mathbf{R_3}$. If this site is not site A, send $\mathbf{R_3}$ to site A.

The only remaining issue is where to perform the join in step 3. There are three possibilities:

1. Plan 1: Send $\mathbf{R_2}$ to site B, and do the join there. Then send the names to site A.
2. Plan 2: Send $\mathbf{R_1}$ to site C, and do the join there. Then send the names to site A.
3. Plan 3: Send $\mathbf{R_1}$ and $\mathbf{R_2}$ to site A, and do the join there.

As before, to determine the best plan we must take into account the sizes of the various tables and the size of the result. We make the following assumptions:

- The lengths of the attributes are
  - `SSnum`: 9 bytes;
  - `Salary`: 6 bytes;
  - `Title`: 7 bytes;
  - `Location`: 10 bytes;
  - `Name`: 15 bytes.

  Thus, the length of each tuple in EMP1 is 30 bytes and in EMP2 is 26 bytes.
- EMP1 (and hence EMP2) has about 100,000 tuples.
- About 5000 employees have a salary of more than \$20,000. Therefore, $\mathbf{R_1}$ has about 5000 tuples (each of length 30 bytes), for a total of 150,000 bytes.
- There are about 50 managers. Therefore, $\mathbf{R_2}$ has about 50 tuples (each of length 26 bytes), for a total of 1300 bytes.
- About 90% of the managers have a salary of more than \$20,000. Therefore, $\mathbf{R_3}$ has about 45 tuples, each of length 15 bytes, for a total of 675 bytes.

We can now evaluate the cost of each plan.

1. If we do the join at site B, we have to send 1300 bytes from site C to site B, and then 675 bytes from site B to site A, for a total of 1975 bytes.
2. If we do the join at site C, we have to send 150,000 bytes from site B to site C, and then 675 bytes from site C to site A, for a total of 150,675 bytes.

3. If we do the join at site A, we have to send 150,000 bytes from site B to site A, and 1300 bytes from site C to site A, for a total of 151,300 bytes.

As you can see, the first plan is substantially better than the other two.[2]

To fully appreciate a well-designed query plan, compare the cost of this plan with the cost of the unoptimized plan in which EMP1 and EMP2 are sent, in their entirety, to site A and the query is evaluated there. In that case, 5,600,000 bytes (= 2,600,000 + 3,000,000) have to be transmitted!

16.3.2 Strategies for a Multidatabase System

An application accessing a multidatabase system does not have a global schema to work with. Instead, a query involving data at several sites must be constructed using a sequence of SQL statements, each of which is formulated over the schema of a particular DBMS and processed at that site. Although global query optimizers do not exist in such an environment, the application designer can use some of the ideas discussed in Section 16.3.1 to choose a suitable sequence of statements for query evaluation. Unfortunately, the designer is limited because of the following considerations:

1. In a multidatabase system, data can be communicated only between a database site and the site at which a query is submitted—site A in the example. With a global query optimizer, on the other hand, database sites cooperate with one another and communicate directly.
2. Even though data cannot be transmitted directly between database sites, we might consider transferring data from one site to another indirectly through site A. This approach is not possible, however. Although site A can receive data from a DBMS (as a result of submitting a SELECT statement), it cannot send data to a DBMS because the application interface is concerned only with processing SQL statements (not receiving data).

This makes it essentially impossible to mimic step 1 of the semi-join procedure (page 700), in which a projection of a table (**P** in that step) is transmitted from one database site to another (see Exercise 16.15 for a somewhat impractical exception to this statement).

Example 16.3.2 (Global Optimization). Let us reconsider the partitioned EMPLOYEE table of the previous section and the query at site A that requests the names of all managers whose salary is more than $20,000. If the query were executed in a system with a global optimizer, we would expect the optimizer to choose plan 1, which has a communication cost of 1975 bytes.

If the same query were executed in a multidatabase system, the application designer could first execute SELECT statements at each site that returned $\mathbf{R}_1$ and $\mathbf{R}_2$

[2] By projecting $\mathbf{R}_2$ at site C on SSnum before sending it to site B, we can further reduce the cost of communication.

to site A. The program would then perform the necessary processing on these tuples to implement the join operation. The communication cost would be the same as plan 3: 151,300 bytes. Although this strategy would not be as efficient as the best strategy that can be chosen by a global query optimizer, it would certainly be an improvement over a naive strategy that brings EMP1 and EMP2 in their entirety to site A, at the cost of 5,600,000 bytes. ■

16.3.3 Tuning Issues: Database Design and Query Planning in a Distributed Environment

As in the centralized case, query planning for distributed databases involves evaluating alternatives, among which are

- Performing operations at different sites
- Sending partial results or entire tables from one site to another during query execution
- Performing semi-joins
- Using the heuristic optimization rules for relational algebra (Section 11.2) to reorder operations

Application designers do not have any significant control over the strategies used by a global query optimizer. However, the designer often does have control over the design of the distributed database, and that design can have a significant effect on query planning by changing the alternatives available to the global query optimizer. This is also true if query planning is done manually by the application designer for a multidatabase system.

In the centralized case, the application designer might change the database schema by, for example, adding indices or denormalizing tables (see Sections 6.13 and 12.2). In the distributed case, the designer might have additional choices, such as

- Placing tables at different sites
- Partitioning tables in different ways and placing the partitions at different sites
- Replicating tables, or data within tables (e.g., denormalizing), and placing the replicas at different sites

As in the centralized case, these choices might speed up certain operations and slow down others. Thus, the designer must evaluate a proposed database design based on the relative frequency of each operation in the application and the importance of throughput and response time for that operation.

In the Internet grocer application, partitioning the INVENTORY relation speeds up local applications involving delivery of merchandise but slows down global applications that require joining the partitions—for example, computing the total inventory for the company. In evaluating these alternatives, the enterprise might decide that the delivery application must execute quickly but that the total inventory application might execute infrequently with no significant demand on its response time.

The application designer might then consider speeding up the global inventory application by replicating the warehouse inventory information in the headquarters database. But this alternative will probably be rejected because the warehouse inventory information is updated frequently—every time a delivery is made—and the communication cost of updating the replicas is much greater than that of performing the global inventory application. Evaluating such tradeoffs is essential in designing an application that executes efficiently and meets the needs of the enterprise.

BIBLIOGRAPHIC NOTES

Our description of distributed query processing is based on the implementations of two systems, SDD-1 [Wong 1977; Bernstein et al. 1981] and System R* [Griffiths-Selinger and Adiba 1980]. The theory of semi-joins is discussed in [Bernstein and Chiu 1981]. Partitioning is discussed in [Chang and Cheng 1980; Ceri et al. 1982]. More in-depth study of a number of issues in distributed databases (especially database design and query processing) can be found in specialized texts, such as [Ceri and Pelagatti 1984; Bell and Grimson 1992; Ozsu and Valduriez 1999].

EXERCISES

16.1 Discuss the advantages to the application designer of designing an application as a homogeneous system in which all databases are supplied by the same vendor.

16.2 Explain why a table might be partitioned in the schema of a centralized system.

16.3 Explain whether or not the following statement is true: the join of two tables obtained by a (vertical or horizontal) partitioning of a table, **T**, can never contain more tuples than are contained in **T**.

16.4 Consider the two examples of query design in a multidatabase system given in Section 16.3.2. Write programs in Java and JDBC that implement both.

16.5 Give an example of a program at site A that requires the join of two tables, one at site B and one at site C. State the assumptions needed to justify the result that, as far as communication costs are concerned, the best implementation is to ship the table at site B to site C, do the join there, and then send the result to site A.

16.6 You are considering the possibility of horizontally partitioning the relation

```
EMPLOYEE (SSN, Name, Salary, Title, Location)
```

by location and storing each partition in the database at that location, with the possibility of replicating some partitions at different sites. Discuss the types of queries and updates (and their frequencies) that might influence your decision.

16.7 Suppose that we have a relation

```
EMPLOYEE2 (SSnum, Name, Salary, Age, Title, Location)
```

which is partitioned as

```
EMP21 (SSnum, Name, Salary)
EMP22 (SSnum, Title, Age, Location)
```

where EMP21 is stored at site B and EMP22 is stored at site C. A query at site A wants the names of all managers in the accounting department whose salary is greater than their age. Design a plan for this query, using the assumptions on page 704 for table and attribute sizes. Assume that the items in the Age column are two bytes long.

16.8 Design a multidatabase query plan and a set of SQL statements that implement the query of the previous exercise.

16.9 Show that step 2 of the method used in Section 16.3.1 to perform a join using a semi-join does in fact generate the semi-join. For simplicity, assume that the join we are attempting is a natural join. That is, prove that

$$\pi_{attributes(T_1)}(T_1 \bowtie T_2) = \pi_{attributes(T_1)}(T_1 \bowtie \pi_{attributes(join\text{-}condition)}(T_2))$$

16.10 Show that step 3 of the method used in Section 16.3.1 to perform a join using a semi-join does in fact generate the join. For simplicity, assume that the join we are attempting is a natural join. In other words, show that

$$(T_1 \ltimes T_2) \bowtie T_2 = (T_1 \bowtie T_2)$$

16.11 Design a query plan for the join example in Section 16.3.1, assuming the same table sizes as in that section, but with the following differences:

a. An application at site B requested the join.
b. An application at site C requested the join.

16.12 Show that the method of designing horizontal partitions described in Section 16.2.1 works as advertised.

16.13 Show that the semi-join operation is not commutative, that is, T_1 semi-joined with T_2 is not the same as T_2 semi-joined with T_1.

16.14 Use the example schema (16.4) on page 703 to design a query for finding the names of all managers (employees with `Title = 'manager'`) whose salary is more than $20,000, but assume that there are three warehouses. Also assume that the total number of employees is 100,000, that 5000 of them make over $20,000, that the total number of managers is 50, and that 90% of the managers make more than $20,000.

16.15 In Section 16.3.2 we pointed out that in a multidatabase system, data could not be communicated directly from one database site to another and that even indirect communication was difficult since a query site cannot send data to a database site.

However, the following "end run" might be considered for computing a semi-join. The query site, A, executes a SELECT statement at the first database site, B, which returns the projection, **P**, used in computing the semi-join. Site A then uses the projection to dynamically construct another SELECT statement whose result set is the semi-join. Using Example 16.3.1 on page 699 of Section 16.3.1 involving tables STUDENT and TRANSCRIPT, give the two queries. Under what circumstances could such an approach be considered?

17

OLAP and Data Mining

This chapter is an introduction to the concepts and techniques from the fields of *online analytical processing* (OLAP), *data warehousing*, and *data mining*. Recall from our discussion in Section 1.4 that while online transaction processing (OLTP) is concerned with using a database to maintain an accurate model of some real-world situation, OLAP and data mining are concerned with using the information in a database to guide strategic decisions. OLAP is concerned with obtaining specific information, while data mining can be viewed as knowledge discovery. Data warehouses are used to accumulate and store the information needed for OLAP and data mining queries.

In Sections 17.2 and 17.3, you will learn about the multidimensional model for OLAP and related notions, such as CUBE and ROLLUP. In Sections 17.7 and beyond, you will be introduced to a number of important techniques, including the a priori algorithm for computing associations, the ID3 and C4.5 algorithms for training decision trees using the information gain measure, the perceptron and back propagation learning algorithms for neural nets, and the K-means and hierarchical algorithms (using dendrograms) for clustering.

17.1 OLAP and Data Warehouses—Old and New

Why is so much free material available on the Internet—all for just filling out a form? In fact, the goodies you receive are not free—you are paying for them by providing information about yourself, and, when you buy on the Internet, you are providing even more information about yourself—your buying habits.

You also provide information about yourself when you purchase items in a department store or supermarket with your credit card. In these cases, you are inputting information into a transaction processing system, and the system is saving that information for future use.

What is done with this information? In many situations, it is combined with what is known about you from other sources, stored in a database, and then

- It might be combined with information about the purchases of other people to help an enterprise plan its inventory, advertising, or other aspects of its future strategy.

- It might be used to produce an individualized profile of your buying (or browsing) habits so that an enterprise can target its marketing to you through the mail or in other ways. Perhaps in the future, the people in your zip code area will see different TV commercials based on information about their purchasing habits. Or perhaps you will see TV commercials personalized for you.

These trends in information gathering and assimilation have serious implications for personal privacy. Do you want strangers to be able to access this information and use it in ways of which you might not approve? However, that is not our concern in this text. Our concern is to understand the techniques that might be used to analyze this data.

The applications that use data of this type are referred to as **online analytic processing**, or **OLAP**, in contrast with **online transaction processing**, or **OLTP**. The two types of applications have different goals and different technical requirements.

- The goal of OLTP is to maintain a database that is an accurate model of some real-world enterprise. The system must provide sufficiently large transaction throughput and low response time to keep up with the load and avoid user frustration. OLTP applications are characterized by
  - Short, simple transactions
  - Relatively frequent updates
  - Transactions that access only a tiny fraction of the database
- The goal of OLAP is to use the information in a database to guide strategic decisions. The databases involved are usually very large and often need not be completely accurate or up to date. Nor is fast response always required. OLAP applications are characterized by
  - Complex queries
  - Infrequent updates
  - Transactions that access a significant fraction of the database

One might say that OLTP is *operational* in that it deals with the everyday operations of the enterprise, while OLAP is *decisional* in that it deals with decision making by the managers of the enterprise.

The example of an OLAP application in Section 1.4 involved managers of a supermarket chain who want to make one-time (not preprogrammed) queries to the database to gather information they need in order to make a specific decision. This illustrates the traditional use of OLAP—ad hoc queries, often made by people who are not highly technical.

The OLAP examples at the beginning of this section describe some of the newer uses. Businesses are using preprogrammed queries against OLAP databases on an ongoing operational basis to customize marketing and other aspects of their business. These queries are often complex and, since they are key to the business and used operationally (perhaps daily or weekly), are designed and implemented by professionals.

In traditional OLAP applications, the information in the OLAP database is often just the data the business happens to gather during day-to-day operations—perhaps in its OLTP systems. In newer applications, the business often makes an active effort to gather—perhaps even to purchase—the additional information needed for its planned application.

As the *A* in OLAP implies, the goal of an OLAP application is to *analyze* data for use in some application. Thus, there are often two separate but related subjects.

- *The analysis to be performed.* For example, a company wants to decide the mix of products to manufacture during the next accounting period. It develops an analysis procedure that requires as input the sales for the last period and the history of sales for the equivalent periods over the past five years.
- *The methods to efficiently obtain the large amounts of data required for the analysis.* For example, how can the company extract the required sales data from databases in its subsidiary departments? In what form should it store this data in the OLAP database? How can it retrieve the data efficiently when needed for the analysis?

The first issue, analysis, is not a database problem since it requires algorithms specific to the particular business in which the company engages. Our interest is primarily in the second issue—database support for these analytical procedures. For our purposes, we assume that the retrieved data is simply displayed on the screen. However, in many situations—particularly in newer applications—this data is input to sophisticated analysis procedures.

Data warehouses. OLAP databases are usually stored in special OLAP servers, often called **data warehouses**, which are structured to support the OLAP queries that will be made against them. OLAP queries are often so complex that if they were run in an OLTP environment, they would slow down OLTP transactions to an unacceptable degree.

We will discuss some of the issues involved in populating a data warehouse in Section 17.6. First, we will look at the kinds of data we might want to store in the warehouse.

17.2 A Multidimensional Model for OLAP Applications

Fact tables and dimension tables. Many OLAP applications are similar to the supermarket example of Section 1.4: analysis of sales of different products in different supermarkets over different time periods. We might describe this sales data with a relational table such as that shown in Figure 17.1. `Market_Id` identifies a particular supermarket, `Product_Id` identifies a particular product, `Time_Id` identifies a particular time interval, and `Sales_Amt` identifies the dollar value of the sales of that product at that supermarket in that time period. Such a table is called a **fact table** because it contains all of the facts about the data to be analyzed.

We can view this data as **multidimensional**. The `Market_Id`, `Product_Id`, and `Time_Id` attributes are the dimensions and correspond to the arguments of a function. The `Sales_Amt` attribute corresponds to the value of the function.

SALES	Market_Id	Product_Id	Time_Id	Sales_Amt
	M1	P1	T1	1000
	M1	P2	T1	2000
	M1	P3	T1	1500
	M1	P4	T1	2500
	M2	P1	T1	500
	M2	P2	T1	800
	M2	P3	T1	0
	M2	P4	T1	3333
	M3	P1	T1	5000
	M3	P2	T1	8000
	M3	P3	T1	10
	M3	P4	T1	3300
	M1	P1	T2	1001
	M1	P2	T2	2001
	M1	P3	T2	1501
	M1	P4	T2	2501
	M2	P1	T2	501
	M2	P2	T2	801
	M2	P3	T2	1
	M2	P4	T2	3334
	M3	P1	T2	5001
	M3	P2	T2	8001
	M3	P3	T2	11
	M3	P4	T2	3301
	M1	P1	T3	1002
	M1	P2	T3	2002
	M1	P3	T3	1502
	M1	P4	T3	2502
	M2	P1	T3	502
	M2	P2	T3	802
	M2	P3	T3	2
	M2	P4	T3	333
	M3	P1	T3	5002
	M3	P2	T3	8002
	M3	P3	T3	12
	M3	P4	T3	3302

FIGURE 17.1 The fact table for the supermarket application.

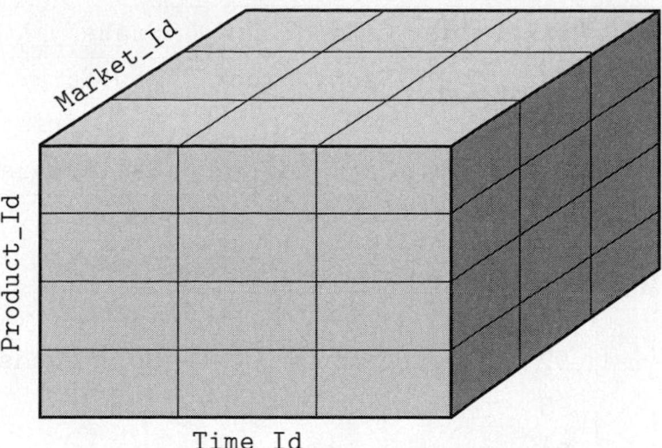

FIGURE 17.2 Three-dimensional cube for the supermarket application.

We can also think of the data in a fact table as being arranged in a multidimensional cube. Thus, in the supermarket example, the data is arranged in the three-dimensional cube shown in Figure 17.2, where the dimensions of the cube are `Market_Id`, `Product_Id`, and `Time_Id` and the vertices, or **cells**, of the cube contain the corresponding `Sales_Amt`. Such a multidimensional view can be an intuitive way to think about OLAP queries and their results.

Additional information about the dimensions can be stored in **dimension tables**, which describe dimension attributes. For the supermarket example, these tables might be called MARKET, PRODUCT, and TIME, as shown in Figure 17.3. The MARKET table describes the market: its city, state, and region. In a more realistic example, the MARKET table would contain a row for each supermarket in the chain, which might include many markets in each city, many cities in each state, and many states in each region.

Star schema. The relations corresponding to the supermarket example can be displayed in a diagram, as in Figure 17.4. The figure suggests a star, with the fact table at the center and the dimension tables radiating from it. This type of schema, called a **star schema**, is very common in OLAP applications. It is interesting to note that a star schema corresponds to a very common fragment of an entity-relation diagram, where the fact table is a relationship and the dimension tables are entities.

If the dimension tables are normalized (so that each might become several tables), the figure gets a bit more complex and is called a **snowflake schema**. However, for two reasons, dimension tables are rarely normalized:

1. They are so small compared with the fact table that the space saved due to the elimination of redundancy is negligible.
2. They are updated so infrequently that update anomalies are not an issue. Moreover, in this situation, decomposing the relations into 3NF or BCNF might lead to significant query overhead, as explained in Section 6.13.

MARKET	Market_Id	City	State	Region
	M1	Stony Brook	New York	East
	M2	Newark	New Jersey	East
	M3	Oakland	California	West

PRODUCT	Product_Id	Name	Category	Price
	P1	Beer	Drink	1.98
	P2	Diapers	Soft Goods	2.98
	P3	Cold Cuts	Meat	3.98
	P4	Soda	Drink	1.25

TIME	Time_Id	Week	Month	Quarter
	T1	Wk-1	January	First
	T2	Wk-24	June	Second
	T3	Wk-52	December	Fourth

FIGURE 17.3 Dimension tables for the supermarket application.

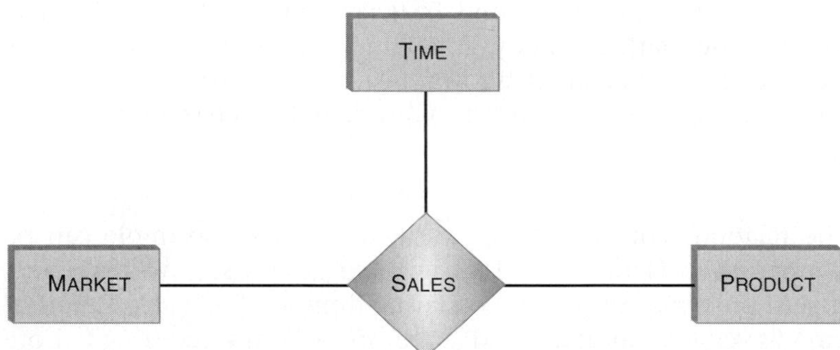

FIGURE 17.4 Star schema for the supermarket example.

Instead of a star schema, many OLAP applications use a **constellation schema**, which consists of several fact tables that might share one or more dimension tables. For example, the supermarket application might maintain a fact table called INVENTORY, with dimension tables WAREHOUSE, PRODUCT, and TIME, as shown in Figure 17.5. Note that the PRODUCT and TIME dimension tables are shared with the SALES fact table, whereas the WAREHOUSE table, which describes where the inventory is stored, is not shared.

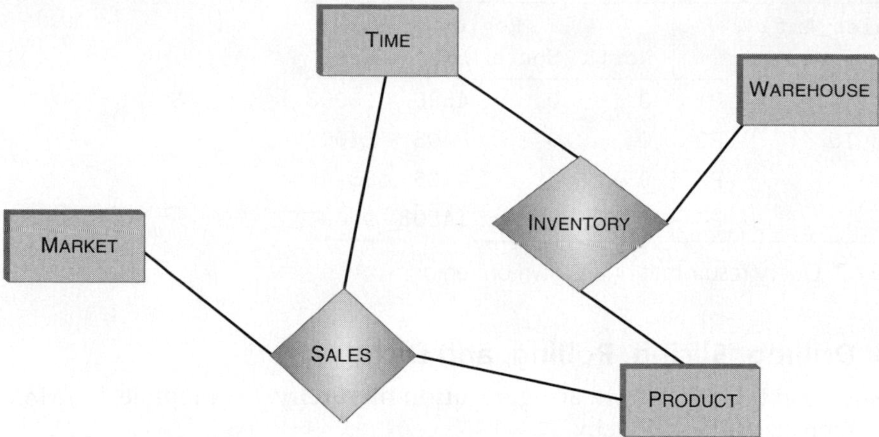

FIGURE 17.5 Constellation schema for the expanded supermarket example.

SUM(Sales_Amt)		Market_Id		
		M1	M2	M3
	P1	3003	1503	15003
Product_Id	P2	6003	2402	24003
	P3	4503	3	33
	P4	7503	7000	9903

FIGURE 17.6 Query result that aggregates `Sales_Amt` on the time dimension.

17.3 Aggregation

Many OLAP queries involve **aggregation** of the data in the fact table. For example, a query that produces the total sales (over time) of each product in each market can be expressed with the SQL statement

```
SELECT      S.Market_Id, S.Product_Id, SUM(S.Sales_Amt)
FROM        SALES S
GROUP BY    S.Market_Id, S.Product_Id
```

which returns the result table shown in Figure 17.6. Here we depict the result table as a two-dimensional cube with the values of the aggregation over `Sales_Amt` placed in the cells. Since this aggregation is over the entire time dimension (i.e., the result does not depend on the time coordinate), it produces a reduced-dimensional view of the data—two dimensions instead of three.

SUM(Sales_Amt)		Region			
		North	South	East	West
	P1	0	0	4506	15003
Product_Id	P2	0	0	8405	24003
	P3	0	0	4506	33
	P4	0	0	14503	9903

FIGURE 17.7 Query result that drills down on regions.

17.3.1 Drilling, Slicing, Rolling, and Dicing

Some dimension tables represent an **aggregation hierarchy**. For example, the MARKET table represents the hierarchy

$$\texttt{Market\_Id} \rightarrow \texttt{City} \rightarrow \texttt{State} \rightarrow \texttt{Region}$$

meaning that supermarkets are in cities, cities are in states, and states are in regions. We can perform queries at different levels of a hierarchy, as shown here:

```
SELECT      S.Product_Id, M.Region, SUM(S.Sales_Amt)
FROM        SALES S,   MARKET M
WHERE       M.Market_Id = S.Market_Id                          17.1
GROUP BY    S.Product_Id, M.Region
```

This produces the table of Figure 17.7, which aggregates total sales per product for each region over all time.

When we execute a sequence of queries that move down a hierarchy—from general to specific, such as moving from aggregation over regions to aggregation over states—we are said to be **drilling down**. Drilling down, of course, requires access to more specific information than is contained in the result of a more general query. Thus, in order to aggregate over states, we must either use the fact table or a previously computed table that aggregates over cities. Thus, we might use the fact table to drill down to states with

```
SELECT      S.Product_Id, M.State, SUM(S.Sales_Amt)
FROM        SALES S,   MARKET M
WHERE       M.Market_Id = S.Market_Id                          17.2
GROUP BY    S.Product_Id, M.State
```

When we move up the hierarchy (for example, from aggregation over states to aggregation over regions), we are said to be **rolling up**. For example, if we were to save the result of executing the query (17.2) as a table called STATE_SALES, then we could roll up the hierarchy using the query

SUM(Sales_Amt)		Quarter			
		First	Second	Third	Fourth
	P1	6500	6503	0	6506
Product_Id	P2	10800	10803	0	10806
	P3	1510	1513	0	1516
	P4	9133	9136	0	6137

FIGURE 17.8 Query result that presents total product sales for each quarter.

```
SELECT      T.Product_Id, M.Region, SUM(T.Sales_Amt)
FROM        STATE_SALES T,   MARKET M
WHERE       R.State = T.State
GROUP BY    T.Product_Id, R.Region
```

While this is not an efficient way to aggregate over regions, it demonstrates the ability to use previously computed results when rolling up. This is an important optimization and has motivated the inclusion in SQL of special features, which we will discuss shortly. It is very common to roll up or drill down using the time dimension—for example, to summarize sales on a daily, monthly, or quarterly basis.

Here is a bit more OLAP terminology. When we view the data in the form of a multidimensional cube and then select a subset of the axes, we are said to be performing a **pivot** (we are reorienting the multidimensional cube). The selected axes correspond to the list of attributes in the GROUP BY clause. Pivoting is usually followed by aggregation on the remaining axes.

As an example, the following query performs a pivot of the multidimensional cube to view it from the product and time dimensions. It finds the total sales (over all markets) of each product for each quarter (of the current year) and produces the table of Figure 17.8:

```
SELECT      S.Product_Id, T.Quarter,  SUM(S.Sales_Amt)
FROM        SALES S,   TIME T
WHERE       T.Time_Id = S.Time_Id                          17.3
GROUP BY    S.Product_Id, T.Quarter
```

If we next ask the same query, but use the GROUP BY clause to group by years instead of by quarters, we are rolling up the time hierarchy.

```
SELECT      S.Product_Id, T.Year, SUM(S.Sales_Amt)
FROM        SALES S,   TIME T
WHERE       T.Time_Id = S.Time_Id
GROUP BY    S.Product_Id, T.Year
```

SQL:1999/2003 and some OLAP vendors support a new SQL clause, ROLLUP, to simplify this process (see Section 17.3.2). However, notice that a corresponding drill-down clause is usually *not* provided. The reason is that rollup is not only a convenience but also an optimization device. If the user first asks to aggregate over quarters and then rolls up the result to years, the OLAP system does not need to compute from scratch but can aggregate to the year using the previously computed aggregation results for each quarter. No such optimization is possible for drilling down. However, OLAP systems typically let the user precompute and cache certain aggregations in order to speed up the drilling down process. For instance, if we are expected to drill down to weeks and quarters, we might ask the system to precompute aggregations of the data cube grouping by weeks in the time dimension. Then when we drill down to weeks or quarters we will not need to sum up the sales figures for each particular value of the `Time_Id` attribute. Instead, when we group by `Week` or `Quarter` we will be summing up the already precomputed weekly sales figures—a much smaller number of items.

> Rollup can be optimized through the reuse of the results of previous requests. Drilling down can be sped up by precomputing and caching certain carefully selected aggregations.

Not all aggregation hierarchies are linear, as is the location hierarchy. The time hierarchy shown in Figure 17.9, for example, is a lattice. Weeks are not fully contained in months—the same week can fall on the boundary for two different months. Thus, we can roll up days into either weeks or months, but we can only roll up weeks into quarters.

Note that all of the above queries access a significant fraction of the data in the fact table. By contrast, the OLTP query to the database at your local supermarket *How many cans of tomato juice are in stock*? accesses only a single tuple.

Slicing and dicing. We can imagine that the hierarchy for each dimension partitions the multidimensional cube into subcubes. Thus, for example, the `Quarter`

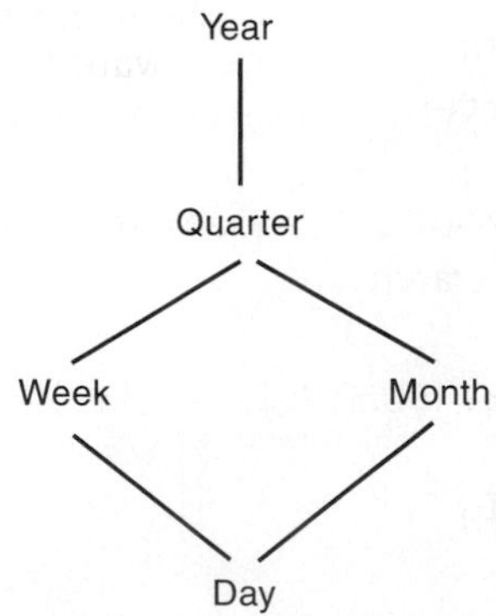

FIGURE 17.9 Time hierarchy as a lattice.

level of the time dimension partitions the cube into subcubes, one for each quarter. Queries that return information about those subcubes are said to **slice and dice**.

- When we pivot, that is, use a GROUP BY clause in a query to specify a level in a hierarchy, we are partitioning the multidimensional cube into subcubes: all the elements in the contained level are grouped together. For example, if we group by product Id and quarter, as in the query (17.3), all transactions for the same product in the same quarter are grouped together. Thus, pivoting creates the effect of **dicing** the data cube into subcubes.
- When we use a WHERE clause that equates a dimension attribute to a constant, we are specifying a particular value for that dimension and so are performing a **slice**.

Typically pivoting and slicing are used together, so it has become known as "slicing and dicing." For example, a query that requests the total product sales in each market in the first quarter

```
SELECT      S.Product_Id, SUM(S.Sales_Amt)
FROM        SALES S, TIME T
WHERE       T.Time_Id = S.Time_Id AND T.Quarter = 'First'
GROUP BY    S.Product_Id
```

is an example of a slice in the time dimension and dice in the product dimension. Thus, pivoting "dices" (partitions) the cube into subcubes along the specified dimensions and slicing selects a cross section that cuts across these subcubes.

17.3.2 The CUBE Operator

Many OLAP queries use the aggregate functions and the GROUP BY clause of the SELECT statement to perform aggregation. However, the standard options for the SELECT statement limit the types of OLAP queries that can be easily formulated in SQL. A number of OLAP vendors (as well as SQL:1999/2003) extend SQL with additional aggregate functions, and some vendors even allow programmers to specify their own aggregate functions.

One extension in this direction is the ROLLUP operator; another is the CUBE operator introduced in [Gray et al. 1997]. Suppose that we want to obtain a table such as that in Figure 17.10. This table is similar to the one in Figure 17.6 except that, in addition, it has totals for each row and each column. To construct such a table, we would need to use four standard SQL SELECT statements to retrieve the necessary information. The following statement returns the data needed for the table entries (without the totals).

```
SELECT      S.Market_Id, S.Product_Id, SUM(S.Sales_Amt)
FROM        SALES S
GROUP BY    S.Market_Id, S.Product_Id
```

SUM(Sales_Amt)		Market_Id			
		M1	M2	M3	Total
	P1	3003	1503	15003	19509
Product_Id	P2	6003	2402	24003	32408
	P3	4503	3	33	4539
	P4	7503	7000	9903	24406
	Total	21012	10908	48942	80862

FIGURE 17.10 Query result for the sales application in the form of a spreadsheet.

The next statement computes the row totals:

```
SELECT      S.Product_Id, SUM(S.Sales_Amt)
FROM        SALES S
GROUP BY    S.Product_Id
```

This statement computes the totals for the columns:

```
SELECT      S.Market_Id, SUM(S.Sales_Amt)
FROM        SALES S
GROUP BY    S.Market_Id
```

and the last statement computes the grand total of 80862 in the lower right corner:

```
SELECT      SUM(S.Sales_Amt)
FROM        SALES S
```

Four statements are required because the table needs four aggregations—by time, by product Id and time, by market Id and time, and by all attributes together. Each such aggregation is produced by a different GROUP BY clause.

Computing all of these queries *independently* is wasteful of both time and computing resources. The first query does much of the work needed for the other three queries, so, if we save the result and then use it to aggregate over `Market_Id` and `Product_Id`, we can compute the second and third queries more efficiently. Efficient computation of such "data cubes" is important in OLAP, and much research has been dedicated to this issue. See, for example, [Agrawal et al. 1996; Harinarayan et al. 1996; Ross and Srivastava 1997; Zhao et al. 1998].

Economy of scale is the main motivation for the CUBE clause [Gray et al. 1997], which is included in the SQL:1999/2003 standard. When CUBE is used in a GROUP BY clause,

```
GROUP BY CUBE(v1, v2, . . . , vn)
```

it is equivalent to a collection of GROUP BYs, one for each of the $2^n - 1$ non-empty subsets of $v1, v2, \ldots, vn$, plus the query that does not have the GROUP BY clause, which corresponds to the empty subset. For example, the statement

```
SELECT     S.Market_Id, S.Product_Id, SUM(S.Sales_Amt)
FROM       SALES S
GROUP BY CUBE(S.Market_Id, S.Product_Id)
```

returns the result set of Figure 17.11, which is equivalent to all four of the above SELECT statements and includes all of the values required for the table of Figure 17.10. Note the NULL entries in the columns that are being aggregated. For example, the

RESULT SET	Market_Id	Product_Id	Sales_Amt
	M1	P1	3003
	M1	P2	6003
	M1	P3	4503
	M1	P4	7503
	M2	P1	1503
	M2	P2	2402
	M2	P3	3
	M2	P4	7000
	M3	P1	15003
	M3	P2	24003
	M3	P3	33
	M3	P4	9903
	M1	NULL	21012
	M2	NULL	10908
	M3	NULL	48942
	NULL	P1	19509
	NULL	P2	32408
	NULL	P3	4539
	NULL	P4	24406
	NULL	NULL	80862

FIGURE 17.11 Result set returned with the CUBE operator.

first NULL in the Product_Id column means that the sales for market M1 are being aggregated over all products.[1]

ROLLUP is similar to CUBE except that instead of aggregating all subsets of its arguments, it creates subsets by moving from right to left. Like CUBE, the ROLLUP option to the GROUP BY clause is included in SQL:1999/2003.

Consider the above SELECT statement in which CUBE has been replaced with ROLLUP:

```
SELECT   S.Market_Id, S.Product_Id, SUM(S.Sales_Amt)
FROM     SALES S                                          17.4
GROUP BY ROLLUP(S.Market_Id, S.Product_Id)
```

The syntax here says that aggregation should be computed first with the finest granularity, using GROUP BY S.Market_Id, S.Product_Id, and then with the next level of granularity, using GROUP BY S.Market_Id. Finally, the grand total is computed, which corresponds to the empty GROUP BY clause. The result set is depicted in Figure 17.12. In a larger example (with more attributes in the ROLLUP clause), the result set table would contain some rows with NULL in the last column, some with NULL in the last two columns, some with NULL in the last three columns, and so on.

Note that the ROLLUP operator of OLAP-extended SQL is a generalization of the idea of rolling up the aggregation hierarchy described on page 718. Moreover, the cost savings from reusing the results of fine-grained aggregations to compute coarser levels of aggregation apply to the general ROLLUP operator. For instance, in query (17.4), aggregations computed for the clause GROUP BY S.Market_Id, S.Product_Id can be reused in the computation of aggregates for the clause GROUP BY S.Market_Id. These aggregates can then be reused in the computation of the grand total.

Materialized views using the CUBE operator. The CUBE operator can be used to precompute aggregations on all dimensions of a fact table and then save them for use in future queries. Thus, the statement

```
SELECT   S.Market_Id, S.Product_Id, SUM(S.Sales_Amt)
FROM     SALES S
GROUP BY CUBE(S.Market_Id, S.Product_Id, S.Time_Id)
```

produces a result set that is the table of Figure 17.1 with the addition of rows corresponding to aggregations on all subsets of the dimensions. The *additional* rows

[1] The use of SQL NULL in this context might be confusing because in this context NULL actually means "all" (it is the aggregation of one of the dimensions).

Result Set	Market_ Id	Product_Id	Sales_Amt
	M1	P1	3003
	M1	P2	6003
	M1	P3	4503
	M1	P4	7503
	M2	P1	1503
	M2	P2	2402
	M2	P3	3
	M2	P4	7000
	M3	P1	15003
	M3	P2	24003
	M3	P3	33
	M3	P4	9903
	M1	NULL	21012
	M2	NULL	10908
	M3	NULL	48092
	NULL	NULL	80862

FIGURE 17.12 Result set returned with the ROLLUP operator.

are shown in Figure 17.13. If this result set is saved as a materialized view (see Section 5.2.9), it can speed up subsequent queries.

Several materialized views can be prepared (with or without the CUBE operator) and used to speed up queries throughout the entire OLAP application. Of course, each such materialized view requires additional storage space, so there is some limit on the number of materialized views that can be constructed. Since updates are infrequent, the view update problem is not an issue.

17.4 ROLAP and MOLAP

We have been assuming that the OLAP data is stored in a relational database as one (or more) star schemas. Such an implementation is referred to as **relational OLAP** (ROLAP).

Some vendors provide OLAP servers that implement the fact table as a **data cube** using some sort of multidimensional (nonrelational) implementation, often with a substantial amount of precomputed aggregation. Such implementations are referred to as **multidimensional OLAP** (MOLAP). Note that in ROLAP implementations, a data cube is a way to think about the data; in MOLAP implementations, the data is actually stored in some representation of a data cube.

RESULT SET	Market_Id	Product_Id	Time_Id	Sales_Amt
	...	...	...	...
	NULL	P1	T1	6500
	NULL	P2	T1	10800
	NULL	P3	T1	1510
	NULL	P4	T1	9133
	NULL	P1	T2	6503
	NULL	P2	T2	10803
	NULL	P3	T2	1513
	NULL	P4	T2	9136
	NULL	P1	T3	6506
	NULL	P2	T3	10806
	NULL	P3	T3	1516
	NULL	P4	T3	6137
	M1	NULL	T1	7000
	M2	NULL	T1	4633
	M3	NULL	T1	4610
	M1	NULL	T2	7004
	M2	NULL	T2	4634
	M3	NULL	T2	16314
	M1	NULL	T3	7008
	M2	NULL	T3	1639
	M3	NULL	T3	16318
	M1	P1	NULL	3003
	M1	P2	NULL	6003
	M1	P3	NULL	4503
	M1	P4	NULL	7503
	M2	P1	NULL	1503
	M2	P2	NULL	2402
	M2	P3	NULL	3
	M2	P4	NULL	7000
	M3	P1	NULL	15003
	M3	P2	NULL	24003
	M3	P3	NULL	33
	M3	P4	NULL	9903
	NULL	NULL	T1	16243
	NULL	NULL	T2	27952

FIGURE 17.13 Tuples added to the fact table by the CUBE operator.

RESULT SET	Market_Id	Product_Id	Time_Id	Sales_Amt
	NULL	NULL	T3	24967
	NULL	P1	NULL	19509
	NULL	P2	NULL	32408
	NULL	P3	NULL	4539
	NULL	P4	NULL	24406
	M1	NULL	NULL	31012
	M2	NULL	NULL	10908
	M3	NULL	NULL	48942
	NULL	NULL	NULL	80862

FIGURE 17.13 (continued)

One use of the CUBE operator is to compute the aggregations needed to load a MOLAP database from an SQL database. Many MOLAP systems also allow the user to specify certain other aggregations that are to be stored as materialized views. Their databases provide efficient implementations of certain (perhaps nonrelational) operations often used in OLAP, such as aggregations at different levels of a hierarchy.

There is no standard query language for MOLAP implementations, but a number of MOLAP (and ROLAP) vendors provide proprietary, sometimes visual, languages that allow technically unsophisticated users to compute tables such as that in Figure 17.10 with a single query, and then to pivot, drill down, or roll up on any table dimension, sometimes with a single click of a mouse.

Not all commercial decision support applications use ROLAP (with star schemas) or MOLAP database servers. Many use conventional relational databases with schemas designed for their particular application. For example, several complex SQL queries used throughout this book can be viewed as OLAP queries (e.g., *List all professors who have taught all courses* . . .). Indeed, any query that uses complicated joins or nested SELECT statements is probably useful only for analysis since its execution time is too long for an OLTP system.

17.5 Implementation Issues

Most of the specialized implementation techniques for OLAP systems are derived from the key technical characteristic of OLAP applications:

> OLAP applications deal with very large amounts of data, but that data is relatively static and updates are infrequent.

Moreover, many of these techniques involve precomputing partial results or indices, which makes them particularly appropriate when queries are known in advance—for example, when they are embedded into an operational OLAP application. They can also be used for ad hoc (nonprogrammed) queries if the database designer or administrator has some idea as to what those queries will be.

One technique is to precompute some often-used aggregations and store them in the database. These include aggregations over some of the dimension hierarchies. Since the data does not change often, the overhead of maintaining the aggregation values is small.

Another technique is to use indices particularly oriented toward the queries that will be made. Since data updates are infrequent, the usual overhead of index maintenance is minimal. Two examples of such indices are *join* and *bitmap* indices.

Star joins and join indices. A join of the relations in a star schema, called a **star join**, can be optimized using a special index structure, called a **join index**, as discussed in Section 9.7.2. All recent releases of major commercial DBMSs are capable of recognizing and optimizing star joins.

Bitmap indices. Bitmap indices, introduced in Section 9.7.1, are particularly useful for indexing attributes that can take only a small number of values. Such attributes occur frequently in OLAP applications. For example, `Region` in the MARKET table might take only four values: `North`, `South`, `East`, and `West`. If the MARKET table has a total of 10,000 rows, a bitmap index on `Region` contains four bit vectors, with a total storage requirement of 40,000 bits or 5K bytes. An index of this size can easily fit in main memory and can provide quick access to records with corresponding values.

17.6 Populating a Data Warehouse

Data for both OLAP and data mining is usually stored in a special database often called a **data warehouse**. Data warehouses are usually very large, perhaps containing terabytes of data that have been gathered at different times from a number of sources, including databases from different vendors and with different schemas. Merging such data into a single OLAP database is not trivial. Additional problems arise when that data has to be periodically updated.

Two important operations must be performed on the data before it can be loaded into the warehouse.

1. *Transformation*. The data from the different source DBMSs must be transformed, both syntactically and semantically, into the common format required by the warehouse.
   (a) *Syntactic transformation*. The syntax used by the different DBMSs to represent the same data might be different. For example, the schema in one DBMS might represent Social Security numbers with the attribute `SSN` while an-

other might use SSnum. One might represent it as a character string, another as an integer.

(b) *Semantic transformation*. The semantics used by the different DBMSs to represent the same data might be different. For example, the warehouse might summarize sales on a daily basis, while one DBMS summarizes them on an hourly basis and another does not summarize sales at all but merely provides information about individual transactions.

2. *Data cleaning*. The data must be examined to correct any errors and missing information. We might think that data obtained from an OLTP database should be correct, but experience indicates otherwise. Moreover, some erroneous data might have been obtained from sources other than an OLTP database—for example, an incorrect zip code on a form filled in on the Internet.

Often the term "data cleaning" is used to describe both types of operations. Although there is no general design theory for performing these operations, a number of vendors supply tools that do a decent job for concrete domains such as postal addresses, product descriptions, and the like.

If no data cleaning is necessary and the sources are relational databases that have schemas sufficiently similar to that of the warehouse, the data can sometimes be extracted from the sources and inserted into the warehouse with a single SQL statement. For example, assume that each store, *M*, in the supermarket chain has an M_SALES table with schema M_SALES(Product_Id, Time_Id, Sales_Amt), which records *M*'s sales of each product for each time period. Then, after time period T4, we can update the fact table (Figure 17.1) stored in the data warehouse with the sales information for market *M* in time period T4 with the statement

```
INSERT INTO SALES(Market_Id, Product_Id, Time_Id, Sales_Amt)
    SELECT Market_Id = 'M', S.Product_Id, S.Time_Id, S.Sales_Amt
    FROM M_SALES  S
    WHERE S.Time_Id = 'T4'
```

If data cleaning or reformatting is needed, the data to be extracted can be represented as nonmaterialized views over the source databases. A cleansing program can then retrieve the data through the views (without requiring knowledge of the individual database schemas) for further processing before inserting it into the warehouse database.

As with other types of databases, an OLAP database must include a **metadata repository** containing information about the physical and logical organization of the data, including its schema, indices, and the like. For data warehouses, the repository must also include information about the source of all data and the dates on which it was loaded and refreshed.

The large volume of data in an OLAP database makes loading and updating a significant task. For the sake of efficiency, updating is usually incremental. Different parts of the database are updated at different times. Unfortunately, however, incremental updating might leave the database in an inconsistent state. It might

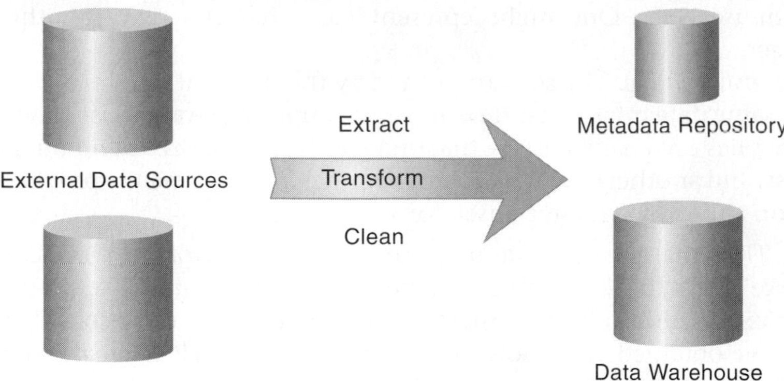

FIGURE 17.14 Loading data into an OLAP database.

not satisfy certain integrity constraints or it might not exactly describe the current state of the enterprise at the current instant. Usually, this is not an important issue for OLAP queries because much of the data analysis involves only summaries and statistical analyses, which are not significantly affected by such inconsistencies.

Figure 17.14 summarizes the processes involved in loading an OLAP database.

17.7 Data Mining Tasks

Data mining is an attempt at knowledge discovery—searching for patterns and structure in large data sets, as contrasted with requesting specific information. If OLAP is about confirming the known, we might say that data mining is about exploring the unknown.

Data mining uses techniques from many disciplines, such as statistical analysis, pattern recognition, machine learning, and artificial intelligence. Our main interest is in understanding these techniques and how they are used to process large data sets. Data mining with its associated data warehousing, data displaying, etc. is sometimes called *Knowledge Discovery in Databases* (KDD).

Among the goals of data mining are

- *Association.* Finding patterns in data that associate instances of that data with other related instances of that data. For example, *Amazon.com* associates the information about books purchased by its customers so that if a particular customer purchases some book, it then suggests other books that this customer might also want to purchase.
- *Classification.* Finding patterns in data that can be used to classify that data (and possibly the people it describes) into certain interesting categories. For example, a company might classify its customers based on their past purchases as either "high-end buyers" or "low-end buyers." This information might then be used to target specific advertisements to those customers.

One important application of classification is for *prediction*. For example, a bank might gather data about the customers who did or did not default on their mortgages over the past five years: their net worth, their income, their marital status, etc. and use that data to classify each customer as a *defaulter* or a *nondefaulter* based on this data. When new customers apply for a mortgage, the bank might use the data on their net worth, income, and marital status to predict whether or not they would default on their mortgage if the application were approved.

- *Clustering*. As with classification, clustering involves finding patterns in data that can be used to classify that data (and possibly the people it describes) into certain interesting categories. However, in contrast with classification, in which the categories are specified by the analyst, in clustering, the categories are discovered by the clustering algorithm.

17.8 Mining Associations

One of the more important applications of data mining is finding associations. An **association** is a correlation between certain values in the database. We gave an example of such a correlation in Section 1.4:

> *In a convenience store in the early evening, a high percentage of customers who bought diapers also bought beer.*

This association can be described using the **association rule**

Purchase_diapers ⇒ *Purchase_ beer* **17.5**

An association can involve more than two items. For example, it might assert that, if a customer buys cream cheese and lox, she is likely to also buy bagels (if the customer buys only cream cheese, she might be planning to use it for a different purpose and therefore not buy bagels).

Purchase_creamcheese AND *Purchase_lox* ⇒ *Purchase_bagels*

To see how the association (17.5) might have been discovered, assume that the convenience store maintains a PURCHASES table, shown in Figure 17.15, which it computes from its OLTP system. Based on this table, the data mining system can compute two measures:

1. *The* **confidence** *for an association.* The percentage of transactions that contain the items on the right side of the association among the transactions that contain the items on the left side of the association. The first three transactions of Figure 17.15 contain diapers, and of these, the first two also contain beer. Hence the confidence for association (17.5) is 66.66%.

PURCHASES	Transaction_Id	Product
	001	diapers
	001	beer
	001	popcorn
	001	bread
	002	diapers
	002	cheese
	002	soda
	002	beer
	002	juice
	003	diapers
	003	cold cuts
	003	cookies
	003	napkins
	004	cereal
	004	beer
	004	cold cuts

FIGURE 17.15 PURCHASES table used for data mining.

2. *The* **support** *for an association.* The percentage of transactions that contain all items (on both the left and right sides) of the association. Two of the four transactions in Figure 17.15 contain both items. Hence the support for association (17.5) is 50%. We also define the support for a single item as the percentage of transactions that contain that item.

The purpose of the confidence factor is to certify that there is certain probability that if a transaction includes all items on the left side of the association—*Purchase_diapers* in (17.5)—then the item on the right side will appear as well—*Purchase_beer*. If the confidence factor is high enough, the convenience store manager might want to put a beer display at the end of the diaper aisle.

However, confidence alone might not provide reliable information. We need to make sure that the correlation it represents is statistically significant. For instance, the confidence for the association *Purchase_cookies* ⇒ *Purchase_napkins* is 100%, but there is only one transaction where napkins and cookies are involved, so this association is most likely not statistically significant. The support of an association deals with this issue by measuring the fraction of transactions in which the association is actually demonstrated.

To assert that the association exists, both of the above measures must be above a certain threshold. Selecting appropriate thresholds is part of the discipline of statistical analysis and is beyond the scope of this book.

It is relatively easy for the system to compute the support and confidence for a particular association. That is an OLAP query. However, it is much more difficult for the system to return all possible associations for which the confidence and support are above a certain threshold. That is a data mining query. The idea of mining for association rules and some early algorithms were first introduced in [Agrawal et al. 1993].

We present an efficient algorithm for retrieving the data needed to determine all associations for which the support is larger than a given threshold, T. As we will see, once we have found those associations it is easy to determine which of them has a confidence factor greater than some given threshold.

Assume that we are trying to find all associations $A \Rightarrow B$ for which the support is greater than T. The naive approach is to compute the support for $A_i \Rightarrow B_j$ for all pairs of distinct items, A_i and B_j. However, if there are n items, $n(n-1)$ pairs have to be tried. This is usually too costly. The situation is even more difficult if we are interested in associations in which the left side contains more than one item, for example A AND $C \Rightarrow B$. Now we would have to compute the support for all triples of items, A_i, B_i, and C_i. It would be still more difficult if we are interested in associations with *any* number of items on the left side.

We call such sets of items (A_i, B_i, . . .) **itemsets**. Our goal is to find all itemsets for which the support is greater than T. The plan is to first find all single items for which the support is greater than T, then use that information to find all pairs of items with support greater than T, and so on. We consider only the case of associations among two items, but the same ideas generalize to associations with more than one item on the left side

The algorithm we use, called the **a priori algorithm**, is based on the following observation, which follows from the fact that if A and B appear together in R rows, then A and B each appear in at least R rows—and perhaps even more.

> *If the support for an association* A ⇒ B *(or an itemset* A, B*) is larger than* T, *then the support for both* A *and* B *separately must be larger than* T.

Based on this observation, the a priori algorithm for pairs of items can be described as follows:

1. *Find all individual items whose support is greater than* T. This requires examining n items. The number of items with high enough support, m, is likely to be much less than n.
2. *Among these* m *items, find all distinct pairs of items whose support is greater than* T. This requires examining $m * (m-1)$ pairs of items. Assume the number of such pairs with high enough support is p.
3. *Compute the confidence factor for these* p *associations.*

If we want to find associations with more than two items, we can use the same ideas. First find single items that have support greater then T, then pairs of items, then triples, and so on.

17.9 Classification and Prediction Using Decision Trees

Classification involves finding patterns in data items that can be used to place those items in specific categories. That categorization can then be used to predict future outcomes.

For example, a bank might gather data from the application forms of past customers who applied for a mortgage and then, based on whether or not those customers later defaulted on their mortgage payments, classify those customers as *defaulters* or *nondefaulters*. When new customers apply for a mortgage, the bank might use the information on their application forms to predict whether or not they might default on their mortgage.

As a simple example, suppose the bank used only three types of information: whether or not the applicant was married, whether or not the applicant had ever defaulted on another mortgage, and the applicant's income at the time of the mortgage application. The information about the past customers would then be stored in a table such as Figure 17.16. The column labels `Married`, `PrevDefault`, and `Income` are called the *attributes* of the table, and the column label `Default` is called the *outcome*. Of course the actual table would have many more attributes and many more rows for different customers, but for the purpose of this example, we assume the table has only these three attributes and these twenty rows.

The bank's goal is to use the information in this table to classify their customers as to whether or not they are *defaulters*. One approach to performing this classification is to make a *decision tree*, such as the one in Figure 17.17.

Classification rules. A decision tree implies a number of **classification rules**. Each rule corresponds to a path from the root of the tree to one of its leaves. Two of the rules for the tree of Figure 17.17 are

```
((PrevDefault = yes) AND (Married = yes)) ⇒ (Default = no)

((PrevDefault = no) AND (Married = yes) AND (Income < 30))
          ⇒ (Default = yes)
```

You might have observed that the entries for `Income` in the table are given as numbers, but the entries for `Income` in the decision tree are for ranges. We will discuss later how we determine appropriate ranges into which to put the `Income` data.

When a table such as Figure 17.16 is used to make a decision tree, the table is called a **training set** because the data in that table is being used to "train" the system as to whether future applicants for a mortgage should be accepted.

CUSTOMER	Id	Married	PrevDefault	Income	Default
	C1	yes	no	50	no
	C2	yes	no	100	no
	C3	no	yes	135	yes
	C4	yes	no	125	no
	C5	yes	no	50	no
	C6	no	no	30	no
	C7	yes	yes	10	no
	C8	yes	no	10	yes
	C9	yes	no	75	no
	C10	yes	yes	45	no
	C11	yes	no	60	yes
	C12	no	yes	125	yes
	C13	yes	yes	20	no
	C14	no	no	15	no
	C15	no	no	60	no
	C16	yes	no	15	yes
	C17	yes	no	35	no
	C18	no	yes	160	yes
	C19	yes	no	40	no
	C20	yes	no	30	no

FIGURE 17.16 The table used to gather information about whether or not the bank's past customers defaulted on their mortgage payments. This table can be used as a training set to make a decision tree.

When a decision tree is developed based on such a table, some of the classification rules derived from the decision tree might not be consistent with the information in the table. For example, the decision tree in Figure 17.16 makes one "mistake." It predicts that

```
((PrevDefault = no) AND (Married = yes) AND (Income ≥ 30))
    ⇒ Default = no)
```

but customer C11 is not correctly classified by that rule—she defaulted. It is naive to expect that the behavior of all the bank's many customers over the past several years could be described by a simple decision tree or a small set of classification rules. The idea is to produce the best possible decision tree (and associated classification rules)

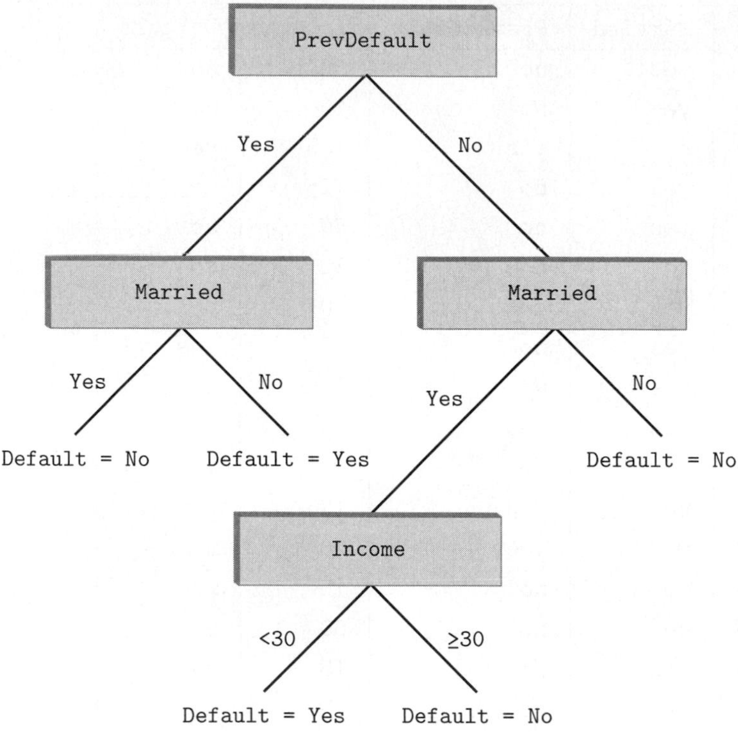

FIGURE 17.17 A decision tree for predicting defaults on a mortgage.

from the training set so that those rules can be used to predict, hopefully with a high success rate, the future behavior of new customers.

One measure of the quality of the decision tree is the percentage of errors that occur when the tree is used to make decisions using all the entries in the training set table, the so-called **training-set error**. Often, some of the historical entries in such a table are not used as part of the training set but are used as a **test set**. After the decision tree has been constructed, the data in the test set is used to test the tree. The percentage of errors using these entries is called the **test-set error**.

Sometimes the test-set error is significantly larger than the training-set error. One reason for this might be that the classification rules implied by the resulting decision tree **overfit** the training data by being tuned to some features peculiar to the particular training set that happened to be selected and not present in the general data. One approach to dealing with such overfitting is to ignore some of the data in the training set—particularly the data that provides the least information about the decision (see the discussion in the next few paragraphs). This can result in the decision tree being **pruned**, that is, all the nodes below a given node (or nodes) are removed, and the best possible decision is made at each such node, again based on the information provided by the remaining data in the training set. We discuss how such pruning might be done later in this section. As we shall see, frequently this pruning is accomplished with still another subset of the historical entries in the table, called the **validation set**, which is disjoint from both the training set and the test set.

Induction on decision trees. A number of algorithms have been developed for producing a decision tree from a training set, and many of these algorithms have been implemented in commercial systems. We discuss one of these algorithms, **ID3** (induction of decision trees) [Quinlan 1986]. The ID3 algorithm is "top down." It starts by selecting an attribute to be used at the top level of the tree to make the first decision and thus produce the second-level nodes in the tree. Each value of that attribute starts a new level of the tree, and the process repeats on each level. A key part of the algorithm is how to pick the attribute on each level that best differentiates the items in the training set.

Intuitively we want to pick the attribute that maximizes the "purity" of the selection (as the devotees of the field would say). A selection is "pure" if it contains mainly instances of one outcome, and it is "impure" if it contains many instances of items that correspond to both outcomes ("yes" and "no" in the example). The measure of purity that is used in the ID3 algorithm is **entropy**, which is defined as

$$-\sum_{i=1}^{n} p_i \log_2 p_i$$

where p_i (the probability that an item has the outcome i) is approximated by the fraction of items that have outcome i. This measure is borrowed from the field of information theory, where it is used to measure randomness or lack of information (the more random a set of data is, the less information it implies). Thus, again intuitively, we can say that we want to select the attribute that gives us the most information about the final decision.

Suppose that half of the entries in a training table have an outcome of "yes" and half have an outcome of "no." Then the entropy for the table would be

$$-(1/2 \log_2 1/2 + 1/2 \log_2 1/2) = 1$$

which is maximally random and corresponds to zero information. By contrast if all the entries have an outcome of "no," the entropy for the table would be

$$-(1 \log_2 1) = 0$$

which is maximally nonrandom and implies a maximum amount of information (that the only decision is "no").

In the table of Figure 17.16, six entries have an outcome of "yes" and fourteen have an outcome of "no," so the entropy of the table is

$$-(6/20 \log_2 6/20 + 14/20 \log_2 14/20) = .881$$

Now we begin to make the decision tree using the table in Figure 17.16 as a training set. Our initial goal is to find what attribute should be used to make the

CUSTOMER	Id	Married	Income	Default
	C3	no	135	yes
	C7	yes	10	no
	C10	yes	45	no
	C12	no	125	yes
	C13	yes	20	no
	C18	no	160	yes

FIGURE 17.18 The table used as the training set at the second level of the tree when `PrevDefault` is "yes."

decision at the top level in the tree. We investigate, one at a time, each of the attributes—`PrevDefault`, `Married`, and `Income`—to see which attribute provides the most information about the outcome.

If the topmost attribute were selected to be `PrevDefault`, the second level of the tree would consist of two nodes, one corresponding to when `PrevDefault` is "yes" and the other to when `PrevDefault` is "no." Each of these nodes would be the topmost node of a subtree of the decision tree. The training sets for these two subtrees would be the two tables: Figure 17.18 (for the subtree where `PrevDefault` is "yes") and Figure 17.19 (for the subtree where `PrevDefault` is "no"). Each of these tables is a subset of the table in Figure 17.16 consisting of those entries where `PrevDefault` has the specified value and with the column for `PrevDefault` omitted.

Now let us investigate how much information would be gained by using `PrevDefault` as the topmost attribute. We start by computing the entropy of each of the resulting subtables. When `PrevDefault` is "yes," four of the six outcomes are "yes" and two are "no," so the entropy of that subtable is

$$-(4/6\ log_2\ 4/6 + 2/6\ log_2\ 2/6) = .918$$

When `PrevDefault` is "no," two of the fourteen outcomes are "yes" and twelve are "no," so the entropy of that subtable is

$$-(2/14\ log_2\ 2/14 + 12/14\ log_2\ 12/14) = .592$$

Since the first subtable has six entries and the second has fourteen entries, the weighted average entropy of the two subtables is

$$(6/20 * .918) + (14/20 * .592) = .690$$

The measure used by the ID3 algorithm to determine which attribute to select is called the **information gain**. The algorithm compares the information gain implied by using each of the attributes and selects the attribute with the largest information gain. The information gain when using some attribute, *A*, as the topmost node in

CUSTOMER	Id	Married	Income	Default
	C1	yes	50	no
	C2	yes	100	no
	C4	yes	125	no
	C5	yes	50	no
	C6	no	30	no
	C8	yes	10	yes
	C9	yes	75	no
	C11	yes	60	yes
	C14	no	15	no
	C15	no	60	no
	C16	yes	15	yes
	C17	yes	35	no
	C19	yes	40	no
	C20	yes	30	no

FIGURE 17.19 The table used as the training set at the second level of the tree when `PrevDefault` is "no."

the tree constructed using a table, T, is the entropy of T minus the average entropy of the subtables determined by *A*:

Information gain$(A,\mathrm{T}) = entropy(\mathrm{T}) - average(entropy(\mathrm{T}_i)*weight(\mathrm{T}_i))$

The average in the computation of the information gain is taken over all subtables T_i of T that are determined by the values of the attribute *A*. The weight of each subtable is the relative contribution of the rows of that subtable to the pool of rows in T: $weight(\mathrm{T}_i) = |\mathrm{T}_i|/|\mathrm{T}|$, where $|\cdot|$ denotes the number of rows in a table. Thus the information gain for the attribute `PrevDefault` is

$$.881 - .690 = .191$$

Note that the attribute that provides the largest information gain is always the attribute whose subtables have the smallest average entropy (since for all calculations of information gain for different attributes, the average entropy corresponding to each attribute is subtracted from the same value of entropy for the complete table).

Now we compute the information gain implied by each of the other attributes. If we repeat the information gain calculation assuming the topmost attribute of the tree is Married, the information gain would be .056.[2] Clearly PrevDefault provides more information gain and would be a better choice for the topmost attribute.

Now consider the possibility of using Income as the topmost attribute. There is a complication since Income has continuous values, whereas a decision tree makes its decision based on discrete values. Therefore, to use an attribute with continuous values, we have to divide its possible values into discrete ranges. This process is called **discretization**. (Actually this approach to dealing with continuous values is not in ID3 but in its extension C4.5 [Quinlan 1986].)

If we decide to divide Income into two ranges, Income $< X$ and Income $\geq X$, we have two choices. We can just pick *some* value of X based on our intuitive knowledge of the application, or we can try *all* values for X that are mentioned in the table and compute the entropy for each to see if any of those ranges provide more information gain than PrevDefault. The second choice is usually preferable. For example, if we try $X = 50$, the information gain would be .035. In fact, it turns out that no value of X provides more information gain than does PrevDefault.

Thus, based on the information-gain measure, we decide to use PrevDefault as the toplevel attribute of the tree. We therefore label the topmost node in the tree PrevDefault and construct a branch descending from that node for each of the possible values of PrevDefault going to a node at the second level. These second-level nodes are each the topmost node of a subtree. The tables of Figures 17.18 and 17.19 are the training sets for these subtrees.

Now we repeat the entire procedure on each of these subtrees. When we use the information gain measure on each of the training tables for these subtrees to determine the attributes to be used to make the decisions at the second level, either of the following situations might (or might not) happen.

1. The attribute selected might be different for the two tables.
2. The range selected for some attributes with continuous values (such as the Income attribute in the example) might be different for the two tables (and different from that in analysis at the topmost level).

In our example, neither of these situations occur, and the attribute with the largest information gain for both second-level nodes is Married. Thus we label both of the second-level nodes Married and construct branches going to nodes at the third level of the tree. The tables to be used as the training sets for these third-level nodes are shown in Figures 17.20, 17.21, 17.22, and 17.23.

Note that in the tables shown in Figures 17.20, 17.21, and 17.23, all entries have the same outcome and therefore the tables have an entropy of 0. Thus these tables correspond to leaf nodes of the decision tree, each labelled with its unique outcome.

[2] The subtable determined by Married = yes has 11 tuples with Default = no and 3 tuples with Default = yes. Therefore, this table's entropy is 0.7496. The subtable determined by Married = no has 3 tuples with Default = no and 3 tuples with Default = yes. Its entropy is therefore 1. The average weighted by the relative number of tuples in these tables ($14/20 = 0.7$ and $6/20 = 0.3$) is thus $0.7 * 0.7496 + 0.3 * 1 = 0.8247$. Therefore, the information gain is $.881 - .8247 = .0563$.

CUSTOMER	Id	Income	Default
	C7	10	no
	C10	45	no
	C13	20	no

FIGURE 17.20 The table used as the training set at the third level of the tree when `PrevDefault` is "yes" and `Married` is "yes."

CUSTOMER	Id	Income	Default
	C3	135	yes
	C12	125	yes
	C18	160	yes

FIGURE 17.21 The table used as the training set at the third level of the tree when `PrevDefault` is "yes" and `Married` is "no."

CUSTOMER	Id	Income	Default
	C1	50	no
	C2	100	no
	C4	125	no
	C5	50	no
	C8	10	yes
	C9	75	no
	C11	60	yes
	C16	15	yes
	C17	35	no
	C19	40	no
	C20	30	no

FIGURE 17.22 The table used as the training set at the third level of the tree when `PrevDefault` is "no" and `Married` is "yes."

We then repeat the procedure on the remaining table, Figure 17.22. The only remaining attribute is `Income`. When we investigate all the possible ranges for `Income`, we find that the maximum information (minimum entropy) is obtained when X is 30. For that value of X, the average entropy is .412. Thus we decide

CUSTOMER	Id	Income	Default
	C6	30	no
	C14	15	no
	C15	60	no

FIGURE 17.23 The table used as the training set at the third level of the tree when `PrevDefault` is "no" and `Married` is "no."

CUSTOMER	Id	Default
	C8	yes
	C16	yes

FIGURE 17.24 The table used as the training set at the fourth level of the tree when `PrevDefault` is "no" and `Married` is "yes" and `Income` is less than 30.

CUSTOMER	Id	Default
	C1	no
	C2	no
	C4	no
	C5	no
	C9	no
	C11	yes
	C17	no
	C19	no
	C20	no

FIGURE 17.25 The table used as the training set at the fourth level of the tree when PrevDefault is "no" and `Married` is "yes" and `Income` is greater than or equal to 30.

to use the ranges, `Income` $<$ 30 and `Income` $\geq$ 30, and obtain the tables shown in Figures 17.24 and 17.25.

The table shown in Figure 17.24 has an entropy of 0 and corresponds to a leaf node labelled with outcome "yes."

However, the table shown in Figure 17.25 does not have an entropy of 0 because all the outcomes are not the same. However, we have run out of attributes and cannot continue the procedure. Thus we say that this table corresponds to a leaf with outcome "no" (because "no" is the most frequently occurring outcome in this table). We have to settle for the fact that this leaf does not make the correct decision for customer C11. That completes the design of the decision tree.

Summary of the ID3 algorithm. The ID3 procedure can be described recursively as follows. Given a table, T, to be used as a training set to construct a decision tree *d*:

1. If T has entropy equal to 0, construct *d* with only a single node, which is a leaf node labelled with the (only) outcome in T.
2. If T has no attributes, construct *d* with only a single node, which is a leaf node labelled with the most frequently occurring outcome in T.
3. Otherwise
   (a) Find the attribute, *A*, in T that provides the maximum information gain. Specifically, find the attribute, *A*, that divides T into *n* subtables, $T_1, T_2, \ldots, T_n$ (assuming that *A* has *n* possible values, $v_1, \ldots, v_n$), such that the information gain is the largest of all the information gains obtained from all the other attributes in T. Each subtable T_i is $\sigma_{a=v_i}(T)$ with the column corresponding to the attribute *A* projected out.
   (b) Label the topmost node in *d* with the name *A*.
   (c) Construct *n* branches descending from that node, where each branch corresponds to one of the *n* values of *A* and is labelled with that value.
   (d) At the end of each branch, for example, the branch corresponding to the value v_i of *A*, start a subtree, d_i, and use T_i as its training set.
   (e) Repeat this procedure on each of the subtrees, $d_1, \ldots, d_n$, starting at step 1.

Brain Teaser: The algorithm ID3 is guaranteed to terminate. Why?

If we are concerned about possible overfitting of the data and want to consider the possibility of pruning the decision tree, one approach is to use the validation set, which (as you might recall) is a subset of the historical data that is disjoint from both the training set and the test set. We first construct the complete decision tree using the training set and compute the training-set error. Then we test the tree with the validation set. If the validation-set error is significantly greater than the training-set error, we can assume that some overfitting has taken place. We then make a series of pruned versions of the tree by deleting each of the leaf nodes. We apply the validation set to each of these pruned versions. If we find that the validation set error has been decreased, we assume that some overfitting has taken place. We then continue the pruning process until the new pruned versions do not have less validation-set error. When we are done, we apply the test set to the final version to compute the test-set error.

The information-gain measure is not the only measure than can be used to produce a decision tree from a training set. Two other measures that have been proposed and used in commercial products are

- **Gain ratio** [Quinlan 1986]. The **gain ratio** is defined as follows:

$$Gain\ Ratio = (Information\ Gain)/SplitInfo$$

where information gain is as defined earlier and

$$SplitInfo = -\sum_{i=1}^{n} |T_i| / |T| \ log_2(|T_i| / |T|)$$

where | T | is the number of entries in the table being decomposed by the attribute and $|T_i|$ is the number of entries in the ith table produced by the decomposition. The idea is to normalize the information-gain measure to compensate for the fact that it favors attributes that have a large number of values.

Since the information gain obtained when using `PrevDefault` is .191, and since there are six entries in the table of Figure 17.18 and fourteen entries in the table of Figure 17.19, the gain ratio for the `PrevDefault` attribute is

$$Gain\ Ratio = .191/(6/20\ log_2(6/20) + 14/20\ log_2(14/20)) = .217$$

- **Gini index** [Breiman et al. 1984]. The **Gini index** is defined as

$$Gini = 1 - \sum_{i=1}^{k} p_i^2$$

where p_i is the probability that a tuple in the training set table has outcome i. Thus, if all of the entries in the training table had outcome "no," the Gini index would be 0, and if half of the entries had outcome "yes" and half had outcome "no," the Gini index would be 1/2.

Since the number of "yes" outcomes in the table of Figure 17.16 is six and the number of "no" outcomes is fourteen, the Gini index of that table is

$$Gini = 1 - ((6/20)^2 + (14/20)^2)) = .42$$

Each measure has its advocates and its share of successes in specific applications.

OPTIONAL

17.10 Classification and Prediction Using Neural Nets

One might say that the decision tree algorithm just discussed is a learning algorithm that *learns* how to make predictions based on the data in its training set. The field of machine learning, which is a subfield of artificial intelligence, provides a number of other techniques that are useful in classification and prediction. Suppose that the mortgage lender wants to determine which applicants are likely to default on their mortgage but believes that the classification depends on a larger number of factors than in the previous example and that these factors should be weighted differently.

To see how a bank might use weights in making a decision, assume it wants to consider only two factors: `PrevDefault` and `Married`. Then it might associate a weight w_1 with the predicate `PrevDefault` = `yes` and a weight w_2 with the predicate `Married` = `yes`. The bank might then evaluate the expression

$$w_1 * x_1 + w_2 * x_2$$

where x_1 has value 1 if `PrevDefault` = `yes` is true and 0 otherwise; x_2 is defined similarly using the predicate `Married` = `yes`. A customer is considered a bad risk if the value of that expression exceeds some threshold, t, that is, if

$$w_1 * x_1 + w_2 * x_2 \geq t.$$

If $w_1 * x_1 + w_2 * x_2 < t$, the customer is considered a good risk. In practice, the lender might want to include a number of other possible factors in this computation. The question is, how should the weights and the threshold be determined?

A technique called **neural nets** allows the lender to use the information in a training set derived from an OLAP database about past customers to "learn" a set of weights that would have predicted their behavior and thus will (hopefully) predict the behavior of new customers. By "learning" we mean that the system uses examples of the characteristics of past customers who did or did not default on their loans to incrementally adjust the weights to give a better prediction of whether or not customers will default.

The above inequality can be viewed as modeling the behavior of a primitive **neuron** (or nerve cell). In general, a neuron can have any number of inputs, $x_1, \ldots, x_n$, and each input has a weight, w_i. The neuron is said to be **activated** if the weighted sum of its inputs, $\Sigma_{i=1}^{n} w_i * x_i$, exceeds or equals some threshold, t, which can be specific to that particular neuron. When a neuron is activated, it **emits** the value 1; otherwise it is said to emit the value 0.

Our discussion of neurons can be simplified if we introduce w_0 so that $w_0 = t$ and rewrite the equation

$$\sum_{i=1}^{n} w_i * x_1 \geq t$$

as

$$\sum_{i=1}^{n} w_i * x_i - w_0 * 1 \geq 0$$

(We can assume there is a new input x_0, which always has a value of -1.) The expression $\sum_{i-1}^{n} w_i * x_i - w_0 * 1$ is sometimes called the **normalized weighted input**. The **activation function** of the neuron is a monotonic function that takes the normalized weighted input, X, and returns a real number, $f(X)$, such that $0 \leq f(X) \leq 1$.

A typical activation function (and the one used above) is a **step function** where $f(X) = 0$, if $X < 0$, and $f(X) = 1$, if $X \geq 0$. The step activation function tells us when the neuron is "active" (emits 1) or "inactive" (emits 0). In general, however, the activation function can be continuous, such as the *sigmoid* function depicted in Figure 17.27, which will be discussed shortly. In such a case the neuron can emit

OPTIONAL

any real number between 0 and 1, and the activation function indicates the "degree of activation" of the neuron.

The perceptron learning algorithm. Based on this notation, we can define a learning algorithm for a single neuron that has the step function activation. This algorithm is sometimes called the **perceptron learning algorithm** because the authors of that algorithm referred to such neuron models as perceptrons.

1. Initially set the values of all the weights and the threshold to some small random number.
2. Apply the inputs corresponding to each item in the training set one at a time to the neuron model. For each input, compute the output of the neuron.
3. If the desired output of the neuron for that input is d and the actual output is y, change each weight, w_i, by Δw_i where

$$\Delta w_i = \eta * x_i * (d - y)$$

   (assuming $x_0 = -1$) where η is some small positive number called the **learning rate**. Note that if for this input, the neuron does not make an error (the desired output equals the actual output), no weights are changed. If the neuron emits a value higher than d, then the weight w_i is decreased in order to try to lower the emitted value (observe that the activation function is monotonically growing). If the emitted value is less than d, then w_i is increased in order to raise the emitted value.
4. Continue the training until some termination condition is met. For example, the data in the training set has been used some fixed number of times, the number of errors has stopped decreasing significantly, the weights have stopped changing significantly, or the number of errors reaches some predetermined level.

If the neuron has n inputs, each of which can be 1 or 0, then there are 2^n possible combinations of these inputs. If we assume that the training set includes each of these 2^n combinations of inputs, the perceptron learning algorithm has the property that if the decision can *always* be correctly made by a single neuron, the values of the weights and threshold will converge to correct values after only a bounded number of weight adjustments [Novikoff 1962].

Neural networks: the sigmoid function. In practice the perceptron learning algorithm is not very useful because for most applications the required decisions cannot be made (even approximately) by a single neuron. Therefore, a network of neurons, such as the one depicted in Figure 17.26, is used.

The network shown has three layers: the input layer, the middle or hidden layer, and the output layer. The input layer does not consist of neurons that can adjust their weights. It just gathers the inputs and presents them to the neurons in the middle layer. The neurons in the middle layer make some intermediate decisions and then send those decisions to the neurons in the output layer, which makes the final decisions.

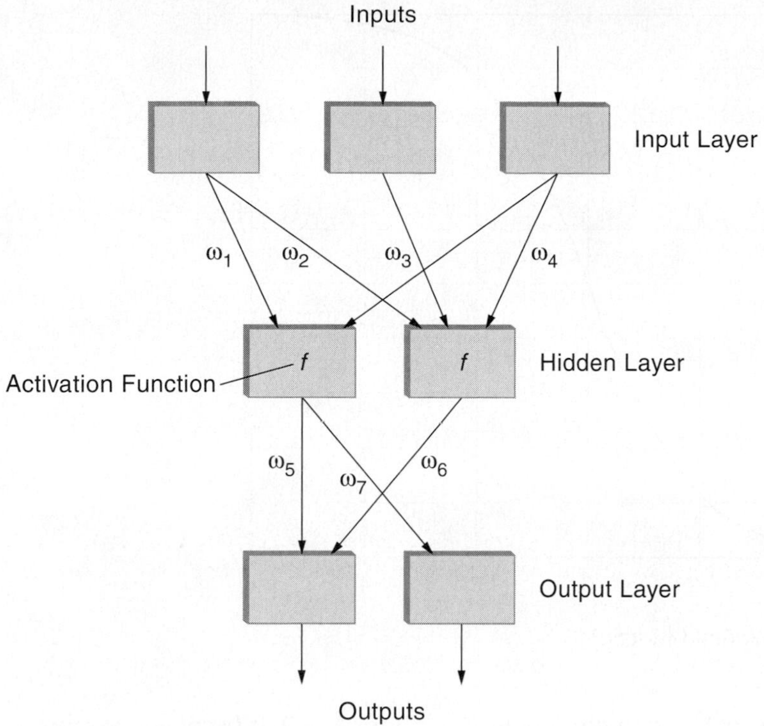

FIGURE 17.26 A neural net.

Learning algorithms for such neural networks are more complex than those for a single neuron because it is not immediately apparent how to adjust the weights of the neurons in the middle layer when one or more of the neurons in the output layer gives an output different than its desired output. More specifically it is not apparent how each such weight in the middle layer affects the output of the network. A mathematical analysis of this situation is difficult because such an analysis usually requires taking derivatives of the activation function, and the step function that we used so far is discontinuous and does not have a derivative. For this reason, neural networks usually use differentiable activation functions.

A commonly used activation function is the **sigmoid function**, shown in Figure 17.27, which is defined as

$$1/(1+e^{-X})$$

where X denotes the normalized weighted input to the neuron:

$$X = \sum_{i=1}^{n} w_i * x_i - w_0 * 1$$

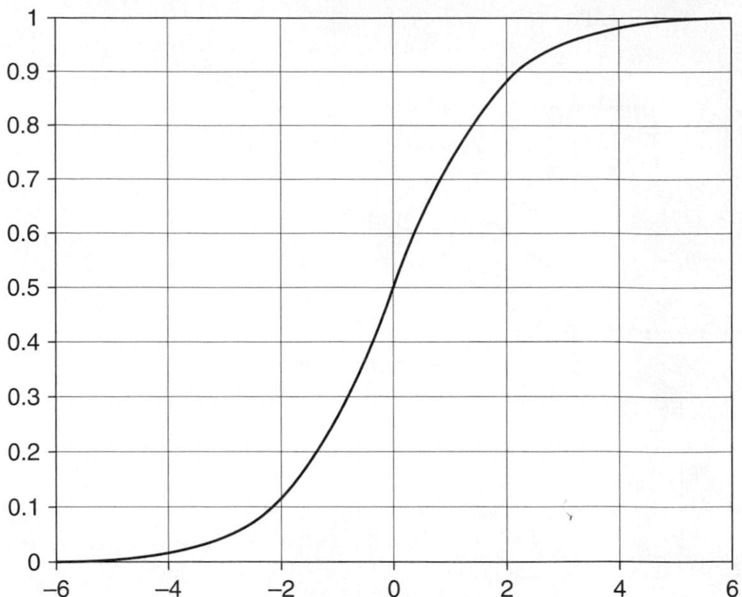

FIGURE 17.27 The sigmoid function.

Note that the value of the sigmoid function is 1/2 for $X = 0$. It becomes asymptotic to 1 for large positive values of X and asymptotic to 0 for large negative values of X. Thus it is a continuous (and differentiable) approximation of the step activation function.

The sigmoid function has an interesting property that we will use later: if the output of the neuron is denoted as y, so that

$$y = 1/(1 + e^{-X})$$

then the partial derivative of y with respect to X is

$$\frac{\partial y}{\partial X} = e^{-X}/(1 + e^{-X})^2 = (1/(1 + e^{-X})) * (1 - (1/(1 + e^{-X}))) = y * (1 - y)$$

and then if we use the definition of X given above, the partial derivative of y with respect to any particular weight, w_i, is

$$\frac{\partial y}{\partial w_i} = \frac{\partial y}{\partial X} * \frac{\partial X}{\partial w_i} = y * (1 - y) * x_i \qquad \textbf{17.6}$$

Using this result, we can now derive the learning procedure for a single neuron that uses the sigmoid activation function. Assume that for some input in the training set, the output of the neuron is y and the desired output is d. The error is then $(d - y)$, and the squared error is $(d - y)^2$. (We could also consider the mean squared error for all the inputs, but now we are just considering a single input.) Consider the squared error as an n-dimensional function of the weights $w_1, \ldots, w_n$. The plan is to take the partial derivative of that function with respect to each of the weights. We will then adjust each weight by some small fraction, η, of the negative of that partial derivative. This is called the **gradient descent** approach to finding the minimum of that function. Thus we change the weight of w_i to $w_i + \Delta w_i$ where

$$\Delta w_i = -\eta \frac{\partial (d-y)^2}{\partial w_i}$$

To see why gradient descent is a good heuristic for finding a local minimum of a function, we need to observe two things:

1. If we change w_i to $w_i + \Delta w_i$, we are moving towards a local minimum of the function $(d-y)^2$. Indeed, if this function is increasing at this value of w_i, the above derivative is positive and so we need to decrease w_i to approach the local minimum. In this case $\Delta w_i < 0$ and $w_i + \Delta w_i$ is an adjustment in the right direction. If the derivative is negative, it means that the function is decreasing, so we need to increase w_i in order to approach the local minimum. In this case $\Delta w_i > 0$ and, again, $w_i + \Delta w_i$ is an adjustment in the right direction. We can imagine that, as we change the weights, we are sliding down a hill.
2. As w_i approaches the local minimum, the value of the derivative decreases to zero and therefore the adjustment step, Δw_i, becomes smaller and smaller. In this way, we avoid overshooting the local minimum by large amounts and the process eventually converges.

The derivative of the square of the error with respect to w_i is

$$\frac{\partial (d-y)^2}{\partial w_i} = -2 * (d-y) * \frac{\partial y}{\partial w_i} = -2 * (d-y) * y * (1-y) * x_i$$

Thus, to adjust the weights and decrease the error, the learning algorithm needs to change w_i by some fraction of the negative of that derivative.

$$\Delta w_i = \eta * x_i * y * (1-y) * (d-y) \qquad \textbf{17.7}$$

(Note that we have incorporated the constant 2 that appears in the derivative into the learning rate η. Note also that we have changed the order of the multipliers to what is common in the literature.)

The back-propagation learning algorithms for neural networks. Next we present a learning algorithm for networks of neurons, each described by the sigmoid activation function. Specifically we discuss one of the most popular learning algorithms for such neural networks: the **back-propagation algorithm**. We present the algorithm for three-layer networks, such as that in Figure 17.26, but this algorithm can be adapted for networks with any number of layers.

It is called the back-propagation algorithm because, for each input in the training set, the algorithm first goes forward to compute the output of each neuron in

OPTIONAL

the output layer. Then it goes backward to adjust the weights in each layer one at a time. It initially adjusts the weights of the neurons in the output layer, and then it uses the result of that adjustment to adjust the weights of the neurons in the middle layer (and, if there are more layers, it goes further backward to adjust the weights in those layers one at a time).

1. Initially set the values of all the weights and thresholds of all the neurons in the network to some small random number.
2. Apply the inputs corresponding to each item in the training set one at a time to the network. For each input, compute the output of each neuron in the output layer.
3. Adjust the value of the weights in each neuron in the output layer. Consider one such neuron, v_{out}, and assume it emits y^{out} (for the given input) while the desired output is d^{out}. We can use the same reasoning for v_{out} as we did for the case of a single neuron earlier. Thus we can apply the equation (17.7) to v_{out} and adjust each weight, w_i^{out}, associated with input x_i^{out}, according to the formula

$$\Delta w_i^{out} = \eta * x_i^{out} * y^{out} * (1 - y^{out}) * (d^{out} - y^{out})$$

For reasons that will become clear in the next step, it is convenient to rewrite this formula as

$$\Delta w_i^{out} = \eta * x_i^{out} * \delta^{out}$$

where

$$\delta^{out} = y^{out} * (1 - y^{out}) * (d^{out} - y^{out}) \qquad \textbf{17.8}$$

4. Adjust the value of the weights in each middle-layer neuron. Consider one such neuron—let us denote it v_{mid}. Assume its output for the given input is y^{mid}. A problem is that we do not know what is the *desired* output of v_{mid}. However we do know the desired outputs of the output-layer neurons to which v_{mid} is connected. We are interested in determining how the input weights in the middle-layer neuron v_{mid} affect the output of the outer-layer neurons. As a simple example, suppose our middle-layer neuron is connected to only one output-layer neuron, such as v_{out} above, and the weight of that connection is $w^{mid/out}$. Suppose that for the given training set input, the output neuron v_{out} emits y^{out} while its desired output is d^{out}. Using the same reasoning as before, for each input weight w_i^{mid} of the middle-layer neuron v_{mid} with input x_i^{mid}, we want to adjust w_i^{mid} by some fraction of the negative of the derivative of $(d^{out} - y^{out})^2$ with respect to w_i^{mid}

$$\Delta w_i^{mid} = -\eta * \frac{\partial (d^{out} - y^{out})^2}{\partial w_i^{mid}}$$

OPTIONAL

Then we note that

$$\frac{\partial(d^{out}-y^{out})^2}{\partial w_i^{mid}} = \frac{\partial(d^{out}-y^{out})^2}{\partial X^{out}} * \frac{\partial X^{out}}{\partial w_i^{mid}}$$

where X^{out} is the X of the output-layer neuron. As before

$$\frac{\partial(d^{out}-y^{out})^2}{\partial X^{out}} = -2 * (d^{out}-y^{out}) * y^{out} * (1-y^{out})$$

Then we observe that the inputs x_k^{out} of the output neuron v_{out} are the outputs of the middle-layer neurons connected to v_{out}. Therefore, we have

$$X^{out} = \sum_k w_k^{mid/out} * y_k^{mid}$$

where the y_k^{mid} are the outputs of all the middle-layer neurons connected to v_{out}, and the $w_k^{mid/out}$ are the corresponding weights of the connection. Note that since v_{mid} is connected to v_{out}, $w^{mid/out}$ is one of these $w_k^{mid/out}$ and y^{mid} is one of these y_k^{mid}. Returning to our derivatives, we can see that $\frac{\partial y_k^{mid}}{\partial w_i^{mid}} \neq 0$ only when y_k^{mid} is y^{mid}, since w_i^{mid} in an input weight to v_{mid} and thus it affects v_{mid}'s output only. We also know from (17.6) that $\frac{\partial y^{mid}}{\partial w_i^{mid}} = x_i^{mid} * y^{mid} * (1-y^{mid})$. Therefore we can then write

$$\frac{\partial X^{out}}{\partial w_i^{mid}} = w^{mid/out} * \frac{\partial y^{mid}}{\partial w_i^{mid}} = w^{mid/out} * x_i^{mid} * y^{mid} * (1-y^{mid})$$

Putting all this together we get

$$\frac{\partial(d^{out}-y^{out})^2}{\partial w_i^{mid}} =$$

$$-2 * (d^{out}-y^{out}) * y^{out} * (1-y^{out}) * w^{mid/out} * x_i^{mid} * y^{mid} * (1-y^{mid})$$

Therefore, we can use the following learning rule for our middle-layer neuron v_{mid} connected to the single output-layer neuron v_{out}. For each weight w_i^{mid} of v_{mid} associated with input x_i^{mid}, adjust that weight using the formula

$$\Delta w_i^{mid} = \eta * x_i^{mid} * \delta^{mid}$$

where δ^{mid} is defined as

$$\delta^{mid} = y^{mid} * (1-y^{mid}) * w^{mid/out} * y^{out} * (1-y^{out}) * (d^{out}-y^{out})$$

OPTIONAL

The formula for δ^{mid} can be rewritten as

$$\delta^{mid} = y^{mid} * (1 - y^{mid}) * w^{mid/out} * \delta^{out}$$

where δ^{out} was previously computed for the output neuron ν_{out} in (17.8). Therefore, δ^{mid} can be computed from δ^{out}, whence the name back propagation.

If the ν_{mid} is connected to several output-layer neurons, we can use the same reasoning based on the negative of the derivative of the sum of the squares of the errors of all the output-layer neurons to which ν_{mid} is connected:

$$\Delta w_i^{mid} = -\eta * \frac{\partial \sum_j (d_j^{out} - y_j^{out})^2}{\partial w_i^{mid}}$$

Here y_j^{out} and d_j^{out} are, respectively, the outputs and the desired outputs of all the output-layer neurons that receive input from ν_{mid}. The computations are a bit more complex, but the result is that the formula for Δw_i^{mid} is the same as when ν_{mid} is connected to a single output-layer neuron except that the formula for δ^{mid} involves the weighted sum of the δ^{out}s of all the output-layer neurons in question:

$$\Delta w_i^{mid} = \eta * x_i^{mid} * \delta^{mid}$$

where

$$\delta^{mid} = y^{mid} * (1 - y^{mid}) * \sum_j (w_j^{wid/out} * \delta_j^{out})$$

5. Continue the training until some termination condition is met. For example, the data in the training set has been used some fixed number of times, the number of errors has stopped decreasing significantly, the weights have stopped changing significantly, or the number of errors reaches some predetermined level.

OPTIONAL

17.11 Clustering

Suppose we examine the addresses of all the people in the United States who have a certain form of lung cancer. We might find that many of those addresses are clustered in a few areas that are near certain chemical plants. We might then conclude that those chemical plants are somehow involved in causing that cancer.

In a more general situation, suppose we are given a set of data items, each with certain attributes, and a similarity measure based on those attributes. In the above example, the items contain information about cancer patients, the attribute is `Address`, and the similarity measure is *nearness* (as measured by Euclidean distance). **Clustering** involves placing those data items into *clusters* such that the items in each cluster are similar to each other and the items in different clusters are less similar. The clusters are usually disjoint. Thus in the example, we are finding clusters of cancer patients who are similar in that they live near each other.

Note that clustering is different than the classification rules and decision trees that we discussed earlier because in those cases the categories into which the data items are to be classified are known in advance. In clustering, the categories are determined by the clustering algorithm.

An important issue in clustering is the similarity measure that is used. When the attributes are numeric, a similarity measure based on Euclidean distance is often used. Thus if two cancer patients have addresses that can be represented using location coordinates as x_1, y_1 and x_2, y_2, the Euclidean distance between them is $\sqrt{(x_1 - x_2)^2 + (y_1 - y_2)^2}$. If the attributes are not numeric, an analyst must develop an appropriate similarity measure. Sometimes this involves converting a nonnumeric attribute into a numeric attribute.

The K-means algorithm. Many algorithms have been proposed for clustering. We first present one of the most popular, the **K-means** algorithm. The inputs to the algorithm are: the dataset of items to be clustered, the desired number of clusters *k*, and the similarity measure. The algorithms proceeds as follows:

1. Select *k* of the items at random as the centers of the (initial versions) of the *k* clusters.
2. Put each item in the dataset into the cluster for which that item is closest to the center, based on the similarity measure. (Initially, when the cluster has only one item, the center is the location of that member.)
3. Recalculate the center of each cluster as the mean of the locations (similarity measures) of all the items in that cluster.
4. Repeat the procedure starting at step 2 until there is no change in the membership in all clusters.

> *Brain Teaser:* The K-means algorithm is guaranteed to eventually terminate. Why?

The final version of the clusters produced by the K-means algorithm is not necessarily unique—there can be several states where equilibrium is achieved. Hence the final version of the clusters might depend on the initial selection of the items in step 1.

As a simple example, consider the table of students' ages and GPAs shown in Figure 17.28. Suppose we are interested in investigating whether older students do better or worse in college than younger ones. As a part of that investigation, we want to cluster these items by age and then see the average GPA in each cluster. Note that the similarity measure (age) is just one-dimensional, so the calculation of distances is particularly easy.

Suppose we want to place the students into two clusters: cluster 1 (younger students) and cluster 2 (older students), so we set *k* equal to 2. Then suppose in step 1 of the algorithm, we randomly select students `S_1` and `S_4` as the centers of our initial clusters. Thus the (initial) centers are at ages 17 and 20.

STUDENT	Id	Age	GPA
	S_1	17	3.9
	S_2	17	3.5
	S_3	18	3.1
	S_4	20	3.0
	S_5	23	3.5
	S_6	26	3.6

FIGURE 17.28 Table of student ages and GPAs for clustering example.

Then we examine each student row and place it in one of the clusters. For example, student S_2 is at a distance of 0 from cluster 1 and at a distance of 3 from cluster 2, so it is placed in cluster 1. On the other hand, student S_5 is at a distance of 6 from cluster 1 and at a distance of 3 from cluster 2, so it is placed in cluster 2. Thus the initial version of the clusters is

Cluster 1: S_1, S_2, S_3
Cluster 2: S_4, S_5, S_6

The new centers of these clusters are

Cluster 1: $(17 + 17 + 18)/3 = 17.333$
Cluster 2: $(20 + 23 + 26)/3 = 23.0$

Then we recompute in which cluster each student is to be placed. The only interesting computation is for student S_4, who is at a distance of 2.677 from the center of cluster 1 and a distance of 3 from the center of cluster 2 and so is placed in cluster 1 (perhaps counter-intuitively since this student was chosen as the initial center of cluster 2). The other students remain in their original clusters. Thus the second version of the clusters is

Cluster 1: S_1, S_2, S_3, S_4
Cluster 2: S_5, S_6

If we now repeat step 2 of the algorithm, the clusters remain the same, and so the algorithm has completed. The average GPA of the students in each cluster is then:

Cluster 1 (younger students): $(3.9 + 3.5 + 3.1 + 3.0)/4 = 3.375$
Cluster 2 (older students): $(3.5 + 3.6)/2 = 3.55$

Whether or not that is a significant difference is a subject for further analysis.

Since the final value of the clusters might depend on the initial selection of items in step 1, some authors suggest that the algorithm be repeated with different initial selections or that a nonrandom selection be made of items that are far apart. Other authors suggest that a better set of final clusters is often obtained if, in step 2, the items are moved one at a time and the cluster centers are recalculated after each move.

In some applications, it might not be obvious what value to use for k. One approach is to try different values of k and calculate the average distance to the center of each cluster as k increases. Usually the average decreases rapidly until the "correct" value of k has been reached and then decreases more slowly.

The hierarchical algorithm. Another algorithm for clustering, in which the value of k need not be selected in advance, is the **hierarchical** algorithm (sometimes called the **agglomerative** hierarchical algorithm). The algorithm proceeds as follows:

1. Start with each item in the dataset as a separate cluster.
2. Select two clusters to merge into a single cluster. The goal is to pick the two clusters that are "closest." Various measures have been proposed for closeness. One measure, and the one we will use, is that the distance between clusters is the distance between their centers. The center of a cluster is the mean (the numeric average) of the locations of all the items in the cluster. We therefore merge the two clusters for which the centers are closest. (Another measure is that the distance between groups is the distance between the "nearest neighbors," the closest two items in each group.)
3. Repeat step 2 until some termination condition is reached. One condition is that some predetermined number of k clusters has been obtained. Another condition might be to continue as long as the average distance to the center of each cluster is decreasing rapidly and terminate when it begins to decrease more slowly. Still another, as we shall see below, is to continue until there is only one cluster and then analyze the result to select an appropriate set of clusters.

One way to implement this algorithm is with a matrix of all the pairwise distances between the clusters. Initially, the matrix contains the pairwise distances between the individual items in the data set. The matrix is then used in step 2 to determine which clusters to merge. After this determination is made, the matrix is updated by inactivating (or deleting) one of the clusters being merged and updating the information about the other cluster (now representing the new cluster) with the distances between that cluster and the other clusters. If there are n items in the dataset, this implementation requires $O(n^2)$ space and $O(n^3)$ time.

If we use this algorithm on the items in the table of Figure 17.28, we would get the following sequence of clusters. Here we denote each cluster by its age attribute and separate different clusters with space.

17 17 18 20 23 26

17, 17 18 20 23 26

17, 17, 18 20 23 26

17, 17, 18, 20 23 26

17, 17, 18, 20 23, 26

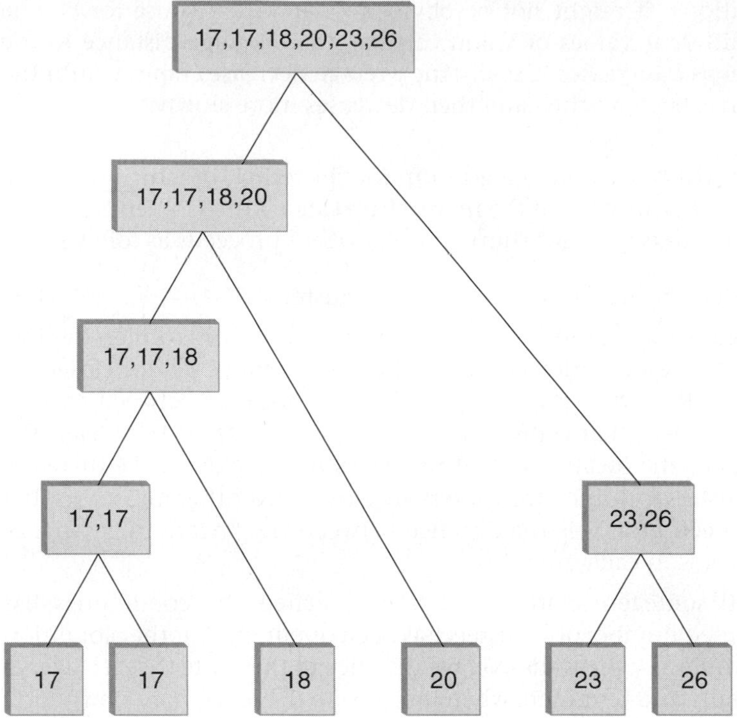

FIGURE 17.29 A dendrogram corresponding to the example of the hierarchical clustering algorithm.

The first row depicts clusters where each item is in a cluster of its own. In the last row we have only two clusters. If we stop at this point, the final set of clusters is the same as with the K-means algorithm. If we continue one more step, we would reduce the set of clusters to a single cluster

17, 17, 18, 20, 23, 26

One way to analyze the results of the hierarchical clustering algorithm is with a tree, usually called a **dendrogram**, that represents the progress of the algorithm, assuming it continues until there is only one cluster. The dendrogram for the above example is shown in Figure 17.29. The cluster generated by each step in the algorithm is denoted by a node in the tree.

Any set of nodes whose children include all the leaves in the tree exactly once represents a possible set of clusters. For example the three nodes denoted as

17, 17, 18   20   23, 26

is a set of clusters that did not appear at any time in the hierarchical algorithm but might be appropriate for certain applications.

The analyst can then analyze such a dendrogram in the light of her knowledge of the application and select a set of clusters that is appropriate for that application.

BIBLIOGRAPHIC NOTES

The term "OLAP" was coined by Codd in [Codd 1995]. A good survey of OLAP appears in [Chaudhuri and Dayal 1997]. A collection of articles on applications and current research in data mining can be found in [Fayyad et al. 1996]. The CUBE operator was introduced in [Gray et al. 1997]. Efficient computation of data cubes is discussed in [Agrawal et al. 1996; Harinarayan et al. 1996; Ross and Srivastava 1997; Zhao et al. 1998]. The idea of mining for association rules and some early algorithms was first introduced in [Agrawal et al. 1993]. The ID3 algorithm for decision trees, including both the information gain and gain ratio measures, was introduced in [Quinlan 1986]. The Gini index was introduced in [Breiman et al. 1984]. A textbook-style coverage of data mining can be found in [Han and Kamber 2001] and [Hand et al. 2001].

EXERCISES

17.1 Is a typical fact table in BCNF? Explain.

17.2 Explain why, in an E-R model of a star schema, the fact table is a relationship and the dimension tables are entities.

17.3 Design another fact table and related dimension tables that a supermarket might want to use for an OLAP application.

17.4 Explain why it is not appropriate to model the database for the Student Registration System as a star schema.

17.5 Design SQL queries for the supermarket example that will return the information needed to make a table similar to that of Figure 17.10, except that markets are aggregated by state, and time is aggregated by months.

a. Use CUBE or ROLLUP operators.
b. Do not use CUBE or ROLLUP operators.
c. Compute the result table.

17.6 a. Design a query for the supermarket example that will return the total sales (over time) for each supermarket.
b. Compute the result table.

17.7 Suppose that an application has four dimension tables, each of which contains 100 rows.

a. Determine the maximum number of rows in the fact table.
b. Suppose that a one-dimension table has an attribute that can take on 10 values. Determine the size in bytes of a bit index on that attribute.

c. Determine the maximum number of tuples in a join index for a join between one of the dimension tables and the fact table.
d. Suppose that we use the CUBE operator on this fact table to perform aggregations on all four dimensions. Determine the number of rows in the resulting table.
e. Suppose that we use the ROLLUP operator on this fact table. Determine the number of rows in the resulting table.

17.8 Design a query evaluation algorithm for the ROLLUP operator. The objective of such an algorithm should be that the results of the previously computed aggregations are *reused* in subsequent aggregations and *not* recomputed from scratch.

17.9 Design a query evaluation algorithm for the CUBE operator that uses the results of the previously computed aggregations to compute new aggregations. (*Hint*: Organize the GROUP BY clauses used in the computation of a data cube into a lattice, that is, a partial order with the least upper bound and the greatest lower bound for each pair of elements. Here is an example of such a partial order: GROUP BY A > GROUP BY A,B > GROUP BY A,B,C and GROUP BY B > GROUP BY B,C > GROUP BY A,B,C. Describe how aggregates computed for the lower parts of the lattice can be used in the computation of the upper parts.)

17.10 Suppose that the fact table of Figure 17.1 has been cubed and the result has been stored as a view, SALES_V1. Design queries against SALES_V1 that will return the tables of Figure 17.10 and Figure 17.7.

17.11 We are interested in building an OLAP application with which we can analyze the grading at our university, where grades are represented as integers from 0 to 4 (4 representing an A). We want to ask questions about average grades for different courses, professors, and departments during different semesters and years. Design a star schema for this application.

17.12 Discuss the difference in storage requirements for a data cube implemented as a multidimensional array and a fact table.

17.13 Give examples, different from those in the text, of syntactic and semantic transformations that might have to be made while loading data into a data warehouse.

17.14 Perform the a priori algorithm on the table of Figure 17.15 to determine all reasonable two-item associations.

17.15 Show that, when evaluating possible associations, the confidence is always larger than the support.

17.16 Apply the gain ratio measure to the table in Figure 17.16 to design a decision tree.

17.17 Apply the Gini measure to the table in Figure 17.16 to design a decision tree.

17.18 Show how the K-mean clustering algorithm would have worked on the table of Figure 17.28 if the original choice for cluster centers had been 17 and 18.

17.19 a. Give an example of a set of three items on a straight line for which the K-mean algorithm, with $k = 2$, would give a different answer for the two clusters depending on the choice of items for the initial clusters.

b. Which of these final clusters would have been obtained by the hierarchical algorithm?

17.20 Suppose the table of Figure 17.16 is stored in a relational database. Use SQL to compute the probabilities needed to compute the information gain when using the `PrevDefault` attribute as the topmost attribute of a decision tree based on that table.

PART FIVE

Transaction Processing

Now we are ready to begin our study of transaction processing.

In Chapter 18 we give a detailed description of the ACID properties of transactions and how transactions differ from ordinary programs.

In Chapter 19 we describe a variety of transaction models. A transaction need not be simply a program wrapped in the ACID properties. It can provide additional features or, alternatively, compromise on the properties in different ways. A workflow represents the ultimate compromise and is discussed in this chapter.

Chapter 20 discusses isolation in general terms and the theory on which it rests. However, for performance reasons, isolation need not be absolute in a relational database. Instead, several degrees of isolation, referred to as isolation levels, are generally offered. While this provides needed flexibility, it adds significantly to the complexity of the design. Chapter 21 discusses this issue at length.

Chapter 22 discusses the implementation of atomicity and durability in situations in which a transaction aborts, the system crashes, or the media on which the database is stored fails.

18

ACID Properties of Transactions

A transaction is a very special kind of program. It executes within an application in which a database models the state of some real-world enterprise. For example, if the enterprise is a bank, then the value of the balance attribute in the row corresponding to your account is the net amount of money held for you in that account by the bank. In fact, since the database is so central to the functioning of the bank, one might say that the database determines the state of the real world.

The job of the transaction is to maintain this model as the state of the enterprise changes. Thus, whenever the state of the real world changes, a transaction is executed that updates the database to reflect that change. The transaction is said to perform a "unit of work" because it does all the work required to update the database to reflect the real-world change.

Specifically a transaction can perform one or more of the following functions:

1. It can update a database to reflect the occurrence of a real-world event that affects the state of the enterprise the database is modeling. An example is a deposit transaction at a bank. The event is that the customer gives the teller cash. After that event occurs, the transaction updates the customer's account information in the database to reflect the deposit.
2. It can ensure that one or more real-world events occur. An example is a withdrawal transaction at an automated teller machine (ATM). The transaction actuates the mechanical device that dispenses the cash, and that event occurs if and only if the transaction successfully completes.
3. It can return information derived from the database about the current state of the enterprise. An example is a transaction that displays a customer's balance.

The difference between the first two functions is that, in the first, the real-world event has already occurred and the transaction simply updates the database to reflect that fact; in the second, the real-world event is triggered from within the transaction.

A single transaction can perform all three functions. For example, a deposit transaction might

1. Update the database in response to a real-world event in which the customer gives cash to the teller

2. Cause the real-world event in which a deposit slip is printed if and only if the transaction successfully completes
3. Return information from the database about the customer's account

Because of the requirement that a transaction processing application must maintain an accurate model of the state of the enterprise, the execution of transactions is constrained by certain properties that do not apply to ordinary programs. For example, the state of the enterprise must be correctly maintained even if the system crashes while transactions are executing or even if hundreds of transactions are attempting to update the database at the same time.

These special properties are frequently referred to using the acronym ACID: Atomic, Consistent, Isolated, Durable. In this chapter, we define these properties (but not in the order of the acronym) and explain why they are needed.

18.1 Consistency

Think of a database as playing both an active and a passive role in relation to the real-world enterprise that it models. In its passive role, it maintains the correspondence between the database state and the enterprise state. For example, the Student Registration System must accurately maintain the identity and number of students who have registered for each course since there is no paper record of the registration. In its active role, it enforces certain rules of the enterprise—for example, the number of students registered for a course must not exceed another number stored in the database, the maximum enrollment for that course. A transaction that attempts to register a student for a course that is already full must not complete successfully.

Consistency is the term that is used to describe these issues, and it has two aspects.

The database must satisfy all integrity constraints. Not all database states are allowable. There are two reasons for this.

1. *Internal consistency.* It is often convenient to store the same information in different forms. For example, we might store the number of students registered for a course as well as a list whose entries name each student registered for the course. A database state in which the length of the list is not equal to the number of registrants is not allowed.
2. *Enterprise rules.* Enterprise rules restrict the possible states of the enterprise. When such a rule exists, the possible states of the database are similarly restricted. The rule relating the number of registrants and the maximum enrollment in a course is one example. A state in which the number of registrants is greater than the maximum enrollment is not allowed.

The restrictions are referred to as **integrity constraints** (or sometimes **consistency constraints**). The execution of each transaction must maintain all integrity constraints. Assuming that all constraints are satisfied when execution starts, the constraints will be satisfied in the new state produced by the transaction when it terminates. (If the constraints are not satisfied when the transaction starts, the transaction is not required to execute correctly and no guarantees can be made about the new state produced by the transaction.)

The database must model the state of the real-world enterprise. The transaction must be **correct** in the sense that it updates the database in such a way as to have the effect stated in its specification. The new database state must reflect the new real-world state—for example, a registration transaction must increment the database variable that stores the number of students registered for a course and must add that student to the list of registrants. A registration transaction that completes successfully but does not update the database leaves the database in a consistent state, but that state does not show the student as registered. Similarly, a deposit transaction that records your deposit as being in someone else's account leaves the database in a consistent state, but that state clearly does not correspond to the state of the real world.

We can determine whether or not all integrity constraints are satisfied by examining the values of the data items in a snapshot of the database (perhaps at a time when no transactions are executing). Unfortunately, this does not tell us whether or not the database state is an accurate reflection of the real-world state of the enterprise. Hence, in addition to the database state being consistent, we require that each transaction must be consistent as well.

> **Transaction consistency**. The transaction designer can assume that, when execution of the transaction is initiated, the database is in a state in which all integrity constraints are satisfied. The designer has the responsibility of ensuring that when execution has completed, the database is once again in a state in which all integrity constraints are satisfied and that the new state reflects the transformation described in the transaction's specification.

Note that we are using the word "consistent" in two ways. The database is consistent when all integrity constraints are satisfied; a transaction is consistent if it maintains the consistency of the database and produces a new database state that satisfies the requirements of the transaction's specifications.

Keep in mind that constructing consistent transactions is the sole responsibility of the application programmer. The remainder of the transaction processing system takes consistency as a given and provides atomicity, isolation, and durability—the properties needed to ensure that concurrent execution of consistent transactions preserves the relationship between the state of the database and the state of the enterprise in spite of failures.

18.1.1 Checking Integrity Constraints

SQL provides some support for maintaining integrity constraints. When the database is designed, certain integrity constraints can be incorporated as SQL assertions, key constraints, and the like. For example, a PRIMARY KEY constraint can eliminate the possibility that two students are recorded in the database with the same student

Id. A CHECK constraint can enforce the relationship between the number of registrants in a class and its maximum enrollment. An ASSERTION can ensure that the room assigned to a particular course is larger than the maximum enrollment. If a transaction updates data that is included in a constraint specified in the schema, the database management system (DBMS) automatically checks that the constraint is not violated and prevents the transaction from completing if that is not the case.

Unfortunately, not all integrity constraints can be encoded in the schema. Even when a constraint can be encoded, the design decision is sometimes made not to do so. Instead, it is checked within the transaction program itself. For example, the constraint that asserts that the maximum enrollment in a class should not be exceeded might be checked by the registration transaction instead of being included in the schema. One reason for such a decision is that constraint checking takes time. When encoded in the schema, constraints are checked automatically whenever a table they reference is modified. As a result, the check might be performed unnecessarily often. By placing constraint checking in the transactions, it can be carried out only in transactions that might cause a violation. For example, a limitation on the number of students who can register for a course cannot be violated by a transaction that deregisters a student. Thus, despite the fact that the number of students in the course is modified, no check need be made (either automatically or otherwise) when this transaction is executed. The advantage of such an approach is that the transaction designer includes constraint-checking code only in transactions where constraint violations can occur.

Checking constraints inside transactions has important drawbacks of its own. It increases the possibility of programming errors and makes it more difficult to maintain the system as rules change. For example, if at some point the limitation on enrollment is changed to say that the number of students in a course should not exceed the room capacity, several transactions might have to be modified, recompiled, and retested. However, if the constraint is specified in the schema, independently of any transaction, changing it is easy and no transaction needs to be modified.

18.1.2 A Transaction as a Unit of Work

The requirement that every transaction preserve integrity constraints limits the designer in specifying the tasks to be done by each of the transactions within an application. To explain this limitation, some authors have defined a transaction as a program that does a "unit of work," meaning that each transaction within an application must do *all* the work required to update the database in a way that maintains the integrity constraints when a real-world event occurs. Thus, for example, it is incorrect to specify that when a student wants to register for a course, two transactions should be executed—one that updates the count of registrants and one that updates the course roster—because neither of these "transactions" is consistent. The "unit of work" in this case requires updating both, and it must be done by a single transaction that then preserves the constraints.

18.2 Atomicity

In addition to consistency, the transaction processing system must provide certain guarantees concerning how transactions are executed. One such guarantee is *atomicity*.

> **Atomicity**. The system must ensure that either the transaction runs to completion or, if it does not complete, it has no effect at all (as if it had never been started).

Conventional operating systems usually do not guarantee atomicity. If during the execution of a (conventional) program, the system crashes, whatever partial changes the program made to files before the crash might still be there when the system restarts. If those changes leave the files in some incorrect state, the operating system takes no responsibility for correcting them.

Such behavior is unacceptable in a transaction processing system. Either a student has or has not registered for a course. Partial registration makes no sense and might leave the database in an inconsistent state. If the system were to crash while a registration transaction was executing, the number of students registered might have been incremented, but the registrant's name might not have been added to the roster, and hence the resulting database state is inconsistent.

If a transaction successfully completes and the system agrees to preserve its effects, we say that it has **committed**. If the transaction does not successfully complete, we say that it has **aborted** and the system must ensure that whatever changes the transaction made to the database are undone, or **rolled back**. A transaction processing system includes sophisticated mechanisms for aborting transactions and rolling back their effects.

The above discussion leads to the following important conclusion:

> Atomic execution implies that every transaction either commits or aborts.

Let us look at another example. A withdrawal transaction at an ATM involves (at least) two actions: The account is debited by the amount of the withdrawal, and the appropriate amount of cash is dispensed. Its atomic execution implies that if the transaction commits, both actions occur; if it aborts, neither occurs. Similarly, the atomic execution of a banking transaction that transfers money between two accounts guarantees that if the transaction commits, both updates occur; if it aborts, neither occurs.

Why transactions abort. A transaction might be aborted for several reasons. One possibility is that the system crashes during its execution (before it commits), or, in the case of a distributed transaction, the system on which one of the databases resides crashes. Other possibilities include the following:

1. Allowing the transaction to complete would cause a violation of an integrity constraint.

2. Allowing the transaction to complete would violate the *isolation requirement,* meaning that there is a possibility of a "bad interaction" with another executing transaction (as described in Section 18.4).
3. The transaction is involved in a deadlock, meaning that two or more transactions are each waiting for the others to complete, and hence none would complete if the system did not abort one of them (as described in Section 20.4.2).

Finally, the transaction itself might decide to abort. For example, the user might push the *cancel* button, or the transaction program might encounter some (application-related) condition that causes it to abandon its computation. Most transaction processing systems have an abort procedure that a transaction can invoke in such cases. Strictly speaking, such a procedure is unnecessary. The transaction can cause the equivalent of an abort by itself, undoing any changes it made to the database and then committing. However, this is a delicate and error-prone task that requires the transaction to remember what database items it has changed and to have sufficient information to enable it to return those items to their previous values. Since the system must contain an abort procedure for dealing with crashes and other conditions anyway, this procedure can be made available to all transactions. The transaction designer can thus avoid having to program the abort.

Programming conventions for bracketing a transaction. Each transaction processing system must provide a set of programming conventions so that the programmer can specify a transaction's boundaries. These conventions differ from one system to another. For example, the start of a transaction might be denoted by a `begin_transaction` command, and its successful completion might be denoted by a `commit` command.

The execution of the `commit` command at run time is a *request* to commit. The system might decide to commit the transaction or, for the reasons previously discussed, to abort it. A `rollback` command is provided so that a transaction can abort itself. In contrast to the request to commit, a request to roll back is always honored by the system.

Before the commit is executed, the transaction must be in an uncommitted state (and can still be aborted). After it is executed, the transaction is in a committed state (and can no longer be aborted). The commit operation must be atomic in the sense that no intermediate state separates the uncommitted and committed states. As a result, if the system crashes while the commit is in progress, on recovery the transaction will be either committed or uncommitted.

18.3 Durability

A second requirement of the transaction processing system is that it not lose information. For example, if you register for a course and your transaction commits, you expect the system to remember that fact despite subsequent hardware or software failures. Even if an ice storm causes a power blackout the next day and the computer crashes (or even if the crash occurs one microsecond after your transaction commits), you still want to be able to attend class. Conventional operating systems usually do not guarantee durability. Backups might be kept, but no assurances are given that the most recent changes are durable. Hardware failures are not restricted to the central processing unit (CPU) and its local memory. The data stored on a mass storage device can also be lost if the device malfunctions. For these reasons, we require *durability*.

> **Durability.** The system must ensure that once the transaction commits, its effects remain in the database even if the computer or the medium on which the database is stored subsequently fails.

Durability can be achieved by storing data redundantly on different backup devices. The characteristics of these devices lead to different degrees of system **availability**. If the devices are fast, the system might provide **nonstop** availability. For example, with **mirrored disks** two identical copies of the database are maintained on different mass storage devices, and updates are made immediately to both devices. Even though one device might fail, the information in the database is still readily available on the other and service can be provided. As a result, the malfunction might be imperceptible to users. The telephone system has this requirement (although in practice the requirement cannot always be met).

If the backup device is slow, service might be unavailable to users for some period of time after a failure while a **recovery** procedure, which restores the database, is executed. Most airline reservation systems are of this type, much to the chagrin of air travelers who want to make reservations when the system is temporarily unavailable. The Student Registration System is also of this type.

In the real world, durability is relative. What kinds of events do we want the committed data in our system to survive?

- CPU crash
- Disk failure
- Multiple disk failures
- Fire
- Malicious attacks

Different costs are involved in achieving durability for each of these events. Each enterprise must decide the degree of durability that is essential to its business, the probability of specific failures that might affect durability, and the level of durability for which it is willing to pay. Many enterprises keep backup copies of their databases in different cities or even in different countries to support a high level of durability.

18.4 Isolation

In discussing atomicity, consistency, and durability, we concentrated on the effect of a single transaction. We next examine the effect of executing a set of transactions. We say that a set of transactions is executed sequentially, or **serially**, if one transaction in it is executed to completion before another is started. Hence, at any given time only one transaction is being processed. The nice thing about serial execution is that, if all transactions are consistent and the database is initially in a consistent state, consistency is maintained. When the first transaction in the set starts, the database is in a consistent state and, since the transaction is consistent, the database will be consistent when the transaction completes. Since the database is consistent when the second transaction starts, it too will perform correctly, and the argument repeats.

Serial execution is adequate for applications that have modest performance requirements, but it is insufficient for applications that have strict requirements on response time and throughput. Fortunately, modern computer systems consist of a collection of processors—CPUs and input/output (I/O) processors—that are capable of the **concurrent execution** of a number of computations and I/O transfers. A transaction, on the other hand, is generally a **sequential program** that alternates between computation on local variables, which requires the use of a CPU, and reading or writing information to or from the database, which requires the use of an I/O device. In either case, the service of only a single processor at a time is needed. Modern computing systems are therefore capable of servicing more than one transaction simultaneously, and we refer to this mode of execution as **concurrent execution**. Concurrent execution is appropriate in a transaction processing system serving many users. In this case, there are many active, partially completed transactions at any given time.

In concurrent execution, the database operations of different transactions are effectively interleaved in time, as shown in Figure 18.1. Transaction T_1 alternately computes (using local variables) and sends requests (SQL statements) to the database system to perform operations on the database. For example, an operation might transfer data between the database and local variables or it might perform some specific update on a database variable. The requests are made in the sequence $op_{1,1}$, $op_{1,2}$. We refer to this as a **transaction schedule**. T_2 behaves in a similar way. Since the executions of the two transactions are not synchronized, the order of operations arriving at the database, called a **schedule**, is an arbitrary merge of the two sequences. In Figure 18.1, this sequence is $op_{1,1}$, $op_{2,1}$, $op_{2,2}$, $op_{1,2}$.

When transactions are executed concurrently, the consistency of each transaction is not sufficient to guarantee that the database remains consistent. For example, although a consistent transaction that starts in a consistent state leaves the database in a consistent state when it commits, its intermediate states during execution need not be consistent. Another (consistent) transaction that reads the values of variables in such an intermediate state can thus behave unpredictably because it assumes that it starts in a consistent state. Suppose, for example, that the registrar periodically executes an audit transaction that prints student and course records. If that transaction executes after a registration transaction updates the course count and before it updates the class roster, the information printed will be inconsistent: the total number of student records indicating enrollment in the course will be one less than the number of students shown in the course record as enrolled in the course. In this example, the database ultimately reaches a consistent state even though the information printed by the audit transaction is inconsistent.

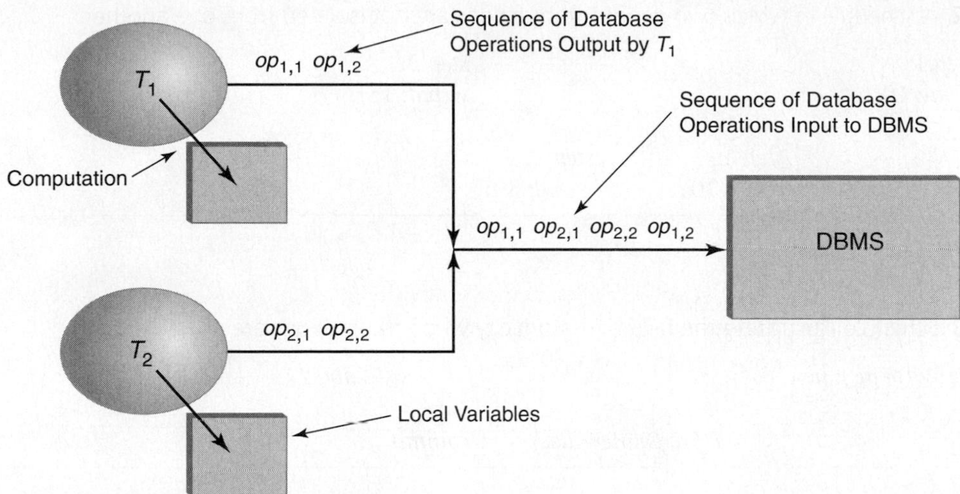

FIGURE 18.1 Database operations output by two transactions in a concurrent schedule might be interleaved in time. Note that the figure should be interpreted as meaning that $op_{1,1}$ arrives first at DBMS followed by $op_{2,1}$, etc.

Concurrent execution can also destroy consistency. In Figure 2.4 on page 23, we showed a concurrent schedule of two registration transactions that destroys consistency. Each transaction read from the database that there were 29 students currently registered in the course, and since the allowable number of students was 30, they each allowed a student to register. After both transactions completed, the count of the number of students registered for the course did not reflect the state of the real world since it said that 30 students were registered when in fact there were 31. In addition, the database state did not satisfy one of the integrity constraints because there were 31 entries on the class roster, although the integrity constraint said there could be no more than 30.

Figure 18.2 illustrates a similar situation. In this case, the execution of two bank deposit transactions is interleaved. Assume that the only integrity constraint asserts that the balance of each account is greater than zero. T_1 is attempting to deposit \$5, and T_2 is attempting to deposit \$20. In its first step, each transaction reads the balance as 10. In their second steps, T_2 writes 30 and T_1 writes 15. Since the final value is 15, T_2's update is lost. Note that the final database state is consistent, because the value of the balance is greater than zero. It is just incorrect: the value of the balance should be 35. If the transactions had executed sequentially, T_1 would have completed before T_2 was allowed to start, T_2 would have read a starting balance of 15, and both updates would have been reflected in the final database.

The failures we have been describing result from the fact that concurrent transactions are accessing shared data—the database (this is exactly the *critical section* problem discussed in the context of operating systems). For this reason, in studying the correctness of concurrent transactions, we are justified in concentrating on the

FIGURE 18.2 A schedule in which two deposit transactions are not isolated from one another.

T_1:	*step* 1: $r(bal: 10)$			*step* 2: $w(bal: 15)$

T_1:	*step* 1: $r(bal: 10)$			*step* 2: $w(bal: 15)$
T_2:		*step* 1: $r(bal: 10)$	*step* 2: $w(bal: 30)$	

FIGURE 18.3 Schedule illustrating the failure of atomicity when transactions are not isolated.

T_1 : *w(prereq: new_list)*			*abort*
T_2:	*r(prereq: new_list)*	*commit*	

operations that access the shared data—the database operations—rather than on the internal operations within the transaction.

Atomicity is also complicated by concurrent execution. For example, in Figure 18.3, T_1 is a transaction that eliminates a prerequisite, $course_1$, from another course, $course_2$. T_1 writes the new list of prerequisites to the database with the operation *w(prereq: new_list)*. The new list is read by the registration transaction T_2, and, based on it, the student is successfully registered. However, after T_2 commits, T_1 aborts and the original list is reinstated. The fact that the student might successfully register for $course_2$ without having taken $course_1$ implies that T_1 has had an effect despite having aborted. Thus, T_1's execution is not atomic.

As these examples demonstrate, we must specify some restriction on concurrent execution that guarantees consistency and atomicity. One such *sufficient* restriction is *isolation*.

Isolation. Even though transactions are executed concurrently, the overall effect of the schedule is the same as if the transactions had executed serially in some order.

The exact meaning of this requirement will be made more clear in Chapters 20 and 21. However, it should be evident that if the transactions are consistent and if the overall effect of a concurrent schedule is the same as that of some serial schedule, the concurrent schedule will maintain consistency. Concurrent schedules that satisfy this condition are called **serializable**.

Note that conventional operating systems usually do not guarantee isolation. Different programs might read and write shared files maintained by the file system. Since the operating system enforces no restriction on the order in which these reads and writes are performed, isolation is not guaranteed when the programs are run concurrently.

18.5 The ACID Properties

The features that distinguish transactions from ordinary programs are frequently abbreviated by the acronym ACID [Haerder and Reuter 1983], which denotes the following four properties of transactions.

- A*tomic*. Each transaction is executed completely or not at all.
- C*onsistent*. The execution of each transaction in isolation maintains database consistency and moves it to a new state that correctly models the new state of the enterprise.
- I*solated*. The concurrent execution of a set of transactions has the same effect as that of some serial execution of that set.
- D*urable*. The results of committed transactions are permanent.

It is the transaction designer's job to design consistent transactions. It is the transaction processing system's job to guarantee that transactions are atomic, isolated, and durable. This guarantee greatly simplifies the designer's task since there is no need to be concerned with failures or concurrent execution.

The ACID properties guarantee that each schedule maintains database consistency in the following sense:

> The ACID properties guarantee that the database is a correct, consistent, and up-to-date model of the real world.

Many applications require such a guarantee of correctness.

ACID properties in the real world. In later chapters, we will show that implementing atomicity, isolation, and durability can cause system performance to suffer. For example,

- Isolation is usually implemented by requiring transactions to obtain locks on the database items they access. These locks prevent other transactions from accessing the items until the locks are released. If locks are held for long periods of time, long waits result and the performance of the system suffers.
- Atomicity and durability are generally implemented by maintaining a log of update operations. Log maintenance involves overhead.
- The atomicity of a distributed transaction requires that the transaction either commit at all sites or abort at all sites. Thus, when the transaction completes at one site it cannot unilaterally commit there. Instead, it must wait until accesses at all sites have completed. Since locks cannot be released until commit time, this might cause a significant delay.

Even though implementation of the ACID properties involves performance penalties, many transaction processing applications are designed to execute in this way. For some applications, however, the penalties are unacceptable—the system cannot achieve the desired throughput or response time. In such situations, isolation is often sacrificed. It is weakened in order to improve performance. For example,

- Some applications do not require exact information about the real world. For example, a decision support system for a nationwide chain of department stores might allow store managers to obtain information about the inventory held in each store. Such information is useful in deciding when to purchase additional merchandise. When transactions are completely isolated, the system produces a snapshot of the inventory of all the stores as it exists at some instant of time. However, managers might be able to make adequate purchasing decisions with an approximate snapshot, in which the inventory reported for some stores is an hour or so old while that reported for others is up to date, or in which a few stores do not supply their inventory at all.
- Some transaction processing applications must model the real world exactly but execute correctly even though transactions are not completely isolated. Complete isolation guarantees that *any* application executes correctly: it is *sufficient* but not *necessary*. *Some* applications model the real world exactly even though some transactions are not isolated. (We will give examples of such applications in Section 21.2.2.)

To improve the performance of such applications, most commercial systems implement weaker levels of isolation that do not guarantee schedules that are equivalent to serial schedules. Designers must choose the level of isolation appropriate for their application. One goal of the following chapters is to explore this issue.

BIBLIOGRAPHIC NOTES

Excellent treatments of transactions and their implementation are given in [Gray and Reuter 1993; Lynch et al. 1994; Bernstein and Newcomer 1997]. The term "ACID" was coined in [Haerder and Reuter 1983], but the individual components of ACID were introduced in earlier papers, for example [Gray et al. 1976; Eswaran et al. 1976].

EXERCISES

18.1 Some distributed transaction processing systems replicate data at two or more sites separated geographically. A common technique for organizing replicated systems is one in which transactions that update a data item must change all replicas. Hence, one possible integrity constraint in a replicated system is that the values of all of the replicas of an item be the same. Explain how transactions running on such a system might violate

a. Atomicity
b. Consistency
c. Isolation
d. Durability

18.2 Consider the replicated system described in the previous problem.

a. What is the impact of replication on the performance of a read-only transaction?

b. What is the impact of replication on the performance of a transaction that both reads and writes the data?
c. What is the impact of replication on the communication system?

18.3 Give three examples of transactions, other than an ATM bank withdrawal, in which a real-world event occurs if and only if the transaction commits.

18.4 The schema of the Student Registration System includes the number of current registrants and a list of registered students in each course.
a. What integrity constraint relates this data?
b. How might a registration transaction that is not atomic violate this constraint?
c. Suppose the system also implements a transaction that displays the current information about a course. Give a nonisolated schedule in which the transaction displays inconsistent information.

18.5 Give three examples of applications in which certain transactions need not be totally isolated and, as a result, might return data which, although not the result of a serializable schedule, is adequate for the needs of the applications.

18.6 Describe a situation in which the execution of a program under your local operating system is not
a. Atomic
b. Isolated
c. Durable

18.7 At exactly noon on a particular day, 100 people at 100 different ATM terminals attempt to withdraw cash from their bank accounts at the same bank. Suppose their transactions are run sequentially and each transaction takes .25 seconds of compute and I/O time. Estimate how long it takes to execute all 100 transactions and what the average response time is for all 100 customers.

18.8 You have the choice of running a single transaction to transfer $300 from one of your savings accounts to another savings account at the same bank or of running two transactions, one to withdraw $300 from one account and a second to deposit $300 in the other. In the first choice the transfer is made atomically; in the second it is not. Describe a scenario in which after the transfer, the sum of the balances in the two accounts is different (from what it was when both transactions started) at the instant the transfer is complete. *Hint:* Other transactions might be executing at the same time that you are doing the funds transfer.

18.9 A distributed transaction consists of subtransactions that execute at different sites and access local DBMSs at those sites. For example, a distributed transaction that transfers money from a bank account at site A to a bank account at site B executes a subtransaction at A that does the withdrawal and then a subtransaction at B that does the deposit.

Such a distributed transaction must satisfy the ACID properties in a global sense: it must be globally atomic, isolated, consistent, and durable. The issue is, if the subtransactions at each site individually satisfy the ACID properties, does the distributed transaction necessarily satisfy the ACID properties? Certainly if the subtransactions at each site are individually durable, the distributed transaction is durable. Give examples of situations in which

a. The subtransactions at each site are atomic, but the distributed transaction is not atomic.

b. The subtransactions at each site are consistent, but the distributed transaction is not consistent.
c. The subtransactions at each site are isolated, but the distributed transaction is not isolated.

18.10 Isolation is a sufficient but not necessary condition to achieve correctness. Consider an application that reserves seats for a concert. Each reservation transaction (1) reads the list of seats that have not yet been reserved, (2) presents them to a potential customer who selects one of them, and (3) marks the selected seat as reserved. An integrity constraint asserts that the same seat cannot be reserved by two different customers. Describe a situation in which two such transactions that reserve two different seats execute in a nonisolated fashion but are nevertheless correct.

18.11 Assume a schedule consists of consistent transactions that execute in an isolated fashion except for one transaction that performs a single update that is lost (as in Figure 18.2). Show that the final state of the database satisfies all integrity constraints but nevertheless is incorrect.

19 Models of Transactions

All of the transactions in the Student Registration System are short and make only a small number of accesses to data stored in a single database server. However, many applications involve long transactions that make many database accesses. For example, in a student billing system a single transaction might prepare the tuition and housing bills for all 10,000 students in a university, and in truly large systems a transaction might access millions of records stored in multiple database servers running at different sites in a network. To deal with such long and complex transactions, many transaction processing systems provide mechanisms for imposing some structure on transactions or for breaking up a single task into several related transactions. In this chapter, we describe some of these structuring mechanisms from the point of view of the application designer. In later chapters, we will describe how the mechanisms can be implemented.

19.1 Flat Transactions

The transaction model we have discussed involves a database on a single server. It has no internal structure and so is called a **flat transaction**, which has the form

```
begin_transaction();
    S;
commit();
```

We introduce the `begin_transaction()` statement here, although, if you recall our discussion of transactions in Section 8.2.3, no such statement exists in the SQL-92 standard (a transaction is implicitly started when the previous transaction ends). It does exist, however, in SQL:1999. In this and later sections in this chapter we talk about transactions in a more general context, and it is useful to describe the abstraction of a transaction explicitly and to use a new syntax for that purpose. `begin_transaction()` informs the DBMS that a new transaction has begun and that the subsequent SQL statements contained in *S* are part of it.

A transaction alternates between computation using local variables and the execution of SQL statements. These statements cause data and status information to be passed between the database and local variables—which include the in and out parameters of the SQL statements and descriptors. The computation completes when the transaction requests that the server commit or abort the changes to the database that have been made. The DBMS guarantees the transaction's atomicity, isolation, and durability.

To understand the limitations of this model, consider the following situations.

1. Suppose that a travel-planning transaction must make flight reservations for a trip from London to Des Moines. The strategy might be to make a reservation from London to New York, then a reservation from New York to Chicago, and finally a reservation from Chicago to Des Moines. Now suppose that, after making the first two reservations, it is found that there are no seats available on the flight from Chicago to Des Moines. The transaction might decide to give up the New York to Chicago reservation and instead choose a route from New York to St. Louis and then to Des Moines.

   There are several options for designing such a transaction. The transaction might abort when it fails to get the Chicago-to-Des Moines reservation, and a subsequent transaction might be used to route the trip through St. Louis. The difficulty with this approach is that the computation to get a reservation from London to New York (and the resulting reservation) will be lost, and the subsequent transaction might find that there are no longer seats available on that flight. Another approach is for the transaction to cancel the New York-to-Chicago reservation and route the trip through St. Louis. While this is a viable approach, in a more involved situation in which a number of computations must be undone, the code for doing this can be quite complex. Furthermore, it seems that with relatively little effort the transaction processing system itself might be able to provide a mechanism for undoing some part of the computation. The system already provides the abstraction of total rollback (abort). What is needed here is a generalization of that abstraction for partial rollback.

2. Since Des Moines does not handle international flights, our traveler must change planes at some point and will probably have to make hotel and auto reservations. Hence, the transaction has to access multiple databases involving different database servers running on machines that might be spread around the world. Despite this multiplicity of database servers, we still want to maintain the ACID abstraction. For example, if we succeed in reserving a seat on the international flight, but the server maintaining the domestic airline's database crashes (making it impossible to arrange a complete trip), we need to abort that reservation. In general, new techniques are needed to guarantee the atomicity, isolation, and durability of transactions that access multiple servers.

3. Arranging a trip includes not only making the necessary reservations but printing and mailing the tickets as well. It is necessary that these jobs get done, but they need not all be done at the same time, particularly since some jobs require mechanical operations and the intervention of humans. Thus, the activities performed by a transaction might be spread out in time as well as in space. Useful here are models that allow a transaction to create other transactions to be executed at a later time. More generally, a model is needed to describe an entire

enterprise-wide activity, involving multiple, related jobs performed at different locations and at different times by both computers and humans.

4. Banks post interest at the end of each quarter. One way to do this is to execute a separate transaction that updates the balance and other relevant account information for each account. If there are 10,000 accounts, 10,000 transactions must be executed. The problem with this approach is that between two successive transactions, the database is in an inconsistent state. Interest has been posted in some accounts but not in others. If at that point an auditor were to run a transaction that summed the balances in all accounts, the total would be a meaningless number. A better approach is to post interest to all accounts in a single transaction. Suppose that this is done with a flat transaction and that after it has posted interest to the first 9,000 accounts, the system crashes. Since the transaction is aborted, all the time and compute cycles it has expended are lost. A model is needed in which a transaction is allowed to preserve partial results in spite of system failures.

The next sections present transaction models that address these and other related issues.

19.2 Providing Structure within a Transaction

With the introduction of flat transactions, the application designer was essentially given an all-or-nothing choice: use flat transactions to get atomicity, isolation, and durability, or design the application without relying on these abstractions. In the remainder of this chapter (and in the following chapters), we will describe models and mechanisms that provide a more refined access to these abstractions. Atomicity, isolation, and durability are made available in different degrees. This flexibility is achieved by introducing structure within a transaction. Structuring implies decomposition. A transaction is broken into parts that relate to each other in various ways. In some cases, the internal structure of a transaction is not visible to other transactions. In other cases it is, and the abstraction of isolation, which is enshrined in ACID, is breached.

In this section we describe models in which the transaction is conceived as a single, tightly integrated unit of work. In Section 19.3 we describe models in which the subtasks of an application are more loosely connected.

19.2.1 Savepoints

Database systems generally provide **savepoints** [Astrahan et al. 1976], which are points in a transaction that serve as the targets of partial rollbacks of the database. A savepoint marks a particular point in the execution of a transaction. The transaction can specify several different savepoints, which are numbered consecutively, so that they can be distinguished and so that the transaction can refer to a specific one at a later time. A savepoint is created using a call to the database server, such as

sp := `create_savepoint()`

The value returned is the savepoint's index, which names the point in the program at which the savepoint was created. A transaction with several savepoints has the form

```
begin_transaction();
      S1;
      sp1 := create_savepoint();
      S2;
      sp2 := create_savepoint();
       . . .
      Sn;
      spn := create_savepoint();
       . . .
      if (condition) {
            rollback(spi);
             . . .
      }
       . . .
commit();
```

A transaction can request a rollback to a particular previously created savepoint using

```
rollback(sp)
```

where the variable *sp* contains the target savepoint's index.

The semantics of rollback is that the values of the database items accessed by the transaction, called its **database context**, are returned to the state they had when the savepoint was created—any database changes that the transaction made after that savepoint was created are undone. The execution of the transaction then continues at the statement after the rollback statement (not the statement after `create_savepoint()`).

For example, the travel-planning transaction might create a savepoint after each individual flight reservation is made. When it is discovered that there are no seats available on the flight from Chicago to Des Moines, the transaction rolls back to the savepoint created after the London-to-New York reservation was made, causing reversal of the database changes made by the New York-to-Chicago reservation. The desired effect is that the database is in the same state it would have been in if the transaction had never attempted to route the passenger through Chicago. We will discuss the implementation of savepoints (and, particularly, how isolation is maintained) in Section 20.8.1.

Note that, although the database is returned to the state it had at the time the savepoint was created, the state of the transaction's local variables is not affected by the rollback call (i.e., the variables are not rolled back). Hence, they might contain values that have been influenced by the values of database items read since the savepoint was created. For example, after creating a savepoint, a transaction might read a database item, *x*, storing its value in local variable $X1$, then calculate a new value in local variable $X2$ and write it back to *x*. If the transaction subsequently rolls back to the savepoint, *x* is restored to its original value and $X2$ has a value that is no longer in the database. The value of $X2$ might influence the subsequent execution of the transaction. This means that rolling back to a savepoint does not create the illusion that execution between savepoint creation and rollback did not occur. Indeed, such an illusion would be inappropriate, since the transaction would then redo the rolled-back computation. The transaction needs to know that rollback has occurred so that a different execution path is taken afterward.

Note that the database state at a savepoint is not durable. If the transaction is aborted or the system crashes, the database is returned to the state it had when the transaction started. Although in one sense an abort can be viewed as a rollback to an (implicitly declared) initial savepoint, there is an important difference between abort and rollback to a savepoint. An aborted transaction does not continue after the abort is executed, whereas a transaction that has been rolled back to a savepoint does continue.

Also, note that after executing the rollback statement `rollback`(sp_i), all savepoints created after sp_i but before the rollback are inaccessible, since it makes no sense to roll back to them later in the computation.

19.2.2 Distributed Transactions

Many transaction processing applications have evolved in similar ways. Over the years an enterprise develops a number of dedicated transaction processing systems to automate individual activities, such as inventory, billing, and payroll. Such systems might have been developed independently, by different groups, at different times, in different locations, using different hardware and software platforms and different database management systems. Each system exports a set of transactions, T_i. These transactions might be stored procedures executed at a database server or applications programs to be executed at user sites. In the latter case the database server exports an SQL interface and the (sub)transaction at that site is the sequence of SQL statements that the application program executes. In many cases, these systems have been operational for years and are known to be reliable. Therefore, management will not allow them to be modified in any way.[1]

As the requirements for automation increase, the enterprise finds it necessary to integrate these systems in order to perform more complex activities. At this point the systems are referred to as **legacy systems** because they are presented to the application designer as complete, unmodifiable units that must be used in building a larger system. Similarly, their transactions are referred to as **legacy transactions**.

[1] In some extreme cases, the person who originally implemented a particular transaction has long since left the company, proper documentation does not exist, and no one else understands how the transaction works.

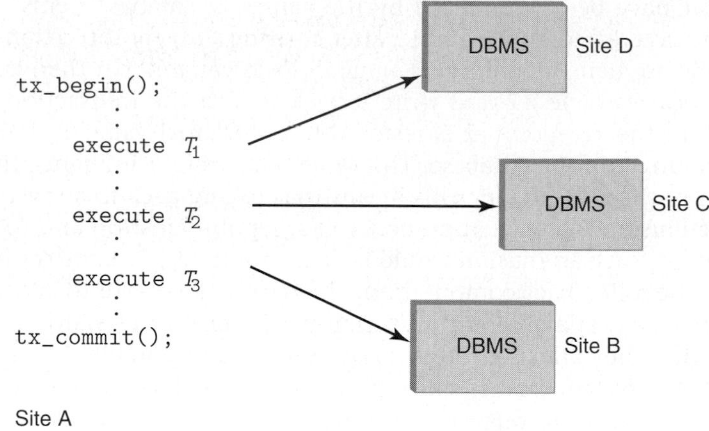

FIGURE 19.1 Distributed transaction invoking legacy transactions at several server sites.

Often the properties of legacy systems make integrating them into a larger system difficult.

For example, the inventory and billing systems might form components of a larger system for automating the sale of an item. Assuming that the servers are accessible through a network, a transaction in an integrated system is a program executed at some network site that invokes the legacy transactions that the servers export. Although it is possible that all of the individual systems reside on the same machine, this is generally not the case. We refer to such a transaction as a **distributed** or **global transaction**.

The situation is illustrated in Figure 19.1, which shows a distributed transaction that invokes three subtransactions. The `execute` statement can be viewed as a call either to a stored procedure at a server or to an application program provided by the legacy system and executed at site A. The figure shows a new syntax for managing the abstraction of a distributed transaction based on the X/Open standard, which we will discuss in Section 23.4. In contrast to `begin_transaction()`, `tx_begin()` is not a call to any particular database server. Instead, it is part of the API of the TP monitor, which controls the entire transaction processing system.

You should understand the advantage of constructing a distributed transaction in this way. The transaction sees billing and inventory as abstractions. Its logic can concentrate on integrating the results produced by the legacy transactions without concerning itself with the schema of the local databases, the details of the billing or inventory process, or issues such as atomicity, concurrency, and durability at each site.

For example, a company might have several warehouses at different sites. At each warehouse a transaction processing system maintains a local database for controlling inventory. The president of the company might want to execute a transaction at the main office (site A in Figure 19.1) that produces information based on the total inventory at all warehouses. That transaction causes legacy transactions (T_1, T_2, and T_3 in the figure) to be executed at each warehouse (sites B, C, and D in the figure) to gather the inventory information. Each legacy transaction communicates its result to the transaction at the main office, which integrates the information and produces a report.

More generally, a distributed transaction might consist of a program that invokes subtransactions at server sites as well as programs at other sites that are themselves distributed transactions (i.e., programs which invoke subtransactions). Hence, a distributed transaction can be viewed as a tree whose leaf nodes are subtransactions at server sites. Furthermore, servers might provide access to resources other than databases (such as files). Each subtransaction is a transaction at the server that it accesses and is therefore ACID. When these servers are database systems, we say that the distributed transaction executes in a multidatabase system. A **multidatabase** (sometimes called a **federated database**) is a loose confederation of databases that contain related information.

We assume that the database at each server, referred to as a local database, has **local integrity constraints**. Since each site maintains atomicity and isolation, these constraints are maintained despite the concurrent execution of the subtransactions of multiple distributed transactions at that site. In addition, the multidatabase, consisting of the combination of all local databases, might have **global integrity constraints** relating data at different sites. We assume that a distributed transaction is globally consistent and hence, when it executes in isolation, maintains those constraints as well.

As an example of a global integrity constraint, assume that a bank maintains local databases at all branch offices and that each database contains an item whose value is the assets of that branch. The bank also maintains a database at its central office that contains an item whose value is the total assets of the bank. A global integrity constraint might assert that the value of the total assets item at the central office is the sum of the values of the assets items at all of the local branches. Note that this constraint is not maintained by individual subtransactions. A deposit at a branch initiates a subtransaction at the branch's database that increments the branch's assets but not the total assets item at the central office. To maintain the global integrity constraint, the deposit subtransaction at the branch must be accompanied by a subtransaction at the central office to increment the total assets item by the same amount.

While it is the responsibility of the distributed transaction to maintain global consistency, the TP monitor might provide mechanisms to ensure that each distributed transaction (including all of its subtransactions) is atomic, isolated, and durable.

- The atomicity of a distributed transaction implies that each subtransaction is atomic at the server it accesses and that either all subtransactions commit or all abort. Thus, when a subtransaction of a distributed transaction, T, completes, it cannot immediately commit because some other subtransaction of T might abort (in which case all of T's subtransactions must also abort). We refer to this all-or-nothing commitment as **global atomicity**.

- Isolation implies not only that each subtransaction is isolated from all other subtransactions executing at the same site (i.e., that each server serializes all the subtransactions that execute at that server) but also that each distributed transaction as a whole is isolated with respect to all others (i.e., that there is some global serialization order among all distributed transactions). Thus, **global serializability** implies that the subtransactions of two distributed transactions, T_1 and T_2, execute in such a way that at all servers it appears that T_1 preceded T_2 or that at all servers it appears that T_2 preceded T_1.
- The durability of a distributed transaction implies the durability of all of its subtransactions.

Global atomicity and isolation are sufficient to ensure that the concurrent execution of a set of distributed transactions has the same effect as if the distributed transactions had executed serially in some order. Since we assume that each distributed transaction taken as a whole is consistent, serializable execution implies that the concurrent schedule is correct. Later, we will discuss different models in which transactions are not necessarily globally atomic or isolated and in which correctness is not guaranteed.

Models of a distributed transaction. A distributed transaction can be viewed as a tree. The root is the program that starts the transaction, and each descendant is a subtransaction that is initiated by the node which is its parent. The tree can be of arbitrary depth. Within that general structure are a number of options.

- The children of a particular subtransaction might or might not be able to execute concurrently.
- The parent of a set of subtransactions might or might not be able to execute concurrently with its children. In the case in which concurrent execution is possible, the parent might or might not be able to communicate with its children.
- In some models, only the root can request that the distributed transaction be committed. In other models, an arbitrary subtransaction can request that the transaction be committed, and it is the transaction designer's responsibility to ensure that only one subtransaction makes the request. In still other models, the right to request commit can be explicitly passed from one subtransaction to another.

A number of possible models exist within these options. Two particular variations predominate and can be viewed as extreme cases.

1. *Hierarchical model.* No concurrency is allowed within the transaction. Having initiated a subtransaction, the parent must wait until the subtransaction completes before proceeding. As a result, the parent can neither create additional subtransactions concurrent with the child nor communicate with it. The transaction is committed by the root. Procedure calling is a natural paradigm for communication within this model. TP monitors generally provide a special form of procedure calling known as **transactional remote procedure call** (TRPC),

which, in addition to invoking a procedure, supports the abstraction of a distributed transaction. TRPC will be discussed in Section 23.5.3.

2. *Peer model.* Concurrency is permitted between a parent and its children and among the children. The hierarchical relationship between a parent and its children is minimized: once created, the child is coequal with, or a peer of, the parent. In particular, a parent and child can communicate symmetrically, and any participant can request that the transaction be committed. **Peer-to-peer communication** is the natural paradigm for communication within the peer model. A pair of subtransactions explicitly establishes a connection and then sends and receives messages over the connection. TP monitors generally support peer-to-peer communication, which we will discuss in Section 23.6.

19.2.3 Nested Transactions

Distributed transactions evolved out of a need to integrate, into a single transactional unit, transactions exported from legacy servers. Since each server supports the transaction abstraction, (sub)transactions separately control their commit/abort decision. As a result, the designer of the distributed transaction has little control over the structure of the distributed transaction. The function of each exported transaction is essentially fixed by the way data is distributed across the servers, and distribution might be controlled by such factors as where the data is generated or where it is accessed most often. This yields a bottom-up design, which might not reflect a clean functional decomposition of the application.

Because it was not conceived as a way of dealing with multiple servers or distributed data, the nested transaction model evolved differently. Its goal is to allow the transaction designer to design a complex transaction from the top down. The transaction is decomposed into subtransactions in a functionally appropriate way (not dictated by the distribution of data). Furthermore, although subtransactions still control their commit/abort decision, the handling of the decision is different. Instead of the all-or-nothing approach of the distributed model, individual subtransactions in the nested model can abort without aborting the entire transaction. Even so, the nested transaction as a whole remains globally isolated and atomic.

A number of concrete models for nested transactions have been proposed. We describe one such model, due to J. Eliot Moss [Moss 1985]. In that model, a transaction and all of its subtransactions can be viewed as a tree. The root of the tree is called the **top-level** transaction, and the terms "parent," "child," "ancestor," "descendent," and "sibling" have their usual meanings. Subtransactions that have no children are called **leaves**. Not all leaves need be at the same level. We assume that the transaction and all of its subtransactions execute at a single site. The semantics of the nested transaction model can be summarized as follows:

1. A parent can create children sequentially so that one child finishes before the next starts, or it can specify that a set of children execute concurrently. The parent does not execute concurrently with the children. It waits until all children in the set complete. Hence, it cannot communicate with its children while they

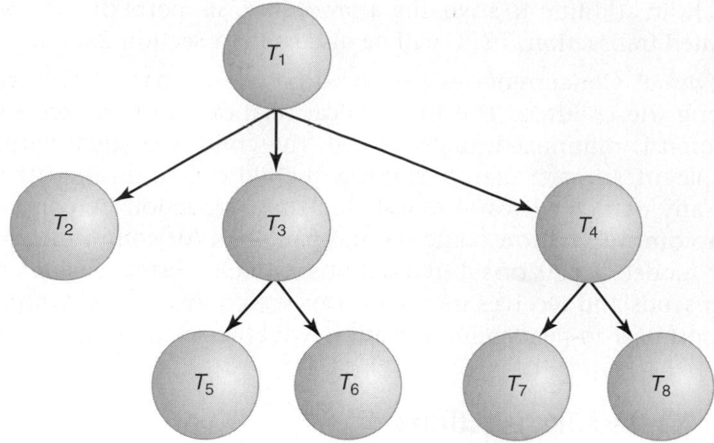

FIGURE 19.2 Structure of a travel planning transaction.

are executing. Once the children have completed, the parent resumes execution and can create additional children. Note that the tree structure depicting a nested transaction (Figure 19.2) does not distinguish children that execute concurrently from those that execute sequentially.

2. A subtransaction (and all of its descendents) appears to execute as a single isolated unit with respect to its concurrent siblings. For example, in Figure 19.2, if T_2 and T_3 execute concurrently, T_2 views the subtree (T_3, T_5, T_6) as a single isolated transaction. It does not see any internal structure. It follows that the effect of the concurrent execution of a set of siblings is the same as if they had executed sequentially in *some* serial order. Thus, the siblings are serializable with respect to each other.

   In some cases, the serialization order of the siblings affects the final state of the database. For example, in a banking application two concurrent siblings whose task is to write checks from the same account produce the same final balance independent of the actual order (assuming that the initial balance of the account was sufficient to cover both checks). However, the check numbers are dependent on the order. Thus, the nested transaction is not deterministic: the same transaction when run at different times can produce different results. If designed correctly, however, all possible results are acceptable to the application.

   We can view all nested transactions executing concurrently as being structured into a single tree with a (fictitious) "mother of all top-level transactions" as a root and all top-level transactions as its children. It then follows that a top-level transaction together with its descendents (taken as a single unit) is isolated with respect to each concurrently executing top-level transaction (and all its descendents). The hierarchical structure within a nested transaction is thus invisible outside of that transaction.

3. Subtransactions are atomic. Each subtransaction can abort or commit independently. The commitment of a subtransaction and its durability are conditional on the commitment of its parent. Hence, a subtransaction is finally committed

and made durable when all of its ancestors (including the top-level transaction) commit, at which point the entire nested transaction is said to have committed. If a subtransaction aborts, all of its children (even those that have committed) are aborted.

4. If a subtransaction aborts, it has the same effect as if it had not executed any database operations. Status is returned to the parent, and the parent can take appropriate action. An aborted subtransaction can thus alter the execution path of the parent transaction and, in this way, can have an impact on the database state. Contrast this to the situation with conventional (flat) transactions, in which an aborted transaction has no effect whatsoever. Also contrast this to distributed transaction, in which the abort of a subtransaction causes the entire transaction to abort.
5. A subtransaction is not necessarily consistent. However, the nested transaction as a whole is consistent.

The implementation of isolation for nested transactions is more complex than that for flat transactions, since concurrency is possible not only between nested transactions but within them as well. We will discuss this issue in Section 20.8.4.

We illustrate the nested transaction model using our travel-planning example. The nested structure of this transaction is shown in Figure 19.2.

Transaction T_1 makes airline reservations for a trip from London to Des Moines. It might first create a subtransaction, T_2, to make a reservation from London to New York and, when that completes, create a second subtransaction, T_3, to make a reservation from New York to Des Moines. T_3, in turn, might create an additional subtransaction, T_5, to make a reservation from New York to Chicago, and T_6, to make a reservation from Chicago to Des Moines. T_5 and T_6 might be specified to execute concurrently. They might access common data (e.g., the customer's bank account), but their execution is serializable.

If T_6 cannot make the reservation from Chicago to Des Moines, it can abort. When T_3 learns of the abort, it can abandon the plan to travel through Chicago and hence also abort (thus causing its other child, T_5, to abort and release the reservation from New York to Chicago). When T_1 learns of the abort, it can create a new subtransaction, T_4, to make reservations from New York to Des Moines through St. Louis (while still maintaining the reservation between London and New York). If T_4 commits, T_1 can commit and its effect on the database will be the sum of the effects of T_2, T_4, T_7, and T_8. The transaction as a whole is viewed as an isolated and atomic unit by other nested transactions.

19.3 Structuring an Application as Multiple Transactions

In a number of situations, it becomes necessary to decompose what might ordinarily be a single transaction into smaller transactions. For example, a long-running transaction might be decomposed so that locks it has acquired can be released at intermediate points, with the goal of improving performance. Or we might want to commit at intermediate points to avoid losing too much work in the event of a crash. In some situations, what might ordinarily be a single transaction involves subtasks that take place at different times. In this section, we discuss methods for providing such structure. We also discuss workflow management systems, which provide a way to view a complex business activity as a set of subtasks that must be executed in some application-dependent way.

19.3.1 Chained Transactions

Often, an application program consists of a sequence of transactions. For example, in a catalog-ordering application there might be a program that consists of a sequence of three transactions: order-entry, shipping, and billing. Between their execution, the program retains information in local variables about the items ordered and the person who ordered them, and it might perform some computations with this information.

A trivial optimization, called **chaining**, automatically starts a new transaction when the previous transaction in the sequence commits, thus avoiding the use of `begin_transaction()` (and the associated overhead of invoking the DBMS) for all but the first transaction in the sequence.[2] When chaining is enabled, an application program consisting of a sequence of transactions has the form

```
begin_transaction();
     S1;
commit();
     S2;
commit();
     . . .
     Sn-1;
commit();
     Sn;
commit();
```

where S_i is the body of the ith transaction, ST_i.

The execution of each commit statement makes the database changes caused by the prior transaction durable. Hence, if a crash occurs during the execution of ST_i, all changes made by $ST_1, \ldots, ST_{i-1}$ are preserved in the database when the system is restarted. Of course, information stored by the application in local variables is lost.

Chaining can be viewed from a different perspective when designing long-running transactions, such as the student billing transaction described earlier. Instead of the automatic start of a new transaction, our concern now is to avoid total rollback if a crash occurs. With chaining, a long-running transaction can be decomposed into a sequence of code fragments, S_1, $S_2, \ldots, S_n$, which are chained together

[2] Actually, `begin_transaction()` can be dispensed with there as well—the first interaction with the server can automatically start a transaction.

as shown above and in which each fragment is a subtransaction. For example, the transaction described earlier that posts interest to 10,000 bank accounts might be decomposed into 10 subtransactions, each of which posts interest to 1,000 accounts.

The following considerations arise when a long-running transaction is decomposed into a chain:

1. The good news is that if a crash occurs during a subtransaction, only the results of that subtransaction are lost since the results of prior subtransactions have already been made durable. (This behavior should be contrasted with that of a transaction using savepoints, where the work of the entire transaction is lost in a crash.) The bad news is that the transaction as a whole is no longer atomic. After recovery, the system assumes no responsibility for restarting the chain from the point at which the crash occurred.
2. Since the subtransactions were originally part of a single transaction, and so perform a single task, they generally need to communicate with each other. They share access to a common set of local variables, so communication can be easily accomplished. For example, if the interest-posting transaction is decomposed as described above, a local variable might contain the index of the last account updated. When a new subtransaction starts, it uses that variable to determine which account to process next. The problem with communication using local variables is that they do not survive a crash, and so, when resuming execution after a crash, a local variable cannot be used to identify the next account to be processed.

   As an alternative, the subtransactions might communicate through database variables. For example, the index of the last account updated by a subtransaction might be stored in a database item before the subtransaction commits. If a crash occurs during execution of the next subtransaction, that database item indicates where posting must resume. Note that in this case the database items used for communication are available to transactions executing in other (concurrent) applications. Care must be taken to ensure that the other applications do not tamper with this information.
3. The database context is not maintained between one subtransaction and the next in a chain. For example, if locks are used to implement isolation, all of the locks held by subtransaction ST_i are released when it commits. Thus, if ST_{i+1} is the next subtransaction in the chain and it accesses an item that ST_i has accessed, the value that ST_{i+1} sees might be different from the value the item had when ST_i committed (because some other transaction—not in the chain—modified the item and committed between the time ST_i committed and the time ST_{i+1} requested access to the item). The point here is that, in contrast to a single long-running transaction, each subtransaction in the chain is isolated but the chained transaction as a whole is not.

   Another component of the database context is the state of any cursor that the transaction has opened. Since `commit` closes cursors, any cursor that ST_i opens is not available to ST_{i+1}.

Although isolation is forfeited, chaining can yield a performance benefit. With locking, a long-running transaction can make the portions of the database that it accesses unavailable for long periods. This can create a performance bottleneck since concurrent transactions are made to wait until the transaction commits and releases the locks it has acquired. By breaking up the transaction into chained subtransactions, locks are released quickly and the bottleneck is eliminated.

4. Our initial view of chaining was one in which a sequence of individual transactions are processed and chaining automatically starts the next transaction in the sequence when the prior transaction completes. In that case, each individual transaction is consistent, so the database is in a consistent state between transactions. When we view chaining as a mechanism for decomposing a single long-running transaction, the situation is different. Although the entire long-running transaction is consistent, the individual subtransactions might not be. This creates a problem, since a subtransaction releases its database context when it commits, making it visible to other, concurrently executing transactions. If these transactions must see a consistent database state, we must require that the subtransactions be consistent. The issue of consistency does not arise with savepoints because the entire transaction is isolated and atomic in that case. Since the database context is not released at a savepoint, no concurrent transaction can see an inconsistent state.

   The consistency of subtransactions is also required in order to deal with crashes. If a crash occurs, the chained transaction does not run to completion and its partial effects are visible to transactions in other applications when the system is restarted. Thus, just as the chained transaction is not isolated, it is also not atomic.

OPTIONAL

An alternate semantics for chained transactions. From a pedagogical point of view, it is interesting to consider an alternate semantics for chained transactions that deals with some of the issues raised by the conventional interpretation. To distinguish this new semantics from its more conventional counterpart, we use the function call `chain()`. A chained transaction now has the form

```
begin_transaction();
    S1;
    chain();
    S2;
    chain();
    ...
    Sn-1;
    chain();
    Sn;
commit();
```

`chain()` commits a subtransaction, ST_i (thus making it durable), and starts a new subtransaction, ST_{i+1}, hence the work lost in a crash is limited to the updates of the subtransaction being executed when the crash occurs. `chain`, however, does not release the database context, and it maintains cursors. When locks are used to implement isolation, any locks held by ST_i are not released but are instead passed on to ST_{i+1}. Thus, if ST_{i+1} accesses an item that ST_i accessed, the value it sees is the same as the value it had when ST_i committed. Since the modifications to the database caused by ST_i are not visible to concurrent transactions, the individual subtransactions need no longer be consistent, and ST_i can leave the database in an inconsistent state if ST_{i+1} has been designed to expect that state. Thus, the chained transaction as a whole is isolated, although performance suffers.

Crash recovery is complicated with this semantics. If recovery simply rolls back the subtransaction that was active at the time of the crash, isolation is not supported since transactions that start after recovery can see an inconsistent state. The chained transaction as a whole cannot be rolled back since earlier subtransactions in the chain have committed. This means that, with the new semantics, a chained transaction must be rolled forward once the first subtransaction has committed. If a crash occurs during the execution of ST_{i+1}, the recovery procedure restarts ST_{i+1} and delivers to ST_{i+1} the database context held by ST_i when it committed (i.e., the database context as it existed at that point, together with the locks held by ST_i). Restarting in this way provides both isolation and atomicity for the chain as a whole. Recall, however, that restarting a transaction is not normally the responsibility of a recovery procedure.

OPTIONAL

19.3.2 Sagas and Compensation

Suppose we use (the conventional notion of) chaining to decompose a single long-running transaction into a sequence of subtransactions, and, after some number of subtransactions have committed, we decide that all the work should be reversed. Unfortunately, atomicity cannot be achieved. Each committed subtransaction released the locks it held on the items it modified when it committed, so the new values were made visible to concurrent transactions, hence we can no longer guarantee that those subtransactions have had no effect.

But suppose we would like to forge ahead anyway and reverse the changes made by the committed subtransactions. We might think that one way to do this is to simply save the original value of each item at the time it was updated and restore that value to the item. We refer to this approach as physical restoration or *physical logging* (see Section 22.2.3). It works for flat or nested transactions since each updated item is locked until the entire transaction commits, hence each item's new value cannot have been accessed by any concurrent transaction.

Unfortunately, undoing changes made by a chained transaction is more complex. Suppose that transaction T_1 is decomposed into a chain of two subtransactions, $ST_{1,1}$, $ST_{1,2}$, and executed concurrently with transaction T_2. If the execution of T_2 is interleaved between the execution of $ST_{1,1}$ and $ST_{1,2}$, then T_2 can access an item, x, updated by $ST_{1,1}$. A problem arises if T_2 also updates x, and the decision to reverse

T_1 is made when $ST_{1,2}$ is executing. If T_2 commits, it would not be correct to simply restore the value x had before the update in $ST_{1,1}$ because the update made by T_2 would be lost. Hence, physical logging does not work in this situation.

A technique used to solve this problem is called **compensation**. Instead of restoring the value of an item updated by a transaction physically, we restore it *logically* by executing a **compensating transaction**. For example, in the student registration application, a *Deregistration* transaction logically reverses the effect of a successful *Registration* transaction. The *Registration* transaction increments the enrollment attribute of a course, and the compensating *Deregistration* transaction decrements the attribute. Compensation does the reversal correctly even if the execution of the *Registration* and *Deregistration* transactions for one student, *A*, are separated by the execution of one or both of these transactions for another student, *B*, although atomicity is not guaranteed. If *A* (temporarily) gets the last seat in the course, *B* will be denied entry before that seat reappears.

In some applications, the compensating transaction need not logically undo all database updates made by the transaction for which it compensates. For example, while a *Reservation* transaction might add a passenger's name to the mailing list the airline uses for advertising purposes, a *Cancellation* transaction might not remove it.

[Garcia-Molina and Salem 1987] proposed a transaction model, called a **Saga**, incorporating compensation and chaining. A compensating subtransaction is designed for each subtransaction in a chained transaction. If a chained transaction, T_i, consists of subtransactions $ST_{i,j}$, $1 \leq j \leq n$, and if $CT_{i,j}$ is a compensating subtransaction for $ST_{i,j}$, an execution of T_i can take two forms. If it completes successfully, the sequence of subtransactions executed is

$$ST_{i,1},\ ST_{i,2}, \ldots, ST_{i,n}$$

If a crash occurs during the execution of $ST_{i,j+1}$, that subtransaction is aborted and the following sequence is executed:

$$ST_{i,1},\ ST_{i,2}, \ldots, ST_{i,j},\ CT_{i,j}, \ldots, CT_{i,1}$$

In the absence of concurrency, all the updates made by T_i are reversed.

However, the atomicity and isolation of T_i is not guaranteed in a concurrent environment. As with chaining, intermediate states are visible to concurrent transactions, and this is true whether or not the Saga completes successfully. So Sagas are neither isolated nor atomic.

The Saga model assumes that all subtransactions are compensatable. Unfortunately, in some applications this is not true. For example, *Reset*(x) resets x to zero. It is not compensatable because the value of x at the time *Reset*(x) is executed has to be retained in order to do the reversal. The existence of noncompensatable subtransactions leads to more problems: compensatable subtransactions do not always work correctly in their presence. For example, a subtransaction that decrements x, *Dec*(x), compensates for a subtransaction that increments x, *Inc*(x). But if *Reset*(x), executed by one Saga, is interleaved between the execution of *Inc*(x) and *Dec*(x), executed by another Saga, compensation does not work. Nevertheless, compensation is a useful tool in several models that we discuss in this chapter and we will treat it in more depth in Chapter 20.

19.3.3 Declarative Transaction Demarcation

The primary goal of the nested and distributed transaction models is to provide rules for commitment when a single transaction is composed of multiple modules. In the case of nested transactions, modules commit conditionally based on their position in the calling hierarchy; in the case of distributed transactions, an all-or-nothing rule applies (either all the subtransactions commit or none do).

A second issue that arises is how the boundaries between transactions are to be specified when an application is constructed from multiple modules. This issue is referred to as **transaction demarcation**. Our assumption up to this point is that transaction demarcation is done explicitly. With chaining, the commit of one transaction in a chain initiates the next. Using the X/Open standard for distributed transactions, the application invokes `tx_begin()` to start a transaction and `tx_commit()` or `tx_rollback()` to end it. The term **programmatic demarcation** is used to describe this approach: the directives that set the boundaries are embedded within the application modules. This approach has an important limitation. By combining the application code with the directives that specify how the code is to be fit into a transaction, the transactional properties of the code, referred to as its **transaction context**, are fixed.

With **declarative demarcation**, the goal is to remove the specification of transaction boundaries from the modules making up the application. This allows the designer of the modules to concentrate on the business rules of the enterprise and not on the possible transactional contexts in which the module might execute. Each module—frequently referred to as a **component** in systems that use declarative demarcation—deals only with application-related issues, such as accessing a database and enforcing enterprise rules. The desired transactional context of each component is described in a separate module, sometimes called a **deployment descriptor**. Then at runtime, the system uses the information in the deployment descriptor to implement the desired transactional context.

Each application provides its own deployment descriptor to specify the transactional context appropriate for each module that executes in that application. For example, a particular component might be used in two different applications. In the first application, the deployment descriptor might specify that when that component is called, a new transaction is to be initiated. In the second application, the deployment descriptor might specify that if that component is called from within a transaction, it is to execute as part of that transaction; if not called from within a transaction, it is to execute without any transactional properties. Thus, with declarative demarcation, the same component can be used in different ways in different applications.

	Status of Calling Method	
`trans-attribute`	`Not in a Transaction`	`In a Transaction`
Required	Starts a New Transaction	Executes within the Transaction
RequiresNew	Starts a New Transaction	Starts a New Transaction
Mandatory	Exception Thrown	Executes within the Transaction
NotSupported	Transaction Not Started	Transaction Suspended
Supports	Transaction Not Started	Executes within the Transaction
Never	Transaction Not Started	Exception Thrown

FIGURE 19.3 The transactional context of a procedure based on the calling context and the `trans-attribute` value associated with the procedure.

Declarative demarcation is particularly relevant for legacy procedures that were created for a nontransactional context. Since no transactional directives are included in the code itself, the procedures can be used without change in a transactional context by providing an appropriate deployment descriptor.

Among the commercial systems that provide declarative demarcation are

- MTS (Microsoft Transaction Service): a TP monitor provided by Microsoft
- J2EE (Java 2 Enterprise Edition): a set of specifications for component-based applications provided by Sun Microsystems, which includes a TP monitor and which has been implemented in commercial products by a number of vendors, including IBM and BEA.

We discuss J2EE, but MTS provides virtually the same capabilities.

In J2EE the transactional context within which a procedure executes is based on the transactional context of the caller and on the value of an **attribute** of that procedure, called the `trans-attribute`, declared in a (separate) file associated with the procedure, called its **deployment descriptor**. The allowable values of the attribute are *Required*, *RequiresNew*, *Mandatory*, *NotSupported*, *Supports*, and *Never*. The possible combinations of the caller's transactional context and the callee's `trans-attribute` value, together with the resulting transactional context of the procedure when it is called are summarized in Figure 19.3.

- *Required*. The procedure must execute within a transaction. If it is called from outside a transaction, a transaction is started. If it is called from within a transaction, it executes within that transaction.
- *RequiresNew*. The procedure must execute within a new transaction. If it is called from outside a transaction, a transaction is started. If it is called from within a transaction, T, the transaction is suspended and a new transaction, T', is started. When the procedure completes, T' commits or aborts, and T resumes.

- *Mandatory*. The procedure must execute within an existing transaction. If it is called from outside a transaction, an exception is thrown. If it is called from within a transaction, it executes within that transaction.
- *NotSupported*. The procedure does not support transactions. If it is called from outside a transaction, a transaction is not started. If it is called from within a transaction, the transaction is suspended until the procedure completes, then the transaction resumes.
- *Supports*. The procedure can execute either within a transaction or not within a transaction, but it cannot cause a new transaction to start. If it is called from outside a transaction, a transaction is not started. If it is called from within a transaction, it executes within that transaction.
- *Never*. The procedure can never execute within a transaction. If it is called from outside a transaction, a transaction is not started. If it is called from within a transaction, an exception is thrown.

Interestingly neither J2EE nor MTS supports nested transactions in their current versions.

In most situations, procedures are specified to have attribute value *Required*. For example, the `Deposit` and `Withdraw` procedures in a banking application would most likely be specified to have attribute value *Required*. These procedures might be used in (at least) two transactional contexts for which the transactional behavior is slightly different.

1. A bank customer wants to perform a deposit to an account and executes a `Deposit` procedure. Since the `trans-attribute` value for the `Deposit` procedure is *Required*, it is executed as a transaction. The same reasoning applies for `Withdraw`.
2. A bank customer wants to perform a transfer of funds from one account to another and executes a `Transfer` procedure with attribute value *Required*. `Transfer` therefore executes as a transaction, T. The transaction calls the `Withdraw` procedure for one account and the `Deposit` procedure for the other. Because the `trans-attribute` values associated with `Deposit` and `Withdraw` are both *Required*, they automatically execute within T (as is appropriate for this application).

An example where the *RequiresNew* attribute might be appropriate is in a procedure that is provided by a business that wants to be paid for its services even if the transaction that called that procedure should subsequently abort.

An example where the *NotSupported* attribute might be appropriate is in a procedure that accesses some file system that does not support any transactional semantics.

In Section 23.10 we discuss J2EE in more detail and, in particular, how declarative transaction demarcation is implemented within J2EE.

19.3.4 Multilevel Transactions

Multilevel transactions are similar in some ways to distributed and nested transactions: a transaction is decomposed into a nested set of subtransactions. Unlike a nested transaction, however, the motivation for a multilevel transaction is increased performance. The goal is to allow more concurrency in the execution of independent transactions. To understand how this is achieved, it is necessary to look ahead a bit.

Isolation is often implemented using locks. When a transaction accesses an item, it locks it, forcing other transactions to wait until the lock is released before accessing the item. This prevents one transaction from seeing the intermediate results of another. If a transaction holds the locks it acquires until it commits, isolation is achieved, but only a limited amount of concurrency is allowed. The resulting performance enhancement, compared with serial execution, is thus limited.

The multilevel model improves on this situation by allowing the individual subtransactions of a multilevel transaction to (unconditionally) commit before the transaction as a whole commits, thus releasing locks and allowing concurrent multilevel transactions that are waiting to progress at an earlier time. This improves performance, but as a result one multilevel transaction can see the partial results produced by another. In contrast, in the nested transaction model the individual subtransactions can only conditionally commit, locks are not released to concurrent nested transactions, and one nested transaction cannot see the partial results of another. Nevertheless, the execution of multilevel transactions is atomic and isolated as we will see.

In this section, we discuss the multilevel transaction model based on the work of [Weikum 1991]. We will describe its implementation in Section 20.8.5, where the advantage of the model with respect to performance will become apparent. As with the nested transaction model, we assume that the subtransactions of a multilevel transaction execute at a single site.

The multilevel transaction model. A multilevel transaction accesses a database over which a sequence of abstractions has been defined. For example, at the lowest level the database might be viewed as a set of pages, which are accessed with read, *Rd*, and write, *Wr*, operations. At the next higher level, we might see the abstraction of tuples, which are accessed using SQL statements. (This is the level of abstraction generally presented by a DBMS.) A yet higher level might see a more application-oriented interface. For example, in the Student Registration System we might define a set of objects representing course sections and manipulate them with abstract operations for moving students between sections: a test and increment operation, *TestInc*, that conditionally adds another student to a section if there is enough room, and a decrement operation, *Dec*, that removes a student from a section.

Given these data abstraction levels, a transaction, *Move*(sec_1, sec_2), that moves a student from section 1 of a large lecture class to section 2, can be structured as shown in Figure 19.4. The application level is the highest level in the figure. *Move* is a program that initiates a transaction by invoking `begin_transaction`, subsequently

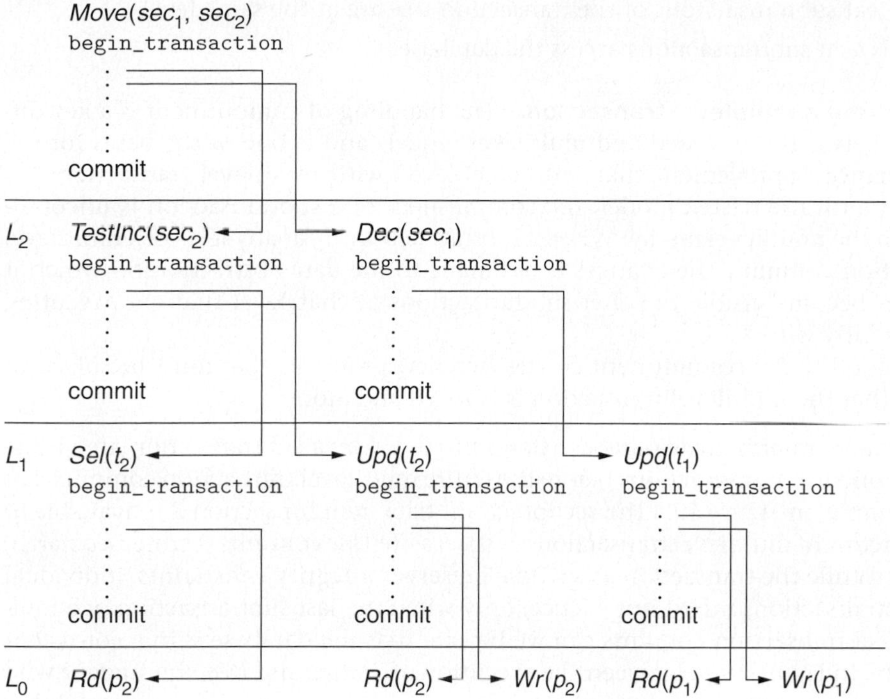

FIGURE 19.4 *Move* transaction viewed in the multilevel model.

invoking *TestInc* to test and increment the count of students in section 2 and, if successful, invoking *Dec* to decrement the count of students in section 1. At level L_2, *TestInc* is implemented by a program that uses a SELECT statement to determine if the student can be allowed in the section and an UPDATE statement that increments the count of students in the section if there is room. *Dec* is implemented by a program in L_2 that uses an UPDATE statement to unconditionally decrement the count of students in a section. We assume that section 1 and section 2 information is stored in tuples t_1 and t_2, respectively. At level L_1, these SQL statements are implemented in programs that read and write database pages. Tuple t_1 is stored in page p_1, and tuple t_2 is stored in page p_2. We ignore accesses to index pages in this example.

An operation invoked at some level can be viewed as a subtransaction at the level below. Thus, an invocation at L_2 of *Upd* causes the execution of a subtransaction at L_1. It, in turn, invokes *Rd* and *Wr*, each of which is implemented as a subtransaction at L_0. Similarly, the invocation of *TestInc* at the application level causes the execution of a subtransaction at L_2, which, in turn, invokes *Sel* and *Upd* at L_1. When a parent subtransaction creates a child subtransaction, it waits until the child completes. In contrast to the nested transaction model, we assume that each subtransaction is a sequential program, and hence children are created in sequence and do not execute concurrently. As a result, a multilevel transaction unfolds sequentially. Two other factors differentiate the multilevel model from the nested model.

1. All leaf subtransactions of the transaction tree are at the same level.
2. Only leaf subtransactions access the database.

Committing a multilevel transaction. The handling of commitment is a key difference between the nested and multilevel models and is one of the bases for the performance improvement that can be achieved with multilevel transactions. In contrast with the nested model, the commitment of a subtransaction is unconditional in the multilevel model. When a subtransaction, T, at any level of a multilevel transaction commits, the changes it has made to the data abstraction on which it operates become visible to other subtransactions at that level that are executing concurrently with T.

Unconditional commitment creates two new problems that must be solved to ensure that the multilevel transaction is isolated and atomic.

- *Isolation.* Intermediate database states produced by a subtransaction are visible to concurrent transactions before the entire multilevel transaction commits. For example, in Figure 19.4 the section count data item for section 2 is available to concurrent multilevel transactions as soon as *TestInc* commits (before *Dec* starts).

  While the transaction as a whole preserves integrity constraints, individual subtransactions might not. Hence, only when the last subtransaction of a multilevel transaction commits can we be sure that the database is in a consistent state. In Figure 19.4, between the execution of *TestInc* and *Dec*, the student who is being moved is counted in both sections. Thus we have to be concerned that concurrent transactions might see inconsistent states.

  Although it appears that multilevel transactions might not be isolated from one another, the implementation of the model, to be described in Section 20.8.5, does guarantee serializability. The transaction *is* isolated in the sense that a schedule produces the same effect as if the multilevel transactions had executed in some serial order.

- *Atomicity.* When a multilevel transaction is aborted, all of the updates it has made to the database must be reversed. However, as we discussed in connection with Sagas (Section 19.3.2), reversal cannot be performed physically: the individual subtransactions of a multilevel transaction commit when they are finished and give up any locks they have obtained, thus allowing concurrent subtransactions to read and write items they have updated.

  For example, consider two concurrent *Move* transactions, M_1 and M_2, executed from a state in which the count of the number of students in section 2 is initially c, as shown in Figure 19.5. The *TestInc* subtransaction of M_2 is executed between the execution of *TestInc* in M_1 and the time M_1 aborts. It is not possible to simply restore the count to c since the increment performed by M_2 (from $c + 1$ to $c + 2$) would be undone as well. Hence, physical logging does not work.

  As with Sagas, this problem is solved using **compensation**. Instead of restoring an old value physically, we reverse it *logically* using a **compensating subtransaction**. *Dec* logically reverses a successful *TestInc*, and hence is a compensating subtransaction. *Inc* (increment) logically reverses *Dec*.

OPTIONAL

In general, to reverse the effects of a subtransaction $ST_{i,j}$ at level L_i, at a point at which its L_{i-1} subtransactions, $ST_{i-1,1}, \ldots, ST_{i-1,k}$, have committed, we execute compensating subtransactions in reverse order: $CT_{i-1,k}, \ldots, CT_{i-1,1}$, where $CT_{i-1,j}$ compensates for $ST_{i-1,j}$. In Figure 19.4, if *TestInc(sec$_2$)* is aborted before *Upd*(t_2) is invoked, nothing need be done (because *Sel*(t_2) needs no compensation), but if it is aborted afterwards, a compensating update statement must be executed that decrements the count in t_2. If *Move* is aborted after *Dec*(*sec*$_1$) commits, compensating subtransactions for it and *TestInc(sec$_2$)* must be executed, in that order.

It might appear that compensation does not guarantee atomicity. For example, a subtransaction of T_2 might be interleaved between the execution of $ST_{i-1,j}$ and $CT_{i-1,j}$ of T_1, allowing it to access results computed in $ST_{i-1,j}$, which are subsequently compensated. However, when we discuss the implementation of multilevel transactions in Section 20.8.5, we will see that interleaving is restricted in a way that guarantees that compensation produces atomicity and serializability. This contrasts with the use of compensation in Sagas, where interleaving is not restricted and atomicity and serializability are not guaranteed. We will discuss other aspects of compensation in Section 20.6.

OPTIONAL

19.3.5 Transaction Scheduling with Recoverable Queues

With chaining, transactions are assembled in a sequence and are processed so that one starts as soon as the previous one completes. Sometimes, however, an application requires that transactions be executed in sequence but not that they be executed as a single unit. Instead, the requirement is that after one transaction completes, the next one will *eventually* be initiated and run to completion. So unlike chaining, a substantial interval might elapse between the completion of one transaction and the start of the next.

For example, a catalog ordering activity might involve three tasks—placing an order, shipping the order, and billing the customer. These tasks might be performed by three separate transactions. The work performed by the shipping and billing transaction can be executed at any convenient time after the order-entry transaction commits. However, it is important that these transactions be executed at some later time, even if the system crashes after the order is taken.

FIGURE 19.5 Schedule demonstrating that undoing the effect of a subtransaction using physical logging does not work.

M_1:		*TestInc*$_1$					*abort*
M_2:				*TestInc*$_2$			
	↑	↑	↑	↑	↑		↑
	count = c	log c	count = $c+1$	log $c+1$	count = $c+2$		Restore count to value logged by M_1

As another example, consider a distributed application in which a transaction, T, at a local site needs to cause some action at a remote site. If the remote action is incorporated into T, the network latency involved in invoking the action and receiving an acknowledgment becomes part of T's response time. If, however, it is not required that the remote action be performed as a single isolated unit together with T, but only that it ultimately be performed, then it can be designed as a separate transaction that T schedules for subsequent execution, and T's response time will not be degraded by network latency.

Applications such as these need some highly reliable mechanism to ensure that the transactions scheduled for future execution are in fact executed. One such mechanism is the **recoverable queue**. A recoverable queue has the semantics of an ordinary queue. Its Application Program Interface (API) allows a transaction to enqueue and dequeue entries. A transaction enqueues an entry describing some work that must be performed (at a later time) if the transaction commits. The information in the entry corresponds to the local state information that must be passed between successive transactions in a chain. At some later time, the entry is dequeued by another transaction that performs the work. This second transaction might be initiated by a server process that repeatedly dequeues entries from the queue and processes them.

To ensure that an entry enqueued by a committed transaction is eventually processed, the queue must be durable. Durability implies that the queue survives failures, so, as with the database itself, the queue must be stored redundantly on mass storage. Transaction atomicity demands that the *enqueue* and *dequeue* operations be coordinated with transaction commitment in the following ways:

- If a transaction enqueues an item and later aborts, the item is removed from the queue.
- If a transaction dequeues an item and later aborts, the item is replaced on the queue.
- An item enqueued by a transaction, T, that has not yet committed cannot be dequeued by another transaction (since we cannot be sure that T will commit).

Note that it would be possible to implement a queue with such properties directly in the database—a transaction wishing to enqueue an entry simply updates the tables used to implement the queue. The problem is that these tables are used heavily by many transactions, and if locking is used to implement isolation, they become a bottleneck, which degrades performance. Hence, it is desirable to implement a queue as a separate module that is treated differently from the point of view of isolation.

Recoverable queues can implement a variety of scheduling policies, including first-in/first-out (FIFO) and priority ordering. Or a process might be allowed to examine entries in the queue and select a particular entry for dequeueing. Note that, even when a queue has FIFO semantics, the entries might not be processed in FIFO order. For example, transaction T_1 might dequeue the head entry, E_1, from a FIFO queue, and at a later time transaction T_2 might dequeue the new head entry, E_2, from the queue. If T_1 subsequently aborts, E_1 is returned to the head of the queue. The

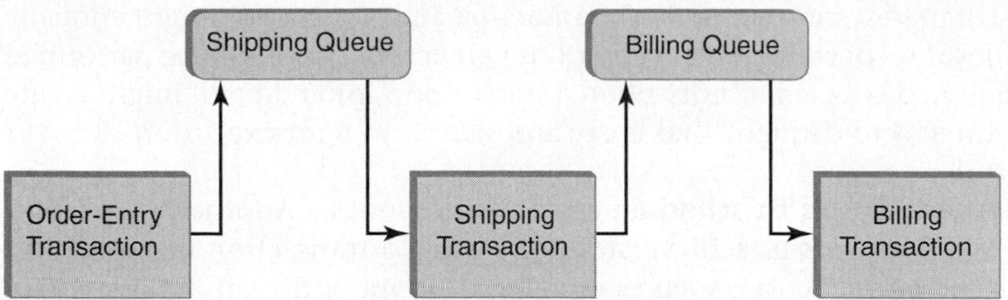

FIGURE 19.6 A system that uses recoverable queues in a pipeline organization.

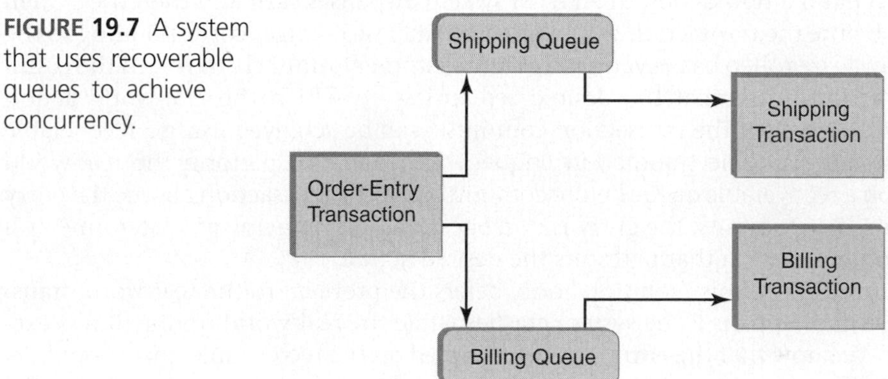

FIGURE 19.7 A system that uses recoverable queues to achieve concurrency.

net effect will be that E_2 has been serviced, before E_1, thereby contradicting the requirements of a FIFO queue.

One way to organize the catalog ordering application is as a pipeline, as shown in Figure 19.6. The order-entry clerk initiates a transaction at the order-entry server, which enters the order, enqueues a shipping entry in a recoverable queue for a shipping transaction, and then commits. At a later time, the shipping server initiates a transaction that dequeues that entry, performs the required operations, enqueues a billing entry in a second recoverable queue for the billing server, and then commits. At a still later time, a billing server initiates a transaction that dequeues the entry, performs the required operations, and then commits. Such an organization is like a pipeline because an entry corresponding to a particular purchase progresses, in sequence, from one queue to the next.

Another way to organize this application is shown in Figure 19.7. An order-entry transaction enqueues entries in both a billing recoverable queue and a shipping recoverable queue and then commits. At a later time, a billing transaction can dequeue the entry from the billing queue and perform the appropriate operations, or a shipping transaction can dequeue the entry from the shipping queue and do its work. In this organization, the billing and shipping transactions for the same order can be executing concurrently. (Of course, the customer might be unhappy if he receives the bill before he receives the shipment.)

In the distributed system example, a transaction at central site A might enqueue an entry in a local recoverable queue describing an action that must be performed at remote site B. At a later time, a distributed transaction initiated at B might create a subtransaction at A to dequeue that entry and send it to B for execution.

Recoverable queues used to schedule real-world events. Another application of the recoverable queue is to achieve atomicity when a transaction is required to perform some real-world action, such as printing a receipt or dispensing cash at an ATM. In contrast to updating a database, real-world actions cannot be rolled back. Once performed by a transaction, they cannot be reversed by an abort (as a result of a system crash, for example). This means that transaction abort is not handled atomically. (What if a transaction in an ATM system dispenses cash and then the system crashes before the transaction commits? The database changes corresponding to the withdrawal are rolled back even though the customer is unlikely to return the cash.)

It might appear that the desired semantics—in which the real-world action occurs if and only if the transaction commits—can be achieved using a recoverable queue as follows. The transaction enqueues a request to perform the real-world action on a recoverable queue before committing. If the transaction aborts, the entry is deleted. If it commits, the entry is durably stored for servicing at a later time by a *real-world* transaction that performs the desired action.

Unfortunately, this "solution" only defers the problem to the real-world transaction. What happens if the system crashes while the real-world transaction is executing? We know that the entry will be preserved on the recoverable queue, but how can we tell whether or not the transaction performed the action before the crash? We need to know this to decide if the real-world transaction should be reexecuted when the system recovers.

One way to solve this problem requires assistance from the physical device that performs the real-world action. Suppose that the device maintains a counter that it increments each time it performs the action, and suppose that the increment and the real world action are done atomically: either both or neither happen. Furthermore, suppose that the counter is readable by the real-world transaction. After performing the action, the real-world transaction, T_{RW}, reads the counter and stores its updated value in the database before committing. When recovering after a crash, the system reads the counter and compares its value to the value stored in the database. If the two are the same, no additional real-world actions have been executed since the last real-world transaction committed. If not, the device counter must have a value that is one greater than the value stored in the database, indicating that a real-world action was performed but that the corresponding real-world transaction, T_{RW}, was aborted as a result of the crash. Hence, the entry that T_{RW} had dequeued was restored to the head of the queue and T_{RW} might or might not have stored the updated value of the counter in the database. Even if it had, that value was rolled back. The system can therefore deduce that the real-world *action* required by the entry at the head of the queue has been performed, but the corresponding real-world *transaction* did not commit. In this case the recovery procedure can simply delete the head entry before restarting the system.

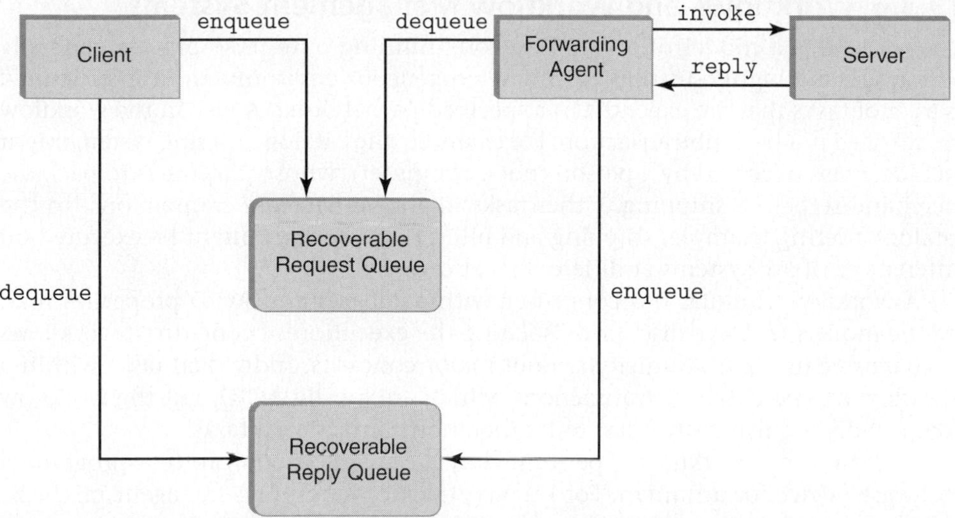

FIGURE 19.8 Use of a forwarding agent to invoke a server.

Recoverable queues used to support a forwarding agent. Another mechanism used in conjunction with recoverable queues is the **forwarding agent**. Consider a client that wants to invoke a service but determines that the target server is not operational. If the required service can be deferred, the client can enqueue the request for later servicing when the target server becomes available. A forwarding agent is a mechanism that can be used to invoke the target server at a later time. It periodically initiates a transaction that dequeues a request-for-service entry from the queue, invokes the target server, and awaits a response. If the transaction does not complete successfully (e.g., if the target server is still not available), it simply aborts and the entry is restored to the queue for later servicing. If the transaction commits, a response entry can be enqueued in a reply queue to be picked up at a later time by the client (see Figure 19.8). Note that the target server cannot (and need not) distinguish between the two circumstances under which it might have been invoked. The service that it performs is independent of whether it was invoked directly by the client or indirectly through the agent.

Recoverable queues as a communication mechanism. A recoverable queue can be viewed as a reliable communication mechanism by which modules communicate with each other. Unlike the communication methods discussed previously, in which the communication is *online* or immediate, communication using queues is *deferred*. This situation is analogous to leaving messages on a telephone answering machine. Since the queue is recoverable, the deferred communication can even take place across a crash of the system.

19.3.6 Workflows and Workflow Management Systems

A **workflow** is a model of a complex, long-running enterprise process generally performed in a highly distributed and heterogeneous environment. It is structured as a set of tasks that are executed in a specified partial order. A task in the workflow model need not be a subtransaction. For example, the catalog ordering system might include a task executed by a person (not a computer), whose purpose is to pack the merchandise before shipping. Other tasks might be database transactions. In the catalog-ordering example, shipping and billing transactions might be executed on different database systems at different locations.

A workflow is much less concerned with databases and ACID properties than are the models we have discussed. Isolating the execution of concurrent workflows or guaranteeing their atomicity are not major concerns. Individual tasks within a workflow can be database transactions, which are locally ACID, but the workflow does not distinguish such tasks from other, nontransactional tasks.

Each task in a workflow is performed by an **agent**, which can be a program, a hardware device, or a human. For keeping track of inventory, the agent might be a software system; for packing merchandise, the agent most likely is a human. A workflow might be performed by a number of agents over a significant period of time.

Each task has a physical status, such as executing, committed, or aborted. A task abort can be due to some system-related condition, for example, a server crash. Or the customer might decide to cancel the task during its execution. The failure of a workflow is not properly called an abort since some tasks might have completed and their results might have become visible.

In addition, the completion of a task might generate some logical status information indicating success or failure. For example, a billing transaction might discover that a customer has a bad credit rating. It completes in this case, but generates a logical failure status that is due to an application-related condition.

The tasks in a workflow have to be coordinated. For example, it might not be possible to schedule a particular task until two or more other tasks have completed (an *AND condition*), or perhaps several tasks can be executed concurrently.

Similarly, at a certain point in the execution of a workflow there might be several tasks that essentially accomplish the same goal, so only one of them should be executed (an *OR condition*). The choice of which to execute can depend on the logical or physical status or output generated by some prior task in the workflow or on the value of some external variable (e.g., the time of day).

A workflow describing the catalog ordering system is shown in Figure 19.9. Task T_1 takes the order. Task T_2 deletes the item from the inventory database and initiates tasks T_3 and T_4 concurrently. T_3 causes the item to be removed from the warehouse, while T_4 performs the billing function. Task T_5 packages the item when it has been removed. After billing and packaging, task T_6 arranges shipping, which can be by airmail (task T_7) or by land (task T_8)—only one of these alternatives is executed. Finally, when the customer signs the delivery papers the database is updated to indicate that the order has been fulfilled (task T_9).

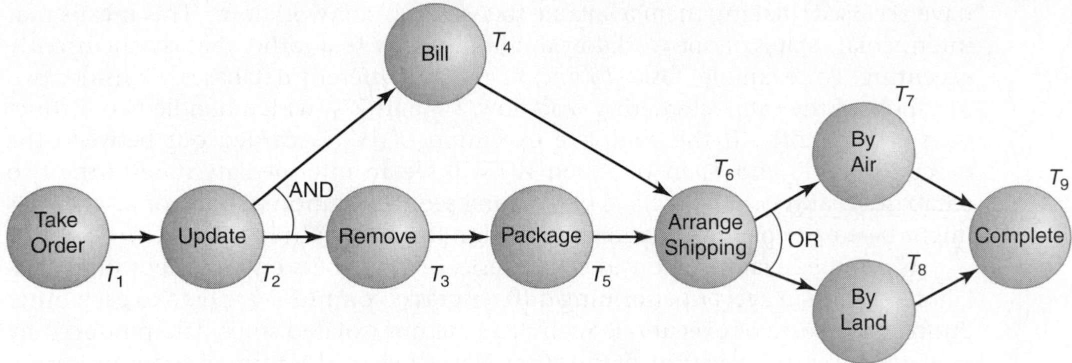

FIGURE 19.9 Workflow showing the execution precedence relationship between tasks of a catalog ordering system.

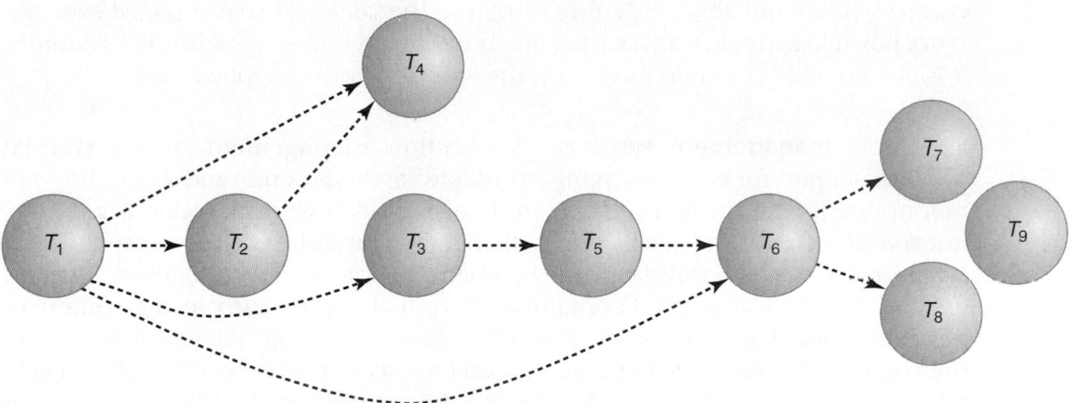

FIGURE 19.10 Flow of data in the catalog ordering system of Figure 19.9.

The results produced by one task frequently must be supplied as input to another, but this flow is not necessarily the same as the control flow. For example, in Figure 19.9 the customer's name and address, gathered during the execution of T_1, are sent to T_4 and T_6, while the identity of the item is sent to T_2 and T_3. T_2 then sends the item's cost to T_4. This flow of data and goods is shown in Figure 19.10. There is also a formatting issue—the data output by one task might have to be reformatted before it can be input to another task. Such issues come up frequently when information must be passed between legacy systems.

The generality of workflows follows partly from the fact that not all tasks are computational and not all agents are software systems. But even if all tasks are computational, the workflow model does not require the ACID properties. Consider isolation: as a workflow is executed, individual tasks might release resources they have accessed, making them available to tasks in other workflows. This means that intermediate states of one workflow might be visible to another that is concurrently executing. For example, tasks T_2 and T_4 update different databases. Consider two instances of the catalog ordering workflow, W_1 and W_2, which handle two distinct sales concurrently. If the complete execution of W_2 is carried out between the execution of T_2 and T_4 in W_1, then W_2 will see an intermediate state of the two databases that it could not have seen in any serial execution of the workflows. This might be an acceptable violation of isolation for this application.

As another example, consider that tasks in a business environment often collaborate: Human agents performing different tasks communicate data to each other during the course of execution. Such tasks are not isolated since data produced by one influences the execution of the other. Nevertheless, this form of communication might be appropriate for some applications.

Finally, it might be appropriate to weaken atomicity since some tasks might not be essential. The catalog-ordering workflow might include a task, T, that adds the customer's name to a mailing list. The failure of T (e.g., the mailing list database crashes) should not abort the entire workflow: the sale must be completed even if it is not possible to send an advertising brochure at a later time. Similarly, if T commits, it is not necessary to undo its effect if the workflow must be rolled back.

Workflow management systems. A **workflow management system (WfMS)** provides support for both specifying a workflow (at design time) and scheduling and monitoring its execution (at execution time). A workflow specification is generally not concerned with the details of a particular task but rather with the way the tasks are sequenced and the way data flows between them. A task can generally be thought of as a black box. It is a self-contained entity that can be used in the context of different types of workflows. For example, a credit-checking task might be used in the context of a mortgage application workflow, as well as a workflow that checks on an applicant applying for a job. Hence the sequencing of tasks in a particular workflow cannot be embedded in the task itself but must be specified externally. This is a major departure from the nested or distributed transaction model where the invocation of one subtransaction (task) is contained within another.

A WfMS might support a GUI that allows the application designer to specify the sequence of tasks in a graphical form as shown in Figure 19.9. Or it might provide a control flow language for this purpose, including the usual programming language constructs, such as conditional statements, while loops, and concurrent execution. In any case, the initiation of a task might be a function of the output or execution state of other tasks.

For example, the designer might specify

initiate T_j when T_k committed **19.1**

where T_j and T_k are tasks. Here T_j starts only if T_k commits. If T_k aborts, T_j is not initiated at all. A specification of the form

```
initiate Tr, Tk when Th committed
```

calls for the concurrent execution of tasks T_r and T_k when T_h commits. Another choice for the designer is

```
initiate Tq when Tk aborted
```

where T_q is a task that performs the same function as T_k in an alternate way. Using this technique, a number of paths leading to the successful completion of a workflow can be specified.

For example, T_k might be a transaction that books a New York-to-Washington air ticket, and T_q might be a transaction that books a New York-to-Washington rail ticket. Alternatively, the workflow might concurrently initiate T_k and T_q with the requirement that T_q commit only if T_k aborts.

The atomicity—or lack thereof—of a workflow is dependent on certain properties of its component tasks. A task can be **retriable**, meaning that, even if it initially aborts, it will eventually commit if retried a sufficient number of times. It is not necessary to specify an alternative path in case a retriable task aborts. It is only necessary to specify that the task be retried until it commits. For example, a deposit transaction is retriable, but a withdraw transaction is not (sufficient funds might never exist). If all tasks of a workflow are retriable, the workflow can always be completed.

The situation is more problematic if a nonretriable task, for which there is no alternate, aborts. The workflow cannot then successfully complete. The effects of tasks that have completed prior to that time must (generally) be reversed. For example, if the workflow has reserved hotels and transportation for a trip, the reservations must be canceled. We faced this problem with Sagas (and multilevel transactions) and saw that compensation, rather than physical restoration, is appropriate. As with Sagas (but in contrast with multilevel transactions), no guarantees are made as to the atomicity or serializability of the workflow when compensation is used.

If a compensating task exists for a task, T, then T is said to be **compensatable**. For example, a compensating task for T_2 in Figure 19.9 restores the item to the appropriate inventory record. If a failure happened during the execution of T_3 and T_4, these tasks are rolled back and compensating tasks are run first for T_2 and then for T_1. In general, compensating tasks are executed for each completed task in reverse order.

A workflow that consists only of compensatable tasks can always be reversed. However, some tasks are neither compensatable nor retriable. For example, a transaction that reserves and pays for a nonrefundable ticket is not compensatable (the ticket is nonrefundable) and not retriable (there is no guarantee that the ticket will ever become available). Such a transaction is often referred to as a **pivot**. (Note that this transaction is not compensatable because of a business rule of the enterprise: certain tickets are nonrefundable. By contrast, with Sagas [and multilevel transactions], we assumed that all subtransactions are compensatable.)

Reversing a workflow after a noncompensatable task has committed is not possible. Instead, atomicity requires that it must be possible to complete the execution at that point. All subsequently executed tasks must be retriable (or appropriate alternate paths must be provided). Hence, for a workflow to be atomic, its execution must consist of the execution of compensatable tasks followed by the execution of retriable tasks. A single pivot task can be executed between the two sets since if the need to undo the workflow occurs during its execution (prior to committing), it can be rolled back.

Workflow control involves automating the execution of a workflow by interpreting its specification. This interpretation can involve a number of issues.

- *Roles, agents, and worklists.* Each agent has an attribute indicating a set of **roles** it can assume, and each task has an associated role. Roles are used by the workflow controller to identify the agents that can perform a task that is ready to be executed. For example, a number of different sales representatives (agents) might be capable of performing task T_1 in Figure 19.9, but billing might be automated and performed by a software system (also an agent). The WfMS might select a particular agent to do the job using an algorithm that balances the load among agents. To facilitate such an assignment, each agent might be associated with a **worklist** enumerating the tasks (from different active workflows) currently assigned to it.
- *Task activation.* The WfMS monitors the physical and logical state of each task and, when a task changes its state (commits or aborts), the WfMS determines whether the initiation condition for a new task has been satisfied (Have all predecessor tasks completed? Is all input information for the task available?). It then selects and notifies the chosen agent and adds the task to its worklist. The WfMS evaluates logical and physical failure situations and initiates compensating tasks as needed.
- *State maintenance.* Assuming that the durability of the result produced by each task is provided by the server that implements the task, the only other issue related to durability concerns the state of the WfMS itself, which maintains the execution state of each active workflow. If this state and the inputs and outputs of the tasks are durable, the execution of the workflows can be resumed after a crash of the WfMS. This is referred to as **forward recovery**.
- *Filters.* Reformatting might be necessary when information from the output of one task is supplied as input to another. The WfMS might provide **filters** for this purpose. Note that the input to a task might be supplied by several prior tasks. The WfMS ensures that all input is present and properly formatted before a task is initiated. Furthermore, a filter might extract information used by the WfMS for the scheduling of subsequent tasks.
- *Recoverable queues.* Recoverable queues might be used by a WfMS as a mechanism for storing information about the tasks of an active workflow and for task sequencing.

The specification of an enterprise process as a workflow is particularly important when the process must satisfy a specific set of complex business rules. For example, management in the enterprise running the catalog-ordering system might have a rule that no merchandise can be shipped to any person who does not pass a credit check. Such rules can be incorporated into the workflow so that management can be sure that, even though many instances of the workflow are initiated in the course of a day (perhaps using human agents with minimum training), each instance is carried out according to the established policy.

Workflows are becoming increasingly important as a way to specify and implement the Web services that enterprises provide to each other and to their customers over the Internet. For example, a travel agency that plans vacations for their customers might utilize a workflow that involves Web services provided by airlines, hotels, tour guides, and credit card companies in various locations throughout the world. The workflow guarantees that all of these services are orchestrated in the way that is required by the travel agency. We discuss a particular workflow management system for Web services in Section 25.6.

BIBLIOGRAPHIC NOTES

The basic idea of a flat transaction has been around for a while. Early descriptions are contained in [Eswaran et al. 1976; Gray 1981; Gray et al. 1976] and an early implementation was presented in [Gray 1978]. A more recent and comprehensive description is found in [Gray and Reuter 1993; Lynch et al. 1994; Bernstein and Newcomer 1997]. Savepoints were introduced in [Astrahan et al. 1976]. A good overview of issues related to distributed transactions over a multidatabase can be found in [Breitbart et al. 1992]. Nested transactions were proposed in [Moss 1985]. Specific models of nested transactions were introduced in [Moss 1985; Beeri et al. 1989; Fekete et al. 1989; Weikum and Schek 1991; Garcia-Molina et al. 1991]. Nested transactions are implemented within the Encina TP monitor [Transarc 1996]. Multilevel transactions have been examined in a number of papers, including [Weikum 1991; Beeri et al. 1989; Beeri et al. 1983; Moss 1985]. A discussion of compensating transactions appears in [Korth et al. 1990]. Sagas were introduced in [Garcia-Molina and Salem 1987]. An excellent overview of a variety of more general transaction models (often referred to as extended transactions) is found in [Elmagarmid 1992] and [Jajodia and Kerschberg 1997]. Additional models are discussed in [Reuter and Wachter 1991; Chrysanthis and Ramaritham 1990; and Elmagarmid et al. 1990].

General overviews of workflow management can be found in [Georgakopoulos et al. 1995; Khoshafian and Buckiewicz 1995; Bukhres and Kueshn, Eds. 1995; Hsu 1995]. Two main issues have received considerable attention: development of the transaction models suitable for workflows and development of languages for workflow specification. Discussions of these issues can be found in [Rusinkiewicz and Sheth 1994; Alonso et al. 1996; Georgakopoulos et al. 1994; Alonso et al. 1997; Worah and Sheth 1997; Kamath and Ramamritham 1996]. If business rules are included as part of the workflow, many complex issues arise. First, the specification language must be rich enough to specify these rules. Second, the workflow must obey the rules, which is a nontrivial achievement. A number of research groups have been investigating formal approaches to workflow specification and algorithms for correct workflow execution. A partial list of this work includes [Orlowska et al. 1996; Attie et al. 1993; Wodtke and Weikum 1997; Singh 1996; Attie et al. 1996; Davulcu et al. 1998; Adam et al. 1998; Hull et al. 1999; Bonner 1999]. Another important issue—*interoperability* among workflows—has been taken up by the Workflow Management Coalition, which has published a number of standards in [Workflow Management Coalition 2000].

EXERCISES

19.1 The banking system described at the end of Section 22.1 can be structured either as a single transaction (with a savepoint after posting interest to each group of 1000 accounts) or as a chained transaction (with a commit point after posting interest to each group of 1000 accounts). Explain the differences in semantics between the two implementations. State when the printing of account statements takes place in each.

19.2 Explain the difference between each of the transaction models with respect to abort, commit, rollback, and isolation in the following cases:

a. A sequence of savepoints in a transaction and a chained transaction
b. A sequence of savepoints in a transaction and a nested transaction consisting of subtransactions that are executed serially
c. A sequence of savepoints in a transaction and a sequence of transactions linked by a recoverable queue
d. A sequence of chained transactions and a nested transaction consisting of subtransactions that are scheduled serially
e. A sequence of chained transactions and a sequence of transactions linked by a recoverable queue
f. A sequence of transactions linked by a recoverable queue and a nested transaction consisting of subtransactions that are executed serially
g. A nested transaction consisting of a set of concurrently executing siblings and a set of concurrently executing peer-related subtransactions of a distributed transaction
h. A nested transaction consisting of subtransactions that execute serially and a multilevel transaction
i. A nested transaction consisting of subtransactions that execute serially and a transaction using declarative demarcation consisting of modules specified with *RequiresNew*

19.3 Decompose the registration transaction in the Student Registration System design (given in Section C.7) into a concurrent nested transaction.

19.4 Redesign the registration transaction in the Student Registration System design (given in Section C.7) as a multilevel transaction.

19.5 Show how the withdraw transaction in an ATM system can be structured as a nested transaction with concurrent subtransactions.

19.6 a. Explain the difference in semantics between the two versions of chaining discussed in the text.
b. Which of these versions is implemented within SQL?
c. Give an example of an application where the second version would be preferable.

19.7 Explain how the Student Registration System could interface with a student billing system using a recoverable queue.

19.8 Give three examples of applications in which isolation is not required and a recoverable queue could be used.

19.9 Explain the difficulties in implementing a print operation in a transaction without the use of a recoverable queue. Assume that the transaction does not mind waiting until printing is complete before committing.

19.10 Consider the real-world transaction for dispensing cash discussed in Section 19.3.5. For each of the critical times—before, during, and after the execution of the real-world transaction—in which the system might crash, describe how the system (after it recovers from the crash) determines whether or not the cash has been dispensed. Discuss some ways in which the cash-dispensing mechanism itself might fail in such a way that the system cannot tell whether or not the cash has been dispensed.

19.11 Explain in what ways the execution of each individual SQL statement in a transaction is like a nested subtransaction.

19.12 Show how the credit card validation transaction described in the first paragraph of Chapter 1 can be structured as a distributed transaction.

19.13 The Student Registration System is to be integrated with an existing student billing system (which also bills for meal plans, dorm rooms, etc.). The databases for the two systems reside on different servers, so the integrated system is distributed. Using your imagination,

a. Give examples of two global integrity constraints that might exist for the global database of this system.
b. Give examples of two transactions that access both databases.

19.14 Describe the process that the admissions office of your university uses to admit new students as a workflow. Decompose the process into tasks, and describe the task interaction using a diagram similar to Figure 19.9.

19.15 Consider a transaction that transfers funds between two bank accounts. It can be structured into two subtransactions: one to debit the first account and the second to credit the second account. Describe how this can be done in (a) the hierarchical model and (b) the peer model.

19.16 Explain how nested transactions can be implemented using savepoints and procedure calls. Assume that the children of each subtransaction do not run concurrently.

19.17 In an application that uses declarative demarcation, one procedure that is called frequently from other procedures is a *logging* procedure that writes appropriate information about the state of the system into a log. What transaction attribute should be used for that procedure?

20

Implementing Isolation

Our university has over 10 thousand undergraduate students, and when the deadline for registration approaches, we might expect hundreds of students to be using the Student Registration System at the same time. The system must ensure that such a large number of concurrent users does not destroy the integrity of the database. Suppose, for example, that because of room size limitations, only 50 students are allowed to register for a particular course (that is one of the integrity constraints of the database), and suppose that 49 have already registered. If two additional students attempt to register concurrently, the system must ensure that no more than one of them succeeds.

One way to ensure the correctness of concurrent schedules is to run transactions serially, one at a time. Thus, when two students try to register for the last opening in a course, the transaction initiated by one of them will execute first, and that student will be registered. Once it has completed, the transaction initiated by the second will execute and that student will be told that the course is full. This type of execution is called **serial**, and the execution of each transaction is said to be **isolated**—the *I* in ACID.

The serial execution of a set of transactions has an important property. Recall that our assumption that transactions are consistent—the *C* in ACID—implies that if the database is in a consistent state and a transaction executes in isolation, it will execute correctly. Since the database has been returned to a consistent state, we can initiate the execution of a second transaction and, because it too is consistent, it will also execute correctly. Hence, if the initial database state is consistent, serial execution of a set of transactions—one transaction at a time—will be correct.

Unfortunately, serial execution is impractical. Databases are central to the operation of many applications and so must be accessed frequently. A system that requires that transactions be executed serially simply cannot keep up with the load. Furthermore, it is easy to see that, in many cases, serial execution is unnecessary. For example, if transaction T_1 accesses tables X and Y and if transaction T_2 accesses tables U and V, the operations of T_1 and T_2 can be arbitrarily interleaved and the end result—including the information returned by the DBMS to the transactions and the final database state—will be identical to the serial execution of T_1 followed by T_2

and also identical to the serial execution of T_2 followed by T_1. Since serial execution is known to be correct, this interleaved schedule must be correct as well.

The interleaved execution of a set of transactions is potentially far more efficient than serial execution of that set. Transaction execution requires the services of multiple system resources—primarily CPU and I/O devices—but a transaction frequently utilizes only one of these resources at a time. With concurrent execution of several transactions, we can potentially utilize a number of these resources simultaneously and hence improve system throughput. For example, while a CPU is doing some computation for one transaction, an I/O device might be providing I/O service for another.

Unfortunately, certain interleaved schedules can cause consistent transactions to behave incorrectly, returning the wrong result to the application and producing inconsistent database states. For that reason, we cannot allow arbitrary interleavings. The first question is how to decide which interleavings are good and which are bad. The next question is how to implement an algorithm that permits the good interleavings and prohibits the bad. We call such an algorithm a **concurrency control**. It schedules database operations requested by concurrently executing transactions in a way that ensures that each transaction is isolated from every other transaction. These are the questions we address in this chapter.

In most commercial transaction processing systems, concurrency control is done automatically and is invisible to the application programmer who designs each transaction as if it will execute in a nonconcurrent environment. Nevertheless, it is important to understand the concepts underlying the operation of concurrency controls because

1. Using a concurrency control to achieve isolation, in contrast to simply allowing arbitrary interleavings, can result in a significant increase in response time and a significant decrease in transaction throughput (measured in transactions per second). Hence, many commercial systems allow the option (sometimes as the default) of running transactions so that they are not completely isolated: various levels of reduced isolation are implemented. Since the designer might be tempted to use one of these options to increase system efficiency, it is important to understand how these reduced levels of isolation can lead to inconsistent databases and incorrect results.
2. Whether the designer chooses to achieve complete isolation or some reduced level of isolation, the overall efficiency of an application can be strongly influenced by the interaction between the concurrency control and the design of both the tables and the transactions within that application.

Isolation is a complex issue, so we break our discussion into two parts. In this chapter, we are primarily interested in isolation in an "abstract" database system. By "abstract" we mean a database in which each data item has a name, and read and write operations name the item that they access. Chapter 24 will be devoted to isolation in a relational database system, in which data is accessed using SQL statements that use conditions to identify rows to be addressed. Studying isolation in abstract databases helps us focus on key issues in concurrency control. The specifics of relational databases will lead to a refinement of the techniques developed for the abstract case.

20.1 Schedules and Schedule Equivalence

The concurrency controls we are interested in will work in any application. We do not discuss concurrency controls that are designed with a specific application in mind. In particular, we are not interested in controls that utilize information about the computation a particular transaction is carrying out. We are interested in controls that must separate good interleavings from bad ones without knowing what the transaction is doing. For example, a transaction might read the value of a variable in the database. If the concurrency control knows that the variable represents a bank account balance and that the transaction will request the read as a first step of a deposit operation, it might be able to use that information in choosing an acceptable interleaving. However, we assume that this information is not available to the concurrency control.

If we cannot use application-specific information, how do we decide which interleavings are correct? The answer lies in our basic assumption that each transaction is consistent and that therefore serial schedules must be correct. From this it follows that any interleaved schedule that has the same effect as that of a serial schedule must also be correct, and this is the correctness criterion we use. We will refine the notion of "has the same effect as that of a serial schedule" later, but you should understand that this is a conservative notion of correctness. As we shall see, for many applications, there will be executions that are correct even though they do not "have the same effect as that of a serial execution."

We assume that a transaction is a program whose data space includes the database and its local variables. While the local variables are accessible only by that transaction, the database is global and accessible by all transactions. The transaction uses different mechanisms to access the two parts of its data space. The local variables are directly accessible by the transaction (i.e., in its virtual memory), but the database is accessible only through calls to procedures provided by the database manager. For example, at a very low level of implementation detail, the transaction asks the database manager to copy a block of data from the database into its local variables—this is a **read request**; or it asks to overwrite a portion of the database with data stored in local variables—this is a **write request**. At this level, we view the database as a collection of data items and do not presume to know anything about the type of information stored in a data item. Also, we make no assumptions as to where the database is stored. Most likely, it is stored on a mass storage device, but in situations in which rapid response is required it can be stored in main memory.

A transaction, then, is a program in which computations made with the local variables are interspersed with requests for access to the database made to the database manager. Since the computation (on local variables) is invisible to the database manager, the manager's view of the execution of a transaction is a sequence

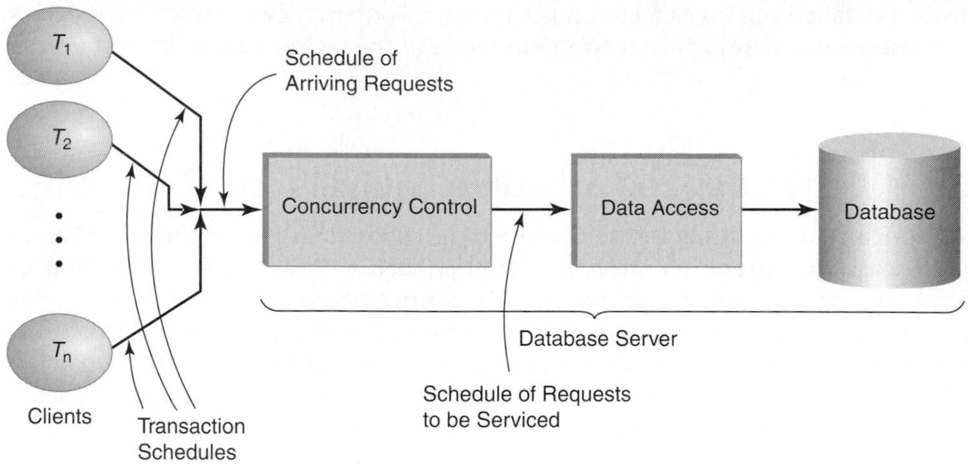

FIGURE 20.1 Role of a concurrency control in a database system.

of read and write requests, which we call a **transaction schedule**. If $p_{i,j}$ is the jth request made by transaction T_i, then

$$p_{i,1}, p_{i,2}, \ldots, p_{i,n}$$

is the transaction schedule of T_i, which consists of n requests to the database manager.

Since transactions execute concurrently, the database manager must deal with a merge of transaction schedules, which we refer to simply as a **schedule**. The database manager has the responsibility of servicing each arriving request. However, doing so in the order of arrival might lead to incorrect behavior. Hence, when a request arrives, a decision must be made as to whether to service it immediately. This decision is made by the manager's concurrency control. If the concurrency control decides that immediately servicing a request might lead to an incorrect schedule, it can delay servicing to a later time or it can abort the requesting transaction altogether.

Hence, the schedule serviced by the database manager might not be the same as the sequence of requests that arrives at the concurrency control. The concurrency control will, in general, reorder the requests. It cannot, of course, reorder the requests of a single transaction. Since we assume that a transaction is a sequential program, it will not submit a request until the previously submitted request has been serviced. The goal of the concurrency control is to reorder requests of *different* transactions in the arriving schedule so as to produce a correct schedule for servicing by the database manager. The system organization is shown in Figure 20.1.

Note that transforming the arriving schedule is not without its costs. A transaction might be either delayed or aborted. Delaying transactions reduces the overall concurrency level within the system and therefore can increase average response time and decrease throughput. Aborting a transaction is worse since it requires that the computation be repeated. Thus, it is important that the concurrency control does no unnecessary transformations, but should recognize as many correct arriving schedules as possible. Concurrency controls are generally incapable of recognizing *all* correct schedules and therefore sometimes perform unnecessary schedule transformations. The goal in designing a concurrency control is to minimize this waste.

We assume that *the execution of each database operation is atomic and isolated with respect to other database operations.* (This assumption might seem trivial for a simple read or write operation in an abstract database but is not so trivial for a complex SELECT operation in a relational database.) Although we have assumed that the concurrency control does not know the semantics of transactions (i.e., the nature of the computations), we assume that it does know the effect of each database operation, which we refer to as **operation semantics**. In this chapter, we are mainly concerned with read and write operations. In the next chapter, we will consider the operations performed on a relational database, such as SELECT and UPDATE.

Equivalence of schedules. Operation semantics is used to determine allowable schedules. To explain how, we must first explain what it means for two schedules to be equivalent. Recall that a schedule is correct if it is equivalent to a serial schedule. So what does it mean for two schedules to be equivalent?

We say that two database operations, p_1 and p_2, **commute** if, for all possible initial database states,

- p_1 returns the same value when executed in either the sequence p_1, p_2 or p_2, p_1
- p_2 returns the same value when executed in either the sequence p_1, p_2 or p_2, p_1
- The database state produced by both sequences is the same

Note that commutativity is symmetric: if p_1 commutes with p_2, then p_2 commutes with p_1.

Suppose that p_1 and p_2 are requests made by different transactions and are successive operations in a schedule, S_1. Then S_1 has the form

$$S_{1,1}, p_1, p_2, S_{1,2}$$

where $S_{1,1}$ is a prefix of S_1, and $S_{1,2}$ is a suffix of S_1. Suppose the two operations p_1 and p_2 commute. Then in schedule S_2,

$$S_{1,1}, p_2, p_1, S_{1,2}$$

all transactions perform the same computations as in schedule S_1 since the values returned to each transaction by read requests are the same in both schedules. Furthermore, both schedules leave the database in the same final state. Hence, we say that schedules S_1 and S_2 are **equivalent**. Operations that do not commute are said to **conflict**. Most important, two operations on different data items always commute. Commutativity is also possible between operations on the same item. For example, two read operations on the same item commute. However, a read and a write on the same item conflict because, although the final state of the item is the same independent of the order of execution, the value returned to the reader depends on the order of the operations. Similarly, two write operations on the same item conflict since the final state of the item depends on the order in which the writes occur.

In any schedule, successive operations that commute with each other and belong to different transactions can always be interchanged to form a new schedule that is equivalent to the original. Since equivalence is transitive we can demonstrate the equivalence of two schedules—both of which are merges of the same set of transaction schedules but which differ substantially in the way the merges are done—using a sequence of such simple interchanges. Unfortunately, demonstrating the equivalence of two schedules by performing such interchanges would be awkward for a concurrency control to do.

The design of most concurrency controls is based on the following theorem, which is an alternate way to demonstrate the equivalence of two schedules:

> **Theorem (schedule equivalence).** Two schedules of the same set of operations are equivalent if and only if conflicting operations are ordered in the same way in both schedules.

Note that we can prove this theorem if we can demonstrate that

> A schedule, S_2, can be derived from a schedule, S_1, by interchanging commuting operations if and only if conflicting operations are ordered in the same way in both schedules.

since we know that two schedules are equivalent if and only if one can be derived from the other by interchanging commuting operations.

The "only if" part of the theorem follows from the observation that the order of conflicting operations is preserved by the interchange procedure. Thus if conflicting operations were ordered differently in both schedules, S_2 could not have been obtained from S_1 using the interchange procedure.

The "if" part is a little more difficult. It can be demonstrated by showing that *any* schedule, S_2 (of the same set of operations as in S_1), in which conflicting operations are ordered the same way as in S_1, can be generated from S_1 using the interchange procedure. To show this, consider the schedule S_1:

$$\ldots, p_i, p_{i+1}, p_{i+2}, \ldots, p_{i+r}, \ldots$$

Suppose that S_2 is a schedule of the same set of operations, and in S_2 conflicting operations are ordered the same way as in S_1. Furthermore, suppose that there exists an i such that for all j satisfying $1 \leq j \leq r-1$, p_i and p_{i+j} are ordered in the same way in both S_1 and S_2, but that p_i and p_{i+r} are ordered differently. Thus, p_{i+r} is the first operation following p_i in S_1 that is ordered differently in S_2, and so p_{i+r} precedes p_i in S_2. Operations p_i and p_{i+r} must commute since conflicting operations are ordered in the same way in S_1 and S_2.

Assume now that there is some k satisfying $1 \leq k \leq r-1$ such that p_{i+r} does not commute with p_{i+k}. Then, in S_2, the operations must be ordered

$$\ldots, p_{i+k}, \ldots, p_{i+r}, \ldots, p_i, \ldots$$

since conflicting operations are ordered in the same way in both schedules. But this contradicts the assumption that p_{i+r} is the first operation following p_i in S_1 that is ordered differently in S_2.

For this reason, the assumption that there exists a k satisfying $1 \leq k \leq r-1$, such that p_{i+r} does not commute with p_{i+k}, is false. Therefore, p_{i+r} commutes with all of the operations in $p_i, \ldots, p_{i+r-1}$, and a series of interchanges of adjacent operations can be used to create a schedule equivalent to S_1 that differs from S_1 only in that p_{i+r} precedes, rather than follows, p_i (as it does in S_2). The interchange procedure can be used repeatedly to reorder the operations that are ordered differently in S_1 and S_2 and thus to transform S_1 into S_2.

20.1.1 Serializability

We have shown that, if conflicting operations are ordered in the same way in two schedules, they are equivalent. Using this rule, we can specify interleaved schedules that are equivalent to serial schedules, and it is these schedules that the concurrency control is designed to permit. We refer to such schedules as serializable [Eswaran et al. 1976].

> A schedule is **serializable** if it is equivalent to a serial schedule in the sense that conflicting operations are ordered in the same way in both.

The notion of a serializable schedule provides the answer to our first question: How are we to decide which interleavings are correct?

> Since a serializable schedule is equivalent to a serial schedule and since we assume that all transactions are consistent, a serializable schedule of any application's transactions is correct.

Serializable schedules are correct for *any* application. However, for a particular application, serializability might be too strong a condition (some nonserializable schedules of that application's transactions might be correct) and can lead to an unnecessary performance penalty. Hence, concurrency controls generally implement a variety of isolation levels, the strongest of which produces serializable schedules. The application designer can choose a level appropriate for the particular application. In this chapter, we deal only with serializable schedules. We will discuss less stringent isolation levels in Chapter 21.

To illustrate serializability, suppose that $p_{1,1}$ and $p_{1,2}$ are two successive database operations requested by transaction T_1, and that $p_{2,1}$ and $p_{2,2}$ are two successive operations requested by transaction T_2. One sequence of interleaved operations is

$$p_{1,1}, p_{2,1}, p_{1,2}, p_{2,2}$$

If $p_{2,1}$ and $p_{1,2}$ commute, this interleaved sequence is equivalent to the serial schedule

$$p_{1,1}, p_{1,2}, p_{2,1}, p_{2,2}$$

and is thus correct.

FIGURE 20.2 (a) *Serializable* schedule; (b) Equivalent *serial* schedule.

T_1:	$r(x)$			$r(y)$	$w(y)$
T_2:		$r(x)$	$w(x)$		

(a)

T_1:	$r(x)$	$r(y)$	$w(y)$		
T_2:				$r(x)$	$w(x)$

(b)

Two transaction schedules are shown in Figure 20.2(a); each displayed on a different line. Time increases from left to right. The total schedule is a merge of the two transaction schedules, with the interleaving indicated spatially. The notation $r(x)$ indicates a read of the data item x; $w(x)$, a write. The value of a data item at any point in the schedule is the value written by the last preceding write or, if there is no preceding write, the initial value.

The schedule in part (a) of Figure 20.2 is interleaved (nonserial) because some of the operations of T_1 occur before those of T_2 and others occur after. The schedule in part (b) is serial, with T_1 completing before T_2 starts and we can denote it as $T_1\ T_2$. The read and write operations on x executed by T_2 in Figure 20.2(a) commute with the read and write operations on y executed by T_1, and so that schedule can be transformed into the schedule in Figure 20.2(b) using a sequence of interchanges of adjacent commutative operations. Hence, the schedule of Figure 20.2(a) is serializable.

Now consider the two schedules from the point of view of the schedule equivalence theorem. The only conflicting operations in the two transactions are $r(x)$ in T_1 and $w(x)$ in T_2. Since they are ordered in the same way in both part (a) and part (b), the theorem tells us that the two schedules are equivalent.

Finally, note that although the schedule of Figure 20.2(a) is equivalent to the serial schedule $T_1\ T_2$ in Figure 20.2(b), it is not equivalent to the serial schedule $T_2\ T_1$.

As another example, the schedule shown in Figure 20.3 is not serializable. Since T_2 wrote x after T_1 read x, T_2 must follow T_1 in any equivalent serial order (because T_2's write does not commute with T_1's read and so cannot be interchanged with it). Similarly, since T_1 wrote y after T_2 read y, T_1 would have to follow T_2 in any equivalent serial order. Since T_1 cannot be both before and after T_2, there is no equivalent serial order.

Although the argument for equivalence between a serializable and a serial schedule is based on commutativity and the reordering of operations, the concurrency control does not necessarily reorder the operations of a serializable schedule before

FIGURE 20.3 Nonserializable schedule.

T_1:	$r(x)$			$w(y)$
T_2:		$r(y)$	$w(x)$	

executing it. Since the effect of the serializable schedule is the same as that of the serial schedule, reordering is not required. If the concurrency control can determine that the (possibly interleaved) sequence of operations that has arrived is the prefix of a serializable schedule no matter what operations might be submitted later, it executes the operations as they arrive. If, however, it cannot be certain of this, some operations have to be delayed. Delay results in reordering. If p_2 arrives after p_1 and the execution of p_1 is delayed, then the order of execution will be p_2, p_1. The concurrency control uses this delaying tactic to produce a (possibly interleaved) schedule that it knows to be serializable. We describe later how this reordering is done.

20.1.2 Conflict Equivalence and View Equivalence

Two schedules are equivalent if conflicting operations are ordered in the same way in both. However, there are actually two different notions of equivalence: the one we have described, called **conflict equivalence** because of its defining property, and a second, called **view equivalence.** Two schedules of the same set of operations are **view equivalent** if they satisfy the following two conditions:

1. Corresponding read operations in each schedule return the same values (therefore, all transactions perform the same calculations and write the same values to the database in both schedules).
2. Both schedules yield the same final database state.

The first condition implies that the transactions in both schedules have the same view of the database—hence the name. The second condition is required since although transactions in both schedules write the same values to the database (since the first condition guarantees that transactions perform the same computations in both schedules), if the writes occur in different orders the two schedules might leave the database in different final states. The second condition restricts the ordering of write statements to the extent of requiring that the final states be the same: the last operation to write each data item must be the same in each schedule.[1]

The condition for conflict equivalence is *sufficient* to ensure view equivalence, but it is *not necessary*; that is, it is stronger than the condition for view equivalence.

[1] Another way to formulate the definition of view equivalence is first to say that there is a hypothetical transaction, T_f, that executes at the end of each schedule and reads all the items written by any transaction in that schedule. Then we can say that two schedules are view equivalent if corresponding read operations in each schedule (including the reads done by T_f) return the same values in both schedules.

FIGURE 20.4 Schedule demonstrating that view equivalence does not imply conflict equivalence.

T_1:		$w(y)$ $w(x)$		
T_2:	$r(y)$		$w(x)$	
T_3:				$w(x)$

Correspondingly, view equivalence is weaker than conflict equivalence. Although two conflict-equivalent schedules are also view equivalent (you are asked to prove this in Exercise 20.6), two view-equivalent schedules are not necessarily conflict equivalent. It might not be possible to derive one from the other by interchanging adjacent operations that commute (but see Exercise 20.39(a) for a special case in which two view-equivalent schedules are also conflict equivalent).

For example, the schedule shown in Figure 20.4 is not conflict equivalent to any serial schedule. The read and write operations on y by T_2 and T_1, respectively, do not commute; hence, if there were a conflict-equivalent serial schedule, T_2 must precede T_1. On the other hand, the two write operations on x by T_1 and T_2 do not commute either and imply that, in a conflict-equivalent serial schedule, T_1 must precede T_2, which is a contradiction. Note, however, that the serial schedule in which the transactions are executed in the order T_2 T_1 T_3 has the same effect as that of the schedule shown in Figure 20.4: x and y have the same final state, and the value returned to T_2 as a result of its read of y is the same in both. The schedule in Figure 20.4 is thus view equivalent to the serial schedule T_2 T_1 T_3 and so is serializable.

Although it might be possible to design concurrency controls based on view equivalence (and perhaps to gain additional concurrency because more serializable schedules are permitted), such controls are difficult to implement. For that reason, concurrency controls are generally based on conflict equivalence. In the remainder of the text, our use of the term "equivalence" will mean conflict equivalence unless we state otherwise.

20.1.3 Serialization Graphs

Another way to think about conflict serializability is based on serialization graphs. A **serialization graph** for a particular schedule, S, of committed transactions is a directed graph in which the nodes are the transactions participating in the schedule and there is a directed edge pointing from the node representing transaction T_i to the node representing transaction T_j,

$$T_i \rightarrow T_j$$

if, in S,

1. Some database operation, p_i, in T_i conflicts with some operation, p_j, in T_j
2. p_i appears before p_j in S

It follows that if a directed edge from T_i to T_j appears in a serialization graph for S, we can conclude that T_i must precede T_j in any schedule that is conflict equivalent to S.

For example, the serialization graph corresponding to the schedule in Figure 20.2(a) consists of the one edge,

$$T_1 \rightarrow T_2$$

because T_2 wrote x after T_1 read x.

The serialization graph for a particular schedule can be used to reason about the serializability of that schedule. For example, the serialization graph for the schedule in Figure 20.3 has two edges,

$$T_1 \rightarrow T_2$$

because T_2 wrote x after T_1 read x, and

$$T_2 \rightarrow T_1$$

because T_1 wrote y after T_2 read y. These two edges form a cycle:

$$T_1 \rightarrow T_2 \rightarrow T_1$$

Thus, we can conclude that, in any equivalent serial schedule, T_1 must precede T_2 and also T_2 must precede T_1. Clearly, this is impossible, so we can conclude that there is no equivalent serial schedule and thus that the schedule of Figure 20.3 is not serializable. More generally, we can state the following result:

> **Theorem (serialization graph).** A schedule is conflict serializable if and only if its serialization graph is acyclic.

To prove this theorem, note that, if the serialization graph for a schedule, S, has a cycle, we can use the above reasoning to show that it is not serializable. Assume, on the other hand, that the graph is acyclic. Let $T_{i_1}, \ldots, T_{i_n}$, be a topological sort[2] of the transactions in the graph, and construct a serial schedule, S^{ser}, which corresponds to this ordering. The schedule S^{ser} is conflict equivalent to S because, if there is an edge from T_r to T_s in the serialization graph, there exists a conflict between an operation, p_r, of T_r and an operation, p_s, of T_s, and p_r precedes p_s in both S and S^{ser}. Since conflicting operations are ordered in the same way in both schedules, they are equivalent (according to the schedule equivalence theorem on page 818) and thus S is conflict serializable.

The serialization graph in Figure 20.5(a) is a somewhat larger example of a graph that has no cycles and hence corresponds to a serializable schedule. The graph

[2] A *topological sort* of an acyclic directed graph is any (total) ordering of the nodes in the graph that is consistent with the ordering implied by the edges in the graph. A given acyclic directed graph might have many topological sorts.

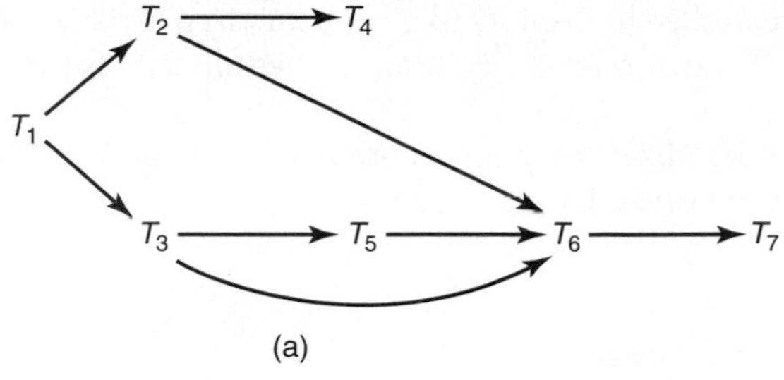

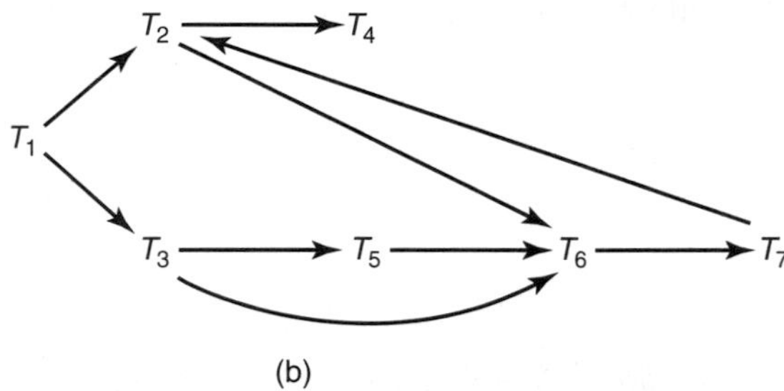

FIGURE 20.5 Two serialization graphs.

has many topological sorts, and hence there are many conflict-equivalent serial schedules of its transactions. Two of these schedules are

$$T_1\ T_2\ T_3\ T_4\ T_5\ T_6\ T_7$$

and

$$T_1\ T_3\ T_5\ T_2\ T_6\ T_7\ T_4$$

The serialization graph in Figure 20.5(b) is obtained from the graph of Figure 20.5(a) by adding the edge $T_7 \rightarrow T_2$. It corresponds to a nonserializable schedule because of the cycle

$$T_2 \rightarrow T_6 \rightarrow T_7 \rightarrow T_2$$

20.2 Recoverability, Cascaded Aborts, and Strictness

Up to this point, our discussion has been motivated by serializability, and we have assumed that all transactions commit. Life gets more complicated when we consider the possibility that a transaction might abort. Additional restrictions must be placed on schedules in that case to ensure atomicity. When a transaction commits, durability requires that any changes it made to the database be made permanent. When a transaction aborts, it must have the same effect as if it had never been initiated. A transaction that has been initiated but has not yet committed or aborted is said to be **active**.

FIGURE 20.6 (a) A nonrecoverable schedule; (b) Its recoverable counterpart.

(a)

T_1: $r(x)\ w(y)$ *commit*
T_2: $w(x)$ *abort*

(b)

T_1: $r(x)\ w(y)$ *abort*
T_2: $w(x)$ *abort*

When a transaction aborts, any changes it made to the database must be nullified. We say that the transaction must be **rolled back**. However, rolling back values the transaction has written to the database might not be sufficient to ensure that the aborted transaction has had no effect. Suppose that T_2 writes a new value to the variable x and that we allow x to be read by transaction T_1 before T_2 terminates, as shown in Figure 20.6(a). The read by T_1 is referred to as a **dirty read**, since T_2 has not committed. If we then allow the sequence of events "T_1 commits, T_2 aborts" to occur, T_2 will have had an effect on T_1 even though we roll x back to the value it had before it was written by T_2. Furthermore, since T_1 has committed, the information it has written to the database—in this case, a new value of y—has been made permanent. This creates a serious problem: that value might be a function of the value that T_1 read from T_2, and hence T_2 has (indirectly) affected the database state even though it has aborted. Thus the execution is not atomic.

Note that, if T_2 does not abort, the schedule in Figure 20.6(a) is serializable. Thus we see that dirty reads can occur in serializable schedules. Since we generally cannot prevent a transaction from aborting, we must design the concurrency control with additional restrictions so that the situation in Figure 20.6(a) cannot happen. Thus, in the above scenario, we cannot allow T_1 to commit until we know what T_2's outcome is. If T_1 had not committed, we could have aborted it when T_2 aborted, as in Figure 20.6(b).

A schedule is said to be **recoverable** [Hadzilacos 1983] if at the time when each transaction, T_1, commits, every other transaction, T_2, that wrote values read by T_1 has already committed. (Thus, if T_2 had aborted, T_1 could have been aborted as well.) A concurrency control is said to be recoverable if it produces only recoverable schedules. We require all concurrency controls to be recoverable. Note that dirty reads are possible in a recoverable schedule.

Dirty reads are undesirable even if transactions do not abort. A transaction, T_2, might update a data item several times, and a dirty read by a concurrent transaction, T_1, might see the intermediate value, as shown in Figure 20.7. Intuitively, we conclude that this cannot be a serializable schedule because intermediate values can never be read in a serial schedule (since the execution of transactions is not

FIGURE 20.7 A nonrecoverable schedule in which a transaction sees an intermediate state.

T_1:		$r(x)$ *commit*	
T_2:	$w(x)$		$w(x)$ *commit*

FIGURE 20.8 Another nonrecoverable schedule.

T_1:		$r(x)$ $r(y)$ *commit*	
T_2:	$w(x)$		$w(y)$ *commit*

FIGURE 20.9 A recoverable schedule that illustrates a cascaded abort. T_3 aborts, forcing T_2 to abort, which then forces T_1 to abort.

T_1:			$r(y)$ $w(z)$			*abort*
T_2:		$r(x)$ $w(y)$			*abort*	
T_3:	$w(x)$			*abort*		

interleaved). The fact that the schedule in Figure 20.7 is not serializable follows from the fact that the read operation of T_1 conflicts with both writes of T_2.

Another example of a dirty read that leads to a nonrecoverable and nonserializable schedule is shown in Figure 20.8. This time, T_2 does not update the same data item twice, but the schedule is nevertheless not serializable because T_1 reads x after T_2 writes it and reads y before T_2 writes it.

Even though a schedule is recoverable, it might have another undesirable property: cascaded aborts. A schedule exhibits **cascaded aborts** if, in order to maintain recoverability, the abort of one transaction causes the abort of one or more other transactions.

Suppose that we allow values written to the database by transaction T_3 to be read by transaction T_2 before T_3 terminates, as shown in Figure 20.9. If T_3 now aborts, T_2 must also abort since it read a value that T_3 wrote. The abort of T_2 forces the abort of T_1 for similar reasons. In a more general case, an arbitrary number of transactions might have to be aborted—an undesirable situation. Thus, it is desirable to have concurrency controls that do not produce schedules containing cascaded aborts.

A concurrency control can eliminate cascaded aborts if it prohibits dirty reads. This condition is more stringent than that for recoverability, which allows T_1 to read a value written by an active transaction, T_2, but does not allow T_1 to commit until after T_2 commits.

However, we choose to require an even stronger condition than simply prohibiting dirty reads; that condition is strictness. A schedule is **strict** [Hadzilacos 1983] if no transaction reads *or writes* a data item written by an active transaction. A write of a data item written by an active transaction is called a **dirty write**. In Figure 20.10, T_2's write on x is dirty. Note that it is not necessary that T_2's write be the next op-

FIGURE 20.10 A schedule that illustrates the difficulty of handling rollback when dirty writes are allowed.

T_1:	$w(x)$		*abort*	
T_2:		$w(x)$		*abort*

eration on x, only that the value overwritten by T_2 be uncommitted. Thus, in the schedule $w_1(x)\ r(x)\ w_2(x)$, the operation $w_2(x)$ is a dirty write even though the (dirty) read $r(x)$ (executed by any transaction) intervenes. A concurrency control is strict if it produces only strict schedules.

Clearly, a strict concurrency control is recoverable and does not exhibit cascaded aborts, but why have we imposed the additional condition on writing? The reason has to do with efficiency in implementing rollback in certain situations. Ordinarily, when we roll back the effect of a write of some data item, x, we expect to restore x to the value it had just before the write occurred. Suppose that we allow the value of x to be changed first by T_1 and then by T_2 (using a dirty write), as shown in Figure 20.10. If T_1 aborts, we do not have to restore the value of x at all since its value is the one written by T_2 and T_2 has not aborted. If T_2 now aborts as well, we have to restore x to the value it had just before T_1's write (not T_2's). Although we could design the system to perform correctly in all such situations, a strict system is much simpler to design since we can always roll back a write simply by restoring x to its value just before the write occurred. In nonstrict systems, the recovery algorithm is more complex, requiring an analysis of the writes made by a number of transactions and requiring the system to retain a sequence of overwritten values that corresponds to the sequence of dirty writes.

Thus if we require that schedules be both serializable and strict (or just serializable and recoverable), if a transaction in that schedule aborts and is rolled back, the resulting execution is atomic as well as serializable.

20.3 Models for Concurrency Control

In this section we give an overview of several ways in which a transaction can interact with a concurrency control and a database. There are two dimensions that can be used to describe this interaction. The first dimension characterizes it as either immediate update or deferred update.

- In an **immediate-update** system, if a transaction's request to write x is granted, the value of x is immediately updated in the database; if its request to read x is granted, the value of x in the database is returned. The situation is shown in Figure 20.11(a). It might appear that a read could return a value written by an as yet uncommitted transaction, which would mean that the concurrency control would not be strict, but we will see that this cannot happen.
- In a **deferred-update** system, if a transaction's request to write x is granted, the value of x in the database is not immediately updated. Instead, the new value

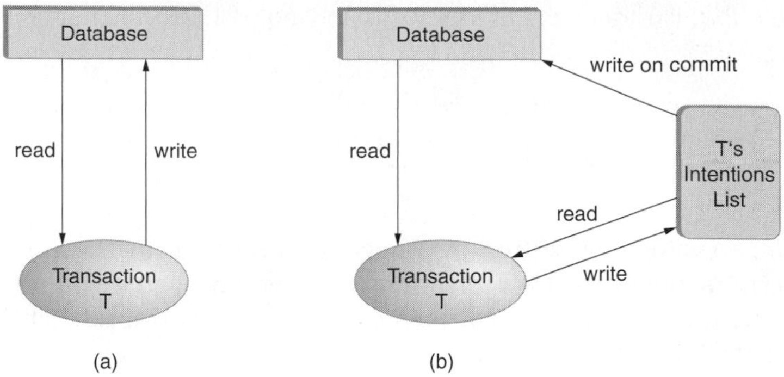

FIGURE 20.11 Dataflow in an (a) immediate-update and (b) a deferred-update concurrency control.

is saved in a buffer maintained by the system for the transaction and called its **intentions list**. If a transaction's request to read x is granted, the system returns the value of x in the database unless the transaction has previously written x, in which case the value x in its intentions list is returned. If and when the transaction commits, its intentions list is used to update the database. The situation is shown in Figure 20.11(b). Note that a value returned by a read is either a value the transaction itself has written or a value written by a committed transaction.

The second dimension deals with how the concurrency control decides whether or not to grant a transaction's request. As shown in Figure 20.1, the goal of a concurrency control is to transform the arriving sequence of requests into a strict, serializable schedule. When a transaction makes a request, the control must decide whether to grant it. The control knows the (partial) schedule of requests that have been granted but has no knowledge of requests that will be arriving in the future. Hence, it must be sure that, no matter what sequence of requests subsequently arrives, the total schedule will be serializable. The control's response to a specific request can be one of the following:

1. Grant the request.
2. Make the requestor wait until some other event occurs.
3. Deny the request (and abort the transaction).

Concurrency controls differ in the kinds of requests that are always granted (response [1] in the above list) and in the kinds of requests that might be delayed or denied. On this basis, concurrency controls can be characterized as either pessimistic or optimistic.

- In a **pessimistic** control, whenever a transaction attempts to perform any database operation, it must request permission. However, the transaction can commit at any time without requesting permission.

- In an **optimistic** control, a transaction can perform any database operation without requesting permission. However, the transaction must request permission to commit.

In both systems, a transaction can abort without requesting permission at any time before it commits.

The design of a pessimistic concurrency control is based on the philosophy that a bad thing is likely to happen: the accesses that transactions make to the database are likely to conflict. Hence, a pessimistic control grants a request only if the request does not cause the schedule to become nonserializable and it is certain that no subsequent request can possibly cause the schedule to become nonserializable as well. The control makes worst-case decisions and hence is called pessimistic. Since the resulting schedules are guaranteed to be serializable, a request to commit can always be granted.

The design of an optimistic control, on the other hand, is based on the philosophy that bad things are not likely to happen: the accesses that transactions make to the database are not likely to conflict. Hence, an optimistic control immediately grants each request for access. When a transaction requests to commit, however, the control must check to make sure that in fact no bad thing has happened—the requests granted to the transaction have caused the schedule to become nonserializable. In that case the transaction cannot be allowed to commit.

An optimistic algorithm might be appropriate for a large database in which transactions typically access only a few items, and those accesses are spread randomly over the database. The more such assumptions are violated, the more likely it is that conflicts will occur, and therefore, requests to commit will have to be denied. In particular, an optimistic algorithm is not appropriate for a database in which **hotspots** exist. These are data items that are heavily accessed in conflicting ways by many transactions.

Concurrency controls are generally characterized by the choices made in these two dimensions. The most commonly implemented concurrency control is the immediate-update pessimistic system, which we describe here in detail. We also discuss, briefly, the deferred-update optimistic system since it is useful in some situations. A deferred-update pessimistic system, which we do not discuss, is also possible.

20.4 A Strategy for Immediate-Update Pessimistic Concurrency Controls

We have required that concurrency controls be strict. A transaction must not be allowed to read or write an item in the database that has been written by another transaction that is still active. We justified this restriction as being necessary to ensure recoverability, to prevent cascaded aborts, and to enable efficient rollback. In this section, we discuss additional issues associated with immediate-update pessimistic systems and propose solutions.

FIGURE 20.12 A schedule that demonstrates that conflicting requests cannot be granted to active transactions if serializability is to be preserved.

T_1 :		$r(x)\ w(y)\ commit$	
T_2 :	$w(x)$		request_$r(y)$

20.4.1 Conflict Avoidance

Suppose that transaction T_2 has written a new value to data item x and that transaction T_1 makes a conflicting request—for example, a request to read x—while T_2 is still active. This is a dirty read, and we have seen that to ensure strictness such a request cannot be granted, but let us ignore strictness for the moment and consider only the requirement of serializability. Since we are assuming an immediate-update system, if T_1's read request is granted, the value written by T_2 will be returned. Hence, if the concurrency control grants the request, it fixes an order between T_1 and T_2 in any serialization: T_1 must follow T_2. If T_1 and T_2 subsequently request access to another data item, y, the concurrency control will have to remember the order it had already fixed between them and ensure that the accesses to y do not contradict that order. Thus, if the accesses to y by T_1 and T_2 fix the order "T_2 must follow T_1 in any serialization," the two contradictory orders preclude any serial order equivalent to the resulting schedule.

The problem in the above scenario is actually more serious than it seems. Suppose that, after the accesses to x, T_1 writes a new value to y, then T_1 commits, and finally T_2 requests to read y, as shown in Figure 20.12. The concurrency control cannot grant the read, since the resulting schedule would not be serializable. Since T_2 cannot complete, it must be aborted, but unfortunately that too is impossible since T_1 has read a result (in x) that T_2 wrote and T_1 cannot be aborted (it has already committed).

The problem can be avoided by delaying T_1's commit, but this only leads to a cascaded abort. To avoid this problem and to ensure serializability, we require that the concurrency control adhere to the following rule:

> The concurrency control grants requests in such a way that each granted request does not determine an ordering among the active transactions.

To enforce this rule, the control will not grant a request to a transaction if it previously granted a conflicting request to another, still active, transaction. In Figure 20.12, T_1's request to read x is delayed until T_2 is no longer active. Keep in mind that, since transactions are sequential programs, delaying a request actually delays the entire transaction. If the rule is enforced, the schedule produced in this case is

$$w_2(x)\ r_2(y)\ commit_2\ r_1(x)\ w_1(y)\ commit_1$$

Note that the rule precludes more than just dirty reads, as in Figure 20.12. Any request that conflicts with a previously granted request of a still active transaction

FIGURE 20.13 Another schedule demonstrating that conflicting requests cannot be granted to active transactions if serializability is to be preserved.

T_1:		$w(x)\ r(y)\ commit$	
T_2:	$r(x)$		request_$w(y)$

	Granted Operation	
Requested Operation	`read`	`write`
`read`		X
`write`	X	X

FIGURE 20.14 The conflict table for an immediate-update pessimistic concurrency control. X denotes conflicting requests.

must be delayed, so the schedule shown in Figure 20.13 is as much a problem from the point of view of the rule as that shown in Figure 20.12.

If the requests made by T_1 and T_2 do not conflict, they can be granted. Requests do not conflict if one of the following conditions is true:

1. The requests refer to different data items.
2. The requests are both read requests.

Figure 20.14 displays the conflict relation in tabular form.

We need to show that a concurrency control based on conflicts produces schedules that are both strict and serializable. The following theorem states that result:

> **Theorem (commit order serialization).** Concurrency controls that do not grant a transaction's request if a conflicting request has already been granted to another still-active transaction produce schedules that are strict and serializable in the order in which the transactions commit (called the **commit order**).

Clearly, all schedules produced by such a concurrency control are strict since no transaction can read or write an item written by another still-active transaction. The more difficult part is to demonstrate serializability in commit order. To do this, we must first deal with the fact that schedules can contain operations of transactions that have not completed (previously we have restricted our discussion to schedules produced by completed transactions). When we say that such a schedule is serializable, we mean that it is equivalent to a schedule in which the operations of committed transactions are not interleaved and occur before those of uncommitted transactions. Henceforth, our notion of a serial schedule includes such schedules.

An inductive argument demonstrates the result. The induction is on the number, i, of committed transactions in a schedule. Consider the base case, $i = 1$. Only one transaction, T_1, has committed, and all others are active. Then the schedule looks as follows: *pre-commit* $commit_1$ *post-commit*, where $commit_1$ is T_1's commit operation, *pre-commit* is the sequence of operations (of all transactions) that occur prior to that, and *post-commit* contains all operations that occur after. Neither *pre-commit* nor *post-commit* contain any commit operations. Since, prior to $commit_1$, all transactions are active, it follows from our assumptions about the concurrency control that no request in *pre-commit* conflicts with any other request in that part of the schedule. Hence, all operations in *pre-commit* commute. In particular, the operations of T_1 (which are all in *pre-commit*) can be interchanged with the operations of all the other transactions to produce an equivalent serial schedule in which all the operations of T_1 precede all the operations of all the other transactions. This demonstrates the base case.

Assume now that all schedules that contain exactly i committed transactions are serializable in commit order. Consider a schedule, S, containing $i+1$ committed transactions, and let T be the last transaction to commit. Let $S = S_1\ S_2$, where S_1 is the prefix of S up to (but not including) T's commit operation. Then S_1 contains i committed transactions and, from the induction hypothesis, is serializable in commit order. Let S_1^{ser} be the serial schedule equivalent to S_1. Thus, S is equivalent to the schedule $S_1^{ser}\ S_2$. S_1^{ser} has the form $S_{1,pre}^{ser}\ S_{1,post}^{ser}$, where $S_{1,pre}^{ser}$ is a serial schedule of the first i committed transactions and $S_{1,post}^{ser}$ is an interleaved schedule containing the operations of T, except its commit, as well as some operations of uncommitted transactions in S. The schedule $S_1^{ser}\ S_2$ has the property that all operations of T follow the ith commit. Furthermore, all operations of T must commute with all operations of any uncommitted transactions in S, so the operations of T can be interchanged in such a way that they follow those of all committed transactions and precede those of all uncommitted transactions. Once again, every pair so interchanged commutes, and thus the resulting schedule is serial and equivalent to S.

Because transactions that access only disjoint data items can be ordered arbitrarily, a serializable schedule can be equivalent to more than one serial schedule but, as we have just shown, one of these serial orders is the commit order.

Although all that we have required is that a schedule be serializable in some order, the user might expect transactions to be executed in commit order. For example, transactions frequently have external actions visible to the user (a deposit transaction outputs a receipt), and the user might expect the equivalent serial order to be consistent with these actions. Hence, a user who initiates T_2 after having observed the external actions of T_1 expects an equivalent serial order in which T_2 executes after T_1 (a withdraw transaction initiated after a receipt has been issued by a deposit transaction should see the result of that deposit in the database). One way to ensure that the order implied by these external actions is the same as the equivalent serial order is to serialize in commit order. Concurrency controls generally serialize transactions in commit order.

20.4.2 Deadlocks

When a transaction makes a request that conflicts with an operation that has been executed by another active transaction, serializability requires that the request not be granted at that time. The requesting transaction might be made to wait until

FIGURE 20.15 Schedule that exhibits deadlock.

T_1:	$w(x)$		request_$r(y)$	
T_2:		$w(y)$		request_$r(x)$

the conflict no longer exists (because the other transaction commits or aborts) and hence is no longer active. However, waiting can lead to a deadlock, as shown in Figure 20.15. When T_1 requests to read y, it is made to wait (until T_2 commits or aborts). When T_2 later requests to read x, it is made to wait (until T_1 commits or aborts). If no action is taken, both transactions will wait forever—a highly undesirable situation.

If you think that such a situation is unlikely to occur, consider the following schedule in which two transactions are each trying to update the same data item (perhaps they are both trying to make a deposit in the same bank account).

$$r_1(x)\ r_2(x)\ \texttt{request\_}w_1(x)\ \texttt{request\_}w_2(x)$$

Again, a deadlock results.

More generally, a **deadlock** is said to exist when there is a cycle of n transactions waiting for each other: T_2 is waiting for T_1, T_3 is waiting for T_2, ..., T_n is waiting for T_{n-1}, and T_1 is waiting for T_n.

Concurrency controls that make transactions wait must have some mechanism for dealing with deadlocks. A common one is for the control to construct a data structure representing the *waits_for* relation: If (T_1, T_2) is an element of *waits_for*, then T_1 is waiting for T_2. *waits_for* can be constructed when a conflict is detected. If T_1's request conflicts with an operation previously granted to an active transaction, T_2, (T_1, T_2) is inserted in *waits_for*. Whenever an element is inserted into *waits_for*, a check is made whether or not adding that element has produced a cycle, in which case a deadlock has been detected. If allowing T_1 to wait causes a deadlock, the concurrency control aborts one of the transactions in the cycle (often T_1).

A second mechanism for dealing with deadlock is **time out**. If the time a transaction waits to perform an operation exceeds some threshold, the control assumes that a deadlock has occurred. As a result, it aborts the transaction.

Finally, a timestamp technique [Rosenkrantz et al. 1978] can be employed to *prevent* (as contrasted with *detect*) deadlock. The concurrency control uses the current value of the clock as the timestamp of a transaction when it is initiated. Assuming that the clock advances more quickly than the rate at which transactions are initiated, each transaction's timestamp is guaranteed to be unique. If a conflict occurs, the concurrency control uses the timestamps of the two transactions involved to make a decision about waits or aborts. For example, it can adopt the policy that an older transaction never waits for a younger one (and can act on this policy by aborting the younger one).

20.5 Design of an Immediate-Update Pessimistic Concurrency Control

The standard technique for implementing an immediate-update pessimistic concurrency control uses **locking**. When a transaction makes a request to perform a database operation on a particular item, the system attempts to obtain an appropriate lock on the item for the transaction. For a read operation it attempts to obtain a **read lock**, and for a write operation it attempts to obtain a **write lock**. The transaction cannot perform the operation until the lock has been granted. A write lock is stronger than a read lock since, once a transaction holds a write lock on an item, it can both read and write the item.

In order to avoid placing an ordering among active transactions, the concurrency control observes the following rules when granting locks.

- The concurrency control grants a read lock on a particular item only if no other active transaction has a write lock on that item. Since it will grant a read lock on an item even though another transaction already has a read lock on that item, a read lock is often referred to as a **shared lock**.
- The concurrency control will grant a write lock on a particular item only if no other active transaction has a read or a write lock on that item. Hence a write lock is often referred to as an **exclusive lock**.

20.5.1 An Implementation Using Lock Sets and Wait Sets

To implement locking, we assume that the concurrency control associates each locked item, x, with a data structure called a **lock set**, $L(x)$, describing the locks held on x by currently active transactions. Given the above rules, it follows that if $L(x)$ is not empty, it can contain either multiple entries describing read locks on x or a single entry describing a write lock on x.

Similarly, we associate each locked item, x, with a data structure called a **wait set**, $W(x)$, which has an entry for each database operation on x that has been requested but for which a lock has not yet been granted. Because of the large number of items stored in a database, it is inefficient to maintain lock and wait sets for those items that are not being referenced. Hence, these sets are generally allocated dynamically for an item when it is first referenced, and the overhead of processing a lock request must include the time for managing the storage used to construct the sets. Generally a hash table is used. $L(x)$ and $W(x)$, if they exist, are found by hashing on x.

Finally we associate with each active transaction, T_i, a data structure called a **lock list**, $\mathcal{L}_i$, which is a list of all the entries the transaction has in lock and wait sets of different data items. Note that the lock list of T_i can have at most one item from a wait set because once a transaction's request is placed in a wait set, the transaction is suspended and it is not resumed until the entry in the wait set has been deleted.

A request by T_i to access x results in a call to a routine in the concurrency control that checks and grants locks. The routine manipulates $L(x)$, $W(x)$, and $\mathcal{L}_i$ by executing the following steps:

1. If T_i already holds a read lock on x and the request is a read, grant the request. If T_i already holds a write lock on x and the request is a read or a write, grant the request.
2. If T_i has not previously been granted an appropriate lock on x, search $L(x)$ for an entry that conflicts with the requested access. For example, if T_i requests to read x, a conflicting entry is a write lock held by T_j, $j \neq i$. If there are no conflicting entries, T_i's request can be granted, but one further situation must be considered.

   Suppose there is a conflicting request in $W(x)$. For example, $W(x)$ might contain an entry describing a request made by T_j to write x, and $L(x)$ might contain an entry describing a read lock held by another transaction, T_k. If T_i has made a read request, it can be serviced immediately since its request does not conflict with the existing lock held by T_k. However, if the scheduling algorithm allows T_i's request to be passed over in this way, it follows that a sequence of read requests can cause T_j to wait indefinitely. We refer to this situation as **starvation** and we say that the algorithm is **not fair**.

   Starvation does not result in nonserializable schedules, but it can be pretty annoying if your transaction is made to wait indefinitely, so concurrency controls are generally fair. One way to ensure fairness is to delay a transaction if its request conflicts with a request in $W(x)$ and to promote entries from $W(x)$ to $L(x)$ in a FIFO fashion (see step 4).

   With this in mind, if T_i's request conflicts with a request in $L(x)$ or $W(x)$, delay the request by inserting an entry identifying T_i and the requested lock type in $W(x)$, link it to $\mathcal{L}_i$, and block T_i. If there are no conflicting entries, grant T_i's request by inserting an entry identifying T_i and the requested lock type in $L(x)$, link the entry to $\mathcal{L}_i$, and resume T_i. We say that T_i *locks* x in this case.
3. A deadlock might result if T_i is made to wait. This would be the case if T_j is (transitively) waiting for T_i. This situation can be detected using the *waits_for* relation described in Section 20.4.2. If a deadlock is detected, abort and restart T_i (or some other transaction in the cycle).
4. When T_i commits or aborts, use $\mathcal{L}_i$ to locate and remove all of T_i's entries in lock sets (since T_i is no longer active). If a lock is removed from $L(x)$ and $W(x)$ is not empty, T_i's lock on x must have conflicted with at least one waiting request, and it might now be possible to grant that request. For example, if T_i held a write lock and there are transactions waiting to acquire read locks, all of their requests can be granted. On the other hand, if T_i held a read lock, and read locks are also held by other transactions, it will not be possible to grant requests in $W(x)$. Several strategies can be used to promote elements of $W(x)$ to $L(x)$ at this point. For example, a fair strategy is one in which requests in $W(x)$ are examined in *FIFO* (first-in-first-out) order. If a request can be granted, move it to $L(x)$ and examine the next request in $W(x)$. If not, examine no further requests. Alternatively, if the first request in the list is a read, grant all reads in the list. If the first request is a write, grant only that request. This algorithm departs from servicing requests in a FIFO order, but it does not result in starvation.

   When the promotion process is complete, $\mathcal{L}_i$ is destroyed.

This concurrency control guarantees that all schedules it permits are serializable since it grants only those requests that commute with requests previously granted to other active transactions.

The locking algorithm has the property that locks are obtained automatically. A transaction does not explicitly request a lock; it simply makes a request to access a data item, and, when the request is granted, the concurrency control automatically records that the transaction holds the appropriate lock. All locks are held until the transaction completes, at which point the control automatically unlocks all data items locked by the transaction. Since write locks are exclusive and held until termination, automatic locking guarantees strict schedules.

Locking to achieve statement-level atomicity and isolation. Whether or not a locking protocol is used to produce transaction isolation, the SQL standard requires that each SQL statement is executed atomically and that its execution is isolated with respect to other concurrently executing SQL statements. To achieve this the DBMS implements an *internal* locking protocol. When executing an SQL statement, in addition to obtaining read and write locks on database items, the DBMS obtains a number of short-duration locks, called **latches**, on various internal data structures, such as cache pages, index pages, lock tables, etc. The DBMS releases the latches when the execution of the SQL statement has completed.

20.5.2 Two-Phase Locking

While the automatic approach to locking is common, some systems allow manual locking and unlocking. In this case, a transaction *explicitly* makes a request to the concurrency control to grant a lock before making a separate request to access the item. As before, an access request is granted only if the concurrency control determines that the requesting transaction currently holds an appropriate lock on the item.

Unlocking can also be manual—except that all locks held by a transaction are released automatically when the transaction terminates. Manual unlocking seems to permit additional flexibility since, if a transaction releases locks prior to termination, concurrent transactions can access data items at an earlier time than that allowed by automatic unlocking. Unfortunately, however, to enforce strictness a transaction cannot release a write lock early. Hence, to enforce strictness early release applies only to read locks.

Furthermore, unless the early release of read locks is done properly, it can lead to nonserializable schedules. For example, consider the schedule shown in Figure 20.16, where $l(x)$ is a request to acquire an appropriate lock on x (read or write) and $u(x)$ is a request to release the lock held on x. T_1 reads x, unlocks it, and then reads y. Between the two accesses, T_2 makes conflicting accesses to both data items. The schedule is not serializable since each transaction must follow the other in any serial order. This situation could not have happened if locks were handled automatically by the concurrency control since locks are not released until

FIGURE 20.16 An example of a non-serializable schedule involving a transaction that is not two-phase.

T_1:	$l(x)\ r(x)\ u(x)$		$l(y)\ r(y)\ u(y)$
T_2:		$l(x)\ l(y)\ r(x)\ w(x)\ r(y)\ w(y)\ u(y)\ u(x)$ *commit*	

commit time. We next show that this situation can be avoided in a manual system by enforcing a protocol called two-phase locking.

A transaction is said to maintain a **two-phase locking** protocol [Eswaran et al. 1976] if it obtains all of its locks before performing any unlocks (it first goes through a locking phase, then an unlocking phase). The schedule of Figure 20.16 is not two-phase since T_1 locks y after unlocking x. Automatic locking is two phase.

> **Theorem (two-phase locking).** A concurrency control that uses a two-phase locking protocol produces only serializable schedules.

A proof of this theorem [Ullman 1982] uses the serialization graph theorem (Section 20.1.3) on page 823: a schedule is conflict serializable if and only if its serialization graph is acyclic. The proof is by contradiction. Assume that the serialization graph for a schedule produced by a two-phase locking concurrency control contains a cycle

$$T_1 \rightarrow T_2 \rightarrow \cdots \rightarrow T_n \rightarrow T_1$$

The edge $T_1 \rightarrow T_2$ implies that T_1 has an operation in the schedule that conflicts with and precedes an operation of T_2. Because the operations conflict, T_1 must have released a lock and T_2 must have acquired a lock between execution of the two operations. A similar situation must exist between T_2 and T_3, and the argument can be carried to the conclusion that T_1 released a lock before T_n acquired a lock. The edge $T_n \rightarrow T_1$ implies that T_n must have released a lock before T_1 acquired a lock. It therefore follows that T_1 acquired a lock after releasing a lock, in violation of the two-phase locking protocol. Hence, we have produced a contradiction, and we can conclude that the serialization graph for all schedules produced by a two-phase locking concurrency control must be acyclic and thus serializable.

When a two-phase locking protocol is used, one possible equivalent serial order is the order in which the transactions performed their first unlock operations. (You are asked to prove this result in Exercise 20.8.) Thus, if the schedule contains transactions T_1 and T_2 and if T_1's first unlock request occurs before T_2's first unlock request, T_1 precedes T_2 in one equivalent serial order. If the transactions hold all locks until commit time, the serialization is in commit order.

The two-phase requirement of the protocol does not distinguish between read and write locks. Serializability is guaranteed as long as locks are treated in a two-phase fashion. However, if write locks are released before commit time, strictness might be compromised and the resulting schedule might not be recoverable. Thus, when manual locking and unlocking are used (and the goal is to produce schedules that are both serializable and strict), write locks should be held until commit time, and read locks can be released early.

Two-phase concurrency controls that hold *all* locks until commit time (for example, automatic locking) are said to satisfy a **strict two-phase locking protocol**. Strict two-phase controls produce schedules that are serializable in commit order.

The word "strict" is (unfortunately) used in two different ways in the database and transaction processing literature. A two-phase locking concurrency control that releases read locks early is a strict concurrency control (because it does not release write locks early) but is not a strict two-phase locking concurrency control (as described in the previous paragraph).

Because the equivalent serial order is determined at run time, two-phase locking is referred to as a **dynamic protocol**, in contrast to **static protocols**, in which the order is determined when transactions are initiated. The timestamp-ordered concurrency control discussed in Section 20.9.1 is an example of a static protocol.

20.5.3 Lock Granularity

We have deliberately referred to the entity being locked as a data item without explaining what a data item is. We now define a **data item** to be any entity in the database that can be locked by a concurrency control algorithm—variable, record, row, table, file, etc. All locking algorithms in this chapter assume that an item has a name that uniquely identifies it. (In Chapter 21, we will see that this is not always the case.) This name is used to reference the item whenever it is accessed.

The size of the entity that is locked determines the **granularity** of the lock. Lock granularity is **fine** if the entity is small and **coarse** otherwise. The coarser the granularity, the more conservative the locking algorithm. Thus, in a DBMS that only supports table locks, an entire table is locked when only one row is accessed. Clearly, serializability is unaffected by lock granularity: as long as the items accessed are locked, a two-phase locking concurrency control produces serializable schedules even if some items are locked unnecessarily. Fine granularity locks have the advantage of allowing more concurrency since transactions need lock only the items they actually access. However, the overhead associated with fine-granularity locking is greater. Transactions generally hold more locks, and therefore more space is required to retain information about these locks. Furthermore, more time is expended in requesting locks for each individual item. Coarse-granularity locking solves these problems when transactions access multiple items in the same locked entity. For example, a transaction might access multiple rows in the same table. A single table lock makes this possible.

Many systems implement page locking as a compromise, locking the page in which the item is stored, not the item itself. The page address becomes the name of the entity that is locked. Page locking is conservative: not only is the item locked, but all other items stored on the same page are locked as well. But it is less conservative than table locking (assuming tables occupy more than one page).

20.6 Objects and Semantic Commutativity

The design of immediate-update pessimistic concurrency controls is based on the commutativity of database operations. In the simple systems we have been discussing, the only operations are read and write, and the only operations on a particular data item that commute are two reads.

If we allow more complex database operations and guarantee that the execution of each complex operation is isolated from the execution of every other complex operation (an important point that we will return to shortly), we can use the semantics of those operations to determine which operations commute and then use that information in the design of the concurrency control. In this section, we discuss object databases (Chapter 14), in which the database operations are methods defined on the objects stored in the database.

As an example of an object database, consider a banking application in which an account object has operations `deposit(x)` and `withdraw(x)` where x is the dollar amount. We assume that the account balance cannot be negative, so `withdraw(x)` returns the value `OK` if there are at least x dollars in the account and the withdraw is successful; it returns `NO` if there are fewer than x dollars in the account and the withdraw is unsuccessful.

The implementation of both of these operations involves a read of the database (to get the account balance) and a write to the database (to store the new value of the balance). A concurrency control operating at the read/write level declares a conflict between the read and write accesses of *any* pair of banking operations executed by different transactions on the same account. For example, if two deposit operations on the same account are executed concurrently, the read request of one will conflict with the write request of the other. Suppose, however, that a concurrency control is prepared to accept (higher-level) requests for method invocations. It can then use the fact that two `deposit()` operations on the same account commute—no matter the order in which they are executed, they return the same information (nothing) and leave the database in the same final state (the account has been incremented by the sum of the deposits). What is wrong with our analysis? Why is the commutativity apparent at the higher level and not at the lower level?

The answer is that, in deciding that two deposit operations commute, we used the fact that the program implementing deposit adds the amount deposited to the current balance, and that addition commutes. We refer to this information as the *semantics* of deposit. Read and write, however, carry very little semantic information. The concurrency control does not know how the information being read is used in the transaction's computation, or the relationship between the information read and the information written.

The lesson here is that more semantic information is available at higher levels, and hence the concurrency control can recognize more commutativity. This allows it to conclude that a larger set of interleaved schedules is equivalent to serial schedules and that less reordering needs to be done. Because reordering involves delays, the use of operation semantics can result in more concurrency and improved performance.

Requested Mode	Granted Mode deposit()	withdraw()
deposit()		X
withdraw()	X	X

FIGURE 20.17 Conflict table for the account object. X denotes conflicts between lock modes.

While two deposit operations commute, `deposit(y)` and `withdraw(x)` on the same account conflict because `withdraw()` might return `OK` if executed after `deposit()` but `NO` if executed before (for example, if the balance was $x - y$ dollars before the operations started). Thus, we can construct the conflict table shown in Figure 20.17 and use that table as the basis of a concurrency control design. The rows and columns in the table correspond to the database operations, and for each such operation there is a corresponding lock that the control can grant. For example, when a transaction wants to invoke `deposit()` on some account, it requests a deposit lock on the account object. If no other transaction holds a withdraw lock on that object, the request is granted; otherwise, the transaction is made to wait. Note that this control achieves more concurrency than one based on read and write operations because the latter does not allow concurrent transactions to execute `deposit` operations on the same object whereas the control based on Figure 20.17 does.

Keep in mind that this analysis is based on the *important* assumption that the programs that implement the operations on an object are isolated—their execution is serializable. For example, the concurrent execution of the programs that implement read and write is serializable. It is not the case that if a (complex) item were concurrently read and written, the read might return the values of some subfields that had been updated by the write and the values of other subfields that had not yet been updated by the write. We will return to this assumption when we discuss the implementation of a multilevel concurrency control in Section 20.8.5.

OPTIONAL

20.6.1 Partial Operations and Backward-Commutativity

We can gain even more concurrency if we incorporate two additional concepts into the concurrency control design. First, we replace a single operation that can have several possible outcomes depending on the initial database state by several operations. For example, we can replace `withdraw(x)` with

- `withdrawOK(x)`, which can be executed when the balance in the account object is greater than or equal to x dollars
- `withdrawNO(x)`, which can be executed when the balance is less than x dollars

We assume that when a transaction submits a request to perform a withdraw operation, the concurrency control checks the balance in the account and determines whether to perform a `withdrawOK()` or a `withdrawNO()`. These new operations are said to be **partial operations** because each is defined only for a subset of initial states. For example, `withdrawNO(x)` is defined only in states in which the balance is less than x. Operations that are defined in all states are said to be **total operations**.

We will say that a schedule is defined in a particular initial state if, when executed starting in that state, all the partial operations it contains are defined. For example, the schedule

$$\texttt{withdrawOK}_1(\texttt{x}),\ \texttt{deposit}_2(\texttt{y}) \quad \textbf{20.1}$$

is defined if the initial account balance, z, satisfies $z \geq x$ and is not defined otherwise.

Second, we can extend the notion of commutativity to partial operations. For example, in all initial states in which (20.1) is defined, the schedule

$$\texttt{deposit}_2(\texttt{y}),\ \texttt{withdrawOK}_1(\texttt{x})$$

is also defined because, after the deposit operation, the balance is $z + y$, which is larger than x, and hence $\texttt{withdrawOK}_1\texttt{(x)}$ must be defined. Furthermore, the final account balance, $z - x + y$, is the same for both schedules. As a result, we say that `deposit()` backward-commutes through `withdrawOK()`.

More precisely, an operation, p, **backward-commutes** through an operation, q, [Weihl 1988] if, in all database states in which the schedule q, p is defined, the schedule p, q is also defined and in both schedules, q and p return the same values and the final state of the database is the same.[3] If p does not backward-commute through q, it is said to **conflict** with q. This definition differs from the definition of commutativity for total operations given in Section 20.1. In that definition, two operations commute if they perform equivalent actions when executed in either order starting from *any initial database state*. By contrast, an operation, p, backward-commutes through an operation, q, if they perform equivalent actions when executed in either order starting from *any initial database state in which the sequence q, p is defined*. Thus, the definition of backward-commute uses the definition of a partial operation.

Note that backward-commutativity is not a symmetric relation: p might backward-commute through q, but q might not backward-commute through p. For example, `deposit()` backward-commutes through `withdrawOK()`, but `withdrawOK()` does not backward-commute through `deposit()` because there might be states in which the schedule

$$\texttt{deposit}_2(\texttt{y}),\ \texttt{withdrawOK}_1(\texttt{x})$$

is defined, but the schedule

$$\texttt{withdrawOK}_1(\texttt{x}),\ \texttt{deposit}_2(\texttt{y})$$

is not. Some partial operations, however, do backward-commute through each other (e.g., two occurrences of `withdrawOK()`).

[3] A related concept, *forward-commutativity*, has also been defined; see Exercise 20.19.

OPTIONAL

Requested Mode	Granted Mode: deposit()	withdrawOK()	withdrawNO()
deposit()			X
withdrawOK()	X		
withdrawNO()		X	

FIGURE 20.18 Conflict table for an account object using partial operations and backward-commutativity. X indicates that the operation corresponding to the row does *not* backward-commute through the operation corresponding to the column.

A concurrency control can use the notion of backward-commutativity on partial operations in the same way it uses standard-commutativity on total operations. For example, if a transaction has a `withdrawOK()` lock on an account object, then a request for a `deposit()` lock on that object by another transaction can be granted because `deposit()` backward-commutes through `withdrawOK()`.

More generally, if a transaction, T_1, has a q lock on an object, then a request by another transaction, T_2, for a p lock on the object can be granted if p backward-commutes through q. Note that since T_2's operation backward-commutes through T_1's operation, the two operations might have been performed in the opposite order and thus the control has not determined an ordering between T_1 and T_2.

On the basis of these ideas, we can expand the conflict table of Figure 20.17 into the conflict table of Figure 20.18. A space at the intersection of a row and column means that the operation corresponding to the row backward-commutes through the operation corresponding to the column, while an X indicates that it does not.

Although both tables exhibit the same number of conflicts, the table of Figure 20.18 allows more concurrency. For example, Figure 20.17 indicates that a `withdraw` request conflicts with both a prior `deposit` and a prior `withdraw`. However, Figure 20.18 indicates that a `withdraw` request conflicts with a prior `deposit` only if it is successful (`withdrawOK`) and conflicts with a prior `withdraw` only if the prior operation was successful and the request will fail (`withdrawNO`).

However, obtaining the additional concurrency involves additional run-time overhead. When a withdraw is invoked, the concurrency control must access the database to determine the value of the account balance so that it knows whether to request a `withdrawOK()` or a `withdrawNO()` lock. This additional overhead does not occur when the control is based on the table of Figure 20.17, which involves total, rather than partial, operations, since total operations commute in all states.

OPTIONAL

20.7 Atomicity, Recoverability, and Compensating Operations

Our concern up to this point has been with serializability, but we also have to consider the issue of recoverability (that is, we must guarantee that the execution is atomic if some transaction aborts). In a system in which the database is accessed with read and write operations, only the write modifies the database state. Since in such a system, a write to a data item, x, conflicts with all other operations on x, once a transaction, T, writes x, no other transaction can access x until T completes (assuming a strict two-phase concurrency control). Hence, if T aborts, it is only necessary to restore x to the value it had before T's write. We have referred to this as physical restoration.

Abort is more complicated in systems that support abstract operations since two abstract operations that modify the same data item (such as two deposit operations) might not conflict. Suppose that T_1 modifies x using operation $p(x)$, and then T_2 makes a request to modify x using a nonconflicting operation, $q(x)$. Since p and q do not conflict, the request can be granted, yielding the schedule $p(x)$, $q(x)$. But suppose T_1 later aborts. We cannot simply restore x to the value it had prior to the execution of p (physical restoration) since in reversing the effect of $p(x)$ we will in addition lose the effect of $q(x)$. We discussed this issue in connection with Sagas in Section 19.3.2 and concluded that compensation was the appropriate way to reverse the effects of a Saga that does not complete successfully.

Unfortunately, the use of compensation in Sagas is not sufficient to guarantee isolated and atomic schedules. However, we are now considering using compensation in a different model, one in which the interleaving of concurrent transactions is controlled using locks. We can do a better job here, but it will require a more precise definition of compensation and, in particular, how it interacts with the concurrency control. (The following analysis is particularly relevant to the implementation of multilevel transactions.)

To get a better understanding of compensation, we can view a database operation as a mapping from database states to database states. Thus, the operation that increments x by 1, $inc(x)$, maps the database state in which x has value 5 to the same state except that x has value 6 (the values of other variables are unaffected). If the mapping implemented by an operation is one-to-one, then there exists an inverse, or compensating, operation that implements a one-to-one mapping from the final state to the initial state. For example, the operation $dec(x)$ compensates for $inc(x)$. Note that the compensating operation has the same parameters as the operation for which it compensates (later we will examine a situation that does not have this property).

Returning to our earlier example, suppose that p has a compensating operation, p^{-1}. If T_1 is aborted using compensation we get the schedule $p(x), q(x), p^{-1}(x)$. How can we be sure that executing p^{-1} after q has modified x will correctly undo the effect of p? Fortunately, our concurrency control schedules q only if it commutes (perhaps backward-commutes) with p (i.e., a q-lock does not conflict with a p-lock), and therefore this schedule is equivalent to the schedule $q(x), p(x), p^{-1}(x)$. But this latter schedule is equivalent to just $q(x)$, and so compensation implemented abort correctly and produced atomicity. What we have demonstrated in this simple example is that recoverability can be achieved using compensation (Section 20.2). Thus, the requirement that nonconflicting operations commute is sufficient to guarantee both serializability and recoverability.

The general case. In the general case, consider a transaction, T, with transaction schedule

$$p_1, p_2, \ldots, p_n \tag{20.2}$$

If T aborts after executing some operation, p_i, it is necessary to execute compensating operations for $p_1, p_2, \ldots, p_i$ in reverse order to abort the effects of T up to that point. The transaction schedule in that case is

$$p_1, p_2, \ldots, p_i, p_i^{-1}, p_{i-1}^{-1}, \ldots, p_1^{-1} \tag{20.3}$$

Thus, there are n possible schedules for aborting T, one for each value of i (depending on when the decision to reverse T is made). All of these schedules have no net effect on the database. When we execute T, we cannot predict which of its $n + 1$ transaction schedules will occur.

When operations were restricted to read and write, an abort operation in a schedule denoted a complex action involving physically undoing all prior changes a transaction had made to the database. In contrast, schedule (20.3) explicitly describes the action of the abort. Our assumption is that when a transaction invokes abort, the concurrency control automatically introduces the appropriate compensating operations into the schedule. The transaction is aborted when its transaction schedule has completed. We refer to the use of compensation here, as well as in Sagas and workflows, as **logical rollback**.

A schedule is recoverable if each aborted transaction has no net effect on the database or on concurrently executing transactions. More precisely, a schedule S is recoverable if, for each aborted transaction, T, in S, S is equivalent to a schedule in which all of T's operations have been deleted.

Consider the following policy for a concurrency control that uses compensation.

1. The control grants compensating operations without checking for conflicts.[4]
2. The control grants forward operations only if they (backward-)commute with all forward operations that have been granted to active transactions (without considering possible conflicts with previously granted compensating operations of active transactions).

We now demonstrate that the policy is correct, in the sense that any schedule produced by the control is recoverable and that, after the recovery has taken place, the resulting schedule of transactions that have not aborted is serializable.

Consider an arbitrary schedule, S, that might have been produced by such a concurrency control and that is the merge of transaction schedules of both committed and aborted transactions (and thus contains both forward and compensating

[4] If the control were to delay a compensating operation because of a conflict, a deadlock might result. This is a possibility whenever a transaction is forced to wait. In such a case the abort could not be completed, causing a violation of the requirement that, in contrast to a request to commit, a request to abort is always granted.

operations). Consider the first compensating operation in S, p_i^{-1}. S has the form

$$S_{prefix}, p_i, S', p_i^{-1}, S_{suffix}$$

where S_{prefix} and S' have no compensating operations and S' is the sequence of operations that separates p_i from p_i^{-1}. Since the concurrency control would not have scheduled an operation in S' unless it commutes with p_i, this schedule is equivalent to the schedule

$$S_{prefix}, S', p_i, p_i^{-1}, S_{suffix}$$

which in turn is equivalent to the schedule

$$S_{prefix}, S', S_{suffix}$$

The transformation has in effect caused p_i and p_i^{-1} to annihilate each other and has thus reduced S to an equivalent schedule that is shorter.

The transformation can now be repeated to eliminate the second compensating operation in S and its matching forward operation. In this manner, all operations of aborted transactions (both forward and compensating) can be eliminated from S, producing an equivalent schedule of the transactions that have not aborted. Therefore, S is recoverable. Furthermore, the resulting schedule is conflict equivalent to a serial schedule. The fact that this type of transformation is always possible demonstrates the correctness of the concurrency control.

A schedule that can be reduced by such a transformation to a serializable schedule of transactions that have not aborted is said to be **reducible**. If a schedule of transactions, in which each transaction is represented by one of its transaction schedules, is reducible, then it is recoverable. All of the schedules produced by the concurrency control described in this section are reducible and hence recoverable.[5]

The undo operation. Unfortunately, not every operation, p, has a compensating operation because not every operation is one-to-one. For example, the operation *Reset*(x), which sets the value of x to 0, does not have a compensating operation since the mapping is many-to-one. Since every value maps to 0, how can a compensating operation know what transformation was performed by the original operation (e.g., change 5 to 0) by just looking at the current state of the object? And if the transformation cannot be deduced, how can it be compensated for?

One way to handle this problem is to simply make a p-lock exclusive: assume that every operation conflicts with an operation, p, that is not compensatable. Then when T_1 gets a p-lock on x as a result of executing $p(x)$, no other transaction can execute an operation on x until T_1 commits or aborts. If T_1 aborts, the value of x can simply be physically restored to the value it had prior to the execution of p since no other transaction has accessed the dirty value.

[5] A more complete discussion of this subject can be found in [Schek et al. 1993].

We can think of physical restoration as being accomplished by an *undo* operation. Undoing an operation such as *Reset*(x) requires that we record some information about the state of x when the operation was executed. For example, if the value of x was 5 at the time *Reset*(x) was executed, we need to remember 5 so that we can return x to that value if the operation must be undone. We can define an undo operation, $p^{undo}(x, s)$, that undoes the execution of an operation $p(x)$. The parameter s contains sufficient information about the state of x at the time $p(x)$ was executed to perform the undo—the complete state does not necessarily have to be saved. *Set*$(x, 5)$ is the undo operation for *Reset*(x) if x had value 5 when *Reset*(x) was executed. This resembles physical logging, an approach used to roll back a transaction that we will discuss in Section 22.2.

Thus an undo operation differs from a compensating operation in that its parameters include information about the database state when the operation it is undoing was executed, while the parameters of a compensating operation contain only the parameters of the operation being compensated.

Although an exclusive lock can be used to guarantee atomicity when p is not compensatable, the question is "Can we get more concurrency?" Stated another way, "If a transaction has a p-lock on x and p is not compensatable, are there *any* operations we can allow another transaction to perform on x"? The answer is "yes," but to understand this, we need to first understand why an undo operation cannot be used in the same way as a compensating operation.

Consider the schedule $p(x),\ q(x)$. If s describes the state of x when p is executed in the schedule, then the undo operation for $p(x)$ is $p^{undo}(x, s)$. Unfortunately, the argument that we used earlier to show that compensation can be used to achieve recoverability does not work for the undo operation. Assume that $q(x)$ backward-commutes with $p(x)$, and that we want to undo the effect of $p(x)$. Why would it be incorrect to append $p^{undo}(x, s)$ to $p(x),\ q(x)$? Since $q(x)$ backward-commutes through $p(x)$, the new schedule is equivalent to $q(x),\ p(x),\ p^{undo}(x, s)$. But in this schedule s might no longer describe the state of x when $p(x)$ is executed, so we cannot expect $p^{undo}(x, s)$ to work correctly.

For example, *Reset*(x) commutes with itself, but, assuming that the initial value of x is 5, the undo operation, *Set*$(x, 5)$, does not work correctly in the schedule $Reset_1(x),\ Reset_2(x),\ Set_1(x, 5)$.

Thus, in order to guarantee recoverability, a stronger condition than simply commutativity is needed in deciding whether a request for a q-lock conflicts with a previously granted p-lock when p is not compensatable. In order to understand the most general form of that condition, we first need to point out that if p is a many-to-one operation, its range might be a proper subset of its domain. This is the case if the domain is finite, but it might also be the case if the domain is infinite. For example, *round* is a many-to-one operation that rounds each real number in its domain to the nearest whole number. Its range, the whole numbers, is a subset of the reals.

As a result, the domain of an undo operation can be a subset of the domain of the operation it undoes, and if that is the case, the undo is a partial operation. For example, the undo operation for *round*(x) is *restore*(x, s). Its domain is the set of whole numbers; it is undefined for other real numbers.

OPTIONAL

The state information, *s*, retained for use in *restore(x,s)* contains the sign of *x* when *round* was executed and the fractional change that was made at that time. The sign is required, since it might be changed by an interleaved execution of some other operation. Thus, if the value of *x* was −9.25 initially, *s* records the fact that *round* added .25 to a negative number. If *x* is still a negative number when *restore* is executed, then .25 has to be subtracted. If it is a positive number, .25 must be added.

Suppose *mag(x)* is the many-to-one operation that produces the magnitude of *x*. Its domain is the set of real numbers and its range is the set of positive real numbers. $mag(x)$ commutes with $round(x)$. Under certain circumstances $mag(x)$ also commutes with *restore(x,s)*. Thus, if the initial state of *x* is a whole number in the schedule $mag(x)$, $restore(x, s)$, the schedule is equivalent to $restore(x, s)$, $mag(x)$. If the initial state is not a whole number, *restore* is undefined. In the schedule $round_1(x)$, $mag_2(x)$, $restore_1(x, f)$, *x* is a whole number when $mag_2(x)$ is executed, and hence the schedule is equivalent to $round_1(x)$, $restore_1(x, s)$, $mag_2(x)$. As a result the undo operation performs correctly.

We can prove the following theorem.

Theorem (undo). A locking concurrency control guarantees serializability and recoverability if the condition used by the control to determine that a request for a *q*-lock that does not conflict with a previously granted *p*-lock held by an active transaction is that

1. *q* backward-commutes through *p* and
2. Either *p* has a compensating operation, or when a *p*-lock is held, p^{undo} backward-commutes through *q*.

We have previously demonstrated the result when a compensating operation exists.[6] Suppose a compensating operation does not exist. To make the argument simple, assume that schedule *S* contains a single undo operation, $p_i^{undo}(x, s)$. Then it must also contain $p_i(x)$ and have the form

$$S_{prefix},\ p_i(x),\ S',\ p_i^{undo}(x, s),\ S_{suffix}$$

T_i must hold a *p*-lock on *x* for the duration of S'. Hence, all the operations in S' commute with $p_i^{undo}(x, s)$, and it follows that *S* is equivalent to the schedule $\hat{S}$

$$S_{prefix},\ p_i(x),\ p_i^{undo}(x, s),\ S',\ S_{suffix}$$

Since *s* describes the state of *x* when p_i is executed in *S*, it also describes the state when p_i is executed in $\hat{S}$. Since $p_i^{undo}(x, s)$ works correctly in $\hat{S}$ and the two schedules are equivalent, it also works correctly in *S*.

In some cases we can decompose an operation that has no compensating operation into two or more partial operations that do have compensating operations. Returning to the example in Section 20.6, the `withdraw(x)` operation does

[6] Note that when *p* has a compensating operation, it is always true that p^{-1} backward-commutes through *q*. See Exercise 20.41.

OPTIONAL

not have a compensating operation because it is many-to-one: for any value of `x` it has two possible results depending on whether the account balance covers the withdrawal. It does have an undo operation `conditionalDeposit(x,y)` where `y` was the account balance when `withdraw(x)` was executed. The semantics of `conditionaldeposit(x,y)` is that if $y \geq x$ (so that the withdrawal succeeded), it deposits x; otherwise it does nothing. However, if we decompose `withdraw(x)` into the two partial operations `withdrawOK(x)` and `withdrawNO(x)`, then `withdrawOK(x)` has a compensating operation, `deposit(x)`, and `withdrawNO(x)` does not need a compensating operation because it has no effect on the database. Note that even though `withdraw(x)` is not a one-to-one operation, its domain and range are identical: the set of all possible account balances.

20.8 Isolation in Structured Transaction Models

In Chapter 19, we introduced a number of transaction models. Having discussed serializability and locking, we can now show how to implement isolation within these models. We will devote all of Chapter 24 to showing how distributed transactions are implemented, so we do not discuss them here.

20.8.1 Savepoints

A savepoint (Section 19.2.1) is a mechanism used within a transaction, T, to achieve partial rollback. It should appear as if the database updates made by the portion of the transaction that were rolled back never happened. After the rollback completes, the items that have been restored can be unlocked and immediately made available (before the transaction completes) to concurrent transactions. Thus we have the following rules for handling savepoints in concurrency controls based on locks:

1. When a savepoint, s, is created, no change is made to any lock set. However, the concurrency control must remember the identity of all locks that T_i acquired prior to creating s, so that if T_i rolls back to s, it can release locks obtained subsequent to the creation. To accomplish this, the control places a marker in the lock list, $\mathcal{L}_i$, containing a number that represents the Id of the savepoint. Lock entries that follow this marker correspond to locks obtained after the creation of s.
2. When the transaction rolls back to s, the locks corresponding to all lock entries following the marker for s in $\mathcal{L}_i$ are released.

It would be a happy result if the above rules preserved isolation in a two-phase locking concurrency control, but this is sadly not the case. A transaction might read a data item, x, after creating a savepoint and then roll back, releasing the read lock. The effect is an early release of a read lock, which allows a non-two-phase schedule to be easily created. To preserve isolation, the second rule can be modified so that write locks are downgraded to read locks and read locks are not released.

20.8.2 Chained Transactions

Chaining can be used to decompose a transaction, T, into smaller subtransactions to avoid total rollback if a crash occurs. In Chapter 19, we discussed two different semantics for how chained transactions deal with the state of database items accessed by the transaction when control moves from one subtransaction in the chain to the next. Using `commit`, the state is not maintained between subtransactions, and, although the individual subtransactions are isolated and serializable, T as a whole is not. Using `chain`, the state is maintained between one subtransaction and the next, and T is isolated and serializable with respect to other transactions.

The `commit` operation is handled in the normal way: all locks are released. For the `chain` operation, locks are not released but are instead passed to the subsequent subtransaction in the chain. Durability is provided in both cases (as described in Chapter 22).

20.8.3 Recoverable Queues

A recoverable queue can be implemented as one or more tables within a database (since the database is durable), but performance suffers. The queue is a hotspot, accessed by many transactions, and, assuming the concurrency control is strict, locks on the queue would be held until commit time, creating bottlenecks.

For this reason, a recoverable queue is implemented as a separate module that uses locks but manages them in a manner suited to the needs of the queue. In one possible implementation, a separate lock is associated with each element on the queue and with the queue's head and tail pointers. A transaction wishing to enqueue or dequeue an element must first obtain a write lock on the tail or head pointer, respectively. A pointer is locked only for the duration of the enqueue or dequeue operation, whereas a lock on an element that is enqueued or dequeued is held until the transaction that performed the enqueue or dequeue operation commits or aborts. Thus, for example, a transaction, T, might dequeue an element from the queue and release the lock on the head pointer. Another transaction can then dequeue the next element before T commits or aborts.

Note that since the queue is implemented as a module separate from the database, the requirements of strictness and two-phase locking can be relaxed. The concurrency control is clearly not strict in the way it manipulates the lock on the pointer, and it need not be two-phase either. The queue is treated as an object with known semantics. Using the fact that it is used for scheduling work, concurrent operations that do not commute are allowed. For example, dequeue operations conflict: if their order is reversed, different elements are returned. However, by implementing the queue in a separate module, the conflict is not visible to the database and hence not taken into account by its concurrency control.

The purpose of the locks used to implement the queue is to guarantee the integrity of the individual enqueue and dequeue operations, not the serializability of the transactions that invoke them. As a result, concurrency is enhanced at the expense of isolation. Concurrent transactions might enqueue and dequeue elements on a set of queues in a variety of orders that would not be possible if serializable execution were enforced.

In contrast to its lock on the head or tail pointer, T always retains a write lock on the element it is accessing until it commits. This guarantees, for example, that after T enqueues an element, no other transaction, T', can dequeue that element until after T commits.

20.8.4 Nested Transactions

Nested transactions support concurrent execution of subtransactions. That is, several subtransactions of a top-level transaction can be executing concurrently and can request conflicting database operations. Hence, in addition to the rules governing the granting of locks to concurrent (nested) transactions, we must introduce new rules governing how locks are granted to the subtransactions of a single (nested) transaction.

The nested transaction model discussed in Section 19.2.3 adheres to the following rules:

1. Each nested transaction in its entirety must be isolated and hence serializable with respect to other nested transactions.
2. A parent subtransaction does not execute concurrently with its children.
3. Each child subtransaction (together with all of its descendants) must be isolated and hence serializable with respect to each of its siblings (together with all of that sibling's descendants).

To implement this we impose the following rules [Beeri et al. 1989]:

1. When a subtransaction of nested transaction, T, requests to read a data item, a read lock is granted if no other nested transaction holds a write lock on that item and all subtransactions of T holding a write lock on that item are its ancestors (and hence are not executing).
2. When a subtransaction of a nested transaction, T, requests to write a data item, a write lock is granted if no other nested transaction holds a read or write lock on that item and all subtransactions of T holding a read lock or a write lock on that item are its ancestors (and hence are not executing).
3. All locks obtained by a subtransaction are held until it aborts or commits. When a subtransaction commits, any locks it obtained that its parent does not hold are inherited by the parent. When a subtransaction aborts, any locks it obtained that its parent does not hold are released.

Since these rules are a superset of the rules that guarantee isolation among concurrent transactions, the schedules of concurrent nested transactions are serializable. To see that these rules enforce the desired semantics among siblings, observe that no lock held within the subtree rooted at one active subtransaction can conflict with a lock held within the subtree rooted at an active sibling. Thus, concurrently active siblings are not ordered by the database operations that have been performed within their subtrees. Therefore the siblings are isolated with respect to each other and hence serializable. They might be serializable in several possible orders, among which is always the order in which they commit (Section 20.4).

20.8.5 Multilevel Transactions

A concurrency control for multilevel transactions can be implemented by two rather elegant generalizations of the conventional, strict two-phase locking concurrency control described in Sections 20.4 and 20.5 [Weikum 1991]. The first generalization makes use of the semantics of the operations at each level; the second relies on the fact that multiple levels are involved.

Operation semantics and commutativity. In Section 20.6, we discussed how the commutativity of operations on objects can be used in the design of conflict tables for immediate-update pessimistic concurrency controls. These ideas form a central part of the multilevel model.

Each level in a system that supports multilevel transactions produces its own (interleaved) schedule. Thus, for example, in Figure 19.4, on page 797, the schedule at level L_2 of the transaction $Move(sec_1,\ sec_2)$ is the sequence $TestInc(sec_2)$, $Dec(sec_1)$. (A reminder: *Move* moves a student from one course section to another; *TestInc* conditionally adds one student to a section; and *Dec* decrements the enrollment in a section.) A more interesting schedule is one that involves the concurrent execution of several multilevel transactions. For example, the L_2 schedule

$$TestInc_1(sec_2),\ TestInc_2(sec_2),\ Dec_2(sec_1),\ Dec_1(sec_1) \qquad \textbf{20.4}$$

involves the interleaved execution of two transactions, $Move_1(sec_1,\ sec_2)$ and $Move_2(sec_1,\ sec_2)$, each of which moves a student from section 1 to section 2. The interesting aspect of this schedule is that since the two decrement operations commute, (20.4) is equivalent to the schedule

$$TestInc_1(sec_2),\ Dec_1(sec_1),\ TestInc_2(sec_2),\ Dec_2(sec_1) \qquad \textbf{20.5}$$

and is thus serializable in the order $Move_1$, $Move_2$. Note that since two *TestInc* operations on the same tuple do not commute, (20.4) is not serializable in the order $Move_2$, $Move_1$ (the initial state might be such that the first to execute succeeds in the increment while the second fails; thus, different results are returned to the caller if the order is reversed).

Suppose now that we examine the schedule (20.4) in terms of the operations that execute at L_1. We see the following:

$$Sel_1(t_2),\ Upd_1(t_2),\ Sel_2(t_2),\ Upd_2(t_2),\ Upd_2(t_1),\ Upd_1(t_1) \qquad \textbf{20.6}$$

As with the banking application discussed in Section 20.6, since update operations on the same tuple do not, *in general*, commute, this schedule is not serializable in either order. A higher-level view, however, shows that the updates implement *Dec*

Requested Mode	Granted Mode `TestInc`	`Dec`
`TestInc`	X	X
`Dec`	X	

FIGURE 20.19 Conflict table for an L_2 concurrency control that schedules *TestInc* and *Dec* operations.

operations, and serializability becomes apparent. Once again, the more semantics available to the concurrency control, the more concurrency it can detect.

A concurrency control for L_2. To take advantage of semantics, we can construct a concurrency control for L_2 that uses a conflict table, C_2, shown in Figure 20.19. The rows and columns of C_2 correspond to operations supported at L_2. For example, a *Move* transaction is a program at the *application* level, L_3, containing invocations of *TestInc* and *Dec*, which are supported at L_2. The concurrency control at L_2 receives these invocations and decides whether they can be serviced using C_2. It grants *TestInc* and *Dec* locks for this purpose. Thus, if *Move* invokes $Dec(sec_2)$, the concurrency control grants a *Dec* lock on sec_2 if no other transaction has a *TestInc* lock on it; otherwise, the *Dec* request must wait. Once the lock has been granted, a program at L_2 can be executed that implements the *Dec* operation by invoking operations at L_1.

Now let us go back to the original example. Although the schedule of (20.4) is serializable in the order $Move_1$, $Move_2$, the two *TestInc* operations do not commute and so impose an ordering on the two transactions. Since the conventional, pessimistic concurrency control (described in Section 20.4) does not grant a request if it imposes an ordering among active transactions, the L_2 scheduler does not produce schedule (20.5). As with a conventional concurrency control, not all conflict-serializable schedules can be recognized. However, consider the following interleaved schedule of transactions $Move_1(sec_1,\ sec_2)$ and $Move_2(sec_1,\ sec_3)$:

$$TestInc_1(sec_2),\ TestInc_2(sec_3),\ Dec_2(sec_1),\ Dec_1(sec_1) \qquad \textbf{20.7}$$

This interleaving is allowed by the L_2 concurrency control since two decrement operations commute. To see that additional concurrency is gained, realize that we have not indicated when the transactions request to commit. Instead of committing immediately after completing $Dec_2(sec_1)$, $Move_2$ might continue to be active for an extended period of time. By recognizing the commutativity of decrement operations, the L_2 concurrency control can avoid delaying Dec_1 until $Move_2$ releases its `Dec` lock on sec_1.

Multilevel concurrency controls. It appears that the strategy for obtaining the best performance is to implement a concurrency control at the highest level, L_n, in the hierarchy (L_2 in Figure 19.4) in order to take advantage of the most semantics. But we have overlooked one important point. In the discussion in Section 20.4 of a conventional, pessimistic concurrency control, we implicitly assumed that the

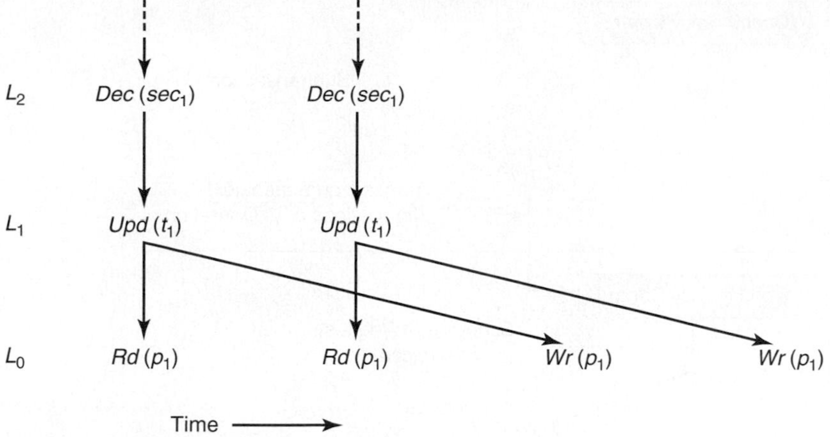

FIGURE 20.20 Decrement operations do not conflict at L_2, but arbitrary interleaving at lower levels can lead to problems.

OPTIONAL

read and write operations scheduled by the concurrency control were isolated with respect to each other. Thus, if the control scheduled a write operation after a read operation, it assumed that the read had completed before the write started. With a multilevel concurrency control, this is true when operations conflict but not necessarily true when they do not. Thus, if a transaction, T, executes $TestInc(sec_1)$ and a second transaction requests the same operation, it will be made to wait until T completes because two *TestInc* operations on the same section conflict. Hence, the two operations will be totally ordered.

However, consider two operations that do not conflict and hence their concurrent execution is permitted by the concurrency control. In Figure 20.20, the L_2 concurrency control has scheduled the concurrent execution of two decrement operations invoked by transaction programs running at L_3. (The programs might invoke other operations as well, but we do not consider them here.) The decrement operation is implemented by a program (subtransaction) in L_2, and that program invokes operations supported by L_1. In this case, each instance of the decrement program makes only a single such invocation—of *Upd*. Each invocation of the *Upd* program in L_1 invokes read and write operations implemented in L_0.

As shown in the figure, each of the update statements reads the same value of the enrollment number stored in tuple t_1, decrements that value, and therefore stores the same value back in t_1. Thus, although two decrement operations have been performed, the enrollment has only been decremented by one. This is an example of the lost update problem introduced in Section 2.3, and the reason it has occurred is that the executions of the two instances of the program that implement the *Upd* operations are not isolated with respect to each other. This violates the assumption made by a concurrency control that each operation that it schedules is isolated (we

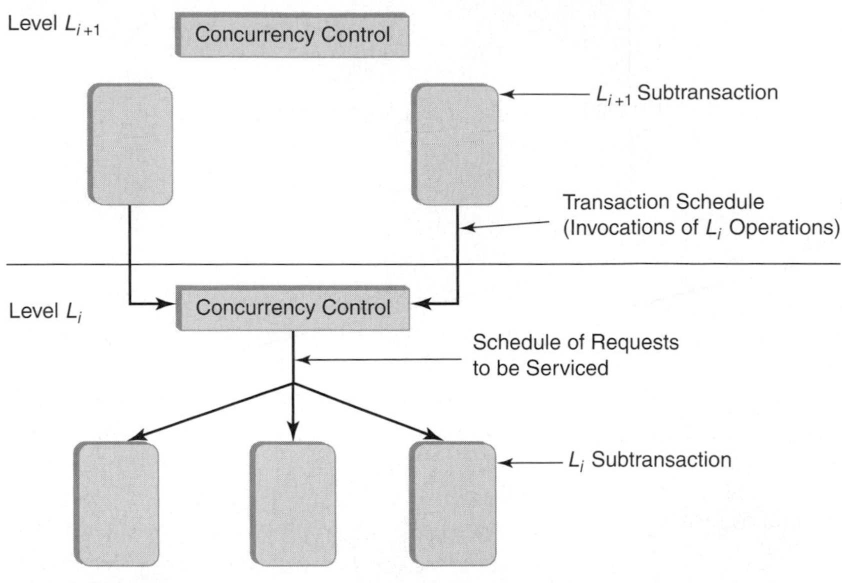

FIGURE 20.21 Relationship between levels in a multilevel concurrency control.

OPTIONAL

discussed this issue on page 840). Operations are implemented by programs, and hence the programs must be serializable.

To overcome this problem, multilevel transactions use a multilevel concurrency control, which guarantees that the operations *at each level* are serializable and hence isolated with respect to each other. A **multilevel concurrency control** is composed of separate controls at each level. Thus, the control at L_i schedules the operation invocations it receives from subtransactions at L_{i+1} in accordance with a conflict table, C_i, which determines whether or not those operations can be executed concurrently. The control grants operation locks as described previously and releases them when the subtransaction at L_{i+1} commits. Figure 20.21 shows this organization.

A goal of a multilevel concurrency control is to guarantee that operations invoked by a program at any level are effectively isolated from each other. In other words, an operation invoked by a transaction at the application level is implemented by a program—think of it as a subtransaction—in L_n. That subtransaction then invokes a sequence of operations, each of which is implemented by a program in L_{n-1}. If the L_n concurrency control determines that op_1 and op_2, invoked by two application transactions, can be executed concurrently, then the subprograms, L_n, that implement these operations will be executed concurrently. These subprograms invoke lower-level operations and create an interleaved schedule at L_{n-1}. To guarantee that op_1 and op_2 are effectively isolated, this interleaved schedule at L_{n-1} must be serializable. That is, it must be equivalent to a serial schedule of the individual sequences. Note that the equivalent serial order is not important since op_1 and op_2

commute and therefore both orders produce the same result. The L_n concurrency control requires only that the schedule at L_{n-1} be equivalent to *some* serial schedule.

To guarantee the isolation of op_1 and op_2 we need a concurrency control at level L_{n-1} that guarantees that schedules at that level are serializable. The argument now repeats. The L_{n-1} control assumes that the operations it schedules are isolated units when in fact they are not. They are subtransactions that produce schedules at L_{n-2}. Hence, a concurrency control at L_{n-2} is needed to guarantee that these subtransactions are serializable.

Let us follow this reasoning, using Figure 20.20 as an example, and see why the L_0 schedule in that figure cannot be produced by a multilevel concurrency control. Two transactions at the application level (not shown in the figure) concurrently invoke $Dec(sec_1)$. The L_2 control sees that the two operations commute, so it grants *Dec* locks on sec_1 to both transactions, allowing two invocations of the L_2 subtransaction that implements *Dec* to run concurrently. Each subtransaction at L_2 is a program that invokes $Upd(t_1)$. Those invocations are passed to the L_1 control. The first L_2 subtransaction is granted an *Upd* lock on t_1, but the second must wait since *Upd* locks conflict. Thus, only a single invocation of the update subtransaction at L_1 is initiated. It invokes read and write operations on p_1. These are passed to the L_0 control, which grants the page locks on p_1 to the update subtransaction and schedules the operations. When the update subtransaction commits, it releases the page locks and returns to the *Dec* subtransaction that invoked it. When *Dec* commits, it releases the *Upd* lock, hence allowing the second invocation of the update subtransaction to commence, and returns to the application transaction that invoked it. In this way, a serializable L_0 schedule (not the schedule shown in Figure 20.20) is produced.

Using the same reasoning as in Section 20.6, we can show that all schedules produced by this concurrency control are recoverable (i.e., compensating operations work correctly and guarantee atomicity when transactions abort).

Using the multilevel model. The multilevel model (Section 20.8.5) of transactions is not widely available to application programmers since a concurrency control has to be provided at each level. If an application is decomposed into levels of abstraction, the application programmer will have to participate in building the concurrency controls for those levels. The model can be used, however, within a DBMS and its implementation utilizes the concept of latches.

Consider the example of granular locking on tuples and pages. An X lock must be acquired on a tuple and an IX lock on the page in which it is stored when the tuple is inserted. But the insert operation must, in addition, update other data structures in the page, for example, the structure that records information about storage allocation within the page. Maintaining locks on these additional items until the transaction completes would unnecessarily reduce concurrency since these locks would prevent other transactions from accessing the page in what might be totally nonconflicting ways.

To alleviate this problem, we can view the procedure that executes an SQL statement within the DBMS as a subtransaction of the transaction that submitted the statement. While the transaction sees the abstraction of tuples, the subtransaction sees the abstraction of page reads and writes. The subtransaction acquires latches on the pages it accesses and releases them when it commits. This ensures the isolation of the subtransaction with respect to concurrent subtransactions (or equivalently, the isolated execution of concurrently processed SQL statements within the DBMS). Since the latches need not be held until the transaction as a whole commits, access by concurrent transactions to other tuples and data structures within the page is possible. The transaction, in turn, retains higher-level locks on the tuples it accesses to ensure appropriate transaction isolation.

The tuple/page hierarchy within a DBMS is one example of an object hierarchy. In Section 20.6 we considered abstract operations on objects and assumed that they were isolated. However, an object in a hierarchy is implemented using lower-level objects, and isolation is not guaranteed. This is a context within which a multilevel control is useful. Using this model, each object implements a concurrency control using the semantics of the operations it supports and allows the concurrent execution of two operations on the object if they commute. The isolation of the procedures within the object that implement these operations is guaranteed by the concurrency controls at the objects that they, in turn, access.

20.9 Other Concurrency Controls

Locking forms the basis of most, but not all, of the concurrency control algorithms in commercial systems. We discuss two nonlocking algorithms in this section: timestamp-ordered concurrency controls and optimistic concurrency controls. The timestamp-ordered algorithm, one of the earliest concurrency control algorithms to be proposed, illustrates the use of timestamps to achieve synchronization. Optimistic concurrency controls are a more recent development and show promise in certain situations. In Section 21.5, we will discuss still another algorithm, multiversion concurrency control, which has been implemented in a number of commercial relational database systems.

20.9.1 Timestamp-Ordered Concurrency Controls

In a **timestamp-ordered concurrency control**, a unique timestamp, $TS(T)$, is assigned to a transaction, T, when it is initiated, and the concurrency control guarantees the existence of an equivalent serial schedule in which transactions are ordered by their timestamps. For this reason, timestamp-ordered controls are **static**; that is, the equivalent serial order is determined at the time they are initiated. Transactions are serialized in their initiation order, not necessarily their commit order.

Unique timestamps can be generated using a clock. The value of the clock at the time the transaction is initiated is taken as the timestamp. As long as the clock ticks faster than the rate at which transactions are initiated, each transaction will get a unique timestamp.[7] We describe an immediate-update version of a timestamp-ordered control; a deferred-update version is also possible.

A timestamp-ordered control stores with each data item, x, the following pieces of information:

- $rt(x)$, the largest timestamp of any transaction that has read x
- $wt(x)$, the largest timestamp of any transaction that has updated x
- $f(x)$, a flag that indicates whether the transaction that last wrote x has committed

The maintenance of this information implies additional overhead and hence is a disadvantage of this scheme. Additional space is required for each separately addressable item in the database. Furthermore, since this information is stored in the database, updates to it must be treated like updates to the data items themselves—they must be recorded on disk and they must be rolled back if the transaction aborts. This means that, in contrast to other controls, a read of a data item x causes a write of $rt(x)$. As a result of this large overhead, timestamp-ordered algorithms have not been widely used.

When a transaction, T_1, makes a request to read x, the concurrency control performs the following actions:

R1. If $TS(T_1) < wt(x)$, some transaction T_2, which must follow T_1 in the equivalent serial (timestamp) order, $(TS(T_2) > TS(T_1))$, has written a new value to x. T_1's read should return a value that x had prior to the write executed by T_2, but that value no longer exists in the database. Thus, T_1 is too old (has too small a timestamp) to read x. It is aborted and restarted (with a new timestamp).

R2. If $TS(T_1) > wt(x)$, there are two cases:

- If $f(x)$ indicates that the value of x is committed, the request is granted. If $TS(T_1) > rt(x)$, the value of $TS(T_1)$ is assigned to $rt(x)$.
- If $f(x)$ indicates that the value of x is not committed, T_1 must wait (to avoid a dirty read).

When T_1 makes a request to write x, the concurrency control performs the following actions:

W1. If $TS(T_1) < rt(x)$, some transaction T_2, which must follow T_1 in the equivalent serial (timestamp) order, has read an earlier value of x. If T_1 is allowed to commit, T_2 should have read the value that T_1 is requesting to write. Thus, T_1 is too old to write x. It is aborted and restarted (with a new timestamp).

[7] In a network in which each site generates its own timestamps using its own local clock, uniqueness is not guaranteed by this algorithm. To guarantee uniqueness, the algorithm is modified by assigning to each site at startup time a unique identifier. Each site appends its identifier to the value of its clock to form a timestamp. Thus, a timestamp at site i is (c_i, id_i), where c_i is the current value of its clock and id_i is i's unique identifier.

*W*2. If $rt(x) < TS(T_1) < wt(x)$, a transaction has stored a new value in x that, in a serial schedule ordered on timestamps, overwrites the value that T_1 is requesting to write (since $TS(T_1) < wt(x)$). Furthermore, no transaction with a timestamp between $TS(T_1)$ and $wt(x)$ previously requested to read x (since $rt(x) < TS(T_1)$).

- If $f(x)$ indicates that x is committed, any subsequent transaction with a timestamp between $TS(T_1)$ and $wt(x)$ that attempts to read x will be aborted (see *R*1). Hence, the value that T_1 is requesting to write will not be read by any transaction and will have no effect on the final database state. The request is thus granted, but the write is not actually performed. This action (not performing the write in this situation) is called the Thomas Write Rule [Thomas 1979].
- If $f(x)$ indicates that x is not a committed value, T_1 must wait (since the transaction that last wrote x might abort and the value that T_1 is requesting to write becomes the current value).

*W*3. If $wt(x), rt(x) < TS(T_1)$, there are two cases:

- If $f(x)$ indicates that the value of x is not a committed value, T_1 is made to wait since granting the request will complicate rollback (see the discussion in Section 20.2).
- If $f(x)$ indicates that the value of x has been committed, the request is granted. The value of $TS(T_1)$ is assigned to $wt(x)$, and the value of $f(x)$ is set to uncommitted. (Later, when T_1 commits, the value of $f(x)$ is set to committed.)

The sequence of requests shown in Figure 20.22 illustrates these rules. Assume that $TS(T_1) < TS(T_2)$, that at time t_0 the read and write timestamps of both x and y are less than $TS(T_1)$, and that both x and y have committed values. Then, at time t_1, rule *R*2 applies, the read request is granted, and $rt(y)$ is set to $TS(T_1)$. At t_2, using *W*3, the write request is granted, $wt(y)$ is set to $TS(T_2)$, and $f(y)$ is set to indicate that y is uncommitted. At t_3, *W*3 again applies, the write request is granted, $wt(x)$ is set to $TS(T_2)$, and since T_2 immediately commits, both $f(x)$ and $f(y)$ indicate committed values. At t_4, *W*2 applies since $rt(x)$ has not changed and $wt(x)$ is now $TS(T_2)$. The request is granted, although the write is not actually performed and $wt(x)$ is not updated.

The sequence is thus accepted by a timestamp-ordered control, but we do not refer to it as a schedule since the control does not submit the final write to the database. Note that the sequence is not conflict equivalent to a serial schedule and would not be accepted by a concurrency control based on conflict equivalence. (However, it is view equivalent to the serial schedule T_1, T_2.) This means that a timestamp-ordered control can accept sequences of requests that are not accepted by a control based on two-phase locking. Exercise 20.30 asks you to provide a schedule accepted by a two-phase locking concurrency control but not a timestamp-ordered control. It follows then that the two controls are incomparable: each can accept (serializable) schedules that will not be accepted by the other.

FIGURE 20.22 Sequence of requests accepted by a timestamp-ordered concurrency control. Assuming that $TS(T_1) < TS(T_2)$ and that the initial values of the read and write timestamps of x and y are smaller than both transactions' timestamps, T_1's final write is not performed.

T_1:		$r(y)$			$w(x)$ *commit*
T_2:			$w(y)$	$w(x)$ *commit*	
	t_0	t_1	t_2	t_3	t_4

20.9.2 Optimistic Concurrency Controls

In general, an optimistic algorithm consists of several steps. In the first, a task is executed under some (optimistic) assumption that simplifies the performance of the task. For example, in a security system the task might be a password check, and the assumption is made that the submitted password is correct. In a concurrency control the task is a transaction, and the assumption is made that conflicts with concurrent transactions will not occur. Hence, we need not be concerned with locking or waiting. Transactions read and write without requesting permission from the concurrency control and thus are never delayed. The second step validates the first step by checking to see if the assumption was actually true. If not, the task must be redone, which implies rollback in the concurrency control case. If the assumption is true, validation results in commitment.

This approach stands in contrast to the pessimistic approach, in which execution of the task is done cautiously. No simplifying assumptions are made in the first step, each request for database access is checked in advance, and appropriate actions are taken immediately if conflicts are detected. Hence, no second (validation) step is required in the pessimistic approach.

Since database accesses during the first step are unchecked and conflicts might actually occur, optimistic concurrency controls [Kung and Robinson 1981] generally use a deferred-update approach to avoid propagating the effects of an incorrectly executed transaction to the database. (If an immediate update approach were used, the updates performed by transactions that later roll back would be visible to concurrent transactions and would result in cascaded aborts.) The new values of the items written are stored in an intentions list and are not used to update the database immediately. Thus, a third step is needed for a transaction that modifies the database and is successfully validated: its intentions list is written to the database.

Since rollback is costly, an optimistic algorithm is appropriate only if conflicts are rare. Note that rollback is more costly with an optimistic algorithm than with a timestamp-ordered algorithm, since the rollback decision is made after the transaction completes. With a timestamp-ordered control a rollback decision is made while the transaction is still executing, which wastes less of the system resources. Rollback can also occur in a pessimistic algorithm because of deadlock. An important advantage of optimistic algorithms is that deadlocks cannot occur since one transaction never waits for another. In comparing the efficiency of optimistic and pessimistic algorithms, the costs of validation, managing the intentions list, locking, and rollback must be considered.

Because the database is not modified during the first step (writes might be requested but are not actually executed), this step is referred to as the **read phase**. The second step is referred to as the **validation phase**, and the third step, as the **write phase**. Thus, a transaction's writes are performed and appear in a schedule during its write phase (write requests during the read phase are not recorded in the schedule). For the sake of simplicity, we initially assume that the validation and write phases form a single critical section, and hence only one transaction can be executing its validation or write phase at a time (but a number of transactions can concurrently be executing their read phase while a single transaction is executing its validation or write phase). We will modify that assumption shortly. The three phases of a transaction are shown in Figure 20.23(a).

The validation phase ensures that S is equivalent to a schedule, S^{ser}, in which committed transactions are executed serially in the order in which they enter validation (i.e., the order in which they commit). The operations of uncommitted transactions follow those of committed transactions in S^{ser}.

There are two cases to consider when validating a transaction, T_1. In case 1 (the simple case), we consider a transaction T_2 that completes its write phase before T_1 starts its read phase, as shown in Figure 20.23(b). Since the two transactions are not concurrently active, all of T_1's operations follow all of T_2's in S. Hence the validation of T_1 against T_2 is always successful, and T_1 follows T_2 in S^{ser}.

Case 2 (the more interesting case) is shown in Figure 20.23(c). Here T_2 completed before T_1 entered validation but was still active when T_1 entered its read phase. If T_1 is successfully validated, then T_2 will precede T_1 in S^{ser}. Hence, validation of T_1 with respect to T_2 requires that if T_1 executes an operation, p, that conflicts with an operation, q, of T_2, p must follow q in S in order for S to be equivalent to S^{ser}.

Suppose that p is a read executed by T_1 during its read phase and that q is a write of the same item executed by T_2 during its write phase. Thus, the transactions have conflicting operations. As shown in Figure 20.23(c), the operations can occur in either order. If p precedes q, the order is contrary to the order in which the transactions enter validation, and hence, if T_1 were allowed to commit, the order would be contrary to the commit order in S^{ser}. Therefore, T_1 must not be successfully validated. It must be aborted. If the operations occurred in the opposite order, T_1 could be allowed to commit (since the order would be consistent with the commit order), but, unfortunately, optimistic controls do not generally record the order in which such operations occur. As a result, validation makes the worst-case assumption that the order is not consistent with the order of entry into validation.

Thus the condition for the validation of T_1 is that the set of items it has read must be disjoint from the set of items written by any transaction whose write phase overlaps T_1's read phase.

Note that when T_1 validates, the only check made concerns T_1's read operations. Validation does not check for conflicts involving T_1's write operations. Although a conflict also occurs if T_1 writes an item that T_2 reads or writes, it follows from Figure 20.23(c) (and the fact that only one transaction at a time can be in its validation or write phases) that if a write of T_1 (during its write phase) conflicts with a read or write of T_2 (during T_2's read or write phases), then the order of the

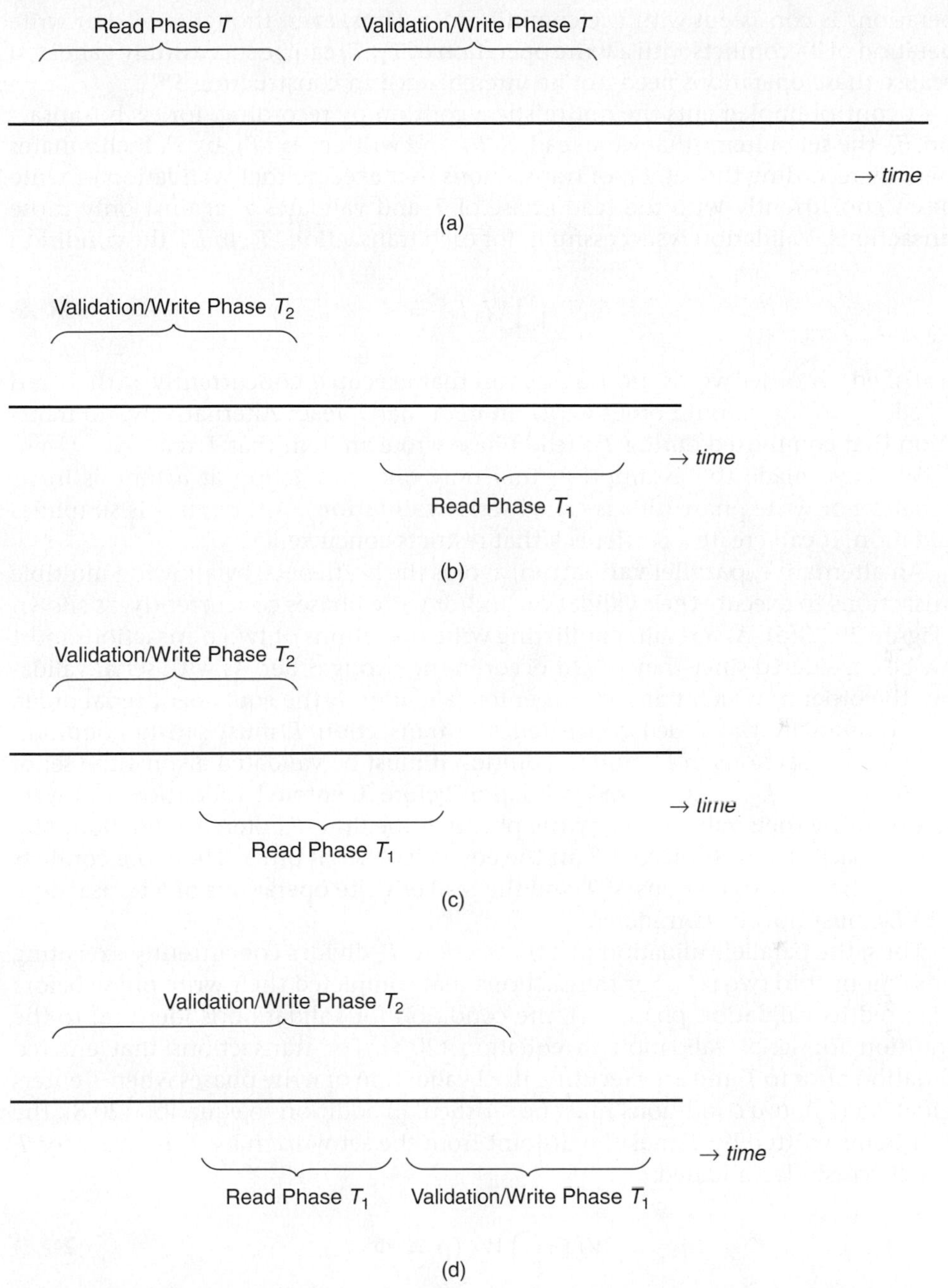

FIGURE 20.23 Transactions in an optimistic concurrency control: (a) the three phases of a transaction, (b) nonconcurrent transactions, (c) T_1 conflicts with T_2 if the set of items read by T_1 overlaps the set of items written by T_2, (d) T_1 conflicts with T_2 if the set of items read or written by T_1 overlaps the set of items written by T_2.

operations is consistent with the commit order. Thus, even though a read or write operation of T_2 conflicts with a write operation of T_1, T_1 can be successfully validated because these operations need not be interchanged in constructing S^{ser}.

A control implements the optimistic algorithm by recording, for each transaction, T, the set of items that were read, $R(T)$, and written, $W(T)$, by T. It eliminates case 1 by recording the set, L_1, of transactions that execute their validation or write phases concurrently with the read phase of T and validates T against only those transactions. Validation is successful if, for each transaction, T_i, in L_1, the condition

$$R(T) \bigcap W(T_i) = \Phi \qquad \textbf{20.8}$$

is satisfied. In other words, no transaction that executed concurrently with T and precedes it in the commit order wrote an item that T read. Alternatively, no transaction that committed during T's read phase wrote an item that T read.

We have made the assumption that only one transaction at a time is in its validation or write phase (this is called **serial validation**). Although this simplifies validation, it can create a bottleneck that restricts concurrency.

An alternative, **parallel validation**, avoids the bottleneck by allowing multiple transactions to execute their validation and/or write phases concurrently, as shown in Figure 20.23(d). As a result, conflicting write operations of two transactions must now be considered since they might occur in the wrong order. As with serial validation, the order in which transactions enter validation is the equivalent serial order. To accommodate the added concurrency, a transaction T must satisfy condition (20.8) for transactions in L_1, and in addition it must be validated against the set of all transactions, L_2, that entered validation before T entered validation and were still executing their validation or write phases at the time T entered validation. Any such transactions must precede T in the equivalent serial order. Therefore conflicts between the write operations of T and the read *or* write operations of a transaction, T_i, in L_2 must now be considered.

Thus, the parallel validation of a transaction, T, divides concurrently executing transactions into two sets. For transactions that completed their write phase before T entered its validation phase (L_1), the condition for validation is identical to the condition for serial validation in equation (20.8). For transactions that entered validation prior to T and are executing their validation or write phases when T enters validation (L_2), *two* conditions must be satisfied. In addition to equation (20.8), the set of items written by T must be disjoint from the set written by T_i in order for T to be successfully validated:

$$W(T) \bigcap W(T_i) = \Phi \qquad \textbf{20.9}$$

Note that a conflict between a write operation of T and a read operation of T_i is not a problem since the order of entry into validation implies that T's write must have followed T_i's read, and therefore the order of the operations in S is consistent with the commit order.

BIBLIOGRAPHIC NOTES

Two excellent books on concurrency controls are [Bernstein et al. 1987; Papadimitriou 1986]. A more theoretical discussion is given in [Lynch et al. 1994].

The concepts of serializability and two-phase locking were introduced in [Eswaran et al. 1976]. The result—that if a schedule is not serializable, there exists an integrity constraint that the schedule makes false—is proved in [Rosenkrantz et al. 1984]. The concepts of recoverability and strictness were introduced in [Hadzilacos 1983]. Backward and forward commutativity were introduced in [Weihl 1988] and are discussed in more detail in [Lynch et al. 1994]. Our implementation of nested transactions is taken from [Beeri et al. 1989] and the implementation of multilevel transactions is taken from [Weikum 1991]. One of the first timestamp-ordered concurrency controls is described in [Thomas 1979], which also introduced the Thomas Write Rule. Optimistic concurrency controls were introduced in [Kung and Robinson 1981]. Intentions lists were first suggested in [Lampson et al. 1981]. A different approach to designing concurrency controls based on the semantics of the application (as opposed to the semantics of the operations) is discussed in [Bernstein et al. 1999b; Bernstein et al. 1999a; Bernstein et al. 1998; Bernstein and Lewis 1996].

EXERCISES

20.1 State which of the following schedules are serializable.

a. $r_1(x)\ r_2(y)\ r_1(z)\ r_3(z)\ r_2(x)\ r_1(y)$
b. $r_1(x)\ w_2(y)\ r_1(z)\ r_3(z)\ w_2(x)\ r_1(y)$
c. $r_1(x)\ w_2(y)\ r_1(z)\ r_3(z)\ w_1(x)\ r_2(y)$
d. $r_1(x)\ r_2(y)\ r_1(z)\ r_3(z)\ w_1(x)\ w_2(y)$
e. $r_1(x)\ r_2(y)\ w_2(x)\ w_3(x)\ w_3(y)\ r_1(y)$
f. $w_1(x)\ r_2(y)\ r_1(z)\ r_3(z)\ r_1(x)\ w_2(y)$
g. $r_1(z)\ w_2(x)\ r_2(z)\ r_2(y)\ w_1(x)\ w_3(z)\ w_1(y)\ r_3(x)$

20.2 Give all possible conflict-equivalent serial orderings corresponding to the serialization graph in Figure 20.5.

20.3 Use a serialization graph to demonstrate that the schedule shown in Figure 20.4 is not conflict serializable.

20.4 Suppose that we declare all of the database integrity constraints in the database schema so that the DBMS will not allow any transaction to commit if its updates violate any of the integrity constraints. Then, even if we do not use any concurrency control, the database always remains consistent. Explain why we must nevertheless use a concurrency control.

20.5 Give an example of a schedule of two transactions that preserves database consistency (the database satisfies its integrity constraints), but nevertheless yields a final database that does not reflect the effect of both transactions.

20.6 Prove that conflict equivalence implies view equivalence.

20.7 Give an example of a schedule in which transactions of the Student Registration System deadlock.

20.8 Prove that with a two-phase locking protocol, one possible equivalent serial order is the order in which the transactions perform their first unlock operation.

20.9 Give an example of a transaction processing system (other than a banking system) that you have interacted with, for which you had an intuitive expectation that the serial order was the commit order.

20.10 Give an example of a schedule that is serializable but not strict.

20.11 Give an example of a schedule that is strict but not serializable.

20.12 Give an example of a schedule produced by a nonstrict two-phase locking concurrency control that is not recoverable.

20.13 Give an example of a schedule produced by a recoverable but nonstrict concurrency control involving three transactions in which a deadlock occurs, causing a cascaded abort of all three.

20.14 Give an example of a schedule produced by a nonstrict two-phase locking concurrency control that is serializable but not in commit order.

20.15 Suppose that the `account` object, the conflict table for which is described in Figure 20.18, has an additional operation, `balance`, which returns the balance in the account. Design a new conflict table for this object, including the new operation.

20.16 Consider the following schedule of three transactions:

$$r_2(y)\ r_1(x)\ r_3(y)\ r_2(x)\ w_2(y)\ w_1(x)\ r_3(x)$$

a. Define a serialization between T_1 and T_2.
b. In what apparent order does T_3 see the database?
c. Is the schedule serializable?
d. Assuming that each transaction is consistent, does the final database state satisfy all integrity constraints?
e. Does the database state seen by T_3 satisfy all integrity constraints? Explain.

20.17

a. Assume that, in addition to the operations `read(x)` and `write(x)`, a database has the operation `copy(x,y)`, which (atomically) copies the value stored in record x into record y. Design a conflict table for these operations for use in an immediate-update pessimistic concurrency control.
b. Assume that, in addition to the operations `read(x)` and `write(x)`, a database has the operation `increment(x,C)`, which (atomically) increments the value stored in record x by the constant C, which might be positive or negative. Design a conflict table for these operations for use in an immediate-update pessimistic concurrency control.

20.18 Suppose that we have a `queue` object that implements an FCFS (first-come-first-served) discipline, with operations `enqueue` and `dequeue`. `enqueue` always succeeds and `dequeue` returns `NO` if the queue is empty and `OK` otherwise. Design a conflict table for this object using partial operations and backward commutativity.

20.19 A pair of (partial) database operations, p and q, are said to **forward-commute** if, in every database state in which both p and q are defined, the sequences p, q and q, p are both defined and, in both sequences, p and q return the same values and the final database state is the same.

a. Describe how forward commutativity can be used in the design of a deferred-update pessimistic concurrency control.

b. Give a conflict table for such a control for the `account` object described in Figure 20.18.

20.20 In Section 20.7 we described a policy for a concurrency control that dealt with both forward and compensating operations and guaranteed that schedules were reducible. Generalize this policy to include undo operations using the conditions on the commutativity described in that section, and show that your generalization preserves reducibility.

20.21 Design a deferred-update pessimistic concurrency control.

20.22 Consider an implementation of chained transactions in which a subtransaction, when it commits, only releases locks on items that will not be accessed by subsequent subtransactions. Explain how this can affect the ACID properties of the overall chained transaction.

20.23 Give the conflict table for each level of the multilevel control described in Section 20.8.5. Each table indicates the conflicts for the operations used to implement the transaction `Move(sec1, sec2)`. Assume that the operation `TestInc` is viewed as two partial operations `TestIncOK` and `TestIncNO`.

20.24 Give an example of a schedule in which a pessimistic concurrency control makes a transaction wait but later allows it to commit, while an optimistic concurrency control restarts the transaction.

20.25 Give an example of a schedule in which a pessimistic concurrency control makes a transaction wait but then allows it to commit, while an optimistic concurrency control allows the transaction to commit without waiting.

20.26 Give an example of a schedule that is acceptable (without any delays caused by locks) by an immediate-update pessimistic strict two-phase locking concurrency control, while an optimistic concurrency control restarts one of the transactions.

20.27 Can a deadlock occur in the timestamp-ordered control described in the text?

20.28 Give an example of a schedule produced by a timestamp-ordered concurrency control in which the serialization order is not the commit order.

20.29 Give an example of a schedule that is strict and serializable but not in commit order and that could have been produced by either a timestamp-ordered concurrency control or a two-phase locking concurrency control.

20.30 Give an example of a schedule that would be accepted by a two-phase locking concurrency control but not by a timestamp-ordered concurrency control.

20.31 Show that the following proposed protocol for a timestamp-ordered concurrency control is not recoverable.

> Store with each data item the maximum timestamp of any (not necessarily committed) transaction that has read that item and the maximum timestamp of any (not necessarily committed) transaction that has written that item.
>
> When a transaction makes a request to read (write) a data item, if the timestamp of the requesting transaction is smaller than the write (read) timestamp in the item, restart the transaction; otherwise, grant the request.

20.32 The *kill-wait* concurrency control combines the concepts of the immediate update concurrency control and the timestamp-ordered control. As in the timestamp-ordered system, when a transaction, T_1 is initiated, it is assigned a timestamp, $TS(T_1)$. However, the system uses the same conflict table as the immediate-update pessimistic control does and resolves conflicts using the rule

> If transaction T_1 makes a request that conflicts with an operation of active transaction, T_2
>
> **if** $TS(T_1) < TS(T_2)$, **then** *abort* T_2, **else** *make* T_1 *wait until* T_2 *terminates.*

where *abort* T_2 is referred to as a *kill* because T_1 kills T_2.

a. Show that the kill-wait control serializes in commit order.
b. Give a schedule produced by a kill-wait control that is not serializable in timestamp order.
c. Explain why deadlock does not occur in a kill-wait control.

20.33 The *wait-die* concurrency control is another control that combines the concepts of the immediate-update concurrency control and the timestamp-ordered control.

> If transaction T_1 makes a request that conflicts with an operation of active transaction T_2
>
> **if** $TS(T_1) < TS(T_2)$, **then** *make* T_1 *wait until* T_2 *terminates,* **else** *abort* T_1.

where *abort* T_1 is referred to as a *die* because T_1 kills itself.

a. Show that the wait-die control serializes in commit order and prevents deadlocks.
b. Compare the fairness of the execution of the kill-wait and wait-die controls.

20.34 Give a complete description of an algorithm for a parallel validation, optimistic concurrency control.

20.35 Describe a serial validation, optimistic concurrency control that uses backward validation and in addition uses timestamps to distinguish the order in which conflicting read and write operations occur. The validation condition in that case need not be conservative, and only conflicts that would violate commit order cause aborts.

20.36 Subroutines can be used in a flat transaction in an attempt to mimic the behavior of a subtransaction in the nested model: whenever a subtransaction aborts, the corresponding subroutine manually undoes any database updates it has performed and returns with status indicating failure. Explain why the nested model allows higher transaction throughput.

20.37 Suppose that transactions T_1 and T_2 can be decomposed into the subtransactions

$$T_1:\ T_{1,1},\ T_{1,2}$$

and

$$T_2:\ T_{2,1},\ T_{2,2}$$

such that the database items accessed by $T_{1,1}$ and $T_{2,1}$ are disjoint from the items accessed by $T_{1,2}$ and $T_{2,2}$. Instead of guaranteeing that all schedules involving T_1

and T_2 are serializable, suppose that a concurrency control guarantees that $T_{1,1}$ is always executed serializably with $T_{2,1}$ and that $T_{1,2}$ is always executed serializably with $T_{2,2}$.

a. Will T_1 always be serializable with T_2? Explain.

b. What minimal additional condition *on the subtransactions* guarantees that the effect of executing T_1 concurrently with T_2 is the same as a serial schedule?

c. Assuming that the condition of (b) holds, what advantage does the new concurrency control have over a concurrency control that guarantees serializability?

20.38 Suppose that transactions T_1 and T_2 can be decomposed into the subtransactions

$$T_1: T_{1,1}, T_{1,2}$$

and

$$T_2: T_{2,1}, T_{2,2}$$

such that each subtransaction individually maintains the consistency constraints of the database. Instead of guaranteeing that all schedules involving T_1 and T_2 are serializable, suppose that a concurrency control guarantees that all subtransactions are always executed serializably.

a. Will T_1 always be serializable with T_2? Explain.

b. Will integrity constraints be maintained by all possible schedules?

c. What possible problems might arise if the concurrency control schedules transactions in this way?

20.39 A **blind write** occurs when a transaction writes a database item it has not read. For example, in the Student Registration System a transaction might compute a student's GPA by reading her course grades, computing the average, and then (blindly) writing the result in the appropriate database item without first reading that item. Some applications have the property that no transactions perform blind writes. Show that for such applications

a. View equivalence is *equivalent* to conflict equivalence.

b. The timestamp-ordered concurrency control described in Section 20.9.1 never uses the Thomas Write Rule.

c. In the timestamp-ordered concurrency control described in the text, for each item, x, that a transaction, T, writes, when T commits, $rt(x) = wt(x) = TS(T)$.

20.40 State which of the following operations has a compensating operation.

a. Give all employees a 10% raise.

b. Give all employees making less than $10,000 a 10% raise.

c. Set the value of a particular item to 12.

d. Insert a new tuple with key 1111 into the database, and set the value of one of its attributes to 12.

e. Set the value of a particular item to the square of its original value.

20.41 Assume an operation p has a compensating operation p^{-1}. Show that if operation q commutes with p, then p^{-1} commutes with q.

20.42 Give an example of a schedule of consistent transactions that is not serializable but maintains the correctness of any integrity constraint that might conceivably be associated with the database.

21

Isolation in Relational Databases

In Chapter 20 we discussed isolation in the context of a simple database model in which data is accessed by read and write commands. We did this in order to concentrate on the problems of serializability and recovery. The simple model, however, is unrealistic. Most databases are relational and are accessed through SQL statements, and this introduces additional issues.

In this chapter we discuss concurrency controls that guarantee serializable schedules in relational databases. However, as we shall see, these concurrency controls often do not provide the performance characteristics required by heavily used systems. Hence, in the real world, less restrictive concurrency controls must often be used. These concurrency controls implement different *levels of isolation*, which do not guarantee serializable schedules. We explore the different isolation levels defined in SQL, how they are implemented, and how they can affect the correctness of transaction systems. We also discuss SNAPSHOT isolation, which is not one of the isolation levels defined in the SQL standard but which is important in the real world because it has been implemented by a number of vendors, including Oracle.

21.1 Conflicts in a Relational Database

Consider a table, ACCOUNTS, in a banking system that contains a tuple for each separate account. We might read all tuples in ACCOUNTS describing accounts controlled by depositor Mary using the SELECT statement

```
SELECT *
FROM ACCOUNTS A
WHERE A.Name = 'Mary'
```
21.1

The expression in the WHERE clause is referred to as the **read predicate** (attribute names are treated as variables in the predicate), and the statement returns all tuples that satisfy the predicate.

The SELECT statement is an operation that reads data in the relational model and corresponds to the read operation in the simple model discussed in Chapter 20.

Conflicts take a different form with such operations. For example, assume that ACCOUNTS has attributes AcctNumber (the key), Name, and Balance. Also assume that there is a table, DEPOSITORS, containing a tuple for each depositor, with attributes Name (the key) and TotalBalance, in which the value of the TotalBalance attribute is the sum of the balances of all that depositor's accounts. An audit transaction, T_1, for Mary might utilize the SELECT statement

```
SELECT SUM(Balance)
FROM ACCOUNTS A
WHERE A.Name = 'Mary'
```

to calculate the sum of the balances in Mary's accounts and then compare it with the result of executing

```
SELECT D.TotalBalance
FROM DEPOSITORS D
WHERE D.Name = 'Mary'
```

Mary should consider taking her business to another bank if the two numbers do not match.

A transaction, T_2, that creates a new account transaction for Mary with initial balance 100, inserts a tuple into ACCOUNTS using the statement

```
INSERT INTO ACCOUNTS
VALUES ('10021', 'Mary', 100)
```
21.2

and then updates TotalBalance by 100 in Mary's tuple in DEPOSITORS using

```
UPDATE DEPOSITORS
SET TotalBalance = TotalBalance + 100
WHERE Name = 'Mary'
```

The operations on ACCOUNTS performed by T_1 and T_2 conflict since INSERT does not commute with SELECT. If INSERT is executed before SELECT, the inserted tuple will be included in the sum; otherwise, it will not. Hence, if T_1 and T_2 are executed concurrently in such a way that T_2 is interleaved between the time T_1 reads ACCOUNTS and the time it reads DEPOSITORS, the audit transaction will fail. (The operations on DEPOSITORS also conflict.)

21.1.1 Phantoms

As with nonrelational databases, we can ensure serializability by using a locking algorithm. In designing such an algorithm, we must first decide what to lock. One approach is to lock tables. They have names, and those names are used in the SQL statements that access them. The SELECT statement can be treated as a read on the data item(s)—table(s)—named in the FROM clause, and DELETE, INSERT, and UPDATE can be treated as writes on the named tables. Therefore the concurrency control algorithms described in Chapter 20 can be used to achieve serializable schedules. As with page locking, table locking is conservative. The problem with this approach is the coarse granularity of the locks. A table might contain thousands (perhaps millions) of tuples. Locking an entire table because one of its tuples has been accessed might result in a serious loss of concurrency.

If, instead of locking tables, we associate a distinct lock with each tuple, lock granularity is fine, but the resulting schedules might not be serializable. For example, suppose that T_1 locks all tuples it has read in ACCOUNTS—those that satisfy the predicate `Name = 'Mary'`. The ability of a transaction to insert a new tuple into a table is not affected by locks held by other transactions on existing tuples in the table. As a result, T_2 can subsequently construct a tuple, t, that satisfies the predicate and describes a new account for Mary and insert it into ACCOUNTS. Hence, the following schedule is possible:

T_1 locks and reads all tuples describing Mary's accounts in ACCOUNTS.

T_2 adds t to ACCOUNTS and locks t.

T_2 locks and updates Mary's tuple in DEPOSITORS.

T_2 commits, releasing all locks that it holds.

T_1 locks and reads Mary's tuple in DEPOSITORS.

Here, T_2 has altered the contents of the set of tuples referred to by the predicate `Name = 'Mary'` by adding t. In this situation, t is referred to as a **phantom** because T_1 thinks it has locked all the tuples that satisfy the predicate but, unknown to T_1, a new tuple, t (that also satisfies the predicate), has been inserted by a concurrent transaction. A phantom can lead to nonserializable schedules and hence invalid results. In the example, the audit transaction finds that `TotalBalance` is not equal to the sum of the account balances.

The problem arises because the SELECT statement does not name a specific item. Instead, it specifies a condition, or predicate, that is satisfied by a number of tuples, some of which might be in a particular table and others of which, like t, might not. While we can set a lock on the tuples that already exist in a table, it is difficult to set a lock on those that do not. To eliminate the possibility of phantoms, we need a locking mechanism that prevents tuples that satisfy a predicate but are not present in the table (that is, phantoms) from being added to the table.

Although we have illustrated the phantom problem using a SELECT statement, the problem also exists with statements that update the database. For example, an UPDATE statement that updates all tuples in a table satisfying predicate P does not commute with an INSERT statement that inserts a tuple satisfying P into the table. Unfortunately, even if the transaction that does the update acquires locks on all updated tuples, a concurrent transaction can still perform the insert.

One approach to preventing phantoms is to lock the entire table—which will certainly prevent any new tuples, including phantoms, from being inserted. As we shall see in Section 21.3.1, however, table locking is not necessary since protocols exist that prevent phantoms but do not require that the entire table be locked. Hence, when commercial DBMSs use the term "tuple locking" (or "page locking") to describe a concurrency control algorithm, you should not assume that they have ignored the phantom problem. They might mean that tuple locks (or page locks) are used as a part of a more elaborate protocol that does guarantee serializability. As in all things, caution is in order—"When all else fails, read the manual." Still, there are many situations in which commercial DBMSs lock an entire table in order to prevent phantoms and achieve serializability.

21.1.2 Predicate Locking

One technique for dealing with phantoms is **predicate locking** [Eswaran et al. 1976]. A predicate, P, specifies a set of tuples. A tuple is in the set if and only if the tuples' attribute values make P true. For example, `Name = 'Mary'` is a predicate that specifies the set of all possible tuples that *might* exist in ACCOUNTS whose `Name` attribute has value `Mary`. This set is a subset of the set, D, of all possible tuples that could ever be stored in ACCOUNTS. Thus, a tuple in which `Name` has value `Jane` is an element D and might be in ACCOUNTS but is not in the subset specified by `Name = 'Mary'`. Note an important point: some of the elements of the subset specified by P might be in ACCOUNTS and some not. For example, the tuple, t, describing Mary's new account satisfies P but is not initially in ACCOUNTS.

Predicates and SQL statements. An SQL statement associates a predicate with each table it accesses. The predicate is used by the statement to identify the tuples on which it operates. Thus, a SELECT statement that accesses a single table—named in its FROM clause—associates the predicate specified in its WHERE clause with that table. The predicate separates those tuples in the table that are in its result set from those that are not. Similarly, a DELETE statement associates the predicate specified in its WHERE with the table it accesses. The predicate identifies the tuples to be deleted.

Things can become more complicated if, for example, the WHERE clause contains a nested SELECT or the FROM clause names several tables. In these cases, several tables might be involved, each with an associated predicate. Although we could describe this more general case, we choose not to complicate the discussion since the goal here is only to present predicate locking as a concept.

The predicate associated with an INSERT statement describes the set of tuples to be inserted. In the simple case in which a single tuple is inserted, the predicate is

$$(\mathtt{A}_1 = \mathtt{v}_1) \wedge (\mathtt{A}_2 = \mathtt{v}_2) \wedge \ldots \wedge (\mathtt{A}_n = \mathtt{v}_n)$$

where $\mathtt{A}_i$ is the ith attribute name and $\mathtt{v}_i$ is the value of the attribute in the inserted tuple. The predicate specifies the set consisting of a single tuple that is to be inserted. For example, the predicate associated with the INSERT statement (21.2) is

```
(AcctNumber='10021') ∧ (Name= 'Mary') ∧ (Balance='100')                21.3
```

More generally, the INSERT might contain a nested SELECT statement and refer to several tables.

```
INSERT INTO TABLE1, (... attribute list ...)
SELECT ... attribute list ...
FROM TABLE2
WHERE P
```

Clearly, P is associated with TABLE2, since the tuples read from that table satisfy P. The predicate associated with TABLE1, however, might be different since the two tables might have different schemas. For example, attributes named in P might not be included in TABLE1, and hence conjuncts referencing those attributes must be deleted. You are asked to investigate this issue in Exercise 21.2.

Finally, an UPDATE statement can be viewed as a DELETE statement followed by an INSERT statement, and hence it has two associated predicates. The first is the predicate P in the UPDATE statement's WHERE clause, which specifies the tuples to be deleted. The SET clause describes how those tuples are to be modified. The resulting set of tuples, described by a predicate, P', are then inserted. For example, the following UPDATE statement posts interest to all of Mary's accounts:

```
UPDATE ACCOUNTS
SET Balance = Balance * 1.05
WHERE Name = 'Mary'
```

In this case, the tuples deleted and the tuples inserted satisfy the same predicate, `Name = 'Mary'`. However, if Mary wants to add her middle initial to her name, we might execute the statement

```
UPDATE ACCOUNTS
SET Name = 'Mary S'
WHERE Name = 'Mary'
```

Now P is `Name = 'Mary'`, but P' is `Name = 'Mary S'`. The predicate associated by the UPDATE with the table is $P \vee P'$.

Predicate locks. Having introduced the idea that an SQL statement associates a predicate with a table, we can now describe a locking technique that eliminates phantoms. When an SQL statement with predicate P accesses table R, it acquires a **predicate lock** on P. The lock is associated with R. You can think of the lock as locking the predicate or, alternatively, as locking *all* tuples satisfying P, whether or not they are in R. The situation is illustrated in Figure 21.1. All of the tuples in D

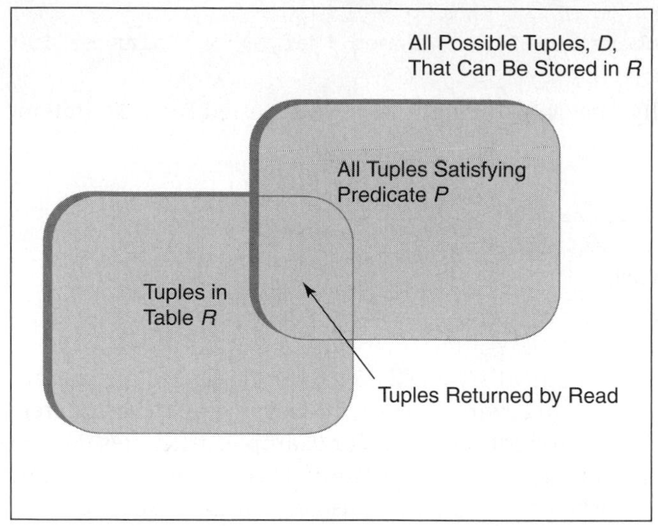

FIGURE 21.1 A SELECT statement accesses table R with predicate P. P specifies a subset of D, the set of all tuples that could possibly be stored in R. Some tuples in the subset might be in R; others might not.

satisfying P are locked. If P appears in the WHERE clause of a SELECT statement, the tuples in the result set are those in the intersection of the sets designated R and P and the predicate lock is a read lock.

Similarly, for a DELETE statement, all tuples in D satisfying P are locked with a predicate write lock, and the tuples in R satisfying P are deleted. In the case of INSERT, the tuples inserted are predicate write locked. For example, when the new account transaction inserts tuple t describing Mary's new account, it obtains a predicate write lock on the predicate (21.3). With the UPDATE statement, the predicate $P \vee P'$ must be write locked.

We now interpret the notion of a conflict somewhat more generally. Instead of requiring that conflicting operations name the same data item, we specify that

> Two operations conflict if at least one is a write and the sets of tuples described by the predicates associated with the operations have non-null intersections.

For example, the SELECT (read) statement (21.1) that returns all tuples satisfying the predicate `Name='Mary'` conflicts with the DELETE (write) statement

```
DELETE
FROM ACCOUNTS
WHERE Balance < 1
```

which deletes all accounts satisfying the predicate `Balance < 1`, since there exist tuples in D satisfying both predicates—for example, the tuple satisfying

```
AcctNumber = '10000' ∧ Name = 'Mary' ∧ Balance = .5
```

Such a tuple *might* be in ACCOUNTS, and hence there exist states of ACCOUNTS for which the order of execution of the two statements yields different results. Thus, the SELECT conflicts with this DELETE. On the other hand, the SELECT does not conflict with

```
DELETE
FROM ACCOUNTS
WHERE Name = 'John'
```

since the predicates associated with the two statements have a null intersection and thus the statements commute. Finally, the statement

```
SELECT *
FROM ACCOUNTS
WHERE Name = 'Mary S'
```

conflicts with the UPDATE statement that adds Mary's middle initial to her `Name` attribute in ACCOUNTS.

Predicate locking solves the phantom problem we introduced earlier. When T_1 reads ACCOUNTS, it obtains a read lock on the predicate `Name = 'Mary'`. Later, when T_2 attempts to insert into ACCOUNTS the tuple t describing Mary's new account, it requests a write lock on predicate (21.3). Since the intersection of the two predicates is not null, a conflict exists and the write lock is not granted. The tuple t is a phantom (it does not exist in ACCOUNTS). Since the predicate lock on `Name = 'Mary'` includes t, it prevents t from being concurrently added.

In an implementation of predicate locking, we associate with each table, R, a lock set, $L(R)$, which contains the locks associated with all requests that have been granted to currently active transactions. Each element of $L(R)$ has a corresponding predicate. When a transaction requests a predicate lock for an operation that conflicts with an element of $L(R)$, the concurrency control makes the transaction wait.

With predicate locking, serializable schedules can be guaranteed at a finer granularity of locking than with table locks since we lock subsets of the set of tuples that might be in R rather than the entire table. Unfortunately, the conflict test—predicate intersection—is expensive to implement. This limits the usefulness of predicate locking and the technique is not used in commercial DBMSs. However, as we discuss in Section 21.3.1, most DBMSs do implement a restricted form of predicate locking that locks indices.

21.2 Locking and the SQL Isolation Levels

Although most commercial DBMSs implement techniques (which we will describe shortly) that guarantee serializability, the resulting performance is inadequate for some applications. Hence, there is considerable incentive to release locks earlier than would be required to guarantee serializability. Early release is possible when

Level	Dirty Reads	Nonrepeatable Reads	Phantoms
READ UNCOMMITTED	Yes	Yes	Yes
READ COMMITTED	No	Yes	Yes
REPEATABLE READ	No	No	Yes
SERIALIZABLE	No	No	No

FIGURE 21.2 Anomalies allowed and disallowed at each isolation level.

weaker levels of isolation [Gray et al. 1976] are used. The SQL standard defines four isolation levels and, as we saw in Section 8.2.3, each transaction can individually choose one of the four. In order of decreasing strength, they are

SERIALIZABLE
REPEATABLE READ
READ COMMITTED
READ UNCOMMITTED

A given DBMS will not necessarily support all isolation levels. It usually provides a particular level as the default and has mechanisms for requesting one of the other supported levels.

SERIALIZABLE corresponds to the notion of serializable execution discussed in this text and is the only level that guarantees correctness for *all* applications. The enhanced performance that can be achieved with weaker levels is obtained at the risk of incorrect execution.

With the exception of SERIALIZABLE, the SQL standard [SQL 1992] specifies the isolation levels in terms of certain undesirable anomalies (sometimes called phenomena) that are to be prevented at each level. An anomaly that is prevented at one level is also prevented at each higher level.

- At READ UNCOMMITTED, dirty reads (see Section 20.2) are possible.
- At READ COMMITTED, dirty reads are not permitted, but successive reads of the same tuple by a particular transaction might yield different values.
- At REPEATABLE READ, successive reads of the same tuple executed by a particular transaction do not yield different values, but phantoms are possible.
- At SERIALIZABLE, phantoms are not permitted. Transaction execution must be serializable.

The anomalies allowed and disallowed are summarized in Figure 21.2.

One might think from the definition of the isolation levels that schedules that do not exhibit dirty reads, nonrepeatable reads, and phantoms are serializable. As we shall see, this is not the case.

SQL isolation levels do not deal with dirty writes, which, as we saw in Section 20.2, are undesirable for several reasons. For example, the schedule in Figure 20.10, page 827, which illustrates a dirty write, does not involve dirty reads, nonrepeatable reads, or phantoms and is, in fact, serializable; hence it does not violate the requirements of any of the isolation levels.

The SQL standard specifies that different transactions in the same application can execute at different levels and each such transaction sees or does not see the anomalies corresponding to its level. For example, when a transaction executing at REPEATABLE READ reads a tuple several times, the same value is always returned even though concurrent transactions are executing at other levels. Similarly, a transaction executing at SERIALIZABLE must see a view of the database that is serialized with respect to the changes made by all other transactions, regardless of their levels.

Independent of the isolation level, the SQL standard requires that a DBMS guarantee that each SQL statement is executed atomically and that its execution is isolated from the execution of other statements.

Locking implementation of the isolation levels. By defining isolation levels in terms of behavior, the SQL standard does not constrain the implementation of a concurrency control. In particular, the definition does not imply that the concurrency control must be implemented using locks. Locks, however, form the basis of most concurrency controls, and hence it is useful to consider how the levels can be supported in a lock-based system. We describe a hypothetical implementation proposed in [Berenson et al. 1995].

Each level is implemented using locks in different ways. Thus, at a particular level, a lock can be conventional (locking an item such as a tuple, page, or table) or a predicate lock. For pedagogical reasons, we will allow predicate locks in our hypothetical implementation even though they are generally not used in practical implementations. This allows us to be more precise about what needs to be locked. A practical implementation would replace predicate locks with table locks or it would use other techniques (see Section 21.3.1).

A lock can be held until commit time—we refer to such a lock as being of **long duration**—or it can be released after the statement that has accessed the item or predicate has been completed, in which case it is of **short duration**. Short-duration locks are not sufficient to guarantee serializability. However, by requiring a transaction to request such a lock, the concurrency control can check whether conflicting locks are held by other transactions and force the requestor to wait in that case. If a lock is not requested (as in READ UNCOMMITTED), the existence of a conflicting lock in a lock set is ignored.

All isolation levels use write locks in the same way. Long-duration write locks are obtained on the predicates associated with UPDATE, INSERT, and DELETE statements.

The implementation of a particular level not only rules out the appropriate undesirable anomalies but possibly other undesirable anomalies as well. Thus, since write locks are of long duration at all levels, dirty writes are ruled out at all levels. Read locks obtained by a SELECT statement are handled differently at each level.

Level	Read Locks
READ UNCOMMITTED	None
READ COMMITTED	Short-duration on tuples returned
REPEATABLE READ	Long-duration on tuples returned
SERIALIZABLE	Long-duration on predicate specified in statement

FIGURE 21.3 Read locks used in the locking implementation of each isolation level. All levels use long-duration write locks on predicates.

- READ UNCOMMITTED. A read is performed without obtaining a read lock. Since reading does not involve the locking mechanism, one transaction might hold a write lock on some item or predicate while another reads it. Thus, a transaction might read uncommitted (dirty) data.
- READ COMMITTED. Short-duration read locks are obtained on each tuple, t, returned by a SELECT. As a result, conflicts with write locks are detected and, since write locks are of long duration, dirty reads are impossible. However, since the read lock on t is released when the read is completed, two successive SELECT statements in a particular transaction that both return t might be separated by the execution of another transaction that updates t and then commits. Hence, the value of t returned by the two statements might be different.
- REPEATABLE READ. Long-duration read locks are obtained on each tuple, t, returned by a SELECT. As a result, a nonrepeatable read of t is not possible. Since the predicate associated with the SELECT is not locked, however, phantoms can occur.
- SERIALIZABLE. All read (and write) locks are long-duration predicate locks, and thus phantoms are not possible. All transactions are serializable.

The use of read locks at each level is summarized in Figure 21.3. Note that, since all write locks are long duration and all levels other than READ UNCOMMITTED acquire read locks before reading an item, a schedule in which all transactions run at levels higher than READ UNCOMMITTED will be strict.

The read locks acquired at the lower isolation levels are weaker than the long-duration predicate read locks used at SERIALIZABLE. This is the source of the performance improvement that these levels can achieve. The management of read locks at a particular level eliminates the anomalies prohibited at that level, independent of whether or not concurrent transactions execute at different levels.

Since all transactions use long-duration predicate write locks, their write operations are serializable. Since, in addition, a transaction, T, running at SERIALIZABLE uses long-duration read predicate locks, *all* of its operations are serializable with respect to the write operations of all other transactions, independent of their isolation level. Hence, T either sees all or none of the updates performed by a concurrent transaction. Transactions executing at lower levels, however, might see the partial results of concurrent transactions and hence do not necessarily see a consistent state. There-

FIGURE 21.4 Schedule involving a read of uncommitted data. T_2 executes at READ UNCOMMITTED.

T_1: $r(t_1:1000)$ $w(t_1:900)$ $r(t_2:500)$ $w(t_2:600)$ *commit*
T_2: $r(t_1:900)$ $r(t_2:500)$ *commit*

---

fore their updates might cause inconsistencies. SERIALIZABLE transactions might see those inconsistencies, and their computations might be affected as a result.

The dangers of executing at lower isolation levels. By allowing transactions to run at isolation levels weaker than SERIALIZABLE, nonserializable schedules can be produced. Thus, a transaction might see inconsistent data and, as a result, might write inconsistent data into the database. To see how this can happen at each of the lower levels, consider the following examples.

- READ UNCOMMITTED. A transaction, T_2, executing at READ UNCOMMITTED might read dirty values produced by another active transaction, T_1. Such values might never be committed and so are meaningless. For example, T_1 might write a value, v, to a data item and later abort. T_2 might read the data item before T_1 aborts and return v to the user. Or T_2 might compute a new value based on v and store it in a different data item, thus corrupting the database since the transaction that produced v aborted.[1] Or T_1 might write v to the data item and then overwrite v with a second value. In this case, v is an intermediate value not meant for external consumption.

  Even if T_1 writes only final values, if T_2 reads them before T_1 commits, problems can arise. For example, in the schedule of Figure 21.4, T_1 is a transaction that transfers \$100 from an account whose balance is stored in tuple t_1 (initially \$1,000) to an account whose balance is stored in tuple t_2 (initially \$500). T_2 is a read-only transaction executing at READ UNCOMMITTED that prints out the balance of all accounts. In Figure 21.4, T_2 reads an uncommitted value of t_1 and hence does not report the \$100 being transferred in either account.

- READ COMMITTED. A transaction, T_1, executing at READ COMMITTED uses short-duration read locks on individual tuples. Hence, as shown in Figure 21.5, it is possible for T_2 to update tuple t and then commit between successive reads in T_1. One might not think that this is too serious an issue since it is unlikely that a transaction will read the same tuple twice. However, incorrect results can occur even when the transaction does not attempt a second read. Figure 21.6 shows a schedule in which T_1 and T_2 are both deposit transactions executing at READ COMMITTED that operate on an account whose balance is stored in tuple t. Since T_1 uses short-duration read locks, it is possible for T_2 to update t and then commit. As a result, the effect of T_2's update is lost. Note that both transactions

[1] To protect against database corruption, transactions running at READ UNCOMMITTED are often required to be read-only.

FIGURE 21.5 Schedule involving a nonrepeatable read. T_1 executes at READ COMMITTED.

$$\begin{array}{llll} T_1: & r(t:1000) & & r(t:2000)\ commit \\ T_2: & & w(t:2000)\ commit & \end{array}$$

FIGURE 21.6 Schedule illustrating the lost-update problem at READ COMMITTED.

$$\begin{array}{llll} T_1: & r(t:1000) & & w(t:1100)\ commit \\ T_2: & & r(t:1000)\ w(t:2000)\ commit & \end{array}$$

FIGURE 21.7 Schedule illustrating that a transaction executing at READ COMMITTED might see an inconsistent view of the database.

$$\begin{array}{llll} T_1: & r(x:10) & & r(y:15)\ \ldots\ commit \\ T_2: & & w(x:20)\ w(y:15)\ commit & \end{array}$$

read committed data. This is an example of the lost-update problem introduced in Chapter 2.

Figure 21.7 shows an example of a transaction, T_1, whose view of the database is inconsistent as a result of being executed at READ COMMITTED. Suppose an integrity constraint states that the values of x and y must satisfy $x \geq y$, but between the reads (after T_1 has released the read lock on x), T_2 changes both values (such that the new values satisfy the integrity constraint) and then commits. T_1 reads the value of x before T_2's update and the value of y afterwards—a view of the database that does not satisfy the constraint ($x = 10,\ \ y = 15$). Since transactions are guaranteed to execute correctly only when they see a consistent view of the database, T_1 might subsequently execute in an unpredictable manner and write erroneous data into the database. Even if T_2's writes were such that the two values read by T_1 happened to satisfy the constraint, the fact that they came from two different versions of the database could cause T_1 to execute incorrectly.

- REPEATABLE READ. Since tuples, but not predicates, have long-duration locks, phantoms can occur. We saw in Section 21.1.1 that this can cause incorrect behavior. Note that the example there also involved a transaction seeing an inconsistent view of the database.

21.2.1 Lost Updates, Cursor Stability, and Update Locks

Figure 21.6 shows a lost update that occurs because short-duration read locks are used at READ COMMITTED. A special case of the lost update problem—when reading is done through a cursor—can be prevented by an isolation level called CURSOR STABILITY, which is provided instead of READ COMMITTED in some implementations of SQL.

When a transaction, T_1, opens an INSENSITIVE cursor over a table, R, a copy of the result set is made and all subsequent FETCH statements through the cursor are done to the copy. Therefore, no matter at which isolation level T_1 is executing, the FETCH statements do not see any subsequent updates to R made by a concurrent transaction, T_2 (or even updates made directly to R by T_1 itself).

However, if T_1 opens a cursor that is not declared INSENSITIVE (for example, if it is KEYSET_DRIVEN), pointers to the tuples in R that are in the result set are returned and all subsequent FETCHs are done through the pointers. If T_1 is executed at READ COMMITTED, it acquires only a short-duration read lock on each tuple fetched. If T_1 and T_2 run concurrently, T_1 might fetch some tuples through the cursor before they are updated by T_2 and others after T_2 has updated them and committed.[2]

An even more troublesome situation might arise if T_1 first reads a tuple and later updates it before moving the cursor. In that case, T_2 might read and update the tuple and commit between T_1's read and write while the cursor is pointing at it. As a result, T_2's update will be lost. The CURSOR STABILITY isolation level prevents such lost updates.

CURSOR STABILITY is an extension of READ COMMITTED. Hence, it provides a level of isolation whose strength lies between READ COMMITTED and REPEATABLE READ. With CURSOR STABILITY, as long as a cursor opened by transaction T_1 points to a particular tuple, that tuple cannot be modified or deleted by another transaction, T_2. Once T_1 moves or closes the cursor, however, T_2 can modify or delete the tuple.

As with the other isolation levels, CURSOR STABILITY can be implemented using long-duration write predicate locks. Read locks are handled as follows:

> CURSOR STABILITY. Short-duration read locks are obtained for each tuple read, except if the tuple is accessed through a cursor. In that case a **medium-duration** read lock is acquired. The lock is retained while the cursor points to the tuple and released when the cursor is moved or closed.

The schedule shown in Figure 21.6 can occur if CURSOR STABILITY is used because we have implicitly assumed that neither T_1 nor T_2 refers to t through a cursor. Suppose, however, that T_1 is posting interest to all accounts in a bank. It accesses each tuple successively through a cursor, first reading the balance in t and then updating t with a new balance. With CURSOR STABILITY, the read lock that T_1 acquires on t is maintained until it requests to update t, at which point the lock is upgraded to a write lock, which is held until T_1 commits (since write locks are of long duration). Hence, it is not possible for another transaction, T_2, to update t between T_1's read and update.

Consider the situation shown in Figure 21.8. Suppose that T_2 is a deposit transaction that accesses t directly through an index and that it executes at READ COMMITTED or CURSOR STABILITY (it makes no difference in this case since it does not use a cursor). T_2 reads t after T_1 has read it. When T_1 requests to update t, its

[2] There might be some confusion here because of the requirement in the SQL standard that each SQL statement is executed in an atomic and isolated fashion. In the case of a cursor, execution of OPEN and FETCH are individually atomic and isolated.

FIGURE 21.8 Schedule illustrating that CURSOR STABILITY is not a panacea.

T_1:	$r(t)$ (through cursor)		$w(t)$ (through cursor)	*commit*		
T_2:		$r(t)$ (through index)			$w(t)$ (through index)	*commit*

read lock can be upgraded to a write lock since T_2's read lock is short duration. Unfortunately, the lost-update problem is not solved. The value T_2 writes (after T_1 commits) is based on the value returned by its previous read, not on the new value written by T_1, so T_1's update is lost.

Before we describe how this problem can be solved, consider another case based on the same sequence of reads and writes as shown in Figure 21.8, only now both transactions execute at CURSOR STABILITY and access t through a cursor. Once again, the situation is not a happy one as both T_1 and T_2 hold their (medium-duration) read locks after reading and a deadlock results when both try to upgrade to write locks. Clearly, CURSOR STABILITY offers only a partial solution to the lost-update problem.

Some commercial DBMSs provide additional mechanisms to deal with these problems.

- In some systems, a transaction, T, can request a write lock on an item at the time it reads the item so that it can update the item later. This avoids the need to upgrade the read lock (and hence avoids the deadlock), but it suffers from the need to lock out all other transactions starting from T's first access, even if the other transactions only want to read the item.
- Some systems provide a new type of lock, called an **update lock**, which can be used by transactions that initially want to read an item but later might want to update it.[3] It allows a transaction to read but not write the item and indicates that the lock is likely to be upgraded to a write lock at a later time. Update locks conflict with one another and with write locks, but not with read locks. For that reason, if T_1 and T_2 both attempt the same sequence of operations as shown in Figure 21.8 and both initially request update locks, the first request will be granted and the other will wait. In this way, both lost updates and deadlocks are avoided. Since update and read locks do not conflict, however, if T_2 wants only to read t, it can acquire a read lock between T_1's read and write since T_1 holds only an update lock in that interval. T_1 must upgrade its update lock to a write lock before it writes the item.
- Some systems provide a version of READ COMMITTED called OPTIMISTIC READ COMMITTED. If T_1 executes at this level, it obtains the same short-duration read lock that would be obtained at READ COMMITTED. However, if T_1 later tries to

[3] An update lock is sometimes called a *read-with-intention-to-write* lock.

write a tuple, t, that it has previously read, it is aborted if some other transaction has modified t and committed between the time T_1 read t and the time it tries to write t. This approach is called "optimistic" because each transaction optimistically assumes that it need not retain read locks on tuples to prevent lost updates.[4] As with other optimistic algorithms, the transaction is aborted if that assumption turns out to be false. Although OPTIMISTIC READ COMMITTED prevents lost updates, problems can still arise (see Exercise 21.13).

21.2.2 Case Study: Correctness and NonSERIALIZABLE Schedules—The Student Registration System

We have shown examples of transactions that behave incorrectly when executed at each isolation level lower than SERIALIZABLE. However, the news is not all bad. The semantics of an application can often be used to demonstrate that when a particular transaction is executed at an isolation level lower than SERIALIZABLE, all of the resulting schedules produce acceptable results. Such transactions can take advantage of the increased concurrency and resulting performance gains that follow from using a lower isolation level.

For example, we might be concerned that some nonserializable schedules allowed by a weak isolation level will result in the violation of an integrity constraint. Recall, however, that many integrity constraints can be declared in the database schema and are automatically checked by the DBMS. Thus, a violation will be detected, and the transaction that caused the violation will be aborted when it requests to commit. Assuming that such schedules do not occur frequently, a net performance gain may result by executing the application at the weaker level.

In addition to schedules that cause violations of schema constraints, we must also be concerned with schedules that

- Produce database states that violate integrity constraints not declared in the schema
- Produce database states that are consistent but incorrect because they do not reflect the desired result of the transaction—for example, a database state resulting from a lost update
- Return data to the user based on a view of the database that is not obtained from a consistent snapshot—for example, by a read-only transaction executing at READ UNCOMMITTED

When we consider whether or not a specific transaction in some application can be executed at a weaker isolation level, we must investigate its interaction with all the other transactions in the same application. Consider the Registration transaction of the Student Registration System, whose requirements and schema were given in Sections B.2 and 4.8. Can it execute correctly at READ COMMITTED? To answer this

[4] This approach is sometimes called *first-committer-wins* because the first transaction to write a tuple is allowed to commit—*wins*—and the second transaction that attempts to write the tuple is aborted—*loses*. We discuss first-committer-wins further in Section 21.5.3.

CASE STUDY

question, we must investigate how each instance of a Registration transaction can interact with other instances of the Registration transaction and with instances of all the other transaction types in the system.

Do not expect the discussion to contain theorems or general principles. This is an area in which experience and creativity count as well as the ability to consider a large number of boring details. That is one reason why people who do this for a living get the big bucks.

To make the discussion concrete, we will assume that the DBMS uses the locking implementation of each isolation level described earlier in this section. Suppose a particular instance of the Registration transaction, T_1, attempts to register a student, *s*, for a course, *c*. To do this, it performs the following sequence of steps (some steps have been omitted):

1. Determine *c*'s prerequisites by reading the table REQUIRES, which has a row for each prerequisite of each course.
2. Check that *s* has satisfied each of *c*'s prerequisites by reading TRANSCRIPT to determine if *s* has taken each prerequisite and received a grade of at least C.
3. Check that the total number of credits that will be taken by *s* will not exceed 20 by reading TRANSCRIPT to determine all the courses in which *s* is already registered.
4. Check that there is enough room in *c* and, if so, increment the current enrollment. To do this, T_1 executes

```
UPDATE CLASS
SET Enrollment = Enrollment + 1
WHERE CrsCode = :courseId AND Enrollment < MaxEnrollment
```

   where the course code of class *c* is stored in the host variable `courseId`, and we assume that CLASS has attributes `MaxEnrollment`, which contains the maximum allowable enrollment in *c*, and `Enrollment`, which contains the number of students currently registered for next semester. (Note that the condition `Enrollment < MaxEnrollment` is actually unnecessary since [as shown in Section 4.8] a constraint that eliminates overenrollment is incorporated in the schema of CLASS. However, we can expect that many students will attempt to enroll in classes that are full, and it is more efficient to check the constraint in the UPDATE statement and abort the transaction immediately.)
5. Insert a row in TRANSCRIPT indicating that *s* is registered for *c*.

Suppose that T_1 is executed at READ COMMITTED. We need to consider the following situations.

- While T_1 is reading REQUIRES in step 1 (using short-duration read locks on rows), a concurrent Course Information transaction, T_2, might update REQUIRES by inserting new rows corresponding to new prerequisites for *c* (together with the enforcement dates for these prerequisites) and then commit.

CASE STUDY

To make the example more interesting, assume that T_1 reads REQUIRES using a DYNAMIC cursor. If T_1 and T_2 execute concurrently, T_1 might see some but not all of the rows that T_2 has inserted. Hence, T_1 is not serializable with respect to T_2.

However, in this situation nonserializability does not cause a problem because it was specified in Section B.3 that new prerequisites do not apply to current registrants. Therefore, in determining *c*'s prerequisites in step 1, T_1 ignores any prerequisites that have been added during the current semester (using the date attribute of each prerequisite row). Thus it makes no difference if T_1 misses some of the prerequisites added by T_2 because it ignores any it does read. For this reason, T_1 executes correctly at READ COMMITTED. Thus this schedule is nonserializable, but nevertheless correct.

Execution is also correct at READ COMMITTED if T_1 uses a KEYSET_DRIVEN cursor because it does not see *any* of the inserted rows and hence it appears as if the transactions are executed serially with T_2 following T_1.

- After T_1 reads TRANSCRIPT in step 2 and gives up the short-duration read locks on the rows it has read, a concurrent Student Grade transaction, T_2, might update TRANSCRIPT by changing a grade in a course *s* has taken. The change might affect a course that is a prerequisite to *c*.

  First we observe that if T_2 changes the grade after T_1 gives up its read locks, T_1 will not see the change. Therefore the effect of the execution of T_2 is the same as if it was serialized after T_1. So far, so good.

  But before we can say that T_2 is serializable after T_1, we must consider how T_1 and T_2 might interact with other transactions in a more complex schedule. For example, after T_2 changes the grade and commits, another transaction, T_3, might read the new grade and then write some item, *x*, and commit. Then T_1 might read *x*.

T_1:	r(grade)		$r(x)$ *commit*
T_2:	w(grade) *commit*		
T_3:		r(grade) $w(x)$ *commit*	

  This schedule is nonserializable since there is a cycle in the serialization graph:

$$T_1 \rightarrow T_2 \rightarrow T_3 \rightarrow T_1$$

  To see if such an interaction can take place, we must analyze all of the possible interactions between T_1 (the Registration transaction), T_2 (the Student Grade transaction), and all of the other transactions in the application—a tedious and error-prone task. If such an interaction can occur, we must analyze its effect on the application.

- It might appear that, as the result of a lost update, the concurrent execution of two Registration transactions attempting to enroll two different students in *c* can cause the MaxEnrollment to be exceeded. This would be possible if each transaction gave up its read locks between the check and increment

CASE STUDY

of `Enrollment`. However, this situation cannot occur because the check and increment are performed in step 4 as part of the isolated execution of a single SQL statement (note that it is not necessary to rely on the protection afforded by long-duration write locks to ensure this).

- Two instances of the Registration transaction are executed concurrently for the same student, *s* (attempting to register for two different courses). In step 3 each instance reads TRANSCRIPT to determine the number of credits for which *s* has already registered. If each executes that step before the other executes step 5 they will both calculate the same number, and in step 5 each will insert a phantom row not seen by the other. If *s* has room for only one additional course, the credit limit will be exceeded.

  The designer of the system might conclude, however, that it is extremely unlikely that a particular student, with room for only one more course, will execute two Registration transactions at the same time and that this particular interleaving of the transactions will occur. Hence the Registration transaction can be safely executed at READ COMMITTED. (If such a conclusion cannot be justified, the Registration transaction would have to be executed at SERIALIZABLE to eliminate the phantoms.)

  Another alternative would be to include the integrity constraint "a student cannot be registered for more than 20 credits in any given semester" in the database schema instead of having it checked within the Registration transaction. Then the system would check that this integrity constraint was not violated, and if the above interleaving occurred, one of the transactions would be aborted. Thus the Registration transaction could be safely executed at READ COMMITTED.

Thus we might decide that the Registration transaction can run correctly at READ COMMITTED. Hence, the read locks acquired in steps 1, 2, and 3 will be released early, improving performance.

We have given an example of an application involving a transaction that can be executed correctly at an isolation level lower than SERIALIZABLE. The cautious designer should, however, assume that lower levels of isolation can produce incorrect results unless it can be demonstrated, using the semantics of the application, that such results are not possible.

Furthermore, note that the errors resulting from choosing an isolation level that is too weak are very difficult to track down. They occur in a schedule in which transactions happen to be interleaved in a particular way. This might happen rarely if the transactions involved are infrequently invoked,[5] and the effects might not become apparent until long after the execution has taken place. For that reason, the system might appear to work correctly for long periods of time until an inconsistent state is suddenly detected. It might be extremely difficult to determine the sequence of events that caused the error.

[5] But note that in a high-performance transaction processing application, a situation that occurs only once in a million transaction executions might occur several times a day.

There is an additional caution from a software-engineering viewpoint. Even though the semantics of the initial version of an application might guarantee only correct schedules at lower isolation levels, the semantics of later versions, in which new transactions are added or older transactions are changed, might not. Thus, the reasoning that leads to the choice of isolation levels should be carefully documented (perhaps in the Design Document) so that the system maintainers can determine whether or not it is still valid for later versions.

21.2.3 Serializable, SERIALIZABLE, and Correct

We have used three terms in describing schedules produced by a concurrency control:

- *Serializable.* Equivalent to a serial schedule.
- SERIALIZABLE. An SQL isolation level. Dirty reads, unrepeatable reads, and phantoms are not allowed, and schedules must be serializable (as stated in the ANSI specifications [SQL 1992]).
- *Correct.* Leaves the database in a state that is consistent, that correctly models the real world, and that satisfies the business rules of the enterprise (as stated in the Specification Document).

These definitions are related as follows (assuming that each transaction is consistent):

- If a schedule is serializable, it is correct.
- If a schedule has been produced by a set of transactions executing at the SERIALIZABLE isolation level, it is serializable (and hence correct).

However, these implications do not go both ways.

- A schedule might be correct, even though it is not serializable.
- A schedule might be serializable, even though it has been produced by transactions executing at isolation levels lower than SERIALIZABLE.

Thus correctness can often be obtained without using the stringent locking protocols required to *guarantee* serializable schedules.

21.3 Granular Locking: Intention Locks and Index Locks

In the previous section, we discussed how the performance of a transaction processing system can be improved through the use of isolation levels weaker than SERIALIZABLE. Performance can also be affected by lock granularity. The good news here, however, is that the choice of granularity *only* affects performance; the choice does not affect correctness. In this section we consider locking algorithms that allow granularity to be adjusted to the needs of the transactions.

The designer of a locking system faces a trade-off between concurrency and overhead in choosing lock granularity. Hence, when implementing a concurrency control for an application that involves some transactions that access large blocks of data (e.g., an entire table) and others that access very small blocks (e.g., a few tuples), it is desirable to use a locking mechanism that allows different granularities.

Granular locking [Gray et al. 1976] is designed to meet this need. A transaction requiring access to a large block of data can lock the block with a single request. A transaction requiring access to small amounts of data within a block can lock each piece individually. In the latter case, several transactions can simultaneously hold locks on small items within the same block.

Managing locks at different levels of granularity presents a new problem. Suppose, for example, a system allows a transaction to lock a record and also to lock specific fields within a record—two locks with different granularity. If transaction T_1 has obtained a write lock on field F within record R, then a request by T_2 for a write lock on the entire record should be denied since it permits T_2 to access F. The problem is to design an efficient mechanism that the concurrency control can use to recognize the lock on F when a lock on R is requested.

The solution is to organize locks hierarchically. Before obtaining a lock on F, T_1 must first obtain a lock on R. The two locks must be acquired in the specified order. Then, when T_2 requests a lock on R, the concurrency control will recognize that a potential conflict exists because T_1 holds a lock on R. But what kind of a lock does T_1 get? Clearly, it would not be a read or write lock since in that case there would be no point in acquiring an additional fine-granularity lock on F, and the effective lock granularity would be coarse.

DBMSs therefore provide a new type of lock, the **intention lock**. Before a transaction can obtain a shared or exclusive lock on an item, it must obtain appropriate intention locks on all containing items in the hierarchy of granularity. Thus, before T_1 can obtain a lock on F, it must first obtain an intention lock on R. Intention locks come in three flavors.

1. If T_1 wants to read a field in R, it must first get an **intention shared** (IS) lock on R. It can then request a shared (S) lock on that field.
2. If T_1 wants to update a field in R, it must first get an **intention exclusive** (IX) lock on R. It can then request an exclusive (X) lock on that field.
3. If T_1 wants to update some fields in R but needs to read all of the fields to determine which ones to update (for example, it wants to change all fields with values less than 100), it must first obtain a **shared intention exclusive** (SIX) lock on R. It can then read all fields in R and request an X lock on the fields it updates. (A SIX lock is a combination of a shared (S) lock and an IX lock on R.)

Although transactions now must acquire additional locks, performance gains are possible since intention locks commute with many other lock types. The conflict table for granular locks is given in Figure 21.9. It indicates, for example, that a request for an IX lock on an item is denied if the item is already S-locked. The justification for this is that the S lock allows all contained items to be read whereas the IX lock allows a transaction to request write locks on some of those items. In contrast, a request for an IX lock is granted if the item is already IS-locked. The justification

Requested Mode	Granted Mode				
	IS	IX	SIX	S	X
IS					X
IX			X	X	X
SIX		X	X	X	X
S		X	X		X
X	X	X	X	X	X

FIGURE 21.9 Conflict table for intention locks. X indicates conflicts between lock modes.

for this is that the IS lock allows some subset of the contained items to be S-locked while the IX lock allows some subset of the contained items to be X-locked. These subsets might be disjoint, and if so there is no conflict. If they are not disjoint, the conflict will be detected at the lower level since the transactions will have to obtain S and X locks on the individual contained items.

In the previous example, T_1 wants to access only F and hence uses fine-grained locking. It acquires an IX lock on R and an X lock on F. T_2 wants to access all fields in R and hence uses course-grained locking. It requests an exclusive lock on R. The lock conflict at R will be detected by the concurrency control using the conflict table of Figure 21.9.

In the general case, the items to be locked are organized in a hierarchy that can be represented as a tree, where the item represented by a node in the tree is contained within the item represented by its parent. Thus, locking an item in the tree implicitly locks all of its descendents. (Locking a record implicitly locks all of its fields.) The general rule is that, before a lock can be obtained on a particular item (which need not be a leaf), an appropriate intention lock must be obtained on all of the containing items (ancestors) in the hierarchy. Thus, in order to lock a particular item in S mode, a transaction must first acquire IS locks on all items on the path to the item from the root, in the order they are encountered. The S lock is acquired last to ensure that the transaction cannot actually access the target object until all locks are in place. Locks are released in the opposite order. Similarly, to obtain an X lock on an item, IX locks must first be obtained on all items on the path from the root to the item.

We intentionally based our example on a system using records and fields, rather than tables and tuples, so that phantoms would not be an issue. In the next section we discuss phantoms in more detail. But consider the following example, which gives a preview of what is to come. A SELECT and an UPDATE statement access a table. In the absence of predicate or granular locks, the UPDATE statement gets a long-duration X lock on the entire table. This prevents the SELECT statement from accessing the table. If the DBMS supports granular locking at the table and row level, the UPDATE statement might acquire a SIX lock on the table and X locks on the rows that satisfy its WHERE clause. These locks prevent concurrent transactions from reading those rows, from changing any rows in the table, and from inserting new rows, but they allow the SELECT statement to read other rows. Thus, granular locking prevents phantoms at the SERIALIZABLE level and uses weaker locks at all isolation levels than nongranular locking. Hence, granular locking has the potential for increasing concurrency.

21.3.1 Index Locks: Granular Locking without Phantoms

We discussed two methods for guaranteeing serializable schedules in a relational database—predicate locking and table locking. We pointed out the deficiencies of each: the computational complexity of predicate locking and the coarse granularity of table locking. The coarse granularity of table locking can be overcome by locking individual tuples, but this can lead to phantoms and nonserializable behavior. Locking the pages on which the tuples are stored (instead of the tuples themselves) is in some ways more efficient but can also lead to phantoms.

A number of DBMSs eliminate phantoms and guarantee serializable schedules by using an enhanced method of granular locking. Recall that the essential requirement for preventing phantoms is that, after a transaction, T_1, has accessed a table, R, using a predicate, P, no concurrently executing transaction, T_2, can insert into R a (phantom) tuple that also satisfies P, until after T_1 terminates. The method depends heavily on whether the access path to R involves an index. If not, all pages have to be scanned and the entire table has to be locked with an S or X lock. If an index is available, however, finer granularity locking is possible.

Assume that the DBMS uses page locking (the method works for tuple locking as well). If no index is available and

- If T_1 has executed a SELECT statement on R, the DBMS must search every page in R to locate the tuples that satisfy P. To perform the search, T_1 acquires an S lock on R. If that lock is held until T_1 commits, T_2 cannot insert a phantom since it would need to acquire a (conflicting) IX lock on R.
- If T_1 has executed a DELETE statement on R, the DBMS must search every page in R to locate the tuples that satisfy P. To perform the search, T_1 first acquires a SIX lock on R and then X locks on the pages containing tuples satisfying P. If these locks are held until T_1 commits, T_2 cannot insert a phantom since it would first need to acquire a (conflicting) IX lock on R.

We consider an UPDATE statement later. Hence, when no index is used, granular locking prevents phantoms.

The situation is more involved if T_1 accesses R through an index. In that case, an entire scan of R is not required. If T_1 executes a SELECT statement on R using predicate P, it acquires only an IS lock on R and S locks on the pages of R containing tuples satisfying P. It locates these pages using the index. Similarly, if T_1 executes a DELETE statement on R using predicate P, it acquires only an IX lock on R and X locks on the pages of R containing tuples satisfying P, which it locates through the index.

Unfortunately, this locking protocol does not prevent phantoms. If T_2 attempts to insert a phantom into R, it can obtain an IX lock on R since an IX lock does not conflict with either the IS or the IX locks obtained by T_1. Hence, there is no conflict at the table level. And if the phantom is stored on a page that is different than the pages locked by T_1, there will be no conflict at the page level either. Thus it will be possible for T_2 to insert the phantom. Some mechanism is needed to prevent this.

For example, the table STUDENT in the schema for the Student Registration System on page 116 has an attribute Address (for simplicity we assume that the address simply designates the town), and T_1 might execute the SELECT statement

```
SELECT *
FROM STUDENT S                                   21.4
WHERE S.Address = 'Stony Brook'
```

If there is an index, ADDRIDX, on Address for the relation STUDENT, it will be used to find the students living in Stony Brook. An IS lock will be acquired on STUDENT, and an S lock will be acquired on all pages containing tuples describing students living in Stony Brook. However, these locks will not prevent T_2 from inserting a tuple, t, describing a new student living in Stony Brook, since T_2 needs to obtain only an IX lock on STUDENT and an X lock on the page in which t is to be inserted (this page might be different from all of the pages in which tuples for students living in Stony Brook are currently stored).

To prevent phantoms in this case, in addition to an appropriate intention lock on the table and page locks on the data pages accessed, a transaction acquires locks on pages of the index structure itself. To understand this, we need to consider the storage structure used for the table. Structures fall into two categories. The first constrains the page(s) into which a tuple, describing a student who lives in Stony Brook, can possibly be stored.[6] A storage structure organized around a clustered index is of this type: the location of a row is controlled by the value its attributes assign to the search key of the index. For example, if ADDRIDX is a clustered B^+ tree with search key Address, then the row must be placed in sorted order based on the value "Stony Brook". A clustered hash index, in which all rows that hash to a particular bucket are placed in the same page, is another example.

If STUDENT is organized in accordance with the second type of storage structure, there is no unique page into which all tuples that describe students living in Stony Brook must be placed. For example, if STUDENT has a clustered index with search key Id, then the row for a student living in Stony Brook might be placed in any page.

The strategy for preventing phantoms depends on the type of the storage structure. If it is of the first type, T_1 can delay T_2 by obtaining a long-duration lock (S or X, depending on whether T_1 is reading or writing) on the page(s) of STUDENT in which all rows that describe students who live in Stony Brook must be stored. Since this is the page into which t must be inserted, T_2 is delayed until T_1 completes. For example, if STUDENT has a clustered hash index with search key Address, and T_1

[6] We have ignored overflow pages. More generally we can consider an overflow page to be an extension of the page to which it is attached.

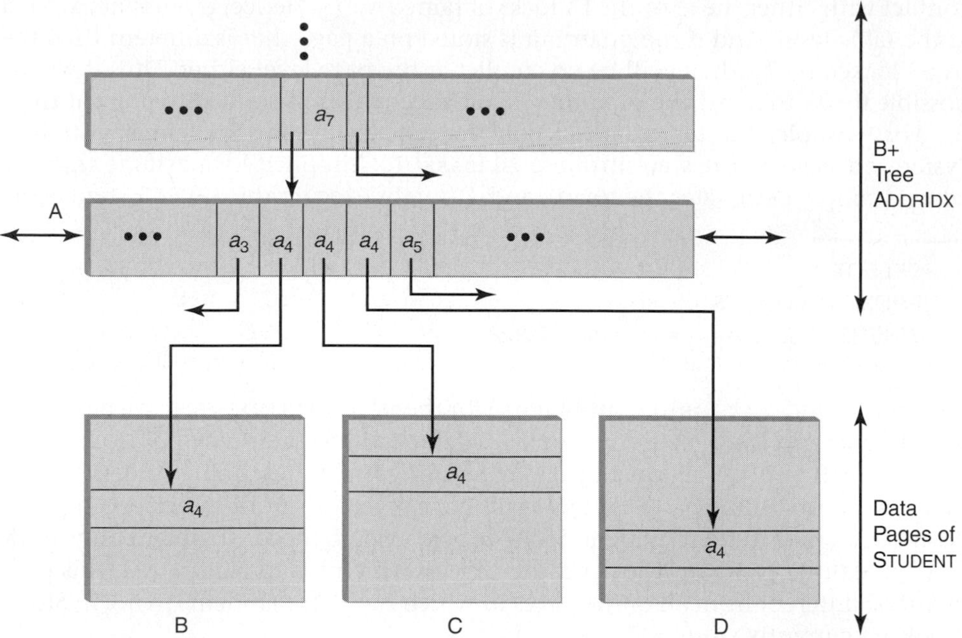

FIGURE 21.10 An unclustered B$^+$ tree secondary index on the STUDENT table.

executes the statement (21.4), it will acquire an S lock on the bucket to which Stony Brook is hashed.

If the storage structure is of the second type, T_1 acquires long-duration read locks on pages of the index it uses in its access path. Figure 21.10 illustrates the case in which a B$^+$ tree with search key `Address` is used as a secondary, unclustered index on STUDENT. Address values are denoted a_i, such that $a_i < a_{i+1}$. We have assumed that a_4 = *"StonyBrook"* and that pages B, C, and D in the STUDENT storage structure contain the tuples describing the students who live there. It is important to note that, since the index is unclustered, pages B, C, and D need not be consecutive in the storage structure. In executing the SELECT statement (21.4), T_1 obtains a long-duration S lock on the leaf page, A, of the index,[7] which contains pointers to pages B, C, and D.

An attempt by T_2 at a later time to insert a new tuple describing a student who lives in Stony Brook requires that a pointer to the data page that will contain the tuple be inserted in every index on STUDENT. In the case of ADDRIDX, the pointer must be inserted in index page A since address values are sorted at the leaf level. Inserting the pointer requires an X lock on A, which generates a conflict with T_1, and so T_2 is forced to wait. The new tuple is thus prevented from becoming a phantom despite the fact that it might ultimately be stored in a data page other than B, C, or D and

[7] More generally, there might be several such leaf pages, but the algorithm is unchanged.

the fact that T_1 and T_2 acquire compatible locks (IS and IX) on STUDENT. The lock on A must be retained by T_1 until it commits.

By locking the index in this fashion, a transaction effectively obtains a predicate lock on a simple predicate: one that specifies a search-key value (such as *key* = *value*) or one that specifies a search key by range (such as *low* ≤ *value* ≤ *high*). A nice feature of this policy, as compared with predicate locking, is that the entire range need not be locked initially. Index leaf pages and data pages are locked as the scan proceeds. Thus, only the first index leaf page is locked for the duration of the scan, whereas a lock on the last one is not acquired until the scan nears completion. If a predicate-locking policy were implemented, the lock on the predicate would be obtained initially and would restrict access to the entire range. We discuss a more efficient way to effectively obtain predicate locks on ranges of search-key values later in this section on page 894.

Although this method eliminates phantoms caused by INSERT statements, several other issues arise with UPDATE statements. Since an UPDATE can be treated as if it were a DELETE (which deletes the tuples to be updated), followed by an INSERT (which inserts the updated tuples), it has the interesting property that it is both subject to phantoms, because of the DELETE part, and the cause of phantoms, because of the INSERT part. If a storage structure of the first type is used, a tuple, t, updated by T_1 might have to be moved to a new page. For example, with hashing, if an attribute of t contained in the hash key is changed, t must be moved to a new bucket. In this case, in order to prevent T_2 from inserting a phantom tuple satisfying the WHERE clause of the UPDATE statement, T_1 must retain a lock on the bucket that originally contained t. In addition, T_1 obtains a lock on the bucket to which t is moved. If a storage structure of the second type based on a clustered index is used and an attribute of t in the search key is changed, the pointer to t must be moved to a new position. T_1 must retain a lock on the index page that originally contained the pointer to prevent a pointer to a phantom tuple from being inserted later. In addition, T_1 obtains a lock on the index page to which the pointer to t is moved. (Since both index pages are modified, these would be X locks.)

We summarize the protocol when no index is used and when a B^+ tree index is used.

Granular locking protocol for relational databases.

- If no index can be used in the execution of an SQL statement
    - A SELECT statement obtains an S lock on the table.
    - An UPDATE or DELETE statement obtains a SIX lock on the table and an X lock on the page(s) containing the tuples to be updated or deleted.
    - An INSERT statement obtains an IX lock on the table and an X lock on the page(s) containing the tuples to be inserted.
- If a B^+ tree index is used on the access path
    - A SELECT statement obtains an IS lock on the table and an S lock on the page(s) containing tuples satisfying the statement's WHERE clause.

- An INSERT, UPDATE, or DELETE statement obtains an IX lock on the table and an X lock on the page(s) containing the tuples to be inserted, updated, or deleted.
- A SELECT, INSERT, UPDATE, or DELETE statement obtains an S lock on the leaf pages of the B^+ tree that were read during the search and X locks on any pages of the B^+ tree that were updated.

If the locks are long duration, the protocol has the property that when an attempt is made to insert a phantom, a lock conflict occurs

- At the table level when indices are not involved
- Along the indexing path when indices are involved

As a result, it does not allow phantoms and produces serializable schedules.

Even when indices are not used, this protocol allows more concurrency than an implementation that eliminates phantoms by using table locks. In this protocol, a transaction, T_1, that executes a write statement that does not use indices requires only an SIX lock on the table (instead of an X lock) and X locks on the pages containing rows that are updated, inserted, or deleted. These locks prevent concurrent transactions from reading those rows and from changing any rows in the table. However, a concurrent transaction, T_2, that uses an index to read rows need only acquire an IS lock on the table, and the IS lock does not conflict with T_1's SIX lock. If the rows to be read by T_2 are not stored in pages that are X-locked by T_1, its access is not delayed (as it would be if the entire table had been X-locked by T_1). Thus, this protocol prevents phantoms with less locking (hence increasing concurrency). If indices are used by the write statement, the protocol achieves even more concurrency.

Granular locking can be used at isolation levels lower than SERIALIZABLE, where phantoms are not an issue. For example, a SELECT statement executing at REPEATABLE READ obtains an IS lock on the table and an S lock on the pages containing tuples satisfying the statement's WHERE clause. In contrast to SERIALIZABLE, however, it does not require long-duration read locks on the leaf pages of indices used by the statement.

Key-range locking. Key-range locking is essentially a refinement of the index locking scheme just described that allows ranges of search-key values to be locked. Instead of locking leaf index pages, it locks index entries at the leaf level. The problem is that an index entry specifies a unique key value. How can we interpret a lock on an entry as a range?

Consider the following example. Suppose the domain of an indexed attribute is the letters from A to Z and, at some particular instant, the index contains keys C, G, P, R, and X. A lock on a leaf index entry can be interpreted as a lock on the half-open interval that starts with the value in the entry and ranges up to, but not including, the value in the next entry. For example, a lock on the entry containing G is interpreted as a lock on all keys in the half-open interval, $[G, P)$, which includes G but not P. We refer to this as a **key-range lock**.

There are two intervals within the range of all key values that need special attention.

- A lock on the last key pointer, X, is interpreted as a lock on X and all larger keys, which we will denote $[X, \infty)$.
- The interval, $[A, C)$, consisting of all keys less than C cannot be specified in this way since A is not present in the index. Hence, an extra lock must be allocated for the initial range if A is not present in the index.

With the additional lock, and in the above example, key-range locking allows the following intervals (which cover the entire range) to be locked:

$$[A, C),\ [C, G),\ [G, P),\ [P, R),\ [R, X),\ [X, \infty)$$

While the lockable intervals are determined by the state of the index, the predicate in an SQL statement specifies an arbitrary interval. To obtain a key-range lock on an arbitrary interval, we lock the minimum set of leaf index entries such that the union of their lock intervals includes the target range. In the example,

- To obtain a lock on all keys, k, such that $H \leq k \leq Q$, we would lock G and P.
- To obtain a lock on all keys, k, such that $H \leq k \leq R$, we would lock G, P, and R.
- To obtain a lock on all keys, k, such that $H \leq k \leq Y$, we would lock G, P, R, and X.

To see how this locking protocol prevents phantoms, we first show how the protocol is used to INSERT a new key, J.

- Obtain a write lock on the key G, thus locking the key range $[G, P)$ that includes J.
- Insert J, thus splitting the interval into two, $[G, J)$ and $[J, P)$.
- Obtain a long-duration write lock on J, thus locking the interval $[J, P)$.
- Release the lock on G.

If as a result of executing a SELECT statement, a transaction holds a key-range lock on any interval that contains J, it would have obtained a long-duration read lock on G. Since the INSERT statement requires a write lock on G, it must wait. Hence phantoms are prevented.

An interesting situation arises if a transaction, T_1, requesting access to an interval, is delayed until another transaction, T_2, that has executed an INSERT statement, has completed. For example, suppose a SELECT statement in T_1 requests to read all entries between U and W. At the time the statement is executed, this requires a lock on R (which locks the interval $[R, X)$). If T_2 is inserting S, it holds a lock on R and T_1 must wait. Since the INSERT splits the interval $[R, X)$ into $[R, S)$ and $[S, X)$, T_1 no longer requires a lock on R when T_2 completes. Instead T_1 needs a lock on S since the interval $[U, W]$ is now included in $[S, X)$. To deal with such situations, a transaction that waits for a key-range lock must reevaluate the entry it is attempting to lock when the leaf level changes. This problem also occurs with index locking. For example, while a transaction waits for a lock on an index page, the page might be split because another transaction has done an INSERT.

Key-range locking has the potential to provide more concurrency than index locking because it operates at a finer granularity. Instead of locking an entire index page, and thus locking the interval implied by all index entries in the page, key-range locking locks only the index entries that cover the interval to be locked. It can be viewed as a special form of predicate locking in which the predicate corresponding to a key range is locked.

Lock escalation. The overhead of granular locking becomes excessive when a transaction accumulates too many fine-grain locks. This overhead takes two forms: the space overhead within the DBMS for recording information about each lock acquired and the time overhead necessary to process each lock request. When a transaction begins acquiring a large number of page (or tuple) locks on a table, it will likely continue to do so. Therefore, it is beneficial to trade in those locks for a single lock on the entire table.

This technique is known as **lock escalation**. A threshold is set in the concurrency control that limits the number of page locks a transaction can obtain on a particular table. When the transaction reaches that limit, the concurrency control attempts to lock the entire table (in the same mode as the page locks). When the table lock is granted, the page locks and the intention lock on the table can be released. Note the danger of deadlock in this scheme. If two transactions are acquiring page locks, at least one of them is a writer, and both reach their threshold, a deadlock results since neither can escalate their locks to a table lock.

OPTIONAL

Locking protocol for B^+ trees. When locks were introduced in Chapter 20, we associated them with data items. In the previous section we saw that by associating locks with index leaf pages we could solve the phantom problem in a neat way. But now you should be suspicious. An index can be regarded as a special table that is implicitly accessed in the course of executing an SQL statement. What about locking the rest of the index?

For example, chaos would result if one transaction was updating (perhaps splitting) a page of a B^+ tree while another was reading it. Figure 21.11(a) is copied from Figure 9.19, and Figure 21.11(b) shows the first stage of the process of splitting index page B to accommodate the insertion of `vera`. A concurrent search for `vince` initiated in this state would yield a negative result. So it appears that index structures must be locked. This is unfortunate from a performance point of view since an index is a heavily used data structure. Although transactions might access the rows of a table in a random way, they all have to traverse the same index, starting from its root, to get there. Hence, locking the index can easily create a bottleneck. What is an application to do?

Clearly, we would like to minimize the amount of locking. Our initial proposal would simply be to associate a lock with each index page and require that a transaction accessing a page hold the lock for the duration of the access. But that does not eliminate the problem illustrated in Figure 21.11(b). If the lock on B is released immediately after the page has been modified, a search for `vince` will still fail.

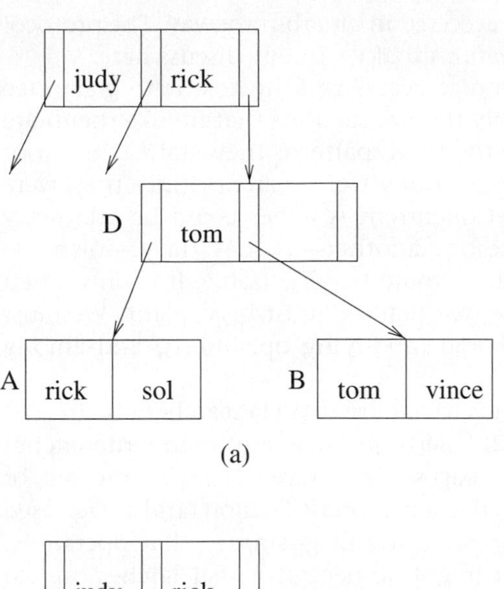

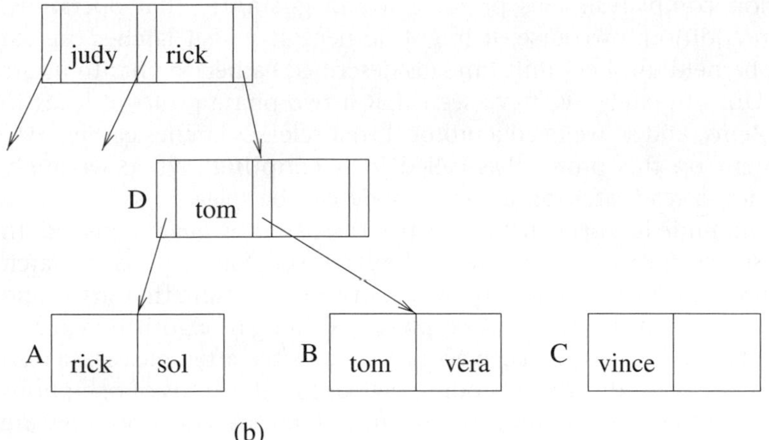

FIGURE 21.11 Two successive intermediate states in the insertion of `vera` into the B^+ tree of Figure 9.19.

Fortunately, there is a way out of this dilemma. Since the information in an index is not directly accessible to the application, the serializability of transactions does not have to include the operations they (implicitly) invoke on indexes. It is sufficient to require only that these operations perform as specified when executed concurrently. We can guarantee this by requiring that the individual operations are serializable. That is, the concurrent execution of a set of index operations is equivalent to a serial execution of the same operations.

A limited set of operations are defined on an index: search, insert, and delete. DBMSs control their interleaving by considering how they might be interleaved and then use latches, and a special protocol for managing the latches, to guarantee that damaging interleavings are prevented. The protocol need not be two phase because

OPTIONAL

the pages and entries of an index are not accessed in an arbitrary way. The protocol used for a B$^+$ tree has some interesting features that we briefly discuss here.

The goal in using latches to synchronize access to a B$^+$ tree is to guarantee that operations on the tree (not necessarily the transactions that invoke them) are serializable. These operations all follow the same pattern: they start at the root and traverse a path to the leaf. If all operations were searches (i.e., they were read-only) there would be no problem. Concurrent searches could be arbitrarily interleaved—that is, they could overtake one another—as they travel down the tree, and we would be guaranteed that they would be serializable. It is only when we introduce operations that modify the tree that we must be vigilant. We must deal with interactions between searches and modifying operations, and among modifying operations.

The simplest protocol we could adopt is to require that (1) searches obtain read latches on all index pages they access, (2) inserts and deletes obtain write latches on all index pages they access (since those pages might have to be split, merged, or modified), and (3) these latches are acquired in a two-phase fashion (and are released when the operation completes). This protocol would guarantee that operations are serializable. In addition, of course, it might be necessary that latches on leaf level index pages be held until commit time (as described earlier) if phantoms are to be prevented. Unfortunately, we have seen that a two-phase protocol leads to performance problems, and so we need a protocol that releases latches earlier.

An improvement on this protocol is called **lock coupling**. When we apply coupling to searches, a read latch on a parent node can be released as soon as a read latch on a child node has been acquired since the parent is never revisited. In Figure 21.11(a) a search for `vince` can release the latch on D as soon as the latch on B has been acquired. For the moment we will continue to require that insert and delete operations obtain write latches in a two-phase fashion. The algorithm violates the two-phase condition since a search can acquire a read latch after releasing a read latch. However, we can take advantage of our knowledge of the kinds of operations that are performed on the tree to demonstrate that, despite the violation, they are serializable (see Exercise 21.19). Lock coupling is sometimes called **crabbing** because it "walks" down the tree in a crab-like fashion.

Coupling provides additional concurrency since a modifying operation that is initiated after a search does not have to wait at the root for the search to finish. It can follow the search down a path and can actually complete if it branches off to a different leaf index page. Thus, in Figure 21.11(a), once a search for `vince` has released the latch on D, an operation that inserts `rob` can move on to A. A search, of course, will be delayed at the root by a modifying operation, so we have to look for a better solution. For example, an insert holds a write latch on the root until the insertion completes.

An obvious improvement would be to apply lock coupling to write latches, but unfortunately, that does not work. Modifying operations have the unpleasant property that they might have to retrace their steps and go back up the tree after descending to a leaf if pages have to be split or merged. With lock coupling this would imply that they would have to reacquire latches that they had previously released.

OPTIONAL

Reacquisition violates serializability: when a modifying operation reacquires a latch on a page it might find that the page has been changed by a concurrent modifying operation.

We can improve concurrency, however, by requiring a modifying operation to acquire update latches instead of write latches as it descends the tree. The update latch could be converted to write latches at a later time (without violating the two-phase requirement) if the operation had to retrace its steps. A search operation can now progress down the same path as a modifying operation and even overtake it since read and update latches do not conflict.

There are still several problems to this approach. For one thing, modifying operations still block each other at the root since update latches conflict. Furthermore, deadlock is now possible. For example, in Figure 21.11(a) the operation that inserts[8] `vera` might hold an update latch on D and a write latch on B. It might then request to upgrade the update latch on D to a write latch in order to insert the pointer to C. A concurrent search for `vince` might hold a read latch on D and request a read latch on B, yielding a deadlock. Despite this problem, update latches appear to be a good idea, since the splits and merges that require modifying operations to retrace their steps back up the tree occur infrequently.

But we are not quite finished. We can alleviate both of these problems by noticing that a modifying operation, as it descends down a path, can place a limit on how far back up the tree it can possibly go. Consider an insert operation, *ins*1. Suppose it traverses a node, *n*, that is not full (such as D in Figure 21.11(a)). It can conclude that it will not need to split *n*, and hence it will not need to modify *n*'s parent. Note that a concurrent insert, *ins*2, cannot fill *n* while *ins*1 is executing further down the tree since *ins*1 holds an update latch on *n* that stops *ins*2 on its descent. This limits the amount of backing up that *ins*1 might have to do. We can take advantage of this observation by modifying the protocol for insert operations. When, on its descent, an insert operation acquires an update latch on a node that is not full, it can release the update latches it holds on *all* ancestor nodes. A similar optimization applies to delete operations.

OPTIONAL

Table partitioning. Table partitioning is a useful technique related to granular locking. Consider again the table STUDENT. An application wishing to extract information about students living in Stony Brook might execute the statement

```
SELECT *
FROM STUDENT S
WHERE S.Address = 'Stony Brook'
```

In an alternative organization of the data, STUDENT is partitioned into separate tables, called **partitions**, one for each town. For example, we might put all of the tuples satisfying the predicate `Address = 'Stony Brook'` in one table, STUD_SB and

[8] See Exercise 21.20 for a treatment of deletes.

all tuples satisfying the predicate `Address = 'Smithtown'` in another, STUD_SM, and so forth. A transaction wishing to retrieve information about students living in Stony Brook now executes

```
SELECT *
FROM STUD_SB
```

Thus, a table lock on the partition is equivalent to a predicate lock on the predicate used to perform the partitioning. This eliminates the need for index locking as a substitute for predicate locking when the predicate is `Address =` *some town*. Since the original table no longer exists, we are not implementing two different granularities of locking. Therefore, a transaction requesting a table lock on a partition need not get an intention lock at a higher level. Partitioning was discussed in more detail in Chapter 16. Its advantage is that since the granularity of partitions is finer than the granularity of the original table, a higher degree of concurrency can be obtained without the overhead of managing intention locks. The disadvantage is that queries that span multiple partitions become more difficult to process. For example, a query that retrieves the tuples of all students living in Stony Brook or Smithtown, or a query that uses a predicate that does not involve the attribute `Address`, must access multiple tables.

OPTIONAL

21.3.2 Granular Locking in an Object Database

Many of the ideas in granular locking for relational databases also apply to object databases. Consider a bank account application. A relational database might have a table ACCOUNTS with tuples representing individual accounts. Similarly an object database might have a class ACCOUNTSCLASS in which individual accounts are represented by object instances of the class. Just as a tuple is contained in a table, we can view an object as being contained in a class. Furthermore, we can use the same lock modes (shared and exclusive and the corresponding intentions modes) and interpret them in an object database in the same way as they are interpreted in a relational database:

- In a relational database, locking a table implicitly locks all the tuples in it.
- In an object database, locking a class implicitly locks all the objects in it.

Thus, in the bank's object database, a granular locking protocol requires that we get the appropriate intention lock on ACCOUNTSCLASS before we can get a lock on a particular account object.

Object databases also support inheritance. Thus, in the bank application, the class hierarchy might include the fact that SAVINGSACCOUNTSCLASS and CHECKINGACCOUNTSCLASS are subclasses of ACCOUNTSCLASS and that ECONOMYCHECKINGACCOUNTSCLASS is a subclass of CHECKINGACCOUNTSCLASS. Since an object in the class ECONOMYCHECKINGACCOUNTSCLASS is also an object of the parent classes

CheckingAccountsClass and AccountsClass, a lock on AccountsClass implicitly locks all the objects in CheckingAccountsClass and EconomyCheckingAccountsClass. Similarly, before we can get a lock on the EconomyCheckingAccountsClass class, we must get the appropriate intention locks on both the CheckingAccountsClass class and the AccountsClass class. Thus, locking a class implicitly also locks

- All of its objects
- All of its descendant classes (and hence all the objects in those classes)

We now summarize our discussion with a (somewhat simplified)[9] protocol for granular locking of object databases.

Granular locking protocol for object databases.

- Before obtaining a lock on an object, the system must get the appropriate intention locks on the class of that object and on all parent classes of that class.
- Before obtaining a lock on a class, the system must get the appropriate intention locks on all parent classes of that class.

With these ideas in mind, we see that much of this discussion on isolation and granular locking for relational databases also applies to object databases.

21.4 Tuning Transactions

Performance is a key issue in the design of systems. In Chapter 12 we described techniques for improving the performance of individual SQL statements. In this section, we list additional techniques that can be used to improve performance at the transaction level.

- Transactions should execute at the lowest level of isolation consistent with the requirements of the application.
- The trade-off between including integrity constraints in the schema, so that the DBMS enforces them, and encoding enforcement in the transactions should be examined carefully. For example, a transaction that modifies a data item named in a constraint might change the item in a way that cannot possibly cause a violation, but if the constraint is part of the schema it will be (unnecessarily) checked when the transaction commits. If such transactions are frequently executed, it might be better to restrict constraint checking to the code of transactions that might cause a violation. On the other hand, such a decision should be weighed

[9] Some DBMSs might allow different granularities—for example, attribute level (individual attributes of an object), or database level. In some DBMSs, a write lock on a class allows the program to change the class declaration, including its methods. Other DBMSs might distinguish between a lock on the class instances, which refers to all of the objects currently in the class (similar to a table lock) and a lock on the class itself, which allows changes to the class definition (similar to a schema lock).

against the potential maintenance overhead. If, at a later time, we need to modify the constraint, the code of all transactions that check this constraint must also be changed and recompiled. This would not be necessary if the constraint were part of the schema.

- By declaring certain integrity constraints in the database schema so that they are automatically checked by the DBMS, it may be possible to execute a transaction at an isolation level lower than that consistent with the requirements of the application. (The transaction would not execute correctly at that isolation level if those integrity constraints were not checked by the DBMS.) This is essentially an optimistic approach in that it assumes that certain interleavings that cause a database to become inconsistent are unlikely. In the (rare) case in which such interleavings occur, the DBMS aborts the transaction when it detects the violation. Keep in mind, however, that errors that do not result in integrity constraint violations will not be detected.
- Transactions should be as short as possible in order to limit the time that locks must be held. It is particularly important to gather all the needed information interactively from the user before initiating the transaction. Since user interactions take a long time, locks should not be held while they are in progress. It is also desirable to decompose a long transaction into a sequence of shorter ones (assuming that this can be done while maintaining consistency). In the extreme case, each SQL statement becomes a single transaction.
- Indices can be used to increase concurrency (because they allow the DBMS to use index locks) as well as to decrease the execution time of certain operations.
- The database should be designed so that the transactions invoked most frequently can be efficiently executed. This might involve *denormalization* (see Section 6.13) to avoid expensive joins.
- Lock escalation is inefficient if the escalation threshold will likely be reached and a table lock will ultimately be acquired. Some databases permit a transaction to explicitly request a table lock before accessing a table (manual locking). Alternatively, if the number of required page (or tuple) locks can be estimated, and it is not too large, the threshold can be set above that value.
- Lock granularity can often be decreased and hence concurrency increased by partitioning one or more of the tables.
- In systems that use page locking, lock conflicts can occur if two transactions access different tuples that happen to be stored on the same page. Putting these tuples on separate pages reduces such conflicts. Similarly, if a single transaction accesses a number of tuples, lock conflicts with other transactions can be reduced if all of those tuples are clustered on a small number of pages.
- A deadlock can occur if one transaction accesses two tables in one order and another transaction accesses them in the opposite order. If possible, transactions that access common resources should all acquire locks on those resources in the same order.

21.5 Multiversion Concurrency Controls

By a **version** or **snapshot** of a database we mean an assignment of values to each database item, x, such that x's value in the version is the value assigned by the last committed transaction that wrote to x. Thus, the value of an item that has been updated by an uncommitted transaction does not appear in the version. Many versions of a database are produced during the execution of a particular schedule of transactions. In a multiversion DBMS, different versions are retained, and the concurrency control need not use the most recent version to satisfy a request to read an item.

In this section, we discuss three multiversion concurrency controls. The advantage of these algorithms is that (in most cases) readers are not required to set read locks. Therefore, a request to read a data item does not have to wait, and a request to write a data item does not have to wait for a reader. This is an important advantage, particularly in the many applications where reading occurs far more frequently than writing. These advantages come at the expense of the additional system complexity required to maintain multiple versions of the database.

Of the three algorithms we discuss, only the first always produces serializable schedules. The other two can produce nonserializable schedules and hence incorrect database states.

Transaction-level read consistency. The first question that must be addressed in specifying a multiversion concurrency control is "What value is returned to a transaction that requests to read an item in the database?" As with the READ COMMITTED isolation level, multiversion algorithms guarantee that only committed data is returned (because, by definition, a version contains only committed data). Recall, however, that at READ COMMITTED nonrepeatable reads can occur. Similarly, with a multiversion control, successive reads by the same transaction might return data from different versions. Thus, the transaction might see an inconsistent view of data. To deal with this situation, some multiversion algorithms guarantee a stronger condition called **transaction-level read consistency**: the data returned by *all* of the SQL statements executed in a transaction comes from the same version of the database. Transaction-level read consistency, however, does not necessarily guarantee serializability.

The next question that must be addressed is "What version of the database is accessed by an SQL statement?" A multiversion control might satisfy a read request with the value of an item obtained from an arbitrary version. For example, assume that transactions T_1 and T_2 are active in a conventional (single-version) immediate-update pessimistic system. If T_1 has written an item and T_2 makes a request to read the item, a conflict exists and T_2 waits. In a multiversion system, T_2's request might be satisfied immediately using a version that was created before T_1's write (note that this need not be the most recently committed version). T_2 then precedes T_1 in any equivalent serial order.

These ideas are illustrated in the following schedule:

$$w_0(y)\ commit_0\ r_2(x)\ w_1(x)\ w_1(y)\ commit_1\ r_2(y) \qquad \textbf{21.5}$$

Assuming transaction T_2 starts after T_0 commits, a control that implements transaction level read consistency might satisfy all read requests submitted by T_2 using the version created by T_0. In that case, the value returned by operation $r_2(y)$ is the value written by $w_0(y)$, which is not the value in the last committed version at the time the read is executed.

21.5.1 Read-Only Multiversion Concurrency Control

In the general case, the design of a multiversion concurrency control that ensures serializable schedules can be quite complex. However, there is a special case called a **Read-Only multiversion concurrency control** that is easier to implement and produces serializable schedules.

A Read-Only multiversion concurrency control distinguishes in advance between two kinds of transactions: **read-only** transactions, which contain no write operations, and **read/write** transactions, which contain both read and write operations.

- Read/write transactions use a conventional, immediate-update, pessimistic concurrency control with a strict two-phase locking protocol for all (read and write) operations. Transactions access the most current version of the item read or written. Hence read/write transactions are provided with transaction-level read consistency and are serializable in commit order.
- All the read operations of a read-only transaction, T_{RO}, are satisfied using the most recent version of the database that existed when T_{RO} made its first read request. Hence, read-only transactions are provided with transaction-level read consistency.

The combined schedule of read-only and read/write transactions is serializable. The equivalent serial order is the commit order of the read/write transactions, with each read-only transaction inserted immediately after the read/write transaction that created the version it read. For example, in schedule (21.5) the equivalent serial order of read/write transactions is T_0, T_1 and the serial order of the complete schedule is T_0, T_2, T_1 since the read-only transaction T_1 read the version produced by T_0. Note that the equivalent serial order is not necessarily the commit order.

To implement this control, the DBMS maintains older versions of each item for use by read-only transactions. We will see in Chapter 22 that DBMSs generally keep version information in their log for recovery purposes, so the maintenance of this information is not unique to multiversion systems. Multiversion systems, however, have the additional requirement of being able to make earlier versions accessible to read-only transactions in an efficient manner. Read/write transactions lock an item as a whole and read the most recent version when it is unlocked.

Read-only transactions do not observe locks, and the only issue is how to provide the appropriate value to satisfy a particular read request. To do this, the system stores with each value of an item a **version number**, which is assigned when the read/write

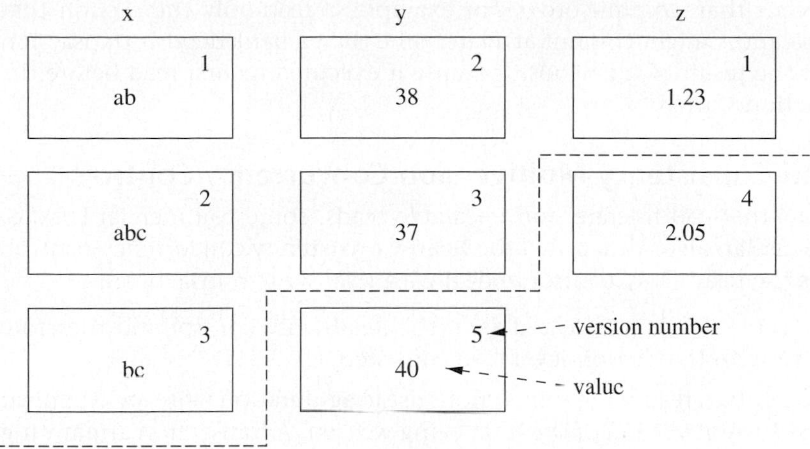

FIGURE 21.12 Satisfying a read request in a multiversion database.

transaction, $T_{R/W}$, that wrote the value commits. To determine what version number to assign, the system maintains a **version counter** (VC) which is incremented when $T_{R/W}$ commits. At that time, the (incremented) value of VC is assigned as the version number of all the items written by $T_{R/W}$. Older versions of the item are retained (perhaps in the log). $T_{R/W}$ has created a new version of the database consisting of the new versions of the items it has updated and the most recent versions (at the time $T_{R/W}$ commits) of all other items. A version contains only committed values.

Each read-only transaction is assigned a **snapshot number**, which is the value of VC that existed when it made its first read request. All subsequent read requests are satisfied using values drawn from the version with that snapshot number.

The situation is illustrated in Figure 21.12. The database consists of three items, x, y, and z. The successive values of each item are tagged with version numbers. For example, there are two versions of z, the first created by the first transaction to commit and the second created by the fourth transaction to commit. Assume that a read-only transaction, T_{RO}, makes its first read request when VC has the value 3. Hence, its snapshot number is 3 and it gets the values of x, y, and z that lie immediately above the dotted line. Versions 4 and 5 of the database might be created while T_{RO} is executing, but it does not see those versions.

Overhead is involved in storing the version numbers. Furthermore, as a practical matter the number of accessible earlier versions might be limited, and hence a (long-running) read-only transaction that draws its information from a very old version might have to be aborted if that version is no longer available.

This control has the highly desirable property that read-only transactions do not have to obtain any locks. For that reason, read-only transactions never have to wait, and read/write transactions never have to wait for read-only transactions. The cost of this property is a more complex concurrency control, the additional storage required to maintain multiple versions tagged with version numbers, and some possible nonintuitive behavior due to the serialization of read-only transactions in an order different than commit order. For example, a read-only transaction that reports bank balances might commit at a later time than a bank deposit transaction but not report the result of the deposit because it executed its first read before the deposit transaction started.

21.5.2 Read-Consistency Multiversion Concurrency Controls

For applications that can tolerate nonrepeatable reads, some commercial DBMSs, such as Oracle, use an algorithm called the **Read-Consistency** concurrency control, which extends the Read-Only control to deal with read/write transactions.

- Read-Only transactions are treated as in the Read-Only control and therefore are provided with transaction-level read consistency.
- Write statements in read/write transactions use long-duration write locks applied to the most current version of the item being written. A transaction attempting to write an item that is write-locked by another transaction must wait.
- Read statements in read/write transactions do not request read locks (read locks are not implemented in this control). Instead, each read request is provided with the value of the most recent version of the requested item (the version that was current when that read request was made).

The Read-Consistency control provides a stronger version of the standard READ COMMITTED isolation level described in Section 21.2 (and is the implementation of READ COMMITTED provided by Oracle). As with the locking implementation of READ COMMITTED, write locks are long duration and reads return committed values. However, the Read-Consistency control provides transaction-level read consistency for read-only transactions, which is not provided by the locking implementation of READ COMMITTED (nor is it required by the ANSI definition of READ COMMITTED).

A nice property of the Read-Consistency control is that no transaction needs to acquire a lock for a read operation. Hence, reads never wait for writes, and writes never wait for reads. As with READ COMMITTED, reads performed by read/write transactions are not repeatable, and so schedules can be nonserializable. For example, the schedule shown in Figure 21.6, which exhibits a lost update, can be produced by this control.

CASE STUDY

21.5.3 Case Study: SNAPSHOT Isolation

Still another variation on the same idea is called SNAPSHOT isolation [Berenson et al. 1995]. Variants of SNAPSHOT isolation have been implemented by a number of database vendors, including Oracle. In fact SNAPSHOT isolation is Oracle's implementation of SET TRANSACTION LEVEL SERIALIZABLE (although the resulting schedules are not necessarily serializable).

SNAPSHOT isolation does not distinguish between read-only and read/write transactions. It is defined as follows:

- All read operations of a transaction are satisfied using the version of the database that was current when the transaction made its first read request. Thus, all transactions are provided with transaction-level read consistency.

- If two transactions, T_1 and T_2, are concurrent (their execution overlaps in time), the set of data items written by T_1 must be disjoint from the set written by T_2. This is called the **disjoint-write property**. If the two transactions attempt to write the same data item, one of them will be aborted. In this definition, a data item can be considered to be either a row or a table (or even an individual attribute within a row), but since tables provide a coarse granularity, which negatively affects performance, we will henceforth assume that a data item is a row.

The disjoint-write property has the important effect of eliminating lost updates. Consider, for example, the lost update shown in Figure 21.6 on page 880. Since T_1 and T_2 are concurrent and their write sets are not disjoint, only one will be allowed to commit.

We describe two implementations of the disjoint-write property, both based on the use of a version counter, VC, that is incremented whenever a transaction that has written an item commits. As before, the incremented value is the version number of the new version created by the transaction. In both implementations, each transaction is assigned a snapshot number (which is the value of VC when it made its first read request). Note that the version number of the version created by T is greater than T's snapshot number.

First-committer-wins implementation. One way to ensure the disjoint-write property is by using a **first-committer-wins** strategy. A transaction, T_1, is allowed to commit only if there is no other transaction that (1) committed between the time T_1 made its first read request and the time it requested to commit, and (2) updated a data item that T_1 also updated. If this is not the case, T_1 aborts. Clearly a concurrency control that implements first-committer-wins ensures the disjoint-write property.

The first-committer-wins property can be implemented without write locks using a deferred-update system. While executing, T_1's updates are stored in an intentions list. When it has completed, it is validated (as in an optimistic concurrency control but with a different validation criterion). Validation is successful if T_1's snapshot number is greater than or equal to the version number of each item that it has updated.

- Suppose that when T_1 requests to commit, the version number of some item that T_1 has updated is greater than T_1's snapshot number. This means that some other transaction, T_2, wrote that item and committed while T_1 was executing. In this case, T_1 must be aborted since T_2 is the first committer—and it wins.
- Suppose that at the time T_1 requests to commit, the version number of all items that T_1 has updated is less than or equal to T_1's snapshot number. Then T_1's intentions list is used to create a new version of the database by appending a new value to each database item named in the list, tagged with the incremented version counter.

As illustrated in Figure 21.12, if T_1's snapshot number is 3, and T_1 has written to x and y, then T_1's request to commit will be denied. Although there are no newer versions of x, a newer version of y was created by a different (committed) transaction while T_1 was executing.

As with the optimistic concurrency control algorithm, this control has the property that no locks are needed; hence, neither reads nor writes ever wait, but transactions might be aborted when they complete.

A locking implementation. The disjoint-write property can also be implemented using an immediate-update locking protocol involving only write locks. This is the implementation provided by Oracle. When a transaction, T_1, requests to write a data item, x

- If no other transaction has a write lock on x,
  - If the version number of x is greater than T_1's snapshot number, T_1 is aborted since a concurrent transaction wrote x and committed before the request (and the first committer wins).
  - If the version number of x is less than or equal to T_1's snapshot number, T_1 is granted a write lock on x and allowed to write it. The lock is retained until T_1 commits or aborts.
- If another transaction, T_2, has a write lock on x, T_1 waits until T_2 terminates.
  - If T_2 commits, T_1 is aborted (T_2 is the first committer and wins).
  - If T_2 aborts, T_1 is granted the lock and allowed to write x (assuming no other transaction is also waiting for that lock).

This control has the property that no read locks are needed. Hence, reads never wait and writes never wait for reads, but transactions might be aborted while waiting for write locks (either because the transaction holding that lock commits or because of a deadlock).

Non-serializable schedules and SNAPSHOT isolation. Although SNAPSHOT isolation eliminates many anomalies, it does not guarantee that all schedules will be serializable, hence transactions can perform incorrectly. For example, in Figure 21.13, T_1 and T_2 are two bank withdrawal transactions that are withdrawing funds from different accounts, with balances a_1 and a_2, owned by the same depositor, d. The bank has a business rule that an individual account balance can be negative, but the sum of the balances in all accounts owned by each depositor must be nonnegative. Thus, if d has only two accounts, the constraint is $a_1 + a_2 \geq 0$. Both T_1 and T_2 are consistent: they read the balances in both accounts before making withdrawals, and thus, when executed in isolation, each maintains the constraint. In the example, each account has \$10 initially and each transaction concludes that it is safe to withdraw \$15 because the combined balance is \$20. However, in the schedule shown, which is allowable in SNAPSHOT isolation (because T_1 and T_2 write to different data items), the final values of a_1 and a_2 are both $-\$5$, thus violating the constraint. Note that this schedule is not serializable because T_2 must be after T_1 (T_2 wrote a_1 after T_1 read it) and T_1 must be after T_2 (T_1 wrote a_2 after T_2 read it). (For a continuation of this example, see Exercise 21.25.)

CASE STUDY

FIGURE 21.13 SNAPSHOT-isolated schedule that is not serializable and leads to an inconsistent database.

$$T_1 : r(a_1 : 10)\ r(a_2 : 10) \qquad\qquad\qquad\qquad\qquad\qquad w(a_2 : -5)\ commit$$
$$T_2 : \qquad\qquad\qquad r(a_1 : 10)\ r(a_2 : 10)\ w(a_1 : -5)\ commit$$

SNAPSHOT isolation and the isolation-level anomalies. Even though the example of Figure 21.13 demonstrates that SNAPSHOT isolation can produce nonserializable schedules, note that these schedules do not exhibit any of the anomalies associated with the lower isolation levels—dirty reads, nonrepeatable reads, and phantoms (as well as dirty writes and lost updates, which are not part of the definitions of the isolation levels).

We need to clarify the statement that SNAPSHOT isolation does not allow phantoms. In a SNAPSHOT-isolated schedule, a transaction, T, might execute a SELECT statement based on a predicate, P, and a concurrent transaction might later insert a tuple, t, that satisfies P (seemingly a phantom). However, t will not be returned in a subsequent execution by T of the same SELECT statement since its result set will be calculated from the same version of the database used by the first execution. On this basis, one might say that t is not a phantom. We give two examples, one where the insertion does not cause an incorrect schedule and one where it does.

- In the example in Section 21.1.1 involving a single-version database and Mary's accounts, the audit transaction, T_1, saw inconsistent data because a phantom was inserted between its two SELECT statements, changing the state of that version. In a multiversion database, a version, once created, never changes. With SNAPSHOT isolation, the result sets for both statements are calculated using one of those versions, hence T_1 does not see the updated value of `TotalBalance`. Therefore, it executes correctly.
- Suppose that the bank database has an integrity constraint stating that no depositor can have more than 10 accounts. To enforce this, an `add_new_account` transaction first executes a SELECT statement using the predicate `Name = 'Mary'` to determine the number of Mary's accounts. If the number is nine or less, it inserts a tuple corresponding to a new account for Mary. If two instances of `add_new_account` execute concurrently, and both have the same snapshot number indicating a version in which Mary has nine accounts, they will both insert a tuple corresponding to a new account. Mary now has 11 accounts, in violation of the constraint. The schedule is nonserializable and incorrect.

There is no agreed-upon definition in the literature of what constitutes a phantom. Some sources say that an isolation level permits phantoms if, when a transaction executes the same SELECT statement twice, the second execution can return a result set containing a (phantom) tuple not contained in the first. Using this definition, phantoms are permitted at REPEATABLE READ but not at SNAPSHOT isolation.

FIGURE 21.14 SNAPSHOT-isolated schedule that is not serializable and does not exhibit any of the named anomalies.

$$
\begin{array}{llllll}
T_1: & r(x) & & w(x)\ commit & & \\
T_2: & & r(x)\ r(y) & & & w(y)\ commit \\
T_3: & & & & r(x)\ r(y)\ w(z)\ commit &
\end{array}
$$

However, the second example illustrates that the effect of phantoms still exists with SNAPSHOT isolation even though, according to the above definition, the insertions do not constitute phantoms. If we had executed the transactions in that example at REPEATABLE READ, the same (nonserializable) schedule would be permitted and we would say that phantoms did occur.

Using the definition of phantoms based on the successive execution of SELECT statements, it follows that SNAPSHOT isolation does not exhibit any of the bad anomalies that define the lower isolation levels. Nevertheless, it does not meet the ANSI definition of SERIALIZABLE [SQL 1992], which states that (in addition to not allowing any of the three anomalies) SERIALIZABLE must provide what is "commonly known as fully serializable execution." This is certainly not the case for SNAPSHOT isolation. Schedules that do not contain the three anomalies of dirty reads, nonrepeatable reads, and phantoms are sometimes called **anomaly serializable**. Thus, SNAPSHOT-isolated schedules are anomaly serializable, but might not be serializable.

This again shows that correctness should not be defined by the absence of certain specific anomalies. Some authors use the term **write skew** to describe the anomaly exemplified by Figure 21.13. But even adding that anomaly to the list should not give you much confidence that the list is complete. For example, the schedule shown in Figure 21.14, which is allowable in SNAPSHOT isolation, is not serializable because its serialization graph has a cycle

$$T_3 \rightarrow T_2 \rightarrow T_1 \rightarrow T_3$$

However, it does not exhibit any of the named anomalies, including write skew.

Figure 21.15 shows another schedule [Fekete et al. 2000] permitted at SNAPSHOT isolation that is not serializable because its serialization graph has the cycle

$$T_3 \rightarrow T_2 \rightarrow T_1 \rightarrow T_3$$

The interesting thing about this example is that it involves a read-only transaction, T_3. The read/write transactions, T_1 and T_2, by themselves, are serializable (T_2 precedes T_1). However T_3 sees a snapshot of the database that never existed. Specifically, T_3 sees the effect of T_1, but not the effect of T_2, even though T_2 precedes T_1 in the (only possible) equivalent serial order.

Correct execution at SNAPSHOT isolation. Even though SNAPSHOT isolation does not guarantee serializable executions, many applications do run serializably at SNAPSHOT isolation. For example, the TPC-C Benchmark (*http://www.tpc.org/tpcc*), which is an application that is used to compare the performance of different vendors'

FIGURE 21.15 Another schedule permitted at SNAPSHOT isolation that is not serializable and does not exhibit any of the named anomalies. This one involves a read-only transaction.

T_1:		$r(x)\ w(x)\ commit$		
T_2:	$r(x)\ r(y)$			$w(y)\ commit$
T_3:			$r(x)\ r(y)\ commit$	

FIGURE 21.16 SNAPSHOT-isolated schedule for a ticket-reservation application. The schedule exhibits write skew and is not serializable but is nevertheless correct.

$T_1 : r(s_1 : U)\ r(s_2 : U)$		$w(s_2 : R)\ commit$
T_2:	$r(s_1 : U)\ r(s_2 : U)\ w(s_1 : R)\ commit$	

DBMSs, has been shown to execute serializably at SNAPSHOT isolation [Fekete et al. 2000].

Many other applications run correctly at SNAPSHOT isolation even though some of their schedules exhibit write skew and are nonserializable. For example, consider an application containing a transaction that reserves a seat for a concert. The transaction examines the status of a number of seats and reserves one. An integrity constraint asserts that the same seat cannot be reserved by more than one person. Suppose that two ticket-reservation transactions execute concurrently and produce the schedule shown in Figure 21.16 (which is virtually identical to the schedule shown in Figure 21.13). Each reads the tuples corresponding to seats s_1 and s_2 and determines that they are both unreserved (U). Then T_1 reserves s_1 by updating its status (to R) in the database; similarly, T_2 reserves s_2. The schedule is correct for this application, even though it exhibits write skew (and hence the schedule is not serializable). Furthermore, if both transactions try to reserve seat s_1, only one will commit because of the disjoint-write property, preserving the integrity constraint. Hence, any schedule of ticket-reservation transactions will execute correctly at SNAPSHOT isolation.

Because of the multiversion aspect of SNAPSHOT isolation, serializable SNAPSHOT-isolated schedules can sometimes yield nonintuitive behavior. For example, the schedule of Figure 21.17 is serializable in the order

$$T_3 \rightarrow T_2 \rightarrow T_1$$

where T_3 precedes T_1 even though it started after T_1 committed.

FIGURE 21.17 SNAPSHOT-isolated schedule that is serializable but in which T_3 precedes T_1 in the equivalent serial order even though it started after T_1 committed.

T_1:	$r(x)$		$w(x)\ commit$		
T_2:		$r(x)\ r(y)$			$w(y)\ commit$
T_3:				$r(y)\ w(z)\ commit$	

In practice, many applications run correctly under SNAPSHOT isolation, particularly if most of the integrity constraints are encoded into the database schema (see Exercise 21.25). However, the cautious designer will perform a careful analysis of the application before making that design decision.

BIBLIOGRAPHIC NOTES

Phantoms and the use of predicate locks to eliminate them were introduced in [Eswaran et al. 1976]. The definition of the SQL isolation levels can be found in [Gray et al. 1976] and in the ANSI SQL standard [SQL 1992]. The locking implementation of the isolation levels is discussed in [Berenson et al. 1995]. [Gray et al. 1976] contains a good discussion of granular locking. Multiversion concurrency controls are discussed in [Bernstein and Goodman 1983; Hadzilacos and Papadimitriou 1985]. The design of a multiversion, optimistic concurrency control is described in [Agrawal et al. 1987]. SNAPSHOT isolation was first discussed in [Berenson et al. 1995]. [Fekete et al. 2000] discusses the conflict aspects of SNAPSHOT isolation and gives a sufficient condition for a SNAPSHOT-isolated schedule to be serializable. They also prove that the TPC-C Benchmark application executes serializably at SNAPSHOT isolation, and they provide the example of nonserializable execution with a read-only transaction. [Bernstein et al. 2000] discusses an approach to proving correctness of schedules at lower isolation levels based on the semantics of the transactions. [Bernstein et al. 1987] contains an excellent summary of many concurrency control algorithms, including index locking. An early version of lock coupling was described in [Shoshani and Bernstein 1969]. Concurrency control in an object database is discussed in [Cattell 1994].

EXERCISES

21.1 Suppose that the transaction processing system of your university contains a table in which there is one tuple for each currently registered student.

a. Estimate how much disk storage is required to store this table.

b. Give examples of transactions that must lock this entire table if a table-locking concurrency control is used.

21.2 Consider an INSERT statement that inserts tuples into table T and that contains a nested SELECT statement having predicate P in its WHERE clause. Assume P is a simple predicate that does not contain a nested SELECT statement and consists of a conjunction of clauses of the form (`Attribute` *op* `constant`). Describe the predicate associated with T.

21.3 Choose a set of transactions for an application of your choice (other than a banking or student registration system). For each isolation level weaker than SERIALIZABLE, give an example of a schedule that produces an erroneous situation.

21.4 Assume that transactions are executed at REPEATABLE READ. Give an example in which a phantom occurs when a transaction executes a SELECT statement that specifies the value of the primary key in the WHERE clause.

21.5 Assume that transactions are executed at REPEATABLE READ. Give an example in which a phantom occurs when a transaction executes a DELETE statement to delete a set of tuples satisfying some predicate, *P*.

21.6 Assume that transactions are executed at REPEATABLE READ. Give an example in which an UPDATE statement executed by one transaction causes a phantom in an UPDATE statement executed in another.

21.7 Consider a schema with two tables, TABLE1 and TABLE2, each having three attributes, `attr1`, `attr2`, and `attr3`, and consider the statement

```
SELECT T1.attr1, T2.attr1
FROM TABLE1 T1, TABLE2 T2
WHERE T1.attr2 = T2.attr2 AND T1.attr3 = 5
          AND T2.attr3 = 7
```

Give an INSERT statement that might cause a phantom.

21.8 Explain the difference between a nonrepeatable read and a phantom. Specifically, give an example of a schedule of the SQL statements of two transactions that illustrate the two cases. Specify an isolation level in each case.

21.9 For each of the locking implementations of the isolation levels, state whether IS locks are required and when they can be released.

21.10 The following procedure has been proposed for obtaining read locks.

> Whenever an SQL statement reads a set of rows that satisfies some predicate in a table, the system first gets an IS lock on the table containing the rows and then gets an S lock on each of the rows.

Explain why this procedure allows phantoms.

21.11 Give an example of a schedule produced by a read-only multiversion concurrency control in which the read/write transactions serialize in commit order while the read-only transactions serialize in a different order.

21.12 Give an example of a schedule of read/write requests that is accepted by a multiversion concurrency control in which transaction T_1 starts after transaction T_2 commits, yet T_1 precedes T_2 in the serial order. Such a schedule can have the following nonintuitive behavior (even though it is serializable): you deposit money in your bank account; your transaction commits; later you start a new transaction that reads the amount in your account and finds that the amount you deposited is not there. (*Hint:* The schedule is allowed to contain additional transactions.)

21.13 Show that the schedule shown in Figure 21.13 for incorrect execution at SNAPSHOT isolation can also occur when executing at OPTIMISTIC READ COMMITTED (Section 21.2.1) and will also be incorrect.

21.14 Give examples of schedules that would be accepted at

a. SNAPSHOT isolation but not REPEATABLE READ

b. SERIALIZABLE but not SNAPSHOT isolation

21.15 A particular read-only transaction reads data that was entered into the database during the previous month and uses that data to prepare a report. What is the weakest isolation level at which this transaction can execute? Explain.

21.16 Explain why a read-only transaction consisting of a single SELECT statement that uses an INSENSITIVE cursor can always execute correctly at READ COMMITTED.

21.17 Suppose that a locking implementation of REPEATABLE READ requires that a transaction obtain an X lock on a table when a write is requested. When a read is requested, a transaction is required to obtain an IS lock on the table and an S lock on the tuples returned. Show that phantoms cannot occur.

21.18 Consider an isolation level implemented using long-duration granular locks on rows and tables. Under what conditions can phantoms occur?

21.19 Show that the algorithm for concurrently accessing a B^+tree in which operations that only search the tree use lock coupling and operations that modify the tree handle write latches in a two-phase fashion guarantees that all operations are carried out successfully.

21.20 In Section 21.3.1 we described an algorithm that allowed the concurrent execution of a search for a unique key and an insert of a row in a B^+ tree. Extend the algorithm to range searches and deletes.

21.21 a. Give an example of a schedule of two transactions in which a two-phase locking concurrency control causes one of the transactions to wait but a SNAPSHOT isolation control aborts one of the transactions.

b. Give an example of a schedule of two transactions in which a two-phase locking concurrency control aborts one of the transactions (because of a deadlock) but a SNAPSHOT isolation control allows both transactions to commit.

21.22 Explain why SNAPSHOT-isolated schedules do not exhibit dirty reads, dirty writes, lost updates, nonrepeatable reads, and phantoms.

21.23 Consider an application consisting of transactions that are assigned different isolation levels. Prove that if transaction T is executed at SERIALIZABLE and transaction T' is any other transaction, then T either sees all changes made by T' or it sees none.

21.24 All of the transactions in some particular application write all of the data items they read. Show that if that application executes under SNAPSHOT isolation, all schedules of committed transactions will be serializable.

21.25 Consider the schedule of two bank withdrawal transactions shown in Figure 21.13 for which SNAPSHOT isolation leads to an inconsistent database. Suppose that the bank encodes, as an integrity constraint in the database schema, the business rule "The sum of the balances in all accounts owned by the same depositor must be nonnegative." Then that particular schedule cannot occur.

Although the integrity constraint is now maintained, the specification of a particular transaction might assert that when the transaction commits, the database state satisfies a stronger condition. Give an example of a stronger condition that a withdrawal transaction might attempt to impose when it terminates and a schedule of two such transactions at SNAPSHOT isolation that causes them to behave incorrectly.

21.26 The following multiversion concurrency control has been proposed.

> Reads are satisfied using the (committed) version of the database that existed when the transaction made its first read request. Writes are controlled by long-duration write locks on tables.

Does the control always produce serializable schedules? If not, give a nonserializable schedule it might produce.

21.27 We have given two different implementations of the READ COMMITTED isolation level: the locking implementation in Section 21.2 and the read-consistency implementation in Section 21.5. Give an example of a schedule in which the two implementations produce different results.

21.28 The granular locking protocol can exhibit a deadlock between two transactions, one of which executes a single SELECT statement and the other a single UPDATE statement. For example, suppose that one transaction contains the single SELECT statement

```
SELECT COUNT (P.Id)
FROM EMPLOYEE P
WHERE P.Age = '27'
```

which returns the number of employees whose age is 27, and the other contains the single UPDATE statement

```
UPDATE EMPLOYEE
SET Salary = Salary * 1.1
WHERE Department = 'Adm'
```

which gives all employees in the administration a 10% raise. Assume that there are indices on both `Department` and `Age` and that the tuples corresponding to the department `Adm` are stored in more than one page as are those corresponding to age 27. Show how a deadlock might occur at isolation levels other than READ UNCOMMITTED.

21.29 Give an example of a schedule executing at SNAPSHOT isolation in which two transactions each introduce a phantom that is not seen by the other transaction, resulting in incorrect behavior. Assume that the data items referred to in the description of SNAPSHOT isolation are rows.

21.30 In an Internet election system, each voter is sent a PIN in the mail. When that voter wants to vote at the election web site, she enters her PIN and her vote, and then a voting transaction is executed.

In the voting transaction, first the PIN is checked to verify that it is valid and has not been used already, and then the vote tally for the appropriate candidate is incremented. Two tables are used: One contains the valid PINs together with an indication of whether or not each PIN has been used and the other contains the names of the candidates and the vote tally for each. Discuss the issues involved in selecting an appropriate isolation level for the voting transaction. Discuss the issues involved in selecting appropriate isolation levels if a new (read-only) transaction is introduced that outputs the entire vote tally table.

21.31 An airlines database has two tables: FLIGHTS, with attributes flt_num, plane_id, num_reserv; and PLANES, with attributes plane_id, and num_seats.

The attributes have the obvious semantics. A reservation transaction contains the following steps:

```
    SELECT F.plane_id, F.num_reserv
    INTO :p, :n
    FROM FLIGHTS F
    WHERE F.flt_num = :f
A.  SELECT P.num_seats
    INTO :s
    FROM PLANES P
    WHERE P.plane_id = :p
B.  . . . check that n < s . . .
C.  UPDATE FLIGHTS F
    SET F.num_reserv = :n + 1
    WHERE F.flt_num = :f
D.  COMMIT
```

Assume that each individual SQL statement is executed in isolation, that the DBMS uses intention locking and sets locks on tables and rows, and that host variable f contains the number of the flight to be booked. The transaction should not overbook the flight.

a. Assuming that the transaction is run at READ COMMITTED, what locks are held at points *A*, *B*, and *D*?

b. The database can be left in an incorrect state if concurrently executing reservation transactions that are running at READ COMMITTED are interleaved in such a way that one transaction is completely executed at point *B* in the execution of another. Describe the problem.

c. In an attempt to avoid the problem described in (b), the SET clause of the UPDATE statement is changed to F.num_reserv = F.num_reserv + 1. Can reservation transactions now be run correctly at READ COMMITTED? Explain.

d. Assuming that the transaction is run at REPEATABLE READ and that the tables are accessed through indices, what table locks are held at points *A*, *B*, and *D*?

e. What problem does the interleaving of (b) cause at REPEATABLE READ? Explain.

f. Does the interleaving of (b) cause an incorrect state if the transaction (either version) is run using SNAPSHOT isolation? Explain.

g. To keep track of each passenger, a new table, PASSENGER, is introduced that has a row describing each passenger on each flight with attributes name, flt_num, seat_id. SQL statements are appended to the end of the transaction (1) to read the seat_id's assigned to each passenger on the flight specified in f and (2) to insert a row for the new passenger that assigns an empty seat to that passenger.

What is the weakest ANSI isolation level at which the transaction can be run without producing an incorrect state (i.e., two passengers in the same seat)? Explain.

21.32 Two transactions run concurrently, and each might either commit or abort. The transactions are chosen from the following:

$$T_1: \ r_1(x)\ w_1(y)$$
$$T_2: \ w_2(x)$$
$$T_3: \ r_3(y)\ w_3(x)$$
$$T_4: \ r_4(x)\ w_4(x)\ w_4(y)$$

In each of the following cases, state (yes or no) whether the resulting schedule is always serializable and recoverable. If the answer is no, give an example of a schedule that is either not serializable or not recoverable.

a. T_1 and T_2 both running at READ UNCOMMITTED
b. T_2 and T_2 both running at READ UNCOMMITTED
c. T_1 and T_2 both running at READ COMMITTED
d. T_1 and T_3 both running at READ COMMITTED
e. T_1 and T_3 both running at SNAPSHOT isolation
f. T_1 and T_4 both running at SNAPSHOT isolation

21.33 Give an example of a schedule that could be produced at SNAPSHOT isolation in which there are two transactions that execute concurrently but do not have the same snapshot number and do not see the same snapshot of the database. (*Hint:* the schedule can contain more than two transactions.)

21.34 A database has two tables:

STUDENT(Id, Name, ···)—Id and Name are both unique
REGISTERED(Id, CrsCode, Credit, ···)—contains one row for each course each student is taking this semester

A transaction type, T, has two SQL statements, $S1$ followed by $S2$ (with local computations between them):

```
S1  SELECT   SUM(R.Credits), S.Id
    INTO     :sum, :id
    FROM     STUDENT S, REGISTERED R
    WHERE    S.Name = 'Joe' AND S.Id = R.Id
    GROUP BY S.Name, S.Id
```

```
S2  UPDATE   Registered
    SET      Credits = Credits + 1
    WHERE    Id = :id AND CrsCode = :crs
```

$S1$ returns the total number of credits for which Joe is registered, together with his Id. T maintains the integrity constraint "no student shall register for more than 20 credits." If Joe has less than 20 credits, T executes $S2$ to increment the number of credits for which Joe has registered in a particular course. Suppose Joe executes two instances of T concurrently at the following isolation levels. In each case say whether or not the named violation of the constraint can occur and, if the answer is yes, explain how (e.g., what locks are or are not held).

a. READ COMMITTED
    lost update
    violation of the integrity constraint
    deadlock

b. REPEATABLE READ
    lost update
    violation of the integrity constraint
    deadlock

c. SNAPSHOT
    lost update
    violation of the integrity constraint
    deadlock

22

Atomicity and Durability

In previous chapters we made the unrealistic assumptions that transactions commit and that the system never malfunctions. The reality is quite different. Transactions can be aborted for a variety of reasons, and hardware and software can fail. Such events must be carefully handled to ensure transaction atomicity. Furthermore, a failure might occur on a mass storage device, causing the loss of information written to the database by committed transactions, thus threatening durability.

In this chapter, we discuss the basic problems that must be solved to achieve atomicity and durability and some techniques to do so. Our description is not meant to reflect the design of any particular failure recovery system. Instead, we emphasize principles that underlie the design of a number of such systems.

22.1 Crash, Abort, and Media Failure

Although the reliability of computer systems has increased dramatically over the years, the probability of a failure is still very real. A failure might be caused by a problem in the processor or in the main memory units (for example, a power loss) or by a bug in the software. Such failures cause the processor to behave unpredictably, perhaps writing spurious information in arbitrary locations in main memory, before finally performing some action that causes it to shut down. We refer to such a failure as a **crash**, and we assume that when a crash occurs, the contents of main memory are lost. For this reason, main memory is referred to as **volatile storage**. It is possible that a failing processor might initiate a spurious write to the mass storage device, but such an event is so unlikely that we assume that the contents of mass storage survive a crash.

In general, a number of transactions will be active when a transaction processing system crashes, which means that the database will be in an inconsistent state. When the system is restarted after a crash, service is not resumed until after a **recovery procedure** is executed to restore the database to a consistent state. The major issue in the design of a recovery procedure is how to deal with a transaction, T, that was active at the time the crash occurred. Atomicity requires either that the recovery procedure cause T to resume execution so that it can complete successfully—called

rollforward—or that any effects that T had prior to the crash be undone—called **rollback**.

Rollforward is often difficult, if not impossible. If T is an interactive transaction, resumption requires the cooperation of the user at the terminal. The user must know which of the updates she requested prior to the crash had actually been recorded in the database, and resume submitting requests from that point. Rolling forward a programmed transaction is further complicated by the fact that the local state (the state of T's local variables) might have been in volatile memory at the time of the crash and hence might be lost. T cannot be resumed from the point at which the crash occurred unless its local state is restored. Thus, in order to roll T forward after a crash, special measures must be taken to periodically save T's local state on a mass storage device during transaction execution.

For these reasons, transactions active at the time of a crash are usually rolled back during recovery in order to achieve atomicity. Note that our primary concern here is with the changes T made to the database before the crash. A transaction might have had other, external, effects such as printing a message on the screen or actuating a controller in a factory. External actions are difficult to reverse, although we discussed one technique for handling them in Section 19.3.5.

The rollback mechanism is required to deal not only with crashes but with transaction aborts as well. A transaction might be aborted for a number of reasons.

- A transaction might be aborted by the user—for example, because he entered incorrect input data.
- A transaction might abort itself—for example, because it encountered some unexpected information in the database.
- A transaction might be aborted by the system—for example, because the transaction has become deadlocked with other transactions, the system does not have sufficient resources to complete it, or allowing it to commit would result in the violation of some integrity constraint.

Media failure. Durability requires that the effects of a transaction on a database not be lost once the transaction has committed. Databases are stored on mass storage devices—usually disks. Since crashes typically do not affect these devices, mass storage is referred to as **nonvolatile** storage. However, mass storage devices are subject to their own forms of failure, which are referred to as **media failures**. A media failure might affect all or some of the data stored on the device. The redundant storage of data is used to ensure a measure of durability in spite of such a failure. The more redundant copies that are kept, the more media failures that can be tolerated. Thus, durability is not absolute. It is related to the value of the data and the amount of money the enterprise is willing to spend on protecting it. A media failure might occur while transactions are executing, so the recovery procedures for media failure must also provide rollback capabilities.

22.2 Immediate-Update Systems and Write-Ahead Logs

The mechanism for rollback is different in immediate- and deferred-update systems. Since immediate-update systems are more common, we deal with them first. Our description of such a system proceeds in stages. In this section, we describe a simple, but impractical system to introduce the major ideas. In later sections we discuss some of the complexities that must be dealt with in commercial systems and describe some of the changes that must be made to the simple system to handle them.

Immediate-update systems maintain a **log**, which is a sequence of records. Records are appended to the log as transactions execute and are never changed or deleted. The log is consulted by the system to achieve both atomicity and durability. For durability, the log is used to restore the database after a failure of the mass storage device on which the database is stored. Hence, the log must be stored on a non-volatile device. Typically, a log is a sequential file on disk. It is often duplexed (and the copies stored on different devices) so that it survives any single media failure. Some DBMSs maintain a single log while others allocate a separate log for each database.

The organization of memory is shown in Figure 22.1. For efficiency, the unit of transfer between the database on mass store and main memory is the page. Recently accessed pages are kept in a cache in main memory. Moreover, information that will eventually be stored in the log is usually first put into a log buffer in main memory. The existence of the cache and log buffer complicates the processing required for rollback and commitment. In this section, we assume that neither a cache nor a log buffer is used but that information is directly read from and written to the database and directly written to the log. We will consider the effect of the log buffer and cache in Section 22.2.1.

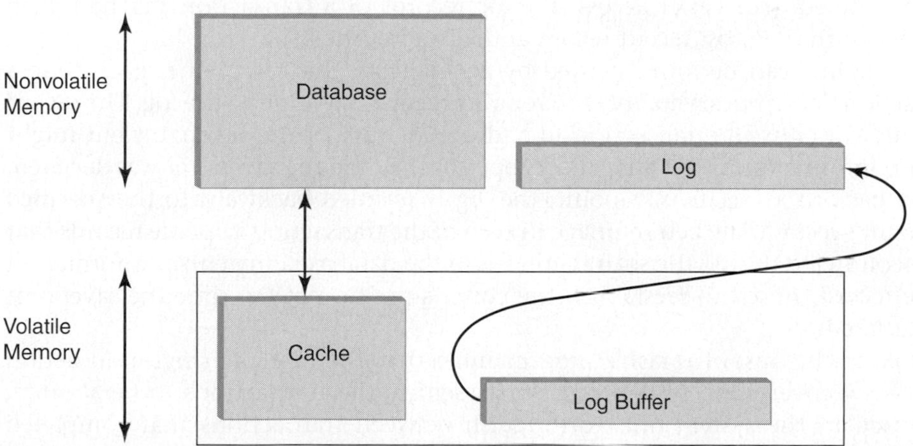

FIGURE 22.1 Organization of memory.

When a transaction executes a database operation that changes the state of the database, the system appends an **update record** to the log (no record need be appended if the operation merely reads the database). An update record describes the change that has been made and, in particular, contains enough information to permit the system to undo that change if the transaction is later aborted. Since the records are appended when the changes are made, the log contains the merge of the update records of all transactions.

In its simplest form, an update record contains the **before-image** of the database item that has been modified—that is, a physical copy of the item before the change was made. If the transaction aborts, the update record is used to restore the item to its original value—hence, the before-image is sometimes referred to as an **undo record**. If the concurrency control enforces serializable execution (i.e., the item was exclusively locked when it was changed) and the concurrency control is strict, the new value could not have been viewed by concurrent transactions, and therefore the aborted transaction will have had no effect on other transactions, and after restoration it will have had no effect on the database either. In addition to the before-image, the update record identifies the transaction that made the change—using a **transaction Id**—and the database item that was changed. We introduce other information contained in the update record as our discussion proceeds.

Because the update record contains a physical copy of the item, this form of logging is referred to as **physical logging**.

If the system aborts a transaction, T, or T aborts itself, rollback using the log is straightforward. The log is scanned backwards starting from the last record appended, and, as T's update records are encountered, the before-images are written to the database, undoing the change.

Since the log might be exceedingly long, it is impractical to search back to the beginning to make sure that all of T's update records are processed. To avoid a complete backward scan, when T is initiated a **begin record** containing its transaction Id is appended to the log. The backward scan can be stopped when T's begin record is encountered. (For easier access, the log records of a transaction can be linked together, with the most recent record at the head of the list.)

Savepoints can be implemented by generalizing this technique. Each time a transaction declares a savepoint, a **savepoint record** is written to the log. The record not only contains the transaction Id and the identity of the savepoint but might contain information about any cursors open at the time the savepoint was declared. To roll back to a specific savepoint, the log is scanned backward to the specified savepoint's record. The before-image in each of the transaction's update records that are encountered during the scan is applied to the database. Any cursor information in the record is used to reestablish the cursor's position at the time the savepoint was declared.

Rollback because of a crash is more complex than the abort of a single transaction since, on recovery, the system must first identify the transactions to be aborted. In particular, the system must distinguish between transactions that completed (committed or aborted) and those that were active at the time the crash occurred. All of the active transactions must be aborted.

When a transaction commits, it writes a **commit record** to the log. If it aborts, it rolls back its updates and then writes an **abort record** to the log. Both records contain the transaction's Id. After writing a commit or abort record, the transaction can release any locks it holds.

Using these records, the identity of the transactions active at the time of the crash can be determined by the recovery procedure. It scans the log backward starting from the last record appended before the crash occurred. If the first record relating to T is an update record, T was active when the crash occurred and must be aborted. If the first record is a commit or abort record, the transaction completed and its update records can be ignored as they are subsequently encountered.

Note that, for durability, it is important to write a commit record to the log when T commits. Because our simplified view assumes that the database is immediately updated when T makes a write request, all database modifications requested by T will be recorded in nonvolatile memory when it requests to commit. However, the commit request itself does not guarantee durability. If a crash occurs after a transaction makes the request, but before the commit record is written to the log, the transaction will be aborted by the recovery procedure and the system will not provide durability. Hence, a transaction has not actually committed until the commit record has been appended to the log on mass storage.

> Appending a commit record to the log is an atomic action (either the record is in the log or it is not in the log), and the transaction is committed if and only if the action has completed.

Checkpoints. One last issue must be addressed with respect to crashes. Some mechanism must be included to avoid a complete backward scan of the log during recovery. Without such a mechanism, the recovery process has no way of knowing when to stop the search for a transaction that was active at the time of the crash since such a transaction might have appended an update record at an early point in the log and then made no further database updates. The recovery process will find no evidence of the transaction's existence unless it scans back to that record. To deal with this situation, the system periodically writes a **checkpoint record** to the log listing the identities of currently active transactions. The recovery process must (at least) scan backward to the most recent checkpoint record. If T is named in that record and the recovery process did not encounter a completion record for T between the checkpoint record and the end of the log, then T was still active when the system crashed. The backward scan must continue until the begin record for T is reached. It terminates when all such transactions are accounted for. Only the most recent checkpoint record is used (a checkpoint record supersedes the one preceding it). The frequency with which these records are written to the log affects the speed of recovery since frequent checkpointing implies that less of the log has to be scanned.

An example of a log is shown in Figure 22.2. As the recovery process scans backward, it discovers that T_6 and T_1 were active at the time of the crash because the last records appended for them are update records. It uses the before-images in these update records (in the sequence they are encountered in the backward scan) to

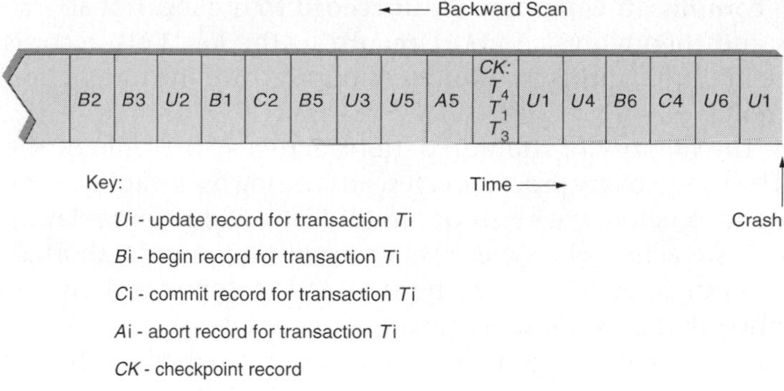

FIGURE 22.2 Log example.

roll back the database items to which they refer. Since the first record it encounters for T_4 is a commit record, it learns that T_4 was not active at the time of the crash and therefore ignores T_4's update records. When it reaches the checkpoint record, it learns that at the time the checkpoint was taken, T_1, T_3, and T_4 were active (T_6 is not mentioned in the checkpoint record since, as indicated by its begin record, it began after the checkpoint was taken). Thus, it concludes that, in addition to T_1 and T_6, T_3 was active at the time of the crash (since it has seen no completion record for T_3). No other transaction could have been active and hence these are the transactions that must be aborted. The recovery process must now continue the backward scan, processing all update records for T_1 and T_3 (there will be no update records for T_6 since its begin record has already been encountered) in the order they are encountered. The scan ends when the begin records for these transactions have been reached.

Write-ahead logging. We have assumed that an update record for a database item, x, is written to the log at the time x is updated in the database. In fact, the update of x and the append of the update record must occur in some order. Does it make a difference in which order these operations are performed? Consider the possibility that a crash occurs at the time the operations are performed. If it happens before either operation is completed, there is no problem. The update record does not appear in the log, but there is nothing for the recovery process to undo since x has not been updated. If the crash happens after both operations are performed, recovery proceeds correctly, as described above. Suppose, however, that x is updated first and that the crash occurs before the update record is appended to the log. Then the recovery process has no way of rolling the transaction back because there is no before-image in the log that the recovery process can use. Recovery thus cannot return the database to a consistent state—an unacceptable situation.

If, on the other hand, the update record is appended first, this problem is avoided. On restart, the recovery process simply uses the update record to restore x. As shown in Figure 22.3, it makes no difference whether the crash occurred before or

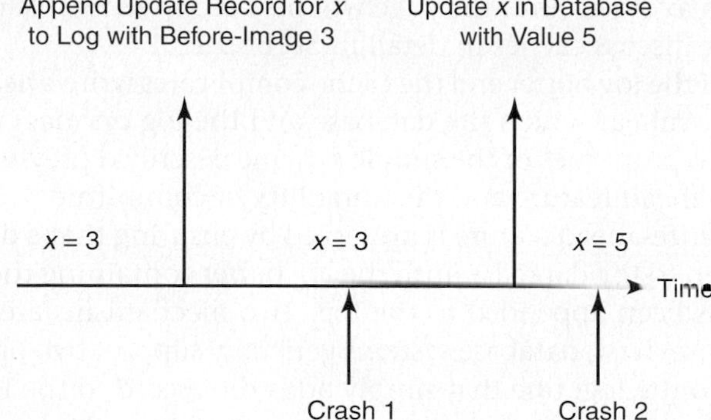

FIGURE 22.3 The recovery procedure can handle database restoration correctly with a write-ahead log.

after the transaction wrote the new value of x to the database. The original value of x was 3, a transaction updated it to 5, and the crash occurred before the transaction committed. If the crash occurred after the update record was appended but before x was updated (Crash 1 in the figure), when the system is restarted the value of x in the database and the before-image in the update record will both be 3. The recovery process uses the before-image to overwrite x—which does not change its value—but the final state after recovery has completed is correct. If the crash occurred after x was updated (Crash 2 in the figure), recovery restores x to 3.

Hence, the update record must always be appended to the log before the database is updated. This is referred to as the write-ahead feature, and the log is referred to as a **write-ahead log**.

22.2.1 Performance and Write-Ahead Logging

While write-ahead logging works correctly, it is unacceptable from a performance point of view since it doubles the number of I/O operations needed to update the database. A log append must now be performed with every database update. To avoid this overhead, database systems generally use a log buffer in volatile memory as temporary storage for log records. The log buffer can be viewed as an extension of the log on mass storage. Log records are appended to the buffer, and periodically it is appended, or **flushed**, to the log, as shown in Figure 22.1. With a log buffer, the cost of writing to the log is prorated over all log records contained in the buffer.

From the point of view of crash recovery, the difference between the log buffer in volatile memory and the log on mass storage is crucial: the log buffer is lost when the system crashes.

Furthermore, our description has ignored the fact that, to improve performance, most database systems support a cache in volatile storage of recently accessed database pages. Thus, when a transaction accesses a database item, x, the database system brings the database page(s) on mass storage containing x into the cache and then copies the value of x into the transaction's local variables. The page is kept in the cache under the assumption that there is a high probability that the transaction will later update x or read another item in the same page. If so, a page transfer will have been avoided since the page will be directly accessible (no I/O required) in the cache. We discuss caches in detail in Section 12.1.[1]

Use of the log buffer and the cache complicates write-ahead logging because they affect the time at which the database and the log on mass storage are actually updated. Two properties of the simple scheme described previously must be preserved: the write-ahead feature and the durability of commitment.

The write-ahead feature is preserved by ensuring that a dirty page in the cache is not written to the database until the log buffer containing the corresponding update record has been appended to the log. Two mechanisms are generally provided for this purpose. First, database systems generally support two operations for appending a record to the log: one that simply adds the record to the log buffer (and relies on the fact that the buffer will ultimately be flushed to the log) and one that adds the record to the buffer and then immediately writes the buffer to the log. The latter operation is referred to as a **forced** operation.

Whereas a normal (unforced) write simply registers a request to write a page to mass storage (the I/O operation is done at a later time), a forced write does not return control to the invoker until the write is complete. Since the log is sequential, when a routine requests a forced write of an update record, of necessity it forces all prior records into the log as well. When the routine resumes execution, it is guaranteed that these records are stored on mass storage. A request can then be safely made to write the corresponding dirty cache page to the database.

The second mechanism involves numbering all log records sequentially with a **log sequence number** (**LSN**), which is stored in the log record. In addition, for each database page, the LSN of the update record corresponding to the most recent update of an item in the page is stored in that page. Thus, if a database page contains database items x, y, and z, and if the item updated most recently is y, the value of the LSN stored in the page is the LSN of the last update record for y.

With the forced write and the LSN, we are in a position to ensure the write-ahead feature. When space is needed in the cache and a dirty page, P, is selected to be written to mass store, the system determines if the log buffer still contains the update record whose LSN is equal to the LSN stored in P. If so, the LSN of P must be greater than the LSN of the last record in the log *on mass storage*. Therefore, the log buffer must be forced to mass storage before the page is written to the database. If not, the update record corresponding to the most recent update to an item in the page has already been appended to the log on mass storage and the page can be written from the cache immediately.

[1] Operating systems often maintain their own cache (e.g., Unix). This can cause problems for DBMSs since not only does the additional caching impact performance (a page brought in from the disk has to be copied from the operating system's cache to the DBMS's cache), but when the DBMS wants to write a page to disk, the page may get no further then the operating system's cache for an indeterminate period of time. We will see shortly that this is a major issue. As a result, DBMSs often use a *raw partition*: a raw disk that can be accessed directly without going through the operating system's file system.

Thus we see that to achieve the write-ahead feature, we must sometimes delay the writing of a cache page containing the new value of an item until the log buffer containing the corresponding update record (which contains the old value of the item) has been written to the log. In addition, to achieve durability, we must ensure that the *new* values of all items updated by *T* are in mass store before *T*'s commit record is appended to the log on mass store. Otherwise, if a crash occurs after the commit record has been appended but before the new values are in mass store, the transaction will have been committed but the new values will have been lost, and hence durability in spite of system crashes has not been achieved.

There are two ways to ensure durability: a **force** policy and a **no-force** policy. With a force policy the force operation is also used for writing pages in the cache. Database pages in the cache that have been updated by *T* are forced out to the database before *T*'s commit record is appended to the log on mass storage. The sequence of events when a transaction is ready to commit is as follows:

1. If the transaction's last update record is still in the log buffer, force it to the log on mass store. This ensures that all old values are durable.
2. If any dirty pages that have been updated by the transaction remain in the cache, force them to the database. This ensures that all new values are durable.
3. Append the commit record to the log buffer. When it is written to the log on mass store (see below) the transaction will be durable.

Figure 22.4 illustrates the sequence of events for a transaction, *T*, that has updated an item, *x*. The update record, with LSN *j* and before-image x_{old}, is in the log buffer, and the updated page, with the new value, x_{new}, and the LSN of the update record, is in the cache. The page is dirty: it has not yet been written to mass storage. Its original version, with value x_{old} and LSN s, $s < j$, is still on mass storage. The update record must be on mass storage (step 1 in the figure) before the dirty page can be written (step 2) to satisfy the write-ahead property. It might be necessary to force the log buffer to ensure this. Similarly, the dirty page must already be on mass storage before the commit record, with $LSN\ k$, $k > j$, can be appended to the log buffer, to ensure that the dirty page gets to mass storage before the commit record does (step 3). It is necessary to force the dirty page to ensure this.

Note that it is not necessary to force the commit record. However, the transaction is not committed until the commit record has been written to the log on mass storage. In some systems, the log buffer is forced when a commit record is appended to the buffer, thus causing the commit to take effect immediately. Other systems do not force the buffer at this time, so a write to the log is avoided, but the commit does not take effect until a later time when the log buffer is flushed. This protocol is referred to as **group commit** since the group of transactions whose commit records are in the log buffer when the next write occurs all commit at once.

A major drawback of the force policy for ensuring durability is that the writing of dirty cache pages and commit are synchronous. The pages modified by a transaction must be written to the database before the transaction can commit. Since page writes are slow, transaction commit is delayed and response time suffers.

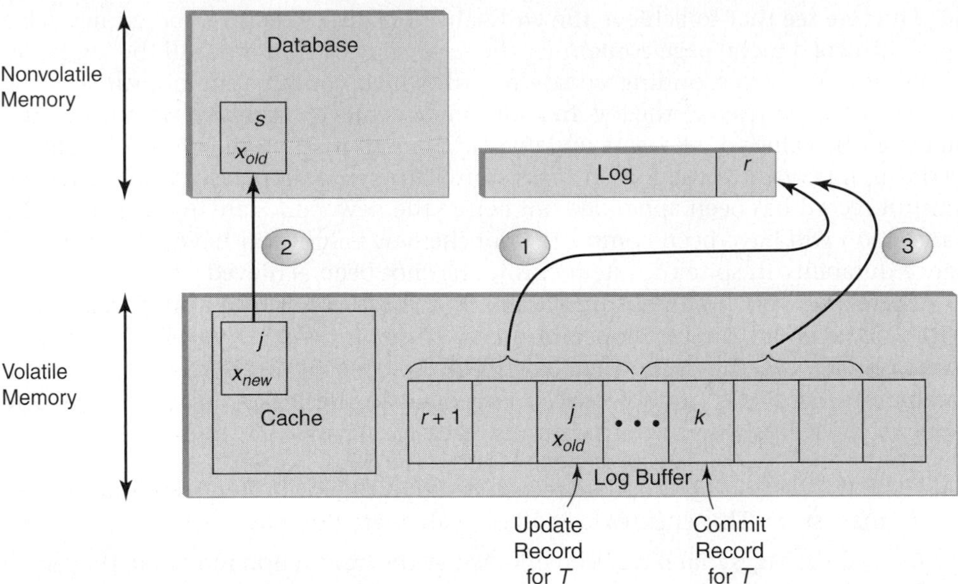

FIGURE 22.4 Implementing durability using a force policy. It might be necessary to force the pages that a transaction has updated out of the cache before the transaction's commit record is written to the log. Before the dirty page updated by T, with LSN value j, can overwrite the earlier version of the page, with LSN s, $s < j$, in the database, it might be necessary to force the log buffer (1) so that the update record with LSN equal to j is on mass storage. After the dirty page has been written, (2) the commit record for T can be appended to the log buffer (3). The log buffer can be written to the log at a later time.

Another disadvantage of the force policy has to do with hotspots—pages that are frequently modified by different transactions (for example, those holding system-related information). An LRU page replacement algorithm might choose not to write such a page out of the cache, but with a force policy the page will be written each time a transaction that has modified the page commits. Thus the force policy conflicts with the efficiency that is being sought by the LRU strategy. The advantage of a force policy, on the other hand, is that no action need be taken to recover a committed transaction after a crash. At the time the transaction's commit record is written to the log on mass store, all of the new values that it has created have been copied to the database on mass storage as well. With a no-force policy, which we describe in the next section, this is not necessarily the case.

22.2.2 Checkpoints and Recovery

In the previous section, we pointed out that the new value of an item, x, updated by a transaction, T, might still be in a dirty page in the cache in volatile memory when T requests to commit. To make T durable, the system must record the new value of x

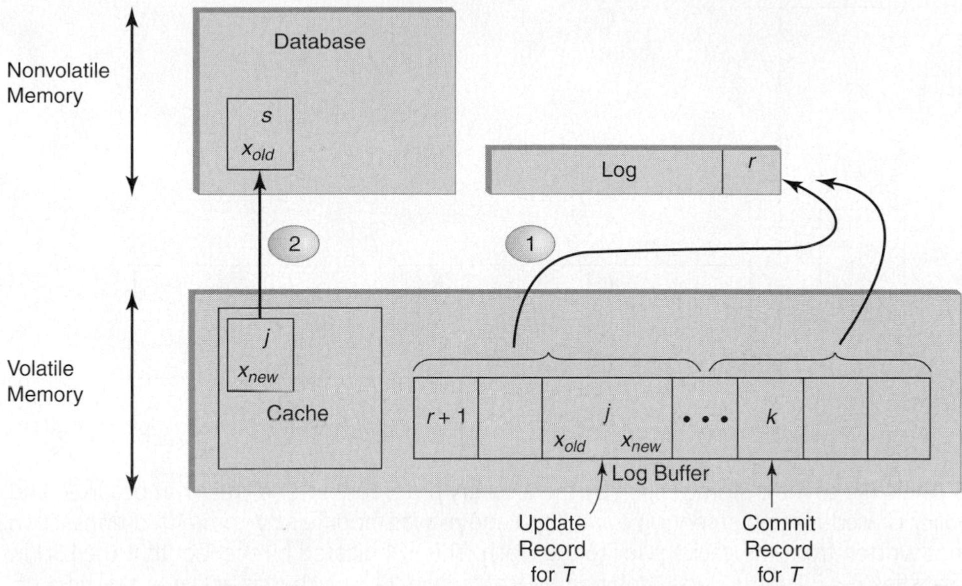

FIGURE 22.5 Implementing durability using an after-image with a no-force policy. The write-ahead feature requires that before a dirty page with LSN j updated by T can overwrite the earlier version of the page, with LSN s, $s < j$, in the database (2), the corresponding update record must be written to the log on mass storage (1). Although the commit record cannot be written before the update record, the relationship between the time the commit record is written and the time the dirty page is written is not constrained.

in nonvolatile memory before T's commit record is made durable by transferring it from the log buffer to the log. A common way of guaranteeing that the new value is in nonvolatile memory is to store after-images (in addition to before-images) in update records in the log.

In its simplest form, an **after-image**—sometimes called a **redo record**—of an updated item is a physical copy of the item's new value. Because all of T's update records precede its commit record in the log, when T's commit record is written to the log on mass storage, the new values of all database items it has created will be on mass storage as well. Then, even if the database page containing x has not been updated on mass storage at commit time and the system crashes after T commits, the new value of x can be installed in the database page on recovery using the after-image as shown in Figure 22.5. The write-ahead feature still requires that the update record be written to the log on mass storage before the dirty page is written to the database, but there is no longer any ordering specified between writing the commit record and writing the dirty page. In particular, the commit record can be written out to the log in durable storage before all the cached pages modified by T have been written.

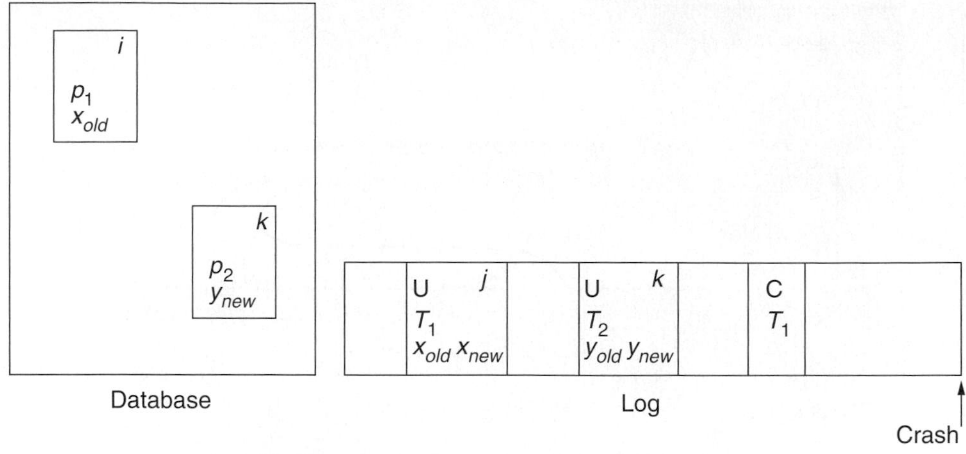

FIGURE 22.6 The state of mass storage seen by the recovery procedure after a crash has occurred and a no-force policy is used for implementing durability. Page p_1 was modified by committed transaction T_1 but was not written from the cache prior to the crash. This is indicated by the fact that the LSN in the page, i, satisfies $i < j$. Page p_2 was modified by transaction T_2, which was active at the time of the crash and was written prior to the crash.

The obvious advantage of a no-force policy is that a transaction can commit without having to wait until all of the pages it has updated have been forced from the cache. The disadvantage is that, when a crash occurs, recovery is complicated by the following possible situations:

- Some pages in the database might contain updates written by uncommitted transactions. These pages must be *rolled back* using the before-images in the log. This problem exists with either a force or a no-force policy.
- Some pages in the database might not yet contain updates made by committed transactions. These pages must be *rolled forward* using the after-images in the log. This problem exists only with a no-force policy.

The situation is shown in Figure 22.6.

We have already dealt with the rollback problem. The question now is how to identify those database pages that must be rolled forward.

One way of doing this is to use a **sharp checkpoint**. Before writing a checkpoint record, *CK*, to the log buffer, processing is halted and all dirty pages in the cache are written to the database. As a result, a recovery process scanning *CK* can conclude that all updates described by updated records in the log prior to *CK* were written to the database before the crash. If *CK* is the most recent checkpoint record, only updates recorded after it in the log *might* not have been written to the database. Using this information, recovery can proceed in three passes.

Pass 1. The log is scanned backward to the most recent checkpoint to determine which transactions were active at the time of the crash (and must be rolled back).

Pass 2. The log is scanned forward (replayed) from the checkpoint. The after-images in all update records (of committed, aborted, *and* active transactions) are used to update the corresponding items in the database. At the end of this pass, the database has been brought up to date with respect to all changes made by all transactions prior to the crash.

Pass 3. The log is scanned backward to roll back all transactions active at the time of the crash. The before-image in each update record of these transactions is used to reverse the corresponding update in the database. This pass completes when the begin records of all the transactions to be rolled back have been reached. The effect is the same as if all active transactions have aborted.

DO-UNDO-REDO is the name given to this general form of recovery. DO refers to the original action of the transaction in updating a data item, UNDO refers to the rollback that occurs in pass 3 if the transaction does not commit, and REDO refers to the rollforward that occurs in pass 2.

There are three things to consider in using this technique.

1. Transactions that update items and abort after the checkpoint pose a special problem. Their updates were rolled back before the abort record was appended to the log (before the crash), and, unfortunately, these updates will be restored to the database during pass 2. To ensure that the recovery process handles these transactions properly, a rollback operation should be treated as an ordinary database update performed by the transaction. An aborted transaction that had updated an item, x, will thus have two records in the log for that item, as shown in Figure 22.7:
   - An update record associated with the update it performed before aborting, with before-image x_{old} and after-image x_{new}
   - A **compensation log record** associated with the reversal of that update during abort processing, with before-image x_{new} and after-image x_{old}

   The compensation log record follows the update record in the log, and the abort record for the transaction follows the last compensation log record. The pass 2 scan first processes the update record and writes its after-image to the database; it then processes the compensation log record and writes its after-image to the database. The final value of x in the database is x_{old}. Since the transaction was not active at the time of the crash, its update and compensation log records are ignored during pass 3. Because compensation log records can be viewed as update records, this technique has the nice property of allowing committed and aborted transactions to be treated in the same way.
2. Some cache pages updated after the last checkpoint record was written might have been written to the database. Hence, in pass 2 some of the update records

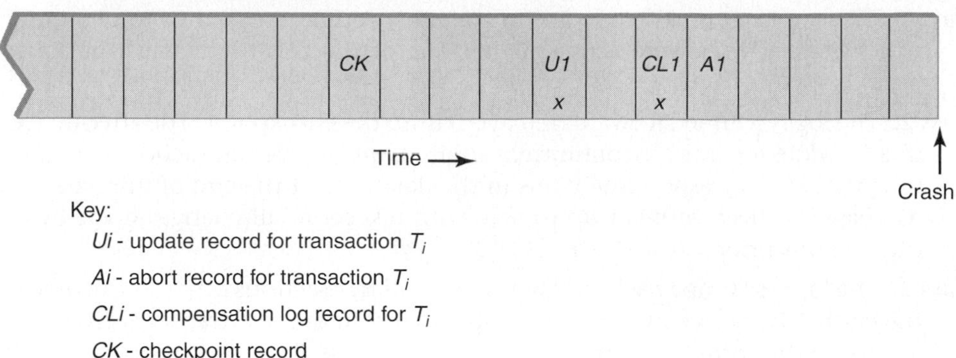

FIGURE 22.7 Log showing records for an aborted transaction that has updated database variable x. The log contains both an update record and a compensation log record for x.

encountered describe updates already transferred to the database. Using the after-images in these records to update the database is unnecessary but not incorrect. In this case, the value of the item in the database and the after-image in the update record are identical, so the use of the after-image has no effect.[2]

3. There is a possibility that the system will crash (again) during recovery, in which case the recovery procedure will be reinitiated. Depending on the pass during which the second crash occurs, a before- or after-image might be applied to a database item a second time. An update using this image, however, is **idempotent**—that is, updating a database item with a particular after-image several times has the same effect as that of a single update. A crash during recovery (or, in fact, several crashes) therefore does not affect the outcome. When recovery finally completes, uncommitted transactions have been aborted and updates made by committed transactions have been recorded in the database.

   Idempotency is an essential feature of physical logging. We have seen its role in several places. It is assumed in the design of the write-ahead log since the application of the before-image to a page that had not yet been updated prior to the crash caused no problem. It is also assumed in the previous bullet, where in pass 2 the application of the after-image to a page that had been updated prior to the crash caused no problem.

Fuzzy checkpoints. The use of sharp checkpoints has one major disadvantage. The system must be halted to write dirty pages from the cache before the checkpoint record is written to the log buffer, and such an interruption of service is unacceptable in many applications. The procedure can be modified slightly to deal with this

[2] Note that several updates of the same database item might have been made after the checkpoint record is written. In that case, the after-image and the item would not be identical. However, after the most recent update record is processed in pass 2, the item will have been brought to the value it had before the crash.

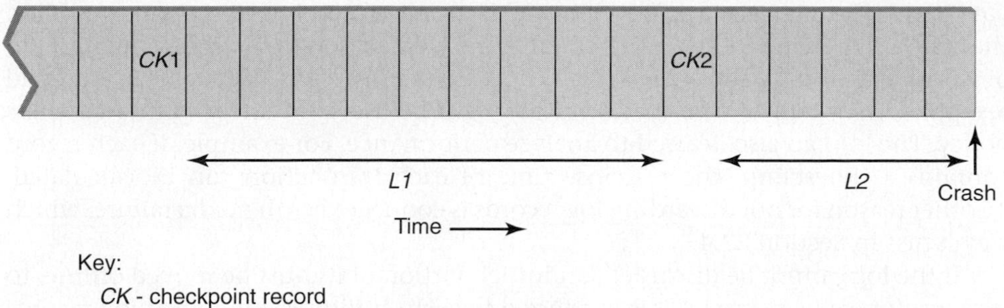

FIGURE 22.8 Use of fuzzy checkpoints.

problem by using **fuzzy checkpoints**. The dirty pages are not written from the cache when a checkpoint record is written to the log; instead, their identity is simply noted (in volatile memory), and they are subsequently written to the database (in the background) during normal processing. The only restriction is that the next checkpoint not be taken until all dirty pages noted at the previous checkpoint have been written.

Fuzzy checkpoints are illustrated in Figure 22.8. At the time *CK*2 is appended to the log buffer, all dirty pages that were in the cache when *CK*1 was appended have been written to the database. The modifications to these pages correspond to update records that appeared in the log prior to *CK*1. A database update corresponding to an update record in region *L*1 of the log creates a dirty page, *P*, that might be in the cache when *CK*2 is appended to the log buffer (*P* might also have been written by that time, but we cannot be sure). If *P* is still in the cache when *CK*2 is appended to the log buffer, its identity is noted. We cannot guarantee that it has been written to the database until the next checkpoint record is appended. Since in the figure the system crashes before that happens, we must make the worst-case assumption that update records in regions *L*1 and *L*2 are not reflected in the database.

In order to bring the database to a state that contains all updates done prior to the crash, pass 2 of the recovery procedure must be modified so that the forward scan starts at *CK*1 instead of *CK*2. Pass 1 still completes at *CK*2 since its purpose is to identify transactions active at the time of the crash. Recovery is now slower than with sharp checkpoints. The trade-off between the speed of recovery and availability during normal operation must now be evaluated to decide whether sharp or fuzzy checkpoints are appropriate for a particular installation.

Archiving the log. We must deal with one other problem so that our description of logging and recovery is (relatively) complete. We have said that log records are appended to the log and never deleted. What happens when mass storage fills with log records? You might think that initial portions of the log can simply be discarded, but log records are often held for substantial periods of time for several reasons.

For one, the log contains information that might be useful for purposes other than recovery. For example, it contains the sequence of updates that brought each data item to its current state. This is useful if the enterprise is called upon to explain the state of an item. For example, an inventory database might record the number of widgets in stock, but the log records how frequently widgets have been sold and resupplied, an item of information that might be useful in streamlining business policy. The log can also be used to analyze performance. For example, if each record contains a timestamp, the response time of each transaction can be calculated. Another reason for not discarding log records is connected with media failure, which we discuss in Section 22.4.

If the log cannot be discarded, an initial portion of it must be moved offline, to tertiary storage (e.g., tape). This is referred to as **archiving**. Only recent log records need to be retained online, and the question now reduces to deciding at what point a portion of the log can be moved. Certainly, records of active transactions must be maintained online in order to handle abort and recovery quickly, so portions of the log containing records whose LSN is less than the LSN of the begin record of the oldest active transaction can be archived. However, the need to recover from media failure introduces other constraints, which we discuss in Section 22.4.

OPTIONAL

22.2.3 Logical and Physiological Logging

Physical logging has an important disadvantage, particularly when it is used in support of relational databases. A simple update might result in changes to a large number of pages in the database. In that case, the before- and after-images can be large and difficult to manage. For example, the insertion of a row into a table might require a complete reorganization of the page to which it is added. In addition to storing the row, the page's header information (which locates the items and the free space within the page) must be updated. Furthermore, similar changes must be made to each index referring to the table. If the index is a B^+ tree, page splitting might occur. All regions affected have to be recorded in the before- and after-images, making the update record large and increasing the I/O overhead necessary to manage the log. *Logical logging* is a technique for overcoming this problem.

With **logical logging**, instead of storing a snapshot of the updated item in the update record, the operation itself and its compensating operation are recorded. For example, the INSERT operation that inserts row *r* into table *T* has a compensating operation that deletes that record. Thus the undo record is <*delete*, *r*, *T*> and the redo record is <*insert*, *r*, *T*>. Rollback and rollforward now consist of applying the appropriate operation instead of simply overwriting the affected area as in physical logging. In this way, logical logging has the potential of reducing the overhead of log maintenance.

Undo operations (Section 20.7) can be used in the same way. For example, the UPDATE operation

```
UPDATE   T
SET      Grade = 'A'
WHERE    StudId= '1234567' AND CRSCODE = 'CS305'
```

does not have a compensating operation (since it is not one to one), but it has an undo operation that updates the value of Grade to what it was before the UPDATE was executed. Thus, if the grade was originally *I*, the undo is an identical update statement except that the set clause is SET Grade = 'I'.

Crash recovery is complicated by the fact that logical operations are not necessarily idempotent. For example, the result of executing the statement

```
UPDATE   T
SET      x = x+5
```

once is not the same as the result of executing it twice. So, in this case, the UPDATE operation is not idempotent. It is thus important to know, when processing an update or compensation log record during pass 2, whether or not the updated database page was flushed before the crash. If so, applying the redo operation in pass 2 can produce an incorrect state. In the above example, if the page on which *x* is stored was written to the database immediately prior to a crash, the logical redo during recovery will cause *x* to be incremented twice.

Fortunately, the problem is easily overcome using the LSN in the page. If during pass 2 it is found that the LSN in a page is greater than or equal to the LSN of an update record for an item in that page (indicating that the page already contains the result of applying the update operation), then the redo operation is not performed.

Unfortunately there is another, more serious, problem. We have implicitly assumed that logical operations are done atomically—for example, either tuple *t* has been inserted in a table or it has not. However, several pages might have to be modified in order to do an insertion, and hence the logical operation is not atomic with respect to failure: the system might crash after some, but not all, pages have been written. Hence, the data might be in an inconsistent state on recovery. Inconsistency here takes a different form. For example, the data page containing *t* might have been written to mass storage, but not the index page that should contain a pointer to *t*. This is different from the state that might be produced by an inconsistent transaction since in this case it is not the data values that are inconsistent but the way they are stored.

The application of a logical operation to an inconsistent state is likely to fail. With the insert example, the application of a logical redo record in pass 2 might result in two copies of *t* in the table. Furthermore, how do we even know whether the logical redo should be applied since the LSN of the data page is greater than or equal to the LSN of the update record for the insert, while the LSN of the index page is smaller? Idempotency guarantees that this is not a problem when physical logging is used. It is also not a problem for logical logging if the logical operation affects only a single page since then execution of the operation is atomic and the LSN in the page indicates whether or not it has happened.

To overcome this problem, **physiological logging** can be used. This technique is a compromise between physical and logical logging (the name is an abbreviation of the more descriptive *physical-to-a-page, logical-within-a-page*). A logical operation that involves multiple page updates is decomposed into multiple, logical, mini-operations in such a way that each mini-operation is confined to a single page (this is the physical dimension to physiological logging) and preserves page consistency. Hence, mini-operations can always be performed on pages, no matter when a failure occurs. The logical operation "Insert t into table T" might be decomposed into the mini-operation "Insert t into a particular page of the file containing T," which is followed by one or more mini-operations such as "Insert a pointer to t into a particular page of an index for T." Each mini-operation gets a separate log record, so recovery will work correctly even if a crash occurs while it is taking place. Since logical mini-operations are not necessarily idempotent, LSNs can be used (as described above) to determine which mini-operations have been applied to a page during pass 2.

In the example above, a mini-operation is a logical operation that is confined to a single page. An update record is created for each of these operations, containing the nature of the mini-operation (e.g., insert), its arguments (e.g., t), and the identity of the page affected. If the mini-operation or its inverse cannot be conveniently represented logically, a physical log record can be used. Thus, physiological logging involves a combination of both physical and logical logging.

22.3 Recovery in Deferred-Update Systems

In a deferred-update system, a transaction's write operation does not update the corresponding data item in the database. Instead, the information to be written is saved in a special area of memory called the transaction's intentions list. The intentions list is *not* stored durably. If the transaction commits, its intentions list is used to update the database. If the transaction aborts, its intentions list is simply discarded. Similarly, if the system crashes, no special action need be taken to abort active transactions since they have made no changes to the database.

To make committed transactions durable, the log and log buffer architecture is used. We assume physical logging for simplicity in the following discussion. When a transaction updates a data item, in addition to saving the new value in the intentions list, the system appends an update record containing an after-image to the log buffer. A before-image is not required in this case since the database item is not updated until after the transaction commits. At that time the transaction must be durable and the changes that it has made will not be undone; hence no before-image is needed. Since there is no before-image, the write-ahead policy does not apply.

At commit time, the system appends a commit record to the log buffer, which it then forces to the log in nonvolatile memory. Since the update records precede the commit record in the log, the force of the commit record guarantees that all update records are also on nonvolatile storage. After the commit operation has completed, the system updates the database from the transaction's intentions list. This corresponds to the write phase in an optimistic concurrency control. It then releases the transaction's locks and writes a **completion record** to the log.

The system might crash between the time the transaction has committed and the time the new values in its intentions list have been written to the database. Since the intentions list is lost, recovery must use the log to complete the installation of the transaction's updates. To speed this process, the system uses a variant of the checkpoint procedure described previously for a pessimistic system. The system periodically appends to the log a checkpoint record that now contains the identities of committed transactions whose intentions lists are currently being used to update the database.

On restart, the recovery process determines the identities of committed transactions whose intentions lists might not have been processed completely when the crash occurred. It does this in pass 1 by scanning the log backward until it gets to the first checkpoint. If the first record it finds for a transaction is a commit record, it knows that the intentions list for that transaction might not have been processed completely. If the first record for a transaction is a completion record, it knows that the intentions list had been processed completely. When the backward scan gets to the first checkpoint, it finds the names of the remaining transactions whose intentions lists had not been processed completely when that checkpoint record had been appended. Then, in pass 2, it uses the update records of the transactions it found in pass 1 to update the database. Recovery is no longer concerned with rolling back database updates performed by transactions that were active at the time of the crash since active transactions do not update the database. Hence, pass 3 is not required.

22.4 Recovery from Media Failure

Durability requires that no information written by a committed transaction be lost. A simple approach to achieving this is to maintain two separate copies of the database on two different nonvolatile devices (perhaps supported by different power supplies) such that simultaneous failure of both devices is unlikely. Mirrored disks are one way to implement this approach. A mirrored disk is a mass storage system in which, whenever a request to write a record is made, the same record is written on two different disks. Thus one disk is an exact copy, a mirror image, of the other. Furthermore, the double write is transparent to the requestor.

A database stored on a mirrored disk will be durable if a single media failure occurs. In addition, the system will remain available if one of the mirrored disks fails since it can continue to operate using the other. When the failed disk is replaced, the system must resynchronize the two. By contrast, when durability is achieved using a log (as described next), recovery from a disk failure might take a significant period of time, during which the system is unavailable to its users.

Even when an immediate update system uses a mirrored disk, it must still use a write-ahead log to achieve atomicity. Thus (in an immediate-update system), before-images are still needed to roll back database items when a transaction aborts, and after-images are still needed to roll forward database items when a transaction commits.

A second approach to achieving durability involves restoring the database from the log when a media failure occurs. One way to do this is to play the log forward *from the beginning* using the after-images in the update records. However, this is impractical because of the size of the log. It will take an enormous amount of time, during which the system is unavailable. A solution is to make an archive copy, or **dump**, of the database periodically.

Recovery using the dump depends on how it was taken. For some applications, the dump can be produced offline. The system is shut down at some convenient time by not allowing new transactions to be initiated and waiting until all active transactions have terminated. A dump is then taken, and when it has been completed, an **end dump** record is written to the log and new transactions can be accepted. To restore the database after a media failure, the system starts with the most recent dump file and then makes two passes through the log records that were appended after the most recent end dump record:

1. A backward pass in which it makes a list of all the transactions that committed after the dump was taken.
2. A forward pass in which it copies into the database the redo records of all of the transactions on the list.

Fuzzy dumps. With many applications, the system cannot be shut down. This calls for a **fuzzy dump**, taken while the system is operating. The fuzzy dump sequentially reads all records in the database, ignoring locks. Thus, transactions can be executing during the dump and can update records and later commit or abort. The dump program can read those records before or after they are written.

Consider an immediate-update system using physical logging. If the two-pass recovery procedure described above were used with a fuzzy dump, the second (forward) pass restores (using after-images in the log) the value of each database item written by a transaction that committed after the dump started, whether or not the dump had in fact read that value. As shown in Figure 22.9(a), the value of x recorded in the dump reflects the effect of T, but the value of y does not. Since T commits after the dump starts, however, the after-images of all changes it has made will be used in reconstructing the database starting from the dump. This is unnecessary for x, but rolls y forward to its proper value. The procedure also handles the case shown in Figure 22.9(b), in which a transaction starts after the dump has completed and later aborts since its update records are ignored in pass 2.

However, the two-pass procedure does not handle two situations correctly:

- The database pages written by a transaction, T, that commits before the dump starts might not be written to the database until after the dump completes. In that case, the dump does not contain the new value written by T, but T is not included in the list of committed transactions, obtained in pass 1, whose update records are used to roll the database forward in pass 2. This happens because the commit record of T precedes the dump record and the forward scan begins with the dump record.

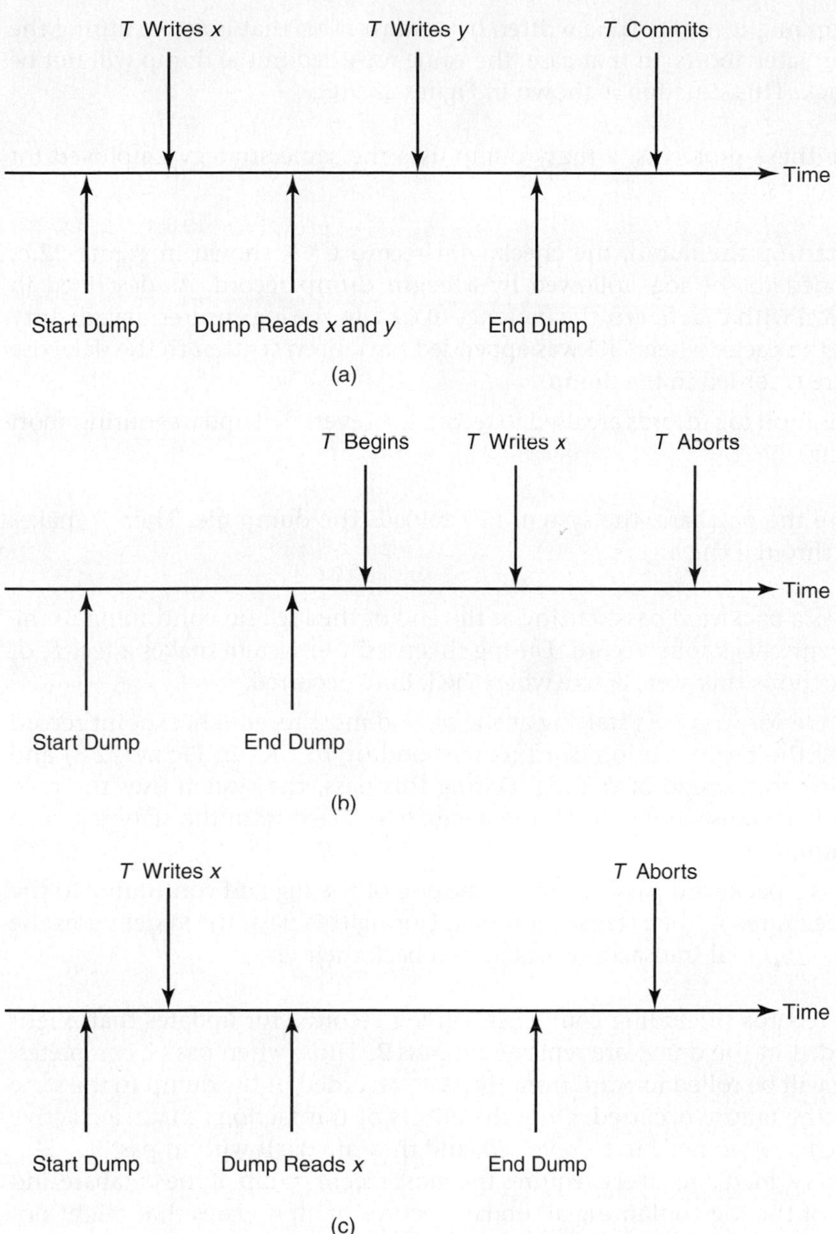

FIGURE 22.9 Effect of transactions being active while a dump is taken.

- The dump might read a value written by a transaction that is active during the dump but later aborts. In that case, the value recorded in the dump will not be rolled back. This situation is shown in Figure 22.9(c).

To overcome these problems, a fuzzy dump uses the same strategy employed for fuzzy checkpoints.

1. Before starting the dump, the checkpoint record *CK*2, shown in Figure 22.8, is appended to the log, followed by a **begin dump** record. As described in connection with that figure, the presence of *CK*2 in the log ensures that all dirty pages in the cache when *CK*1 was appended have been written to the database and so are recorded in the dump.
2. Compensation log records are used to record the reversal of updates during abort processing.

To restore the database, the system first reloads the dump file. Then it makes three passes through the log.

Pass 1. This is a backward pass starting at the end of the log and continuing to the most recent checkpoint record. During this pass, the system makes a list, *L*, of all transactions that were active when the failure occurred.

Pass 2. This is a forward pass starting at the second most recent checkpoint record preceding the begin dump record (corresponding to *CK*1 in Figure 22.8) and continuing to the end of the log. During this pass, the system uses the redo records of all transactions to roll the database forward from the state recorded in the dump.

Pass 3. This is a backward pass starting at the end of the log and continuing to the earliest begin record of a transaction in *L*. During this pass, the system uses the undo records of all transactions in *L* to roll back their effect.

All redo records (including compensation log records) for updates that might not be included in the dump are replayed in pass 2. Thus, when pass 2 completes, the database will be rolled forward from the state recorded in the dump to the state it had when the failure occurred. Only the effects of transactions that were active when the media failed need to be reversed, and they are dealt with in pass 3.

In summary, media recovery requires the most recent dump of the database and that portion of the log containing all update records of all updates that might not be in the dump. Note that the required portion of the log will generally be greater than the portion required for crash recovery. Both portions must include the begin record of the oldest active transaction. However, crash recovery additionally requires that the log contain the two most recent checkpoint records, while media recovery requires the two checkpoint records preceding the start of the dump. Furthermore, if the most recent archived copy of the database is damaged, the same algorithm can be used to restore an earlier copy.

With physiological logging, instead of unconditionally applying before- and after-images during passes 2 and 3, the LSN is used, as described in Section 22.2.3, to determine whether or not an operation should be applied.

BIBLIOGRAPHIC NOTES

One of the first discussions on logging and recovery technology is in [Gray 1978]. Much of the current technology is based on the implementations of System R [Gray et al. 1981] and Aries (Algorithm for Recovery and Isolation Exploiting Semantics) [Mohan et al. 1992]. Excellent summaries of the technology are in [Haerder and Reuter 1983; Bernstein and Newcomer 1997; Gray and Reuter 1993]. A more abstract view of failures, in which recovery and serializability are integrated into a single model, is described in [Schek et al. 1993].

EXERCISES

22.1 Describe the contents of each of the following log records and how that record is used (if at all) in rollback and in recovery from crashes and media failure.

a. Abort record
b. Begin record
c. Begin dump record
d. Checkpoint record
e. Commit record
f. Compensation log record
g. Completion record
h. Redo record
i. Savepoint record
j. Undo record

22.2 Suppose that the concurrency control uses table locks and that a transaction performs an operation that updates the value of one attribute of one tuple in one table. Does the update record have to contain images of the entire table or just the one tuple?

22.3 Suppose that a dirty page in the cache has been written by two active transactions and that one of the transactions commits. Describe how the caching procedure works in this case.

22.4 Suppose that the database system crashes between the time a transaction commits (by appending a commit record to the log) and the time it releases its locks. Describe how the system recovers from this situation.

22.5 Explain why the log buffer need not be flushed when an abort record is appended to it.

22.6 Explain why the LSN need not be included in pages stored in the database when physical logging is used together with a cache and log buffer.

22.7 Suppose that each database page contained the LSN of the commit record of the last transaction that has committed and written a database item in the page, and suppose that the system uses the policy that it does not flush the page from the cache until the LSN of the oldest record in the log buffer is greater than the LSN of the page. Will the write-ahead policy be enforced?

22.8 The second step of the sharp checkpoint recovery procedure is as follows: The log is scanned forward from the checkpoint. The after-images in all update records are used to update the corresponding items in the database. Assuming a locking concurrency control in which locks are held until commit time, show that the updates can be performed in either of the following orders:

a. As each update record is encountered in the forward scan, the corresponding database update is performed (even though the update records for different transactions are interleaved in the log).
b. During the forward scan, the update records for each transaction are saved in volatile memory, and the database updates for each transaction are all done at once when the commit record for that transaction is encountered during the forward scan.

22.9 In the sharp checkpoint recovery procedure, explain whether or not the system needs to obtain locks when it is using the after-images in the log to update the database.

22.10 Consider the following two-pass strategy for crash recovery using a sharp checkpoint and physical logging: (1) The first pass is a backward pass in which active transactions are rolled back. Active transactions are identified as described in Section 22.2. The pass extends at least as far as the begin record of the oldest active transaction or the most recent checkpoint record, whichever is earlier in the log. As update records for these transactions are encountered in the scan, their before-images are applied to the database. (2) The second pass is a forward pass from the most recent checkpoint record to roll forward, using after-images, all changes made by transactions that completed since the checkpoint record was written (compensation log records are processed in the same way as ordinary update records so that aborted transactions are handled properly). Does the procedure work?

22.11 In order for logical logging to work, a logical database operation must have a logical inverse operation. Give an example of a database operation that has no inverse. Suggest a procedure involving logical logging that can handle this case.

22.12 Consider using the crash recovery procedure described in Section 22.2 (intended for physical logging) when logical logging is used. Explain how the procedure has to be modified to handle crashes that occur during recovery. Assume that the effect of each update is confined to a single page.

22.13 Explain why, in a deferred-update system, the write-ahead feature that is a part of immediate-update systems is not used when a database item is updated.

22.14 Explain why in a deferred-update system, the system does not first copy the intentions list into the database and then append the commit record to the log.

22.15 Assume that the system supports SNAPSHOT isolation. Describe how a sharp (nonfuzzy) dump could be taken without shutting down the system.

22.16 a. Explain how the log is implemented in your local DBMS.
b. Estimate the time in milliseconds to commit a transaction in your local DBMS.

22.17 The LSN stored in a page of the database refers to an update record in the log describing the most recent update to the page. Suppose that a transaction has performed the last update to a page and later aborts. Since its update to the page is reversed, the LSN in the page no longer refers to the appropriate update record. Why is this not a problem in the description of logging in the text?

22.18 An airlines reservation system has demanding performance and availability standards. Do the following play a role in enhancing performance? Do they enhance availability? Explain your answers.

a. Page cache
b. Log buffer
c. Checkpoint record
d. Physiological logging
e. Mirrored disk

PART SIX

Distributed Applications and the Web

In this part we will discuss some of the newest and most exciting applications of databases and transaction processing systems: systems that operate in distributed environments and, in particular, on the Internet.

In Chapter 23 we will discuss the back-end implementations of transaction processing systems: the various architectures used in the implementation, including two- and three-tiered systems and the TP monitor. Then we will describe how these architectures can be implemented on the Internet and how Web applications servers are built using J2EE.

In Chapter 24 we will discuss how the ACID properties are (or are not) implemented in a distributed environment. The chapter also contains a description of protocols that support data replication.

In Chapter 25 we will describe the emerging front-end standards for business-to-business interactions over the Internet: the XML based interfaces that enable servers to interact smoothly over the Web without human intervention. The role of transactions in these standards is highlighted.

In Chapter 26 we will introduce encryption techniques and describe how they are used in the implementation of security in Internet interactions, including SSL and certificates. We will then discuss a number of XML-based encryption protocols.

23

Architecture of Transaction Processing Systems

Transaction processing systems are among the largest software systems in existence. They must be built to respond to a wide spectrum of applications, so the demands on them vary greatly. At one extreme are single-user systems accessing a local database. At the other extreme are multiuser systems in which a single transaction can access a heterogeneous set of resource managers that are distributed across a network, and in which thousands of transactions can be executing each second. Many such systems have critical performance requirements and are the foundation of vital enterprises.

To create and maintain such a complex system, a functional decomposition into modules that perform distinct tasks is essential. In this chapter, we discuss the modular structure of these systems, taking a historical perspective. We start with the earliest and simplest systems and then move forward in time and complexity, introducing new elements one step at a time. We describe the various tasks that must be performed, show how they are mapped into modules, and explain how these modules communicate in each organization.

Some of the largest and most sophisticated transaction processing systems are on the Internet. At the end of the chapter, we describe how the architectures described earlier in the chapter are implemented in this context.

23.1 Transaction Processing in a Centralized System

Due to hardware limitations, the earliest transaction processing systems were centralized. All modules resided on a single computer—for example, a single PC or workstation servicing a single user, or a mainframe computer with many connected terminals servicing multiple users concurrently. We consider these two cases separately.

23.1.1 Organization of a Single-User System

Figure 23.1 shows how a single-user transaction processing system might be organized on a PC or workstation. The user module performs **presentation and application services**. Presentation services displays forms on the screen, and it handles the flow of information from and to the user through the forms. A typical cycle of

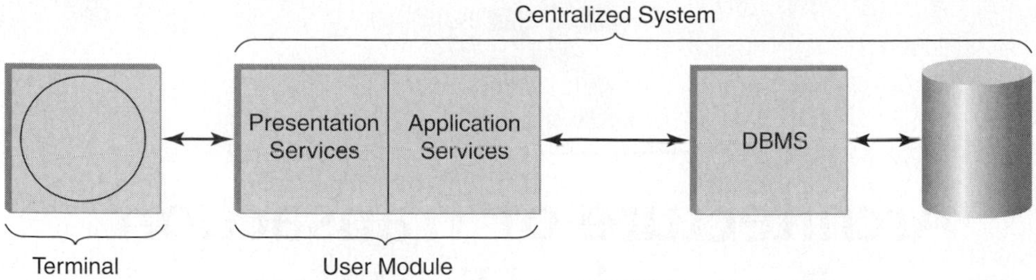

FIGURE 23.1 Single-user transaction processing system.

activity might start with presentation services displaying a form on which the user enters information in textboxes and then submits a request for service by making an appropriate click. Presentation services recognizes the click, and it calls application services to satisfy the request, passing to it the information that has been input. Application services checks the integrity constraints not specified in the schema and executes a sequence of steps in accordance with the rules of the enterprise.

Application services must communicate with the database server. For example, the application service that registers a student for a course in the Student Registration System has to make sure that the student has taken the prerequisite courses and must add the student's name to the class roster. Its requests to access the database might be implemented in embedded SQL statements that are sent to the database server.

Note that the user does not interact directly with the database server. Instead the user invokes programs that act as intermediaries. To allow a user direct access to the database server—for example, by specifying the SQL statements to be executed directly from the terminal—is dangerous since a careless or malicious user could easily destroy the integrity of the database by writing erroneous data. Even allowing the user read-only access to the data has drawbacks. For one thing, it is generally not a simple matter to formulate an SQL query to return the information a user might want to see. For another, there might be information in the database that some users are not allowed to see. Grade information for a particular student that must not be given to any other student but can be made available to a faculty member is one example.

These problems can be solved by requiring that the user access the database indirectly through application services. Since the application services is implemented by the application programmer, one can hope that its accesses to the server are correct and appropriate.

Although a program within application services can be viewed as a transaction, the full power of a transaction processing system is not required in this case. For example, with a single-user system only one transaction is invoked at a time, so isolation is automatic. Mechanisms might still be needed to implement atomicity and durability, but they can be relatively simple for the same reason.

Although one can argue that single-user systems are too simple to be included in the category of transaction processing systems, they illustrate two of the essential services that must be provided in all of the systems we will be discussing: presentation services and application services. In particular, one advantage of separating presentation services from application services is that the designers of one need not be concerned with the details of the other. Thus the designers of application services can concentrate on the business rules of the enterprise and do not have to be concerned with the details of dealing with the presentation of the input and output. In fact the hardware or software drivers involved with presentation services can be changed without having any effect on the application services software (assuming the interface between the two services remains the same).

23.1.2 Organization of a Centralized Multiuser System

Transaction processing systems supporting an enterprise of any size must permit multiple users to have access to them from multiple locations. Early versions of such systems involved the use of terminals connected to a central computer. In situations in which the terminals and the computer were confined to a small area (for example a single building), communication could be supported over hard-wired connections. More frequently, however, the terminals were located at remote sites and communicated with the computer over telephone lines. In either case, a major difference between these early systems and current multiuser systems is that the terminals were "dumb." They had no computing capability. They served as I/O devices that presented a simple, generally textual interface to the user. In terms of Figure 23.1, presentation services (beyond those built into the terminal hardware) were minimal and had to be executed at the central site. While such systems could be spread over a substantial geographical area, they were not considered distributed since all of the computing and intelligence resided at a single site.

The introduction of multiuser transaction processing systems motivated the development of transactions and the need for the ACID properties. Since multiple users interact with the system concurrently, there must be a way to isolate one user's interaction from another. Because the system is now supporting a major enterprise, as contrasted with an individual's database, issues of atomicity and durability become important.

Figure 23.2 shows the organization of early multiuser transaction processing systems. A user module, containing both presentation and application services, is associated with each user and runs at the central site. Since a number of users execute concurrently, each user module is executed in a separate process. These processes run asynchronously and can submit requests for service to the database server at any time. For example, while the server is servicing a request from one application to execute an SQL statement, a different application might submit a request to execute another SQL statement. Sophisticated database servers are capable of servicing many such requests simultaneously, with the guarantee that each SQL statement will be executed as an isolated and atomic unit.

As we have seen, however, such a guarantee is not sufficient to ensure that the interactions of different users are appropriately isolated. To provide isolation, the application program needs the abstraction of a transaction. A transaction support

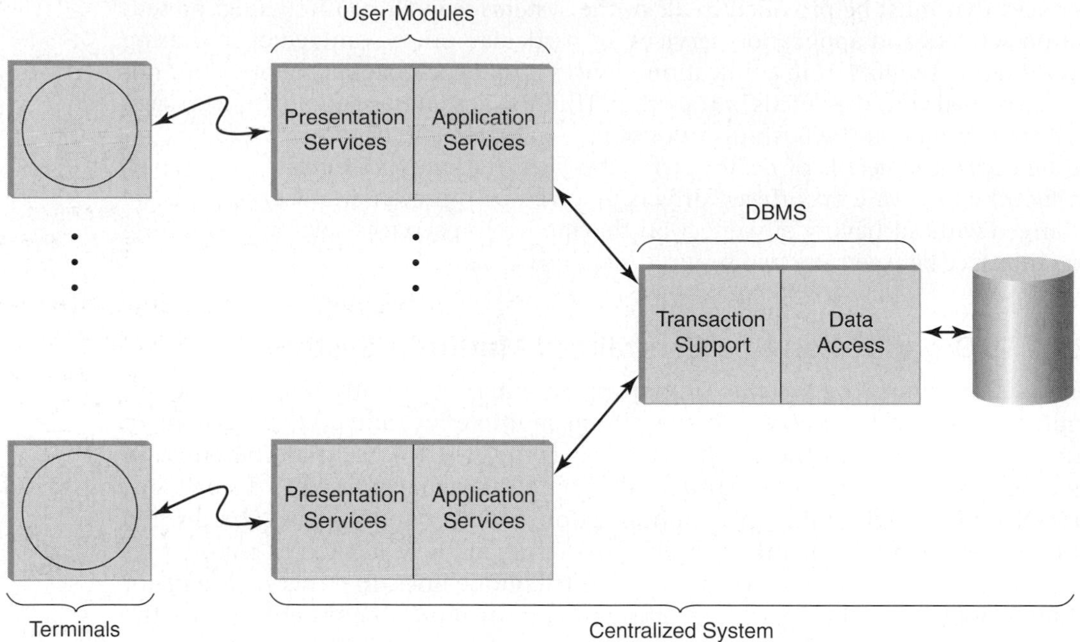

FIGURE 23.2 Multiuser centralized transaction processing system.

module is therefore provided within the database server to implement commands such as `begin_transaction`, `commit`, and `rollback` and to provide atomicity, isolation, and durability. This module includes the concurrency control and the log. Since presentation, application, and database services are all supplied at the same site, this organization is referred to as a **single-tiered model**.

23.2 Transaction Processing in a Distributed System

Modern transaction processing systems are generally implemented on distributed hardware involving multiple independent computers at geographically distinct sites. The ATM machine is separate from the bank's computer, and a computer at a ticket agent's site is separate from the airline's main reservation system. In some cases, an application might communicate with several databases, each stored on a different computer. The computers are connected in a network, and modules located at any site can exchange messages in a uniform way.

The architecture of these systems is based on the client/server model. With distributed hardware, the client and server modules need not reside at the same site. The location of the database servers might depend on a number of factors, including

- *Minimization of communication costs or response time.* For example, in an industrial system consisting of a central office, warehouses, and manufacturing facilities, if most of the transactions accessing employee records are initiated at the central office, these records might be kept at that location and the inventory records kept at the warehouses.
- *Ownership and security of data.* For example, in a distributed banking system with a computer at each branch office, a branch might insist that the information about its accounts be kept locally in its own computer.
- *Availability of computational and storage facilities.* For example, a sophisticated database server can reside only at a site that includes extensive mass storage facilities.

When a transaction processing system is distributed, its *database portion* might still be *centralized;* that is, it might utilize a single database server residing on a single computer. Alternatively, the database might be *distributed;* that is, it might utilize multiple database servers residing on the same or different computers. Thus, a transaction processing system can be distributed but have a centralized database.

23.2.1 Organization of a Distributed System

The organization of a distributed transaction processing system evolved from the multiuser system shown in Figure 23.2. As a first step, terminals are replaced by client computers, so the user module, responsible for presentation and application services, now resides on a client computer and communicates with the database server. This is referred to as a **two-tiered model**. Figure 23.3 shows the organization of a distributed transaction processing system with a centralized database. Application programs on client machines initiate transactions, which, as shown in Figure 23.2, are handled by the transaction support module on the database server to ensure atomicity and isolation.

The database server might export an SQL interface so that an application program on the client computer can send a request to the database server to execute a particular SQL statement. However, several important problems arise when client machines directly use such an interface. One problem has to do with the integrity of the database. As with a single-user system, our concern is that the client machines, which reside at client sites, might not be secure and hence might not be trustworthy. An erroneous or malicious application program, for example, can destroy database integrity by submitting an improper update statement.

Another significant problem relates to network traffic and the ability of the system to handle a large number of clients. A user wishing to scan a table might execute SQL statements that cause all of the rows of the table to be transferred from the database server to the client machine. Since these machines can be widely separated, considerable network traffic might be required even though the result of the transaction might involve only a few of the rows transferred. Unfortunately, the network can support only a small number of clients if such requests have to be processed in this way.

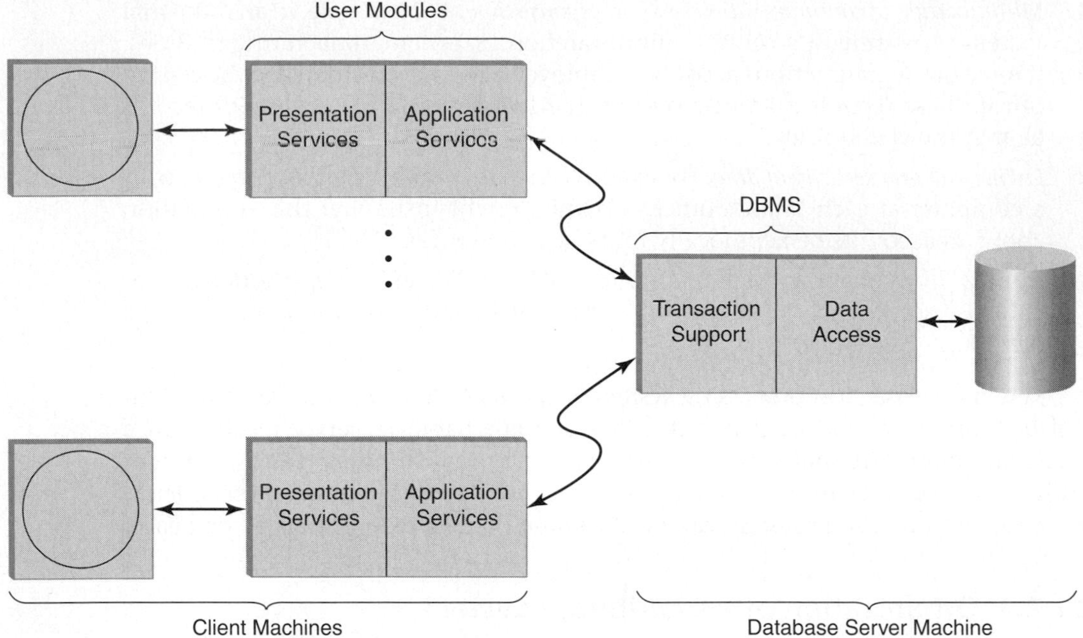

FIGURE 23.3 Two-tiered multiuser distributed transaction processing system.

Stored procedures. One way to address this problem is through stored procedures. Instead of submitting individual SQL statements, the application program on the client computer requests that a particular stored procedure be executed by the database server. In effect, the application program is now provided with a high-level, or more abstract, database interface. For example, a database server for a bank might make `deposit()` and `withdraw()` stored procedures available to application programs.

Stored procedures have several important advantages.

- They are assumed to be correct and their integrity can be maintained at the database server. Application programs executed on client computers are prohibited from submitting individual SQL statements. Since the only way the client computer can access the database is through the stored procedures, the consistency of the database is protected.
- The designer of the application program does not have to know the schema of the database in order to design and build the application programs. And if, at some later time, the schema of the database has to be changed for some reason, the stored procedures that access the database might have to be recoded, but none of the application programs that call those procedures need to be changed.
- The SQL statements of a stored procedure can be compiled and prepared in advance and therefore can be executed more efficiently than interpreted code.

- The service provider can more easily authorize users to perform particular application-specific functions. For example, only a bank teller, not a customer, can issue a certified check. Managing authorization at the level of individual SQL statements is difficult. A withdraw transaction might use the same SQL statements and access the same tables as a transaction that produces a certified check. The authorization problem can be solved by denying the customer direct access to the database and instead allowing him permission to execute the withdraw stored procedure, but not the certified check stored procedure.
- By offering a more abstract service, the amount of information that must be communicated through the network is reduced. Instead of transmitting the intermediate results of individual SQL statements between the application program on the client machine and the database server, all processing of intermediate results is now done by the stored procedure at the database server, and only the initial arguments and final results pass through the network. This is how the table scan described above can be performed. Data communication is thus reduced, and a larger number of clients can be served. However, the database server must be powerful enough to handle the additional work that the execution of stored procedures entails.

The three-tiered model. The idea of providing higher-level services to the client computer can be carried one step further. Figure 23.4 shows a **three-tiered model** of a distributed transaction processing system, which contrasts with the two-tiered system of Figure 23.3. The user module has been divided into a presentation server and an application server that execute on different computers. Presentation services, at the client site, assembles the information input by the user, makes certain validity checks on the information (e.g., type checking), and then sends a request message to the application server, executing elsewhere in the network.

The application server executes the application program corresponding to the requested service. As before, this program implements the rules of the enterprise, checking conditions that have to be satisfied in order for the request to be executed and invoking the appropriate stored procedures at the database server to carry it out. The application program views the servicing of a user request as a sequence of tasks. Thus, in the design of the Student Registration System given in Section C.7.2, the registration transaction performs (among others) the tasks of checking that the course is offered, that the student has taken all of the course prerequisites, and that the student has not registered for too many courses, before finally performing the task of registering the student.

Each task might require the execution of a complex program, and each program might be a distinct stored procedure on the database server. The application program controls transaction boundaries by invoking `begin_transaction` and `commit` and hence can cause the procedures to be executed within a single transaction. Moreover, it encourages task reuse. If tasks are chosen to perform generally useful functions, they can be invoked as components of different application programs. In the general case, the transaction is distributed, having the application program as a root, and the

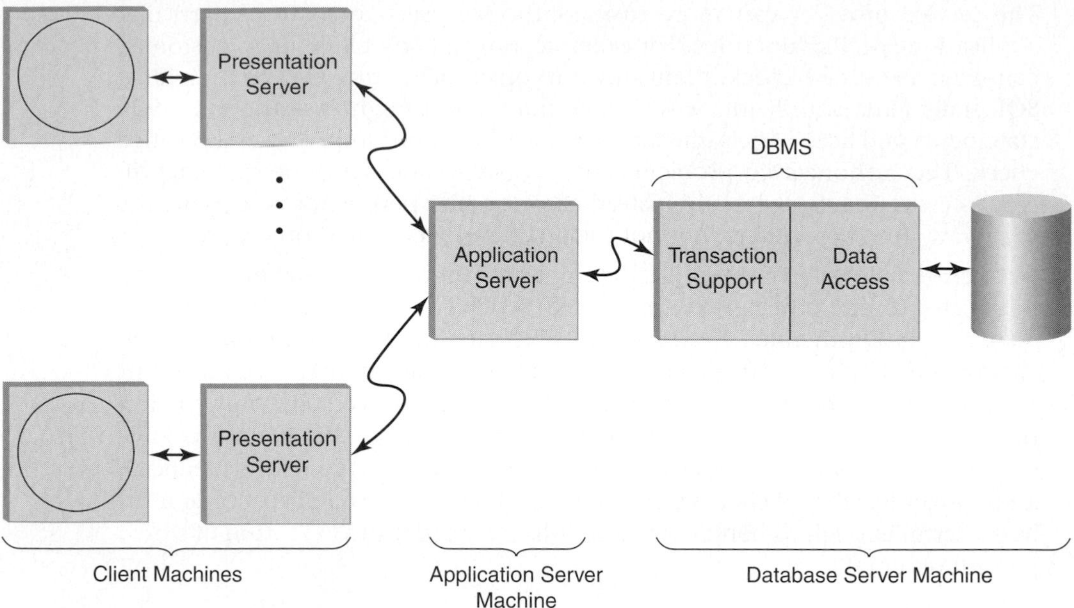

FIGURE 23.4 Three-tiered distributed transaction processing system.

stored procedures are the component subtransactions executing on different servers. In this case, more elaborate transaction support, which we discuss in Section 23.4, is required.

The application can be thought of as a workflow (Section 19.3.6), consisting of a set of tasks that must be performed in some specified order (although all tasks in this case are computational). The application server can be thought of as a workflow controller, controlling the flow of tasks required to implement the user's request.

Figure 23.4 shows a single application server with multiple clients. Since the servicing of a single client request might take a substantial amount of time, a number of client requests might be pending at the same time. Hence, the application server must handle requests concurrently in order to maintain an adequate level of performance. It might do this by allocating a process for each user. Unfortunately, processes carry substantial overhead, and thus the number of processes that can be used in this way is limited. Hence, application servers are often constructed using a multithreaded process (instead of multiple processes), with each user assigned to a different thread. Overhead is reduced since thread switching is much more efficient than process switching. Furthermore, since the information needed to describe each thread within a multithreaded process is much less than the information needed to describe a process, the total amount of information that must be maintained is greatly reduced. The application server can maintain a pool of threads to avoid dynamic thread creation, and it can allocate a thread to a user as needed.

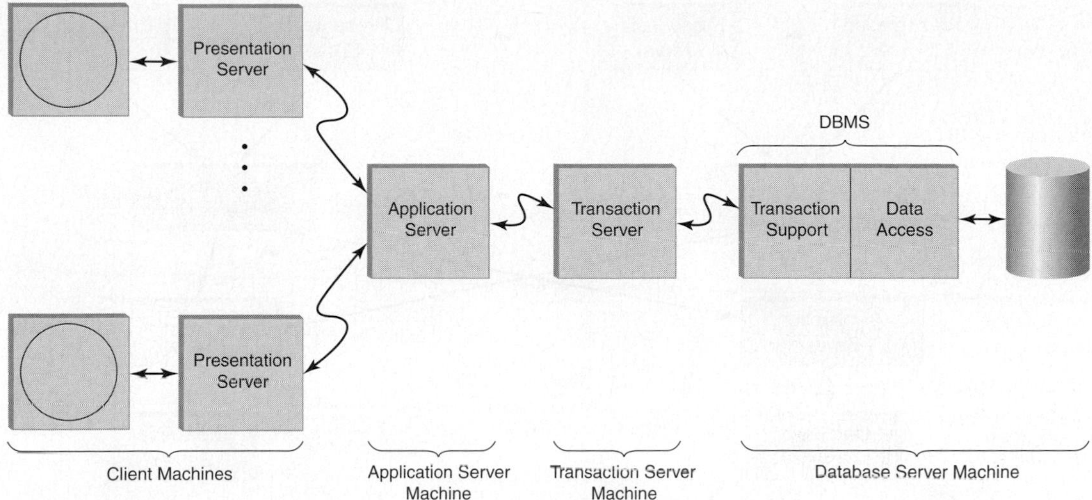

FIGURE 23.5 Three-tiered distributed transaction processing system with tasks executed in a transaction server.

Multiple instances of the application server might exist—particularly if there are many clients. Each instance might reside on a separate computer, and each computer might be connected to a distinct subset of the clients. For example, an application server and the clients it services might be geographically close to one another. Alternatively, a client might connect to any application server.

In some organizations, the stored procedures, which implement the tasks invoked by the application program, are moved out of the database server and executed in a separate module called a **transaction server**, as shown in Figure 23.5. The transaction server is generally located on a computer physically close to the database server in order to minimize network traffic, whereas the application server is located near or at the user site. The transaction server now does the bulk of the work since it submits the SQL statements to the database server and processes the data returned. The application server is primarily responsible for sending requests to the transaction servers.

Although not shown in Figure 23.5, there might be multiple instantiations of the transaction server. This is an example of a **server class**, which is used when it is expected that the server will be heavily loaded. Instances of the class might run on different computers connected to the database server in order to share the transaction load arising from concurrently executing workflows. More generally, there might be multiple database server machines storing different portions of the enterprise's database—for example, a billing database on one server and a registration database on another. A particular transaction server might then be capable of executing only a subset of the tasks and be connected to a subset of the database servers. In that case, the application server must invoke the appropriate

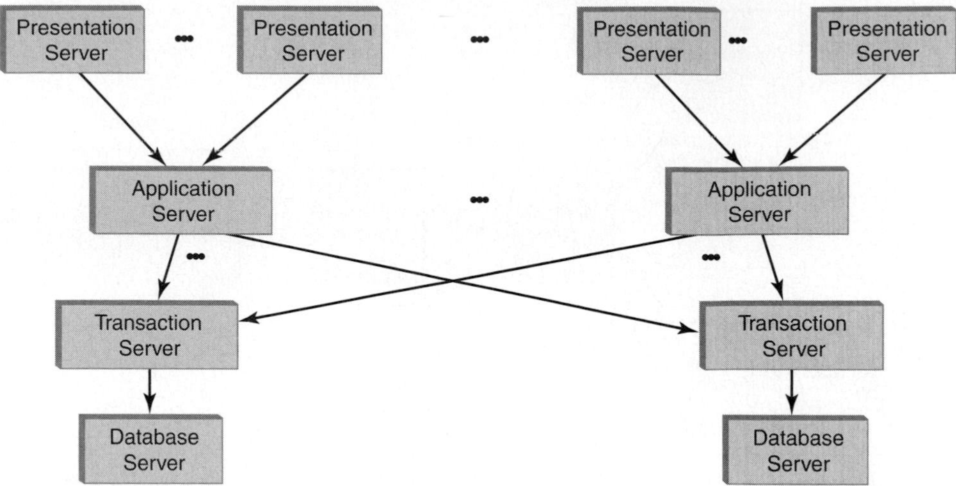

FIGURE 23.6 Interconnection of presentation, application, and transaction servers in a three-tiered architecture.

transaction server to get a particular task done. This selective invocation is frequently referred to as **routing**. An application program acting as a distributed transaction routes requests to multiple transaction servers, as shown in Figure 23.6.

Separating the transaction server from the database server is useful in the following situations:

1. Different components of an enterprise use different sets of procedures to access a common database. Separating these sets on different transaction servers allows each component to more easily control its own procedures. For example, the accounting system and the personnel system of a large corporation might use completely different procedures that access the same data.
2. A single procedure must access several different databases on different server machines.
3. The database server must handle requests arising from a large user population and hence can become a bottleneck. Moving stored procedures off the database machine eases this load.

Among the advantages of separating the client machines from the application server machine are these:

1. The client computers can be smaller (and hence cheaper). This is particularly important in applications involving hundreds, and perhaps thousands, of client machines.
2. System maintenance is easier since changes in enterprise rules (causing changes to the workflow program) can be localized to the application server computer instead of to all client computers.

3. The security of the system is enhanced since individual users do not have physical access to the application server computer and so cannot easily change the application programs.

Case Study: The three-tiered architecture and levels of software abstraction. From a software-engineering viewpoint, one approach to designing a complex application is to structure it hierarchically, as a sequence of levels of abstraction. Each level is built using the abstractions implemented in the level preceding it. In terms of our implementation of the Student Registration System, the lowest level is the conceptual level supported by the DBMS, which supplies the abstraction of individual SQL statements. The middle level consists of the methods `checkCourseOffering()`, `checkCourseTaken()`, `checkTimeConflict()`, `checkPrerequisites()`, and `addRegisterInfo()` (described in Section C.7.3), which uses the SQL statements. The next level of abstraction is the complete transactions, such as `Register()`. Note that by using the middle level, transactions are shielded from database-related concerns (i.e., the actual SQL queries). The top level of abstraction includes the modules for interacting with the user, for instance, a GUI that allows the student to fill out the forms required for course registration.

We now see that a correspondence can be established between the levels of abstraction in the application design and the three-tiered architecture. In the Student Registration System, presentation services software sees the abstraction of the total registration interaction provided by the application server. The application server, in turn, sees the abstraction of the individual checking tasks provided by the transaction server, which in turn uses the conceptual level abstraction provided by the DBMSs.

CASE STUDY

23.2.2 Sessions and Context

Each of the architectures we have discussed involves **sessions** between clients and servers. A session exists between two entities if they are communicating with one another to perform some job and each maintains some state information, or **context**, concerning its role in that job. Two types of sessions are particularly important in the context of transaction processing systems: communication sessions and client/server sessions. We discuss them next.

Communication sessions. In the two-tiered model, presentation/application servers communicate with database servers; in the three-tiered model, presentation servers communicate with application servers, which in turn communicate with database (or transaction) servers. The handling of a client request often involves the efficient and reliable exchange of multiple messages between communicating modules. In this case, communication sessions are generally established. A communication session requires that each communicating entity maintains context information, such as the sequence numbers of the messages transmitted in each direction (for reliably transmitting messages), addressing information, encryption keys, and the current direction of communication. Context information is stored in a data structure called a **context block**.

Messages must be exchanged just to set up and take down a communication session, which makes the cost of these activities nontrivial. As a result, it is wasteful for the presentation server to create a communication session each time a client makes a request or for the application server to create a session each time it has to get service from a database server. Instead, long-term communication sessions are created between servers. Each session is **multiplexed**: it carries messages for many concurrently executing clients.

One advantage of using a three-tiered model is made apparent by Figure 23.6. A large transaction processing system might involve thousands of client machines and multiple database servers. In the worst case, each client in a two-tiered model would have a (long-term) connection to each database server and the total number of connections would be the product of these two numbers—a potentially large number. The overhead of establishing these connections and the storage costs for context blocks within each database server would become excessive.

By introducing the application level, each client now needs to establish a single connection to an application server and the application server needs to establish connections to the database servers. However, a connection between an application server and a database server can be shared—multiplexed—by multiple transactions running on behalf of multiple users on that application server. In the best case only a single connection exists between an application server and a database server. Then, if there are n_1 client machines, n_2 application servers, and n_3 database servers, the worst-case number of connections in a two-tiered architecture is $n_1 * n_3$, whereas the number of connections in a three-tiered architecture is $n_1 + (n_2 * n_3)$. Since n_2 is much less than n_1, a substantial reduction in the number of connections results. Hence, a three-tiered architecture scales better as the system grows to handle a large client population.

Client/server sessions. A server may need to maintain context information about each client for which it provides a service. Consider a database server servicing a client that accesses a table through a cursor. The client executes a sequence of SQL statements (OPEN, FETCH) to create a result set and retrieve its rows. Context has to be maintained by the server so that it can process these statements. Thus, for a FETCH statement, the server must know which row was returned last. Alternatively, the server managing a store's Web site maintains shopping-cart context for each client. A typical client interaction involves a sequence of requests that update the state of the cart. Furthermore, the server does not want to have to authenticate the client and determine what it is authorized to do each time a request is made. Hence, authentication and authorization information can also be stored in the context.

The context used by the server for a particular client/server session can be maintained in a number of different ways.

- *Stored locally at the server.* The server can maintain its client context locally. Each time the client makes a request, the server looks up the client's context and interprets the request using that context. Notice that this approach works well if the client always calls the same server, but care must be taken if the requested service is provided by an arbitrary instance of a class of servers. In that case, successive requests might be serviced by different instances, and context stored locally by one will not be available to another. Furthermore, if the number of clients is large and sessions are long, the server will be maintaining context for many clients simultaneously and session maintenance may be a serious burden.

- *Context stored in a database.* The server can store each client's context in a database. This approach can avoid the problem of server classes, if all instances of the class can access the same database.
- *Context stored at the client.* The context can be passed back and forth between client and server. The server returns its context to the client after servicing a request. The client does not attempt to interpret the context but simply saves it and passes it back to the server when it makes its next request. This approach relieves the server of the need to store the context and also avoids the problem of server classes. Sensitive information in the context that should not be accessible to the client can be encrypted.

When context information is stored on the server or in a database, the server has the problem of locating a client's context when a request from that client arrives. Frequently this problem is solved using a **context handle**, which is a pointer to where the server has stored the client's context. The handle is passed by the server to the client with each server response and is returned by the client to the server in the next request. The interpretation of the handle is totally under the control of the server. The client should not modify it in any way. One example of a context handle is the **cookie** used for client/server applications over the Internet. Sometimes cookies contain some context information as well as a pointer to additional information stored at the server site.

We have so far focused only on the context associated with a sequence of requests made by a client to a particular server and have overlooked the important issue that context must also be associated with a transaction as a whole (which can include multiple requests to *different* servers and hence might encompass multiple sessions). The need for this is illustrated in Figure 23.7, in which a client has set up one session with server $S1$ and another session with server $S2$; both servers have used server $S3$ to fulfill the client's requests. The problem is that issues such as isolation and atomicity are associated with the transaction as a whole and not with any particular session. For example, locks (discussed in Chapter 20) are used to implement isolation. $S3$ must use transaction context to determine that a lock acquired in handling a request from $S1$ for a particular transaction can be used in servicing a request from $S2$ for the same transaction.

When a user logs on at a client machine, a client/server session, with associated context, is established between the client and the application server to handle the user. A thread in the application server (a multithreaded process) is allocated to support the server's end of the session. Client context can be stored in the thread's private stack, and the process's global data, data shared among all threads, can store

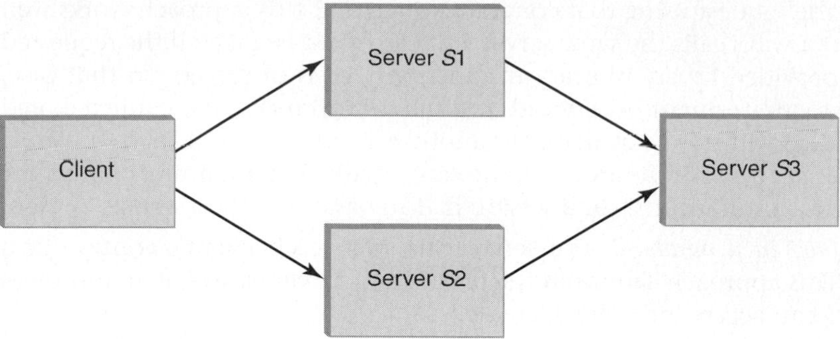

FIGURE 23.7 Transaction context must be maintained when two servers access the same server on behalf of a single transaction.

the state of any resources maintained by the server for use by all clients. Multiplexed communication sessions between the application server and transaction servers are an example of such a resource.

23.2.3 Queued Transaction Processing

The two-tiered model shown in Figure 23.3 is referred to as **data centered**, whereas the three-tiered model shown in Figure 23.5 is referred to as **service centered**. In both, the client and server engage in **direct transaction processing**. The client invokes a server and then waits for the result. The service is provided as quickly as possible and a result is returned. The client and server are thus synchronized.

With **queued transaction processing**, the client enqueues a request on a queue of pending requests to the server and then performs other tasks. The request is dequeued when the server is ready to provide the service. A request from a presentation server, for example, is often enqueued in front of an application server until an application server thread can be assigned to handle the requests. Later, when the service is completed, the server can enqueue the result on a separate result queue. The result is dequeued still later by the client. The client and server are thus unsynchronized.

With recoverable queues, queue operations are transactional. The handling of a request in a queued transaction processing system might involve three transactions, as shown in Figure 23.8. The client executes transaction T_1 to enqueue the request prior to service; the server then executes transaction T_2, which dequeues the request, services it, and enqueues the result on the reply queue; and the client finally executes transaction T_3 to dequeue the result from the reply queue. Figure 23.8 should be compared with Figure 19.8 on page 803. The main difference is that in Figure 19.8 a forwarding agent is used to dequeue the request from the request queue and invoke a (passive) server whereas in Figure 23.8 the server (actively) dequeues the request.

Queued transaction processing offers a number of advantages. The client can input a request at times when the server is busy or down. Similarly, the server can return results even if the client is unprepared to accept them. Furthermore, if the

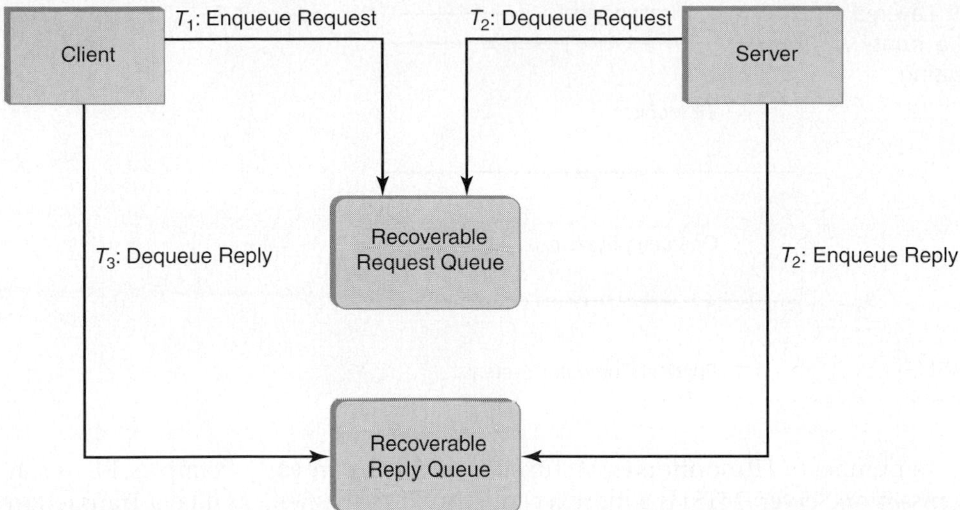

FIGURE 23.8 Queued transaction processing involves two queues and three transactions.

server crashes while the request is being serviced, the service transaction is aborted and the request is restored to the request queue. It is serviced when the server is restarted, without any intervention by the client. Finally, when multiple servers become available, the queue can be integrated into an algorithm that balances the load on all servers.

23.3 The TP Monitor: An Overview

A TP monitor is a collection of software modules that augment the services provided by an operating system. An operating system creates the abstraction of concurrently executing *processes* that can communicate with one another using a message-passing facility, and provides them with shared access to the physical resources of the computer system. The TP monitor extends this to create the abstraction of *transactions* that execute concurrently in a distributed environment. As shown in Figure 23.9, a TP monitor can be viewed as a layer of software between the operating system and the application routines.

Examples of the services provided by a TP monitor are

- Communication protocols of various kinds
- Security of distributed applications, including authentication and encryption
- Atomicity, isolation, and durability of distributed transactions

These services can be provided in an application-independent way; they have general utility and hence can be used in many different distributed applications.

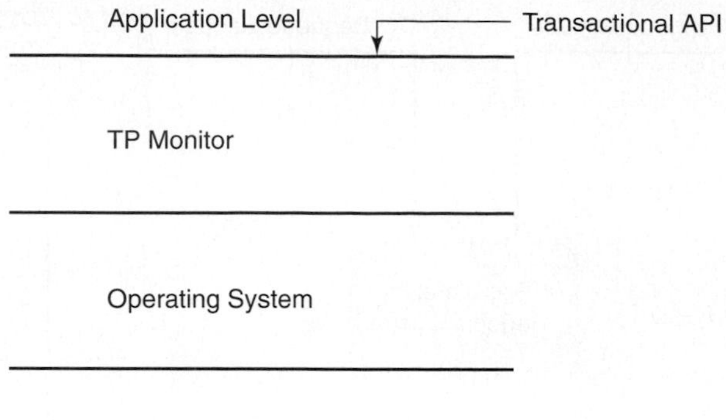

FIGURE 23.9 Layered structure of a transaction processing system.

A number of TP monitors exist. Tuxedo and Encina are early examples. Microsoft Transaction Server (MTS) is a more recent entry into the field, and Java Transaction Service (JTS) is a specification of a Java-based TP monitor. All of them include or specify a set of application-independent services that, though needed in a transaction processing system, are not usually provided by an operating system.

Homogeneous and heterogeneous transaction processing systems. Early transaction processing systems were **homogeneous**, involving the hardware and software of a single vendor. Such systems utilized interfaces designed by the vendor—**proprietary interfaces**—that enabled its products to be interconnected in a variety of ways. Even when these interfaces were published, it was difficult to incorporate products from other vendors into the system because different vendors used different interfaces.

Many current transaction processing systems are **heterogeneous**, involving the products of multiple vendors: hardware platforms, operating systems, database managers, and communication protocols. Homogeneous systems have evolved into heterogeneous systems for the following reasons:

- Newer applications often require the interconnection of older, legacy systems produced by different vendors that had previously operated independently. For example, over the years each department in a company might have developed its own purchasing system. Now the company requires a company-wide purchasing system that interconnects all local systems.
- There are more vendors supplying hardware and software components, and users demand the ability to incorporate the best components available regardless of the supplier.

The implementation of heterogeneous systems requires vendors to agree on (1) standardized, nonproprietary interfaces—**open interfaces**—that define the content and format of the information that must be exchanged in an interaction and (2) communications software to transmit that information. If a legacy system that uses a nonstandard, proprietary interface is to be included, a **wrapper** program can be written as a bridge between interfaces.

Homogeneous transaction processing systems are frequently referred to as **TP-Lite**. Heterogeneous transaction processing systems tend to be more complex since there is more emphasis on strict boundaries between the various functions, and are referred to as **TP-Heavy**. We will be discussing TP-Heavy systems in what follows.

TP monitors are particularly important in the architectures of heterogeneous systems, where the abstraction of a transaction must be implemented and maintained in the context of the interconnection of a number of different systems, possibly from different vendors.

Middleware. To promote the development of open distributed systems in general—and transaction processing systems in particular—various software products have been developed that are frequently referred to as middleware. **Middleware** is software that supports the interaction of clients and servers, often in heterogeneous systems. Many of the modules provided by a TP monitor fall under the general heading of middleware.

JDBC and ODBC (Sections 8.5 and 8.6) are two examples of middleware that allow an application to interact with database servers from a variety of vendors. CORBA (Section 14.6), another example, allows applications to access objects distributed through a network.

23.3.1 The Services Provided by a TP Monitor

The following services are generally provided by a TP monitor.

Communication. The TP monitor supports the abstractions used by application program modules to communicate with one another. The application views these abstractions as an API. The abstractions are implemented within the TP monitor using the lower-level message-passing facility provided by the operating system. Two abstractions often provided are remote procedure call and peer-to-peer communication. Remote procedure call is commonly used by application programs due to its simplicity and its natural relationship to the client/server model. Peer-to-peer communication is more complex, but more flexible. System level modules tend to communicate in this way in order to use the flexibility to optimize performance. Communication with most DBMSs is done through peer-to-peer connections. We discuss communication in Section 23.5.

Global atomicity and isolation. One goal of a TP monitor is to guarantee global atomicity and isolation. The subtransactions of a distributed transaction might execute at a variety of different resource managers. Frequently these are database managers that implement atomicity and isolation locally for individual subtransactions. Unfortunately, local isolation and local atomicity do not guarantee global isolation and global atomicity. To guarantee these properties globally, the actions of the resource managers must be coordinated.

The TP monitor is responsible for providing this coordination. In a TP-Lite system, coordination might be integrated into the vendor's resource managers, while in a TP-Heavy system coordination is generally the responsibility of a separate, off-the-shelf module called a **transaction manager**. When a distributed transaction requests to commit, the transaction manager engages in an exchange of messages with the resource managers, called an **atomic commit protocol**, to ensure that they either all commit their subtransactions or all abort them. We discuss transaction managers in more detail in Section 23.4.

In order for a transaction manager to coordinate the individual resource managers participating in a distributed transaction, it must be informed whenever the transaction invokes a new resource manager. Thus, each time the application initiates a new subtransaction (by communicating with a resource manager for the first time), the transaction manager must be informed. Hence, the transaction manager's role is tied in with the communication abstraction used by the application. Support for global atomicity thus involves both the transaction manager and the communication facility. This is a complex issue, which we will discuss separately in Section 23.5.3.

In contrast to database managers, some resource managers might provide no local support for isolation and atomicity. For example, a transaction might access files maintained by a file server. Access to them should be isolated and atomic. Thus, if the transaction updates two files, no concurrent transaction should see one update and not the other. If the file server does not support isolation, a transaction might use a lock manager provided by the TP monitor. The manager implements general purpose locks. An application can associate a lock in the lock manager with a file in the file server. A transaction that accesses a file should set the corresponding lock (by calling the lock manager) before calling the file server to do the access. This corresponds to the manual locking discussed in Section 20.5. If all transactions follow this protocol, accesses to the file can be synchronized in the same way as accesses to data items in a database server that provides a concurrency control.

Similarly, if the file server does not log before-images, it does not support atomicity. In that case the TP monitor might provide a log manager that the transaction can explicitly use to durably store the images so that changes made by an aborted transaction can be rolled back.

Load balancing and routing. Large transaction processing systems use server classes. If the servers in a class are distributed across a network, availability increases and, since they can execute concurrently, performance is improved. When a client invokes a service supported by a server class, the TP monitor can route the call to any of the servers in the class. Some TP monitors use load balancing as a criterion in this choice. They might use a round robin or randomizing algorithm to distribute the load across the servers, or they might keep information on the number of sessions (perhaps as measured by the number of peer-to-peer connections) that each server in the class is handling and choose the one whose load is the smallest. Load balancing can be integrated with queueing when queued transaction processing is provided.

Recoverable queues. In addition to supporting queued transaction processing, recoverable queues are generally useful for asynchronous communication between application modules and are provided by many TP monitors.

Security services. The information used in a transaction processing system often needs to be protected. Encryption, authentication, and authorization are the foundation of protection and for that reason are often supported by TP monitors. We will discuss these services in Chapter 26.

Threading. We have seen (for example, in connection with an application server) that threads reduce the overhead of handling a large number of clients in a transaction processing system. Unfortunately, not all operating systems support multithreaded processes. Some TP monitors provide their own threading to deal with this. In such cases, the operating system schedules a process for execution, unaware that the process contains monitor code to support threads internally. The code selects the particular thread to be executed next.

Supporting servers. TP monitors provide a variety of servers that are useful in a transaction processing system. For example, a timing server might keep clocks on different computers synchronized; a file server might be provided as a general utility.

Nested transactions. Some TP monitors provide support for nested transactions.

Since we have introduced a number of terms in this chapter that are often confused, we will review their definitions at this point in our discussion.

- A **transaction server** executes the application subroutines that implement the basic units of work from which an application program is built.
- A **transaction manager** is a resource manager that supports the atomic execution of distributed transactions.
- A **TP monitor** includes the transaction manager, transaction servers, and the underlying middleware necessary to tie together the modules of the transaction processing system.
- A **transaction processing system** includes the TP monitor as well as the application code and the various resource managers, such as DBMSs, that make up the total system.

23.4 The TP Monitor: Global Atomicity and the Transaction Manager

A major issue in the implementation of distributed transactions is global atomicity. While atomicity at any particular server can be implemented by that server, global atomicity requires the cooperation of all servers involved in the transaction: either they all agree to commit their subtransactions or they all agree to abort them. Cooperation is achieved through the use of a protocol.

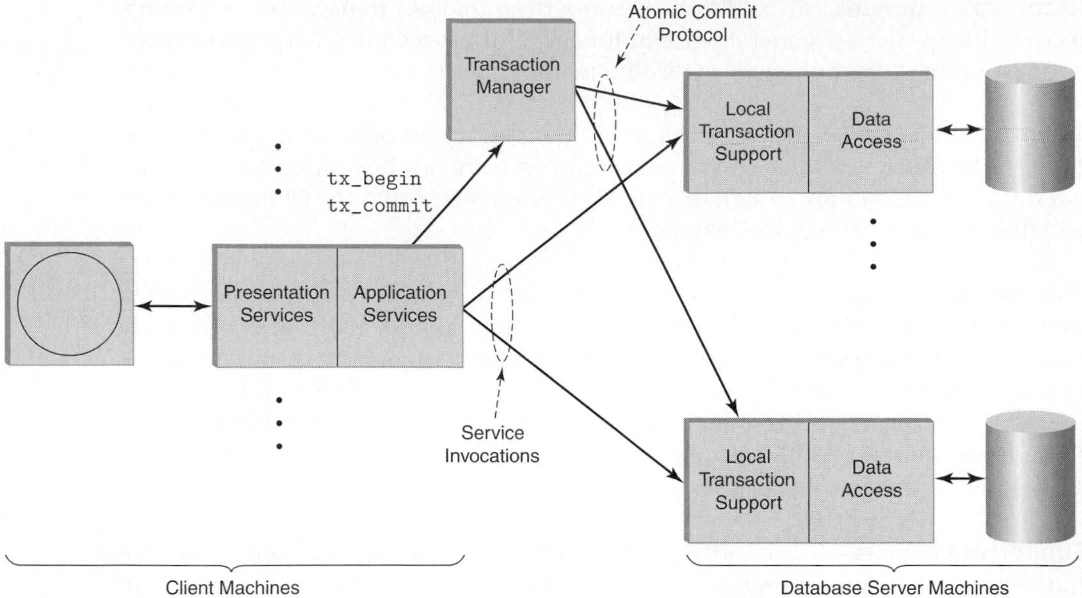

FIGURE 23.10 Two-tiered multidatabase transaction processing system in which a transaction can access several database servers.

The algorithm for implementing global atomicity can be integrated into the individual servers in a TP-Lite system. In TP-Heavy systems, the algorithm is often implemented in a separate middleware module, shown in Figure 23.10, called a transaction manager. For simplicity, the figure shows a two-tiered system, but three tiers are frequently involved.

In both cases, the module for supporting global atomicity responds to commands from the application program (perhaps an application server) that set the boundaries of a distributed transaction, and coordinates the commitment of its subtransactions. To do this, it must know when the transaction as a whole and each of its subtransactions are initiated. Here we describe the process as it works in TP-Heavy systems, which, because of their heterogeneity, rely on interface standards. One such standard is the X/Open standard API.

X/Open was defined by X/Open Company Limited, an independent worldwide organization supported by many of the largest information systems suppliers and software companies. Part of this API is the `tx` interface, which supports the transaction abstraction and includes `tx_begin()`, `tx_commit()`, and `tx_rollback()`. These procedures are called from the application and implemented in the transaction manager. To be specific in describing concepts related to distributed transactions, we base our discussion on this standard.

The application calls `tx_begin` when it wants the transaction manager to know that it is starting a distributed transaction. The transaction manager records the existence of a new distributed transaction and returns an identifier that uniquely names it. Hence, the transaction manager can be regarded as a resource manager in which the resource managed is the set of transaction identifiers. Later, when the application requests service from a server the transaction manager is informed of the existence of the new subtransaction at the server's site.

The application calls `tx_commit` to inform the transaction manager of the distributed transaction's successful completion. The transaction manager then communicates with each server hosting a subtransaction in such a way that either all subtransactions commit or all abort, thus making the distributed transaction globally atomic. An atomic commit protocol controls the exchange of messages for this purpose. In this role, the transaction manager is frequently referred to as the **coordinator**. (We will discuss the most commonly used atomic commit protocol in Section 24.2.)

Each of the `tx` procedures is a function that returns a value that indicates the success or failure of the requested action. In particular, the return value of `tx_commit()` indicates whether the distributed transaction actually committed or aborted and the reason for an abort. For example, the distributed transaction might be aborted if the transaction manager discovers that one of the database servers has crashed or that communication to that server has been interrupted.

23.5 The TP Monitor: Remote Procedure Call

The general distributed transaction model presented in Section 19.2.2 involves a set of related computations performed by a number of modules, which might be located at different sites in a network and which communicate with one another. For example, an application module might request service from a database server, or the application itself might be distributed and one application module might call for the services of another.

Consider a course-registration application program, *A*1 (perhaps executing in the context of a transaction on an application server), that invokes a stored procedure on a database server, *D*1, to register a student in a course, and then invokes a procedure in a remote application program, *A*2, to bill that student. *A*2 might in turn invoke a stored procedure on a different database server, *D*2, to record the charge. Both *D*1 and *A*2 are viewed as servers by *A*1 (and *D*2 is viewed as a server by *A*2), but only *D*1 and *D*2 are resource managers in the sense that they control resources whose state must be made durable. Hence, only *D*1 and *D*2 need participate in the atomic commit protocol. If *A*1 is executing in the context of a transaction, *T*, we say that *T* **propagates** from *A*1 to *A*2 and *D*1[1] as a result of the invocations made in *A*1.

Although message passing underlies all communication, a TP monitor generally offers an application several higher-level communication abstractions. The one

[1] Some TP monitors permit violations of this general rule. For example, *A*1 can specify that *A*2 not be included in *T*. Similarly, *A*2 can itself specify that it not be included in *T*. In addition, commands have been defined that permit a routine to temporarily exclude itself from the current transaction and then resume its participation at a later time.

chosen might depend on the structure of the application. In some cases there is a strict hierarchical relationship between the modules. For example, a client module might request service from a server module and then wait for a reply. In this case, a procedure-calling mechanism is particularly convenient. In other applications a module might treat the other modules it interacts with as peers. In that case, the peer-to-peer communication paradigm is appropriate. Often legacy modules are involved, and their mode of communication is fixed.

In this section, we discuss communication using remote procedure call, and in Section 23.6 we discuss peer-to-peer communication. In Section 23.7 we discuss event communication, which is particularly appropriate for handling exceptional situations.

A network-wide message-passing facility can support communication between modules, but it suffers from the deficiency that the interface it presents to the modules is not convenient to use. Invoking operating system primitives for sending and receiving a message is neither elegant nor simple. Users prefer the procedural interface of a high-level language and benefit from the type checking automatically provided by a compiler. For these reasons, it is desirable to create a procedure-calling facility that makes invoking a procedure in a possibly remote module similar to calling a local procedure (one linked into the caller's code). Such a facility supports **remote procedure call**, or RPC [Birrell and Nelson 1984, 1990].

Using RPC, a distributed computation takes on a tree structure since a called procedure in one module can in turn invoke a procedure in another. The procedure that initiates the computation as a whole is referred to as the **root**.

The execution of a remote procedure is handled by a thread in the target module. Local variables are allocated in the thread's stack. When the procedure returns, the stack is deallocated and hence cannot be used to store the context of the distributed computation in anticipation of future calls. For this reason, RPC communication is referred to as **stateless**. If context must be maintained over several calls, the called procedure must store it globally or it must be passed back and forth using a context handle (see Section 23.2.2).

23.5.1 Implementation of Remote Procedure Call

RPC is implemented using **stubs**. A client stub is a routine linked to a client. A server stub is a routine linked to a server. The routines serve as intermediaries between the client and server as shown in Figure 23.11. A client calls a server procedure using that procedure's globally unique name. The name is a character string known to the users of the system. The call does not invoke the procedure directly, however. Instead, it invokes the client stub, which locates the server (using directory services, which we will describe shortly) and sets up a connection to it. The stub generally converts the arguments from the format used by the client to the format expected by the server and then packs them, together with the name of the called procedure, into an invocation message, a process called **marshaling of arguments**, and uses the message-passing facility provided by the operating system to send the message

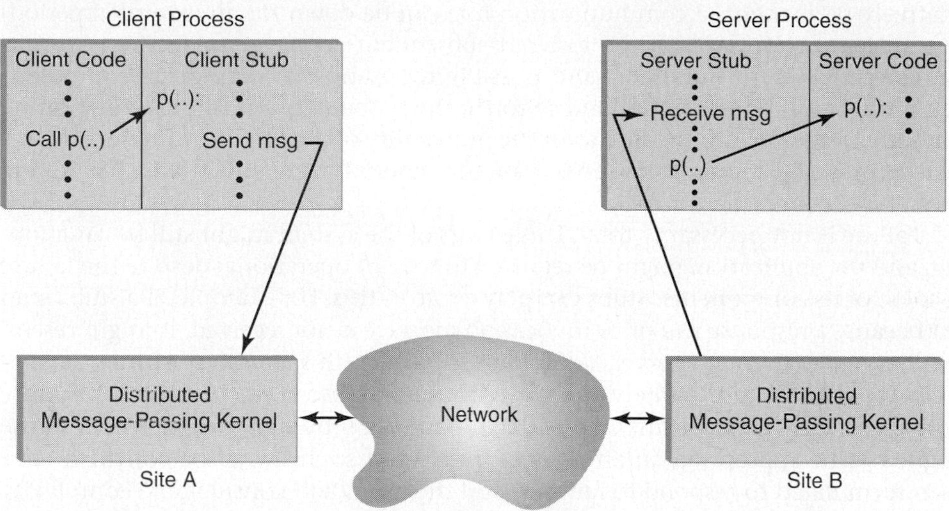

FIGURE 23.11 Use of stubs to support remote procedure call.

to the server. In its message-passing role, the operating system is often referred to as a **distributed message-passing kernel**.

In the figure, the server happens to be on a different machine. The server stub receives invocation messages from all clients. It extracts the arguments in a particular message and invokes the appropriate procedure using a standard (local) procedure call. The result of the call is returned to the server stub, which sends it back to the client stub using the message-passing facility, and the client stub returns it to the client (recall that the client stub was invoked by the client application using a conventional procedure call). Thus, RPC is a high-level communication facility implemented by the procedure call mechanism coupled with the operating systems' message-passing facility.

The stub mechanism has several advantages. Only the stubs interface to the operating system. It appears to the client and to the server that they are communicating with each other directly through a conventional procedure call. Furthermore, the stub mechanism makes a call to a server on a local machine and a call to a server on a remote machine appear identical to the client: in both cases it appears as an invocation of a local procedure linked into the client code. Hence, the client code need not be aware of the physical location of the server. It uses the same mechanism to communicate with a local server as with a remote server. Finally, if modules are moved, the client and server code need not be changed. This feature is generally referred to as **location transparency**.

In connecting clients to servers, stubs must deal with the possibility of failure. Failure in a single-site system is relatively infrequent and generally comes in the form of a crash. Failures in a distributed system can include not only the crash of a particular computer but also a communication failure. Such a failure might be relatively permanent (a communication line can be down for an extended period) or transient (a message can be lost but subsequent messages might be transmitted correctly). With hundreds, and possibly thousands, of connected computers, communication lines, routers, and so forth, the probability that all are functioning correctly is significantly smaller than the probability of a single site functioning correctly. Since RPC requires the services of a number of these units, failure handling plays a more prominent role.

Failure is not necessarily total. Large parts of the system might still be functioning, and the application might be required to remain operational despite the failure of some of its components. Stubs can play a role in this. For example, if a stub times out because a response to a prior invocation message is not received, it might resend the message to the same server, or perhaps to a different server in the same class, or abort the client. Unfortunately, there might be a number of reasons why a response is not received—message loss, server crash—and an action appropriate in one case might not be appropriate in another. A number of sophisticated algorithms have been formulated to respond to failures, and these can add considerable complexity to the stub.

In addition to adding to the complexity of the stub, network failures can compromise location transparency since the nature of the failure might be visible to the application through the RPC interface. For example, if the caller is informed that the server is unavailable, it is apparent that the called procedure is remote. Other issues that affect location transparency are the absence of global variables and the fact that parameters are not passed by reference. Finally, since multiple machines are now involved, new security issues might arise. We discuss some of these security issues in Section 26.4.1.

23.5.2 Directory Services

A server is known to its clients by its interface. The interface is published and contains the information a client needs to invoke the server's procedures: procedure names and descriptions of parameters. As discussed in Sections 14.5.1 and 14.6, an interface definition language (IDL) is a high-level language that is used to describe the interface. An IDL compiler compiles the interface description into a header file and server-specific client and server stubs. The header file must be included with the application program when it is compiled, and the client stub is linked to the client code in the resulting module. The use of an IDL file to describe the server interface encourages the development of open systems. The client and server can be built by different vendors as long as they agree on the interface through which they communicate.

The server interface, however, does not specify the identity and location of a server process that will actually execute the procedure. The location might not be known at compile time, or it might change dynamically. Furthermore, the server might be implemented as a class, with instances executing on different nodes in a network. The system must therefore provide a run-time mechanism to bind a client to a server dynamically.

Binding can be achieved by requiring that a server, *S*, when it is ready to provide service to clients, register with some central naming service available to all clients. Such a service is often provided by a separate **name**, or **directory**, **server**.

To register, *S* supplies to the directory server its globally unique name (the character string used by clients) and network address, the interfaces it supports, and the communication protocol(s) it uses to exchange messages with clients (these are the messages used to implement RPC communication). For example, *S* might accept messages requesting service only over a TCP connection. This is an example of a server (*S*) acting as a client with respect to another server (the directory server).

The client stub submits a server name or the identification of a particular interface to the directory server and requests the network address and communication protocol to be used to communicate with a server having that name or supporting that interface. Once this information has been provided, the client stub can communicate directly with the server.

Although the directory server is itself a server, it must have some special status since clients and servers have to be able to connect to it without having to use another directory server (to avoid the chicken-and-egg problem). Hence, it should reside at a well-known network address that can be determined without using a directory server.

A directory server can be a complex entity. One source of that complexity is a result of the central role it plays in distributed computing. If the directory server fails (perhaps because the host on which it resides crashes), clients can no longer locate servers and new distributed computations cannot be established. To avoid such a catastrophe, directory service itself might be distributed and/or replicated across the network. However, this raises new problems: making sure that replicas are up to date and that a client anywhere in the network can locate a directory server that has the information it requires.

The **Distributed Computing Environment** (DCE) [Rosenberry et al. 1992] is an example of middleware that supports distributed systems such as TP monitors.[2] Among the services it provides are RPC between modules running on different operating system platforms. Directory services are provided in connection with this as well as other basic features, such as the security services that we will discuss in Chapter 26.

23.5.3 The Transaction Manager and Transactional RPC

The transaction manager's role in implementing global atomicity is illustrated in Figures 23.12 and 23.13. The X/Open system calls `tx_begin()`, `tx_commit()`, and `tx_rollback()` to invoke procedures within the transaction manager (*TM*) that initiate and terminate transactions. When an application initiates a transaction, *T*, it invokes `tx_begin()`. As shown in Figure 23.12, *TM* returns a transaction identifier, *tid*, that uniquely identifies *T*. The transaction identifier is retained in the client stub.

[2] The TP monitor Encina is based on DCE.

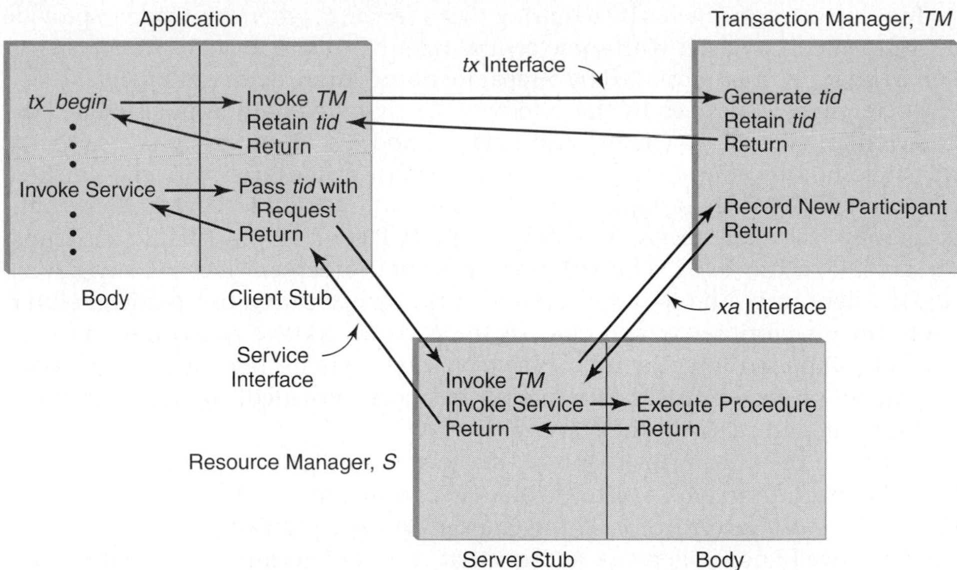

FIGURE 23.12 Communication with the transaction manager to implement transactional remote procedure call.

Subsequently, whenever the client invokes a resource manager, *S*, the client stub appends *tid* to the call message to identify the calling transaction to *S*. If this is the first request by *T* to *S*, the server stub at *S* notifies *TM* that it is now performing work for *T* by calling *TM*'s procedure `xa_reg()` and passing *tid*. Thus, *TM* can record the identities of all resource managers that participate in *T*. *S* is referred to as a **cohort** of *T*. `xa_reg()` is part of X/Open's `xa` interface between a transaction manager and a resource manager. When a transaction manager and a resource manager both support the `xa` interface, they can be connected in support of distributed transactions even though they are the products of different vendors.

Note that the standard defines both the `tx` interface, between an application and a transaction manager, and the `xa` interface, between a transaction manager and a resource manager, but it does not define an interface between an application and a resource manager. That interface is defined by the resource manager itself.

Since procedure calling is a synchronous communication mechanism (the caller waits until the callee has completed), when a subtransaction completes its computation, all subtransactions it has invoked have also completed. Hence, when the root of the transaction tree finishes its computation, the entire distributed transaction is complete and the root can request that the transaction be committed by calling the transaction manager procedure `tx_commit()`, as shown in Figure 23.13. (If the client wishes to abort *T*, it calls `tx_rollback()`.) The transaction manager must then make sure that termination is globally atomic—either all servers invoked by *T* commit or all abort. It does this by engaging in an atomic commit protocol in which

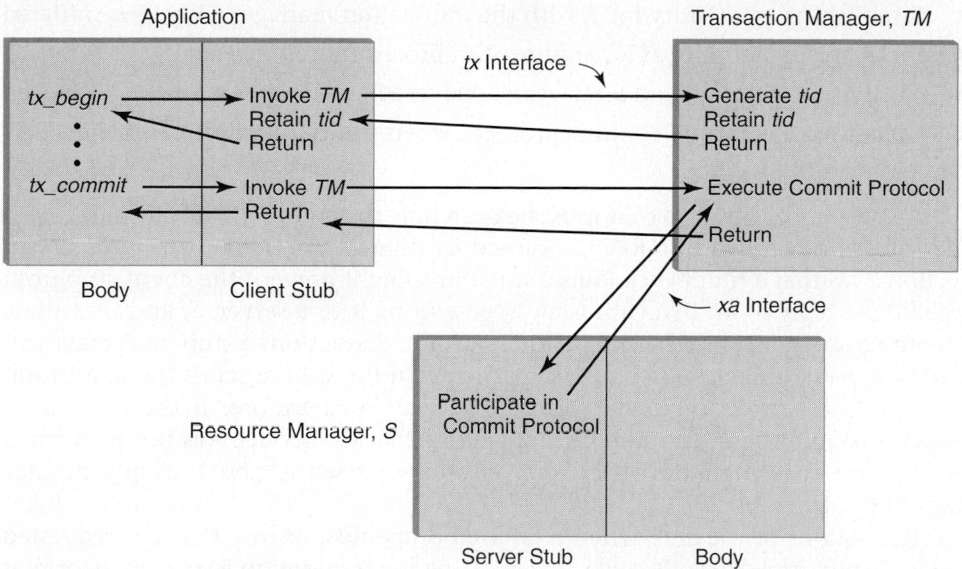

FIGURE 23.13 Communication with the transaction manager to perform an atomic commit protocol.

it serves as coordinator and the resource managers serve as cohorts. The most widely used atomic commit protocol, *two-phase commit*, will be described in Section 24.2.

To execute a commit protocol, the transaction manager must communicate with all cohorts (e.g., *S*), as shown in Figure 23.13. It does this by using callbacks that the resource managers have registered with it. In addition to the normal service interface that a resource manager presents to an application, it offers a set of **callbacks** to the transaction manager. These are resource manager procedures that the transaction manager can use for a variety of purposes. Each resource manager might offer different callbacks depending upon the services it is capable of performing. Those that can engage in an atomic commit protocol register callbacks for that purpose.[3] If a cohort does not register such callbacks, it cannot participate in the protocol and global atomicity cannot be guaranteed.

The procedure-calling mechanism we have just discussed (involving the use of *tid* and the xa interface) is thus an enhanced version of the RPC mechanism and is one ingredient used to implement global atomicity. This mechanism is provided by the TP monitor and referred to as a **transactional remote procedure call**, or **TRPC**.[4]

Global atomicity is implemented by the stubs and the transaction manager. It involves the following:

[3] Callbacks to support distributed savepoints are another example.

[4] TRPC can be implemented as an enhancement of the authenticated RPC to be discussed in Section 26.6.

- Establishing an identity for T with the transaction manager when T is initiated
- Including T's identity as an argument in procedure call messages
- Notifying the transaction manager whenever a new resource manager is invoked
- Executing the atomic commit protocol when the transaction completes (Section 24.2)

An additional obstacle that must be overcome to achieve global atomicity (and that must be handled by TRPC) is caused by failures in the network. We saw in Section 23.5 that a number of failure situations might prevent the client stub from receiving a reply to an invocation message sent by it to a server, S, and that these situations are indistinguishable to the client stub. The actions a stub might take can lead to several different outcomes. In particular, if the stub re-sends the invocation message, the service might be performed twice. Furthermore, if the invocation message is not re-sent, the stub cannot assume that the service was not performed since the message might have been received and processed at S, but the reply message might have been lost.

The actions of the stub when a failure occurs must ensure that the requested service is performed exactly once at S, allowing the transaction to continue, or that the requested service is not performed at all and (assuming that the service cannot be provided at a different server) the transaction is aborted. Thus, the stub ensures what is called **exactly once semantics.**

The situation is further complicated by the fact that S might have invoked another server, S', in performing the requested service. If the site at which S executes has crashed, and S' executes elsewhere in the network, an **orphan** results: The task at S' has no parent process (i.e., S) to which it reports. The stub has the nontrivial job of guaranteeing exactly once semantics under these circumstances.

23.6 The TP Monitor: Peer-to-Peer Communication

With remote procedure call, a client sends a request message to a server to invoke a procedure and waits for a reply. Hence, communication is synchronous. The subtransaction is performed at the server and a reply message is sent when service is completed. The request/reply pattern of communication is asymmetric, and the client and server do not execute concurrently.

In contrast, **peer-to-peer communication** is symmetric. Once a connection is established, both parties use the same send and receive commands to converse. It is also more flexible since any pattern of messages between peers can be supported. The send is an asynchronous operation, meaning that the system buffers the message that has been sent and then returns control to the sender. Unlike RPC, the sender can thus execute concurrently with the receiver. The sender might perform some computation or send additional messages, and thus a stream of messages might flow from the sender to the receiver before the receiver replies. As with RPC, peer-to-peer communication is supported by a lower-level message-passing protocol (such as TCP/IP or SNA).

As usual, flexibility comes at the price of added complexity. Each party must be prepared to deal with the pattern of messages used by the other, which means that there is now more room for error. For example, if each process is in a state in which it is expecting a message from the other before it can continue, deadlock results. Peer-to-peer communication is often supported by TP monitors not only because of its added flexibility, but also because many database servers (often running on mainframes) use this mode of communication.

23.6.1 Establishing a Connection

A variety of peer-to-peer protocols exist. Our discussion in this section is based on IBM's commonly used SNA protocol LU6.2 [IBM 1991] and an API that interfaces to it.

To begin a conversation, a module must first set up a connection to the program with which it wishes to communicate. This is done with an `allocate()` command that has as an argument the target program's name. A new instance of the program is created to handle the other end of the conversation. In contrast to RPC, location transparency is not a goal: the requester explicitly provides the address of the receiving program.

Returning to the example of a distributed computation in Section 23.5, *A*1 might set up a peer-to-peer connection to *A*2. A new instance of the billing program is initiated to receive the messages sent by *A*1 over the connection.

While connections in LU6.2 are half duplex, connections generally might be half or full duplex. With **half duplex**, messages can flow in either direction over the connection, but at any given time one module, *A*, is the sender (the connection is currently in **send mode** for *A*) and the other module, *B*, is the receiver (the connection is currently in **receive mode** for *B*). *A* sends an arbitrary number of messages to *B* and then passes send permission to *B*. This makes *B* the sender and *A* the receiver. When *B* finishes sending messages, it passes send permission back to *A* and the process repeats. This contrasts with a **full duplex** connection, in which either party can send at any time. With half duplex, the current direction of the connection is a part of its context.

When a program in module *A*, executing as part of a transaction, sets up a connection to a program instance in module *B*, the transaction propagates from *A* to *B*. Once the connection has been established, *A* and *B* are equal partners and all messages over the connection pertain to that transaction. Client/server context can be conveniently stored at each end of the connection in local variables, allowing each arriving message to be interpreted by the receiving program with respect to the context. For this reason, protocols built using peer-to-peer interactions are often **stateful**.

A module can engage in an arbitrary number of different peer-to-peer connections concurrently. Because any module participating in the transaction can set up a new connection to any other module, the general structure of a distributed transaction is typically that of an acyclic graph, as shown in Figure 23.14, in which nodes represent the transaction's participants and links represent connections. The graph

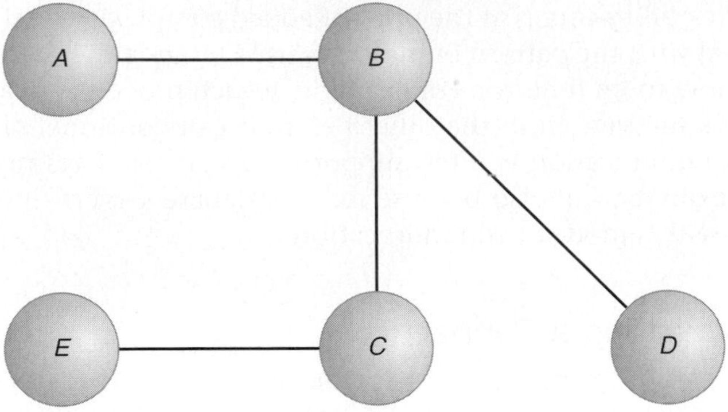

FIGURE 23.14 Set of modules communicating through peer-to-peer connections.

is acyclic because a new instance of a program is created whenever a connection is set up. Hence, nodes in the graph represent program instances, and it is not possible for a program to set up a connection to an existing instance. In the figure, for example, *C* and *D* might represent different instances of the same program. No node occupies a unique position analogous to the root node of a procedure-calling hierarchy.

23.6.2 Distributed Commitment

The rules governing commitment are consistent with the equal status of the participants in a transaction that uses peer-to-peer connections: any node can request to commit the transaction. In contrast to the hierarchical model of distributed transactions, where only the root module can request to commit (and therefore, since communication is synchronous, all subtransactions must have completed at that time) transactional peers are not synchronized. When a participant decides to commit, its transactional peers might still be executing and not yet ready to commit. Hence, an integral part of committing a transaction in the peer-to-peer model is ensuring that all participants have completed. As a result, the atomic commit protocol must both guarantee that all participants have completed and that they either all commit or all abort. The following description is based on [Maslak et al. 1991].

In a properly organized transaction, a single module, *A*, initiates the commit. All of *A*'s connections must be in send mode at this time. *A* initiates the commit by declaring a **syncpoint**, which causes a **syncpoint message** to be sent over each of *A*'s connections. *A* then waits until the commit protocol completes.

Participant *B*, connected to *A*, might not have completed its portion of the transaction when it receives the syncpoint message. When *B* has completed and all of its connections (other than the connection to *A*) are in send mode, it also declares a syncpoint, which causes a syncpoint message to be sent over all of its connections (other than the connection to *A*). In this way, syncpoint messages spread through the transaction graph. A node having only one connection is a leaf node in the tree (e.g., *E* in the figure). After receiving a syncpoint message, it also declares a syncpoint when it completes, although no additional syncpoint messages result.

Eventually, each peer has declared a syncpoint, and all are synchronized at their syncpoint declarations. When a leaf node declares a syncpoint, a response message is sent back up the tree to the root. When all leaves have responded, the root can conclude that the entire transaction has completed. A description of the atomic commit protocol in the context of peer-to-peer communication is provided in Section 24.2.3.

The syncpoint protocol requires that only one module initiate it and that a module declare a syncpoint only if (1) all of its connections are in send mode and it has not yet received a syncpoint message, or (2) all but one of its connections are in send mode and it has received one syncpoint message over the connection in receive mode. If the protocol is not used correctly, the transaction is aborted. For example, if two participants initiate the protocol by declaring a syncpoint, syncpoint messages converge on some intermediate node over two connections. This violates the protocol and causes the transaction to abort.

The implementation of global atomicity uses a module similar to the transaction manager, called a **syncpoint manager**. In a manner similar to the technique used with RPC, each time *A* invokes a resource manager for the first time, the syncpoint manager is informed of a new participant in the transaction. Similarly, if *A* sets up a connection to *B*, the syncpoint manager is informed. The syncpoint manager must direct the atomic commit protocol among the participants of the transaction (in this case, *A* is included as a participant).

23.7 The TP Monitor: Event Communication

When modules communicate using RPC, the callee, or server, is structured to accept service requests. It exports procedures that clients can call and whose purpose is to service the requests. When no request is being processed, the server is idle, waiting for the next invocation. The situation is similar when peer-to-peer communication is used. In this case, the server accepts a connection and executes a receive command. Once again, however, when no service has been requested, the server is idle.

Both procedural and peer-to-peer communication are useful in designing modules whose primary purpose is to service requests from other modules. However, these modes of communication are often inappropriate for a module that must deal with an exceptional situation but cannot simply wait for that situation to occur because it has other things to do.

For example, suppose that a module, M_1, repeatedly reads and records the temperature in a furnace. A second module, M_2, which controls the flow of fuel to the furnace (and perhaps executes on a different computer), might want to be informed of the exceptional case in which the temperature reaches a certain limit. (Perhaps M_2 shuts down the furnace in that case.) Since M_2 must function as a controller, it needs a way to find out when the exceptional case occurs. One way to implement this requirement is for M_2 to periodically call on M_1, using procedural communication, and request that it return the current recorded temperature. Another is for M_2, using a peer-to-peer connection, to periodically send a message to M_1 requesting the temperature. These approaches are referred to as **polling**. If it is unlikely that the value will ever reach the limit, polling is wasteful of resources since M_2 is constantly making requests but the replies indicate that no action need be taken. If M_2 must respond quickly when the value reaches the limit, polling is even more wasteful since in this case more-frequent communication is required.

As a second example, consider a point-of-sale system in which an application module, M, on a sales terminal responds to service requests from customers input at the keyboard. If the system is about to be taken offline temporarily, an out-of-service message must be printed on the terminal. Unfortunately, if M is designed to respond only to inputs from the keyboard, it will not recognize communication coming from the central site and cannot be notified to print the message. Once again, a convenient mechanism for responding to exceptional situations is needed.

In the point-of-sale system, it might be possible to redesign M, using a standard client/server paradigm, to respond to a request from the central site (in addition to requests coming from the keyboard). However, this might not be sufficient if the response to the central site is time critical. If the required response time is less than the time allotted to service a keyboard request, the central site might be forced to wait for a time that exceeds the maximum response time. Hence, an interrupt mechanism is necessary.

Exceptional situations are referred to as **events**. Some TP monitors provide an **event communication** mechanism with which one module that recognizes an event can conveniently notify another module, M, to handle that event. Notification might take the form of an interrupt, causing M to execute an event-handling routine.[5]

The module that agrees to be interrupted uses the event-handling API of the TP monitor to **register** an **event handler** (or callback) that it wishes to execute when notified of an event. In Figure 23.15, M has registered the handler `foo` with the TP monitor. Since M does not wait for the event to occur but continues to engage in its usual activities, event notification is said to be **unsolicited**.

The system interrupts M when an event it is to handle occurs. It saves M's current state and passes control to `foo`. When `foo` exits, the system, using the saved state, returns control to the point at which M was interrupted. M can thus respond immediately when the event occurs. This response is asynchronous because it cannot be determined in advance when the event will occur and thus at what point during M's execution (i.e., between which pair of instructions) `foo` will be executed. While fast response is often important, careful design is required to ensure that the execution of the handler does not interfere with the interrupted computation.

As depicted in Figure 23.15, the event-generating module, N, invokes **notify** of the event API to indicate to the system that an event has occurred and that the module M is to be interrupted. This process is often called **notification**. Assuming

[5] Our discussion is based on event communication in the Tuxedo transaction processing system [Andrade et al. 1996].

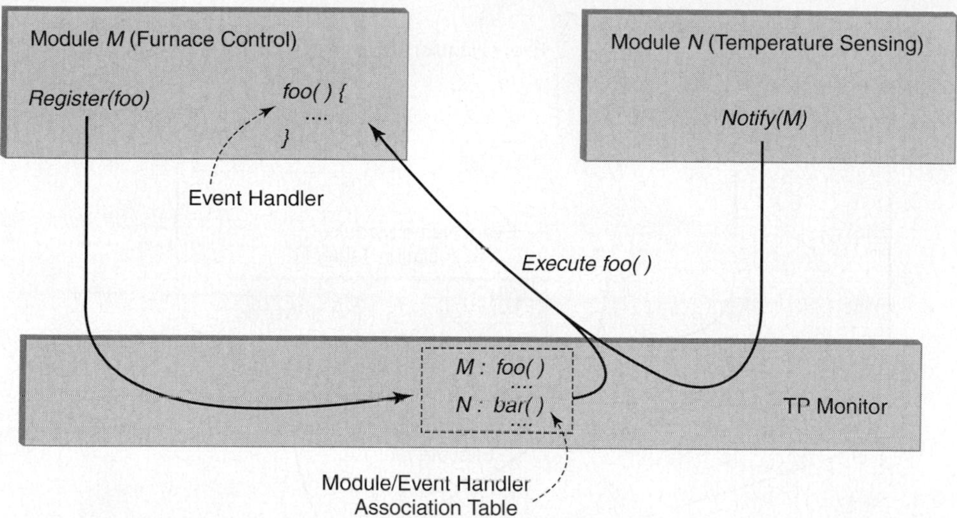

FIGURE 23.15 Event processing that links an event-generating module with an event-handling module.

that a handler has been registered by *M*, the TP monitor causes it to be executed. The API might allow a message to be passed to *M* by the event-generating module as an argument.

23.7.1 Event Broker

While the event communication described in the previous section is useful, it has one important drawback. The event-generating module must know the identity of the modules to be notified (there can be more than one). In an application in which the modules that respond to events might change, it is desirable to make the target event-handling modules transparent to the event-generating module. This can be done with an event broker.

An **event broker** is a server provided by a TP monitor, which functions as an intermediary between event-generating and event-handling modules. When an event broker is used, each event is given a name. An event-handling module, *M*, after registering an event-handling routine, *foo*, with the TP monitor, **subscribes** to an event, *E*, by calling the broker using the event API. The name of the event is supplied as an argument. The broker then records the association between the named event and *M*. An event can have more than one subscriber, in which case a list of event-handling modules is associated with it. When the event occurs, the event-generating module, *N*, **posts** the event with the broker (again using the broker's API and passing the name of the event an argument). The broker then notifies all modules that previously subscribed to the event. The situation just described

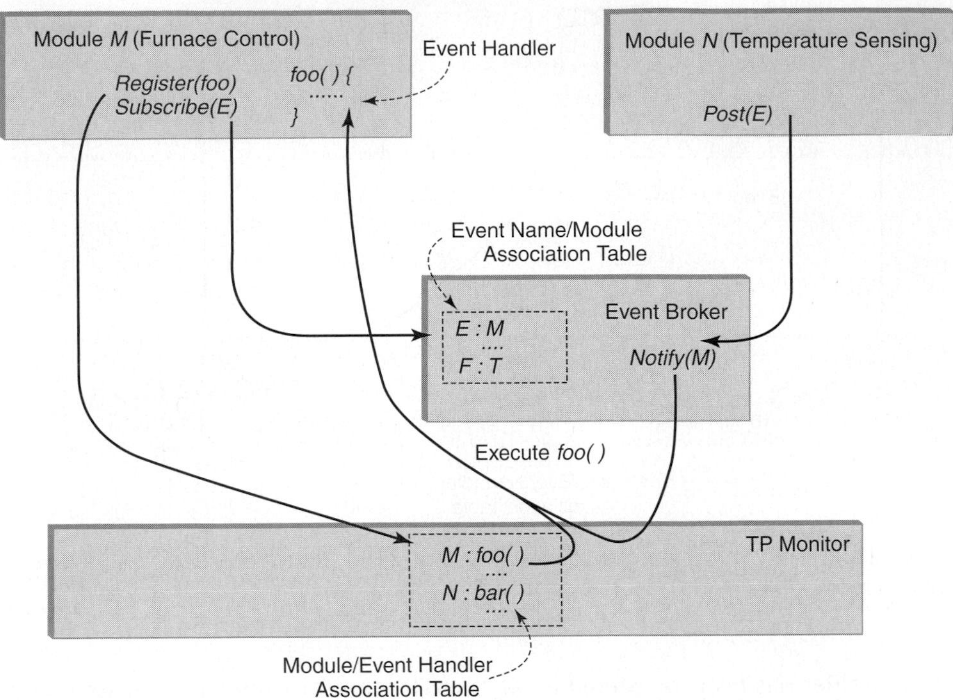

FIGURE 23.16 Use of an event broker to process event postings.

is shown in Figure 23.16. Although the figure looks similar to Figure 23.15, notice that the broker keeps an association between named events and event-handling modules, and uses `notify` to communicate with an event-handling module. The association between the event-handling module and the event-handling routine is kept in the TP monitor, as before.

As with other forms of communication, communication through events can cause a transaction to propagate from one module to another. For example, if the action `post(Event)` was performed as part of a transaction in the event-generating module, the resulting handler execution can become part of that transaction as well. In some situations, however, the handler's execution should not be part of the transaction that posted the event. For example, a transaction performing some database activities might find an uncorrectable database error, which requires it to abort. Before aborting, the transaction might want to post an event to notify the database administrator of the error. The event handler should not be a part of the transaction. If it were, it would be aborted when the transaction aborts and the database administrator would not be notified. The rules governing when transactions propagate as a result of event postings are a part of the protocol implemented by the transaction processing system.

23.8 Storage Architectures

One of the goals of the various architectures we have been discussing is to increase transaction throughput. Many large systems require a throughput of thousands of transactions per second. There is one bottleneck to achieving such throughput that we have not yet discussed: disk I/O. Although processor and memory speeds continue to increase significantly every year, disk-access speeds increase much less rapidly and are still measured in milliseconds. It is hard to achieve a throughput of a thousand transactions per second when each disk access takes a time measured in thousandths of a second.

Disk caches. One approach to increasing throughput involves the use of the disk cache maintained by the DBMS. A disk cache is a region in main memory in which recently accessed database pages are stored. If at some later time, a transaction either reads or updates an item on a page that is stored in the cache, a disk access will have been avoided and a hit will be said to have occurred.

We discussed disc caches in detail in Section 12.1. Here we just note that to obtain a high throughput, many designers consider it mandatory to obtain a hit rate of over 90% (90% of the accesses can be satisfied from the cache). To achieve such a hit rate, the cache size must often be a significant percentage of the size of the database. In some large applications, the cache size is measured in tens of gigabytes.

RAID systems and disk striping. Even if a 95% cache hit rate can be achieved, the remaining 5% of accesses that require disk I/O can considerably slow down the system. Another way to increase throughput is through the use of RAID systems with disk striping. A **Redundant Array of Independent Disks (RAID)** system consists of a set of disks configured to appear to the operating system to be a single disk with increased throughput and reliability compared to the throughput and reliability of the individual disks making up the RAID. The increased throughput is obtained by partitioning—or striping—each file across several disks, and the increased reliability is obtained using some form of redundant storage.

We discussed RAID systems in detail in Section 9.1.1. Here we just remind you that (1) a number of different levels of RAID systems have been defined, depending on the type of data striping and redundancy they provide; and (2) the levels usually recommended for high performance transaction processing applications are Level 5 with a write cache (block-level striping of both data and parity information) and Level 10 (a striped array of mirrored disks).

Direct attached storage. It is often the case that the database is spread over several disks or RAID systems, directly connected to a DBMS. This might be done because the database is too large to fit on a single disk or because the system can achieve higher throughput if it can access several disks concurrently. For example, different tables might be stored on different disks. When several transactions access the tables, or when one transaction wants to perform a join on the tables, the accesses can be done concurrently. Alternatively, a single table might be explicitly partitioned (in the schema) into several tables, each of which is stored on a different disk (a subset of the rows or columns is stored on each disk). Then, for example, operations that require a complete table scan can be done concurrently. We discussed partitioning as a way to do database tuning in Sections 12.2.4 and 12.5 and as a way to distribute data in a distributed database system in Section 16.2.

Network attached storage and storage area networks. Instead of having the disks, RAID systems, or other storage devices connected directly to the DBMS, they might be put on a network connected to the DBMS. We discuss two different architectures of this type.

- In **network attached storage** (NAS), the storage devices are directly connected to a file server—sometimes called an **appliance**—instead of to the DBMS. The file server is a resource manager that provides a general-purpose storage facility. It offers its services to clients and other servers (e.g., DBMSs) through a network. Thus, the files stored on the appliance can be shared among all the applications and servers on the network.
- In a **storage area network** (SAN), a DBMS or file server communicates with its storage devices through a separate, high-speed network. The network operates at about the speed of the bus on which a storage device might be directly connected to the server. The server accesses the devices using the same commands (and at the same speed) as if it were connected directly to them. Clients and other servers communicate with the server through a separate (conventional) network similar to the one on which a NAS might be connected.

Both NAS and SAN networks can scale to a much larger number of storage devices than if those devices were directly connected to a server. Scaling with NAS involves adding additional file servers. Scaling with SAN, in addition, involves adding more storage devices on the high-speed network.

SANs are generally thought to be preferable for high-performance transaction processing applications because they allow the DBMS to manage the storage devices directly instead of accessing files indirectly through a file server.

A NAS might be more appropriate for an application that requires a large amount of file sharing among different servers. One example might be the Web site for a national newspaper with an archiving service, in which a number of servers need to share access to a large set of Web pages that might be requested by clients.

23.9 Transaction Processing on the Internet

The growth of the Internet has stimulated the development of many Internet services involving distributed transactions and heterogeneous systems. These services are provided by servers, called Web servers, that are capable of communicating over the Web. Often Web servers have throughput requirements of thousands of transactions per second. The systems generally fall into two categories: **customer-to-business** (C2B) and **business-to-business** (B2B). You are probably familiar with C2B systems.

These are the ones which you, as a customer, interact with over the Internet. For example, you might buy a book at *Amazon.com*. Your interaction involves fetching pages from Amazon's Web site that are displayed by your Web browser, entering data in input boxes, and clicking on links and buttons.

B2B systems are more complex since they are fully automated. A program on one business's Web site communicates with a program on another business's Web site with no human intervention (and without the use of a browser). Instead of simply purchasing a few items, a B2B system might involve complex agreement protocols and substantial commercial transactions.

Internet services can be decomposed into two parts. Front-end systems deal with the interface that the system offers to customers and businesses. How is the system described to users? How is it invoked? Back-end systems deal with implementing the application that actually provides the service.

In the next subsection we discuss the architecture of C2B systems in which the front end is provided by a Web browser and the back end is provided using the architecture discussed earlier in this chapter. Section 23.10 then describes how the back end of C2B systems can be implemented using commercial Web application servers. The same back-end implementation can be used for B2B systems, but with a different front end. B2B front-ends are discussed extensively in Chapter 25.

23.9.1 Architectures for C2B Transaction Processing Systems on the Internet

Web transaction processing systems often make use of two Java constructs: the applet and the servlet. When a Web server supporting C2B interactions sends a page to a customer's browser, it can include with the page one or more programs, called **applets**, written in Java.[6] Applets execute in a programming environment supplied with the browser. They can animate the page, respond to certain events (such as mouse clicks), and interact with the user and the network in other ways.

The browser displays the page when it is received and possibly executes specified applets. The page might include buttons, text boxes, and the like, to be filled in by the user. Associated with the page, but usually hidden from the user, is (1) the URL of a Web server (perhaps different from the one that sent the page) to which the user-supplied information is to be transmitted, and (2) the name of an application on that server to process the information.

While applets are client-side applications, a **servlet** is a Java program on the server that makes use of standard Java servlet API that supports many of the activities needed by server-side applications. For example, methods are provided for reading and writing the information on an HTML page. A servlet has a lifetime that extends beyond the interactions of any single user. When a servlet is started, it creates a number of threads. The threads are allocated dynamically to serve requests for service as they arrive. Requests are generally submitted using the HTTP protocol

[6] Or they might include Microsoft's ActiveX Controls, which are typically written in Visual Basic.

(discussed in Section 25.3) and might be sent by a browser or by another application on the Web. The servlet can concurrently handle as many requests as there are threads.

Servlets are not the only way used to interact with Web servers. An older mechanism involves **CGI scripts**. CGI is technically inferior to servlets but has the advantage that scripts can be written in any language, while servlets must be written in Java. Another mechanism that is quickly gaining momentum is **.NET**. Like CGI, applications can be written in any language, but for the moment the .NET infrastructure is available only for the Windows platform. Java servlets, on the other hand, can be made platform independent.

We discuss three possible ways in which a transaction processing system can be organized to provide C2B service over the Internet.

1. *Two-tiered.* The browser acts as both a presentation and an application server, and the database server resides at the Internet site containing the Web server. The servlet thread at the Web server responds to a request from a browser with an HTML page (with which the user interacts), together with the application program written as a Java applet. After the user fills in the appropriate fields on the page, the applet, which implements the enterprise rules, executes from within the browser. The applet might initiate a transaction and then submit SQL statements or call stored procedures for processing by the database server. The applet communicates with the database server using JDBC (see Section 8.5). This model is similar to that of Figure 8.9, page 295. The JDBC driver might be downloaded from the Web server with the Java applet, in which case it sets up a network connection to the database server. Or the driver might reside on the Web server and receive commands from the browser as data through the servlet thread.
2. *Three-tiered.* The browser acts as the presentation server, and the servlet thread on the Web server acts as the application server. When the Web server is contacted, a servlet thread sends the browser an HTML page with which the user interacts. When the user fills in the page and submits it to the server, a servlet thread, which implements the enterprise rules, is assigned to that interaction. Now the servlet thread, instead of the applet, might initiate a transaction on the database server, as in Figure 23.4. When the servlet thread completes, it can return an HTML page to the browser.
3. *Four-tiered.* Most high-throughput applications use the architecture shown in Figure 23.17 in which there are three tiers at the server site (these, in fact, can be three different sites) and one tier at the browser site. The browser connects to the servlet thread on the Web server, which then processes the information returned by the browser. The Web server might respond to the browser with a new page, or it might invoke an appropriate program on the application server to process the user's request. The application server executes on a different computer, which might be separated from the Web server by a **firewall** to protect it from receiving spurious messages from other sources. The application program might initiate transactions involving data on the database server, which might

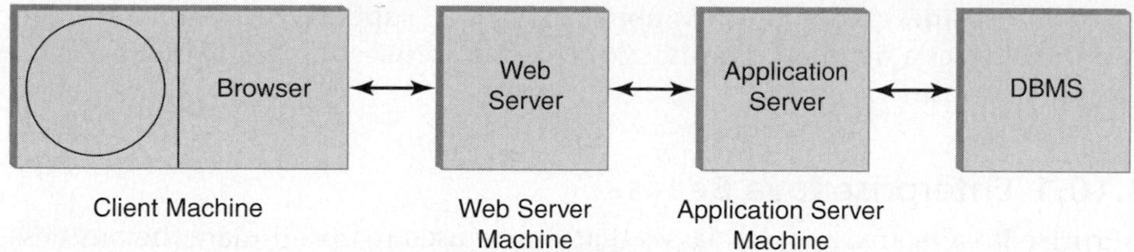

FIGURE 23.17 An Internet-based client connected to a four-tiered transaction processing system.

be separated from the application server computer by a (different) firewall.[7] When the application program completes and returns information to the servlet thread, the thread prepares the appropriate HTML page and returns it to the browser. The application server views the browser and the Web server together as its presentation server.

This architecture is particularly appropriate for high-throughput applications because it allows multiple application servers. The Web server might include a load-balancing module that selects a particular application server to support a user session. An application server might access multiple database servers throughout the enterprise (for example, inventory, shipping, and billing databases) and in other enterprises (for example, for credit card approval). For really high-throughput applications, there might also be multiple Web servers, with an extra layer of HTTP routers that are connected directly to the Internet, whose job is to relay an HTTP request to a particular Web server.

To further increase throughput, systems using this architecture might cache appropriate information on all tiers. For example, the Web server might cache commonly used HTML pages, and the application server might cache commonly used entity beans (see below).

23.10 Web Application Servers—J2EE

A number of vendors provide products called **Web application servers**, which include modules that can be used to build transaction processing systems for the Web. Web application servers provide similar functionality to TP monitors and include services that are particularly oriented toward Web applications. Unfortunately, the terminology is confusing since Web application servers are frequently called simply "application servers" and we have been using that term to describe only the middle tier of a transaction processing system. To avoid any confusion, we will continue to use the term "Web application server" to refer to the commercial products.

Most commercial Web application servers are built using the technology of Java 2 Enterprise Edition (J2EE). Only Microsoft's Web application server is based on .NET technology. J2EE includes a set of Java classes, called *beans*, that can be adapted to

[7] Firewalls can also be used in three-tiered and other Web architectures.

support the business methods of an application. J2EE supports Java servlets and in addition provides a number of transaction-oriented services especially designed for Web applications.

23.10.1 Enterprise Java Beans

Enterprise Java beans are Java classes that can be used to encapsulate the business methods of an enterprise. They are generally invoked by a servlet and execute within an infrastructure of services provided by J2EE. The infrastructure supports transactions, persistence, concurrency, authorization, etc. In particular, it implements the declarative model of transaction demarcation discussed in Section 19.3.3. This allows the bean programmer to focus on the business rules and methods of the enterprise rather than on the system-level aspects of the application.

There are three types of enterprise Java Beans: *entity beans*, *session beans*, and *message-driven beans*. We discuss them in the following paragraphs.

Entity beans. Each **entity bean** represents a persistent business object whose state is stored in a database. Typically, each entity bean corresponds to a database table, and each instance of that bean corresponds to a row in the table. For example, in a banking application, there might be an entity bean called ACCOUNT, with fields that include `accountId`, `ownerName`, `socSecNum`, and `balance` and with methods that include `Deposit` and `Withdraw`. The ACCOUNT bean might correspond to a database table called ACCOUNT with attributes `accountId`, `ownerName`, `socSecNum`, and `balance`. Each instance of the ACCOUNT bean corresponds to a row in the ACCOUNT table. Each entity bean must have a primary key. For the ACCOUNT bean, the primary key might be `accountId`.

Entity beans can be used in an application program just like any other object. However, any changes made to an entity bean by the program are *persistent* in that they are propagated to the corresponding item in the database. Thus, in the banking application, any changes to the `balance` field of an instance of the ACCOUNT bean are propagated to the `balance` attribute in the corresponding row in the ACCOUNT table.

Persistence can be managed either by the bean itself, using SQL code written by the application programmer, or automatically by the system. Every entity bean must execute within the context of a transaction, and that transaction must be managed by the system. We will discuss these issues later in this section. Because the state of an entity bean is saved in a database, its lifetime extends beyond any one interaction and even survives system crashes.

Session beans. A **session bean** is instantiated when a client initiates an interaction with the system. It maintains the context, or state, of the client's session and supplies the methods that implement client requests. An example of a session bean is SHOPPINGCART, which provides the services of adding items to a "shopping cart" as the customer scans a catalog and then of purchasing the selected items. Each such service is provided by one or more business methods of the bean. Examples of such methods might be `AddItemToShoppingCart` and `CheckOut`. The context maintained

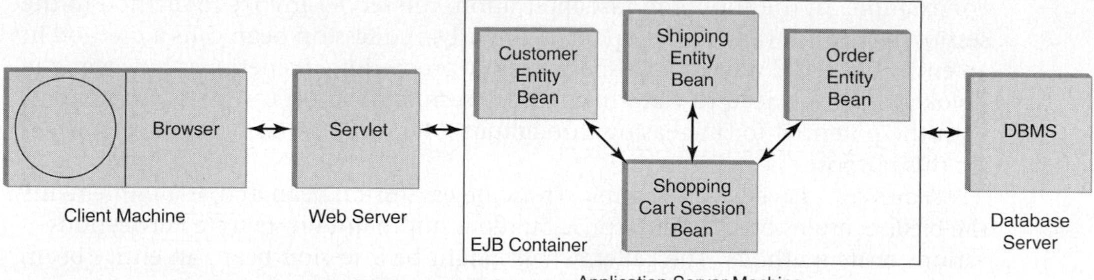

FIGURE 23.18 A four-tiered Internet-based architecture for the shopping-cart transaction.

by an instance of SHOPPINGCART would identify the items in the client's shopping cart.

Session beans can also be stateless, in which case they do not maintain context between requests. An example of a stateless session bean is STOCKQUOTE, an instance of which responds to a sequence of individual requests from a client for stock quotations. In this case no context is needed. All the information required to satisfy a request is contained in the parameters of the method call.

The lifetime of a session bean is just one session. The state of the bean is not persistent beyond that session and does not survive system crashes. In the shopping cart application, we might say that customers get their own shopping carts, which are returned after they leave the store.

Session beans can use the services of entity beans. When the customer wants to complete an order by purchasing the items in the shopping cart, the `CheckOut` method is called. It, in turn, calls methods in the appropriate entity beans, CUSTOMER, ORDER, and SHIPPING, to record the purchase in the corresponding database tables.

A session bean can also call other session beans, perhaps on other J2EE servers, if it needs to use their services. For example, to transfer funds between accounts at different banks, the session bean at the first bank might need to use the services of a session bean at the second bank.

A method in a session bean can be transactional. For example, the `CheckOut` method in SHOPPINGCART might execute as a transaction. Transactions can be managed either by the bean itself using standard JDBC code or automatically by the system as described later in this section.

An architecture for a four-tiered implementation of the shopping application is shown in Figure 23.18. The browser accesses a servlet on the Web server. The servlet calls the appropriate method in the SHOPPINGCART session bean on the application server. The method in SHOPPINGCART calls appropriate methods in the entity beans, which then make their state persistent in the database on the database server. Each instance of a purchase is executed as a transaction.

Message-driven beans. All of the communication we have discussed so far involves invoking methods in session or entity beans and is therefore synchronous.

For example, in the shopping cart application, the servlet invokes a method in the session bean and waits for a response. Similarly, the session bean calls a method in an entity bean and waits for a response before proceeding. Sometimes, however, the invoker does not need to wait. In that case communication can be asynchronous, with the potential for increasing throughput. **Message-driven beans** are provided for this purpose.

A message-driven bean is similar to a stateless session bean in that it implements the business rules of some enterprise but does not maintain its state between invocations of its methods. The caller, which might be a session bean, an entity bean, another message-driven bean, or any system or component that uses **Java Message Service** (JMS), invokes the message-driven bean by sending it a message. The message is buffered on a JMS message queue. When a message arrives on a message queue, the system calls an appropriate message-driven bean to process that message. Thus a message-driven bean acts as a message **listener**, waiting for the arrival of a message. JMS message queues have the same semantics as the recoverable queues discussed in Section 23.2.3. The sender does not wait, and the message-driven bean does not return a result when it completes. Thus, message-driven beans provide a mechanism that allows applications to operate asynchronously.

For example, a method in the session bean for the shopping-cart application might send an asynchronous message to the shipping-department application telling it to ship the purchased items. The session bean method can then terminate. The shipping department might have a message queue, ShippingMessageQueue, on which it receives such messages and a message-driven bean, SHIPPINGMESSAGEQUEUELISTENER, which processes messages according to the business rules of the enterprise. Each message-driven bean must have an `onMessage` method that is invoked automatically when a message is received. The method performs the service requested in the message and can call methods in other beans for this purpose.

A message-driven bean is stateless: after an instance of the bean has completed processing one message, its state is deallocated and the bean can be immediately reused to process another message on the queue from the same or a different application. As with a session bean, methods in a message-driven bean can be transactional, and that transaction can be managed either by the bean itself or by the system.

Structure of an enterprise Java bean. Every enterprise Java bean has an `ejb-name`. For example, the name of the shopping-cart session bean might be SHOPPINGCART. An entity or session bean consists of a number of parts: (1) the bean class, which contains the implementation of the business methods of the enterprise; (2) a deployment descriptor, which contains metadata describing the bean; and (3) various interfaces. As described in more detail below, clients access the bean only through these interfaces. The interfaces contain the signatures of the business methods, whose implementations are in the bean class, and signatures of other methods, whose purpose is to control various life-cycle issues (e.g., creation and destruction of the bean). In contrast to the methods in the bean class, the system provides the implementation of the methods whose declaration is given in the interfaces. A

FIGURE 23.19 A portion of a deployment descriptor describing authorization properties.

```
<method-permission>
     <role-name>teller</role-name>
     <method>
          <ejb-name>Account</ejb-name>
          <method-name>Withdraw</method-name>
     </method>
</method-permission>
```

message-driven bean consists of only a bean class and a deployment descriptor (no interfaces) since clients can access it only through its message queue.

- The **bean class** contains the business methods of an enterprise. For example, the bean class of SHOPPINGCART might be called SHOPPINGCARTBEAN and might contain business methods `AddItemToShoppingCart` and `CheckOut`. The bean programmer must provide application code for these business methods.
- The **deployment descriptor** contains declarative metadata describing the bean. For an entity bean, the descriptor can specify persistence information (i.e., how it relates to a database table), transactional information (i.e., what is the transactional semantics when a method is called), and authorization information (i.e., who is allowed to invoke a method). For a session or message-driven bean, the deployment descriptor can describe its transactional and authorization properties. For example, the deployment descriptor for the `Withdraw` method of an ACCOUNT entity bean must specify that it is to be executed as a transaction, and it might specify that it can be invoked on behalf of either the owner of the account or a teller. It might also specify that its persistence is to be managed by the bean programmer (rather than automatically).

  Deployment descriptors are written in XML and can be quite complex. Fortunately, most Web application servers provide graphic tools that can be used to build deployment descriptors by filling in various forms on the screen. Figure 23.19 shows part of a deployment descriptor that specifies that the `Withdraw` method in the ACCOUNT bean can be executed by a teller. We discuss how persistence and transactional properties are specified later in this section.
- The **remote interface** is used by clients to access an entity or session bean that is executing on the server. Remote access is provided by Java's RMI (Remote Method Interface), which has facilities similar to RPC. For each method in the bean class, the signature of a corresponding method is declared in the remote interface. The client calls the interface method rather than directly calling the bean method. Hence, the interface method acts as a proxy for the associated bean method. The interface method executes on the server along with the corresponding bean method. It implements the semantics specified in the deployment descriptor and then calls the bean method. For example, if the deployment

descriptor specifies that a bean method is to be executed as a transaction, the corresponding interface method initiates a transaction and then calls the bean method. When the call returns, the interface method commits or aborts the transaction. The remote interface for the SHOPPINGCART session bean might also be called SHOPPINGCART. It contains methods `AddItemToShoppingCart` and `CheckOut`. The bean programmer must supply declarations for these interface methods, but the system provides the implementation based on information in the deployment descriptor.

- The (optional) **local interface** is used by local components (i.e., components in the same container—see below) to access methods within an entity or session bean without the overhead of RMI. For example, beans local to the ACCOUNT entity bean might want to use its `Deposit` and `Withdraw` methods, so signatures corresponding to these methods would be included in the local interface. The local interface for the ACCOUNT entity bean might be called LOCALACCOUNT. As with the remote interface, the methods in the local interface act as proxies for the methods in the bean class. When a local interface method is called, it implements the semantics specified in the deployment descriptor and then calls the corresponding bean method. The bean programmer must supply declarations for these interface methods, but the system provides the implementation.

  The semantics of local and remote interfaces are not identical. For remote interfaces, parameters are passed by value/result; for local interfaces, they are passed by reference.

- A **home interface** declares the signatures of methods that control the life cycle of a bean. Methods for creating and removing beans fall in this category. In this context, the home interface is often referred to as a **factory** since it produces new instances of the bean. Any remote client of the bean can call these home interface methods.

  For example, the home interface for the SHOPPINGCART session bean class might be called SHOPPINGCARTHOME. A client that wants to establish a new shopping session calls the `create()` method of SHOPPINGCART to create a new instance of the bean to use in the session. Create is a static method. That is, it operates on the class as a whole, not on an individual instance. The client later calls a `remove()` method to remove the instance when the session is completed.

  The home interface for the ACCOUNT entity bean class might be called ACCOUNTHOME. A client that wants to establish a new account calls the create method of ACCOUNTHOME to create a new instance of the bean (a new row in the table) corresponding to the new account.

  The home interface for an entity bean also declares signatures of finder methods that can be used to locate one or more instances of a particular bean and return references to them. A finder method is also a static method. For example, a client that wants to deposit money in a particular account might first use the method `findByPrimaryKey()` to obtain a reference to the particular instance of the entity bean corresponding to the primary key supplied as an argument. It can then use the reference to invoke the methods of that instance. The bean

FIGURE 23.20 A portion of a deployment descriptor for a session bean showing how the various interfaces of the bean are named and declaring that the bean is stateful and executes container-managed transactions.

```
<enterprise-beans>
    <session>
        <ejb-name>ShoppingCart</ejb-name>
        <remote>ShoppingCart</remote>
        <local>LocalShoppingCart</local>
        <home>ShoppingCartHome</home>
        <local-home>LocalShoppingCartHome</local-home>
        <ejb-class>ShoppingCartBean</ejb-class>
        <session-type>stateful</session-type>
        <transaction-type>container</transaction-type>
        ......
    </session>
    ......
</enterprise-beans>
```

programmer can declare other finder methods as well, for example, to find all the accounts corresponding to a particular `ownerName`.

- The (optional) **local home interface** is used by local clients (within the same container) to access life-cycle (and finder) bean methods. The home interface for the ACCOUNT entity bean class might be called LOCALACCOUNTHOME.

Figure 23.20 shows a portion of a deployment descriptor of the SHOPPINGCART session bean that specifies the names of the various interfaces of the bean. Note that `ejb-name` specifies the name of the bean, while `ejb-class` is the bean class that contains the implementation of the business methods implemented by the bean. The deployment descriptor also specifies that the session bean is stateful and that the transactions it executes are container-managed (as discussed later).

By contrast, Figure 23.21 shows a similar portion of a deployment descriptor of the SHIPPINGMESSAGEQUEUELISTENER message-driven bean. Note that a message-driven bean has no remote, local, or home interfaces, but instead the descriptor contains information about the bean's message queue. The EJB 2.1 specification allows message-driven beans to accept messages from messaging services other than JMS. In the figure, the `<messaging-type>` attribute states that the bean is using JMS, the `<message-destination-type>` attribute states that the bean uses a JMS Queue (corresponding to point-to-point JMS messaging) rather than a Topic (corresponding to publish/subscribe messaging), and the `<message-destination-link>` is a link to the name of the queue. Later, in Figure 23.23, we show a portion of a deployment descriptor of an entity bean.

FIGURE 23.21 A portion of a deployment descriptor for a message-driven bean.

```
<enterprise-beans>
  <message-driven>
    <ejb-name>ShippingMessageQueueListener</ejb-name>
    <ejb-class>ShippingMessageQueueListenerBean</ejb-class>
    <messaging-type>javax.jms.MessageListener</messaging-type>
    <transaction-type>container</transaction-type>
    <message-destination-type>javax.jms.Queue</message-destination-type>
    <message-destination-link>ShippingMessageQueue</message-destination-link>
    ......
  </message-driven>
......
</enterprise-beans>
```

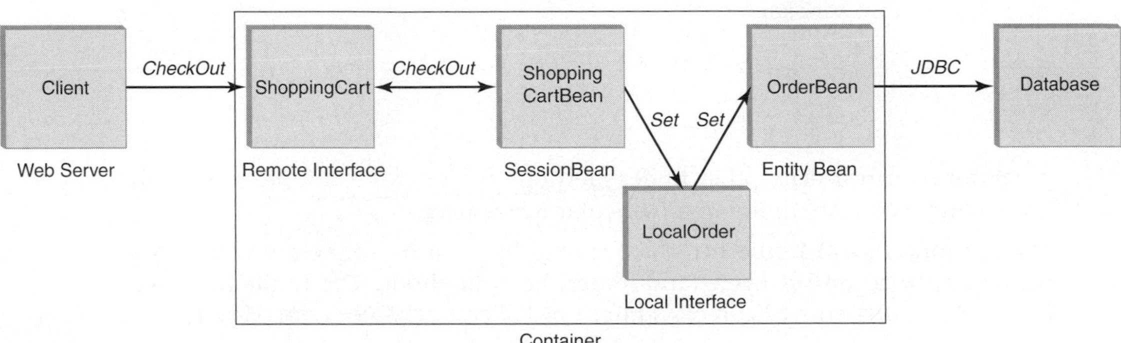

FIGURE 23.22 The remote and local interfaces within the container for one interaction in the SHOPPINGCART session bean.

23.10.2 The EJB Container

Enterprise Java beans execute in a special environment called an **EJB container**, which is provided by the Web application server. An EJB container can support multiple beans. The container provides system-level support for the beans, based partly on the metadata in their deployment descriptors.

The interface methods, together with the methods of the beans, execute in the context of the container. The client invokes an interface method instead of directly invoking the corresponding bean method. The interface method implements the semantics specified in the deployment descriptor when the call is made and then calls the bean method. The situation is shown in Figure 23.22. The methods of the home interface also execute in the context of the container.

Persistence of entity beans: container-managed persistence. The persistence of an entity bean can be managed either by the bean itself, using JDBC code written by the bean programmer—**bean-managed persistence**—or automatically by the EJB container based on information in the bean's deployment descriptor—**container-managed persistence**. We discuss container-managed persistence (CMP) in what follows and deal with bean-managed persistence later in the section.

With CMP, the container explicitly creates and maintains connections to the database, relieving the client of this responsibility. The deployment descriptor is used to specify the connection protocol to connect to that database. However, deployment descriptor formats for these purposes are vendor specific, and we do not discuss them here.

With CMP, the container handles all the database accesses; the bean contains no code to access the database. The programmer must declaratively specify the persistent fields within the bean's deployment descriptor. The default assumption is that the name of the entity bean is the same as the name of the corresponding table and that the fields of an entity bean and the attributes in the corresponding database table have the same names. The bean name and field names (together with relationships, which we discuss later) are part of the **abstract schema** of the bean.

The term "abstract" is used to distinguish the schema of the bean from the physical schema of the underlying database. Since the bean methods are written in terms of the abstract schema and do not contain the code to connect to or access the database, the bean becomes portable: it can be connected to a different database by appropriately modifying the deployment descriptor. However, J2EE only describes the default mapping of the abstract schema of the bean to the physical schema of the database, one which is based on the identity of the names. It does not say how such a mapping should be described in the deployment descriptor when the names in the abstract and the physical schemas differ. Each vendor can provide a proprietary method to describe such mappings.

The deployment descriptor specifies the fields that are to be persistent and managed by the container. For example, Figure 23.23 shows a portion of a deployment descriptor for the ACCOUNT entity bean showing that the `balance` and `accountId` fields are container managed and that the `accountId` field is the primary key.

With CMP, the bean programmer must declare in the entity bean a `get` method and a `set` method for each persistent field. For example, the methods for the `balance` field of the ACCOUNT entity bean are

```
public abstract float getBalance( );
public abstract void setBalance(float Balance);
```

The name of an access method must start with `get` or `set` followed by the capitalized name of the persistent field. When the bean is deployed in the EJB container, the container generates the appropriate code for these methods. In a similar fashion, the signatures of the methods in the home interface must be provided by the bean programmer, but the bodies are provided automatically when the bean is deployed.

`get` and `set` methods can be included in the local and remote interface of the bean so that fields can be manipulated by bean clients. Thus, when a client wants to make a withdrawal from the bank, the client's session bean can either call the

FIGURE 23.23 A portion of a deployment descriptor for an entity bean showing how fields are specified as container managed and which field represents the primary key.

```
<enterprise-beans>
    <entity>
        <ejb-name>Account</ejb-name>
        <remote>Account</remote>
        <local>LocalAccount</local>
        <home>AccountHome</home>
        <local-home>LocalAccountHome</local-home>
        <ejb-class>AccountBean</ejb-class>
        <persistence-type>Container</persistence-type>
        <cmp-field>
            <field-name>balance</field-name>
        </cmp-field>
        <cmp-field>
            <field-name>accountId</field-name>
        </cmp-field>
        <primkey-field>accountId</primkey-field>
        ......
    </entity>
......
</enterprise-beans>
```

`Withdraw` method in the entity bean (assuming such a method exists) or it might directly call the `getBalance` and `setBalance` methods of the entity bean to do the same thing. Of course, this second alternative reveals to the session bean information about the internal organization of the database (an attribute name) that might better be kept concealed. Note that, if the session bean calls the `Withdraw` method in the entity bean, the `Withdraw` method will call the same `getBalance` and `setBalance` methods since that is the only way to access the `balance` field of the bean: with CMP, the fields cannot be accessed directly using SQL statements.

The `set` method does not immediately cause the database to be updated. The method that actually updates the database is called `ejbStore`. The implementation of `ejbStore` is also generated by the container. Recall that an entity bean can be used only in the context of a transaction. When that transaction commits, `ebStore` is automatically called by the container to perform the appropriate updates.

Container-managed relationships. For entity beans that have CMP, the container can also provide a **container-managed relationship** (CMR). In addition to fields that represent data items, such as `balance`, entity beans can have fields that represent relationships between entity beans. These are the relationships we first introduced in Section 4.3. They can be one-to-one, one-to-many, or many-to-many, and they can be unidirectional or bidirectional.

For example, the entity beans ACCOUNT and BANKCUSTOMER might be related through a relationship called ACCOUNTSIGNERS. The relationship might be implemented in ACCOUNT using a relationship field signers. The value of signers in a particular instance of ACCOUNT contains references to the instances of BANKCUSTOMER corresponding to customers who can sign checks for the account. If the relationship is bidirectional, BANKCUSTOMER will also have a relationship field, perhaps named canSignFor. Its value, in a particular instance of BANKCUSTOMER, contains references to the instances of ACCOUNT corresponding to accounts for which that customer can sign. ACCOUNTSIGNERS is a many-to-many relationship since multiple customers can sign for a single account and multiple accounts can be signed for by a single customer. The relationship allows an application to locate related entities starting from either a customer or an account.

If a relationship is declared to be container managed in the deployment descriptor, the container will implement the relationship in the tables of the database. Figure 23.24 shows a portion of the deployment descriptor for the relationship ACCOUNTSIGNERS. Note that a relationship has an ejb-relation-name, and each participant in the relationship has an ejb-relationship-role-name. A new field is declared in both ACCOUNT and BANKCUSTOMER indicating the bidirectionality. The field types are Java collections, indicating that the relationship is many-to-many. If the relationship had been unidirectional, only one new field would have been declared.

The container will create a new table to store a many-to-many relationship such as signers. For a one-to-one relationship, it will create an appropriate foreign key in both tables participating in the relationship.

The bean programmer must declare within both entity beans participating in the relationship the appropriate get and set methods for the relationship fields. For example, for ACCOUNT

```
public abstract Collection getSigners( );
public abstract void setSigners(Collection BankCustomers):
```

Note the use of collections to handle the "many" part of the relationship. Thus the getSigners method returns the collection of references to the entity beans corresponding to BANKCUSTOMERS who can sign checks for the account. The setSigners method sets the signers relationship field in the ACCOUNT entity bean to be the collection of references to the BANKCUSTOMER entity beans specified in the method's parameter. Similarly, a getCanSignFor and setCanSignFor method would be provided for BANKCUSTOMER.

The container generates the code for the get and set methods, including code to maintain the referential integrity of the relationship (Section 3.2.2) as specified in the deployment descriptor.

CMRs can be specified only among entity beans that are in the same container. The get and set methods for relationships are invoked through the local interface of the bean, not the remote interface.

FIGURE 23.24 A portion of a deployment descriptor describing a relationship.

```
<ejb-relation>
    <ejb-relation-name>AccountSigners</ejb-relation-name>
    <ejb-relationship-role>
        <ejb-relationship-role-name>account-has-signers
            </ejb-relationship-role-name>
        <multiplicity>many</multiplicity>
        <relationship-role-source>
            <ejb-name>Account</ejb-name>
        </relationship-role-source>
        <cmr-field>
            <cmr-field-name>signers</cmr-field-name>
            <cmr-field-type>java.util.Collection</cmr-field-type>
        </cmr-field>
    </ejb-relationship-role>
    <ejb-relationship-role>
        <ejb-relationship-role-name>customers-sign-accounts
            </ejb-relationship-role-name>
        <multiplicity>many</multiplicity>
        <relationship-role-source>
            <ejb-name>BankCustomer</ejb-name>
        </relationship-role-source>
        <cmr-field>
            <cmr-field-name>canSignFor</cmr-field-name>
            <cmr-field-type>java.util.Collection</cmr-field-type>
        </cmr-field>
    </ejb-relationship-role>
</ejb-relation>
```

EJB Query Language: finder methods and select methods. For CMP, the code for the method `findByPrimaryKey()` is automatically generated by the container, based on the entry in the deployment descriptor giving the name of the primary key. The container will also generate the code for other finder methods declared in the home interface, based on queries specified in the deployment descriptor using a query language, **EJB QL** (EJB Query Language). EJB QL is based on SQL but is embedded in XML.

Figure 23.25 shows a portion of a deployment descriptor for a finder method `findByName` that might be included in either or both the remote and the local home interface of ACCOUNT. It contains a query to be used as the basis of the method. `ownerName` is one of the fields of ACCOUNT. The query returns a collection, each element of which maps to the remote or local interface (depending on whether the finder method is declared in the remote home interface or the local home interface of the bean) of an instance of ACCOUNT. Hence, a client can use the result of the query

FIGURE 23.25 A portion of a deployment descriptor describing an EJB QL query.

```
<query>
    <query-method>
        <method-name>findByName</method-name>
        <method-params>
            <method-param>string</method-param>
        </method-params>
    </query method>
    <ejb-ql>
        select object(A) from Account A where A.ownerName = ?1
    </ejb-ql>
</query>
```

to invoke the methods of any entity bean referred to in the collection. The name of the owner of each bean in the collection is the value of the positional parameter denoted ?1. The keyword OBJECT denotes the fact that its argument, the variable A, ranges over instances of a class.

EJB QL can also be used to specify queries for select methods. A **select method** is more general than a get (which can return only the value of a field of a particular instance of a bean) and finder methods (which can return only collections of references to instances of the bean that contains the finder method). In addition to mimicking a finder method, a select method can return a collection of field values (this corresponds to a result set) or an aggregation over field values. For example, a bank might enforce a business rule that allows the balance in a depositor's account to be negative, as long as the sum of the balances in all accounts owned by that depositor is positive. Hence, the withdraw method, in addition to updating the balance field of a particular account, needs to sum up the balance fields of other accounts having the same social security number. It does this using a select method based on the query

```
SELECT SUM S.balance
  FROM ACCOUNT A
  WHERE A.socSecNum = ?1
```

Note that the keyword OBJECT is not used in the SELECT clause since S.balance is not a range variable.

In addition, a select method can return a collection of references to instances of related entity beans using a relationship field of the bean containing the select method. This requires the use of path expressions, and we do not discuss it here.

Select methods are static methods (since they must access all instances). They can be invoked only from within a method of the entity bean itself, and hence they are not declared in any interface. Furthermore, they implement only a subset of the semantics of SQL's SELECT statements. For example, the current version of the

EJB specifications (version 2.1) does not allow select methods to perform joins, but later versions might allow them. As with finder methods, with CMP, the container generates the code for a select method.

Persistence of entity beans: bean-managed persistence. With bean-managed persistence (BMP), the bean programmer must provide the JDBC statements to access the database. One reason why a system designer might decide to use BMP is to map an entity bean to a view involving several tables instead of mapping the bean to a single table. CMP could not automatically deal with such a mapping.

Whether persistence is bean managed or container managed, clients of the bean must use the life-cycle methods in the bean's home interface: for example, the create, remove, and finder methods. For BMP, the container does not automatically generate the code for these methods. Code must be provided by the bean designer that uses SQL explicitly. Thus, the user-defined `create` method might involve an SQL INSERT statement, a remove method might involve an SQL DELETE statement, and finder methods might involve an SQL SELECT statement.

Even when designers choose BMP, they might build beans using `get` and `set` methods. But in this case the container does not automatically generate the code for these methods, and the designer must manually generate the programs for these methods using JDBC calls. Or the designer can choose not to use `get` and `set` at all and directly access the bean fields using JDBC.

As with CMP, the container automatically calls `ejbStore` when a transaction involving a bean commits. However, with BMP, the container does not automatically generate the code for `ejbStore`. The bean programmer can provide a program for `ejbStore` to perform the necessary updates or can provide a null program for `ejbStore` and perform the updates with standard JDBC calls within the bean methods.

Setting transaction boundaries. Two issues have to be dealt with if bean execution is to be transactional: transaction boundaries have to be set (this is primarily an issue of atomicity), and concurrency has to be managed (this is primarily an issue of isolation). We will deal with boundaries in this subsection and concurrency in the next.

A session or message-driven bean can initiate a transaction by explicitly executing an appropriate command, in which case we refer to the transaction as having **bean-managed demarcation**. Alternatively, transaction initiation for such beans can be automatically done by the EJB container when a bean method is called based on information in the bean's deployment descriptor. Such a transaction is referred to as having **container-managed demarcation**. Container-managed demarcation is an example of the use of declarative transaction demarcation, as described in Section 19.3.3.

An entity bean, on the other hand, cannot start a transaction explicitly (i.e., it cannot be specified to have bean-managed demarcation): transaction demarcation is required and must be container managed.

With bean-managed demarcation, the bean programmer must explicitly specify within the bean the appropriate JDBC or JTA statements to start and commit (or abort) the transaction. An interesting aspect of the J2EE specification asserts that if a method in a stateful session bean with bean-managed demarcation initiates a transaction but does not commit or abort it, the transaction persists so that execution of the next method of the bean that is invoked becomes part of the same transaction. This continues until some method commits or aborts the transaction.

With container-managed demarcation, the programmer must declaratively specify in the deployment descriptor the circumstances under which a transaction is to be initiated (see below). This can be done for each individual method of the bean separately or for the bean as a whole.[8] The proxy routines in the remote and local interface are automatically generated in conformance with this information and execute within the container. Assuming a transaction is to be initiated, the interface method creates a transaction and then calls the corresponding bean method. When the method returns, the interface method can request that the transaction be committed or aborted.

In the case of container-managed demarcation for a message-driven bean, the transaction is initiated by the container *before* the `onMessage` method is called. As a result, the transaction includes the step of removing the message from the queue. Hence, if the transaction aborts, the message is returned to the queue and will be serviced later by another instance of the bean. By contrast, with bean-managed demarcation, the transaction is initiated explicitly during the execution of the `onMessage` method *after* the message has been removed from the queue. Thus if the transaction should abort, the message that initiated the transaction will not be put back on the queue, and hence the transaction will not be reexecuted.

The designer can specify in the deployment descriptor how the bean is to participate in a transaction. The possibilities (*Required*, *RequiresNew*, *Mandatory*, *NotSupported*, *Supports*, and *Never*) are described in detail in Section 19.3.3 and are summarized in Figure 19.3 on page 794. Certain restrictions exist on their use.

- For message-driven beans, only *Required* and *NotSupported* are allowed. If the method in the calling module (the module that sent the message) is part of a transaction then, based on the semantics of JMS, the message will not actually be placed (i.e., be visible) on the message queue until that transaction commits (see Section 23.2.3). Thus a message-driven bean is never called by a client from within a transaction that is active when the bean is started. This explains why only *Required* and *NotSupported* are allowed with message-driven beans.
- For stateless session beans, *Mandatory* is *not* allowed. If it were, and the bean was called from a client that is not in a transaction, the bean would throw an exception; hence the restriction.

[8] This type of declarative demarcation of transactions is also provided by the Microsoft MTS (Microsoft Transaction Service), which is part of .NET.

- For entity beans, only *Required*, *RequiresNew*, and *Mandatory* are allowed (since an entity bean must always execute within a transaction).

For example, a session bean might explicitly start a transaction (hence bean-managed demarcation) and then call an entity bean whose deployment descriptor specifies container-managed demarcation with attribute value *Required*. As a result, the method executed in the entity bean would be part of the same transaction, and the transaction as a whole would be characterized as having bean-managed demarcation. If the attribute value in the entity bean were *RequiresNew*, a new transaction having container-managed demarcation would be initiated when the entity bean is called and would commit on return.

The following element is a portion of a deployment descriptor stating that the `Checkout` method of the SHOPPINGCART session bean is to utilize container-managed transaction demarcation with attribute *Required*.

```
<container-transaction>
    <method>
        <ejb-name>ShoppingCart</ejb-name>
        <method-name>Checkout</method-name>
    </method>
    <trans-attribute>Required</trans-attribute>
</container-transaction>
```

Whether the demarcation is bean managed or container managed, the container includes a transaction manager, which acts as a coordinator for a two-phase commit protocol. For example, a single session bean might access several entity beans associated with multiple databases in the same container. The container's transaction manager would coordinate the beans at commit time. Alternatively, a session bean might call methods of other session beans, which might execute in different containers, and all of these session beans might access entity beans associated with different databases. In this case, the transaction managers of the set of containers involved would participate in the protocol as shown in Figure 24.4.

A transaction with container-managed demarcation is aborted and rolled back if a system exception is thrown or if a session or entity bean aborts itself by calling the `setRollbackOnly` method. A transaction with bean-managed demarcation aborts itself by explicitly calling the appropriate JDBC or JTA statements.

Managing transactional concurrency. By its nature, an instance of a message-driven bean is executed on behalf of only one client at a time: the client that sent the message. Furthermore, whenever a session or entity bean is called, the caller gets its own instance of that bean. Hence, beans are not multithreaded, and access to variables local to a bean does not require synchronization.

Concurrently executing instances of entity beans, however, can conflict with one another since a number of such beans might refer to the same row in a database table. Database accesses are handled in the normal way by the DBMS's concurrency control. The programmer might be satisfied with the default level of concurrency provided by the DBMS, or he can specify the level explicitly in the deployment descriptor or—for bean-managed demarcation—using the appropriate JDBC commands.

The J2EE standard does not say when the changes made by a transaction are to be propagated to the database. In most implementations, the changes are propagated when the transaction commits by `ejbStore`. However, this can lead to deadlocks (if a transaction first obtains a read lock when a `get` is executed and, at commit time, requests write locks to do the propagation). Some vendors of Web Application Servers allow the descriptor to specify that propagation is to occur at an earlier time. For example, propagation might be done at `set` time.

Some vendors offer alternatives to the J2EE approach to concurrency just discussed, which make use of delayed propagation. In one such alternative the container plays a role in controlling the isolation level. An optimistic algorithm is implemented. The container sets the isolation level at the DBMS to READ COMMITTED so that a transaction does not obtain any long-term read locks. When a `get` occurs, the value is read from the database into the entity bean, and when a `set` occurs the value is saved in the entity bean (and not written into the database). The entity bean is thus being used as an element of an intentions list (Section 20.9.2). When the transaction completes, the container performs a validation check to ensure that no item that the transaction read was written *since the read took place*. If the transaction passes the validation check, the updated items are then copied from the entity bean into the database. For example, the check might be performed as part of `ejbStore`.

Note that this is not the same validation check made in the optimistic concurrency control discussed in Section 20.9.2. In that control, when a transaction completes, a validation check is made to determine whether an item it read was changed by a concurrent transaction *any time within its read phase*. Both validation methods produce serializable schedules.

If instead, the validation checked only that the items that had been read *and then written* by the transaction had not been changed after the read took place, that would have been an implementation of OPTIMISTIC READ COMMITTED (Section 21.2.1) and would not necessarily yield serializable schedules.

23.10.3 Using Java Beans

Part of the vision underlying enterprise Java beans is that they could be reused. For example, Sam's Software Company might be in the business of supplying components to enterprises that want to build Internet business applications. Sam's might be selling a set of beans for shopping-cart applications, including a SHOPPINGCART session bean. Henry's Hardware Store, which wants to implement an Internet shopping-cart application, might purchase those beans from Sam's. Henry's system might use all the beans they purchased from Sam's, except that, instead of using SHOPPINGCART exactly, the system creates a child session bean, HENRYSSHOPPINGCART. Some of the methods in SHOPPINGCART have been changed to reflect Henry's business rules. Henry's programmers might also edit the deployment descriptors of some of the beans to make them conform to Henry's needs and map them to Henry's database.

The job of implementing Henry's system has been drastically reduced. Henry's programmers need be concerned mainly with Henry's business rules, not with the technical details of the operational environment in which the system will run. After obtaining, and perhaps modifying, the beans, the major remaining job is to assemble the beans and deploy them within a Web application server.

Once Henry's system is complete, it can run on any computer using any Web application server that supports J2EE. Note, however, that while all commercial Web application servers that support J2EE provide all the features of the current J2EE standard, they each also provide a number of additional proprietary features. Any application that uses those features might not be portable between Web application servers.

Web application servers usually supply graphical tools for creating skeleton versions of servlets, and enterprise Java beans for specifying their properties, for assembling these components, and for deploying them in an application. Among the other services provided by Web application servers are

- *Transaction oriented services.* These services include Java Transaction API (JTA), Java Transaction Services (JTS), Java Messaging Service (JMS), Java Database Connectivity (JDBC), and so on.
- *Services usually offered by TP monitors.* These services include access to a transaction manager, load balancing, multithreading, security services, communication protocols, and so on.
- **Support for business-to-business XML-based Web services.** These services include support for XML, SOAP, UDDI, WSDL, etc. We discuss these services in Chapter 25.

Our goal here is not to make you an expert in J2EE or any particular commercial Web application server, but to make you aware that such tools can considerably simplify the implementation of Web-based transaction processing systems. Understanding the principles described in this text will make it easier to understand and correctly use the detailed information provided in technical manuals.

BIBLIOGRAPHIC NOTES

Much of the material on transaction processing systems in this chapter was drawn from two books. [Gray 1978] is encyclopedic in its coverage of transaction processing systems, and the student is urged to go to this excellent source for additional information. Another excellent source is [Bernstein and Newcomer 1997]. [Gray 1978] gets down to implementation details, but Bernstein and Newcomer focus on a higher level of coverage of much of the same material. Their work includes a very useful discussion of the two-tiered and three-tiered models and a description of several TP monitors. Additional information on Tuxedo can be found in [Andrade et al. 1996]. Material on Encina can be found in [Transarc 1996]. RPCs were introduced by [Birrell and Nelson 1984]. A description of IBM's LU6.2, the most commonly used peer-to-peer protocol, can be found in [IBM 1991]. A general discussion of communication techniques, including RPC, can be found in [Peterson and Davies 2000]. The discussion of the handling of exceptional situations is based on the model used in the Tuxedo system [Andrade et al. 1996]. Description of the X/Open model for distributed transaction processing can be found in [*X/Open CAE Specification Structured Transaction Definition Language (STDL)* 1996] and [*X/Open Guide Distributed Transaction Processing: Reference Model*, Version 3 1996b].

Vast literature exists on programming Web applications (including database applications) using Java servlets. A few recent titles include [Hall 2000; Hunter and Crawford 1998; Sebesta 2001; Berg and Virginia 2000].

Documentation for J2EE version 1.4 can be found at *http://java.sun.com/j2ee/download.html*. Documentation on Enterprise Java Beans version 2.1 is at *http://java.sun.com/products/ejb/docs.html*.

EXERCISES

23.1 Explain the advantages to a bank in providing access to its accounts database only through stored procedures such as `deposit()` and `withdraw()`.

23.2 Explain why the three-level organization of a transaction processing system (including transaction servers) is said to be scalable to large enterprise-wide systems. Discuss issues of cost, security, maintainability, authentication, and authorization.

23.3 Explain what happens in a three-level architecture for a transaction processing system if the presentation server crashes while the transaction is executing.

23.4 Explain why the *cancel* button on an ATM does not work after the *submit* button has been pressed.

23.5 Explain the advantages of including a transaction server in the architecture of a transaction processing system.

23.6 Give an example of a transaction processing system you use that is implemented as a distributed system with a centralized database.

23.7 Give an example in which a transaction in a distributed database system does not commit atomically (one database manager it accessed commits, and another aborts) and leaves the database in an inconsistent state.

23.8 Explain whether the system you are using for your project can be characterized as TP-Lite or TP-Heavy.

23.9 List five issues that arise in the design of heterogeneous distributed transaction processing systems that do not arise in homogeneous distributed systems.

23.10 Explain the difference between a TP monitor and a transaction manager.

23.11 Give three examples of servers, other than transaction servers, database servers, and file servers, that might be called by an application server in a distributed transaction processing system.

23.12 Describe the architecture of the student registration system used by your school.

23.13 State two ways in which transactional remote procedure calls differ from ordinary remote procedure calls.

23.14 Suppose that a transaction uses TRPC to update some data from a database at a remote site and that the call successfully returns. Before the transaction completes, the remote site crashes. Describe informally what should happen when the transaction requests to commit.

23.15 Explain the difference between the `tx_commit()` command used in the X/Open API and the COMMIT statement in embedded SQL.

23.16 Propose an implementation of distributed savepoints using the `tx` and `xa` interfaces to the transaction manager. Assume that each subtransaction (including the transaction as a whole) can declare a savepoint, and that when it does so, it forces its children to create corresponding savepoints. When a (sub)transaction rolls back to a savepoint, its children are rolled back to their corresponding savepoints.

23.17 Give three advantages of using an application server architecture in a client server system.

23.18 Give an example of an event, different from that given in the text, in which the callback function should not be part of the transaction.

23.19 Explain how peer-to-peer communication can be used to implement remote procedure calling.

23.20 Explain some of the authentication issues involved in using your credit card to order merchandise over the Internet.

23.21 Implement a Web tic-tac-toe game in which the display is prepared by a presentation server on your browser and the logic of the game is implemented within a servlet on the server.

23.22 Print out the file of cookies for your local Web browser.

23.23 Consider a three-tiered system interfacing to a centralized DBMS, in which $n1$ presentation servers are connected to $n2$ application servers, which in turn are connected to $n3$ transaction servers. Assume that for each transaction, the application server, on average, invokes k procedures, each of which is executed on an arbitrary transaction server, and that each procedure, on average, executes s SQL statements that must be processed by the DBMS. If, on average, a presentation server handles r requests per second (each request produces exactly one transaction at the application server), how many SQL statements per second are processed by the DBMS and how many messages flow over each communication line?

23.24 In Section 23.10 we discuss an optimistic concurrency control that uses a different validation check than the concurrency control described in Section 20.9.2. Give an example of a schedule that would be allowed by the validation check of Section 23.10 but not by the validation check of Section 20.9.2.

24

Implementing Distributed Transactions

Many transaction processing applications must access databases at multiple sites, perhaps scattered throughout the world. For example, in our university, much of the information about the research contracts obtained by our faculty is maintained in a database located in the state capital, several hundred miles away. We discussed the database and query design issues related to distributed database systems in Chapter 16. In this chapter, we discuss transaction-related issues. In particular, we might require that transactions that access such distributed databases maintain the same correctness conditions as the local transactions we have been discussing—namely the ACID properties.

24.1 Implementing the ACID Properties

A **distributed transaction**, *T*, is a transaction that accesses databases at multiple sites in a network. The portion of a distributed transaction that executes at a particular site is called a **subtransaction**. For example, a database manager might export stored procedures that *T* can invoke as subtransactions. Or *T* might submit individual SQL statements to be executed by the database manager, in which case the sequence of SQL statements submitted by *T* becomes *T*'s subtransaction at that manager. *T* might invoke subtransactions so that they execute in sequence (one completes before another starts) or concurrently (several can execute at the same time and perhaps communicate with one another while they are executing).

Distributed database systems are useful when the organizations they support are themselves distributed and each component maintains its own portion of the data. Communication costs can be minimized by placing data at the site at which it is most frequently accessed, and system availability can be increased since the failure of a single site need not prevent continued operation at other sites. For example, the Student Registration System might be implemented as a distributed system. Student information might be stored on one computer and course information on a different computer. The two computers might be located in different buildings on campus.

We refer to the individual database managers that execute subtransactions of a distributed transaction as **cohorts** of that transaction. A database manager is a

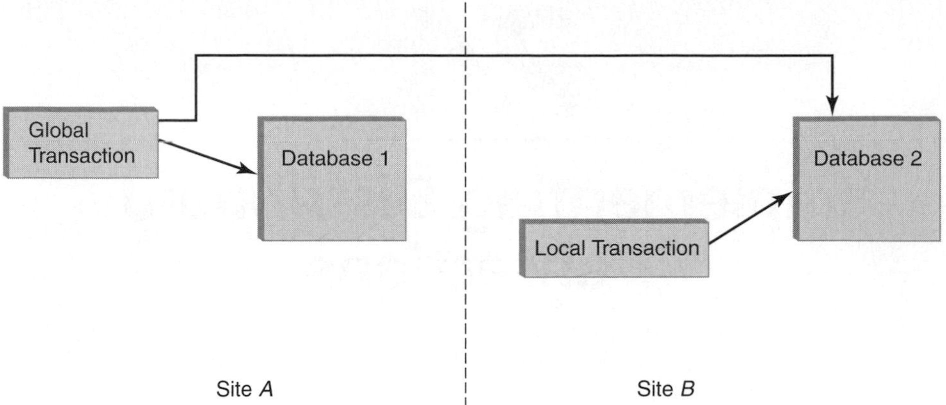

FIGURE 24.1 Data access paths for a distributed transaction.

cohort of each distributed transaction for which it is executing a subtransaction and might be a cohort of a number of distributed transactions simultaneously.

We would like each distributed transaction to satisfy the ACID properties. The module responsible for doing much of the work necessary to implement these properties is called the **coordinator**. In most systems, the transaction manager is the coordinator.

In addition to serving as a cohort of a distributed transaction, a database manager might execute a stored procedure or a series of SQL statements for an application that does not require the services of any other database manager. Such an application is invoking a (single-site) transaction rather than a subtransaction of a distributed transaction. Since the database manager does not distinguish between these two cases, we frequently refer to a subtransaction as simply a transaction. The data access paths for a distributed transaction are shown in Figure 24.1.

Consider the nationwide distribution system of a hardware manufacturing company. The company maintains a network of warehouses at different sites throughout the country, and each site has its own local database, which stores information about that site's inventory. A customer at some site might initiate a transaction requesting 100 dozen widgets. The transaction might read the data item containing the number of widgets currently in the local warehouse and find that there are only 10 dozen, which it (tentatively) reserves, and then access data at one or more of the other warehouses to reserve the additional 90 dozen widgets. After all 100 dozen have been located and reserved, the data items at each of the sites are decremented and appropriate shipping orders generated. If 100 dozen cannot be located, the transaction releases all reserved widgets and commits, returning failure status to the customer. In this way, either all sites at which widgets have been reserved decrement their local databases or none do.

Physical failures are more complex when transactions are distributed. We saw in Chapter 22 that a crash is a common type of failure. In a centralized system, all the modules involved in the transaction fail when the computer crashes. With distributed transactions, the crash of some computer in the network can cause some subset of modules to fail while the rest continue to execute. Special protocols must be designed to handle this new failure mode.

A similar situation arises when a communication failure causes the network to become **partitioned**. In this case, operational sites cannot communicate with one another. We discuss how to deal with such failures in Section 24.2.2. We assume that a distributed transaction can abort (and hence must be recoverable) and that once it commits, the system must ensure that all database changes it has made (at all sites) are durable.

If we assume that each site supports the ACID properties locally and ensures that there are no local deadlocks, then the distributed transaction processing system also must ensure the following:

- *Atomic termination.* Either all cohorts of a distributed transaction must commit or all must abort.
- *No global deadlocks.* There must be no global (distributed) deadlocks involving multiple sites.
- *Global serialization.* There must be a (global) serialization of all transactions (distributed and otherwise).

We discuss each of these issues in this chapter (Sections 24.2, 24.4, and 24.5). We also consider data replication and issues related to the distribution of data in a network (Sections 24.7 and 24.8).

24.2 Atomic Termination

To ensure global atomicity, a distributed transaction can commit only if all of its subtransactions commit. Even though a subtransaction has successfully completed all of its operations and is ready to commit, it cannot unilaterally decide to do so because some other subtransaction of the same distributed transaction might abort (or might already have aborted). In that case, the entire distributed transaction must be aborted. Thus, when a subtransaction has completed successfully, it must wait for all others to complete successfully before it can commit.

The coordinator executes an **atomic commit protocol** to guarantee global atomicity. The communication paths related to the protocol are shown in Figure 24.2. When an application program initiates a distributed transaction, T, it notifies the coordinator, thus setting the initial transaction boundary. Each time T invokes the services of a resource manager for the first time, that manager informs the coordinator that it has joined the transaction. When T completes, the application informs the coordinator, thus setting the final transaction boundary. The coordinator then initiates the atomic commit protocol.

Atomicity requires that, when T completes, either all cohorts must commit their changes or all must abort. In processing T's request to commit, therefore, the

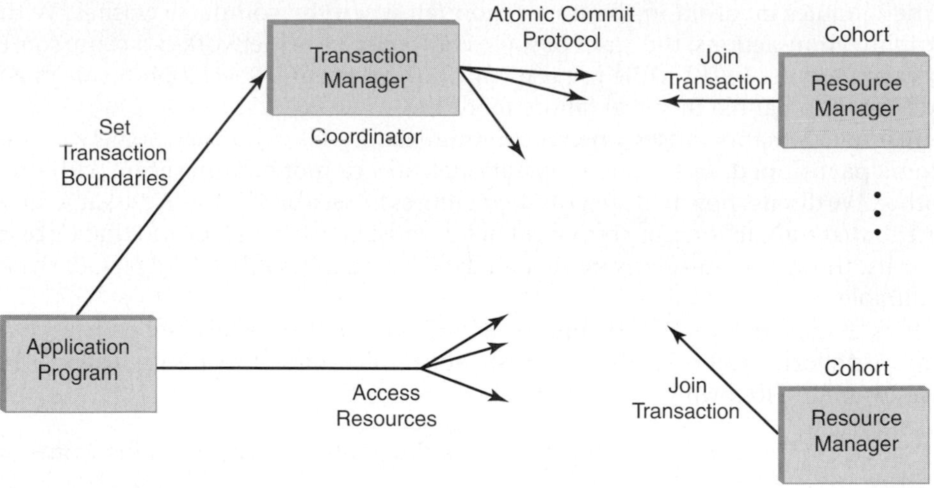

FIGURE 24.2 Communication paths in an atomic commit protocol.

coordinator must first determine if all cohorts agree to do so. Some of the reasons a cohort might be unable to commit are

- The schema at a cohort site might specify deferred constraint checking (see Section 8.3). When the subtransaction at the site completes, the database manager might determine that a constraint is violated and abort the subtransaction.
- The database manager at a cohort site might use an optimistic concurrency control. When the subtransaction at the site completes, the manager performs the validation procedure. If validation fails, the manager aborts the subtransaction.
- A subtransaction at a site, *S*, might have been aborted by the concurrency control at *S* or because of a (local) deadlock or a (local) conflict with other subtransactions at *S*.
- The cohort site might have crashed and so is unable to respond to the protocol messages sent by the coordinator.
- Some communication lines might have failed, preventing the cohort from responding to the protocol messages sent by the coordinator.

24.2.1 The Two-Phase Commit Protocol

A number of atomic commit protocols have been proposed, but the one that is in common use is called the **two-phase commit protocol** [Gray 1978; Lampson and Sturgis 1979] (in Exercise 24.8 we describe another atomic commit protocol). The protocol is initiated by the coordinator when the transaction requests to commit. To perform the protocol, the coordinator needs to know the identities of all the cohorts of the transaction. Therefore, when the transaction is initiated, the coordinator allocates a **transaction record** for the transaction in volatile memory. Furthermore, each time a resource manager joins the transaction, its identification is appended to that transaction record. We discussed this situation in Section 23.5.3 for RPC communication and in Section 23.6 for peer-to-peer communication. Thus, when the transaction requests to commit, the transaction record contains a list of all its cohorts.

We describe the protocol as a series of messages exchanged between the coordinator and the cohorts. When the transaction requests to commit, the coordinator starts the first phase of the two-phase commit protocol by sending a **prepare message** to each cohort. The purpose of this message is to determine whether the cohort is willing to commit and, if so, to request that it prepare to commit by storing all of the subtransaction's update records on nonvolatile storage.[1] Having the update records in nonvolatile storage guarantees that if the coordinator subsequently decides that the transaction should be committed, the cohort will be able to do so, even if it crashes after responding positively to the *prepare message*.

If the cohort is willing to commit, it ensures that its update records are on nonvolatile storage by forcing a **prepared record** to its log. It is then said to be in the **prepared state** and can reply to the *prepare message* with a **vote message**.

The vote is **ready** if the cohort is willing to commit and **aborting** if it had aborted at an earlier time or is unable to commit for one of the reasons cited previously. Once a cohort votes "ready," it cannot change its mind since the coordinator uses the vote to decide whether the transaction as a whole is to be committed. The cohort is said to have entered an **uncertain period** because it does not know whether the subtransaction will ultimately be committed or aborted by the coordinator. It must await the coordinator's decision, and during that waiting period it is blocked in the sense that it cannot release locks and the concurrency control at the cohort database cannot abort the subtransaction. This is an unfortunate situation that we will return to in Section 24.6. If the cohort votes "aborting," it aborts the subtransaction immediately and exits the protocol. Phase 1 of the protocol is now complete.

The coordinator receives, and records in the transaction record, each cohort's vote. If all votes are "ready," it decides that T can be committed globally, records the fact that the transaction has committed in the transaction record, and forces a **commit record**—containing a copy of the transaction record—to its log.

As with single-resource transactions, T is committed once that commit record is safely stored in nonvolatile memory. All update records for all cohorts are in nonvolatile memory at that time because each cohort forced a prepare record before voting. Note that we are assuming that the transaction manager and each of the cohort database managers have their own independent logs.

The coordinator then sends each cohort a **commit message** telling it to commit. It is now apparent why the coordinator's commit record must be forced. If a *commit message* were sent to a cohort before the commit record was durable, the coordinator might crash in a state in which the message had been sent but the record was not

[1] A cohort site where only reads have been performed can implement a simplified version of the protocol. See Exercise 24.12.

durable. Since each cohort commits its subtransaction when the *commit message* is received, this would result in an inconsistent state: the distributed transaction is uncommitted, but the cohort's subtransaction is committed. Commit processing at the cohort is carried out as described in Section 22.2 and involves the forcing of a commit record to the database manager's log (to indicate that the subtransaction is committed), lock release, and local cleanup. After a cohort performs these actions, it sends a **done message** back to the coordinator indicating that it has completed the protocol.

When the coordinator receives a *done message* from each cohort, it appends a **completion record** to the log and deletes the transaction record from volatile memory. The protocol is then complete. For a committed transaction, the coordinator executes two writes to its log, only one of which is forced. The cohort forces two records in the commit case: the prepare record and the commit record. The number of forced writes is a factor in evaluating the efficiency of a protocol since each time a routing forces an I/O operation it must wait until the operation completes.

If the coordinator receives any "aborting" votes, it deallocates *T*'s record in volatile storage and sends an **abort message** to each cohort that voted to commit (cohorts that voted to abort have already aborted and exited from the protocol). The coordinator does not record the abort in its log because this protocol has the presumed abort property, which we discuss in Section 24.2.2. On receiving the *abort message*, the database manager aborts the cohort and writes an **abort record** in its log. The arrival of the *commit* or *abort message* at the cohort ends its uncertain period.

The sequence of messages exchanged between the application, the coordinator (transaction manager), and cohort (resource manager) is shown in Figure 24.3.

Summary of the two-phase commit protocol. We summarize the two-phase commit protocol here:

Phase 1

1. The coordinator sends a *prepare message* to all cohorts.
2. Each cohort waits until it receives a *prepare message* from the coordinator. If it is prepared to commit, it forces a prepared record to its log, enters a state in which it cannot be aborted by its local control, and sends "ready" in the *vote message* to the coordinator.

   If it cannot commit, it appends an abort record to its log. Or it might already have aborted. In either case, it sends "aborting" in the *vote message* to the coordinator, rolls back any changes the subtransaction has made to the database, releases the subtransaction's locks, and terminates its participation in the protocol.

Phase 2

1. The coordinator waits until it receives votes from all cohorts. If it receives at least one "aborting" vote, it decides to abort, sends an *abort message* to all cohorts

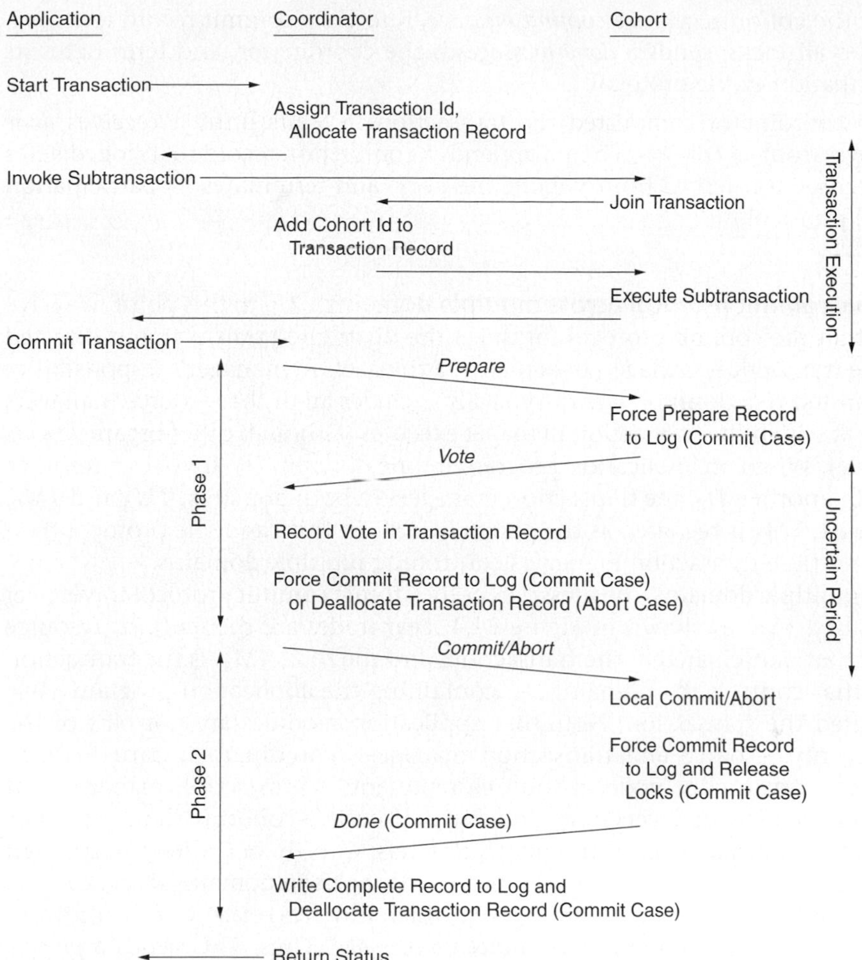

FIGURE 24.3 Exchange of messages in a two-phase commit protocol.

that voted "ready," deallocates the transaction record in volatile memory, and terminates its participation in the protocol.

If all votes are "ready," the coordinator decides to commit (and stores that fact in the transaction record), forces a commit record (which includes a copy of the transaction record) to its log, and sends a *commit message* to each cohort.

2. Each cohort that voted "ready" waits to receive a message from the coordinator. If a cohort receives an *abort message*, it rolls back any changes the subtransaction has made to the database, appends an abort record to its log, releases the subtransaction's locks, and terminates its participation in the protocol.

If the cohort receives a *commit message*, it forces a commit record to its log, releases all locks, sends a *done message* to the coordinator, and terminates its participation in the protocol.

3. If the coordinator committed the transaction, it waits until it receives *done messages* from all cohorts. Then it appends a completion record to its log, deletes the transaction record from volatile memory, and terminates its participation in the protocol.

The atomic commit protocol across multiple domains. Up to this point, we have assumed that the commit protocol for the entire distributed transaction is directed by a single transaction manager. In actuality, a transaction manager's responsibility is often limited to a **domain**, which typically includes all of the resource managers at the site at which the transaction manager executes (although other organizations are possible). When an application program in one domain, D_A, invokes a resource manager in another, D_B, the transaction managers in both domains, TM_A and TM_B, are informed. TM_A is regarded as the parent of TM_B in this case. The protocol then involves multiple transaction managers controlling multiple domains.

With multiple domains, the messages of the atomic commit protocol travel over the edges of a tree, as shown in Figure 24.4. Leaf nodes are the (cohort) resource managers that participated in the transaction, and the root, TM_A, is the transaction manager that controls the domain, D_A, containing the application program, *App*, that initiated the transaction. Note that application modules are not part of the tree since only resource and transaction managers (coordinators) participate in the protocol. An interior node in the tree represents a transaction manager that coordinates resource managers in its domain and acts as a cohort with respect to its parent transaction manager. In the figure, *App* has, directly or indirectly (through other application programs), invoked resource managers in domains *B* and *C*.

App sends its request to commit to TM_A, which initiates phase 1 of the protocol among its children by sending each a *prepare message*. Thus, TM_A sends a *prepare message* to both local resource managers (e.g., RM_A) and both remote transaction managers (e.g., TM_B). When a transaction manager receives a *prepare message*, it initiates phase 1 of the protocol among its children by sending each a *prepare message*. For example, when TM_C receives the *prepare message* from TM_A, it sends a *prepare message* to each of its two (resource manager) children.

On the basis of the votes TM_C receives from its children, it responds with an appropriate vote to TM_A. Thus, if it receives "ready" votes from both resource managers, it forces a prepared record (including the transaction record containing information about its direct descendents) to its log and responds with a "ready" vote. If TM_A commits, TM_B will be able to commit its descendents in the tree, even if it should crash during the uncertain period and be restarted later.

If TM_A also receives "ready" votes from TM_B and the two resource managers in D_A, it enters phase 2 of the protocol by committing the transaction and sending a *commit message* to each of its children. TM_B and TM_C then initiate phase 2 of the protocol by relaying the *commit message* to their children. While the figure shows a

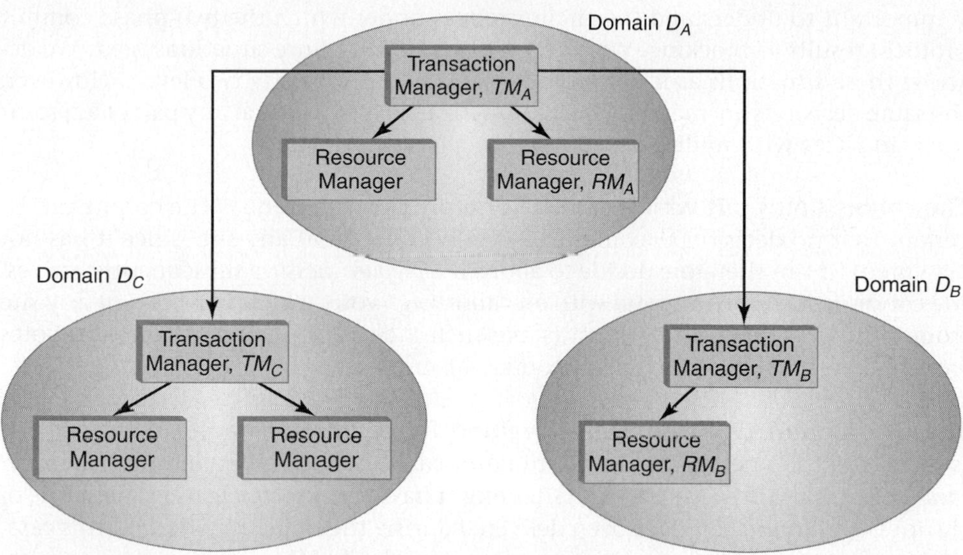

FIGURE 24.4 Distributed transaction structured as a tree.

tree with only two coordinator levels, a general distributed transaction might have an arbitrary number of levels.

TM_B acts as the representative of the resource managers in D_B with respect to TM_A and thus is a cohort with respect to (coordinator) TM_A. Hence, TM_A must be informed that TM_B is one of its cohorts, and TM_B must bc informed of its dual role with respect to RM_B and TM_A. In the X/Open model of distributed transactions, the responsibility for spreading this information is placed on a server called the **communication resource manager**, and the interface between a transaction manager and the communication resource manager in its domain is called the xa+ interface.

24.2.2 Dealing with Failures in the Two-Phase Commit Protocol

The two-phase commit protocol includes measures for dealing with various kinds of failures that might occur in a distributed system.

- A **timeout protocol** is executed if a site times out while waiting for a message. (A timeout might occur either because the sending site has crashed, the message is lost, or the message delivery system is slow.)
- A **restart protocol** is executed by a site recovering from a crash.

If a site cannot complete the commit protocol until some failure is repaired, we say that the site is **blocked**. When a site blocks, the decision to commit or abort is delayed for an arbitrary period of time. This delay is particularly undesirable at a cohort site that uses a locking concurrency control since items that the subtransaction has locked remain unavailable to other transactions at that site. For this reason, it is important to understand the circumstances under which the two-phase commit protocol results in blocking. We consider the various failure situations next. We describe these situations as if the protocol tree contains exactly two levels. However, the same decisions are made between a parent and its children at any pair of adjacent levels in a tree with multiple levels.

The cohort times out while waiting for a prepare message. The cohort can be certain that no decision to commit has yet been taken at any site (since it has not yet voted). It can therefore decide to abort. If a *prepare message* subsequently arrives, the cohort can simply respond with an "aborting" vote, which will prevent any site from reaching a commit decision (since such a decision requires "commit" votes from all sites). In this way, global atomicity is preserved.

The coordinator times out while waiting for a vote message. This situation is similar to the one above. The coordinator can decide to abort and send an *abort message* to all cohorts. Note that all sites might have sent *commit messages*, but one of the messages might not have been delivered during the timeout period. In this case, the coordinator aborts the transaction, even though all of the cohorts are operational and voted to commit—a counterintuitive situation.

The cohort times out while waiting for a commit or abort message. This situation is more serious since the cohort has voted "ready" and is in its uncertain period. It is blocked until it can determine if the coordinator has made a decision and, if so, what that decision is. The cohort cannot unilaterally choose to commit or abort since the coordinator might have made a different choice, thus violating unanimity.

The cohort can attempt to communicate with the coordinator, requesting the transaction's status. If this is not possible (the coordinator has crashed or the network is partitioned), the cohort can try to communicate with other cohorts. (To facilitate such communication, the coordinator can provide a list of all cohorts in the *prepare message*, which the cohort can store in the prepare record that it writes to the log.) If the cohort finds a cohort that has not yet voted, both decide to abort. This is safe since the coordinator cannot have decided to commit if any cohort has not yet voted. If it finds a cohort that has aborted or committed, it makes the same decision. If all other cohorts it finds are also in their uncertain period, it remains blocked until communication can be established with the coordinator or a cohort that has committed or aborted.

The coordinator times out while waiting for a done message. The coordinator communicates with the cohort requesting the *done message*. When a *done message* has been received from each cohort, it deallocates the transaction record.

The coordinator crashes. When the coordinator restarts after a crash, it searches its log. If, for some transaction, T, it finds a commit record but no completion record, it must be in phase 2 of the protocol for T. The coordinator restores T's transaction record (found in T's commit record) to volatile memory and resumes the protocol by sending a *commit message* to each cohort since the crash might have occurred before the *commit messages* were sent. If the coordinator does not find a commit record for some transaction, two possibilities exist.

1. The protocol was still in phase 1 when the crash occurred.
2. The coordinator has aborted the transaction.

The coordinator cannot distinguish between these two cases since in both it has not written any records to its log. Fortunately, it does not need to distinguish between them since in the first case the transaction is aborted and hence the two cases can be treated identically: the coordinator takes no action with respect to T. If the first case has occurred, and a cohort queries the coordinator concerning the status of T, the coordinator will reply with an *abort message* since it will not find a transaction record for T in volatile memory. This is allowable because the transaction was in phase 1 of the protocol when the coordinator crashed, and hence the coordinator had not made any decision before the crash. The second case is also handled correctly since no action is the correct course if T had previously aborted. This reasoning is part of the presumed abort protocol described next.

The cohort crashes or times out while in the prepared state—the presumed abort property. When a cohort restarts after a crash, it searches its log. If it finds a prepared record but no commit or abort record, it knows that it was in the prepared state at the time of the crash. It requests the transaction's status from the coordinator. The coordinator might also have been restarted (see above), or the cohort might have crashed while the coordinator remained active. If the coordinator finds the transaction record for the transaction in volatile memory, the coordinator can immediately respond to the request. However, if it does not find a transaction record, it presumes (without checking its log) that the transaction has aborted and reports that to the cohort. This feature of the protocol is referred to as **presumed abort**[2] [Mohan et al. 1986].

The presumed abort feature works because the absence of a transaction record indicates that one of the following is true:

- The coordinator has committed the transaction, received *done messages* from all cohorts, and deleted the transaction record from volatile memory.
- The coordinator has crashed, and its restart protocol found commit and completion records for the transaction in its log.
- The coordinator has aborted the transaction and deleted the transaction record.

[2] One dictionary definition of the word *presume* is "to expect or assume, to regard as probably true as in 'innocence is presumed until guilt is proven.'" However, in this case the coordinator knows that the transaction has aborted.

- The coordinator has crashed, and its restart protocol did not find any records for the transaction in its log (it aborted the transaction or was in phase 1 of the protocol when it crashed).

Since the cohort is still in the prepared state (and hence has not sent a *done message*), the first and second possibilities are ruled out. Therefore the coordinator can report that the transaction has aborted. This same reasoning applies if the cohort times out in its prepared state and requests the transaction's status from the coordinator. (Note that, when the commit protocol is used across multiple domains, each coordinator in the protocol tree can use the presumed abort property to respond to requests from its cohorts.)

Note that we have implicitly taken advantage of the fact that the cohort forces the commit record to the log before it sends the *done message*. If the record were not forced, it would be possible for the cohort to crash after sending the message but before the commit record is appended to its log. In that case (assuming all other cohorts send *done messages*), the coordinator will have committed the transaction and deleted the transaction record. But when the cohort is restarted, it believes it is in the prepared state (since there is no commit record in its log), and the coordinator will respond "abort" to the cohort's query, causing a violation of global atomicity.

Timeout Protocol for the Two-Phase Commit Protocol.

- *TO1. Cohort times out while waiting for a prepare message*. The cohort decides to abort.
- *TO2. Coordinator times out while waiting for a vote message*. The coordinator decides to abort, sends an *abort message* to each cohort from which it received a "ready" vote, deletes the transaction record from volatile memory, and terminates its participation in the protocol.
- *TO3. Cohort times out while waiting for a commit/abort message*. The cohort attempts to communicate with the coordinator to determine the outcome of the transaction. If it can communicate with the coordinator, the coordinator can use the presumed abort property to formulate its answer. If the cohort cannot communicate with the coordinator, it attempts to communicate with another cohort. If it finds one that has committed or aborted, it makes the same decision. If it finds one that has not yet voted, they both decide to abort. Otherwise the cohort blocks.
- *TO4. Coordinator times out while waiting for a done message*. The coordinator sends a message to the cohort requesting that the *done message* be sent. It maintains the transaction record in its volatile memory until it has received a *done message* from each cohort.

Restart protocol for the two-phase commit protocol. The protocol for restarting a coordinator or cohort site after a crash can be built on the crash recovery procedure described in Section 22.2.

- *RES*1. If the restarted site is a cohort site and, for some transaction, the site's crash recovery procedure finds a commit or abort record in its log, that transaction has completed, and the procedure takes no additional actions beyond those discussed in Section 22.2.
- *RES*2. If the restarted site is a cohort and, for some transaction, the site's crash recovery procedure finds a begin transaction record in its log but does not find a prepared record (and hence the cohort has not yet voted), the procedure takes no additional actions beyond those discussed in Section 22.2 (i.e., it aborts the subtransaction).
- *RES*3. If the restarted site is a cohort and, for some transaction, the site's crash recovery procedure finds a prepared record but no commit or abort record in its log (and hence the cohort might have sent a ready vote before the crash), the crash occurred during the cohort's uncertain period. The crash recovery procedure acquires locks on all items that the transaction updated (these items are named in the update records in the log) so that when the system is restarted, the items are inaccessible to other transactions, and then it restores the updates. The cohort then follows the protocol TO3.
- *RES*4. If the restarted site is the coordinator and, for some transaction, it finds a commit record but no completion record in its log, the crash occurred after the coordinator had committed the transaction but before it had received a *done message* from each cohort. When the coordinator is restarted, the transaction record is restored to volatile memory from the commit record. The coordinator then follows the protocol TO4.

The presumed commit property. Although the two-phase commit protocol with the presumed abort property has been chosen as the X/Open standard, it is not the only protocol for implementing global atomicity. In particular, it is interesting to consider a protocol that implements a **presumed commit** property.

The goal of the protocol with presumed commit is to eliminate the *done messages* that committed cohorts send with presumed abort after they have completed commit processing. Recall that after the coordinator sends *commit messages*, it keeps the transaction record in its volatile memory until it has received a *done message* from each cohort. The coordinator knows that after it receives a *done message* from a cohort, that cohort will never again request status, so when it receives *done messages* from all cohorts, it can delete the transaction record. If, on the other hand, the coordinator aborts the transaction, it sends *abort messages* to the cohorts and immediately deletes the transaction record, so there is no need for a cohort to reply with a *done message*. If a cohort queries the coordinator and no transaction record is found, the coordinator presumes that the transaction has aborted and sends an *abort message*.

Our plan is to reverse this situation. When the coordinator commits a transaction and sends a *commit message* to each cohort, it immediately deletes the transaction record from volatile memory, and thus a cohort does not have to reply with

OPTIONAL

a *done message*. When the coordinator aborts a transaction and sends an *abort message* to each cohort, it retains the transaction record until each replies with a *done message*. Since most transactions commit, fewer *done messages* will be sent. This is an advantage that presumed commit has over presumed abort.

With this strategy, when a cohort times out or restarts in the prepared state and queries the coordinator concerning the status of the transaction, if the coordinator finds no transaction record in its volatile memory, it can presume that the transaction has committed. If the transaction had aborted, the transaction record would be present (since not all cohorts have responded with *done messages*). In either case the coordinator can report the transaction's status to the cohort.

We need to argue that the strategy works. The argument rests on the requirement that the only times at which the transaction record can be deleted from the coordinator's volatile memory are when the transaction commits or when, in the abort case, all *done messages* have been received. However, there is a problem. If the coordinator crashes before it has made a decision to commit or abort, the contents of volatile memory will be lost. Since no information about the transaction exists in the coordinator's log, it will not be able to reconstruct the transaction record when it recovers. If one of the cohorts then queries the coordinator, it will incorrectly report that the transaction has committed.

To fix this problem, the coordinator forces a **start record**, including a copy of the transaction record, to its log at the beginning of the first phase of the protocol. Now if the coordinator crashes before deciding commit or abort, its restart procedure will find the start record, but no commit or abort record, in the log. The procedure can then deduce that a decision has not yet been made and choose to abort the transaction and restore the transaction record, indicating the abort, to volatile memory. The start record must be forced to ensure that before any cohort can enter the prepared state (and perhaps send a query message) the transaction record can be restored to volatile memory if the coordinator crashes.

To understand how the coordinator's actions relate to the cohort's actions, consider the following cases:

- *The coordinator crashes before deciding*. If the coordinator crashed before sending a *prepare message*, the cohort will timeout and abort. This is consistent with the fact that the coordinator has chosen to abort the transaction. If the coordinator crashed after sending a *prepare message* but before deciding, the cohort will respond with a *vote message* and will timeout waiting for a *commit* or *abort message*. It will then send a query to the coordinator. The coordinator's restart procedure will have reconstructed the transaction record in volatile memory and, when the query is processed, will reply that the transaction has aborted.
- *The coordinator crashes after deciding to abort*. In this case the coordinator might have sent one or more *abort messages*, and hence, instead of a query, the coordinator might receive *done messages*. The coordinator then waits to receive *done messages* from all cohorts before deleting the transaction record. If it times out waiting for a particular cohort's *done message*, it requests that that cohort send a *done message* when the cohort completes abort processing. Note that it is

OPTIONAL

not necessary for the coordinator to force an abort record if it decides to abort. If the coordinator crashes before the abort record is appended to its log, its restart procedure will find a start record, but no commit or abort record, in the log and correctly consider the transaction to be aborted.

- *The coordinator crashes after deciding to commit.* We still require that the coordinator force a commit record when it decides to commit the transaction in order to ensure that the transaction is committed before *commit messages* are sent. If the coordinator subsequently crashes, its restart procedure will conclude that the transaction has committed and will not reconstruct the transaction record.

We must also consider the forcing question on the cohort side. If the transaction aborts, the cohort must force an abort record to its log before sending the *done message*. If it were not forced, the cohort might crash after the *done message* was sent but before the abort record was appended. Thus, the cohort will appear to be in the prepared state when it recovers. Unfortunately, if the coordinator received *done messages* from all cohorts, it would have deleted the transaction record. A subsequent query by the cohort would elicit an incorrect (presumed) commit response from the coordinator.

A protocol with the presumed commit property has the advantage that when a transaction commits (the usual situation), no *done* messages are sent. This can speed up the protocol. However, it has the disadvantage that in both the commit and the abort cases, the coordinator is required to force a start record. This can slow the protocol.

In summary, when a transaction commits using the presumed abort protocol

- The coordinator makes one forced log write (the commit record) and sends two messages to the cohorts (*prepare* and *commit*).
- A cohort makes two forced log writes (a prepared record and a commit record) and sends two message (*ready* and *done*).

By contrast, when a transaction commits using the presumed commit protocol

- The coordinator makes two forced log writes (the start record and the commit record) and sends two messages to the cohorts (*prepare* and *commit*).
- A cohort makes two forced log writes (a prepared record and a commit record) and sends one message (*ready*).

Although it appears that the costs and benefits of the two protocols are similar, there is a substantial difference if the transaction is structured as a tree as in Figure 24.4. With presumed commit, each local transaction manager in the tree must force a start record to its log when it enters the first phase of the protocol. If the tree is deep, a large number of forced writes must be done in sequence (as the tree is descended). These forced writes can incur a substantial amount of execution time. This is one reason why the presumed abort protocol was selected as the X/Open standard.

Formats and protocols: the X/Open standard. The two-phase commit protocol ties together software modules, such as DBMSs and a transaction manager, that

OPTIONAL

might have been provided by different vendors. If these modules are to communicate effectively, and if application programs are to communicate with them, they must agree on communication conventions, sometimes called the **format and protocols (FAP)**. Standardization of the FAP promotes **interoperability** among products of different vendors.

The X/Open standard permits interoperability by defining a set of function calls for exchanging protocol messages and the formats of those messages. With X/Open, the names of functions called by applications and implemented in the transaction manager (coordinator) are prefixed with `tx`—for example, `tx_begin()` is the function called to start a transaction and `tx_commit()` to commit it. Similarly, X/Open function calls from the transaction manager to resource managers and vice versa are prefixed with `xa`. Thus, when a resource manager (cohort) wants to join a transaction, it calls `xa_reg()`. When the transaction manager wants to send a *prepare message* to a resource manager it calls `xa_prepare()`, and the value returned is a "ready" or "aborting" vote. If all votes are "ready," the transaction manager sets the return value of the application program's call of `tx_commit()` to commit and calls each of the resource managers with `xa_commit()`. If one or more of the return values of `xa_prepare()` is "aborting," the transaction manager sets the return value of the application's call of `tx_commit()` to "abort" and calls each of the resource managers with `xa_abort()`.

24.2.3 The Peer-to-Peer Atomic Commit Protocol

A variation of the two-phase commit protocol achieves the atomic commitment of transactions that use peer-to-peer communication.[3]

In Section 23.6 we introduced the syncpoint manager as the module that coordinated the atomic commit protocol in a manner analogous to the way the transaction manager coordinates the atomic commit protocol when RPC communication is used. We assumed that all participants in a distributed transaction resided in the same domain, and hence a single syncpoint manager sufficed. In general, however, multiple domains, and hence multiple syncpoint managers, will be involved.

A syncpoint manager, SM_A, associated with an application program, A, keeps a record of all application programs and resource managers in its domain, D_A, with which A has directly communicated. Similarly, if A sets up a connection to B in its domain, D_B, SM_A is informed of the fact that SM_B is participating in the transaction.

Assuming that A initiates the commit protocol by declaring a syncpoint, all of its connections must be in send mode. SM_A assumes the root position in a tree similar to the one pictured in Figure 24.4 and starts phase 1 of the protocol by sending a *prepare message* to each resource manager that A has invoked and a *syncpoint message* over each of its connections to other application programs. Then A waits until the protocol completes. When the *syncpoint message* arrives at some other application program, B, that program might not have completed its portion of the transaction. When it does and all of its connections (other than the connection to A) are in send

[3] This description is based on [Maslak et al. 1991].

mode, it also declares a syncpoint. This causes SM_B to send a *prepare message* to each resource manager that B has invoked and a *syncpoint message* to each program (other than A) with which B has communicated. Then B waits until the protocol completes. In this way, *syncpoint message* spreads to all modules that have participated in the transaction.

Assuming that all peers want to commit, each eventually declares a syncpoint, all are synchronized at their syncpoint declarations, and the associated resource managers are in a prepared state. "Ready" *vote messages* propagate up the tree, and phase 1 of the two-phase commit protocol completes. Then phase 2 starts, and the transaction is committed by the tree of syncpoint managers. Commit status is also returned to each program, which can then continue its execution by starting a new transaction.

If a peer decides to abort, local rollback is initiated and abort status is sent to all resource managers, causing them to roll back as well. Abort status is also returned to each program, which can then continue executing by starting a new transaction.

24.3 Transfer of Coordination

Generally, the transaction manager associated with the site at which the transaction is initiated becomes the coordinator. It communicates with the cohorts to carry out the atomic commit protocol. The cohorts might be resource managers, but more generally they are transaction managers in a distributed transaction tree.

There are several reasons why basing coordination at the initiator site might not be an optimal arrangement. For one thing, the initiator site might not be the most reliable site involved in the transaction. For example, the transaction might be initiated as the result of some action at a point-of-sales terminal and involve servers in the store's main office and at the customer's bank. It might be safer to have coordination located at one of these servers. In order to allow this, the protocol can be modified so that coordinator status is transferred from one participant to another.

A second reason for transferring coordination has to do with optimizing the number of messages to be exchanged during the protocol. The two-phase commit protocol (with the presumed abort property) involves the exchange of four messages between the coordinator and each cohort. It is possible to improve on this. For example, the following modified protocol involves two participants, P_1 and P_2, that can be thought of either as transaction managers (each of which controls a set of cohort resource managers) or servers.

1. P_1 initiates the protocol by entering the prepared state (if P_1 is a transaction manager, its cohorts are all in their prepared states). It then sends a message to P_2, which simultaneously says that P_1 is prepared to commit and requests that P_2 both prepare and commit the transaction as a whole. Thus, the message is a combination of a "ready" vote and a *prepare message* and has the effect of transferring the coordinator role to P_2.
2. P_2 receives the message and, assuming it is willing to commit, enters the prepared state. Since it knows that P_1 is prepared, P_2 can decide to commit the

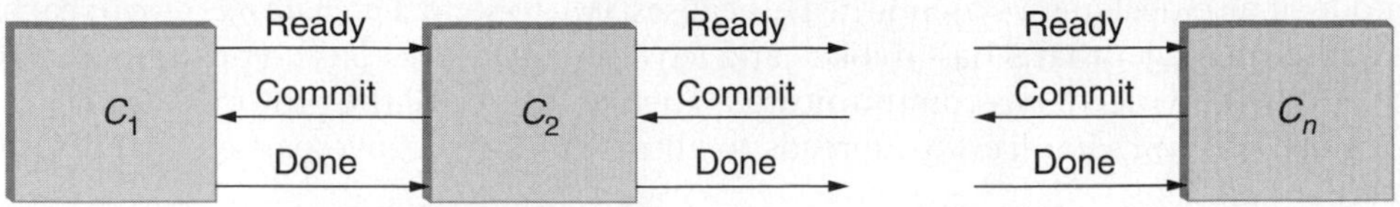

FIGURE 24.5 The linear commit protocol.

transaction as a whole and take the actions necessary to commit the transaction locally. It responds to P_1 with a *commit message*.

3. P_1 receives the message, commits locally, and responds with a *done message* to P_2.

The *done message* is required because of the presumed abort property: P_2, acting as the new coordinator, must remember the transaction's outcome in case the *commit message* it sent to P_1 is not received. It can then respond to a query from P_1 asking about the transaction's outcome. The *done message* indicates to P_2 that it can delete the transaction record from volatile memory. The fact that the protocol has completed with an exchange of only three messages (instead of four) shows that the number of messages exchanged can be optimized.

24.3.1 The Linear Commit Protocol

The **linear commit protocol** is a variation of the two-phase commit protocol that uses transfer of coordination. The cohorts are assumed to be interconnected in a (linear) chain as shown in Figure 24.5. Assume that the leftmost cohort, C_1, initiates the protocol. When it is ready to commit, it goes into the prepared state and sends a *ready message* to the cohort on its right, C_2, indicating that it is ready to commit and transferring coordination to C_2. After the message is received, if C_2 is willing to commit, it also goes into the prepared state and relays the message to the cohort on its right, again transferring coordination. The process continues until the message reaches the rightmost cohort, C_n. If C_n agrees to commit, it commits and sends a *commit message* to C_{n-1}, which commits and propagates the message down the chain until it reaches C_1, which then commits. Finally, a *done message* is propagated up the chain from C_1 to C_n to complete the protocol. The *done message* is required to allow C_{i+1}, acting as coordinator for C_i, to delete the transaction record from its volatile memory.

If, after receiving the first protocol message, a cohort wants to abort the transaction, it aborts and sends *abort messages* to the cohorts on its left and right. Those cohorts abort and forward the *abort message* further along the chain until it reaches both ends. The logging, timeout, and recovery protocols used to achieve atomicity for various types of failure are similar to those for the two-phase commit protocol (see Exercise 24.9).

The linear commit protocol involves fewer messages than the two-phase commit protocol and hence saves on communication costs. If n is the number of cohorts, the linear commit requires $3(n - 1)$ messages, whereas the two-phase commit requires $4n$ messages (a separate coordinator is involved). On the other hand, the two-phase commit completes after a sequence of four message exchanges (independent of the number of cohorts) since the coordinator communicates with all cohorts in parallel. The linear commit requires a sequence of $3(n - 1)$ exchanges because messages are sent serially.

24.3.2 Two-Phase Commit without a Prepared State

The basic idea in transfer of coordination can be used to adapt the two-phase commit protocol to situations in which (exactly) one of the cohorts, C, does not support the two-phase commit protocol (for example, if C does not understand the *prepare message* and does not have a prepared state, which might be the case if C is an older legacy system). In this case the coordinator executes phase 1 of the protocol with the cohorts that do support a prepared state in the normal way. If all of these cohorts agree to commit, the coordinator requests that C commit its subtransaction (this is not the *commit message*, which is part of the two-phase commit protocol). This effectively allows C to decide whether the transaction as a whole will be committed, but C is not smart enough to realize this. If C responds to the coordinator that it has committed, the coordinator sends *commit messages* to the other cohorts and completes phase 2 of the protocol. If C responds that it has aborted, the coordinator sends abort messages to the other cohorts.

Note that C does not actually function as a coordinator since it does not take the steps necessary to handle failures: it does not maintain a transaction record for the distributed transaction, nor does it understand a *done message*. Thus, it cannot respond to queries from other cohorts if a failure occurs. Hence, coordination is not completely transferred.

24.4 Distributed Deadlock

Pessimistic concurrency controls that employ waiting are subject to deadlock. Assuming that the concurrency control at each site does not permit a deadlock locally, we want to ensure that the overall system is not subject to distributed deadlock. For example, a simple distributed deadlock between two distributed transactions, T_1 and T_2, both of which have cohorts (subtransactions) at sites A and B, will result if the concurrency control at site A makes T_1's cohort, T_{1A}, wait for T_2's cohort, T_{2A}, while the concurrency control at site B makes T_2's cohort, T_{2B}, wait for T_1's cohort, T_{1B}.

Note that in the general model of a distributed transaction, the cohorts can run concurrently, whereas a transaction accessing a single database is purely sequential. Hence, in the above example, T_{2A} not only holds some resource for which T_{1A} is waiting but can actually progress since it is not delayed by the fact that T_{2B} is waiting. Deadlock still occurs, however, since T_2 cannot release its locks until it commits globally, which will not happen if T_{2B} is waiting. Ultimately, in such a situation, all progress in the deadlocked transactions stops.

In general, a distributed deadlock cannot be eliminated by aborting and restarting a single cohort. The statements executed by a cohort are really a subsequence of the statements executed by the transaction as a whole. They cannot be reexecuted because other cohorts might already have executed statements that logically follow them. For example, T_{1A} might have sent a message to T_{1B} containing some results that it had computed before the deadlock occurred. Restarting T_{1A} without restarting T_{1B} makes no sense since the message will be resent, so the entire distributed transaction must be restarted.

The techniques to detect a distributed deadlock are simple extensions of those discussed in Section 20.4.2. In one, the system constructs a distributed *waits_for* relation and searches for cycles whenever a cohort is made to wait. For example, a cohort of T_1 informs its coordinator that it is waiting for a cohort of T_2. T_1's coordinator then sends a **probe** message to T_2's coordinator. If T_2's coordinator has also been informed by one of its cohorts that it is waiting for a cohort of T_3, the probe message is relayed by the coordinator of T_2 to the coordinator of T_3. A deadlock is detected if the probe returns to T_1's coordinator.

Another technique uses timeout: whenever the wait time experienced by a cohort at some site exceeds some threshold, the concurrency control at that site assumes that a deadlock exists and aborts the cohort.

Finally, the timestamp technique [Rosenkrantz et al. 1978] described in Section 20.4.2 can be used for distributed transactions with one small generalization. To ensure that timestamps created at one site are different from timestamps created at all other sites, each site is assigned a unique identifier. A coordinator at site *A* creates a timestamp for a distributed transaction, *T*, by concatenating *A*'s site identifier to the right of the value obtained from *A*'s clock. When *T* creates a cohort at some site, it sends along the value of its timestamp. With a single, unique timestamp associated with all of *T*'s cohorts, the strategy of never allowing an older transaction to wait for a younger transaction eliminates distributed deadlocks.

24.5 Global Serialization

In a centralized system, the goal of a concurrency control is to respond to requests to access items in the database so as to produce a specified level of isolation. With a distributed transaction, multiple DBMSs are involved, each of which might be supporting a different isolation level. Under such circumstances, the isolation between concurrent distributed transactions is poorly defined. Suppose, however, that we consider the problem of implementing globally serializable schedules. A simple (albeit impractical) approach is to provide a single control at some central site. All requests (at any site) are sent to this site, which maintains the data structures for implementing the locks for data items at all sites.

Such a system is just a centralized concurrency control in which the data is distributed. Unfortunately, this approach has significant drawbacks: it requires excessive communication (with the delays that this implies), the central site is a bottleneck, and the entire system is vulnerable to the failure of that site.

A better approach, and the one generally followed, is for each site to maintain its own concurrency control. Whenever a (sub)transaction makes a request to perform an operation at some site, the concurrency control at that site makes a decision based only on local information available to it, without communicating with any other site. Each concurrency control separately uses the techniques previously described to ensure that the schedule it produces is equivalent to at least one serial schedule of transactions and subtransactions of distributed transactions at its site. The overall design of the system must then ensure that distributed transactions are serialized globally—that is, that there is at least one equivalent serial ordering on which all sites agree.

Our concern, since the sites operate independently and might even employ different concurrency control algorithms, is that there might be no ordering on which all sites agree. Consider distributed transactions T_1 and T_2 that might have subtransactions at sites A and B. At site A, T_{1A} and T_{2A} might have conflicting operations and be serialized in the order T_{1A}, T_{2A}, while at site B, conflicting subtransactions of the same two transactions might be serialized T_{2B}, T_{1B}. In that case, there is no equivalent serial schedule of T_1 and T_2 as a whole.

We can ensure that local serializability at each site implies global serializability using nothing more than the individual concurrency controls and the two-phase commit protocol. Specifically it can be shown that

> If the concurrency controls at each site independently use either a strict two-phase locking or an optimistic algorithm, and the system uses a two-phase commit protocol, every global schedule is serializable (in the order in which their coordinators have committed them). [Weihl 1984]

While we do not prove that result here, it is not hard to see the basic argument that can be generalized into a proof. Suppose that sites A and B use strict two-phase locking concurrency controls, that a two-phase commit algorithm is used to ensure global atomicity, and that transactions T_1 and T_2 are as described above. We argue by contradiction. Suppose that the conflicts described above occur (so that the transactions are not serializable) and that both transactions commit. T_{1A} and T_{2A} conflict on some data item at site A, so T_{2A} cannot complete until T_{1A} releases the lock on that item. Since the concurrency control is strict and a two-phase commit algorithm is used, T_{1A} does not release the lock until after T_1 has committed. Since T_2 cannot commit until after T_{2A} completes, T_1 must commit before T_2. But if we use the same reasoning at site B, we conclude that T_2 must commit before T_1. Hence, we have derived a contradiction, and it follows that both transactions cannot have committed. In fact, the conflicts we have assumed at sites A and B yield a deadlock, and one of the transactions will have to be aborted.

You might think that virtually all systems use one of the specified concurrency control algorithms and thus satisfy the theorem. But many applications execute at isolation levels lower than SERIALIZABLE and hence do not satisfy the theorem.

24.6 When Global Atomicity Cannot Be Guaranteed

In practice, there are a number of situations in which an atomic commit protocol cannot be completed and hence global atomicity cannot be guaranteed.

- *A cohort site does not participate in two-phase commit.* A particular site might not support the protocol. For example, a resource manager might be a legacy system that does not support a prepared state. Alternatively, a site might elect not to participate to avoid the degradation of performance that can occur with blocking. A transaction is blocked during the uncertain period and holds locks that prevent other transactions from accessing the locked items. Since the site cannot control the length of the uncertain period, it is no longer independent: factors that control access to locked resources are controlled elsewhere. For example, the length of the uncertain period depends on the speed with which other cohorts respond to *prepare messages* and the efficiency of the message-passing system. If the coordinator crashes or the network becomes partitioned, a cohort might remain blocked for a substantial period of time.

  Cohort sites that elect to participate in the protocol often deal with this problem by unilaterally deciding to commit or abort a blocked subtransaction in order to release locks. Such a decision is referred to as a **heuristic decision**. Unfortunately, assigning a technical name does not change the fact that global atomicity might be compromised as a result of such an action. A heuristic decision might cause global inconsistency in the database (a subtransaction that updated a data item at one site might commit, but a subtransaction of the same distributed transaction at a different site that updated a related data item might abort). Such inconsistencies can sometimes be resolved in an ad hoc manner by communication among the database administrators at the different sites. Although heuristic decisions do not preserve global atomicity, they are the only way to resolve an important practical problem.

  A cohort site might not participate for reasons unrelated to performance. For example, the site might charge a fee to execute a subtransaction and, when the subtransaction completes and returns a result, might demand the fee even if the overall distributed transaction subsequently aborts. Therefore, the site administrator might insist that the subtransaction commit as soon as it completes, without waiting for the distributed transaction to commit or abort globally.

- *The language does not support two-phase commit.* On the application side, some database query languages allow a transaction to connect to multiple DBMSs but do not support two-phase commit. When a transaction completes, it sends individual (independent) commit commands to each DBMS. Thus, the all-or-none commit provided by a two-phase commit protocol is not enforced, and so the transaction is not guaranteed to be globally atomic. For example, most versions of embedded SQL do not support two-phase commit. However, JDBC and ODBC both provide APIs for implementing two-phase commit: JTS (Java Transaction service) for JDBC and MTS (Microsoft Transaction Server) for ODBC.

- *The system does not support two-phase commit.* Support of the two-phase commit protocol requires that the system middleware include a coordinator (transaction manager) and that the application, coordinator, and servers agree on conventions for exchanging protocol messages. For example, the X/Open standard specifies APIs for this purpose (e.g., the `tx` and `xa` interfaces). For many applications, such system support is not available, and so the two-phase commit cannot be implemented.

24.6.1 Weaker Commit Protocols

If sites do not participate in a two-phase commit protocol (or some other atomic commit protocol), the execution of distributed transactions is not guaranteed to be isolated or atomic. Nevertheless, systems might have to be designed under this constraint. In such cases, the application designer must carefully assess how this affects the correctness of the database and the ultimate utility of the application to its clients.

When the two-phase commit is not supported, or for some other reason is not used, one of the following weaker commit protocols might be used.

- In the **one-phase commit protocol**, the application program does not send commit commands to any site until all subtransactions have completed. If any abort, the distributed transaction is aborted. If all complete successfully, it sends a separate commit command to each site. Some sites might commit, and some might abort. A distributed transaction implemented with embedded SQL might operate in this fashion.
- In the **zero-phase commit protocol**, each subtransaction commits as soon as it completes. Hence, some sites might commit and some might abort.
- In the **autocommit protocol**, a commit operation is performed immediately (automatically by the system) after each SQL statement. Autocommit is the default in ODBC and JDBC.

None of these protocols guarantees global atomicity since subtransactions (or operations) might commit at some sites and abort at others. However, we can say that if (1) the concurrency control at each site uses either a strict two-phase locking or an optimistic algorithm, (2) the application program uses a one-phase commit protocol, and (3) the subtransactions at all sites commit, then all global schedules are serializable (in the order in which the application programs have committed them) and all global and local integrity constraints are maintained.

The same reasoning that justifies a similar result for the two-phase commit applies here—with the added restriction that the subtransactions at all sites must commit. If some subtransactions abort (so that distributed transactions are not necessarily atomic) the parts of the transactions that do commit are serializable.

With the zero-phase commit protocol, a subtransaction might commit and release locks at one site before another subtransaction is initiated and acquires locks at another site. Hence, from a global perspective, locking is not two-phase. As a result, global serializability is not guaranteed, even if the subtransactions at all sites commit. Transactions might be serializable in different orders at different sites. Each subtransaction maintains the local integrity constraint at the site at which it executes, but the schedule of distributed transactions does not necessarily maintain global integrity constraints.

The zero-phase commit protocol holds locks for a shorter period of time than does the one-phase commit protocol, and hence can provide better performance. Zero-phase commit might therefore be appropriate for applications in which there are no global integrity constraints and so global serializability is not an issue.

An example where zero-phase commit might be used is the Internet grocer application described in Section 16.2.3. The company has a headquarters site that registers customers and accepts purchase orders, and a number of warehouse sites throughout the country from which the groceries are delivered to the customers. Information about each customer is stored both at the headquarters site and the local warehouse site from which that customer's grocery orders will be delivered.

A customer registration transaction might consist of two subtransactions, executed in sequence: the first creates a customer record at the headquarters site, and the second creates a corresponding record at the appropriate warehouse site. The transaction can be viewed as having a zero-phase commit protocol since the first subtransaction is allowed to commit before the second is initiated. The reason for this design is to allow rapid response to the customer who is registering online. Although a global integrity constraint asserts that a customer recorded at a warehouse site is also recorded at headquarters, the fact that it is temporarily violated is viewed as acceptable because the record at the warehouse site is not needed until the customer makes an order, presumably at a later time. Note also that the (sub)transaction at the warehouse site is retriable: even if it should abort the first time it is executed, it will eventually commit if retried. Thus, the integrity constraint will ultimately be satisfied. We return to this example in Section 24.7.2 on asynchronous replication (the customer record is replicated in two databases).

The autocommit protocol holds locks for the shortest possible time and hence yields the best performance, but it does not guarantee even local serializability at each site. For this reason, it is not guaranteed to maintain either global or local integrity constraints.

In the one-phase and zero-phase commit protocols, if the application program requests that a subtransaction at some site be committed and it is aborted instead, the program is notified of the abort and might be able to take alternate action—perhaps retrying the subtransaction or initiating a new subtransaction at a different site. For some applications, this feature can be a significant advantage compared with the two-phase commit protocol in which, when a subtransaction at any site aborts, the entire distributed transaction aborts.

24.7 Replicated Databases

A common technique for dealing with failures is to replicate portions of a database at different sites in the network. Then if a site crashes or becomes separated from the network because of a partition, the portion of the database being maintained by that site can still be accessed by contacting a different site that holds a replica. We say that the **availability** of the data has been increased.

Replication can also improve the efficiency of access to data (hence increasing transaction throughput and decreasing response time) since a transaction can access the nearest replica, perhaps one that exists at the site at which the transaction is executing. For example, in the Internet grocer application discussed in Section 16.2.3, the company has a table describing its customers that is replicated at its headquarters site and at the local warehouse from which a customer's orders are delivered. Transactions involving the delivery of merchandise execute at the warehouse site and use the replica stored there, while transactions involving monthly mailings to all customers execute at headquarters and use the replica stored there.

Of course, replication has its costs. First, more storage is required. Second, the system becomes more complex since we must properly manage access to replicated data. For example, if we allow two transactions to access and perhaps to update different replicas of the same item, each might be unaware of the effects of the other, resulting in a problem similar to the lost update problem. Thus, a replicated system must ensure that the replicas of a data item are properly updated and that an appropriate value is supplied to a transaction that requests to read an item. In the Internet grocer application, the replicated customer information needs to be updated only when the customer information changes—for example, a change of address, which occurs infrequently.

An item is said to be **totally replicated** if a replica exists at every site. It is said to be **partially replicated** if replicas exist at some, but not all, sites.

If the DBMS itself does not support replication, the application itself can replicate data items. The DBMS is then unaware of the fact that distinct items at different sites are replicas of one another. If $x1$ and $x2$ are replicas of a data item, each transaction must explicitly maintain the integrity constraint $x1 = x2$. A transaction that accesses a replicated data item must specify which replica it wants by addressing a specific DBMS. A transaction that updates a replicated item must explicitly initiate subtransactions to update each replica.

Instead of requiring transactions to manage replication, most commercial DBMSs provide a special subsystem for this purpose—a **replica control**—which makes replication invisible to the application. The replica control knows where all replicas of a data item are located. When a transaction requests to read or write an item, it does not specify a particular replica. The request is processed by the replica control, which automatically translates it into a request to access the appropriate replica(s) and passes the request to the local concurrency control (if the replica is local) and/or to the remote site(s) at which the replica resides. We assume that concurrency controls implement a locking protocol, so when replicas are accessed they are locked in the same way as are ordinary data items: a shared lock for read access; an exclusive lock for write access. The concurrency control is unaware that a data item might actually be a copy of another data item at a different site. The relationship between the replica control and the concurrency control is shown in Figure 24.6.

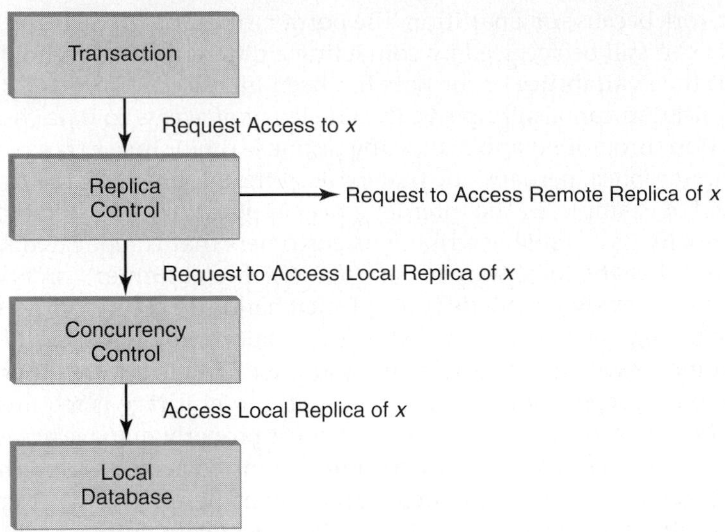

FIGURE 24.6 Relationship between replica control and concurrency control in a replicated database.

Replica controls in commercial DBMSs attempt to maintain some form of **mutual consistency**. With **strong mutual consistency**, every committed replica of an item always has the same value as every other committed replica. Unfortunately, performance considerations often make this goal impractical to achieve, and so most replica controls maintain the more modest goal, **weak mutual consistency**: all committed replicas of an item *eventually* have the same value, although, at any particular time, some might have different values. A variety of algorithms are used to maintain these goals.

The simplest replica control system is referred to as a **read-one/write-all** system. When a transaction requests to read a data item, the replica control can return the value of any one—presumably the nearest—of its replicas. With a fully replicated system, transactions that do not update replicated data items need not make any remote accesses and hence can respond rapidly to the user. When, however, a transaction requests to update a data item, the replica control must execute an algorithm that (eventually) causes all replicas of the item to be updated. This is the difficult case, and different algorithms have different characteristics. Generally speaking, read-one/write-all systems yield an improvement in performance over nonreplicated systems (where reads might have to access distant data items) if reads occur substantially more frequently than updates.

When a transaction requests to read a data item, the replica read is locked and the lock is held to commit time. Write locks are also held to commit time. The only issue is: what replicas are write locked and when? Read-one/write-all systems come in two varieties in this regard: synchronous update and asynchronous update. We discuss synchronous-update systems in Section 24.7.1 and asynchronous-update systems in Section 24.7.2.

24.7.1 Synchronous-Update Replication Systems

In a **synchronous-update system**, when a transaction updates a data item, the replica control locks and updates all of the replicas before the transaction commits. As a result, strong mutual consistency is maintained, transactions execute serializably, and database consistency is preserved. Synchronous replication is also referred to as **eager** replication since replicas are updated immediately.

Locking can be done in one of two ways.

1. *Pessimistically.* All necessary locks are acquired before the transaction proceeds beyond the statement that requested the access.
2. *Optimistically.* Only a single replica is locked and updated when the statement is executed. The other replicas are locked and updated later but before the transaction commits.

In either form, a new type of deadlock, **one-item deadlock**, is possible. This occurs if two updaters of the same item run concurrently and each succeeds in locking a subset of the item's replicas. Such deadlocks can be resolved with the usual protocols.

When a transaction commits, we must guarantee that each updated replica of an item is durable. It is not sufficient to simply commit the transaction at the site at which it was initiated (and release its locks) and send commit messages to replica sites since a replica site might crash before receiving the message. In that case, if the replica is not updated when the site recovers, a read request for the item by another transaction that uses that replica will not return the correct value.

The two-phase commit protocol can be used to overcome this problem. The cohorts are the replica sites that the transaction has accessed.[4] The prepared state is necessary to guarantee that all updates are durable before the transaction actually commits.

Unfortunately, eager replication has the effect of requiring the transaction to acquire additional locks, which increases the probability of deadlock. Furthermore, the response time is greatly increased due to the time required to handle lock requests for remote replicas and the fact that the transaction cannot complete until durability at all replica sites is ensured. These factors negatively impact performance, and for this reason synchronous replication has limited applicability.

The quorum consensus protocol. Although synchronous-update read-one/write-all replication can increase availability for readers, it does not help updaters. Because of the write-all requirement, the update cannot be completed if any site has crashed. We now describe a variant of synchronous replication in which no operation need access all replicas, so a data item might still be available even though some replica is inaccessible. To achieve this goal, we no longer insist on maintaining (even weak) mutual consistency. As a result, replica values are no longer identical. Despite this, the goal is the same as for read-one/write-all replication: all schedules resulting

[4] A replica site at which only reads have been performed can give up its read locks as soon as it receives the *prepare message*. See Exercise 24.12.

from the use of a quorum consensus replica control should be equivalent to serial schedules in which there is only one copy of each data item.

The basic idea of the **quorum consensus** protocol [Gifford 1979] is that when a transaction makes a request to read or write a replicated item, the concurrency control first locks some subset of the replicas, called a **read quorum** or a **write quorum** respectively, before granting the request. In the read case, the value returned to the transaction is then constructed from the values of the replicas in the read quorum. In the write case, all the replicas in the write quorum are then updated with the value to be written.

If the number of replicas in a read quorum is p and the number of replicas in a write quorum is q, we require that $p + q > n$ and $q > n/2$, where n is the total number of replicas. This ensures that there is a nonempty intersection between any read quorum and any write quorum and between any two write quorums of a particular item. As a result, whenever concurrent transactions execute conflicting operations on a replicated item, a lock request made by one of them will not be granted at the site of at least one replica, and one of the operations will be forced to wait. Note that the read-one/write-all system can be viewed as a quorum consensus protocol in which the number of replicas in a read quorum is one and in a write quorum is n.

With a quorum consensus algorithm it is possible to trade off the availability and the cost of the operations on an item. The smaller the value of p, the more available an item for reading and the lower the cost of a read. Similarly, the smaller the value of q, the more available an item is for writing and the lower the cost of a write. The availabilities of read and write are related, however. The more available and efficient read is, the less available and efficient write is and vice versa.

When a write request is granted, only the items in the write quorum are updated. Mutual consistency is not maintained since replicas not in the write quorum are not updated. As a result, replicas of an item will generally have different values, only some of which are current. We assume that, when each transaction commits, it is assigned a unique timestamp and that each replica of an item has the timestamp of the (committed) transaction that last wrote it. Since each read quorum intersects each write quorum, each read quorum intersects the write quorum assembled by the most recent writer. Therefore, at least one replica in each read quorum has the current value.

The problem is: how can the replica control identify such a replica? If the clocks at each site are exactly synchronized, this is not hard to do. Suppose that transactions T_1 and T_2 both update the same item, and T_1's update is first. Since their write quorums intersect, T_2's update must occur after T_1 commits (if T_1 and T_2 were concurrent, T_2 would have been forced to wait). Thus, since timestamps are assigned at commit time, T_2's timestamp must be greater than T_1's timestamp, and it follows that in any read quorum a replica with the largest timestamp in the quorum has the current value of the item.

Unfortunately, clocks at different sites are not exactly synchronized, and the consensus algorithm must take this into account. A technique for doing this is the subject of Exercise 24.21.

We can now summarize the quorum consensus protocol. We assume that an item, *R*, is stored as a set of replicas in the system and that each replica contains a value and a timestamp. We also assume an immediate-update pessimistic concurrency control and a strict two-phase commit protocol. Finally, we require that the timestamps of transactions are consistent with their commit order.

Quorum Consensus Replica Control Protocol.

1. When a transaction executing at site *A* makes a request to read or write a particular item, the replica control at *A* sends the request to a read or write quorum of sites containing the replica. If the concurrency control at all quorum sites can grant the appropriate lock on the replica, the requested operation is performed and a reply is returned to the replica control at *A*. If the request is a read, the reply contains the value of the replica and its timestamp.
2. When replies have been received by the replica control at *A* from a quorum of sites, the transaction can proceed. If the request was a read, the replica control at *A* returns to the transaction the value of the replica in the quorum with the largest timestamp.
3. A transaction commits using the two-phase commit protocol, where the cohorts are all of the sites at which it holds a read or write lock.[5] The coordinator obtains a timestamp for the transaction using its local clock and sends it with the prepare message. If the transaction commits, each cohort at which a write occurred updates its replica with the value of the timestamp before unlocking it.

As long as the control can assemble the necessary quorums for all operations, the protocol can proceed even when failures have occurred. When a site fails and is subsequently restarted, some of its replicas might have very old timestamps. The site need take no special recovery action, however, since the values contained in these replicas will not be used by any transaction until after they have been overwritten by some later transaction, at which time they will be current.

We have described the quorum consensus algorithm because it is an elegant solution to the replication problem. It has not, however, received wide acceptance among vendors of database systems.

24.7.2 Asynchronous-Update Replication Systems

In an **asynchronous-update system**, when a transaction updates a data item, the replica control updates some but not all of the replicas before the transaction commits. Most often, only a single replica is updated. The other replicas are updated after the transaction commits, and hence only weak mutual consistency is maintained. These later updates might be triggered by the commit operation or perhaps executed periodically at fixed time intervals. Asynchronous replication is referred to as **lazy** since replicas are not updated immediately. The updates are not done as a

[5] As before, a replica site at which only reads have been performed can release its read locks as soon as it receives the *prepare message*.

FIGURE 24.7 Schedule illustrating the possibility of inconsistent views with lazy replication. T_1 updates x and y at sites A and B. T_{ru} propagates the updates after T_1 commits. Because propagation is asynchronous, T_2 sees the new value of y but the old value of x.

T_1:	$w(x_A)$	$w(y_B)$	*commit*				
T_2:			$r(x_C)$	$r(y_B)$	*commit*		
T_{ru}:						$w(x_C)$	*commit*

part of the transaction itself so that, in contrast to synchronous-update replication, *the system as a whole might not be serializable and transactions might see an inconsistent state.*

For example, Figure 24.7 shows a schedule in which transaction T_1 updates x_A—the copy of x at site A, and y_B—the copy of y at site B. After T_1 commits, transaction T_2 reads y_B—hence getting the new value of y—and the replica of x at site C, x_C, that has not yet been updated. Thus, T_2 sees a (possibly) inconsistent view of the database. Later, a replica update transaction, T_{ru}, that updates all replicas of x and y, including x_C, is executed.

In the context of replication, **capture** refers to the process by which the replica control recognizes that an update of a data item by an application has occurred and that the new value must be propagated to all replicas whose value has not been updated. Capture can take two forms: the log can be monitored and updates to replicated items noted for later propagation; or triggers can be set in the database to record the changes. **Apply** refers to the process by which replica sites are informed of the updates they must perform to keep their replicas current.

Different applications are best served by different forms of asynchronous replication. In some cases, the emphasis is on keeping the replicas as tightly synchronized as possible. Although serializability is not ensured, the goal is to minimize the interval between the time one replica is updated and the time the update is applied to the other replicas. A distributed application that maintains account or customer service records might fall in this category, which is variously referred to as **group**, **peer-to-peer**, or **multimaster** replication. In other cases, tight synchronization is not crucial. For example, an organization might have a large sales force in the field that periodically logs in to a central site and downloads a reasonably up-to-date view of the data. The form of replication that is frequently used in this case is **primary copy** replication. A third form of replication is referred to as **procedural** and applies when large blocks of data must be updated.

Primary copy replication. In this approach to replication, a particular replica of a data item is designated the **primary copy** [Stonebraker 1979], and other replicas are **secondary copies**. Secondary copies are created by **subscribing** to the changes made at the primary copy. Although a transaction can read any copy, it can update only the primary. In one approach, if transaction T at site A wants to update data item x, it must obtain an exclusive lock on the primary copy of x, x_p, and update it. Even if there is a secondary copy at A, x_A, the secondary is not updated immediately. As a result, if two transactions want to update x, the first must commit before the lock on x_p can be granted to the second. Thus, the write operations of transactions are serialized, but read operations are not. In another approach, the application simply transmits updates to the primary copy to be processed later.

T's updates are asynchronously and nonserializably propagated to secondary copies (including x_A) after it commits. Since T and the apply step do not constitute a single isolated unit, replicas are updated in a nonserializable fashion. Since reads can be satisfied using arbitrary replicas, concurrent transactions might see an inconsistent view of the database (as shown in Figure 24.7) and function incorrectly as a result.

With primary copy replication, all updates are funneled through the primary copy. If T updates x, the site at which x_p exists executes replica-update transaction(s) to implement the apply step after T commits. A single update transaction might update all replicas (as in Figure 24.7), or an individual update transaction for each replica might be used. If the update transactions at each replica site are executed in the same order as that in which the primary copy is updated, the replica control system guarantees weak mutual consistency.

In a variant of primary copy replication, if T at site A requests to update x, and x_A is not the primary copy, it locks both the primary copy of x and x_A and updates them as part of the transaction. Other secondary copies are updated as previously described after T commits. In this way, the user at A can execute subsequent transactions that read x_A without having to wait for the update to propagate back from the primary to A.

In an alternate approach to the apply step, instead of propagating updates from the primary copy when a transaction commits, the replica control system at a site periodically broadcasts the current values of primary copies at its site to other sites. The broadcast should be transactionally consistent, containing all of the updates performed by committed transactions on primary copies of data items at the site since the last broadcast.

In some implementations, each secondary site can declare a view of the primary item, and only that view is transmitted. This is particularly useful if the secondary sites communicate with the primary site through a low-bandwidth (e.g., telephone) connection and it is therefore important that only relevant data be replicated at each site.

In still another approach to the apply step, updates are not automatically propagated from the primary site, and replica sites explicitly request that their view be refreshed. This is referred to as a **pull strategy** since the secondary sites pull the data from the primary sites. In contrast, in the **push strategy** of the algorithms we have described up to this point, the primary site pushes data out to the secondary. Push strategies reduce the interval in which replica values are outdated. In either case, all replicas of an item will eventually contain the same value, so weak mutual consistency is supported.

A pull strategy might be appropriate when secondary sites are mobile computers (perhaps hand-held) used by a large sales force in the field. A salesperson might update his replica when he connects to the network. Since bandwidth is small,

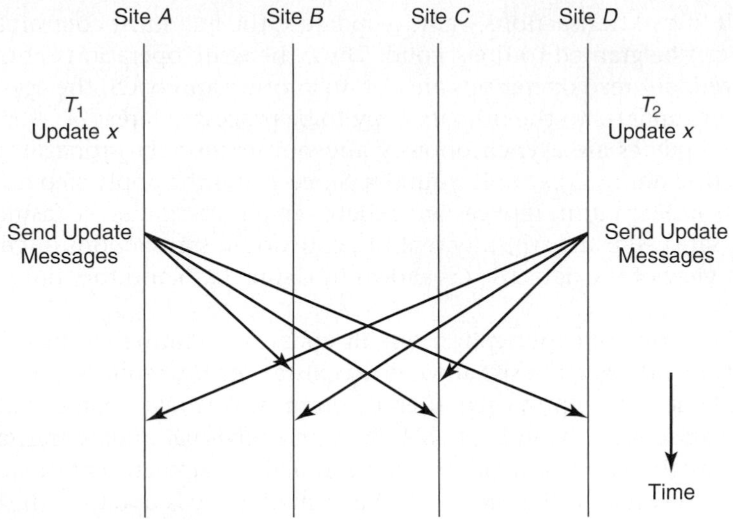

FIGURE 24.8 With group replication, updates might reach replicas in different orders, leading to violation of mutual consistency.

he defines a view that includes only information pertaining to his sales region. In this application, the replicas can be slightly (for example, minutes or hours) old. Read accesses predominate. A write occurs only when a new contract is signed, and the new information is sent to the primary first and broadcast to (or pulled by) all secondaries later. If the update occurs while the secondary is disconnected, it must be saved until a connection is established.

Group replication. In contrast to primary copy replication, with group replication an update can be made to any replica—presumably the nearest one. (Thus, if a database is totally replicated, read/write as well as read-only transactions can be completed using only data at the local site.) The updates made by a transaction, T, are later propagated to the other replicas. Since propagation is asynchronous, global serializability cannot be guaranteed.

As with primary copy replication, group replication can lead to nonserializable, and hence incorrect, schedules. For example, a schedule similar to the one shown in Figure 24.7 is possible. In addition, without further refinement, it might not even support weak mutual consistency. Figure 24.8 illustrates a situation in which two concurrent transactions, T_1 and T_2, executing at sites A and D, respectively, update replicas of data item x locally. As shown, the order of arrival of the messages that propagate those updates might be different at different replica sites. Since the final value of a replica is the value in the last message received, mutual consistency might not be preserved. In the terminology of replication, a **conflict** has occurred and the replica control system must employ a **conflict resolution** strategy to guarantee **convergence** and preserve mutual consistency.

One algorithm that guarantees weak mutual consistency associates a unique timestamp with each update and with each replica. An update's timestamp is the time at which the update was requested, and a replica's timestamp is the timestamp of the last update applied to it. Weak mutual consistency can be ensured if a replica site simply discards an arriving update when its timestamp is less than that of the replica's timestamp. This is an example of the Thomas Write Rule [Thomas 1979] we discussed in Section 20.9.1. With this algorithm, the value of each replica eventually converges to the value contained in the update with the largest (most recent) timestamp. Although the rule guarantees weak mutual consistency, lost updates are possible: two transactions read and update different replicas, but only the result of one survives. For this reason, the algorithm might not be appropriate for some applications.

Unfortunately, no algorithm exists that correctly merges the effects of different transactions in such situations for all applications. In some applications, the appropriate conflict resolution strategy is obvious. For example, if a directory is replicated and concurrent transactions append distinct entries to different replicas, the final value of all of the directory's replicas should contain both entries. Thus, a conflict-resolution strategy for a particular application can often be devised. In the general case, a replica control system can notify the user when it detects a conflict and allow the user to resolve it. Since there is no conflict-resolution strategy that is guaranteed to be correct, some commercial systems provide several alternative ad hoc strategies, including "Oldest update wins," "Youngest update wins," "Update from the highest priority site wins," and "User provides a procedure for conflict resolution."

Procedural replication. This form of replication is useful when updates need to be applied to many items in a batch-oriented fashion—for example, if interest has to be posted to each bank account and bank records are replicated at several sites. If each update were separately transmitted over a network, communication costs would be high. An alternative is to replicate a stored procedure at each secondary site and invoke that procedure at all replicas when the data is to be updated.

Summary. *The trade-off between synchronous- and asynchronous-update systems is one of correctness versus performance*. Many commercial DBMSs provide both types of replication. The designer should be aware that asynchronous updates can produce nonserializable schedules that might be incorrect and yield an inconsistent database.

In some applications, however, asynchronous updates are acceptable. For example, in Section 24.6.1 we described an Internet grocer application in which information about a customer was stored at both the headquarters site and at a warehouse site. We did not assume that a customer's record was identical at the two sites and treated the registration transaction as two separate subtransactions using a zero-phase commit. If, however, the records were identical, the database could be viewed as replicated and an asynchronous-update algorithm would produce the same result: the record would be created by a transaction at headquarters site, and, after the transaction had committed, it would be propagated to the warehouse site. As with the zero-phase commit, the response time seen by the user is minimized.

24.8 Distributed Transactions in the Real World

Although the theory underlying distributed transaction processing systems might seem complex, its final results are surprisingly simple and practical. If the concurrency control at each site is either a strict two-phase locking (pessimistic) control or an optimistic control (hence schedules are locally serializable), a two-phase commit protocol is used (hence transactions are globally atomic), and synchronous-update replication is used (hence, strong mutual consistency is maintained), distributed transactions will be globally serializable. Global deadlocks, which might arise as the result of waits imposed by pessimistic controls, can be resolved using timestamps, waits-for graphs, or timeout.

Atomicity and isolation are the properties of a transaction processing system that guarantee that if the transactions of an application are consistent, the application will run correctly. We have now seen that, in order to improve performance, distributed transaction processing systems frequently do not support atomicity and isolation completely. Transactions at a site might not run at the SERIALIZABLE isolation level, the two-phase commit protocol might not be used in committing distributed transactions, or an asynchronous-update technique might be used to support replication. Whether these compromises cause incorrect behavior is very much dependent on the semantics of the application. For this reason, in building a particular transaction processing system, these issues must be considered carefully.

BIBLIOGRAPHIC NOTES

A comprehensive discussion of distributed transactions can be found in [Gray and Reuter 1993]. [Ceri and Pelagatti 1984] is more theoretical in its orientation.

The two-phase commit protocol was introduced in [Gray 1978; Lampson and Sturgis 1979]. The presumed abort property for the two-phase commit protocol was discussed in [Mohan et al. 1986]. A more powerful commit protocol, called three-phase commit, was introduced in [Skeen 1981]. The wound-wait and kill-wait systems, which use a timestamp technique to avoid deadlocks, were introduced in [Rosenkrantz et al. 1978]. A proof that the two-phase commit protocol, together with two-phase locking local concurrency controls, guarantees global serializability was given in [Weihl 1984]. The quorum consensus protocol was introduced in [Gifford 1979]. Primary copy replication was introduced in [Stonebraker 1979], and the Thomas Write Rule is from [Thomas 1979].

EXERCISES

24.1 Describe the recovery procedure if a cohort or coordinator crashes at the following states within the two-phase commit protocol:

a. Before the coordinator sends the *prepare message*

b. After a cohort has voted but before the coordinator has decided commit or abort

c. After the coordinator has decided to commit but before the cohort has received the *commit message*

d. After the cohort has committed, but before the coordinator has entered the completion record in the log

24.2 Explain why a cohort does not have to force an abort record to the log during the two-phase commit protocol.

24.3 Explain how the fuzzy dump recovery procedure must be expanded to deal with prepared records in the log (assuming the site engages in the two-phase commit protocol).

24.4 Describe the two-phase commit protocol when one or more of the database managers is using an optimistic concurrency control.

24.5 Describe the presumed abort feature in the case in which multiple domains are involved.

24.6 Describe how the two-phase commit protocol can be expanded to deal with a cohort site that uses a timestamp-ordered concurrency control.

24.7 Give schedules of distributed transactions executing at two different sites such that the commit order is different at each site but the global schedule is serializable.

24.8 Phase 1 of the *Extended Two-Phase Commit Protocol* is identical to Phase 1 of the two-phase commit protocol we have described. Phase 2 of the extended protocol is as follows:

> *Phase Two.* If the coordinator received at least one "aborting" vote during Phase 1, it decides to abort, deallocates the transaction record from its volatile memory, sends an *abort message* to all cohorts that voted "ready," and terminates the protocol. If all votes are "ready," the coordinator enters its uncertain period, forces a *willing_to_commit record* (which contains a copy of the transaction record) to its log, and sends a *commit message* to each cohort. Note that the transaction is not yet committed.
>
> If a cohort receives an *abort message*, it decides to abort, rolls back any changes it made to the database, appends an abort record to its log, releases all locks, and terminates. If a cohort receives a *commit message*, it decides to commit, forces a commit record to its log, releases all locks, sends a *done message* to the coordinator, and terminates the protocol.
>
> The coordinator waits until it receives the first *done message* from a cohort. Then it decides to commit, forces a commit record to its log, and waits until it receives a *done message* from all cohorts. Then it writes a completion record to its log, deletes the transaction record from its volatile memory, and terminates.

Describe timeout and restart procedures for this protocol. Show that this protocol blocks only when the coordinator and at least one cohort crash (or a partition occurs) or when all cohorts crash. Give an example where the transaction aborts even though all cohorts voted "ready."

24.9 Design a logging, timeout, and restart procedure for the linear commit protocol. Do not assume the existence of a separate coordinator module. Assume that all communication between cohorts is carried on along the chain.

24.10 Consider a distributed transaction processing system that uses a serial validation optimistic concurrency control at each site and a two-phase commit protocol. Show that deadlocks are possible under these conditions.

24.11 Prove that if all sites use optimistic concurrency controls and if a two-phase commit protocol is used, distributed transactions are globally serializable.

24.12 If a cohort in a distributed transaction has performed only read operations, the two-phase commit protocol can be simplified. When the cohort receives the *prepare message*, it gives up its locks and terminates its participation in the protocol. Explain why this simplification of the protocol works correctly.

24.13 Consider the following atomic commit protocol that attempts to eliminate the blocking that occurs in the two-phase commit protocol. The coordinator sends a *prepare message* to each cohort containing the addresses of all cohorts. Each cohort sends its vote directly to all other cohorts. When a cohort receives the votes of all other cohorts it decides to commit or abort in the usual way.

a. Assuming no failures, compare the number of messages sent in this protocol and in the two-phase commit protocol. Assuming that all messages take the same fixed amount of time to deliver, which protocol would you expect to run faster? Explain.

b. Does the protocol exhibit blocking when failures occur?

24.14 The *kill-wait* concurrency control of Exercise 20.32 is based on locking. When it is used in a distributed system, it is referred to as the *wound-wait* protocol. We assume that a distributed transaction uses RPC to communicate among cohorts so that when the two-phase commit protocol starts, all cohorts have completed. The *kill* primitive is replaced by a *wound* primitive.

> If the cohort of transaction, T_1, at some site makes a request that conflicts with an operation of the cohort of an active transaction, T_2, at that site, then
>
> **if** $TS(T_1) < TS(T_2)$ **then** *wound* T_2 **else** *make* T_1 *wait*

where *wound* T_2 means that T_2 is aborted (as in the *kill-wait* protocol), unless T_2 has entered the two-phase commit protocol, in which case T_1 waits until T_2 completes the protocol.

Explain why this protocol prevents a global deadlock among transactions.

24.15 Suppose the nested transaction model were extended so that subtransactions were distributed over different sites in a network. At what point in the execution of a distributed nested transaction would a cohort enter the prepared state? Explain your reasoning.

24.16 In the text we state that if, in a distributed database system, each site uses a strict two-phase locking concurrency control (all locks are held until commit time) and the system uses a two-phase commit protocol, transactions will be globally serializable. Does the result also hold if the concurrency controls are not strict—read locks are released early—but are two phase?

24.17 Explain how to implement synchronous-update replication using triggers.

24.18 Design a quorum consensus protocol in which, instead of a timestamp field, each item has a version number field, which is updated whenever the item is written.

24.19 Consider a quorum consensus protocol in which an item is stored as five replicas and the size of each read and write quorum is three. Give a schedule that satisfies the following conditions:

> Three different transactions write to the item. Then two of the replica sites fail, leaving only three copies—*all of which contain different values.*

Explain why the protocol continues to execute correctly.

24.20 Consider a quorum consensus protocol in which an item is stored as n replicas, and the size of read and write quorums are p and q respectively.

a. What is the maximum number of replica sites that can fail and still have the protocol work correctly?

b. What is the minimum value that p and q can have such that $p = q$?

c. Select p and q so that the maximum number of replica sites can fail and still have the protocol work correctly. For this selection, how many sites can fail?

24.21 The quorum consensus replication algorithm requires that the timestamps of transactions be consistent with their commit order. In the absence of synchronized clocks, this requirement is not easily met. Propose an alternate algorithm for tagging replicas that can be used with quorum consensus. (*Hint:* Instead of assigning timestamps to transactions, assign version numbers to individual replicas.)

24.22 Describe an application of replicated data items in which serializability is not needed.

24.23 In what way is the checkbook you keep at home for your checking account like an asynchronous-update replication system?

24.24 Give an example of a nonserializable schedule produced by a primary copy asynchronous-update replication system.

24.25 The following variant of the primary copy asynchronous-update replication protocol has been proposed for totally replicated systems.

a. A transaction executing at site A updates only the replicas at A before it commits (it needed to access no other site since replication is total).

b. After the transaction commits, a second transaction is initiated to update the primary copies of all items updated at A.

c. After the transaction in step (b) has completed, each primary site propagates the update made at that site to all secondaries (including the one at site A). Updates made to a primary copy by several transactions are propagated to secondaries in the order in which the primary was updated.

Explain why, in step (b), all primaries must be updated in a single transaction and, in step (c), the update is propagated to site A.

24.26 Explain how triggers can be used to implement primary copy replication.

24.27 Describe a design of a logging protocol for distributed savepoints.

24.28 In the presumed commit version of the two-phase commit protocol described in the text, when the protocol starts, the coordinator forces a start record to its log. Describe a situation in which, if the coordinator had not forced this record to its log, the protocol would not work correctly.

25

Web Services

25.1 The Basic Idea

Web services are one of the most exciting new application areas on the Internet. On hearing this, you might ask

> What's all the fuss about? It's easy to obtain a Web service. For example, if I want to make a reservation on an airline flight, I first go to Google to find the Web addresses of the airline. Then I go to their Web site, make a few clicks to read their schedule, a few more clicks to find the flight I want, and a final click to charge the reservation I want to my credit card. Done!

All well and good, but now consider another scenario in which that approach does not work so well:

> You are a travel agent, and you want to schedule a trip for a client. First you want to get quotes on fares from a number of airlines for that date and time. Then you want to make the airline reservation on the cheapest airline. After that, you want to perform similar activities to make hotel reservations and reserve a car. Actually, you are performing these services for about twenty-five clients at the same time.
>
> You certainly do not want to do all this by making individual clicks on a Web page. You want the services to be performed by a program that reads a local file to determine the required activities and then sends messages over the Internet to other programs at the sites of the airlines, the hotels, and the car rental agencies.

This is the type of scenario for which Web services are oriented. They are, in general, business-to-business (B2B) systems, in contrast to the customer-to-business (C2B) systems with which you might be more familiar.

B2B systems are widely viewed as one of the fastest-growing areas of Web applications with a huge market potential. They open up exciting opportunities for businesses to

- Provide their services to an expanding world-wide market
- Outsource nonessential functions to other businesses and concentrate on core services

- Obtain services they need for their business from a world-wide network of possible service providers
- Establish partnerships with businesses from around the world to provide combined services that are better and less expensive than any one business could provide

And, most importantly, the costs of obtaining or providing these services, the so-called *transaction costs*, are sharply reduced compared with conventional methods. Thus, in the travel agency example, the transaction costs of obtaining the airline and hotel reservations by computer-to-computer communication are essentially zero compared with the costs of a human obtaining those reservations using the telephone or sitting at a computer terminal.

Web services can be regarded as the next step in several trends related to software integration. In Chapter 19 we discussed distributed transactions as a mechanism for integrating independent functions within the same enterprise. While Web services provide a model for doing the same thing, the ultimate goal is to provide integration beyond enterprise boundaries, where the modules being integrated have been developed by completely independent organizations. This type of integration should be possible as the field matures and standards take hold. Furthermore, whereas standards like CORBA (see Section 14.6) are oriented toward fine-grained integration at the level of objects, Web services are oriented toward coarse-grained integration at the level of entire services.

In this section, we briefly discuss some of the issues that arise in providing a service of this type.

- How can a company that wants to provide a particular service describe it to potential users? Such a description must include the format of the messages required to invoke the service and the address of the site at which the service is provided. The description must be understandable by both people and programs.
- How can a company that wants to obtain a particular service discover what companies provide it and, for each provider, find the information necessary to invoke that service? The service description must be discoverable by both people and programs.
- How can we ensure that an invocation message sent by the service requester will be understood by the service provider since the programs might be written in different languages, and the data types recognized by the languages might not be consistent? Furthermore, the programs might be executing under different operating systems on computers produced by different vendors. This issue is called **interoperability**.

The following technologies characterize and support Web services. But we want to caution you that this field is changing very rapidly. By the time you read this, many details of the proposed standards that we discuss might change. We are presenting a snapshot of a rapidly changing field.

- **XML** (Extensible Markup Language). Web services are described using XML, and the bodies of the various messages exchanged between services are XML documents. The use of XML allows the description to be independent of the hardware or software platforms involved and hence addresses the interoperability issue. For example, when a C++ program invokes a Web service, the arguments are converted into an XML format before they are passed to the service. When the invocation message reaches the service site, the arguments are converted to the format expected by the service, which might be implemented in Java. Thus the Java program can understand the data sent by the C++ program. We discussed XML in Chapter 15.
- **SOAP.**[1] The messages used by Web services are generally sent using the SOAP protocol. SOAP messages are XML documents and are exchanged using both synchronous, *request/response*, and asynchronous, *one-way*, communication. The original emphasis of SOAP was to support RPC and the transfer of parameter values with a request/response message pattern, but the protocol is increasingly used simply to support the exchange of arbitrary XML documents using both message patterns. It is anticipated that such document transmission will ultimately be its dominant use. This use of SOAP to transmit XML documents is often referred to as a **document-centric** approach. SOAP messages are frequently carried as the data portion of HTTP messages. We briefly discuss HTTP (Section 28.3) before giving a more complete discussion of SOAP (Section 28.4).
- **WSDL** (Web Services Description Language). A Web service can be described by the operations it makes available to other services and the information it exchanges when those operations are invoked. WSDL is used for such descriptions and hence provides the functionality of an Interface Definition Language, IDL (see Section 23.5.2). For example, an operation that provides fare quotes for an airline receives a request from a travel agent. The request contains an XML document listing flight numbers and dates. The service responds with an XML document containing the requested fares. The WSDL description of the operation includes the name of the operation, the messages exchanged during the operation, and an itemization of the data contained in each message.

  In addition, the WSDL description specifies a message transport that can be used to carry the information, how the data items are mapped to the format of the messages used by that transport, and the address of the service. This information is generally referred to as a **binding** and hence WSDL can be thought of as "IDL with binding." Frequently, the transport is SOAP over HTTP.

  We sometimes say that the service *exposes* or *exports* a WSDL interface. By that we mean that the implementation of the service is hidden from its users, while its interface is published so that potential users can access it. The WSDL description itself is in the form of an XML document.

[1] Although the term SOAP started out as an acronym for Simple Object Access Protocol, it is now simply accepted as a name with no further meaning. Whatever the original intention, invoking object methods is now the least important use of the protocol

Although WSDL allows the specification of request/response message exchanges, the emphasis in the Web services community is moving toward loosely coupled, one-way, asynchronous interactions that allow more flexibility. Message delays, failures, and the uncertainty of linking up with a module whose implementation is under the control of an unrelated organization make this form of coupling more appropriate. This philosophy differentiates Web services from the more tightly coupled, synchronous, RPC-oriented approach taken by CORBA (see Section 14.6).

- **BPEL** (Business Process Execution Language). The implementation of a complex Web service will generally involve synchronous and/or asynchronous interactions with the client and with other Web services. For example, the travel service might receive a client request, obtain price quotes from a number of airlines services, order tickets from one of them, interact with the client's credit card company, and finally send the tickets to the client. Hence, the service can be viewed as a workflow that communicates with other services. We discussed workflows in Section 19.3.6. The individual messages exchanged with these services are described in the WSDL documents they export, and the sequence in which these interactions (think tasks) take place amounts to a workflow. BPEL describes that workflow. It is a full-blown programming language with an emphasis on communication. A BPEL description of a workflow is in the form of an XML document.
- **UDDI** (Universal Description, Discovery, and Integration). UDDI addresses the problem of publishing and discovering Web services. It provides a registry (database) in which both of the following are included:
  - Companies that want to provide Web services can publish information about their services (including a WSDL description of how the service can be invoked).
  - Companies that want to utilize services available on the Web can search the database to discover companies that provide such services.

  The information stored in the UDDI registry is contained in XML documents.
- **WS-Coordination**. Complex Web services might require some aspects of transactional atomicity. WS-Coordination provides a framework for coordinating the termination of a set of Web services.

Security is important when interacting with Web services. Messages might have to be encrypted, and the various principals involved in requesting and supplying Web services might have to be authenticated. We discuss security for Web services in Section 26.14.

Front-end systems, back-end systems, and transaction processing. Many enterprises doing business over the Web implement the services they provide with transaction processing systems such as those we discussed in Chapter 23. For example, the implementation of an operation `getFareOp` that provides price quotes for airline reservations might involve the execution of a transaction that accesses a database that stores fares. In the context of Web services, such a transaction processing system is called a **back-end system**. By contrast, the systems we will discuss in this chapter are called **front-end systems**. Front-end systems describe how services are described and invoked, while back-end systems describe how they are implemented.

A back-end system can be exposed on the Web by equipping it with a WSDL interface. We can think of that interface as a simple front-end system and the combination of the front end and the back end as an extension of the transaction processing systems we discussed in Chapter 23.

In the C2B systems described in Section 23.9, the front-end systems cause Web pages to be displayed by the client's browser, and HTTP is used for communication. If the system is implemented in J2EE (Section 23.10), an HTTP message is received by a servlet, which interprets it and then calls a session bean in the back end to implement the service. Similarly, a B2B system is invoked by a SOAP message. The message is received by a SOAP-processing module that interprets it and then (again assuming J2EE) calls a session bean in the back end that implements the service.

Frequently, the implementation of an operation exported by a Web service involves the use of operations exported by other services. Hence, one service integrates the functionality of other services. This integration can be expressed as a BPEL program that invokes the other services. A system that performs this integration is also referred to as a front-end system, but in this case the front-end system is not directly connected to a back-end system. Instead, it invokes back-end systems and other front-end systems through their WSDL interfaces. Hence, to expand on our comparison of front-end and back-end systems, front-end systems are concerned with how Web services are exposed on the Web, how they are invoked, and how they integrate other services. Back-end systems are concerned with how the basic functionality (e.g., database transactions) are implemented.

Thus, Web services are provided by systems that combine front ends and back ends in a variety of ways. Such systems can be viewed as extensions of the transaction processing systems we discussed in Chapter 23. Furthermore, just as an invocation of a back-end system might require transactional properties, the invocation of a front-end system that integrates the operations of other Web services might also require transactional properties. WS-Coordination is designed for this purpose. Thus the material in this chapter also extends the discussion of workflows, distributed transactions, and atomic commit protocols in Chapters 19 and 24.

25.2 Web Basics

Before starting a discussion of Web services it is useful to set the stage by reviewing a few relevant facts about the Internet that supports these services. The Internet is a collection of interconnected computers that communicate by exchanging messages. Each computer is directly connected to a subset of neighboring machines through network links. A message is passed using a store-and-forward technique in which it moves from machine to neighboring machine as it travels from source to destination.

A hierarchical set of protocols supports communication, with each level in the hierarchy implementing a communication abstraction based on the services provided by lower levels. The physical level provides the abstraction of sending bits over the communication devices. The link level transmits packets between neighboring nodes using the services of the physical level. The network level implements an end-to-end abstraction by moving an entire message from source to destination using the services of the link level.

Our story starts at the next level, called the **transport level**, which provides the basic end-to-end service of moving data from source to destination in a way that insulates higher levels from having to deal with the idiosyncrasies of the intervening networks and provides certain quality-of-service guarantees. Such guarantees might be concerned with reliability, throughput, and delay.

A **connection-oriented** transport level is one in which a connection between two endpoints is set up before any data is transmitted and then removed when communication has completed. The connection is established by reserving resources at the endpoints, and perhaps at intermediate nodes as well, so that data can be moved in a way that is consistent with the guarantees. Data structures are set up at the endpoints to store the state of the connection: who is entitled to send data next, what is the sequence number to be used, etc. In some implementations, a path between the endpoints, consisting of a sequence of intermediate nodes, might be determined at the network level and physical resources along the path are reserved: bandwidth on communication lines and buffer space in nodes.

By maintaining state information, the connection-oriented approach is in a position to provide such features as reliability (lost data can be detected), sequencing (data segments are received in the same order as they are sent), and flow control (the rate at which data is sent can be controlled). For example, the sequence number stored at an endpoint enables the receiver to detect missing or out-of-order data. On the other hand, the connection set-up and take-down costs are not trivial. Hence, the connection-oriented approach is most suitable in situations in which large amounts of data must be transferred.

Our interest in this issue arises from the fact that Web communication is generally based on the **Transmission Control Protocol** (TCP), which is a transport level connection-oriented protocol. The **Hypertext Transfer Protocol** (HTTP) is built on top of TCP and is designed specifically for Web communication. HTTP messages are contained in TCP data that travels over TCP connections. Indeed, you can think of the Web as a set of clients and servers on the Internet that communicate using HTTP. Hence, before we start discussing Web services, we need to spend a little time discussing HTTP.

25.3 Hypertext Transfer Protocol

HTTP is a connection-oriented protocol that supports the exchange of messages with arbitrary content (not just HTML pages) between a source and a destination. It has a request/response structure and was originally designed to support simple interactions between a client (browser) and a Web server. The client sends a request message containing a Uniform Resource Locator (URL), more generally, a Uniform Resource Identifier (URI) that identifies a page to a Web server, and the server responds with a response message containing the page.

Request and response messages have different formats. The first line of a request message, referred to as the **request line**, has the form

method URL HTTP_version

The *URL* field identifies an item in the network and consists of three parts: the protocol, the host name, and the local name of an item at that host. For example, in the URL `http://www.yourbusiness.com/pages/display`, the prefix `http` identifies the protocol used to access an item, `www.yourbusiness.com` identifies the machine hosting the item, and `/pages/display` names an item at that machine.

The *method* field names the method to be invoked at the server that receives the message. Some commonly used methods are

- GET—requests the page identified by the URL
- HEAD—requests information *about* the page identified by the URL (the page is not transmitted)
- POST—contains information to be used at the server, which can include much more than just a URL. (We describe an important use of this below.)

The request line can be followed by one or more **header lines** having the form

field_name : value

Each header line supplies a different type of information to the server as identified by the field name. For example, a `From` field provides the sender's e-mail address, a `Content-Type` field describes the format of the data being sent, an `Accept` field specifies an acceptable response format, and an `If-Modified-Since` field (which might be used when a GET method is invoked) instructs the server to respond with the page identified in the URL only if it has been modified since the time (value) supplied. A `SOAPAction` header line is used if the data carried by the HTTP message is a SOAP message. It identifies the SOAP processor at the server that is to receive the message. The last header line is followed by an empty line, and any data follows that.

A simple client/server interaction starts when the user clicks on a link on a page displayed by a browser. The browser, using the services of a directory server (Chapter 23), translates the host name in the URL associated with the link into an Internet host address. The complete address consists of the host address followed by a TCP port number, which is an internal address within the host. The default port number for HTTP messages is 80, which identifies a process at the server, frequently referred to as an HTTP processor, that processes HTTP messages. The browser then sets up a TCP connection to the server and sends an HTTP message specifying the GET method to request the page identified in the URL.

The response message begins with a status line having the form

HTTP_version status_code reason

The *reason* is a human readable explanation of the three-digit *status code* that encodes the outcome of the request. As with the request message, it can be followed by one or more header lines. For example, an `Expires` header gives the time at which the accompanying page should be considered stale, and a `Last-Modified` header gives the time the page was last modified. If a page has been requested, it follows the header fields.

Returning to our example and assuming the server can locate the requested page, the server sends a response message containing the page, and the browser displays the page, completing the interaction. In Version 1.0 of the protocol, the server then disconnects. This might seem wasteful since the user is likely to request additional pages but is done because the server can maintain a limited number of connections and has no idea of whether, or when, the user will send another message. The implication is that each client/server interaction has to pay the price of connection setup and takedown. This is described as the "stateless" aspect of the protocol, meaning that no connection information is maintained at either end between interactions. Version 1.1 of HTTP improves on this by allowing the TCP connection to stay in place for possible future interactions. The problem, however, is to decide how long to keep the connection open, since the user might go to lunch at that point. A timeout mechanism can be used for this purpose, with the result that a new connection might have to be set up if another interaction does not occur soon enough.

One of the powerful features of HTTP is that it allows the user to do more than simply follow links from one Web page to another. More generally, the user can invoke programs on the server (although this is not the technique generally used for Web services). In this case the HTML page displayed by the browser contains a form element. For example, the form might be opened by the tag

```
<FORM  action="http://www.yourbusiness.com/servlets/placeorder"
        method="POST">
```

and have input boxes that the browser displays and into which the user enters data, which serve as parameters to the program to be invoked at the server. The `action` and `method` attributes are used for this purpose. The value of `action` specifies where the parameters are to be submitted: in this case the program which handles the data has the local name `/servlets/placeorder` on the destination server `www.yourbusiness.com`. Note that the destination might be different from the server that supplied the page. If the appropriate TCP connection does not exist, the client must set it up prior to sending the message. The value of `method` specifies the method field in the request line of the HTTP message used to invoke the program. The convention for transmitting the parameters depends on the method. If it is POST, the parameters are encoded in the data part of the request message; if it is GET, they are encoded as a suffix to the URL in the request line. The URL in this case might be

```
http://www.yourbusiness.com/servlets/placeorder?box1="12"&box2="Nov"
```

where 12 and Nov are the data supplied by the user in input fields number 1 and 2.

25.4 SOAP: Message Passing

Web services are based on XML, and SOAP has been generally accepted by Web service implementors as the communication protocol for transmitting information in XML format between SOAP-enabled clients (as opposed to ordinary browsers). The information might be an arbitrary XML document, in which case it is referred to as **document-style SOAP**. Alternatively, the information might describe the invocation of a remote procedure, in which case it is referred to as **RPC-style SOAP**. SOAP itself, however, is simply a protocol for transmitting a single message, so the invocation of a remote procedure will involve the use of two RPC-style SOAP messages. In this case, SOAP prescribes a particular XML format for the messages.

XML is the essential ingredient here since it supports interoperability. In addition to being a simple mechanism for transmitting XML data, SOAP provides for extensibility, error handling, and flexible data encoding. The World Wide Web Consortium (W3C) sets the standards in the Web services area. At the time that this chapter was written, Version 1.2 of SOAP had achieved the status of a recommendation by W3C. A protocol recommended by W3C is essentially a standard. We will discuss that version here.

SOAP describes how a message is to be formatted but does not specify how it is to be delivered. The message must be embedded in a transport level protocol for this purpose, and HTTP is commonly used: the SOAP message becomes the body of an HTTP message and is sent to the destination. At the next lower level in the protocol hierarchy, the HTTP message becomes data in a TCP stream sent over a connection. Assuming that the destination is **SOAP enabled**, an HTTP listener (at port 80) passes the body of the HTTP message on to the SOAP processor—a program that understands SOAP and is capable of processing the message.

An embedding of a SOAP message in HTTP is shown in Figure 25.1. Our example concerns an airline, SlowHawk, and will be used throughout the chapter. In this case, the SOAP message is carried in the data part of an HTTP message invoking the POST method. The destination URL has been split between the request line, which contains the argument `/fareService/getFareOp` (identifying a procedure to be invoked), and the `Host` header line that provides the host address, `www.SlowHawk.com`, of the service. Since a SOAP message is being sent, the `Content-Type` field is set to `application/soap+xml` (as opposed to `text/html`, which is appropriate for a browser). The `SOAPAction` header contains a URI that identifies the operation that the message is intended to invoke. It can be used in message routing or by a firewall

FIGURE 25.1 SOAP embedded in HTTP.

```
POST /fareService/getFareOp HTTP/1.1
Host: www.SlowHawk.com
Content-Type: application/soap+xml
Content-Length: 1000
SOAPAction: http://www.SlowHawk.com/fareService/getFareOp
```

. . . A SOAP message, such as the one in Figure 25.2, goes here . . .
. . . The `Content-Length` *header assumes that the message length is 1000. . . .*

FIGURE 25.2 The structure of a SOAP message.

```
<s:Envelope xmlns:s="http://www.w3.org/2003/05/soap-envelope">
  <s:Header>
    <!-- The header element is optional -->
    <!-- If present, header blocks go here -->
  </s:Header>
  <s:Body>
    <!-- An XML document goes here -->
  </s:Body>
</s:Envelope>
```

---

for message filtering. The `SOAPAction` header is required when the HTTP message contains a SOAP message.

While HTTP is a common way to transmit SOAP messages, the messages can also be transmitted in other ways. For example, the message can be sent as the body of an e-mail message using the Simple Mail Transfer Protocol (SMTP). The technique used to transmit SOAP messages is referred to as a **binding**. It was a goal of the SOAP developers to allow for flexible binding. For example, a particular Web service might provide two bindings: a customer can submit a SOAP request using HTTP or e-mail. The design of the SOAP message format is not dependent on the choice of binding.

The structure of a SOAP message is shown in Figure 25.2. It consists of an optional header element and a mandatory body element wrapped in an `Envelope` element. The name space describing the `Envelope` tag, *http://www.w3.org/2003/05/soap-envelope*, not only identifies the XML document as a SOAP message but also identifies the version. Different versions use different namespaces. A receiving SOAP processor can decide, based on the namespace URI, whether it is capable of processing the message. The tags `Envelope`, `Header`, and `Body` are defined in that namespace. The header element supports extensibility, which we will discuss later.

SOAP specifies a structure for a single message. Often Web services will need to exchange multiple messages. They may do this in a conversational mode in which there is no fixed pattern. The decision as to who sends a message next might be dynamically determined based on the XML documents exchanged. The XML documents form the body of the SOAP messages.

Alternatively, there might be a predetermined pattern. For example, having sent a particular message, the sender expects to get two responses back. The simplest pattern is the request/response pattern, which is natural for procedure invocation and is referred to as RPC-style SOAP. We discuss it next. It is important to note that remote procedures do not have to be invoked using this format and that request/response communication is not restricted to the invocation of remote procedures. A request/response exchange might simply be transmitting XML documents.

25.4.1 SOAP and Remote Procedure Call

Suppose the GoSlow Travel Agency uses a service provided by the SlowHawk airline to obtain quotes on airline fares. SlowHawk offers a method `getFareOp` that returns the quote and makes a reservation that will be held for a short period of time while the client decides whether or not to use it. GoSlow invokes `getFareOp` using the RPC-style SOAP request message shown in Figure 25.3. The response message from the method is shown in Figure 25.4. Request and response information is contained in the `Body` of the messages. A complete description of this information might be provided using an Interface Definition Language, but this is not part of SOAP.

FIGURE 25.3 The RPC-style SOAP request message for `getFareOp`.

```
<s:Envelope xmlns:s="http://www.w3.org/2003/05/soap-envelope"
    xmlns:xs="http://www.w3.org/2001/XMLSchema"
    xmlns:xsi="http://www.w3.org/2001/XMLSchema-instance">
  <s:Body>
    <n:getFareOp xmlns:n="http://www.goslow.com/wsdl/trips"
      s:encodingStyle="http://schemas.xmlsoap.org/soap/encoding">
      <n:custId xsi:type="xs:string">
        xyz123
      </n:custId>
      <n:destination xsi:type="xs:string">
        Chicago
      </n:destination>
      <n:departureDate xsi:type="xs:date">
        2004-12-27
      </n:departureDate>
      <n:returnDate xsi:type="xs:date">
        2005-1-04
      </n:retur
    </n:get
  </s:Body
</s:Envelope
```

FIGURE 25.4 The RPC-style SOAP response message from getFareOp.

```
<s:Envelope xmlns:s="http://www.w3.org/2003/05/soap-envelope"
    xmlns:xs="http://www.w3.org/2001/XMLSchema"
    xmlns:xsi="http://www.w3.org/2001/XMLSchema-instance">
  <s:Body>
    <n:getFareOpResponse xmlns:n="http://www.goslow.com/wsdl/trips"
      s:encodingStyle="http://schemas.xmlsoap.org/soap/encoding">
      <n:custId xsi:type="xs:string">
        xyz123
      </n:custId>
      <n:tripNo xsi:type="xs:float">
        10997890
      </n:tripNO>
      <n:cost xsi:type="xs:float">
        327.98
      </n:cost>
    </n:getFareOpResponse>
  </s:Body>
</s:Envelope>
```

The organization of the information is self-evident. The name of the element in the request body is the same as the method name (getFareOp), and the name of the element in the response body is (by convention) the method name with Response appended to the end (e.g., getFareOpResponse). The names of the child elements in the request message must be the same as the names of the input parameters of the method, and they appear in the same order. The names of the child elements in the response message are the same as the names of the output parameters of the method, and they appear in the same order. All of these names are drawn from the namespace http://www.goslow.com/wsdl/trips, which we will see in Figure 25.21 when we discuss WSDL. If a child element appears in both the request and response structures, it is an in/out parameter. An additional child element, with tag result, is used in the response message if the method returns a value, but that is not needed here. We will discuss the encodingStyle attribute at the end of this section.

In this example the arguments involve only the simple data types float, date, and string. Since these correspond to types in XML Schema, the arguments are easy to send. The sender transforms the arguments from the binary representation used by the client's host language to the ASCII strings required in the XML representation within SOAP.

In general, however, a structured type, such as an array or record, might be passed as an argument. The sender and the receiver must agree on the XML format to be used in the SOAP messages to describe that type. For example, are the elements of an array to be sent as a sequence of rows or a sequence of columns? What tags will be used? The sender then must convert its internal data into the ASCII string corresponding to that format when sending the message, and the receiver must convert from that format into its internal format after receiving the message. The conversion at the sender is called **serialization**, and at the receiver it is called **deserialization**.

Serialization/deserialization is not so easily done—since the client and server might be implemented in different languages on different platforms, and as a result there is no guarantee that the deserialization tool at the server will understand how the serialization was done at the client. There are several techniques for dealing with this problem. We describe one here and return to this issue in Section 25.5.2.

SOAP defines a data model that can be used to represent arbitrary data structures and then specifies rules for transforming instances of that model into the serialized ASCII strings contained in SOAP messages. For example, an instance of the model might represent a particular array of values, and the SOAP data model specifies how it should be represented as an ACSII string. It is up to the client and server to map an instance of a type specified in the client's or server's language into an instance of the model. Since the rules specify the serialization of each model instance, each client's and server's type instance is, as a result, mapped to a serialized string. The client and server must provide serialization and deserialization programs that implement that mapping.

The fact that SOAP rules have been used to serialize the request message of Figure 25.3 is indicated by the value of the `encodingStyle` attribute of the `getFareOp` element. In order to be completely flexible, however, SOAP allows applications to define their own set of rules to perform this function. Thus, with one set of rules an array might be serialized as a sequence of rows using one set of tags, while in another it might be serialized as a sequence of columns using a different set of tags. The set of rules that have been used are identified by the `encodingStyle` attribute. In most cases the standard SOAP encoding rules are indicated.

There must be a serializer and a deserializer program for every data type in the request and response messages. Many vendors supply programs that implement the SOAP encoding rules for the simple and structured types defined in the SOAP standard for languages such as Java and C++ (that is, they serialize and deserialize the data types in Java or C++ into the ASCII corresponding to the types defined in the SOAP standard). The `encodingStyle` attribute can be attached to any element other than the `Envelope`, `Header`, and `Body` elements, and its value specifies the style the sender used to serialize the data in that element. RPC-style messages in which data is encoded using the rule set named in the most local `encodingStyle` attribute are referred to as **RPC/encoded**.

25.4.2 SOAP Extensibility

The designers of SOAP were keenly aware that in the rapidly developing Web environment new infrastructure facilities would constantly be emerging. Thus, although today we might invoke the `getFareOp` method by simply supplying the method name and arguments as shown in Figure 25.3, later we might introduce security and require that the requester be authenticated before the method is invoked, or we might want to charge for the service and require that a billing routine be executed first. Encryption and logging are other examples. The key thing to note is that the information required to invoke the method does not change. However, additional information might be required by the new infrastructure service that is essentially orthogonal to the invocation information. Thus, the name and password necessary for authentication and the credit card number necessary for billing are unrelated to the method name and arguments required for invocation.

Extensibility refers to the fact that the information that must be supplied to an infrastructure service can be added without making any change to the body of the message that contains the information for the ultimate destination (e.g., the invocation information). SOAP provides the `Header` element for this purpose. A header can contain any number of child elements called **header blocks**, each of which carries information for a particular infrastructure service. Since XML allows an element to declare its own namespace, a development group can design the structure of a block for a particular service without worrying about interference from other groups developing blocks for other services. This not only illustrates the utility of the namespace concept, but also shows the advantage of being able to associate a namespace with an individual element (and its associated scope).

Figure 25.5 shows the request message of Figure 25.3 with the addition of a header block to accommodate an authentication service. The block uses the namespace `www.SlowHawk.com/authentication/` in which the tags `authinfo`, `name`, and `password` are defined.

Having inserted the authentication information into the message, we next have to describe how the authentication server gets to perform its function before `getFareOp` is invoked. This issue is complicated by the fact that the authentication server might reside at a node, referred to as an **intermediary**, that is different from the node at which `getFareOp` is executed. The off-loading of infrastructure services is helpful when a Web service is heavily used. In this case the message must be routed through the intermediary, which accesses the header block on its way through, performs the infrastructure service, and then relays the message to the next (perhaps final) destination. Hence, the client must send the message to the intermediary, not to the destination server.

For example, `SlowHawk` might receive requests through a proxy machine that acts as an intermediary by performing authentication. The proxy scans the header looking for blocks that it should process. Each block is identified by its tag and namespace and can optionally have an attribute, `role`, that identifies the purpose of the block. The block should be processed by an intermediary designed to fulfill that purpose. Correspondingly, each SOAP node assumes certain roles and processes those blocks whose role attribute matches one of its functions.

A role value of `next` in a header block acts as a wild card: all intermediaries assume this role. Hence, a header block with role `next` should be processed by any intermediary that receives the message. Blocks that do not have a role specified are intended for the final destination.

The processing of a header block is mediated by the block's `mustUnderstand` attribute, which indicates whether or not an intermediary that assumes the role

FIGURE 25.5 A SOAP message for invoking `getFareOp` that uses an intermediate authentication server.

```
<s:Envelope xmlns:s="http://www.w3.org/2003/05/soap-envelope"
      xmlns:xs="http://www.w3.org/2001/XMLSchema"
      xmlns:xsi="http://www.w3.org/2001/XMLSchema-instance">
  <s:Header>
    <auth:authinfo xmlns:auth="www.SlowHawk.com/authentication/"
        s:role="SlowHawk.proxy.com"
        s:mustUnderstand="true">
      <auth:name> John Smith </auth:name>
      <auth:password> doggie </auth:password>
    </auth:authinfo>
    <!-- Other header blocks go here -->
  </s:Header>
  <s:Body>
    <n:getFareOp xmlns:n="http://www.goslow.com/wsdl/trips"
      s:encodingStyle="http://schemas.xmlsoap.org/soap/encoding">
      <n:custId xsi:type="xs:string">
        xyz123
      </n:custId>
      <n:destination xsi:type="xs:string">
        Chicago
      </n:destination>
      <n:departureDate xsi:type="date">
        2004-12-27
      </n:departureDate>
      <n:returnDate xsi:type="xs:date">
        2005-01-04
      </n:returnDate>
    </n:getFareOp>
  </s:Body>
</s:Envelope>
```

stated in the block is required to process the block. If it has value `true` and an intermediary that assumes the role is unwilling to process the block (perhaps because of its contents), the message is aborted and a fault message is returned to the sender. Header blocks that do not contain `mustUnderstand="true"` (i.e., the value is `false` or the attribute is not present) are regarded as optional. In that case, if an intermediary that assumes the role does not process the block, the block is simply ignored. A header block dealing with priority might be treated in this way.

A message might travel through a number of intermediaries on its way to its final destination. At each node the header is scanned and the appropriate blocks are processed. After processing a block, the intermediary might delete it and send

FIGURE 25.6 The SOAP message that the intermediary sends to the final destination.

```
<s:Envelope xmlns:s="http://www.w3.org/2003/05/soap-envelope"
      xmlns:xs="http://www.w3.org/2001/XMLSchema"
      xmlns:xsi="http://www.w3.org/2001/XMLSchema-instance">
  <s:Header>
      <ident:userId xmlns:ident="www.SlowHawk.com/authentication/">
        <ident:Id> 123456789 </ident:Id>
      </ident:userId>
  </s:Header>
  <s:Body>
    <n:getFareOp xmlns:n="http://www.goslow.com/wsdl/trips"
      s:encodingStyle="http://schemas.xmlsoap.org/soap/encoding">
      <n:custId xsi:type="xs:string">
        xyz123
      </n:custId>
      <n:destination xsi:type="xs:string">
        Chicago
      </n:destination>
      <n:departureDate xsi:type="date">
        2004-12-27
      </n:departureDate>
      <n:returnDate xsi:type="xs:date">
        2005-01-04
      </n:returnDate>
    </n:getFareOp>
  </s:Body>
</s:Envelope>
```

the message forward. The intermediary can also reinsert the header block (perhaps with new contents) or add new header blocks intended for nodes further down the chain. The final destination processes all headers with unspecified roles, as well as the message body. Notice that the destination need not be aware that any processing by intermediaries has taken place.

The message that the intermediary sends to the destination is shown in Figure 25.6. The authentication header block shown in Figure 25.5 has been deleted, and a new block has been added containing the (authenticated) `Id` determined by the proxy. In this case the destination uses `Id` to determine if the client is authorized to invoke `getFareOp`. Since the new block will be processed by the destination, it does not contain a `role` attribute.

WS-Addressing. As we have described it up to this point, a SOAP message does not contain the address of the intended receiver. The address must be provided separately by the program that constructs the SOAP message to the program that

FIGURE 25.7 WS-Addressing header blocks for the message of Figure 25.3.

```
<wsa:Action>http://www.SlowHawk.com/wsdl/trips/getFarePT/itineraryMsg
</wsa:Action>
<wsa:To> ··· URI identifying final destination ··· </wsa:To>
<wsa:MessageId> ··· unique message identifier ··· </wsa:MessageId>
```

implements the transport protocol that will carry the message and is included in the transport header. For example, the address is contained in the HTTP header in Figure 25.1. Furthermore, it might also be necessary to separately specify to the transport protocol the identity of the particular processor at the destination address that should receive the message. With HTTP this is the value in the `SOAPAction` header line. Providing this information separately is awkward since it makes the sending of a SOAP message dependent on the particular transport protocol in use: the information has to be provided in different ways to different protocols. This runs counter to a fundamental goal of the Web services architecture: it should be transport-neutral.

Furthermore, when security is an issue, spreading the message-relevant data over two protocols means that two different security mechanisms must be used. Techniques for securing a SOAP message, which we will discuss in Chapter 26, do not secure information provided outside the message.

For these reasons, it is desirable to make SOAP transport-neutral. All the information needed to send a SOAP message should be contained in the message itself. In this way, the message can be constructed in a uniform way by the sender and delivered to any transport protocol, which can then use the information in a transport-specific way.

WS-Addressing makes this possible by introducing header blocks into the SOAP message containing the missing information.[2] Additional blocks to be inserted in the header of the message of Figure 25.3 are shown in Figure 25.7. The prefix `wsa` identifies the WS-Addressing namespace, *http://schemas.xmlsoap.org/ws/2004/08/addressing*. The address of the destination is provided by the `To` element. The `Action` element identifies the purpose of the message for the receiving SOAP processor. The purpose is determined by the application semantics. For example, the message might be a request to invoke a particular operation. The *recommended* way to identify the purpose of a message is to provide a URI that refers to the WSDL declaration of the information it carries—more precisely, that identifies the declaration of the WSDL message carried by the SOAP message. This is done by concatenating the target namespace of the WSDL document with the port type and the message name (details that will be clarified when we discuss Figure 25.22.) The value of the `Action`

[2] This discussion is based on the specification document submitted to W3C for approval entitled "Web Services Addressing (WS-Addressing)," August 10, 2004.

element should be identical to the value in the SOAPAction header line when the SOAP message is carried by HTTP.

While these two elements are required, a number of optional elements are also defined. The MessageId element provides a unique identifier for the message. In some situations it is useful to relate one message to another—for example a response to a prior request might want to identify that request. A RelatesTo header element is defined for this purpose, and in this case it would contain the identifier of the request.

Finally, WS-Addressing introduces the complex type EndpointReferenceType. An instance of the type contains all the information needed to address a message to an endpoint. For example, a sender might pass to a receiver an endpoint reference for an endpoint to which the receiver should send a reply (or a fault) message. (The endpoint might have a different address than the sender's.) The sender might use a ReplyTo header block, which takes an endpoint reference as its value.

The following is an example of an endpoint reference:

```
<wsa:EndpointReference
        xmlns:wsa="http://schemas.xmlsoap.org/ws/2004/08/addressing"
        xmlns:gs="http://www.goslow.com/wsdl/trips">
    <wsa:Address> <!-- a URI goes here --> </wsa:address>
    <wsa:PortType> gs:tripPT </wsa:PortType>
    <wsa:ReferenceProperties>
        <gs:Id> 16022875 </gs:Id>
    </wsa:ReferenceProperties>
</wsa:EndpointReference>
```

The value of the Address attribute is the URI of the destination and is the only required item. Information about the WSDL description of the endpoint can be provided. The portType element is an example of this (the service and port can also be named).

The ReferenceProperties element has child elements that are used to provide further identification of the message's target (beyond just the URI) at the destination (e.g., a shopping cart identifier). For example, a transaction might send a message to a receiver containing an endpoint reference to be used for a reply. It might include its Id in the reference. The Id will simply be copied by the receiver into a SOAP header block when a reply message is constructed (its value is not used by the receiver). The header block will be used when the reply arrives back at the sender to identify the transaction. Thus an endpoint identifies a target at some level of granularity. In some contexts this identification can be done with just a URL. In others, more is involved.

The endpoint reference might also supply policy information (e.g., should the message be encrypted, and if so, how).

After all this discussion, we can finally discuss how a process knows how to address a SOAP message. If the destination is known in advance, the information needed in the two SOAP header blocks that must be included in the message, `To` and `Action`, can be stored statically in the sending process. Or it can be retrieved from a WSDL specification (which we will discuss in Section 25.5). But suppose this is not the case? Suppose the process receives in a message an endpoint reference that it wants to use to address another message? The `Address` element of the reference is copied to the `To` header block in the new message. The value of the `Action` header block is obtained from the WSDL specification (see page 1066). The children of `ReferenceProperties` are copied verbatim as header blocks in the message and are used at the destination site to further direct the message.

This leaves open the question of how a node on the message path knows whether to relay the message on to an intermediary or send it to the final destination and, if it is to be sent to an intermediary, which one? The current approach to this is referred to as **next hop** routing: each node on the path makes this decision based on the destination address, information in header blocks, and information stored locally.

25.4.3 SOAP Faults

SOAP explicitly provides a mechanism for communicating information back to the sender about faults that arise while an intermediary or the final destination is processing the message. Faults are divided into categories. For example, a `VersionMismatch` fault indicates that the namespace identifying the `Envelope` tag is not understood by the receiver (the receiver does not understand the version of SOAP used by the sender). A `MustUnderstand` fault indicates that an intermediary was not prepared to process a block addressed to it in which the value of the `mustUnderstand` attribute was `true`. A `Sender` fault indicates that there is a problem with the contents of the message, and a `Receiver` fault indicates that the problem is not with the message.

Although a SOAP body can contain an arbitrary XML document, we have seen that when a message is used to invoke a remote procedure, the body takes on a particular format. Similarly, SOAP provides an explicit format for a fault message. It contains a fault code, which places the fault in an appropriate category, a human-readable explanation of the fault, the identity of the node at which the fault occurred, and an optional element in which application-specific information can be provided.

25.4.4 SOAP Binding

A SOAP message is transmitted between two sites using a transport protocol. Since the transport is typically HTTP, we will say a few words about that particular binding. But keep in mind that other transport protocols can be used. SOAP does not require any particular transport.

When bound to HTTP, SOAP messages can be sent using either GET or POST. With POST, the SOAP envelope becomes the data part of an HTTP request message. When RPC-style SOAP is used to format the SOAP message (for example the message in Figure 25.3), a procedure is being invoked and results are generated which are returned in a SOAP response message. The SOAP response (for example the message in Figure 25.4) is carried in the data part of the HTTP response.

With document-style SOAP, communication can be one-way or request/response. In the latter case the sender transmits an XML document and the receiver responds with an XML document. However, the response is not built into the SOAP protocol as with RPC-style SOAP: two separate messages are involved, and each is carried in an HTTP request message. Keep in mind, that whenever an HTTP request message is transmitted, an HTTP (not a SOAP) response is generated automatically. This can serve as an acknowledgment that the XML document contained in the request has been received.

A nice feature of the HTTP binding when RPC-style SOAP is being transmitted, is that it provides a way to automatically associate the response with the corresponding request. This is important if an application is concurrently communicating with multiple servers and is referred to as **correlation**. In that case the application might have several requests outstanding. When a response arrives, it is necessary to associate it with the corresponding request. Since HTTP uses TCP, correlation follows from the fact that the response arrives in the HTTP response message on the same connection over which the request was sent.

With other transports (for example, email), correlation might not be automatic and it might be necessary to include a `MessageId` header block in the request message and a `RelatesTo` header block in the associated response message containing the same unique Id so that the two messages can be matched. The use of such header blocks is particularly appropriate if the application is communicating with several other services in conversational mode.

SOAP utilizes the HTTP GET method in the special case in which the application simply wants to retrieve a resource, that is, the server is accessed in read-only mode. This usage is a SOAP-level version of the interaction that occurs when a browser requests an HTML page: the browser sends an HTTP request message invoking the GET method, and the page is returned in the HTTP response message. A SOAP interaction of this sort is essentially the same except that a SOAP message is returned in the HTTP response instead of an HTML page. Since a SOAP message can contain an arbitrary XML document, this is appropriate when the application wants to process the information instead of displaying it. Since the interaction simply retrieves a SOAP message (XML document) identified by a URI—the only information that has to be sent to the target server in the request is that URI.

The HTTP binding supports this type of SOAP interaction by using an HTTP GET request that identifies the desired SOAP message (XML document) in the URI field and has an `Accept` field with value `application/soap+xml` to indicate that a SOAP message is expected in the response. The request message has no SOAP content. For example, a request to fetch SlowHawk's schedule for flights to Boston might have the form

```
GET /fareService/schedules?destination="Boston"  HTTP/1.1
Host: www.SlowHawk.com
Accept: application/soap+xml
```

Note that when GET is used, only the HTTP response message contains a SOAP message, while with POST, SOAP messages might be contained in both the HTTP request and in the response.

25.5 WSDL: Specifying Web Services

We have seen how SOAP can be used to encapsulate XML data exchanged by Web services, but how does one *describe* that service and how the data is exchanged? That is the problem addressed by WSDL (Web Services Description Language), which is under active development. At the time that this chapter was written, Version 1.1 was a W3C working draft and Version 2.0 was already under consideration. Since BPEL, which we discuss in Section 25.6, is based on Version 1.1, we will primarily be concerned with that version. Version 2.0 has some interesting features, which we will point out at the end of Section 25.5.

WSDL describes message exchange at two levels:

- The **abstract level** describes the (abstract) interface supported by a Web service. It gives the names of *operations* supported by the Web service, the *messages* used to invoke them, and the data types of the different items in the messages. It groups related operations into what it calls a *port type*. The abstract level can be viewed as an Interface Definition Language.
- The **concrete level** specifies how the abstract level is implemented. It gives a Web address at which the operations of a port type can be invoked and specifies how the messages that are exchanged through that address are *bound* to a specific transport protocol (for example, HTTP). It also groups Web addresses (and hence bindings of port types) together into something it refers to as a *service*.

25.5.1 The Abstract Level

In many respects describing a service at the abstract level is like describing an object in an object-oriented language. The abstract level defines the following elements:

- Optional **type** definitions in the XML Schema format. These types are used to specify message parts, as described below. See Section 15.3 for a detailed exposition of schema documents in XML.
- **Port types**. A port type provides an abstract description of a collection of operations. This description is analogous to an object interface.
- **Operations**. An operation is analogous to a method of an object. A description of an operation includes a set of messages that the operation expects as input and

returns as output. An operation can also return a *fault* message if an execution of the operation ends abnormally.

- **Messages.** Messages are used to invoke operations and return results. Messages are described independently of operations, and each operation refers to messages that describe its input, output, and faults. A message can have multiple **parts**. Each part is described by a type and is an input or output parameter of an operation.

An operation together with its messages and their parts corresponds to the signature of a method.

The overall structure of a WSDL specification at the abstract level is depicted in Figure 25.8. The italicized symbols are names of types, messages, port types, and operations, which are chosen by the user. Nonitalicized symbols are part of the WSDL syntax. The template shows the main components of an abstract level WSDL specification, how the namespaces are defined and used to identify the types and messages introduced by a WSDL document, and how user-defined types are used to give structure to messages. For instance, the template shows a two-part message where the structure of the first part is defined by a complex type defined in the same WSDL document, and the second part's type is a standard XML Schema type. We discuss each component of an abstract WSDL specification below.

Message descriptions. Operations are invoked by messages. An example of a message description used in `getFareOp` is given in Figure 25.9. Each message can contain a number of parts. By decomposing the (abstract) message into parts it is possible to place different items of data in different positions within the (concrete) message of the transport protocol that carries the data. Thus, one part might be mapped to a SOAP header block while another might be stored in the body of a SOAP message. Each part has a type. We have assumed that all the declarations in this example appear in an XML document whose default namespace is *http://schemas.xmlsoap.org/wsdl/*, which declares tags such as `part`, `message`, etc.

The types in the `getFareOp` example are simple, but other applications might require complex types, which can be declared in the WSDL document or in an application-specific schema document.

Note that the message in Figure 25.9 is the WSDL declaration of the contents of the SOAP message in Figure 25.3 even though the names do not correspond. The name in Figure 25.3, `getFareOp`, is the name of the procedure being called, as required in RPC-style messages. The name in Figure 25.9, `itineraryMsg`, can be arbitrarily chosen. It would be a mistake to call it `getFareOp`, since that name is used for the operation that uses the message, as shown in Figure 25.10.

Operations. An operation is described by the messages it exchanges and the pattern in which the exchange takes place. An operation used in the GoSlow example is shown in Figure 25.10. Different patterns are appropriate for different operations. Version 1.1 of WSDL supports two patterns. Version 2.0 provides more flexibility (see Section 25.5.4).

FIGURE 25.8 Skeleton of an abstract level WSDL description.

```
<definitions targetNameSpace="myNamespace"
      xmlns="http://www.w3.org/2003/06/wsdl"
      xmlns:xs="http://www.w3.org/2001/XMLSchema"
      xmlns:myPrefix="myNamespace">
   <types>
      <schema xmlns="http://www.w3.org/2001/XMLSchema"
            xmlns:myPrefix="myNamespace"
            targetNameSpace="myNamespace">
         <complexType name="myType1"> ··· </complexType>
            ...
      </schema>
   </types>
      ...
   <message name="myMessage1">
      <part name="part1" type="myPrefix:myType1"/>
      <part name="part2" type="xs:string"/>
   </message>
   <message name="myMessage2">
      <part name="anotherPart1" type="···"/>
   </message>
      ...
   <portType name="myPortType">
      <operation name="myOperation">
         <input message="myPrefix:myMessage1"/>
         <output message="myPrefix:myMessage2"/>
         <fault message="···"/>
      </operation>
   </portType>
   ...
   <!-- Concrete level declarations go here -->
</definitions>
```

FIGURE 25.9 An abstract description of a WSDL message.

```
<message name="itineraryMsg">
   <part name="custId" type="xs:string"/>
   <part name="destination" type="xs:string"/>
   <part name="departureDate" type="xs:date"/>
   <part name="returnDate" type="xs:date"/>
</message>
```

FIGURE 25.10 The operation getFareOp.

```
<operation name="getFareOp">
  <input message="gs:itineraryMsg"
    wsa:Action="http://www.SlowHawk.com/wsdl/trips/getFarePT
    /itineraryMsg"/>
  <output message="gs:itineraryRespMsg"
    wsa:Action="http://www.SlowHawk.com/wsdl/trips/getFarePT
    /itineraryRespMsg"/>
  <fault name="invalidArgFault"
    wsa:Action="http://www.SlowHawk.com/wsdl/trips/getFarePT
    /invalidArgFaultMsg"
    message="gs:invalidArgFaultMsg"/>
</operation>
```

- *Request/response*. An input message (of the type specified by the operation's `input` child element) is sent by the requester, and an output message (of the type specified by the operation's `output` child element) is returned by the provider. WSDL does not specify whether the communication is synchronous (the requester waits until it receives the output message) or asynchronous (the requester does not wait but continues its execution after sending the message and separately receives the output message at a later time). Thus, the request/response pattern might be used synchronously to implement an RPC interaction, or it might be used asynchronously to implement an interchange of e-mail messages.

  The (optional) `fault` element identifies the declaration of a message that is returned to the invoker if a fault occurs. The provider responds to an input message with either the output message or a message of the type specified in the `fault` element (but not both).

  Figure 25.10 gives an example of an RPC operation, `getFareOp`, supported by SlowHawk. The fact that both input and output messages are specified indicates that the operation uses a request/response message-exchange pattern. For simplicity we have assumed that the WSDL declarations for both GoSlow and SlowHawk are combined in the same document (more realistically, each organization would publish its own WSDL document). The document is shown in Figures 25.21–25.23. We have assumed that the target namespace of the document containing all these declarations is `http://www.goslow.com/wsdl/trips` and that this namespace is denoted with the prefix gs. Hence, the operation declaration is referencing message declarations that appear elsewhere in the same document.

  The `wsa:Action` attribute in the message element is the WS-Addressing extension of WSDL that was referred to on page 1060. Its value, a URI, identifies the purpose of the message and is used as the value of the `Action` header block of the SOAP message that carries the WSDL message. The attribute is optional: it can be explicitly specified for a message of the port type (as is done in the

FIGURE 25.11 The getFarePT port type.

```
<portType name="getFarePT">
    <operation name="getFareOp">
        ...
    </operation>
    <!--other operations, if implemented, would be declared here -->
</portType>
```

figure), or a WS-Addressing default procedure can be used to construct a value. In the figure the value shown is actually the default value. Keep in mind that WSDL is transport-neutral. We have described how the value of `Action` is used by SOAP. It might be used differently if SOAP is not used, or it might be ignored.

Messages are defined separately from operations because a particular message might be used in different operations. For example, we have used the name `itineraryMsg` (rather than `getFareOpMsg`) for the input message type of the operation `getFareOp` because we will be using this type of message in several different operations.

- *One-way*. An input message (of the type specified by the `input` child) is sent by the requester, and no response is returned by the provider. (Recall, however, that if HTTP is used to transport the message, an HTTP acknowledgment will be received by the HTTP processor at the requester's site.) Hence, the operation specifies only an input message. No fault messages are allowed with this pattern. This style is often used to invoke a Web service asynchronously. The requester does not wait for a response. However the provider might respond at a later time with a message directed to an operation supported by the requester. We will see examples of such services in Sections 25.6.

Port types. A port type groups together related operations. For example, SlowHawk might support the port type, `getFarePT`, shown in Figure 25.11. In this case there is only one operation, but the figure indicates where other operations would be declared if they were present.

25.5.2 The Concrete Level

The concrete level describes how port types and their operations are bound to transport protocols and Web locations. The concrete level defines the following elements:

- A **binding** describes how the abstract messages used by the operations of a port type are mapped to concrete messages that are transmitted by a particular transport protocol. For example, if the message is to be sent using SOAP over HTTP, the binding describes how the message parts are mapped to elements in the SOAP body and header and what the values of the attributes are. In addition, the binding describes how values are to be serialized within a message.

FIGURE 25.12 Outline of a complete WSDL document.

```
<definitions targetNamespace=" . . . "
             <!-- specification of other namespaces -->
             xmlns="http://www.w3.org/2003/06/wsdl/">
  <!-- Abstract level specification -->
    <types>
        <!-- XML Schema types used in this document -->
    </types>
    <message>  . . . </message>
        <!-- other messages are specified here -->
    <portType> . . . </portType>
        <!-- other port types are specified here -->
  <!-- End of the abstract level -->
  <!-- Concrete level specification -->
    <binding> . . . </binding>
        <!-- other bindings are specified here -->
    <service>
        <port> . . . </port>
        <!-- other ports are specified here -->
    </service>
        <!-- other services are specified here -->
  <!-- End of the concrete level -->
</definitions>
```

- A **port** maps a binding to a Web address. In the context of WSDL, an endpoint corresponds to a port. A port specifies the address at which the operations of a port type, using a particular transport protocol, can be invoked.
- A **service** is a collection of related ports.

The overall structure of a WSDL document, which includes both the abstract and concrete levels, is shown in Figure 25.12. We next discuss the components of the concrete WSDL specification in more detail.

Services. A service gives a name to a set of ports. Each port specifies the address at which the operations of a particular port type can be invoked together with the binding to be used. Since, as we shall see shortly, the binding specifies a port type, the port effectively ties the port type to an address. Taken together, the ports of a service host a set of related operations that are offered to customers.

Consider the following declaration:

```
<service name="getFareService">
     <port name="getFareRPCPort"
              binding="gs:GetFareRPCBinding">
```

```
            <soap:address location=
                  "http://www.SlowHawk.com/fareservice1"/>
        </port>
        <!-- other ports go here -->
    </service>
```

The port getFareRPCPort identifies a particular binding—getFareRPCBinding—and the Web address at which messages that use that binding are to be sent. The service getFareService groups getFareRPCPort with other related ports. The prefix gs indicates that the service is declared in the same WSDL document as the abstract elements.

A service supported by a server might contain several ports for the same port type—but provided through different bindings. This allows a requester to choose the most convenient way to communicate with that server. Alternatively, different implementations of the same port type might be referenced by ports of different services supported by different servers. For example, the travel industry might specify a standard port type for making airplane reservations, and different airlines might provide different reservation services, each of which implements the port type. In this case the implementations of the port types at the different servers should provide semantically equivalent behavior.

RPC-style binding. A binding element is the most complex aspect of a WSDL document. Its structure must be flexible enough to accommodate the message formats used by a variety of different transports. We will describe three different bindings for getFarePT. We first consider SOAP over HTTP since it is widely used and it illustrates many features of a binding element.

Suppose we want the operations of getFarePT to be invoked with RPC-style SOAP messages sent using HTTP. Then we might declare the binding getFareRPC-Binding, shown in Figure 25.13, for that purpose. The name of the port type being bound is indicated by the type attribute of the outer binding element.

The child soap:binding is an example of an extension of WSDL that provides information specific to a SOAP binding. We assume that the prefix soap is associated with *http://schemas.xmlsoap.org/wsdl/soap/*—the namespace used by all SOAP-related elements and attributes of WSDL. In our discussions they all will be identified with the soap prefix.

It is important to keep in mind that the elements input and output inside a binding element, such as the one in Figure 25.13, are *not* in themselves SOAP messages and neither are the similarly named elements in an abstract level description of an operation, as in Figure 25.10. Instead, these are descriptions from which the actual SOAP messages are *constructed*. We will explain how this is done shortly.

The soap:binding element specifies the message format (via the style attribute) and transport (via the transport attribute) to use. In Figure 25.13, the transport is SOAP over HTTP, and the format is rpc. Hence, we expect a message that looks like Figure 25.3. If, instead, the style attribute had value document, the message body would have a different structure, which we will discuss later in this

FIGURE 25.13 An RPC/encoded SOAP binding for `getFarePT`.

```
<binding name="getFareRPCBinding" type="gs:getFarePT">
  <soap:binding style="rpc"
    transport="http://schemas.xmlsoap.org/soap/http/"/>
  <operation name="gs:getFareOp">
    <input>
      <soap:body
        use="encoded"
        namespace="http://www.goslow.com/wsdl/trips"
        encodingStyle="http://schemas.xmlsoap.org/soap/encoding/"/>
    </input>
    <output>
      <soap:body
        use="encoded"
        namespace="http://www.goslow.com/wsdl/trips"
        encodingStyle="http://schemas.xmlsoap.org/soap/encoding/"/>
    </output>
  </operation>
</binding>
```

section. Another possible transport is SOAP over SMTP. It can be used to deliver SOAP messages by email and will also be discussed later in this section.

Binding-related details of each operation of a port type are described in the `operation` child element of `binding`. (This use of the word "operation" should be contrasted with the signature of an operation, which is described at the abstract level of WSDL using the `operation` child element of `portType`.) `getFarePT` contains only one operation, `getFareOp`. The `name` attribute gives the name of the operation. The `operation` element contains a description of each of the messages the operation can send or receive. Thus, the `input` child element describes the input message and the `output` child describes the output message. A `fault` child would describe the fault message, but it is omitted in our example.

OPTIONAL

RPC-style binding and SOAP messages. We have seen that the binding uses the elements `input`, `output`, and `fault` to describe messages at the concrete level, but these elements do not actually name any messages. The question therefore is, Which messages do these elements refer to? The answer is that descriptions at the concrete level are related to the descriptions at the abstract level through the operation that they both describe. For instance, in Figure 25.13 the `input` and `output` elements describe the operation `getFareOp`. The abstract level description of this operation appears in Figure 25.10, from which we know that the `input` element refers to the message `itineraryMsg` and the `output` element to `itineraryRespMsg`.

Since the binding style in this case is `rpc`, RPC-style SOAP messages will be constructed (similar to the messages in Figures 25.3 and 25.4). Thus, each part of `itineraryMsg` is a parameter of the operation `getFareOp`, and the information returned is stored in the body of the message `itineraryRespMsg`. Since all of this information is stored in the SOAP body, the `input` and `output` elements in Figure 25.13 contain only a `soap:body` child—another SOAP-related element of WSDL. With other types of bindings, some information might be carried in a SOAP header, and a `soap:header` child would be included to describe this.

We are now ready to explain how an actual SOAP message is constructed from a WSDL binding and an abstract message description—in the example, how the SOAP message in Figure 25.3 is obtained. Let *N* be the element tagged `getFareOp` in Figure 25.3. It is the child of the `Body` element in the envelope of the SOAP message being constructed. *N*'s tag is obtained from the `name` attribute of the `operation` element of the `binding` element. The `namespace` attribute of `soap:body` provides the value for the `xmlns` attribute in *N*'s opening tag. It designates the target namespace of the WSDL document in which the message is declared (see Figures 25.3 and 25.21). Similarly, the `encodingStyle` attribute of `soap:body` provides the value for the `encodingStyle` attribute in *N*'s opening tag.

Next, the abstract WSDL message is identified as explained earlier. In our case, it is the message `itineraryMsg` described in Figure 25.9. Finally, each part of `itineraryMsg` describes a parameter of the operation and yields a child element of *N*. The part's name, specified in the WSDL (abstract level) message declaration, becomes the child's tag.

RPC-style binding and parameter serialization. The next question is how the values of the parameters to an operation are serialized in the SOAP message being constructed. In the WSDL message declaration, each part has an associated type, which might be complex. In that case the type declaration, which we will refer to as an **abstract type** declaration, will be an element of some WSDL schema. (Figure 25.8 on page 1065 shows a skeleton of abstract level type declarations.)

Earlier (page 1055), we pointed out that if the SOAP communication is specified as RPC/encoded, the serialization of a parameter in a SOAP message is generated by a serializer program at the client. How can we be sure that the string generated by the client's SOAP serializer corresponds to the abstract type declaration in the WSDL file? In fact, it might not! And if it does not, does that mean that it is incorrect? Again, the answer is no! Then how can a receiver determine that a received message is correct? The `use` attribute is provided for this purpose. It has two possible values: `encoded` and `literal`.

- If the `use` attribute of the `soap:body` element in the binding has the value `encoded`, then the values of the parameters are serialized using the encoding mechanism specified in the `encodingStyle` attribute of the element (which becomes the encoding style attribute used in the SOAP message). This situation is depicted in Figure 25.13. An **RPC/encoded** binding specifies that the parameters of an RPC-style message are to be serialized through the set of rules specified in the `encodingStyle` attribute. Note that in Figure 25.3 (which is an RPC/encoded SOAP message) each parameter child has a type attribute. Using this attribute

OPTIONAL

FIGURE 25.14 An RPC/literal SOAP binding for the getFarePT.

```
<service name="GetFareService">
  <port name="GetFareDocPort" binding="gs:GetFareDocBinding">
    <soap:address location="http://www.SlowHawk.com/fareservice2/"/>
  </port>
</service>

<binding name="GetFareDocBinding" type="gs:GetFarePT">
  <soap:binding style="rpc"
       transport="http://schemas.xmlsoap.org/soap/http"/>
  <operation name="gs:getFareOp">
    <input>
      <soap:body
        use="literal"
        namespace="http://www.goslow.com/wsdl/trips"/>
    </input>
    <output>
      <soap:body
        use="literal"
        namespace="http://www.goslow.com/wsdl/trips"/>
    </output>
  </operation>
</binding>
```

OPTIONAL

the receiver can determine the specific encoding rule that was used to serialize the argument.[3]

- If the use attribute of the soap:body element in the binding has the value literal, the parameter element in the SOAP message body is an ASCII string that is a literal instance of the part's type as specified in the message declaration. This binding is referred to as **RPC/literal** and is illustrated in Figure 25.14.

  In some cases the instance is directly available. For example, if the value of the parameter is XML data, it will already be an instance of the type. In other cases it might be necessary to explicitly construct an instance of the type. For example, the arguments produced by a procedure call in a Java program must be converted from binary to the ASCII strings that corresponds to the type definitions. We addressed this issue earlier (page 1054) when we introduced the

[3] The specification of the type attribute is useful in cases in which subtypes of a parameter's base type have been declared (perhaps using XML's type extension feature) to carry additional information for particular argument values. For example, if the destination is a city with multiple airports, the destination part might have to include an additional element identifying a specific airport. Although the message declaration specifies that the parameter is of the base type, a specific invocation might pass a value of the subtype.

use of rules to serialize data. In this case we are also serializing data, with the difference that instead of using rules in accordance with some encoding style, the serialization constructs an instance of the type.

Although with RPC/literal the serialized arguments are literal instances of schema types, the SOAP `Body` *as a whole* is not described by a (single) schema. Instead it is constructed as described in connection with Figure 25.3: the procedure name is the tag of the child of the `Body` element, and it has child elements for each parameter tagged with that parameter's name. Thus, with both RPC/literal and RPC/encoded, the `Body` is not an instance of a schema (even though with RPC/literal the parameter values are instances of schema types).

As an example of where RPC/encoded and RPC/literal bindings give different strings for particular parameters, suppose a procedure has n parameters, all of the same abstract type. The body of an RPC-style SOAP request message produced by a serializer will generally contain n child elements, each of which is an instance of the type. Each instance is the value of a parameter and, correspondingly, the value of a `part` of the request message.

But suppose in a particular invocation the values of all the parameters are the same. Then the serializer might be smart enough to encode the request message differently. The message will still contain a child element for each parameter. But instead of a child being an instance of the abstract type, it is a pointer to a single instance of the type stored as a separate element elsewhere in the message. That instance contains the value being passed to all parameters. Clearly the request message contains the proper information to invoke the procedure *if it is interpreted correctly*. However, if the deserializer is expecting parts that conform to the abstract type declaration, it will be greatly disappointed.

The problem, then, boils down to this. In some cases each argument is an exact, or *literal*, instance of the parameter type specified in the WSDL message declaration. In other cases, each argument is produced by a serializer that *encodes* data in accordance with some rules, and hence the argument is not necessarily an instance of the schema type specified for the parameter in the message declaration. There might be several forms that the argument can take, all semantically correct. RPC-style SOAP often uses the encoding approach. The deserializer can validate the message if it knows (1) that it has been encoded, (2) the encoding style rules that were used (since it will then know all the forms the parameter might take), and (3) the type of the argument.

OPTIONAL

Document-style binding. With an RPC-style binding, the information transmitted between a client and a server consists of the parameters of a procedure call. However, Web services are becoming increasingly document-centric, and the information transmitted consists of XML documents rather than procedure parameters.

For example, an operation, `sendInvoiceOp`, of port type `invoicePT` might send an invoice using a one-way pattern. The message, `sendInvoiceMsg`, that carries the invoice might have one `part`, named `invoice` (which is the actual document to be sent) whose type describes instances of invoices. The appropriate WSDL declarations could be

```
<types>
    <schema xmlns="http://www.w3.org/2001/XMLSchema"
           xmlns:inv="http://www.invoicesource.com/invoice"
           targetNameSpace="http://www.invoicesource.com/invoice">
            ...
        <complexType name="invoiceType"> ··· </complexType>
    </schema>
</types>
    ...
<message name="sendInvoiceMsg">
    <part name="invoice" type="inv:invoiceType"/>
</message>
    ...
<portType name="invoicePT">
    <operation name="sendInvoiceOp">
        <input message="inv:sendInvoiceMsg"/>
    </operation>
</portType>
```

The binding in this case is shown in Figure 25.15. Document-style communication is indicated in the `soap:binding` element, and the value of the `use` attribute of the `input` element is set to `literal`, which indicates that no encoding is involved. Hence this binding is referred to as a **document/literal** binding.

In this example, the WSDL message declaration has a single part and the `Body` of the corresponding SOAP message contains an invoice—an XML document whose

FIGURE 25.15 A document/literal SOAP binding for the `invoicePT`.

```
<binding name="sendInvBinding" type="inv:invoicePT">
    <soap:binding style="document"
        transport="http://schemas.xmlsoap.org/soap/http"/>
    <operation name="inv:sendInvoiceOp">
        <input>
            <soap:body
                use="literal"
                namespace=
                    "http://www.invoicesource.com/invoice"/>
        </input>
    </operation>
</binding>
```

schema is given by the part's type, `invoiceType`, and is specified in the message declaration.

```
<s:Envelope xmlns:s="http://www.w3.org/2003/05/soap-envelope">
     <s:Body>
          <!-- an instance of invoiceType goes here -->
     </s:Body>
</s:Envelope>
```

To ensure compatibility with older specifications (and not for technical reasons), WSDL constructs a message using a document-style binding differently than it does using an RPC-style binding. The difference is that with a document-style binding, the part's name (`invoice`) does not appear as a tag in the SOAP message. In contrast, with RPC-style binding, each message part gives a name to a child element in the message body. But with both document/literal and RPC/literal, the part itself is an instance of the schema that describes the part's type.

Document-style binding generalized. The document/literal binding can also be used with multipart messages. But, again, in order to ensure backward compatibility, a new strategy is used to specify the types of the parts. Although we did not discuss it before, types for message parts can be specified indirectly: the `part` child of the `message` element can use an `element` attribute (instead of a `type` attribute) whose value is the name of an element declared elsewhere. In this case, the type of the part is the type of that element. For example, if you want to send two invoices, the relevant WSDL declarations would be

```
<types>
     <schema ··· >
          <element name="firstInvoice" type="inv:invoiceType"/>
          <element name="secondInvoice" type="inv:invoiceType"/>
          <complexType name="invoiceType">
               <!-- the complex type definition goes here -->
          </complexType>
     </schema>
</types>
     ...
<message name="sendInvoiceMsg">
     <part name="invoice1" element="inv:firstInvoice"/>
     <part name="invoice2" element="inv:secondInvoice"/>
</message>
```

Now the `Body` element of the SOAP envelope will contain two child elements:

```
<s:Envelope xmlns:s="http://www.w3.org/2003/05/soap-envelope">
     <s:Body>
```

```
            <firstInvoice ··· >
                <!-- an instance of invoiceType goes here -->
            </firstInvoice>
            <secondInvoice ··· >
                <!-- an instance of invoiceType goes here -->
            </secondInvoice>
        </s:Body>
    </s:Envelope>
```

The children are instances of the schema elements `firstInvoice` and `second-Invoice`, and the tag names come from the names of the elements rather than the parts (as would be the case with RPC-style messages).

With RPC-style binding, part types can be specified with either a `type` or an `element` attribute, and, in fact, the same message can contain some parts with one specification and some with the other. Not so with the document-style binding: it can specify a multipart message *only* if all of its parts use the `element` attribute.

So far we have seen only bindings that use the HTTP transport. As an alternative, Figure 25.16 shows a document/literal binding of `getFarePT` to SOAP over SMTP. In this figure, the port `GetFareSMTPPort` can be used to communicate with the service by email. The address to which the email is to be sent is specified in

OPTIONAL

FIGURE 25.16 A document/literal SMTP binding for `getFarePT`.

```
<service name="GetFareService">
    <port name="GetFareSMTPPort" binding="gs:GetFareSMTPBinding">
        <soap:address location="mailto:fareservice@SlowHawk.com"/>
    </port>
</service>

<binding name="GetFareSMTPBinding" type="gs:GetFarePT">
    <soap:binding style="document"
        transport="http://schemas.xmlsoap.org/soap/smtp"/>
    <operation name="gs:getFareOp">
        <input>
            <soap:body
                use="literal"
                namespace="http://www.goslow.com/wsdl/trips"/>
        </input>
        <output>
            <soap:body
                use="literal"
                namespace="http://www.goslow.com/wsdl/trips"/>
        </output>
    </operation>
</binding>
```

FIGURE 25.17 Description of the GetFareService.

```
<service name="GetFareService">
    <port name="GetFareRPCPort" binding="gs:"GetFareRPCBinding">
        <soap:address location=
            "http://www.SlowHawk.com/fareservice1/"/>
    </port>
    <port name="GetFareDocPort" binding="gs:GetFareDocBinding">
        <soap:address location=
            "http://www.SlowHawk.com/fareService2/"/>
    </port>
    <port name="GetFareSMTPPort" binding="gs:GetFareSMTPBinding">
        <soap:address location=
            "mailto:fareservice@SlowHawk.com"/>
    </port>
    <port name="GetFareGETPort" binding="gs:GetFareGETBinding">
        <soap:address location=
            "http://www.SlowHawk.com/fareservice3/"/>
    </port>
    <port name="GetFarePOSTPort" binding="gs:GetFarePOSTBinding">
        <soap:address location=
            "http://www.Fare.com/fareservice4/"/>
    </port>
</service>
```

the `location` attribute of the `soap:address` element of the port. The fact that the binding describes both an input and an output element shows that, although document/literal is a natural way to bind one-way communication, there is no reason why it cannot be used for request/response communication as well.

A Web service can provide ports with the same functionality but different bindings. Some might use HTTP and some SMTP; some might use the RPC-style and some the document-style messages. For instance, SlowHawk Airline might make the port type `GetFarePT` available through a number of different bindings with the corresponding ports gathered together under a single service. This is shown in Figure 25.17.

As Web services become more document-centric, the document/literal binding is likely to become the prevalent form of messaging. One might wonder if document/encoded is possible as a binding style. The Web services community has not yet figured out what this might mean, so it is not likely to make an appearance any time soon.

25.5.3 Putting It All Together

A WSDL description of a Web service has as its root a `definitions` element. Its children are the various elements we have discussed. An outline of a WSDL document is

OPTIONAL

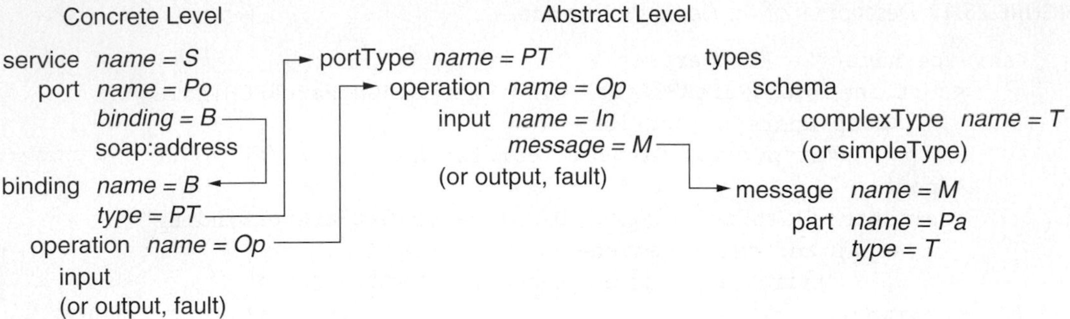

FIGURE 25.18 An overview of the relationships among the WSDL components. Attributes are italicized to distinguish them from elements.

shown in Figure 25.12. An example of such a document for GoSlow is given in Figures 25.21, 25.22 and 25.23. In this example, declarations for distinct Web services are lumped together in a single WSDL document to avoid complexity. In real life, each service would supply a *separate* WSDL document describing the operations it exports.

Figure 25.18 is an overview of some of the main elements of WSDL and the connections among them. The top-level elements are `service`, `binding`, `message`, `type`, and `portType`. The indented items denote information represented by child elements. The level of indentation denotes the level of nesting of the various elements and attributes.

25.5.4 WSDL Version 2.0

A number of changes are being considered in WSDL Version 2.0.[4] Some names will likely be different. A `portType` will be called an `interface`, and a `port` will be called an `endpoint`. Messages have been eliminated. An operation will describe a message by referring directly to a type declaration in the `types` component of the WSDL document.

An interface now takes the form shown in Figure 25.19. Two interesting new features are shown in the figure. The first is the `pattern` attribute of the `operation` element. It permits a variety of **message exchange patterns** (MEPs) to be specified for the operation. We have seen two patterns in WSDL Version 1.1: request/response and one-way. The `pattern` attribute allows an arbitrary number of patterns to be specified. A message exchange pattern is denoted by a URI.

An MEP is not a part of the WSDL document. Instead, it is described separately in terms of placeholders (think formal parameters) such as `In` and `Out` to denote a message sent to or received from the server and assigned a URI. Each of the actual

[4] This description is based on the working draft entitled "Web Services Description Language (WSDL) Version 2.0 Part 1: Core Language," August 3, 2004, *http://www.w3.org/TR/wsdl20*.

FIGURE 25.19 A `getFareIF` interface that inherits operations from another interface (WSDL Version 2.0).

```
<interface name="getFareIF" extends="reservationIF">
    <fault name="invalidArgFault"
        element="invalidArgFaultElem"/>
    <operation name="getFareOp"
        pattern="http://www.w3.org/2004/03/wsdl/in-out">
        <input messageLabel="In"
            element="gs:itineraryElem"/>
        <output messageLabel="Out"
            element="gs:itineraryRespElem"/>
        <outfault ref="invalidArgFault"
            messageLabel="Out"/>
    </operation>
    <!-- other operations are specified here -->
</interface>
```

messages exchanged by the operation—the `input` and `output` children of the operation element in the port type declaration—have a corresponding `messageLabel` attribute that identifies its placeholder in the description of the MEP.

A set of patterns has been predefined. `In-Out`, which is used in Figure 25.19, is one of them. It corresponds to the standard request/response pattern. The `messageLabel` attribute of `input` indicates that it corresponds to the `In` placeholder Some of the other patterns are `In-Only` (corresponding to one-way), `Robust In-Only` (`In-Only` with the possibility that the server responds with a fault message), and `In-Optional-Out` (which is like `In-Out` except that the response from the service is optional).

The structure of the `input` (or `output`) message (described by `message` and `part` elements in Version 1.1) is determined by the element in some schema document referred to by the `element` attribute. Faults are treated a little differently. A `fault` child of `interface` (there may be several) identifies, with its `element` attribute, the message that will be sent when a particular fault occurs. To allow for the fact that several operations within a particular interface might raise the same fault, `fault` is not local to an operation. Instead, any operation that raises the fault has an `outfault` child element that references `fault`. Its `messageLabel` attribute identifies the placeholder of the message in the MEP that the fault message is associated with. The fault message might be associated with the output message and *replace* that message if a fault occurs (as in the `In-Out` pattern). Alternatively, the fault might be associated with the input message and be *triggered by* that message if a fault occurs (as in the `Robust In-Only` pattern).

The second feature, indicated by the `extends` attribute of the `interface` element, allows an interface to inherit operations from other interfaces in an inheritance hierarchy based on the IsA relationship (Sections 4.4, 4.6.3, and 14.3.1). In the example, getFareIF extends the interface reservationIF in the sense that getFareIF contains getFareOp and, in addition, all the operations of reservationIF. For example, reservationIF might include a getScheduleOp operation, which returns the schedule of flights.

25.6 BPEL: Specifying Business Processes

In Section 25.5 we discussed how WSDL can be used to specify an interface that a server can present to the world. For example, SlowHawk's interface exposed the operation getFareOp that a client can invoke to obtain the airfare for a particular flight.

However, B2B interactions are generally more complex than this simple example. They do not consist of just a single operation invocation. Instead, there might be a lengthy exchange of information involving a sequence of operation invocations between a client and a server. Furthermore, the server might invoke other servers—hence becoming a client itself—in order to satisfy the initial request. In addition, the server has to maintain state during the processing of the interaction. The contents of a message received has to be interpreted in the context of events that have occurred up to that point, for example messages that were previously received. The state will, in general, determine the future behavior of the server.

We illustrate this situation with an example that expands on the getFarePT discussed earlier. Suppose our goal is to implement a full-blown travel agency service, GoSlow. GoSlow exports a port type containing three operations:

1. makeTripOp that takes a customer Id, a destination, a departure date, and a return date as input parameters and returns a trip number and a cost
2. acceptTripOp that takes a customer Id, a trip number and credit card information as input and returns a complete itinerary
3. cancelTripOp that takes a customer Id and a trip number as input parameters and returns an acknowledgement

When a client invokes makeTripOp, GoSlow's job is to make air and hotel reservations. To do this, GoSlow invokes getFareOp at the airline server, SlowHawk, to reserve a flight and gets back a reservation number and the cost. It also invokes getRoomOp at the hotel server, RoachHeaven, to reserve a room and gets back a reservation number and the cost. GoSlow then computes the total cost, assigns a trip number, and then returns both to the client. The state maintained by GoSlow at this point would include the client identification, reservation numbers, and cost. The client then invokes either acceptTripOp or cancelTripOp to confirm the reservations and pay for or cancel the reservations.

You can think of GoSlow as implementing a workflow. It receives a client request, makes reservations, responds to the client, then waits for either a confirmation or cancellation, and so forth. It is also an example of what has come to be called a **business process**, since it represents the way GoSlow does one aspect of its business. We will refer to it here as simply a process. GoSlow publishes its WSDL interface and interacts with other processes (for example, SlowHawk) through their WSDL interfaces. Interactions might use request/response (perhaps implementing RPC) or one-way messaging.

What is new here? First, there is a protocol that the client must follow. After invoking `makeTripOp`, the client must invoke either `acceptTripOp` or `cancelTripOp`. Unfortunately, WSDL does not provide GoSlow with a way of describing this protocol to the client. WSDL can only describe the individual exported operations in isolation.

One way to describe a protocol for a business process such as GoSlow is to publish GoSlow's program. But the client does not need or want all the details. A skeletal program that shows that GoSlow first accepts an invocation of `makeTripOp` and then accepts an invocation of either `acceptTripOp` or `cancelTripOp` is sufficient.

This approach has another important advantage. A skeletal program can show how GoSlow manipulates some of its local variables, and the values of these variables can be used to describe data-dependent protocols. For example, if a client accepts a trip made by GoSlow by invoking `acceptTripOp`, it must specify whether it will pay using a credit or a debit card. GoSlow's future actions, including the services it subsequently invokes, might depend on this information, which is a part of GoSlow's state. Therefore, the sequence of interactions followed by GoSlow is data dependent.

Thus, the program description goes well beyond the information presented through WSDL in that it shows the sequence in which operations are invoked and accepted and how that sequence is affected by the state of the process. The process is said to **orchestrate**[5] the use of the operations published in WSDL files.

Languages for describing business processes are currently a hot topic in the Web services community. In this section we present one such language, Business Process Execution Language for Web Services Version 1.1 (BPEL4WS, or simply BPEL). BPEL is undergoing standardization at the time of the writing of this text, but it is a leading contender and illustrates the issues that are addressed in an orchestration language. Version 1.1 of BPEL is based on Version 1.1 of WSDL.

Before getting into the details of the BPEL language, we need to distinguish between two levels of process[6] description. At one level we have what is called an **executable process** that contains all the details of the process, including a full description of the process state and how it is manipulated. At the other extreme we have what is called an **abstract process** that (should) contain only those aspects of the process that are necessary to describe its interface to other processes and is therefore not executable. You can think of an abstract process as (roughly) a projection of the corresponding executable process.

An abstract process differs from an executable process in two important ways. First, it is concerned with the protocol-relevant parts of the state. For example, the type of meal that you order on the flight is probably not protocol-relevant since the sequence of messages exchanged is not likely to depend on whether or not you are

[5] A buzz word in the Web services community that refers to the way the conductor of an orchestra organizes the services provided by the musicians into a coherent product.

[6] A better word would be program, but we will stay with BPEL terminology.

a vegetarian. Hence, your choice of meal ought not to be accessed by the abstract version of GoSlow. However, the protocol might be sensitive to whether you are paying with a credit card or a debit card: the sequence of messages exchanged might depend on the mode of payment. So this item must be accessible to the abstract process. Thus, if a client process has requested credit card payment, it can tell from the abstract process the sequence of messages that will follow.

A protocol-relevant item of data is referred to as a **property**. BPEL effectively prevents abstract processes from using data other than properties to affect the flow of control of the protocol. We discuss this restriction on page 1093.

Secondly, although the price of a ticket might be protocol-relevant (a ticket costing more than $1000 might require a special method of payment), the algorithm used to calculate the price might be complex, embarrassing to the airline, and have no impact on the flow of messages. Hence, the algorithm is coded into the executable version of the process but need not appear in the abstract version. BPEL uses what it calls **opaque assignment** to gloss over such details. Opaque assignment is permitted only in abstract processes, and it will be explained in more detail on page 1091. Its use implies a difference in the data manipulation techniques available to the two kinds of processes.

BPEL can be used to describe both an abstract and an executable version of the same business process. While the designers do not claim that the executable version of BPEL is a complete language for the purposes of implementing a business process on a particular platform, they do assert that it "defines a portable execution format for business processes that rely exclusively on Web service resources and XML data."[7]

25.6.1 Communication

Communication is central to Web services, so it is a good place to start our discussion of BPEL. In Section 25.5.1 we described several patterns of communication. BPEL provides three activities (the BPEL terminology for statements) for controlling communication.

1. An **invoke** activity names a particular operation and one or two variables. If a single variable is named, the operation specifies one-way communication, whereas if two variables are named the operation specifies request/response communication. In both cases the activity causes the value of the first variable to be sent in the operation's input message. If two variables are named, the invoker waits until the output message is returned and assigned to the second variable and then resumes execution. Waiting is appropriate if a procedure is being invoked. Hence, BPEL imposes a synchronous programming style on the use of the operation. If only a single variable is named in the activity, the invoker resumes as soon as the input message is sent.

[7] See *Business Process Execution Language for Web Services* Version 1.1, March 31, 2003, *http://www.106.ibm.com/developerworks/webservices/library/ws-bpel*.

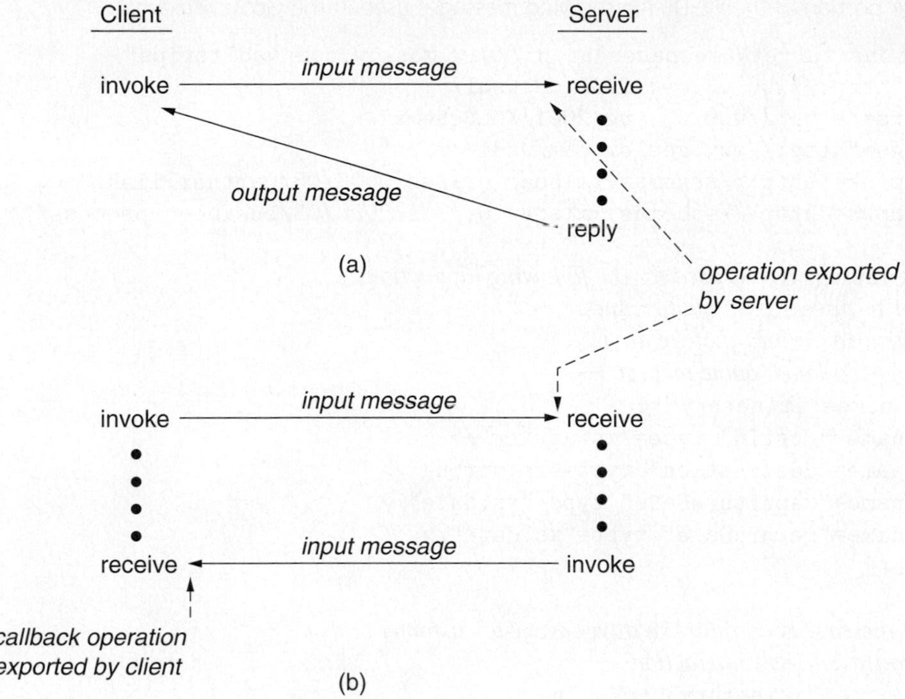

FIGURE 25.20 Common patterns of communication: (a) request/response and (b) one-way.

2. A **receive** activity is used to receive a message that has been sent either synchronously or asynchronously by an `invoke`. The process waits until the message arrives.
3. A **reply** activity is used to send a response to a request/response-style invocation that was previously received. The process resumes execution immediately.

The two common patterns of communication—request/response and one-way—are shown in Figure 25.20. Figure 25.20(a) illustrates synchronous request/response communication. In Figure 25.20(b) the client invokes an operation but does not wait for a response. Hence, if a response is forthcoming, it is sent asynchronously by the server to a port type exported by the client. This response is often referred to as a **callback**.

Having described communication in general terms we are now in a position to get more specific. A listing of a portion of the WSDL file for the GoSlow example is shown in Figures 25.21 to 25.23. For simplicity we have assumed that the declarations for all the Web services involved in the example are contained in a single file. More realistically, the declarations for each service would be provided in a separate file provided by that service.

FIGURE 25.21 A portion of the WSDL file showing messages used in the GoSlow example.

```
<definitions targetNamespace="http://www.goslow.com/wsdl/trips"
  xmlns="http://www.w3.org/2003/06/wsdl/"
  xmlns:xs="http://www.w3.org/2001/XMLSchema"
  xmlns:gs="http://www.goslow.com/wsdl/trips"
  xmlns:plnk="http://schemas.xmlsoap.org/ws/2003/05/partner-link/"
  xmlns:bpws="http://schemas.xmlsoap.org/ws/2003/03/business-process/">

<!-- This message type is used for the following interactions:
  customer to travel agent: quote request
  travel agent to airline: quote request
  travel agent to hotel: quote request -->
<message name="itineraryMsg">
  <part name="custId" type="xs:string"/>
  <part name="destination" type="xs:string"/>
  <part name="departureDate" type="xs:date"/>
  <part name="returnDate" type="xs:date"/>
</message>

<!-- This message is used for the travel-agent-to-customer and
  airline-to-travel-agent interactions -->
<message name="itineraryRespMsg">
  <part name="custId" type="xs:string"/>
  <part name="tripNo" type="xs:string"/>
  <part name="cost" type="xs:float"/>
</message>


<!-- A message for the customer to travel agent interaction: OK -->
<message name="acceptTripMsg">
  <part name="custId" type="xs:string"/>
  <part name="cardNo" type="xs:string"/>
  <part name="credDeb" type="xs:string"/>
  <part name="tripNo" type="xs:string"/>
</message>

<!-- A fault message used in the travel agent to airline interaction -->
<message name="invalidArgFaultMsg">
  <part name="custId" type="xs:string"/>
  <part name="faultString" type="xs:string"/>
</message>

<!-- Omitted messages: cancelTripOp, invalidCustFaultMsg,
  badPayFaultMsg, etc. -->
```

FIGURE 25.22 A continuation of the WSDL file shown in Figure 25.21 containing port types used in the GoSlow example.

```
<portType name="tripPT">        <!-- provided by GoSlow -->
  <operation name="makeTripOp">
    <input message="gs:itineraryMsg"/>
    <output message="gs:itineraryRespMsg"/>
    <fault name="invalidCustFault"
      message="gs:invalidCustFaultMsg"/>
  </operation>
  <operation name="acceptTripOp">
    <input message="gs:acceptTripMsg"/>
    <output message="gs:acceptTripRespMsg"/>
    <fault name="badPayFault"
        message="gs:badPayFaultMsg"/>
  </operation>
  <operation name="cancelTripOp">
    <input message="gs:cancelTripMsg"/>
    <output message="gs:cancelTripRespMsg"/>
  </operation>
</portType>

<portType name="hotelCallbackPT">      <!-- provided by GoSlow -->
  <!-- hotel calls back to confirm or deny -->
  <operation name="receiveResOp">
    <input message="gs:receiveResMsg"/>
  </operation>
</portType>

<portType name="getFarePT">       <!-- provided by SlowHawk -->
  <operation name="getFareOp">
    <input message="gs:itineraryMsg"
      wsa:Action="http://www.SlowHawk.com/wsdl/trips/getFarePT
      /itineraryMsg"/>
    <output message="itineraryRespMsg"
      wsa:Action="http://www.SlowHawk.com/wsdl/trips/getFarePT
      /itineraryRespMsg"/>
    <fault name="invalidArgFault"
      message="gs:invalidArgFaultMsg"
      wsa:Action="http://www.SlowHawk.com/wsdl/trips/getFarePT
      /invalidArgFaultMsg"/>
  </operation>
</portType>
```

FIGURE 25.22 (continued)

```
<portType name="roomResPT">      <!-- provided by RoachHeaven -->
    <operation name="getRoomOp">
        <input message="gs:itineraryMsg"/>
    </operation>
    <operation name="cancelRoomOp"
        <input message="gs:cancelRoomMsg"/>
    </operation>
</portType>
```

We have omitted some elements at the abstract level of WSDL to avoid excess detail. We have also omitted all elements at the concrete level since they are not directly accessible to a BPEL process. For example, BPEL does not provide mechanisms to directly access a binding. The fact that binding information is not accessible ensures that the same process description can be reused with different transports. However, even though the concrete declarations are not accessible, lower-level modules of the executable version of a process use bindings when the process communicates with other processes. The bindings provide the information needed to format and address messages that are sent and to process messages that are received.

Partner link types. Each process uses WSDL declarations at the abstract level to describe the elementary communication activities in which it is willing to engage. But to specify the activities precisely, we need, in addition, a way to describe the connections between processes. For example, GoSlow is a process that requests a hotel reservation by invoking an operation on the port type `roomResPT`, which is provided by some other process. It expects that that process will respond by invoking an operation on the port type `hotelCallbackPT`, which GoSlow provides. Similarly, RoachHeaven provides a port type `roomResPT` to receive a reservation request from another process and expects to respond using a port type `hotelCallbackPT` provided by that process. Clearly, GoSlow and RoachHeaven satisfy a necessary condition to do business since they each provide the port types needed by the other. (On the other hand, the condition is not sufficient since it says nothing about the sequence in which operations over these port types are invoked and accepted.)

WSDL has been extended to enforce this condition through the introduction of **partner link types**. The fact that the tag `partnerLinkType` comes from a namespace (prefixed `plnk`) different from the WSDL namespace is an indication that an extension of WSDL is involved. A `partnerLinkType` has a name and one or two roles. Each role is named and describes one end of a possible connection by specifying one port type that must be provided by the process at that end. For example, the partner link type `GoSlowRoachLT` in Figure 25.23 has been declared to support a room reservation interaction and specifies that the process providing the hotel service must provide the `roomResPT` port type, and the process requesting a reservation must provide the `hotelCallbackPT` port type.

FIGURE 25.23 A continuation of the WSDL file shown in Figures 25.21 and 25.22 containing properties, property aliases, and partner link types used in the GoSlow example.

```
<bpws:property name="Id" type="xs:string"/>     <!-- properties -->
<bpws:property name="payType" type="xs:string"/>

<bpws:propertyAlias propertyName="gs:Id"      <!-- property aliases -->
    messageType="gs:itineraryMsg" part="custId"/>

<bpws:propertyAlias propertyName="gs:Id"
    messageType="gs:itineraryRespMsg" part="custId"/>

<bpws:propertyAlias propertyName="gs:payType"
    messageType="gs:acceptTripMsg" part="credDeb"/>

<plnk:partnerLinkType name="custGoSlowLT">    <!-- partner Link Types -->
    <!-- link between customer and travel agency -->
    <plnk:role name="travelService">
        <plnk:portType name="gs:tripPT"/>
    </plnk:role>
</plnk:partnerLinkType>

<plnk:partnerLinkType name="GoSlowHawkLT">
    <!-- link between travel agency and airline -->
    <plnk:role name="airline">
        <plnk:portType name="gs:getFarePT"/>
    </plnk:role>
</plnk:partnerLinkType>

<plnk:partnerLinkType name="GoSlowRoachLT">
    <!-- link between travel agency and hotel -->
    <plnk:role name="hotel">
        <plnk:portType name="gs:roomResPT"/>
    </plnk:role>
    <plnk:role name="roomReq">
        <plnk:portType name="gs:hotelCallbackPT"/>
    </plnk:role>
</plnk:partnerLinkType>
<!-- declarations of bindings, ports and services would go here -->
</definitions>
```

As a special case, if only one end of the connection needs to supply a port type for the interaction, only one role needs to be specified in the partner link. In this case any process can communicate with the process that assumes that role. For example, any process can be a customer of GoSlow. A customer does not need to provide a port type if it does not expect a response or if the operation it invokes uses a request/response pattern of communication.

Properties. An abstract process is concerned with the protocol-relevant items in a message. For example, the part `credDeb` of the `acceptTripMsg` message indicates whether the customer intends to pay with a credit card or a debit card. This information is protocol-relevant since GoSlow communicates differently with its partners depending on the mode of payment. BPEL insists that any protocol-related item—an item used by an abstract process—be specified using a property declaration. This restriction on abstract processes guarantees that their control flow, and hence the protocol that they implement, is based on properties (we will return to this point on page 1094).

A **property declaration** introduces a global property name and an associated XML Schema type. The property is associated with a data item of the same type using a **property alias**. In Figure 25.23, a `property` declaration introduces the global property name `payType`, and a `propertyAlias` declaration associates that name with the `credDeb` part of the `acceptTripMsg` message. More generally, a property alias can be used to associate a property with any element or attribute *within* a message part using XPath expressions.

We will see shortly that a customer Id is also protocol-relevant. It might be contained in several messages, and it might be given different part names in each, but it always has the same significance with respect to application logic. For example, the message `itineraryMsg` associated with GoSlow's port type `tripPT` has the part `custId` that is used to convey the customer's Id. Since GoSlow and SlowHawk would normally create separate WSDL files to describe their services and would design their messages separately, SlowHawk might use a part named `clientId` to convey the same information (we do not do this here to keep the example simple). By aliasing both these parts to the property name `Id`, GoSlow (and particularly its abstract version) can be written entirely in terms of `Id`. This makes it easier to understand and highlights the semantics of the protocol.

Thus, properties serve two functions. They are used to limit the access of abstract processes to protocol-relevant data, and they also provide a uniform way to refer to protocol-relevant data.

25.6.2 Processes

Our first version of (a fragment of) the GoSlow process is shown in Figure 25.24. We are interested primarily in communication, so an abstract process is shown, as indicated by the `abstractProcess` attribute of the `process` element. GoSlow communicates with three processes—the customer, SlowHawk, and RoachHeaven—

FIGURE 25.24 An elementary version of the GoSlow process expressed in BPEL.

```
<process name="GoSlowProcess"
  targetNamespace="http://www.goslow.com/wsdl/trips-bp"
  xmlns="http://schemas.xmlsoap.org/ws/2003/03/business-process/"
  xmlns:gs="http://www.goslow.com/wsdl/trips"
  abstractProcess="yes">

<partnerLinks>
  <partnerLink name="customer" partnerLinkType="gs:custGoSlowLT"
    myRole="travelService"/>
  <partnerLink name="airProvider" partnerLinkType="gs:GoSlowHawkLT"
    partnerRole="airline"/>
  <partnerLink name="hotelProvider" partnerLinkType="gs:GoSlowRoachLT"
    myRole="roomReq" partnerRole="hotel"/>
</partnerLinks>

<variables>
  <variable name="itineraryVar" messageType="gs:itineraryMsg"/>
  <variable name="itineraryRespVar" messageType="gs:itineraryRespMsg"/>
  <variable name="getFareVar" messageType="gs:itineraryMsg"/>
  <variable name="acceptTripVar" messageType="gs:acceptTripMsg"/>
  <variable name="invalidArgFaultVar"
      messageType="gs:invalidArgFaultMsg"/>
</variables>
<sequence>
  <receive partnerLink="customer" portType="gs:tripPT"
    operation="makeTripOp" variable="itineraryVar"/>
  <assign>
    <copy>
      <from variable="itineraryVar"/>
      <to variable="getFareVar"/>
    </copy>
  </assign>
  <invoke partnerLink="airProvider" portType="gs:getFarePT"
    operation="getFareOp" inputVariable="getFareVar"
    outputVariable="itineraryRespVar"/>
  <assign>
    <copy>
      <from opaque="yes"/>
      <to variable="itineraryRespVar" part="cost"/>
    </copy>
  </assign>
  <reply partnerLink="customer" portType="gs:TripPT"
    operation="makeTripOp" variable="itineraryRespVar"/>
  <!-- Second half of protocol goes here (Figure 25.26) -->
</sequence>

</process>
```

which are referred to as **partners**, and for this communication, partner links are needed.

Partner links. A partner link type describes a requirement on the port types supported by two processes that interact, but it does not identify the processes. Many pairs of processes might meet that requirement. There is a need for a mechanism that can be used by a process to claim one end of such a connection. The partner link is used for that purpose. Partner link declarations are part of BPEL rather than WSDL since they are specific to a particular process's participation in an interaction.

Each `partnerLink` element in Figure 25.24 specifies a partner link type, the role (of that partner link type) played by GoSlow, `myRole`, and the role played by the process at the other end of the link, `partnerRole`. The individual communication activities within the process refer to a `partnerLink` in order to specify the source or target of a message.

It might be necessary for one or both of a pair of processes to support several port types in order to interact. Since a partner link type names a single port type at each end, several partner links must be used. In that case, the language supports a `partners` element that allows partner links to be grouped together with the effect that a suitable partner has to support all the partner links in the group.

Variables. Variables are defined next. They are used for storing messages that have been received or sent, as well as arbitrary data. Their values form a part of the state of the process. The type of each variable can be a message type, an XML simple type, or an XML schema element. They are declared, respectively, using statements of the form

```
<variable name="..." messageType="..."/>
<variable name="..." type="..."/>
<variable name="..." element="..."/>
```

A variable of message type has the part structure of the named type, and each part can be an arbitrary XML document. Hence, a data item in the variable is identified with the variable name, the part name, and an XPath query that returns a single node.

Basic activities. The `sequence` tag introduces the main body of the process and says that the enclosed activities are to be executed sequentially (`sequence` is actually a structured rather than a basic activity, but we need it here). In order to discuss communication concepts in an orderly way, we have ignored the hotel reservation in this version of the process and we will also assume that only one customer at a time invokes `makeTripOp`. Here we illustrate request/response-style communication both between the customer and GoSlow and between GoSlow and SlowHawk. One-way communication will be discussed in Section 25.6.3.

The first activity in the `sequence` receives an invocation by specifying the desired partner link, port type, and operation, and the local variable into which the input message is to be placed. Simply specifying the port type is not sufficient. An operation must be specified since a port type can include several operations. A partner link must also be specified since a particular port type might be used by several other processes through different partner links. For example, port type *PT* might occupy a role in two distinct partner link types, *PLT*1 and *PLT*2. A process might declare two partner links, one based on *PLT*1 and the other based on *PLT*2, and in each claim the role corresponding to *PT* as `myrole`. Hence the process must specify in the `receive` activity over which partner link it wants to receive a message.

Note that several partner links might be based on the *same* partner link type. For example, GoSlow might communicate with two different airlines, each of which provides a port of type `getFarePT`. It would have a different partner link for each, but each link would be based on the same partner link type.

The data sent by the customer is received by GoSlow in `itineraryVar`, and we could have used this variable in the `invoke` statement that follows (as `inputVariable="itineraryVar"`). We choose not to do this so we can illustrate the **assign** activity. A simple form of `assign` appears next. It copies the contents of one variable, `itineraryVar`, to another variable, `getFareVar`, of the same message type.

Next GoSlow invokes `getFareOp` and waits for a response. Note that the activity specifies variables to accommodate the message sent (`getFareVar`) and the response message (`itineraryRespVar`).

Finally, GoSlow performs an *opaque* initialization of the variable `itineraryRespVar` (explained below) and then replies to the customer.

Note that Figure 25.24 is only a fragment of the GoSlow process. We will add some missing pieces soon.

Opaque assignment. Processes (abstract and executable) can engage in arbitrarily complex computations that result in the assignment of a value to an item. In order to omit from an abstract process the details of a computation that appears in a corresponding executable process, BPEL allows an abstract process (but not an executable process) to execute opaque assignments. An opaque assignment statement assigns to an item a nondeterministically chosen value from the item's domain. The value chosen is an example of a result that might be produced by the computation. Thus the computation in the executable process can be replaced by opaque assignment in the corresponding abstract process.

An example of opaque assignment is shown in the assign statement following the invocation of `getFareOp` in Figure 25.24. To keep the example short we have assumed that the response to the invocation of `getFareOp` received by GoSlow from SlowHawk and the response to `makeTripOp` sent by GoSlow to the customer utilize the same variable, `itineraryRespVar`. However, the value of `cost` in the two processes differ. GoSlow presumably adds to the airfare reported by SlowHawk the cost of the hotel (we have not considered the hotel yet) and its commission. The computation for doing this is hidden in the abstract process using opaque assignment.

It might be argued that since an abstract process is not executable, opaque assignment serves no purpose. Why not simply omit the computation of the executable process without replacing it with an opaque assignment? You can do this (and we have omitted without replacement other computations), but replacement preserves the structure of the executable process. Furthermore, replacement of computations that assign new values to properties allows us to check that protocol-relevant data is properly initialized (`cost` is not protocol-relevant, but it illustrates opaque assignment). Finally, by nondeterministically choosing the value to be assigned from the domain of the target variable, it is possible to use an abstract process to emulate the message sequences that an executable business process might produce. For example, a property whose value has been assigned opaquely can be used in the condition of a switch construct (Section 25.6.3), which determines the flow of control of the business process.

Other types of the `assign` activity are available to both abstract and executable processes, but since their purpose is to support computation, their use in abstract processes is discouraged (but not prohibited). Hence, although an abstract process can utilize all of the variants of the `assign` activity allowed to executable processes and more (i.e., opaque assignment), the intent is that most of the computation that appears in an executable process is omitted from its abstract counterpart.

25.6.3 Structured Activities

BPEL is a complex language, and it is not our intention to cover all of its features. However, it's interesting to see a few of the structured activities that are used to control the flow of execution. We have already discussed the `sequence` activity.

Flow. Concurrency is provided with the `flow` activity. Figure 25.25 shows a reimplementation of the GoSlow fragment corresponding to Figure 25.24, except we have now introduced the hotel service. The `flow` activity causes all the activities nested within it to be executed concurrently. In this case there are two activities, `invoke` (for obtaining an airline reservation) and `sequence` (for obtaining a hotel reservation). Hence, requests for air and hotel reservations are processed at the same time. Control exits from `flow` when all nested activities terminate.

The protocol for reserving a room, shown in Figure 25.25, is different from the protocol for reserving a flight since RoachHeaven expects to communicate with its clients asynchronously. The declaration of the operation `getRoomOp` in the WSDL file specifies only an input variable, and the corresponding invocation of the operation by GoSlow does not wait for a response. Instead, RoachHeaven responds by asynchronously invoking a callback operation provided by GoSlow on port type `hotelCallbackPT`. GoSlow must explicitly execute a `receive` activity to get this response.

Note that we do not show the assignment activities in Figure 25.25. Full assignments (assignment to all parts) must be included in the corresponding executable process, but in many cases even assignment to properties can be omitted in abstract processes. Furthermore, mention of the variables used by communication activities (e.g., `receive`, `reply`, `invoke`) can also be omitted in abstract processes. We will not cover the rules that govern all the possibilities.

FIGURE 25.25 Introducing concurrency into the GoSlow process.

```
<sequence>
  <receive partnerLink="customer" portType="gs:tripPT"
    operation="makeTripOp"/>
  <flow>
    <invoke partnerLink="airProvider" portType="gs:getFarePT"
      operation="getFareOp"/>
    <sequence>
      <invoke partnerLink="hotelProvider" portType="gs:roomResPT"
        operation="getRoomOp"/>
      <receive partnerLink="hotelProvider" portType="gs:hotelCallbackPT"
        operation="receiveResOp"/>
    </sequence>
  </flow>
  <reply partnerLink="customer" portType="gs:tripPT"
      operation="makeTripOp"/>
  <!-- Second half of protocol goes here (Figure 25.26) -->
</sequence>
```

Pick. GoSlow operates in an asynchronous environment that does not allow it to predict the sequence of events to which it must respond. For example, GoSlow has no way of knowing if, after the customer receives GoSlow's reply to its invocation of makeTripOp, the customer will invoke acceptTripOp or cancelTripOp. Hence, GoSlow must be prepared to receive both invocation messages (although only one will arrive). The pick control construct is provided for this purpose, and its use is illustrated in Figure 25.26. The fragment shown is meant to be inserted after the reply statement in Figures 25.24 or 25.25.

The pick control construct contains a set of nested clauses, each of which corresponds to an event that might occur. At run time, the clause corresponding to the first event to occur is executed, and the pick is then exited. Hence, in contrast to flow, only one clause gets executed. An event is either the arrival of a message, accepted by an onMessage clause, or a timeout, accepted by an onAlarm clause. At least one onMessage clause is required. In the example, GoSlow is willing to accept an invocation of either acceptTripOp or cancelTripOp and times out if neither arrives within a specified time interval. Note the similarity between onMessage and receive.

Switch. Figure 25.26 elaborates on the first onMessage clause to illustrate the switch activity. This activity consists of a list of case clauses followed by an optional otherwise clause.

The value of the condition attribute of a case clause is a Boolean expression conforming to XPath 1.0 syntax. Compliant implementations of the current version of

FIGURE 25.26 The second half of the GoSlow process.

```
<pick>
  <onMessage partnerLink="customer" portType="gs:tripPT"
          operation="acceptTripOp" variable="acceptTripVar">
    <switch>
      <case condition=
            "getVariableProperty('acceptTripVar','gs:payType')=credit">
        <sequence>
          <!-- handle credit payment -->
        </sequence>
      </case>
      <case condition=
            "getVariableProperty('acceptTripVar','gs:payType')=debit">
        <sequence>
          <!-- handle debit payment -->
        </sequence>
      </case>
      <otherwise>
        <throw faultName="payFault"/>
      </otherwise>
    </switch>
  </onMessage>

  <onMessage partnerLink="customer" portType="gs:tripPT"
      operation="cancelTripOp" variable="cancelTripVar">
      <!-- handle cancellation -->
  </onMessage>

  <onAlarm for="timeout interval">
    <!-- handle time out -->
  </onAlarm>
</pick>
```

BPEL are required to support the XPath language. How does an XPath expression access data in a BPEL process? The answer to this question has important implications concerning the difference between an abstract and an executable process.

BPEL introduces two extension functions to XPath that can be used in an XPath expression to enable it to access BPEL data: `getVariableProperty` and `getVariableData`. `getVariableProperty` returns the value of a property. Recall that a property is aliased to an item embedded in an XML document that forms a message part. `getVariableData` returns the value of an *arbitrary* item embedded in a message part (not just one that is pointed to by a property). Abstract processes are not permitted to use `getVariableData`, while executable processes can use both.

Since these functions are the only way to access data from within conditions, the control flow of an abstract process, and hence the sequence with which it executes communication activities, can be dependent only on properties. Thus, if an abstract process gives a complete description of a process's protocol, that protocol must be entirely dependent on properties.[8]

The conditions in `switch` clauses are evaluated in order, and the first clause whose condition has value true is executed, and then the `switch` activity is exited. If all conditions are false, the `otherwise` clause is executed. If no `otherwise` clause is present, the `switch` is exited normally.

Since the protocol depends on the payment type, the `switch` activity in Figure 25.26 tests the property `payType` (using `getVariableProperty`) when `acceptTripOp` is invoked. If `payType` (which actually refers to the part `credDeb` in `acceptTripMsg`—see Figure 25.23) has a value other than `credit` or `debit`, a fault is thrown. We deal with faults in Section 25.6.6.

While. For brevity we omit a discussion of the `while` activity. As you might expect, it has a body that is repeatedly executed until an XPath condition becomes false.

25.6.4 Links

The design of BPEL has been influenced from two different directions. Influence from the programming languages community is shown in the traditional structured control constructs that we have discussed and that are provided in the language. A second influence comes from the workflow community, since a BPEL process can be thought of as a workflow. In this community a workflow is traditionally viewed as a graph that can take an arbitrary (not necessarily structured) form. The graph consists of nodes representing tasks (perhaps representing the invocation or execution of an operation) and edges representing precedence relations describing the order in which tasks are to be executed. The link construct is introduced into BPEL to accommodate this view.

A precedence relationship is implicit in the `sequence` activity. It specifies that the nested activities are to be executed in the order given. In contrast, the `flow` activity does not specify any constraints on the order in which activities in different branches are to be executed. Thus, in Figure 25.25 the invocation of `getFareOp` in the first branch can be arbitrarily interleaved between the asynchronous invocation of `getRoomOp` and the callback response in the second branch. This is acceptable in this application since there is no relationship between making an airline reservation and a hotel reservation.

However, in a more complex application, a precedence relationship might exist between tasks on different sequential branches. For example, making a hotel

[8] Note that an abstract process can access an arbitrary part of a variable (whether or not it contains properties) using assignment, so it would not be accurate to say that an abstract process can access only properties. But an assignment to an item that is not a property does not affect control flow due to this restriction.

reservation might involve getting price quotes from several hotels and then choosing the hotel based on how much money is left in the travel budget after the cost of the airline ticket has been deducted. In that case, while price quotes can be obtained in the second branch concurrently with the invocation of `getFareOp` in the first, the choice of hotel and the confirmation of the hotel reservation in the second depends on the completion of `getFareOp` in the first.

A **link** provides a means to introduce a precedence relationship that restricts the unconstrained concurrency of activity execution in different branches of a `flow` activity. Each link has a name and is declared local to the flow. It synchronizes the execution of exactly one source activity and one target activity within the flow. The source activity is identified by a `source` element within the activity that names the link. The target activity is identified by a `target` element within the activity naming the same link. The implication of a link between a source activity and a target activity is that the source must complete before execution of the target starts. A typical situation is shown in Figure 25.27. Although activities A and B are in different branches of the `flow`, B cannot be started until A has completed.

While the basic concept of a link is simple, the situation gets dramatically more involved when we consider this type of synchronization in more detail.

- Source and target activities need not be at the same level of nesting. For example a target activity might constitute one branch of the `flow` while the corresponding source might be nested arbitrarily deeply within control constructs in another branch. But certain restrictions—which we do not discuss—apply.

FIGURE 25.27 The use of a link to synchronize activities within a `flow`.

```
<flow>
    <link name="AtoB"/>
    <sequence>
        <invoke ··· />
        <invoke name="A" ··· >
            <source linkName="AtoB"/>
        </invoke>
        <invoke ··· />
    </sequence>
    <sequence>
        <invoke ··· />
        <invoke name="B" ··· >
            <target linkName="AtoB"/>
        </invoke>
        <invoke ··· />
    </sequence>
</flow>
```

- In some cases even though execution of the activity that is the source of a link completes, it might not be appropriate to initiate the target activity. To introduce this flexibility, a source activity can have an associated `transitionCondition`, which is a function of variables accessible to the source activity and produces a positive or negative **link status**. This status is used in conjunction with the `joinCondition` discussed next.
- An activity can be the target of several links. Such an activity can have a `joinCondition` attribute, which is a Boolean expression over the status of those links. It specifies the condition that must be satisfied in order for the activity to be initiated, and it is evaluated when the status of all the incoming links has been determined. For example, the activity might be initiated if the status of any one of the incoming links is positive. Alternatively, the condition might stipulate that the status of all incoming links must be positive.
- What happens if the activity that is the source of a link is not executed? For example, the activity might be on a branch of a `switch` statement that is not chosen in a particular execution of the process. Since the `joinCondition` at the target activity cannot be evaluated until the status of all the target's incoming links have been determined, this causes a problem. To deal with this situation, if an activity will not be executed, the switch statement sets the status of all its outgoing links to negative.
- If the `joinCondition` of an activity evaluates to false, the activity will not be executed and a `joinFailure` fault is thrown. In applications where this situation is not considered abnormal, the fault can simply be suppressed. In this case the status of all of the activity's outgoing links is set to negative, and as a result the fact that the activity is not executed is propagated to other activities that are targets of its outgoing links. This is referred to as **dead-path-elimination**.

Links provide an alternate way of controlling the sequencing of activities in a workflow. In fact one could envision a workflow in which each activity constitutes a different branch of an enormous `flow` and the activities are interconnected by a network of links that specify the order in which they are to execute. This is essentially the graphical view of a workflow in which control constructs, which also specify the precedence of task execution, are not used. Hence, BPEL provides the designer with two distinct ways of specifying precedence, which can be used in conjunction with one another.

25.6.5 BPEL and WS-Addressing

Each communication statement in a BPEL process explicitly names the port type and operation that is to be invoked at the destination. Hence, we say that a BPEL process is *statically dependent* on the abstract WSDL interface. Each communication statement also names a partner link, but it does not identify the process at the other end of the link. In the GoSlow example our assumption has been that GoSlow deals with only a single airline, SlowHawk. Hence, the partner role, `airline`, of its partner link, `airProvider`, can be initialized at deployment time to refer to SlowHawk.

More generally, the port type getFarePT might be supported by a number of airlines, and GoSlow must determine the airline appropriate for a particular trip dynamically. Thus, there is a need to provide a mechanism in BPEL to specify at run time the process referred to by a partner link.

BPEL relies on WS-Addressing and the endpoint reference type (which contains all the information necessary to address a message) to provide this mechanism. If, as in the GoSlow example, the endpoint reference corresponding to the partner role of a partner link is known in advance, it can be associated with that role at deployment time.[9] If this is not the case, the appropriate endpoint reference can be assigned to the role at run time.

For example, a dynamic version of GoSlow might maintain a database listing all the airlines supporting getFareOp, their endpoint references, and the destination cities that they reach. When a customer requests a trip to a particular destination, GoSlow can access the database to select an appropriate airline. Assuming that the endpoint reference of the selected airline is stored in part airEPR of variable airInfo, GoSlow can assign the reference to the partnerRole of airProvider using the following form of the assignment activity designed to manipulate partner links

```
<assign>
    <copy>
        <from variable="airInfo" part="airEPR"/>
        <to partnerLink="airProvider"/>
    </copy>
</assign>
```

The to child need not specify which role of airProvider is the target of the assignment, since myRole cannot be changed. (This is the subject of Exercise 25.11.) Similarly, the endpoint reference associated with either role of a partner link can be assigned to a variable.

Having initialized airProvider to refer to the selected airline, GoSlow can invoke getFareOp using the invoke statement shown in Figure 25.24. Thus, the target address is determined (dynamically) at run time, but the operation and port type are determined (statically) at design time.

Endpoint references are manipulated opaquely by BPEL: their contents cannot be accessed using the BPEL language itself. However, in the executable version of BPEL, lower-level modules that manipulate messages sent by a BPEL program use endpoint references to determine message destinations (and, in some situations, bindings as well).

[9] It might seem that an endpoint reference, whose main component is a URI, would be associated with a port rather than a partner link. Recall, however, that BPEL is independent of the concrete level of WSDL where ports are defined. As a result BPEL does not deal with ports.

25.6.6 Handling Errors

Web services interactions typically involve a number of processes, implemented by different organizations, executing at independent sites spread across the Internet. Hence, the interaction generally takes a significant amount of time, and failures are not uncommon. In addition to the other failure modes one would expect in a conventional distributed application, the fact that components are developed by different organizations makes it more likely that messages contain unexpected and/or undesired data. These are the problems that one would expect in a loosely coupled environment, and BPEL provides a flexible structure for dealing with them.

Fault and compensation handlers are used to reverse the effects of partially completed interactions. The execution of these handlers is tied in with the concept of scopes. A **scope** is a feature of most programming languages (think `begin/end` blocks) and serves to define the execution context of an activity. A scope can have a name and local declarations and encloses a (possibly complex) activity to be executed. Declarations include, among other items, local variables, fault handlers, and a compensation handler. (Note, however, that properties do not have scope—they are always global to the entire process.) Scopes can be nested in the usual way to create a global/local execution environment for the activity.

Compensation. A process invokes the services of other processes in the course of performing an interaction. Even if the computation performed by each process is a transaction, it is unlikely that the interaction will use a two-phase commit protocol to ensure global atomicity since the organizations involved are independent, and interactions are lengthy. Using a two-phase commit causes locks to be held for long periods and sites to lose control over when locks are released (see Section 24.6). If two-phase commit is not used, individual sites might commit during an interaction that ultimately fails. We saw in Section 20.7 that compensation is a technique for recovering in such a case.

A compensation handler can be declared local to a scope. The implication is that, in BPEL's view, a scope encapsulates a basic unit of work that either completes successfully or fails, and that compensation can be used to reverse the effects of a successfully completed scope at a later time. Furthermore, at most one compensation handler can be declared. The implication is that, in BPEL's view, how success is achieved is a detail hidden within the scope. There is only one kind of success, and the details of how it is to be reversed are hidden within the compensation handler.

A simple scenario that illustrates the use of compensation is shown in Figure 25.28. Scope *B* is nested immediately within scope *A*. It is an activity in the sequence of activities that constitute scope *A*. Scope *B* contains the invocation of a Web service, *reserveOp*. Suppose that after exiting from scope *B* normally (*reserveOp* has completed successfully), a fault occurs in *activities-2* that requires the reversal of *reserveOp*. When the fault is raised, control will be passed to a fault handler (we will discuss fault handlers in the next subsection) local to scope *A* (assuming that such a handler has been declared). Reversal can be done by invoking—from within that handler—the compensation handler local to scope *B*.

FIGURE 25.28 A simple process fragment illustrating compensation.

```
<scope name="A">
    <sequence>
        <!-- activities-1 -->
        <scope name="B">
            <compensationHandler>
                <invoke ..cancelOp.. >
            </compensationHandler>
            <invoke ..reserveOp.. >
        </scope>
        <!-- activities-2 -->
    </sequence>
</scope>
```

Compensation is not automatic. The application programmer must explicitly code the body of the handler. Thus, more generally, scope *B* might invoke several operations, not all of which require compensation. Identifying those that require compensation, determining the correct compensating operation for each, and deciding on the order in which compensating operations are invoked are all decisions that the application programmer must make and encode in the body of the handler.

A handler is invoked using the `compensate` activity, which names the scope to which the handler is local (the scope to be compensated for). For example, the compensation handler local to scope *B* is invoked from scope *A* using `<compensate scope="B"/>`. Compensation can only be invoked if execution of scope *B* has terminated normally—that is, the unit of work has been successfully completed. In BPEL terminology, the compensation handler local to a scope is **installed** when normal exit from the scope has occurred. Uninstalled handlers cannot be invoked.

Scope *B* terminates abnormally if a fault occurs during its execution. The nature of the fault and the point at which it was raised within the scope determine the actions to be taken to reverse the partial execution. Hence, in contrast to compensation, reversal after a fault depends on the specific details of the event. We will discuss faults shortly.

Compensation applies only to the scope's external effects—the effects of the operations it has invoked at other sites. On entry, a scope's compensation handler is given a snapshot of the process's state at the time control exited (normally) from the scope. Since it can access only the snapshot and not the variables themselves, compensation cannot affect the state of the process and applies only to external activities.

When the compensation handler completes, control returns to the point following the `compensate` activity that called it. That still leaves open one question. Where in the process can a `compensate` activity be placed? In BPEL, compensation handles failure, and failure is detected when a fault occurs. Hence, a `compensate` activity can appear only within a fault handler or a compensation handler. (The execution of compensation handlers can be nested if nested scopes have to be reversed. You will see an example of this shortly.)

Faults. Faults signal failure and start the process of reversing the effects of an interaction. A fault might be raised in a process if it gets a fault response to an operation that it has invoked synchronously. Alternatively, a process might explicitly execute a `throw` activity if it recognizes that an anomalous situation has arisen. An example of this is shown in Figure 25.26. Finally, a **standard** fault—a fault recognized by the BPEL processor such as `joinFailure`—might occur.

When a fault, *f*, is raised in a scope, *S*, all activities within *S* are immediately terminated. Since *S* might enclose a `flow`, terminating an activity might imply cutting off a concurrent activity at an arbitrary point. For example, one branch of a flow might execute a synchronous `invoke` while another faults. Although the `invoke` is terminated, the invoked server might still be servicing the request.

When termination is complete and if *S* has declared a fault handler for *f*, control is passed to it. Based on the nature of *f*, the handler can invoke compensation handlers for scopes immediately enclosed in *S* that have completed normally and clean up after other, immediately enclosed, activities (this is complicated by the fact that the handler might not know how far *S* had progressed when *f* occurred). While processing *f*, the fault handler might throw a fault (possibly *f*), which will be raised in the immediately enclosing scope.

If *S* has not declared a handler for *f* locally, *f* is raised in the immediately enclosing scope and on up the line until a handler is found or the process is terminated abnormally. Assuming that some handler, *F*, processes *f* without throwing another fault, control ultimately exits from *F*. If *F* is local to scope *S′* (which might be *S*), control resumes in the scope that immediately encloses *S′*, at the activity immediately following *S′*.

Whether a fault handler local to scope *S* throws a fault or simply exits from that handler, *S* is said to have exited abnormally. Hence, if a compensation handler has been declared local to *S* it is *not* installed—compensation cannot be invoked for a scope that has not terminated normally. This makes sense since compensation applies to a unit of work that has completed successfully.

To illustrate these points, consider the interaction between GoSlow and SlowHawk. The `reply` activity that SlowHawk might use to respond to a faulty invocation of `getFareOp` by GoSlow is

```
<reply partnerLink="myCustomer" portType="mygs:getFarePT"
     operation="getFareOp" variable="myFaultVar"
     faultName="invalidArgFault"/>
```

This version of the `reply` activity is different from the one used in Figure 25.24. In this case the fault named in the `faultName` attribute is being reported. Furthermore, the value returned is of type `invalidArgFaultMsg` (see Figure 25.22) instead of `itineraryRespMsg`, which is the type used for a normal return. (Note that the

FIGURE 25.29 Catching a fault in GoSlow.

```
<invoke partnerLink="airProvider" portType="gs:getFarePT"
        operation="getFareOp" inputVariable="itineraryVar"
        outputVariable="itineraryRespVar"/>
    <catch faultName="gs:invalidArgFault"
        faultVariable="invalidArgFaultVar>
        <sequence>
            <invoke partnerLink="hotelProvider"
                portType="gs:roomResPT"
                operation="cancelRoomOp"/>
            <reply partnerLink="customer"
                portType="gs:tripPT"
                operation="makeTripOp"
                faultName="invalidCustFault"/>
            <!-- other activities -->
        </sequence>
    </catch>
</invoke>
```

variable, partner link, and prefix mygs are declared locally to SlowHawk, but that mygs refers to the WSDL definitions of Figures 25.21–25.23.)

The reply raises an invalidArgFault at the point in GoSlow where getFare is invoked. In general, a fault handler is declared local to a scope using a catch element, but in this case it is convenient to attach the catch directly to the invocation (i.e., the invoke activity implicitly defines a scope). As a result, the invocation of getFareOp in Figure 25.24 is modified, as shown in Figure 25.29, in order to handle invalidArgFault. When the fault is raised in GoSlow, the value of myFaultVar is assigned to invalidArgFaultVar, and the handler code is the sequence within the catch. If a room reservation was made prior to the fault, cancelRoomOp is invoked. After replying to the customer, the handler might raise a fault that causes GoSlow to terminate.

If there were several invocations of getFareOp within GoSlow, it might be better to declare a single catch element local to a scope that contains all the invocations rather than declaring catch elements local to each invoke. A fault thrown by any invocation winds up in this handler. In either case, the handler cancels the room reservation and returns a fault to the customer.

The throw activity is illustrated in Figure 25.26. GoSlow raises the fault payFault if the customer has supplied a value of payType other than credit or debit as a parameter of acceptTripOp. We can expect that GoSlow would declare a handler for payFault in a scope that contains the throw. The handler would execute a reply to return a badPayFault to the customer (see Figure 25.22).

In general, several fault handlers (including possibly a <catchAll> handler) can be declared local to a scope to handle different faults. All are children of a single

<faultHandlers> element. The rules for determining the appropriate handler for a specific case are detailed and uninteresting.

Typically, the body of the fault handler invokes a compensation handler for each immediately enclosed scope, *S*, that has completed normally. One possible situation is shown in Figure 25.30. Fault $f2$ occurs in $scope_2$ and is handled by the `catch` element local to that scope. The handler cleans up locally, compensates for $scope_3$ and $scope_4$ (which have completed normally), and then throws the fault $f1$.

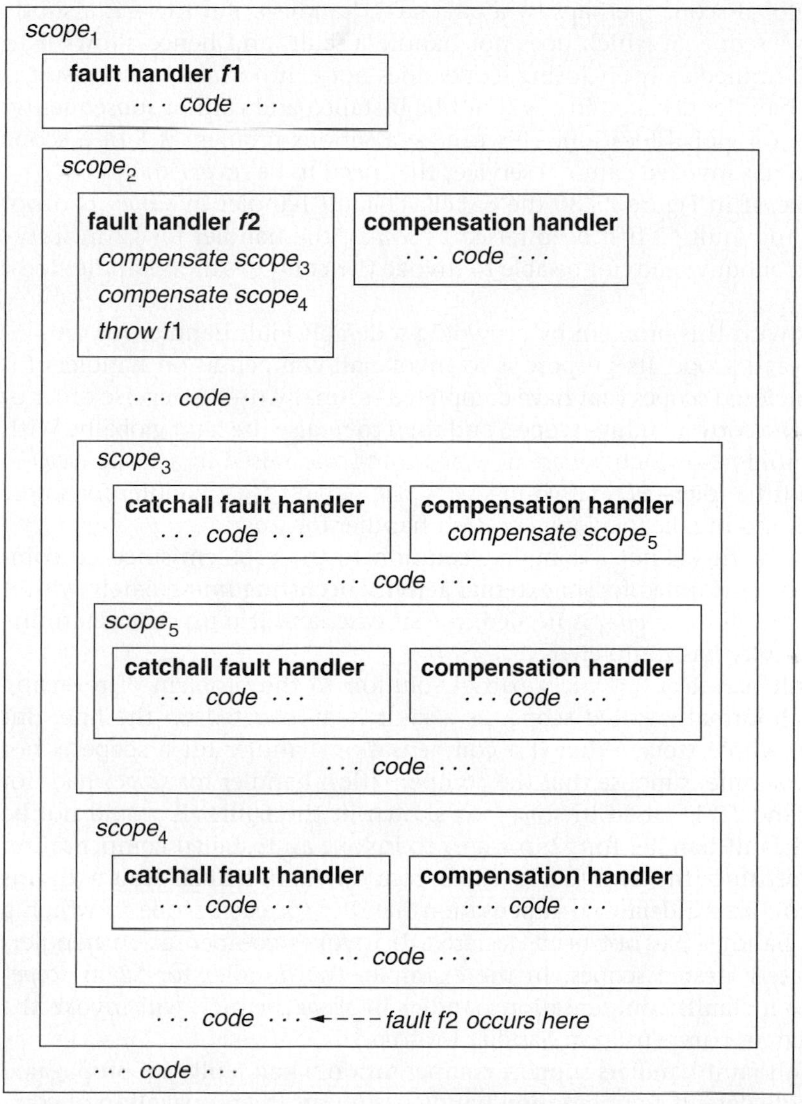

FIGURE 25.30 Example of the interaction between fault and compensation handlers.

$scope_2$ exits abnormally and $f1$ is handled in $scope_1$. The compensation handler for $scope_3$ compensates for $scope_5$.

Default handlers. If a business process contains an activity `throw f`, it is clear that the application programmer should provide a handler for f. Similarly, a fault response to an invocation, such as `invalidArgFault`, should be anticipated by the invoker and provided for. But what about a standard fault (for example, `joinFailure`)? The programmer might be excused for not providing handlers for all standard faults in a particular scope and simply allow them to be passed up and handled in a global scope (perhaps by a `catchall` handler). But there is a subtle problem here. A scope, S, which does not handle a fault, and hence allows it to be raised in the immediately enclosing scope, does not exit normally. As a result, a compensation handler declared in S will not be installed and cannot subsequently be invoked from a global location. This can be a serious problem if S or a scope nested within S has invoked external services that need to be reversed.

For example, if in Figure 25.30 the `catchall` fault handler in $scope_3$ had not been declared and fault $f2$ had been raised in $scope_3$, the handler for $f2$ in $scope_2$ would get control but would not be able to invoke the compensation handler local to $scope_3$.

BPEL deals with this problem by providing a default fault handler for unhandled faults in each scope. Its purpose is to invoke all compensation handlers for immediately enclosed scopes that have completed normally (in the reverse order of completion of the corresponding scopes) and then to reraise the fault globally. With this feature, before $f2$—which we are now assuming was raised in a scope ($scope_3$) that has no fault handler—is reraised in $scope_2$, the default fault handler for $scope_3$ will get control and invoke the compensation handler for $scope_5$.

Unfortunately, this is not a complete solution to the problem since no compensation will be performed for an external activity occurring immediately within $scope_3$. A fault handler in $scope_3$ is needed in that case, and it must first determine that such an activity has completed.

Default fault handlers provide a partial solution to the problem of reversing the effects of abnormally exited scopes as a fault is propagated up the line. But that is not the whole story. What if a compensation handler for a scope is not declared? For example, suppose that the compensation handler for $scope_3$ had not been declared and $f2$ is raised in $scope_2$, as shown in the figure. It would not be possible for the fault handler for $f2$ in $scope_2$ to invoke an installed compensation handler for $scope_5$ since the latter is not visible from the former. BPEL deals with this problem by providing a default compensation handler for each scope in which a compensation handler has not been declared. It invokes compensation handlers in all immediately nested scopes. In the example, the handler for $f2$ in $scope_2$ can invoke the (default) compensation handler in $scope_3$, which will invoke the (explicitly declared) compensation handler for $scope_5$.

Thus, default fault handlers support compensation when faults are propagated up the line, while default compensation handlers support the propagation of compensation down the line.

25.6.7 Handling Multiple Requests

There is a major deficiency in the way GoSlow has been implemented in the previous sections. It can handle only one customer interaction. Of course, we could modify it to handle multiple requests, one at a time, by simply placing the process in a `while` loop. However, we would like it to handle interactions concurrently, as a multithreaded server. BPEL provides two features to support this goal.

Multiple customer interactions can be handled concurrently by creating multiple instances of the process, one for each interaction. Ordinarily, the first activity of such a process is a `receive` that receives a request from a customer, as in Figure 25.24. In BPEL the `receive` can contain a `createInstance` attribute. If its value is set to `yes`, the reception of a message creates a new instance of the process to handle the arriving message. The default value is `no`. This is the only way a new instance of a process can be created.

For example, if the initial `receive` statement in GoSlow is replaced by

```
<receive partnerLink="customer" portType="gs:tripPT"
      operation="makeTripOp" variable="itineraryVar"
      createInstance="yes"/>
```

then each customer request will be handled by a separate instance of GoSlow and these instances can execute concurrently.

There are a few restrictions on the use of this feature. The `receive` must be the initial activity in the process. This makes sense since the activity that is enabled when the new instance is created is the activity following the `receive`. If an activity preceded the `receive`, it would not be executed in the new instance.

The restriction is not meant to exclude the possibility that there are several initial activities. This might be necessary in the case in which there are several distinct requests that a customer might submit. For example, in addition to `tripPT`, GoSlow might support a port type containing operations that allow customers to query a database of possible destinations. We want a new instance of GoSlow to be created for either type of request, but we cannot know in advance which type will arrive next. One way to handle this is to have `pick` be the initial activity and to set the `createInstance` attribute to `yes` in each of its `onMessage` clauses. Thus the restriction is relaxed to allow either a `pick` or a `receive` to be the first activity.

Creating process instances to provide concurrency introduces a new problem. How does a customer address the correct instance? This is not a problem if the customer's interaction consists of a single, synchronous invocation of an operation on a server, and the server does not invoke other servers in the process of handling the request. In that case, the customer's invocation message creates the new instance of the server, and when the instance replies, the interaction is over. The customer does not have to send a subsequent message.

Consider, however, a customer's interaction with GoSlow. Assuming the customer books the trip, this involves two invocations: first `makeTripOp` and then `acceptTripOp`. If two customers concurrently book a trip, a distinct instance of

GoSlow will be created for each. The problem is to decide to which instance an invocation message for acceptTripOp sent by one of the customers should be delivered.

The solution to this problem relies on the likelihood that there is some identifying item of information contained in the messages that are exchanged in a particular interaction. For example, the customer's Id is contained in all the messages of a trip interaction. If the run-time infrastructure hosting the business processes associates a process instance with an Id value, it can identify the target instance of a particular message by examining the Id value the message carries. An order number and social security number are other examples of identifying items of data.

Unfortunately, the infrastructure has no way of knowing which parts of a message are identifying items. Hence, in order to implement this solution, BPEL provides the application programmer with a construct to specify those parts.

In a more general situation, the messages of an interaction might be identified by several such items. For example, if GoSlow had to allow for the possibility that a single customer might run several trip-booking interactions concurrently, the messages of an interaction would have to be identified by both a trip number and a customer Id. Finally, it might be the case that different identifying items are used in different messages of the same interaction. For example, the messages in GoSlow's conversation with SlowHawk might all contain a purchase order number, not the customer's Id, while the messages in GoSlow's conversation with the customer might all contain the customer's Id but not the purchase order number—but all these messages belong to the same interaction.

Clearly, handling all these situations is a complex business. Let us look at a simple case. BPEL allows a process to declare a **correlation set** local to a scope. This is a set of properties such that all messages having the same values of all the properties in the set are part of the same interaction and hence are handled by the same instance. Thus, a correlation set identifies a particular instance of a process among a set of instances of that process, and a correlation set and a port together uniquely identify a process instance among all process instances at a host machine.

For example, in the case of GoSlow, we might include the following correlation set in the declarations of Figure 25.24:

```
<correlationSets>
    <correlationSet name="custCorr"
        properties="gs:Id"/>
</correlationSets>
```

In the general case, the value of the properties attribute might be a list of properties (e.g., trip number, customer Id), but in this case, the value of the property Id is sufficient to distinguish the messages of one interaction from the messages of another.

Having defined a correlation set we can use it in a communication activity. For example, in order to adapt GoSlow to concurrently handle customers, we modify the receive activity in Figure 25.24 as follows:

```
<receive partnerLink="customer" portType="gs:tripPT"
         operation="makeTripOp" variable="itineraryVar"
         createInstance="yes">
     <correlations>
         <correlation set="custCorr" initiate="yes"/>
     </correlations>
</receive>
```

The value yes assigned to the createInstance attribute of the receive indicates that a new instance of GoSlow is to be created when a message is received. The correlations child lists the correlation set(s) that should be used to match an arriving message to an instance. The value yes assigned to the initiate attribute of the correlation element (its default value is no) indicates, in addition, that values in the received message should be used to initialize the properties of the correlation set associated with the instance. Thus, the new version of the receive activity creates a new instance of GoSlow. It associates with it a new instance of the correlation set custCorr when a message arrives, and it initializes the correlation set instance with the value of Id in the arriving message.

Instance creation and correlation set initialization do not necessarily go hand in hand. A single instance might sequentially engage in several conversations (one conversation ends before the next starts) using the same correlation set. In this case a new conversation starts with a receive activity that initializes the correlation set, but the receive does not create a new instance. However, BPEL imposes the restriction that a set can be initialized only once. Hence, the instance of the process would have to exit the scope (and deallocate the set) and then reenter the scope in which the set is declared, and the correlation set will be initialized anew.

In general, the <correlations> element introduces one or more correlation sets. Each set is a list of properties, and each property in the set identifies (through a propertyAlias association) an item in the arriving message. Once a correlation set has been initialized, other receive activities in the instance that name the same correlation set will accept only messages containing that value.

In the GoSlow example, in addition to modifying the receive that accepts the invocation of makeTripOp to create a new instance and initialize a correlation set, the onMessage clause of the pick in Figure 25.26 (which is effectively a receive activity) must be modified in a corresponding way:

```
<onMessage partnerLink="customer" portType="tripPT"
         operation="acceptTripOp" variable="acceptTripVar">
     <correlations>
         <correlation set="custCorr"/>
```

```
        </correlations>
        <!-- the switch activity goes here -->
    </onMessage>
```

Here it is not appropriate to create a new instance, so the `createInstance` attribute of `onMessage` has the value `no` (by default). Furthermore, it is not appropriate to initialize the correlation set, so the `initiate` attribute of the `correlation` element also has the value `no` (by default). Hence, the activity only accepts invocations of `acceptTrip` carrying a value of `Id` equal to the value associated with the instance when the instance was created by the `receive` statement.

Having introduced correlation sets it is now possible to state two fairly intuitive rules that relate to it. First, it should never be the case that (at execution time) a process has two receive type statements (a `receive` statement or an `onMessage` clause of a `pick`) enabled at the same time with the same partner link, port type, operation, and correlation set(s). For example, this might happen (in an erroneous process) if the statements were embedded in two branches of a `flow`. Such a situation would imply that an arbitrary decision would have to be made at run time to choose the statement that accepts a particular arriving message. The semantics of a process that violates this restriction are not defined.

The second rule states that it should never be the case that a process has accepted more than one outstanding synchronous request from a particular partner link, port type, operation, and correlation set(s). If this rule were violated—perhaps by executing identical `receive` statements on different branches of a `flow`—the target of a subsequently executed `reply` would not be uniquely specified.

25.6.8 Front-End and Back-End Systems

Now that we have seen some of the details of BPEL and WSDL, we can return to our discussion of front-end and back-end systems. Figure 25.31 shows how these systems might communicate in the course of a B2B interaction. A front-end system (for example, the one at the right of the figure) might be implemented in BPEL (or another language that mimics a BPEL specification). In providing service, it might invoke other front-end systems (for example, the one at the top of the figure) and back-end systems (for example, the one at the bottom of the figure). The back-end system might be a transaction processing system implemented as described in Chapter 23. Both the front-end and the back-end systems expose WSDL interfaces and are invoked using SOAP messages.

For example, GoSlow and SlowHawk might be implemented in BPEL in two front-end systems. An invocation of `makeTripOp` at GoSlow results in a nested invocation of `getFareOp` at SlowHawk to obtain the required fare. Although we did not discuss `getFareOp`, it might, in turn, invoke a transaction exported by a back-end transaction processing system. GoSlow's operation `acceptTripOp` accepts credit or debit card information and performs the processing necessary to complete a reservation. This might involve invoking an operation `approveOp` at the card company's site, which might involve the services of banking and database systems

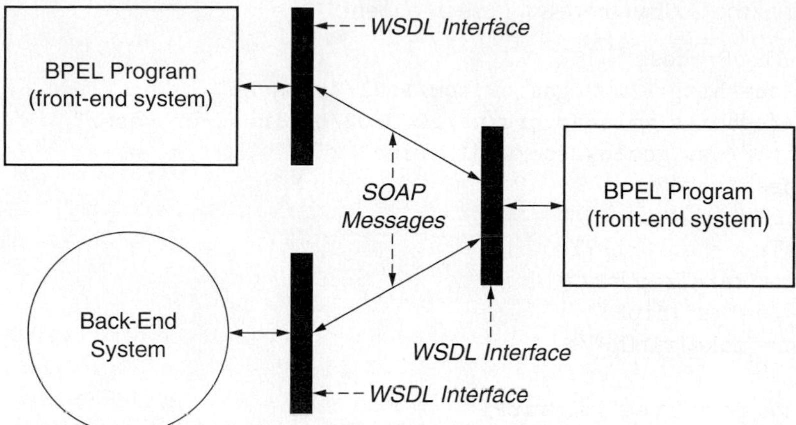

FIGURE 25.31 An example of interconnected Web services.

elsewhere. Hence, `approveOp` is implemented in a front-end system at the card company, which invokes these other, back-end, systems. Finally, `acceptTripOp` invokes a (local) back-end transaction processing system on the GoSlow server to record information about the reservation.

25.6.9 Interacting with a Web Service: Projection of a BPEL Process

Suppose you are a potential client of GoSlow and want to find out how to interact with it to plan a trip. Unfortunately, GoSlow's WSDL interface is not sufficient for that purpose since it contains only the operations and messages you must use but says nothing about how you must sequence the messages in order to complete an interaction. In this case the sequencing is trivial (`makeTripOp` followed by either `acceptTripOp` or `cancelTripOp`), but in a more realistic situation a more complex interaction might be required.

The information you want can be found in the executable BPEL process in GoSlow's front-end, but that contains more information than you need. An abstract version of the process is sufficient, but even that contains more information than necessary since, for example, you do not care how GoSlow interacts with other services (e.g., SlowHawk) to provide the service you requested, what properties GoSlow uses, how GoSlow processes fault conditions, how GoSlow maintains your state, and so on.

The information you need can be provided by a **projection** of the abstract process that contains only the communication with the customer, together with the control structures pertinent to that communication. Such a projection, or view, of the abstract GoSlow process (Figures 25.24 and 25.26) is shown in Figure 25.32. From this you can easily see what messages you must interchange and in what order.

FIGURE 25.32 A projection of the GoSlow process for use by a client.

```
<process name="GoSlowProcess"
    targetNamespace="http://www.goslow.com/wsdl/trips-bp"
    xmlns="http://schemas.xmlsoap.org/ws/2003/03/business-process/"
    xmlns:gs="http://www.goslow.com/wsdl/trips"
    abstractProcess="yes">
<sequence>
    <receive portType="gs:tripPT"
        operation="makeTripOp"/>
    <reply portType="gs:TripPT"
        operation="makeTripOp"/>
    <pick>
        <onMessage portType="gs:tripPT"
                operation="acceptTripOp">
                    ...
        </onMessage>
        <onMessage portType="gs:tripPT"
                operation="cancelTripOp">
                    ...
        </onMessage>
    </pick>
</sequence>
</process>
```

Projections can also be made for the various partners that provide the services used by GoSlow, for example the SlowHawk airline. The partners can use such projections, together with the corresponding projections of their own BPEL processes, to ensure that the processes are compatible (that they send and receive matching messages at the appropriate times). Projections might become an important use case for BPEL as an increasing number of enterprises seek to develop business processes that interact smoothly with each other.

25.7 UDDI: Publishing and Discovering Information about Services

Now that we have explained how a business, for example, Company A, can use WSDL to describe the services it is willing to perform, there remains the problem of how another business, Company B, that might want to use that service can discover that Company A provides the service and then obtain its WSDL description. This is the problem addressed by UDDI (Universal Description, Discovery, and Integration). As with the other protocols we have discussed, UDDI is still under active development. We give a brief overview of version 3.0, which at the time this book was written was a technical committee specification.

UDDI provides a means by which service providers can publish information about the services they provide and requesters can find information about which providers provide the services they want and how to obtain those services. More specifically UDDI provides

- A *Registry* (*database*) that contains information about
  - Business entities
  - Informal descriptions of the services provided by those entities
  - Various categorizations of those entities and services that can be used as the basis for searches in the registry
  - WSDL descriptions of those services
- *Inquiry and Publisher Interfaces* (*query and update languages*) that
  - Requestors can use to find and retrieve information from the registry
  - Providers can use to enter information into the registry

In some respects, a UDDI registry can be viewed as a telephone book, and the information stored in it can be characterized the same way telephone book information is characterized (except that the last characterization is new).

- *White page information.* Name, Address, Contact Person, Web site, etc.
- *Yellow page information.* Type of Business, Locations, Products, Services, Categorizations
- *Green page information.* Technical information about business services, including pointers to WSDL descriptions of the services

25.7.1 Data Structures in the UDDI Registry

A UDDI registry is a database, and so we start with a diagram that helps describe the data structures in a registry. Figure 25.33 shows an overview of the data structures that appear in a UDDI registry that is being used to describe a service.

There are four "top-level" data structures in the registry: `businessEntity`, `businessService`, `bindingTemplate`, and `tModel`. Each top-level structure has a unique key called its **universal unique identifier** (uuid).[10] For example in Figure 25.34, we show a `businessEntity` whose `businessKey` is denoted as `uuid:123BZK`. (`publisherAssertion` is not a top-level data structure and does not have a uuid. We will discuss its use later in this section.)

For simplicity, we have omitted some of the optional elements within the data structures. The `businessEntity` and `businessService` structures can contain optional categorization elements that describe the business entity and its services.

[10] The system assigns the uuid to ensure uniqueness. Version 3 of UDDI allows services to propose their own keys, which do not have to be in the form of uuids and which the system checks for uniqueness. We do not discuss this possibility any further.

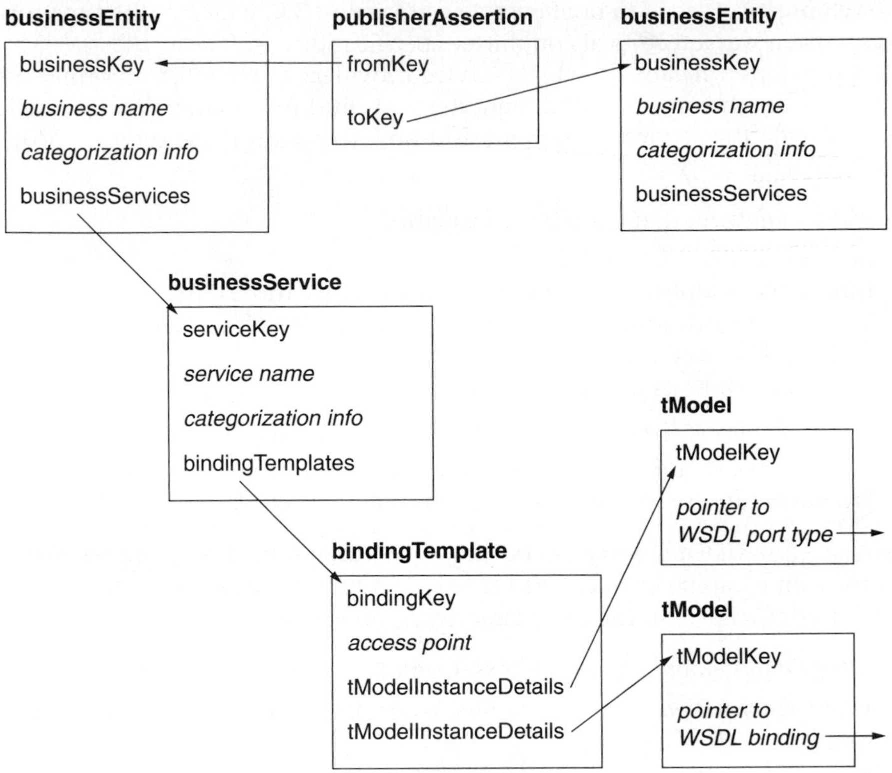

FIGURE 25.33 Overview of the data structures in a UDDI registry.

Using these elements, the registry can be searched for specific businesses or services based on international or industry categorization standards. Examples of such standards are the U.S. government's NAICS (National American Industry Classification System) and the International Standards Organization's ISO 3166 geographic categorization. Individual industries can also publish their own standard categories, which can be included in these optional elements.

The UDDI registry structures are:

- **businessEntity.** The `businessEntity` is the highest-level data structure in the registry. It contains white page information about the business (for example, a travel agency)
    - The name of the business, address, contact persons, etc.
    - Optional categorization information that can be used in searches to find the business
    - One or more `businessService` data structures, each of which describes a different service the business provides

FIGURE 25.34 A simple example of a businessEntity data structure.

```
<businessEntity businessKey="uuid:123BZK">
    <name> SlowHawk </name>
    <description> Airline </description>
    <contacts> . . . </contacts>
    <businessServices>
        <businessService> . . . </businessService>
    </businessServices>
    <categoryBag>
        <!-- We expand this example later -->
    </categoryBag>
</businessEntity>
```

FIGURE 25.35 A simple example of a businessService data structure.

```
<businessService serviceKey="uuid:123SRK">
    <name> Fare Service </name>
    <description> Provides fares for specific flights </description>
    <bindingTemplates>
        <bindingTemplate> . . . </bindingTemplate>
    </bindingTemplates>
    <categoryBag> . . . </categoryBag>
</businessService>
```

Figure 25.34 shows a simple example of a businessEntity data structure. The businessKey is a unique identifier for the business. The businessServices element contains one or more businessService data structures that describe the services provided by that business. This example does not have any of the optional categorization elements. Figure 25.38, which we discuss later, is an expansion of this figure that does contain such categorization elements.

- **businessService.** A businessService data structure contains yellow page information about one specific service a particular business provides
  - The name, unique identifier, and informal description of that service
  - One or more bindingTemplate data structures, each of which describes a different binding for that service
  - Optional categorization information that can be used in searches to find the service

  Figure 25.35 shows a simple example of a businessService data structure. Again, this example does not have any of the optional categorization elements.

FIGURE 25.36 A simple example of a `bindingTemplate` data structure.

```
<bindingTemplate bindingKey="uuid:123BNK"/>
  <description> GetFare SOAP binding </description>
  <accessPoint useType="endPoint"/>
    http://www.SlowHawk.com
  </accessPoint>
  <tModelInstanceDetails>
    <tModelInstanceInfo tModelKey="uuid:3456TMK">
      <description> WSDL port type of GetFare </description>
    </tModelInstanceInfo>
    <tModelInstanceInfo tModelKey="uuid: . . . ">
      <description> WSDL RPC/encoded binding of getFare </description>
    </tModelInstanceInfo>
  </tModelInstanceDetails>
</bindingTemplate>
```

- **bindingTemplate.** A `bindingTemplate` data structure contains green page information about one specific binding of one specific service a particular business provides.[11]
  - The unique identifier and informal description of the binding
  - The Web address at which that binding can be accessed (provided in the `port` declaration local to the WSDL description of the service)
  - One or more `tModelKeys` that point to `tModel` data structures, which provide technical details about that binding for that service. (We explain why there are often two such keys when we discuss `tModels` in the next bullet.)

  Thus, the `bindingTemplate` data structure relates a service to a binding of that service. Figure 25.36 shows a simple example of a `bindingTemplate` data structure.
- **tModel (technical model).** A `tModel` data structure contains green page information describing the technical details of a service. In particular a `tModel` contains (within `overviewDoc`) a pointer to a file containing the WSDL description of the service. Specifically, a `tModel` data structure contains
  - The name and informal description of the technical information represented by the `tModel`
  - A pointer to the location of the WSDL information represented by the `tModel`

[11] We have used the word "binding" in several contexts in this chapter. A SOAP binding maps a SOAP message to a particular transport protocol. A WSDL binding maps an abstract message described in a port type to a concrete message sent using a particular transport protocol to a particular port. A UDDI `bindingTemplate` maps the name of a service to its WSDL description.

FIGURE 25.37 A simple example of a `tModel` data structure.

```
<tModel tModelKey="uuid:3456TMK">
    <name> getFarePT </name>
    <description> WSDL port type of getFare Service </description>
    <overviewDoc>
        <overviewURL>
            http://www.SlowHawk.com/GetFarePTDescription
        </overviewURL>
    </overviewDoc>
</tModel>
```

Figure 25.37 shows a simple example of a `tModel` data structure.

According to the published "best practices" for using a UDDI registry to store information about WSDL services, a `bindingTemplate` should contain two different `tModelKeys` that point to two different `tModels` for a specific service. One `tModel` points to a file containing the WSDL description of the port type of that service, and the other points to a file containing the WSDL description of the `binding`.

One reason for having two `tModels` for the same service is that the port type might be shared by many businesses that provide the same service. For example, the airline industry might define a standard `getFare` service described by a generic port type, and many individual airlines might provide that service, each with its own binding. Thus the `bindingTemplates` of each of the services provided by the different airlines would point to the same `tModel` for the port type and different `tModels` for their individual bindings. The services of all the airlines would be semantically equivalent, but would be implemented differently.

Another reason for having two `tModels` is that a single provider might support two or more different bindings of the same service, each described by a different `bindingTemplate`. Each of these `bindingTemplates` would point to the same `tModel` that describes the port type of that service and different `tModels` that correspond to the different bindings.

Actually, `tModel` data structures have a number of different uses in UDDI registries in addition to pointing to WSDL files.

- They are used to point to files containing categorization information. Such `tModels` might be referenced by `businessEntity`, `businessService`, or `publisherAssertion` data structures.
- They are used to point to files containing complex search criteria that can be used by the `find` methods in the query language, which are discussed in Section 25.7.2.

Figure 25.38 is an expansion of Figure 25.34 that includes categorization information involving a `tModel`. The `categoryBag` items can contain one or

FIGURE 25.38 An example of a `businessEntity` data structure that includes a `categoryBag` that refers to a `tModel`.

```
<businessEntity businessKey="uuid:123BZK">
    <name> SlowHawk </name>
    <description> Airline </description>
    <contacts> . . . </contacts>
    <businessServices>
        <businessService> . . . </businessService>
    </businessServices>
    <categoryBag>
        <keyedReference
            keyName="Scheduled Passenger Air Transportation"
            keyValue="481111"
            tModelKey="uuid:C0B9FE13-179F-413D-8A5B-5004DB8E5BB2"/>
    </categoryBag>
</businessEntity>
```

more `keyedReference` elements. Within each `keyedReference` element is a `tModelKey`, whose uuid points to a `tModel` that contains information about a particular categorization. The `keyValue` gives a particular key within that categorization, and the `keyName` is an informal human-readable name for the meaning of that key. This key can then be used in a search for that business entity, as shown later in Figure 25.41.

In Figure 25.38, the uuid `C0B9FE13-179F-413D-8A5B-5004DB8E5BB2` in the `tModelKey` corresponds to the North American Industry Classification System (NAICS), and the `keyValue 481111` corresponds to "Scheduled Passenger Air Transportation Industry" within that classification.

- **publisherAssertion.** A `publisherAssertion` data structure represents relationships between pairs of `businessEntity` structures. For example, one `businessEntity` might be a subsidiary or a partner of the other. The data structure contains
  - A `fromKey` and a `toKey`, which are `businessKeys` that point to the two `businessEntity` data structures for which a relationship is being defined
  - A description of the relationship (within the `keyedReference`)

  Figure 25.39 shows a simple example of a `publisherAssertion` data structure. It states that the business entity with the key `uuid:123BZK` (which according to Figure 25.38 is SlowHawk) is a parent business of the entity with the key `uuid:123SUB`.

Using these data structures, a requester can find all of the WSDL services provided by a business, and for each of these services all of the bindings for that service, and for each binding the detailed WSDL description of that binding. To actually find this information, the requester can use the *Inquiry Interface*, discussed next.

FIGURE 25.39 A simple example of a `publisherAssertion` data structure.

```
<publisherAssertion>
     <fromKey> uuid:123BZK </fromKey>
     <toKey> uuid:123SUB </toKey>
     <keyedReference
          tModelReference="uuid: . . . "
          keyName="subsidiary"
          keyValue="parent-child" />
</publisherAssertion>
```

25.7.2 The Inquiry Interface (Query Language)

The **Inquiry Interface** can be used by requesters to obtain information from a UDDI registry. The messages in the Inquiry Interface are shown in Figure 25.40. There are two kinds of messages: `get` messages and `find` messages.

The `get` messages take as input the key value of a data structure and return as output a copy of the data structure. Thus, if the requester knows the value of the key of a particular data structure (the `businessKey`, `serviceKey`, `bindingKey` or `tModelKey`), he can obtain a copy of that data structure with the appropriate `get` message.

If the requester does not know the appropriate key value, he can retrieve information about the different data structures using the appropriate `find` message based on various search criteria. Included with this retrieved information are key values, which can be used in subsequent `get` messages.

We discuss the `find_business` message in some detail. The others are similar. A simple example of `find_business` message is

```
<find_business xmlns="urn:uddi-org:api_v3">
     <name>SlowHawk</name>
</find_business>
```

This example uses a simple search criterion—the name of the business. UDDI offers a large and expandable set of search criteria, including name, identifier, key, category, etc. and a large number of search qualifiers including, exact match, approximate match, case-sensitive match, etc.

A slightly more complex example of a `find_business` message is shown in Figure 25.41. Here, we are searching for businesses based on a key value of `481111` as specified by the categorization corresponding to the `uuid` in the `tModel` (`C0B9FE13-179F-413D-8A5B-5004DB8E5BB2`), which we have already noted is the North American Industry Classification System. The results of the find operation are sorted alphabetically by name in descending order. We assume the `businessEntitys` are described with `categoryBags` as in Figure 25.38. Note that in order to formulate this query, the requester had to know both the `keyValue` for the passenger airline

FIGURE 25.40 The messages in the Inquiry Interface.

`get_businessDetail`
Returns a businessDetailMessage *containing information about all the* businessEntities *that satisfy the specified* businessKeys

`get_serviceDetail`
Returns a serviceDetailMessage *containing information about all the* businessServices *that satisfy the specified* serviceKeys

`get_bindingDetail`
Returns a bindingDetailMessage *containing information about all the* bindingTemplates *that satisfy the specified* bindingKeys

`get_tModelDetail`
Returns a tModelListDetailMessage *containing information about all the* tModels *that satisfy the specified* tModelKeys

`find_business`
Returns a businessListMessage *containing information about all the* businessEntities *that satisfy a particular criterion*

`find_service`
Returns a serviceListMessage *containing information about all the* businessServices *that satisfy a particular criterion*

`find_tModel`
Returns a tModelListMessage *containing information about all the* tModels *that satisfy a particular criterion*

`find_binding`
Returns a bindingDetailMessage *containing information about all the* bindingTemplates *that satisfy a particular criterion*

`find_relatedBusiness`
Returns a relatedBusinessesListMessage *containing information about all the* businessEntities *related to a given* businessEntity *based on a particular criterion*

FIGURE 25.41 An example of `find_business` message based on a search key.

```
<find_business xmlns="urn:uddi-org:api_v3">
    <findQualifiers>
        <findQualifier>sortByNameDesc</findQualifier>
    </findQualifiers>
    <categoryBag>
        <keyedReference
            keyName="Scheduled Passenger Air Transportation"
            keyValue="481111"
            tModelKey="uuid:C0B9FE13-179F-413D-8A5B-5004DB8E5BB2"/>
    </categoryBag>
</find_business>
```

FIGURE 25.42 A simple example of a `businessList`.

```
<businessList  . . . />
    <businessInfos>
        <businessInfo businessKey="uuid:123BZK"/>
            <name>SlowHawk</name>
            <serviceInfos>
                <serviceInfo serviceKey="uuid:123SRK"/>
                    <name> Fare Service </name>
                </serviceInfo>
                <serviceInfo serviceKey= . . . />
                    <name>  . . . </name>
                </serviceInfo>
            </serviceInfos>
        </businessInfo>
    </businessInfos>
</businessList>
```

industry (481111) and the `tModelKey` for the NAICS (`uuid:C0B9FE13-179F-413D-8A5B-5004DB8E5BB2`). Such information might be separately available in published sources or over the Internet.

Figure 25.42 shows a simple example of the `businessList` returned by a call to `find_business`. It includes the `businessKey` of SlowHawk and the `name` and `serviceKey` of its services (assuming SlowHawk provides only two services).

WSDL services have been defined for the inquiry and publisher interfaces `InquireSoap` and `PublishSoap`. We give an example of `InquireSoap` here and one of `PublishSoap` in Section 28.7.3. Figure 25.43 shows the `InquireSoap` port type definition for `find_business`, and Figure 25.44 shows the message definitions. The

FIGURE 25.43 The WSDL port type definition for `find_business`.

```
<portType name="InquireSoap">
    <operation name="find_business"
        <input message="tns:find_business"/>
        <output message="tns:businessList"/>
        <fault name="error"
            message="tns:dispositionReport"/>
    </operation>
</portType>
```

FIGURE 25.44 The message definitions for `find_business`.

```
<message name="find_business">
    <part name="body"
        element="uddi:find_business"/>
</message>

<message name="businessList">
    <part name="body"
        element="uddi:businessList"/>
</message>
```

bodies of the messages are just the corresponding UDDI structures for the messages, as described in the `element` attribute of the `part` child in the `message` definition.

We do not discuss the `get` messages. They are basically quite simple. An example of a `get_businessDetail` message is

```
<get_businessDetail>
    <businessKey> uuid:123BZK </businessKey>
</get_businessDetail>
```

This query returns a `businessEntity` data structure corresponding to the `businessKey` that was supplied as input.

25.7.3 The Publisher Interface (Update Language)

The **Publisher Interface** can be used by businesses to store and update information in a UDDI registry. The messages in the Publisher Interface are shown in Figure 25.45. (The last three messages are retrieval, not update, messages.)

One part of each message is an authentication token so that only the appropriate party can access the registry through this interface. Furthermore, the Publisher

FIGURE 25.45 The messages in the Publisher Interface.

save_business
 Creates or updates businessEntity

delete_business
 Deletes businessEntity

save_service, delete_service

save_binding, delete_binding

save_tModel, delete_tModel

set_publisherAssertions
 Sets all the assertions for a publisher

add_publishersAssertions
 Adds one or more assertions to a publisher's collection

delete_publisherAssertions
 Deletes one or more assertions from a publisher's collection

get_publisherAssertions
 Returns the set of publisherAssertions *for a publisher*

get_assertionStatusReport
 Returns status of current and outstanding publisherAssertions *for a publisher*

get_registeredInfo
 Returns list of all businessEntity *and* tModel *data controlled by a publisher*

Interface requires that the messages be sent in encrypted form so that no other parties can read or alter the messages that are sent.

The PublishSoap port type for save_business is shown in Figure 25.46. Figure 25.47 shows the definition of the messages, and Figure 25.48 shows the XML schema for the save_business element included in these messages.

One part of the save_business element is a businessEntity element (or a subset of such an element). If this is a new businessEntity (not an updating of an old one), the registry assigns some elements to it, for example, a unique businessKey and authorizedName, which cannot be included in the input message,

FIGURE 25.46 The PublishSoap port type for save_business.

```
<portType name="PublishSoap">
    <operation name="save_business"
        <input message="tns:save_business"/>
        <output message="tns:businessDetail"/>
        <fault name="error"
                method="tns:dispositionReport"/>
    </operation>
</portType>
```

FIGURE 25.47 The message definitions for save_business.

```
<message name="save_business">
    <part name="body"
        element="uddi:save_business"/>
</message>

<message name="business_detail">
    <part name="body"
        element="uddi:business_detail"/>
</message>
```

FIGURE 25.48 The schema for save_business.

```
<complexType name="save_business">
    <sequence>
        <element ref="uddi:authInfo"/>
        <element maxOccurs="unbounded" minOccurs="0"
        ref="uddi:businessEntity"/>
        <element maxOccurs="unbounded" minOccurs="0"
        ref="uddi:uploadRegister"/>
    </sequence>
    <attribute name="generic" type="string" use="required"/>
</complexType>
```

but which will appear in the output message.[12] If it is an update of an existing element, it might be only a subset of that element, in which case only the elements in the subset are changed. The output message is the updated businessEntity. The

[12] As we have noted, version 3.0 of UDDI allows the service to propose its own key, which the system then checks for uniqueness.

remaining `save` messages are defined similarly. The `delete` messages take as inputs authentication information and the key to the structure to be deleted.

25.7.4 Some Final Observations about UDDI

One feature of UDDI that we have not discussed is a *subscription service* by which businesses that are service requesters can be notified whenever the information about a particular service is changed in the registry. This information would obviously be useful for requesters who use the same service on a periodic basis.

A related feature, which was added in version 3, is a new data structure, `operationalInfo`, that contains historical information about each publishing operation, such as when information about some service was added or modified. Then there is a new operation, `get-operationalInfo`, to retrieve that information.

Many companies offer a variety of tools for inquiry and publishing in UDDI registries. Some offer GUIs that involve filling in various fields on a form and submitting that form. Others offer Java APIs for querying and updating a UDDI registry. These APIs involve defining an object corresponding to the query or update, filling in certain attributes in that object, and then calling the appropriate procedure.

25.8 WS-Coordination: Transactional Web Services

Coordination refers to the act of organizing a number of independent entities to achieve some goal. The goal might be related to security, replication, etc., but our interest is in organizing the termination of transactions and workflows. An example of this is the two-phase commit protocol: the coordinator supervises the cohorts, and the goal is atomic termination.

Termination control is a concern in the Web services area. For example, it might be appropriate for an operation (or some portion of an operation) exported by a Web service to be atomic. This is easy to do if the operation does not invoke other Web services since atomicity can be implemented by a back-end server. However, if the operation does invoke other services—for example, GoSlow's operation `makeTripOp` invokes SlowHawk and RoachHeaven (Figure 25.25 on page 1093)—it will be more difficult to achieve atomicity. Coordination will be required, and complete atomicity might not be possible.

The first thing to note is that BPEL does not support transactions. It does provide for compensation, but this is only a tool that is useful in *implementing* transactional support. Second, the transaction manager that is supplied by a TP monitor is not oriented to the Web services environment. The X/Open standard is not based on XML or SOAP. Furthermore, X/Open assumes a more integrated environment. For example, with RPC communication it is assumed that stubs exist at server sites to automatically register a subtransaction when it is invoked.

WS-Coordination fills this gap. It provides a general framework for supporting coordination among Web services for a variety of purposes. Although it has not yet been accepted as a standard, we discuss it here since its initial application will be to support termination protocols. We also discuss two protocols that can be executed within the WS-Coordination framework: WS-AtomicTransaction and WS-BusinessActivity.[13]

WS-Coordination can be viewed as an XML-based tool for organizing a number of independent applications into a coordinated activity. It allows an application to activate a coordination context that describes the coordination type it wants to impose on an activity and to pass the context to the participating applications. It allows each application to register for a protocol that controls its role in that coordination type. Finally, it provides a framework within which the execution of the protocol is supported. These terms will be made clear in the following discussion.

WS-Coordination. WS-Coordination assumes the existence of coordinator sites on the Web. An application, App_1 (for example, GoSlow), that wants to initiate a coordinated activity first uses the **activation service** of a coordinator, C_1, to create a **coordination context** for a particular type of activity. For example, App_1 might create an activity with coordination-type atomic transaction in order to provide for the all-or-nothing termination of a distributed interaction. A coordination type is identified by a URI, and WS-Coordination is extensible in the sense that as new coordination types are needed, they can easily be added. Nothing in WS-Coordination depends on the characteristics of a particular coordination type.

The context returned by the activation service to the application describes the activity and can be sent in a message to another application that might join the activity. It contains a unique identifier for the activity (the equivalent of a transaction identifier—see page 972), the coordination type, and an endpoint reference (see the discussion of WS-Addressing on page 1058) of a **registration service** within C_1.

App_1 can then invoke C_1's registration service through the endpoint reference, passing the context as an argument and specifying a protocol that it wishes to use in participating in the activity. Each activity type has an associated set of protocols. Each participant can choose a protocol that it will use to participate in the activity. For example, a module participating in an activity being coordinated as an atomic transaction might register for a two-phase commit protocol (we will see other possibilities shortly). The registration service responds by returning an endpoint reference for a **protocol service** that implements the requested protocol and that is used for exchanging protocol messages with the application at execution time. This is the endpoint that a participant in an atomic transaction protocol would use to send *prepared* or *committed* messages.

The role of WS-Coordination as a framework for coordination is now apparent. The protocol to be executed is controlled by the protocol service. Each protocol service has its own specification. Its goal, and the details of the messages exchanged to achieve that goal, are protocol dependent and are separately specified. Thus, creating an atomic transaction involves using WS-Coordination together with a protocol service that supports WS-AtomicTransaction. WS-Coordination's responsibility is

[13] This section is based on the version of WS-Coordination, WS-AtomicTransaction, and WS-BusinessActivity dated November, 2004.

simply to create a coordination context for the activity, register the participants in the activity, and distribute endpoint references to the protocol service.

For example, App_1 might create an activity with coordination type atomic transaction. This establishes C_1 as the root coordinator of the activity. App_1 might then use the registration endpoint reference in the coordination context returned by C_1 to register for a particular protocol, p_1, associated with atomic transactions. It also sends the context, as a SOAP header element, in an application message to App_2, inviting it to join the activity. App_1 might be GoSlow, and App_2 might be SlowHawk. App_2 joins by registering with C_1 or with a different coordinator, C_2, for a protocol, p_2, passing the activity's context as an argument. In the latter case, C_2 communicates with C_1 (using the endpoint reference in the context). As a result, it becomes a subordinate coordinator as in Figure 24.4 and acts as an intermediary between C_1 and App_2.

Similarly, if App_1 (or App_2) invokes a server, R_1 (such as a DBMS), it sends the context to R_1. R_1 registers with C_1 or with a different coordinator. It is important to relate WS-Coordination to the implementation of the two-phase commit protocol described in Section 24.2.1. There registration is implicit: when a server is invoked, the coordinator is automatically notified through the *xa* interface, and there is only one protocol available. WS-Coordination offers more flexibility in activity types and protocols but requires more involvement of the participants. Participants must explicitly pass contexts in application messages and register for protocols.

WS-AtomicTransaction. An atomic transaction is appropriate for a short-lived activity involving participants who trust one another and who operate within a tightly coupled organization. The activity should be short-lived since atomicity requires that participants keep resources locked until termination completes. Trust is required since an untrustworthy participant can cause the entire transaction to abort, wasting the efforts of the other participants.

The AtomicTransaction activity type offers three protocols. Different participants in the same activity can register for different protocols. The protocol service must keep track of the identities of the participants and the protocols for which they have registered.

- *Completion protocol.* One participant, usually the application that creates the activity (App_1 in our example), registers for this protocol and becomes the application that initiates the commit protocol by sending a commit message to the coordinator. When the protocol completes, this participant will be notified by the coordinator of the outcome.
- *Durable2PC protocol.* This is the standard two-phase commit protocol with presumed abort that was discussed in Section 24.2. A module that registers for this protocol exchanges *prepare, vote, commit,* and *done* messages with its coordinator as described there.
- *Volatile2PC protocol.* This is identical to Durable2PC, but its implementation satisfies the following condition. The coordinator sends *prepare* messages to

participants registered for Volatile2PC first, before sending them to those registered for Durable2PC. Only when *vote* messages have been returned from all Volatile2PC participants are *prepare* messages sent to participants registered for Durable2PC.

Why are both Volatile2PC and Durable2PC needed? The protocols address an issue caused by the presence of caching servers on the Web. These servers act as intermediaries between content servers and clients that access the content. Performance is enhanced and bottlenecks avoided by storing recently accessed content on a caching server. A client transaction reads and updates content in the cache, greatly reducing the need to access the content server. However, a problem arises when the transaction completes but the updated content in the cache has not yet been transferred back to the content server. The updated content must be transferred back to the content server before the transaction is allowed to commit.

There is nothing new here. This is exactly the problem discussed in Section 22.2.1, but the context is different. In that case the DBMS managed both the cache and durable storage and could arrange to delay the commit until all of the dirty pages created by a transaction had been flushed from the cache to the database. In the Web case, the cache and the database are managed by different Web servers. If all prepare messages were sent at the same time, the content server might vote commit without being in the prepared state: it might not be aware that a dirty page created by the transaction is present in the cache. Since a cache server does not support durability, a crash might result in the loss of a dirty page.

Delaying prepare messages to participants registered for Durable2PC solves this problem. The cache server registers for Volatile2PC and does not send a vote message to the coordinator until all of an activity's dirty content has been sent to the content server. Then when the content server receives a prepare message, it is aware of all of the activity's dirty content and can make it durable before voting.

A participant can register for multiple protocols. For example, it might register for both Completion and Durable2PC if it wants to both initiate termination and participate in the termination decision.

The atomic commit protocol is virtually identical to the one described in Chapter 24. The protocol service acts as the coordinator. If the participant that registered for the Completion protocol requests to rollback, the coordinator simply sends `rollback` messages to all the cohorts (cohorts do not reply to this message). If the request is to commit, the following steps are taken:

1. The coordinator sends *prepare* messages to all the cohorts who registered for the Volatile2PC protocol, and each cohort can reply with either a *prepared* message,[14] an *aborted* message, or a *readOnly* message (the standard implements the read-only optimization discussed in Section 24.2.1).

[14] In Chapter 24 this was referred to as a *ready* message. We will follow the terminology used in the WS-AtomicTransaction specification.

2. If all the Volatile2PC cohorts respond with either *prepared* or *readOnly* messages, the coordinator sends *prepare* messages to all the cohorts who registered for the Durable2PC protocol. Each such cohort can reply with either a *prepared*, *aborted*, or *readOnly* message.
3. If all the cohorts respond with either *prepared* or *readOnly* messages, the coordinator decides to commit and sends a *commit* message to all the cohorts that responded with `prepared` messages. The cohorts reply with *committed* messages[15]. The coordinator can forget about the activity when all *committed* messages have been received. If any cohort responded with an *aborted* message, the coordinator decides to abort and sends *rollback* messages to all the cohorts that responded `prepared`. The cohorts do not reply (as explained in the presumed abort protocol).

To deal with timeout and recovery issues, the specification uses the presumed abort protocol (Section 24.2.2), and the coordinator and cohorts must perform the logging described in that protocol. The specification provides a *replay* message that a cohort can send to the coordinator during a recovery or timeout protocol to determine the status of the activity.

The protocol illustrates the use of some of the WS-Addressing header elements discussed on page 1060. For example, a register message must contain a `MessageId` and `ReplyTo` header, while a response to the message must contain a `RelatesTo` header.

WS-BusinessActivity. The concept of an atomic transaction is well established, and while WS-AtomicTransaction has not been accepted as a standard, its specification is fairly stable. The concept of a business activity, on the other hand, is a subject of considerable debate, and its specification is still undergoing change. Despite this, we include a description of the latest business activity proposal because it sheds light on the issues involved in relaxing the ACID requirements of a transaction.

The general Web environment encompasses a number of features that render the atomic transaction model inappropriate for many activities.

- Message delays and communication with humans can lengthen the execution time of an interaction.
- Since a server might be providing service to a wide variety of clients, server loading is unpredictable, making the time it takes for a server to respond to an invocation unpredictable.
- Servers are controlled by different organizations that might not trust one another. An untrustworthy participant can abort an entire transaction or cause unreasonable delays.
- Site and communication failures are more likely.

[15] In Chapter 24 these were referred to as *done* messages.

- It might be necessary to allow a participant to withdraw from an activity before the activity completes. For example, a server might not be willing to participate in the two-phase commit protocol. It might simply execute an operation and withdraw from the activity, making its state visible to subsequently invoked operations and making the implementation of isolation impossible. Thus, the set of participants is dynamic.

For all of these reasons, a more flexible and less ambitious termination protocol is required for many activities.

The concept of a business activity, specified in WS-BusinessActivity, has been proposed to deal with such issues. It is instructive to think of a business activity as composed of a nested set of subtransactions, each of which might be implemented using WS-AtomicTransaction. A subtransaction is generally confined to a single, tightly-coupled organizational domain and moves the business activity from one "consistent" state to another.

The termination of a business activity is more complex than an atomic transaction. With atomic transactions, atomicity dictates an all-or-nothing discipline: if a participant fails for any reason, the entire transaction is aborted. The sequence of messages in the two-phase commit protocol that does the termination is completely defined and can be separated from application logic. As a result, a protocol service for an atomic transaction can be provided by an off-the-shelf coordinator.

Business activities are different. For one thing, compensation can be used to undo the effect of a committed participant. Secondly, the failure of one participant does not necessarily imply that all others must compensate their effects. Furthermore, a variety of application-level failure conditions might arise, and the activity might need to respond differently to each. As a result, separating application logic from the protocol service does not always work in this situation. For example, the decision as to whether compensation is required when a particular participant faults might depend on the semantics of the application. Hence the application must explicitly deal with the fault. Furthermore, if one participant aborts, the application might decide to invoke a different participant to accomplish the same or a related task. This is similar to the nested transaction model (Section 19.2.3) in which if one subtransaction aborts, the parent transaction can use application logic to decide to invoke a different subtransaction to accomplish the task.

As a result, in some situations the protocol service must be integrated into the application code. This allows the application to decide how coordination should be accomplished. The mechanism for making this happen is readily available: the endpoint returned when a participant registers can target an application module.

WS-BusinessActivity defines two coordination types. The `AtomicOutcome` coordination type requires that all participants must either complete successfully or all must compensate their effects. With the `MixedOutcome` coordination type, some participants might complete successfully while others might compensate.

Within each coordination type, two termination protocols are supported. Participants in the same activity can register for different protocols.

- *BusinessAgreementWithParticipantCompletion*. The participant notifies the coordinator when it has completed its participation. For example the participant might have been asked to provide some specific service. The participant notifies the coordinator when that service has been completed.
- *BusinessAgreementWithCoordinatorCompletion*. The coordinator notifies the participant when its services are no longer required. For example, the participant might be providing a sequence of services for a particular business activity (e.g., a sequence of stock quotes), and the participant does not know and hence needs to be notified when no further quotes will be requested.

Suppose a participant in an activity with coordination type `MixedOutcome` registers for the *BusinessAgreementWithParticipantCompletion* protocol. The participant might notify the coordinator that it has completed by sending a *Completed* protocol message. This indicates that it has completed successfully, and effectively tells the coordinator that it is in the prepared state. Alternatively, the participant might send an *Exit* protocol message (indicating that it is withdrawing from the protocol) or a *Fault* protocol message (indicating that it has failed). The protocol service can respond to a *Completed* message with either *Close* (indicating that the participant should commit) or *Compensate* (indicating that the participant should reverse its action). The choice might depend on an arbitrary application-related condition in which case the coordination logic must be integrated with the application.

Alternatively, a rule for how the choice is to be made might be specified in the coordination context (using an extension element). For example, a majority rule would specify that a *Close* message should be sent if a majority of the participants complete successfully. In this case integration is not required and an off-the-shelf protocol service can be used.

The coordinator can also initiate termination of a participant using the *cancel* message.

The following example illustrates a typical situation. A buyer service might invoke the activation service of a coordinator to create a coordination context for a business activity having the `MixedOutcome` coordination type. The service might then pass the context on to three suppliers (participants) in application messages that request quotes. The suppliers register for the *BusinessAgreementWithParticipant-Completion* protocol and might use the coordinator's registration service for this purpose.

We assume that the buyer implements the protocol service and hence coordinates the termination protocol for the three participants. A state diagram that describes all possible message sequences between the coordinator and one particular participant in the *BusinessAgreementWithParticipantCompletion* protocol is shown in Figure 25.49. Protocol states are shown in ovals, solid arrows are messages sent by the coordinator, and dashed arrows are messages sent by the participant.

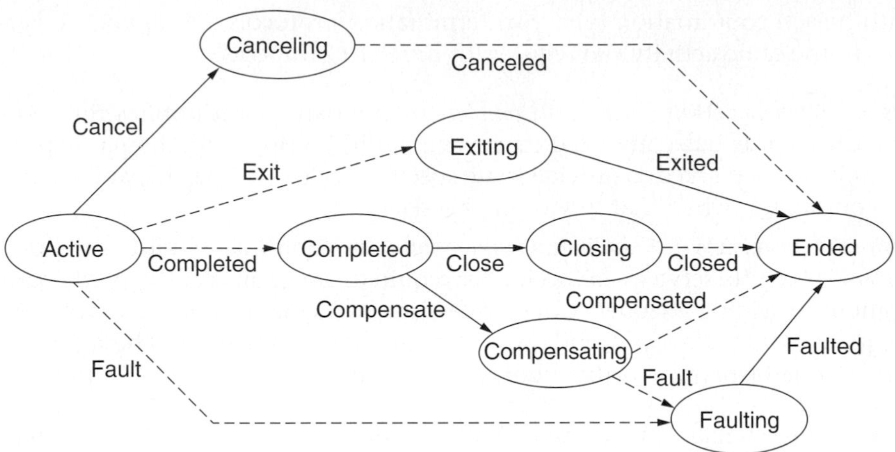

FIGURE 25.49 State diagram for the BusinessAgreementWithParticipantCompletion protocol. Protocol states are shown in ovals, solid arrows are messages sent by the coordinator, and dashed arrows are messages sent by the participant.

Supplier *A* might suffer some failure and declare its completion with a *Fault* protocol message. Suppliers *B* and *C* might perform some computation, update their databases, and declare their completion with *Completed* protocol messages containing quotes. The buyer decides to select the quote from *B*. Hence, acting as coordinator and executing the protocol service described in the figure, the buyer sends a *Compensate* protocol message to *C* and a *Close* protocol message to *B*. *C* responds with a *Compensated* message, and *B* responds with a *Closed* message. These sequences of messages correspond to paths shown in the figure.

The sequence of messages described in this example represent one possible sequence allowed in the protocol. There are a number of other possible sequences between the buyer and *A*, *B*, and *C*. The choice of the sequence depends on the application logic. For example, *B* detects a fault, and the buyer decides to do business with *A* and not *C*, etc. Hence, in contrast to WS-AtomicTransaction, application logic has been combined with coordination. The integration of the protocol service with the buyer's application code in the example allows this to happen. However, combining the protocol service with the application is not mandatory. With a different application, an endpoint reference to a protocol service implemented by an off-the-shelf coordinator could be returned to the participants.

The state diagram for the *BusinessAgreementWithCoordinatorCompletion*, shown in Figure 25.50, is almost identical to that in Figure 25.49 except for the *Complete* message and the *Completing* state. The coordinator sends this message when it needs to notify a participant that its services are no longer required. This corresponds to asking the participant to enter the prepared state.

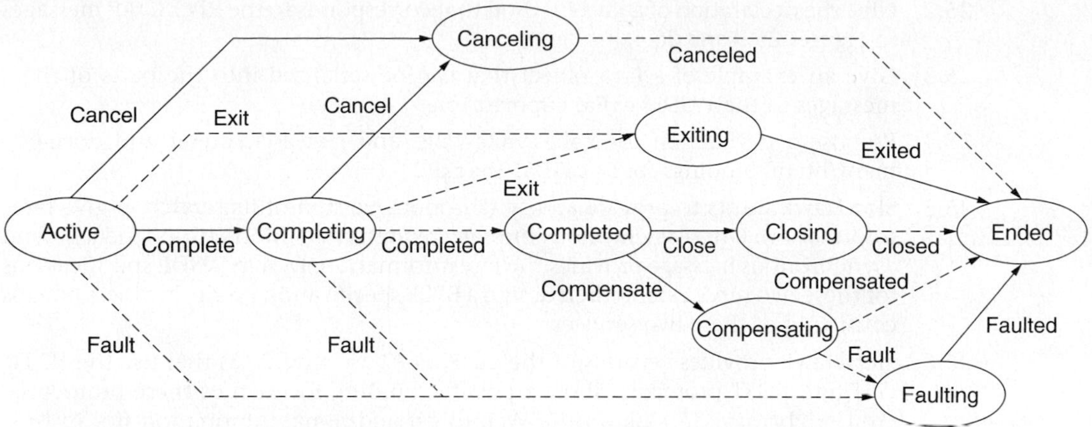

FIGURE 25.50 State diagram for the BusinessAgreementWithCoordinatorCompletion protocol. Protocol states are shown in ovals, solid arrows are messages sent by the coordinator, and dashed arrows are messages sent by the participant.

BIBLIOGRAPHIC NOTES

Material on the protocols discussed in this chapter can be found at the Web sites of the appropriate standardization organizations or the companies developing them.

- *HTTP http://www.w3.org/Protocols/#Specs*
- *SOAP http://www.w3.org/TR/SOAP/*
- *WS-Addressing http://www.w3.org/Submission/2004/SUBM-ws-addressing-20040810/*
- *WSDL http://www.w3.org/TR/wsdl/*
- *BPEL http://www.ibm.com/developerworks/library/ws-bpel/*
- *UDDI http://uddi.org/pubs/uddi-v3.00-published-20020719.htm*
- *WS-Coordination http://xmlcoverpages.org/WS-Coordination200411.pdf*
- *WS-AtomicTransaction http://xmlcoverpages.org/WS-AtomicTransaction200411.pdf*
- *WS-BusinessActivity http://xmlcoverpages.org/WS-BusinessActivity200411.pdf*

EXERCISES

25.1 SOAP extensibility relates to the use of intermediaries and SOAP headers to add features to a Web service that is invoked using SOAP messaging. Give an example of an extension and how an intermediary and header would be used to implement it.

25.2 Give the declaration of a Java method that corresponds to the RPC SOAP messages in Figures 25.3 and 25.4.

25.3 Give an example of a Java object that can be serialized into the parts of the messages in the WSDL`getFareOperation`.

25.4 Propose a declaration for `receiveResMsg`, and give RPC/literal and document/literal bindings for `hotelCallbackPT`.

25.5 SlowHawk wants to provide an asynchronous version of its service to give fare information. One asynchronous message requests fare information, and a second asynchronous message provides the fare information. Design WSDL specifications for these two services, and then design a BPEL specification for the business process consisting of these two services.

25.6 SlowHawk provides versions of the `getFarePT` (Section 25.5) that use the HTTP GET and POST protocols. Show a possible binding for each of these protocols. (You might have to look on the Web to get additional information not in the text.)

25.7 A stock brokerage company offers a `getQuote` service in which a requester sends a `getQuoteRequest` message containing a stock symbol and the brokerage company responds with a `GetQuoteResponse` message containing the current quotation for that stock. Suppose all that is known is the name of the brokerage company? Describe informally the sequence of UDDI queries you would use to find out the details of the RPC SOAP messages needed to invoke that service.

25.8 Two BPEL processes are said to be **compatible** if there are no communication deadlocks: every send in one process is received by the other, and every receive in one process has a corresponding send in the other. Give an example of two noncompatible processes for which every receive in one of the processes has a corresponding send in the other, but there is a communication deadlock.

25.9 Design the outline of a BPEL process that the vendor can use to describe the following business process:

> When you buy something over the Internet, you send the vendor the name, catalog number, and price of the item you want. Then the vendor sends you a form to fill out, containing the name, catalog number, and price of the item and requesting your name, address, credit card number, and expiration date. You return the form to the vendor. The vendor then sends your name, credit card number, and the price of the item to the credit card company to be approved. After it is approved, the vendor sends you a confirmation message. Then it sends a message to the warehouse to ship the item.

25.10 Explain which parts of the business process in the previous example should be part of an ACID transaction (Section 25.8).

25.11 Design the outlines of BPEL processes for two sites that are performing the following bidding workflow:

> Site 1 decides to offer an item for sale at some offering price and sends that offer in a message to site 2. When site 2 receives that message, it decides whether it wants to accept that offer or make a new bid (at some lower price). It sends that information, either new bid or accept, in a message to site 1. When

site 1 receives that message, it decides whether it wants to accept that bid or make a new offer (at a higher offering price). It then sends that information in a message to site 2. The bidding continues, sending messages back and forth, until one of the sites, s_a decides to accept a bid or offer and sends that information in a message to the other site, s_b. After sending that accept message, s_a exits the process, and after receiving the accept message, s_b also exits the process.

25.12 Explain why an assignment of an endpoint reference to `myRole` of a `partnerLink` makes no sense.

25.13 Show the changes to GoSlow that will be required if customers invoke `makeTripOp` using a one-way pattern and pass an endpoint reference for a callback.

25.14 Give an example of a business activity (Section 25.8) involving a travel agency in which a `compensate` message will be sent after an activity has completed.

25.15 Scope *S*3 is nested in scope *S*2 which is nested in scope *S*1. Assume that fault handlers for fault *f* exist in each scope and that compensation handlers *C*2 and *C*3 have been declared in *S*2 and *S*3. In each of the following cases, either explain how the specified sequence of events might happen or why the sequence is impossible

a. Suppose *f* is raised in *S*2 after *S*3 has exited normally and *C*2 is entered before *C*3.

b. Suppose *f* is raised in *S*2 after *S*3 has exited normally and *C*3 is entered.

c. Suppose *f* is raised in *S*1 after *S*2 has exited normally and *C*2 is entered before *C*3.

d. Suppose *f* is raised in *S*1 after *S*2 has exited normally and *C*3 is entered before *C*2.

e. Suppose *f* is raised in *S*1 after *S*2 has exited normally, no handler for *f* has been declared in *S*1. Describe the sequence of events that occurs.

f. Suppose *f* is raised in *S*1 after *S*2 has exited normally, no handler for *f* has been declared in *S*1, and no compensation handler has been declared in *S*2. Describe the sequence of events that occurs.

g. Suppose *f* is raised in *S*1 after *S*2 has exited normally, no handler for *f* has been declared in *S*1, and no compensation handler has been declared in *S*2. Describe the sequence of events that occurs.

25.16 Correlation sets can be associated with `invoke` statements (as well as `receive` statements) using

```
<invoke partnerLink="···" portType="···"
     operation="···" inputVariable="···">
     <correlations>
          <correlation set="···" initiate="yes/no"/>
     <\monocorrelations>
</invoke>
```

Give a circumstance under which it might be useful to do this.

26

Security and Electronic Commerce

Security is a major issue in the design of applications that deal with privileged information or that support systems on which life and property depend. In most applications the participants in a transaction must identify each other, with a high degree of certainty, and they might want to ensure that no third party is observing or modifying the information being exchanged.

Security issues are particularly important for transactions executed over the Internet because it is relatively easy for imposters to pretend to be other than who they actually are and for eavesdroppers to listen in on the exchanges between participants. And with the increasing amount of electonic commerce (both customer-to-business and business-to-business), server sites want to be able to reassure their users that interactions are secure.

26.1 Authentication, Authorization, and Encryption

Authentication refers to the process by which the identity of a participant is established. When you perform a transaction at an automated teller machine (ATM), the system establishes your identity using the information on your ATM card and your personal identification number (PIN). Furthermore, you may want to establish that you are talking to a real ATM and not a machine that looks like an ATM but is actually a "Trojan horse" designed to obtain your PIN. Similarly, when you are considering executing an Internet transaction with Macy's and you have to supply your credit card number to the server, you want to make certain that you are actually talking to that server and not to three students in a dorm room pretending to be Macy's.

Authorization refers to the process that determines the mode in which a particular client is allowed to access a specific resource controlled by a server. The client is assumed to have been previously authenticated. Authorization can be individual (*you* are allowed to withdraw money from your bank account) or group-wide (*all tellers* are allowed to write certified checks), and it is specified in terms of the services that the server offers. For example, "withdraw money from a specified account," or "write a certified check."

Encryption is used to protect information stored at a particular site or transmitted between sites from being accessed by unauthorized users. A variety of highly sophisticated algorithms exist to transform this information into a bit stream that is intelligible only to selected users.

Since encryption plays an important role in authentication and authorization, we quickly review its general structure first. Then we discuss authentication and authorization and how all three concepts are applied in electronic commerce transactions. Finally we discuss how these concepts are incorporated into XML.

26.2 Encryption

The general model of an encryption system is shown in Figure 26.1. The information to be sent is generally a string of characters referred to as **plaintext**. It is encrypted by a program (or device) that transforms it into **ciphertext**, and it is the ciphertext that is actually transmitted. At the receiving end, the ciphertext is decrypted by another program (or device) that transforms it back into the original plaintext.

The goal of an encryption system is to protect information from an **intruder**. Intrusion is generally assumed to take two forms: **passive**, in which an intruder can only copy information in transit; and **active**, in which an intruder can, in addition, modify information in transit, resend previously sent messages that it has copied, or send new messages. While no practical encryption system can completely defend against an intruder with unlimited computational resources (which can be used to analyze the ciphertext), the goal is to make intrusion so difficult that it becomes extremely unlikely that an intruder will succeed.

There are a variety of encryption algorithms, and it is generally assumed that the intruder knows the particular algorithm used in the system under attack. However, each algorithm is parameterized by one or more **keys**, which control the encryption and decryption process. Recovery of the plaintext from the ciphertext without the

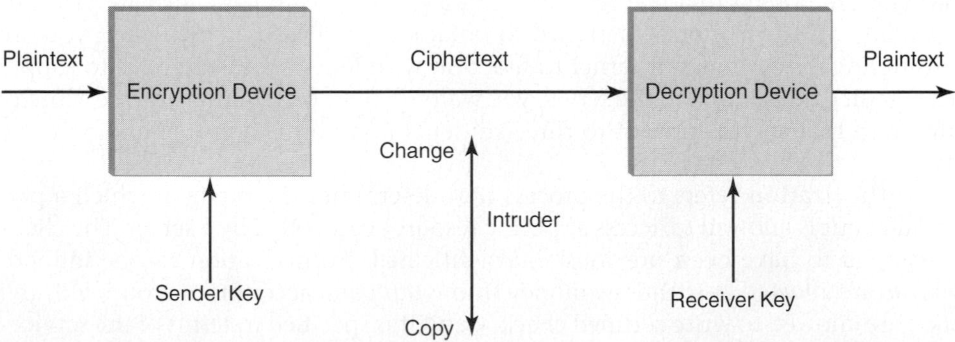

FIGURE 26.1 Model of an encryption system.

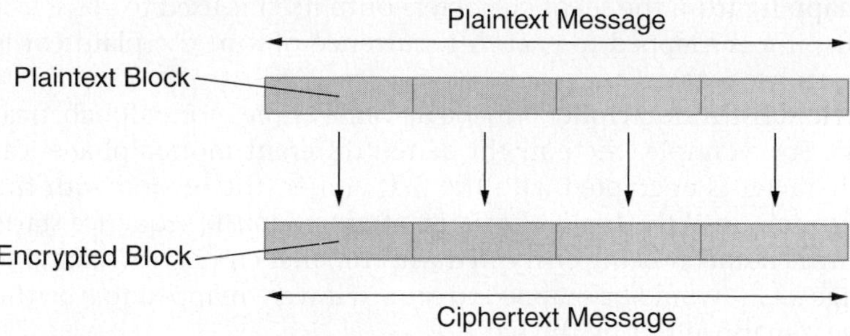

FIGURE 26.2 Encryption using a block cipher.

decryption key is exceedingly difficult. Hence, the strength of the technique depends on keeping the decryption key secret.[1]

We use the notation

$$ciphertext = K_{sender}[plaintext]$$

to denote that the ciphertext is the plaintext encrypted by the sender with the key K_{sender}. The complete encryption system, including encryption and decryption, can be represented with the notation

$$plaintext = K_{receiver}[K_{sender}[plaintext]]$$

which states that, if the plaintext is first encrypted with K_{sender} and then decrypted with $K_{receiver}$, the result will be the original plaintext.

Symmetric cryptography. With **symmetric cryptography**, the same key is used for both encryption and decryption ($K_{sender} = K_{receiver}$). The key is known only to the two communicating processes (since it can be used to decrypt the ciphertext) and is used by both to encrypt and decrypt a back-and-forth exchange of messages referred to as a **session**. In this context, the key is often referred to as a **session key**. Generally, each session gets a new session key.

Several common techniques are used in symmetric cryptography. With a **block cipher**, the plaintext is divided into fixed-size blocks, which are then mapped in a one-to-one fashion into ciphertext blocks as shown in Figure 26.2. The particular mapping is a function of the encryption algorithm and key. The sequence of ciphertext blocks is the encrypted message. Since the mapping is one to one, the plaintext can be recovered.

A **substitution cipher** is one type of block cipher. A variety of substitution ciphers have been proposed for mapping plaintext blocks. For example, a **monoalphabetic** (sometimes called *simple*) substitution cipher has a block size of one character,

[1] A truly unbreakable encryption system is the **one-time pad** [Stallings 1999; Schneier 1995], which uses a randomly generated key that is as long as the message and is used for one message and then discarded.

and a one-to-one mapping from the set of characters onto itself is used to construct the ciphertext. Thus, if *a* is mapped to *c*, each occurrence of *a* in the plaintext is replaced by *c* in the cipher text.

A **polyalphabetic** substitution cipher is made up of multiple monoalphabetical substitution ciphers. For example, there might be ten different monoalphabetical ciphers. The first character is encrypted with the first cipher, the second with the second cipher, and so on, until the tenth character, after which the sequence starts over with the eleventh character being encrypted with the first cipher. For example, the plaintext message *aa* . . . would be mapped to *cr* . . . if *a* were mapped to *c* by the first cipher and *a* were mapped to *r* by the second.

A **polygram** substitution cipher is one in which the block size is more than one. For example, if the block size is three, the block *cde* might be encrypted as *zyy*, *cxy* as *rst*, and *dce* as *dtr*. Then the plaintext message *cdecxy* would be mapped to *zyyrst*.

A **transposition** cipher is also a block cipher, but in contrast to a substitution cipher, the order of the characters in each plaintext block is altered to produce the ciphertext block—the reordering is the same on each plaintext block and is described by the key. For example, with a block size of three, the key "312" indicates that the characters in each block are to be reordered such that the first character in the ciphertext block is to be the third character in the plaintext block, the second character in the ciphertext block is to be the first character in the plaintext block, and the third character in the ciphertext block is to be the second character in the plaintext block. Then the plaintext message *cdecxy* would be mapped to *ecdycx*.

Ciphers that map plaintext blocks into ciphertext blocks are subject to a frequency analysis attack. It is assumed that the intruder knows the block size and can measure the frequency with which each plaintext block is used in normal (unencrypted) communication. The intruder can then compare that with the frequency with which ciphertext blocks appear in an encrypted stream. By matching ciphertext and plaintext blocks with similar frequency characteristics, the intruder can greatly reduce the number of alternatives that must be tested to determine which plaintext block maps into a particular ciphertext block. The longer the encrypted stream the intruder can monitor, the more accurate the frequency estimate of the ciphertext blocks and the greater the reduction in computation that will result. The frequency analysis attack renders many substitution ciphers with small block sizes of little use since accurate frequency profiles for small plaintext blocks are available.

ANSI's **Data Encryption Standard** (DES) is a symmetric encryption technique that uses a sequence of stages to encrypt a block of plaintext. As shown in Figure 26.3, each stage encrypts the output of the previous stage. All stages use a 64-bit block size, and each uses either a substitution or a transposition cipher. The result of combining these two cipher techniques is sometimes referred to as a **product cipher**. DES uses a 56-bit key as input to a key generator to produce a different 48-bit subkey for each of the stages.[2] The standard is in wide use, for example, within the banking and financial services industry.

[2] The key has been criticized by cryptographic experts as being too small.

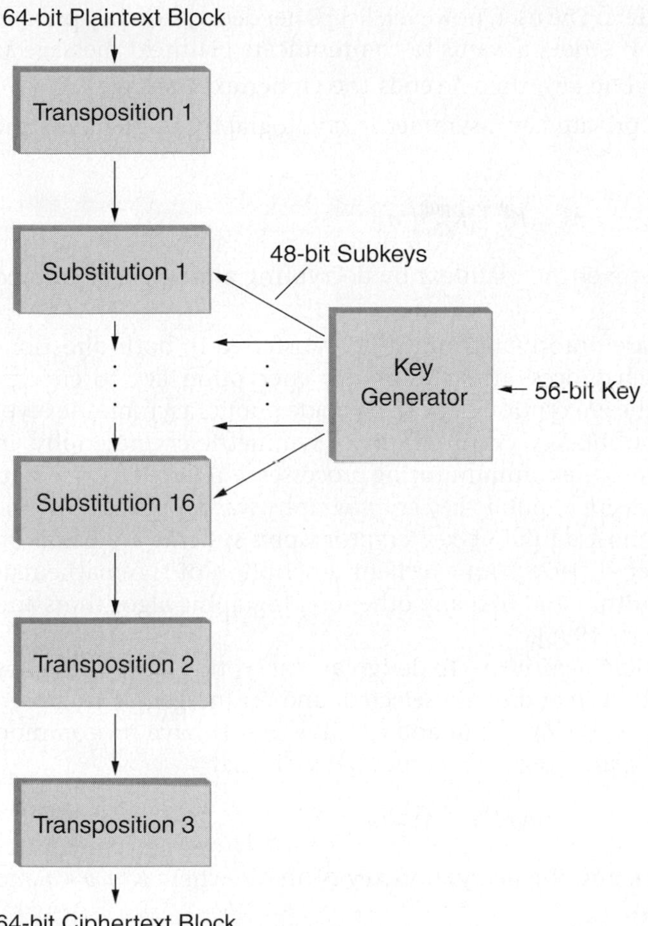

FIGURE 26.3 The processing of a plaintext block using DES.

A **bit stream cipher**, is an example of an encryption technique that is not based on blocks. The ciphertext stream is the result of taking the bit-by-bit exclusive OR of the plaintext stream and a pseudorandom sequence of bits produced by a random number generator. The key in this case is the initial seed supplied to the generator. By using the key with the same generator at the receiving end, the same pseudorandom sequence can be produced to decrypt the ciphertext, once again using a bit-by-bit exclusive OR.

Asymmetric cryptography. In contrast to symmetric cryptography, **asymmetric cryptography** associates with each user an encryption key and a decryption key. The encryption key is not a secret. A user distributes her encryption key openly to anyone who might want to send her a message. It is therefore referred to as a public key, and it is known to potential intruders. The user, however, keeps her decryption key private: it is known only to herself. If sender S wants to communicate plaintext message M to user C and K_C^{pub} is C's public key, then S sends the ciphertext message $K_C^{pub}[M]$. Furthermore, if K_C^{priv} is C's private key, asymmetric cryptography implements the relationship

$$M = K_C^{priv}[K_C^{pub}[M]]$$

which asserts that C can recover the plaintext by decrypting a message encrypted with K_C^{pub} using K_C^{priv}.

If, as is generally the case, information must be transferred in both directions between two processes, each process uses the other's encryption key to encrypt messages it sends. Because the encryption key can be made public, asymmetric cryptography is referred to as **public-key cryptography**. (Symmetric cryptography, in which the key is known only to the communicating processes, is referred to as **secret-key cryptography**.) The concept of public-key cryptography was proposed in [Diffie and Hellman 1976], but almost all public-key cryptography systems are based on the RSA algorithm [Rivest et al. 1978]. An excellent description of the mathematics underlying the RSA algorithm and of many other cryptographic algorithms and protocols is given in [Schneier 1995].

We briefly describe the RSA algorithm. To design an encryption/decryption key pair, two large prime numbers, p and q, are selected, and an integer, d, is chosen that is relatively prime to $(p-1)*(q-1)$ (d and $(p-1)*(q-1)$ have no common factors other than 1). Finally, an integer e is computed such that

$$e * d \equiv 1 \ (mod\ (p-1)*(q-1))$$

The encryption key is (e, N), and the decryption key is (d, N), where $N = p * q$ and is referred to as the modulus.

For example, (using small prime numbers) we might select p and q to be 7 and 13. Then N is 91, and $(p-1)*(q-1)$ is 72. We can choose d to be 5 (which is relatively prime to 72) and e to be 29 because $e * d$ equals 145 and

$$145 \equiv 1 \ (mod\ 72)$$

Then the encryption key is (29, 91), and the decryption key is (5, 91).

The message to be encrypted is broken into blocks such that each block, M, can be treated as an integer between 0 and $(N-1)$. To encrypt M into the ciphertext block, B, we perform the calculation

$$B = M^e \ (mod\ N)$$

To decrypt B, we perform

$$M = B^d \ (mod\ N)$$

The protocol works correctly because

$$M = (M^e \ (mod\ N))^d \ (mod\ N) \ = \ M^{e*d} \ (mod\ N) \qquad \textbf{26.1}$$

More information on public key cryptography is provided in [Schneier 1995].

Returning to the example, assume M is 2. Then to encrypt M, we compute

$$2^{29} \ (mod\ 91) = 32$$

Thus the encrypted message, B, is 32. To decrypt B, we compute

$$32^5 \ (mod\ 91) = 2$$

which is the plaintext message M.

Although d and e are mathematically related, factoring N (a large integer) to obtain p and q (and ultimately d and e) is extremely difficult. Hence, only the receiver can decrypt messages sent to it.

Public-key encryption is a very powerful technique, but it is more computationally intensive than symmetric cryptography (exponentiation of large numbers to large powers is expensive, although not nearly as expensive as factoring a large number, which would be necessary to break the encryption). For that reason, it is generally used to encrypt a few small blocks of information, exchanged as part of a protocol, rather than large blocks of data, which are generally encrypted using symmetric techniques.

26.3 Digital Signatures

One very important use of asymmetric cryptography is to implement **digital signatures**. As with a conventional signature attached to a document, a digital signature works in two ways. It can be used by the sender, C, of a document to prove that he authored the document, and it can be used by the receiver of the document as evidence that C authored it. The latter case is referred to as **nonrepudiation**: once you send a signed check, you cannot, at a later time, deny that you authorized a money transfer. A digital signature also serves a third, very important purpose. Once a document is signed, it cannot be modified without invalidating the signature. Hence, a digital signature guarantees data integrity.

As with public-key cryptography, the concept was first described in [Diffie and Hellman 1976], but, like public-key systems, most digital signature systems are based on the RSA algorithm [Rivest et al. 1978] or on other algorithms developed specifically for signatures.

Digital signatures based on encryption algorithms utilize a property of many asymmetric encryption algorithms—the roles of the public and private keys can be reversed: the private key can be used to encrypt plaintext, and the resulting ciphertext can be decrypted using the corresponding public key

$$M = K_C^{pub}[K_C^{priv}[M]] = K_C^{priv}[K_C^{pub}[M]] \qquad \textbf{26.2}$$

Assuming (26.2), a simple-minded signature algorithm is one in which C signs a document, M, by encrypting it with her private key, K_C^{priv}. If the receiver can recover meaningful information (e.g., an ASCII string) by decrypting a message using K_C^{pub}, the receiver can conclude that the message could have been generated only by C since only C knows K_C^{priv}. (Someone else might actually have sent the message, but only C could have generated it.) This technique assumes that the receiver knows C's public key, K_C^{pub}. The process of distributing public keys and related issues are discussed in Sections 26.4 and 26.8.

Note that since anyone can decrypt the message with the public key, the message is not hidden. Message hiding is not the purpose of a digital signature protocol.

A problem with this technique is that encrypting and decrypting an entire message using a public-key algorithm can be computationally intensive and time consuming. To reduce this time, some function, f, of M is computed—generally a hash—that produces a result that is considerably smaller than M itself. $f(M)$ is sometimes called a **message digest** of M. f effectively divides the set of all messages into equivalence classes: all the messages that are mapped to a particular digest value are in the same class. f is assumed to be known to intruders as well as to the communicants. $f(M)$ is encrypted with K_C^{priv} and referred to as a digital signature, which is transmitted along with M.

Thus, C sends two items, $K_C^{priv}[f(M)]$ and M, to the receiver. The receiver decrypts the first item using K_C^{pub} and then compares the outcome with the result of applying f to the second item. If the two are the same, the receiver should be able to conclude that M could have been generated only by C. To safely allow such a conclusion, however, we must deal with some other issues.

Consider an intruder that listens to and copies a signed transmission, (K_C^{priv} $[f(M)]$, M), from C.

1. The intruder might use the signature $K_C^{priv}[f(M)]$ to sign a different message, M', in an attempt to fool a receiver into believing that C sent M'. The intruder can succeed in this attack if it can construct M' such that $f(M) = f(M')$. To prevent this attack, f is required to be a **one-way function**: f has the property that, given an output, y, constructing an argument, x, such that $f(x) = y$ is computationally infeasible. For example, a one-way message digest function might produce an output string that satisfies the following properties:
   (a) All values in the range of f are equally likely.
   (b) If any bit of the message is changed, every bit in the message digest has a 50% chance of changing.

   Property (a) guards against the possibility of finding an M' such that $f(M) = f(M')$ simply because f maps a large percentage of messages to $f(M)$. Property (b) ensures that $f(M)$ and $f(M')$ are not the same simply because M and M' are related or similar messages.

   Under these conditions, it is extremely difficult for the intruder to construct a message M' such that $f(M') = f(M)$ and hence to find a message, M', to which the signature $K_C^{priv}[f(M)]$ can be attached. Furthermore, the intruder cannot forge the signature that can be used with M', $K_C^{priv}[f(M')]$, since it does not know K_C^{priv}.

2. The intruder might attempt to copy and then resend a signed message a second time,[3] in what is referred to as a **replay attack**. A replay attack can be dealt with by having the signer construct a timestamp (using the technique described in Section 24.4) and include it in M. Since the digital signature is calculated over the entire message, the intruder cannot change the timestamp. Assuming that clocks at all sites in the network are roughly synchronized, if the receiver keeps a list of the timestamps of all recently received messages and rejects arriving messages containing timestamps in the list (recall that timestamps are globally unique), it can detect a message's second arrival. The key point here is that a particular timestamp is never used twice. Hence, a replay attack can also be dealt with if each message has a unique sequence number.

It should now be clear how a digital signature guarantees the integrity of the message. Although the message is transmitted in the clear, and hence can be read by an intrude, it cannot be changed by the intruder since the signature of the changed message would be different. (If privacy is desired, the signed message can be encrypted with another key.) Similarly, nonrepudiation is guaranteed. The signer cannot deny having constructed the message since the digital signature accompanying the message could have been constructed only with the signer's private key. For these reasons, digital signatures are often used in commercial security protocols.

26.4 Key Distribution and Authentication

With both symmetric and asymmetric cryptography, before two parties can communicate they must agree on the encryption/decryption key(s) to be used. Since doing so often involves communicating keys in messages, this phase of a protocol is called **key distribution**. In most situations, key distribution also involves authentication. At the same time that the parties agree on a key, they also make sure of each other's identity.

One might think that key distribution is easy for asymmetric algorithms since the receiver's encryption key is public knowledge. That is, if C wants to send an encrypted message to S, it simply sends a request in the clear (unencrypted) to S requesting S's public key. S can then send its public key (in the clear) to C. Life is not so simple, however. An intruder might intercept S's message to C and substitute its own public key. If C uses that key, the intruder can decrypt all messages sent from C to S. For this reason, key distribution is complicated by authentication when public-key encryption is used. C must be able to authenticate the sender of the key.

[3] This attack might be of some value if the message were a request by C to transfer money into the intruder's bank account.

The problem of key distribution with asymmetric encryption is generally dealt with using certificates, which we discuss in Section 26.8.

A similar situation exists with symmetric encryption. A session key must be created and distributed to the two communicating processes before a session can be started. It becomes a part of the communication context and is discarded when the session completes. Once again, a process using a session key wants to be certain of the identity of the other process that has a copy of that key.

It follows that, in addition to addressing the key distribution problem, we must also be concerned with authentication. Intuitively, when we speak of a client, we think of the individual on whose behalf the client process is running, and we use these concepts interchangeably.

One goal of authentication is to enable a server to positively identify the client that is the source of a message that it has received so that it can decide whether to grant the requested service. For example, should the requestor be allowed to withdraw money from Jody's bank account? Another goal is to enable a client to authenticate the server before sending it any important information. For example, am I sending my credit card number to Macy's or to a Macy's impersonator?

To model these situations, we speak of **principals**. A principal might be a person or a process, and the purpose of authentication is to demonstrate that a principal is who it claims to be. Generally, a person demonstrates that she is who she claims to be by providing something that only she possesses. The simplest, and least secure, of these is a password, in which case the individual possesses some unique knowledge. Unfortunately, passwords often have to be short and relevant (e.g., a pet's name) to be remembered and therefore can frequently be compromised by an intruder willing to try enough candidates. Also, if a password is sent over the network, it might be intercepted and thereby compromised.

Security can be enhanced by requiring a *physical* item that only the individual possesses, for example a token card. An even more secure technique involves the use of some biological identifier such as a fingerprint or voiceprint. Unfortunately, the cost of biological mechanisms is high, and any computer representation of such characteristics might be copied.

Although passwords play a role in key distribution and authentication protocols, the protocols involve a number of new techniques that employ the exchange of encrypted messages. Since the protocols involve the exchange of only a few short messages, the cost of encrypting and decrypting them is generally not significant. Hence, the protocols can be based on either symmetric encryption (e.g., Kerberos, as discussed in Section 26.4.1) or public-key encryption (e.g., SSL, as discussed in Section 26.8). However, because of the heavy computational requirements of public-key encryption, the actual exchange of data generally uses symmetric techniques based on session keys.

26.4.1 The Kerberos Protocol: Tickets

As an example of a protocol that uses symmetric cryptography to authenticate a client to a server and distribute a (symmetric) session key for subsequent data exchange, we describe a simplified version of the widely used **Kerberos** system designed at MIT [Steiner et al. 1988; Neuman and Ts'o 1994]. Kerberos is an off-the-shelf middleware module that can be incorporated into a distributed computing system and might be provided by a TP monitor or a Web application server.

The Kerberos protocol involves the use of an intermediary process, called a **key server**. (Actually Kerberos calls its key server the Key Distribution Server, or KDS.) The key server creates session keys on demand and distributes them in such a way that they are known only to the communicating processes. For this reason, it is referred to as a **trusted third party**.

Each user wishing to participate in the protocol registers a symmetric **user key** with the key server, *KS*. User keys are not session keys. They are used only in the key distribution protocol at the start of a session.

Assume that a client, *C*, wants to communicate with a server, *S*. *C* and *S* have previously registered user keys $K_{C,KS}$ and $K_{S,KS}$, respectively, with *KS*. $K_{C,KS}$ is known only to *C* and *KS*. Similarly, $K_{S,KS}$ is known only to *S* and *KS*. *KS* is trusted by *C* in the sense that *C* assumes that *KS* will never communicate $K_{C,KS}$ to any other process and that the data structure it uses to store $K_{C,KS}$ is protected from unauthorized access. Similarly, *KS* is trusted by *S*.

Kerberos introduces the concept of a **ticket** to distribute a session key. To understand the role of a ticket, consider the following sequence of steps, illustrated in Figure 26.4, which forms the heart of the protocol. (As with the other protocols described here, we omit some minor details.)

1. *C* sends to *KS* a message, *M*1 (in the clear), requesting a ticket to be used to authenticate *C* to *S*. *M*1 contains the names of the intended communicants (*C*, *S*).

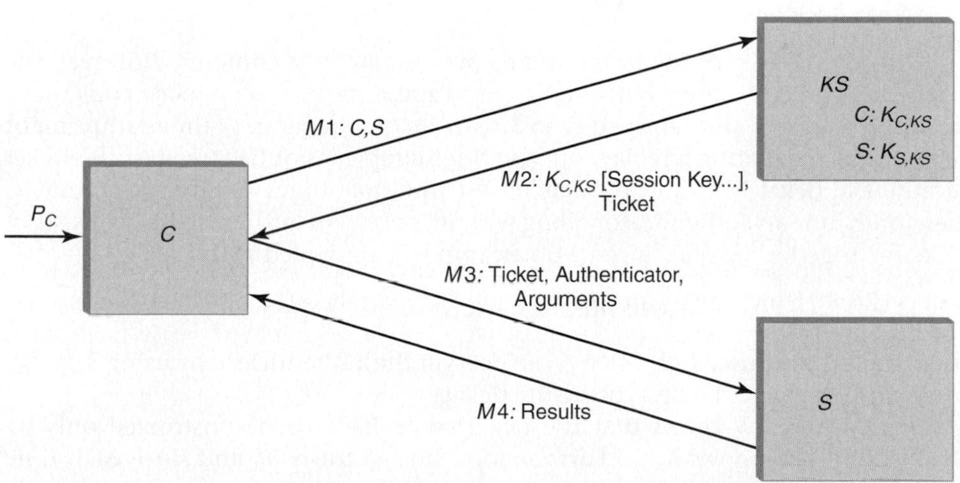

FIGURE 26.4 Sequence of messages used to authenticate a client in symmetric encryption.

2. When *KS* receives *M*1, the following takes place:
   (a) *KS* (randomly) constructs a session key, $K_{sess,C\&S}$.
   (b) *KS* sends to *C* a message, *M*2, containing two items:
      (i) $K_{C,KS}[K_{sess,C\&S},\ S,\ LT]$
      (ii) $K_{S,KS}[K_{sess,C\&S},\ C,\ LT]$—the actual ticket
      where *LT* is the *lifetime* (the time interval) over which the ticket is valid.
3. When *C* receives *M*2, it performs the following steps:
   (a) *C* recovers $K_{sess,C\&S}$ from the first item using $K_{C,KS}$ (it cannot decrypt the ticket).
   (b) *C* saves the ticket until it is ready to request some service from *S*.

Observe that *KS* does not know the actual source of *M*1: it could have been sent by an intruder, *I*, posing as *C*. However, *KS* encrypts *M*2, making the information returned accessible only to *C* and *S*.

Rather than store its user key, $K_{C,KS}$, in some protected way, *C* constructs it when needed using the principal's password, P_C, which is supplied to *C* at login time. This is done with the help of a one-way function, *f*.

$$K_{C,KS} = f(P_C)$$

Thus, only *C* (using *f*) can construct $K_{C,KS}$, and hence only *C* can retrieve $K_{sess,C\&S}$ from the first item in *M*2: the message sent by *KS* to the process claiming to be *C*. Note that the protocol does not send P_C across the network and so avoids the possibility that it might be copied. Furthermore, since *C* does not store $K_{C,KS}$ in the system, the possibility that it might be stolen is reduced.

Later, when *C* wants to request service from *S*, the following takes place:

4. *C* sends to *S* a message, *M*3, containing the arguments of the request, (which might or might not be encrypted using $K_{sess,C\&S}$), the ticket, and an authenticator (see below).

Only *S* can decrypt the ticket and recover the items it contains. However, the ticket (containing *C*) alone is not sufficient to authenticate *C* to *S* since *I* could have copied it in step 2 and replayed it to *S* with its own request. A timestamp might be useful in preventing a replay, but the timestamp cannot be stored in the ticket because the ticket is meant to be used by *C* multiple times during its lifetime. *C* therefore sends an authenticator along with its ticket. An **authenticator** consists of *C*'s name together with a (current) timestamp, *TS*, encrypted with $K_{sess,C\&S}$:

$$authenticator = K_{sess,C\&S}[C,\ TS]$$

and is meant to be used only once. *S* can decrypt the authenticator by using $K_{sess,C\&S}$ (which it determines by decrypting the ticket).

At this point, *S* knows that the ticket could have been constructed only by *KS* since only *KS* knows $K_{S,KS}$. Furthermore, since *S* trusts *KS* and since each time $K_{sess,C\&S}$ is transmitted it is encrypted by either $K_{C,KS}$ or $K_{S,KS}$, *S* knows that only *C* (and *KS*) knows $K_{sess,C\&S}$. The authenticator contains some plaintext (e.g., *C*) encrypted by $K_{sess,C\&S}$, that can be compared with the contents of the ticket (which also contains C). If they match, S concludes that C must have constructed the authenticator. To authenticate C to S (i.e., to be sure that the invocation actually comes from C), however, several possible attacks must be ruled out.

1. I attempts a replay attack in which it copies both the ticket and the authenticator from $M3$ and uses them at a later time. To combat this, we must make it impossible for an authenticator (in contrast to a ticket) to be used more than once. A new authenticator (with a unique timestamp) is constructed by C for each of its requests. The authenticator is *live* if its timestamp is within the lifetime (LT) of the accompanying ticket. To ensure that a copy of an authenticator is of no value, and that S can defend itself against a replay, S uses the following protocol:
   (a) If the received authenticator is not live, S rejects it.
   (b) S maintains a list of authenticators it has received that are still live. If the received authenticator is live, S compares it against the list and rejects it if a copy is found. By maintaining lifetime information, S can limit the number of authenticators it has to keep on the list.
2. I intercepts $M3$ (it does not reach S) and tries to use the ticket and authenticator for its own request for service. However, if C has chosen to encrypt the arguments of its request with $K_{sess,C\&S}$, then I cannot substitute its own arguments because it does not know $K_{sess,C\&S}$. Sending the entire intercepted message at a later time accomplishes nothing for I since it simply causes C's original request to be serviced.
3. I intercepts $M1$ (it does not reach KS) and substitutes the message (C, I). KS responds to C with a ticket encrypted with $K_{I,KS}$. I's goal in this attack is to copy the message $M3$ that it hopes that C will subsequently send to S. Since the ticket is encrypted with I's private key, I can extract the session key. In this case S will not be able to decrypt the ticket, but I can determine private information about C contained in the arguments that C sends to S. The protocol defends against this attack by including the server's name in the first item of $M2$, which in this case will be I instead of S. C uses this information to determine the identity of the process that can decrypt its request message.

A number of distinct levels of protection can be offered by this protocol. The client can request that authentication occur only when a connection to the server is first established. Or it can request authentication on each call for service. Or it can request that $K_{sess,C\&S}$ be used to encrypt the arguments of the invocation (in $M3$) and the results returned (in $M4$) as well as to encrypt the authenticator.

We have given arguments to demonstrate how Kerberos defends against a variety of attacks an intruder might attempt. Be under no illusions as to whether our discussion constitutes a proof that Kerberos is secure—it does not. Such proofs are the subject of ongoing research.

Single sign-on. Kerberos provides a property, referred to as **single sign-on**, that is becoming important as client interactions become increasingly complex. Complex interactions frequently involve access to multiple resources and hence multiple servers. Each server needs to authenticate the client and, in the worst case, has its own interface for doing so. If the client uses the same password for all servers, security can be compromised; if the client uses different passwords, he must remember all of them. In either case he must engage in multiple authentication protocols, and the system administrator must keep the authentication information associated with each server current as client information changes.

With single sign-on, the client needs to authenticate itself only once. Kerberos provides this property by concentrating authentication in an **authentication server**, *AS* (similar to *KS*), which authenticates *C* at login time using the password supplied by the client, as described earlier. Since the identity of the servers the client intends to access might not be known at this time, it is not possible for *AS* to construct the appropriate tickets (since each ticket must be encrypted with a particular server's key). Instead, it returns a **ticket-granting ticket** to *C*, which is used for requesting service from a particular server, called the **ticket-granting server**, *TGS*—also part of Kerberos. Later *C* can request the specific tickets it needs (for example, a ticket for *S*) from *TGS* using the ticket-granting ticket.

The authentication server generates a session key, $K_{sess,C\&TGS}$, that *C* can use to communicate with *TGS*, and returns to *C* (in a format similar to that of *M*2 in the simplified protocol).

- $K_{C,AS}[K_{sess,C\&TGS}, TGS, LT]$—$K_{sess,C\&TGS}$ is a session key for communicating with *TGS*
- $K_{TGS,AS}[K_{sess,C\&TGS}, C, LT]$—the ticket-granting ticket for *TGS*

where $K_{C,AS}$ and $K_{TGS,AS}$ are keys that *AS* and *TGS* have registered with *AS*.

Later, when *C* wants to access a particular server, *S*, it sends a copy of the ticket-granting ticket together with the server's name (and an authenticator) to *TGS*. *TGS* then returns to *C* (again in a format similar to that of *M*2).

- $K_{sess,C\&TGS}[K_{sess,C\&S}, S, LT]$—$K_{sess,C\&S}$ is a session key for communicating with *S*.
- $K_{S,AS}[K_{sess,C\&S}, C, LT]$—This is the ticket for *S* (note that *S*'s private key, $K_{S,AS}$, is available to *TGS*).

C thus obtains a different ticket for each server it accesses. It engages in a single authentication protocol, and since the use of tickets is invisible at the user level, the user interface is simplified. Also, since authentication is concentrated in a single server, the administration of authentication information is simplified.

26.4.2 Nonces

Suppose two processes, P_1 and P_2, share a session key, K_{sess}, and P_1 sends an encrypted message, *M*1, to P_2 and expects an encrypted reply, *M*2. When P_1 receives *M*2, how can P_1 be sure that it was constructed by P_2? It might seem that P_1 can just decrypt *M*2 using K_{sess} and see if the result makes sense. Often, however, determining whether a string makes sense requires human intervention, and in some cases even that does not help. Consider the case in which $M2$ simply contains a data string (an arbitrary string of bits—perhaps the weight of some device) calculated by P_2. An intruder might substitute a random string for $M2$. When P_1 decrypts that string using K_{sess}, it might produce another string that looks like a data string. Unfortunately, P_1 cannot determine whether or not the string is correct without repeating P_2's calculation (which it is not in a position to do). Alternatively, the intruder might replay an earlier message sent during the same session and hence encrypted with K_{sess}. In some cases, such a replay might be a possible correct response to $M1$ (two devices could have the same weight), and hence P_1 is fooled into accepting it.

A nonce can be used to solve this problem. A **nonce** is a bit string created by one process in a way that makes it highly unlikely that another process can create the same string. For example, a randomly created bit string of sufficient length created in one process probably will not be created later by another process. Nonces have a variety of uses, one of which is related to authentication.

To solve the above problem, P_1 includes a nonce, N, in $M1$, and P_2 includes $N + 1$ in $M2$. On receipt of $M2$, P_1 knows that the sender must have decrypted $M1$, since $N + 1$, not a simple replay of N, is returned. This implies that the sender knows K_{sess} and is therefore P_2.

In Kerberos, the timestamp TS (which is already part of the authenticator) can be used as a nonce so that no additional items need be added. The server can include $TS + 1$ in $M4$.

Nonces are often used in cryptographic protocols for a completely different reason. Appending a large random number to the plaintext before encrypting a message makes it considerably harder for an intruder to decrypt the message by guessing parts of its contents—for example, guessing the expiration date or some of the redundant information in a credit card number—and using that information to reduce the cost of a brute-force search to discover the key. This use of a nonce is sometimes referred to as adding **salt** to a message. A number of the protocols we discuss later use salted messages, but we omit that part of the protocol in our discussion. In some protocols, a nonce used for this purpose is called a **confounder**.

26.5 Authorization

Having authenticated a client, the server must next decide whether the requested service should be granted. Thus, when a request arrives from a client to access a particular object, the authorization component of the system must decide whether the principal should be allowed the requested access to that object. This is referred to as an **authorization policy**. The modes in which an object can be accessed depend on the type of the object being protected.

If, for example, the resource is a file, the modes of access might be read, write, append, and execute. Operating systems typically control access to files stored in their file system by first requiring that principals authenticate themselves (at login

Id	r	w	a	x
11011	1	1	0	0
00000	1	0	0	0

FIGURE 26.5 Access control list for a file.

time) and then checking that each access to a file has been previously authorized by the file's owner. The data structure that is generally used to record the system's protection policy (in Windows and many versions of UNIX) is the **access control list** (ACL).

Each file has an associated ACL, and each entry on the ACL identifies a principal and contains a bit for each possible access mode. The ith bit corresponds to the ith access mode and indicates whether or not that principal is allowed to access the file in that way. Figure 26.5 shows an ACL for a file. The first five bits contain an Id. Each of the following bits corresponds to an access mode: read, write, append, and execute. The figure indicates that the user with Id 11011 has permission to read and write the file associated with the list.

As a practical matter, it is necessary to introduce the notion of a **group**. For example, it would be awkward to list all principals separately in the ACL of a file that is universally readable. A group is simply a set of principals, and an ACL entry can correspond to it. The access permissions contained in the entry are allowed to all group members. Thus, as illustrated in Figure 26.5, a file that is universally readable but writable only by its owner might have an ACL consisting of two entries: one for the owner with Id 11011 and read and write bits set and one for the group containing all principals with only the read bit set. The Id 00000 identifies the group consisting of all users. With the introduction of groups, several entries in an ACL might refer to a particular principal (e.g., a principal might belong to several groups). In this case, the principal is granted the union of the permissions in each such entry.

The structure for storing and enforcing an authorization policy in a transaction processing system is only a minor generalization of the ACL/group structure used by operating systems to protect files. Resources are controlled by servers, so a server (instead of the operating system) is responsible for storing the ACL and enforcing the authorization policy on the resources it controls. Servers export certain methods, making them available for invocation by clients. These methods constitute the modes of access to the resources encapsulated within the server. In short, the authorization policy is formulated in terms of the methods a particular principal can invoke and the particular resources on which to invoke them. In the Student Registration System, for example, the method that changes a grade cannot be invoked by a student, the method that changes the personal information describing a student (e.g., a student's address) can be invoked only by that student, and the method that sets a limit on class enrollment can be invoked by any faculty member.

ACLs can be used in support of this generalization. In one approach, the Student Registration System server might use a single ACL containing an entry for the student group and an entry for the faculty group. The permission bits in each entry correspond to the methods that can be invoked by the clients. An entry needs to have only enough bits so that each exported method can be associated with a distinct bit. In this case, the faculty group is granted permission for the grade change and class enrollment methods, and the student group is granted permission for the personal information method. The additional requirement that the personal information of a particular student be changed only by that student has to be checked separately. The ACL is checked by the server when a method is invoked, and, if the necessary permission has not been granted, an error code is returned to the caller.

Alternatively, we might regard the server as managing a number of distinct resources—class records, personal records—and allocate a separate ACL for each record. In this case, a finer granularity of protection can be enforced. For example, the ACL for a student's personal record contains an entry for that student only.

The SQL GRANT statement is one way that a client can specify an authorization policy for a table. In this case, the access modes correspond to various types of SQL statements. An SQL server might implement the policy using ACLs, in which case the GRANT statement causes a modification to the ACL associated with the table specified in the statement.

Each server is generally responsible for providing its own authorization module because the objects it controls and the access to them are specific to that server. By contrast, a principal's identity and group membership can be general to all servers. The authorization module within each server, referred to as a **reference monitor**, is responsible for constructing, retrieving, and interpreting access control lists. Middleware modules for doing this might be provided by a TP monitor.

26.6 Authenticated Remote Procedure Call

A goal of many distributed applications that require authentication and authorization is to hide the complexities of the required protocols from the principal. Once the principal has executed the login procedure, service invocation should be simple, and authentication and authorization should be invisible (unless a violation is detected). One way to achieve this goal is by implementing authentication in the RPC stubs, as shown in Figure 26.6, and by presenting the abstraction of an **authenticated RPC** to clients and servers. This is the approach used in the DCE (distributed computing environment) model of distributed computation.

In this approach, middleware provides an API that the client can use to log in and to invoke servers. The API interfaces to the stub, which engages in the exchange of messages (for example, the messages of Figure 26.4). The key server is now referred to as the **security server** since it implements authentication and plays a role in implementing authorization as well. It keeps track of all groups to which each principal belongs and includes (in a ticket sent to a principal) a list of that principal's group Ids. Security servers can be obtained as off-the-shelf middleware modules.

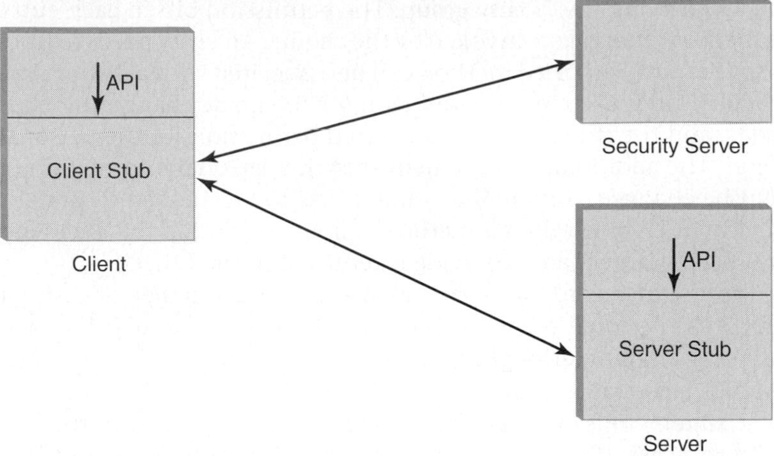

FIGURE 26.6 Relationship between stubs and authentication.

Each server is responsible for securely storing a copy of its server key, $K_{S,KS}$, locally and making it available to the server stub when an invocation message arrives. The stub can then decrypt the ticket contained in the message to determine the client's identity and the groups to which the client belongs.

The server stub API provides calls that the server can use to retrieve the client's identity and group membership information contained in the ticket from the server stub. Authorization for each client call is provided within the server proper (not the server's stub) by the reference monitor, using the client's (authenticated) identity and group membership information and the access control lists contained within the server.

26.7 Electronic Commerce

Security issues are particularly critical when transactions are executed over the Internet. Authentication is important to prevent one site from successfully impersonating another. Encryption is important to prevent eavesdropping. In addition, there is a general sense of suspicion between the parties participating in Internet transactions, perhaps because there is no face-to-face interaction and because impressive looking Web sites can be produced by fly-by-night operations.

In Chapter 25 we distinguished two kinds of electronic commerce transactions: customer-to-business (C2B) and business-to-business (B2B). The security requirements of the two are similar, but we assume that customers have only the security software that comes with their browsers, while businesses can have more sophisticated and specialized protection, such as their own public and private encryption keys, which customers (usually) do not have.

26.8 The Secure Sockets Layer Protocol: Certificates

Servers (perhaps representing businesses) that want to authenticate themselves to other parties as part of an Internet transaction can use a **certification authority** (**CA**), which acts as a trusted third party. A number of companies are in the business of being certification authorities.

A CA uses public-key encryption to generate **certificates**, which certify the association between a principal's name (e.g., Macy's) and its public key. The certificate contains (among other items) the principal's name and public key, and it is signed with the private key of the CA. Since the CA's public key is well known (and is most likely prestored in the user's browser), any process in the system can determine the validity of the certificate. Hence, if a client wants to communicate securely with Macy's, it can encrypt a message using the public key found in a valid certificate containing the name "Macy's" and be certain that only a process with knowledge of Macy's private key will be able to decrypt the message. Certificates thus solve the problem of distributing public keys reliably, which is the key distribution problem for asymmetric encryption. They are used in the protocols described below.

Any Internet server, *S*, that wants to obtain a certificate from a CA first generates a public and private key and then sends the public key, plus other information, to the CA. The CA uses various means to verify the server's identity (perhaps looking it up in Dun and Bradstreet and communicating with personnel at the server's place of business by phone and ordinary mail) and then issues it a certificate containing, among other items,

- The CA's name
- *S*'s name
- *S*'s URL
- *S*'s public key
- Timestamp and expiration information

The CA signs the certificate and sends the signed certificate to *S* in the clear, perhaps by e-mail. *S* then verifies its correctness (for example, that the public key stored in the certificate is *S*'s public key). Note that a certificate is public information readily available to an intruder. It is, however, of no use to an intruder because a client who wishes to communicate with *S* will use *S*'s public key to encrypt a message. Since *S*'s private key is not contained in the certificate, only *S* can decrypt the message.

The SSL protocol. The **Secure Sockets Layer** (SSL) protocol [Netscape 2000] uses certificates to support secure communication and authentication over the Internet between a client and an Internet server (or between servers). By using certificates, SSL is able to eliminate the need for an online key server (as in Kerberos), which can be a bottleneck in transaction systems that process thousands of transactions per second.[4]

A goal of SSL is to authenticate a server to a client. Since this is done using a certificate, each server that wants to be authenticated must first obtain a certificate. Clients, on the other hand, are not generally registered with certification authorities and hence do not have certificates or the encryption keys associated with them.[5] A logged-in client is typically represented by a browser, which (usually) does not have a private key of its own. Rather, the browser contains the public keys of all certification authorities that have made arrangements with that browser's vendor. The browser does not actually communicate with a CA during the SSL protocol; nor does a CA know any private information about a browser.

The SSL protocol authenticates the server to the client and establishes a session key for their use. A browser engages in the SSL protocol when it connects to a server whose URL begins with *https:* (instead of *http:*), which indicates an SSL-encrypted HTTP protocol.

Assume that a browser, *C*, connects to a server, *S*, that claims to represent a particular enterprise, *E* (for example, Macy's). In this case, the protocol consists of the following steps:

1. *S* sends *C* a copy of its certificate signed by the CA—in the clear.
2. *C* validates the certificate's signature using the CA's public key (included in its browser) and hence knows that the public key in the certificate belongs to the enterprise named in the certificate.
3. *C* generates and sends to *S* a session key encrypted with the public key in the certificate.[6]

Note that *C*, not *S*, generates the session key because, at this point in the protocol, *C* can communicate securely with *S* using the public key in the certificate, but *S* cannot communicate securely with *C* (nor is there an online key server, as in Kerberos, to generate the session key). Once the session key has been established, *C* and *S* can use it to exchange encrypted messages.

The steps in the protocol described above are performed invisibly to the application program in a layer of the communication hierarchy between the data transport (TCP/IP) and application levels. However, one small problem remains that requires user participation. Suppose an intruder intervenes and supplies its own (valid) certificate. Before sending any messages encrypted with the public key contained in the certificate, the user should verify that it describes the correct server. This is eas-

[4] Note, however, that certificates have a potentially significant disadvantage in that, once a certificate has been granted to a server by a CA, it is difficult to revoke it later if necessary. By contrast, an online key server can easily stop providing keys for a particular server.

[5] SSL has an optional authentication protocol for clients that do have certificates.

[6] SSL is actually slightly more complex. *C* generates and sends to *S* a **pre-master secret** from which *C* and *S* independently, using the same algorithm, generate two session keys—one for communication in each direction. This adds an additional measure of security. The pre-master secret is also used by *C* and *S* to verify the integrity of messages in the application part of the protocol.

ily done since the name of the certificate owner is contained in the certificate itself (and has not been altered because the certificate was signed by the CA). The user can determine the name by clicking on the security icon displayed by the browser.

If the browser uses the session key to communicate a credit card number to *S*, the user can have considerable confidence that that communication is secure. The browser itself generated the session key, which it communicated to *S* using *E*'s public key, and the user knows that *E*'s public key is genuine because it was obtained from a certificate that could have been generated only by the CA. The user trusts the CA to have verified *E*'s identity and included the correct information about *E* in the certificate and trusts the browser vendor to have included the correct public key for each CA and a correct implementation of the SSL protocol in the browser. The user must also trust that its browser has not been corrupted, perhaps by some malicious program it downloaded at some earlier time.

At this point, the protocol has authenticated the server to the client, but the client has not been authenticated to the server. For many applications, client authentication is not necessary. For example, most servers will accept a credit card purchase from any browser that can supply the credit card number, without determining that the browser actually represents the card owner. (Most telephone-order catalog companies accept orders under similar conditions.)

For other applications, *S* does want to ensure that it is talking to a particular client (for example, before a stock broker's server sends a client its private portfolio information or accepts a stock trading transaction). One way to provide such authentication is for client and server to agree on a password, which the server stores and the client supplies after the session key has been established. Another way is for the client to have a certificate as well so that both client and server can be authenticated.

26.9 Passport: Single Sign-On

In Section 26.4.1 we discussed the difficulty that arises when a user has to interact with several different applications that require password authentication. Kerberos is an example of a protocol that implements single sign-on to solve this problem. Similarly, Microsoft Passport is an Internet protocol that uses an authentication server, *A*, to implement single sign-on. *A* stores the password of each customer, *C*, and a symmetric encryption key, $K_{S,A}$, for each server, *S*, that has registered for its service. It also stores a symmetric key, K_A for its own use. In simplified form, the protocol consists of the following steps:

1. When *S* wants to authenticate *C*, it sends a page to *C*'s browser that contains *A*'s address. The page is **redirected** (redirected pages are not displayed) from *C* to *A* (by setting the attribute `http-equiv= "refresh"`). In other words, the effect is as if, after receiving the page, *C* had clicked on *A*'s address, forwarding the page to *A*.
2. *A* sends a page to *C*'s browser requesting *C*'s password.

3. C enters its password and clicks the submit button. An SSL session is established between C and A, and C sends its password to A using the session key established as a part of the SSL protocol.
4. A verifies that the password is correct.
5. A sends a page and a cookie to C. The page states that C has been authenticated and is redirected to S. It is encrypted with $K_{S,A}$, and hence S can verify that it came from A. The cookie also states that C has been authenticated. It is encrypted with K_A and placed on C's browser. Its use will be explained below.
6. S sends a page to C that includes a (second) cookie to be placed on C's browser encrypted with a key known only to S. Thus if C returns to S's site, S can retrieve the cookie and determine that C was previously authenticated.

Suppose that C later visits a different server, S', that also offers Passport authentication, and S' asks A to authenticate C. After step 1 of the procedure, A can retrieve the cookie it previously put in C's browser and hence knows that C has been previously authenticated. A can now implement single sign-on. A skips steps 2 through 4 (it does not have to ask again for C's password) and executes an abbreviated version of step 5 (it does not have to place another cookie on C's browser).

A's cookie is similar to a Kerberos ticket, but the Passport protocol does not have the extra security offered by a Kerberos authenticator and hence is subject to some of the attacks that the authenticator addresses.

For example, A leaves a cookie on C's browser after C completes its interaction with S. If C's interaction originates from a public terminal (for example in a public library), a subsequent user of the terminal might (perhaps inadvertently) be authenticated as C. Kerberos deals with this type of threat by requiring that the client construct an authenticator, and this requires that the client know information contained in the ticket (the session key). In Passport, however, the cookie can be used on behalf of a client without the client demonstrating any knowledge of its contents. To circumvent this problem, most sites have a button that C can use to remove A's cookie from the browser.

Paying with a credit card using single sign-on. Microsoft also has a related service, called E-Wallet, by which a user can store information, including a credit card number, mailing address, etc., on an E-Wallet server. Then the procedure described above is used to authenticate C to both S and the E-Wallet server. (Only a single password need be entered.) After the authentication has been completed, specified items from the E-Wallet server are sent to the merchant (in encrypted form) as a part of the purchase interaction. Thus the user does not have to re-enter credit card information and mailing address for each purchase with each merchant.

Verified by Visa is another protocol that provides single sign-on for paying with a credit card. In this protocol, the customer first enters a credit card number on the merchant's Web page. The page is sent (in an SSL session) to the merchant who initiates an authentication protocol similar to the first four steps of the Passport protocol. The goal of the protocol is to authenticate to the merchant that the customer is authorized to use that credit card. In this case, the authentication is performed by an authentication server operated by the bank that issued the card. That server checks that the password corresponds to the credit card number and that the credit card number is valid. One advantage of the system is that the customer can use the same password for all Visa purchases.

Note that in both the E-Wallet and Verified by Visa protocols, the merchant learns the credit card number of the customer.

26.10 Keeping Credit Card Numbers Private

Many merchants use the SSL protocol in customer purchase transactions. After the session key is established, the customer sends the details of the items to be purchased and the credit card information to the merchant's server, which completes the transaction by having the credit card approved at some other site representing the credit card company. One drawback of this protocol is that the merchant learns the client's credit card number. We saw that this was the case in both the Passport and Verified by Visa protocols.

Of course, in most non-Internet customer-merchant transactions, the merchant learns the customer's credit card number as well. When you go to a restaurant, for example, you give your credit card to a waitress who gets the transaction approved and returns a receipt for you to sign. How do you know she has not copied your credit card number?

However, revealing the credit card number to the merchant is particularly problematic in electronic commerce because only the number, not the card itself, is needed to make a purchase. This makes it easier for a criminal to make purchases without the cardholder's knowledge. Furthermore, the anonymous nature of electronic commerce does not promote a trusting relationship between merchant and customer. Hence Internet customers are more comfortable if merchants do not learn their credit card numbers. Also, on many sites, such as eBay, the "merchant" is not an established company but just an ordinary person who is selling, for example, her old record collection. The customer does not want that person to learn her credit card number.

One simple approach to this problem is to use a trusted third party to whom the customer has already given her credit card number and the merchant has already set up an account. When the customer wants to make a purchase, she tells the trusted third party to make a charge against her credit card and credit the merchant with the money. The most popular trusted third party of this type is PayPal, which currently has millions of registered users who execute hundreds of thousands of transactions per day, corresponding to billions of dollars in payments.

The PayPal protocol handles customer-to-customer (C2C) interactions. It allows one customer, C_1, to send money to another customer, C_2, who she identifies to PayPal by his email address. Perhaps C_1 just purchased an item from C_2 on an auction site. An important requirement is that the money can be transferred using C_1's credit card without C_2 seeing any of C_1's credit card information.

C_1 and C_2 must have previously registered with PayPal, which maintains accounts for them. Registration is accomplished at the PayPal site by submitting SSL encrypted forms that contain, among other information, C_1's name, email address, credit card information, and a password. To send money to C_2

1. C_1 logs onto the PayPal site, authenticates herself with her password (using SSL), and requests that PayPal use her credit card account to send the money to C_2, who she identifies with an email address.
2. PayPal executes a transaction that takes money from C_1's credit card account, deposits the money in C_2's PayPal account, and sends C_2 an email notifying him of the transaction. (This notification is why the protocol has been characterized, somewhat inaccurately, as "sending money by email.")

Once the money is in C_2's PayPal account, he can leave it there to use for later purchases through PayPal or he can request that PayPal send him a check for the amount.

OPTIONAL

26.11 The Secure Electronic Transaction Protocol: Dual Signatures

Another protocol in which the merchant does not learn the credit card number of the customer is the **Secure Electronic Transaction** (**SET**) protocol [VISA 2000], jointly developed by Visa and MasterCard. SET is particularly oriented toward customer-to-business (C2B) interactions. While SSL is a **session-level security protocol**, which guarantees secure communication for the duration of a session, SET is a **transaction-level security protocol**, which guarantees security for a purchasing transaction, including an atomic commit.

The SET protocol is quite complex, with many signatures and much cross checking to increase overall security. Here we present a simplified version that demonstrates the mechanisms by which the credit card number is hidden from the merchant and how the purchasing transaction is committed atomically.

The protocol involves two new ideas:

1. Each customer has his own certificate and hence his own public and private keys. These keys are used to provide one of the unique features of the protocol, the **dual signature**, which considerably increases the security of the transaction. The customer's certificate also contains a message digest of his credit card number and its expiration date. Recall that information in the certificate is unencrypted. Hence, only the digest (not the credit card number itself) can be included. The digest is used to verify that the credit card number supplied by the customer corresponds to a card belonging to the customer.
2. A new server, the **payment gateway**, G, operates on behalf of the credit card company. Thus, SET is a three-way protocol, involving the customer, the mer-

chant, and the payment gateway, which acts as a trusted third party during the protocol and performs the commit operation at the end of the transaction.

The basic idea of the protocol is that customer C sends merchant M a two-part message: the first part contains the purchase amount and C's credit card information encrypted with G's public key (so that M cannot see the credit card information); the second part contains the purchase amount and the details of the purchase (but not the credit card information) encrypted with M's public key. M then forwards the first part of the message to G, which decrypts it, approves the credit card purchase, and commits the transaction.

In one possible attack on a protocol such as this in which there is a two-part message, an intruder attaches the first part of one message to the second part of another. For example, having intercepted the messages for Joe's and Mary's purchases, an intruder can attach the first part of Joe's message to the second part of Mary's, hoping to force Joe to pay for Mary's goods. One way to thwart this type of attack is to have M associate a unique Id with each transaction and to require that C include it in both parts of the message. An attempt to unite the parts of different messages then becomes easily detectable. This does not solve the problem of a dishonest merchant, however, who associates the same Id with two different purchases so that the parts of the two resulting messages can be combined. A new mechanism is needed to overcome this type of problem. That mechanism is the dual signature, described next.

Before SET begins, C and M negotiate the terms of a purchase. The protocol begins with a handshake in which C and M exchange certificates and authenticate each other. C sends its certificate to M, and M sends both its certificate and G's certificate to C, at which point C and M know each other's and G's public key. Then the purchase transaction begins.

1. M sends a signed message to C containing a (unique) transaction Id (which is used to guard against replay attacks). C uses the public key in M's certificate to check the signature and hence knows that the message came from M and was not altered in transit.
2. C sends a message to M containing two parts plus the dual signature:
   (a) The transaction Id, C's credit card information, and the dollar amount of the order (but not a description of the items purchased)—encrypted with G's public key:
   $$m_1 = K_G^{pub}[trans\_Id,\ credit\_card\_inf,\ \$\_amount]$$
   (b) The transaction Id, the dollar amount of the order, a description of the items purchased (but not C's credit card information)—encrypted with M's public key:
   $$m_2 = K_M^{pub}[trans\_Id,\ \$\_amount,\ desc]$$

OPTIONAL

The dual signature has three fields:

(a) The message digest, MD_1, of the first part of the message:

$$MD_1 = f(m_1)$$

where $f()$ is the message digest function

(b) The message digest, MD_2, of the second part of the message:

$$MD_2 = f(m_2)$$

(c) C's signature of the concatenation of MD_1 and MD_2:

$$K_C^{pri}[f(MD_1 \cdot MD_2)]$$

Thus, the complete dual signature is

$$dual\_signature = MD_1,\ MD_2,\ K_C^{pri}[f(MD_1 \cdot MD_2)]$$

and the complete message sent from C to M is $(m_1,\ m_2,\ dual\_signature)$.

The dual signature binds the two parts of the message. So, for example, an attempt by an intruder or M to associate m_2' with m_1 does not work since its message digest, MD_2', will be different from MD_2. Although MD_2' can be substituted for MD_2 in the dual signature, $K_C^{pri}[f(MD_1 \cdot MD_2)]$ cannot be used as the signature for $MD_1 \cdot MD_2'$, and only C can compute the correct dual signature for the reconstructed message.

3. M decrypts the second part of the message with its private key (but it cannot decrypt the first part, which contains the credit card number). The merchant then

(a) Uses the dual signature to verify that m_2 has not been altered in transit. It first computes the message digest of m_2 and checks that it is the same as the second field of the digital signature (MD_2). It then uses the public key in C's certificate to check that the third field is the correct signature for the concatenation of the first two fields.

(b) Verifies the transaction Id, the dollar amount of the order, and the description of the items purchased.

Next M sends a message to G containing two parts:

(a) m_1 and the dual signature it received from C:

$$m_3 = m_1,\ dual\_signature$$

(b) The transaction Id and the dollar amount of the order—signed with M's private key and encrypted with G's public key:

$$m_4 = K_G^{pub}[trans\_Id,\ \$\_amount,\ K_M^{pri}[f(trans\_Id,\ \$\_amount)]]$$

The complete message sent from M to G is $(m_3,\ m_4)$, together with copies of C's and M's certificates.

OPTIONAL

4. G decrypts the message using its private key.
   (a) It uses the dual signature and the public key in C's certificate to verify that m_1 was prepared by C and was not altered (as in step 3a).
   (b) It uses the message digest of the credit card information in C's certificate to verify the credit card information supplied in m_1.
   (c) It uses M's signature in m_4 and the public key in M's certificate to verify that m_4 was not altered.
   (d) It checks that the transaction Id and the dollar amount are the same in m_1 and m_4 (to verify that M and C agreed on the purchase).
   (e) It checks that the Transaction Id was never submitted before (to prevent a replay attack).
   (f) It does whatever is necessary to approve the credit card request.

   Then G returns a signed *approved* message to M. At this point, the transaction is committed.
5. When M receives the *approved* message, it knows that the transaction has committed. It sends a signed message to C: *transaction complete*. C then knows that the transaction has committed.

Note how the protocol deals with some other attacks.

1. M cannot attempt to substitute different goods since the dual signature is over the description agreed to by C. By forwarding the dual signature on to G, M has committed itself to that description.
2. C cannot use m'_1, copied from a message submitted by a different customer in an attempt to get that customer to pay for C's purchase by attaching it to m_2. In that case, the dual signature does not help since it is computed by C. However, m'_1 and m_2 would have different transaction Ids, so the transaction will be rejected by G.

The atomic commit protocol for SET. When G commits the transaction, it logs appropriate data to make the transaction durable. M might also wish to commit its subtransaction when it receives the approved message from G. Many customers might not want to perform a formal commit, but the exchange of messages between C, M, and G can be viewed as a linear commit protocol and in that context

- The messages sent from C to M in step 2 and from M to G in step 3 are *vote messages*. Before sending them, C and M must be in a prepared state.
- The messages sent from G to M in step 4 and from M to C in step 5 are *commit messages*. G and M must enter appropriate *commit records* into their logs before sending those messages.

Note that G is a trusted third party, trusted by the other two participants to perform the commit.

26.12 Goods Atomicity, Certified Delivery, and Escrow

Some Internet transactions involve the actual delivery of the purchased items. Transactions involving the purchase of downloaded software are in this category. Such transactions[7] should be **goods atomic** in that the goods are delivered if and only if they have been paid for. In the context of the SET protocol, "paid for" means that the purchase has been approved by the payment gateway; in the context of the electronic cash protocols described in Section 26.13, it means that the electronic cash has been delivered to the merchant and accepted by the bank.

Transactions involving the purchase of physical goods are usually not goods atomic. The customer orders the goods, and the transaction commits, after which (in most cases) the merchant ships the goods. In Internet commerce, however, the customer might not trust the merchant to send (download) the goods after the transaction commits.

Goods atomicity is not really a new concept. The only original idea is that the event of delivering the goods is part of the transaction in which the goods are paid for. The requirement that the goods be delivered if and only if they are paid for is just the usual definition of atomic transaction execution. The hard part of implementing goods atomicity is that delivery cannot be rolled back, which means that if the goods are delivered before the transaction commits and the transaction subsequently aborts, there is no way to undo the delivery, and the execution is not atomic.

OPTIONAL

In Section 19.3.5, we considered a situation similar to goods atomicity in which cash is dispensed by an ATM if and only if the withdraw transaction at the bank commits. We discussed how a recoverable queue could be used for that purpose. Both cash dispensing and goods atomicity involve an external event that is supposed to take place if and only if the transaction commits.

The concept of goods atomicity and a protocol for implementing it were developed in connection with the NetBill system [Cox et al. 1995]. The protocol is in some ways similar to SET in that it involves a client, a merchant, and a trusted third party that effectively consummates a credit card transaction through a linear commit protocol. Rather than describe NetBill, we describe how to implement goods atomicity as an enhancement of the SET protocol.

After C and M have agreed on the terms of a transaction, but before C sends a confirmation to M (step 2 of SET), M sends (downloads) the goods to C, encrypted with a new symmetric key, $K_{C,M}$, that M has constructed for this purpose. M also sends a message digest of the encrypted goods so that C can verify that the encrypted goods were correctly received. Note that C cannot use the goods at this point since it does not know $K_{C,M}$.

The description, *desc*, that C sends to M (in m_2) includes both a specification of the goods and the message digest of the encrypted goods, signed with C's private key. In effect, C is acknowledging that it has received (in encrypted form) the

[7] The term "transaction" is used loosely in this context. The actual delivery of the goods might occur after the transaction commits but is part of the protocol in which the transaction is embedded.

goods corresponding to the digest. As in step 2 of SET, the complete message is (m_1, m_2, *dual_signature*), and this is C's vote to commit. If, on receiving the message from C, M agrees that the description it has received from C is accurate, it constructs the message (m_3, m_4) as in step 3 of SET, but includes two additional items in m_4:

1. $K_{C,M}$
2. The message digest of the encrypted goods signed with C's private key, which it received from C in step 2, signed again (countersigned) with M's private key

M then sends the message to G (step 3 of SET).

An unscrupulous merchant cannot change the terms of the transaction (perhaps to show a higher price) since the dual signature constructed by C contains the price information. By adding its signature to the message (in m_4) and forwarding it to G, M commits itself to the transaction. Once again, this message is M's vote to commit.

When G receives the doubly signed message from M (step 4 of SET), it knows that both parties are prepared to commit to the terms of the transaction. As with SET, if G is satisfied with the credit card information supplied by C, it commits the transaction, durably stores m_3, m_4, and the dual signature, and sends an *approved* message to M. M, in turn, sends a *transaction complete* message containing $K_{C,M}$ to C, so C can decrypt the goods.

This protocol is goods atomic for the following reasons:

- If a failure occurs before G commits the transaction, no money is transferred and C does not get the goods since it does not get $K_{C,M}$.
- If a failure occurs after the commit, the money is transferred, G has a (durable) copy of $K_{C,M}$, and C has an encrypted copy of the goods. C can get $K_{C,M}$ either from M or—if for some reason M does not send $K_{C,M}$—from G since G knows that the transaction has committed and C's certificate identifies it as the principal who constructed the dual signature.

An important feature of the protocol is that when the transaction commits, G has a copy of $K_{C,M}$, and hence C can decrypt the goods even if M "forgets" to send the *transaction complete* message containing $K_{C,M}$.

Certified delivery. Another issue in the delivery of goods over the Internet is **certified delivery**. A goods-atomic transaction guarantees delivery to the customer, but we would like to have the additional assurance that the right goods are delivered. How can M defend itself against a charge that the goods it sent do not meet the agreed-upon specifications, and how can C be assured that the specific goods ordered are received? In particular, if there is a dispute between M and C about the delivered goods and that dispute is to be resolved by an arbiter, how can M and C present their respective cases to the arbiter? For example,

- Suppose that after decrypting the delivered goods, C finds that they do not meet their specifications and wants her money back. C can demonstrate to the arbiter that the software does not work, but how can she show that this software is in fact the same software that M sent?

OPTIONAL

OPTIONAL

- Suppose that C is trying to cheat M, and the nonworking software she demonstrates to the arbiter is not the same software that M sent. How can M unmask this attempted fraud?

The enhanced SET protocol meets the requirements of certified delivery. Recall that G durably stored m_3, m_4, and the dual signature when the transaction committed. The dual signature constructed by C was over the specification of the goods contained in m_2. By forwarding the signature on to G, M confirms that the specification is accurate (since it can decrypt m_2 to examine the specification and it can check that the signature is over m_2).

- C can demonstrate to an arbiter that the encrypted goods she claims to have received from M are actually the goods that were sent by M by simply running the digest function against the goods and comparing the result to the digest in m_4 stored by G. The arbiter can then decrypt the goods using $K_{C,M}$ and test them. C can also provide m_2 (containing the specifications) and demonstrate that the dual signature was on m_2 and hence agreed to by M. The arbiter is now in a position to judge C's claim.
- M can defend himself against a claim that the received goods do not meet their specifications since M can also produce m_2. Once again the arbiter can determine that the goods have not been tampered with and then test them against their specifications.

Escrow services. Another application requiring goods atomicity is the purchase of actual (nonelectronic) goods over the Internet from an unknown person or an auction site. The goods cannot be downloaded but must be sent by a shipping agent. One participant in the transaction might be suspicious that the other will not abide by the conditions of the purchasing agreement. How can both parties be sure that the transaction is goods atomic and that the goods will be delivered if and only if they are paid for?

One approach that comes close to meeting these requirements uses a trusted third party called an **escrow agent**. A number of companies are in the business of being escrow agents on the Internet. The basic idea is that, after the customer and the merchant have agreed on the terms of the purchase, instead of paying the merchant, the customer pays the escrow agent, which holds the money until the goods have been delivered and accepted by the customer. Only then does the escrow agent forward the payment to the merchant.

We sketch a simplified form of an escrow protocol,[8] leaving out many of the details involving authentication, encryption, and so forth. The protocol involves a customer, C, a merchant, M, and an escrow agent, E. It begins after C and M have reached agreement on the terms of the purchase.

1. C sends E the agreed-upon payment, perhaps using one of the secure payment methods described in this chapter.

[8] The protocol described is based on the i-Escrow protocol [i-Escrow 2000].

2. *E* durably stores the payment and other information needed for the rest of the protocol and commits the transaction.
3. *E* notifies *M* that the payment has been made.
4. *M* sends *C* the goods using some traceable shipping agent (such as FedEx or UPS), which agrees to make available to *E* the status information on the shipment (including confirmation of delivery).
5. When *C* receives the goods, she inspects them to see if they match her order. This inspection must be completed by the end of a stipulated period, which starts when the goods have been delivered as documented by the shipping agent's tracking mechanism.
   (a) If *C* is satisfied with the goods, the following take place:
      (i) *C* notifies *E* that the goods have been received and are satisfactory.
      (ii) *E* forwards the payment to *M*.
   (b) If *C* is not satisfied with the goods, the following take place:
      (i) *C* notifies *E* that the goods have been received and are not satisfactory.
      (ii) *C* returns the goods to *M* using some traceable shipping agent.
      (iii) *M* receives the goods and notifies *E*.[9]
      (iv) *E* returns the payment to *C*.
   (c) If, by the end of the inspection period, *C* does not notify *E* as to whether or not she is satisfied with the goods, *E* forwards the payment to *M*.[10]

This protocol reasonably approximates both goods atomicity and certified delivery. For example, *C* has a stipulated inspection period to determine whether or not the goods delivered are the goods ordered. As with the previous goods-atomicity protocol, this one relies on a third party, which is trusted by both *C* and *M*, to perform certain specified activities after the transaction commits.

26.13 Electronic Cash: Blind Signatures

The Internet purchasing transactions we have discussed so far use a credit card, which, along with a check, is an example of **notational money**. That is, your actual assets are represented by the balance in your bank account; your credit card or check is a *notation* against those assets. At the time you make a purchase, you provide a notation that identifies you and the cost of the goods you are purchasing; the merchant trusts that you will abide by the purchasing agreement and eventually pay for the purchases with real money—that there is enough money in your checking account or that you are in good standing with your credit card company. In either case, your bank balance will eventually be decremented to reflect your purchase.

[9] *M* can inspect the returned goods to see if they are as specified and must complete this inspection by the end of a stipulated inspection period. We omit what happens if *M* finds the returned goods unsatisfactory.

[10] *M* might not send the goods to *C* in step 4, or *C* might not return the goods to *E* in step 5b(ii). Again, these situations can be resolved using the shipping agent's tracking mechanism.

OPTIONAL

In contrast to notational money, cash is backed by the government. Although it does not have intrinsic value (it is, after all, just a piece of paper) the public's trust in the stability of the government causes it to be treated as if it had intrinsic value (i.e., as if it were gold). Thus, the merchant knows that he can deposit cash in his account or use it to purchase other goods without having to trust the customer. Cash is often referred to as **token money**. In the world of the Internet, token money is **electronic** or **digital** cash.

Token money offers the participants in a transaction certain advantages over notational money.

- *Anonymity*. Since the customer is not required to provide a signed record to complete a cash transaction, such a transaction can be performed anonymously. Neither the bank nor the credit card company knows the customer's identity. By contrast, a credit card company keeps records of all customers' purchases, and a bank has access to canceled checks. These records might be made available at a later time to the government, to a court proceeding, or even to someone hoping to pry into an individual's personal life.
- *Small-denomination purchases*. For each credit card transaction, the credit card company charges a fixed fee plus a percentage of the purchase price. Thus, credit cards are not appropriate for purchases involving only a small amount of money, yet many Internet vendors would like to charge a few cents for a page of information they supply to browsers. Small-denomination electronic cash would be useful for such transactions.

Hence, there is a need to support transactions based on electronic cash. Such transactions should satisfy the requirement of **money atomicity**: money should not be created or destroyed. However, since electronic cash is represented by a data structure in the system, there are several ways in which money atomicity might be violated. For example,

- A dishonest customer or merchant can make a copy of the data structure and use both the original and the copy.
- Money can be created or destroyed if a failure occurs (e.g., a message is lost or the system crashes). For example, a customer who has sent a copy of the data structure to a merchant cannot determine whether the message was received by the merchant and so decides to reuse the data structure in a different purchase—even though the money was actually received. Alternatively, the message might not have been received, but the customer does not reuse the data structure, failing to realize that the payment has not been made.

What follows is a discussion of an electronic cash protocol designed to support the purchase of arbitrary (not necessarily electronic) goods. Goods atomicity is not a feature of this protocol; instead, the customer trusts that the merchant will send the goods after the transaction commits.

OPTIONAL

Tokens and redundancy predicates. This protocol is based on the Ecash protocol [Chaum et al. 1988]. Cash is represented by electronic tokens of various denominations. Each token consists of a unique serial number, *n*, encrypted with a private key known only to the bank. The terminology here is confusing since it is often said that, in electronic cash protocols, the bank "signs" the serial number to create the token. Here, the meaning of signing differs from that given in Section 26.3, in which a signed item consists of the item followed by an encryption of its digest. In this section, when we say that the bank signs a serial number, we mean that the bank encrypts the serial number with a private key, and the result is a token.

How does this scheme prevent intruders from creating counterfeit tokens? After all, a token is just a bit string of a certain length. The fact that the bit string is the encryption of a serial number provides no protection. You might think that we could test the token for validity by decrypting it with the bank's public key and examining the result. However, that key can be applied to any valid or invalid token, yielding a bit string, and we have no way of distinguishing a bit string that is a valid serial number from one that is not.

To prevent intruders from creating counterfeit tokens, we use a technique that requires serial numbers to be bit strings that have some special property that distinguishes them from arbitrary bit strings. For example, it might be required that the first half of the serial number be created at random and the second half be a scrambled form of the first half using a fixed and known scrambling function. Formally, we say that there is some well-known predicate, *valid*, called a **redundancy predicate**, such that, for all valid serial numbers, *n*, the predicate *valid*(*n*) is true.

Although it is assumed that the counterfeiter knows the redundancy predicate and the bank's public key for decrypting tokens, she does not know the bank's private key and so cannot produce tokens by encrypting a valid serial number. Hence, in counterfeiting tokens she faces the problem of finding a (fake) token that decrypts to a bit string that satisfies *valid*. The counterfeiter can use a trial-and-error technique to do this, but it is extremely unlikely that the result of decrypting an arbitrarily chosen bit string will satisfy *valid* if the bit string is long enough and if *valid* is such that the number of bit strings of that length that satisfy *valid* is a small percentage of the total number of bit strings of that length.

In its scheme for minting tokens, the bank keeps a set of public/private key pairs and chooses serial numbers that satisfy *valid*. It signs all serial numbers used in creating tokens of a particular denomination, *j*, with the same private key, K_j^{priv}, from the set and uses a different private key for each denomination. The bank does not keep a list of the serial numbers of the tokens that it has created, but if the numbers are large enough and the number of tokens minted at each denomination is limited, the probability that the bank will choose the same serial number twice can be made vanishingly small. The bank does keep a list of the serial numbers of all tokens deposited and therefore can reject a copy of a token that was deposited already. In this way, it can detect an attempt to use a duplicated token. Any customer or merchant can check the validity and denomination of a token by decrypting it with K_j^{pub} and applying *valid* to the result.

OPTIONAL

A simple digital cash protocol. If anonymity is not an issue, the customer, *C*, the merchant, *M*, and the bank, *B*, can use the following simple digital cash protocol.

Creating tokens

1. *C* authenticates himself to *B* and sends a message requesting to withdraw some specified amount of cash, in the form of tokens, from his account.
2. *B* debits *C*'s account and mints the requested tokens by making up a serial number, n_i, for each token, such that *valid*(n_i) is true. It then encrypts n_i with the private key, K_j^{priv}, corresponding to the token's denomination *j*, to produce the token $K_j^{priv}[n_i]$.
3. *B* sends the tokens to *C*, encrypted with a session key generated for *B* and *C*'s use in the usual manner. A token cannot be sent in the clear because an intruder can copy it and spend the copy before *C* has a chance to spend the original. (In that case, the original token will be rejected by *B* when it is later deposited by *C*). At this point, the token-creation transaction is committed.
4. *C* receives the tokens and stores them in his "electronic wallet."

OPTIONAL

Spending tokens

1. When *C* wants to use some of his tokens to purchase goods from *M*, he establishes a session with *M* and generates a session key in the usual manner. He then sends a message to *M* containing a purchase order for the goods and the appropriate number of tokens, all encrypted with the session key.
2. Upon receiving the message from *C*, *M* decrypts the tokens and checks that they are valid and are sufficient to purchase the requested goods. *M* then sends the tokens to *B*, encrypted with a session key.
3. Upon receiving the message from *M*, *B* decrypts the tokens and checks that they are valid. It then checks its list of deposited tokens to ensure that the received tokens have not already been deposited. *B* then adds the received tokens to its list of deposited tokens, credits *M*'s account with the amount of the tokens, commits the transaction, and sends a *complete* message to *M*.
4. Upon receiving the *complete* message from *B*, *M* performs local commit actions and then sends a *complete* message (and the goods purchased) to *C*.

(This protocol does not guarantee goods atomicity or certified delivery. *M* might not send the goods to *C*.) As with the SET protocol, the exchange of messages among *B*, *M*, and *C* can be viewed as a linear commit protocol.

An anonymous protocol and blinding functions. The simple digital cash protocol does not provide anonymity to the customer because the bank can record the serial numbers of the tokens withdrawn by the customer. When those tokens are deposited by a merchant, the bank could conclude that the merchant sold something to that customer. This exposes some information about the customer's activities that she might prefer to keep private. To provide anonymity, the protocol is modified so that the customer (not the bank) makes up a serial number, n, that satisfies $valid(n)$, scrambles it, and then submits it to the bank. The bank creates the token by signing the scrambled serial number (it does not know what the serial number is), using a private key appropriate to the denomination being withdrawn. Such a signature is called a **blind signature** [Chaum et al. 1988]. The bank does not know the serial number, so it cannot trace it back to the customer when the token is later deposited by the merchant. When the customer receives the blinded token from the bank, it unscrambles it to obtain the token.

To implement a blind signature, the protocol uses a **blinding function**, b (sometimes called a **commuting function**). The function b and its inverse, b^{-1}, have two properties:

1. Given $b(n)$, it is very difficult to determine n.
2. b commutes with the encryption function used by the bank involving the (private) denomination key K_j^{priv}. That is,

   $$K_j^{priv}[b(n)] = b(K_j^{priv}[n])$$

   and as a result

   $$b^{-1}(K_j^{priv}[b(n)]) = b^{-1}(b(K_j^{priv}[n])) = K_j^{priv}[n]$$

   Therefore C can recover the token from the blinded token.

Creating tokens

1. C creates a valid serial number, n, satisfying $valid(n)$.
2. C selects a blinding function, b (known only to C), and **blinds** the serial number by computing $b(n)$.
3. C authenticates himself to B and sends a message containing $b(n)$, requesting to withdraw from his account some specified amount of cash in the form of tokens. (As in the simple digital cash protocol, the message is encrypted with a session key.) Since B does not know the blinding function, it cannot determine n.
4. B signs $b(n)$ with a private key, K_j^{priv}, appropriate to the token's denomination, creating the blinded token $K_j^{priv}[b(n)]$. It debits C's account accordingly and then returns the blinded token to C, again using a session key. Although B cannot check that C had selected a valid serial number (satisfying $valid(n)$), C has no reason to construct an invalid number because he knows that B will debit his account by the amount of the token and that the token's validity will be checked when he attempts to spend it. At this point, the token creation transaction is committed.
5. C **unblinds** the blinded token by using $b^{-1}(K_j^{priv}[b(n)])$ to obtain $K_j^{priv}[n]$, which is the requested token consisting of a signed valid serial number.

OPTIONAL

Creating a blinding function. The protocol requires that C create his own blinding function, b, unknown to B. This might seem a difficult task, but it is actually quite easy in the context of the RSA algorithm for public key cryptography. In one scheme for doing this, C first generates a random number, u, that is relatively prime[11] to the modulus N of the bank's keys (see Section 26.2). Because u is relatively prime to N, it has a **multiplicative inverse**, u^{-1}, with respect to N, such that

$$u * u^{-1} \equiv 1 \ (mod\ N)$$

To blind the serial number, n, C computes

$$K_j^{pub}[u] * n \ (mod\ N)$$

and sends the result to B. Hence, the blinding function can be viewed simply as multiplication by a random number.

The signed result, sr, returned by B to C is

$$sr = K_j^{pri}[K_j^{pub}[u] * n]$$

Using equation (26.1) on page 1141, it follows that

$$sr = u * K_j^{pri}[n] \ (mod\ N)$$

Informally, we can say that, to unblind the token, C "divides sr by u," but actually C uses the multiplicative inverse, u^{-1}, to recover the token

$$K_j^{pri}[n] = u^{-1} * sr \ (mod\ N)$$

The serial number n can now be obtained using K_j^{pub}.

Spending tokens. The protocol for spending and validating tokens involves the same steps as those in the simple protocol previously described. Fortunately, we did not assume that B kept a list of the serial numbers of the tokens it generated because, with the anonymous protocol, it does not know what these numbers are. When M submits the token to B for redemption, B simply assumes that, if the serial number satisfies *valid*, it earlier (blindly) signed that serial number. As before, B keeps a list of the serial numbers of tokens that have been deposited, so it will not accept the same token twice.

Money atomicity. The question is whether the electronic cash protocols achieve money atomicity. Money atomicity has two aspects:

1. Money might be created (outside of any transaction) if a process can make a copy of a token and then spend it. However, the bank will uncover this attempted fraud when it checks the serial number against its list of previously submitted

[11] Euclid's algorithm can be used to test whether the random number is relatively prime to N (see [Stalling 1997]).

OPTIONAL

tokens. Counterfeiting is another way of creating money, but, as we saw earlier, success in this is unlikely.

2. Money might be destroyed as the result of a failure, but such problems can generally be dealt with.
   (a) In the token generation transaction, the bank debits the customer's account, sends the token, and then commits, but the communication system loses the token, and it is never delivered to the customer. However, these protocols have the interesting property that, if the customer claims never to have received a token that the bank sent, the bank can simply send the customer a copy of the (blinded) token that it retrieves from its log. Even if the customer is dishonest and now has two copies of the token, only one can be spent.
   (b) In the token-spending transaction, the system crashes after the customer sent the token but before she received a message that the transaction committed. The customer does not know whether the transaction committed before the crash and hence whether the token was actually spent. If she attempts to spend the token again, she might be accused of fraud. However, she can later ask the bank whether a particular token was spent (i.e., is in the list of spent tokens), but this might compromise her anonymity.

26.14 Security in XML-Based Web Services

Increasingly, Web services require security. The integrity and privacy of data might have to be guaranteed, and principals might have to be authenticated. Many of these proposals for security protocols are still in an early stage of development and are likely to change. In this section we briefly discuss the basic ideas underlying some of them, leaving out details and a number of possible variations and optional features.

Web services security is built on the techniques described in previous sections. For example, public-key and symmetric encryption techniques, digital signatures, certificates, and Kerberos are used. The new issue is how to integrate them into the Web environment, and this means expressing them in XML and developing standards that all the players in the Web services world agree on. We consider two related problems: First, how do you encrypt and/or sign information contained in an XML document or a SOAP message? And second, how do you exchange security related information?

26.14.1 Encryption and Signatures—XML Encryption and XML Signature

XML Encryption. *XML Encryption*[12] is concerned with the encryption of XML data. It addresses a number of problems. How do we fit encrypted data into the XML model? How do we transmit to the receiver of encrypted XML data information

[12] We describe the *W3C Recommendation* of December 10, 2002, which can be found at *http://www.w3.org/TR/2002/REC-xmlenc-core-20021210*.

about how the encryption was done? Finally, an XML document will generally contain a variety of elements describing many aspects of an interaction. The elements are supplied by and directed to a variety of different entities. To make sure a receiver accesses only information relevant to it, each element might have to be encrypted in a different way. How is this to be done?

Suppose an XML document describing a purchase contains the buyer's name and credit card information:

```
<Payment xmlns = "http:// ...">
    <Name>John Doe</Name>
    <CreditCard Limit="5000" Currency="USD">
        <Number>1234 5678 9012 3456</Number>
        <Issuer>Bank of XY</Issuer>
        <Expiration>04/09</Expiration>
    </CreditCard>
</Payment>
```

While the name must be accessible to the merchant, we might want to reserve for the credit card company access to the credit card information. The result of encrypting the credit card information using XML Encryption is shown in Figure 26.7.

The `credit card` element has been replaced by an `EncryptedData` element. Its `Type` attribute indicates that an entire element (including its tag) within the document has been encrypted. The actual encrypted value of the `credit card` element is in the `CipherValue` element. The `EncryptionMethod` element gives information about the method used for encryption. The value of its `Algorithm` attribute is a URI that identifies the encryption algorithm, in this case a Triple DES algorithm. The `KeyName` element gives information that can be used to identify the

FIGURE 26.7 An encrypted element within an XML document.

```
<PaymentInfo xmlns = "http:// ...">
  <Name>John Doe</Name>
  <EncryptedData Type="http://www.w3.org/2001/04/xmlenc#Element"
     xmlns="http://www.w3.org/2001/04/xmlenc#"/>
    <EncryptionMethod
     Algorithm="http://www.w3.org/2001/04/xmlenc#tripledes-cbc"/>
    <ds:KeyInfo xmlns:ds="http://www.w3.org/2000/09/xmldsig#">
     <ds:KeyName>keyABC</ds:KeyName>
    </ds:KeyInfo>
    <CipherData>
     <CipherValue>Zx23XAbc4</CipherValue>
    </CipherData>
  </EncryptedData>
</PaymentInfo>
```

decryption key (perhaps the name of a file accessible to the receiver containing the key). The assumption is that the key is properly protected, and the receiver can produce the key given this information. The `EncryptionMethod` and `KeyName` elements are both optional and can be omitted if the user is expected to know that information.

In this example, the entire element has been encrypted, including its tag. In some circumstances it is desirable not to encrypt the tag. For example, executing an XPath search might be inhibited if tags are encrypted. More interestingly, since an intruder might be able to guess the tag, security is compromised. The intruder knows the clear text corresponding to a portion of the cipher text. Hence, among the possible values of the `Type` attribute is one which indicates that tags are not encrypted.

In some situations the same element might be encrypted more than once. For example, in a medical record the details of a particular malady might be accessible to the medical staff only while more general medical information might be accessible to the accounting department (for billing purposes) as well. To handle this, the details might be encrypted using a particular key or technique known only to the medical staff and then all the medical information (including the details) might be encrypted using a different key or technique known to both the medical staff and the accountants. As a result, the details are doubly encrypted and accessible only to the medical staff. For example, in Figure 26.7 we might encrypt both the `Name` element and the `EncryptedData` element and embed the result as `CipherData` in another `EncryptedData` element.

In Figure 26.7 the symmetric key used to decrypt the element is known to the receiver, and the sender simply identifies it using the `KeyName` child. Alternatively, the sender might transmit the key, in encrypted form, along with the element. In this case the key might be encrypted using the public key of the receiver. The `EncryptedKey` element defined in XML Encryption is used for this purpose. An example of this case will be given shortly. These alternatives illustrate the fact that the basic encryption techniques can be used in a variety of ways to satisfy the needs of different applications.

XML Signature. *XML Signature*[13] is concerned with signatures on XML data. As with XML Encryption, either an entire XML document or an individual element in a document can be signed. A simple signature element is shown in Figure 26.8

The `SignedInfo` element groups together all the information about the signature except the signature itself. A single signature can be used to sign multiple data items stored in different places. To do this, `SignedInfo` contains one or more `Reference` elements, each of which identifies an item through its URI attribute.

In Figure 26.8 the initial character of the value of the `URI` attribute of the `Reference` element, `#`, indicates that the data is an element elsewhere in the same document: the element with tag `MsgBody`. (In Figure 26.10 we present a complete

[13] We describe the *W3C Recommendation* of February 12, 2002, which can be found at *http://www.w3.org/TR/2002/REC-xmldsig-core-20020212*.

FIGURE 26.8 A simple signature element.

```
<Signature Id="A Simple Signature"
      xmlns="http://www.w3.org/2000/09/xmldsig#">
  <SignedInfo>
    <CanonicalizationMethod
      Algorithm="http://www.w3.org/TR/2001/REC-xml-c14n-20010315"/>
    <SignatureMethod
      Algorithm="http://www.w3.org/2000/09/xmldsig#rsa-sha1"/>
    <Reference URI="#MsgBody">
      <Transforms ··· </Transforms>
      <DigestMethod
        Algorithm="http://www.w3.org/2000/09/xmldsig#sha1"/>
      <DigestValue>dER4boXp453tr56Y</DigestValue>
    </Reference>
  </SignedInfo>
  <SignatureValue>zi990CrnT9zopr0o</SignatureValue>
</Signature>
```

SOAP message containing both the data and its signature. It includes the element MsgBody being referred to here.) In other cases we might be signing data external to the document—for example a file attached to a message of a page accessible on the Web. For example, the attribute value *http://www.mycompany.audit#personnel* indicates that the personnel element contained in the indicated Web page has been signed.

The Reference element also gives us the first step used to compute the signature: the method used to compute the digest of the data is specified as the value of the Algorithm attribute of the DigestMethod child element, and the resulting digest value is given in the DigestValue child. (Since the Transforms element is a distraction from our description of the signature algorithm, we defer discussing it until later in this section on page 1175.)

The second step of the signature algorithm signs the SignedInfo element (*not* the data) in the traditional way. A digest of the SignedInfo element is computed, and the result is signed with the private key of the sender. The specific algorithm that does this is the value of the Algorithm attribute of the SignatureMethod element.

Hence, XML Signature uses *two* digests to compute a signature. Note that the double digest has all the properties of a digest as described in Section 26.3: all digest values are equally likely, and if any bit of the data is changed, all bits of the digest have a 50% chance of changing.

A nice feature of the double digest algorithm is that by signing the SignedInfo element instead of just the data, the sender guarantees that an intruder cannot change the information describing the signature algorithm that was used to sign the data. What would be the point of such an attack? Suppose an intruder could substitute in the SignedInfo element the name of a different digest function, D_2, for the digest function, D_1, used by the sender, and suppose that D_1 maps the item to be signed to the digest value *dv*. If the set of items mapped to *dv* by D_1 is a subset of the set mapped by D_2 to *dv*, then the receiver will not be able to detect the substitution (since the value *dv* will be encrypted in both cases). However, the likelihood that the intruder will be able to attach the signature to different data successfully is increased. Hence, the intruder has weakened the integrity guarantee provided by the digital signature.

Producing a digest of the `SignedInfo` element is not as simple as it appears. The element is embedded within an XML document. When computing the signature, the sender must extract the data first and, in the process, spaces or tab characters might be inserted or deleted. Similarly, when the receiver checks the signature, the data must be extracted from the received document. If this extraction is done differently, the string checked by the receiver might not be the same as the string signed by the sender. Although semantically the XML content of the data will be the same, the digest function is sensitive to the exact string. Two strings that differ by only a single space character will have completely different digests (see Section 26.3). Hence the digest computed by the receiver will not match the digest computed by the sender.

One way to deal with this problem is to convert the `SignedInfo` element into a canonical form—**canonicalize** it. This guarantees a unique representation of the element with respect to these issues. Both the sender and the receiver canonicalize the element using the algorithm specified in the element `CanonicalizationMethod` before computing the digest.

Reading from the top of the `Signature` element

- The `CanonicalizationMethod` element identifies the canonicalization algorithm to be applied to the `SignedInfo` element.
- The `SignatureMethod` element identifies the signature algorithm to be used to sign the `signedInfo` element (for example RSA-SHA1).
- The `Reference` element identifies the data to be signed and contains the `DigestMethod` and the `DigestValue`.
- The `DigestMethod` element identifies the digest algorithm to be used on the data.
- The `DigestValue` element gives the result of executing the digest algorithm on the data to be signed.
- The `SignatureValue` element gives the result of signing the `SignedInfo` element.

Note that the `SignatureValue` element is not a child of the `SignedInfo` element. This is fortunate because otherwise we would be in the awkward situation of having to know the value of the signature before we actually compute it.

Finally, in more complicated applications, certain transformations might have been performed by the sender on the data referenced by a `Reference` element *before* the message digest was computed. In other words, the received data is not exactly the data that the sender signed. For example, the data might bave been canonicalized (do not be confused here—we are talking about the data itself, not the `SignedInfo` element) before being digested. Or, the data might have been compressed or encrypted. Another case occurs when an XML document includes an element that was not digested. For example, the element might contain information that is subject to modification as the data is moved from one site to another. If the element is processed by the digest function, then any subsequent change to its value will invalidate the signature. In order to accommodate this problem the sender might have deleted the element before computing the digest—although the element is contained in the data sent.

In order to validate the signature, the receiver must know what transformations were performed when the signature was computed by the sender. It can then repeat those transformations, in the same order, to the received data as a first step (before computing the digest) of the signature validation process. The transformations are identified in the `Transforms` child of a `Reference` element. `Transforms` contains an ordered list of `Transform` children, each one of which describes a particular transformation that was performed.

One last point needs to be considered: suppose the receiver does not know the public key to be used in checking the signature. The sender might want to transmit this information, and XML Signature provides several ways in which this can be done. For example, the sender might provide a string that identifies the key. This might be the case if the receiver has several public keys on file and uses the string to identify the appropriate one. This type of information is transmitted in a `KeyInfo` child of the `Signature` element

```
<KeyInfo>
  <KeyName>
    ··· the identifier goes here ···
  </KeyName>
</KeyInfo>
```

Another alternative is to send a certificate. We will see an example of that shortly.

26.14.2 Encrypting and Signing SOAP Messages— WS-Security

XML Encryption and XML Signature supply a complete solution to the problem of encrypting and signing an XML document. However, if the document in question is a SOAP message, additional conventions must be introduced so that a SOAP processor can utilize these tools. The protocol that we describe is referred to as **WS-Security**.[14] WS-Security defines a security header block, tagged `wsse:Security`, which can be placed in the header of a SOAP message and which contains security related information. For example, the information might be a security token (which might contain a certificate or a Kerberos ticket), a timestamp (which can be used for dealing with replays), a signature, or an encrypted key. These items can be used in

[14] The discussion is based on the *OASIS Standard 200401*, March 2004.

a variety of ways to create a level of security appropriate to a particular application. We discuss two simple examples.

- **Sending encrypted data.** In Figure 26.9 the encrypted data is the entire child element (including its tag) of the body of a SOAP message. The header block contains an EncryptedKey element describing the key that was used to encrypt

FIGURE 26.9 An encrypted SOAP message.

```
<s:Envelope
  xmlns:s="http://www.w3.org/2001/12/soap-envelope"
  xmlns:ds="http://www.w3.org/2000/09/xmldsig#"
  xmlns:wsse="http://schemas.xmlsoap.org/ws/2002/04/secext"
  xmlns:xenc="http://www.w3.org/2001/04/xmlenc#">
  <s:Header>
    <wsse:Security>
      <xenc:EncryptedKey>
        <xenc:EncryptionMethod Algorithm="..."/>
        <ds:KeyInfo>
          <wsse:KeyIdentifier
            MnH5x7...
          </wsse:KeyIdentifier>
        </ds:KeyInfo>
        <xenc:CipherData>
          <xenc:CipherValue>jh54Da...</xenc:CipherValue>
        </xenc:CipherData>
        <xenc:ReferenceList>
          <xenc:DataReference URI="#bodyID"/>
        </xenc:ReferenceList>
      </xenc:EncryptedKey>
    </wsse:Security>
  </s:Header>
  <s:Body>
    <xenc:EncryptedData Id="bodyID"
        Type="http://www.w3.org/2001/04/xmlenc#Element">
      <xenc:EncryptionMethod
        Algorithm="http://www.w3.org/2001/04/xmlenc#tripledes-cbc"/>
      <xenc:CipherData>
        <xenc:CipherValue>Kiu87Cde...</xenc:CipherValue>
      </xenc:CipherData>
    </xenc:EncryptedData>
  </s:Body>
</s:Envelope>
```

the data. In this case, the data was encrypted with a symmetric key. The `Algorithm` attribute of the `EncryptionMethod` child of `encryptedKey` identifies the method that was used to encrypt the key. The `CipherData` element contains the key in encrypted form. So, in order to decrypt the data, the receiver must first decrypt the key. Fortunately, the sender has supplied some information about how that can be done using the `KeyIdentifier` child of the `KeyInfo` element. The value of that child uniquely identifies a key that the receiver can access to decrypt the encrypted key. So the assumption here is that the sender and receiver have exchanged some key information prior to the sending of this message.

The `ReferenceList` child contains a list of items encrypted by the (encrypted) key. In this case, the list contains a single `DataReference` child whose `URI` refers to the `EncryptedData` element in the message with `Id` value `BodyID` (recall that the # means that the data is an element within the same XML document).

- **Sending signed data.** In Figure 26.10 the body contains the (unencrypted) data, and the header contains its signature. The `Signature` element is the same as that shown in Figure 26.8 with the exception that a `KeyInfo` child that contains information about the key to be used by the receiver to check the signature has been added. The assumption is that in this application the receiver does not know the public key to use. Hence, a certificate containing that key is included in a `BinarySecurityToken` header block, and a reference to it is included in the `SecurityTokenReference` element. Both of these elements are defined in the WS-Security schema. A security token might simply contain a user's name, or it might contain binary information like a certificate or a Kerberos ticket. A token reference might involve a URI (as in this case) or a `KeyIdentifier` (as described in connection with Figure 26.9 and embedded in a `KeyInfo` element).

  The `Id` attribute of `Body` assigns the name `MsgBody` to the data, and the signature shown in Figure 26.8 refers to that item.

General considerations. A SOAP message can pass through a number of intermediaries before getting to its final destination. A header block is addressed to an intermediary using the `role` attribute and contains individual processing instructions for the intermediary. This allows different security header blocks to be addressed to different intermediaries. For example, an intermediary might be a signature verifier, which verifies the signature of the data in the body. The signature would be included as a `Security` header block addressed to that site. After verifying the signature, the verifier might add an additional header block asserting that verification was successful and pass the message on to the final destination.

Alternatively, different intermediaries along a path might sign or encrypt different (perhaps overlapping) portions of a message, adding new security header blocks as the message progresses. For example, a salesperson might send an order in the body of a SOAP message and include a security header block with his signature. When the order is processed in the shipping department, a shipping header might be added and the shipping department might sign both that header and the body.

FIGURE 26.10 A signed SOAP message.

```
<s:Envelope xmlns:S="http://www.w3.org/2001/12/soap-envelope"
    xmlns:ds="http://www.w3.org/2000/09/xmldsig#">
  <s:Header>
    <wsse:Security
      xmlns:wsse="http://schemas.xmlsoap.org/ws/2002/04/secext"
      xmlns:wsu="...">
      <wsse:BinarySecurityToken>
        ValueType="...#X509v3"
        wsu:Id="X509Token"
        EncodingType="...">
        AsD4Fg567...
      </wsse:BinarySecurityToken>
      <ds:Signature>
        <!-- The SignedInfo and SignatureValue elements in Figure 26.8 appear here. -->
        <KeyInfo>
          <wsse:SecurityTokenReference>
            <wsse:Reference URI="#X509Token"/>
          </wsse:SecurityTokenReference>
        </KeyInfo>
      </ds:Signature>
    </wsse:Security>
  <s:Header>
  <s:Body Id="MsgBody">
    <!-- The data being signed appears here -->
  </s:Body>
</s:Envelope>
```

The message might then be passed to another department that functions in a similar way, adding new information, signatures, and perhaps encryption. The new blocks should be prepended so that the order in which these operations have taken place is implicit in the order of the blocks, making it possible to reverse the operations at a later time. In addition, care should be taken if modifications to previously signed data are made.

An interesting security breach may be possible if an element that is embedded in a larger XML document and that uses globally defined namespace prefixes is signed. If the global information (that is not included in the signature) is tampered with, the meaning of the signed element might change even though its integrity is guaranteed by the signature. The problem can be avoided if the prefixes are declared within the signed element.

A `Timestamp` element can be included in a security header block to indicate to the receiver the freshness of the message. Alternatively, it might be used in detecting replay attacks. In that case it should be signed by the sender to prevent alteration.

The important thing to note about WS-Security is that it does not specify a particular security policy. Rather, it supplies a toolbox of mechanisms that an application can use to convey security-related information and thereby to construct a policy suitable to its needs.

26.14.3 SAML: Authentication, Authorization, and Single Sign-On

SAML (Security Assertion Markup Language)[15] addresses the issue of specifying and exchanging security-related data—called **statements**—in a loosely coupled environment. Statements currently fall into three categories:

1. **Authentication statement.** Describes an authentication event that happened sometime in the past. For example, Joe was authenticated using method *M* at time *T*.
2. **Attribute assertion.** Provides the value of an attribute that describes a particular subject. For example, the value of the attribute "department" associated with Joe is Accounting.
3. **Authorization decision statement.** Gives the result of an authorization decision concerning a particular subject. For example, Joe is authorized to take action *A* with respect to resource *R*.

A number of use cases have been identified which illustrate the role SAML can play. Some of these are illustrated in Figure 26.11. The single sign-on use case is shown in (a). The user is authenticated at *site* 1, and an authentication statement is created. Later the user contacts *site* 2 and uses the statement to avoid re-authenticating. An authorization use case is shown in (b). The user requests access to a resource at *site* 1, and authorization decisions are made at *site* 2. *Site* 1 requests an authorization decision statement from *site* 2. Since *site* 2 is making decisions about *site* 1's resources and understands its access modes, it is likely that the two sites are in the same security domain. In (c) *site* 1 invokes a transaction at *site* 2 on behalf of the user. For example, *site* 1 might maintain credit information about the user that it passes to *site* 2 in an attribute statement.

In all of these cases, SAML distinguishes between the **asserting party**, the party that creates the statement, and the **relying party**, the party that uses the statement. The asserting party is referred to as a **SAML authority**.

To get a better idea of how SAML works, look at Figure 26.12. It shows a SAML **assertion**, which is an element that contains one or more SAML statements all pertaining to a single subject. In this case. a single authentication statement is included. In addition to the statements themselves, the assertion provides a number of other items of information. The time the assertion was constructed is an attribute of the `Assertion` element. The SAML authority that created the assertion is given as an `Issuer` child. The `Subject` child identifies the entity the statements describe:

[15] The discussion is based on the description of SAML V2.0 contained in *OASIS Draft 10,* April 2004

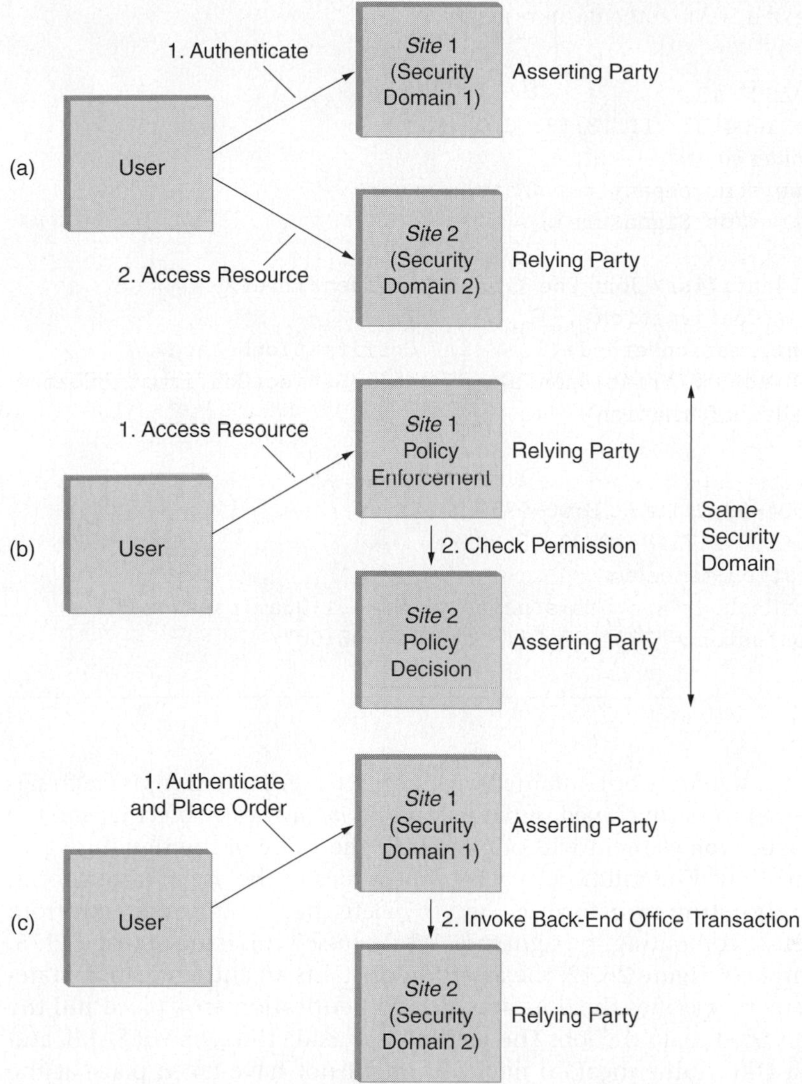

FIGURE 26.11 Use cases for SAML protocol: (a) single sign-on; (b) authorization; (c) invoking a transaction.

in this case, John Doe. The `Conditions` child specifies conditions on the use of the assertion: in this case, the time interval during which the assertion can be used.

Note that the `Signature` child contains the authority's signature. It guarantees the integrity of the assertion and allows the relying party to authenticate the authority using the authority's public key. A good question that you might ask at this

FIGURE 26.12 An example of a SAML authentication assertion.

```
<saml:Assertion
    AssertionID="ABCE-123"
    IssueInstant="2004-03-21T113:13:00-05:00"
    <!– other attributes go here – – >
  <saml:Issuer> www.somecompany.com </saml:Issuer>
  <ds:Signature> ··· </ds:Signature>
  <saml:Subject>
      <saml:NameIdentifier> John Doe </saml:NameIdentifier>
      <saml:SubjectConfirmation>
        <saml:ConfirmationMethod> ··· </saml:ConfirmationMethod>
        <saml:SubjectConfirmationData> ··· </saml:SubjectConfirmationData>
      <saml:SubjectConfirmation>
  </saml:Subject>
  <saml:Conditions
    NotBefore="2004-03-21T113:13:00-05:00"
    NotAfter="2004-03-21T113:18:00-05:00"/>
  <saml:AuthenticationStatement
    AuthenticationMethod="urn:oasis:names:tc:SAML:1.0:am:password"
    AuthenticationInstant="2004-03-21T113:13:00-05:00"/>
</saml:Assertion>
```

point is, how can a signature be contained within the element that it signs (such signatures are referred to as enveloped signatures)? That is, how can you compute the digest of the `Assertion` element without knowing the value of the signature that is contained within it? The solution to this problem lies in the use of a transform. The **enveloped signature transform** is used to delete the signature element from the assertion before computing the signature. We discussed this issue on page 1175.

In the example of Figure 26.12, the assertion contains an authentication statement. The statement specifies the time at which authentication took place and the method that was used to do the job. The method is outside the scope of SAML and is specified by a URI. Authentication might or might not have taken place at the authority's site. An additional (optional) child element is provided to specify the location. Note that SAML itself is not doing the authentication; an assertion simply reports on an authentication event that occurred sometime in the past.

One additional feature is needed if assertions are to be useful The relying party receives the assertion from a sender. For example, the assertion might state that its subject has been authenticated in some way. How does the relying party know that the sender represents that subject? The assertion might have been copied by an intruder who is now trying to use it to masquerade as the subject.

The additional feature is provided by the `SubjectConfirmation` child of the `Subject` element. This child element provides information that can be used by the relying party to confirm that the assertion was received from a sender representing the subject and that therefore the relying party can use the assertion in satisfying the sender's request. The `ConfirmationMethod` identifies the method that the relying party can use for this purpose, and the `SubjectConfirmationData` optionally provides some information that the method will use. For example, the data might be the public key of the subject, and the method might involve requiring the sender to demonstrate knowledge of the corresponding private key (by some specified interchange of encrypted messages using those keys).

The `SubjectConfirmation` element is required, independent of the type of SAML statements contained in the assertion. If the protocol is being used for single sign-on, however, you might legitimately ask if the required confirmation does not defeat the purpose of single sign-on since the subject is being asked to confirm its identity at each site despite the fact that the assertion already contains an authentication statement. The answer to this question is twofold. First, the same confirmation procedure is used at all sites so that the problem of requiring the subject to authenticate itself differently at each site—possibly with different passwords—is avoided. Hence, once the authentication statement has been created, subsequent confirmations can be hidden below the application level. This is also the approach used by Kerberos, where the use of the ticket-granting ticket need not be part of the application. Secondly, the confirmation method need not be a complete authentication protocol. In the above example, the sender does not have to present a certificate. The relying party has the authentication statement and hence already knows the association between the public key and the subject's identity. It can simply request the sending site to demonstrate knowledge of the private key.

SAML envisions that there will ultimately be **SAML Authority sites** on the Web: Authentication Authorities, Authorization Authorities, and Assertion Authorities, among others. Authority sites will act as trusted third parties that maintain repositories of authentication, authorization, and attribute assertions. For example, a site such as Yahoo, MSN, or AOL could act as an authentication authority with various servers acting as relying parties.

A site can send an assertion it has created to an appropriate Authority, which can store it in its repository. For example, when a user is authenticated by some site, the site can send the authentication assertion to an Authentication Authority. Later, other sites can query the Authentication Authority to obtain the assertion.

Alternatively, a client might authenticate itself with a vendor, who creates an authentication statement that it later sends to a supplier. After receiving the statement, the supplier might query an Authorization or Attribute Authority to obtain additional information about a customer.

As with the other proposed standards introduced in this section, we have discussed only a small fraction of the SAML protocol. A complete description would include SAML bindings (in particular, the conventions for embedding assertions in SOAP messages) and SAML protocols (the conventions used for communicating assertions). We refer the interested reader to the latest SAML document available on the Web. (See Bibliographic Notes.)

Discussion: single sign-on. Why do we need SAML single sign-on? A number of approaches to single sign-on already exist. For example, Passport centralizes authentication in an authentication server, a trusted third party that uses passwords for authentication. The server places and retrieves an encrypted cookie containing authentication information at the user's site and uses the cookie to avoid re-authentication each time the user accesses a new server.

In contrast, SAML does not actually do authentication and hence does not enforce a particular authentication procedure. A server can use an arbitrary procedure and then create an authentication statement that identifies the procedure used. The statement is passed in an assertion directly from one server to another, and the second server can judge from the assertion whether to trust the authentication done by the first. If not, it performs its own authentication. Hence, a trusted third party is not required.

Kerberos is similar to Passport in that it uses a trusted third party and stores tickets—which roughly correspond to encrypted cookies—at user sites. It is an integrated protocol that implements two-way authentication, key distribution, and encryption. SAML does not do any of these things. It simply provides an XML framework within which other protocols can be used to provide authentication.

Finally, SSL does not support single sign-on. If a client has a certificate, it supports client authentication as well as server authentication. However, a server that has authenticated a client cannot transfer that authentication to a different server. This is one of the use cases for which SAML was designed.

BIBLIOGRAPHIC NOTES

Much of the material in this chapter is well covered by [Stallings 1999]. The concept of public-key cryptography was first presented by [Diffie and Hellman 1976], but almost all public-key cryptography systems are based on the RSA algorithm [Rivest et al. 1978]. [Schneier 1995] does a good job of describing the mathematics underlying the RSA algorithm and of many other cryptographic algorithms and protocols. Like public-key cryptography, the concept of digital signatures was introduced in [Diffie and Hellman 1976], but, again, most digital-signature systems are based on the RSA algorithm [Rivest et al. 1978] or on other algorithms developed specifically for signatures and not appropriate for encryption. The Kerberos system is discussed in [Steiner et al. 1988; Neuman and Ts'o 1994] and forms the basis of security as provided in DCE [Hu 1995].

Descriptions of the SET and SSL protocols can be found at appropriate sites on the Web, which at publication time were [Netscape 2000] for SSL and [VISA 2000] for SET. The NetBill system was introduced in [Cox et al. 1995]. [Chaum et al. 1988] introduced the Ecash protocol and blind signatures. The escrow agent protocol is based on the i-Escrow system available through eBay and described at publication time on its Web site [i-Escrow 2000].

Material on Web security can be found on the Web sites of the standards committees or the companies developing them. For XML Encryption: *http://www.w3*

.org/TR/xmlenc-core/. For XML Signature: *http://www.w3.org/TR/xmldsig-core/*. For WS-Security: *http://www.oasis-open.org/committees/tc_home.php?wg_abbrev=wss*. For SAML: *http://www.oasis-open.org/committees/tc_home.php?wg_abbrev=security*.

EXERCISES

26.1 Discuss some security issues involved in executing transactions over the Internet.

26.2 Anyone who uses a computer keyboard should be able to easily solve the following simple substitution cipher:

Rsvj ;ryyrt od vjsmhrf yp yjr pmr pm oyd tohjy pm yjr lrunpstf/

26.3 Explain why, in general, short encryption keys are less secure than long keys.

26.4 Why is it necessary, in the Kerberos protocol, to include *S* in the message sent from *KS* to *C* (i.e., message *M*2)? Describe an attack that an intruder can use if *S* is not included.

26.5 Explain how timestamps are used to defend against a replay attack in a security protocol.

26.6 Explain how nonces are used to increase security when encrypting messages that are short or that include fields for which the plaintext might be known to an intruder.

26.7 In a system using public-key cryptography, site *B* wants to fool *C* by impersonating *A*. *B* waits until *A* requests to communicate with *B*. *A* does this by sending an "I want to communicate" message to *B*, stating its name (*A*) and encrypted with *B*'s public key. Then *B* springs the trap. It sends an "I want to communicate" message to *C* claiming it is *A* and encrypted with *C*'s public key. To ensure that it is actually communicating with *A*, *C* replies (to *B*) with a message obtained by encrypting a large random number, *N*, with *A*'s public key. If *C* gets a response containing $N + 1$ encrypted with *C*'s public key, it would like to conclude that the responder is *A* because only *A* could have decrypted *C*'s message. *C* gets such a response. However, this conclusion is wrong because the response comes from *B*. Explain how this could have happened. (*Hint:* The protocol can be corrected if the encrypted text of each message includes the name of the sender.)

26.8 Suppose an intruder obtains a copy of a merchant's certificate.

a. Explain why the intruder cannot simply use that certificate and pretend he is the merchant.

b. Explain why the intruder cannot replace the merchant's public key with his own in the certificate.

26.9 Suppose that you use the SSL protocol and connect to a merchant site, *M*. The site sends you *M*'s certificate. When the SSL protocol completes, how can you be sure that the new session key can be known only to *M* (perhaps an intruder has sent you a copy of *M*'s certificate)? Can you be sure that you are connected to *M*?

26.10 Using your local Internet Browser

a. Describe how you can tell when you are connected to a site that is using the SSL protocol.

b. Suppose you are connected to a site that is using the SSL protocol. Describe how you can determine the name of the CA that supplied the certificate used by that site.
c. Determine how many bits are in the keys that your browser uses for SSL encryption.

26.11 Suppose that you obtained a certificate of your own. Explain how you could use that certificate to deal with situations in which an intruder might steal your credit card number.

26.12 Suppose that an intruder puts a virus on your computer that alters your browser. Describe two different ways that the intruder could then impersonate some server site *S* that you might attempt to communicate with—even though you use the SSL protocol—and obtain your credit card number.

26.13 A merchant using the SSL protocol (without SET) might implement a credit card transaction as follows: The customer purchases an item, and the merchant asks him to send his credit card information encrypted using the session key established with the SSL protocol. When the merchant receives that information, she initiates a separate transaction with the credit card company to have the purchase approved. When that transaction commits, the merchant commits the transaction with the customer.

Explain the similarities and differences of this protocol to SET.

26.14 Assume that the merchant in the SET protocol is dishonest. Explain why he cannot cheat the customer.

26.15 Explain why a trusted third party is used in the certified delivery protocol.

26.16 Describe a restart procedure that the merchant's computer can use to deal with crashes during the SET protocol.

26.17 Explain why MD_2 in the SET protocol (Section 26.11) must be a part of the dual signature.

26.18 Explain why a forger could not simply submit an arbitrary random number as a token in the electronic cash protocol.

26.19 Assume that, in the anonymous electronic cash protocol, the bank is honest but the customer and the merchant might not be.

a. After receiving the tokens from the bank, the customer later claims that she never received them. Explain what the bank should then do and why it is correct.
b. After receiving the message containing the purchase order and the tokens from the customer, the merchant claims never to have received the message. Explain what the customer should do and why.

26.20 Describe the methods used in each of the following protocols to prevent a replay attack:

a. Kerberos authentication
b. SET
c. Electronic cash

Bibliography

Abiteboul, S., Buneman, P., and Suciu, D. (2000). *Data on the Web*. Morgan Kaufmann, San Francisco.

Abiteboul, S., Hull, R., and Vianu, V. (1995). *Foundations of Databases*. Addison-Wesley, Boston, MA.

Abiteboul, S., and Kanellakis, P. (1998). Object identity as a query language primitive. *Journal of the ACM* **45**(5): 798–842.

Abiteboul, S., Quass, D., McHugh, J., Widom, J., and Wiener, J. (1997). The Lorel query language for semistructured data. *International Journal on Digital Libraries* **1**(1): 68–88.

Adam, N., Atluri, V., and Huang, W. (1998). Modeling and analysis of workflows using Petri nets. *Journal of Intelligent Information Systems* **10**(2): 131–158.

Agrawal, D., Bernstein, A., Gupta, P., and Sengupta, S. (1987). Distributed optimistic concurrency control with reduced rollback. *Distributed Computing* **2**(1): 45–59.

Agrawal, R., Imielinski, T., and Swami, A. (1993). Database mining: A performance perspective. *IEEE Transactions on Knowledge and Data Engineering* **5**(6): 914–925.

Agrawal, S., Agrawal, R., Deshpande, P., Gupta, A., Naughton, J., Ramakrishnan, R., and Sarawagi, S. (1996). On the computation of multidimensional aggregates. *Proceedings of the International Conference on Very Large Data Bases (VLDB)*, Mombai, India, 506–521.

Aho, A., and Ullman, J. (1979). Universality of data retrieval languages. *ACM Symposium on Principles of Programming Languages (POPL)*, 110–120.

Alagic, S. (1999). Type-checking OQL queries in the ODMG type systems. *ACM Transactions on Database Systems* **24**(3): 319–360.

Alonso, G., Agrawal, D., Abbadi, A. E., Kamath, M., Günthör, R., and Mohan, C. (1996). Advanced transaction models in workflow contexts. *Proceedings of the International Conference on Data Engineering (ICDE)*, New Orleans, LA, 574–581.

Alonso, G., Agrawal, D., Abbadi, A. E., and Mohan., C. (1997). Functionality and limitations of current workflow management systems. *IEEE-Expert, Special Issue on Cooperative Information Systems* **1**(9).

Andrade, J. M., Carges, M. T., Dwyer, T. J., and Felts, S. D. (1996). *The TUXEDO System, Software for Constructing and Managing Distributed Business Applications*. Addison-Wesley, Boston, MA.

Apt, K., Blair, H., and Walker, A. (1988). Towards a theory of declarative knowledge. In *Foundations of Deductive Databases and Logic Programming*, ed. J. Minker. Morgan Kaufmann, San Francisco, 89–148.

Arisawa, H., Moriya, K., and Miura, T. (1983). Operations and the properties of non-first-normal-form relational databases. *Proceedings of the International Conference on Very Large Data Bases (VLDB)*, Florence, 197–204.

Armstrong, W. (1974). Dependency structures of database relations. *IFIP Congress*, Stockholm, 580–583.

Astrahan, M., Blasgen, M., Chamberlin, D., Eswaran, K., Gray, J., Griffiths, P., King, W., Lorie, R., McJones, P., Mehl, J., Putzolu, G., Traiger, I., and Watson, V. (1976). System R: A relational approach to database management. *ACM Transactions on Database Systems* **1**(2): 97–137.

Astrahan, M., Blasgen, M., Gray, J., King, W., Lindsay, B., Lorie, R., Mehl, J., Price, T., Selinger, P., Schkolnick, M., Traiger, D. S. I., and Yost, R. (1981). A history and evaluation of System R. *Communications of the ACM* **24**(10): 632–646.

Attie, P., Singh, M., Emerson, E., Sheth, A., and Rusinkiewicz, M. (1996). Scheduling workflows by enforcing intertask dependencies. *Distributed Systems Engineering Journal* **3**(4): 222–238.

Attie, P., Singh, M., Sheth, A., and Rusinkiewicz, M. (1993). Specifying and enforcing intertask dependencies. *Proceedings of the International Conference on Very Large Data Bases (VLDB)*, Dublin, 134–145.

Atzeni, P., and Antonellis, V. D. (1993). *Relational Database Theory*. Benjamin-Cummings, San Francisco.

Avron, A., and Hirshfeld, J. (1994). Query evaluation, relative safety, and domain independence in first-order databases. *Methods of Logic in Computer Science* **1**: 261–278.

Bancilhon, F., Delobel, C., and Kanellakis, P., eds. (1990). *Building an Object-Oriented Database System: The Story of 02*. Morgan Kaufmann, San Francisco.

Bancilhon, F., and Spyratos, N. (1981). Update semantics of relational views. *ACM Transactions on Database Systems* **6**(4): 557–575.

Batini, C., Ceri, S., and Navathe, S. (1992). *Database Design: An Entity-Relationship Approach*. Benjamin-Cummings, San Francisco.

Bayer, R., and McCreight, E. (1972). Organization and maintenance of large ordered indices. *Acta Informatica* **1**(3): 173–189.

Beeri, C., and Bernstein, P. (1979). Computational problems related to the design of normal form relational schemes. *ACM Transactions on Database Systems* **4**(1): 30–59.

Beeri, C., Bernstein, P., and Goodman, N. (1978). A sophisticate's introduction to database normalization theory. *Proceedings of the International Conference on Very Large Data Bases (VLDB)*, San Mateo, CA, 113–124.

Beeri, C., Bernstein, P., and Goodman, N. (1989). A model for concurrency in nested transaction systems. *Journal of the ACM* **36**(2): 230–269.

Beeri, C., Bernstein, P., Goodman, N., Lai, M.-Y., and Shasha, D. (1983). A concurrency control theory for nested transactions. *Proceedings of the 2nd ACM Symposium on Principles of Distributed Computing*, Montreal, Canada, 45–62.

Beeri, C., Fagin, R., and Howard, J. (1977). A complete axiomatization for functional and multivalued dependencies in database relations. *Proceedings of the ACM SIGMOD International Conference on Management of Data*, Toronto, Canada, 47–61.

Beeri, C., and Kifer, M. (1986a). Elimination of intersection anomalies from database schemes. *Journal of the ACM* **33**(3): 423–450.

Beeri, C., and Kifer, M. (1986b). An integrated approach to logical design of relational database schemes. *ACM Transactions on Database Systems* **11**(2): 134–158.

Beeri, C., and Kifer, M. (1987). A theory of intersection anomalies in relational database schemes. *Journal of the ACM* **34**(3): 544–577.

Beeri, C., Mendelson, A., Sagiv, Y., and Ullman, J. (1981). Equivalence of relational database schemes. *SIAM Journal of Computing* **10**(2): 352–370.

Bell, D., and Grimson, J. (1992). *Distributed Database Systems*. Addison-Wesley, Boston, MA.

Berenson, H., Bernstein, P., Gray, J., Melton, J., O'Neil, E., and O'Neil, P. (1995). A critique of ANSI SQL isolation levels. *Proceedings of the ACM SIGMOD International Conference on Management of Data*, San Jose, CA, 1–10.

Berg, C., and Virginia, C. (2000). *Advanced Java 2 Development for Enterprise Applications*, 2nd ed. Prentice Hall, Englewood Cliffs, NJ.

Bernstein, A. J., Gerstl, D., Leung, W.-H., and Lewis, P. M. (1998). Design and performance of an assertional concurrency control system. *Proceedings of the International Conference on Data Engineering* (ICDE), Orlando, FL, 436–445.

Bernstein, A. J., Gerstl, D., and Lewis, P. (1999). Concurrency control for step decomposed transactions. *Information Systems* **24**(8): 673–698.

Bernstein, A. J., Gerstl, D., Lewis, P., and Lu, S. (1999). Using transaction semantics to increase performance. *International Workshop on High Performance Transaction Systems*, Pacific Grove, CA, 26–29.

Bernstein, A. J., and Lewis, P. M. (1996). High-performance transaction systems using transaction semantics. *Distributed and Parallel Databases* **4**(1).

Bernstein, A. J., Lewis, P., and Lu, S. (2000). Semantic conditions for correctness at different isolation levels. *Proceedings of the International Conference on Data Engineering*, San Diego, CA, 507–566.

Bernstein, P. (1976). Synthesizing third normal form from functional dependencies. *ACM Transactions on Database Systems* **1**(4): 277–298.

Bernstein, P., and Chiu, D. (1981). Using semi-joins to solve relational queries. *Journal of the ACM* **28**(1): 28–40.

Bernstein, P., and Goodman, N. (1983). Multiversion concurrency control—Theory and algorithms. *ACM Transactions on Database Systems* **8**(4): 465–483.

Bernstein, P., Goodman, N., Wong, E., Reeve, C., and Rothnie, J. (1981). Query processing in a system for distributed databases (SDD-1). *ACM Transactions on Database Systems* **6**(4): 602–625.

Bernstein, P., Hadzilacos, V., and Goodman, N. (1987). *Concurrency Control and Recovery in Database Systems*. Addison-Wesley, Boston, MA.

Bernstein, P., and Newcomer, E. (1997). *Principles of Transaction Processing*. Morgan Kaufmann, San Francisco.

Birrell, A., and Nelson, B. (1984). Implementing remote procedure calls. *ACM Transactions on Computer Systems* **2**(1): 39–59.

Biskup, J., Menzel, R., and Polle, T. (1996). Transforming an entity-relationship schema into object-oriented database schemas. In *Advances in Databases and Information Systems, Workshops in Computing*, eds. J. Eder and L. Kalinichenko. Springer-Verlag, Moscow, Russia, 109–136.

Biskup, J., Menzel, R., Polle, T., and Sagiv, Y. (1996). Decomposition of relationships through pivoting. *Proceedings of the 15th International Conference on Conceptual Modeling*. In vol. 1157 of *Lecture Notes in Computer Science*. Springer-Verlag, Heidelberg, Germany, 28–41.

Biskup, J., and Polle, T. (2000a). *Constraints in Object-Oriented Databases* (manuscript).

Biskup, J., and Polle, T. (2000b). Decomposition of database classes under path functional dependencies and onto constraints. *Proceedings of the Foundations of Information and Knowledge-Base Systems*. In vol. 1762 of *Lecture Notes in Computer Science*. Springer-Verlag, Heidelberg, Germany, 31–49.

Blaha, M., and Premerlani, W. (1998). *Object-Oriented Modeling and Design for Database Applications*. Prentice Hall, Englewood Cliffs, NJ.

Blakeley, J., and Martin, N. (1990). Join index, materialized view, and hybrid-hash join: A performance analysis. *Proceedings of the International Conference on Data Engineering (ICDE)*, Los Angeles, 256–263.

Blasgen, M., and Eswaran, K. (1977). Storage access in relational databases. *IBM Systems Journal* **16**(4): 363–378.

Bonner, A. (1999). Workflow, transactions, and datalog. *ACM SIGACT-SIGMOD-SIGART Symposium on Principles of Database Systems (PODS)*, Philadelphia, PA, 294–305.

Booch, G. (1994). *Object-oriented Analysis and Design with Applications*. Addison-Wesley, Boston, MA.

Booch, G., Rumbaugh, J., and Jacobson, I. (1999). *The Unified Modeling Language User Guide*. Addison-Wesley, Boston, MA.

Bourret, R. (2000). Namespace myths exploded. *http://www.xml.com/pub/a/2000/03/08/namespaces/index.html*.

Bradley, N. (2000a). *The XML Companion*. Addison-Wesley, Boston, MA.

Bradley, N. (2000b). *The XSL Companion*. Addison-Wesley, Boston, MA.

Bray, T., Hollander, D., and Layman A. (1999). Namespaces in XML. *http://www.w3.org/TR/1999/REC-xml-names-19990114/*.

Breiman, L.,Freidman, J. J., Olshen, R. A., and Stone, C. L. (1984). *Classification and Regression Trees Technical Report*. Wadsworth International, Monterey, CA.

Breitbart, Y., Garcia-Molina, H., and Silberschatz, A. (1992). Overview of multidatabase transaction management. *VLDB Journal* **1**(2): 181–240.

Bukhres, O., and Kueshn, E., eds. (1995). *Distributed and Parallel Databases—An International Journal*, Special Issue on Software Support for Workflow Management.

Buneman, P., Davidson, S., Hillebrand, G., and Suciu, D. (1996). A query language and optimization techniques for unstructured data. *Proceedings of the ACM SIGMOD International Conference on Management of Data*, Montreal, Canada, 505–516.

Cattell, R. (1994). *Object Database Management* (rev. ed.). Addison-Wesley, Boston, MA.

Cattell, R., and Barry, D., eds. (2000). *The Object Database Standard: ODMG 3.0*. Morgan Kaufmann, San Francisco.

Ceri, S., Negri, M., and Pelagatti, G. (1982). Horizontal partitioning in database design. *Proceedings of the International ACM SIGMOD Conference on Management of Data*, Orlando, FL, 128–136.

Ceri, S., and Pelagatti, G. (1984). *Distributed Databases: Principles and Systems*. McGraw-Hill, New York.

Chamberlin, D., Robie, J., and Florescu, D. (2000). Quilt: An XML query language for heterogeneous data sources. In *Lecture Notes in Computer Science*. Springer-Verlag, Heidelberg, Germany. *http://www.almaden.ibm.com/cs/people/chamberlin/quilt_lncs.pdf*.

Chang, S., and Cheng, W. (1980). A methodology for structured database decomposition. *IEEE-TSE* **6**(2): 205–218.

Chaudhuri, S. (1998). An overview of query optimization in relational databases. *ACM SIGACT-SIGMOD-SIGART Symposium on Principles of Database Systems (PODS)*, Seattle, 34–43.

Chaudhuri, S., and Dayal, U. (1997). An overview of data warehousing and OLAP technology. *SIGMOD Record* **26**(1): 65–74.

Chaudhuri, S., Krishnamurthy, R., Potamianos, S., and Shim, K. (1995). Optimizing queries with materialized views. *Proceedings of the International Conference on Data Engineering (ICDE)*, Taipei, Taiwan, 190–200.

Chaum, D., Fiat, A., and Noar, M. (1988). Untraceable electronic cash. *Advances in Cryptology: Crypto'88 Proceedings*. In *Lecture Notes in Computer Science*. Springer-Verlag, Heidelberg, Germany, 319–327.

Chen, I.-M., Hull, R., and McLeod, D. (1995). An execution model for limited ambiguity rules and its application to derived data update. *ACM Transactions on Database Systems* **20**(4): 365–413.

Chen, P. (1976). The entity-relationship model—Towards a unified view of data. *ACM Transactions on Database Systems* **1**(1): 9–36.

Chrysanthis, P., and Ramaritham, K. (1990). ACTA: A framework for specifying and reasoning about transaction structure and behavior. *Proceedings of the ACM SIGMOD International Conference on Management of Data*, Atlantic City, NJ, 194–205.

CLIPS (2003). CLIPS: A tool for building expert systems. *http://www.ghg.net/clips/CLIPS.html*.

Cochrane, R., Pirahesh, H., and Mattos, N. (1996). Integrating triggers and declarative constraints in SQL database systems. *Proceedings of the International Conference on Very Large Data Bases (VLDB)*, Bombay, India, 567–578.

Codd, E. (1970). A relational model of data for large shared data banks. *Communications of the ACM* **13**(6): 377–387.

Codd, E. (1972). Relational completeness of data base sublanguages. *Data Base Systems*. In vol. 6 of *Courant Computer Science Symposia Series*. Prentice Hall, Englewood Cliffs, NJ.

Codd, E. (1979). Extending the database relational model to capture more meaning. *ACM Transactions on Database Systems* **4**(4): 397–434.

Codd, E. (1990). *The Relational Model for Database Management, Version 2*. Addison-Wesley, Boston, MA.

Codd, E. (1995). Twelve rules for on-line analytic processing. *Computerworld*, April 13.

Copeland, G., and Maier, D. (1984). Making Smalltalk a database system. *Proceedings of the ACM SIGMOD International Conference on Management of Data*, Boston, 316–325.

Cosmadakis, S., and Papadimitriou, C. (1983). Updates of relational views. *ACM SIGACT-SIGMOD-SIGART Symposium on Principles of Database Systems (PODS)*, Atlanta, GA, 317–331.

Cox, B., Tygar, J., and Sirbu, M. (1995). Netbill security and transaction protocol. *Proceedings of the 1st USENIX Workshop on Electronic Commerce*, New York, vol. 1.

Date, C. (1992). Relational calculus as an aid to effective query formulation. In *Relational Database Writings*, eds. C. Date and H. Darwen. Addison-Wesley, Boston, MA.

Date, C., and Darwen, H. (1997). *A Guide to the SQL Standard*, 4th ed. Addison-Wesley, Boston, MA.

Davulcu, H., Kifer, M., Ramakrishnan, C. R., and Ramakrishnan, I. V. (1998). Logic based modeling and analysis of workflows. *ACM SIGACT-SIGMOD-SIGART Symposium on Principles of Database Systems (PODS)*, Seattle, WA, 25–33.

Deutsch, A., Fernandez, M., Florescu, D., Levy, A., and Suciu, D. (1998). XML-QL: A query language for XML. *Technical Report W3C. http://www.w3.org/TR/1998/NOTE-xml-ql-19980819/*.

Deutsch, A., Fernandez, M., and Suciu, D. (1999). Storing semistructured data with `stored`. *Proceedings of the ACM SIGMOD International Conference on Management of Data*, Philadelphia, PA, 431–442.

DeWitt, D., Katz, R., Olken, F., Shapiro, L., Stonebraker, M., and Wood, D. (1984). Implementation techniques for main-memory database systems. *Proceedings of the ACM SIGMOD International Conference on Management of Data*, Boston, 1–8.

Diffie, W., and Hellman, M. (1976). New directions in cryptography. *IEEE Transactions on Information Theory* **IT-22**(6): 644–654.

Di Paola, R. A. (1969). The recursive unsolvability of the decision problem for the class of definite formulas. *Journal of ACM* **16**(2): 324–327.

DOM (2000). Document Object Model (DOM). *http://www.w3.org/DOM/*.

Eisenberg, A. (1996). New standard for stored procedures in SQL. *SIGMOD Record* **25**(4): 81–88.

Elmagarmid, A., ed. (1992). *Database Transaction Models for Advanced Applications*. Morgan Kaufmann, San Francisco.

Elmagarmid, A., Leu, Y., Litwin, W., and Rusinkiewicz, M. (1990). A multidatabase transaction model for interbase. *Proceedings of the International Conference on Very Large Data Bases (VLDB)*, Brisbane, Australia, 507–518.

Eswaran, K., Gray, J., Lorie, R., and Traiger, I. (1976). The notions of consistency and predicate locks in a database system. *Communications of the ACM* **19**(11): 624–633.

Fagin, R. (1977). Multivalued dependencies and a new normal form for relational databases. *ACM Transactions on Database Systems* **2**(3): 262–278.

Fagin, R., Nievergelt, J., Pippenger, N., and Strong, H. (1979). Extendible hashing—A fast access method for dynamic files. *ACM Transactions on Database Systems* **4**(3): 315–344.

Fayyad, U., Piatetsky-Shapiro, G., Smyth, P., and Uthurusamy, R., eds. (1996). *Advances in Knowledge Discovery and Data Mining*. The MIT Press, Cambridge, MA.

Fekete, A., Liarokapis, D., O'Neil, E., O'Neil, P., and Shasha, D. (2000). Making snapshot isolation serializable. *http://www.cs.umb.edu/ poneil/publist.html*.

Fekete, A., Lynch, N., Merritt, M., and Weihl, W. (1989). Commutativity-based locking for nested transactions. *Technical Report MIT/LCS/TM-370.b*. Laboratory for Computer Science, Massachusetts Institute of Technology, Cambridge, MA.

Flach, P. A., and Savnik, I. (1999). Database dependency discovery: A machine learning approach. *AI Communications* **12**(3): 139–160.

Florescu, D., Deutsch, A., Levy, A., Suciu, D., and Fernandez, M. (1999). A query language for XML. *Proceedings of the Eighth International World Wide Web Conference*, Toronto, Canada.

Fowler, M., and Scott, K. (2003). *UML Distilled,* 3rd ed. Addison-Wesley, Boston, MA.

Frohn, J., Lausen, G., and Uphoff, H. (1994). Access to objects by path expressions and rules. *Proceedings of the International Conference on Very Large Data Bases (VLDB)*, Santiago, Chile, 273–284.

Fuh, Y.-C., Dessloch, S., Chen, W., Mattos, N., Tran, B., Lindsay, B., DeMichiel, L., Rielau, S., and Mannhaupt, D. (1999). Implementation of SQL3 structured types with inheritance and value substitutability. *Proceedings of the International Conference on Very Large Data Bases (VLDB)*, Edinburgh, Scotland, 565–574.

Garcia-Molina, H., Gawlick, D., Klien, J., Kleissner, K., and Salem, K. (1991). Modeling long-running activities as nested Sagas. *Quarterly Bulletin of the IEEE Computer Society Technical Committee on Data Engineering* **14**(1): 14–18.

Garcia-Molina, H., and Salem, K. (1987). Sagas. *Proceedings of the ACM SIGMOD International Conference on Management of Data*, San Francisco, 249–259.

Garcia-Molina, H., Ullman, J., and Widom, J. (2000). *Database System Implementation*, Prentice Hall, Englewood Cliffs, NJ.

Georgakopoulos, D., Hornick, M., Krychniak, P., and Manola, F. (1994). Specification and management of extended transactions in a programmable transaction environment. *Proceedings of the International Conference on Data Engineering (ICDE)*, Houston, 462–473.

Georgakopoulos, D., Hornick, M., and Sheth, A. (1995). An overview of workflow management: From process modeling to infrastructure for automation. *Journal on Distributed and Parallel Database Systems* **3**(2): 119–153.

Gifford, D. (1979). Weighted voting for replicated data. *Proceedings of the ACM 7th Symposium on Operating Systems Principles*, Pacific Grove, CA, 150–162.

Gogola, M., Herzig, R., Conrad, S., Denker, G., and Vlachantonis, N. (1993). Integrating the E-R approach in an object-oriented environment. *Proceedings of the 12th International Conference on the Entity-Relationship Approach*, Arlington, TX, 376–389.

Gottlob, G., Paolini, P., and Zicari, R. (1988). Properties and update semantics of consistent views. *ACM Transactions on Database Systems* **13**(4): 486–524.

Graefe, G. (1993). Query evaluation techniques for large databases. *ACM Computing Surveys* **25**(2): 73–170.

Gray, J. (1978). Notes on database operating systems. *Operating Systems: An Advanced Course*. In vol. 60 of *Lecture Notes in Computer Science*, Springer-Verlag, Berlin, 393–481.

Gray, J. (1981). The transaction concept: Virtues and limitations. *Proceedings of the International Conference on Very Large Data Bases (VLDB)*, Cannes, 144–154.

Gray, J., Chaudhuri, S., Bosworth, A., Layman, A., Reichart, D., and Venkatrao, M. (1997). Data cube: A relational aggregation operator generalizing group-by, cross-tab, and sub-totals. In *Data Mining and Knowledge Discovery*, eds. Fayyad et al., The MIT Press, Cambridge, MA.

Gray, J., Laurie, R., Putzolu, G., and Traiger, I. (1976). Granularity of locks and degrees of consistency in a shared database. *Modeling in Data Base Management Systems*, Elsevier, North Holland.

Gray, J., McJones, P., and Blasgen, M. (1981). The recovery manager of the System R database manager. *Computer Surveys* **13**(2): 223–242.

Gray, J., and Reuter, A. (1993). *Transaction Processing: Concepts and Techniques*. Morgan Kaufmann, San Francisco.

Griffiths-Selinger, P., and Adiba, M. (1980). Access path selection in distributed database management systems. *Proceedings of the International Conference on Data Bases*, Aberdeen, Scotland, 204–215.

Griffiths-Selinger, P., Astrahan, M., Chamberlin, D., Lorie, R., and Price, T. (1979). Access path selection in a relational database system. *Proceedings of the ACM SIGMOD International Conference on Management of Data*, Boston, 23–34.

Gulutzan, P., and Pelzer, T. (1999). *SQL-99 Complete, Really*. R&D Books, Gilroy, CA.

Gupta, A., and Mumick, I. (1995). Maintenance of materialized views: Problems, techniques, and applications. *Data Engineering Bulletin* **18**(2): 3–18.

Gupta, A., Mumick, I., and Ross, K. (1995). Adapting materialized views after redefinitions. *Proceedings of the ACM SIGMOD International Conference on Management of Data*, San Jose, CA, 211–222.

Gupta, A., Mumick, I., and Subrahmanian, V. (1993). Maintaining views incrementally. *Proceedings of the ACM SIGMOD International Conference on Management of Data*, Washington, DC, 157–166.

Hadzilacos, V. (1983). An operational model for database system reliability. *SIGACT-SIGMOD-SIGART Symposium on Principles of Database Systems (PODS)*, Atlanta, 244–256.

Hadzilacos, V., and Papadimitriou, C. (1985). Algorithmic aspects of multiversion concurrency control. *SIGACT-SIGMOD-SIGART Symposium on Principles of Database Systems (PODS)*, Portland, OR, 96–104.

Haerder, T., and Reuter, A. (1983). Principles of transaction-oriented database recovery. *ACM Computing Surveys* **15**(4): 287–317.

Hall, M. (2000). *Core Servlets and JavaServer Pages (JSP)*. Prentice Hall, Englewood Cliffs, NJ.

Han, J., and Kamber, M. (2001). *Data Mining: Concepts and Techniques*. Morgan Kaufmann, San Francisco.

Hand, D. J., Mannila, H., and Smyth, P. (2001) *Principles of Data Mining*. MIT Press, Cambridge, MA.

Harinarayan, V., Rajaraman, A., and Ullman, J. (1996). Implementing data cubes efficiently. *Proceedings of the ACM SIGMOD International Conference on Management of Data*, Montreal, Canada, 205–216.

Harrison, G. (2001) *Oracle SQL: High-Performance Tuning,* 2nd ed. Prentice Hall, Upper Saddle River, NJ.

Henning, M., and Vinoski, S. (1999). *Advanced CORBA Programming with C++*. Addison-Wesley, Boston, MA.

Hsu, M. (1995). Letter from the special issues editor. *Quarterly Bulletin of the IEEE Computer Society Technical Committee on Data Engineering,* Special Issue on Workflow Systems. **18**(1): 2–3.

Hu, W. (1995). *DCE Security Programming*. O'Reilly and Associates, Sebastopol, CA.

Huhtala, Y., Karkkainen, J., Porkka, P., and Toivonen, H. (1999). TANE: An efficient algorithm for discovery of functional and approximate dependencies. *The Computer Journal* **42**(2): 100–111.

Hull, R., Llirbat, F., Simon, E., Su, J., Dong, G., Kumar, B., and Zhou, G. (1999). Declarative workflows that support easy modification and dynamic browsing. *Proceedings of the ACM International Joint Conference on Work Activities Coordination and Collaboration (WACC),* San Francisco, 69–78.

Hunter, J., and Crawford, W. (1998). *Java Servlet Programming*. O'Reilly and Associates, Sebastopol, CA.

IBM (1991). System network architecture (SNA) logical unit 6.2 (LU6.2): Transaction programmer's reference manual for LU6.2. *Technical Report GC30-3084*. IBM, White Plains, NY.

i-Escrow (2000). i-Escrow. *http://www.iescrow.com.*

ILOG (2003). ILOG JRules. *http://www.ilog.com/products/jrules/*.

Ioannidis, Y. (1996). Query optimization. *ACM Computing Surveys* **28**(1): 121–123.

Ito, M., and Weddell, G. (1994). Implication problems for functional constraints on databases supporting complex objects. *Journal of Computer and System Sciences* **49**(3): 726–768.

Jacobson, I., Christerson, M., Jonsson, P., and Övergaard, G. (1992). *Object-Oriented Software Engineering: A Use Case Driven Approach*. Addison-Wesley, Boston, MA.

Jaeschke, G., and Schek, H.-J. (1982). Remarks on the algebra of non-first-normal-form-relations. *ACM SIGACT-SIGMOD-SIGART Symposium on Principles of Database Systems (PODS),* Los Angeles, 124–138.

Jajodia, S., and Kerschberg, L., eds. (1997). *Advanced Transaction Models and Architectures,* Kluwer Academic Publishers, Dordrecht, Netherlands.

Jess (2003). The Rule Engine for the Java Platform. *http://herzberg.ca.sandia.gov/jess/*.

Kamath, M., and Ramamritham, K. (1996). Correctness issues in workflow management. *Distributed Systems Engineering Journal* 3(4): 213–221.

Kanellakis, P. (1990). Elements of relational database theory. In *Handbook of Theoretical Computer Science*, vol. B, *Formal Models and Semantics*, ed. J. V. Leeuwen. Elsevier, Amsterdam, 1073–1156.

Kantola, M., Mannila, H., Raäihä, K.-J., and Siirtola, H. (1992). Discovering functional and inclusion dependencies in relational databases. *International Journal of Intelligent Systems* **7**(7): 591–607.

Kay, M. (2000). *XSLT Programmer's Reference*. Wrox Press, Paris.

Keller, A. (1985). Algorithms for translating view updates to database updates for views involving selections, projections, and joins. *ACM SIGACT-SIGMOD-SIGART Symposium on Principles of Database Systems (PODS)*, Portland, OR, 154–163.

Khoshafian, S., and Buckiewicz, M. (1995). *Introduction to Groupware, Workflow, and Workgroup Computing*. John Wiley & Sons, New York.

Kifer, M. (1988). On safety, domain independence, and capturability of database queries. *Proceedings of the 3rd International Conference on Data and Knowledge Bases*, Jerusalem, Israel, 405–415.

Kifer, M., Bernstein, A. J., and Lewis, P. M. (2004). *Databases and Transaction Processing: An Application-Oriented Approach*. Addison-Wesley, Boston, MA.

Kifer, M., Kim, W., and Sagiv, Y. (1992). Querying object-oriented databases. *Proceedings of the ACM SIGMOD International Conference on Management of Data*, Washington, DC, 393–402.

Kifer, M., and Lausen, G. (1989). F-Logic: A higher-order language for reasoning about objects, inheritance and schema. *Proceedings of the ACM SIGMOD International Conference on Management of Data*, Portland, OR, 134–146.

Kifer, M., Lausen, G., and Wu, J. (1995). Logical foundations of object-oriented and frame-based languages. *Journal of the ACM* **42**(4): 741–843.

Kitsuregawa, M., Tanaka, H., and Moto-oka, T. (1983). Application of hash to database machine and its architecture. *New Generation Computing* **1**(1): 66–74.

Knuth, D. (1973). *The Art of Computer Programming: Vol III, Sorting and Searching,* 1st ed., Addison-Wesley, Boston, MA.

Knuth, D. (1998). *The Art of Computer Programming: Vol III, Sorting and Searching*, 3rd ed., Addison-Wesley, Boston, MA.

Korth, H., Levy, E., and Silberschatz, A. (1990). A formal approach to recovery by compensating transactions. *Proceedings of the International Conference on Very Large Data Bases*, Brisbane, Australia, 95–106.

Kung, H., and Robinson, J. (1981). On optimistic methods for concurrency control. *ACM Transactions on Database Systems* **6**(2): 213–226.

Lacroix, M., and Pirotte, A. (1977). Domain-oriented relational languages. *Proceedings of the International Conference on Very Large Data Bases (VLDB)*, Tokyo, Japan, 370–378.

Lampson, B., Paul, M., and Seigert, H. (1981). *Distributed Systems: Architecture and Implementation (An Advanced Course)*. Springer-Verlag, Heidelberg, Germany.

Lampson, B., and Sturgis, H. (1979). Crash recovery in a distributed data storage system. *Technical Report*. Xerox Palo Alto Research Center, Palo Alto, CA.

Langerak, R. (1990). View updates in relational databases with an independent scheme. *ACM Transactions on Database Systems* **15**(1): 40–66.

Larson, P. (1981). Analysis of index sequential files with overflow chaining. *ACM Transactions on Database Systems* **6**(4): 671–680.

Litwin, W. (1980). Linear hashing: A new tool for file and table addressing. *Proceedings of the International Conference on Very Large Databases (VLDB)*, Montreal, Canada, 212–223.

Lynch, N., Merritt, M., Weihl, W., and Fekete, A. (1994). *Atomic Transactions*. Morgan Kaufmann, San Francisco.

Maier, D. (1983). *The Theory of Relational Databases*. Computer Science Press. Rockville, MD. (Available through Books on Demand: *http://www.umi.com/hp/Support/BOD/index.html*.)

Makinouchi, A. (1977). A consideration on normal form of not-necessarily-normalized relations in the relational data model. *Proceedings of the International Conference on Very Large Data Bases (VLDB)*, Tokyo, Japan, 447–453.

Mannila, H., and Raäihä, K.-J. (1992). *The Design of Relational Databases*. Addison-Wesley, Workingham, UK.

Mannila, H., and Raäihä, K.-J. (1994). Algorithms for inferring functional dependencies. *Knowledge Engineering* **12**(1): 83–99.

Maslak, B., Showalter, J., and Szczygielski, T. (1991). Coordinated resource recovery in VM/ESA. *IBM Systems Journal* **30**(1): 72–89.

Masunaga, Y. (1984). A relational database view update translation mechanism. *Proceedings of the International Conference on Very Large Data Bases (VLDB)*, Singapore, 309–320.

Melton, J. (1997). *Understanding SQL's Persistent Stored Modules*. Morgan Kaufmann, San Francisco.

Melton, J., Eisenberg, A., and Cattell, R. (2000). *Understanding SQL and Java Together: A Guide to SQLJ, JDBC, and Related Technologies*. Morgan Kaufmann, San Francisco.

Melton, J., and Simon, A. (1992). *Understanding the New SQL: A Complete Guide*. Morgan Kaufmann, San Francisco.

Microsoft (1997). *Microsoft ODBC 3.0 Software Development Kit and Programmer's Reference*. Microsoft Press, Seattle.

Minker, J. (1997). *Logic and databases: past, present, and future*. *AI Magazine* **18**(3): 21-47.

Missaoui, R., Gagnon, J.-M., and Godin, R. (1995). Mapping an extended entity-relationship schema into a schema of complex objects. *Proceedings of the 14th International Conference on Object-Oriented and Entity Relationship Modeling*, Brisbane, Australia, 205–215.

Mohan, C., Haderle, D., Lindsay, B., Pirahesh, H., and Schwartz, P. (1992). Aries: A transaction recovery method supporting fine-granularity locking and partial rollbacks using write-ahead logging. *ACM Transactions on Database Systems* **17**(1): 94–162.

Mohan, C., Lindsay, B., and Obermarck, R. (1986). Transaction management in the R* distributed database management system. *ACM Transactions on Database Systems* **11**(4): 378–396.

Mohania, M., Konomi, S., and Kambayashi, Y. (1997). Incremental maintenance of materialized views. *Database and Expert Systems Applications (DEXA)*. Springer-Verlag, Heidelberg, Germany.

Mok, W., Ng, Y.-K., and Embley, D. (1996). A normal form for precisely characterizing redundancy in nested relations. *ACM Transactions on Database Systems* **21**(1): 77–106.

Moss, J. (1985). *Nested Transactions: An Approach to Reliable Computing*. The MIT Press, Cambridge, MA.

Netscape (2000). SSL-3 specifications. *http://home.netscape.com/eng/ssl3/index.html*.

Neuman, B. C., and Ts'o, T. (1994). Kerberos: An authentication service for computer networks. *IEEE Communications* **32**(9): 33–38.

Novikoff, A. (1962). On Convergence Proofs for Perceptrons. *Proceedings of the Symposium on Mathematical Theory of Automata*, New York, 615–621.

O'Neil, P. (1987). Model 204: Architecture and performance. *Proceedings of the International Workshop on High Performance Transaction Systems*. In vol. 359 of *Lecture Notes in Computer Science*. Springer-Verlag, Heidelberg, Germany, 40–59.

O'Neil, P., and Graefe, G. (1995). Multi-table joins through bitmapped join indices. *SIGMOD Record* **24**(3): 8–11.

O'Neil, P., and Quass, D. (1997). Improved query performance with variant indexes. *Proceedings of the ACM SIGMOD International Conference on Management of Data*, Tucson, AZ, 38–49.

Orfali, R., and Harkey, D. (1998). *Client/Server Programing with Java and CORBA*. John Wiley, New York.

Orlowska, M., Rajapakse, J., and ter Hofstede, A. (1996). Verification problems in conceptual workflow specifications. *Proceedings of the International Conference on Conceptual Modeling*. In vol. 1157 of *Lecture Notes in Computer Science*, Springer-Verlag, Heidelberg, Germany.

Ozsoyoglu, Z., and Yuan, L.-Y. (1985). A normal form for nested relations. *ACM SIGACT-SIGMOD-SIGART Symposium on Principles of Database Systems (PODS)*, Portland, OR, 251–260.

Ozsu, M., and Valduriez, P. (1999). *Principles of Distributed Database Systems* (2nd ed.) Prentice Hall, Englewood Cliffs, NJ.

Papadimitriou, C. (1986). *The Theory of Concurrency Control*. Computer Science Press, Rockville, MD.

Paton, N., Diaz, O., Williams, M., Campin, J., Dinn, A., and Jaime, A. (1993). Dimensions of active behavior. *Proceedings of the Workshop on Rules in Database Systems*, Heidelberg, Germany, 40–57.

Peterson, L., and Davies, B. (2000). *Computer Networks: A Systems Approach*, 2nd ed. Morgan Kaufmann, San Francisco.

Peterson, W. (1957). Addressing for random access storage. *IBM Journal of Research and Development* **1**(2): 130–146.

Pope, A. (1998). *The CORBA Reference Guide*. Addison-Wesley, Boston, MA.

PostgreSQL. (2000). PostgreSQL. *http://www.postgresql.org*.

Pressman, R. (2002). *Software Engineering: A Practitioner's Approach*, 5th ed. McGraw-Hill, New York.

Przymusinski, T. C. (1988). *On The Declarative Semantics of Deductive Databases and Logic Programs*. In *Foundations of Deductive Databases and Logic Programming*, ed. J. Minker. Morgan Kaufmann, Los Altos, CA, 193–216.

Quinlan, J. (1986). Induction of Decision Trees. *Machine Learning* **1**(1): 81–106.

Ram, S. (1995). Deriving functional dependencies from the entity-relationship model. *Communications of the ACM* **38**(9): 95–107.

Ramakrishnan, R., Srivastava, D., Sudarshan, S., and Seshadri, P. (1994). The CORAL deductive database system. *VLDB Journal* **3**(2): 161–210.

Ramakrishnan, R., and Ullman, J. (1995). A survey of deductive databases. *Journal of Logic Programming* **23**(2): 125–149.

Ray, E. (2001). *Learning XML*. O'Reilly and Associates, Sebastopol, CA.

Reese, G. (2000). *Database Programming with JDBC and Java*. O'Reilly and Associates, Sebastopol, CA.

Reuter, A., and Wachter, H. (1991). The contract model. *Quarterly Bulletin of the IEEE Computer Society Technical Commmttee on Data Engineering* **14**(1): 39–43.

Rivest, R., Shamir, A., and Adelman, L. (1978). On digital signatures and public-key cryptosystems. *Communications of the ACM* **21**(2): 120–126.

Robie, J., Chamberlin, D., and Florescu, D. (2000). Quilt: An XML query language. *XML Europe*. *http://www.almaden.ibm.com/cs/people/chamberlin/robie_XML_Europe.pdf*.

Robie, J., Lapp, J., and Schach, D. (1998). XML query language (XQL). *Proceedings of the Query Languages Workshop*, Boston. *http://www.w3.org/TandS/QL/QL98/pp/xql.html*.

Rosenberry, W., Kenney, D., and Fisher, G. (1992). *Understanding DCE*. O'Reilly and Associates, Sebastopol, CA.

Rosenkrantz, D., Stearns, R., and Lewis, P. (1978). System level concurrency control for distributed database systems. *ACM Transactions on Database Systems* **3**(2): 178–198.

Rosenkrantz, D., Stearns, R., and Lewis, P. (1984). Consistency and serializability in concurrent database systems. *SIAM Journal of Computing* **13**(3): 505–530.

Ross, K., and Srivastava, D. (1997). Fast computation of sparse datacubes. *Proceedings of the International Conference on Very Large Data Bases (VLDB)*, Athens, Greece, 116–125.

Roth, M., and Korth, H. (1987). The design of non-1nf relational databases into nested normal form. *Proceedings of the ACM SIGMOD International Conference on Management of Data*, San Francisco, 143–159.

Rumbaugh, J., Blaha, M., Premerlani, W., Eddy, F., and Lorenzen, W. (1991). *Object-Oriented Modeling and Design*. Prentice Hall, Englewood Cliffs, NJ.

Rusinkiewicz, M., and Sheth, A. (1994). Specification and execution of transactional workflows. In *Modern Database Systems: The Object Model, Interoperability, and Beyond*, ed. W. Kim. ACM Press, New York, 592–620.

Sagonas, K., Swift, T., and Warren, D. (1994). XSB as an efficient deductive database engine. *Proceedings of the ACM SIGMOD International Conference on Management of Data*, Minneapolis, MN, 442–453.

Savnik, I., and Flach, P. (1993). Bottom-up induction of functional dependencies from relations. *Proceedings of the AAAI Knowledge Discovery in Databases Workshop (KDD)*, Ljubliana, Slovenija, 174–185.

Schach, S. (1999). *Software Engineering*, 5th ed. Aksen Associates, Homewood, IL.

Schek, H.-J., Weikum, G., and Ye, H. (1993). Towards a unified theory of concurrency control and recovery. *ACM SIGACT-SIGMOD-SIGART Conference on Principles of Database Systems (PODS)*, Washington, DC, 300–311.

Schneier, B. (1995). *Applied Cryptography: Protocols, Algorithms, and Source Code in C*. John Wiley, New York.

Sciore, E. (1983). Improving database schemes by adding attributes. *ACM SIGACT-SIGMOD-SIGART Symposium on Principles of Database Systems (PODS)*, New York, 379–383.

Sebesta, R. (2001). *Programming the World Wide Web*. Addison-Wesley, Boston, MA.

SGML (1986). Information processing—Text and office systems—Standard Generalized Markup Language (SGML). *ISO Standard 8879*. International Standards Organization, Geneva, Switzerland.

Shasha, D., and Bonnet, P. (2003). *Database Tuning: Principles, Experiments, and Troubleshooting Techniques*. Morgan Kaufman, San Francisco.

Shipman, D. (1981). The functional data model and the data language DAPLEX. *ACM Transactions on Database Systems* **6**(1): 140–173.

Shoshani, A., and Bernstein, A. J. (1969). Synchronization in a parallel accessed data base. *Communications of the ACM* **12**(11).

Signore, R., Creamer, J., and Stegman, M. (1995). *The ODBC Solution: Open Database Connectivity in Distributed Environments*. McGraw-Hill, New York.

Singh, M. (1996). Synthesizing distributed constrained events from transactional workflow specifications. *Proceedings of the International Conference on Data Engineering*, New Orleans, LA, 616–623.

Skeen, D. (1981). Nonblocking commit protocols. *Proceedings of the ACM SIGMOD International Conference on Management of Data*, Ann Arbor, MI, 133–142.

Spaccapietra, S., ed. (1987). *Entity-Relationship Approach: Ten Years of Experience in Information Modeling, Proceedings of the Entity-Relationship Conference*, Elsevier, North Holland.

SQL (1992). ANSI X3.135-1992, *American National Standard for Information Systems—Database Language—SQL*. American National Standards Institute, Washington, DC.

SQLJ (2000). SQLJ. *http://www.sqlj.org*.

Stallings, W. (1999). *Cryptography and Network Security: Principles and Practice*, 2nd ed. Prentice Hall, Englewood Cliffs, NJ.

Stallman, R. (2000). GNU coding standards. *http://www.gnu.org/prep/standards.html*.

Standish (2000). Chaos. *http://standishgroup.com/visitor/chaos.htm*.

Staudt, M., and Jarke, M. (1996). Incremental maintenance of externally materialized views. *Proceedings of the International Conference on Very Large Data Bases (VLDB)*, Bombay, India, 75–86.

Steiner, J. G., Neuman, B. C., and Schiller, J. I. (1988). Kerberos: An authentication service for open network systems. *USENIX Conference Proceedings*, Dallas, TX, 191–202.

Stonebraker, M. (1979). Concurrency control and consistency of multiple copies of data in INGRES. *IEEE Transactions on Software Engineering* **5**(3): 188–194.

Stonebraker, M. (1986). *The INGRES Papers: Anatomy of a Relational Database System*. Addison-Wesley, Boston, MA.

Stonebreaker, M., and Kemnitz, G. (1991). The POSTGRES next generation database management system. *Communications of the ACM* **10**(34): 78–92.

Summerville, I. (2000). *Software Engineering*, 5th ed. Addison-Wesley, Boston, MA.

Sun (2000). JDBC data access API. *http://java.sun.com/products/jdbc/*.

Sybase (1999). Sybase adaptive server enterprise performance and tuning guide. *http://sybooks.sybase.com/onlinebooks/group-as/asg1200e/aseperf*.

Teorey, T. (1999). *Database Modeling and Design: The E-R Approach*. Morgan Kaufmann, San Francisco.

Thalheim, B. (1992). *Fundamentals of Entity-Relationship Modeling*. Springer-Verlag, Berlin.

Thomas, R. (1979). A majority consensus approach to concurrency control for multiple copy databases. *ACM Transactions on Database Systems* **4**(2): 180–209.

Topor, R., and Sonenberg, E. (1988). On domain independent databases. In *Foundations of Deductive Databases and Logic Programming*, ed. J. Minker. Morgan Kaufmann, Los Altos, CA, 217–240.

Transarc (1996). Encina monitor programmer's guide and reference. *Technical Report ENC-D5008-06*. Transarc Corporation, Pittsburgh, PA.

Ullman, J. (1982). *Priniciples of Database Systems*. Computer Science Press, Rockville, MD.

Ullman, J. (1988). *Principles of Database and Knowledge-Base Systems,* volumes 1 and 2. Computer Science Press, Rockville, MD.

Vaghani, J., Ramamohanarao, K., Kemp, D., Somogyi, Z., Stuckey, P., Leask, T., and Harland, J. (1994). The Aditi deductive database system. *The VLDB Journal* **3**(2): 245–288.

Valduriez, P. (1987). Join indices. *ACM Transactions on Database Systems* **12**(2): 218–246.

Van Gelder, A. (1992). The Well-Founded Semantics of Aggregation. *ACM SIGACT-SIGMOD-SIGART Symposium on Principles of Database Systems (PODS)*, San Diego, CA, 127–138.

Van Gelder, A., Ross, K. A., and Schlipf, J. S. (1991). The well-founded semantics for general logic programs. *Journal of the ACM* **38**(3): 620–650.

Van Gelder, A., and Topor, R. (1991). Safety and translation of relational calculus queries. *ACM Transactions on Database Systems* **16**(2): 235–278.

Venkatrao, M., and Pizzo, M. (1995). SQL/CLI—A new binding style for SQL. *SIGMOD Record* **24**(4): 72–77.

Vincent, M. (1999). Semantic foundations of 4nf in relational database design. *Acta Informatica* **36**(3): 173–213.

Vincent, M., and Srinivasan, B. (1993). Redundancy and the justification for fourth normal form in relational databases. *International Journal of Foundations of Computer Science* **4**(4): 355–365.

VISA (2000). SET specifications. *http://www.visa.com/nt/ecomm/set/intro.html*.

Weddell, G. (1992). Reasoning about functional dependencies generalized for semantic data models. *ACM Transactions on Database Systems* **17**(1): 32–64.

Weihl, W. (1984). *Specification and Implementation of Atomic Data Types*. Ph.D. thesis, Department of Computer Science, Massachusetts Institute of Technology, Cambridge, MA.

Weihl, W. (1988). Commutativity-based concurrency control for abstract data types. *IEEE Transactions on Computers* **37**(12): 1488–1505.

Weikum, G. (1991). Principles and realization strategies of multilevel transaction management. *ACM Transactions on Database Systems* **16**(1): 132–180.

Weikum, G., and Schek, H. (1991). Multi-level transactions and open nested transactions. *Quarterly Bulletin of the IEEE Computer Society Technical Committee on Data Engineering* **14**(1): 55–66.

Whalen, G., Garcia, M., DeLuca, S., and Thompson, D. (2001). *Microsoft SQL Server 2000 Performance Tuning Technical Reference*. Microsoft Press, Redmond, WA.

Widom, J., and Ceri, S. (1996). *Active Database Systems*. Morgan Kaufmann, San Francisco.

Wodtke, D., and Weikum, G. (1997). A formal foundation for distributed workflow execution based on state charts. *Proceedings of the International Conference on Database Theory (ICDT)*, Delphi, Greece, 230–246.

Wong, E. (1977). Retrieving dispersed data from SDD-1: A system for distributed databases. *Proceedings of the 2nd International Berkeley Workshop on Distributed Data Management and Data Networks*, Berkeley, CA, 217–235.

Wong, E., and Youssefi, K. (1976). Decomposition—A strategy for query processing. *ACM Transactions on Database Systems* **1**(3): 223–241.

Worah, D., and Sheth, A. (1997). Transactions in transactional workflows. In *Advanced Transaction Models and Architectures*, eds. S. Jajodia and L. Kerschberg. Kluwer Academic Publishers, Dordrecht, Netherlands, 3–45.

Workflow Management Coalition (2000). WfMC standards. *http://www.aiim.org/wfmc/standards/docs.htm*.

XML (1998). Extensible Markup Language (XML) 1.0. *http://www.w3.org/TR/REC-xml*.

XMLSchema (2000a). XML Schema, part 0: Primer. *http://www.w3.org/TR/xmlschema-0/*.

XMLSchema (2000b). XML Schema, parts 1 and 2. *http://www.w3.org/XML/Schema*.

X/Open (1996a). *X/Open CAE Specification Structured Transaction Definition Language (STDL)*. X/Open Co., Ltd., London.

X/Open (1996b). *X/Open Guide Distributed Transaction Processing: Reference Model, Version 3*. X/Open Co., Ltd., London.

XPath (2003). XML Path Language (XPath), version 2.0. *http://www.w3.org/TR/xpath/*.

XPointer (2000). XML pointer language (XPointer), version 1.0. *http://www.w3.org/TR/xptr/*.

XQuery (2004). XQuery 1.0: An XML query language. Eds. S. Boag, D. Chamberlin, M. F. Fenrandez, D. Florescu, T. Robie, and T. Simeon. *http://www.w3.org/TR/xquery*.

XSB (2003). The XSB system. *http://xsb.sourceforge.net/*.

XSLT (1999). XSL transformations (XSLT), version 1.0. *http://www.w3.org/TR/xslt/*.

Zaniolo, C. (1983). The database language GEM. *Proceedings of the ACM SIGMOD International Conference on Management of Data*, San Jose, CA, 423–434.

Zaniolo, C., and Melkanoff, M. (1981). On the design of relational database schemata. *ACM Transactions on Database Systems* **6**(1): 1–47.

Zhao, B., and Joseph, A. (2000). XSet: A lightweight XML search engine for Internet applications. *http://www.cs.berkeley.edu/~ravenben/xset/*.

Zhao, Y., Deshpande, P., Naughton, J., and Shukla, A. (1998). Simultaneous optimization and evaluation of multiple dimensional queries. *Proceedings of the ACM SIGMOD International Conference on Management of Data*, Seattle, WA, 271–282.

Zloof, M. (1975). Query by example. *NCC*. AFIPS Press, Montvale, NJ.

Index

- | in XPath, 636
- -- in SQL, 152
- ≠ in indexing, 448
- _ in SQL, 154
- {} in XQuery, 652
- # in SQLJ, 303
- $ in OQL, 560
- % in SQL, 154
- > and < in XPath, 635
- * in SQL, 152
- + in Java and JDBC, 297
- .NET, 984, 985
- : to specify
  - host variable in embedded SQL, 270
  - host variable in SQLJ, 305
- ? parameter
  - in dynamic SQL, 288
  - in JDBC, 297
  - in ODBC, 309

- abort. *See* compensation; rollback
  - definition of, 22, 767
  - of distributed transaction, 783
  - in embedded SQL, 274
  - implemented with log, 922
  - in JDBC, 302
  - of multilevel transaction, 798
  - of nested transaction, 786
  - in ODBC, 313
  - in peer-to-peer communication, 1021
  - presumed. *See* two-phase commit protocol
  - reasons for, 767, 920
  - of transactions
    - with abstract operations, 842
    - with real-world actions, 802
    - with recoverable queues, 800
    - with savepoints, 781
  - in two-phase commit, 1010
  - undo operation, 845
  - in workflow, 807
- aborting message. *See* two-phase commit protocol
- abort message. *See* two-phase commit protocol
  - in linear commit protocol, 1022
- abort record, 922. *See* two-phase commit protocol
- ABSOLUTE row selector, 280
- absolute XPath expression, 629
- abstract data type, 531
- Abstract Object Data Model, 523
- abstract operations
  - backward commutativity, 841
  - commutativity, 839
  - compensation for, 842
  - concurrency control for, 841
  - definition of, 839
  - forward commutativity, 841, 864
  - object methods as, 839
- abstract process. *See* BPEL
- acceptance test, C-10
- access control in SQL, 63, 176
- access control list, 1149
- Access DBMS, 474, 484
- access error in SQL, 301
- access path. *See* query execution plan
  - binary search as, 393
  - cost, 324
  - covering relational operator, 393
  - definition of, 321, 393
  - file scan as, 393
  - index as, 346, 393
  - and locking, 890
  - in query execution plan, 267
  - selectivity of, 394
- ACID Properties
  - definition of, 24, 773
  - of distributed transactions, A-23, 783, 1007
  - has negative effect on performance, 773
  - related to correctness, 25, 773
  - of a transaction processing system, 25, 773
- ACL. *See* access control list
- activation function in neural nets, 745
- active database, 251
- actor in use case, B-2, B-3
- AFTER triggers, 258
- after image, A-21, 929
- agent in workflow, 804, 808
- agglomerative hierarchical algorithm, 755
- aggregate function
  - in SQL, 164

aggregate function *(continued)*
in SQL/XML, 674
aggregation. *See* SQL
in OLAP, 717
in SQL/XML, 674
in UML, 104
algorithm. *See* protocol
ALL operator, 162
ALLOCATE DESCRIPTOR statement, 290
alpha test, C-10
ALTER TABLE statement, 60
AND condition in workflow, 804
anomaly
deletion, 194
dirty read, A-7, 824, 876
dirty write, 826, 876
insertion, 194
lost update, A-7, 24, 771, 880, 907
nonrepeatable read, A-7, 876
phantom, A-9, 871, 876
serializable, 910
at SNAPSHOT isolation, 908
update, 194
write skew, A-14, 910
anonymous type in XML Schema, 616
ANY operator, 162
API
for authentication, 1151
JDBC as, 294
ODBC as, 307
for peer-to-peer communication, 975
for transactions, 966
X/Open Standard, 966, 1020
applet, 983
appliance, 982
application programmer, 8
application server
definition of, 953
multithreaded, 954
routing, 955
servlet as, 984
Web, 985
as workflow controller, 954
application services, 947
archiving
of database, 937
of log, 934
arity of a relation, 35
Armstrong's Axioms
augmentation, 201
definition of, 202
reflexivity, 201
soundness and completeness, 202
transitivity, 202
assign construct in BPEL, 1091
association class in UML, 97
association in UML, 97
association rule, 731
associations in data mining, 731
asymmetric cryptography. *See* cryptography
definition of, 1139
used in certificates, 1153
used in digital cash, 1166
used in digital signatures, 1141
used in the SSL protocol, 1154
asynchronous-update replication. *See* replication
atomic commit protocol, 963. *See* two-phase commit protocol
definition of, 967
atomic conditions
in DRC, 476
in TRC, 464
atomicity
complicated by concurrent execution, 772
of data, 36
definition of, 21, 767
global, 783, 965, 1007
goods, 1162
implementation of, A-18, 920
maintained by compensation, 842
money, 1166, 1170
provided by TP monitor, 963
for real-world events with recoverable queue, 802
statement-level, A-11, 836, 855, 877, 881, 896
ATOMIC in SQL/PSM, 283
atomic termination. *See* two-phase commit protocol
attribute
assertion, 1183
closure, 204
domain of, 37, 71
of entity, 71
naming problem, 136
in ODMG, 550
of relation, 35, 37
for relationship, 73
set valued, 71, 515
augmentation rule, 201
authenticated RPC, 1151
authentication
assertion, 1183
definition of, 1135
on the Internet, 1154
SAML, 1180
in a session, 957
using asymmetric cryptography, 1154
using Kerberos, 1144
using a password, 1144
using SSL, 1154
using symmetric cryptography, 1144
authentication server, 1148, 1155
authenticator, 1146
authorization
assertion, 1183
definition of, 1135, 1149
SAML, 1180
in a session, 957
in SQL, 63
authorization Id in SQL, 63
autocommit
in JDBC, 301
in ODBC, 312
protocol, 1027
availability, A-22
as applied to durability, 768
increased by replication, 1028
as system requirement, 6

AVG function, 164

B2B services
security for, 1171
B2B systems
back-end systems for, 983
definition of, 982
issues in providing, 1044
publishing and discovering with BPEL, 1110
specifying with BPEL, 1080
transactions for, 1123
back-end systems, 1108
architectures for, 983, 985
for B2B systems, 983
definition of, 983, 1046
back propagation algorithm for neural nets, 749
backward commutativity, 841
balanced tree. *See* B^+ tree
definition of, 354
base relation
in Datalog, 497
basic type, 526
BCNF. *See* normal form, Boyce-Codd
beans. *See* enterprise Java beans
enterprise Java, 986
message-driven, 987
BEFORE triggers, 257
before image, A-18, 922, 964
BEGIN DECLARE SECTION, 270
begin dump record, 940
begin record, A-19, 922
best-matching template in XSLT, 644
beta test, C-10
binary large object. *See* blob
binary search
as access path, 393
of sorted file, 333
binding. *See* SOAP; WSDL
bindingTemplate in UDDI, 1113
bitmap index
definition of, 375
for join, 376
for OLAP applications, 728
for star join, 404
bit stream cipher, 1138
black box test, C-7
blinding function, 1169
blind signature, 1168
blind write, 867
blob, 519
block cipher, 1137
blocking. *See* two-phase commit protocol
bound variable, 464
Boyce-Codd normal form. *See* normal form
BPEL
abstract process, 1081
restrictions on data access, 1088, 1094
assign activity, 1091
business process, 1080
callback, 1083, 1086, 1092
compensation, 1099
correlation set, 1106
createInstance, 1105
default handlers, 1104
executable process, 1081, 1094
fault handler, 1099
flow construct, 1092
implements workflows, 1080, 1095
invoke, 1082
links, 1095
multiple requests, 1105
opaque assignment, 1082, 1091
partner, 1086
pick construct, 1092
projection of a process, 1109
property, 1082, 1088, 1094
receive, 1082
reply, 1082
role, 1086
scope, 1099
sequence construct, 1090
switch construct, 1093
and transactions, 1123
variable, 1090
for Web services, 1046
browser, 1047, 1049
as presentation server, 984
in SSL security protocol, 1154
B tree, 354
B^+ tree
as access path, 393
as balanced tree, 354
concurrent access, 898
crabbing, 898
definition of, 353
deletions in, 357
fillfactor in, 358
insertions in, 355
lock coupling, 898
locking
in granular locking protocol, 891
protocol, 896
as main index, 353
range search on, 353
as secondary index, 353
sibling, 358
sibling pointer, 353
splitting pages, 355
bucket
definition of, 364
level in extendable hashing, 370
splitting
in extendable hashing, 368
in linear hashing, 371
bulk insertion. *See* insertion
businessEntity in UDDI, 1112
business process. *See* BPEL
Business Process Execution Language. *See* BPEL
business rules
implemented by transaction, 947, 953
implemented with workflow, 809
businessService in UDDI, 1113
business-to-business systems. *See* B2B systems

C2B systems, 1047
architectures for, 983
definition of, 982

C2B systems *(continued)*
  implemented with Web Application Servers, 985
C4.5 algorithm, 740
CA. *See* certification authority
cache, A-21
  buffer pools, 435
  clean page, 434
  complicates rollback and commitment, 921
  controller, 328
  definition of, 434
  dirty page, 434, 926, 928, 1126
  disk, 325, 981
  hit, 325, 435
  least-recently-used algorithm, 434
  and logging, 925
  miss, 435
  most-recently-used algorithm, 435
  page replacement algorithm, 434
  prefetching, 329, 436
  procedure, 434
  write-back, 329
  write-gathering, 329
  and WS-AtomicTransaction, 1126
`CallableStatement` class in JDBC, 302
callback, 1083
  in atomic commit protocol, 973
  in BPEL, 1086, 1092
  definition of, 973
  in event handler, 978
call-level interface
  definition of, 268
  JDBC as, 294
  in object databases, 547
  ODBC as, 307
  in SQL:1999, 268
CALL statement, 285
candidate key. *See* primary key
  compared with search key, 337
  definition of, 42
  in foreign-key constraint, 45
  specifying in SQL, 47
  in XML, 622
canonicalization. *See* XML Signature
capture in replicated systems, 1034
CARDINALITY
  function in SQL:2003, 542
cardinality constraint
  in E-R model, 76
cardinality of a relation, 35
Cartesian product operator, 135
cascaded aborts, 826
catalog functions in ODBC, 312
catalog in SQL, 62
`catch` clause in Java, 301
CDATA, 595
centralized database, 951
certificate
  electronic commerce, 1153
  WS-Security, 1176
certification authority, 1153
certified delivery, 1163
CGI scripts, 984
`chain()`, 790
chained transactions
  alternative semantics of, 790
  and cursors, 789
  and database context, 789
  implementation of, 849
  increased performance with, 789
  semantics of, 788
  in SQL, 274
CHECK clause, 49
checkpoint
  in deferred-update systems, 936
  fuzzy, 932
  in fuzzy dump, 940
  sharp, 930
checkpoint record, A-19, 923
checksum, 325, 1142
child
  of nested transaction, 785
  in object databases, 549
  in XML, 583
chunk, 326
cipher. *See* cryptography
  bit stream, 1138
  block, 1137
  monoalphabetic, 1137
  polyalphabetic, 1138
  polygram, 1138
  product, 1138
  simple, 1137
  substitution, 1137
  transposition, 1138
ciphertext, 1136
class
  in CODM, 525
  extent of, 525
  in UML, 96
`Class` class in JDBC, 295
class diagram
  in UML, 96
classification hierarchy, 79
classification in data mining, 730, 734, 744
classification rule, 734
CLI. *See* call-level interface
client/server model
  organization of transaction processing system, 950
`close()` method in JDBC, 297
closed-world assumption, 145
clustered index
  B^+ tree as, 353
  definition of, 340
  ISAM index as, 350
  as main index, 340
  range search on, 341
clustering in data mining, 730, 752
cluster in SQL, 63
coding techniques, C-13
CODM
  class in, 525
  domain of type in, 527
  introduction to, 523
  IsA relationship in, 525
  oid in, 524
  subclass in, 525
  subtype in, 526
  type in, 526

value in, 524
cohort. *See* two-phase commit protocol
collection value, 530
column. *See* attribute
in relational table, 14, 35
column-accessor method in SQLJ, 305
comment
in XQuery, 650
comments
in code, C-13
in SQL, 152
in XML, 584
commit
based on commit record, 923
in chained transaction, 788
definition of, 22, 767
of distributed transaction, 783
in embedded SQL, 274
group, 927
in JDBC, 302
of multilevel transaction, 798
of nested transaction, 786
in ODBC, 313
in peer-to-peer communication, 976, 1020
in quorum consensus protocol, 1032
with real-world actions, 802
with recoverable queue, 800
for replicated data, 1031
COMMIT AND CHAIN statement, 274
commit message. *See* two-phase commit protocol
in linear commit protocol, 1022
commit() method in JDBC, 302
commit order
with distributed databases, A-27, 1025
not guaranteed with non-strict two-phase locking, 837
not guaranteed with timestamp concurrency control, 856
with optimistic concurrency control, 862
with strict two-phase locking, A-6, 831
with two-phase commit, A-27, 1025
commit protocol. *See* two-phase commit protocol
in peer-to-peer communication, 976, 1020
commit record, 922. *See* two-phase commit protocol
COMMIT statement, 274
Common Object Request Broker Architecture. *See* CORBA
communication. *See* HTTP; peer-to-peer communication; remote procedure call; SOAP
asynchronous, 987
event, 978
full duplex, 975
half duplex, 975
HTTPS protocol, 1154
session, 957
using recoverable queues, 803
communication protocols, 1047
communication resource manager, 1013
communication services provided by TP monitor, 963
commuting function, 1169
commuting operations
for abstract operations, 839
backward
and compensation, 842
definition of, 841
definition of, 817
forward, 841, 864
on objects, 839, 851
for read and write operations, A-2
compensatable task. *See* workflow
compensation. *See* abort
for abstract operations, 842
with backward commutativity, 842
in BPEL, 1099
and concurrency control, 844
correctly preserves atomicity, 842, 855
definition of, 842
and logical logging, 934
in multilevel transactions, 792, 798, 855
in object databases, 842
related to recoverable schedules, 843
in Sagas, 792
in workflows, 807
compensation log record
and checkpoints, 931
definition of, 931
and dumps, 940
completeness
of Armstrong's axioms, 202
of MVD inference rules, 236
completion record. *See* two-phase commit protocol
composition
in UML, 104
compositor, 609
Conceptual Object Data Model. *See* CODM
conceptual schema, 32, 957
concurrency. *See* enterprise Java beans
bean-managed, 1000
container-managed, 1000
concurrency control. *See* multilevel transaction; multiversion concurrency control; optimistic concurrency control
with abstract operations, 841
and compensating operations, 844
deferred-update, 827
definition of, A-4, 814
design of, 834
for distributed systems, A-26, 1024
dynamic, 838, 856
immediate-update, 827
kill-wait, 866, 1040
in multi-user system, 949

concurrency control *(continued)*
for nested transactions, 850
for object databases, 841
operation semantics in, 817
optimistic, 859
pessimistic, 828
for quorum consensus replication, 1032
Read-Consistency multiversion, 906
Read-Only multiversion, 904
recoverable, 825
static, 838, 856
strict, 826
for synchronous-update replication, 1031
timestamp-ordered, 856
wait-die, 866
wound-wait, 1040
concurrency control services in CORBA, 573
condition handler in SQL/PSM, 283
confidence in an association, 731
configuration management, 9
conflict. *See* commuting operations
for abstract operations, 842
in asynchronous replication, A-29
based on backward commutativity, 842
based on operation semantics, 842
definition of, 817
of lock requests, A-5, 831, 839, 841
for object databases, 842
in predicate locking, 874
for read and write operations, 817
in replica control, 1037
conflict equivalence, 821, 863, 867
conflict table
based on backward commutativity, 842
based on operation semantics, 839
for intention locking, A-16, 888
for two-phase locking, A-5, 831
confounder in cryptography, 1149
`Connection` class in JDBC, 294
connection-oriented protocol. *See* protocol
CONNECT statement, 273
consistency
definition of, 21, 765
destroyed by concurrent execution, 22, 770
mutual, A-28, 1029
in primary copy replication, 1035
preserved by quorum consensus replication, 1031
preserved by synchronous-update replication, 1031
related to correctness, 765
related to integrity constraints, 20, 764
strong mutual, A-28, 1029
produced by synchronous-update replication, 1031
weak mutual, A-28, 1029
achieved using timestamps, 1036
in group replication, 1036
consistency constraint. *See* integrity constraint
constellation schema, 716
constraint. *See* integrity constraint
adding or dropping in SQL, 60
candidate key, 42
domain, 37
foreign-key, 38
inclusion dependency, 45
interrelational, 38
intra-relational, 38
key, 41
primary key, 42
reactive, 56
semantic, 40, 45
in SQL, 47
static, 40
superkey, 42
and triggers, 57
type, 37
container. *See* enterprise Java Beans
context. *See* session
database
with alternate chaining, 791
with recoverable queue, 799
with savepoints, 779
of a session, 957, 975, 986
session key as part of, 1144
and threads, 959
context handle, 959, 968
context object in CORBA, 565
cookie, 959
coordinator. *See* two-phase commit protocol
in digital cash protocol, 1168
in SET protocol, 1160
CORBA, 562
architecture of, 562
concurrency control services in, 573
CORBAservices, 569
dynamic invocation API, 567
general inter-ORB protocol, 568
GIOP, 568
IIOP, 568
implementation repository, 565
interface definition language, 563
interface repository, 564
Internet inter-ORB protocol, 568
language mappings, 564
location transparency in, 562
and middleware, 963
naming services in, 571
object query services in, 571
object reference, 567
object transaction services in, 572
ORB, 564
OTS in, 572

persistent state service in, 569
recoverable objects in, 573
relation to Web services, 1044, 1045
server skeleton in, 565
static method invocation in, 565
transaction objects in, 573
transaction services in, 572
correctness
definition of, 765
for distributed transactions, 1007
with non-SERIALIZABLE isolation levels, 883, 887
with non-serializable schedules, 887
related to
ACID properties, 25, 773, 1007
consistency, 765
integrity constraints, 20, 764
serial execution, A-1, 22, 769, 813
serializable execution, 24, 772, 819, 887
SERIALIZABLE isolation level, 876, 887
correlated nested query, 158, 449
correlation. *See* SOAP
correlation set in BPEL, 1106
correspondences. *See* E-R Model
covering index. *See* index-only queries
covering of relational operators, 393
crabbing, 898
crash. *See* failure
definition of, A-18, 919
rollback for, 922
CREATE ASSERTION statement, 49
CREATE DOMAIN statement, 53
CREATE INDEX statement, 339
createInstance in BPEL, 1105
CREATE RECURSIVE VIEW statement, 490
`create_savepoint()`, 779
CREATE SCHEMA statement, 62
`createStatement()` method in JDBC, 296
CREATE TABLE statement, 46
CREATE TRIGGER statement, 58
CREATE VIEW statement, 59, 174
critical path, C-11
critical section
in database access, 771
validation phase as, 859
cross product operator. *See* Cartesian product operator
cryptography. *See* asymmetric cryptography; cipher; symmetric cryptography
asymmetric, 1139
levels of protection, 1147
model, 1136
one time pad, 1136
principal, 1144
public-key, 1140
secret-key, 1140
SOAP, 1176
symmetric, 1137
XML, 1171
CUBE operator, 722
CURRENT_DATE, 118
current() in XSLT, 647
current node in XPath, 631
cursor
and chaining, 789
dynamic, 310, 884
in dynamic SQL, 293
in embedded SQL, 277
and impedance mismatch, 520
INSENSITIVE, 277
and isolation levels, 880
in JDBC, 297
key_set driven, 310
lost update when using, 880
in ODBC, 309
and savepoints, 922
static, 310
updatable, 279
updating and deleting through, 279, 299
CURSOR STABILITY
definition of, A-13, 880
implementation of, 881
incorrect execution with, 882
customer-to-business systems. *See* C2B systems
cylinder of disk, 322

DAS, 981
data
self-describing, 579
semistructured, 581
data atomicity, 36
database. *See* multidatabase; relational database
active, 251
archive of, 937
context
with recoverable queue, 799
with savepoints, 779
deductive, 488, 490
definition of, 3
design of distributed, 706
distributed, 688
dump. *See* dump
federated. *See* multidatabase
global, A-23, 783
heterogeneous, 688
homogeneous, 688, 691
instance, 38
local, 783
query language
definition of, 127
relational algebra as, 128
relational calculus as, 461
SQL as, 147
schema, 38
version, 903
database administrator, 9
database context, 780, 789
database designer, 8
database management system, 4
database manipulation language, 948
data-centered design, 960
data cleaning, 729
data cube, 725

data definition language. *See* SQL
definition of, 33
of SQL, 46
Data Encryption Standard, 1138
data independence
conceptual, 33
physical, 33
Datalog
query, 497
rule, 497
Datalog*, 496
data manipulation language. *See* SQL
definition of, 34
of SQL, 147
data mining, 11, 247
associations in, 731
C4.5 algorithm, 740
classification in, 730, 734, 744
clustering in, 730, 752
confidence in an association, 731
decision trees in, 734
definition of, 730
dendrogram in, 756
entropy in, 737
hierarchical algorithm in, 755
ID3 algorithm, 737
itemset in, 733
K-means algorithm in, 753
machine learning, 744
neural nets in, 744
predication in, 730, 734, 744
a priori algorithm in, 733
support for an association, 732
training sets in, 734
data model. *See* data definition language; data manipulation language; relational database; storage definition language
conceptual schema, 32, 33
constraints, 33
definition of, 33
external schema, 33
physical schema, 31
view abstraction level, 33
data partitioning. *See* partitioning
data warehouse, 10, 178, 713, 728
DCE, 568, 971, 1151
DDL. *See* data definition language
deadlock
avoidance
by rearranging operations, 902
with timestamps, 833, 866, 1024, 1040
definition of, A-8, 832
detection
with probe chasing, 1024
with timeout, A-8, 833, 1024
with waits_for graph, A-8, 833, 1024
distributed, A-27, 1023
global, A-26, 1007
one-item, 1031
decision support system, 9
decision trees in data mining, 734
declarations in embedded SQL, 270
declarative demarcation. *See* transaction demarcation
declarative language, 127
DECLARE CURSOR statement, 277
deductive database, 488, 490
deferred consideration of triggers, 253
deferred mode for integrity constraints, 56, 285
deferred-update systems
definition of, 827
optimistic concurrency control for, 859
recovery in, 936
for SNAPSHOT isolation, 907
degree of relationship, 75
DELETE statement, 184
deletion anomaly, 194
dendrogram in data mining, 756
denormalization, 245, 444
dense index, 342
dependency
functional, 198
join, 230
multivalued, 231
Dependency Chart, C-11
dependency graph
in Datalog, 507
deployment descriptor. *See* enterprise Java beans
derived partitioning, 694
derived relation
in Datalog, 497
DES. *See* Data Encryption Standard
DESCRIBE INPUT statement, 290
DESCRIBE OUTPUT statement, 290
descriptor area in dynamic SQL, 290
deserialization. *See* SOAP
Design Document
definition of, C-1
format of, C-4
readers, C-1
design review, C-6
diagnostics area, 271
Diagnostics Pack for Oracle, 451
DIAGNOSTICS SIZE, 274
dice in OLAP, 720
digital cash
definition of, 1165
protocol for, 1168
digital signature
based on RSA algorithm, 1141
definition of, 1141
guarantees message integrity, 1141, 1143
guarantees nonrepudiation, 1141, 1143
message digest in, 1142
dimension table, 715
Direct Attached Storage, 981
direct element constructor
in XQuery, 652
direct execution of SQL, 267
directory in extendable hash index, 367
directory server. *See* server
direct transaction processing, 960
dirty page. *See* cache

dirty read
  definition of, A-7
  in non-recoverable schedules, 824
  with READ COMMITTED, 876
dirty write
  definition of, 826
  prevented at each isolation level, 876
DISCONNECT statement, 273
discretization, 740
disjoint-write property
  definition of, 906
  eliminates lost updates, 907
  implementation of, 908
  with SNAPSHOT isolation, 906
disjunctive normal form, 395
disk
  block, 325
  cache, 325
  chunk, 326
  cylinder, 322
  page, 325
  platter, 322
  read/write head, 322
  rotational latency, 323
  sector, 322
  seek time, 323
  striping, 326
  track, 322
  transfer time, 323
Distributed Computing Environment, 971, 1151
distributed database. *See* distributed transaction; multidatabase
  definition of, 688, 951
  distributing the data, 691
  global join in, 698
  with global schema, 689
  heterogeneous, 688, 690
  homogeneous, 688, 690, 691
  integrated, 689
  location transparency in, 691
  partitioning in, 691
  partition transparency in, 695
  query design for multidatabase, 705
  query optimization in, 698
  replication in, 691, 1028
  replication transparency in, 691
  semantic integration of, 690
  semijoin in, 699
  in transaction processing system, 1005
distributed deadlock, 1023
distributed join, 698
distributed system, 951. *See* distributed transaction
distributed transaction, 781, 1044. *See* two-phase commit protocol
  and application server, 953
  architecture of, 955
  atomic commit protocol tree. *See* two-phase commit protocol
  atomic termination of. *See* two-phase commit protocol
  autocommit for, 1027
  cohort. *See* two-phase commit protocol
  coordinator. *See* two-phase commit protocol
  deadlock in, 1023
  definition of, A-23, 781, 1005
  global serialization of, 1024
  linear commit for, 1022
  non-ACID properties, A-26
  one-phase commit for, 1027
  peer-to-peer atomic commit for, 1020
  related to nested transaction, 785
  replication in, 1028
  using embedded SQL, ODBC, and JDBC, 1026
  zero-phase commit for, 1027
division operator
  in relational algebra, 144
  in SQL, 160
DML. *See* data manipulation language
document-centric approach to Web services, 1045
document object model, 627
document type definition, 582, 594
DOM, 627
domain. *See* two-phase commit protocol
  of attribute, 36, 37, 71
  constraint, 37
  definition of, 14
  independence, 486
  specifying in SQL, 48
  of type, 527
  user defined, 37
domain relational calculus, 474
domain variable, 474
done message. *See* two-phase commit protocol
DO-UNDO-REDO, 931
drilling down in OLAP, 718
driver
  in JDBC, 294
  in ODBC, 307
driver manager
  in JDBC, 294
  in ODBC, 307
DriverManager class in JDBC, 294
DROP ASSERTION statement, 61
DROP COLUMN statement, 60
DROP CONSTRAINT statement, 61
DROP DOMAIN statement, 61
DROP INDEX statement, 340
DROP SCHEMA statement, 62
DROP TABLE statement, 61
DROP VIEW statement, 176
DTD, 582, 594
dual signature, 1158
dumb terminals, 949
dump
  of database, A-22, 937
  fuzzy, A-23, 938
  off line, 938
durability
  definition of, 22, 769
  implementation of, A-18, 920

dynamic concurrency control, 838, 856
dynamic constraint, 40
DYNAMIC cursor, 310
dynamic invocation API in CORBA, 567
dynamic parameter, 288
dynamic SQL
  ? parameter in, 288
  cursor in, 293
  definition of, 286
  descriptor area, 290
  prepared statements in, 287
  SQLDA, 290
  stored procedures in, 293
dynaset, 310

eager replication, 1031
early release of locks
  at lower isolation levels, 875
  with manual locking, 836
ECA rule, 251
Ecash protocol, 1166
EJB. *See* enterprise Java beans
  ejbStore, 994
  QL, 995
  Query Language, 995
electronic cash
  definition of, 1165
  protocol for, 1168
Electronic commerce, 1152
element constructor
  computed, 661
embedded SQL
  : in, 270
  abort in, 274
  commit in, 274
  cursor in, 277
  declarations in, 270
  definition of, 147, 268
  does not support two-phase commit, 276, 1026
  host language variables in, 270
  integrity constraints in, 285
  isolation levels in, 274
  in Java, 303
  status processing in, 271
  stored procedures in, 282
  transactions in, 274
empty element. *See* XML
Encina. *See* transaction processing system
encryption. *See* cryptography
  definition of, 1135
  SOAP, 1176
  XML, 1171
end dump record, 938, 940
endpoint
  in WSDL, 1078
entailment
  definition of, 200
  of join dependencies, 231
enterprise Java beans
  abstract interface, 993
  bean-managed demarcation, 998
  concurrency, 1000
  container, 991
  container-managed demarcation, 998
  container-managed relationships, 994
  context, 986
  declarative demarcation, 986. *See* transaction demarcation
  definition of, 986
  deployment descriptor, 989
  EJB Query Language, 995
  entity beans, 986
  home interface, 990
    `create` method, 990
    `findByPrimaryKeymethod`, 990
    `remove` method, 990
  local home interface, 991
  local interface, 990
  message-driven beans, 987
  parameter passing, 990
  persistence, 992, 998
  remote interface, 990
  as reusable components, 1001
  select methods, 997
  session beans, 986
  transaction, 998
entity
  attribute, 71
  definition of, 70
  domain of attribute, 71
  key constraint of, 72
  translation into relational model, 86
  type, 71
entity beans. *See* enterprise Java beans
Entity-Relationship Model. *See* E-R Model
entropy in making decision trees, 737
equality search
  on B^+ trees, 353
  definition of, 333
  on hash indices, 364
  on indexed files, 337
  on sorted files, 333
equi-join operator, 138
equivalent schedule. *See* schedule
E-R Model
  attribute in, 71
  correspondences, 77
  definition of, 70
  entity in, 70
  E-R diagram, 72
  identifying relationship in, 84
  IsA hierarchy in, 90
  and join dependency, 230
  key in, 72
  and object databases, 122
  participation constraint, 81
  relationship attribute, 73
  relationships in, 73
  for Student Registration System, 111
  translation into relational model
    entity, 86
    IsA hierarchy, 90
    participation constraints, 92
    relationships, 88
  weak entity in, 84
error processing. *See* status processing

Error Report Form, C-9
ER/Studio, 123
ERwin, 123
escalation. *See* lock
ESCAPE clause in SQL, 154
escape syntax
 in JDBC, 302
 in ODBC, 313
escrow agent, 1164
event
 broker, 979
 causing a trigger to fire, 58, 251
 as communication mechanism, 977, 978
 handler, 978
 as request by a transaction, 251, 254
event-condition-action rule, 251
exactly once semantics, 974
EXCEPT function in SQL:2003, 542
exception handling in JDBC, 300
exclusive part-of relationship
 in conceptual modeling, 83
EXEC SQL as prefix in embedded SQL, 269
executable process. *See* BPEL
EXECUTE statement, 288
EXECUTE IMMEDIATE statement, 289
`executeQuery()` method in JDBC, 296
`executeUpdate()` method in JDBC, 296
existential quantifier, 464
EXISTS operator in SQL, 159
extendable hash indexing, 367
extensible markup language. *See* XML
extensible stylesheet language, 637. *See* XSLT
extent of class, 525
external actions
 certified delivery, 1162
 and commit order, 832
 electronic cash, 1165
 escrow agent, 1164
 goods atomicity, 1162
 implemented by recoverable queue, 802
external schema, 33
external sorting, 384
EXTRACT, 118

fact table in OLAP, 713
failure. *See* crash
 causing partition, 1006
 in centralized system, 969
 in distributed system, 969, 1006
 kinds of, 919
 media, 920, 937
 in RPC, 970
 in workflow, 807
fairness in concurrency control, 834
fan-out of index, 349
FAP, 1019
fault handler in BPEL, 1099
federated database. *See* multidatabase
FETCH statement, 277, 280
FIFO policy
 in concurrency control, 835
 in recoverable queue, 800
Fifth Normal Form, 235
file scan as access path, 393
file structures, 31
fillfactor
 in B^+ tree, 358
 definition of, 335
 in hash index, 366
 in ISAM index, 352
filter in workflow, 808
find message in UDDI, 1117
FIRST row selector, 280
first-committer-wins
 definition of, 907
 eliminates lost updates, 907
 implementation of, 907
 with READ COMMITTED, 882
 with SNAPSHOT isolation, 907
`flatten` operator, 555
flat transaction, 777
flow construct in BPEL, 1092
flushing buffers, 925, 1126
forced operation
 in deferred-update systems, 936
 to ensure write-ahead in log, 926
 in two-phase commit, 1009
 when committing, 926
 write, 926, 1010
forced write, A-24
force policy for durability, 926
foreign-key
 definition of, 43
 in Java entity beans, 995
 specifying in SQL, 53
 violation of constraint, 56
 in XML, 625
foreign key constraint
 definition of, 38
 and indices, 443
 in translating E-R model, 89
 and triggers, 57
formats and protocols, 1019
`forName()` method in JDBC, 295
forward commutativity, 841
forwarding agent, 802, 960
forward recovery in workflow, 808
fourth normal form. *See* normal form
four-tiered transaction processing system, 984
free variable, 464
frequency analysis, 1138
front-end systems
 definition of, 983
 implemented with WSDL and BPEL, 1046, 1108
full duplex communication, 975
fully inverted index, 340
function
 message digest, 1142
 one-way, 1142
functional dependency
 and Armstrong's axioms, 202
 and Boyce-Codd normal form, 208
 definition of, 198
 and entailment, 200

functional dependency *(continued)*
  as an integrity constraint, 198
  satisfaction of, 198
  and third normal form, 210
  trivial, 201
  and update anomalies, 199
fuzzy checkpoint, 932
fuzzy dump, A-23, 938

Gain Ratio in decision trees, 743
Gantt chart, C-11
GemStone object DBMS, 543
generalization in UML, 101
GET. *See* HTTP
`getConnection` method in JDBC, 296
GET DESCRIPTOR statement, 291
GET DIAGNOSTICS statement, 272
`getMetaData()` method in JDBC, 300
Gini Index in decision trees, 743
glass box test, C-8
global atomicity. *See* atomicity
global database. *See* multidatabase
global deadlock. *See* deadlock
global element in XML Schema
  definition of, 616
  referencing of, 620
global integrity constraint. *See* integrity constraint
global join. *See* join
global schema. *See* schema
global serialization. *See* serializable
global transaction. *See* distributed transaction
goods atomicity
  definition of, 1162
  implementation of, 1162
  trusted third party in, 1162
GRANT statement
  and access control list, 1151
  definition of, 63
granularity of triggers, 254
granular locking in object databases. *See* locking
granular locking in relational databases. *See* locking
green page information in UDDI, 1111
group authorization, 1150
GROUP BY clause, 167, 721
group commit, 927
grouping in SQL, 167
group replication, 1034, 1036
guard in UML state diagram, C-3

half duplex communication, 975
handshake in SET, 1159
handshake in SSL, 1154
hash in cryptography, 1142
hash index
  as access path, 393
  bucket splitting
    in extendable, 368
    in linear, 371
  definition of, 364
  directory in extendable, 367
  does not support range or partial key search, 365
  dynamic, 366
  equality search in, 364
  extendable, 367
  fillfactor in, 366
  linear, 371
  locking, 891
  static, 366
hash-join, 402
HAVING clause, 168
HEAD. *See* HTTP
heap file
  definition of, 329
  efficiency of access, 330
heterogeneous system. *See* distributed database; transaction processing system
heuristic decision, 1026
hierarchical algorithm in data mining, 755
hint. *See* tuning
histograms. *See* tuning
home interface. *See* enterprise Java beans
homogeneous system. *See* distributed database; transaction processing system
horizontal partitioning, 692
host language, 267
host language variables
  in embedded SQL, 270
  in JDBC, 297
  in ODBC, 309
hotspot, 829, 927
HTML, 983
HTTP, 1048
  built on TCP, 1048
  GET, 1049, 1062
  HEAD, 1049
  and HTML forms, 1050
  invoking methods with, 1050
  POST, 1049, 1061
  request message, 1048, 1061
  response message, 1048, 1050, 1061
  SOAPAction, 1049, 1051, 1058
  SOAP binding for, 1061
  and TCP, 1049, 1050
HTTPS protocol, 1154
hypertext transfer protocol. *See* HTTP

ID3 algorithm, 737
ID attribute type in XML, 596
idempotent operations
  in logical logging, 935
  in physical logging, 932
identifying relationship in E-R, 84
IDL
  in CORBA, 563
  definition of, 970
  in ODMG, 547
  relation to WSDL, 1045
  in RPC, 970
  and SOAP, 1053
IDREF, 596
IDREFS, 596
immediate consideration of triggers, 253
immediate mode for integrity constraints, 56, 285

immediate-update concurrency control
definition of, 827
to implement SNAPSHOT isolation, 908
locking in, 834
recovery in, 921
rollback in, 921
impedance mismatch
definition of, 520
and ODMG, 520, 545
and persistent objects, 523
in SQL, 277, 520
and SQL:1999/2003, 520
implementation repository in CORBA, 565
IMPORT SCHEMA
in XQuery, 662
IN operator, 157
inclusion dependency, 45
incremental development, C-15
index
automatic creation of, 339
bitmap, 375, 728
B^+ tree, 353
choosing an, 377
clustered, 340
definition of, 321, 337
dense, 342
entry, 337
fan-out of, 349
hash, 364
integrated, 338
inverted, 340
ISAM, 350
join, 376, 403, 728
leaf entry, 348
leaf level, 349
location mechanism, 347
locking, 891
locking B^+ Tree, 891
locking hash index, 891
locking ISAM, 891
multilevel, 347, 348
partial key search on, 345
and performance, 902
primary, 340
search key of, 337
secondary, 340
separator, 348
separator level, 349
simple example of, 18
sparse, 342
tree, 347
two-level, 348
unclustered, 340
index-only queries, 346, 440
index sequential access method. *See* ISAM index
Information gain in making decision trees, 738
Information_Schema in SQL, 63
inheritance
in object databases, 540
in WSDL, 1079
inner join
in SQL, 173
InquireSoap in UDDI, 1119
Inquiry Interface in UDDI, 1117
INSENSITIVE cursor. *See* cursor
INSERT statement, 182
insertion
anomaly, 194
bulk, 183
inspection period, 1164
instance
of database, 38
of object database, 529
of relation, 35
instance-document, 599
integrated distributed database system, 689
integrated index, 338
integration test, C-7
integrity constraint
checking in decomposed tables, 211
deferred mode in, 56, 285
definition of, 20, 38, 764
dynamic, 40
in embedded SQL, 285
enforced by triggers, 255
in E-R model, 70
foreign-key, 43
functional dependencies as, 198
global, A-23, 783
immediate mode in, 56, 285
interrelational, 38
intra-relational, 38
key, 41
local, A-23, 783
primary key, 42
referential integrity, 43
related to business rules, 20, 764
in the relational model, 37
semantic, 40, 45
static, 40
and triggers, 57
intention lock. *See* lock
intentions list
aborting with, 936
in deferred-update system, 827
in J2EE, 1001
in optimistic concurrency control, 859
in SNAPSHOT isolation, 907
interface
in WSDL, 1078
interface definition language. *See* IDL
interface definition in ODMG, 547
intermediary. *See* SOAP
Internet
authentication on, 1154
certified delivery protocol, 1162
electronic cash protocol, 1165
goods atomicity protocol, 1162
secure communication over, 1153
SET protocol, 1158
SSL protocol, 1153
transaction processing on, 982
INTERSECT function in SQL:2003, 542
intersection anomaly, 240
intersection operator, 133
inverted index, 340
invoke in BPEL, 1082
ISAM index
definition of, 350
deletions from, 351

ISAM index *(continued)*
insertions in, 352
locking, 891
searching, 351
IsA relationship
in CODM, 525
in E-R model, 79, 90
and limitations of SQL, 518
in WSDL, 1079
IS A SET
predicate in SQL:2003, 542
IS lock, A-15, 888
isolation
definition of, 24, 772
related to serializable schedules, A-2
related to serial schedules, 24, 772
statement-level, A-11, 836, 855, 877, 881, 896
isolation levels
concurrent execution at multiple levels, 878
CURSOR STABILITY. *See* CURSOR STABILITY
definition of, A-11, 875
in embedded SQL, 274
examples of correct behavior with, 883
examples of incorrect behavior with, 879
in JDBC, 301
locking implementations of, A-11, 877
in ODBC, 312
OPTIMISTIC READ COMMITTED. *See* OPTIMISTIC READ COMMITTED
READ COMMITTED. *See* READ COMMITTED
READ UNCOMMITTED. *See* READ UNCOMMITTED
REPEATABLE READ. *See* REPEATABLE READ
SERIALIZABLE. *See* SERIALIZABLE
SNAPSHOT. *See* SNAPSHOT; SNAPSHOT isolation
IS VALID ACCORDING TO SCHEMA predicate in SQL/XML, 671, 678
itemset, 733
iterator
in CORBA, 572
in ODMG, 561
in SQLJ, 305
IX lock, A-15, 888

J2EE, 985. *See* enterprise Java beans; Java 2 Enterprise Edition
Java. *See* enterprise Java beans
applets in, 983
J2EE, 985
JMS, 987
servlet in, 983
Java 2 Enterprise Edition, 985. *See* enterprise Java beans
Java binding
in ODMG, 560
placeholder in, 560
Java Data Objects Specification, 520, 546
Java Message Service, 987
Java Transaction API, 302, 998
Java Transaction Service. *See* JTS
JDBC
+ concatenation symbol in, 297
? parameters in, 297
abort in, 302
autocommit in, 301
`CallableStatement` class, 302
called by SQLJ, 303
`Class` class, 295
`close()` method, 297
commit() method, 302
`Connection` class, 294
`createStatement()` method, 296
cursor in, 297
description of, 294
does not support two-phase commit, 302
driver in, 294
`DriverManager` class, 294
driver manager in, 294
escape syntax in, 302
exception handling in, 300
`executeQuery()` method, 296
`executeUpdate()` method, 296
`forName()` method, 295
forward-only result set, 299
`getConnection()` method, 296
`getMetaData()` method, 300
isolation levels in, 301
and middleware, 963
`PreparedStatement` class, 297
prepared statements in, 297
`prepareStatement()` method, 297
`ResultSet` class, 294
`ResultSetMetaData` class, 300
`rollback()` method, 302
scroll-insensitive result set, 299
scroll-sensitive result set, 299
`setAutoCommit()` method, 301
`setTransactionIsolation()` method, 301
`setXXX()` functions, 297
`Statement` class, 294
status processing in, 300
stored procedures in, 302
supports two-phase commit, 1026
transactions in, 301
updatable cursors in, 299
used in Internet transaction processing, 984
JDBC-ODBC bridge, 294
JMS, 987
join. *See* index
computing
with block-nested loops, 397
with index-nested loops, 398
with nested loops, 397
dependency
definition of, 230
and lossless, 230
satisfaction of, 230
distributed, 698

global, 698
hash, 402
left outer, 142
operator
definition of, 137
equi-join, 138
natural join, 140
theta-join, 138
order, 454
outer, 142, 655
right outer, 142
semijoin, 699
sort-merge, 400
star, 403, 728
join index. *See* index
JTA, 302, 998
JTS
supports two-phase commit, 302, 1026
as TP monitor, 302, 961

KDD, 730
KDS, 1145
Kerberos, 1144, 1176
single sign-on, 1184
key. *See* search key of index
in cryptography
definition of, 1136
distribution, definition of, 1143
distribution for asymmetric cryptography, 1153
distribution server in Kerberos, 1145
distribution for symmetric cryptography, 1144, 1145
key server, 1145
private, 1139
public, 1139
for SSL, 1154
user key in Kerberos, 1145
in E-R Model
on entity type, 72
on relationship type, 75
in relational model, 41
in SQL
candidate, 42
constraint on relation, 41
foreign, 43
primary, 42
in XML, 622
key-range lock, 894
KEYSET_DRIVEN cursor
in embedded SQL, 279
in JDBC, 299
in ODBC, 310
kill-wait concurrency control, 866, 1040
K-means algorithm in data mining, 753
Knowledge Discovery in Databases, 730

language binding in ODMG, 545
LAST row selector, 280
latch, A-11, 855, 897. *See* lock
definition of, 836
latency of disk, 323, 334
lazy replication, 1033
leaf level of index tree, 349
leaf transaction, 785
learning rate for a neural network, 746
left outer join
in SQL, 173
legacy system, 781, 962
legacy transactions, 781
legal instance
of database, 38
of relation, 37
of schema, 198, 231
LET-clause in XQuery, 663
lifetime of system, 7
LIKE predicate in SQL, 154
linear commit protocol, 1022. *See* two-phase commit protocol
in digital cash protocol, 1170
in goods atomic protocol, 1162
in SET protocol, 1161
linear hashing, 371
links in BPEL, 1095
listener
message-driven bean as, 988
literal in ODMG, 548
load balancing, 960, 964
local database, 783
local home interface. *See* enterprise Java beans
local integrity constraint. *See* integrity constraint
local interface. *See* enterprise Java beans
local schema, 688
location transparency, 562, 689, 691, 950, 969, 970
lock. *See* latch; locking
conflict table, A-5, 831, 888
escalation, 896
and performance, 902
exclusive, A-15, 834, 888
granularity, 838, 871, 887, 890
definition of, A-15
and performance, 902
index, 887, 891
intention, A-16, 888
intention exclusive, A-15, 888
intention shared, A-15, 888
internal, 896
IS, A-15, 888
IX, A-15, 888
key-range, 894
long-duration, 877
page, A-9, 838
predicate, 872, 893, 894
read, A-4, 834, 877, 888
shared, A-15, 834, 888
shared intention exclusive, A-16, 888
short-duration, 836, 877, 896
SIX, A-16, 888
table, A-9, 870
tuple, A-9, 871
update, 882
write, A-4, 834, 877, 888
lock coupling, 898
locking. *See* lock; two-phase locking
early release
at lower isolation levels, 875
with manual locking, 836
granularity

locking *(continued)*
  granularity *(continued)*
    object database, 900
  manual, 836, 964
  protocol
    for B^+ trees, 896
    for chained transactions, 849
    for distributed transactions, 1024
    for granular locking, 888
    for immediate-update pessimistic concurrency controls, 834
    for index locking, 893
    for intention locking, 888
    for multiversion concurrency controls, 904
    for nested transactions, 850
    for object databases, 901
    for quorum consensus replication, 1032
    for READ COMMITTED isolation level, A-12, 878
    for READ UNCOMMITTED isolation level, A-12, 877
    for recoverable queues, 849
    for REPEATABLE READ isolation level, A-12, 878
    for savepoints, 848
    for SERIALIZABLE isolation level, A-12, 878, 893
    for synchronous-update replication, 1031
  in relational databases, A-9, 869
lock list, 834
lock manager, 964
lock set, 834
log
  after image. *See* after image
  archiving of, 934
  before image. *See* before image
  definition of, A-18, 921
  logical, 934
  overflow, 933
  physical, 798, 845, 922, 934
    and idempotency, 932
  physiological, 935
  placement of, 452
  to recover from media failure, 937
  write-ahead, A-21, 925
    with cache page and log buffer, 926
    with mirrored disk, 937
    used to implement atomicity and durability, A-18
log buffer, A-21, 921, 925
log manager, 964
log sequence number, 926, 935
long-duration lock, 877
lossless decomposition
  definition of, 213
  and join dependency, 230
  in partitioning, 693
lossy decomposition, 213
lost update
  in asynchronous replication, A-29
  definition of, A-7, 880
  eliminated with disjoint-write property, 907
  eliminated with first-committer-wins, 907
  eliminated with SNAPSHOT isolation, A-14, 907
  example of, 24, 771
  and multilevel concurrency control, 853
  at READ COMMITTED, 879
  when reading through a cursor, 880
LSN. *See* log sequence number
LU6.2 protocol, 975

machine learning, 247, 744
main index
  B^+ tree as, 353
  definition of, 340
  ISAM index as, 350
  is clustered index, 340
manual locking, 836, 964
marshaling, 565, 968. *See* remote procedure call
mass storage, 322, 920
materialized view, 177
MAX function, 164
media failure, 920, 937
MEMBER OF predicate in SQL:2003, 542
merge replication, 1036
merging, 384
message syncpoint, 976
message authentication code in SSL, 1155
message digest, 1142, 1174
message-driven beans. *See* enterprise Java beans
message exchange pattern in WSDL, 1078
method signature, 528
Microsoft Transaction Server. *See* MTS
middleware
  for authentication, 1151
  definition of, 963
  and distributed databases, 690
  Kerberos as, 1144
MIN function, 164
minimal cover, 222
minimality property of key constraint, 41
mirrored disk, A-22, 327, 768, 937
module test, C-7
MOLAP, 725
money atomicity, 1166, 1170
monitor. *See* TP monitor
  reference, 1151
monoalphabetic cipher, 1137
MTS
  supports two-phase commit, 313, 1026
  as TP monitor, 961
  uses declarative demarcation, 794
multidatabase
  definition of, A-23, 688, 783
  query planning for, 705
multidimensional data, 713
multilevel index, 347, 348
multilevel transaction
  compensation in, 798, 855

concurrency control, 854
definition of, 796
implementation of, 851
in the implementation of the DBMS, 855
multimaster replication, 1034
multiple attributes in search key, 344
multiple requests in BPEL, 1105
multiplicity of an attribute in UML, 96
multiplicity constraint in UML, 98
multiset
returned by relational operators, 151
in SQL:2003, 540
MULTISET function in SQL:2003, 541
multivalued dependency
definition of, 231
splitting the left-hand side of, 240
multiversion concurrency control. *See* SNAPSHOT isolation
definition of, 903
Read Consistency, 906
Read-Only, 904
SNAPSHOT isolation, A-13, 906
mutator method. *See* SQL:1999/2003
mutual consistency. *See* consistency
MVD. *See* multivalued dependency

named type in XML Schema, 616
name() in XSLT and XPath, 647
name of a DTD, 595
name server. *See* server
namespace. *See* XML namespace
naming problem for attributes, 136
naming services in CORBA, 571
NAS, 982
natural join operator, 140
navigation axis in XPath, 632
negation
stratified, 507
nested query
definition of, 157
in FROM clause, 162
in SELECT clause, 652
and tuning, 440
in WHERE clause, 157
nested relation, 522
nested transaction
allows subtransactions to abort, 785
commit and abort of, 786
definition of, 785
implementation of, 850
related to distributed transaction, 785
top-level, 785
and WS-BusinessActivity, 1128
Network Attached Storage, 982
neural net
activation function
sigmoid, 747
gradient descent, 748
neural nets
activation function, 745
step function, 745
back propagation algorithm, 749
for learning, 744
learning rate, 746
perceptron learning algorithm for a single neuron, 746
weighted input, 745
neuron
activation of, 745
emission of value, 745
NEXT row selector, 280, 305
`next()` function in JDBC, 297
node() in XSLT and XPath, 648
no-force policy for durability, 926
non-1NF data model, 522
non-ACID properties
in distributed transaction, 1027
reasons for, 773
relation to correctness, 773
in workflow, 805
nonce
for authentication, 1148
as confounder, 1149
definition of, 1148
as salt, 1149
non-exclusive part-of relationship
in conceptual modeling, 83
nonrepeatable read, A-7, 876
non-repudiation. *See* digital signature
non-serializable execution
at lower isolation levels, 879, 883
reasons for, 773, 875
related to correctness, 773, 887
in replicated databases, 1035
in workflow, 805
non-stop availability, 768
non-volatile storage, 920
normal form
1NF, 207
2NF, 207
3NF, 207
4NF, 207, 231
Boyce-Codd, 207
algorithm for, 219
definition of, 208
properties of, 211
definition of, 207
and E-R diagrams, 87
fifth, 235
first, 207
fourth, 207, 229, 231
of relation schema, 197
second, 207
third, 207
algorithm for, 222
definition of, 210
properties of, 211
normalization theory, 197
notational money, 1165
notification in event processing, 978
NOT in SQL, 154
NULL in SQL
definition of, 48
and indexing, 448
in query processing, 181

O_2, 523
object
  backward commuting operations on, 841
  commuting operations on, 839, 851
  compared with entity, 70
  fault, 522
  Id, 523
  locking, 901
  partial operations on, 840
  persistent, 522, 546
  in SQL:1999/2003, 530
Object Constraint Language in UML, 96
object databases
  concurrency control for, 839
  schema, 528
Object Definition Language. *See* ODL
object fault in an object database, 523
object id. *See* oid
Object Manipulation Language, 557
Object Query Language, 552
object query services in CORBA, 571
object reference in CORBA, 567
object-relational database, 529
object request broker, 564
ObjectStore object DBMS, 543
object transaction services in CORBA, 572
observer method. *See* SQL:1999/2003
OCL in UML, 96
ODBC, 268
  ? parameters in, 309
  abort in, 313
  autocommit in, 312
  catalog functions in, 312
  commit in, 313
  cursor in, 309
  description of, 307
  does not support two-phase commit, 313
  driver in, 307
  driver manager in, 307
  dynamic cursor in, 310
  escape syntax in, 313
  isolation levels in, 312
  keyset_driven cursor in, 310
  and middleware, 963
  prepared statements in, 309
  RETCODE, 312
  `SQLAllocConnect()`, 307
  `SQLAllocEnv()`, 307
  `SQLAllocStmt()`, 308
  `SQLBindCol()`, 309
  `SQLColAttributes()`, 312
  `SQLColumns()`, 312
  `SQL_COMMIT`, 313
  `SQLConnect()`, 307
  `SQLDescribeCol()`, 312
  `SQLDisconnect()`, 308
  `SQLError()`, 312
  `SQLExecDirect()`, 308
  `SQLExecute()`, 309
  `SQLFetch()`, 310
  `SQLFreeConnect()`, 308
  `SQLFreeEnv()`, 308
  `SQLFreeStmt()`, 308
  `SQLGetData()`, 310
  `SQLPrepare()`, 309
  `SQL_ROLLBACK`, 313
  `SQLSetConnectionOption()`, 312
  `SQLSetStmtOption()`, 310
  `SQLTables()`, 312
  `SQLTransact()`, 313
  static cursor in, 310
  status processing in, 312
  stored procedures in, 313
  supports two-phase commit, 1026
  transactions in, 312
ODL
  and impedance mismatch, 546
  in ODMG, 546, 547
ODMG
  architecture of, 543
  attributes in, 550
  data model of, 523
  `flatten` operator in, 555
  and impedance mismatch, 520, 545
  interface definition in, 547
  Java binding in, 560
  language bindings in, 558
  literal in, 548
  Object Definition Language, 546
  Object Manipulation Language, 557
  Object Query Language, 552
  path expressions in, 553
  persistence capable class in, 559
  relationship in, 550
  transactions in, 557
oid
  compared with primary key, 523
  definition of, 523
OLAP, 10, 178, 445, 712
OLTP, 10, 445, 712
OMG, 562
OML in ODMG, 557
one-item deadlock, 1031
one-phase commit protocol, 1027
one time pad, 1136
one-way function, 1142
online analytic processing. *See* OLAP
online transaction processing. *See* OLTP
opaque assignment in BPEL, 1091
open interface, 962
OPEN statement, 277
operating system
  abstraction created, 961
  interaction with DBMS, 925
  message passing facility, 961, 963, 968
  threading, 965
operation semantics
  definition of, 817
  used in concurrency control, 851
optimistic concurrency control
  and deferred-update system, 936

definition of, 828
implementation of, 859
and J2EE, 1001
OPTIMISTIC READ COMMITTED, 882
optimistic update, 1031
OQL
definition of, 552
nested query in, 555
OQS in CORBA, 571
Oracle DBMS
implements READ COMMITTED, 906
implements SNAPSHOT isolation, 906
Oracle Designer, 123
ORB in CORBA, 564
OR condition in workflow, 804
ORDER BY clause, 170, 279
orphan, 974
OTS in CORBA, 572
outer join, 142. *See* join
in SQL, 173
out parameter in embedded SQL, 271
overfitting
in decision trees, 736, 743
overflow chain, 335
overflow page
in clustered index, 342
in hash index, 366
in ISAM index, 352
in sorted file, 335

page
dirty, 928, 1126
locking. *See* lock
page buffer, A-21
page of disk data, 325
page id in index entry, 337
page lock. *See* lock
page number, 330
parallel query processing, 452
parallel validation, 862
in parameter in embedded SQL, 271
parameter passing
in dynamic SQL, 288
in embedded SQL, 270
in enterprise Java beans, 990
in JDBC, 297
in ODBC, 309
parsed character data, 594
partial key search
on B^+ tree, 353
definition of, 345
not supported by hash index, 365
partial operations, 840
partial sorting, 384
participation constraint, 81
partitioning
definition of, 691
derived, 694
in distributed databases, 691
horizontal, 446, 692
to increase concurrency, 452, 899
lossless, 693
in storage architecture, 981
transparency, 695
for tuning, 446
using IsA hierarchy, 80
vertical, 447, 693
partition of networks, 1006
partner in BPEL, 1086
partner link
in BPEL, 1090
part-of relationship
in conceptual modeling, 83
in UML, 104
PASSING AS SEQUENCE
in SQL/XML, 673
PASSING AS VALUE
in SQL/XML, 673
Passport, 1155
single sign-on, 1156, 1184
password for authentication, 1144, 1146, 1155
path expression
definition of, 518
in ODMG, 553
in SQL:1999/2003, 534
payment gateway, 1158
PayPal, 1157
PCDATA, 594
peer-to-peer communication
atomic commit for, 976, 1020. *See* protocol
definition of, 974
is stateful, 975
in peer model of distributed transactions, 785
prepared state in, 1020
syncpoint in, 976, 1020
peer-to-peer replication, 1034
perceptron learning algorithm for a single neuron, 746
persistence. *See* enterprise Java beans
bean-managed, 992, 998
capable class in ODMG, 559
container-managed, 992
persistent object, 522, 523, 546
persistent state service in CORBA, 569
Persistent Stored Modules. *See* PSM language
PERT chart, C-11
pessimistic concurrency control, 828
pessimistic update, 1031
phantom
definition of, A-9, 871
related to SNAPSHOT isolation, 909
with REPEATABLE READ, 876
with tuple or page locks, 871
phenomenon. *See* anomaly
physical restoration, 791, 798, 842, 844, 845. *See* log
physical schema, 31
physiological logging. *See* log
pick construct in BPEL, 1092
pipeline
in query processing, 418, 425
in system organization, 801
pivoting in OLAP, 719
pivot in workflow model, 807
placeholder, 288

plaintext, 1136
platter of disk, 322
Poet object DBMS, 543
polling, 977
polyalphabetic cipher, 1138
polygram cipher, 1138
POST. *See* HTTP
posting of an event, 979
PowerDesigner, 123
preamble of procedure, C-13
precompiler for embedded SQL, 268
precondition of procedure, C-5
predicate
  definition of, 14
  locking, 872, 893, 894
predication in data mining, 730, 734, 744
prefetching. *See* cache
pre-master secret in SSL, 1154
preparation of SQL statement
  definition of, 267
  in dynamic SQL, 287
  in embedded SQL, 268
  in JDBC, 297
  in ODBC, 309
  in stored procedures, 285
PREPARE statement, 287
prepared record. *See* two-phase commit protocol
prepared state. *See* two-phase commit protocol
PreparedStatement class in JDBC, 297
prepared statements
  in dynamic SQL, 287
  in embedded SQL, 268
  in JDBC, 297
  in ODBC, 309
  in stored procedures, 285
prepared-to-commit state. *See* two-phase commit protocol
  in goods atomic protocol, 1162
  in peer-to-peer communication, 1020
  in SET protocol, 1161
prepare message. *See* two-phase commit protocol
PREPARE statement, 287
prepareStatement() method in JDBC, 297
presentation server
  definition of, 953
  Internet browser as, 984
presentation services, 947
presumed abort property. *See* two-phase commit protocol
presumed commit property. *See* two-phase commit protocol
primary copy replication. *See* replication
primary key. *See* candidate key
  definition of, 42
  and insertion anomaly, 210
  specifying in SQL, 47
  in XML, 622
PRIMARY KEY
  and foreign key constraint, 53
primitive value, 524, 530
principal in cryptography, 1144
à priori algorithm in data mining, 733
PRIOR row selector, 280
private key, 1139
probe chasing, 1024
procedural language, 127
procedure cache. *See* cache
procedures. *See* stored procedures, 282
processing instruction. *See* hint
  in XML, 584
  xml-stylesheet, 638
product cipher, 1138
profile in UML, 97
programmatic demarcation. *See* transaction demarcation
projection of a BPEL process, 1109
projection of MVD, 233
Project Management Plan, C-16
project manager, C-10, 8
project meetings, C-11
project operator
  computing, 388
  definition of, 131
Project Plan, C-10
propagation of transaction. *See* transaction
property. *See* BPEL
property declaration
  in BPEL, 1088
proprietary interface, 962
protocol
  atomic commit, 976, 1007, 1020, 1022
  authentication
    based on asymmetric cryptography, 1153
    based on symmetric cryptography, 1144
  autocommit, 1027
  blind signature, 1165
  certified delivery, 1162, 1164
  commit in peer-to-peer communication, 976, 1020
  connection-oriented, 1048
  CORBA Inter-ORB, 568
  digital signature, 1141
  disjoint-write, 908
  dual signature, 1158
  electronic cash, 1165
  escrow agent, 1164
  FAP, 1019
  first-committer-wins, 907
  fuzzy checkpoint, 932
  fuzzy dump, 938
  goods atomicity, 1162, 1164
  granular locking in object databases. *See* locking
  granular locking in relational databases. *See* locking
  group commit, 927
  https, 1154
  immediate-update pessimistic concurrency control, 834
  index locking, 893
  intention locking, 888
  Kerberos, 1144
  key distribution
    based on asymmetric cryptography, 1153

based on symmetric cryptography, 1144
linear commit, 1022
locking for B^+ tree, 896
locking for different isolation levels, 877
locking in object databases, 901
logging, 921
logical and physiological logging, 934
LU6.2, 975
nested transactions, 850
one-phase commit, 1027
optimistic concurrency control, 859
PayPal, 1157
peer-to-peer
  atomic commit, 976, 1020
  communication, 974
physical logging, 934
quorum consensus, 1031
Read-Consistency multiversion concurrency control, 906
Read-Only multiversion concurrency control, 904
recovery in deferred-update systems, 936
recovery in immediate-update systems, 921
recovery from media failure, 937
replication, 1031
rollback in immediate-update systems, 921
Secure Electronic Transaction, 1158
Secure Sockets Layer, 1153
SET, 1158
SNA, 974
SNAPSHOT isolation, 906
SSL, 1153
TCP, 974
timestamp-ordered concurrency control, 856
two-phase commit. *See* two-phase commit protocol
two-phase locking. *See* two-phase locking
X/Open Standard, 1020
zero-phase commit, 1027
pruning a decision tree, 736, 743
PSM language. *See* stored procedures
  and SQL-92, 283
  and SQL:1999/2003, 532
  and triggers, 257
public-key cryptography. *See* asymmetric cryptography; cryptography
publisherAssertion in UDDI, 1116
publishing
  in SQL/XML, 671
PublishSoap in UDDI, 1121
pull in replication, 1035
push in replication, 1035

QA test, C-7
QBE. *See* Query-by-Example
quantified predicate in SQL:1999, 163
quantifier
  existential, 464
  implicit, 478
    in QBE, 479
  universal, 464
query
  in database, 4
  in Datalog, 497
  execution plan, 128, 267
  index-only, 346, 440
  processing, 128
  recursive, 490
  result, 276
  stratified, 507
Query Analyzer for SQL Server, 451
Query-By-Example
  based on DRC, 474
  description of, 479
  implicit quantification in, 479
  join in, 480
query execution plan, 384. *See* access path
  cost of, 414
  for database systems, 705
  definition of, 410
  for distributed systems, 698
  logical, 424
query language, 127
  for OLAP queries, 10
  relational calculus as, 461
  SQL as, 147
query optimization
  definition of, 128
  for distributed systems, 698
  index-only strategy, 440
  for multidatabase systems, 705
query optimizer, 384
  cost based, 410, 453
  definition of, 409
  rule based, 410
query tree
  definition of, 414
  left-deep, 425
queue. *See* recoverable queue
queued transaction processing. *See* transaction processing system
quorum consensus protocol, 1031

RAID systems, 326, 981
range query, 391, 439
range search
  in B^+ tree, 353
  on clustered index, 341
  definition of, 333
  with ISAM index, 351
  not supported by hash index, 365
  of sorted file, 335
Rational Rose, 123
raw partition, 925
reactive constraint
  definition of, 56
  implemented with triggers, 57
READ COMMITTED
  definition of, A-11, 876

READ COMMITTED *(continued)*
example of incorrect execution with, 879
with first-committer-wins, 882
implemented with multiversion concurrency control, 906
implemented in Oracle DBMS, 906
locking implementation of, A-12, 878
optimistic, 882
Read-Consistency multiversion concurrency control, 906
read lock. *See* lock
read-one/write-all replication. *See* replication
Read-Only multiversion concurrency control, 904
read phase, 859
read quorum, 1032
read request, 815
READ UNCOMMITTED
definition of, A-11, 876
example of incorrect execution with, 879
locking implementation of, A-12, 877
read-with-intention-to-write lock, 882
ready message, 1022. *See* two-phase commit protocol
real-world actions. *See* external actions
receive in BPEL, 1082
receive mode in peer-to-peer communication, 975
record
abort, A-19, 922
begin, A-19, 922
begin dump, 940
checkpoint, A-19, 923
commit, A-19, 922
compensation log, 931
completion, 936
end dump, 938, 940
redo, 929
undo, A-18
update, A-18, 921
recoverable
concurrency control, 825
related to compensating actions, 843
related to reducible, 845
schedule, 825
recoverable objects in CORBA, 573
recoverable queue
as communication mechanism, 803
FIFO ordering in, 800
implementation of, 849
priority ordering in, 800
provided by TP monitor, 964, 965
in queued transaction processing, 960
semantics of, 800
used to implement forwarding agent, 802
used to implement real-world action, 802
used to schedule transactions, 799, 988, 999
used in workflows, 808
recoverable server in CORBA, 573
recovery
in deferred-update systems, 936
definition of, 768
from disk failure, A-22
in immediate-update systems, 921
from media failure, 937
using fuzzy dump, 938
using log, 937
procedure, 919
using fuzzy checkpoints, 932
using log, A-22, 923
using sharp checkpoints, 929
recurrence equations, 490
recursive query
and aggregation in SQL, 495
and negation in SQL, 493
in SQL, 490
redirect in HTTP, 1155
redo record, 929
reducible schedule, 845
reduction factor in query optimization, 422
redundancy predicate, 1167
redundant attribute, 222
redundant FD, 222
reference
data type in SQL:1999/2003, 533, 538
monitor, 1151
type, 526
value, 524
referential integrity, 43, 995
reflexivity rule, 201
registry in UDDI, 1111
relation
attribute
definition of, 35
domain of, 37
name of, 37
constraint
candidate key, 42
domain, 37
dynamic, 40
foreign-key, 43
integrity, 37, 38
interrelational, 40
intra-relational, 40
key, 41
primary key, 42
semantic, 40, 45
superkey, 42
type, 37
definition of, 14, 35
instance, 35
nested, 522
schema, 37
tuple, 35
union-compatible, 133
relational algebra
Cartesian product, 135
cross product, 135
description of, 128
division, 144
equi-join, 138
intersection, 133
join, 137

natural join, 140
project, 131
renaming, 136
select, 128
set difference, 133
set operators, 133
theta-join, 138
union, 133
relational calculus, 461
relational database, 35
definition of, 38
introduction to, 14
limitations of, 515
locking in, A-9, 869
as subset of CODM, 530
relational expression, 133
relational model. *See* relational database
relational operator, 15
Cartesian product, 135
cross product, 135
division, 144
equi-join, 138
intersection, 133
join, 137
natural join, 140
project, 131
renaming, 136
select, 128
set difference, 133
theta-join, 138
union, 133
relationship. *See* enterprise Java beans
attribute, 73
binary, 75
container-managed in J2EE, 994
definition of, 73
degree of, 75
key of, 75
in ODMG, 550
role
definition of, 73
name of, 73
schema of, 75
ternary, 75
translation into relational model, 88
type, 73
relationship instance
definition of, 73
RELATIVE row selector, 280
relative XPath expression, 629
reliability, 6
Remote Method Interface. *See* RMI
remote procedure call. *See* transactional remote procedure call; WSDL
authenticated, 1151
as communication mechanism, 968
compared to peer-to-peer communication, 974
in CORBA, 562
definition of, 968
failure in, 970
implemented with stubs, 968
is stateless, 968
marshaling, 968
and subtransactions, 971
used in client/server systems, 950, 968
renaming operator, 136
REPEATABLE READ
definition of, A-11, 876
example of incorrect execution with, 880, 909
locking implementation of, A-12, 878
repeating groups, 446
replay attack, 1143, 1147
replica control. *See* replication
definition of, A-28, 1029
quorum consensus, 1033
replication
asynchronous-update, A-28, 1030
capture in, 1034
conflict resolution strategy in, 1036
convergence in, 1036
definition of, A-28, 1028
of directory server, 971
eager, 1031
group, A-29, 1036
lazy, 1033
merge, 1036
multimaster, 1034
mutual consistency. *See* consistency
partial, 1029
peer-to-peer, 1034
primary copy, A-30, 1034
procedural, 1034
pull in, 1035
push in, 1035
quorum consensus protocol, 1031
read-one/write-all, A-28, 1030
secondary copy, 1034
subscription in, 1034
synchronous-update, A-28, 1030
total, 1029
transparency, 691
reply in BPEL, 1082
Requirements Document, B-1
response time, 7
restart
in chained transactions, 791
restart protocol. *See* two-phase commit protocol
result set
definition of, 276
forward-only, 299
scroll-insensitive, 299
scroll-sensitive, 299
`ResultSet` class in JDBC, 294
`ResultSetMetaData` class in JDBC, 300
RETCODE, 312
retriable task. *See* workflow
RETURNING CONTENT
in SQL/XML, 673
RETURNING SEQUENCE
in SQL/XML, 673
revision history, C-13
REVOKE statement, 65
rid
definition of, 330

rid *(continued)*
in index entry, 337
right outer join
in SQL, 173
risk management plan, C-17
RMI, 990
ROLAP, 725
role
in BPEL, 1086
in E-R model, 73, 550
in workflow, 808
rollback. *See* abort; compensation
for abort, 922
for crash, 922
in deferred-update systems, 936
definition of, 22, 767, 919
in immediate-update systems, 921
in JDBC, 302
in ODBC, 313
to savepoint, 779
using log, A-19, 922
using logical log, 934
ROLLBACK AND CHAIN statement, 274
ROLLBACK statement. *See* SQL
rollforward
definition of, 919
using logical log, 934
rolling up in OLAP, 718
ROLLUP operator, 724
root element in XML, 583
root node in XPath, 629
rotational latency of disk, 323
routing by an application server, 955
row. *See* tuple
in relational table, 14, 35
row id. *See* rid
row-level granularity, 254
ROW type constructor in SQL:1999/2003, 531
row type in SQL:1999/2003, 531
ROW value constructor in SQL:1999/2003, 531
RPC. *See* remote procedure call
RSA encryption algorithm
in asymmetric encryption, 1140
in signatures, 1141
rule
in Datalog, 497
run in external sort, 385

safe triggers, 264
Sagas, 791
salt in cryptography, 1149
SAML, 1180
SAN, 982
SAS, 981
savepoint
definition of, 779
locking implementation of, 848
rollback implementation of, 922
scaling for large systems, 954, 958
schedule. *See* serializable
definition of, 23, 770, 815
equivalence of, A-2, 817, 818, 821
non-serializable, A-1
recoverable, 825
reducible, 845
serial, A-1, 22, 769, 813, 819
strict, 826
schema
conceptual, 32, 33
of database, 38
of entity type, 72
external, 33
global, 689
legal instance of, 198, 231
local, 688
of object database, 528
physical, 31
of relation, 35, 37
of relationship, 75
snowflake, 715
specified by CREATE TABLE command, 46
in SQL, 62
star, 715
schema valid document, 599
scope in BPEL, 1099
SDL. *See* storage definition language
search key of index
compared with candidate key, 337
definition of, 337
with multiple attributes, 344
secondary copy replication, 1034
secondary index
B^+ tree as, 353
definition of, 340
is unclustered index, 340
sector of disk, 322
Secure Electronic Transaction Protocol, 1158
Secure Sockets Layer protocol, 1153
security
assertion, 1183
definition of, 7
mechanism
in Kerberos, 1144
in SSL, 1153
server, 1151
services provided by TP monitor, 965
for Web services, 1171
security mechanism
for electronic cash, 1165
in SET, 1158
seek time of disk, 323
SELECT DISTINCT statement, 151
selection-condition
in relational algebra, 129
in XPath queries, 634
selectivity of access path, 394
select operator
computing, 390
definition of, 128
SELECT statement
definition of, 148
expressions in, 152
self-describing data, 579
self-referencing column, 533
Semantic Web, 497
semijoin, 699
semistructured data, 581

send mode in peer-to-peer
communication, 975
separator in index file, 347
sequence construct in BPEL, 1090
sequence diagram, B-15
sequence number in cryptography,
1143
serializable. *See* non-serializable
execution
anomaly, 910
in commit order, A-6, 831
definition of, A-2, 24, 772, 819
execution of distributed
transactions, 783
execution of global transactions,
1007, 1025
of global transactions, A-26
order produced by two-phase
locking, 837
produced by concurrency
control
optimistic, 859
pessimistic, 834
Read-Only multiversion, 904
timestamp-ordered, 856
using granular locking, 893
produced by quorum consensus
algorithm, 1031
produced by synchronous-
update replication,
1031
related to reducible, 845
related to SERIALIZABLE, 887
with two-phase commit, 1025
SERIALIZABLE isolation level
definition of, A-11, 876
locking implementation of,
A-12, 878, 893
related to serializable, 887
serialization. *See* SOAP
serialization graph, 822
serial schedule. *See* schedule
serial validation, 862
server. *See* application server;
transaction server
authentication, 1148, 1155
directory, 970, 1049
key, 1145
name, 970
security, 1151
storage, 982
ticket-granting, 1148
timing, 965
Server Attached Storage, 981
server class. *See* transaction server
and context storage, 958
definition of, 955
and load balancing, 964
server skeleton in CORBA, 565
service-centered design, 960
servlet
as application server, 984
definition of, 983
session. *See* context
definition of, 957
and load balancing, 964
multiplexed, 958
and threads, 959
session bean. *See* enterprise Java
beans
session key
definition of, 1137
distribution of, 1144
establishing in Kerberos, 1144
establishing in SSL, 1154
set
constructor in SQL, 157
difference operator
computing, 388
definition of, 133
function in SQL:2003, 542
operations in SQL, 154
type, 526
value, 524
valued attribute, 515
`setAutoCommit()` method in
JDBC, 301
SET CONNECTION statement, 273
SET DESCRIPTOR statement, 291
SET protocol, 1158
SET TRANSACTION statement, 274
`setTransactionIsolation()`
method in JDBC, 301
set-valued attribute
in E-R, 71
shared intention exclusive lock,
A-16, 888
sharp checkpoint, 930
short-duration lock, 836, 877, 896
sibling pointers in B^+ tree, 353
signature. *See* XML Signature
blind, 1168
in cryptography, 1141
dual, 1158
of method, 528
in SAML, 1180
SOAP, 1176
signature of method, 547
simple cipher, 1137
Simple Mail Transfer Protocol. *See*
SMTP
Simple Object Access Protocol. *See*
SOAP
single sign-on, 1184
Internet, 1155
Kerberos, 1147
SAML, 1180, 1183
single-tiered transaction
processing system, 949
SIX lock, A-16, 888
SLI. *See* statement-level-interface
slice in OLAP, 720
slot number, 330
SMTP
binding in WSDL, 1076
SNA protocol, 974
snapshot, 903. *See* version
number
in SNAPSHOT isolation, 906
returned by insensitive cursor,
277, 310
SNAPSHOT isolation
and anomalies, 908
definition of, A-13, 906
disjoint-write property, 906
example of correct execution
with, 909, 911
example of incorrect execution
with, 908
first-committer-wins, 907

SNAPSHOT isolation *(continued)*
implementation of, 906
implemented by Oracle DBMS, 906
is anomaly serializable, 910
and phantoms, 909
snapshot number, 907
TPC-C Benchmark executes serializably at, 910
write skew at, 910
snapshot number
in Read-0nly multiversion concurrency controls, 905
in SNAPSHOT isolation, 907
snowflake schema, 715
SOAP. *See* WS-Addressing
body, 1052
data model, 1055
deserialization, 1054
document-style, 1051, 1062
encodingStyle, 1055
encryption and signature, 1176
envelope, 1052
extensibility, 1055
faults, 1061
header, 1052, 1056, 1059, 1125, 1178
HTTP binding, 1061
intermediary, 1056, 1178
message correlation, 1062
message structure, 1052
mustUnderstand, 1056, 1061
request message, 1053
response message, 1053
role, 1056
RPC/encoded, 1055
RPC-style, 1051, 1053, 1061
serialization, 1054, 1072
for Web services, 1045
WS-Addressing, 1058, 1066, 1127
WS-Security, 1176
Software Engineering. *See* Design Document; Requirements Document; Specification Document; Statement of Objectives; Waterfall model
coding techniques, C-13
database design, 69
design review, C-6
Entity-Relationship Diagram, 70
incremental development, C-15
levels of abstraction, 957
methodology, B-1
Project Plan, C-10
sequence diagram, B-15
Standish Report, 8
state diagrams, C-2
Test Plan Document, C-7
UML, B-2, C-2, 95
use case, B-2
sorted file
binary search of, 333
definition of, 333
range search of, 335
sorting
avoidance, 448
external, 384
partial, 384
sort-merge join, 400
soundness
of Armstrong's axioms, 202
of MVD inference rules, 236
sparse index, 342
Specification Document, B-2, C-1
spread of a transaction. *See* transaction
SQL. *See* dynamic SQL; embedded SQL
-- to start comments, 152
% in pattern matching, 154
_ in pattern matching, 154
* in SELECT, 152
access control in, 63, 176
access error in, 301
aggregate function, 164
aggregation, 167
ALL, 162
ALLOCATE DESCRIPTOR, 290
ALTER TABLE, 60
ANY, 162
AVG, 164
base relation, 174
BEGIN DECLARE SECTION, 270
CALL, 285
CHECK, 49
comments, 152
COMMIT, 274
COMMIT AND CHAIN, 274
CONNECT, 273
COUNT, 164, 444
CREATE ASSERTION, 49
CREATE DOMAIN, 53
CREATE INDEX, 339
CREATE SCHEMA, 62
CREATE TABLE, 46
CREATE TRIGGER, 58
CREATE VIEW, 59, 174
CURRENT_DATE, 118
data definition language, 46
DECLARE CURSOR, 277
DELETE, 184
DESCRIBE INPUT, 290
DESCRIBE OUTPUT, 290
diagnostics area, 271
DIAGNOSTICS SIZE, 274
direct execution of, 267
DISCONNECT, 273
division, 160
DROP ASSERTION, 61
DROP COLUMN, 60
DROP CONSTRAINT, 61
DROP DOMAIN, 61
DROP INDEX, 340
DROP SCHEMA, 62
DROP TABLE, 61
DROP VIEW, 176
ESCAPE, 154
EXECUTE, 288
EXECUTE IMMEDIATE, 289
EXISTS, 159
EXTRACT, 118
FETCH, 277, 280
FOREIGN KEY, 53
GET DESCRIPTOR, 291
GET DIAGNOSTICS, 272
GRANT, 63
GROUP BY, 167, 450
grouping, 167

HAVING, 168
IN, 157
INSERT, 182
join in, 149
LIKE, 154, 448
limitations of, 517
MAX, 164
MIN, 164
nested query, 157, 162
NOT, 154
NULL, 48, 181
null value, 48, 181
OPEN, 277
ORDER BY clause, 279
PREPARE, 287
PRIMARY KEY, 47, 53
PUBLIC, 63
query sublanguage, 147
restrictions on GROUP BY and HAVING, 172
REVOKE, 65
ROLLBACK, 274
ROLLBACK AND CHAIN, 274
SELECT, 148
expressions in SELECT clause, 152
expressions in WHERE clause, 152
SELECT DISTINCT, 151
set comparison operators, 162
SET CONNECTION, 273
set constructor, 157
set operations, 154
SET TRANSACTION, 274
SQLERROR, 271
SQLSTATE, 271, 285
START TRANSACTION, 274
static, 268
SUM, 164
UNIQUE, 47
UPDATE, 185
view, 174
access control, 176
materialized, 177
as subroutine, 174
and tuning, 449
updatable, 187
update, 185
WHENEVER, 271
WITH RECURSIVE, 492
SQL-92. *See* SQL
as basis for SQLJ, 303
SQL:1999
CREATE RECURSIVE VIEW, 490
history of, 147
new features, 46
triggers in, 256
SQL:1999/2003
CREATE METHOD, 532
EXECUTE privilege, 536
and impedance mismatch, 520
mutator method, 535
objects in, 530, 533
observer method, 535
REF, 533, 538
ROW type constructor, 531
self-referencing column in, 533
tuple value, 530
typed table in, 533
UNDER, 532
use of path expression, 534
user-defined types, 531
SQL:2003, 46, 294
MULTISET, 540
UNNEST, 541
SQLAllocConnect() function in ODBC, 307
SQLAllocEnv() function in ODBC, 307
SQLAllocStmt() function in ODBC, 308
SQLBindCol() function in ODBC, 309
SQL/CLI, 307
SQLColAttributes() function in ODBC, 312
SQLColumns() function in ODBC, 312
SQL_COMMIT in ODBC, 313
SQLConnect() function in ODBC, 307
SQL-connection, 273
SQLDA in dynamic SQL, 290
SQLDescribeCol() function in ODBC, 312
SQLDisconnect() function in ODBC, 308
SQLERROR, 271, 312
SQLException in Java, 301
SQLExecDirect() function in ODBC, 308
SQLExecute() function in ODBC, 309
SQLFetch() function in ODBC, 310
SQLFreeConnect() function in ODBC, 308
SQLFreeEnv() function in ODBC, 308
SQLFreeStmt() function in ODBC, 308
SQLGetData() function in ODBC, 310
SQLJ, 303
SQLPrepare() function in ODBC, 309
SQL/PSM language, 256
SQL_ROLLBACK in ODBC, 313
SQL-schema, 62
SQL-server, 273
SQL-session, 273
SQLSetConnectionOption() function in ODBC, 312
SQLSetStmtOption() function in ODBC, 310
SQLSTATE, 271, 285
SQLTables() function in ODBC, 312
SQLTransact() function in ODBC, 313
SQL/XML, 668
goal of, 628
as query language, 582
SSL protocol, 1153
Staff Allocation Chart, C-11
Standish Report, 8
star join
computed using bitmapped join index, 728

star join *(continued)*
  computing using bitmapped join index, 404
  definition of, 403
star schema, 715
start record. *See* two-phase commit protocol
START TRANSACTION statement, 274
starvation in concurrency control, 834
state diagram, C-2
stateful, 975
stateless, 968
state maintenance in workflow, 808
Statement class in JDBC, 294
statement-level atomicity and isolation, A-11, 836, 855, 877, 881, 896
statement-level granularity, 254
statement-level-interface, 268, 547, 558
Statement of Objectives, B-1, 13
static concurrency control. *See* concurrency control
static constraint, 40
STATIC cursor in ODBC, 310
static method invocation in CORBA, 565
static protocol, 856
static SQL. *See* embedded SQL
statistics. *See* tuning
status processing
  in embedded SQL, 271
  in JDBC, 300
  in ODBC, 312
stereotype in UML, 97
Storage Area Network, 982
storage definition language, 34
storage servers, 982
storage structure
  B^+ tree as, 353
  definition of, 321
  hash index as, 364
  heap file as, 329
  ISAM index as, 350
  sorted file as, 333
stored procedures. *See* PSM language
  advantages of, 282, 951
  in dynamic SQL, 293
  in embedded SQL, 282
  in JDBC, 302
  in ODBC, 313
  recompilation of, 454
  in two- and three-level architectures, 951, 953
stratification
  in Datalog, 508
stratified negation, 494
stress test, C-8
strict. *See* two-phase locking
  concurrency control, 826
strict two-phase locking. *See* two-phase locking
string value of XPath expression, 634
striping, 326
strong mutual consistency. *See* consistency
stub
  appends transaction identifier, 971
  in authenticated RPC, 1151
  as implementation of RPC, 968
Student Registration System
  code for registration transaction, C-22
  database design for, 111
  deliverables for, B-12
  Design Document, C-17, 111
  design of Registration Transaction, C-20
  E-R Diagram for, 111
  integrity constraints for, B-7, C-18, 113
  Requirements Document, B-5, 111
  schema for, 111
  sequence diagram for, B-15
  Specification Document, B-16
  Statement of Objectives, 13
  Test Plan Document, C-7
  use cases for, B-7
subclass in CODM, 525
SUBMULTISET OF
  predicate in SQL:2003, 542
subscription
  to an event, 979
  in primary copy replication, 1034
subscription service in UDDI, 1123
substitution cipher, 1137
subtransaction
  compensatable, 792
  of distributed transaction, A-23, 783, 971
  of nested transaction, 785
subtype in CODM, 526
SUM function, 164
superkey, 42
supertable, 540
support for an association, 732
symmetric cryptography. *See* cryptography
  authentication in, 1144
  definition of, 1137
synchronous-update replication. *See* replication
syncpoint
  declaration of, 1020
  definition of, 976
  manager, 977, 1020
  message, 1020
system
  architecture, 9
  integrated distributed database, 689
  multidatabase, 688
  status, 9
system administrator, 9
system analyst, 8
system catalog, 46

table. *See* partitioning; relation
  in relational database, 14, 35
table locking. *See* lock
tag
  local name of, 590

in XML, 582
target namespace. *See* XML
namespace; XML Schema
target of query, 461
task activation in workflow, 808
task dependency in project plan,
C-10
TCP protocol, 974, 1048
template in XSLT, 641
termination
atomic, 1007
test
acceptance, C-10
alpha, C-10
beta, C-10
black box, C-7
glass box, C-8
stress, C-8
Testing Protocol Document, C-9
Test Plan Document
definition of, C-7
as script, C-9
test set, 736
test set error in decision trees, 736,
743
theta-join operator, 138
third normal form. *See* normal
form
Thomas Write Rule, 858, 867,
1036
thread
in application server, 954
in Java servlet, 983
in TP monitor, 965
three-tiered transaction processing
system, 953, 984
throughput, 7
`throws` clause in Java, 301
ticket, 1145, 1148
ticket-granting server, 1148
ticket-granting ticket, 1148
timeout
to detect deadlock, A-8, 833,
1024
stub, 970
timeout protocol. *See* two-phase
commit protocol
timestamp
assigned to transactions, 856
on authenticator, 1146
to avoid deadlock, 833, 866,
1024, 1040
in cryptography, 1143
used in replication, 1036
timestamp-ordered concurrency
control, 856
timing server provided by TP
monitor, 965
tModel in UDDI, 1114
token money, 1165
tokens as electronic cash, 1166
top-level transaction, 785
topological sort, 823
total operations, 840
TPC-C Benchmark
executes serializably at
SNAPSHOT isolation, 910
TP-Heavy, 963, 965
TP-Lite, 963, 965
TP monitor, 5, 782. *See* peer-
to-peer communication;
remote procedure call;
transaction manager
and access control lists, 1151
API for, 1020
creates abstraction of
transaction, 961
definition of, 961
in JTS, 302
load balancing with, 964
in MTS, 313
peer-to-peer communication,
974
providing threading, 965
and remote procedure call, 967
supporting servers, 965
support of nested transactions,
965
track of disk, 322
training set error in decision trees,
736, 743
training sets in data mining, 734
transaction. *See* enterprise Java
beans
abstraction of, 773
active, 824
chained, 788
definition of, 4
description of, 20, 763
distributed. *See* distributed
transaction
in embedded SQL, 274
extended, 809
flat, 777
global. *See* distributed
transaction
in JDBC, 301
nested, 785
in ODBC, 312
older, 833, 1024
propagation, 967, 975, 980
read-only, 904
read/write, 904
as unit of work, 766
younger, 833, 1024
transactional objects in CORBA,
573
transactional remote procedure
call, 784, 971. *See* remote
procedure call
transactional server in CORBA,
573
transaction context, 793
transaction costs in Web services,
1044
transaction demarcation, 986
declarative, 793
programmatic, 793
and the transaction manager,
966
using enterprise Java beans, 998
transaction id, A-18, 922
transaction-level read consistency
definition of, 903
produced by Read-Only
multiversion concurrency
control, 904
produced by SNAPSHOT
isolation, 906

transaction manager, 972. *See* TP monitor; two-phase commit protocol
  in CORBA, 573
  definition of, A-24, 965
  and global isolation and atomicity, 963
  and Web services, 1123
transaction monitor. *See* TP monitor
transaction processing system
  centralized, 947
  definition of, 5
  distributed, 950
  Encina, 961, 971
  four-tiered, 984
  guarantees provided by, 767
  heterogeneous, 962
  homogeneous, 962
  on the Internet, 982
  JTS, 961
  MTS, 961
  multi-user, 949
  queued, 960
  single-tiered, 949
  single user, 947
  three-tiered, 953, 984
  Tuxedo, 961, 978
  two-tiered, 951, 984
transaction record. *See* two-phase commit protocol
transaction schedule. *See* schedule
transaction server, 955
transaction services in CORBA, 572
transfer of coordination, 1021
transfer time of disk, 323
transformation for populating a data warehouse, 728
transitivity rule, 202
Transmission Control Protocol. *See* TCP
transparency
  location, 689, 691
  in partitioning, 695
  replication, 691
transport protocol, 1048
transposition cipher, 1138
tree index. *See* B^+ tree and ISAM index
  location mechanism for, 347
  two interpretations of, 347
tree of transactions in nested transactions, 785
triggering graph, 264
triggers
  activation of, 252
  after, 254, 258
  before, 254, 257
  conflicts of, 255
  consideration of, 252
  deferred consideration, 253
  definition of, 251
  execution of, 253
  firing of, 251
  granularity of, 254
  immediate consideration, 253
  to implement active database, 251
  to implement reactive constraints, 57
  instead of, 254, 261
  and integrity constraints, 255
  safe, 264
  in SQL, 57
  in SQL:1999, 58, 256
trivial functional dependency, 201
TRPC. *See* transactional remote procedure call
trusted third party
  certification authority as, 1153
  escrow agent as, 1164
  in goods atomicity, 1162
  for key distribution, 1145
  for single password protocols, 1155
`try` clause in Java, 301
tuning, 433
  cache, 434
  denormalization, 444
  hint, 454
  histograms, 453, 454
  indices, 437
  statistics, 453, 454
  tools, 451
tuple
  definition of, 14, 35
  locking, 871. *See* lock
  type, 526
  value, 524, 530
  variable, 461
tuple lock. *See* lock
tuple relational calculus, 461
Tuxedo. *See* transaction processing system
two-level index, 348
two-phase commit protocol, A-24, 1008. *See* embedded SQL; JDBC; JTS; linear commit protocol, peer-to-peer communication; MTS; ODBC; transaction manager; WS-Coordination; X/Open Standard
  aborting message, A-24, 1009
  abort message, A-25, 1010, 1014
  abort record, A-25, 1010
  atomic termination, A-24, 1007
  blocking, A-24, 1009, 1013, 1014, 1026
  and callbacks, 973
  cohort, A-24, 1005, 1008
    restart protocol, 1016
    time out, 1016
    and transaction manager, 971
  commit message, A-25, 1009
  commit record, A-24, 1009, 1014
  completion record, A-25, 1009, 1014
  coordinator, A-24, 1005, 1008
    for distributed systems, 965
    for linear commit, 1022
    for peer-to-peer commit, 1021
    restart protocol, 1016
    syncpoint manager as, 1021
    time out, 1016
    transaction manager as, 965
    in WS-Coordination, 1124
  domain, 1012, 1020

done message, A-25, 1009
with no prepared state, 1023
prepared record, A-24, 1009
prepared state, A-24, 1009
prepared-to-commit state, 1009, 1014
prepare message, A-24, 1009, 1012
presumed abort property, 1014, 1015
presumed commit property, 1017
protocol tree, 1012
in quorum consensus, 1033
ready message, A-24, 1009
reasons for not participating in, 1026
restart protocol, 1013
and serializability, A-26, 1025
simplified for read-only cohorts, 1009, 1031, 1040
start record, 1018
in synchronous replication, 1031
timeout protocol, 1013, 1016
transaction record, 1008
uncertain period, A-24, 1009, 1014
vote message, A-24, 1009, 1012
and Web services, 1099
two-phase locking
and B^+ trees, 898
can produce non-recoverable schedules, 837
definition of, A-4, 837
equivalent serial order produced by, 837
necessary and sufficient for serializability, 837
strict, A-4, 838
two-tiered transaction processing system, 951, 984
`tx_begin()`
as call to transaction manager, 966, 971
definition of, 966
`tx_commit()`
as call to transaction manager, 966, 971
definition of, 966
in two-phase commit, 1020
`tx` interface, 966
`tx_rollback()`
as call to transaction manager, 966, 971
definition of, 966
type
basic, 526
in CODM, 526
constraint, 37
reference, 526
set, 526
tuple, 526

UDDI
add message, 1120
bindingTemplate, 1113
businessEntity, 1112
businessService, 1113
data structures in, 1111
delete message, 1120
find message, 1117
get message, 1117, 1120
green page information, 1111
InquireSOAP, 1119
Inquiry Interface, 1117
publisherAssertion, 1116
Publisher Interface, 1120
PublishSOAP, 1121
registry, 1111
save message, 1120
set message, 1120
subscription service, 1123
tModel, 1114
for Web services, 1046
white page information, 1111
yellow page information, 1111
UML, 574
actor, B-2
aggregation in, 104
association, 97
association class, 97
class diagram, 96
composition in, 104
generalization, 101
for modeling databases, 69
multiplicity of an attribute in, 96
multiplicity of a role, 98
Object Constraint Language in, 96
OCL in, 96
profile in, 97
sequence diagram, B-15
state diagram, C-2
stereotype in, 97
use case, B-3
use case diagram, B-2
uncertain period. *See* two-phase commit protocol
unclustered index
B^+ tree as, 353
definition of, 340
as secondary index, 340
undo operation, 845. *See* compensating
undo record, A-18
Unified Modeling Language, 574. *See* UML
uniform resource identifier. *See* URI
uniform resource locator. *See* URL
union-compatible relations, 133
union operator
computing, 388
definition of, 133
UNIQUE
key constraint, 47
in XML, 622
uniqueness property of key constraint, 41
unit of work, 766
Universal Description, Discovery, and Integration. *See* UDDI
universal quantifier, 464
universal unique identifier, 1111
UNNEST function in SQL:2003, 541
UPDATE statement, 185
in database, 4

update anomaly, 194
update lock, 882, 899
update record, A-18, 921
URI
  definition of, 590
  in SOAP message, 1052
URL, 296, 590, 983, 1049
use case, B-3
use case diagram, B-3
use case diagram in UML, B-2
user, 8
user-defined type
  in SQL:1999/2003, 531
user key in Kerberos, 1145
USING clause, 288
uuid, 1111

validation phase, 859
validation set, 736, 743
value
  in CODM, 524
  collection, 530
  primitive, 524, 530
  reference, 524
  set, 524
  in SQL:1999/2003, 530
  tuple, 524, 530
variable
  in BPEL, 1090
Verified by Visa, 1156
version. *See* snapshot
  counter in multiversion concurrency controls, 904
  of a database, A-13, 903
  number in multiversion concurrency controls, 904
vertical partitioning, 693
view. *See* SQL view
  produced by a global schema, 690
  in the relational model, 33
view equivalence, 821, 863, 867
Visual Explainer for DB/2, 451
visual query language. *See* Query-By-Example
volatile storage, 919
vote message. *See* two-phase commit protocol

wait-die concurrency control, 866
wait set, 834
waits_for graph, A-8, 833, 1024
Waterfall model, B-1
weak entity in E-R, 84
weak mutual consistency. *See* consistency
Web. *See* Internet
Web application server, 985
Web server, 982
Web Service Description Language. *See* WSDL
weight of an attribute, 416
WfMS, 806
WHENEVER statement, 271
WHERE clause. *See* SQL
white page information in UDDI, 1111
WITH RECURSIVE clause, 492
workflow, 1046
  abort in, 807
  agent in, 804
  AND condition in, 804
  and BPEL, 1080
  compensatable task, 807
  compensation in, 807
  controller, 954
  definition of, 804
  failure in, 807
  management system, 806
  OR condition in, 804
  pivot, 807
  retriable task, 807
  in transaction processing, 954
Workflow Management Coalition, 809
worklist in workflow, 808
World Wide Web. *See* Internet
World Wide Web Consortium, 1051
wound-wait concurrency control, 1040
wrapper
  as a bridge between interfaces, 962
write
  blind, 867
  dirty, 826
  forced, 926
  lock. *See* lock
  phase, 859
  quorum, 1032
  skew, A-14, 910
write-ahead log. *See* log
write-back cache. *See* cache
write-gathering cache. *See* cache
write lock. *See* lock
write request, 815
WS-Addressing, 1058, 1066
  and BPEL, 1097
  endpoint reference, 1060, 1098, 1124
WS-AtomicTransaction. *See* WS-Coordination
WS-Coordination, 1046, 1123. *See* two-phase commit protocol
  activation service, 1124
  coordination context, 1124
  protocols, 1124
  protocol service, 1124
  registration service, 1124
  and two-phase commit protocol, 1124, 1125
  WS-AtomicTransaction, 1125
    Completion protocol, 1125
    Durable two-phase commit protocol, 1125
    Volatile two-phase commit protocol, 1125
  WS-BusinessActivity, 1127
    compensation, 1128
    two-phase commit protocol, 1127
  and X/Open, 1123, 1125
WSDL, 1063
  abstract level, 1063
  binding, 1045, 1067
  concrete level, 1063, 1067
  document/literal, 1073

document style SOAP binding, 1069
endpoint, 1067, 1078
fault element, 1066
inheritance, 1079
interface in, 1078
IsA relationship in, 1079
message, 1063
message exchange pattern in, 1078
operation, 1063
part, 1064
port, 1067
port type, 1063, 1067
remote procedure call, 1064
RPC/encoded, 1071. *See* SOAP
RPC/literal, 1072
RPC style SOAP binding, 1069
service, 1067
SMTP binding, 1076
Version 2.0, 1078
for Web services, 1045
WS-Security, 1176

xa_abort(), 1020
xa_commit(), 1020
xa interface, 971, 1020
xa_prepare(), 1020
xa_reg(), 971
XML
comments in, 584
definition of, 581
for Web services, 1045
XMLAGG in SQL/XML, 674
XML attribute
of type ID, 588, 596
of type IDREF, 588, 596
of type IDREFS, 588, 596
xmlns, 590
XML document
schema valid, 599
type definition, 594
valid, 594
well-formed, 589
XML element, 583
ancestor of, 583
attribute of, 583
child of, 583
content of, 583
descendant of, 583
empty, 584
parent of, 583
XMLELEMENT in SQL/XML, 671
XML Encryption, 1171
XML namespace, 1179
declaration, 590
default, 592
definition of, 589
prefix, 592
in schema document, 599
target namespace, 600
xmlns, 590
xmlns. *See* XML attribute; XML namespace
XMLPARSE
in SQL/XML, 677
XML processor, 583
XML-QL, 649
XMLQUERY in SQL/XML, 672
XML as data type in SQL/XML, 670
XML schema, 582
anonymous type in, 616
global element, 616, 620
instance-document, 599
named type in, 616
target namespace, 600
XML signature, 1173
canonicalization, 1175
message digest, 1174
transforms, 1175, 1181
XML stylesheet
definition of, 583
processing instruction, 584, 638
XML tag, 583
X/Open, 573, 781, 966, 971, 1007, 1013, 1019, 1026, 1123
XPath
description of, 628
expression, 634
goal of, 628
as query language, 582
selection condition, 634
XPointer, 636
XQL, 649
XQuery
computed element constructor, 661
count, 658
description of, 649
direct element constructor, 652
empty, 658
expression, 658
function, 658
goal of, 628
IF-THEN-ELSE, 658
as query language, 582
sum, 658
user-defined function, 658
XSL, 637. *See* XSLT
XSLT
best-matching template, 644
copy-of, 638
description of, 637
for-each, 639
goal of, 628
if, 639
as query language, 582
template, 641
value-of, 639
XSL transformation. *See* XSLT

yellow page information in UDDI, 1111

zero-phase commit protocol, 1027